REEDS

PRACTICAL BoatOwner

BRITAIN'S BIGGEST SELLING YACHTING MAGAZINE   SAIL AND POWER

SMALL CRAFT ALMANAC

2012

D0488918

EDITORS

Andy Du Port & Rob Buttress

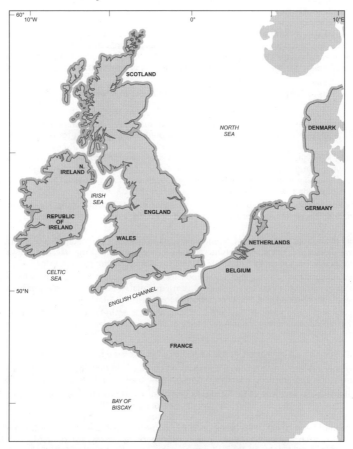

THE UNITED KINGDOM AND IRELAND
PLUS DENMARK TO THE GIRONDE

REEDS
PRACTICAL Boat Owner
BRITAIN'S BIGGEST SELLING YACHTING MAGAZINE · SAIL AND POWER

SMALL CRAFT ALMANAC
2012

Editors: Andy Du Port & Rob Buttress

The Editors would like to thank the many official bodies who have kindly provided essential information in the preparation of this Almanac. They include the UK Hydrographic Office, Trinity House, Northern Lighthouse Board, Irish Lights, HM Nautical Almanac Office, HM Stationery Office, HM Customs, Meteorological Office and the Maritime and Coastguard Agency.

Information from the Admiralty List of Lights, Admiralty Tide Tables and the Admiralty List of Radio Signals is reproduced with the permission of the UK Hydrographic Office and the Controller of HMSO. Extracts from the following are published by permission of the Controller of HM Stationery Office: International Code of Signals, 1969; Meteorological Office Weather Services for Shipping. Phases of the Moon and Sun/Moon rising and setting times are derived from the current editions of the Channel and Eastern Almanacs, and are included by permission of HM Nautical Almanac Office. UK and Foreign tidal predictions are supplied by the UK Hydrographic Office, Taunton TA1 2DN. Acknowledgment is also made to the following authorities for permission to use tidal predictions stated: Danish Safety Administration, Farvandsvæsnet: Esbjerg. SHOM, France: Dunkerque, Dieppe, Le Havre, Cherbourg, St Malo, Brest, Pointe de Grave, Authorisation (No 173/2011). Rijkswaterstaat, The Netherlands: Vlissingen, and Hoek van Holland. BSH, Hamburg and Rostock: Helgoland, Wilhelmshaven and Cuxhaven (BSH 11123/2008-07). Vlaamse Hydrografie, Belgium: Zeebrugge. **Warning**: The UK Hydrographic Office has not verified the reproduced data and does not accept any liability for the accuracy of reproduction or any modifications made thereafter.

Corrections Any necessary corrections will be published on the website www.reedsalmanacs.co.uk. Data in this almanac is corrected up to Edition 26/2011 of the *Admiralty Notices to Mariners*.

IMPORTANT SAFETY NOTE AND LEGAL DISCLAIMER

This Almanac is intended as a navigational aid only and to assist with basic planning for your passage. The information, charts, maps and diagrams in this Almanac should not be relied on for navigational purposes and should always be used in conjunction with current official hydrographic data. Whilst every care has been taken in its compilation, this Almanac may contain inaccuracies and is no substitute for the relevant official hydrographic charts and data, which should always be consulted in advance of, and whilst, navigating in the relevant area. Before setting out you should also check local conditions with the harbourmaster or other appropriate office responsible for your intended area of navigation.

Before using any waypoint or coordinate listed in this Almanac it must first be plotted on an appropriate official hydrographic chart to check its usefulness, accuracy and appropriateness for the prevailing weather and tidal conditions.

To the extent that the editors or publishers become aware that corrections are required, these will be published on the website www.reedsalmanacs.co.uk. Readers should therefore regularly check the website for any such corrections. Data in this Almanac is corrected up to Edition 26/2011 of the Admiralty Notices to Mariners.

The publishers, editors and their agents accept no responsibility for any errors or omissions, or for any accident, loss or damage (including without limitation any indirect, consequential, special or exemplary damages) arising from the use or misuse of, or reliance upon, the information contained in this Almanac.

The decision to use and rely on any of the data in this Almanac is entirely at the discretion of, and is the sole responsibility of, the Skipper or other individual in control of the vessel in connection with which it is being used or relied upon.

Correspondence Letters on nautical matters should be addressed to info@reedsalmanacs.co.uk

Practical Boat Owner is published monthly by IPC Magazines Ltd, Blue Fin Building, 110 Southwark Street, London SE1 0SU. For subscription enquiries and overseas orders call +44 (0)844 848 0848 or visit www.pbo.co.uk/ipbjm.

Almanac manager: Chris Stevens
Cartography & production: Chris Stevens
Adlard Coles Nautical
50 Bedford Square, London WC1B 3DP

Tel: +44 (0)207 631 5600
www.reedsalmanacs.co.uk

Foreword

I find I'm using my Small Craft Almanac more than ever these days, referring often to the tidal stream atlases, the tidal gates information, and the tide tables themselves. On a recent cruise in France, with just a quick glance into the almanac, I found out the sources of weather forecasts, I found phone numbers for marinas to check they had space, and I knew just who to call in an emergency.

The editors at Reeds are respected worldwide for their expertise and we at Practical Boat Owner magazine are delighted to be their partners in bringing sailors in the UK and further afield this invaluable sailors' companion.

Keep it at home for planning, then pop it in your kitbag for use on passage. Designed to fit neatly into your chart-table, bookshelf or any small space onboard, the Reeds PBO Small Craft Almanac will, we hope, assist you in safe and successful cruising in 2012.

Sarah Norbury
Editor
Practical Boat Owner
Britain's biggest-selling yachting magazine

Contents

ABBREVIATIONS

AC, ACA	Admiralty chart, chart agent
AC	Shore power (electrical)
ACN	Adlard Coles Nautical
Al	Alternating lt
ALL	Admiralty list of lights
ALRS	Admiralty list of radio signals
ASD	Admiralty sailing directions (Pilot)
ATT	Admiralty tide tables
ATT	Atterisage (landfall/SWM) buoy
Bcn, Bn	Beacon
Bkwtr	Breakwater
BST	British summer time (DST)
CD	Chart datum
Cf	Compare, cross-refer to
CG	Coastguard
Ch	Channel (VHF)
chan.	Channel (navigational)
COG	Course over the ground
CROSS	Centre régional opérationnel de surveillance et sauvetage (MRCC)
CRS	Coast radio station(s)
DF	Direction finding
Dia	Diaphone (fog signal)
Dir Lt	Directional light
DSC	Digital selective calling
DST	Daylight saving time
DZ	Danger zone (buoy)
E	East
ECM	East cardinal mark (buoy/beacon)
ED	Existence doubtful, European datum
EPIRB	Emergency pos'n indicating radio bn
F	Fixed light. Beaufort wind force
FFL	Fixed and flashing lt
Fl	Flashing light
FM	Frequency modulation
FV	Fishing vessel
G	Green. Gravel
GMDSS	Global maritime distress & safety system
H, Hrs, h	Hour(s)
H24	Continuous
HAT	Highest astronomical tide
Hbr	Harbour
Hd	Head, headland
HF	High frequency
HJ	Day service, sunrise to sunset
HO	Office hours, Hydrographic office
ht	Height
HW	High water
HX	No fixed hours
Hz	Hertz
IALA	Int'l association of lt ho authorities
IDM	Isolated danger mark (buoy/bcn)
IMO	Int'l maritime organisation
Inmarsat	Int'l maritime satellite system
IPTS	Int'l port traffic signals
Is, I	Island, Islet
Iso	Isophase light
ITZ	Inshore traffic zone
Kn	Knot(s)
Lanby	Large automatic navigational buoy
Lat	Latitude
LB	Lifeboat
Ldg	Leading (lt)
LF	Low frequency
Long	Longitude
LT	Local time
Lt(s)	Light(s)
Lt F	Light float
Lt Ho	Lighthouse
Lt V	Light vessel
LW	Low water
M	Sea mile(s)
m	Metre(s)
MCA	Maritime & Coastguard Agency
Météo	Météorologie/weather
MF	Medium frequency
MHWN	Mean HW neaps
MHWS	Mean HW springs
MHz	Megahertz
MLWN	Mean LW neaps
MLWS	Mean LW springs
MMSI	Maritime mobile service identity
Mo	Morse
MRCC	Maritime rescue co-ordination centre
MRSC	Maritime rescue sub-centre (not in UK)
MSI	Maritime safety information
N	North
NCM	North cardinal mark (buoy/bcn)
Oc	Occulting light
PHM	Port-hand mark (buoy/bcn)
Pt(e), (a)	Point(e), Punta
Q	Quick flashing
R	Red. River
Ra	Coast radar station
Racon	Radar transponder beacon
RG	Emergency RDF station
R/T	Radiotelephony
S	South
s	second(s) of time
SAR	Search and rescue
SCM	South cardinal mark (buoy/bcn)
SHM	Starboard-hand mark (buoy/bcn)
Sig Stn	Signal station
SMS	Short message service (texting)
SNSM	Société nationale de sauvetage en mer (French LB service)
SOG	Speed over the ground
SOLAS	Safety of life at sea (Convention)
SPM	Special mark (buoy/bcn)
SRR	SAR Region
SSB	Single sideband (radio)
Stn	Station
SWM	Safe water mark, landfall buoy
Tfc	Traffic
TSS	Traffic separation scheme
UQ	Ultra quick flashing lt
UT	Universal time
VHF	Very high frequency
VNF	Voie navigable de France (canals)
VQ	Very quick flashing lt
VTS	Vessel traffic service
W	West, White
WCM	West cardinal mark (buoy/bcn)
WGS	World geodetic system (datum)
WIP	Work in progress
WPT	Waypoint
Y	Yellow, orange, amber

GENERAL VOCABULARY. See also weather vocabulary on page 105

ENGLISH	GERMAN	FRENCH	SPANISH	DUTCH
ASHORE				
Ashore	An Land	A terre	A tierra	Aan land
Airport	Flughafen	Aéroport	Aeropuerto	Vliegveld
Bank	Bank	Banque	Banco	Bank
Boathoist	Bootskran	Travelift	Travelift	Botenlift
Boatyard	Bootswerft	Chantier naval	Astilleros	Jachtwerf
Bureau de change	Wechselstelle	Bureau de change	Cambio	Geldwisselkantoor
Bus	Bus	Autobus	Autobús	Bus
Chandlery	Yachtausrüster	Shipchandler	Efectos navales	Scheepswinkel
Chemist	Apotheke	Pharmacie	Farmacia	Apotheek
Dentist	Zahnarzt	Dentiste	Dentista	Tandarts
Doctor	Arzt	Médecin	Médico	Dokter
Engineer	Motorenservice	Ingénieur/mécanique	Mecánico	Ingenieur
Ferry	Fähre	Ferry/transbordeur	Ferry	Veer/Pont
Garage	Autowerkstatt	Station service	Garage	Garage
Harbour	Hafen	Port	Puerto	Haven
Hospital	Krankenhaus	Hôpital	Hospital	Ziekenhuis
Mast crane	Mastenkran	Grue	Grúa	Masten kraan
Post office	Postamt	Bureau de poste/PTT	Correos	Postkantoor
Railway station	Bahnhof	Gare de chemin de fer	Estación de ferrocanil	Station
Sailmaker	Segelmacher	Voilier	Velero	Zeilmaker
Shops	Geschäfte	Boutiques	Tiendas	Winkels
Slip	Slip	Cale	Varadero	Helling
Supermarket	Supermarkt	Supermarché	Supermercado	Supermarkt
Taxi	Taxi	Taxi	Taxis	Taxi
Village	Ort	Village	Pueblo	Dorp
Yacht club	Yachtclub	Club nautique	Club náutico	Jacht club
NAVIGATION				
Abeam	Querab	A côté	Por el través	Naast
Ahead	Voraus	Avant	Avante	Voor
Astern	Achteraus	Arrière	Atrás	Achter
Bearing	Peilung	Cap	Maración	Peiling
Buoy	Tonne	Bouée	Boya	Boei
Binoculars	Fernglas	Jumelles	Prismáticos	Verrekijker
Channel	Kanal	Chenal	Canal	Kanaal
Chart	Seekarte	Carte	Carta náutica	Zeekaart
Compass	Kompass	Compas	Compás	Kompas
Compass course	Kompass Kurs	Cap du compas	Rumbo de aguja	Kompas koers
Current	Strömung	Courant	Coriente	Stroom
Dead reckoning	Koppelnavigation	Estime	Estimación	Gegist bestek
Degree	Grad	Degré	Grado	Graden
Deviation	Deviation	Déviation	Desvio	Deviatie
Distance	Entfernung	Distance	Distancia	Afstand
Downstream	Flußabwärts	En aval	Río abajo	Stroom afwaards
East	Ost	Est	Este	Oost
Ebb	Ebbe	Jusant	Marea menguante	Eb
Echosounder	Echolot	Sondeur	Sonda	Dieptemeter
Estimated position	Gegißte Position	Point estimé	Posición estimado	Gegiste positie
Fathom	Faden	Une brasse	Braza	Vadem
Feet	Fuß	Pieds	Pie	Voet
Flood	Flut	Flot	Flujo de marea	Vloed
Handbearing compass	Handpeilkompass	Compas de relèvement	Compás de marcaciones	Handpeil kompas

ENGLISH	GERMAN	FRENCH	SPANISH	DUTCH
Harbour guide	Hafenhandbuch	Guide du port	Guia del Puerto	Havengids
High water	Hochwasser	Peine mer	Altamer	Hoog water
Latitude	Geographische Breite	Latitude	Latitud	Breedte
Leading lights	Feuer in Linie	Alignement	Luz de enfilación	Geleide lichten
Leeway	Abdrift	Dérive	Hacia sotavento	Drift
Lighthouse	Leuchtturm	Phare	Faro	Vuurtoren
List of lights	Leuchtfeuer Verzeichnis	Liste des feux	Listude de Luces	Lichtenlijst
Log	Logge	Loch	Corredera	Log
Longitude	Geographische Länge	Longitude	Longitud	Lengte
Low water	Niedrigwasser	Basse mer	Bajamar	Laag water
Metre	Meter	Mètre	Metro	Meter
Minute	Minute	Minute	Minuto	Minuut
Nautical almanac	Nautischer Almanach	Almanach nautique	Almanaque náutico	Almanak
Nautical mile	Seemeile	Mille nautique	Milla marina	Zeemijl
Neap tide	Nipptide	Morte-eau	Marea muerta	Dood tij
North	Nord	Nord	Norte	Noord
Pilot	Lotse	Pilote	Práctico	Loods/Gids
Pilotage book	Handbuch	Instructions nautiques	Derrotero	Vaarwijzer
RDF	Funkpeiler	Radio gonio	Radio-gonió	Radio richtingzoeker
Radar	Radar	Radar	Radar	Radar
Radio receiver	Radio, Empfänger	Récepteur radio	Receptor de radio	Radio ontvanger
Radio transmitter	Sender	Emetteur radio	Radio-transmisor	Radio zender
River outlet	Flußmündung	Embouchure	Embocadura	Riviermond
South	Süd	Sud	Sud, Sur	Zuid
Spring tide	Springtide	Vive-eau	Marea viva	Springtij/ springvloed
Tide	Tide, Gezeit	Marée	Marea	Getijde
Tide tables	Tidenkalender	Annuaire des marées	Anuario de mareas	Getijdetafel
True course	Wahrer Kurs	Vrai cap	Rumbo	Ware Koers
Upstream	Flußaufwärts	En amont	Río arriba	Stroom opwaards
VHF	UKW	VHF	VHF	Marifoon
Variation	Mißweisung	Variation	Variación	Variatie
Waypoint	Wegpunkt	Point de rapport	Waypoint	Waypoint/Route punt
West	West	Ouest	Oeste	West

OFFICIALDOM

Certificate of registry	Schiffszertifikat	Acte de franchisation	Doc de matrícuia	Zeebrief
Check in	Einklarieren	Enregistrement	Registrar	Check-in
Customs	Zoll	Douanes	Aduana	Douane
Declare	Verzollen	Déclarer	Declarar	Aangeven
Harbour master	Hafenmeister	Capitaine du port	Capitán del puerto	Havenmeester
Insurance	Versicherung	Assurance	Seguro	Verzekering
Insurance certificate	Versicherungspolice	Certificat d'assurance	Certificado deseguro	Verzekeringsbewijs
Passport	Paß	Passeport	Pasaporte	Paspoort
Police	Polizei	Police	Policía	Politie
Pratique	Verkehrserlaubnis	Pratique	Prático	Verlof tot ontscheping
Prohibited area	Sperrgebiet	Zone interdite	Zona de prohibida	Verboden gebied
Register	Register	Liste de passagers	Lista de tripulantes/rol	Register
Ship's log	Logbuch	Livre de bord	Cuaderno de bitácora	Logboek
Ship's papers	Schiffspapiere	Papiers de bateau	Documentos del barco	Scheepspapieren
Surveyor	Gutachter	Expert maritime	Inspector	Opzichter

Chapter 1 – Navigation

PASSAGE PLANNING AND SOLAS V

All passages by any vessel that goes to sea *must* be planned. 'Going to sea' is defined as proceeding beyond sheltered waters. Even in very familiar waters every passage, however short, should be properly planned. Before you set sail you need to determine where you are going, how to get there and what factors may influence the plan.

Full passage planning requirements may be found in Chapter V of the International Convention for Safety of Life at Sea (SOLAS), but more digestible guidance for small craft is in the MCA's Pleasure Craft Information Pack at: **www.mcga.gov.uk/c4mca/pleasure_craft_information_packdec07-2.pdf.**

Although the passage plan does not have to be recorded on paper, in the event of legal action a written plan is clear proof that the required planning has been completed; it can also be referred to during the passage. A suggested passage planning form is overleaf. When completed this would constitute, with due consideration of the points below, a reasonable passage plan. The blank form may be photocopied and modified to suit individual needs.

Although spot checks on small craft are unlikely, the MCA could, following an accident or incident, take action under the Merchant Shipping Act if it could be proved that the skipper did not have a reasonable passage plan.

Passage planning considerations

All passage plans should at least consider the following:

• **Weather.** Before setting out check the weather forecast and know how to get regular updates during the passage.

• **Tides.** Check tidal predictions and determine if there are any limiting depths at your port of departure, during the passage and at the port of arrival (and at alternative ports, if applicable). Tidal streams will almost certainly affect the plan.

• **Vessel.** Confirm she is suitable for the intended trip, is properly equipped, and has sufficient fuel, water and food on board.

• **Crew.** Take into account your crew's experience, expertise and stamina. Cold, tiredness and seasickness can be debilitating – and skippers are not immune.

• **Navigation.** Make sure you are aware of all navigational dangers by consulting up to date charts, pilot books and this Almanac. Never *rely* on GPS for fixing your position.

• **Contingency plan.** Consider bolt holes which can be entered *safely* in an emergency, if the weather deteriorates or mutiny threatens.

• **Information ashore.** Make sure someone ashore knows your plans, when they should become concerned and what action to take if necessary. Be sure to join the Coastguard Voluntary Identification Scheme (Form CG66).

"The winds and waves are always on the side of the ablest navigators." (Edward Gibbon)

Passage planning form

The following notes amplify some of the items on the form:

• The height of tide affects the depth, and tidal streams may hinder sensible progress – off headlands or in narrow passages, for example. On longer passages, which cross main tidal streams, determine the net effect of the streams and calculate a course to steer – more efficient than trying to maintain a track.

• Note which harbours and marinas have restricted times of access due to bars, sills or locks. These may affect your ETA and, probably, your ETD.

• Prepare a detailed pilotage plan for entry/exit of any unfamiliar harbour; a sketch is invaluable.

• Squinting into the setting sun can make pilotage very difficult. At night, light from a full moon can help enormously.

• Know when you expect to see lights at night – a good check on progress. See table of dipping/rising lights.

• Look up and note relevant VHF channels and/or phone numbers for ports of departure and arrival.

NAVIGATION

PASSAGE PLANNING FORM

DATE:........................ FROM: .... TO: .... DIST: ....M

ALTERNATIVE DESTINATION(S): ....

WEATHER FORECAST: ....
....

FORECASTS AVAILABLE DURING PASSAGE: ....
....

TIDES

DATE:..................................	DATE:..................................	DATE: ....
PLACE:.................................	PLACE:	PLACE: ....
HW	HW	HW ....
LW	LW	LW ....
HW	HW	HW ....
LW	LW	LW ....
COEFFICIENT:	....	....
HEIGHT OF TIDE AT:	....	....
.... hrs ....m	.... hrs ....m	............hrs ....m

DEPTH CONSTRAINTS: ....

TIDAL STREAMS AT: ....

TURNS .... AT .... TOTAL SET (FM .... TO ....): ....° ....M

TURNS .... AT .... TOTAL SET (FM .... TO ....): ....° ....M

NET TIDAL STREAM FOR PASSAGE: ....° ....M

ESTIMATED TIME: ....hrs ETD: .... ETA: ....

SUN/MOON	SUNRISE:	SUNSET:	
	MOONRISE:	MOONSET:	PHASE: ....

WAYPOINTS	NO	NAME	TRACK/DISTANCE (TO NEXT WAYPOINT)
	....	....	.... / ....
	....	....	.... / ....
	....	....	.... / ....
	....	....	.... / ....
	....	....	.... / ....

DANGERS   CLEARING BEARINGS/RANGES/DEPTHS
....
....
....

LIGHTS/MARKS EXPECTED ....
....
....
....

COMMUNICATIONS	PORT/MARINA	VHF	☎ ....
	PORT/MARINA	VHF	☎ ....

NOTES (CHARTS PREPARED & PAGE NUMBERS OF RELEVANT PILOTS/ALMANACS/ETC): ....
....
....

DISTANCES (M) ACROSS THE ENGLISH CHANNEL

ENGLAND ⟍ FRANCE/CI	Longships	Falmouth	Fowey	Plymouth bkwtr	Salcombe	Dartmouth	Torbay	Weymouth	Poole Hbr Ent	Needles Lt Ho	Nab Tower	Littlehampton	Shoreham	Brighton	Newhaven	Eastbourne	Folkestone	Dover
Le Conquet	112	112	123	125	125	137	144	172	188	194	212	230	240	245	249	261	295	301
L'Aberwrac'h	102	97	106	107	105	117	124	153	168	174	192	211	219	224	228	239	275	280
Roscoff	110	97	101	97	91	100	107	130	144	149	165	184	193	197	200	211	246	252
Trébeurden	120	105	106	102	94	102	109	129	142	147	164	181	190	194	197	208	244	249
Tréguier	132	112	110	101	94	98	102	116	128	132	147	162	170	174	177	188	224	229
Lézardrieux	142	121	118	107	94	100	105	115	126	130	140	157	165	169	172	184	219	224
St Q.-Portrieux	159	137	135	124	111	115	121	127	135	135	146	162	171	174	178	189	225	230
St Malo	172	149	146	133	118	120	124	125	130	130	143	157	166	170	173	184	220	225
St Helier	155	130	123	108	93	95	100	99	104	104	115	132	140	144	147	158	194	199
St Peter Port	139	113	104	89	73	70	75	71	79	83	97	112	120	124	127	135	174	179
Braye (Alderney)	146	116	106	89	72	69	71	54	60	62	73	91	100	103	106	114	153	159
Cherbourg	168	138	125	107	92	87	88	66	64	63	68	81	90	92	96	102	140	145
St Vaast	194	164	150	132	116	111	112	83	76	72	71	80	87	88	90	96	132	138
Ouistreham	229	198	185	167	151	146	147	117	107	100	86	91	92	91	90	92	125	130
Deauville	236	205	192	174	158	153	154	122	111	104	88	89	88	87	85	87	120	125
Le Havre	231	200	187	169	153	148	148	118	105	97	82	82	83	82	79	80	115	120
Fécamp	242	212	197	179	163	157	157	120	105	96	75	71	68	65	62	62	90	95
Dieppe	268	237	222	204	188	180	180	142	125	117	91	80	75	70	64	63	70	75
Boulogne	290	258	242	224	208	198	195	153	135	127	97	81	71	66	59	47	28	25
Calais	305	272	257	239	223	213	210	168	150	141	111	96	86	81	74	62	26	22

NOTES

1. This Table applies to Areas 1–3, and 14–16, each of which also contains its own internal Distance Table. Approximate distances in nautical miles are by the most direct route, while avoiding dangers and allowing for Traffic Separation Schemes.

2. For ports within the Solent, add the appropriate distances given in Area 2 to those shown above under either Needles Lighthouse or Nab Tower.

AREA 1 *South West England - Isles of Scilly to Anvil Point*

SELECTED LIGHTS, BUOYS & WAYPOINTS

Positions are referenced to WGS84

ISLES OF SCILLY TO LAND'S END

Bishop Rock ☆ Fl (2) 15s 44m **20M**; part obsc 204°-211°, obsc 211°-233° and 236°-259°; Gy ○ twr with helo platform; *Racon T, 18M, 254°-215°*; 49°52'·37N 06°26'·74W. Round Rk ⚓ 49°53'·10N 06°25'·19W. Old Wreck ⚓ VQ; 49°54'·26N 06°22'·81W.

ST AGNES and ST MARY'S

Peninnis Hd ⚡ Fl 20s 36m 9M; 231°-117° but part obsc 048°-083° within 5M; W ○ twr on B frame, B cupola; 49°54'·28N 06°18'·21W.

Spanish Ledge ⚓ Q (3) 10s; *Bell;* 49°53'·94N 06°18'·86W.

Bartholomew Ledges ⚓ QR 12m; 49°54'·37N 06°19'·89W.

N Bartholomew ⚓ Fl R 5s; 49°54'·49N 06°19'·99W.

Bacon Ledge ⚓ Fl (4) R 5s; 49°55'·22N 06°19'·26W.

Ldg lts 097·3°: Front, Iso RW (vert) 2s; W △, 49°55'·12N 06°18'·50W. Rear, Oc WR (vert) 10s; Or X on W bcn.

St Mary's Pool pier ⚡ Fl WRG 2s 5m 4M; 070°-R-100°-W-130°-G-070°; 49°55'·11N 06°19'·00W.

Crow Rock ⚓ Fl (2) 10s; 49°56'·26N 06°18'·49W.

Hats ⚓ VQ (6) + L Fl 10s; 49°56'·21N 06°17'·14W.

AROUND TRESCO, BRYHER and ST MARTIN'S

Tresco Flats, Hulman ⚓ Fl G 4s, 49°56'·29N 06°20'·31W.

Little Rag Ledge ⚓ Fl (2) R 5s, 49°56'·43N 06°20'·43W.

Bryher, Bar Quay ⚓ Q (3) 10s, 49°57'·37N 06°20'·84W.

Spencers Ledge ⚓ Q (6) + L Fl 15s; 49°54'·78N 06°22'·06W.

Steeple Rock ⚓ Q (9) 15s; 49°55'·46N 06°24'·24W.

Round Island ☆ Fl 10s 55m **18M**, also shown in reduced vis; 021°-288°; W ○ twr; *Horn (4) 60s; Racon M, 10M;* 49°58'·74N 06°19'·39W.

St Martin's, Higher Town quay ⚡ Fl R 5s, 49°57'·45N 06°16'·84W.

SCILLY TO LAND'S END

Seven Stones Lt V 🚢 Fl (3) 30s 12m **15M**; R hull; *Horn (3) 60s; Racon O, 15M;* 50°03'·63N 06°04'·32W.

Wolf Rock ☆ Fl 15s 34m **16M**; H24; *Horn 30s; Racon T, 10M;* 49°56'·72N 05°48'·57W.

Longships ☆ Fl (2) WR 10s 35m **W15M**, R11M; 189°-R-327°-W- 189°; also shown in reduced vis; Gy ○ twr with helicopter platform; *Horn 10s;* 50°04'·01N 05°44'·81W.

Carn Base ⚓ Q (9) 15s; 50°01'·48N 05°46'·18W.

Runnel Stone ⚓ Q (6) + L Fl 15s; *Bell;* 50°01'·18N 05°40'·36W.

LAND'S END TO PLYMOUTH

Tater-du ☆ Fl (3) 15s 34m **20M**; 241°-072°; W ○ twr. FR 31m 13M, 060°-072° over Runnel Stone; *Horn (2) 30s;* 50°03'·14N 05°34'·67W.

NEWLYN

Low Lee ⚓ Q (3) 10s; 50°05'·56N 05°31'·38W.

S Pier ⚡ Fl 5s 10m 9M; W ○ twr; 253°-336°; 50°06'·18N 05°32'·57W.

N Pier ⚡ F WG 4m 2M; 238°-G-248°, W over hbr; 50°06'·18N 05°32'·62W.

PENZANCE

S Pier ⚡ Fl WR 5s 11m **W17M**, R12M; 159°-R (unintens)-224°-R-268°-W-344·5°-R-shore; 50°07'·06N 05°31'·68W.

Mountamopus ⚓ Q (6) + L Fl 15s; 50°04'·62N 05°26'·25W.

Lizard ☆ Fl 3s 70m **26M**; H24; 250°-120°, partly visible 235°-250°; W 8-sided twr; *Horn 30s;* 49°57'·61N 05°12'·13W.

Manacle ⚓ Q (3) 10s; *Bell;* 50°02'·81N 05°01'·91W.

FALMOUTH

St Anthony Head ☆ Iso WR 15s 22m, **W16M**, R14M, H24; 295°-W-004°-R (over Manacles)-022°-W-172°; W 8-sided twr; *Horn 30s;* 50°08'·46N 05°00'·96W.

Black Rock Fl (2) 10s 3M; B IDM bcn twr; 50°08'·72N 05°02'·00W.

Black Rock ⚓ Fl R 2·5s; 50°08'·68N 05°01'·74W.

Castle ⚓ Fl G 2·5s; 50°08'·99N 05°01'·62W.

St Mawes ⚓ Q (6) + L Fl 15s; 50°09'·10N 05°01'·42W.

The Governor ⚓ VQ (3) 5s; 50°09'·15N 05°02'·40W.

West Narrows ⚓ Fl (2) R 10s; 50°09'·39N 05°02'·07W.

East Narrows ⚓ Fl (2) Q 10s; 50°09'·43N 05°01'·90W.

The Vilt ⚓ Fl (4) G 15s; 50°09'·99N 05°02'·28W.

Northbank ⚓ Fl R 4s; 50°10'·34N 05°02'·26W.

St Just ⚓ QR; 50°10'·44N 05°01'·72W.

Mylor appr chan ⚓ Fl G 6s; 50°10'·79N 05°02'·70W. ⚓ Fl R 5s.

Messack ⚓ Fl G 15s; 50°11'·31N 05°02'·22W.

Carrick ⚓ Fl (2) G 10s; 50°11'·59N 05°02'·74W.

Pill ⚓ Fl (3) G 15s; 50°12'·05N 05°02'·40W.

Turnerware Bar ⚓ Fl G 5s; 50°12'·40N 05°02'·15W.

Inner Harbour

N Arm ⚡ QR 5m 3M; 50°09'·42N 05°03'·20W.

Visitors Yacht Haven ⚡ 2 FR (vert); 50°09'·27N 05°03'·91W.

Falmouth Marina ⚓ VQ (3) 5s; 50°09'·91N 05°04'·99W.

DODMAN POINT and MEVAGISSEY

Naval gunnery targets SSE of Dodman Point:

'A' ⚓ Fl Y 10s; 50°08'·53N 04°46'·37W.

'B' ⚓ Fl Y 5s; 50°10'·30N 04°45'·00W.

'C' ⚓ Fl Y 2s; 50°10'·40N 04°47'·51W.

Gwineas ⚓ Q (3) 10s; *Bell;* 50°14'·48N 04°45'·40W.

Mevagissey, Victoria Pier ⚡ Fl (2) 10s 9m 12M; *Dia 30s;* 50°16'·15N 04°46'·92W.

FOWEY

Cannis Rock ⚓ Q (6) + L Fl 15s; *Bell;* 50°18'·38N 04°39'·95W.

Fowey ⚡ L Fl WR 5s 28m W11M, R9M; 284°-R-295°-W-028°-R-054°; W 8-sided twr, R lantern; 50°19'·63N 04°38'·83W.

St Catherine's Pt ⚡ Fl R 2·5s 15m 2M; 150°-295°; 50°19'·69N 04°38'·66W.

Lamp Rock ⚓ Fl G 5s 3m 2M; vis 357°-214°; 50°19'·70N 04°38'·41W. Whitehouse Pt ⚡ Iso WRG 3s 11m W11M,

R/G8M; 017°-G-022°- W-032°-R-037°; R col; 50°19'·98N 04°38'·28W.

POLPERRO, LOOE, EDDYSTONE and WHITSAND BAY

Udder Rock ⚓ VQ (6) + L Fl 10s; *Bell;* 50°18'·93N 04°33'·85W.

POLPERRO, W pier ⚹ FW 4m 4M; FR when hbr closed in bad weather; 50°19'·86N 04°30'·96W.

Spy House Pt ⚹ Iso WR 6s 30m 7M; W288°-060°, R060°-288°; 50°19'·81N 04°30'·69W.

LOOE, Ranneys ⚓ Q (6) + L Fl 15s; 50°19'·85N 04°26'·37W.

Mid Main ⚓ Q (3) 10s 2M; 50°20'·56N 04°26'·94W.

Banjo Pier ☆ Oc WR 3s 8m **W15M**, R12M; 207°-R267°-W-313°-R-332°; 50°21'·06N 04°27'·06W.

White Rock ⚹ Fl R 3s 5m 2M; 50°21'·03N 04°27'·09W.

Eddystone ☆ Fl (2) 10s 41m **17M**. Same twr, Iso R 10s 28m 8M; vis 110·5°-130·5° over Hand Deeps; Gy twr, helicopter platform; *Horn 30s; Racon T, 10M;* 50°10'·84N 04°15'·94W.

Hand Deeps ⚓ Q (9) 15s; 50°12'·68N 04°21'·10W.

PLYMOUTH

PLYMOUTH SOUND, WESTERN CHANNEL

Draystone ⚓ Fl (2) R 5s; 50°18'·85N 04°11'·07W.

Knap ⚓ Fl G 5s; 50°19'·56N 04°10'·02W.

Plymouth bkwtr W head, ⚹ Fl WR 10s 19m W12M, R9M; 262°-W-208°-R-262°; W ○ twr. Same twr, Iso 4s 12m 10M; vis 033°-037°; *Horn 15s;* 50°20'·07N 04°09'·52W.

Maker ⚹ Fl (2) WRG 10s 29m, W11M, R/G6M; 270°-G330°-W-004°-R-050°; W twr, R stripe; 50°20'·51N 04°10'·87W.

Queens Ground ⚓ Fl (2) R 10s; 50°20'·29N 04°10'·08W.

New Ground ⚓ Fl R 2s; 50°20'·47N 04°09'·43W.

Melampus ⚓ Fl R 4s; 50°21'·15N 04°08'·72W.

PLYMOUTH SOUND, EASTERN CHANNEL

Wembury Pt ⚹ Oc Y 10s 45m; occas; 50°19'·01N 04°06'·63W.

West Tinker ⚓ VQ (9) 10s; 50°19'·25N 04°08'·64W.

East Tinker ⚓ Q (3) 10s; 50°19'·20N 04°08'·30W.

Whidbey ⚓ Oc (2) WRG 10s 29m, W8M, R/G6M, H24; 000°-G-137·5°-W-139·5°-R-159°; Or and W col; 50°19'·53N 04°07'·27W.

The Breakwater, E head ⚓ L Fl WR 10s 9m W8M, R6M; 190°-R-353°-W-001°-R-018°-W-190°; 50°20'·01N 04°08'·24W.

Staddon Pt ⚓ Oc WRG 10s 15m W8M, R/G5M; H24. 348°-G-038°-W-050°-R-090°; W structure, R bands; 50°20'·17N 04°07'·54W.

Withyhedge Dir ⚹ 070° (for W Chan): WRG 13m W13M, R/G5M; H24; 060°-FG-065°-Al WG (W phase increasing with brg) -069°-FW-071°-Al WR (R phase increasing with brg)-075°-F R-080°; W ▽, orange stripe on col. Same col, Fl (2) Bu 5s; vis 120°-160°; 50°20'·75N 04°07'·44W.

SMEATON PASS (W of Mt Batten and S of The Hoe)

Ldg lts 349°. Front, Mallard Shoal ⚓ Q WRG 5m W10M, R/G3M; W △, Or bands; 233°-G-043°- R-067°- G-087°-W-099°-R-108° (ldg sector); 50°21'·60N 04°08'·33W. Rear, 396m from front, Hoe ⚓ Oc G 1·3s 11m 3M, 310°-040°; W ▽, Or bands; 50°21'·81N 04°08'·39W.

S Mallard ⚓ VQ (6) + L Fl 10s; 50°21'·51N 04°08'·30W.

W Mallard ⚓ QG; 50°21'·57N 04°08'·36W.

S Winter ⚓ Q (6) + L Fl 15s; 50°21'·40N 04°08'·55W.

NE Winter ⚓ QR; 50°21'·54N 04°08'·50W.

NW Winter ⚓ VQ (9) 10s; 50°21'·55N 04°08'·70W.

ENTRANCE TO THE CATTEWATER

QAB (Queen Anne's Battery) ldg lts ⚹ 048·5°. Front, FR; Or/W bcn; 50°21'·84N 04°07'·84W. Rear, Oc R 8s 14m 3M; 139m NE.

Fishers Nose ⚹ Fl (3) R 10s 6m 4M; 50°21'·80N 04°08'·01W. Also F Bu ≠ 026·5° with F Bu 50°22'·00N 04°07'·86W, for Cobbler Chan.

DRAKE CHANNEL, THE BRIDGE and THE NARROWS

Asia ⚓ Fl (2) R 5s; 50°21'·47N 04°08'·85W.

St Nicholas ⚓ QR; 50°21'·55N 04°09'·20W.

N Drakes Is ⚓ Fl R 4s; 50°21'·52N 04°09'·38W.

E Vanguard ⚓ QG; 50°21'·47N 04°09'·70W.

W Vanguard ⚓ Fl G 3s; 50°21'·49N 04°09'·98W.

Devils Point ⚓ QG 5m 3M; Fl 5s in fog; 50°21'·59N 04°10'·04W. Battery ⚓ Fl R 2s; 50°21'·52N 04°10'·21W.

The Bridge Channel

No 1, ⚓ QG 4m; 50°21'·03N 04°09'·53W. No 2, ⚓ QR 4m. No 3, ⚓ Fl (3) G 10s 4m. No 4, ⚓ Fl (4) R 10s 4m; 50°21'·09N 04°09'·63W.

Mount Wise, Dir ⚹ 343°: WRG 7m, W13M, R/G5M; H24. 331°-FG-338°-Al WG-342° (W phase increasing with brg)-FW-344°-Al WR-348° (R phase increasing with bearing)-FR-351°. In fog, 341·5°-FW-344·5°; 50°21'·96N 04°10'·33W.

Ocean Court Dir Q WRG 15m, W11M, R/G3M; 010°-G-080°-W-090°-R-100°; 50°21'·85N 04°10'·11W.

PLYMOUTH TO START POINT

RIVER YEALM Sand bar ⚓ Fl R 5s; 50°18'·59N 04°04'·12W.

SALCOMBE

Sandhill Pt Dir ⚹ 000°: Fl WRG 2s 27m W10M, R/G7M; 182·5°-G-357·5°-W-002·5°-R-182·5°; R/W ◊ on W mast, rear daymark; 50°13'·77N 03°46'·67W. Front daymark, Pound Stone R/W ⚓.

Bass Rk ⚓ Fl R 5s; 50°13'·47N 03°46'·71W.

Wolf Rk ⚓ Fl G 5s; 50°13'·53N 03°46'·58W.

Blackstone Rk ⚓; 50°13'·61N 03°46'·51W.

Ldg lts 042·5°, front Fl 1·8s, rear Fl 4·8s 5/45m 8M. Front 50°14'·53N 03°45'·31W.

Start Pt ☆ Fl (3) 10s 62m **25M**; 184°-068°. Same twr: FR 55m 9M; 210°-255° over Skerries Bank; *Horn 60s;* 50°13'·34N 03°38'·54W.

START POINT TO PORTLAND BILL

DARTMOUTH

Kingswear Dir ⚹ 328°: Iso WRG 3s 9m 8M; 318°-G-325°-W-331°-R-340°; W ○ twr; 50°20'·82N 03°34'·09W.

Mewstone ⚓ VQ (6) + L Fl 10s; 50°19'·92N 03°31'·89W.

West Rock ⚓ Q (6) + L Fl 15s; 50°19'·86N 03°32'·47W.

Homestone ⚓ QR; 50°19'·61N 03°33'·55W.

Castle Ledge ⚓ Fl G 5s; 50°19'·99N 03°33'·11W.

Checkstone ⚓ Fl (2) R 5s; 50°20'·45N 03°33'·81W.

Dir ⚓ 104·5°: FW 5m 9M; vis 102°-107°; 50°20'·65N 03°33'·80W.

BRIXHAM

Berry Head ☆ Fl (2) 15s 58m **19M**; vis 100°-023°; W twr; 50°23'·98N 03°29'·01W. R lts on radio mast 5·7M NW, inland of Paignton.

Victoria bkwtr ⚓ Oc R 15s 9m 6M; W twr; 50°24'·33N 03°30'·78W.

Fairway Dir ⚓ 159°: Iso WRG 5s 4m 6M; 145°-G-157°-W-161°-R-173°; 50°23'·83N 03°30'·57W.

No. 1 ▲ Fl G; 50°24'·30N 03°30'·89W.

No. 2 ▱ Fl R; 50°24'·32N 03°30'·83W.

PAIGNTON and TORQUAY

▲ QG (May-Sep); 50°27'·42N 03°31'·80W, 85m off Haldon Pier.

Haldon Pier (E) ⚓ QG 9m 6M; 50°27'·43N 03°31'·73W.

Princess Pier (W) ⚓ QR 9m 6M; 50°27'·46N 03°31'·73W.

TEIGNMOUTH

Outfall ▱ Fl Y 5s; 50°31'·97N 03°27'·77W, 288°/1·3M to hbr ent.

Bar ▲ Fl G 2s; 50°32'·44N 03°29'·25W.

Trng wall, middle ⊥ Oc R 6s 4m 3M; 50°32'·33N 03°29'·93W.

The Point ⊥ Oc G 6s 3M & FG (vert); 50°32'·42N 03°30'·05W.

RIVER EXE to SIDMOUTH and AXMOUTH

Exe ⊛ Mo(A) 10s; 50°35'·92N 03°23'·75W.

No. 1 ▲ 50°36'·07N 03°23'·78W.

No. 2 ▱ 50°36'·03N 03°23'·91W.

Ldg lts 305°. Front, Iso 2s 6m 7M, 50°36'·99N 03°25'·34W. Rear, Q 12m 7M, 57m from front. No. 10 ▱ Fl R 3s; 50°36'·73N 03°24'·77W.

No. 12 Warren Pt ▱ 50°36'·91N 03°25'·41W.

Sidmouth ⚓ Fl R 5s 5m 2M; 50°40'·48'N 03°14'·43W.

Axmouth jetty ⚓ Fl G 4s 7m 2M; 50°42'·12N 03°03'·29W.

LYME REGIS

Outfall ↉ Q (6) + L Fl 15s; 50°43'·17N 02°55'·66W.

Ldg lts 284°: Front, Victoria Pier ⚓ Oc WR 8s 6m, W9M,

R7M; 284°-R-104°-W-284°; Bu col; 50°43'·19N 02°56'·17W. Rear, FG 8m 9M.

WEST BAY (BRIDPORT)

W pier root, Dir ⚓ 336°: F WRG 5m 4M; 165°-G-331°-W-341°-R-165°; 50°42'·62N 02°45'·89W.

W pier outer limit ⚓ Iso R 2s 5m 4M; 50°42'·51N 02°45'·83W.

E pier outer limit ⚓ Iso G 2s 5m 4M; 50°42'·53N 02°45'·80W.

PORTLAND BILL TO ANVIL POINT

Portland Bill lt ho ⚓ Fl (4) 20s 43m **25M**. vis 221°-244° (gradual change from 1 Fl to 4 Fl); 244°-117° (shows 4 Fl); 117°-141° (gradual change from 4 Fl to 1 Fl). W ○ twr; Dia 30s; 50°30'·85N 02°27'·39W. Same twr, FR 19m 13M; 271°-291° over Shambles.

W Shambles ↄ Q (9) 15s; Bell; 50°29'·78N 02°24'·41W.

E Shambles ↄ Q (3) 10s; Bell; 50°30'·78N 02°20'·08W.

PORTLAND HARBOUR

Outer Bkwtr Fort Head (N end) ⚓ QR 14m 5M; 013°-268°; 50°35'·11N 02°24'·87W.

NE Bkwtr (A Hd) ⚓ Fl 2·5s 22m 10M; 50°35'·16N 02°25'·07W.

NE Bkwtr (B Hd) ⚓ Oc R 15s 11m 5M; 50°35'·65N 02°25'·88W.

N Arm (C Hd) ⚓ Oc G 10s 11m 5M; 50°35'·78N 02°25'·95W.

WEYMOUTH

Ldg lts 239·6°: both FR 5/7m 7M; Front 50°36'·46N 02°26'·87W, S Pier hd ⚓ Q 10m 9M; 50°36'·58N 02°26'·49W. IPTS 190m SW.

LULWORTH RANGE TO ANVIL POINT

Targets off St Alban's Hd: DZ 'A' ▱, Fl Y 2s, 50°33'·34N 02°06'·52W.

DZ 'B' ▱, Fl Y 10s, 50°32'·11N 02°05'·92W.

DZ 'C' ▱, Fl Y 5s, 50°32'·76N 02°04'·56W.

Anvil Pt ⚓ Fl 10s 45m 9M; vis 237°-076° (H24); W ○ twr and dwelling; 50°35'·51N 01°57'·60W. Measured mile close west.

		1	2	3	4	5	6	7	8	9	10	11	12	13	14	15	16	17
1	Longships	**1**																
2	Scilly (Crow Rock)	22	**2**															
3	Penzance	15	35	**3**														
4	Lizard Point	23	42	16	**4**													
5	Falmouth	39	60	32	16	**5**												
6	Mevagissey	52	69	46	28	17	**6**											
7	Fowey	57	76	49	34	22	7	**7**										
8	Looe	63	80	57	39	29	16	11	**8**									
9	Plymouth (bkwtr)	70	92	64	49	39	25	22	11	**9**								
10	River Yealm (ent)	72	89	66	49	39	28	23	16	4	**10**							
11	Salcombe	81	102	74	59	50	40	36	29	22	17	**11**						
12	Start Point	86	103	80	63	55	45	40	33	24	22	7	**12**					
13	Dartmouth	95	116	88	72	63	54	48	42	35	31	14	9	**13**				
14	Torbay	101	118	96	78	70	62	55	50	39	38	24	15	11	**14**			
15	Exmouth	113	131	107	90	82	73	67	61	51	49	33	27	24	12	**15**		
16	Lyme Regis	126	144	120	104	96	86	81	74	63	62	48	41	35	30	21	**16**	
17	Portland Bill	135	151	128	112	104	93	89	81	73	70	55	49	45	42	36	22	**17**

DISTANCE TABLES

Approx distances in nautical miles are by the most direct route allowing for dangers and TSS.

SWANAGE TO ISLE OF WIGHT

SWANAGE
Pier Hd ☆ 2 FR (vert) 6m 3M; 50°36'·56N 01°56'·95W.
Peveril Ledge ⚓ QR; 50°36'·41N 01°56'·10W.

POOLE BAR and SWASH CHANNEL
Poole Bar (No. 1) ▲ QG; *Bell*; 50°39·29N 01°55'·14W.
(Historic wreck) ⚓ Fl Y 5s; 50°39'·70N 01°54'·86W.
South Hook (No. 11) ⚓ 50°39'·70N 01°55'·20W.
No. 2 ⚓ Fl R 2s; 50°39'·23N 01°55'·24W.
No. 3 ▲ Fl G 3s; 50°39'·76N 01°55'·49W.
No. 4 ⚓ Fl R 2s; 50°39'·72N 01°55'·60W.
Training Bank ⚓ 2 FR (vert); 50°39'·82N 01°55'·86W.
No. 6 ⚓ Fl R 4s; 50°40'·14N 01°55'·91W.
No. 5 ▲Fl G 5s; 50°40'·19N 01°55'·81W.
Hook Sands (No. 7) ▲ Fl G 3s; 50°40'·50N 01°56'·16W.
Channel (No. 8) ⚓ Fl R 2s; 50°40'·45N 01°56'·27W.
No. 10 ⚓ Fl R 4s; 50°40'·84N 01°56'·86W.
Swash (No. 9) ⚓ Q (9) 15s; 50°40'·88N 01°56'·70W.

EAST LOOE CHANNEL
East Hook ⚓ 50°40'·58N 01°55'·23W.
East Looe 1 ▲ Fl G 5s; 50°41'·09N 01°55'·82W.
East Looe 2 ⚓ Fl R 4s; 50°41'·07N 01°55'·83W.
East Looe 3 (Limit 10 knots) ▲ Fl G 3s; 50°41'·11N 01°56'·16W.
East Looe 4 (Limit 10 knots) ⚓ Fl R 2s; 50°41'·09N 01°56'·17W.
North Hook ⚓ Fl (2) R 5s; 50°41'·01N 01°56'·44W.

BROWNSEA ROADS
No. 12 ⚓ Q R; 50°40'·94N 01°57'·17W.
No.14 ⚓ Fl R 2s; 50°41'·03N 01°57'·32W.
N Haven ⚓ Q (9) 15s 5m; 50°41'·15N 01°57'·17W.
Brownsea ⚓ Fl (2) 3s 10s; 50°41'·14N 01°57'·39W.
Brownsea Island Dir lt 299°F WRG & 2FR(vert); 296·5°-G-297·8°-AltWG-298·8°-W-299·2°-AltWR-300·2°-R-301·5°; 50°41'·16N 01°57'·67W (only shown for commercial vessels); 2FR(vert); 301·5°-296·5° (shown H24).

MIDDLE SHIP CHANNEL
Bell (No. 15) ⚓ Q (6) + L Fl 15s; 50°41'·36N 01°57'·12W.
No. 16 ⚓ VQ R; 50°41'·43N 01°57'·25W.
No. 17 ▲ Fl G 3s; 50°41'·68N 01°57'·02W.
Aunt Betty (No. 22) ⚓ Q (3)10s; 50°41'·97N 01°57'·25W.
Diver (No. 25) ⚓ Q (9) 15s; 50°42'·29N 01°58'·32W.

NORTH CHANNEL
Salterns Marina Outer Bkwtr Hd ☆ 2 FR (vert) 2M; Tfc sigs; 50°42'·23N 01°57'·10W.
Parkstone YC platform ☆ Q 8m 1M; hut on dolphin; 50°42'·37N 01°58'·08W.
Stakes (No. 29) ⚓ Q (6) + L Fl 15s; 50°42'·43N 01°59'·00W.

POOLE BAY
Bournemouth Rocks ⚓ 50°42'·32N 01°53'·40W.
Lightwave ⚓ 50°41'·50N 01°51'·68W.
Christchurch Ledge ⚓ 50°41'·57N 01°41'·55W (Apr-Oct).
⚓ (x2) Fl (5) Y 20s; 50°37'·98N 01°43'·02W; (265° 2.6M from Needles F'wy)

WESTERN APPROACHES TO THE SOLENT

NEEDLES CHANNEL
Needles Fairway ⚓ L Fl 10s; *Whis*; 50°38'·24N 01°38'·98W.
SW Shingles ⚓Fl R 2·5s; 50°39'·29N 01°37'·52W.
Bridge ⚓ VQ (9) 10s; ***Racon (T) 10M***; 50°39'·63N 01°36'·88W.

Needles 50°39'·73N 01°35'·50W; Oc (2) WRG 20s 24m **W17M**, R14M, R13M G14M; ○ Twr, R band and lantern; vis: shore-R-300°-W-083°-R (unintens)-212°-W-217°-G-224° (H24). *Horn (2) 30s.*

Shingles Elbow ⚓ Fl (2) R 5s; 50°40'·37N 01°36'·05W.
Mid Shingles ⚓ Fl (3) R 10s; 50°41'·21N 01°34'·66W.
Warden ▲ Fl G 2·5s; *Bell*; 50°41'·48N 01°33'·55W.
NE Shingles ⚓ Q (3) 10s; 50°41'·96N 01°33'·41W.

Hurst Point ☆ 50°42'·48N 01°33'·03W; FL (4) WR 15s 23m W13M, R11M; W ○ Twr; vis:080°-W(unintens)-104°, 234°-W-244°-R-250°-W-053°. Same structure, Iso WRG 4s 19m **W21M, R18M, G17M**; vis: 038·8°-G-040·8°-W-041·8°-R- 043·8°; By day W7M, R5M, G5M.

NORTH CHANNEL
North Head ▲ Fl (3) G 10s; 50°42'·69N 01°35'·52W.

THE WESTERN SOLENT

Note: Numerous yellow yacht racing buoys are laid throughout the Solent (seasonal, Mar-Dec). Most, but not all, are lit Fl Y 4s.

SOLENT MARKS
Sconce ⚓ Q; *Bell*; 50°42'·53N 01°31'·43W.
Black Rock ▲ Fl G 5s; 50°42'·57N 01°30'·59W.
Lymington Bank ⚓ Fl (2) R 5s; *Bell*; 50°43'·10N 01°30'·85W.
Solent Bank ⚓ Fl (3) R 10s; 50°44'·23N 01°27'·37W.
Hamstead Ledge ▲ Fl (2) G 5s; 50°43'·87N 01°26'18W.
Newtown River ⚓ Q (9) 15s; 50°43'·75N 01°24'·96W.
W Lepe ⚓ Fl R 5s; 50°45'·24N 01°24'·09W.
Salt Mead ▲ Fl (3) G 10s; 50°44'·51N 01°23'·04W.
Gurnard Ledge ▲ Fl (4) G 15s; 50°45'·51N 01°20'·59W.
E Lepe ⚓ Fl (2) R 5s; *Bell*; 50°45'·93N 01°21'·07W.
Lepe Spit ⚓ Q (6) + L Fl 15s; 50°46'·78N 01°20'·64W.
Gurnard ⚓ Q; 50°46'·22N 01°18'·84W.

YARMOUTH
East Fairway ⚓ Fl R 2s. 50°42'·62N 01°29'·95W.
Poole Belle ⚓ Fl Y 5s; 50°42'·54N 01°30'·17W.
Pier Head, centre, ☆ 2 FR (vert) 2M; G col. High intensity FW (occas); 50°42'·51N 01°29'·97W.
Ldg Lts 187·6° Front FG 5m 2M; 50°42'·36N 01°30'·06 W. Rear, 63m from front, FG 9m 2M; both W ◇.

LYMINGTON
Jack in the Basket ⚓ Fl R 2s 9m; 50°44'·27N 01°30'·57W.
Ldg Lts 319·5°, Or posts. Front, FR 12m 8M; 50°45'·19N 01°31'·65W. vis: 309·5°-329·5°. Rear, FR 17m 8M.
Cross Boom No. 2 ⚓ Fl R 2s 4m 3M; R □ on pile; 50°44'·36N 01°30'·58W.
No. 1 ⚓ Fl G 2s 2m 3M; G △ on pile; 50°44'·41N 01°30'·48W.

Lymington Yacht Haven ldg lts 244°. Front FY 4m; R △; 50°45'·09N 01°31'·53W. Rear, 22m from front, FY 6m; R ▽.

BEAULIEU RIVER

Millennium Dir lt 334°. ⚡ Oc WRG 4s 13m W4M, R3M, G3M; vis: 318°-G-330°-W-337°-R-348°; 50°47'·12N 01°21'·90W.
Beaulieu Spit, E end ⌶ Fl R 5s 3M; R dolphin, W band; 50°46'·85N 01°21'·76W.
No. 1 ⌶ 50°46'·91N 01°21'·70W.
No 2 ⌶ 50°46'·92N 01°21'·78W.

COWES

South Bramble ▲ Fl G 2·5s; 50°46'·98N 01°17'·72W.
Prince Consort ⌀ VQ; 50°46'·42N 01°17'·55W.
Prince Consort Shoal ⬙ Fl (4) Y 10s; 50°46'·29N 01°17'·71W.
No. 1 ▲ Fl G 3s; 50°46'·07N 01°18'·03W.
No. 2 ◔ QR; 50°46'·07N 01°17'·87W.
E. Cowes Bkwtr Hd ⚡ Fl R 3s 3M; 50°45'·88N 01°17'·52W.

CENTRAL SOLENT AND SOUTHAMPTON WATER

Note: Numerous yellow yacht racing buoys are laid throughout the Solent (seasonal, Mar-Dec). Most, but not all, are lit Fl Y 4s.

SOLENT MARKS

Lepe Spit ⌀ Q (6) + L Fl 15s; 50°46'·78N 01°20'·64W.
NE Gurnard ◔Fl (3) R 10s; 50°47'·06N 01°19'·42W.
W Bramble ⌀ VQ (9) 10s; *Bell*; **Racon (T) 3M**; 50°47'·20N 01°18'·65W.
Thorn Knoll ▲Fl G 5s; 50°47'·50N 01°18'·44W.
Bourne Gap ◔ Fl R 3s; 50°47'·83N 01°18'·34W.
West Knoll ◔ Fl Y 2·5s; 50°47'·43N 01°17'·84W.
North Thorn ▲ QG; 50°47'·91N 01°17'·84W.
Stanswood Outfall ⌶ Iso R 10s 6m 5M; 4 FR Lts; 50°48'·26N 01°18'·82W.

CALSHOT REACH

East Knoll ▲ 50°47'·96N 01°16'·83W.
CALSHOT SPIT ⬗ Fl 5s 5m 10M; R hull, Lt Twr amidships; *Horn (2) 60s*; 50°48'·35N 01°17'·64W.
Calshot ⌀ VQ; *Bell*; 50°48'·44N 01°17'·03W.
Castle Point ◔ IQ R 10s; 50°48'·71N 01°17'·67W.
Reach ▲ Fl (3) G 10s; 50°49'·05N 01°17'·65W .
Black Jack ◔ Fl (2) R 4s; 50°49'·13N 01°18'·09W.
Hook ⌀ QG; *Horn (1) 15s*; 50°49'·52N 01°18'·30W.
Coronation ▲ Fl Y 5s; 50°49'·55N 01°17'·62W.
Bald Head ▲ Fl G 2·5s; 50°49'·80N 01°18'·06W.

RIVER HAMBLE

Hamble Pt ⌀ Q (6) + L Fl 15s; 50°50'·15N 01°18'·66W.
Hamble Common Dir lt 351·7°, Oc (2) WRG 12s 5m W4M; R4M;   G4M;   vis: 348·7°-G-350·7°-W-352·7°-R-354·7°; 50°51'·00N 01°18'·84W.
Sailing Club Dir lt 028·9° ⚡ Iso WRG 6s 5m W4M, R4M, G4M: vis: 025·9°-G-027·9°-W-029·9°-031·9°; 50°51'·10N 01°18'·34W.

SOUTHAMPTON WATER

Fawley Marine Terminal. SE end ⚡ 2 FR (vert) 9m 10M; 50°50'·06N 01°19'·42W.
Greenland ▲ Iso G 2s; 50°51'·11N 01°20'·38W.
Cadland ◔ Fl R 3s; 50°51'·02N 01°20'·54W.

Lains Lake ◔ Fl (2) R 4s; 50°51'·59N 01°21'·65W.
Hound ▲ Fl (3) G 10s; 50°51'·68N 01°21'·52W.
Netley ▲ Fl G 3s; 50°52'·03N 01°21'·81W.
Deans Elbow ◔ Oc R 4s; 50°52'·16N 01°22'·76W.
NW Netley ▲ Fl G 7s; 50°52'·31N 01°22'·73W.
Weston Shelf ▲ Fl (3) G 15s; 50°52'·71N 01°23'·26W.

HYTHE

Hythe Pier Hd ⚡ 2 FR (vert) 12m 5M; 50°52'·49N 01°23'·61W.
Hythe Marina Ent ⌀ Q (3) 10s; 50°52'·63N 01°23'·88W.
Hythe Knock ◔ Fl R 3s; 50°52'·83N 01°23'·81W.

SOUTHAMPTON and RIVER ITCHEN

Swinging Ground No. 1 ▲ Oc G 4s; 50°53'·00N 01°23'·44W.
E side. No. 1 ⌶ QG; 50°53'·15N 01°23'·40W.
No. 2 ⌶ Fl G 5s 2M; 50°53'·29N 01°23'·38W.
No. 3 ⌶ Fl G 7s; 50°53'·48N 01°23'·28W.
No. 4 ⌶ QG 4m 2M; 50°53'·62N 01°23'·16W.

SOUTHAMPTON and RIVER TEST

Queen Elizabeth II Terminal, S end ⚡ 4 FG (vert) 16m 3M; 50°53'·00N 01°23'·71W.
Gymp ◔ QR; 50°53'·17N 01°24'·30W.
Town Quay Ldg Lts 329°, both F 12/22m 3/2M.
Gymp Elbow ◔ Oc R 4s; 50°53'·50N 01°24'·68W.
Dibden Bay ⌀ Q; 50°53'·70N 01°24'·92W.

THE EASTERN SOLENT

Note: Numerous yellow yacht racing buoys are laid throughout the Solent (seasonal, Mar-Dec). Most, but not all, are lit Fl Y 4s.

SOLENT MARKS

West Ryde Middle ⌀ Q (9) 15s; 50°46'·48N 01°15'·79W.
Norris ◔ Fl (3) R 10s; 50°45'·97N 01°15'·51W.
North Ryde Middle ◔ Fl (4) R 20s; 50°46'·61N 01°14'·31W.
South Ryde Middle ▲ Fl G 5s; 50°46'·13N 01°14'·16W.
Peel Bank ◔ Fl (2) R 5s; 50°45'·49N 01°13'·35W.
SE Ryde Middle ⌀ VQ (6)+L Fl 10s; 50°45'·93N 01°12'·10W.
NE Ryde Middle ◔ Fl (2) R 10s; 50°46'·21N 01°11'·88W.
Mother Bank ◔ Fl R 3s; 50°45'·49N 01°11'·21W.
Browndown ▲ Fl G 15s; 50°46'·57N 01°10'·95W.
Fort Gilkicker ⚡ Oc G 10s 7M; 50°46'·43N 01°08'·47W.
N Sturbridge ⌀ VQ; 50°45'·33N 01°08'·23W.
Ryde Sands ⌶ Fl R 10s; 50°44'·54N 01°07'·19W.
Ryde Sands ⌶ L Fl R 12s; 50°44'·16N 01°05'·99W.
No Man's Land Fort; 50°44'·40N 01°05'·70W.
No Man's ◔ Iso R 2s; 50°44'·44N 01°05'·60W.
Horse Sand Fort ⚡ Iso G 2s 21m 8M; 50°45'·01N 01°04'·34W.
Saddle ▲ VQ (3) G 10s; 50°45'·20N 01°04'·98W.

NORTH CHANNEL and HILLHEAD

Calshot ⌀ VQ; *Bell (1) 30s*; 50°48'·44N 01°17'·03W.
Hillhead ◔ Fl R 2·5s; 50°48'·07N 01°16'·00W.
E Bramble ⌀ VQ (3) 5s; 50°47'·23N 01°13'·64W.

WOOTTON CREEK

Wootton Beacon ⌀ Q 1M; (NB); 50°44'·53N 01°12'·13W.
Dir lt. Oc WRG 10s vis: 220·8°-G-224·3°-W-225·8°-R-230·8°; 50°44'·03N 01°12'·86W.

RYDE

Ryde Pier ☆, NW corner, N and E corner marked by 2 FR (vert). In fog FY from N corner, vis: 045°-165°, 200°-320°; 50°44'·34N 01°09'·72W.

Leisure Hbr E side ☆ 2 FR (vert) 7m 1M. FY 6m shown when depth of water in Hbr greater than 1m; 2 FY 6m when depth exceeds 1·5m; 50°43'·99N 01°09'·29W.

PORTSMOUTH APPROACHES

Horse Sand ▲ Fl G 2·5s; 50°45'·53N 01°05'·27W.

Outer Spit ⚏ Q (6) + L Fl 15s; 50°45'·58N 01°05'·50W.

Mary Rose ⚏ Fl Y 5s; 50°45'·80N 01°06'·20W.

Boyne ▲ Fl G 5s; 50°46'·15N 01°05'·26W.

Spit Refuge ⚏ Fl R 5s; 50°46'·15N 01°05'·46W.

Spit Sand Fort ☆ Fl R 5s; 18m 7M. 50°46'·24N 01°05'·94W.

Castle (NB)▲ Fl (2) G 6s; 50°46'·45N 01°05'·38W.

Southsea Castle N corner ☆ Iso 2s 16m 11M, W stone Twr, B band; vis: 337°-071°; 50°46'·69N 01°05'·33W.

Southsea Castle Dir lt 001·5° WRG 11m W13M, R5M, G5M; same structure; vis: 351·5°-FG-357·5°-Al WG (W phase incr with brg), 000°-FW-003°-AlWR(R phase incr with brg), 005·5°-FR-011·5°; 50°46'·69N 01°05'·33W.

Ridge ⚏ Fl (2) R 6s; 50°46'·44N 01°05'·65W.

No. 1 Bar (NB) ▲ Fl (3) G 10s; 50°46'·77N 01°05'·81W.

No. 2 ⚏ Fl (3) R 10s; 50°46'·69N 01°05'·97W.

No. 3 ▲ QG; 50°47'·08N 01°06'·24W.

No. 4 ⚏ QR; 50°47'·01N 01°06'·36W.

BC Outer ⚏ Oc R 15s; 50°47'·32N 01°06'·68W.

PORTSMOUTH HARBOUR

Fort Blockhouse ☆ Dir lt 320°; WRG 6m W13M, R5M, G5M; vis: 310°- Oc G-316°-Al WG(W phase incr with brg), 318·5°-Oc-321·5°- Al WR (R phase incr with brg), 324°-Oc R-330°. 2 FR (vert) 20m E; 50°47'·37N 01°06'·74W.

Ballast ⚏ Fl R 2·5s; 50°47'·62N 01°06'·83W.

Hbr Ent Dir lt (NB) (Fuel Jetty) ☆ WRG 2m 1M; vis: 322·5°-Iso G 2s -330°-Al WG-332·5°-Iso 2s(main chan) -335°-Al WR-337·5°-Iso R 2s-345° (Small Boat Chan) H24; 50°47'·85 N01°06'·98W.

EASTERN APPROACHES to THE SOLENT

Outer Nab 1 ⚏ VQ (9) 10s; 50°38'·18N 00°56'·88W.

Outer Nab 2 ⚏ VQ (3) 5s; 50°38'·43N 00°57'·70W.

Nab Tower ☆ 50°40'·08N 00°57'·15W; Fl 10s 27m **16M**, *Horn (2) 30s; Racon (T) 10M.*

N 2 ⚏ Fl Y 2·5s. 6M; 50°41'·03N 00°56'·74W.

N 1 ⚏ Fl Y (4)10s; 50°41'·26N 00°56'·52W.

N 4 ⚏ Fl Y 7·5s; 50°41'·50N 00°57'·02W.

N 3 ⚏ Fl (3) Y 15s; 50°41'·63N 00°56'·74W.

N 5 ⚏ Fl Y 5s; 50°41'·99N 00°56'·97W.

N 7 ⚏ Fl Y 2·5s; 50°42'·35N 00°57'·20W.

New Grounds ⚏ VQ (3) 5s; 50°41'·84N 00°58'·49W.

Nab End ⚏ Fl R 5s; *Whis;* 50°42'·63N 00°59'·49W.

Dean Tail ▲ Fl G 5s; 50°42'·99N 00°59'·17W.

Dean Tail S ⚏ Q (6) + L Fl 10s; 50°43'·04N 00°59'·57W.

Dean Tail N ⚏ Q; 50°43'·13N 00°59'·57W.

Horse Tail ▲ Fl (2) G 10s; 50°43'·23N 01°00'·23W.

Nab East ⚏ Fl (2) R 10s; 50°42'·86N 01°00'·80W.

Dean Elbow ▲ Fl (3) G 15s; 50°43'·69N 01°01'·88W.

St Helens ⚏ Fl (3) R 15s; 50°43'·36N 01°02'·41W.

Horse Elbow ▲QG; 50°44'·26N 01°03'·88W.

Cambrian Wreck ⚏ 50°44'·43N 01°03'·43W.

Warner ⚏ QR; *Whis;* 50°43'·87N 01°03'·99W.

BEMBRIDGE

St Helen's Fort ☆ (IOW) Fl (3) 10s 16m 8M; large ○ stone structure; 50°42'·30N 01°05'·05W.

Bembridge Tide Gauge ⚏ Fl Y 2s 1M; 50°42'·46N 01°05'·02W.

SOUTH EAST COAST of the ISLE of WIGHT

St Catherine's Point ☆ 50°34'·54N 01°17'·87W; Fl 5s 41m **25M**; vis: 257°-117°; FR 35m 13M (same Twr) vis: 099°-116°.

Ventnor Haven W Bwtr ☆ 2 FR (vert) 3M; 50°35'·50N 01°12'·30W.

Sandown Pier Hd ☆ 2 FR (vert) 7m 2M; 50°39'·05N 01°09'·18W.

W Princessa ⚏ Q (9) 15s; 50°40'·16N 01°03'·65W.

Bembridge Ledge ⚏ Q (3) 10s; 50°41'·15N 01°02'·81W

1	Portland Bill	**1**																
2	Weymouth	8	**2**															
3	Swanage	22	22	**3**														
4	Poole Hbr ent	28	26	6	**4**													
5	Needles Lt Ho	35	34	14	14	**5**												
6	Lymington	42	40	20	24	6	**6**											
7	Yarmouth (IOW)	40	39	18	22	4	2	**7**										
8	Beaulieu River ent	46	45	25	29	11	7	7	**8**									
9	Cowes	49	46	28	27	14	10	9	2	**9**								
10	Southampton	55	54	34	34	20	16	16	9	9	**10**							
11	R. Hamble (ent)	53	51	32	34	18	12	13	6	6	5	**11**						
12	Portsmouth	58	57	37	35	23	19	19	12	10	18	13	**12**					
13	Langstone Hbr	61	59	39	39	25	21	21	14	12	21	18	5	**13**				
14	Chichester Bar	63	62	42	42	28	23	24	17	15	23	18	8	5	**14**			
15	Bembridge	59	58	38	39	24	18	19	13	10	18	15	5	6	8	**15**		
16	Nab Tower	64	63	43	44	29	23	24	18	15	24	19	10	7	6	6	**16**	
17	St Catherine's Pt	45	44	25	25	12	19	21	27	15	36	29	20	20	19	17	15	**17**
18	Littlehampton	79	79	60	61	46	44	45	38	36	45	42	31	28	25	28	22	35	**18**

DISTANCE TABLES

Approx distances in nautical miles are by the most direct route allowing for dangers and TSS.

NAVIGATION

LANGSTONE and APPROACHES

Eastney Pt Fraser Trials Range ☆ FR, Oc (2) Y 10s, and FY Lts (occas) when firing taking place; 50°47'·19N 01°02'·22W.

Winner ⌁; 50°45'·10N 01°00'·10W.

Roway Wk ⌁ Fl (2) 5s; 50°46'·11N 01°02'·28W.

Langstone Fairway ⌁ L Fl 10s; 50°46'·32N 01°01'·36W.

Eastney Pt Outfall ☆ QR 2m 2M; 50°47'·23N 01°01'·68W.

East Milton ⌁ Fl (4) R 10s; 50°48'·16N 01°01'·76W.

NW Sinah ▲ Fl G 5s; 50°48'·14N 01°01'·58W.

CHICHESTER ENTRANCE

West Pole (tripod) ⌁ Fl R 5s 14m 7M; 50°45'·45N 00°56'·59W.

Bar ⌁ Fl(2) R 10s 10m 4M; 50°46'·02N 00°56'·38W.

Eastoke ⌁ QR; 50°46'·68N 00°56'·11W.

West Winner ⌁ QG; Tide gauge. 50°46'·88N 00°55'·98W.

EMSWORTH CHANNEL

Fishery ⌁ Q (6) + L Fl 15s; 50°47'·38N 00°56'·07W.

NW Pilsey ▲ Fl G 5s; 50°47'·50N 00°56'·20W.

Verner ⌁ Fl R 10s; 50°48'·20N 00°56'·63W.

Marker Pt ⌁ Fl (2) G 10s 8m; 50°48'·91N 00°56'·72W.

Emsworth ⌁ Q (6) + L Fl 15s; tide gauge; 50°49'·66N 00°56'·76W.

THORNEY CHANNEL

Camber ⌁ Q (6) + L Fl 15s; 50°47'·87N 00°54'·06W.

Pilsey ⌁ Fl (2) R 10s ; 50°47'·98N 00°54'·24W.

Thorney ⌁ Fl G 5s; 50°48'·20N 00°54'·28W.

CHICHESTER CHANNEL

NW Winner ▲ Fl G 10s; 50°47'·19N 00°55'·92W.

N Winner ⌁ Fl (2) G 10s; 50°47'·31N 00°55'·83W.

Mid Winner ▲ Fl (3) G 10s; 50°47'·38N 00°55'·69W.

Stocker ⌁ Fl (3) R 10s; 50°47'·45N 00°55'·52W.

Copyhold ⌁ Fl (4) R 10s; 50°47'·50N 00°54'·93W.

East Head Spit ▲ Fl (4) G 10s; 50°47'·45N 00°54'·82W.

Snowhill ▲ Fl G 5s; 50°47'·52N 00°54'·34W.

Sandhead ⌁ Fl R 10s; 50°47'·67N 00°54'·25W.

Chalkdock ⌁ Fl (2) 10s; 50°48'·49N 00°53'·30W.

AREA 3 *South East England – Selsey Bill to North Foreland*

SELECTED LIGHTS, BUOYS & WAYPOINTS

Positions are referenced to WGS84

OWERS TO BEACHY HEAD

SELSEY BILL and THE OWERS

S Pullar ⌁ VQ (6) + L Fl 10s; 50°38'·84N 00°49'·29W.

Pullar ⌁ Q (9) 15s; 50°40'·47N 00°50'·09W.

Boulder ▲ Fl G 2·5s; 50°41'·56N 00°49'·09W.

Street ⌁ QR; 50°41'·69N 00°48'·89W.

Owers ⌁ Q (6) + L Fl 15s; *Bell*; *Racon (O) 10M*; 50°38'·59N 00°41'·09W.

E Borough Hd ⌁ Q (3) 10s *Bell*; 50°41'·54N 00°39'·09W.

LITTLEHAMPTON

West Pier Hd ⌁ QR 7m 6M; 50°47'·88N 00°32'·46W.

Training Wall Hd ⌁ QG 10m 2M; 50°47'·87N 00°32'·38W.

Ldg Lts 346°. Front, E Pier Hd ☆ FG 6m 7M; B col. Rear, 64m from front, Oc WY 7·5s 9m10M; W twr; vis: 290°-W-356°-Y-042°; 50°48'·09N 00°32'·51W.

Outfall ⌁ Fl Y 5s; 50°46'·27N 00°30'·53W.

Littlehampton ☆ Fl (5) Y 20s 9m 5M; 50°46'·19N 00°29'·54W.

WORTHING and SHOREHAM

Outfall ⌁ Fl R 2·5s 3m; 50°48'·38N 00°20'·34W.

Express ⌁ Fl Y 5s; (Apr-Oct); 50°47'·28N 00°17'·09W.

W Bkwtr Head ☆ Fl R 5s 7m 7M; 50°49'·49N 00°14'·89W.

Ldg Lts 355°. Middle Pier Front, Oc 5s 8m 10M; W watch-house, R base; tidal Lts, tfc sigs; *Horn 20s*. **Rear**, 192m from front, Fl 10s 13m **15M**; Gy twr vis: 283°-103°; 50°49'·75N 00°14'·88W.

Outfall ⌁ 50°49'·47N 00°14'·39W.

Shoreham Outfall ⌁ Q (6) + L Fl 15s; 50°47'·88N 00°13'·72W.

BRIGHTON and BRIGHTON MARINA

Black Rk Ledge ⌁ Fl Y 4s; 50°48'·07N 00°06'·46W.

W Bkwtr Hd ☆ QR 10m 7M; W ○ structure, R bands;

Horn (2) 30s; 50°48'·50N 00°06'·38W.

E Bkwtr Hd ☆ QG 8m 7M and Fl (4) WR 20s 16m W10M, R8M; W pillar, G bands; vis: 260°-R-295°-W-100°; 50°48'·47N 00°06'·37W.

Saltdean Outfall ⌁ Fl Y 5s; 50°46'·72N 00°02'·13W.

NEWHAVEN

Bkwtr Head ☆ Oc (2) 10s 17m 12M; 50°46'·56N 00°03'·50E.

E Pier Hd ☆ Iso G 10s 12m 6M; W twr; 50°46'·81N 00°03'·59E.

OFFSHORE MARKS

CS 1 ⌁ Fl Y 2·5s; *Whis*; 50°33'·69N 00°03'·92W.

GREENWICH ⌁ 50°24'·54N 00°00'·10E; Fl 5s 12m **15M**; Riding light FW; R hull; *Racon (M) 10M*; *Horn 30s* .

CS 2 ⌁ Fl Y 5s; 50°39'·14N 00°32'·60E.

CS 3 ⌁ Fl Y 10s; 50°52'·04N 01°02'·18E.

BEACHY HEAD TO DUNGENESS

Beachy Head ☆ 50°44'·03N 00°14'·49E; Fl (2) 20s 31m 8M; W round twr, R band and lantern; vis: 248°-101°; (H24).

Royal Sovereign ☆ Fl 20s 28m 12M; W ○ twr, R band on W cabin on col; *Horn (2) 30s*; 50°43'·45N 00°26'·09E.

Royal Sovereign ⌁ QR; 50°44'·23N 00°25'·84E.

EASTBOURNE and SOVEREIGN HARBOUR

SH ⌁ L Fl 10s; 50°47'·40N 00°20'·71E.

Martello Tower ☆ Fl (3) 15s 12m 7M.; 50°47'·24N 00°19'·83E.

Dir lt 258°Fl WRG 5s 4m 1M; vis: 252·5°-G-256·5°-W-259·5°-R-262·5°; 50°47'·28N 00°19'·71E.

S Bkwtr Hd ☆ Fl (4) R 12s 3m 6M; 50°47'·30N 00°20'·03E.

St Leonard's Outfall ⌁ Fl Y 5s; 50°49'·31N 00°31'·95E.

HASTINGS

Ldg Lts 356·3°. Front, FR 14m 4M; 50°51'·29N 00°35'·38E. Rear, West Hill, 357m from front, FR 55m 4M; W twr.

RYE

Rye Fairway, L Fl 10s; 50°54'·04N 00°48'·04E.

W Groyne Hd No. 2 ☆ Fl R 5s 7m 6M; 50°55'·58N 00°46'·55E.

E Arm Hd No. 1 ♦ Q (9) 15s 7m 5M; G △; Horn 7s; 50°55'·73N 00°46'·46E.

Dungeness Outfall ♦ Q (6) + L Fl 15s; 50°54'·45N 00°58'·21E.

Dungeness ☆ 50°54'·81N 00°58'·56E; Fl 10s 40m **21M**; B ○ twr, W bands and lantern, floodlit; Part obsc 078°-shore; (H24). F RG 37m 10M (same twr); vis: 057°-R-073°-G-078°-196°-R-216°; Horn (3) 60s; FR Lts shown between 2·4M and 5·2M WNW when firing taking place. QR on radio mast 1·2M NW.

DUNGENESS TO NORTH FORELAND

FOLKESTONE

Hythe Flats Outfall ◌ Fl Y 5s; 51°02'·52N 01°05'·32E.

Breakwater Head ☆ Fl (2) 10s 14m **22M**; Dia (4) 60s; 51°04'·56N 01°11'·69E.

DOVER

Admiralty Pier Extension Head ☆ 51°06'·69N 01°19'·66E; Fl 7·5s 21m **20M**; W twr; vis: 096°-090°, obsc in The Downs by S Foreland inshore of 226°; Horn 10s; Int Port Tfc sigs.

S Bkwtr W Hd ☆ 51°06'·78N 01°19'·80E;Oc R 30s 21m **18M**; W twr.

Knuckle ☆ 51°07'·04N 01°20'·49E; Fl (4) WR 10s 15m **W15M**, R13M; W twr; vis: 059°-R-239°-W-059°.

N Head ☆ Fl R 2·5s 11m 5M; 51°07'·20N 01°20'·61E.

Eastern Arm Hd ☆ Fl G 5s 12m 5M; Horn (2) 30s; Int port tfc sigs; 51°07'·31N 01°20'·59E.

OFFSHORE MARKS

Bullock Bank ♦ VQ; 50°46'·94N 01°07'·60E.

Ridens SE ♦ VQ (3) 5s; 50°43'·47N 01°18'·87E.

Colbart SW ♦ VQ (6) + L Fl 10s; 50°48'·86N 01°16'·30E.

South Varne ♦ Q (6) + L Fl 15s; 50°55'·64N 01°17'·30E.

Mid Varne ♦ VQ(9)10s; 50°58'·94N 01°19'·88E.

East Varne ♦ VQ(3)5s; 50°58'·22N 01°20'·90E.

Colbart N ♦ VQ; 50°57'·45N 01°23'·29E

VARNE ⌐ 51°01'·29N 01°23'·90E; Fl R 5s 12m **15M**; Racon (T) 10M; Horn 30s.

CS 4 ♦ Fl (4) Y 15s; 51°08'·62N 01°33'·92E.

MPC ♦ Fl Y 2·5s; **Racon (O) 10M**; 51°06'·12N 01°38'·20E.

SW Goodwin ♦ Q (6) + L Fl 15s; 51°08'·50N 01°28'·88E.

S Goodwin ◌ Fl (4) R 15s; 51°10'·60N 01°32'·26E.

SE Goodwin ◌ Fl (3) R 10s; 51°12'·99N 01°34'·45E

E GOODWIN ⌐ 51°13'·26N 01°36'·37E; Fl 15s 12m **23M**; R hull with lt twr amidships; **Racon (T) 10M**; Horn 30s.

E Goodwin ♦ Q (3) 10s; 51°15'·67N 01°35'·69E.

NE Goodwin ♦ Q (3) 10s; **Racon (M) 10M**. 51°20'·31N 01°34'·16E.

DEAL and THE DOWNS

Trinity Bay VQ (9) 10s; 51°11'·60N 01°29'·00E.

Deal Bank ◌ QR; 51°12'·92N 01°25'·57E.

Goodwin Fork ♦ Q (6) + L Fl 15s; Bell; 51°14'·38N 01°26'·70E.

Downs ◌ Fl (2) R 5s; Bell; 51°14'·50N 01°26'·22E.

GULL STREAM

W Goodwin ▲ Fl G 5s; 51°15'·61N 01°27'·38E.

S Brake ◌ Fl (3) R 10s; 51°15'·77N 01°26'·82E.

NW Goodwin ♦ Q (9) 15s; 51°16'·73N 01°28'·60E.

Brake ◌ Fl (4) R 15s; Bell; 51°16'·98N 01°28'·19E.

N Goodwin ▲ Fl G 2·5s; 51°18'·12N 01°30'·35E.

Gull Stream ◌ QR; 51°18'·26N 01°29'·69E.

Gull ♦ VQ (3) 5s; 51°19'·57N 01°31'·30E.

Goodwin Knoll ▲ Fl (2) G 5s; 51°19'·57N 01°32'·20E.

RAMSGATE CHANNEL

B2 ▲ Fl (2) G 5s; 51°18'·26N 01°23'·93E.

W Quern ♦Q (9) 15s; 51°18'·98N 01°25'·39E.

RAMSGATE

RA ♦ Q(6) + L Fl 15s; 51°19'·60N 01°30'·13E.

E Brake ◌ Fl R 5s; 51°19'·47N 01°29'·20E.

No. 1 ▲QG; 51°19'·56N 01°27'·29E.

No. 2 ◌ Fl (4) R 10s; 51°19'·46N 01°27'·28E.

No. 3 ▲ Fl G 2·5s; 51°19'·56N 01°26'·61E.

No. 4 ◌ QR; 51°19'·46N 01°26'·60E.

N Quern ♦ Q; 51°19'·41N 01°26'·11E.

No. 5 ♦ Q (6) + L Fl 15s; 51°19'·56N 01°25'·91E.

No. 6 ◌ Fl (2) R 5s; 51°19'·46N 01°25'·91E.

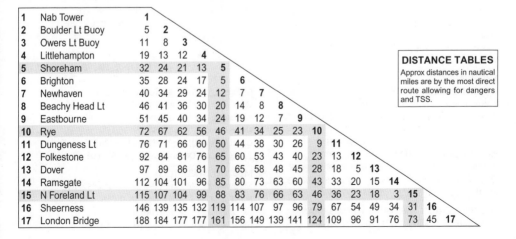

		1	2	3	4	5	6	7	8	9	10	11	12	13	14	15	16	17
1	Nab Tower	1																
2	Boulder Lt Buoy	5	2															
3	Owers Lt Buoy	11	8	3														
4	Littlehampton	19	13	12	4													
5	Shoreham	32	24	21	13	5												
6	Brighton	35	28	24	17	5	6											
7	Newhaven	40	34	29	24	12	7	7										
8	Beachy Head Lt	46	41	36	30	20	14	8	8									
9	Eastbourne	51	45	40	34	24	19	12	7	9								
10	Rye	72	67	62	56	46	41	34	25	23	10							
11	Dungeness Lt	76	71	66	60	50	44	38	30	26	9	11						
12	Folkestone	92	84	81	76	65	60	53	43	40	23	13	12					
13	Dover	97	89	86	81	70	65	58	48	45	28	18	5	13				
14	Ramsgate	112	104	101	96	85	80	73	63	60	43	33	20	15	14			
15	N Foreland Lt	115	107	104	99	88	83	76	66	63	46	36	23	18	3	15		
16	Sheerness	146	139	135	132	119	114	107	97	96	79	67	54	49	34	31	16	
17	London Bridge	188	184	177	177	161	156	149	139	141	124	109	96	91	76	73	45	17

DISTANCE TABLES
Approx distances in nautical miles are by the most direct route allowing for dangers and TSS.

South Bkwtr Hd ⚓ VQ R 10m 5M; 51°19'·46N 01°25'·41E.
N Bkwtr Hd ⚓ QG 10m 5M; 51°19'·56N 01°25'·47E.
Western Marine terminal Dir lt 270° ⚓, Oc WRG 10s
10m 5M; B △, Or stripe; vis: 259°-G-269°-W- 271°-R-281°;
51°19'·51N 01°24'·85E. Rear 493m from front Oc 5s 17m
5M; B ▽, Or stripe; vis: 263°-278°.

BROADSTAIRS and NORTH FORELAND

Broadstairs Knoll ⌇ Fl R 2·5s; 51°20'·88N 01°29'·48E.
Pier SE End ☆ 2 FR (vert) 7m 4M; 51°21'·50N 01°26'·74E.
Elbow ⚓ Q; 51°23'·23N 01°31'·59E.

North Foreland ☆ 51°22'·49N 01°26'·70E; Fl (5) WR 20s
57m **W19M, R16M, R15M**; W 8-sided twr; vis: shore-W-
150°-R(**16M**)-181°-R(**15M**)-200°-W-011°; H24.

OFFSHORE MARKS

F1 ⚓ Fl (4) Y 15s; 51°11'·21N 01°44'·91E.
South Falls ⚓ Q (6) + L Fl 15s; 51°13'·84N 01°43'·93E.
Mid Falls ⚓ Fl (3) R 10s; 51°18'·63N 01°46'·99E.
Inter Bank ⚓ Fl Y 5s; *Bell; Racon (M) 10M*; 51°16'·47N
01°52'·23E.
F2 ⚓ Fl (4) Y 15s; 51°20'·41N 01°56'·19E.

AREA 4 *East England – North Foreland to Berwick-upon-Tweed*

SELECTED LIGHTS, BUOYS & WAYPOINTS | Positions are referenced to WGS84

THAMES ESTUARY – SOUTHERN

(Direction of buoyage generally East to West)

APPROACHES to THAMES ESTUARY

Foxtrot 3 ⌑ 51°24'·20N 02°00'·40E; Fl 10s 12m **15M**;
Racon (T) 10M; *Horn 10s*.
Falls Hd ⚓ Q; 51°28'·23N 01°49'·89E.
Drill Stone ⚓ Q (3) 10s; 51°25'·88N 01°42'·89E.
Thanet NW ⚓ Q(9) 15s; 51°26'·80N 01°33'·80E.
NE Spit ⚓ VQ (3); *Racon (T) 10M*; 5s; 51°27'·93N
01°29'·89E.
East Margate ⌇ Fl R 2·5s; 51°27'·03N 01°26'·40E.
Elbow ⚓ Q; 51°23'·23N 01°31'·59E.
Foreness Pt Outfall ⌇ Fl R 5s; 51°24'·61N 01°26'·02E.
Longnose ⌀ 51°24'·15N 01°26'·08E.
Longnose Spit ⚓ Fl R 2·5s 5m 2M; 51°23'·93N 01°25'·68E.

MARGATE and GORE CHANNEL

SE Margate ⚓ Q (3) 10s; 51°24'·05N 01°20'·40E.
S Margate ▲ Fl G 2·5s; 51°23'·83N 01°16'·65E.
Hook Spit ▲ QG; 51°24'·08N 01°12'·09E.
E Last ⌇ QR; 51°24'·01N 01°12'·05E.

HERNE BAY

Beltinge Bay Bn ⚓ Fl Y 5s; 51°22'·73N 01°08'·63E.
Landing Stage ☆ Q 18m 4M, (isolated); 51°22'·91N
01°06'·89E.
N Pier Hd ☆ 2 FR (vert); 51°22'·43N 01°07'·27E.

WHITSTABLE

Whitstable Street ⌀ ; 51°24'·00N 01°01'·54E. (See The
Swale.)
Oyster ⌇ Fl (2) R 10s; 51°22'·14N 01°01'·16E.
W Quay Dn ☆ Fl G 5s 2m.

THE SWALE

Whitstable Street ⌀ Fl R 2s; 51°24'·00N 01°01'·54E.
Columbine ▲ Fl G 2s; 51°24'·26N 01°01'·34E.
Columbine Spit ▲ Fl (3) G 10s; 51°23'·86N 01°00'·03E.
Ham Gat ▲ Q G; 51°23'·08N 00°58'·32E.
Pollard Spit ⌇ Q R; 51°22'·98N 00°58'·57E.
Sand End ▲ Fl G 5s; 51°21'·43N 00°55'·90E.
Receptive Point ▲ Fl G 10s; 51°20'·86N 00°54'·41E.
Queenborough Spit ⚓ Q (3) 10s; 51°25'·81N 00°43'·93E.
South Oaze ⌇ Fl R 2s; 51°21'·34N 00°56'·01E.

QUEENS CHANNEL and FOUR FATHOMS CHANNEL

E Margate ⌇ Fl R 2·5s; 51°27'·03N 01°26'·40E.

Spaniard ⚓ Q (3) 10s; 51°26'·23N 01°04'·00E.
Spile ▲ Fl G 2·5s; 51°26'·43N 00°55'·70E.

PRINCES CHANNEL

Tongue Sand E ⚓ VQ (3) 5s; 51°29'·48N 01°22'·21E.
Tongue Sand N ⚓ Q; 51°29'·68N 01°22'·03E.
Princes Outer ⚓ VQ (6) + L Fl 10s; 51°28'·89N
01°20'·43E.
Princes North ▲ Q G; 51°29'·25N 01°18'·35E.
Princes South ⌇ Q R; 51°28'·74N 01°18'·26E.
Princes No.1 ▲ Fl (4) G 15s; 51°29'·23N 01°16'·02E.
Princes No.2 ⌇ Fl (2) R 5s; 51°28'·81N 01°13'·08E.
Princes No.3 ▲ Fl (2) G 5s; 51°29'·33N 01°13'·10E.
Princes No.4 ⌇ Fl (3) R 10s; 51°28'·83N 01°09'·90E.
Princes No.5 ▲ Fl (3) G 10s; 51°29'·39N 01°10'·00E.
Princes Mid ⚓ Fl Y 5s; 51°29'·19N 01°09'·00E.
Shivering Sand Twr N ⚓ Q; 51°30'·01N 01°04'·76E.
Shivering Sand Twr S ⚓ Q (6) + L Fl 15s; *Bell*; 51°29'·75N
01°04'·83E.
Princes No.8 ⌇ Fl (2) R 5s; 51°29'·14N 01°03'·00E.
Princes Inner ⚓ Fl Y 2·5s; 51°29'·59N 01°03'·47E.

FOULGER'S GAT and KNOB CHANNEL

The N Edinburgh Channel is not buoyed. Fisherman's Gat
is a commercial ship channel; Foulger's Gat, suitable for
leisure craft, is marked at each end with SWMs.

Long Sand Inner ⌇ Mo 'A' 15s; 51°38'·80N 01°25'·60E.
Long Sand Outer ⌇ L Fl 10s; 51°35'·90N 01°26'·00E.
SE Knob ▲ Fl G 5s; 51°30'·89N 01°06'·41E.
Knob ⚓ Iso 5s; *Whis*; 51°30'·69N 01°04'·28E.

OAZE DEEP

Oaze Deep ▲ Fl (2) G 5s; 51°30'·03N 01°00'·70E.
Red Sand Trs N ⌇ Fl (3) R 10s; *Bell*; 51°28'·73N
00°59'·32E.
N Oaze ⌇ QR; 51°30'·03N 00°57'·65E.
Oaze ⚓ Fl (4) Y 10s; 51°29'·06N 00°56'·93E.
W Oaze ⚓ Iso 5s; 51°29'·06N 00°55'·43E.
Oaze Bank ▲ Q G 5s; 51°29'·36N 00°56'·95E.
Cant ⚓ (unlit); 51°27'·77N 00°53'·36E.
East Cant ⌇ QR; 51°28'·53N 00°55'·60E.

MEDWAY, SHEERNESS

Medway ⚓ Mo (A) 6s; 51°28'·83N 00°52'·81E.
No. 1 ▲ Fl G 2·5s; 51°28'·55N 00°50'·50E.
No. 2 ⚓ Q; 51°28'·33N 00°50'·52E.
No. 7 ▲ Fl G 10s; 51°27'·91N 00°47'·52E.

No. 9 ⚓ Fl G 5s; 51°27'·74N 00°46'·61E.

No. 11 ⚓ Fl (3) G 10s; 51°27'·51N 00°45'·80E.

Grain Hard ⚓ Fl G 5s; 51°26'·98N 00°44'·17E.

Isle of Grain ✰ Q 20m 13M; R & W ◊ on R twr; 51°26'·70N 00°43'·38E.

Queenborough Spit ⚓ Q (3) 10s; 51°25'·81N 00°43'·93E.

RIVER THAMES

SEA REACH, NORE and YANTLET

No. 1 ⚓ Fl Y 2·5s; *Racon (T) 10M*;   51°29'·45N 00°52'·57E.

No. 2 ⚓ Iso 5s; 51°29'·40N 00°49'·75E.

No. 3 ⚓ Oc 10s; 51°29'·33N 00°46'·54E.

No. 4 ⚓ Fl Y 2·5s; 51°29'·61N 00°44'·18E.

No. 5 ⚓ Iso 5s; 51°29'·95N 00°41'·44E.

No. 6 ⚓ Iso 2s; 51°30'·03N 00°39'·83E.

No. 7 ⚓   Fl Y 2·5s; *Racon (T) 10M*; 51°30'·10N 00°37'·04E.

Nore Swatch ⚓ Fl (4) R 15s; 51°28'·28N 00°45'·55E.

Mid Swatch ⚓ Fl G 5s; 51°28'·68N 00°44'·16E.

W Nore Sand ⚓ Fl (3) R 10s; 51°29'·41N 00°40'·85E.

East Blyth ⚓ Fl (2) R 10s; 51°29'·72N 00°37'·80E.

Mid Blyth ⚓ Q; 51°30'·08N 00°32'·38E.

LEIGH-ON-SEA and SOUTHEND-ON-SEA

Leigh ⚓ ; 51°31'·07N 00°42'·56E.

Southend Pier E End ✰ 2 FG (vert) 7m; *Horn Mo (N) 30s, Bell (1)*

SE Leigh ⚓ Q (6) + L Fl 15s; 51°29'·42N 00°47'·07E.

GRAVESEND

Shornmead ✰ Fl (2) WR 10s 12m 11/7M , W11M, W7M, R11M; vis 070°-W-084°-R(Intens)-089°-W(Intens)-094°-W-250°; 51°26'·92N 00°26'·24E.

Northfleet Upper ✰ Oc WRG 10s 30m **W16M**, R12M, G12M; vis:126°-R-149°-W-159°-G-268°-W-279°; 51°26'·93N 00°20'·06E.

THAMES TIDAL BARRIER

Span B (51°29'·73N 00°02'·23E) is used for small craft/yachts Eastbound and Span G (51°29'·91N 00°02'·21E) is used for small craft/yachts Westbound. Spans B, C, D, E, F & G are navigable. Spans C to F are for larger vessels. All spans display a F GR ✰. A **Green** ➝ indicates span open for navigation. A **Red X** indicates span closed to navigation. In low visibility fixed lights are shown either side of those spans which are displaying a **Green** ➝.

THAMES ESTUARY – NORTHERN

KENTISH KNOCK

Kentish Knock ⚓ Q (3) 10s; 51°38'·08N 01°40·43E.

S Knock ⚓ Q (6) + L Fl 15s; *Bell*; 51°34'·13N 01°34'·29E.

KNOCK JOHN CHANNEL

No. 7 ⚓ Fl (4) G 15s; 51°32'·03N 01°06'·40E.

No. 5 ⚓ Fl (3) G 10s; 51°32'·49N 01°07'·75E.

No. 4 ⚓ QR 10s; 51°32'·33N 01°07'·90E.

No. 2 ⚓ Fl (3) R 10s; 51°33'·11N 01°09'·85E.

No. 3 ⚓ Q (6) + L Fl 15s; 51°33'·23N 01°09'·70E.

No. 1 ⚓ Fl G 5s; 51°33'·75N 01°10'·72E.

Knock John ⚓ Fl (2) R 5s; 51°33'·61N 01°11'·37E.

BLACK DEEP

No. 12 ⚓ Fl (4) R 15s; 51°33'·83N 01°13'·50E.

No. 11 ⚓ Fl (3) G 10s; 51°34'·33N 01°13'·40E.

No. 10 ⚓ Fl (3) R 10s; 51°34'·74N 01°15'·60E.

No. 9 ⚓ Q (6) + L Fl 15s; 51°35'·13N 01°15'·09E.

No. 8 ⚓ Q (9) 15s; 51°36'·36N 01°20'·43E.

No. 7 ⚓ QG. 51°37'·08N 01°17'·69E.

No. 6 ⚓ Fl R 2·5s; 51°38'·53N 01°24'·41E.

No. 5 ⚓ VQ (3) 5s; 51°39'·53N 01°23'·00E.

No. 4 ⚓ Fl (2) R 5s; 51°41'·42N 01°28'·49E.

Long Sand Bcn ⚓ ; 51°41'·48N 01°29'·49E.

No. 3 ⚓ Fl (3) G 15s; 51°42'·39N 01°26'·66E.

No. 1 ⚓ Fl G 5s, 51°44'·03N 01°28'·09E.

No. 2 ⚓ Fl (4) R 15s; 51°45'·63N 01°32'·20E.

Sunk Head Tower ⚓ Q; *Whis*; 51°46'·63N 01°30'·51E.

Black Deep ⚓ QR; 51°47'·79N 01°36'·31E.

Trinity ⚓ Q (6) + L Fl 15s; 51°49'·03N 01°36'·39E.

Long Sand Head ⚓ VQ; *Whis*; 51°47'·90N 01°39'·42E.

FISHERMANS GAT

Outer Fisherman ⚓ Q (3) 10s; 51°33'·89N 01°25'·01E.

Fisherman No. 1 ⚓ Fl G 2·5s; 51°34'·53N 01°23'·57E.

Fisherman No. 2 ⚓ Fl R 2·5s; 51°34'·35N 01°23'·01E.

Fisherman No. 3 ⚓ Fl G 5s; 51°34'·72N 01°22'·94E.

Fisherman No. 4 ⚓ Fl (2) R 5s; 51°35'·25N 01°21'·35E.

Fisherman No. 5 ⚓ Fl (2) G 5s; 51°35'·52N 01°21'·75E.

Inner Fisherman ⚓ Q R; 51°36'·07N 01°19'·87E.

BARROW DEEP

SW Barrow ⚓ Q(6) + L Fl 15s; *Bell*; 51°32'·29N 01°00'·31E.

Barrow No. 14 ⚓ Fl R 2·5s; 51°31'·83N 01°00'·43E.

Barrow No. 13 ⚓ Fl (2) G 5s; 51°32'·82N 01°03'·07E.

Barrow No. 12 ⚓ Fl (2) R 5s; 51°32'·77N 01°04'·13E.

Barrow No.11 ⚓ Fl (3) G 10s; 51°34'·08N 01°06'·70E.

Barrow No. 9 ⚓ VQ (3) 5s; 51°35'·34N 01°10'·30E.

Barrow No. 8 ⚓ Fl (2) R 5s; 51°35'·03N 01°11'·40E.

Barrow No. 6 ⚓ Fl (4) R 15s; 51°37'·30N 01°14'·69E.

Barrow No. 5 ⚓ Fl G 10s; 51°40'·03N 01°16'·20E.

Barrow No. 4 ⚓ VQ (9) 10s; 51°39'·88N 01°17'·48E.

Barrow No. 3 ⚓ Q (3) 10s; *Racon (M)10M*; 51°42'·02N 01°20'·24E.

Barrow No. 2 ⚓ Fl (2) R 5s; 51°41'·98N 01°22'·89E.

WEST SWIN and MIDDLE DEEP

Blacktail (W) ⚓ ; 51°31'·46N 00°55'·19E.

Maplin ⚓ Q G (sync with W Swin); *Bell*; 51°33'·66N 01°01'·40E.

W Swin ⚓ Q R (sync with Maplin); 51°33'·40N 01°01'·97E.

Maplin Edge ⚓ Fl G 2.5s; 51°35'·33N 01°03'·64E.

Maplin Bank ⚓ Fl (3) R 10s; 51°35'·50N 01°04'·70E.

EAST SWIN and KING'S CHANNEL

NE Maplin ⚓ Fl G 5s; *Bell*; 51°37'·43N 01°04'·90E.

W Hook Middle ⚓ 51°39'·18N 01°07'·97E.

S Whitaker ⚓ Fl (2) G 10s; 51°40'·17N 01°09'·11E.

N Middle ⚓ Q; 51°41'·35N 01°12'·61E.

W Sunk ⚓ Q (9) 15s; 51°44'·33N 01°25'·80E.

Gunfleet Spit ⚓ Q (6) + L Fl 15s; *Bell*; 51°45'·33N 01°21'·70E.

WHITAKER CHANNEL and RIVER CROUCH

Whitaker ⚓ Q (3) 10s; *Bell*; 51°41'·43N 01°10'·51E.

Whitaker No. 6 ⌷ Q; 51°40'·69N 01°08'·06E.

Swin Spitway ⌷ Iso 10s; *Bell*; 51°41'·95N 01°08'·35E.

Ron Pipe ⌷ 51°40'·54N 01°03'·48E.

Swallow Tail ▲ 51°40'·51N 01°04'·70E.

Ridge ⌷ Fl R 10s; 51°40'·13N 01°04'·87E.

Foulness ⌷ Fl (2) R 10s; 51°39'·92N 01°04'·12E.

Sunken Buxey ⌷ Q; 51°39'·54N 01°00'·59E.

Buxey No. 1 ⌷ VQ (6) + L Fl 10s; 51°39'·18N 01°01'·01E.

Buxey No. 2 ⌷ Q; 51°38'·98N 01°00'·15E.

Outer Crouch ⌷ Q (6) + L Fl 15s; 51°38'·38N 00°58'·48E.

GOLDMER GAT and WALLET

NE Gunfleet ⌷ Q (3) 10s; 51°49'·93N 01°27'·79E.

Wallet No. 2 ⌷ Fl R 5s; 51°48'·88N 01°22'·99E.

Wallet No. 4 ⌷ Fl (4) R 10s; 51°46'·53N 01°17'·23E.

Wallet Spitway ⌷ L Fl 10s; *Bell*; 51°42'·86N 01°07'·30E.

Knoll ⌷ Q; 51°43'·88N 01°05'·07E.

Eagle ⌷ QG; 51°44'·13N 01°03'·82E.

N Eagle ⌷ Q; 51°44'·71N 01°04'·32E.

NW Knoll ⌷ Fl (2) R 5s; 51°44'·35N 01°02'·17E.

Colne Bar ⌷ Fl (2) G 5s; 51°44'·61N 01°02'·57E.

Bench Head ⌷ Fl (3) G 10s; 51°44'·69N 01°01'·10E.

RIVER BLACKWATER

The Nass ⌷ VQ (3) 5s 6m 2M; 51°45'·83N 00°54'·83E.

Thirslet ⌷ Fl (3) G 10s; 51°43'·73N 00°50'·39E.

No. 1 ▲ ; 51°43'·44N 00°48'·02E.

RIVER COLNE and BRIGHTLINGSEA

Inner Bench Head No. 2 ⌷ Fl (2) R 5s; 51°45'·96N 01°01'·74E.

Colne Pt No. 1 ▲ Fl G 3s; 51°46'·01N 01°01'·92E.

No. 8 ⌷ Fl R 3s; 51°46'·90N 01°01'·30E.

No. 9 ▲ Fl G 3s; 51°47'·36N 01°01'·07E.

Ldg lts 041°. Front, FR 7m 4M; W ☐, R stripe on post; vis: 020°-080°; 51°48'·39N 01°01'·20E. Rear, 50m from front, FR 10m 4M; W ☐, R stripe on post. FR lts are shown on 7 masts between 1·5M and 3M NW when firing occurs.

WALTON BACKWATERS

Pye End ⌷ L Fl 10s; 51°55'·03N 01°17'·90E.

No. 2 ⌷ Fl (2) 5s; 51°54'·62N 01°16'·80E.

Crab Knoll No. 3 ▲ Fl G 5s; 51°54'·41N 01°16'·41E.

HARWICH APPROACHES

(Direction of buoyage North to South)

MEDUSA CHANNEL

Medusa ⌷ Fl G 5s; 51°51'·23N 01°20'·35E.

Stone Banks ⌷ FlR 5s; 51°53'·19N 01°19'·23E.

Pennyhole ⌷ ; 51°53'·55N 01°18'·00E (Mar–Sep).

CORK SAND and ROUGH SHOALS

S Cork ⌷ Q (6) + L Fl 15s; 51°51'·33N 01°24'·09E.

SE Roughs Tower ⌷ Q (3) 10s; 51°53'·64N 01°28'·94E.

NW Roughs Tower ⌷ VQ (9) 10s; 51°53'·81N 01°28'·77E.

Cork Sand ⌷ Fl (3) R 10s; 51°55'·51N 01°25'·42E.

HARWICH CHANNEL

Sunk Inner ⌷ Iso 3s 11m 12M; *Racon T*; *Horn 30s*; 51°51'·03N 01°34'·89E.

S Threshold ⌷ Fl (4) Y 10s; 51°52'·20N 01°33'·14E.

S Shipwash ⌷ 2 By(s) Q (6) + L Fl 15s; 51°52'·71N 01°33'·97E.

Outer Tidal Bn ⌷ Mo (U) 15s 2m 3M; 51°52'·85N 01°32'·34E.

E Fort Massac ⌷ VQ (3) 5s; 51°53'·36N 01°32'·79E.

W Fort Massac ⌷ VQ (9) 10s; 51°53'·36N 01°32'·49E.

Walker ⌷ QR; 51°53'·79N 01°33'·90E.

N Threshold ⌷ Fl Y 5s; 51°54'·49N 01°33'·47E.

SW Shipwash ⌷ Q (9)15s; 51°54'·75N 01°34'·21E.

Haven ⌷ Mo (A) 5s; 51°55'·76N 01°35'·56E.

W Shipwash ⌷ Fl (2) R 10s; 51°57'·13N 01°35'·89E.

NW Shipwash ⌷ Fl R 5s; 51°58'·98N 01°37'·01E.

Harwich App (HA) ⌷ Iso 5s; 51°56'·75N 01°30'·66E.

Cross ⌷ Fl (3) Y 10s; 51°56'·23N 01°30'·48E.

Harwich Chan No. 1 ⌷ Fl Y 2·5s; *Racon (T) 10M*; 51°56'·13N 01°27'·06E.

Harwich Chan No. 3 ⌷ Fl (3) Y 10s; 51°56'·04N 01°25'·54E.

Harwich Chan No. 5 ⌷ Fl (5) Y 10s; 51°55'·96N 01°24'·01E.

Harwich Chan No. 7 ⌷ Fl (3) Y 10s; 51°55'·87N 01°22'·49E.

S Bawdsey ⌷ Q (6) + L Fl 15s; *Whis*; 51°57'·23N 01°30'·19E.

Washington ▲ QG; 51°56'·52N 01°26'·59E.

Felixstowe Ledge ▲ Fl (3) G 10s; 51°56'·30N 01°23'·72E.

Wadgate Ledge ⌷ Fl (4) G 15s; 51°56'·16N 01°21'·99E.

Platters ⌷ Q (6) + L Fl 15s; 51°55'·64N 01°20'·97E.

Rolling Ground ▲ QG; 51°55'·55N 01°19'·75E.

Beach End ▲ Fl (2) G 5s; 51°55'·62N 01°19'·21E.

Cork Sand Yacht Bn ⌷ VQ 2M; 51°55'·21N 01°25'·20E.

Rough ⌷ VQ; 51°55'·19N 01°31'·00E.

Pitching Ground ⌷ Fl (4) R 15s; 51°55'·43N 01°21'·05E.

Inner Ridge ⌷ QR; 51°55'·38N 01°20'·20E.

Deane ⌷ L Fl R 6s; 51°55'·36N 01°19'·28E.

Landguard ⌷ Q; 51°55'·45N 01°18'·84E.

RIVERS STOUR AND ORWELL

RIVER STOUR and HARWICH

Shotley Spit ⌷ Q (6) + L Fl 15s; 51°57'·21N 01°17'·69E.

Shotley Marina Lock E side Dir lt 339·5° 3m 1M (uses Moiré pattern); Or structure; 51°57'·46N 01°16'·60E.

Guard ⌷ Fl R 5s; *Bell*; 51°57'·07N 01°17'·86E.

RIVER ORWELL and IPSWICH

Suffolk Yacht Harbour. Ldg lts Front Iso Y 1M; 51°59'·73N 01°16'·09E. Rear Oc Y 4s 1M.

HARWICH TO ORFORDNESS

FELIXSTOWE, R DEBEN and WOODBRIDGE HAVEN

Woodbridge Haven ⌷ Mo(A)15s; 51°58'·20N 01°23'·85E.

Deben ⌷ ; 51°59'·30N 01°23'·53E.

RIVERS ORE and ALDE

Orford Haven ⌷ L Fl 10s; *Bell*. 52°01'·62N 01°28'·00E.

OFFSHORE MARKS

S Galloper ⌷ Q (6) L Fl 15s; *Racon (T) 10M*; 51°43'·98N 01°56'·43E.

N Galloper ⌷ Q; 51°49'·84N 01°59'·99E.

S Inner Gabbard ⌷ Q (6) + L Fl 15s. 51°49'·92N 01°51'·89E.

N Inner Gabbard ⌷ Q; 51°59'·20N 01°56'·00E.

Outer Gabbard ⌷ Q (3) 10s; *Racon (O) 10M*; 52°04'·19E.

NHR-SE ▲ Fl G 5s; 51°45'·39N 02°39'·89E.

SHIPWASH and BAWDSEY BANK

E Shipwash ⌷ VQ (3) 5s; 51°57'·08N 01°37'·89E.

NW Shipwash ⌀ Fl R 5s; 51°58'·98N 01°37'·01E.
N Shipwash ⌀ Q 7M; *Racon (M) 10M; Whis*; 52°01'·73N 01°38'·27E.
S Bawdsey ⌀ Q (6) + L Fl 15s; *Whis*; 51°57'·23N 01°30'·22E.
Mid Bawdsey ▲ Fl (3) G 10s; 51°58'·88N 01°33'·59E.
NE Bawdsey ▲ Fl G 10s; 52°01'·73N 01°36'·09E.

CUTLER and WHITING BANKS
Cutler ▲ QG; 51°58'·51N 01°27'·48E.
SW Whiting ⌀ Q (6) + L Fl 10s; 52°00'·96N 01°30'·69E.
Whiting Hook ⌀ Fl R 10s; 52°02'·98N 01°31'·82E.
NE Whiting ⌀ Q (3) 10s; 52°03'·61N 01°33'·32E.

ORFORD NESS TO WINTERTON

(Direction of buoyage is South to North)
Orford Ness ☆ 52°05'·03N 01°34'·46E; Fl 5s 28m **20M**; W ○ twr, R bands. F WRG 14m **W17M**, R13M, **G15M** (same twr). vis: R shore-210°, 038°-R-047°-G-shore; *Racon (T) 18M*.
FR 13m 12M vis: 026°- 038° over Whiting Bank.
Aldeburgh Ridge ⌀ QR; 52°06'·49N 01°36'·95E.

SOUTHWOLD
Southwold ☆ 52°19'·63N 01°40'·89E; Fl (4) WR 20s 37m **W16M, R12M**, R14M; vis 204°-R (intens)- 215°-W-001°.

LOWESTOFT and APPR VIA STANFORD CHANNEL
E Barnard ⌀ Q (3) 10s; 52°25'·14N 01°46'·38E.
Newcome Sand ⌀ QR; 52°26'·28N 01°46'·97E.
S Holm ⌀ VQ (6) + L Fl 10s; 52°27'·05N 01°47'·15E.
Stanford ⌀ Fl R 2·5s; 52°27'·35N 01°46'·67E.
SW Holm ▲ Fl (2) G 5s; 52°27'·87N 01°46'·99E.
Kirkley ☆ Oc WRG 10s 17m, W8M, R6M, G6M, vis: 210°-G-224°-W-229°-R-313°; 52°27'·71N 01°44'·54E.
Claremont Pier ⚡ Fl R 5s 5m 3M; 52°27'·89N 01°44'·87E.
Outer Hbr S Pier Hd ⚡ Oc R 5s 12m 6M; *Horn (4) 60s*; Tfc sigs; 52°28'·29N 01°45'·36E.
N Newcome ⌀ Fl (4) R 15s; 52°28'·39N 01°46'·37E.
Lowestoft ☆ 52°29'·22N 01°45'·35; Fl 15s 37m **23M**; W twr; part obscd 347°- shore.

LOWESTOFT NORTH ROAD and CORTON ROAD
Lowestoft Ness SE ⌀ Q (6) + L Fl 15s; 52°28'·84N 01°46'·25E.
Lowestoft Ness N ⌀ VQ (3) 5s; *Bell*; 52°28'·89N 01°46'·23E.
W Holm ▲ Fl (3) G 10s; 52°29'·80N 01°47'·09E.
NW Holm ▲ Fl (4) G 15s; 52°31'·93N 01°46'·70E.

GREAT YARMOUTH APPROACH via HOLM CHANNEL
E Newcome ⌀ Fl (2) R 5s; 52°28'·51N 01°49'·21E.
Holm Approach ⌀ Q (3) 10s; 52°30'·88N 01°50'·22E.
Holm Sand ⌀ Q (9) 15s; 52°33'·18N 01°46'·54E.
S Corton ⌀ Q (6) + L Fl 15s; *Bell*; 52°32'·94N 01°49'·12E.
NE Holm ⌀ Fl R 2·5s; 52°32'·69N 01°48'·48E.
Mid Corton ▲ Fl G 2·5s; 52°33'·62N 01°48'·01E.
N Holm ⌀ Q. 52°33'·93N 01°47'·23E.

GREAT YARMOUTH and GORLESTON
W Corton ▲ Fl (3) G 10s; 52°34'·12N 01°47'·50E.
Gorleston South Pier Hd ⚡ Fl R 3s 11m 11M; vis: 235°-340°; 52°34'·33N 01°44'·28E.
N Pier Hd ⚡ QG 8m 6M; vis: 176°-078°; *Horn(3) 60s*; 52°34'·38N 01°44'·38E.

GREAT YARMOUTH TO THE WASH

(Direction of buoyage ⌂ South to North)

YARMOUTH and CAISTER ROADS/COCKLE GATEWAY
SW Scroby ▲ Fl G 2·5s; 52°35'·13N 01°46'·69E.
Scroby Elbow ▲ Fl (2) G 5s; *Bell*; 52°36'·55N 01°46'·26E.
Yarmouth Outfall ⌀ Q R; 52°37'·58N 01°45'·70E.
Mid Caister ⌀ Fl (2) R 5s; *Bell*; 52°38'·99N 01°45'·66E.
NW Scroby ▲ Fl (3) G 10s; 52°40'·36N 01°46'·31E.
N Caister ⌀ Fl (3) R 10s; 52°40'·77N 01°45'·65E.
Hemsby ⌀ Fl R 2·5s; 52°41'·80N 01°46'·00E.
N Scroby ⌀ VQ; 52°41'·39N 01°46'·47E.
Cockle ⌀ VQ (3) 5s; *Bell*; 52°44'·03N 01°43'·59E.

OFFSHORE ROUTE
Cross Sand ⌀ L Fl 10s 6m 5M; *Racon (T) 10M*; 52°37'·03N 01°59'·14E.
E Cross Sand ⌀ Fl (4) R 15s; 52°38'·55N 01°53'·55E.
NE Cross Sand ⌀ VQ (3) 5s; 52°44'·22N 01° 53'·80E.
Smith's Knoll ⌀ Q (6) + L Fl 15s 7M; *Racon (T) 10M*; 52°43'·52N 02°17'·89E.
S Winterton Ridge ⌀ Q (6) + L Fl 15s; 52°47'·21N 02°03'·44E.
E Hammond Knoll ⌀ Q (3) 10s; 52°52'·32N 01°58'·64E.
Hammond Knoll ⌀ Q (9) 15s; 52°49'·68N 01°57'·54E.
Newarp ⌀ L Fl 10s 7M; *Racon (O) 10M*; 52°48'·37N 01°55'·69E.
S Haisbro ⌀ Q (6) + L Fl 15s; *Bell*; 52°50'·82N 01°48'·29E.
Mid Haisbro ▲ Fl (2) G 5s; 52°54'·22N 01°41'·59E.
N Haisbro ⌀ Q; *Racon (T) 10M*; 53°00'·22N 01°32'·29E.
Happisburgh ☆ Fl (3) 30s 41m 14M; 52°49'·21N 01°32'·18E.

(Direction of buoyage ⌂ East to West)

CROMER
Cromer ☆ 52°55'·45N 01°19'·01E; Fl 5s 84m **21M**; W 8-sided twr; vis: 102°-307° H24; *Racon (O) 25M*.
Tayjack Wk ⌀ Fl R 2·5s; 52°57'·61N 01°15'·37E.
E Sheringham ⌀ Q (3) 10s; 53°02'·21N 01°14'·84E.
W Sheringham ⌀ Q (9) 15s; 53°02'·95N 01°06'·72E.

BLAKENEY
Blakeney Fairway (SWM) ⌀; 52°59'·31N 00°57'·83E (approx).
Blakeney Overfalls ⌀ Fl (2) R 5s; *Bell*; 53°03'·01N 01°01'·37E.

WELLS-NEXT-THE-SEA/BRANCASTER STAITHE
Wells Leading Buoy ⌀ Fl(2) R 5s; 52°59'·64N 00°50'·36E.
Bridgirdle ⌀ Fl R 2·5s; 53°01'·73N 00°43'·95E.

APPROACHES TO THE WASH
S Race ⌀ Q (6) + L Fl 15s; *Bell*; 53°07'·81N 00°57'·34E.
E Docking ⌀ Fl R 2·5s; 53°09'·82N 00°50'·39E.
N Race ▲ Fl G 5s; *Bell*; 53°14'·98N 00°43'·87E.
N Docking ⌀ Q; 53°14'·82N 00°41'·49E.
Scott Patch ⌀ VQ (3) 5s; 53°11'·12N 00°36'·39E.
S Inner Dowsing ⌀ Q (6) + L Fl 15s; *Bell*; 53°12'·12N 00°33'·69E.
Boygrift Tower ⚡ Fl (2) 10s 12m 5M; 53°17'·63N 00°19'·24E.
Burnham Flats ⌀ Q (9) 15s; *Bell*; 53°07'·53N 00°34'·89E.

THE WASH
West Ridge ⌀ Q (9) 15s; 53°19'·06N 00°44'·47E.

N Well ⚓ L Fl 10s; *Bell*; **Racon (T) 10M**; 53°03'·02N 00°27'·90E.

Roaring Middle ⚓ L Fl 10s 7m 8M; 52°58'·64N 00°21'·08E.

CORK HOLE/KING'S LYNN

Sunk ⚓ Q (9) 15s; 52°56'·29N 00°23'·40E.

Seal Sand ⚓ Q; *Bell*; 52°56'·00N 00°20'·00E.

WISBECH CHANNEL/RIVER NENE

Beacons are moved as required.

Masts on W side of River Nene to Wisbech carry FG Lts and those on E side QR or FR Lts.

FREEMAN CHANNEL

Boston Roads ⚓ L Fl 10s; 52°57'·66N 00°16'·04E.

Boston No. 1 ▲ Fl G 3s; 52°57'·88N 00°15'·16E.

Alpha ⚓ Fl R 3s; 52°57'·65N 00°14'·99E.

No. 3 ▲ Fl G 6s; 52°58'·08N 00°14'·07E.

No. 5 ▲ Fl G 3s; 52°58'·51N 00°12'·72E.

Freeman Inner ⚓ Q (9) 15s; 52°58'·59N 00°11'·36E.

Delta ⚓ Fl R 6s; 52°58'·38N 00°11'·25E.

BOSTON LOWER ROAD

Boston No. 7 ▲ Fl G 3s; 52°58'·62N 00°10'·00E.

Boston No. 9 ▲ Fl G 3s; 52°57'·58N 00°08'·36E.

Black Buoy ⚓ Fl (2) R 6s; 52°56'·82N 00°07'·74E.

Tabs Head ⚓ Q WG 4m 1M; R □ on W mast; vis: W shore - 251°- G - shore; 52°56'·00N 00°04'·91E.

BOSTON, NEW CUT AND RIVER WITHAM

Ent N side, Dollypeg ⚓ QG 4m 1M; B △ on Bn; 52°56'·13N 00°05'·03E.

New Cut ⚓ Fl G 3s; △ on pile; 52°55'·98N 00°04'·67E.

New Cut Ldg Lts 240°. Front, No. 1, F 5m 5M; 52°55'·85N 00°04'·40E. Rear, 90m from front, F 8m 5M.

WELLAND CUT/RIVER WELLAND

SE side ⚡ Iso R 2s; NW side Iso G 2s. Lts QR (to port) and QG (to stbd) mark the chan upstream; 52°55'·72E 00°04'·68E.

(Direction of buoyage ⚲ North to South)

BOSTON DEEP/WAINFLEET ROADS

Scullridge ▲ ; 52°59'·76N 00°13'·86E.

Friskney ▲ ; 53°00'·59N 00°16'·76E.

Long Sand ▲ ; 53°01'·27N 00°18'·30E.

Pompey ▲ ; 53°02'·19N 00°19'·26E.

Swatchway ▲ ; 53°03'·81N 00°19'·70E.

Off Ingoldmells Point ⚡ Fl Y 5s 22m 5M; Mast; *Mo (U) 30s*; 53°12'·49N 00°25'·85E.

THE WASH TO THE RIVER HUMBER

(Direction of buoyage ⚲ South to North)

Dudgeon ⚓ Q (9) 15s 7M; **Racon (O) 10M**; 53°16'·62N 01°16'·90E.

E Dudgeon ⚓ Q (3) 10s; 53°19'·72N 00°58'·69E.

Mid Outer Dowsing ▲ Fl (3) G 10s; 53°24'·82N 01°07'·79E.

N Outer Dowsing ⚓ Q; 53°33'·52N 00°59'·59E; *Racon (T) 10M*.

B.1D Platform Dowsing ⌗ 53°33'·68N 00°52'·63E; Fl (2) 10s 28m **22M**; Morse (U) R 15s 28m 3M; *Horn (2) 60s*.

RIVER HUMBER APPROACHES

W Ridge ⚓ Q (9) 15s; 53°19'·04N 00°44'·50E.

Inner Dowsing ⚓ Q (3) 10s 7M, **Racon (T) 10M**; *Horn 60s*; 53°19'·10N 00°34'·80E.

Protector ⚓ Fl R 2·5s; 53°24'·84N 00°25'·12E.

DZ No. 4 ⚓ Fl Y 5s; 53°27'·15N 00°19'·06E.

DZ No. 3 ⚓ Fl Y 2·5s 53°29'·30N 00°19'·21E.

Rosse Spit ⚓ Fl (2) R 5s 53°30'·56N 00°16'·60E.

Haile Sand No. 2 ⚓ Fl (3) R 10s; 53°32'·42N 00°13'·18E.

Humber ⚓ G lt float L Fl 10s 7M; **Racon (T) 7M**; 53°38'·70N 00°21'·24E.

N Binks ▲ Fl G 4s; 53°36'·01N 00°18'·28E.

S Binks ▲ Fl G 2s 53°34'·74N 00°16'·55E.

SPURN ⚓ Q (3) 10s 10m 8M; **Racon (M) 5M**; 53°33'·56N 00°14'·20E.

SE CHEQUER ⚓ VQ (6) + L Fl 10s 6m 6M; 53°33'·38N 00°12'·55E.

Chequer No. 3 ⚓ Q (6) + L Fl 15s; 53°33'·07N 00°10'·63E.

No 2B ⚓ Fl R 4s; 53°32'·33N 00°09'·10E.

Tetney ⚓ 2 VQ Y (vert); *Horn Mo (A)60s*; QY on 290m floating hose; 53°32'·35N 00°06'·76E.

RIVER HUMBER/GRIMSBY/HULL

Binks No. 3A ▲ Fl G 4s; 53°33'·92N 00°07'·43E.

Spurn Pt ⚓ Fl G 3s 11m 5M; 53°34'·37N 00°06'·47E.

BULL ⚓ VQ 8m 6M; 53°33'·54N 00°05'·70E.

Bull Sand ⚓ Q R ; 53°34'·45N 00°03'·69E.

North Fort ⚓ Q; 53°33'·80N 00°04'·19E.

South Fort ⚓ Q (6) + L Fl 15s; 53°33'·65N 00°03'·96E.

Haile Sand Fort ⚡ Fl R 5s 21m 3M; 53°32'·07N 00°01'·99E.

Haile Chan No. 4 ⚓ Fl R 4s; 53°33'·64N 00°02'·84E.

Middle No. 7 ⚓ VQ (6) + L Fl 10s; 53°35'·80N 00°01'·50E.

Grimsby Royal Dock ent E side ⚡ Fl (2) R 6s 10m 8M; Dn; 53°35'·08N 00°04'·04W.

Killingholme Lts in line 292°. Front, Iso R 2s 10m 14M. 53°38'·78N 00°12'·96W. Rear, 219m from front, F WRG 22m 3M; vis: 289·5°-G-290·5°-G/W-291·5°-W-292·5°-R/W-293·5° (H24).

RIVER HUMBER TO WHITBY

Canada & Giorgios Wreck ⚓ VQ (3) 5s; 53°42'·37N 00°07'·16E.

BRIDLINGTON

SW Smithic ⚓ Q (9) 15s; 54°02'·41N 00°09'·21W.

N Pier Hd ⚡ Fl 2s 12m 9M; *Horn 60s*; (Tidal Lts) Fl R or Fl G; 54°04'·77N 00°11'·19W.

N Smithic ⚓ VQ; *Bell*; 54°06'·22N 00°03'·90W.

Flamborough Hd ☆ 54°06'·98N 00°04'·96W; Fl (4) 15s 65m **24M**; W ○ twr; *Horn (2) 90s*.

FILEY/SCARBOROUGH/WHITBY

Filey Brigg ⚓ Q (3) 10s; *Bell*; 54°12'·74N 00°14'·60W.

Scarborough E Pier Hd ⚡ QG 8m 3M; 54°16'·88N 00°23'·36W.

Scarborough Pier ⚡ Iso 5s 17m 9M; W ○ twr; vis: 219°-039° (tide sigs); *Dia 60s*; 54°16'·91N 00°23'·40W.

Whitby ⚓ Q; *Bell*; 54°30'·33N 00°36'·58W.

Whitby High ☆ 54°28'·67N 00°34'·10W; Ling Hill Fl WR 5s 73m **18M**, R16M; W 8-sided twr and dwellings; vis: 128°-R-143°-W- 319°.

WHITBY TO THE RIVER TYNE

RUNSWICK/REDCAR
Salt Scar ⚓ 54°38'·12N 01°00'·12W VQ; *Bell*.
Luff Way Ldg Lts 197°. Front, on Esplanade, FR 8m 7M; vis: 182°-212°; 54°37'·10N 01°03'·71W. Rear, 115m from front, FR 12m 7M; vis: 182°-212°.
High Stone. Lade Way Ldg Lts 247°. Front, Oc R 2·5s 9m 7M; 54°37'·15N 01°03'·92W. Rear, 43m from front, Oc R 2·5s 11m 7M; vis: 232°-262°.

TEES APPROACHES/HARTLEPOOL
Tees Fairway ⚓ Iso 4s 8m 8M; *Racon (B) unknown range; Horn (1) 5s*; 54°40'·94N 01°06'·48W.
Bkwtr Hd S Gare ☆ 54°38'·85N 01°08'·27W; Fl WR 12s 16m **W20M, R17M**; W ○ twr; vis: 020°-W-274°-R-357°; Sig Stn; *Horn 30s*.
Ldg Lts 210·1° Front, FR 18m 13M; 54°37'·22N 01°10'·20W. **Rear**, 560m from front, FR 20m **16M**.
Longscar ⚓ Q (3) 10s; *Bell*; 54°40'·86N 01°09'·89W.
The Heugh ☆ 54°41'·79N 01°10'·56W; Fl (2) 10s 19m**19M**; W twr.
Hartlepool Marina Lock Dir Lt 308° Dir Fl WRG2s 6m 3M; vis: 305·5°-G-307°-W-309°-R-310·5°; 54°41'·45N 01°11'·92W.

SEAHAM/SUNDERLAND
Seaham N Pier Hd ⚓ Fl G 10s 12m 5M; W col, B bands; 54°50'·26N 01°19'·26W.
Sunderland Roker Pier Hd ☆ 54°55'·28N 01°21'·15W; Fl 5s 25m **23M**; W □ twr, 3 R bands and cupola: vis: 211°-357°; *Siren 20s*.
Old N Pier Hd ⚓ QG 12m 8M; metal column; 54°55'·13N 01°21'·61W.
DZ ⚓ 54°57'·04N 01°18'·90W and ⚓ 54°58'·61N 01°19'·90W; both Fl Y 2·5s.

TYNE ENTRANCE/NORTH SHIELDS
Ent North Pier Hd ☆ 55°00'·88N 01°24'·18W; Fl (3) 10s 26m **26M**; Gy □ twr, W lantern; *Horn 10s*.
Herd Groyne Hd Ldg Lt 249°, Oc RG 10s 13m, R11M, G11M; R pile structure, R&W lantern; vis: 224°-G-246·5°, 251·5°-R-277°; FR (unintens) 080°-224°. Same structure Dir Oc 10s 14m **19M**; vis: 246·5°-W-251·5°; *Bell (1) 5s*; 55°00'·49N 01°25'·44W.

RIVER TYNE TO BERWICK-UPON-TWEED

CULLERCOATS and BLYTH
Cullercoats Ldg Lts 256°. Front, FR 27m 3M; 55°02'·06N 01°25'·91W. Rear, 38m from front, FR 35m 3M.
Blyth Ldg Lts 324°. Front ⚓, F Bu 11m 10M; 55°07'·42N 01°29'·82W. Rear ⚓, 180m from front, F Bu 17m 10M. Both Or ⚓ on twr.
Blyth E Pier Hd ☆ 55°06'·98N 01°29'·21W; Fl (4) 10s 19m **21M**, W twr; same structure FR 13m 13M, vis:152°-249°; Horn (3) 30s.

COQUET ISLAND, AMBLE and WARKWORTH
Coquet ☆ 55°20'·03N 01°32'·39W; Fl (3) WR 20s 25m **W19M, R15M**; W □ twr, turreted parapet, lower half Gy; vis: 330°-R-140°-W-163°-R-180°-W-330°; sector boundaries are indeterminate and may appear as Alt WR; *Horn 30s*.
Amble N Pier Head ⚓ Fl G 6s 12m 6M; 55°20'·39N 01°34'·25W.

SEAHOUSES, BAMBURGH and FARNE ISLANDS
N Sunderland ⚓ Fl R 2·5s; 55°34'·62N 01°37'·12W.
Bamburgh Black Rocks Point ☆ 55°36'·99N 01°43'·45W; Oc(2) WRG 8s 12m **W14M**, R11M, G11M; W bldg; vis: 122°-G-165°-W- 175°-R-191°-W- 238°-R- 275°-W- 289°-G-300°.
Inner Farne ⚓ Fl (2) WR 15s 27m W10M, R7M; W ○ twr; vis: 119°- R - 280° - W -119°; 55°36'·92N 01°39'·35W.
Longstone ☆ **W side** 55°38'·62N 01°36'·65W; Fl 20s 23m **24M**; R twr, W band.
Swedman ⚓ Fl G 2·5s; 55°37'·65N 01°41'·63W.

HOLY ISLAND
Ridge ⚓ Q (3) 10s; 55°39'·70N 01°45'·97W.
Plough Rock ⚓ Q (9) 15s; 55°40'·24N 01°46'·00W.
Old Law E Bn ⚓ (Guile Pt) Oc WRG 6s 9m 4M; vis: 180·5°-G-258·5°-W-261·5°-R-shore.
Heugh ⚓ Oc WRG 6s 24m 5M; vis: 135°-G-308°-W-311-R-shore; 55°40'·09N 01°47'·99W.
Plough Seat ⚓ QR; 55°40'·37N 01°44'·97W.
Goldstone ⚓ QG; 55°40'·25N 01°43'·64W.

BERWICK-UPON-TWEED
Bkwtr Hd ⚓ Fl 5s 15m 6M; vis: 201°-009°, (obscured 155°-201°); W ○ twr, R cupola and base; FG (same twr) 8m 1M; vis 009°-G-155°; 55°45'·88N 01°59'·06W.

1	Ramsgate	1			11	31	61	78	91	107	126	189	205	205	232	Berwick-upon-Tweed	11
2	Sheerness	34	2			10	27	42	65	81	102	157	176	185	203	Amble	10
3	Gravesend	56	22	3			9	16	36	51	70	138	149	156	180	Sunderland	9
4	London Bridge	76	45	23	4			8	24	39	58	122	137	140	169	Hartlepool	8
5	Burnham-on-Crouch	44	34	53	76	5			7	16	35	88	114	121	143	Whitby	7
6	Brightlingsea	41	28	47	71	22	6			6	20	81	98	105	130	Scarborough	6
7	Harwich	40	50	65	83	31	20	7			5	58	83	87	114	Bridlington	5
8	River Deben (ent)	45	55	71	89	35	23	6	8			4	72	75	113	Hull	4
9	Southwold	62	80	95	113	58	46	30	23	9			3	34	83	Boston	3
10	Lowestoft	72	90	105	123	68	56	40	33	10	10			2	85	King's Lynn	2
11	Great Yarmouth	79	97	112	130	76	63	52	41	18	7	11			1	Great Yarmouth	1

25

AREA 5 *E Scotland – Berwick-upon-Tweed to C Wrath & N Isles*

SELECTED LIGHTS, BUOYS & WAYPOINTS

Positions are referenced to WGS84

BERWICK-UPON-TWEED TO BASS ROCK

BURNMOUTH
Ldg lts 241°. Front, FR 29m 4M; 55°50'·53N 02°04'·25W. Rear, 45m from front, FR 35m 4M. Both on W posts (unclear by day).

EYEMOUTH
Blind Buss ↲ Q; 55°52'·80N 02°05'·25E.
Ldg Lts 174°. Front, W Bkwtr Hd ✧, FG 9m 6M; 55°52'·47N 02°05'·29W. Rear, elbow 55m from front, FG 10m 6M.

ST ABBS to DUNBAR and BASS ROCK
St Abbs Hd ☆ 55°54'·96N 02°08'·29W; Fl 10s 68m **26M**; W twr; *Racon (T) 18M*.
Barns Ness Tower (Lt ho disused 36m); 55°59'·22N 02°26'·76W.
Bayswell Hill Ldg Lts 198°. Front, Oc G 6s 15m 3M; W △ on Or col; 188° -G(intens)-208°; 56°00'·25N 02°31'·21W. Rear, Oc G 6s 22m 3M; ▽ on Or col; synch with front,188°-G(intens)-208°.
Bass Rock, S side, ☆ Fl (3) 20s 46m 10M; W twr; vis: 241°- 107°; 56°04'·61N 02°38'·48W.

FIRTH OF FORTH AND SOUTH SHORE
(Direction of buoyage East to West)

NORTH BERWICK
Outfall ↲ Fl Y; 56°04'·29N 02°40'·89W.
Fidra ☆ 56°04'·39N 02°47'·13W; Fl (4) 30s 34m **15M**; W twr; obsc by Bass Rock, Craig Leith and Lamb Island.

PORT SETON, COCKENZIE, FISHERROW and S CHANNEL
Port Seton, E Pier Hd ✧ Iso WR 4s 10m W9M, R6M; vis: shore - R - 105°- W - 225°- R - shore; *Bell (occas)*; 55°58'·40N 02°57'·23W.
Fisherrow E Pier Hd ✧ Oc 6s 5m 6M; 55°56'·79N 03°04'·11W.
Narrow Deep ↺ Fl (2) R 10s; 56°01'·46N 03°04'·59W.
Herwit ▲ Fl (3) G 10s; 56°01'·05N 03°06'·52W.
North Craig ↲ Q (3) 10s 56°01'·02N 03°03'·52W.
Craigh Waugh ↲ Fl (2) 10s;56°00'·26N 03°04'·47W.
Diffuser Hds (Outer) ↲ 55°59'·81N 03°07'·84W.

LEITH and GRANTON
Leith Approach ↺ Fl R 3s; 55°59'·95N 03°11'·51W .
East Bkwtr Hd ✧ Iso R 4s 7m 9M; 55°59'·48N 03°10'·94W.
GrantonE Pier Head ✧ Fl R 2s 5m 6M; 55°59'·28N 03°13'·27W.

NORTH CHANNEL and MIDDLE BANK
Inchkeith Fairway ↺ Iso 2s; *Racon (T) 5M*; 56°03'·49N 03°00'·10W.
No. 1 ▲ Fl G 9s; 56°03'·22N 03°03'·71W.
No. 2 ↺ Fl R 9s; 56°02'·90N 03°03'·72W.
No. 3 ▲ Fl G 6s; 56°03'·22N 03°06'·10W.
No. 4 ↺ Fl R 6s; 56°02'·89N 03°06'·11W.
No. 5 ▲ Fl G 3s; 56°03'·18N 03°07'·88W.
No. 6 ↺ Fl R 3s; 56°03'·05N 03°08'·44W.
No. 8 ↺ Fl R 9s 56°02'·95N 03°09'·62W.

Inchkeith ☆ 56°02'·01N 03°08'·17W; Fl 15s 67m 14M; stone twr.
Pallas Rock ↲ VQ (9) 10s 56°01'·50N 03°09'·30W.
East Gunnet ↲ Q (3) 10s; 56°01'·41N 03°10'·38W.
West Gunnet ↲ Q (9) 15s 56°01'·34N 03°11'·06W.
No. 7 ▲ QG; *Racon (T) 5M*; 56°02'·80N 03°10'·97W.
No. 9 ▲ Fl G 6s; 56°02'·32N 03°13'·48W.
No. 10 ↺ Fl R 6s; 56°02'·07N 03°13'·32W.
No. 11 ▲ Fl G 3s 56°02'·08N 03°15'·26W.
No. 12 ↺ Fl R 3s; 56°01'·78N 03°15'·15W.
No. 13 ▲ Fl G 9s; 56°01'·77N 03°16'·94W.
No. 14 ↺ Fl R 9s; 56°01'·52N 03°16'·82W.
Oxcars ☆ Fl (2) WR 7s 16m W13M, R12M; W twr, R band; vis: 072°-W-087°- R-196°-W-313°-R-072°; 56°01'·36N 03°16'·84W.
Inchcolm E Pt ☆ Fl (3) 15s 20m 10M; Gy twr; part obsc by land 075°-145·5°; 56°01'·72N 03°17'·83W.
No. 15 ▲ Fl G 6s; 56°01'·39N 03°18'·95W.

MORTIMER'S DEEP
Hawkcraig Point Ldg Lts 292°. Front, Iso 5s 12m 14M; W twr; vis: 282°-302°; 56°03'·03N 03°17'·07W. Rear, 96m from front, Iso 5s 16m 14M; W twr; vis: 282°-302°.
Inchcolm S Lts in line 066°. Front, 84m from rear, Q 7m 7M; W twr; vis: 062·5°-082·5°; 56°01'·78N 03°18'·28W. Common Rear, Iso 5s 11m 7M; W twr; vis: 062·5°-082·5°; 56°01'·80N 03°18'·13W. N Lts in line 076·7°. Front, 80m from rear, Q 7m 7M; W twr; vis: 062·5°-082·5°.

APPROACHES TO FORTH BRIDGES
No. 17 ▲ Fl G 3s; 56°01'·23N 03°19'·84W.
No. 16 ↺ Fl R 3s; 56°00'·87N 03°19'·60W.
No. 19 ▲ Fl G 9s; 56°00'·71N 03°22'·47W.
Beamer Rk ✧ Fl 3s 6m 9M; W twr, R top; 56°00'·28N 03°24'·74W.

PORT EDGAR
W Bkwtr Hd ✧ Fl R 4s 4m 8M; 55°59'·86N 03°24'·78W. W blockhouse.

FIRTH OF FORTH – NORTH SHORE (INWARD)

BURNTISLAND
W Pier Outer Hd ✧ Fl (2) R 6s 7m; W twr; 56°03'·22N 03°14'·26W.
E Pier Outer Hd ✧ Fl (2) G 6s 7m 5M; 56°03'·24N 03°14'·17W.

ABERDOUR, BRAEFOOT BAY and INCHCOLM
Hawkcraig Pt ✧ (see **MORTIMER'S DEEP** above).
Braefoot Bay Terminal, W Jetty. Ldg Lts 247·3°. **Front**, Fl 3s 6m **15M**; W △ on E dolphin; vis: 237·2°-257·2°; 56°02'·16N 03°18'·71W; 4 dolphins with 2 FG (vert). **Rear**, 88m from front, Fl 3s 12m **15M**; W ▽ on appr gangway; vis: 237·2°-257·2°; synch with front.

INVERKEITHING BAY
St David's ↲ Fl G 5s 3m 7M; Or □, on pile; 56°01'·37N 03°22'·29W.
Channel ▲ QG; 56°01'·43N 03°23'·02W.

HM NAVAL BASE, ROSYTH

Main Chan Dir lt 323·5°. Bn 'A' Oc WRG 7m 4M; R ☐ on W post with R bands; vis: 318°-G-321°-321°-W-326°-R-328° (H24); 56°01'·19N 03°25'·61W.

Dir lt 115°, Bn 'C' Oc WRG 6s 7m 4M; W ▽ on W Bn; vis: 110°- R -113° W -116·5° - G -120°; 56°00'·61N 03°24'·25W.

S Arm Jetty Hd ⚓ L Fl (2) WR 12s 5m W9M; R6M; vis: 010°-W-280°-R-010°; 56°01'·09N 03°26'·58W.

RIVER FORTH

ROSYTH to GRANGEMOUTH

Dhu Craig ▲ Fl G 5s; 56°00'·74N 03°27'·23W.

Blackness ⚓ QR; 56°01'·06N 03°30'·30W.

Tancred Bank ⚓ Fl (2) R 10s; 56°01'·58N 03°31'·91W.

Dods Bank ⚓ Fl R 3s; 56°02'·03N 03°34'·07W.

Bo'ness ⚓ Fl R 10s; 56°02'·23N 03°35'·38W.

Torry ⚓ Fl G 10s 5m 7M; G ○ structure; 56°02'·46N 03°35'·28W.

Bo'ness Bcns ⚑ 2 QR 3m 2M; 56°01'·85N 03°36'·22W.

Bo'ness Hbr ⚓ ; 56°01'·26N 03°36'·46W.

GRANGEMOUTH

Grangemouth App No. 1 ⚓ Fl (3) 10s 4m 6M;56°02'·12N 03°38'·10W.

Hen & Chickens ▲ Fl (3) G 10s; 56°02'·35N 03°38'·08W.

FIRTH OF FORTH – NORTH SHORE (OUTWARD)

KIRKCALDY and METHIL

Kirkaldy E. Pier Hd ⚓ Fl WG 10s 12m 8M; vis: 156°-G-336°-W-156°; 56°06'·78N 03°08'·90W.

Methil Outer Pier Hd ⚓ Oc G 6s 8m 5M; W twr; vis: 280°-100°; 56°10'·76N 03°00'·48W.

ELIE and ST MONANS

Elie Ness ☆ 56°11'·04N 02°48'·77W; Fl 6s 15m **17M**; W twr.

St Monans Bkwtr Hd ⚓ Oc WRG 6s 5m W7M, R4M, G4M; vis: 282°-G-355°-W-026°-R-038°; 56°12'·20N 02°45'·94W.

PITTENWEEM and ANSTRUTHER EASTER

Pittenweem, Ldg Lts 037° Middle Pier Hd. Front, FR 4m 5M. Rear, FR 8m 5M. Both Gy Cols, Or stripes; 56°12'·69N 02°43'·69W.

Pittenweem, E Bkwtr Hd ⚓ Fl (2) RG 5s 9m R9M, G6M; vis: 265°-R-345°-G-055°; Horn 90s (occas); 56°12'·63N 02°43'·74W.

Anstruther, Ldg Lts 019°. Front FG 7m 4M; 56°13'·28N 02°41'·76W. Rear, 38m from front, FG 11m 4M, (both W masts).

MAY I, CRAIL, ST ANDREWS and FIFE NESS to MONTROSE

Isle of May ☆ 56°11'·12N 02°33'·46W(Summit); Fl (2) 15s 73m **22M**; ☐ twr on stone dwelling.

Crail, Ldg Lts 295°. Front, FR 24m 6M (not lit when hbr closed); 56°15'·46N 02°37'·84W. Rear, 30m from front, FR 30m 6M.

Fife Ness ☆ 56°16'·74N 02°35'·19W; Iso WR 10s 12m **W21M, R20M**; W bldg; vis: 143°-W-197°-R-217°-W-023°.

N Carr ⚓ Q (3) 10s 3m 5M; 56°18'·05N 02°32'·94W.

Bell Rk ☆ 56°26'·08N 02°23'·21W; Fl 5s 28m **18M**; Racon (M) 18M.

St Andrews N Bkwtr Bn ⚓ Fl G 3M 56°20'·36N 02°46'·77W.

RIVER TAY, TAYPORT, DUNDEE and PERTH

Tay Fairway ⚓ L Fl 10s; Bell; 56°28'·30N 02°36'·60W.

Middle ▲ Fl G 3s; 56°28'·08N 02°38'·24W.

Middle ⚓ Fl (2) R 6s 56°27'·65N 02°38'·23W.

Abertay N ⚓ Q (3) 10s; Racon (T) 8M; 56°27'·39N 02°40'·36W.

Abertay S (Elbow) ⚓ Fl R 6s 56°27'·13N 02°39'·83W.

Tayport High Lt Ho ☆ 56°27'·17N 02°53'·96W; Dir lt 269°; Iso WRG3s 24m **W22M, R17M, G16M**; W twr; vis: 267°-G-268°-W-270°-R-271°.

ARBROATH

Ldg lts 299·2°. Front , FR 7m 5M; W col; 56°33'·29N 02°35'·16W. Rear, 50m from front, FR 13m 5M; W col.

MONTROSE

Scurdie Ness ☆ 56°42'·10N 02°26'·24W; Fl (3) 20s 38m **23M**; W twr; Racon (T) 14-16M.

Outer Ldg Lts 271·5°; Front, FR 11m 5M; W twin pillars, R bands; 56°42'·21N 02°27'·41W; Rear, 272m from front, FR 18m 5M; W twr, R cupola.

Inner Ldg Lts 265°; Front FG 21m 5M; Rear FG 33m 5M.

MONTROSE TO RATTRAY HEAD

JOHNSHAVEN and GOURDON HARBOUR

Johnshaven, Ldg Lts 316°. Front, FR 5m; 56°47'·62N 02°20'·26W. Rear, 85m from front, FG 20m; shows R when unsafe to enter hbr.

Gourdon Hbr, Ldg Lts 358°. Front, FR 5m 5M; W twr; shows G when unsafe to enter; Siren (2) 60s (occas); 56°49'·69N 02°17'·24W. Rear, 120m from front, FR 30m 5M; W twr.

Todhead Lighthouse (disused), white tower, 13m.

STONEHAVEN to GIRDLE NESS

Outer Pier Hd ⚓ Iso WRG 4s 7m 5M; vis: 214°-G-246°-W-268°-R-280°; 56°57'·59N 02°12'·00W.

Girdle Ness ☆ Fl (2) 20s 56m **22M**; obsc by Greg Ness when brg more than about 020°; Racon (G) 25M; 57°08'·34N 02°02'·91W.

ABERDEEN

Fairway ⚓ Mo (A) 5s; Racon (T) 7M; 57°09'·31N 02°01'·95W.

Torry Ldg Lts 235·7°. Front, FR or G 14m 5M; R when ent safe, FG when dangerous to navigation; vis: 195°-279°; 57°08'·37N 02°04'·51W. Rear, 205m from front, FR 19m 5M; W twr; vis: 195°-279°.

S Bkwtr Hd ⚓ Fl (3) R 8s 23m 7M; 57°08'·69N 02°03'·34W.

N Pier Hd ⚓ Iso G 4s 11m 10M; W twr; 57°08'·74N 02°03'·69W. In fog FY 10m (same twr) vis: 136°-336°; Bell (3) 12s.

PETERHEAD and RATTRAY HEAD

Buchan Ness ☆ Fl 5s 40m **28M**; W twr, R bands; Racon (O) 14-16M; 57°28'·23N 01°46'·51W.

Kirktown Ldg lts 314°. Front, Oc R 6s 14m 10M; Or △ on lattice mast; 57°30'·22N 01°47'·21W. Rear, Oc R 6s 21m 10M (sync with front); Or ▽ on lattice mast.

S Bkwtr Hd ⚓ Fl (2) R 12s 24m 7M; 57°29'·79N 01°46'·54W.

N Bkwtr Hd ⚓ Iso RG 6s 19m 11M; W tripod; vis: 171°-R-236°-G-171°; Horn 30s; 57°29'·84N 01°46'·32W.

Rattray Hd ☆ 57°36'·61N 01°49'·03W; Fl (3) 30s 28m **24M**; W twr; *Racon (M) 15M*.

RATTRAY HEAD TO INVERNESS

Rattray Hd ☆ 57°36'·61N 01°49'·03W Fl (3) 30s 28m **24M**; W twr; *Racon (M) 15M*; *Horn (2) 45s*.

FRASERBURGH

Fraserburgh Ldg lt 291°; Iso R 2s 12m 9M; 57°41'·57N 02°00'·13W. Rear, 75m from front, Iso R 2s 17m 9M.
Fraserburgh, Balaclava Bkwtr Head ⚡ Fl (2) G 8s 26m 6M; dome on W twr; vis: 178°-326°; 57°41'·51N 01°59'·70W.
Kinnaird Hd ☆ 57°41'·87N 02°00'·26W Fl 5s 25m **22M**; vis: 092°-297°.

MACDUFF, BANFF and WHITEHILLS

Macduff Pier Hd ⚡ Fl (2) WRG 6s 12m W9M, R7M; W twr; vis: shore-G-115°-W-174°-R-210°; 57°40'·25N 02°30'·02W.
Macduff Ldg Lts 127°, Front FR 44m 3M; 57°40'·12N 02°29'·75W. Rear, 60m from front, FR 55m 3M; both Or △ on mast.
Banff Ldg Lts 295°, Front Fl R 4s; 57°40·30N 02°31·36W. Rear, QR; both vis: 210°-345°.
Whitehills Pier Hd ⚡ 57°40'·80N 02°34'·88W Fl WR 3s 7m W9M, R6M; W twr; vis: 132°-R-212°-W-245°.

PORTSOY and FINDOCHTY

Portsoy Pier Ldg Lts 173°, Front Fl G 4s 20m 3M; post; 57°41'·09N 02°41'·40W; Rear Q G 22m 3M; R △ on BW post.
Findochty Middle Pier Ldg Lts 166°, Front FR 6m 3M; 57°41'·90N 02°54'·20W. Rear FR 10m 3M.

BUCKIE

West Muck ⚡ QR 5m 7M; tripod; 57°41'·06N 02°58'·01W.
N Pier 60m from Hd ☆ 57°40'·9N 02°57'·5W Oc R 10s 15m **15M** W twr.

LOSSIEMOUTH, HOPEMAN and BURGHEAD

Lossiemouth S Pier Hd ⚡ Fl R 6s 11m 5M; *Siren 60s*; 57°43'·42N 03°16'·69W.
Covesea Skerries ☆ 57°43'·47N 03°20'·45W Fl WR 20s 49m **W24M, R20M**; W twr; vis: 076° - W - 267° - R - 282°.
Hopeman Ldg Lts 081°, Front,FR 3m; 57°42'·71N 03°26'·18W. Rear, 10m from front, FR 4m.
Burghead N Bkwtr Hd ⚡ Oc 8s 7m 5M; 57°42'·09N 03°30'·03W.

FINDHORN, NAIRN and INVERNESS FIRTH

Findhorn Landfall ⚓ LF 10s 57°40'·34N 03°38'·77W.
Nairn E Pier Hd ⚡ Oc WRG 4s 6m 5M; 8-sided twr; vis: shore-G-100°-W-207°-R-shore; 57°35'·62N 03°51'·65W
Riff Bank E ⚓ Fl Y 10s 3m 5M 57°38'·38N 03°58'·18W.

SOUTH CHANNEL

Riff Bank S ⚓ Q (6) + L Fl 15s; 57°36'·73N 04°00'·97W.
Chanonry ☆ 57°34'·44N 04°05'·57W Oc 6s 12m **15M**; W twr; vis: 148°-073°.
Munlochy ⚓ L Fl 10s; 57°32'·91N 04°07'·65W .
Petty Bank ⚓ Fl R 5s 57°31'·58N 04°08'·98W.
Meikle Mee ⚑ Fl G 3s 57°30'·26N 04°12'·02W.
Longman Pt ⚓ Fl WR 2s 7m W5M, R4M; vis: 078°-W-258°-R-078°; 57°29'·99N 04°13'·31W.

Craigton Point ⚡ Fl WRG 4s 6m W11M, R7M, G7M; vis: 312° - W - 048° - R - 064° - W - 085°- G - shore; 57°30'·05N 04°14'·09W.
Bridge Centre, Or △; *Racon (K) 6M*; 57°29'·97N 04°13'·79W.

INVERNESS and CALEDONIAN CANAL

R. Ness Outer ⚓ QR 3m 4M; 57°29'·83N 04°13'·93W.
Carnarc Pt ⚡ Fl G 2s 8m 4M; G f'work twr; 57°29'·72N 04°14'·25W.
Clachnaharry, S Tr'ng Wall Hd ⚓ Iso G 4s 5m 2M; tfc sigs; 57°29'·43N 04°15'·86W.

INVERNESS TO DUNCANSBY HEAD

CROMARTY FIRTH and INVERGORDON

Fairway ⚓ L Fl 10s; *Racon (M) 5M*; 57°39'·96N 03°54'·19W.
Cromarty Bank ⚑ Fl (2) G 10s; 57°40'·66N 03°56'·78W.
Buss Bank ⚓ Fl R 3s 57°40'·97N 03°59'·54W.
Cromarty - The Ness (Lt ho disused W tr 13m); 57°40'·98N 04°02'·20W
Nigg Oil Terminal Pier Hd ⚡ Oc G 5s 31m 5M; Gy twr; floodlit; 57°41'·54N 04°02'·60W.

DORNOCH FIRTH to LYBSTER

Tarbat Ness ☆ 57°51'·88N 03°46'·76W Fl (4) 30s 53m **24M**; W twr, R bands; *Racon (T) 14-16M*.
Lybster, S Pier Hd ⚡ Oc R 6s 10m 3M; 58°17'·79N 03°17'·41W.
Clyth Ness Lt Ho (unlit); W twr, R band; 58°18'·64N 03°12'·74W.

WICK

S Pier Hd ⚡ Fl WRG 3s 12m W12M, R9M, G9M; W 8-sided twr; vis: 253°-G-270°-W-286°-R-329°; *Bell (2) 10s* (occas); 58°26'·34N 03°04'·73W.
Dir lt 288·5° F WRG 9m W10M, R7M, G7M; col, N end of bridge; vis: 283·5°-G-287·2°-W-289·7°-R-293·5°; 58°26'·54N 03°05'·34W
Noss Hd ☆ 58°28'·71N 03°03'·09W Fl WR 20s 53m **W25M, R21M**; W twr; vis: shore-R-191°-W-shore.

DUNCANSBY HEAD TO CAPE WRATH

Duncansby Hd ☆ 58°38'·65N 03°01'·58W Fl 12s 67m **22M**; W twr; *Racon (T)*.
Pentland Skerries ☆ 58°41'·41N 02°55'·49W Fl (3) 30s 52m **23M**; W twr.
Lother Rock ⚡ Fl 2s 13m 6M; *Racon (M) 10M*; 58°43'·79N 02°58'·69W.
Swona ⚡ Fl 8s 17m 9M; vis: 261°-210°; 58°44'·25N 03°04'·24W.
Swona N Hd ⚡ Fl (3) 10s 16m 10M; 58°45'·11N 03°03'·10W.
Stroma ☆, Swilkie Point 58°41'·75N 03°07'·01W Fl (2) 20s 32m **26M**; W twr.
Dunnet Hd ☆ 58°40'·28N 03°22'·60W Fl (4) 30s 105m **23M**.

THURSO, SCRABSTER and CAPE WRATH

Thurso Ldg Lts 195°. Front, FG 5m 4M; Gy post; 58°35'·96N 03°30'·76W. Rear, FG 6m 4M; Gy mast.
Scrabster Q. E. Pier Hd ⚡ Fl (2) 4s 8m 8M 58°36'·66N 03°32'·31W.

Strathy Pt ☆ 58°36'·04N 04°01'·12W Fl 20s 45m **26M**; W twr on W dwelling. F.R. on chy 100° 8·5M.

Sule Skerry ☆ 59°05'·09N 04°24'·38W Fl (2) 15s 34m **21M**; W twr; *Racon (T)*.

North Rona ☆ 59°07'·27N 05°48'·91W Fl (3) 20s 114m **24M**.

Sula Sgeir ⚡ Fl 15s 74m 11M; ☐ structure; 59°05'·61N 06°09'·57W.

Loch Eriboll, White Hd ⚡ Fl WR10s 18m W13M, R12M; W twr and bldg; vis: 030°-W-172°-R-191°-W-212°; 58°31'·01N 04°38'·90W.

Cape Wrath ☆ 58°37'·54N 04°59'·94W Fl (4) 30s 122m **22M**; W twr.

ORKNEY ISLANDS

Tor Ness ☆ 58°46'·78N 03°17'·86W Fl 5s 21m **17M**; W twr.

Cantick Hd (S Walls, SE end) ☆ 58°47'·23N 03°07'·88W Fl 20s 35m 13M; W twr.

SCAPA FLOW and APPROACHES

Long Hope, S Ness Pier Hd ⚡ Fl WRG 3s 6m W7M, R5M, G5M; vis: 082°-G- 242°-W- 252°-R-082°; 58°48'·05N 03°12'·35W.

Hoxa Head ⚡ Fl WR 3s 15m W9M, R6M; W twr; vis: 026°-W-163°-R-201°-W-215°; 58°49'·31N 03°02'·09W.

Nevi Skerry ⚓ Fl (2) 6s 7m 6M; 58°50'·67N 03°02'·70W.

Rose Ness ⚡ 58°52'·33N 02°49'·97W Fl 6s 24m 8M; W twr.

Barrel of Butter ⚡ Fl (2) 10s 6m 7M; 58 53'·40N 03°07'·62W.

Cava ⚡ Fl WR 3s 11m W10M, R8M; W ○ twr; vis: 351°-W-143°-196°-W-251°-R-271°-R-298°; 58°53'·21N 03°10'·70W .

Houton Bay Ldg Lts 316°. Front ⚓ Fl G 3s 8m. Rear ⚓, 200m from front, FG 16m; vis: 312°- 320°; 58°54'·97N 03°11'·56W.

CLESTRAN SOUND and HOY SOUND

Graemsay Is Hoy Sound Low ☆ Ldg Lts 104°. **Front**, 58°56'·42N 03°18'·60W Iso 3s 17m **15M**; W twr; vis: 070°-255°. **High Rear**, 1·2M from front, Oc WR 8s 35m **W20M, R16M;** W twr; vis: 097°-R-112°-W-163°-R-178°-W-332°; obsc on Ldg line within 0·5M.

Skerry of Ness ⚡ Fl WG 4s 7m W7M, G4M; vis: shore -W-090°- G-shore; 58°56'·95N 03°17'·83W.

STROMNESS

Ldg Lts 317°. Front, FR 29m 11M; post on W twr; 58°57'·61N 03°18'·15W. Rear, 55m from front, FR 39m 11M; vis: 307°-327°; H24.

AUSKERRY

Copinsay ☆ 58°53'·77N 02°40'·35W Fl (5) 30s 79m **21M**; W twr.

Auskerry ☆ 59°01'·51N 02°34'·34W Fl 20s 34m **20M**; W twr.

Helliar Holm, S end ⚡ Fl WRG 10s 18m W14M, R11M, G11M; W twr; vis: 256°-G-276°-W-292°-R-098°-W-116°-G-154°; 59°01'·13N 02°54'·09W.

Balfour Pier Shapinsay ⚡ Fl (2) WRG 5s 5m W3M, R2M, G2M; vis: 270°-G-010°-W-020°-R-090°; 59°01'·86N 02°54'·49W.

KIRKWALL

Thieves Holm, ⚡ Q.R8M; 59°01'·09N 02°56'·21W.

Pier N end ☆ 58°59'·29N 02°57'·72W Iso WRG 5s 8m **W15M**, R13M, G13M; W twr; vis: 153°-G-183°-W-192°-R-210°.

WIDE FIRTH
Linga Skerry ⚓ Q (3) 10s; 59°02'·39N 02°57'·56W.
Boray Skerries ⚓ Q (6) + L Fl 15s; 59°03'·65N 02°57'·66W.
Skertours ⚓ Q; 59°04'·11N 02°56'·72W.
Galt Skerry ⚓ Q; 59°05'·21N 02°54'·20W.
Brough of Birsay ☆ 59°08'·19N 03°20'·41W Fl (3) 25s 52m **18M**.
Papa Stronsay NE end, The Ness Fl(4)20s 8m 9M; W twr; 59°09'·34N 02°34'·93W.

SANDAY ISLAND and NORTH RONALDSAY
Quiabow ⬆ Fl (2) G 12s; 59°09'·82N 02°36'·30W.
Start Pt ☆ 59°16'·69N 02°22'·71W Fl (2) 20s 24m **18M**.
Kettletoft Pier Hd ⚡ Fl WRG 3s 7m W7M, R5M, G5M; vis: 351°-W- 011°-R-180°-G-351; 59°13'·80N 02°35'·86W.
N Ronaldsay ☆ NE end, 59°23'·34N 02°22'·91W Fl 10s 43m **24M**; R twr, W bands; *Racon (T) 14-17M*.

EDAY and EGILSAY
Calf Sound ⚡ Fl (3) WRG 10s 6m W8M, R6M, G6M; W twr; vis: shore-R-215°-W-222°-G-301°-W-305°; 59°14'·21N 02°45'·82W.
Backaland Pier ⚡ 59°09'·43N 02°44'·88W Fl R 3s 5m 4M; vis: 192°-250°.
Egilsay Graand ⚓ Q (6) + L Fl 15s; 59°06'·86N 02°54'·42W.

WESTRAY and PIEROWALL
Noup Head ☆ 59°19'·86N 03°04'·23W Fl 30s 79m **20M**; W twr; vis: about 335°-282° but partially obsc 240°-275°.
Pierowall E Pier Head ⚡ Fl WRG 3s 7m W11M, R7M, G7M; vis: 254°-G-276°-W-291°-R-308°-G-215°; 59°19'·35N 02°58'·53W.
Papa Westray, Moclett Bay Pier Head ⚡ Fl WRG 5s 7m W5M, R3M, G3M; vis: 306°-G-341°-W-040°-R-074°; 59°19'·60N 02°53'·52W.

SHETLAND ISLES
FAIR ISLE
Skadan South ☆, 59°30'·84N 01°39'·16W Fl (4) 30s 32m **22M**; W twr; vis: 260°-146°, obsc inshore 260°-282°.
Skroo ☆ N end 59°33'·13N 01°36'·58W Fl (2) 30s 80m **22M**; W twr; vis: 086·7°-358°.

MAINLAND, SOUTH
Sumburgh Head ☆ 59°51'·21N 01°16'·58W Fl (3) 30s 91m **23M**.
Mousa, Perie Bard ⚡ Fl 3s 20m 10M; 59°59'·84N 01°09'·51W.

BRESSAY and LERWICK
Bressay, Kirkabister Ness ☆ 60°07'·20N 01°07'·29W; Fl (2) 20s 32m **23M**.
Maryfield Ferry Terminal ⚡ Oc WRG 6s 5m 5M; vis: W008°-R013°-G-111°-008°; 60°09'·43N 01°07'·45W.
North Ness ⚡ Iso WG 4s 4m 5M; vis: shore-W-158°-G-216°-W-301°; 60°09'·57N 01°08'·77W
Loofa Baa ⚓ Q (6) + L Fl 15s 4m 5M; 60°09'·72N 01°08'·79W.
Soldian Rock ⚓ Q (6) + L Fl 15s 60°12'·51N 01°04'·73W.

N ent Dir lt 215°, Oc WRG 6s 27m 8M; Y △, Or stripe; vis: 211°-R-214°-W-216°-G-221°; 60°10'·47N 01°09'·53W.

Rova Hd ⚓ 60°11'·46N 01°08'·60W Fl (3) WRG 18s 12m W12M, R9M, G9M; W twr; vis: 090°-R-182°-W-191°-G-213°-R-241°-W-261·5°-G-009°-R-040°. Same structure and synchronised: Fl (3) WRG 18s 14m **W16M**, R13M, G13M; vis: 176·5°-R-182°-W-191°-G-196·5°.

Dales Voe ⚓ Fl (2) WRG 8s 5m W4M, R3M, G3M; vis: 220°-G-227°-W-233°-R-240°; 60°11'·79N 01°11'·23W.

Hoo Stack ⚓ Fl (4) WRG 12s 40m W7M, R5M, G5M; W pylon; vis: 169°-R-180°-W-184°-G-193°-W-169°. Same structure, Dir lt 182°. Fl (4) WRG 12s 33m W9M, R6M, G6M; vis: 177°- R-180°-W-184°-W-187°; synch with upper lt; 60°14'·96N 01°05'·38W.

Mull (Moul) of Eswick ⚓ Fl WRG 3s 50m W9M, R6M, G6M; W twr; vis: 028°-R-200°-W-207°-G-018°-W-028°; 60°15'·74N 01°05'·90W.

Inner Voder ⚓ Q (9) 15s; 60°16'·43N 01°05'·18W.

WHALSAY and SKERRIES

Symbister Ness ⚓ Fl (2) WG 12s 11m W8M, G6M; W twr; vis: shore-W-203°-G-shore; 60°20'·43N 01°02'·29W.

Suther Ness ⚓ Fl WRG 3s 10m W10M, R8M, G7M; vis: shore -W-038°-R-173°-W-206°-G-shore; 60°22'·12N 01°00'·20W.

Bound Skerry ☆ 60°25'·47N 00°43'·72W Fl 20s 44m **20M**; W twr.

South Mouth. Ldg Lts 014°. Front, FY3m 2M; 60°25'·33N 00°45'·01W. Rear, FY 12m 2M.

Muckle Skerry ⚓ Fl (2) WRG 10s 15m W7M, R5M, G5M; W twr; vis: 046°-R-192°-R-272°-G-348°-W-353°-R-046°; 60°26'·41N 00°51'·84W.

YELL SOUND

S ent, Lunna Holm ⚓ Fl (3) WRG 15s 19m W10M, R7M, G7M; W ○twr; vis: shore-R-090°-W-094°-G-209°-W-275°-R-shore; 60°27'·34N 01°02'·52W.

Firths Voe ☆, N shore 60°27'·21N 01°10'·63W Oc WRG 8s 9m **W15M**, R10M, G10M; W twr; vis: 189°-W-194°-G-257°-W-261°-R-339°-W-066°.

Linga Is. Dir lt 150° ⚓ Q (4) WRG 8s 10m W9M, R9M, G9M; vis: 145°-R-148°-W-152°-G-155°. Q (4) WRG 8s 10m W7M, R4M, G4M; same structure; vis: 052°-R-146°; 154°-G-196°-W-312°; synch; 60°26'·80N 01°09'·13W.

The Rumble Bn ⚓ R Bn; Fl 10s 8m 4M; *Racon (O)*; 60°28'·16N 01°07'·26W.

Yell, Ulsta Ferry Term. Bkwtr Hd ⚓ Oc RG 4s 7m R5M, G5M; vis: shore-G-354°, 044°-R-shore. Same structure; Oc WRG 4s 5m W8M, R5M, G5M; vis: shore-G-008°-W-036°-R-shore; 60°29'·74N 01°09'·52W.

Toft Ferry Terminal ☆,Dir lt 241° (H24); Dir Oc WRG 10s 8m **W16M**, R10M, G10M; vis: 236°-G-240°-W-242°-R-246°; By day W2M, R1M, G1M. 60°27'·96N 01°12'·34W.

Ness of Sound, W side ⚓ Fl (3) WRG 12s 18m W9M, R6M, G6M; vis: shore-G-345°-W-350°-R-160°-W-165°-G-shore;60°31'·34N 01°11'·28W.

Brother Is. Dir lt 329°. Fl (4) WRG 8s 16m W10M, R7M, G7M; vis: 323·5°-G-328°-W-330°-R-333·5°; 60°30'·95N 01°14'·11W.

Mio Ness ⚓ Q (2) WR 10s 12m W7M, R4M; W ○ twr; vis: 282° - W - 238° - R - 282°; 60°29'·66N 01°13'·68W.

Tinga Skerry ⚓ Q (2) G 10s 9m 5M. W ○ twr; 60°30'·48N 01°14'·86W.

YELL SOUND, NORTH ENTRANCE

Bagi Stack ⚓ Fl (4) 20s 45m 10M; 60°43'·53N 01°07'·54W.

Gruney Is ⚓ Fl WR 5s 53m W8M, R6M; W twr; vis: 064°-R-180°-W-012°; *Racon (T) 14M*; 60°39'·15N 01°18'·17W.

Pt of Fethaland ☆ 60°38'·05N 01°18'·70W Fl (3) WR 15s 65m **W24M, R20M**; vis 080°-R-103°-W-160°-206°-W-340°.

Muckle Holm ⚓ Fl (4) 10s 32m 10M 60°34'·83N 01°16'·01W.

Little Holm ⚓ Iso 4s 12m 6M; W twr; 60°33'·42N 01°15'·88W.

Outer Skerry ⚓ Fl 6s 12m 8M; 60°33'·04N 01°18'·32W.

Quey Firth ⚓ Oc WRG 6s 22m W12M, R8M, G8M; W twr; vis: shore (through S & W)-W-290°-G-327°-W-334°-W-shore; 60°31'·43N 01°19'·58W.

Lamba, S side ⚓Fl WRG 3s 30m W8M, R5M, G5M; W twr; vis: shore-G-288°-W-293°-R-327°-W-044°-R-140°-W-shore. Dir lt 290·5° Fl WRG 3s 24m W10M, R7M, G7M; vis: 285·5°-G-288°-W-293°-W-295·5°; 60°30'·73N 01°17'·84W.

SULLOM VOE

Gluss Is ☆ Ldg Lts 194·7° (H24). **Front**, 60°29'·77N 01°19'·44W F 39m **19M**; □ on Gy twr; H24. **Rear**, 0·75M from front, F 69m **19M**; □ on Gy twr.; H24. Both Lts 9M by day.

Little Roe ⚓ Fl (3) WR 10s 16m W5M, R4M; W structure, Or band; vis: 036°-R-095·5°-W-036°; 60°29'·99N 01°16'·46W.

Skaw Taing ⚓ Ldg Lts 150·5°. Front, Oc WRG 5s 21m W8M, R5M, G5M; Or and W structure; vis: 049°-W-078°-G-147°-W-154°-R-169°-W-288°; 60°29'·10N 01°16'·86W. Rear, 195m from front, Oc 5s 35m 8M; vis: W145°-156°.

Ness of Bardister ⚓ Oc WRG 8s 20m W9M, R6M, G6M; Or &W structure; vis: 180·5°-W-240°- R-310·5°-W-314·5°-G-030·5°; 60°28'·19N 01°19'·63W.

Fugla Ness. Lts in line 212·3°. Rear, 60°27'·25N 01°19'·74W Iso 4s 45m 14M. Common front 60°27'·45N 01°19'·57W Iso 4s 27m 14M; synch with rear Lts. Lts in line 203°. Rear, 60°27'·26N 01°19'·81W Iso 4s 45m 14M.

Sella Ness ☆ Dir lt 133·5° 60°26'·76N 01°16'·66W Oc WRG 10s 19m **W16M**, R3M, G3M; vis: 123·5° -G- 130·5°-Al WG(white phase increasing with brg)-132·5°-W-134·5°-Al WR(R phase inc with brg)-136·5°-R-143·5°; H24. By day Oc WRG 10s 19m W2M, R1M,G1M as above.

EAST YELL, UNST and BALTA SOUND

Whitehill ⚓ Fl WR 3s 24m W9M, R6M; vis: shore-W-163°-R-211°-W-352°-R-shore.

Balta Sound ⚓Fl WR 10s 17m 10M, R7M; vis: 249°-W-008°-R-058°-W-154°; 60°44'·48N 00°47'·56W.

Holme of Skaw ⚓ Fl 5s 8m 8M; 60°49'·87N 00°46'·33W.

Muckle Flugga ☆ 60°51'·32N 00°53'·14W Fl (2) 20s 66m **22M**.

Yell. Cullivoe Bkwtr Hd ⚓ Fl (2) WRG 10s 3m 4M; vis: 080°-G- 294°-W-355°-R-080°; 60°41'·91N 00°59'·66W.

Head of Mula ⚓Fl WRG 5s 48m W10M, G7M, R7M; metal

framework twr; vis: 292°-G-357°-W-002°-R-157°-W-161·5; 60°44'·48N 00°47'·56W.

MAINLAND, WEST

Esha Ness ☆ 60°29'·34N 01°37'·65W Fl 12s 61m **25M**.

Ness of Hillswick ⚲ Fl (4) WR 15s 34m W9M, R6M; vis: 217°-W-093°-R-114°; 60°27'·21N 01°29'·80W.

Muckle Roe, Swarbacks Minn ⚲ Fl WR 3s 30m W9M, R6M; vis: 314°-W-041°-R-075°-W-137°; 60°20'·98N 01°27'·07W.

W Burra Firth Outer ⚲ Oc WRG 8s 27m W9M, R7M, G7M; vis: 136°-G-142°-W-150°-R-156°. H24; 60°17'·79N 01°33'·56W.

W Burra Firth Inner ☆ 60°17'·78N 01°32'·17W F WRG 9m **W15M**, R9M, G9M; vis: 095°-G-098°-W-102°-105°; H24.

Ve Skerries ⚲ Fl (2) 20s 17m 11M; W twr; *Racon (T) 15M*; 60°22'·36N 01°48'·78W.

Papa Stour Housa Voe Dir lt 228° ⚲ F WRG 2m W9M, R7M, G7M; vis: 219°- G-226°- W-230°-R-239°; 60°19'·58N 01°40'·47W.

Rams Head ⚲ Fl WRG 8s 16m W9M, R6M; G6M; W house; vis: 265°-G-355°-W-012°-R-090°-W-136°, obsc by Vaila I when brg more than 030°; 60°11'·96N 01°33'·47W.

North Havra ⚲ Fl(3) WRG 12s 24m W11M, R8M, G8M; W twr; vis: 001°-G-053·5°-W-060·5°-R-182°, 274°- G-334°-W-337·5°-R -001°; 60°09'·85N 01°20'·31W.

SCALLOWAY

Bullia Skerry ⚲ Fl 5s 5m 5M; steel pillar & platform 60°06'·55N 01°21'·57W.

Point of the Pund ⚲ Fl WRG 5s 20m W7M, R5M, G5M; W twr; vis: 350°-R-090°-G-111°-R-135°-W-140°-G-177°, 267°-W-350°; 60°07'·99N 01°18'·31W.

Whaleback Skerry ⚲ Q; 60°07'·95N 01°18'·90W.

Blacks Ness Pier SW corner ⚲ Oc WRG 10s 10m W11M, G8M, R8M; vis: 052°-G-063·5°-W-065·5°-R-077°; 60°08'·02N 01°16'·59W.

Fugla Ness ⚲ Fl (2) WRG 10s 20m W10M, R7M, G7M; W twr; vis: 014°-G-032°-W-082°-R-134°-W-shore; 60°06'·38N 01°20'·85W.

FOULA

South Ness ☆ 60°06'·75N 02°03'·87W Fl (3) 15s 36m **18M**; W twr; vis: obscured 123°-221°.

		c1	c2	c3	c4	c5	c6	c7	c8	c9	c10	c11	c12		
1	Berwick-upon-Tweed	1	11	155	79	47	76	104	144	126	120	125	145	Cape Wrath	11
2	Eyemouth	10	2	10	95	124	120	148	190	170	162	156	160	Lerwick	10
3	Dunbar	26	17	3	9	50	46	74	114	104	90	95	115	Kirkwall	9
4	Port Edgar	58	50	34	4	8	31	59	99	89	75	80	100	Scrabster	8
5	Methil	45	36	20	20	5	7	29	69	58	44	50	72	Wick	7
6	Fife Ness	38	29	17	34	16	6	6	43	32	26	44	74	Helmsdale	6
7	Dundee	58	49	37	54	36	20	7	5	13	34	59	90	Inverness	5
8	Montrose	59	51	43	61	43	27	27	8	4	23	48	79	Nairn	4
9	Stonehaven	72	66	60	78	60	44	45	20	9	3	25	56	Lossiemouth	3
10	Aberdeen	82	78	73	90	72	56	57	32	13	10	2	33	Banff/Macduff	2
11	Peterhead	105	98	93	108	94	78	80	54	35	25	11	1	Peterhead	1

AREA 6 *NW Scotland – C Wrath to Oban including The Western Isles*

SELECTED LIGHTS, BUOYS & WAYPOINTS

Positions are referenced to WGS84

CAPE WRATH TO LOCH TORRIDON

Cape Wrath ☆ 58°37'·54N 04°59'·99W Fl (4) 30s 122m **22M**; W twr.

LOCH INCHARD and LOCH LAXFORD

Kinlochbervie Dir lt 327° ☆. 58°27'·49N 05°03'·08W WRG 15m **16M**; vis: 326°-FG-326·5°-Al GW-326·75°-FW-327·25°-Al RW-327·5°-FR-328°.

Creag Mhòr Dir lt 147°; Iso WRG 2s 16m 4M; vis: 136·5°-R -146·5°-W-147·5°-G-157·5°; 58°26'·99N 05°02'·45W.

Stoer Head ☆ 58°14'·43N 05°24'·07W Fl 15s 59m **24M**; W twr.

LOCH INVER, SUMMER ISLES and ULLAPOOL

Soyea I ⚲ Fl (2) 10s 34m 6M; 58°08'·56N 05°19'·67W.

Glas Leac ⚲ Fl WRG 3s 7m 5M; vis: 071°- W-078°-R-090°-103°- W-111°, 243°-W-247°-G-071°; 58°08'·68N 05°16'·36W.

Rubha Cadail ⚲ Fl WRG 6s 11m W9M, R6M, G6M; W twr; vis: 311°-G-320°-W-325°-R-103°-W-111°-G-118°-W-127°-R-157°-W-199°; 57°55'·51N 05°13'·40W.

Ullapool Pt ⚲ Iso R 4s 8m 6M; W twr; vis: 258°-108°; 57°53'·59N 05°09'·93W.

Cailleach Head ⚲ Fl (2) 12s 60m 9M; W twr; vis: 015°-236°; 57°55'·81N 05°24'·23W.

LOCH EWE and LOCH GAIRLOCH

Fairway ⚲ L Fl 10s; 57°51'·98N 05°40'·09W.

Rubha Reidh ☆ 57°51'·52N 05°48'·72W Fl (4) 15s 37m **24M**.

Glas Eilean ⚲ Fl WRG 6s 9m W6M, R4M; vis: 080°-W-102°-R-296°-W-333°-G-080°; 57°42'·79N 05°42'·42W.

OUTER HEBRIDES – EAST SIDE

LEWIS

Butt of Lewis ☆ 58°30'·89N 06°15'·84W Fl 5s 52m **25M**; R twr; vis: 056°-320°.

Tiumpan Head ☆ 58°15'·66N 06°08'·29W Fl (2) 15s 55m **25M**; W twr.

Broad Bay Tong Anch. Ldg Lts 320°, Oc R 8s 8m 4M; 58°14'·48N 06°19'·98W. Rear, 70m from front, Oc R 8s 9m 4M.

STORNOWAY

Arnish Point ☆ Fl WR 10s 17m W9M, R7M; W ○ twr; vis: 088°-W-198°-R-302°-W-013°; 58°11'·50N 06°22'·16W.

Sandwick Bay, NW side ⚡ Oc WRG 6s 10m 9M; vis: 334°-G-341°-W-347°-R-354°; 58°12'·20N 06°22'·11W.

No. 1 Pier SW corner ⚡ Q WRG 5m 11M; vis: shore-G-335°-W-352°-R-shore; 58°12'·36N 06°23'·43W.

Creed Estuary ⚡ Iso WRG 10s 24m 5M; vis: 277°-G-282°-W-290°-R-295°; 58°12'·03N 06°23'·47W.

No. 3 Pier ⚡ Q (2) G 10s 7m 2M 58°12'·31N 06°23'·28W.

Glumaig Hbr ⚡ Iso WRG 3s 8m 3M; 58°11'·27N 06°22'·9W; grey framework twr; vis: 150°-G-174°-W-180°-R-205°.

LOCH ERISORT, LOCH SHELL and EAST LOCH TARBERT

Shiants ⬥ QG; 57°54'·57N 06°25'·70W.

Sgeir Inoe ⬥ Fl G 6s; *Racon (M) 5M*; 57°50'·93N 06°33'·93W.

Eilean Glas (Scalpay) ☆ 57°51'·41N 06°38'·55W Fl (3) 20s 43m **23M**; W twr, R bands; *Racon (T) 16-18M*.

Sgeir Graidach ⚓ Q (6) + L Fl 15s; 57°50'·36N 06°41'·37W.

Sgeir Ghlas ⚡ Iso WRG 4s 9m W9M, R6M, G6M; W ○ twr; vis: 282°-G-319°-W-329°-R-153°-W-164°-G-171°; 57°52'·36N 06°45'·24W.

Tarbert ⚡ 57°53'·82N 06°47'·93W Oc WRG 6s 10m 5M.

SOUND OF HARRIS, LEVERBURGH and BERNERAY

No.1 ⬥ QG; 57°41'·20N 07°02'·67W.

No. 3 ⬥ Fl G 5s; 57°41'·86N 07°03'·44W.

No. 4 ⬥ Fl R 5s; 57°41'·76N 07°03'·63W.

Suilven ⬥ Fl (3)R 10s; 57°41'·68N 07°04'·36W.

Cabbage ⬥ Fl (2) R 6s; *Racon (T) 5M (3cm)*; 57°42'·13N 07°03'·96W.

Leverburgh Ldg Lts 014·7°. Front, Q 10m 4M 57°46'·23N 07°02'·04W. Rear, Oc 3s 12m 4M.

Jane's Tower ⚓ Q (2) G 5s 6m 4M; vis: obscured 273°-318°; 57°45'·76N 07°02'·12W.

Leverburgh Reef ⚓ Fl R 2s 4m 57°45'·97N 07°01'·86W.

Leverburgh Pier Hd ⚡ Oc WRG 8s 5m 2M; Gy col; vis: 305°-G-059°-W-066°-R-125°; 57°46'·01N 07°01'·62W.

NORTH UIST

Fairway ⬥ L Fl 10s; 57°40'·23N 07°01'·39W.

Valley Island ⚡ Fl WRG 3s 4m 8M; vis: 206°-W-085°-G-140°-W-145°-R-206°; 57°39'·69N 07°26'·42W.

Griminish Hbr Ldg Lts 183°. Front, QG 6m 4M; 57°39'·38N 07°26'·75W. Rear, 110m from front, QG 7m 4M.

LOCH MADDY and GRIMSAY

Weaver's Pt ⚡ 57°36'·49N 07°06'·00W Fl 3s 24m 7M; W hut.

Glas Eilean Mòr ⚡ 57°35'·95N 07°06'·70W Fl (2) G 4s 8m 5M.

Vallaquie I ⚡ Fl (3) WRG 8s 11m W7M, R5M, G5M; W pillar; vis: shore-G-205°-W-210°-R-240°-G-254°-W-257°-R-shore; 57°35'·50N 07°09'·40W.

Lochmaddy Ldg Lts 298°. Front, Ro-Ro Pier 2 FG (vert) 8m 4M. Rear, 110m from front, Oc G 8s 10m 4M; vis: 284°-304°; 57°35'·76N 07°09'·36W.

Grimsay No. 1 ⬥ Fl (2) R 8s; 57°28'·26N 07°11'·82W.

SOUTH UIST and LOCH CARNAN

Landfall ⚓ L Fl 10s; 57°22'·27N 07°11'·52W.

Ldg Lts 222°. Front Fl R 2s 7m 5M; W ◇ on post; 57°22'·00N 07°16'·34W. Rear, 58m from front, Iso R 10s 11m 5M; W ◇ on post.

Ushenish ☆ (S Uist) 57°17'·89N 07°11'·58W Fl WR 20s 54m **W19M, R15M**; W twr; vis: 193°-W-356°-R-018°.

LOCH BOISDALE

MacKenzie Rk ⬥ Fl (3) R 15s 3m 4M; 57°08'·24N 07°13'·71W.

Calvay E End ⚡ Fl (2) WRG 10s 16m W7M, R7M, G7M; W twr; vis: 111°-W-190°-G-202°-W-286°-R-111°; 57°08'·53N 07°15'·38W.

Gasay I ⚡ Fl WR 5s 10m W7M, R7M; W twr; vis: 120°-W-284°-R-120°; 57°08'·93N 07°17'·39W.

Ro-Ro Jetty Head ⚡ Iso RG 4s 8m 2M; vis: shore-G-283°-R-shore; 2 FG (vert) 8m 3M on dn; 57°09'·12N 07°18'·22W.

LUDAIG and ERISKAY

Ludaig Bwtr ⚡ 2 FR (vert) 6m 3M; 57°06'·17N 07°19'·49W.

Acairseid Mhor Ldg Lts 285°. Front, Oc R 6s 9m 4M; 57°03'·89N 07°17'·25W. Rear, 24m from front, Oc R 6s 10m 4M.

BARRA, CASTLEBAY and VATERSAY SOUND

Drover Rocks ⚓ Q (6) + L Fl 15s; 57°04'·08N 07°23'·54W.

Binch Rock ⚓ Q (6) + L Fl 15s; 57°01'·60N 07°17'·12W.

Curachan ⚓ Q (3) 10s; 56°58'·56N 07°20'·51W.

Ardveenish ⚡ Oc WRG 6m 9/6M; vis: 300°-G-304°-W-306°-R-310°; 57°00'·21N 07°24'·43W.

Bo Vich Chuan ⚓ Q (6) + L Fl 15s; *Racon (M) 5M*; 56°56'·15N 07°23'·31W.

Channel Rk ⚡ Fl WR 6s 4m W6M, R4M; vis: 121·5°-W-277°-R-121·5°; 56°56'·24N 07°28'·94W.

Sgeir a Scape ⬥ Fl (2) 8s; 56°56'·25N 07°27'·21W.

Rubha Glas. Ldg Lts 295°. Front ⚓ FBu 9m 6M; Or △ on W twr; 56°56'·77N 07°30'·64W. Rear ⚓, 457m from front, FBu 15m 6M; Or ▽ on W twr; vis: 15° and 8° respectively either side of ldg line.

Barra Hd ☆ 56°47'·11N 07°39'·26W Fl 15s 208m **18M**; W twr; obsc by islands to NE.

Flannan I ☆, Eilean Mór Fl (2) 30s 101m **20M**; W twr; 58°17'·32N 07°35'·23W, obsc in places by Is to W of Eilean Mór.

Rockall ⚡ Fl 15s 19m 8M (unreliable); 57°35'·76N 13°41'·27W.

Gasker Lt ⚡ Fl (3) 10s 38m 10M; 57°59'·05N 07°17'·20W.

Whale Rock ⚓ Q (3) 10s 5m 5M; *Racon (T)*; 57°54'·40N 07°59·91W.

Haskeir I ☆ 57°41'·98N 07°41·36W Fl 20s 44m **23M**; W twr; *Racon (M) 17–15M*.

Monach Isles ☆ Fl (2) 15s 47m **18M**; R brick twr; 57°31'·55N 07°41'·68W.

EAST LOCH ROAG

Aird Laimishader Carloway ⚡ Fl 6s 63m 8M; W hut; obsc on some brgs; 58°17'·06N 06°49'·50W.

Ardvanich Pt ⚡ Fl G 3s 4m 2M; 58°13'·48N 06°47'·68W.

Tidal Rk ⚡ Fl R 3s 2m 2M (synch with Ardvanich Pt above); 58°13'·45N 06°47'·57W.

Grèinam ☆ Fl WR 6s 8m W8M, R7M; W Bn; vis: R143°-169°, W169°-143°; 58°13′·30N 06°46′·16W.

NORTH UIST and SOUTH UIST
Vallay I ☆ Fl WRG 3s 8M; vis: 206°-W-085°-G-140°-W-145°-R-206°; 57°39′·70N 07°26′·34W.

Falconet twr ☆ FR 25m 8M (3M by day); shown 1hr before firing, changes to Iso R 2s 15 min before firing until completion; 57°22′·04N 07°23′·58W.

ST KILDA
Ldg Lts 270°. Front, Oc 5s 26m 3M; 57°48′·32N 08°34′·31W. Rear, 100m from front, Oc 5s 38m 3M; synch.

LOCH TORRIDON TO MALLAIG

LITTLE MINCH and W SKYE
Eugenie Rock ₤ Q 6 + LF 15s; 57°46′·47N 06°27′·28W.
Eilean Trodday ☆ Fl (2) WRG 10s 52m W12M, R9M, G9M; W Bn; vis: W062°-R088°-130°-W-322°-G-062°; 57°43′·64N 06°17′·89W.
Uig, Edward Pier Hd ☆ 57°35′·09N 06°22′·29W Iso WRG 4s 9m W7M, R4M, G4M; vis: 180-W-006°-G-050°-W-073°-R-180°.
Waternish Pt ☆ Fl 20s 21m 8M; W twr; 57°36′·48N 06°37′·99W.
Loch Dunvegan, Uiginish Pt ☆ Fl WRG 3s 16m W7M,R5M,G5M; W metal-framed Twr; vis: 041°-G-132°-W-145°-R-148°-W-253°-R- 263°-W-273°-G-306°, obsc by Fiadhairt Pt when brg > 148°; 57°26′·84N 06°36′·53W.
Neist Point ☆ 57°25′·41N 06°47′·30W Fl 5s 43m **16M**; W twr.
Loch Harport, Ardtreck Pt ☆ 57°20′·38N 06°25′·80W Fl 6s 18m 9M; small W twr.

RONA, LOCH A'BHRAIGE and INNER SOUND
Na Gamhnachain ₤ Q; 57°35′·89N 05°57′·71W.
Rona NE Point ☆ 57°34′·68N 05°57′·56W Fl 12s 69m **19M**; W twr; vis: 050°-358°.
Loch A'Bhraige, Sgeir Shuas ☆ Fl R 2s 6m 3M; vis: 070°-199°; 57°35′·02N 05°58′·61W.
Ldg Lts 136·5°. Front, ↓ Q WRG 3m W4M, R3M; vis: 135°-W- 138°-R- 318°-G-135°; 57°34′·41N 05°58′·09W. Rear, ↓ Iso 6s 28m 5M.
Ru Na Lachan ☆ Oc WR 8s 21m 10M; twr; vis: 337°-W-022°- R-117°-W-162°; 57°29′·02N 05°52′·15W.

SOUND OF RAASAY, PORTREE and CROWLIN ISLANDS
Sgeir Mhór ₄ Fl G 5s; 57°24′·57N 06°10′·53W.
Eilean Beag ☆ Fl 6s 32m 6M; W Bn; 57°21′·21N 05°51′·42W.

RAASAY and LOCH SLIGACHAN
Suisnish ☆ 2 FG (vert) 8m 2M; 57°19′·87N 06°03′·91W.
Eyre Point ☆ Fl WR 3s 6m W9M, R6M; W twr; vis: 215°-W-266°-R- 288°-W-063°; 57°20′·01N 06°01′·29W.

KYLEAKIN and KYLE OF LOCH ALSH
Carragh Rk ▲ Fl (2) G 12s; *Racon (T) 5M*; 57°17′·18N 05°45′·36W.
Bow Rk ₂ Fl (2) R 12s; 57°16′·71N 05°45′·85W.
Fork Rks ▲ Fl G 6s; 57°16′·85N 05°44′·93W.
Black Eye Rk ₂ Fl R 6s; 57°16′·72N 05°45′·31W.
Eileanan Dubha East ☆ Fl (2) 10s 9m 8M; vis: obscured 104°-146°; 57°16′·56N 05°42′·32W.
8 Metre Rock ☆ Fl G 6s 5m 4M; 57°16′·60N 05°42′·69W.

String Rock ₂ Fl R 6s; 57°16′·50N 05°42′·89W.
Sgeir-na-Caillich ☆ Fl (2) R 6s 3m 4M; 57°15′·59N 05°38′·90W.

SOUND OF SLEAT
Kyle Rhea ☆ Fl WRG 3s 7m W8M, R5M, G5M; W Bn; vis: shore-R-219°-W-228°-G-338°-W-346°-R-shore; 57°14′·22N 05°39′·93W.
Sandaig I, NW point ☆ Fl 6s 13m 8M; W twr; 57°10′·05N 05°42′·29W.
Ornsay, SE end ☆ 57°08′·59N 05°46′·88W Oc 8s 18m **15M**; W twr; vis: 157°-030°.
Pt. of Sleat ☆ Fl 3s 20m9M; W twr; 57°01′·08N 06°01′·08W.

MALLAIG and LOCH NEVIS ENTRANCE
Sgeir Dhearg ▲ QG; 57°00′·74N 05°49′·50W.
Northern Pier E end ☆ Iso WRG 4s 6m W9M, R6M, G6M; Gy twr; vis: 181°-G-185°-W-197°-R-201°. Fl G 3s 14m 6M; same structure; 57°00′·47N 05°49′·50W.
Sgeir Dhearg ☆ 57°00′·63N 05°49′·61W Fl (2) WG 8s 6m 5M; Gy Bn; vis: 190°-G-055°-W-190°.

SMALL ISLES AND WEST OF MULL

CANNA and RUM
Canna, E end Sanday Is ☆ Fl 10s 32m 9M; W twr; vis: 152°-061°; 57°02′·82N 06°28′·02W.
Loch Scresort ₤ Q; 57°00′·79N 06°14′·61W.

HYSKEIR, EIGG, MUCK and ARISAIG
Humla ▲ Fl G 6s 3m 4M 57°00′·46N 06°37′·39W.
Hyskeir ☆ 56°58′·14N 06°40′·87W Fl (3) 30s 41m **24M**; W twr. *Racon (T) 14-17M*.
SE point Eigg (Eilean Chathastail) ☆ Fl 6s 24m 8M; W twr; vis: 181°-shore; 56°52′·25N 06°07′·28W.
Eigg, Sgeir nam Bagh (Ferry Terminal) ☆ Dir 245°; Fl WRG 3s 9m W14, R11, G11; H24; steel pole; vis: 242·5°-G-244°-W-246°-R-247·5°. 2FR(vert) on same structure; 56°52′·80N 06°07′·60W.
Isle of Muck (Port Mor) ☆ Dir Fl WRG 3s 7m W14, R11, G11, by day W1, R1, G1; steel twr; vis: 319·5°-G-321°-W-323°-R-324·5°; 56°49′·96N 06°13′·64W.
Bogha Ruadh☆ Fl G 5s 4m 3M; 56°49′·56N 06°13′·05W.
Bo Faskadale ▲ Fl (3) G 18s; 56°48′·18N 06°06′·37W.
Ardnamurchan ☆ 56°43′·63N 06°13′·58W Fl (2) 20s 55m **24M**; Gy twr; vis: 002°-217°.
Cairns of Coll, Suil Ghorm ☆ Fl 12s 23m 10M; W twr; 56°42′·26N 06°26′·75W.

TIREE, COLL and ARINAGOUR
Loch Eatharna, Bogha Mór ▲ Fl G 6s; 56°36′·65N 06°30′·90W.
Roan Bogha ₤ Q (6) + L Fl 15s 3m 5M; 56°32′·23N 06°40′·18W.
Placaid Bogha ▲ Fl G 4s; 56°33′·22N 06°44′·06W.
Scarinish ☆, S side of ent 56°30′·01N 06°48′·27W Fl 3s 11m **16M**; W □ twr; vis: 210°-030°.
Cairn na Burgh More (Treshnish Is), Fl (3) 15s 36m 8M; solar panels on framework tr; 56°31′·05N 06°22′·95W.
Gott Bay Ldg Lts 286·5°. Front FR 8m; 56°30′·61N 06°47′·82W. Rear 30m from front FR 11m.
Cairn na Burgh More (Treshnish Is), Fl (3) 15s 36m 8M; solar panels on framework tr; 56°31′·05N 06°22′·95W.

Skerryvore ✡ Fl 10s 46m **23M**; Gy twr; *Racon (M) 18M*.
56°19'·36N 07°06'·88W

LOCH NA LÀTHAICH (LOCH LATHAICH)

Eileanan na Liathanaich, SE end ✸ Fl WR 6s 12m W8M,
R6M; vis: R088°- W108°-088°; 56°20'·56N 06°16'·38W.
Loch Eatharna, Pier Head ✸ Dir Oc WRG 7s 6m 2M; vis:
316°-G-322°-W-328°-R-334°; 56°36'·86N 06°31'·29W.
Dubh Artach ✡ 56°07'·94N 06°38'·08W Fl (2) 30s 44m **20M**;
Gy twr, R band.

SOUND OF MULL

LOCH SUNART, TOBERMORY and LOCH ALINE

Ardmore Pt ✸ Fl (2) 10s 18m 13M; 56°39'·37N
06°07'·70W.

New Rks ▲ Fl G 6s 56°39'·05N 06°03'·30W.

Rubha nan Gall ✡ 56°38'·33N 06°04'·00W Fl 3s 17m **15M**;
W twr.

Eileanan Glasa (Dearg Sgeir) ✸ 56°32'·25N 05°54'·80W
Fl 6s 7m 8M; W ○ twr.

Fiunary Spit ▲ 56°32'·66N 05°53'·17W Fl G 6s.

Lochaline Ldg Lts 356°. Front, F 2m; 56°32'·39N
05°46'·49W. Rear, 88m from front, F 4m; both H24.

Ardtornish Pt ✸ Fl (2) WRG 10s 8m W8M, R6M, G6M; W
twr; vis: G shore- 302°-W-308°-R-342°-W-057°-R-095°-W-
108°-G-shore; 56°31'·10N 05°45'·23W.

Craignure Ldg Lts 240·9°. Front, FR 10m; 56°28'·26N
05°42'·28W. Rear, 150m from front, FR 12m; vis: 225·8°-
255·8°.

MULL TO CALEDONIAN CANAL AND OBAN

Lismore ✡, SW end 56°27'·34N 05°36'·45W Fl 10s 31m
17M; W twr; vis: 237°-208°.

Lady's Rk ⌓ Fl 6s 12m 5M; 56°26'·92N 05°37'·05W.

Duart Pt ✸ Fl (3) WR 18s 14m W5M, R3M; vis: 162°-W-261°-R-
275°-W-353°-R-shore; 56°26'·84N 05°38'·77W.

LOCH LINNHE

Corran Shoal ⌐ QR 56°43'·69N 05°14'·39W.

Ent W side, Corran Pt ✸ Iso WRG 4s 12m W10M, R7M,
G7M; W twr; vis: shore-R-195°-W-215°-G-020-W-030°-
R-shore; 56°43'·25N 05°14'·54W.

Corran Narrows NE ✸ Fl 5s 4m 4M; W twr; vis: S shore-214°;
56°43'·62N 05°13'·90W .

Clovullin Spit ⌐ Fl (2) R 15s; 56°42'·29N 05°15'·56W.

Cuil-cheanna Spit ▲ Fl G 6s; 56°41'·17N 05°15'·72W.

FORT WILLIAM and CALEDONIAN CANAL

Corpach, Caledonian Canal Lock ent ✸ Iso WRG 4s 6m
5M; W twr; vis: G287°- W310°- R335°-030°; 56°50'·52N
05°07'·44W.

LYNN OF LORN

Sgeir Bhuidhe Appin ⌓ Fl (2) WR 7s 8m W9M R6M; W Bn;
vis: W013·5°- R184°-220°; 56°33'·63N 05°24'·65W.

Appin Point ▲ Fl G 6s; 56°32'·69N 05°25'·97W.

Dearg Sgeir, off Aird's Point ⌓ Fl WRG 2s 2m W3M,
R1M, G1M; vis: 196°-R-246°-W-258°-G-041°-W-058°-R-
093°-W-139°; 56°32'·20N 05°25'·22W.

Rubha nam Faoileann (Eriska) ⌓ QG 2m 2M; G col; vis
128°-329°; 56°32'·20N 05°24'·11W.

Branra Rk ⌕ Fl(2) 10s 3m 5M; B twr, R band; 56°32'·02N
05°26'·60W.

DUNSTAFFNAGE BAY/OBAN

N spit of Kerrera ✸ Fl R 3s 9m 5M; W col, R bands;
56°25'·49N 05°29'·56W.

Dunollie ✸ Fl (2) WRG 6s 6m W8M, R6M, G6M; vis:
351°-G- 020°- W-047°-R-120°-W-138°-G-143°; 56°25'·37N
05°29'·05W.

Corran Ledge ⌕ VQ (9) 10s; 56°25'·19N 05°29'·11W.

OBAN TO LOCH CRAIGNISH

Kerrera Sound, Dubha Sgeirean ✸ Fl (2) 12s 7m 5M; W
○ twr; 56°22'·81N 05°32'·27W.

Bogha Nuadh ⌕ Q (6) + LFl 15s; 56°21'·69N 05°37'·88W.

Bono Rock ⌕ Q (9) 15s; 56°16'·21N 05°41'·22W.

Fladda ✸ Fl (2) WRG 9s 13m W11M, R9M, G9M; W twr;
vis: 169°-R-186°-W-337°-G-344°-W-356°-R-026°; 56°14'·89N
05°40'·83W.

Dubh Sgeir (Luing) ✸ Fl WRG 6s 9m W6M, R4M. G4M; W
twr; vis: W000°- R010°- W025°- G199°-000°; *Racon (M)
5M*; 56°14'·76N 05°40'·20W.

The Garvellachs, Eileach an Naoimh, SW end ✸ Fl 6s 21m
9M; W Bn; vis: 240°-215°; 56°13'·04N 05°49'·06W.

LOCH MELFORT and CRAOBH HAVEN

Melfort Pier ✸ Dir FR 6m 3M; (Apr -Nov); 56°16'·14N
05°30'·19W.

▲ 56°12'·88N 05°33'·59W.

Craobh Marina Bkwtr Hd ✸ Iso WRG 5s 10m, W5M,
R3M, G3M; vis:114°-G-162°-W-183°-R-200°; 56°12'·78N
05°33'·52W.

1	Cape Wrath	**1**															
2	Ullapool	54	**2**														
3	Stornoway	53	45	**3**													
4	East Loch Tarbert	75	56	33	**4**												
5	Portree	83	57	53	42	**5**											
6	Kyle of Lochalsh	91	63	62	63	21	**6**										
7	Mallaig	112	82	83	84	42	21	**7**									
8	Eigg	123	98	97	75	54	35	14	**8**								
9	Castlebay (Barra)	133	105	92	69	97	76	59	46	**9**							
10	Tobermory	144	114	115	87	74	53	32	20	53	**10**						
11	Loch Aline	157	127	128	100	87	66	45	33	66	13	**11**					
12	Fort William	198	161	162	134	121	98	75	63	96	43	34	**12**				
13	Oban	169	138	139	111	100	77	56	44	77	24	13	29	**13**			
14	Loch Melfort	184	154	155	117	114	93	69	61	92	40	27	45	18	**14**		
15	Craobh Haven	184	155	155	117	114	92	70	60	93	40	27	50	21	5	**15**	
16	Crinan	187	157	158	129	112	95	74	63	97	42	30	54	25	14	9	**16**
17	Mull of Kintyre	232	203	189	175	159	143	121	105	120	89	87	98	72	62	57	51	**17**

DISTANCE TABLES

Approx distances in nautical
miles are by the most direct
route allowing for dangers
and TSS.

AREA 7 *SW Scotland – Oban to Kirkcudbright*

SELECTED LIGHTS, BUOYS & WAYPOINTS

Positions are referenced to WGS84

COLONSAY TO ISLAY

COLONSAY
Scalasaig, Rubha Dubh ☆ Fl (2) WR 10s 8m W8M, R6M; W bldg; vis: shore-R- 230°-W-337°-R-354°; 56°04'·01N 06°10'·90W.

SOUND OF ISLAY
Rhubh' a Mháil (Ruvaal) ☆ 55°56'·18N 06°07'·46W Fl (3) 15s 45m **19M**; W twr.
Carragh an t'Struith ☆ Fl 3s 8m 9M; W twr; vis: 354°-180°; 55°52'·30N 06°05'·78W.
Carraig Mòr ☆ Fl (2) WR 6s 7m W8M, R6M; W twr; vis: shore-R- 175°-W-347°-R-shore; 55°50'·42N 06°06'·13W.
McArthur's Hd ☆ Fl (2) WR 10s 39m W14M, R11M; W twr; W in Sound of Islay from NE coast,159°-R-244°-W-E coast of Islay; 55°45'·84N 06°02'·90W.

PORT ELLEN and LOCH INDAAL
Carraig Fhada ☆ Fl WRG 3s 20m W8M, R6M, G6M; W ☐ twr; vis: W shore- 248°-G-311°-W-340°-R-shore; 55°37'·22N 06°12'·71W.
Rubh'an Dùin ☆ Fl (2) WR 7s 15m W11M, R8M; W twr; vis: shore-R-218°-W-249°-R-350°-W-shore; 55°44'·70N 06°22'·28 W.
Orsay Is, **Rhinns of Islay** ☆ 55°40'·40N 06°30'·84W Fl 5s 46m **24M**; W twr; vis: 256°-184°.

JURA TO MULL OF KINTYRE

SOUND OF JURA, CRAIGHOUSE, L SWEEN and GIGHA
Na Cùiltean ☆ Fl 10s 9m 9M; 55°48'·64N 05°54'·90W.
Gamhna Gigha ☆ Fl (2) 6s 7m 5M; 55°43'·78N 05°41'·08W.

WEST LOCH TARBERT
Dunskeig Bay ☆ Q (2) 10s 11m 8M; 55°45'·22N 05°35'·00W.
Eileen Tráighe (off S side) ↓ Fl (2) R 5s 5m 3M; R post; 55°45'·37N 05°35'·75W.

MULL OF KINTYRE
Mull of Kintyre ☆ 55°18'·64N 05°48'·25W Fl (2) 20s 91m **24M**; W twr on W bldg; vis: 347°-178°.

CRINAN CANAL and ARDRISHAIG
Crinan, E of lock ent ☆ Fl WG 3s 8m 4M; W twr, R band; vis: shore-W-146°-G-shore; 56°05'·48N 05°33'·37W.
Ardrishaig Bkwtr Hd ☆ L Fl WRG 6s 9m 4M; vis: 287°-G-339°-W- 350°-R-035°; 56°00'·76N 05°26'·59W.

LOCH FYNE TO SANDA ISLAND

EAST LOCH TARBERT
Eilean na Beithe ☆ Fl WRG 3s 7m 5M; vis: G036°- W065°-R078°-106°; 55°52'·68N 05°19'·62W.

KILBRANNAN SOUND, CRANNAICH and CARRADALE BAY
Port Crannaich Bkwtr Hd ☆ Fl R 10s 5m 6M; vis: 099°-279°; 55°35'·60N 05°27'·84W.

CAMPBELTOWN LOCH to SANDA ISLAND
Davaar N Pt ☆ 55°25'·69N 05°32'·42W Fl (2) 10s 37m **23M**; W twr; vis: 073°-330°.

Sanda Island ☆ 55°16'·50N 05°35'·01W Fl 10s 50m **15M**; W twr; vis: 242°-121°.
Patersons Rock ≈ Fl (3) R 18s; 55°16'·90N 05°32'·48W.

KYLES OF BUTE TO RIVER CLYDE

KYLES OF BUTE and CALADH
Ardlamont Point No. 47 ≈ W Fl R 4s; 55°49'·59N 05°11'·76W.
Ardmaleish Point No. 41 ↓ Q (3) 10s; 55°53'·02N 05°04'·70W.
Bogany Point No. 36 ≈ Fl R 4s; 55°50'·78N 05°01'·41W.

FIRTH OF CLYDE
Toward Pt ☆ 55°51'·73N 04°58'·79W Fl 10s 21m **22M**; W twr.
No. 34 ↓ Q (3) 10s; 55°51'·44N 04°59'·11W.
Skelmorlie ↓ Iso 5s; 55°51'·65N 04°56'·34W.

WEMYSS and INVERKIP
Cowal ↓ L Fl 10s; 55°56'·00N 04°54'·83W.
The Gantocks ↓ Fl R 6s 12m 6M; ○ twr; 55°56'·45N 04°55'·08W.

DUNOON
Cloch Point ☆ Fl 3s 24m 8M; W ○ twr, B band, W dwellings; 55°56'·55N 04°52'·74W.

LOCH LONG and LOCH GOIL
Loch Long ↓ Oc 6s; 55°59'·15N 04°52'·42W.
Baron's Pt No. 3 ☆ Oc (2) Y 10s 5m 3M; 55°59'·18N 04°51'·12W.
Ravenrock Pt ☆ Fl 4s 12m 10M; W twr on W col. Dir lt 204°, WRG 9m (same twr); vis: 201·5°-F R-203°-Al WR(W phase incr with brg)-203·5°-FW-204·5°-Al WG(G phase incr with brg)-205°-FG-206·5°; 56°02'·14N 04°54'·39W.
Port Dornaige ☆ Fl 6s 8m 11M; W col; vis: 026°-206°; 56°03·75N 04°53'·65W.
Rubha Ardnahein ☆ Fl R 5s 3m 3M; vis: 132°-312°; 56°06'·15N 04°53'·60W.
The Perch, Ldg Lts 318° Front, F WRG 3m 5M; vis: 311°-G-317°-W- 320°-R-322°. Same structure, Fl R 3s 3m 3M; vis: 187°-322°; 56°06'·90N 04°54'·31W. Rear, 700m from front, F 7m 5M; vis: 312°-322·5°.
Cnap Pt ☆ Ldg Lts 031°. Front, Q 8m 10M; W col; 56°07'·40N 04°49'·97W. Rear, 87m from front F 13m; R line on W twr.

GOUROCK
Ashton ↓ Iso 5s; 55°58'·10N 04°50'·65W.
Rosneath Patch ↓ Fl (2) 10s 5m 10M; 55°58'·52N 04°47'·45W.

ROSNEATH, RHU NARROWS and GARELOCH
Ldg Lts 356°. **Front, No. 7N** ↓ 56°00'·05N 04°45'·36W Dir lt 356°. WRG 5m **W16M**, R13M, G13M; vis: 353°-Al WG- 355°- FW-357°-Al WR-000°-FR-002°.
Dir lt 115° WRG 5m **W16M**, R13M, G13M; vis: 111°-Al WG-114°-FW- 116°-Al WR-119°-FR-121°. Passing lt Oc G 6s 6m 3M; G △ on G pile . Rear, Ardencaple Castle Centre ☆ 56°00'·54N 04°45'·43W 2 FG (vert) 26m 12M; twr on Castle NW corner; vis: 335°-020°.

No. 8N Lt Bn ⚓ 55°59'·09N 04°44'·21W Dir lt 080° WRG 4m; **W16M**, R13M,G13M;vis: 075°-FG-077·5°-Al WG-079·5°-FW-080·5°-AltWR-082·5°-FR-085°. **Dir lt 138°** WRG 4m **W16M**, R13M, G13M; vis: 132°-FG-134°-Al WG- FW137°-139°-Al WR-142°. Passing lt Fl Y 3s 6m 3M.

Gareloch No. 1 Lt Bn ⚲ VQ (4) Y 5s 9m; Y 'X' on Y structure; 55°59'·12N 04°43'·89W.

No. 3N Lt Bn ⚓ 56°00'·07N 04°46'·72W Dir lt 149° WRG 9m **W16M**, R13M, G13M F & Al; vis: 144°-FG-145°-Al WG-148°-FW-150°-Al WR-153°-FR-154°. Passing lt Oc R 8s 9m 3M.

Rosneath DG Jetty ⚲ 2 FR (vert) 5M; W col; vis: 150°-330°; 56°00'·39N 04°47'·51W.

Rhu Pt ⚓ Q (3) WRG 6s 9m W10M, R7M, G7M; vis: 270°-G-000°-W-114°-R-188°; 56°00'·95N 04°47'·19W.

Dir lt 318° WRG **W16M**, R13M,G13M; vis: 315°-Al WG-317°-F-319°-Al WR-321°-FR-325°.

Limekiln No. 2N Lt Bn ⚓ 56°00'·67N 04°47'·64W Dir lt 295° WRG 5m **W16M**, R13M, G13M F & Al; R ☐ on R Bn; vis: 291°-Al WG- 294°-FW- 296°-Al WR-299°-FR-301°.

Mamberg Dir lt 331°, Q(4)WRG 8s 10m 14M; vis: 328·5°-G-330°-W-332°-R-333°; H24; 56°03'·74N 04°50'·47W.

GREENOCK and PORT GLASGOW

Anchorage Lts in line 196°. Front, FG 7m 12M; Y col; 55°57'·62N 04°46'·58W. Rear, 32m from front, FG 9m 12M. Y col.

Lts in line 194·5°. Front, FG 18m; 55°57'·45N 04°45'·91W. Rear, 360m from front, FG 33m.

Steamboat Quay, W end ⚲ FG 12m 12M; B&W chequered col; vis 210°-290°; 55°56'·25N 04°41'·44W. From here to Glasgow Lts on S bank are Fl G and Lts on N bank are Fl R.

CLYDE TO MULL OF GALLOWAY

LARGS and FAIRLIE

Approach ⚲ L Fl 10s; 55°46'·40N 04°51'·85W.
Fairlie Patch ▲ Fl G 1·5s; 55°45'·38N 04°52'·34W.

MILLPORT and GREAT CUMBRAE

Ldg Lts 333°. Pier Head front, 55°45'·04N 04°55'·85W FR 7m 5M. Rear, 137m from front, FR 9m 5M.
Mountstuart ⚲ L Fl 10s; 55°48'·00N 04°57'·57W.
Runnaneun Pt (Rubha'n Eun) ⚲ Fl R 6s 8m 12M; W twr; 55°43'·79N 05°00'·23W.
Little Cumbrae Is, Cumbrae Elbow ⚲ Fl 6s 28m 14M; W twr; vis: 334°-193°; 55°43'·22N 04°58'·06W.

ARDROSSAN

Approach Dir lt 055°, WRG 15m W14M, R11M, G11M; vis: 050°-F G-051·2°-Alt WG(W phase inc with Brg)- 053·8°-FW-056·2°-Alt WR(R phase inc with brg)-058·8°-FR-060°; 55°38'·66N 04°49'·22W. Same structure FR 13m 6M; vis: 325°-145°.
Lt ho Pier Hd ⚲ Iso WG 4s 11m 9M; W twr; vis: 035°-W-317°-G-035°; 55°38'·47N 04°49'·57W.

IRVINE

Ldg Lts 051°. Front, FG 10m 5M; 55°36'·40N 04°41'·57W. Rear, 101m from front, FR 15m 5M; G masts, both vis: 019°-120°.

TROON

Troon Approach ⚓ Fl R 2s 4m 3M; 55°33'·06N 04°41'·35W.
W Pier Hd ⚲ Fl (2) WG 5s 11m 9M; W twr; vis: 036°-G-090°-W-036°; 55°33'·07N 04°41'·02W.
Lady I ⚲ Fl 2s 19m 11M; W Tr R vert stripes; *Racon (T) 13-11M*; 55°31'·63N 04°44'·05W.

ARRAN, RANZA, LAMLASH and BRODICK

Pillar Rk Pt ☆ (Holy Island), 55°31'·04N 05°03'·67W Fl (2) 20s 38m **25M**; W ☐ twr.
Holy I SW end ⚲ Fl G 3s 14m 10M; W twr; vis: 282°-147°; 55°30'·73N 05°04'·21W.
Pladda ☆ 55°25'·50N 05°07'·12W Fl (3) 30s 40m **17M**; W twr.

AYR and AILSA CRAIG

S Pier Hd ⚲ Q 7m 7M; R twr; vis: 012°-161°. Also FG 5m 5M; vis: 012°-082°; 55°28'·17N 04°38'·74W.
Ldg Lts 098°. Front, FR 10m 5M; Tfc sigs; 55°28'·15N 04°38'·38W. Rear, 130m from front Oc R 10s 18m 9M.
Turnberry Point ☆, near castle ruins 55°19'·56N 04°50'·71W Fl 15s 29m **24M**; W twr.
Ailsa Craig ☆ 55°15'·12N 05°06'·52W Fl 4s 18m **17M**; W twr; vis: 145°-028°.

GIRVAN

S Pier Hd ⚲ 2 FG (vert) 8m 4M; W twr; 55°14'·72N 04°51'·90W.

LOCH RYAN and STRANRAER

Milleur Point ⚓ Q; 55°01'·28N 05°05'·66W.
Fairway ⚲ Iso 4s; 54°59'·77N 05°03'·82W.
Forbes Shoal ⚲ QR; 54°59'·47N 05°02'·96W.

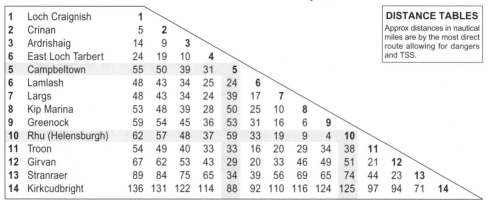

		1												
1	Loch Craignish	1												
2	Crinan	5	2											
3	Ardrishaig	14	9	3										
6	East Loch Tarbert	24	19	10	4									
5	Campbeltown	55	50	39	31	5								
6	Lamlash	48	43	34	25	24	6							
7	Largs	48	43	34	24	39	17	7						
8	Kip Marina	53	48	39	28	50	25	10	8					
9	Greenock	59	54	45	36	53	31	16	6	9				
10	Rhu (Helensburgh)	62	57	48	37	59	33	19	9	4	10			
11	Troon	54	49	40	33	33	16	20	29	34	38	11		
12	Girvan	67	62	53	43	29	20	33	46	49	51	21	12	
13	Stranraer	89	84	75	65	34	39	56	69	65	74	44	23	13
14	Kirkcudbright	136	131	122	114	88	92	110	116	124	125	97	94	71	14

DISTANCE TABLES
Approx distances in nautical miles are by the most direct route allowing for dangers and TSS.

Loch Ryan W ⚓QG;54°59'·23N 05°03'·24W .
Cairn Pt ⚡ Fl (2) R 10s 14m 12M; W twr; 54°58'·46N 05°01'·85W.
Cairnryan ⚡ Fl R 5s 5m 5M; 54°57'·77N 05°00'·99W.
Stranraer No.1 ⚓ Oc G 6s; 54°56'·67N 05°01'·32W.
No. 3 ⚓ QG; 54°55'·87N 05°01'·60W.
No. 5 ⚓ Fl G 3s; 54°55'·08N 05°01'·86W.
E Pier Hd ⚡ 2 FR (vert) 9m; 54°54'·61N 05°01'·60W.
Corsewall Point ☆ 55°00'·41N 05°09'·58W Fl (5) 30s 34m **22M**; W twr; vis: 027°-257°.
Black Head Old Lighthouse (disused); W tower, 22m; 54°51'·70N 05°08'·80W.

PORTPATRICK

Ldg Lts 050·5°. Front, FG (occas); 54°50'·50N 05°07'·02W. Rear, 68m from front, FG 8m (occas).
Crammag Hd ☆ 54°39'·90N 04°57'·92W Fl 10s 35m **18M**; W twr.

Mull of Galloway ☆, SE end 54°38'·08N 04°51'·45W Fl 20s 99m **28M**; W twr; vis: 182°-105°.

MULL OF GALLOWAY and WIGTOWN BAY

Port William Ldg Lts 105°. Front, Pier Hd Fl G 3s 7m 3M; 54°45'·66N 04°35'·28W. Rear, 130m from front, FG 10m 2M.
Whithorn Ldg Lts 335°. Front, Oc R 8s 7m 7M; Or ♦; 54°42'·01N 04°22'·05W. Rear, 35m from front, Oc R 8s 9m 7M; Or ♦, synch.
Little Ross ⚡ Fl 5s 50m 12M; W twr; obsc in Wigtown B when brg more than 103°; 54°45'·93N 04°05'·10W.

KIRKCUDBRIGHT BAY and KIPPFORD

Little Ross NNE end of Is ⚡ Fl (2) 5s 21m 5M; Stone bcn; 54°46'·06N 04°05'·02W.
Hestan I, E end ⚡ Fl (2) 10s 42m 9M; 54°49'·95N 03°48'·53W.

AREA 8 *NW England & Wales – Kirkcudbright & Isle of Man to Swansea*

SELECTED LIGHTS, BUOYS & WAYPOINTS

Positions are referenced to WGS84

SOLWAY FIRTH TO BARROW-IN-FURNESS

SILLOTH and MARYPORT

Lees Scar ⚡ Fl G 5s 11m 4M; W piles; 54°51'·78N 03°24'·79W.
Groyne Hd ⚡ 2 FG (vert) 4m 4M; Fl Bu tfc signals close by; 54°52'·14N 03°23'·93W.
Maryport S Pier Hd ⚡.Fl 1·5s 10m 6M; 54°43'·07N 03°30'·64W.

WORKINGTON and HARRINGTON

N Workington ⚓ Q; 54°40'·10N 03°38'·18W.
S Workington ⚓ VQ (6) + L Fl 10s; 54°37'·01N 03°38'·58W.
South Pier ⚡ Fl 5s 11m 5M; R bldg; 54°39'·12N 03°34'·67W.
Ldg Lts 131·8°. Front, FR 10m 3M; 54°38'·92N 03°34'·19W. Rear, 134m from front, FR 12m 3M.

WHITEHAVEN

W Pier Hd ⚡ Fl G 5s 16m 8M; W ○ twr; 54°33'·17N 03°35'·92W.
N Pier Hd ⚡ Fl R 5s 8m 10M; W ○ twr; 54°33'·17N 03°35'·75W.
Saint Bees Hd ☆ 54°30'·81N 03°38'·23W Fl (2) 20s 102m **18M**; W○ twr; obsc shore-340°.

RAVENGLASS

Blockhouse ⚡ FG; (Eskdale Range); 54°20'·16N 03°25'·34W.
Selker ⚓ Fl (3) G 10s; *Bell;* 54°16'·14N 03°29'·58W.

BARROW-IN-FURNESS

Lightning Knoll ⚓ L Fl 10s; 53°59'·83N 03°14'·28W.
Halfway Shoal ⚓ QR 19m 10s; R&W chequer Bn; 54°01'·46N 03°11'·88W.
Isle of Walney ☆ 54°02'·92N 03°10'·64W Fl 15s 21m **23M**; stone twr; obsc 122°-127° within 3M of shore.
Walney Chan Ldg Lts 040·7°. No.1 Front ⚓, Q 7m 10M; B Pile; 54°03'·19N 03°09'·22W. No. 2 Rear ⚓, 0·61M from front, Iso 2s 13m 10M; Pile.
Rampside Sands Ldg Lts 005·1°. No. 3 Front ⚓, Q 9m10M; W ○ twr; 54°04'·41N 03°09'·79W. No. 4 Rear ⚓, 0·77M from front, Iso 2s 14m 6M; R col, W face.

ISLE OF MAN

Whitestone Bank ⚓ Q (9) 15s; 54°24'·58N 04°20'·41W.
Point of Ayre ☆ 54°24'·94N 04°22'·13W Fl (4) 20s 32m **19M**; W twr, two R bands, *Racon (M) 13-15M*.
Low Lt Ho (unlit), RW twr, B base, 54°25'·03N 04°21'·86W.

PEEL

Peel Bkwtr Hd ⚡ Oc 7s 11m 6M; W twr; 54°13'·67N 04°41'·69W.

PORT ERIN and PORT ST MARY

Ldg Lts 099·1°. Front, 54°05'·23N 04°45'·57W FR 10m 5M; W twr, R band. Rear, 39m from front, FR 19m 5M; W col, R band.
Calf of Man Lighthouse (disused), white 8-sided tower.
Chicken Rk ⚡ Fl 5s 38m **21M**; twr; 54°02'·27N 04°50'·32W.
Alfred Pier Hd ⚡ Oc R 10s 8m 6M; 54°04'·33N 04°43'·82W.

CASTLETOWN and DERBY HAVEN

Dreswick Pt ⚡ Fl (2) 30s 23m 12M; W twr; 54°03'·29N 04°37'·45W.
New Pier Hd ⚡ Oc R 15s 8m 5M; 54°04'·33N 04°38'·97W.
Derby Haven, Bkwtr SW end ⚡Iso G 2s 5m 5M; W twr, G band; 54°04'·58N 04°37'·06W.

DOUGLAS

Douglas Head ☆ 54°08'·60N 04°27'·95W Fl 10s 32m **24M**; W twr; obsc brg more than 037°. FR Lts on radio masts 1 and 3M West.
No. 1 ⚓ Q (3) G 5s; 54°09'·04N 04°27'·68W.
Princess Alexandra Pier Hd ⚡ Fl R 5s 16m 8M; R mast; *Whis (2) 40s;* 54°08'·84N 04°27'·85W.
Ldg Lts 229·3°, Front ⚓, Oc Bu 10s 9m 5M; W △ R border on mast; 54°08'·72N 04°28'·25W. Rear ⚓, 62m from front, Oc Bu 10s 12m 5M; W ▽ on R border; synch with front.

Victoria Pier Hd ☆ Iso G 10s 10m 3M; W col; vis: 225°-327°; Intnl Port Tfc Signals; 54°08'·84N 04°28'·08W.

Conister Rk Refuge twr Q 3M; vis: 234°-312°; 54°09'·03N 04°28'·12W.

LAXEY to RAMSEY

Laxey Pier Hd ☆ Oc R 3s 7m 5M; W twr, R band; obsc when brg less than 318°; 54°13'·50N 04°23'·43W.

Maughold Head ☆ 54°17'·72N 04°18'·58W Fl (3) 30s 65m **21M**.

Bahama ⚓ VQ (6) + L Fl 10s; 54°20'·01N 04°08'·57W.

Queens Pier Dn ☆ Fl R 5s; 54°19'·28N 04°21'·95W.

King William Bank ⚓ Q (3) 10s; 54°26'·01N 04°00'·08W.

BARROW TO RIVERS MERSEY AND DEE

MORECAMBE

Lightning Knoll ⚓ L Fl 10s; 53°59'·84N 03°14'·28W.

Morecambe ⚓ Q (9) 15s; 53°52'·01N 03°24'·10W.

Lune Deep ⚓ Q (6) + L Fl 15s; *Racon (T)*; 53°56'·07N 03°12·90W.

Lts in line about 090°. Front, FR 10m 2M; G mast; 54°04'·41N 02°52'·63W. Rear, 140m from front, FR 14m 2M; G mast.

HEYSHAM

SW Quay Ldg Lts 102·2°. Front ⚓, both F Bu 11/14m 2M; Or & B ♦ on masts; 54°01'·91N 02°55'·22W.

RIVER LUNE, GLASSON DOCK and FLEETWOOD

R Lune ⚓ Q (9) 15s; 53°58'·63N 03°00'·03W.

Fairway No. 1(Fleetwood) ⚓ 53°57'·67N 03°02'·03W Q; *Bell*.

Fleetwood Esplanade Ldg Lts 156°. Front, Iso G 2s 14m 9M; 53°55'·71N 03°00'·56W. Rear, 320m from front, Iso G 4s 28m 9M. Both vis on Ldg line only. (H24) (chan liable to change).

RIVER RIBBLE

Gut ⚓ L Fl 10s; 53°41'·74N 03°08'·98W.

Perches show Fl R on N side, and Fl G on S side of chan. S side, 14¼M Perch ☆ Fl G 5s 6m 3M; 53°42'·75N 03°04'·90W.

Jordan's Spit ⚓ Q (9) 15s; 53°35'·76N 03°19'·28W. FT ⚓ Q; 53°34'·56N 03°13'·20W.

RIVER MERSEY and LIVERPOOL

Bar ⚓ Fl.5s 12M; *Racon (T) 10M*; 53°32'·01N 03°20'·98W.

Q1 ⚓ VQ; 53°31'·00N 03°16'·72W.

Q2 ⚓ VQ R; 53°31'·47N 03°14'·95W.

Q3 ▲ Fl G 3s; 53°30'·95N 03°15'·10W.

Formby ⚓ Iso 4s; 53°31'·13N 03°13'·48W.

C4 ⚓ Fl R 3s; 53°31'·82N 03°08'·51W.

Crosby ⚓ Oc 5s; 53°30'·72N 03°06'·29W.

C14 ⚓ Fl R 3s; R hull; 53°29'·91N 03°05'·34W.

Brazil ▲ QG; 53°26'·85N 03°02'·23W.

RIVER DEE, MOSTYN and CONNAH'S QUAY

HE1 ⚓ Q (9) 15s; 53°26'·33N 03°18'·08W.

HE2 ▲ Fl G 2·5s; 53°24'·90N 03°12'·88W.

Mostyn Dir Lt 174°. ☆ 53°19'·33N 03°16'·12W Iso WRG 2s 16m 7M

vis: 174·8°-G-176·8°-W-177·8°-R-179·8°; H24.

WALES – NORTH COAST AND INNER PASSAGE

South Hoyle Outer ⚓ Fl R 2·5s; 53°21'·47N 03°24'·70W.

Prestatyn ▲ QG; 53°21'·51N 03°28'·51W.

Inner Passage ⚓ Fl R 5s; 53°21'·91N 03°31'·95W.

Mid Patch Spit ⚓ QR; 53°22'·25N 03°32'·67W.

North Hoyle Wind Farm (30 turbines, see 9.10.5) centred on 53°25'·00N 03°27'·00W. NW, NE, SW, SE extremities (F.R Lts) Fl Y 2.5s 5M Horn Mo (U) 30s.

Mast ☆ Mo (U) 15s 12m 10M & 2FR (vert); Horn Mo (U) 30s; Mast (80); 53°28'·84N 03°30'·50W.

W Constable ⚓ Q (9) 15s; *Racon (M) 10M*; 53°23'·14N 03°49'·26W.

N Constable ⚓ VQ; 53°23'·76N 03°41'·42W.

RHYL, LLANDUDNO and CONWY

River Clwyd Outfall ▲ 53°19'·59N 03°30'·63W.

Llandudno Pier Hd ☆ 2 FG (vert) 8m 4M; 53°19'·90N 03°49'·51W.

Great Ormes Hd Lt Ho, (unlit) 53°20'·56N 03°52'·17W.

Conwy Fairway ⚓ L Fl 10s; 53°17'·95N 03°55'·58W.

C1 ▲ Fl G 10s; 53°17'·83N 03°54'·58W.

C2 ⚓ Fl (2) R 10s; 53°17'·94N 03°54'·52W.

River Conwy ent, S side, ☆ L Fl G 15s 5m 2M; 53°18'·03N 03°50'·86W.

ANGLESEY

Point Lynas ☆ 53°24'·98N 04°17'·35W Oc 10s 39m **18M**; W castellated twr; vis: 109°-315°; *Horn 45s;* H24.

AMLWCH to HOLYHEAD BAY

Main Bkwtr ☆ Fl G 15s 11m 3M; W mast; vis: 141°-271°; 53°25'·02N 04°19'·91W.

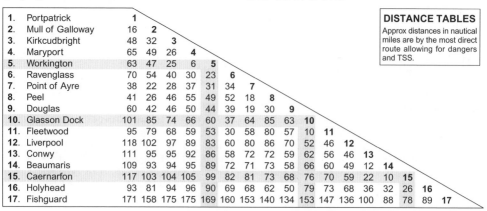

		1	2	3	4	5	6	7	8	9	10	11	12	13	14	15	16	17
1.	Portpatrick	**1**																
2.	Mull of Galloway	16	**2**															
3.	Kirkcudbright	48	32	**3**														
4.	Maryport	65	49	26	**4**													
5.	Workington	63	47	25	6	**5**												
6.	Ravenglass	70	54	40	30	23	**6**											
7.	Point of Ayre	38	22	28	37	31	34	**7**										
8.	Peel	41	26	46	55	49	52	18	**8**									
9.	Douglas	60	42	46	50	44	39	19	30	**9**								
10.	Glasson Dock	101	85	74	66	60	37	64	85	63	**10**							
11.	Fleetwood	95	79	68	59	53	30	58	80	57	10	**11**						
12.	Liverpool	118	102	97	89	83	60	80	86	70	52	46	**12**					
13.	Conwy	111	95	95	92	86	58	72	72	59	62	56	46	**13**				
14.	Beaumaris	109	93	94	95	89	72	71	73	58	66	60	49	12	**14**			
15.	Caernarfon	117	103	104	105	99	82	81	73	68	76	70	59	22	10	**15**		
16.	Holyhead	93	81	94	96	90	69	68	62	50	79	73	68	36	32	26	**16**	
17.	Fishguard	171	158	175	175	169	160	153	140	134	153	147	136	100	88	78	89	**17**

DISTANCE TABLES

Approx distances in nautical miles are by the most direct route allowing for dangers and TSS.

Furlong ◣ Fl G 2·5s; 53°25'·41N 04°30'·47W.
Archdeacon Rock ⌕ Q; 53°26'·71N 04°30'·87W.
Victoria Bank ⌕ VQ; 53°25'·61N 04°31'·37W.
Coal Rk ⌕ Q (6) + L Fl 15s; 53°25'·91N 04°32'·79W.
Ethel Rk ⌕ VQ; 53°26'·64N 04°33'·67W.
The Skerries ☆ 53°25'·27N 04°36'·55W Fl (2) 15s 36m
20M; W ○ twr, R band; *Racon (T) 25M*. Iso R 4s 26m 10M;
same twr; vis: 233°-252°; *Horn (2) 60s*. H24 in periods of
reduced visibility.
Langdon ⌕ Q (9) 15s; 53°22'·74N 04°38'·74W.
Bolivar ◣ FL G 2·5s; 53°21'·51N 04°35'·33W.
Wk ⌕ Fl (2) R 10s; 53°20'·43N 04°36'·60W.

HOLYHEAD to SOUTH STACK
Bkwtr Head ⚡ Fl (3) G 10s 21m 14M; W ☐ twr, B band; Fl
Y vis: 174°-226°; *Siren 20s*; 53°19'·31N 04°37'·16W.
Spit ◣ Fl G 3s; 53°19'·79N 04°37'·15W.
South Stack ☆ 53°19'·31N 04°41'·98W Fl 10s 60m **24M**;
(H24); W ○ twr; obsc to N by N Stack and part obsc in
Penrhos bay; *Horn 30s*. Fog Det lt vis: 145°-325°.

MENAI STRAIT TO BARDSEY ISLAND
Ten Feet Bank ⌕ QR; 53°19'·47N 04°02'·82W.
Dinmor ◣ QG; 53°19'·34N 04°03'·32W.
Trwyn-Du ⚡ Fl 5s 19m 12M; W ○ castellated twr, B
bands; vis: 101°-023°; *Bell (1) 30s*, sounded continuously;

53°18'·77N 04°02'·44W. FR on radio mast 2M SW.

APPROACHES to BEAUMARIS and BANGOR
(Direction of buoyage ⇗ NE to SW)
Perch Rock ⌕ Fl R 5s; 53°18'·73N 04°02'·09W.

PORT DINORWIC and CAERNARFON
Port Dinorwic Pier Hd ⚡ 53°11'·18N 04°12'·64W F WR 5m
2M; vis: 225°-R- 357°-W-225°.

(Direction of buoyage ⇗ SW to NE)
Caernarfon N Pier Hd ⚡ 2 FG (vert) 5m 2M; 53°08'·72N
04°16'·56W.
Abermenai Point ⚡ Fl WR 3·5s 6m 3M; W mast; vis:
065°-R-245°-W-065°; 53°07'·62N 04°19'·72W.
C1 ◣ Fl G 5s; 53°07'·50N 04°24'·76W.
C2 ⌕ Fl R 10s; 53°07'·60N 04°24'·85W.
Llanddwyn I ⚡Fl WR 2·5s 12m W7M, R4M; W twr; vis:
280°-R- 015°-W-120°; 53°08'·05N 04°24'·79W .

PORTH DINLLÄEN
CG Stn ⚡ FR when firing taking place 10M N; 52°56'·82N
04°33'·89W.
Careg y Chwislen ⌕ 52°56'·99N 04°33'·51W.
Bardsey I ☆ 52°44'·97N 04°48'·02W Fl (5) 15s 39m **26M**;
W ☐ twr, R bands; obsc by Bardsey Is 198°-250° and in
Tremadoc B when brg < 260°.

AREA 9 *S Wales & SW England – Swansea to Padstow*
SELECTED LIGHTS, BUOYS & WAYPOINTS
| Positions are referenced to WGS84 |

CARDIGAN BAY
Bardsey I ☆ 52°45'·00N 04°47'·98W Fl (5) 15s 39m **26M**;
W ☐ twr, R bands; obsc by Bardsey I 198°-250° and in
Tremadoc B when brg less than 260°.
St Tudwal's ⚡ Fl WR 15s 46m W14, R10M; vis:
349°-W-169°-R- 221°-W-243°-R-259°-W-293°-R-349°; obsc
by East I 211°-231°; 52°47'·92N 04°28'·30W.

PWLLHELI and PORTHMADOG
Pwllheli App ⌕ Iso 2s; 52°53'·02N 04°23'·07W.
Porthmadog Fairway ⌕ L Fl 10s; 52°52'·97N 04°11'·18W.

BARMOUTH and ABERDOVEY
Diffuser ⌕ Fl Y 5s; 52°43'·19N 04°05'·38W.
Barmouth Outer ⌕ L Fl 10s; 52°42'·62N 04°04'·83W.
Aberdovey Outer ⌕ Iso 4s; 52°32'·00N 04°05'·56W.
Cynfelyn Patches, Patches ⌕ Q (9) 15s; 52°25'·83N
04°16'·41W.

ABERYSTWYTH, ABERAERON and NEW QUAY
Aberystwyth S Bkwtr Hd ⚡ Fl (2) WG 10s 12m 10M; vis:
030°-G- 053°-W-210°; 52°24'·40N 04°05'·52W.
Ldg Lts 133°. Front, FR 4m 5M; 52°24'·37N 04°05'·39W.
Rear, 52m from front, FR 7m 6M.
Aberaeron N Pier ⚡ Fl (4) WRG 15s 10m 6M;
vis: 050°-G-104°-W-178°-R-232°; 52°14'·61N 04°15'·87W.
Carreg Ina ⌕ Q; 52°13'·25N 04°20'·75W.
New Quay Pier Hd ⚡ Fl WG 3s 12m W8M, G5M; G △; vis:
135°-W- 252°-G-295°; 52°12'·95N 04°21'·35W.

CARDIGAN and FISHGUARD
Cardigan Channel ⌕ Fl (2) 5s; 52°06'·44N 04°41'·43W.

Fishguard N Bkwtr Hd ⚡ Fl G 4·5s 18m 13M; *Bell (1) 8s*;
52°00'·76N 04°58'·23W.
Strumble Head ☆ 52°01'·79N 05°04'·43W Fl (4) 15s 45m
26M; vis: 038°-257°; (H24).

BISHOPS and SMALLS
South Bishop ☆ 51°51'·14N 05°24'·74W Fl 5s 44m **16M**;
W ○ twr; *Horn (3) 45s; Racon (O)10M*; (H24).
The Smalls ☆ 51°43'·27N 05°40'·19W Fl (3) 15s 36m **18M**;
Racon (T); *Horn (2) 60s*. Same twr, Iso R 4s 33m 13M; vis:
253°-285° over Hats & Barrels Rk; both Lts shown H24 in
periods of reduced visibility.
Skokholm I ☆, 51°41'·64N 05°17'·22W Fl WR 10s 54m
W18M, R15M; vis: 301°-W-154°-R-301°; partially obsc
226°-258°.

WALES – SOUTH COAST – BRISTOL CHANNEL
MILFORD HAVEN
St Ann's Head ☆ 51°40'·87N 05°10'·42W Fl WR 5s 48m
W18M, R17M, R14M; W 8-sided twr; vis: 233°-W-247°-
R-285°-R(intens)- 314°-R-332°-W131°, partially obscured
between 124°-129°; *Horn (2) 60s*.
W Blockhouse Point ⌕ Ldg Lts 022·5°. Front, F 54m 13M;
B stripe on W twr; vis: 004·5°-040·5°; intens on lead. By day
10M; vis: 004·5°-040·5°; *Racon (Q)*; 51°41'·31N 05°09'·56W.
Watwick Point Common Rear ☆, 0·5M from front, F 80m
15M; vis: 013·5°-031·5°. By day 10M; vis: 013·5°-031·5°;
Racon (Y).
W Blockhouse Point ⌕ Q WR 21m W9M, R7M; R lantern on
W base: vis: 220°-W-250°-R-020°-W-036°-R-049°; 51°41'·31N
05°09'·56W.

Dale Fort ⚔ Fl (2) WR 5s 20m W5M, R3M; vis: 222°-R-276°-W-019°; 51°42'·16N 05°09'·01W.

Gt Castle Hd ⚓ F WRG 27m W5M, R3M, G3M; vis: 243°-R-281°-G- 299°-W-029°; also Dir WRG (040°) 038·25°-G-039°-Al WG-039·5°-W-040·5°-AlWR-041°-R-041·75°; 51°42'·67N 05°07'·07W (not used in conjunction with the following front light) also Ldg Lts 039·7° **Front**, Oc 4s 27m **15M**; vis: 031·2°-048·2°. **Rear**, 890m from front. 05°06'·60W Oc 8s 53m **15M** (by day 10M) vis: 031·2°-048·2°.

St Ann's ⚔ Fl R 2·5s; 51°40'·25N 05°10'·51W.

Mid Channel Rks ⚓ Q (9) 15s; 51°40'·18N 05°10'·14W.

Sheep ▲ QG; 51°40'·06N 05°08'·31W.

Millbay ⚓ Fl (2) R 5s; 51°41'·05N 05°09'·45W.

W Chapel ▲ Fl G 10s; 51°40'·98N 05°08'·67W.

E Chapel ⚓ Fl R 5s; 51°40'·87N 05°08'·15W.

Rat ▲ Fl G 5s; 51°40'·80N 05°07'·86W.

Angle ⚓ VQ; 51°41'·63N 05°08'·27W.

Thorn Rock ⚓ Q (9) 15s; 51°41'·53N 05°07'·76W.

Turbot Bank ⚓ VQ (9) 10s; 51°37'·41N 05°10'·08W.

ODAS Fl(5) Y 20s; 51°36'·70N 05°08'·70W

St Gowan ⚓ Q (6) + L Fl 15s, **Racon (T) 10M**; 51°31'·93N 04°59'·77W.

TENBY to SWANSEA BAY

Caldey I ⚔ Fl (3) WR 20s 65m W13M, R9M; vis: R173°-W212°- R088°-102°; 51°37'·90N 04°41'·08W.

Woolhouse ⚓ Q (6) + L Fl 15s; 51°39'·35N 04°39'·69W.

Burry Port Inlet ⚔ 51°40'·62N 04°15'·06W Fl 5s 7m **15M**.

W. Helwick (W HWK) ⚓ Q (9) 15s; **Racon (T) 10M**; 51°31'·40N 04°23'·65W Q.

E. Helwick ⚓ VQ (3) 5s; *Bell*; 51°31'·80N 04°12'·68W.

SWANSEA BAY and SWANSEA

Ledge ⚓ VQ (6) + L Fl 10s; 51°29'·93N 03°58'·77W.

Mixon ⚓ Fl (2) R 5s; *Bell*; 51°33'·12N 03°58'·78W.

Outer Spoil Gnd ⚓ Fl Y 2·5s; 51°32'·11N 03°55'·73W.

Grounds ⚓ VQ (3) 5s; 51°32'·81N 03°53'·47W.

Mumbles ☆ 51°34'·01N 03°58'·27W Fl (4) 20s 35m **15M**; W twr; *Horn (3) 60s*.

SW Inner Green Grounds ⚓ Q (6) + L Fl 15s; *Bell*; 51°34'·06N 03°57'·03W.

Lts in line 020°. Front: E Breakwater head, Oc G 4s 5m 2M & 2FG(vert) 10m 6M; 51°36'·38N 03°55'·62W. Rear, 3·1ca from front: FG 6M.

SWANSEA BAY, RIVER NEATH and PORT TALBOT

Neath App Chan ▲ Fl G 5s; 51°35'·71N 03°52'·83W.

Cabenda ⚓ VQ (6) + L Fl 10s; **Racon (Q)**; 51°33'·36N 03°52'·23W.

Ldg Lts 059·8° (occas). Front, Oc R 3s 12m 6M; 51°34'·92N 03°48'·10W. Rear, 400m from front, Oc R 6s 32m 6M.

BRISTOL CHAN – NORTH SHORE (E PART)

W Scar ⚓ Q (9) 15s, Bell, **Racon (T) 10M**; 51°28'·31N 03°55'·57W.

South Scar (S SCAR) ⚓ Q (6) + L Fl 15s; 51°27'·61N 03°51'·58W.

E. Scarweather ⚓ Q (3) 10s; *Bell*; 51°27'·98N 03°46'·76W.

PORTHCAWL

Fairy ⚓ Q (9) 15s; *Bell*; 51°27'·86N 03°42'·07W.

Porthcawl Bkwtr Hd ⚔ 51°28'·39N 03°41'·98W F WRG 10m W6M, R4M, G4M; vis: 302°-G-036°-W-082°-R-122°.

W Nash ⚓ VQ (9) 10s ; *Bell*; 51°25'·99N 03°45'·95W.

Nash ☆ 51°24'·03N 03°33'·06W Fl (2) WR 15s 56m **W21M, R16M**; vis: 280°-R-290°-W-100°-R-120°-W-128°.

Breaksea ⚓ L Fl 10s; *Racon (T) 10M*;   51°19'·88N 03°19'·08W.

BARRY

W Bkwtr Hd ⚔ Fl 2·5s 12m 10M; 51°23'·46N 03°15'·52W.

N. One Fathom ⚓ Q; 51°20'·94N 03°12'·17W.

Mackenzie ⚓ QR; 51°21'·75N 03°08'·24W.

Flat Holm ☆, SE Pt 51°22'·54N 03°07'·14W Fl (3) WR 10s 50m **W15M**, R12M; W ○ twr; vis: 106°-R-140°-W-151°-R-203°-W-106°; (H24).

CARDIFF and PENARTH ROADS

Lavernock Outfall ⚓ Fl Y 5s; 51°23'·95N 03°09'·50W.

Ranie ⚓ Fl (2) R 5s; 51°24'·23N 03°09'·39W.

S Cardiff ⚓ Q (6) + L Fl 15s; *Bell*; 51°24'·18N 03°08'·57W.

Mid Cardiff ▲ Fl (3) G 10s; 51°25'·60N 03°08'·09W.

Cardiff Spit ⚓ QR; 51°24'·57N 03°07'·12W.

N Cardiff ▲ QG; 51°26'·52N 03°07'·19W.

PENARTH and CARDIFF

Wrach Chan Dir lt 348·5°. Oc WRG 10s 5m; W3M, R3M, G3M; vis: 344·5°-G-347°-W-350°-R-352°; H24; 51°27'·16N 03°09'·75W.

Outer Wrach ⚓ Q (9) 15s; 51°26'·20N 03°09'·46W.

Tail Patch ▲ QG; 51°23'·53N 03°03'·65W.

Hope ⚓ Q (3) 10s; 51°24'·84N 03°02'·68W.

NW Elbow ⚓ VQ (9) 10s; *Bell*; 51°26'·28N 02°59'·93W.

EW Grounds ⚓ L Fl 10s 7M; *Whis*; *Racon (T) 7M*; 51°27'·12N 02°59'·95W.

NEWPORT DEEP, RIVER USK and NEWPORT

Newport Deep ▲ Fl (3) G 10s; *Bell*; 51°29'·36N 02°59'·12W.

East Usk ☆ 51°32'·40N 02°58'·01W; Fl (2) WRG 10s 11m W11M,R10M, G10M; vis: 284°-W-290° -obscured shore-324°-R- 017°-W-037°-G-115°-W-120°. Also Oc WRG 10s 10m W11M, R9M, G9M; vis: 018°-G-022°-W- 024°-R-028°. Julians Pill Ldg Lts 062°. Front, FG 5m 4M; 51°33'·30N 02°57'·94W. Rear, 61m from front, FG 8m 4M.

BRISTOL CHAN – SOUTH SHORE (E PART)

BRISTOL DEEP

N Elbow ▲ QG; *Bell*; 51°26'·97N 02°58'·65W.

S Mid Grounds ⚓ VQ (6) + L Fl 10s; 51°27'·62N 02°58'·68W.

E Mid Grounds ⚓ Fl R 5s; 51°27'·75N 02°54'·98W.

Clevedon ⚓ VQ; 51°27'·39N 02°54'·93W.

Welsh Hook ⚓ Q (6) + L Fl 15s; 51°28'·53N 02°51'·86W.

Avon ▲ Fl G 2·5s; 51°27'·92N 02°51'·73W.

Black Nore Point W round tower on lattice base. 51°29'·09N 02°48'·05W.

Newcome ⚓ 51°30'·01N 02°46'·71W Fl (3) R 10s.

Denny Shoal ⚓ VQ (6) + L Fl 10s; 51°30'·15N 02°45'·45W.

Firefly ▲ Fl (2) G 5s; 51°29'·96N 02°45'·35W.

Portishead Point ☆ 51°29'·68N 02°46'·42W Q (3) 10s 9m **16M**; B twr, W base; vis: 060°-262°; *Horn 20s*.

PORTISHEAD

Pier Hd ⚓ Iso G 2s 5m 3M; 51°29'·69N 02°45'·27W.

Seabank. Lts in line 086·8°. Front, IQ 13m 5M; vis: 070·3°-

103·3°; by day 1M vis: 076·8°-096·8°; 51°30'·07N 02°43'·81W. Dir WG 6m 5M; vis: 089·7°-FG-090·6°-AltWG-090·8°-FW-093·6°. Rear, 500m from front, IQ 16m 5M; vis: 070·3°-103·3°; by day 1M, vis: 076·8°-096·8°.

Knuckle Lts in line 099·6°, Oc G 5s 6m 6M; 51°29'·94N 02°43'·67W. Rear, 165m from front, FG 13m 6M; vis: 044°-134°.

AVONMOUTH

Royal Edward Dock N Pier Hd ☆ Fl 4s 15m 10M; vis: 060°-228·5°; 51°30'·49N 02°43'·09W.

King Road Ldg Lts 072·4°. N Pier Hd ☆ Front, Oc R 5s 5m 9M; W obelisk, R bands; vis: 062°-082°; 51°30'·49N 02°43'·09W. Rear ☆, 546m from front, QR 15m 10M; vis: 066°- 078°.

RIVER AVON, CUMBERLAND BASIN and AVON BRIDGE

S Pier Hd ☆ Oc RG 30s 9m 10M and FBu 4m 1M; vis: 294°-R-036°-G-194°; 51°30'·37N 02°43'·10W. Bell(1) 10s.

Ldg Lts 127·2°. Front ⚓, Iso R 2s 6m 3M, vis: 010°-160°; 51°30'·10N 02°42'·59W. Rear⚓ , Iso R 2s10m 3M, vis: 048°-138°.

BRISTOL CHANNEL (SOUTH SHORE)

WESTON-SUPER-MARE

Pier Hd ☆ 2 FG (vert) 6m; 51°20'·88N 02°59'·26W.

E Culver ⚓ Q (3) 10s; 51°18'·00N 03°15'·44W.

W Culver ⚓ VQ (9) 10s; 51°17'·47N 03°19'·00W.

Gore ⚓ Iso 5s; Bell; 51°13'·94N 03°09'·79W.

BURNHAM-ON-SEA and RIVER PARRETT

Ent ☆ Fl 7·5s 7m 12M; vis: 074°-164°; 51°14'·89N 03°00'·36W;

Dir lt 076°. F WRG 4m W12M, R10M, G10M; vis: 071°-G- 075°-W-077°- R-081°.

DZ No. 1 ⚓ Fl Y 2·5s; 51°15'·28N 03°09'·49W.

DZ No. 2 ⚓ Fl Y 10s; 51°13'·77N 03°19'·86W.

DZ No. 3 ⚓ Fl Y 5s; 51°16'·34N 03°14'·98W.

WATCHET, MINEHEAD and PORLOCK WEIR

Watchet W Bkwtr Hd ☆ Oc G 3s 9m 9M; 51°11'·03N 03°19'·74W.

Watchet E Pier ☆ 2 FR (vert) 3M; 51°11'·01N 03°19'·72W.

Minehead Bkwtr Hd ☆ Fl (2) G 5s 4M; vis: 127°-262°; 51°12'·81N 03°28'·36W.

Lynmouth Foreland ☆ 51°14'·73N 03°47'·21W Fl (4) 15s 67m 18M; W ◯ twr; vis: 083°-275°; (H24).

LYNMOUTH and WATERMOUTH

River Training Arm ☆ 2 FR (vert) 6m 5M;   51°13'·90N 03°49'·83W.

Harbour Arm ☆ 2 FG (vert) 6m 5M; 51°13'·92N 03°49'·84W.

Sand Ridge ⚓ Q G; 51°15'·01N 03°49'·77W.

Copperas Rock ⚓ Fl G 2·5s; 51°13'·78N 04°00'·60W.

Watermouth☆OcWRG5s1m3M;W△;vis:149·5°-G-151·5°-W-154·5°-R-156·5°; 51°12'·93N 04°04'·60W.

ILFRACOMBE to BAGGY POINT

Ldg Lts 188°. Front, Oc 10s 8m 3M; 51°12'·53N 04°06'·65W. Rear, Oc 10s 6m 3M.

Horseshoe ⚓ Q; 51°15'·02N 04°12'·96W.

Bull Point ☆ 51°11'·94N 04°12'·09W Fl (3) 10s 54m 20M; W ◯ twr, obscd shore-056°. Same twr; FR 48m 12M; vis: 058°-096°.

Morte Stone ⚓ Fl G 5s; 51°11'·30N 04°14'·95W.

Baggy Leap ⚓ Fl (2) G 10s; 51°08'·92N 04°16'·97W.

BIDEFORD, RIVERS TAW and TORRIDGE

Bideford Fairway ⚓ L Fl 10s; Bell; 51°05'·25N 04°16'·25W.

Bideford Bar ⚓ Q G; 51°04'·89N 04°14'·62W.

Instow ☆ Ldg Lts 118°. Front, 51°03'·62N 04°10'·66W Oc 6s 22m 15M; vis: 103·5°-132°. Rear, 427m from front, Oc 10s 38m 15M; vis: 103°-132·5°; (H24).

Crow Pt ☆ Fl WR 2. 5s 8m W6M R5M; vis: 225°-R-232°-W-237°-R-358°-W- 015°-R-045°; 51°03'·96N 04°11'·39W.

LUNDY

Near North Point ☆ 51°12'·10N 04°40'·65W Fl 15s 48m 17M; vis: 009°-285°.

South East Point ☆ 51°09'·72N 04°39'·37W Fl 5s 53m 15M; vis: 170°-073°; Horn 25s.

Hartland Point ☆ 51°01'·29N 04°31'·59W Fl (6) 15s 37m 22M; (H24).

NORTH CORNWALL

BUDE, PADSTOW and NEWQUAY

Compass Point twr 50°49'·71N 04°33'·42W.

Stepper Point (Padstow) ☆ L Fl 10s 12m 4M; 50°34'·12N 04°56'·72W.

Trevose Head ☆ 50°32'·94N 05°02'·13W Fl 7·5s 62m 21M; Horn (2) 30s.

North Pier Hd (Newquay) ☆ 2 FG (vert) 5m 2M; 50°25'·07N 05°05'·19W.

HAYLE and ST IVES

The Stones ⚓ Q; 50°15'·64N 05°25'·51W.

Godrevy I ☆ Fl WR 10s 37m W12M, R9M; vis: 022°-W-101°-R-145°-W-272°; 50°14'·54N 05°24'·04W.

Hayle App ⚓ QR; 50°12'·26N 05°26'·30W.

St Ives App ⚓ 50°12'·85N 05°28'·42W

Pendeen ☆ 50°09'·90N 05°40'·32W Fl (4) 15s 59m 16M; vis: 042°-240°; in bay between Gurnard Hd and Pendeen it shows to coast; Horn 20s.

1	Aberystwyth	1		12	64	66	122	164	192	224	254	286	299	318	361		Kilrush	12
2	Fishguard	40	2		11	13	69	111	139	171	201	233	246	265	308		Dingle	11
3	Milford Haven	84	48	3		10	56	102	131	165	188	227	242	252	295		Valentia	10
4	Tenby	107	71	28	4		9	42	70	102	132	164	177	196	239		Baltimore	9
5	Swansea	130	94	55	36	5		8	35	69	95	135	150	168	202		Kinsale	8
6	Cardiff	161	125	86	66	46	6		7	34	65	100	115	133	172		Youghal	7
7	Sharpness	192	156	117	106	75	33	7		6	32	69	84	102	139		Dunmore East	6
8	Avonmouth	175	139	100	89	58	20	18	8		5	34	47	66	108		Rosslare	5
9	Burnham-on-Sea	169	133	94	70	48	53	50	33	9		4	15	36	75		Arklow	4
10	Ilfracombe	128	92	53	35	25	44	74	57	45	10		3	21	63		Wicklow	3
11	Padstow	142	106	70	70	76	97	127	110	98	55	11		2	48		Dun Laoghaire	2
12	Longships	169	133	105	110	120	139	169	152	140	95	50	12		1		Carlingford Lough	1

AREA 10 *Ireland – Clockwise from Lambay Island*

SELECTED LIGHTS, BUOYS & WAYPOINTS

Positions are referenced to WGS84

LAMBAY ISLAND TO TUSKAR ROCK

MALAHIDE and LAMBAY ISLAND
Taylor Rks ⚓ Q; 53°30'·21N 06°01'·87W.
Burren Rocks ⚓ Fl G 5s; 53°29'·35N 06°02'·35W.
Malahide approach ⚓ L Fl 10s; 53°27'·12N 06°06'·87W.

HOWTH
Rowan Rocks ⚓ Q (3) 10s; 53°23'·88N 06°03'·27W.
E Pier Hd ☆ Fl (2) WR 7·5s 13m W12M, R9M; W twr; vis: W256°- R295°-256°; 53°23'·66N 06°04'·03W.
Baily ☆ 53°21'·70N 06°03'·14W Fl 15s 41m **26M**; twr. Fog Det Lt VQ.
Rosbeg E ⚓ Q (3) 10s; 53°21'·02N 06°03'·45W.
Rosbeg S ⚓ Q (6) + L Fl 15s; 53°20'·22N 06°04'·17W.

PORT OF DUBLIN
Dublin Bay ⚓ Mo (A) 10s; *Racon (M)*; 53°19'·92N 06°04'·64W.
No. 1 ▲ Fl (3) G 5s; 53°20'·30N 06°05'·56W.
No. 3 ▲ IQ G; 53°20'·57N 06°06'·76W.
No. 4 ⚓ IQ R; 53°20'·48N 06°06'·93W.
No. 5 ▲ Fl G 2s; 53°20'·64N 06°08'·60W.
No. 6 ⚓ Fl R 2s; 53°20'·56N 06°08'·75W.
Great S Wall Hd Poolbeg ☆ Fl R 4s 20m 10M *(synchro with N.Bull)*; R ○ twr; Horn (2) 60s; 53°20'·53N 06°09'·08W.
N Bull ☆ Fl G 4s 15m 10M; G ○ twr; 53°20'·70N 06°08'·98W.
N Bank ☆ 53°20'·69N 06°10'·59W Oc G 8s 10m **16M**; G □ twr.

DUN LAOGHAIRE
E Bkwtr Hd ☆ Fl (2) R 8s 16m **17M**; twr, R lantern; 53°18'·15N 06°07'·62W. Fog Det Lt VQ.
Outfall ⚓ Fl Y 5s; 53°18'·41N 06°08'·35W.
Muglins ☆Fl R 5s 14m 11M; 53°16'·52N 06°04'·58W.

OFFSHORE MARKS
Bennett Bank ⚓ Q (6) + L Fl 15s; 53°20'·17N 05°55'·11W.
Kish Bank ☆ 53°18'·64N 05°55'·48W Fl (2) 20s 29m **21M**; W twr, R band; *Racon (T) 15M*.
N Kish ⚓ VQ; 53°18'·56N 05°56'·44W.
E Kish ⚓ Fl (2) R 10s; 53°14'·35N 05°53'·56W.
E Codling ⚓ Fl (4) R 10s; 53°08'·54N 05°47'·11W.
W Codling ▲ Fl G 10s; 53°06'·97N 05°54'·51W.
S Codling ⚓ VQ (6) + L Fl 15s; 53°04'·74N 05°49'·76W.
Breaches Shoal ⚓ Fl (2) R 6s; 53°05'·67N 05°59'·81W.
North India ⚓ Q; 53°03'·12N 05°53'·46W.
South India ⚓ Q (6) + L Fl 15s; 53°00'·36N 05°53'·31W.
Codling ⚓ Q(3) 10s; *Racon (G) 10M*.

WICKLOW to ARKLOW
Wicklow ⚓ Fl (4) Y 10s; 52°59'·54N 06°01'·29W.
E Pier Hd ☆ Fl WR 5s 11m 6M; W twr, R base and cupola; vis: 136°-R-293°-W-136°; 52°58'·99N 06°02'·07W.
W Packet Quay Hd ☆ Fl WG 10s 5m 6M; vis: 076°-G-256°-W-076°; 52°58'·88N 06°02'·08W.
Wicklow Hd ☆ 52°56'·84N 05°58'·47W Fl (3) 15s 37m **23M**; W twr.
Horseshoe ⚓ Fl R 3s; 52°56'·84N 05°58'·47W.

N Arklow ⚓ Q; 52°53'·86N 05°55'·21W.
Arklow Bank Wind Farm from 52°48'·47N 05°56'·57W to 52°46'·47N 05°57'·11W, N and S Turbines Fl Y 5s14m 10M + Fl W Aero lts. AIS transmitters. Other turbines Fl Y 5s. See 9.12.5.

ARKLOW to WEXFORD
S Pier Hd ☆ Fl WR 6s 11m 13M; twr; vis: R shore- W223°-R350°-shore; 52°47'·61N 06°08'·22W.
Roadstone Bkwtr Hd ☆ QY; 52°46'·65N 06°08'·23W.
S Arklow ⚓ Q(6) + LFl 15s; *Racon (O) 10M*; 52°40'·20N 05°58'·89W.
No. 2 Glassgorman ⚓ Fl (4) R 10s; 52°45'·35N 06°05'·34W.
No. 1 Glassgorman ⚓ Fl (2) R 6s; 52°37'·69N 06°07'·34W.
N Blackwater ⚓ Q; 52°32'·22N 06°09'·51W.
No. 6 Rusk ⚓ Fl R 3s; 52°32'·65N 06°10'·41W.
No. 4 Rusk ⚓ Fl (2) R 5s; 52°31'·07N 06°10'·86W.
No. 2 Rusk ⚓ Fl (2) R 5s; 52°28'·64N 06°12'·61W.
No. 1 Rusk ▲ Fl (2) G 5s; 52°28'·54N 06°11'·80W.
W Blackwater ▲ Fl G 6s; 52°25'·87N 06°13'·56W.
SE Blackwater ⚓ Q (3) 10s, *Racon (M) 10M*; 52°25'·62N 06°08'·42W.
S Blackwater ⚓ Q (6) + L Fl 15s; 52°22'·76N 06°12'·87W.
North Long ⚓ Q; 52°21'·44N 06°17'·04W.
West Long ▲ QG; 52°18'·18N 06°17'·96W.
Lucifer ⚓ VQ (3) 5s; 52°17'·02N 06°12'·67W.

ROSSLARE
S Long ▲ Fl (2) G 6s (sync with Splaugh); 52°14'·74N 06°15'·80W.
Splaugh ⚓ Fl (2) R 6s (sync with S Long); 52°14'·37N 06°16'·76W.
South Holdens ▲ Fl G 3s; 52°15'·14N 06°17'·24W. (Synch with Calmines)
Calmines ⚓ Fl R 3s; 52°15'·01N 06°17'·77W. (Synch with S Holdens).
W Holdens ▲ Fl (3) G 10s; 52°15'·77N 06°18'·74W.
Rosslare Pier Hd ☆ Oc WRG 5s 15m W13M, R10M, G10M; R twr; vis:098°-G-188°-W-208°-R-246°-G-283°-W-286°-R-320°; 52°15'·43N 06°20'·29W.
Ballygeary ☆Oc WR 1·7s 7m 4M vis: shore-R-152°-W-200°-W(unintens)-205°; 52°15'·25N 06°20'·48W.

TUSKAR ROCK TO OLD HEAD OF KINSALE

Tuskar ☆ 52°12'·17N 06°12'·42W Q (2) 7·5s 33m **24M**; W twr; *Racon (T) 18M*.
S Rock ⚓ Q (6) + L Fl 15s; 52°10'·80N 06°12'·84W.
Fundale ⚓ Fl (2) R 10s; 52°11'·04N 06°19'·78W.
Barrels ⚓ Q (3) 10s; 52°08'·32N 06°22'·05W.

KILMORE
Kilmore Quay SWM ⚓ Iso 10s; (Apr-Sep); 52°09'·20N 06°35'·30W.
Kilmore Bkwtr Hd ☆ Q RG 7m 5M; vis: 269°-R-354°-G-003°-R-077°; 52°10'·20N 06°35'·15W.
Ldg lts 007·9°, Front 52°10'·37N 06°35'·08W Oc 4s 3m 6M. Rear, 100m from front, Oc 4s 6m 6M; sync with front.
Coningbeg ⚓ Q(6)+LFl 15s, Racon, AIS; 52°03'·20N 06°38'·57W.

'M5' ODAS 35 ⌐ 51°41'·40N 06°42'·24W; Fl (5) Y 20s.

WATERFORD

Hook Hd ☆ 52°07'·32N 06°55'·85W Fl 3s 46m **23M**; W twr, two B bands; *Racon (K) 10M*. Fog Det Lt VQ.

Waterford ⊿ Fl R 3s. Fl (3) R 10s; 52°08'·95N 06°57'·00W.

Duncannon Dir lt ⚡ F WRG 13m 10M, white tower on fort, 359·5°-FG-001·2°-Alt GW-001·7°-FW-002·4°-Alt WR-002·9°-FR-004·5°; 52°13'·23N 06°56'·25W; Oc WR 4s 13m 9 WM R 7M on same tower, 119°-R-149°-W-172°.

Passage Pt ⚡ Fl WR 5s 7m W6M, R5M; R pile structure; vis: W shore- R127°-302°; 52°14'·26N 06°57'·77W.

Cheek Pt ⚡ Q WR 6m 5M; W mast; vis: W007°-R289°-007°; 52°16'·12N 06°59'·38W.

Sheagh ⚡ Fl R 3s 29m 3M; Gy twr; vis: 090°-318°; 52°16'·29N 06°59'·34W.

Snowhill Point Ldg lts 255°. Front, Fl WR 2·5s 5m 3M; vis: W222°- R020°- W057°-107°; 52°16'·39N 07°00'·91W. Rear, Flour Mill, 750m from front, Q 12m 5M.

Queen's Chan Ldg lts 098°. Front, QR 8m 5M; B twr; W band; vis: 030°-210°;52°15'·32N 07°02'·38W. Rear, 550m from front, Q 15m 5M; W mast.

Beacon Quay ⚡ Fl G 3s 9m; vis: 255°-086°; 52°15'·50N 07°04'·21W.

Cove ⚡ Fl WRG 6s 6m 2M; W twr; vis: R111°- G161°-W234°-111°; 52°15'·05N 07°05'·16W.

Smelting Ho Pt ⚡ Q 8m 3M; W mast; 52°15'·15N 07°05'·27W.

Ballycar ⚡ Fl RG 3s 5m; vis: G127°- R212°-284°; 52°15'·06N 07°05'·51W.

DUNMORE EAST

East Pier Head ☆ 52°08'·93N 06°59'·37W Fl WR 8s 13m **W17M**, R13M; Gy twr, vis: W225°- R310°-004°.

W Wharf ⚡ Fl G 2s 6m 4M; vis: 165°-246°; 52°08'·97N 06°59'·45W.

DUNGARVAN

Ballinacourty Pt ⚡ Fl (2) WRG 10s 16m W10M, R8M, G8M; W twr; vis: G245°- W274°- R302°- W325°-117°; 52°04'·69N 07°33'·18W.

Helvick ⊿ Q (3) 10s; 52°03'·61N 07°32'·25W.

Mine Head ☆ 51°59'·52N 07°35'·25W Fl (4) 30s 87m **20M**; W twr, B band; vis: 228°-052°.

YOUGHAL

Bar Rocks ⊿ Q (6) + L Fl 15s; 51°54'·85N 07°50'·05W.

Blackball Ledge ⊿ 51°55'·34N 07°48'·53W Q (3) 10s.

W side of ent ☆ 51°56'·57N 07°50'·53W Fl WR 2·5s 24m **W17M**, R13M; W twr; vis: W183°- R273°- W295°- R307°-W351°-003°.

BALLYCOTTON

Ballycotton ☆ 51°49'·52N 07° 59'·09W Fl WR 10s 59m **W21M, R17M**; B twr, within W walls, B lantern; vis: 238°-W-048°-R-238°; Fog Det Lt VQ.

The Smiths ⌐ Fl (3) R 10s; 51°48'·62N 08°00'·71W.

Power ⊿ Q (6) + L Fl 15s; 51°45'·59N 08°06'·67W.

CORK

Cork ⊿ L Fl 10s; *Racon (T) 7M*; 51°42'·92N 08°15'·60W.

Daunt Rock ⌐ Fl (2) R 6s; 51°43'·52N 08°17'·65W.

Fort Davis Ldg lts 354·1°. Front, 51°48'·82N 08°15'·80W

Dir WRG 29m **17M**; vis: FG351·5°-AlWG352·25°-FW353°-AlWR355°-FR355·75°-356·5°. Rear, Dognose Quay, 203m from front, Oc 5s 37m 10M; Or 3, synch with front.

Roche's Pt ☆ 51°47'·59N 08°15'·29W Fl WR 3s 30m **W20M, R16M**; vis: shore-R-292°-W-016°-R-033°, 033°- W (unintens)-159°-R-shore.

Outer Hbr Rk E2 ⌐ Fl R 2·5s; 51°47'·52N 08°15'·67W.

Chicago Knoll E1 ▲ Fl G 5s; 51°47'·66N 08°15'·54W.

W1 ▲ Fl G 10s; 51°47'·69N 08°16'·05W.

W2 ⌐ Fl R 10s; 51°47'·69N 08°16'·34W.

White Bay Ldg lts 034·6°. Front, Oc R 5s 11m 5M; W hut; 51°48'·53N 08°15'·22W. Rear, 113m from front, Oc R 5s 21m 5M; W hut; synch with front.

Spit Bank Pile ⚡ Iso WR 4s 10m W10M, R7M; W house on R piles; vis: R087°- W196°- R221°- 358°; 51°50'·72N 08°16'·45W.

KINSALE and OYSTER HAVEN

Bulman ⊿ Q (6) + L Fl 15s; 51°40'·14N 08°29'·74W.

Charle's Fort ⚡ Fl WRG 5s 18m W9M, R6M, G7M; vis: G348°-W358°- R004°-168°; H24; 51°41'·74N 08°29'·97W.

OLD HEAD OF KINSALE TO MIZEN HEAD

Old Head of Kinsale ☆, S point 51°36'·28N 08°32'·03W Fl (2) 10s 72m **20M**; B twr, two W bands.

COURTMACSHERRY

Barrel Rock ⊥ 51°37'·01N 08°37'·30W.

Black Tom ▲ Fl G 5s; 51°36'·41N 08°37'·95W.

Wood Pt (Land Pt) ⚡ Fl (2) WR 5s 15m 5M; vis: W315°-R332°-315°; 51°38'·16N 08°41'·00W.

Galley Head ☆ summit 51°31'·80N 08°57'·19W Fl (5) 20s 53m **23M**; W twr; vis: 256°-065°.

GLANDORE and CASTLETOWNSHEND

Reen Point ⚡ Fl WRG 10s 9m W5M, R3M, G3M; W twr; vis: Gshore- W338°- R001°-shore; 51°30'·98N 09°10'·50W.

Kowloon Bridge ⊿ Q (6) + L Fl 15s; 51°27'·58N 09°13'·75W.

BALTIMORE and FASTNET

Barrack Pt ⚡ Fl (2) WR 6s 40m W6M, R3M; vis: R168°-W294°-038°; 51°28'·33N 09°23'·65W.

Loo Rock ▲ Fl G 3s; 51°28'·43N 09°23'·45W.

Fastnet ☆, W end 51°23'·35N 09°36'·19W Fl 5s 49m **27M**; Gy twr, *Racon (G) 18M*. Fog Det Lt VQ.

SCHULL and LONG ISLAND CHANNEL

Ldg lts 346° Front, Oc 5s 5m 11M, W mast; 51°31'·68N 09°32'·43W. Rear, 91m from front, Oc 5s 8m11M; W mast.

CROOKHAVEN

Rock Is Pt ⚡ L Fl WR 8s 20m W13M, R11M; W twr; vis: W over Long Is B to 281°-R-340°; inside harbour 281°-R-348°- towards N shore; 51°28'·59N 09°42'·29W.

MIZEN HEAD TO DINGLE BAY

Mizen Head ☆ 51°27'·00N 09°49'·24W Iso 4s 55m **15M**; vis: 313°-133°.

Sheep's Hd ☆ 51°32'·60N 09°50'·95W Fl (3) WR 15s 83m **W18M, R15M**; W bldg; vis: 007°-R-017°-W-212°.

BANTRY BAY, CASTLETOWN BEARHAVEN, WHIDDY ISLE, BANTRY and GLENGARIFF

Roancarrigmore ☆ 51°39'·19N 09°44'·83W Fl WR 3s 18m **W18M**, R14M; W □ twr, B band; vis: 312°-W-050°-

R-122°-R (unintens)- 242°-R-312°. Reserve lt W8M, R6M obsc 140°-220°.

Ardnakinna Pt ☆ 51°37'·11N 09°55'·08W Fl (2) WR 10s 62m **W17M**, R14M; W ○ twr; vis: 319°-R- 348°-W-066°-R-shore.

Castletown Dir lt 023·25° ⚟ Oc WRG 5s 7m W15M, R12M, G12M; W hut, R stripe; vis: 019·5°-G-023°-W-023·5°-R-027°; 51°38'·79N 09°54'·30W.

Castletown Ldg lts 010°. Front, Oc 3s 4m 1M; W col, R stripe; vis: 005°-015°; 51°39'·16N 09°54'·40W. Rear, 80m from front, Oc 3s 7m 1M; W with R stripe; vis: 005°-015°.

Bull Rock ☆ 51°35'·51N 10°18'·08W Fl 15s 83m **21M**; W twr; vis: 220°-186°.

KENMARE RIVER, DARRYNANE and BALLYCROVANE

Darrynane Ldg lts 034°. Front, Oc 3s 10m 4M; 51°45'·90N 10°09'·20W. Rear, Oc 3s 16m 4M.

Skelligs Rock ☆ 51°46'·12N 10°32'·51W Fl (3) 15s 53m **19M**; W twr; vis: 262°-115°; part obsc within 6M 110°-115°.

VALENTIA and PORTMAGEE

Fort (Cromwell) Point ☆ 51°56'·02N 10°19'·27W FlWR 2s 16m **W17M, R15M**; W twr; vis: 304°-R-351°,102°-W-304°; obsc from seaward by Doulus Head when brg more than 180°.

Dir lt 141° ⚟ Oc WRG 4s 25m W11M, R8M, G8M (by day: W3M, R2M, G2M); W twr, R stripe; vis:136°-G-140°-W-142°-R-146°; 51°55'·51N 10°18'·42W.

DINGLE BAY TO LOOP HEAD

DINGLE BAY, VENTRY and DINGLE

Ldg lts 182° Oc 3s. Front 52°07'·41N 10°16'·59W, rear 100m behind.

Inishtearaght ☆, W end Blasket Islands 52°04'·55N 10°39'·68W Fl (2) 20s 84m **19M**; W twr; vis: 318°-221°; *Racon (O).*

BRANDON BAY, TRALEE BAY and FENIT HARBOUR

Little Samphire Is ☆ 52°16'·26N 09°52'·91W Fl WRG 5s 17m **W16M**, R13M; G13M; Bu ○ twr; vis: 262°-R-275°, 280-R-090°-G-140°-W-152°-R-172°.

Great Samphire I ⚟ QR 15m 3M; vis: 242°-097°; 52°16'·15N 09°51'·82W.

Fenit Hbr Pier Hd ⚟ 2 FR (vert) 12m 3M; vis: 148°-058°; 52°16'·24N 09°51'·55W.

SHANNON ESTUARY

Ballybunnion ⚓ VQ; *Racon (M) 6M*; 52°32'·52N 09°46'·93W.

Kilstiffin ⚬ Fl R 3s; 52°33'·80N 09°43'·83W.

Kilcredaun Head ⚬, W twr; 52°34'·78N 09°42'·58W.

Tail of Beal ⚓ Q (9) 15s; 52°34'·39N 09°40'·75W.

Carrigaholt ⚬ Fl (2) R 6s; 52°34'·92N 09°40'·51W.

Beal Spit ⚓ VQ (9) 10s; 52°34'·82N 09°39'·98W.

Beal Bar ⚓ Q; 52°35'·18N 09°39'·23W.

Doonaha ⚬ Q (3) R 5s; 52°35'·46N 09°38'·50W.

Letter Point ⚬ Fl R 7s; 52°35'·44N 09°35'·89W.

Asdee ⚬ Fl R 5s; 52°35'·09N 09°34'·55W.

Rineanna ⚬ QR; 52°35'·59N 09°31'·24W.

North Carraig ⚓ Q; 52°35'·60N 09°29'·76W.

Scattery Is, Rineanna Pt ⚟ Fl (2) 8s 15m 10M; W twr; vis: 208°-092°; 52°36'·32N 09°31'·03W.

KILRUSH

Marina Ent Chan Ldg lts 355°. Front, Oc 3s; 52°37'·99N 09°30'·27W. Rear, 75m from front, Oc 3s.

Tarbert Is N Point ⚟ Q WR 4s 18m W14M, R10M; W ○ twr; vis: W069°- R277°- W287°-339°; 52°35'·52N 09°21'·83W.

Tarbert (Ballyhoolahan Pt) Ldg lts 128·2° ⚓. Front,Iso 3s 13m 3M; △ on W twr; vis: 123·2°-133·2°; 52°34'·35N 09°18'·80W. Rear, 400m from front, Iso 5s 18m 3M; G stripe on W Bn.

Garraunbaun Pt ⚟ Fl (3) WR 10s 16m W8M, R5M; W □ col, vis: R shore - W072°- R242°- shore; 52°35'·62N 09°13'·94W.

Rinealon Pt ⚟ Fl 2·5s 4m 7M; B col, W bands; vis: 234°-088°; 52°37'·12N 09°09'·82W.

FOYNES

W Chan Ldg lts 107·9° (may be moved for changes in chan). Front, Oc 4s 34m 12M;52°36'·91N 09°06'·59W . Rear, Oc 4s 39m 12M.

RIVER SHANNON

Beeves Rock ⚟Fl WR 5s 12m W12M, R9M; vis: 064·5°-W-091°-R- 238°-W-265°-W(unintens)-064·5°; 52°39'·01N 09°01'·35W .

North Channel Ldg lts 093°. Front, Tradree Rock Fl R 2s 6m 5M; W Trs; vis: 246°-110°; 52°41'·00N 08°49'·87W. Rear 0·65M from front, Iso 6s 14m 5M; W twr, R bands; vis: 327°-190°.

N side, Ldg lts 061°. Front, 52°40'·72N 08°45'·27W, Crawford Rock 490m from rear, Fl R 3s 6m 5M. Crawford No. 2, Common Rear, Iso 6s 10m 5M; 52°40'·85N 08°44'·88W.

Ldg lts 302·1°, Flagstaff Rock, 670m from rear, Fl R 7s 7m 5M; 52°40'·66N 08°44'·40W.

Ldg lts 106·5°. Meelick Rk, Front Iso R 4s 6m 5M; 52°40'·24N 08°42'·32W. Meelick No. 2, rear 275m from front Iso R 4s 9m 5M; both W beacons.

LOOP HEAD

Loop Head ☆ 52°33'·68N 09°55'·96W Fl (4) 20s 84m **23M**.

LISCANNOR BAY TO SLYNE HEAD

GALWAY BAY and INISHMORE

Eeragh, Rock Is ☆ 53°08'·90N 09°51'·40W Fl 15s 35m **18M**; W twr, two B bands; vis: 297°-262°.

Straw Is ☆ 53°07'·06N 09°37'·85W Fl (2) 5s 11m **15M**; W twr.

Killeany Ldg lts 192°. Front, Oc 5s 6m 3M; W col on W □ base; vis: 142°-197°, 53°06'·25N 09°39'·74W. Rear, 43m from front, Oc 5s 8m 2M; W col on W □ base; vis: 142°-197°.

Inishmaan, Ldg lts 199°, Oc 6s 8M; 53°06'·08N 09°34'·77W.

Inisheer ☆ 53°02'·78N 09°31'·58W Iso WR 12s 34m **W20M, R16M**; vis: 225°-W(partially vis >7M)-231°, 231°-W-245°-R-269°-W-115°; *Racon (K) 13M*.

Finnis Rock ⚓ Q (3) 10s; 53°02'·82N 09°29'·14W.

Black Hd ⚟ Fl WR 5s 20m W11M, R8M, W □ twr; vis: 045°- R268°-276°; 53°09'·26N 09°15'·83W.

GALWAY

Margaretta Shoal ▲ Fl G 3s; *Whis;* 53°13'·68N 09°05'·99W.

Leverets ☆ Q WRG 9m 10M; B ☐ twr, W bands; vis: 015°-G-058°-W-065°-R-103°-G-143·5°-W-146·5°-R-015°; 53°15'·33N 09°01'·90W.

Rinmore ☆ Iso WRG 4s 7m 5M; W ☐ twr; vis: 359°-G-008°-W-018°-R-027°; 53°16'·12N 09°01'·97W.

Appr Chan Dir lt 325°, WRG 7m 3M; vis: 322·25°-FG-323·75°-AlGW-324·75°-FW-325·25°-AlRW-326·25°-FR-331·25°-FlR-332·25°; 53°16'·12N 09°02'·83W.

GALWAY TO SLYNE HEAD

Spiddle Pier Hd ☆ Fl WRG 3·5s 11m W6M, R4M, G4M; Y col; vis: 102°-G-282°-W-024°-R-066°; 53°14'·42N 09°18'·55W.

Cashla Bay Ent, W side ☆ Fl (3) WR 10s 8m W6M, R3M; W col on concrete structure; vis: 216°-W-000°-R-069°; 53°14'·23N 09°35'·20W.

Lion Pt Dir lt Iso WRG 5s 6m (H24), G6M, W8M, R6M,(night), G2M, W3M, R2M(day); vis: 005°-G-008·5°-W-011·5°-R-015°; 53°15'·84N 09°33'·95W.

Rossaveel Pier Ldg lts 116° Front, 53°16'·02N 09°33'·38W Oc 3s 7m 3M; W mast. Rear, 90m from front, Oc 3s 8m 3M.

Kiggaul Bay ☆ Fl WRG 3s 5m W5M, R3M, G3M; vis: 310°-G-329°-W-349°-R-059°; 53°14'·03N 09°43'·02W.

Croaghnakeela Is ☆ Fl 3·7s 7m 5M; W col; vis: 034°-045°, 218°-286°, 311°-325°; 53°19'·40N 09°58'·21W.

Inishnee ☆ Fl (2) WRG 10s 9m W5M, R3M, G3M; W col on W ☐ base; vis: 314°-G-017°-W-030°-R-080°-W-194°; 53°22'·75N 09°54'·53W.

Slyne Head, North twr, Illaunamid ☆ 53°23'·99N 10°14'·06W Fl (2) 15s 35m **19M**; B twr.

SLYNE HEAD TO EAGLE ISLAND

CLIFDEN BAY and INISHBOFIN

Carrickrana Rocks Bn, large W Bn; 53°29'·24N 10°09'·48W.

Cleggan Point ☆ Fl (3) WRG 15s 20m W6M, R3M, G3M; W col on W hut; vis: shore-W-091°-R-124°-G-221°; 53°34'·49N 10°07'·73W.

Inishlyon Lyon Head ☆ Fl WR 7·5s 13m W7M, R4M; W post; vis: 036°-W-058°-R-184°-W-325°-R-036°; 53°36'·74N 10°09'·56W.

Gun Rock ☆ Fl (2) 6s 8m 4M; W col; vis: 296°-253°; 53°36'·59N 10°13'·23W.

CLEW BAY and WESTPORT

Roonagh Quay Ldg lts 144°. Front 53°45'·75N 09°54'·23W. Rear, 54m from front, both Iso 10s 9/15m.

Cloughcormick ↓ Q (9) 15s; 53°50'·56N 09°43'·20W.

Achillbeg I S Point ☆ 53°51'·51N 09°56'·85W Fl WR 5s 56m **W18M, R18M, R15M;** W ☐ twr on ☐ building; vis: 262°-R-281°-W-342°-R- 060°-W- 092°-R(intens)-099°-W-118°.

ACHILL SOUND

Ldg lts 330°, 53°52'·50N 09°56'·91W Whitestone Point, Front and rear both Oc 4s 5/6m; W ◊, B stripe.

Achill I Ldg lts 310°, Purteen, Oc 8s 5m; 53°57'·83N 10°05'·93W (PA). Rear, 46m from front Oc 8s 6m.

BLACKSOD BAY

Blacksod ↓ Q (3) 10s; 54°05'·89N 10°03'·01W.

Blacksod Pier Root ☆ Fl (2) WR 7·5s 13m W12M, R9M; W twr on dwelling; vis: 189°-R-210°-W-018°; 54°05'·91N 10°03'·63W.

Carrigeenmore ↓ VQ(3) 5s 3M; 54°06'·56N 10°03'·4W.

Black Rock ☆ 54°04'·03N 10°19'·25W Fl WR 12s 86m **W20M, R16M;** W twr; vis: 276°-W-212°-R-276°.

Eagle Is, W end ☆ 54°17'·02N 10°05'·56W Fl (3) 15s 67m **19M**; W twr.

EAGLE ISLAND TO RATHLIN O'BIRNE

BROAD HAVEN BAY

Rinroe Pt ☆ Fl (2) 10s 5m 3M; 54°17'·83N 09°50'·59W.

Gubacashel Point ☆ Iso WR 4s 27m **W17M**, R12M; 110°-R-133°-W-355°-R-021° W twr; 54°16'·06N 09°53'·33W.

KILLALA

Inishcrone Pier Root ☆ Fl WRG 1·5s 8m 2M; vis: 098°-W-116°-G- 136°-R-187°; 54°13'·21N 09°05'·79W.

Ldg lts 230°. Rinnaun Point, Front No. 1, Oc 10s 7m 5M; ☐ twr; 54°13'·21N 09°05'·79W. Rear, 150m from front, No. 2 Oc 10s 12m 5M; ☐ twr.

Dir lt 215°, Inch I, Fl WRG 2s 6m 3M; ☐ twr; vis: 205°-G-213°-W- 217°-R-225°; 54°13'·29N 09°12'·30W.

Ldg lts 196°. Kilroe, Front, 54°12'·63N 09°12'·33W Oc 4s 5m 2M; ☐ twr. Rear,120m from front, Oc 4s 10m 2M; ☐ twr.

Ldg lts 236°. Pier, Front, Iso 2s 5m 2M; W ◊ on twr; 54°13'·02N 09°12'·84W. Rear, 200m from front, Iso 2s 7m 2M; W ◊ on pole.

SLIGO

Black Rock ☆ Fl WR 5s 24m 10/8M; vis: 130°-W-107°-R-130° (R sector covers Wheat and Seal rks); W twr, B band; 54°18'·45N 08°37'·06W.

Lower Rosses, (N of Cullaun Bwee) ☆ Fl (2) WRG 10s 8m 10M; W hut on piles; vis: 061°-G-066°-W-070°-R-075°; shown H24; 54°19'·72N 08°34'·41W.

Ldg lts 125°. Front, Metal Man Fl (3) 6s 13m 7M. Rear, Oyster I, 365m from front, fL (3) 6s 13m 7M (synchronised); H24.

Wheat Rock ↓ Q (6) + LFl 15s; 54°18'·84N 08°39'·10W.

DONEGAL BAY and KILLYBEGS

St John's Pt ☆ Fl 6s 30m 14M; W twr; 54°34'·16N 08°27'·64W.

Bullockmore ↓ Qk Fl (9) 15s; 54°33'·98N 08°30'·14W.

Rotten I ☆ 54°36'·97N 08°26'·41W Fl WR 4s 20m **W15M,** R11M; W twr; vis: W255°- R008°- W039°-208°.

New Landing Dir lt 338°, Oc WRG 6s 17m; vis: 328°-G-334°-Al WG-336°-W-340°-Al WR-342°-R-348°; 54°38'·14N 08°26'·38W.

Killybegs Outer ↓ VQ (6) + L Fl 10s; 54°37'·92N 08°29'·15W.

RATHLIN O'BIRNE TO BLOODY FORELAND

S of ARAN and RUTLAND S CHANNEL

Rathlin O'Birne, W side ☆ Fl WR 15s 35m **W18M**, R14M; W twr; vis: 195°-R-307°-W-195°; *Racon (O) 13M*, vis 284°-203°. 54°39'·80N 08°49'·94W.

Dawros Head ☆ L Fl 10s 39m 4M; 54°49'·63N 08°33'·64W.

Wyon Point ☆ Fl (2) WRG 10s 8m W6M, R3M; W ☐ twr; vis: shore-G-021°-W-042°-R-121°-W-150°-R-shore; 54°56'·51N 08°27'·54W.

BURTONPORT
Ldg lts 068·1°. Front , FG 17m 1M; Gy Bn, W band; 54°58'·95N 08°26'·40W. Rear, 355m from front, FG 23m 1M; Gy Bn, Y band.

N SOUND OF ARAN and RUTLAND N CHANNEL
Rutland I Ldg lts 137·6°. Front, 54°58'·97N 08°27'·68W Oc 6s 8m 1M; W Bn, B band. Rear, 330m from front, Oc 6s 14m 1M.
Inishcoo Ldg lts 119·3°. Front, Iso 6s 6m 1M; W Bn, B band; 54°59'·43N 08°29'·63W. Rear, 248m from front, Iso 6s 11m 1M.
Ldg lts 186°. Front, Oc 8s 8m 3M; B Bn, W band; 54°58'·94N 08°29'·27W. Rear, 395m from front, Oc 8s 17m 3M; B Bn.
Aranmore, Rinrawros Pt ☆ 55°00'·90N 08°33'·66W Fl (2) 20s 71m **27M**; W twr; obsc by land about 234°-007° and about 013°. Auxiliary lt Fl R 3s 61m 13M, same twr; vis: 203°-234°.

OWEY SOUND to INISHSIRRER
Cruit Is. Owey Sound Ldg lts 068·3°. Front, Oc 10s; 55°03'·06N 08°25'·85W. Rear, 107m from front, Oc 10s.
Rinnalea Point ☆ 55°02'·59N 08°23'·72W Fl 7·5s 19m 9M; ☐ twr; vis: 132°-167°.
Gola I s Ldg lts 171·2°. Front, Oc 3s 9m 2M; W Bn, B band; 55°05'·11N 08°21'·07W. Rear, 86m from front, Oc 3s 13m 2M; B Bn, W band; synch with front.
Glassagh. Ldg lts 137·4°. Front, Oc 8s 12m 3M; 55°06'·83N 08°18'·97W. Rear, 46m from front, Oc 8s 17m 3M; synch.
Inishsirrer, NW end ☆ Fl 3·7s 20m 4M; W☐ twr vis: 083°-263°; 55°07'·40N 08°20'·93W.

BLOODY FORELAND TO INISHTRAHULL
BLOODY FORELAND to SHEEPHAVEN
Bloody Foreland ☆ Fl WG 7·5s 14m W6M, G4M; vis: 062°-W-232°-G-062°; 55°09'·51N 08°17'·03W.
Tory Island ☆ 55°16'·36N 08°14'·97W Fl (4) 30s 40m **27M**; B twr, W band; vis: 302°-277°; *Racon (M) 12-23M*; H24.
West Town Ldg lts 001° ☆ Iso 2s 9m 7M △ on Y structure R stripe; 55°15'·79N 08°13'·50W. Rear Iso 2s 11m 7M ▽ ditto (synchronised).
Ballyness Hbr. Ldg lts 119·5°. Front, Iso 4s 25m 1M; 55°09'·06N 08°06'·98W. Rear, 61m from front, Iso 4s 26m 1M.
Portnablahy Ldg lts 125·3°. Front Oc 6s 7m 2M; B col, W bands; 55°10'·79N 07°55'·65W. Rear, 81m from front, Oc 6s 12m 2M; B col, W bands.

MULROY BAY
Limeburner ℓ Q Fl; 55°18'·54N 07°48'·40W.
Ravedy Is ☆ Fl 3s 9m 3M; twr; vis: 177°-357°; 55°15'·14N 07°46'·90W.

LOUGH SWILLY, BUNCRANA and RATHMULLAN
Fanad Head ☆ 55°16'·57N 07°37'·91W Fl (5) WR 20s 39m **W18M**, R14M; W twr; vis 100°-R-110°-W-313°-R-345°-W-100°.
Swilly More ▲ Fl G 3s; 55°15'·12N 07°35'·79W.
Dunree ☆ Fl (2) WR 5s 46m W12M, R9M; vis: 320°-R-328°-W-183°-R-196°; 55°11'·88N 07°33'·25W.
Buncrana Pier near Hd ☆ Iso WR 4s 11m W13M, R10M; R

twr, W band; vis: R shore- over Inch spit, 052°-W-139°-R-shore over White Strand Rock; 55°07'·60N 07°27'·86W.
Rathmullan Pier Hd ☆ Fl G 3s 5M; vis: 206°-345°; 55°05'·70N 07°31'·66W.
Inishtrahull ☆ 55°25'·86N 07°14'·62W Fl (3) 15s 59m **19M**; W twr; obscd 256°-261° within 3M; *Racon (T) 24M 060°-310°*. Fog Det Lt VQ.

INISHTRAHULL TO RATHLIN ISLAND
LOUGH FOYLE
Foyle ℓ L Fl 10s; 55°15'·32N 06°52'·60W.
Tuns ⚲ Fl R 3s; 55°14'·00N 06°53'·46W.
Inishowen Dunagree ☆ 55°13'·56N 06°55'·75W Fl (2) WRG 10s 28m **W18M**, R14M, G14M; W twr, 2 B bands; vis: 197°-G-211°-W-249°-R-000°. Fog Det lt VQ 16m vis: 270°.
Greencastle S Bkwtr Dir lt 042·5°. Fl (2) WRG 3s 4m W11M, R9M, G9M; vis 307°-G- 040°-W-045°-R-055°; 55°12'·17N 06°59'·13W.
McKinney's ⚲ Fl R 5s; 55°10'·9N 07°00'·5W.
Moville ℓ Fl WR 2·5s 11m 4M; W house on G piles vis: 240°-W-064°-R-240°; 55°10'·98N 07°02'·13W.

RIVER BANN, COLERAINE and PORTRUSH
River Bann Ldg lts 165°. Front, Oc 5s 6m 2M; W twr; 55°09'·96N 06°46'·23W. Rear, 245m from front, Oc 5s 14m 2M; W ☐ twr.
W Mole ☆ Fl G 5s 4m 2M; Gy mast; vis: 170°-000°; 55°10'·25N 06°46'·45W.
Portstewart Point ☆ Oc R 10s 21m 5M; R☐ hut; vis: 040°-220°; 55°11'·33N 06°43'·26W.
N Pier Hd ☆ Fl R 3s 6m 3M; vis: 220°-160°; 55°12'·34N 06°39'·58W.

RATHLIN ISLAND
Rathlin W 0·5M NE of Bull Pt ☆ 55°18'·05N 06°16'·82W Fl R 5s 62m **22M**; W twr, lantern at base; vis: 015°-225°; H24. Fog Det Lt VQ.
Drake Wreck ℓ 55°17'·00N 06°12'·48W Q (6) + L Fl 15s.
Manor House ☆ Oc WRG 4s 5M; vis: 020°-G-023°-W-026°-R-029°; 55°17'·52N 06°11'·73W.
Rue Pt ☆ Fl (2) 5s 16m 14M; W 8-sided twr, B bands; 55°15'·53N 06°11'·47W.
Altacarry Head Rathlin East ☆ 55°18'·09N 06°10'·29W Fl (4) 20s 74m **26M**; W twr, B band; vis: 110°-006° and 036°-058°; *Racon (G) 15-27M*.

FAIR HEAD TO LAMBAY ISLAND
RED BAY, CARNLOUGH and LARNE
Red Bay Pier ☆ Fl 3s 10m 5M; 55°03'·93N 06°03'·21W.
Carnlough Hbr N Pier ☆ Fl G 3s 4m 5M; 54°59'·59N 05°59'·29W.
East Maiden ☆ Fl (3) 15s 29m **23M**; W twr, B band; *Racon (M) 11-21M*. Auxiliary lt Fl R 5s 15m 8M; 54°55'·74N 05°43'·65W; same twr; vis:142°-182° over Russel and Highland Rks.
N Hunter Rock ℓ Q; 54°53'·04N 05°45'·13W.
S Hunter Rock ℓ VQ (6) + L Fl 10s; 54°52'·69N 05°45'·22W.
Larne No. 1 ▲ QG; 54°51'·68N 05°47'·67W.
Chaine Twr ☆ Iso WR 5s 23m **W16M**, R12M; Gy twr; vis: 232°-W-240°-R-000° (shore); 54°51'·27N 05°47'·90W.

Ent Ldg lts 184°, No. 11 Front, 54°49'·60N 05°47'·81W Oc 4s 6m 12M; W 2 with R stripe on R pile structure; vis: 179°-189°. No. 12 Rear, 610m from front, Oc 4s 14m 12M; W 2 with R stripe on R ☐ twr; synch with front, vis: 5° either side of Ldg line.

CARRICKFERGUS
Black Hd ☆ 54°45'·99N 05°41'·33W Fl 3s 45m **27M**; W 8-sided twr.
Cloghan Jetty ⚓ 54°44'·10N 05°41'·58W QG. Marina Ent Appr ⚸ Dir Oc WRG 3s 5m 3M; vis: G308°- W317·5°-R322·5°-332°; 54°42'·58N 05°48'·78W.

BELFAST LOUGH and BANGOR
Belfast Fairway ⬩ Iso 4s; *Racon (G)*; 54°41'·71N 05°46'·24W.
Mew I ☆ NE end 54°41'·91N 05°30'·79W Fl (4) 30s 37m; B twr, W band; *Racon (O) 14M*. Fog Det Lt VQ.

DONAGHADEE, BALLYWATER and PORTAVOGIE
Donaghadee ☆, S Pier Hd 54°38'·70N 05°31'·86W Iso WR 4s 17m **W18M**, R14M; W twr; vis: shore-W-326°-R-shore; *Siren 12s*. Ballywalter, Bkwtr Hd Fl WRG 3s 4m 9M; vis: 240°-G-267°-W-277°-R-314°; 54°32'·68N 05°28'·83W.
Skulmartin ⚓ L Fl 10s; 54°31'·82N 05°24'·80W.
Portavogie Bkwtr Hd ⚸ Iso WRG 5s 9m W10M, R8M, G8M; ☐ twr; vis: shore-G-258°-W-275°-R-348°; 54°27'·44N 05°26'·14W.
Plough Rock ⚓ 54°27'·40N 05°25'·12W Fl R 3s.
South Rock ⬩ Fl (3) R 30s 7M 54°24'·49N 05°22'·02W.

STRANGFORD LOUGH
Strangford ⚓ L Fl 10s; 54°18'·61N 05°28'·67W.
Bar Pladdy ⬩ Q (6) + L Fl 15s; 54°19'·34N 05°30'·51W.
Dogtail Pt Ldg lts 341° Front, Oc (4) G 10s 2m 5M; 54°20'·79N 05°31'·83W. Rear, Gowlands Rk, 0·8M from front, Oc (4) G 10s 6m 5M.
Swan Is ⚸ Fl (2) WR 6s 5m; W col; vis: 115°-W-334°-R-115°; 54°22'·38N 05°33'·16W.
Strangford East Ldg lts 256°. Front, Oc WRG 5s 6m W9M, R6M, G6M: vis: 190°-R-244°-G-252°-W- 260°-R-294°; 54°22'·29N 05°33'·27W. Rear, 46m from front, Oc R 5s 10m 6M; vis: 250°-264°.
Portaferry Pier Hd ⚸ Oc WR 10s 9m W9M, R6M; Or mast; vis: W335°- R005°- W017°-128°; 54°22'·82N 05°33'·03W.

ARDGLASS
Inner Pier Hd ⚸ Iso WRG 4s 10m W8M, R7M, G5M; twr; vis:

shore-G-308°-W-314°-R-shore; 54°15'·79N 05°36'·33W.

DUNDRUM BAY
St John's Point ☆ 54°13'·61N 05°39'·30W Q (2) 7·5s 37m **25M**; B twr, Y bands. **Auxiliary Light** ☆ Fl WR 3s 14m **W15M**, R11M; same twr, vis: 064°-W-078°-R-shore; Fog Det lt VQ 14m vis: 270°.
DZ East ⚲ 54°13'·51N 05°46'·23W.
DZ Middle ⚲ 54°13'·01N 05°48'·57W.
DZ West ⚲ 54°13'·35N 05°50'·07W.

ANNALONG
E Bkwtr Hd ⚸ Oc WRG 5s 8m 9M; twr; vis: 204°-G-249°-W-309°-R-024°; 54°06'·51N 05°53'·73W.

KILKEEL
Pier Hd ⚸ Fl WR 2s 8m 8M; vis: R296°-W313°-017°; 54°03'·46N 05°59'·30W.

CARLINGFORD LOUGH and NEWRY RIVER
Hellyhunter ⬩ Q (6) + L Fl 15s; *Racon*; 54°00'·35N 06°02'·10W
Haulbowline ☆ 54°01'·19N 06°04'·74W Fl (3) 10s 32m **17M**; Gy twr; reserve lt 15M.
Ldg lts 310·4° Front, Oc 3s 7m 11M; R △ on twr; vis: 295°-325°; 54°01'·80N 06°05'·43W. Rear, 457m from front, Oc 3s 12m 11M; R ▽ on twr; vis: 295°-325°; both H24.
Newry River Ldg lts 310·4°. Front, 54°06'·37N 06°16'·51W. Rear, 274m from front. Both Iso 4s 5/15m 2M; stone cols.

DUNDALK
Imogene ⚓ Fl (2) R 10s; 53°57'·41N 06°07'·02W.
Pile Light ☆ 53°58'·56N 06°17'·70W Fl 15s 10m **21M**; W Ho; vis: 124°-W-151°-R-284°-W-313°-R-124°.
Dunany ⚓ Fl R 3s; 53°53'·56N 06°09'·47W.

DROGHEDA to LAMBAY ISLAND
Port Approach Dir lt 53°43'·30N 06°14'·73W WRG 10m **W19M, R15M**, G15M; vis: 268°-FG-269°-Al WG-269·5°-FW-270·5°-Al WR-271°-FR-272°; H24.
Balbriggan ⚸ Fl (3) WRG 10s 12m W13M, R10M, G10M; W twr; vis: 159°-G-193°-W-288°-R-305°; 53°36'·76N 06°10'·80W.
Rockabill ☆ 53°35'·82N 06°00'·25W Fl WR 12s 45m **W17M, R13M**; W twr, B band; vis: 178°-W-329°-R-178°.
Skerries Bay Pier Hd ⚸ Oc R 6s 7m 7M; W col; vis: 103°-154°; 53°35'·09N 06°06'·49W.

		1	2	3	4	5	6	7	8	9	10	11	12	13	14	15
1	Strangford Lough	1														
2	Bangor	34	2													
3	Carrickfergus	39	6	3												
4	Larne	45	16	16	4											
5	Carnlough	50	25	26	11	5										
6	Portrush	87	58	60	48	35	6									
7	Lough Foyle	92	72	73	55	47	11	7								
8	L Swilly (Fahan)	138	109	104	96	81	48	42	8							
9	Burtonport	153	130	130	116	108	74	68	49	9						
10	Killybegs	204	175	171	163	148	115	109	93	43	10					
11	Sligo	218	189	179	177	156	123	117	107	51	30	11				
12	Eagle Island	234	205	198	193	175	147	136	123	72	62	59	12			
13	Westport	295	266	249	240	226	193	187	168	120	108	100	57	13		
14	Galway	338	309	307	297	284	253	245	227	178	166	163	104	94	14	
15	Kilrush	364	335	332	323	309	276	270	251	203	191	183	142	119	76	15

DISTANCE TABLES
Approx distances in nautical miles are by the most direct route allowing for dangers and TSS.

AREA 11 *West Denmark – Skagen to Rømø*

SELECTED LIGHTS, BUOYS & WAYPOINTS

Positions are referenced to WGS84

SKAGEN TO THYBORØN

SKAGEN

Skagen W ☆ Fl (3) WR 10s 31m **W17M**/R12M; 053°-W-248°-R-323°; W ○ twr; 57°44'·94N 10°35·70E.

Skagen ☆ Fl 4s 44m **23M**; Gy ○ twr; *Racon G, 20M*; 57°44'·14N 10°37'·81E.

Skagen No 1A ⚓ L Fl 10s; *Racon N*; 57°43'·46N 10°53'·55E. (Route T)

Skagen No. 2 ⚓ L Fl 10s; 57°37'·61N 11°05'·51E. (Route T)

Skagens Rev ⚓ Q; 57°45'·97N 10°43'·74E.

⚓ Q (3) 10s; 57°43'·87N 10°42'·31E.

Skagen Harbour

Ldg Its 334·5°, both Iso R 4s 13/22m 8M. Front, 57°43'·06N 10°35'·45E; mast. Rear, 57°43'·19N 10°35'·34E; twr.

E bkwtr ⚡ Fl G 3s 8m 5M; G twr; *Horn (2) 30s*; 57°42'·88N 10°35'·66E.

W bkwtr ⚡ Fl R 3s 8m 5M; R twr; 57°42'·84N 10°35'·60E.

HIRTSHALS

Hirtshals ☆ F Fl 30s 57m **F 18M; Fl 25M**; W ○ twr, approx 1M SSW of hbr ent; 57°35'·10N 09°56'·55E.

Ldg Its 166°, both Iso R 2s 10m 11M; R △ on twr; 57°35'·69N 09°57'·64E; marina ent is close N of this lt. Rear, Iso R 4s 18m 11M; R ▽ on twr; 330m from front.

Approach chan ⚓ Fl (3) G 10s; 57°36'·18N 09°56·94E.

⚓ Fl R 3s; 57°36'·44N 09°57'·67E.

⚓ Fl (5) Y 20s; 57°36'·43N 09°57'·72E.

⚓ Fl G 5s; 57°36'·11N 09°57·14E.

Outer W mole ⚡ Fl G 3s 14m 6M; G mast; *Horn 15s*; 57°35'·97N 09°57'·37E.

W mole spur ⚡ Fl G 5s 9m 4M; G mast; 57°35'·77N 09°57'·51E.

E mole ⚡ Fl R 5s 9m 6M; G mast; 57°35'·85N 09°57'·61E.

LØKKEN

Lee bkwtr ⚡ Fl 5s 5m 5M; 57°22'·39N 09°42'·11E.

TRANUM STRAND (Firing ranges)

Tranum No. 1 ☆ Al Fl WR 4s 22m W7·5M, R7M; twr; by day Q; shown when firing in progress; 57°12'·43N 09°30'·34E.

Tranum No. 2 ☆ light as per No.1; 57°10'·57N 09°26'·22E.

LILD STRAND

Bragerne ⚓ Fl G 5s; 57°10'·67N 08°56'·35E.

Ldg Its 138°, three ⚡: F 12/22m 7/8M; 127°-149°; 3 masts. Front 57°09'·22N 08°57'·75E. Landing place *Siren 30s, fishing.*

HANSTHOLM

Hanstholm ☆ Fl (3) 20s 65m **26M**; shown by day in poor vis; W 8-sided twr; 57°06'·77N 08°35'·92E, approx 1M S of the hbr ent.

Hanstholm ⚓ LFl 10s; 57°08'·06N 08°34'·87E.

Ldg Its 142·6°, both Iso 2s 37/45m 13M; synch; 127·6°-157·6°; R △ on mast. Front, 57°07'·12N 08°36'·15E. Rear, 170m from front, R ▽ on mast.

Note: The 4 outer/inner mole heads are floodlit.

W outer mole ⚡ Fl G 3s 11m 9M; G pillar; 57°07'·56N 08°35'·45E. E outer mole ⚡ Fl R 3s 11m 9M; R pillar; 57°07'·61N 08°35'·57E.

Roshage ⚡ Fl 5s 7m 5M; 57°07'·75N 08°37'·25E (1M E of hbr).

NØRRE VORUPØR

Mole ⚡ Fl G 5s 6m 4M; 57°57'·74N 08°21'·679E.

Ldg Its, both Iso R 4s 20/30m 9M, indicate safest landing place for FVs; vis 22·5° either side of Idg line; synch. Front 57°57'·46N 08°22'·10E. Rear, 80m from front.

Lodbjerg ☆ Fl (2) 20s 48m **23M**; ○ twr; 56°49'·40N 08°15'·76E.

THYBORØN

Landfall ⚓ L Fl 10s; *Racon T, 10m*; 56°42'·54N 08°08'·69E.

Agger Tange Idg Its 082°: Front, Iso WRG 4s 8m W11M, R/G8M; 074·5°-G-079·5°-W-084·5°-R-089·5°; R △ on bcn; 56°42'·97N 08°14'·14E. Rear, Iso 4s 17m 11M; 075°-089°; synch; R ▽ on Gy twr; 804m from front.

Off Havmolen ⚓ 56°43'·25N 08°12'·52E.

Approach ☆ Fl (3) 10s 24m 12M; intens 023·5°-203·5°; also lit by day in poor vis; lattice twr; 56°42'·49N 08°12'·91E (S side of ent).

Langholm Idg Its 120°, both Iso 2s 7/13m 11M; synch; 113°-127°. Front, R △ on R hut, 56°42'·45N 08°14'·54E. Rear, R ▽ on Gy twr.

Thyborøn Havn ⚡ Oc (2) WRG 12s 6m W11M, R/G8M; 122·5°-G-146·5°-W-150°-R-211·3°-G-337·5°-R-340°-R-344°; W twr R band; 56°42'·35N 08°13'·39E (680m N of ent to Yderhavn and Basins).

1	Skagen	**1**																
2	Hirtshals	33	**2**															
3	Hanstholm	85	52	**3**														
4	Thyborln	114	84	32	**4**													
5	Torsminde	141	108	56	24	**5**												
6	Hvide Sande	162	179	77	45	24	**6**											
7	Esbjerg	200	174	122	90	76	54	**7**										
8	Fanl	210	177	125	93	79	57	3	**8**									
9	Rlml	233	200	148	116	94	73	30	33	**9**								
10	H rnum	248	215	163	131	108	86	70	73	29	**10**							
11	Husum	275	247	195	163	152	131	95	98	68	45	**11**						
12	Kiel/Holtenau	261	233	281	249	232	208	180	183	189	126	129	**12**					
13	Bremerhaven	306	285	233	201	185	163	127	129	107	83	82	123	**13**				
14	Wilhelmshaven	414	296	242	310	184	162	125	128	106	82	82	123	45	**14**			
15	Helgoland	259	238	186	154	141	119	83	85	63	39	47	104	44	43	**15**		
16	Cuxhaven	304	284	232	200	162	138	110	113	85	56	66	70	58	56	38	**16**	
17	Wangerooge	283	262	210	178	168	147	109	112	94	68	52	108	38	27	24	42	**17**
18	Hamburg	338	317	265	233	216	192	163	167	139	99	113	90	81	110	88	54	61	**18**

DISTANCE TABLES
Approx distances in nautical miles are by the most direct route allowing for dangers and TSS.

Yderhavn, N mole ☆ Fl G 3s 6m 4M; G pedestal; 56°42′·02N 08°13′·52E.
S mole ☆ Fl R 3s 6m 4M; R pedestal; 56°41′·97N 08°13′·53E.

LIMFJORD (TO 08°42′E)

Sælhundeholm Løb, into Nissum Bredning ('Broad').
No. 1 Fl (2) G 5s; 56°41′·14N 08°14′·17E.
No. 3 Fl G 3s; 56°40′·75N 08°13′·79E.
No. 7 Fl G 3s; 56°40′·31N 08°13′·52E.
No. 11 Fl G 3s; 56°39′·83N 08°13′·59E.
No. 16 Fl R 3s; 56°38′·51N 08°13′·89E.
No. 18 Fl (2) R 5s; 56°38′·20N 08°14′·34E.
No. 21 Fl G 3s; 56°38′·98N 08°14′·71E.
No. 26 Fl R 3s; 56°38′·71N 08°15′·38E.
No. 29 Fl G 3s; 56°38′·40N 08°15′·94E.
Q; 56°38′·06N 08°16′·70E.

APPROACHES TO LEMVIG (Marina and Havn)

Toftum Dir ☆ 120°, Iso WRG 4s 24m, W12M, R/G 8M; 110°-G-120°-W-137°-R-144°; hut; 56°33′·09N 08°18′·33E.
Rønnen Fl G 3s; 56°36′·71N 08°21′·74E.
Rønnen L Fl 10s; 56°35′·58N 08°21′·62E.
Søgard Mark ldg lts 243·5°: both FR 20/30m 5M; vis 90° either side of ldg line. Front, R △ on W bcn; 56°34′·39N 08°17′·29E. Rear, R ▽ on W post; 235m from front.
Chan 56°33′·27N 08°18′·31E.
Ldg lts, W of hbr 177·7°, both FR 8/20m 5M; 153°-203°. Front R △ on twr; 56°33′·04N 08°18′·16E. Rear, R ▽ on W post; 184m from front.
Vinkel Hage marina, N mole ☆ FG 3m 5M; 56°33′·09N 08°18′·33E.
S mole, FR 3m 4M. Marina is 9ca N of the Havn on the W side.
Ostre Havn 56°33′·17N 08°18′·40E. Havn ent, FG/FR 4m 5M.

THISTED HAVN (Marina)

Outer W mole ☆ Fl R 3s 4m 2M; 56°57′·10N 08°41′·90E.
Outer E mole ☆ Fl G 3s 4m 2M; 56°57′·10N 08°41′·95E.
Thisted Bredning ☆ Aero 3 Fl R 1·5s (vert; 45m apart) 183m 10M; TV mast; 56°58′·52N 08°41′·15E, 1·55M NNW of hbr ent.

THYBORØN TO BLÅVANDS HUK

Bovbjerg ☆ Fl (2) 15s 62m 16M; 56°30′·79N 08°07′·18E.
Wave recorder buoy Fl (5) Y 20s; 56°28′·49N 08°03′·35E.

THORSMINDE HAVN

(All Lat/Longs for this harbour are approximate)
Lt ho ☆ F 30m 13M; Gy twr; 56°22′·34N 08°06′·99E.
Groyne, N ☆ Fl 5s 8m 5M; Gy hut; 56°22′·46N 08°06′·82E.
N mole ☆ Iso R 2s 9m 4M; R hut; 56°22′·36N 08°06′·62E.
S mole ☆ Iso G 2s 9m 4M; G hut; 56°22′·26N 08°06′·92E.
West hbr, W mole ☆ FG 5m 2M; Gy post; 56°22′·36N 08°07′·12E.
E mole ☆ FR 5m 2M; Gy post; 56°22′·26N 08°07′·18E.
NW dolphin ☆ FG 5m 4M; Gy post; 56°22′·26N 08°07′·22E.
SE dolphin ☆ FG 5m 4M; Gy post; 56°22′ 26N 08°07′ 26E.
Lock, E side ☆ Iso 4s 12m 4M; Gy mast; 020°-160°; 56°22′·36N 08°07′·22E.
Road bridge ☆ Iso 4s 5m 4M; 200°-340°; 56°22′·36N 08°07′·26E.

HVIDE SANDE

Lyngvig ☆ Fl 5s 53m **22M**; W ○ twr; 56°02′·95N 08°06′·17E.
N outer bkwtr ☆ Fl R 3s 7m 8M; R hut; 55°59′·94N 08°06′·55E.
N mole ☆ Fl R 5s 10m 6·5M; R floodlit edifice; 55°59′·98N 08°06′· 84E.
S mole ☆ Fl G 5s 10m 6M; 55°59′·93N 08°06′·88E.
Lt ho ☆ F 27m 14M; Gy twr; 56°00′·00N 08°07′·35E.
Nordhavn, E pier ☆ FG 4m 4M; 56°00′·16N 08°07′·42E.
W pier ☆ 2 FR 3m 2M; W posts; 060°-035°; 56°00′·07N 08°07′·12E.
Sydhavn, W pier ☆ FG 4m 2M; 56°00′·06N 08°07′·52E.
E Pier ☆ FR 4m 2M; Gy post; 56°00′·06N 08°07′·53E.
Lock entrance ldg lts 293·5°: both FR 11/14m 2M; 201·6°-021·6°. Front, R △ on Gy tr, 56°00′·0N 08°07′·8E. Rear, R ▽ on Gy twr, 72m from front.
Fjordhavn ldg lts 246·6° (both vis 7·5° either side of ldg line): Front, Iso G 2s 4m 4M; Or △ on mast; 56°00′·5N 08°07′·9E. Rear, Iso G 4s 6m 4M, Or ▽ on mast, 128m from front.

HORNS REV (marks westward from coast)

Oskbøl firing range. Two lights (4M apart), both AIFl WR 4s 35m **16M**, R13M, (by day Q 10M), are shown when firing is in progress: North ☆ 55°37′·3N 08°07′·1E. South ☆ 55°33′·6N 08°04′·7E.
Range safety buoys: Fl Y 5s; 55°42′·32N 08°06′·92E. Fl Y 3s; 55°38′·63N 07°50′·91E. Fl Y 3s; 55°37′·35N 07°56′·98E. 55°36′·02N 08°02′·49E.
Blåvands Huk ☆ Fl (3) 20s 55m **23M;** W□twr; 55°33′·46N 08°04′·95E.
Horns Rev is encircled by:
Tuxen Q; 55°34′·22N 07°41′·92E on the N side.
Vyl Q (6) + L Fl 15s; 55°26′·22N 07°49′·99E on the S side.
No. 2 L Fl 10s; 55°28′·74N 07°36′·49E on the SW side.
Horns Rev W Q (9) 15s; 55°34′·47N 07°26′·05E, off the W end.
Slugen Channel (crosses Horns Rev ESE/WNW)
L Fl G 10s; 55°33′·99N 07°49′·38E.
Fl G 3s; 55°32′·26N 07°53′·65E.
Fl (2) R 5s; 55°31′·46N 07°52′·88E.
Fl (2) G 5s; 55°30′·52N 07°59′·20E.
Fl (3) R 10s; 55°29′·42N 08°02′·56E.
Søren Bovbjergs Dyb (unlit N/S side channel off Slugen Chan)
55°33′·57N 07°55′·55E.
55°32′·80N 07°55′·30E.
55°32′·19N 07°56′·29E.
55°31′·24N 07°57′·46E.
Wind farm in □ 2·7M x 2·5M, centred on 55°29′·22N 07°50′·21E: 80 turbines all R lts, the 12 perimeter turbines are lit Fl (3) Y 10s.
NE turbine, ***Racon (U)***; 55°30′·28N 07°52′·63E & transformer platform, 2 Mo (U) 15s 9m 5M, 55°30′·52N 07°52′·53E.
SW turbine, ***Racon (U)***; 55°28′·11N 07°48′·26E.
Horns Rev II wind farm in U2M x 6M, centred on 55°36′·08N 07°34′·78E: 91 turbines all R lts, the 12 perimeter turbines are lit Fl (3) Y 10s.
2 Met masts, both 70m, ☆ 2 Mo (U) 15s 12m 5M and Aero QR: 151B (55°29′·21N 07°54′·72E) and 151C (55°29′·24N 07°58′·52E).

BLÅVANDS HUK TO RØMØ

APPROACHES TO ESBJERG

Grådyb ↟ L Fl 10s; *Racon G, 10M*; 55°24'·63N 08°11'·59E.

Sædding Strand 053·8° triple ldg lts: valid up to Nos 7/8 buoys; H24: **Front** Iso 2s 13m **21M**; 052°-056°; R bldg; 55°29'·74N 08°23'·87E.

Middle Iso 4s 26m **21M**; 051°-057°; R twr, W bands; 55°29'·94N 08°24'·33E, 630m from front.

Rear F 37m **18M**; 052°-056°; R twr; 55°30'·18N 08°24'·92E, 0·75M from front.

No. 1 ↟ Q; 55°25'·49N 08°13'·89E.

No. 2 ⚲ Fl (3) R 10s; 55°25'·62N 08°13'·73E.

No. 3 ▲ Fl G 3s; 55°25'·93N 08°14'·84E.

No. 4 ⚲ Fl R 3s; 55°26'·02N 08°14'·72E.

Tide Gauge ☆ Fl (5) Y 20s 8m 4M; 55°26'·05N 08°15'·93E.

No. 5 ▲ Fl G 5s; 55°26'·32N 08°15'·83E.

No. 6 ⚲ Fl R 5s; 55°26'·44N 08°15'·70E.

No. 7 ↟ Q; 55°26'·76N 08°16'·91E.

No. 8 ⚲ Fl (2) R 5s; 55°26'·89N 08°16'·81E.

Ldg lts 067°, valid up to Nos 9/10 buoys. Both FG 10/25m **16M**, H24. Front, Gy tripod; rear, Gy twr, 55°28'·76N 08°24'·70E.

No. 9 ▲ Fl (2) G 10s; 55°27'·04N 08°18'·21E.

No.10 ⚲ Fl (2) R 10s; 55°27'·20N 08°18'·04E.

Ldg lts 049°, valid up to No 16 buoy/Jerg. Both FR 16/27m **16M**, H24. Front, W twr; rear, Gy twr, 55°29'·92N 08°23'·75E.

No. 11 ▲ Fl G 3s; 55°27'·71N 08°19'·59E.

No. 12 ⚲ Fl R 3s; 55°27'·88N 08°19'·39E.

No. 13 ▲ Fl G 5s; 55°28'·40N 08°20'·99E.

No. 14 ⚲ Fl R 5s; 55°28'·57N 08°20'·73E.

Jerg ☆ Fl G 3s 7m 5M; G twr, Y base; 55°28'·88N 08°22'·00E.

No. 16 ↟ Q (6) + L Fl 15s; 55°29'·04N 08°21'·80E.

No. 15A ▲ Fl (2) G 5s; 55°29'·01N 08°22'·47E.

No 18 ⚲ Fl (2) R 5s; 55°29'·19N 08°22'·71E.

Fovrfelt N ☆ Oc (2) WRG 6s 7m W6M, R/G4M; 066·5°-G-073°-W-077°-R-085·5°; 327°-G-331°- W-333·5°-R-342°; Y twr; 55°29'·29N 08°23'·79E.

Fovrfelt ☆ Fl (2) R 10s 11m 6M; R twr; 55°29'·03N 08°23'·75E.

No 15B ▲ Fl (2) G 10s; 55°28'·83N 08°23'·65E.

ESBJERG HAVN

Strandby, shelter mole, NW corner ☆ Oc WRG 5s 6m W13M, R/G9M; 101·7°-G-105·5°-W-109·5°-R-111·7°; W bldg, R band; 55°28'·76N 08°24'·63E.

Industrifiskerihavn, W mole ☆ Fl R 5s 6m 4M; R structure; 55°28'·52N 08°24'·96E.

E mole ☆ Fl G 5s 6m 4M; G structure; 55°28'·52N 08°25'·03E.

Nordsøkai ↓ Q (9) 15s 5m; Y twr, B band; 55°28'·45N 08°25'·04E.

Konsumfiskerihavn, W mole ☆ FlR 3s 6m; 203°-119°; R twr; 55°28'·31N 08°25'·33E. Yacht hbr in SSE part of Basin II.

E mole ☆ Fl G 3s 6m; 023°-256°; G tr; 55°28·31N 08°25·40E.

Trafikhavn, NW corner, ☆ Oc (2) WRG 12s 6m W13M, R/G9M; 118°-G-124·5°-W-129°-R-131°; W bldg, R band; 55°28·22N 08°25·43E.

N mole ☆ FR 8m 5M; 232°-135°; R bldg; 55°28'·13N 08°25'·46E.

S mole ☆ FG 8m 4M; 045°-276°; G bldg; 55°28'·08N 08°25'·51E.

No. 22 ⚲ Fl (2) R 5s; 55°27'·62N 08°25'·50E.

Sønderhavn (industrial) W mole ☆ FR 9m 4M;

55°27'·49N 08°26'·12E. E mole ☆ FG 9m 4M; 55°27'·43N 08°26'·31E.

Aero ☆ 3 x Fl 1·5s (vert, 82m apart) 251m 12M, H24; on chimney; 55°27'·27N 08°27'·32E (1200m ESE of Sønderhavn ent).

FANØ

Slunden outer ldg lts 242°, both Iso 2s 5/8m 3M; 227°-257°. Front, twr; 55°27'·20N 08°24'·53E. Rear, twr, 106m from front.

E shore, reciprocal ldg lts 062°, both FR 10/13m 3M; 047°-077°. Front, twr; 55°27'·65N 08°26'·01E. Rear, twr, 140m from front.

No. 1 ☆ Fl (2) G l0s 5m 2M; G pile; 55°27'·45N 08°25'·28E.

No. 2 ☆ Fl (2+1) Y 5s 5m 2M; Y pile; 55°27'·42N 08°25'·32E.

No. 3 ☆ Fl G 3s 5m 2M; G pile; 55°27'·39N 08°25'·07E.

No. 4 ☆ Fl R 3s 5m 2M; R pile; 55°27'·35N 08°25'·10E.

Nordby ldg lts 214°, both FR 7/9m 4M; 123·7°-303·7°. Front , W mast;55°26'·94N 08°24'·44E. Rear, Gy twr, 84m from front.–Kremer Sand ☆ FG 5m 3M; G dolphin; 55°27'·3N 08°24'·9E.

Næs Søjord ☆ FR 5m 3M; R pile; 55°27'·27N 08°24'·86E.

Nordby marina 55°26'·65N 08°24'·53E.

KNUDEDYB

G ↟ 55°20'·50N 08°24'·28E.

K ↟ 55°18'·92N 08°20'·06E.

No. 2 ⚓ 55°18'·82N 08°21'·33E.

No. 4 ⚓ 55°18'·81N 08°22'·21E.

No. 6 ⚓ 55°18'·38N 08°24'·63E.

No. 10 ⚓ 55°18'·68N 08°28'·50E.

Knoben ⚓ 55°18'·71N 08°30'·60E.

JUVRE DYB

No. 4 ⚓ 55°13'·76N 08°24'·73E.

No. 6 ⚓ 55°13'·41N 08°26'·60E.

No. 8 ⚓ 55°12'·69N 08°26'·83E.

No. 10 ⚓ 55°12'·55N 08°28'·72E.

Rejsby Stjært ↟ 55°13'·15N 08°30'·55E.

OUTER APPROACH (Lister Tief) TO RØMØ

See also Area 15 for details of lights on Sylt.

Rode Klit Sand ↟ Q (9) 15s, 55°11'·11N 08°04'·88E, (130°/9M to Lister Tief ↟).

Lister Tief ↟ Iso 8s, *Whis*; 55°05'·32N 08°16'·80E.

No. 1 ↥ 55°05'·21N 08°18'·20E.

No. 3 ↟ Fl G 4s; 55°04'·75E 08°18'·73E.

No. 2 ⚲ Fl (3) R 10s; 55°04'·23N 08°22'·32E.

No. 9 ↟ Fl (2) G 9s; 55°03'·76N 08°23'·05E.

Lister Landtief No 5 ↥ 55°03'·68N 08°24'·73E.

No. 4 ⚲ FL (2) R 5s; 55°03'·84N 08°25'·29E.

G1 ↟ Fl Y 4s; 55°03'·27N 08°28'·32E.

RØMØ DYB and HAVN

No. 1 ▲ Fl (2) G 10s; 55°03'·23N 08°30'·30E.

No. ☆ Fl (2) R 10s 5m 3M; R pole; 55°03'·50N 08°31'·10E.

No. 14 ☆ Fl R 3s 6m 2M; R pole; 55°03'·85N 08°32'·55E.

No. 20 ☆ Fl R 5s 5m 2M; R pole; 55°04'·79N 08°34'·13E.

No. 9 ↥ 55°04'·79N 08°34'·63E.

No. 11 ↥ 55°05'·17N 08°34'·69E.

Rømø Hbr:

S mole ☆ Fl R 3s 7m 2M; Gy twr; 55°05'·19N 08°34'·31E.

N mole ☆ Fl G 3s 7m 2M; Gy twr; 55°05'·23N 08°34'·30E.

Inner S mole ☆ FR 4m 1M; 55°05'·2N 08°34'·2E.

Inner N mole ☆ FG 4m 1M; 55°05'·3N 08°34'·2E.

AREA 12 *Germany (North Sea coast) – List to Emden*

SELECTED LIGHTS, BUOYS & WAYPOINTS

Positions are referenced to WGS84

DANISH BORDER TO BÜSUM

SYLT
Lister Tief ⚓ Iso 8s; *Whis;* 55°05'·33N 08°16'·79E.
List West (Ellenbogen) ⚡ Oc WRG 6s 19m W14M, R11M, G10M; 040°-R-133°-W-227°-R-266·4°-W-268°-G-285°-W-310°- W(unintens)-040°; W twr, R lantern; 55°03'·15N 08°24'·00E.
List Hafen, S mole ⚡ FR 5m 4M; 218°-353°; R mast; 55°01'·01N 08°26'·51E.
Hörnum ☆ Fl (2) 9s 48m **20M**; 54°45'·23N 08°17'·47E.
Vortrapptief ⚓ Iso 4s; 54°34'·88N 08°12'·97E, toward Hörnum.
S mole ⚡ FR 7m 4M; 54°45'·57N 08°17'·97E.

AMRUM ISLAND
Rütergat ⚓ Iso 8s; 54°30'·08N 08°12'·32E.
Amrum ☆ Fl 7·5s 63m **23M**; R twr, W bands; 54°37'·84N 08°21'·23E.
Wriakhorn Cross ⚡ L Fl (2) WR 15s 26m W9M, R7M; 297·5°-W-319·5°-R-330°-W-005·5°-R-034°; 54°37'·62N 08°21'·22E.
Amrum Hafen ldg lts 272° TE 2011.

FÖHR ISLAND
Nieblum Dir lt showing over Rütergat. ☆ Oc (2) WRG 10s 11m **W19M, R/G15M**; 028°-G-031°-W-032·5°-R-035·5°; R twr, W band; 54°41'·10N 08°29'·20E.
Ohlörn ⚡ Oc (4) WR 15s 10m 13/10M, 208°-W-237·5°-R-298°- W-353°- R-080°; R twr, Gy lantern; 54°40'·85N 08°34'·00E (SE Föhr).
Wyk Hbr outer ent, FR 54°41'·55N 08°34'·69E; and FG.

DAGEBÜLL
Dagebüll Iso WRG 8s 23m **W18M, R/G15M**; 042°-G-043°-W-044·5°- R-047°; 54°43'·82N 08°41'·43E. FW lts on ent moles.

LANGENESS ISLAND
Nordmarsch ⚡ L Fl (3) WR 20s 13m W14M, R11M; 268°-W-279°-R-306°-W-045°-R-070°-W-218°; dark brown twr; 54°37'·58N 08°31'·85E.

SCHLÜTTSIEL
No. 2/SA 26 ⚓ 54°36'·84N 08°38'·95E. Hbr ent ▲ 54°40'·89N 08°45'·10E.

RIVER HEVER
Hever ⚓ Iso 4s; *Whis;* 54°20'·41N 08°18'·82E.
Westerheversand ☆ Oc (3) WRG 15s 41m **W21M, R17M, G16M**; 012·2°-W-069°-G-079·5°-W-080·5° (ldg sector for Hever)-R-107°-W-233°-R-248°; R twr, W bands; 54°22'·37N 08°38'·36E.
Norderhever No. 1 ⚓ Fl (2+1) R 15s; 54°22'·46N 08°30'·83E.

PELLWORM ISLAND
Pellworm ☆ Oc WRG 5s 38m **20M, R 16M, G 15M**; 037·5°-G-040°-W-042·5°-R-045°; R twr, W band; 54°29'·78N 08°39'·98E.

NORDSTRAND
Suderhafen, S mole ⚓ 54°28'·07N 08°55'·62E.

HUSUM
⚓ Fl G 4s, 54°28'·80N 08°58'·60E, start of access chan. Ldg lts 090°, both Iso G 8s 7/9m 3M.

RIVER EIDER
Eider ⚓ Iso 4s; 54°14'·54N 08°27'·61E.
St Peter ☆ L Fl (2) WR 15s 23m **W15M**, R12M; 271°-R-280·5°-W-035°-R-055°-W-068°-R-091°-W-120°; 54°17'·24N 08°39'·10E.
Eiderdamm lock, N mole, W end ⚡ Oc (2) R 12s 8m 5M; W twr.

BÜSUM
Süderpiep ⚓ Iso 8s; *Whis;* 54°05'·82N 08°25'·70E.
Büsum ☆ Iso WRG 6s 22m **W19M**, R12M; 248°-W-317°-R-024°-W-148°; 54°07'·60N 08°51'·48E.
E mole ⚡ Oc (3) G 12s 10m 4M; vis 260°-168°; G twr; 54°07'·19N 08°51'·65E.

GERMAN BIGHT TO RIVER ELBE
GB Light V ⚓ Iso 8s 12m **17M**; R hull marked G-B; *Horn Mo (R) 30s; Racon T, 8M;* 54°10'·80N 07°27'·60E.

HELGOLAND
Helgoland ☆ Fl 5s 82m **28M**; brown □ twr, B lantern, W balcony; 54°10'·91N 07°52'·93E.
Vorhafen. Ostmole, S elbow ⚡ Oc WG 6s 5m W6M, G3M; 203°-W-250°-G-109°; G post; fog det lt; 54°10'·31N 07°53'·94E.

RIVER ELBE (LOWER)

APPROACHES
Nordergründe N ⚓ VQ; 53°57'·06N 08°00'·12E.
Elbe ⚓ Iso 10s; *Racon T, 8M;* 53°59'·95N 08°06'·49E.
No.1 ⚓ QG; 53°59'·21N 08°13'·20E.
No.25 ⚓ QG; 53°56'·62N 08°38'·25E.
Neuwerk ☆, S side, L Fl (3) WRG 20s 38m **W16M**, R12M, G11M; 165·3°-G-215·3°-W-238·8°-R-321°; 343°-R-100°; 53°54'·92N 08°29'·73E.

CUXHAVEN
No. 31 ⚓ Fl G 4s; 53°51'·93N 08°41'·21E.
Yacht hbr ent, F WR and F WG lts; 53°52'·43N 08°42'·49E.

OTTERNDORF
No. 43 ⚓ Oc (2) G 9s; 53°50'·23N 08°52'·24E.
Medem ⚡ Fl (3) 12s 6m 5M; B △, on B col; 53°50'·15N 08°53'·85E.

BRUNSBÜTTEL
No. 57a ⚓ Fl G 4s; 53°52'·62N 09°07'·93E, 030°/ 8 cables to lock.
Alter Vorhafen ent, mole 1 ⚡ F WG 14m W10M, G6M; 266·3°-W-273·9°-G-088·8°, floodlit; 53°53'·27N 09°08'·59E.

RIVER ELBE (BRUNSBÜTTEL TO HAMBURG)
Some of the more accessible yacht hbrs are listed below, but not the many ldg lts and dir lts which define the main river fairway.

FREIBURG
Reede 1 ⚓ Oc (2) Y 9s; 53°50'·41N 09°19'·45E, off ent.

STÖRLOCH
Stör ldg lts 093·8°, both Fl 3s 7/12m 6M; synch. Front, 53°49'·29N 09°23'·91E; △ on R ○ twr. Rear, 200m east; ▽ on white mast.

51

GLÜCKSTADT

Glückstadt ldg lts 131·8°, both Iso 8s 15/30m **19/21M**; intens on ldg line; W twrs, R bands. **Front** ☆, 53°48'·31N 09°24'·24E. **Rear** ☆, 0·68M from front.

Rhinplatte Nord ⚓ Oc WRG 6s 11m W6M, R4M, G3M; 122°-G-144°-W-150°-R-177°- W-122°; 53°48'·09N 09°23'·36E.

N mole ⚓ Oc WRG 6s 9m W9M R7M, G6M; 330°-R-343°-W-346°-G-008°; 123°-G-145°-W-150°-R-170°; W twr with gallery; 53°47'·12N 09°24'·53E.

N pier hd ⚓ FR 5m 5M; 53°47'·10N 09°24'·50E. (S mole hd, FG).

KRUCKAU

S mole Oc WRG 6s 8m, W6M, R4M, G3M; 116·3°-W-120·7° (ldg sector)-R-225°-G-315°-R-331·9°-W-335·4° (ldg sector)-335·4°-G-116·3°; B dolphin; 53°42'·85N 09°30'·72E.

PINNAU

Ldg lts 112·7°, both Iso 4s8/13m 6M. Front, 53°40'·08N 09°34'·02E.

STADE

Stadersand ⚓ Iso 8s 20m 14M; 53°37'·69N 09°31'·64E (at ent).

HAMBURG YACHT HARBOUR, WEDEL

Both entrances show FR & FG, May to Oct; 53°34'·25N 09°40'·77E.

CITY SPORTHAFEN

Brandenburger Hafen Ent ⚓ Iso Or 2s; 53°32'·52N 09°58'·81E.

WESER ESTUARY

ALTE WESER

Schlüsseltonne ⚓ Iso 8s; 53°56'·25N 07°54'·76E.

Alte Weser ☆ F WRG 33m **W23M, R19M, G18M**; 288°-W-352°-R-003°-W-017° (ldg sector for Alte Weser)-G-045°-W-074°-G-118°- W-123° (ldg sector for Alte Weser)- R-140°-G-175°-W-183°-R-196°-W-238°; R ○ twr, 2 W bands, B base; *Fog det lt; Horn Mo (AL) 60s;* 53°51'·79N 08°07'·65E.

16/A15 ⬢ Fl (2+1) R 15s; 53°49'·66N 08°06'·44E (junction with Neuwe Weser).

NEUE WESER

Tegeler Plate, N end ☆ Oc (3) WRG 12s 21m **W21M, R17M, G16M**; 329°-W-340°-R-014°-W-100°-G-116°- W-119° (ldg sector for Neuer Weser)-R-123°-G-144°-W-147° (ldg sector

for Alte Weser)-R-264°; R ○ twr, gallery, W lantern, R roof; Fog det lt; 53°47'·87N 08°11'·45E.

BREMERHAVEN

No. 61 ⚓ QG; 53°32'·26N 08°33'·93E (Km 66·0).

Vorhafen N pier ⚓ FR 15m 5M; 245°-166°; F in fog; 53°32'·15N 08°34'·50E.

RIVER JADE

1b/Jade 1: Oc G 4s; 53°52'·40N 07°44'·00E.

Mellumplate ☆ FW 28m **24M**; 116·1°-116·4° (ldg sector for outer part of Wangerooger Fahrwasser); R ☐ twr, W band; 53°46'·28N 08°05'·51E.

No.19 ⚓ QG; 53°47'·10N 08°01'·83E.

No. 31/P-Reede/W Siel 1 ⚓ Oc (3) G 12s; 53°41'·59N 08°04'·51E.

HOOKSIEL

No. 37/Hooksiel 1 ⚓ IQ G 13s; 53°39'·37N 08°06'·58E.

Vorhafen ent ⚓ L Fl R 6s 9m 3M; 53°38'·63N 08°05'·25E.

WILHELMSHAVEN

Fluthafen N mole ⚓ F WG 9m,W6M, G3M; 216°-W-280°-G-010°-W-020°-G-130°; G twr; 53°30'·86N 08°09'·32E.

EAST FRISIAN ISLANDS

NORTH EDGE OF INSHORE TRAFFIC ZONE

TG19/Weser 2 ⚓ Fl (2+1) G 15s; 53°54'·99N 07°44'·52E.

TG13 ⚓ Oc (3) G 12s; 53°50'·85N 07°15'·43E.

TG7 ⚓ Fl (2) G 9s; 53°47'·24N 06°49'·65E.

TG1/Ems ⚓ IQ G 13s; 53°43'·36N 06°22'·24E.

WANGEROOGE

Harle ⚓ Iso 8s; 53°49'·26N 07°48'·92E.

Wangerooge, W end ☆ Fl R 5s 60m **23M**; R ○ twr, 2 W bands; 53°47'·40N 07°51'·37E.

Buhne H ⚓ VQ (9) 10s; 53°46'·86N 07°49'·65E.

D4 ⚓ ; 53°46'·25N 07°51'·89E, off hbr ent.

SPIEKEROOG

Otzumer Balje ⚓ Iso 4s; 53°47'·98N 07°37'·12E (often moved).

Spiekeroog ⚓ FR 6m 4M; 197°-114°; R mast; 53°45'·0N 07°41'·3E.

LANGEOOG

Accumer Ee ⚓ Iso 8s; 53°46·96N 07°25·91E (frequently moved).

W mole head ⚓ Oc WRG 6s 8m W7M, R5M, G4M; 064°-G-070°-W-074°-R-326°-W-330°-G-335°-R-064°; R basket on R mast; *Horn Mo (L) 30s* (0730-1800LT); 53°43'·42N 07°30'·13E .

BALTRUM

Groyne hd ⚓ Oc WRG 6s 6m; W6M, R4M, G3M; 074·5°-G-090°-W-095°-R-074·5°; 53°43'·3N 07°21'·7E.

1	Esbjerg	**1**																
2	H rnum Lt (Sylt)	47	**2**															
3	Husum	95	48	**3**														
4	Hamburg	163	112	113	**4**													
5	Kiel/Holtenau	179	128	129	90	**5**												
6	Brunsb ttel	126	75	76	37	53	**6**											
7	Cuxhaven	110	63	66	54	70	17	**7**										
8	Bremerhaven	127	80	82	81	131	78	58	**8**									
9	Wilhelmshaven	125	78	82	110	123	70	56	45	**9**								
10	Hooksiel	116	69	73	101	117	64	47	36	9	**10**							
11	Helgoland	83	38	47	88	104	51	38	44	43	35	**11**						
12	Wangerooge	109	60	52	61	108	55	42	38	27	19	24	**12**					
13	Langeoog	119	72	77	114	130	77	60	47	43	34	35	21	**13**				
14	Norderney	123	77	85	81	137	84	69	62	53	44	44	29	18	**14**			
15	Emden	165	129	137	174	190	137	120	115	106	97	85	80	63	47	**15**		
16	Borkum	133	97	105	104	163	110	95	88	80	71	67	55	46	31	32	**16**	
17	Delfzijl	155	119	127	159	173	120	105	100	89	83	81	65	56	41	10	22	**17**
18	Den Helder	187	192	198	229	245	192	175	180	159	150	153	148	130	115	125	95	115	**18**

DISTANCE TABLES

Approx distances in nautical miles are by the most direct route allowing for dangers and TSS.

NORDERNEY

Norderney ☆ Fl (3) 12s 59m **23M**; unintens 067°-077° and 270°-280°; R 8-sided twr; 53°42'·58N 07°13'·83E.
Dovetief ⚓ Iso 4s; 53°45'·47N 07°12'·70E.
Schluchter ⚓ Iso 8s; 53°44'·48N 07°02'·27E.
W mole head ⚡ Oc (2) R 9s 13m 4M; 53°41'·9N 07°09'·9E.

JUIST

Juist-N ⚓ VQ; 53°43'·82N 06°55'·42E.
Training wall, S end ⚡ Oc (2) R 9s 7m 3M; 53°39'·65N 06°59'·81E.

MAINLAND HARBOURS: R. JADE TO R. EMS

HARLESIEL

Carolinensieler Balje, Leitdamm ⚡ L Fl 8s 7m 6M; G mast; 53°44'·13N 07°50'·10E.
Ldg lts 138°, both Iso 6s 12/18m 9M, intens on ldg line; Front 53°40'·70N 07°34'·50E. Rear 167m from front.
N mole head ⚡ Iso R 4s 6m 7M; 53°42'·58N 07°48'·64E.

NEUHARLINGERSIEL

Training wall head ⚡ Oc 6s 6m 5M; 53°43'·22N 07°42'·30E.

BENSERSIEL

E training wall head ⚡ Oc WRG 6s 6m W5M, R3M, G2M; 110°-G-119°-W-121°-R-110°; R post & platform; 53°41'·80N 07°32'·84E.

DORNUMER-ACCUMERSIEL

W bkwtr head, approx 53°41'·04N 07°29'·30E.

NESSMERSIEL

N mole head ⚡ Oc 4s 6m 5M; G mast; 53°41'·9N 07°21'·7E.

NORDDEICH

W trng wall head ⚡ FG 8m 4M, 021°-327°; G framework twr; 53°38'·62N 07°09'·0E.

GREETSIEL

Meßstation lt bcn, Fl Y 4s 15m 3M; 53°32'·94N 07°02'·18E.

RIVER EMS

APPROACHES

GW/EMS ⬚ Iso 8s 12m **17M**; *Horn Mo (R) 30s (H24)*; *Racon T, 8M*; 54°09'·96N 06°20'·72E.
Borkumriff ⚓ Oc 4s; *Racon T, 8M*; 53°47'·44N 06°22'·05E.
Osterems ⚓ Iso 4s; 53°41'·91N 06°36'·17E.
Riffgat ⚓ Iso 8s; 53°38'·96N 06°27'·10E.
Westerems ⚓ Iso 4s; *Racon T, 8M*; 53°36'·93N 06°19'·39E.
H1 ⚓ 53°34'·91N 06°17'·97E.

BORKUM

Borkum Grosser ☆ Fl (2) 12s 63m **24M**; brown ○ twr; 53°35'·32N 06°39'·64E. Same twr; ⚡ F WRG 46m **W19M, R/G15M**; 107·4°-G-109°-W-111·2°- R-112·6°.
Fischerbalje ⚡ Oc (2) 16s 15m 3M; 260°-W-123°. Fog det lt; R/W ○ twr on tripod; 53°33'·18N 06°42'·90E.
Schutzhafen, E mole hd ⚡ FG10m 4M; 53°33'·48N 06°45'·02E. W mole hd, FR 8m 4M.

RIVER EMS (LOWER)

No. 27 ⚓ Fl G 4s; 53°30'·24N 06°47'·52E.
No. 35 ⚓ Fl G 4s; 53°27'·03N 06°52'·80E.
No. 37 ⚓ QG; 53°26'·01N 06°54'·85E.
No. 41 ⚓ Fl (2) G 9s; 53°24'·25N 06°56'·68E.
No. 49 ⚓ Oc (2) G 9s; 53°19'·95N 06°59'·71E.

KNOCK

Knock ⚡ F WRG 28m W12M,R9M, G8M; 270°-W-299°-R-008·3°-G-023°-W-026·8°-R-039°-W-073°-R-119°-W-154°; fog det lt; Gy twr, white conical radar antenna; 53°20'·32N 07°01'·40E.

EMDEN

No. 59 ⚓ Oc (2) G 9s; 53°19'·41N 07°03'·86E.
No. 65 ⚓ Fl (2) G 9s; 53°19'·82N 07°06'·56E.
Outer hbr, W pier ⚡ FR 10m 4M; R 8-sided twr; *Horn Mo (ED) 30s*; 53°20'·06N 07°10'·49E.
E pier ⚡ FG 7m 5M; G mast on pedestal; 53°20'·05N 07°10'·84E.

AREA 13 *Netherlands & Belgium – Delfzijl to Nieuwpoort*

SELECTED LIGHTS, BUOYS & WAYPOINTS

| Positions are referenced to WGS84 |

TSS OFF NORTHERN NETHERLANDS

TERSCHELLING-GERMAN BIGHT TSS

TG1/Ems ⚓ IQ G 13s; 53°43'·33N 06°22'·24E.
TE5 ⚓ Fl (3) G 10s; 53°37'·79N 05°53'·69E.
TE1 ⚓ Fl (3) G 10s; 53°29'·58N 05°11'·31E.

OFF VLIELAND TSS

VL-CENTER ⬚ Fl 5s 12M; *Racon C, 12–15M*; 53°26'·93N 04°39'·88E. VL7 ⚓ L Fl G 10s; 53°26'·40N 04°57'·60E.
VL1 ⚓ Fl (2) G 10s; 53°10'·96N 04°35'·31E.

DELFZIJL TO HARLINGEN

DELFZIJL

PS3/BW26 ⚓ Fl (2+1) G 12s; 53°19'·25N 07°00'·32E.
W mole ⚡ FG; 53°19'·01N 07°00'·27E.
Ldg lts 203° both Iso 4s. Front, 53°18'·63N 07°00'·17E.

SCHIERMONNIKOOG AND LAUWERSOOG

WG (Westgat) ⚓ Iso 8s; *Racon N*; 53°32'·00N 05°58'·54E.

WRG ⚓ Q; 53°32'·87N 06°03'·24E.
AM ⚓ VQ; 53°30'·95N 05°44'·72E.
Schiermonnikoog ☆ Fl (4) 20s 43m **28M**; dark R ○ twr. Same twr: F WR 29m **W15M**, R12M; 210°-W-221°-R-230°. 53°29'·20N 06°08'·79E.
Lauwersoog W mole ⚡ FG; *Horn (2) 30s*; 53°24'·68N 06°12'·00E.

ZEEGAT VAN AMELAND

BR ⚓ Q; 53°30'·66N 05°33'·52E.
TS ⚓ VQ; 53°28'·15N 05°21'·53E.
WA ⚓ 53°28'·35N 05°28'·64E. (Westgat buoys are all unlit)
Ameland, W end ☆ Fl (3) 15s 57m **30M**; 53°26'·89N 05°37'·42E.

NES

VA2-R1 ⚓ VQ(6) + L Fl 10s; 53°25'·71N 05°45'·88E.
Reegeul R3 ⚡ Iso G 4s; 53°25'·80N 05°45'·93E.
R7 ⚡ QG; 53°25'·91N 05°46'·21E.

HET VLIE (ZEEGAT VAN TERSCHELLING)

ZS (Zuider Stortemelk) ⚓ Iso 4s; *Racon T*; 53°19'·58N 04°55'·77E.

ZS1 ▲ VQ G; 53°19'·22N 04°57'·58E.

ZS5 ▲ L Fl G 8s; 53°18'·53N 05°01'·10E.

ZS11-VS2 ⚐ Q (9) 15s; 53°18'·66N 05°05'·95E.

SCHUITENGAT TO WEST TERSCHELLING

VL 4/SG 1 ⚐ 53°19'·17N 05°10'·45E; buoys are frequently moved.

SG 3 ▲ 53°19'·38N 05°10'·51E.

SG 19 ▲ L Fl G 5s; 53°20'·89N 05°12'·42E.

SG 23 ▲ L Fl G 8s; 53°21'·17N 05°13'·28E.

NOORD MEEP/SLENK TO WEST TERSCHELLING

WM3 ▲ Iso G 2s; 53°17'·45N 05°12'·28E.

NM 4-S 21 ⚐ VQ (3) 5s; 53°19'·02N 05°15'·47E.

SG 15-S 2 ⚐ Q (9) 15s; 53°20'·44N 05°11'·70E.

Brandaris Twr ☆ Fl 5s 54m **29M**; Y ☐ twr partly obscured by dunes; 53°21'·62N 05°12'·86E.

W Terschelling W hbr mole ⚡ FR 5m 5M; R post, W bands; *Horn 15s*; 53°21'·26N 05°13'·09E. E pier hd ⚡ FG 4m 4M.

VLIELAND

VS3 (Vliesloot) ▲ VQ G; 53°18'·27N 05°06'·25E.

VS14 ⚑ Iso R 4s; 53°17'·58N 05°05'62E.

VS16-VB1 ⚏ Fl (2+1) R 10s; 53°17'·62N 05°05'·19E.

E/W mole hds ⚡ FG and ⚡ FR; 53°17'·68N 05°05'·51E.

Ldg lts 282° ⚑ Iso 4s 10/16m 1M, synch; 53°17'·75N 05°04'·47W (100m apart); mainly for the ferry terminal at E Vlieland.

E Vlieland (Vuurduin) ☆ Iso 4s 54m **20M**; 53°17'·75N 05°03'·49E.

APPROACHES TO HARLINGEN (selected marks):

VLIESTROOM buoys are frequently moved.

VL1 ▲ QG; 53°18'·99N 05°08'·82E. VL 2 ⚑ QR; 53°19'·40N 05°09'·19E.

IN 1 ▲ VQ G; 53°16'·07N 05°09'·70E (Inschot).

BLAUWE SLENK

BS-IN2 ⚐ VQ (3) 5s; 53°15'·99N 05°10'·32E.

BS13 ▲ QG; 53°13'·31N 05°17'·13E. BS19 ▲ VQ G; 53°11'·90N 05°18'·28E.

BS23 ▲ L Fl G 8s; 53°11'·42N 05°19'·60E.

POLLENDAM

Ldg lts 112°, both Iso 6s 8/19m 13M (H24); B masts, W bands. Front, 53°10'·52N 05°24'·19E. Use only between P2 and P6.

P2 ⚡ Iso R 2s; 53°11'·47N 05°20'·38E on the training wall, as are P4, Iso R 8s; P6, Iso R 4s; P8, Iso R 8s; and P10, Iso R 2s. Yachts should keep outboard of P1 thru 7 SHM buoys. P1 ▲ Iso G 2s; 53°11'·39N 05°20'·32E. P7 ▲ VQ G; 53°10'·68N 05°23'·45E.

HARLINGEN

S mole hd ⚡ FG 9m; *Horn (3) 30s*; 53°10'·56N 05°24'·18E.

N mole hd ⚡ FR 9m 4M; R/W pedestal; 53°10'·59N 05°24'·32E.

TEXEL AND THE WADDENZEE

APPROACHES TO EIERLANDSCHE GAT

Eierland ☆ Fl (2) 10s 52m **29M**; R ○ twr; 53°10'·93N 04°51'·31E.

EG ⚐ VQ (9) 10s; 53°13'·36N 04°47'·08E.

MOLENGAT (from the N)

MG ⚐; RW bands; 53°03'·88N 04°40'·18E.

MG1 ⚑; 53°02'·89N 04°40'·86E.

MG5 ▲ Iso G 4s; 53°01'·26N 04°41'·74E.

MG13 ▲ Iso G 8s; 52°59'·16N 04°42'·35E.

S14-MG17 ⚐ VQ (6) + L Fl 10s; 52°58'·50N 04°43'·60E.

OUDESCHILD

T12 ⚑ Iso R 8s; 53°02'·23N 04°51'·52E.

Oudeschild Dir ☆ Oc 6s; intens 291°; 53°02'·40N 04°50'·94E; leads 291° into hbr between N mole head FG 6m; and S mole head ⚡ FR 6m; *Horn (2) 30s* (sounded 0600-2300); 53°02'·33N 04°51'·17E.

APPROACHES TO KORNWERDERZAND SEALOCK

DOOVE BALG (From Texelstroom eastward)

T23 ▲ VQ G; 53°03'·60N 04°55'·85E, 066°/3M from Oudeschild.

T29 ▲ 53°03'·25N 05°00'·05E.

D1 ⚑ Iso G 4s; 53°02'·18N 05°03'·42E.

D21 ⚑ Iso G 8s; 53°03'·55N 05°15'·71E.

BO2-WG1 ⚐ Q (6) + L Fl 10s; 53°05'·00N 05°17'·91E.

BOONTJES (From Harlingen southward)

BO40 ⚑ Iso R 4s; 53°09'·87N 05°23'·29E.

BO28 ⚑ Iso R 8s; 53°07'·81N 05°22'·49E.

BO9/KZ2 ⚐ Q; 53°04'·95N 05°20'·24E.

KORNWERDERZAND SEALOCK

W mole ⚡ FG 9m 7M; *Horn Mo(N) 30s*; 53°04'·78N 05°20'·03E.

E mole ⚡ FR 9m 7M; 53°04'·70N 05°20'·08E.

W mole elbow ⚡ Iso G 6s 6m 7M; 53°04'·61N 05°19'·90E.

APPROACHES TO DEN OEVER SEALOCK

MALZWIN and VISJAGERSGAATJE CHANS TO DEN OEVER

MH4-M1 ⚐ VQ (9) 10s; 52°58'·09N 04°47'·52E, close N Den Helder.

M15 ▲ QG; 52°59'·39N 04°55'·48E (hence use DYC 1811.3).

VG1-W2 ⚏ Fl (2+1) G 10s; 52°59'·00N 04°56'·85E.

O9 ▲ Iso G 8s; 52°56'·63N 05°02'·38E.

DEN OEVER SEALOCK

Ldg lts 131°, both Oc 10s 6m 7M; 127°-137°. Front, 52°56'·32N 05°02'·98E. Rear, 280m from front.

E end of swing bridge, ⚡ Iso WRG 5s 14m 10/7M; 226°-G-231°-W-235°-R-290°-G-327°-W-335°-R-345°; 52°56'·12N 05°02'·52E.

ZEEGAT VAN TEXEL AND DEN HELDER

OFFSHORE MARKS W and SW OF DEN HELDER

NH (Noorderhaaks) ⚐ VQ; 53°00'·24N 04°35'·37E.

MR ⚐ Q (9) 15s; 52°56'·77N 04°33'·82E.

ZH (Zuiderhaaks) ⚐ VQ (6) + L Fl 10s; 52°54'·65N 04°34'·72E.

Vinca G wreck ⚐ Q (9) 15s; *Racon D*; 52°45'·93N 04°12'·31E.

SCHULPENGAT (from the SSW)

Schulpengat Dir ☆ 026·5°, Dir WRG, Al WR, Al WG, **W22M R/G18M**, church spire; 025.1°-FG-025.6°-AlWG-026.3°-FW-026.7°-Al WR-027.4°-F R-027.9°; shown H24.

Schilbolsnol ☆ F WRG 27m **W15M**, R12M, G11M; 338°-W-002°-G-035°-W(ldg sector for Schulpengat)-038°-R-051°-W-068°; post; 53°00'·50N 04°45'·70E (on Texel).

SG ⚐ Mo (A) 8s; *Racon Z*; 52°52'·90N 04°37'·90E.

S1 ▲ Iso G 4s; 52°53'·53N 04°38'·82E.

S7 ▲ QG; 52°56'·25N 04°40'·92E. S6A ⚑ QR; 52°56'·52N 04°40'·51E.

S10 ⌖ Iso R 8s; 52°57'·59N 04°41'·57E. S14-MG17 ⌖, see Molengat.

S11 ▲ Iso G 8s; 52°57'·55N 04°43'·25E.

Huisduinen ⌖ F WR 26m W14M, R11M; 070°-W-113°-R-158°-W-208°; ☐ twr; 52°57'·14N 04°43'·30E (abeam S10 PHM buoy).

Kijkduin ☆ Fl (4) 20s 56m **30M**; vis 360°, except where obsc'd by dunes on Texel; brown twr; 52°57'·33N 04°43'·58E (mainland).

MARSDIEP and DEN HELDER

T1 ▲ Fl (3) G 10s; 52°57'·99N 04°44'·62E.

T3 ▲ Iso G 8s; 52°58'·07N 04°46'·42E.

Den Helder ldg lts 191°, both Oc G 5s 15/24m 14M, synch. Front, vis 161°-221°; B ▽ on bldg; 52°57'·37N 04°47'·08E.

Marinehaven, W bkwtr head ⌖ QG 11m 8M; *Horn 20s*; 52°57'·95N 04°47'·07E (Harssens Island).

W side, ⌖ Fl G 5s 9m 4M (H24); 180°-067°; 52°57'·78N 04°47'·08E.

Yacht hbr (KMYC), ent ⌖ FR & FG; 165m SW of ⌖ Fl G 5s, above.

E side, MH6 ⌖ Iso R 4s; 52°57'·99N 04°47'·41E.

Ent E side, ⌖ QR 9m 4M (H24); 52°57'·77N 04°47'·37E.

DEN HELDER TO AMSTERDAM

Zanddijk Grote Kaap ⌖ Oc WRG 10s 30m W11M, R8M, G8M; 041°-G-088°-W-094°-R-131°; brown twr; 52°52'·86N 04°42'·88E.

Petten ⌖ VQ (9) 10s; 52°47'·33N 04°36'·78E (Power stn outfall).

Egmond-aan-Zee ☆ Iso WR 10s 36m **W18M**, R14M; 010°-W-175°-R-188°; W ○ twr; 52°36'·99N 04°37'·16E.

Wind farm approx 6·4M W of Egmond-aan-Zee is marked by: a Meteomast, Mo (U) 15s 11m 10M; 52°36'·36N 04°23'·41E; and by L Fl Y 15s; Horn Mo (U) 30s on 5 of the peripheral wind turbines.

IJMUIDEN

Baloeran ⌖ Q (9) 15s; 52°29'·21N 04°32'·00E.

IJmuiden ⌖ Mo (A) 8s; *Racon Y, 10M*; 52°28'·45N 04°23'·92E.

Ldg lts 100·5° (FW 5M by day; 090·5°-110·5°). **Front** ☆ F WR 30m **W16M**, R13M; 050°-W-122°-R-145°-W-160°; (Tidal and traffic sigs); dark R ○ twrs; 52°27'·70N 04°34'·47E. **Rear** ☆ Fl 5s 52m **29M**; 019°-199° (FW 5M by day; 090·5°-110·5°); 560m from front.

S bkwtr hd ⌖ FG 14m 10M (in fog Fl 3s); *Horn (2) 30s*; W twr, G bands; 52°27'·82N 04°31'·93E.

N bkwtr hd ⌖ FR 15m 10M; 52°28'·05N 04°32'·55E.

IJM 1 ▲ Iso G 4s; 52°27'·75N 04°33'·59E.

S outer chan ⌖ Iso G 6s, 52°27'·75N 04°33'·81E. ⌖ Iso R 6s, 52°27'·84N 04°34'·39E (Forteiland). Kleine Sluis 52°27'·84N 04°35'·43E.

AMSTERDAM

IJ8 ⌖ Iso R 8s (for Sixhaven marina); 52°22'·86N 04°54'·37E. Oranjesluizen, N lock 52°22'·93N 04°57'·60E (for IJsselmeer).

AMSTERDAM TO ROTTERDAM

Noordwijk-aan-Zee ☆ Oc (3) 20s 32m **18M**; W ☐ twr; 52°14'·88N 04°26'·02E.

SCHEVENINGEN

Lighthouse ☆ Fl (2) 10s 48m **29M**; 014°-244°; brown twr; 52°06'·23N 04°16'·13E, 5ca E of hbr ent.

Ldg lts 156°, both Iso 4s 18/22m 14M, H24; synch; Gy masts. Front 52°05'·87N 04°15'·54E; rear 489m from front. Intens at night.

SCH ⌖ Iso 4s; 52°07'·76N 04°14'·12E.

KNS ⌖ Q (9)15s; 52°06'·41N 04°15'·32E.

W mole ⌖ FG 12m 9M; G twr, W bands; 52°06'·23N 04°15'·16E.

E mole ⌖, FR 12m 9M; R twr, W bands; 52°06'·24N 04°15'·37E.

Inner ldg lts 131°: both Iso G 4s synch; Gy posts. Front 52°05'·81N 04°15'·89E. Rear, 34m from front.

NOORD HINDER N & S TSS and JUNCTION

NHR-N ⌖ L Fl 8s; *Racon K, 10M*; 52°10'·91N 03°04'·76E.

Noord Hinder ⌖ Fl (2) 10s; *Horn (2) 30s*; *Racon T, 12-15M*; 52°00'·10N 02° 51'·11E.

NHR-S ⌖ Fl Y 10s; 51°51'·37N 02°28'·72E.

NHR-SE ▲ Fl G 5s; 51°45'·42N 02°39'·96E.

Birkenfels ⌖ Q (9) 15s; 51°38'·98N 02°31'·75E.

Twin ⌖ Fl (3) Y 9s; 51°32'·00N 02°22'·59E.

Garden City ⌖ Q (9) 15s; 51°29'·20N 02°17'·54E.

APPROACHES TO HOEK VAN HOLLAND

Europlatform ⌖ Mo (U) 15s; W structure, R bands; helicopter platform; *Horn Mo(U) 30s*; 51°59'·89N 03°16'·46E.

Goeree ☆ Fl (4) 20s 32m **28M**; R/W chequered twr on platform; helicopter platform; *Horn (4) 30s*; *Racon T, 12-15M*; 51°55'·42N 03°40'·03E.

Maasvlakte ☆ Fl (5) 20s 67m **28M**, H24; 340°-267°; W twr, B bands; 51°58'·20N 04°00'·84E, 1·5M SSW of Maas ent.

Maas Center ⌖ Iso 4s; *Racon M, 10M*; 52°00'·92N 03°48'·79E.

SB-M ⌖ Fl(2)Y 10s; *Racon Z*; 52°00·08N 03°53·18E

MO ⌖ Mo (A) 8s; 52°00'·95N 03°58'·07E.

MN3 ▲ Fl (3) G 10s; 52°04'·47N 03°58'·76E.

MN1 ▲ Fl G 5s; 52°02'·07N 04°00'·83E.

HOEK VAN HOLLAND

Maasmond ldg lts 112° (for deep draught vessels): both Iso 4s 30/46m **21M**; 101°-123°, synch; W twr, B bands. **Front**, 51°58'·88N 04°04'·88E (NW end of Splitsingsdam). **Rear**, 0·6M from front.

Indusbank N ⌖ VQ; 52°02'·89N 04°03'·57E.

MVN ⌖ VQ; 51°59'·61N 04°00'·20E.

MV ⌖ Q (9) 15s; 51°57'·45N 03°58'·45E.

Maas 1 ▲ L Fl G 5s; 51°59'·35N 04°01'·68E.

Nieuwe Waterweg ldg lts 107°: both Iso R 6s 29/43m **18M**; 099.5°-114.5°; R twr, W bands. Front, 51°58'·55N 04°07'·52E. Rear, 450m from front.

Noorderdam Head ⌖ FR 25m 10M (In fog Al Fl WR 6s; 278°-255°); R twr, W bands; 51°59'·67N 04°02'·80E.

Nieuwe Zuiderdam ⌖ FG 25m 10M, 330°-307°; (In fog Al Fl WG 6s); G twr, W bands; 51°59'·14N 04°02'·49E.

ROTTERDAM

Maassluis ⌖ FG 6m; 51°54'·94N 04°14'·81E; and FR.

Vlaardingen ⌖ FG 51°53'·99N 04°20'·95E; and FR.

Spuihaven, W ent ⌖ FR; 51°53'·98N 04°23'·97E.

Veerhaven, E ent ⌖ FG; 51°54'·42N 04°28'·75E; and FR.

City marina ent, 51°54'·64N 04°29'·76E.

APPROACHES TO HARINGVLIET

Buitenbank , Iso 4s; 51°51'·16N 03°25'·71E.

Hinder ⌖ Q (9) 15s; 51°54'·55N 03°55'·42E.

SH ⌖ VQ (9) 10s; 51°49'·49N 03°45'·79E.

Westhoofd ☆ Fl (3) 15s 55m **30M**; R ☐ tr; 51°48'·79N 03°51'·85E.

Ooster ⌀ Q (9) 15s; 51°47'·90N 03°41'·27E.

SLIJKGAT

SG ⌀ Iso 4s; 51°51'·95N 03°51'·42E.

SG 2 ⌀ Iso R 4s; 51°51'·71N 03°53'·45E.

SG 5 ▲ Iso G 4s; 51°50'·91N 03°55'·44E.

SG 11 ▲ Iso G 4s; 51°50'·81N 03°58'·52E.

P1 ▲ Iso G 4s; 51°51'·30N 04°01'·12E.

P3 ▲ Iso G 8s; 51°51'·12N 04°01'·45E.

P9 ▲ Iso G 8s; 51°49'·98N 04°02'·15E.

STELLENDAM

N mole ⚡ FG; *Horn (2) 15s*; 51°49'·88N 04°02'·03E.

Buitenhaven ⚡ Oc 6s; 51°49'·73N 04°01'·75E.

APPROACHES TO OOSTERSCHELDE

OUTER APPROACHES

Schouwenbank ⌀ Mo (A) 8s; *Racon O, 10M*; 51°44'·94N 03°14'·32E.

Middelbank ⌀ Iso 8s; 51°40'·86N 03°18'·20E.

MW ⌀ Q (9) 15s; 51°44'·55N 03°24'·04E (Schouwendiep).

MD 3 ▲ Fl G 5s; 51°42'·70N 03°26'·98E.

SW Thornton ⌀ Iso 8s; 51°30'·98N 02°50'·90E.

Rabsbank ⌀ Iso 4s; 51°38'·25N 03°09'·93E.

Westpit ⌀ Iso 8s; 51°33'·65N 03°09'·92E.

ZSB ⌀ VQ (9) 10s; 51°36'·57N 03°15'·62E.

OG1 ▲ QG; 51°36'·14N 03°20'·08E.

WESTGAT, OUDE ROOMPOT and ROOMPOTSLUIS

West Schouwen ☆ Fl (2+1)15s 57m **30M**; Gy twr, R diagonals on upper part; 51°42'·52N 03°41'·50E, 5·8M N of Roompotsluis.

OG-WG ⌀ VQ (9) 10s; 51°37'·18N 03°23'·82E.

WG1 ▲ Iso G 8s; 51°38'·00N 03°26'·24E.

WG4 ⌀ L Fl R 8s; 51°38'·62N 03°28'·78E.

WG7 ▲ Iso G 4s 51°39'·40N 03°32'·67E.

WG-GB (Geul van de Banjaard) ⚲ 51°39'·72N 03°32'·69E.

OR1 ⚡ 51°39'·15N 03°33'·59E.

OR5 ▲ Iso G 8s; 51°38'·71N 03°35'·53E.

OR11 ▲ Iso G 4s; 51°36'·98N 03°38'·40E.

OR12 ⌀ Iso R 4s; 51°37'·27N 03°39'·25E.

OR-R ⌀ VQ (3) 5s; 51°36'·41N 03°38'·96E.

Roompotsluis ldg lts 073·5°, both Oc G 5s; synch. Front, 51°37'·33N 03°40'·75E. Rear, 280m from front.

N bkwtr ⚡ FR 7m; 51°37'·31N 03°40'·09E.

WESTKAPELLE TO VLISSINGEN

OOSTGAT

Ldg lts 149·5°: Front, Noorderhoofd Oc WRG 10s 20m; W13M, R/G10M; 353°-R-008°-G-029°-W-169°; R ○ twr, W band; 51°32'·40N 03°26'·21E, 0·73M from rear (Westkapelle).

Westkapelle ☆, rear, Fl 3s 50m **28M**; obsc'd by land on certain brgs; ☐ twr, R top; 51°31'·75N 03°26'·83E.

Kaloo ⌀ Iso 8s; 51°35'·55N 03°23'·24E. Chan is well buoyed/lit.

OG5 ▲ Iso G 8s; 51°33'·95N 03°25'·92E.

OG-GR ⌀ VQ (3) 5s; 51°32'·74N 03°24'·71E.

Molenhoofd ⚡ Oc WRG 6s 10m; 306°-R-329°-W-349°-R-008°-G-034·5°-W-036·5°-G-144°-W-169°-R-198°; W mast R bands; 51°31'·58N 03°26'·05E.

Zoutelande FR 21m 12M; 321°-352°; R ☐ twr; 51°30'·28N 03°28'·41E.

Kaapduinen, ldg lts 130°: both Oc 5s 25/34m 13M; synch; Y ☐ twrs, R bands. Front, 115°-145°; 51°28'·47N 03°30'·99E. Rear, 107·5°-152·5°; 220m from front.

Fort de Nolle ⚡ Oc WRG 9s 11m W6M, R/G4M; 293°-R-309°-W-324·5°-G-336·5°-R-014°-G-064°-R-099·5°-W-110·5°-G-117°-R-130°; W col, R bands; 51°26'·94N 03°33'·12E.

Ldg lts 117°: Front, Leugenaar, Oc R 5s 6m 7M; intens 108°-126°; W&R pile; 51°26'·43N 03°34'·14E.

Rear, Sardijngeul Oc WRG 5s 8m W12M, R9M, G8M; synch; 245°-R-272°-G-282.5°-W-123°-R-147°; R △, W bands on R & W mast; 550m from front; 51°26'·30N 03°34'·56E.

OFFSHORE: W HINDER TSS TO SCHEUR CHAN

West Hinder ☆ Fl (4) 30s 23m 13M; *Horn Mo (U) 30s*; *Racon W*; 51°23'·30N 02°26'·27E.

WH Zuid ⌀ Q (6) + L Fl 15s; 51°22'·78N 02°26'·25E.

Oost-Dyck ⌀ Q; 51°21'·38N 02°31'·12E.

Bergues N ⌀ Q; 51°19'·96N 02°24'·53E.

Oost-Dyck West ⌀ Q (9) 15s; 51°17'·15N 02°26'·32E.

Oostdyck radar twr; ⚡ Mo (U) 15s 15m 12M on 4 corners; *Horn Mo (U) 30s*; *Racon O*. R twr, 3 W bands, with adjacent red twr/helipad; 51°16'·49N 02°26'·83E.

AN ⌀ Fl (4) R 20s; 51°23'·45N 02°36'·92E.

AZ ▲ Fl (3) G 10s; 51°21'·15N 02°36'·92E.

KB2 ⌀ VQ; 51°21'·04N 02°42'·20E.

KB ⌀ Q; *Racon K*; 51°21'·03N 02°42'·80E.

MBN ⌀ Q; 51°20'·82N 02°46'·29E.

SWA ⌀ Q (9) 15s; 51°22'·28N 02°46'·34E.

VG ⌀ Q ; 51°23'·38N 02°46'·21E, Vaargeul 1.

VG1 ▲ VQ G; 51°25'·03N 02°49'·04E.

VG2 ⌀ Q (6) + L Fl R 15s; *Racon V*; 51°25'·96N 02°48'·16E.

VG3 ▲ QG; 51°25'·05N 02°52'·85E.

VG5 ▲ Fl G 5s; 51°24'·63N 02°57'·90E.

VG7 ⌀ Q ; 51°24'·53N 02°59'·90E.

Goote Bank ⌀ Q (3) 10s; 51°26'·95N 02°52'·72E.

A1 ⌀ Iso 8s; 51°22'·36N 02°53'·33E.

A1bis ⌀ L Fl 10s; 51°21'·68N 02°58'·02E.

WESTERSCHELDE APPROACHES

SCHEUR CHANNEL

S1 ▲ Fl G 5s; 51°23'·14N 03°00'·12E.

S3 ⌀ Q; 51°24'·30N 03°02'·92E.

MOW 0 ⊙ Fl (5) Y 20s; *Racon S, 10M*; 51°23'·67N 03°02'·75E.

S5 ▲ Fl G 5s; 51°23'·70N 03°06'·30E.

S7 ▲ Fl G 5s; 51°23'·98N 03°10'·42E.

S9 ▲ QG; 51°24'·42N 03°14'·99E.

S12 ⌀ Fl (4) R 10s; 51°24'·67N 03°18'·22E.

S-W ⌀ Q; 51°24'·13N 03°18'·22E, here Wielingen chan merges.

S14 ⌀ Fl R 5s; 51°24'·58N 03°19'·67E.

WIELINGEN CHANNEL

BVH ⌀ Q (6) + L Fl R 15s; 51°23'·13N 03°12'·04E.

MOW3 tide gauge ⚡ Fl (5) Y 20s; *Racon H, 10M*; 51°23'·38N 03°11'·92E.

W ▲ Fl (3) G 15s; 51°23'·27N 03°14'·92E.

W1 ▲ Fl G 5s; 51°23'·48N 03°18'·22E.

Fort Maisonneuve ⌀ VQ (9) 10s; wreck; 51°24'·20N 03°21'·50E.

W3 ▲ Iso G 8s; 51°23'·96N 03°21'·49E.

W5 ▲ Iso G 4s; 51°24'·31N 03°24'·50E.

W7 ▲ Iso G 8s; 51°24'·60N 03°27'·23E.

W9 ⚓ Iso G 4s; 51°24'·96N 03°30'·43E.

Nieuwe Sluis ☆ Oc WRG 10s 26m W14M, R11M, G10M; 055°-R-089°-W-093°-G-105°-R-134°-W-136·5°-G-156·5°-W-236·5°-G-243°-W-254°-R-292°-W-055°; B 8-sided twr, W bands; 51°24'·41N 03°31'·29E.

Songa ⚓ QG; 51°25'·16N 03°33'·66E.

W10 ⚓ QR; 51°25'·85N 03°33'·28E.

VLISSINGEN

Koopmanshaven, W mole root, ☆ Iso WRG 3s 15m W12M, R10M, G9M; 253°-R-277°-W-284°-R-297°- W-306·5°-G-013°-W-024°-G-033°-W-035°-G-039°-W-055°-G-084·5°-R-092°-G-111°-W-114°; R pylon; 51°26'·37N 03°34'·52E.

Sardijngeul Oc WRG 5s; 51°26'·30N 03°34'·56E: see OOSTGAT last 3 lines. E mole head, ☆ FG 7m; W mast; 51°26'·32N 03°34'·67E.

Buitenhaven ent, W side ☆ FR 10m 5M; also Iso WRG 4s: W073°-324°, G324°-352°, W352°-017°, G017°-042°, W042°-056°, R056°-073°; W post, R bands; tfc sigs; 51°26'·38N 03°36'·06E.

Buitenhaven ent, E side ☆ FG 7m 4M; 51°26'·41N 03°36'·38E.

Schone Waardin ☆ Oc WRG 9s 10m W13M, R10M, G9M; 235°-R-271°-W-288°-G-335°-R-341°-G-026°-W-079°-R-091°; R mast, W bands; 51°26'·54N 03°37'·91E (1M E of Buitenhaven ent).

BRESKENS

ARV-VH ⚓ Q; 51°24'·71N 03°33'·89E.

VH2 (Vaarwaterlangs Hoofdplaat) ⚓ 51°24'·34N 03°33'·90E.

Yacht hbr, W mole ☆ FG 7m; in fog FY; Gy post; 51°24'·03N 03°34'·06E. E mole ☆ FR 6m; Gy mast; 51°23'·95N 03°34'·09E.

WESTERSCHELDE: TERNEUZEN TO PAAL

TERNEUZEN

Nieuw Neuzenpolder ldg lts 125°, both Oc 5s 6/16m 9/13M; intens 117°-133°; synch. Front, W col, B bands; 51°20'·97N 03°47'·24E. Rear, B & W twr; 365m from front.

Oost Buitenhaven E mole ☆ FR 5M; 51°20'·56N 03°49'·19E.

Former ferry hbr (W part) & marinas (E part), W mole head ☆ FG, Gy mast; 51°20'·57N 03°49'·64E. E mole, FR.

W mole ☆ Oc WRG 5s 15m W9M, R7M, G6M; 090°-R-115°-W-120°-G-130°-W-245°-G-249°-W-279°-R-004°; B & W post; 51°20'·54N 03°49'·58E, close SW of ☆ FG.

HANSWEERT

W mole ☆ Oc WRG 10s 9m W9M, R7M, G6M; (in fog FY); 288°-R-311°-G-320°-W-332·5°-G-348·5°-W-042·5°-R-061·5°-W-078°-G-099°-W-114·5°-R-127·5°-W-288°; R twr, W bands; 51°26'·41N 04°00'·53E.

BELGIUM: ZANDVLIET TO ANTWERPEN

ZANDVLIET

Dir ☆ 118·3°,WRG 20m W4M, R/ G3M; 116·63°-Oc G-117·17°- FG-117·58°-Alt GW-118·63°-F-118·63°-Alt RW-119·18°-FR-119·58°- Oc R-120·13°; 51°20'·61N 04°16'·47E, near Zandvliet locks.

ANTWERPEN

Royerssluis, ldg lts 091°, both FR. Ent FR/FG (for Willemdok ④).

No. 109 ⚓ Iso G 8s; 51°13'·88N 04°23'·87E, (off Linkeroever ④).

Linkeroever marina ⚓ F WR 9m W3M, R2M; shore-W-283°-R-shore; B ⊙, R lantern; 51°13'·91N 04°23'·70E. Marina ent, FR/FG.

COASTAL MARKS

SWW ⚓ Fl (4) R 20s; 51°21'·95N 03°00'·94E; Wandelaar.

WBN ⚓ QG; 51°21'·50N 03°02'·59E; Wandelaar.

Oostende Bank N ⚓ Q; 51°21'·20N 02°52'·93E.

Wenduine Bank E ⚓ QR; 51°18'·83N 03°01'·64E.

Wenduine Bank W ⚓ Q (9) 15s; 51°17'·23N 02°52'·76E.

Nautica Ena wreck ⚓ Q; 51°18'·08N 02°52'·79E.

Oostendebank E ⚓ Fl (4) R 20s; 51°17'·35N 02°51'·91E.

Oostendebank W ⚓ Q (9)15s; 51°16'·20N 02°44'·74E.

LST 420 ⚓ Q (9)15s; 51°15'·45N 02°40'·61E.

MBN ⚓ Q; 51°20'·82N 02°46'·27E.

Middelkerke Bank ⚓ Fl G 5s; 51°18'·19N 02°42'·75E.

Middelkerke Bank S ⚓ Q (9) 15s; 51°14'·73N 02°41'·89E.

D1 ⚓ Q (3) 10s; 51°13'·95N 02°38'·59E.

BT Ratel ⚓ Fl (4) R 15s; 51°11'·63N 02°27'·92E; Buiten Ratel.

ZEEBRUGGE TO THE FRENCH BORDER

ZEEBRUGGE

A2 ⚓ Iso 8s; 51°22'·41N 03°07'·05E.

Ldg lts 136°, both Oc 5s 22/45m 8M; 131°-141°; H24, synch; W cols, R bands. Front, 51°20'·71N 03°13'·11E. Rear, 890m SE.

SZ ⚓ Q (3) 10s; 51°23'·30N 03°08'·65E (Scheur Channel).

Z ⚓ QG; 51°22'·48N 03°09'·95E.

WZ ⚓ Q (9) 15s; 51°22'·57N 03°10'·72E.

W outer mole ☆ Oc G 7s 31m 7M; G vert strip lts visible from seaward; 057°-267°; *Horn (3) 30s*; IPTS; 51°21'·74N 03°11'·17E.

E outer mole ☆ Oc R 7s 31m 7M; R vert strip lts visible from seaward; 087°-281°; *Bell 25s*; 51°21'·78N 03°11'·86E.

Ldg lts 154°: Front, Oc WR 6s 20m 3M; 135°-W-160°-R-169°; W pylon, R bands; 51°20'·33N 03°12'·89E. Rear, Oc 6s 38m 3M, H24, synch; Iden twr; 51°19'·99N 03°13'·13E.

Leopold II mole ☆ Oc WR 15s 22m, **W20M, R18M**; 068°-W-145°-R-212°-W-296°; IPTS; *Horn (3+1) 90s*; 51°20'·85N 03°12'·17E.

Entrance to Marina and FV hbr 51°19'·88N 03°11'·85E.

BLANKENBERGE

Promenade pier Fl (3) Y 20s, 8m 4M; 51°19'·28N 03°08'·18E.

Lt ho ☆ Fl (2) 8s 30m **20M**; 065°-245°; W twr, B top; 51°18'·75N 03°06'·85E.

Ldg lts 134°, both FR 5/9m 3/10M, R cross (X) topmarks on masts; front 51°18'·70N 03°08'·82E; rear 81m from front.

E pier ☆ FR 12m 11M; 290°-245°; W ○ twr; *Bell (2) 15s*; 51°18'·91N 03°06'·55E.

W pier ☆ FG 14m 11M; intens 065°-290°, unintens 290°-335°; W ○ twr; 51°18'·89N 03°06'·42E.

OBST 4 – OBST 14 are eleven ⚓s Q approx 3ca offshore, marking Spoil Ground between Blankenberge and Oostende.

OOSTENDE

Oostendebank East ⚓ Fl (4) R 20s; 51°17'·35N 02°51'·91E.

Wenduinebank West ⚓ Q (9) 15s; 51°17'·23N 02°52'·76E.

Buitenstroombank ⚓ Q; 51°15'·17N 02°51'·71E.

Binnenstroombank ⚓ Q (3) 10s; 51°14'·47N 02°53'·65E.

Ldg lts 143°: both Iso 4s (triple vert) 36/46m 4M, 068°-218°; X on metal mast, R/W bands. Front, 51°13'·80N 02°55'·89E.

Oostende lt ho ☆ Fl (3) 10s 65m **27M**; obsc 069·5°-071°; Gy twr, 2 sinusoidal Bu bands; 51°14'·18N 02°55'·84E.
E pier ⚡ F R 8m 5M; 51°14'·52N 02°55'·18E; WIP until 2012 is marked by 1 NCM buoy Q; 2 SPM buoys QY; and 3 PHM buoys QR. IPTS, tidal and storm sigs are shown from sig mast 51°14'·25N 02°55'·44E, plus QY when chan closed for ferry.
W pier ⚡ FG 12m 10M, 057°-327°; *Bell 4s*; W ○ twr 51°14'·31N 02°55'·03E.

NIEUWPOORT
Zuidstroombank ≈ Fl R 5s; 51°12'·28N 02°47'·37E.
Weststroombank ≈ Fl (4) R 20s; 51°11'·34N 02°43'·03E.
Wreck 4 ⚓ Q (6) + L Fl 15s; 51°10'·90N 02°405'·03E.
Nieuwpoort Bank ⚓ Q (9) 15s; 51°10'·16N 02°36'·09E.
Oostduinkerke ⚓ Q; 51°09'·15N 02°39'·44E.

Lt ho ☆ Fl (2) R 14s 28m **16M**; R/W twr; 51°09'·27N 02°43'·79E.
E pier ⚡ FR 11m 10M; vis 025°-250° & 307°-347°; W ○ twr; 51°09'·41N 02°43'·08E.
W pier ⚡ FG 10m 9M; vis 025°-250° & 284°-324°; W ○ twr; IPTS from root; 51°09'·35N 02°43'·00E.
⚡ QG 51°08'·65N 02°44'·31E marks the Y-junction where the channel forks stbd for KYCN and port for WSKLM and VVW-N.

WESTDIEP and PASSE DE ZUYDCOOTE
Den Oever wreck 2 ⚓ Q; 51°08'·11N 02°37'·43E.
Wreck 1 ⚓ Q; 51°08'·32N 02°35'·03E (adjacent to ≈ next line).
Wave recorder ≈ Fl (5) Y 20s; 51°08'·25N 02°34'·98E.
Trapegeer ▲ Fl G 10s; 51°08'·41N 02°34'·36E.
E12 ⚓ VQ (6) + L Fl 10s; 51°07'·89N 02°30'·68E.
French waters, for continuity (see also Area 17):
CME ⚓ Fl Q (3) 10s; 51°07'·30N 02°30'·00E.
E11 ⚓ Fl G 4s; 51°06'·90N 02°30'·90E.
E10 ⚓ Fl (2) R 6s; 51°06'·30N 02°30'·47E.
E9 ⚓ Fl (2) G 6s; 51°05'·64N 02°29'·68E.
E8 ⚓ Fl (3) R 12s; 51°05'·16N 02°28'·67E.

1	Delfzijl	**1**															
2	Terschelling	85	**2**														
3	Harlingen	102	19	**3**													
4	Den Oever	110	34	21	**4**												
5	Den Helder	115	39	30	11	**5**											
6	Amsterdam	159	83	81	62	51	**6**										
7	IJmuiden	146	70	68	49	38	13	**7**									
8	Scheveningen	171	95	93	74	63	38	25	**8**								
9	Rotterdam	205	129	127	108	97	72	59	34	**9**							
10	Hook of Holland	185	109	107	88	77	52	39	14	20	**10**						
11	Stellendam	201	125	123	104	93	68	55	30	36	16	**11**					
12	Roompotsluis	233	157	155	136	125	100	87	50	68	48	32	**12**				
13	Vlissingen	228	152	150	131	120	99	86	61	67	47	45	24	**13**			
14	Zeebrugge	239	163	161	142	131	106	93	68	74	54	50	28	16	**14**		
15	Blankenberge	244	168	166	147	136	111	98	73	79	59	55	33	21	5	**15**	
16	Oostende	239	163	161	142	131	110	106	81	87	67	72	40	29	13	9	**16**
17	Nieuwpoort	262	186	184	165	154	129	116	91	97	77	83	51	39	23	18	9	**17**

DISTANCE TABLES
Approx distances in nautical miles are by the most direct route allowing for dangers and TSS.

AREA 14 *North France – Dunkerque to Cap de la Hague*

SELECTED LIGHTS, BUOYS & WAYPOINTS

Positions are referenced to WGS84

OFFSHORE MARKS: W Hinder to Dover Strait
Fairy South ⚓ VQ (6) + L Fl 10s; 51°21'·20N 02°17'·31E.
Fairy West ⚓ VQ (9) 10s 6M; 51°23'·86N 02°09'·30E.
Hinder 1 ⚓ Fl (2) 6s; 51°20'·80N 02°10'·93E.
Bergues ⚓ Fl G 4s 7m 4M; 51°17'·14N 02°18'·63E.
Bergues S ⚓ Q (6) + L Fl 15s; 51°15'·09N 02°19'·42E.
Ruytingen E ⚓ VQ; 51°14'·55N 02°17'·93E.
Ruytingen N ⚓ VQ 4M; 51°13'·16N 02°10'·28E.
Ruytingen SE ⚓ VQ (3) 15s; 51°09'·20N 02°08'·94E.
Ruytingen NW ⚓ Fl G 4s 3M; 51°09'·11N 01°57'·30E.
Ruytingen W ⚓ VQ 4M; 51°06'·93N 01°50'·45E.
Ruytingen SW ⚓ Fl (3) G 12s 3M; 51°05'·00N 01°46'·84E.
Sandettié N ⚓ VQ 6M; 51°18'·47N 02°04'·81E.
Sandettié E ⚓ Fl R 4s 7m 3M; 51°14'·88N 02°02'·65E.

DUNKERQUE TO BOULOGNE
PASSE DE ZUYDCOOTE
E12 ⚓ VQ (6) + L Fl 10s; 51°07'·89N 02°30'·68E (Belgium).
CME ⚓ Q (3) 10s; 51°07'·30N 02°30'·00E.
E11 ⚓ Fl G 4s; 51°06'·90N 02°30'·90E.
E10 ⚓ Fl (2) R 6s; 51°06'·30N 02°30'·47E.
E9 ⚓ Fl (2) G 6s; 51°05'·64N 02°29'·68E.
E8 ⚓ Fl (3) R 12s; 51°05'·16N 02°28'·68E. (E7 does not exist)

PASSE DE L'EST
E6 ⚓ QR; 51°04'·90N 02°27'·00E.
E4 ⚓ Fl R 4s; 51°04'·49N 02°24'·54E.
E1 ⚓ Fl (2) G 6s; 51°04'·06N 02°23'·10E.
E2 ⚓ Fl (2) R 6s; 51°04'·35N 02°22'·31E.
⚓ Q (6) + L Fl 15s; 51°04'·28N 02°21'·73E.

DUNKERQUE PORT EST
E jetty ☆ Fl (2) R 6s 12m 10M; R □, W pylon; 51°03'·59N 02°21'·20E.
W jetty ☆ Fl (2) G 6s 35m 11M; W twr, brown top; 51°03'·63N 02°20'·95E.
Ldg lts 137·5°, front Q7m11M 51°02'·98N 02°22'·05E, rear, Q10m11M, 114m from front, both W cols, R tops, synched.
Inner W jetty ⚓ Q 11m 9M; 51°03'·33N 02°21'·43E.
Dunkerque lt ho ☆ Fl (2) 10s 59m **26M**; 51°02'·93N 02°21'·86E.

DUNKERQUE INTERMEDIATE CHANNEL
DW30 ⚓ QR; 51°04'·14N 02°20'·16E.
DW29 ⚓ QG; 51°03'·83N 02°20'·25E.
DW16 ⚓ Fl (2) R 6s; 51°03'·31N 02°08'·98E.
DKB ⚓ VQ (9) 10s; 51°02'·95N 02°09'·26E.

DW12 ⚓ Fl (3) R 12s; 51°03'·19N 02°05'·57E.
DW11 ⚓ Fl (3) G 12s; 51°02'·88N 02°05'·77E. (DW10-7 omitted)

GRAVELINES
W jetty ☆ Fl (2) WG 6s 9m W8M, G6M; 317°-W-327°-G-085°-W-244°; Y ○ twr, G top; 51°00'·94N 02°05'·49E.

PASSE DE L'OUEST
DW6 ⚓ VQ R; 51°02'·60N 02°01'·01E.
DW5 ⚓ QG; 51°02'·20N 02°00'·92E.
DKA ⚓ L Fl 10s; 51°02'·55N 01°56'·96E.
RCE (Ridens de Calais East) ⚓ Iso G 4s; 51°02'·44N 01°53'·24E.
Dyck ⚓ Fl 3s; *Racon B*; 51°02'·99N 01°51'·79E.
RCA (Ridens de Calais Approach) ⚓ Q; 51°00'·90N 01°48'·72E.

CALAIS
E jetty ☆ Fl (2) R 6s 12m **17M**; (in fog two Fl (2) 6s (vert) on request); Gy twr, R top; *Horn (2) 40s;* 50°58'·39N 01°50'·45E.
W jetty ⚓ Iso G 3s 12m 9M; (in fog Fl 5s on request); W twr, G top; *Bell 5s;* 50°58'·24N 01°50'·40E.
Calais ☆ Fl (4) 15s 59m **22M**; vis 073°-260°; W 8-sided twr, B top; 50°57'·68N 01°51'·21E (440m E of marina entry gate).

CALAIS, WESTERN APPROACH
Calais Approach ⚓ VQ (9) 10s 8m 8M; 50°58'·89N 01°45'·11E.
CA2 ⚓ Fl R 4s; 50°58'·15N 01°45'·68E.
CA4 ⚓ Fl (2)R 6s; 50°58'·38N 01°48'·65E.
CA6 ⚓ Fl (3) R 12s; 50°58'·63N 01°49'·92E.
Les Quénocs ⚓ VQ; 50°56'·85N 01°41'·12E.
CA1 ⚓ Fl G 4s; 50°57'·64N 01°46'·14E (0·5M NNW of Sangatte). Sangatte ⚓ Oc WG 4s 13m W8M, G5M; 065°-G-089°-W-152°-G-245°; W pylon, B top; 50°57'·19N 01°46'·50E.
Abbeville wreck ⚓ VQ (9) 10s; 50°56'·08N 01°37'·58E.
Cap Gris-Nez ☆ Fl 5s 72m **29M**; 005°-232°; W twr, B top; *Horn 60s;* 50°52'·09N 01°34'·96E.

OFFSHORE MARKS: DOVER STRAIT TSS, French side
Colbart N ⚓ Q 6M; 50°57'·46N 01°23'·29E.
Colbart SW ⚓ VQ (6) + L Fl 10s 8m; 50°48'·87N 01°16'·32E.
ZC2 (Zone Côtière) ⚓ Fl (2+1) Y 15s 5M; 50°53'·54N 01°30'·89E.
ZC1 ⚓ Fl (4) Y 15s 4MN; 50°44'·99N 01°27'·21E.
Ridens SE ⚓ VQ (3) 5s 6M; 50°43'·48N 01°18'·87E.
Bassurelle ⚓ Fl (4) R 15s 6M; *Racon B, 5-8M;* 50°32'·74N 00°57'·69E.
Vergoyer N ⚓ VQ 5M; *Racon C, 5-8M;* 50°39'·67N 01°22'·21E; (temp ext)
Vergoyer NW ⚓ Fl (2) G 6s 4M; 50°37'·16N 01°17'·85E.
Vergoyer E ⚓ VQ (3) 5s 6M; 50°35'·76N 01°19'·70E.
Vergoyer W ⚓ Fl G 4s 4M; 50°34'·66N 01°13'·57E.
Vergoyer SW ⚓ VQ (9) 10s 6M; 50°27'·01N 01°00'·03E.

BOULOGNE TO DIEPPE

BOULOGNE
Bassure de Baas ⚓ VQ; 50°48'·53N 01°33'·05E.
Approches Boulogne ⚓ VQ (6) + L Fl 10s 8m 6M; 50°45'·31N 01°31'·07E.
Digue N (detached) ⚓ Fl (2) R 6s 10m 7M; 50°44'·71N 01°34'·18E.
Digue S (Carnot) ☆ Fl (2+1) 15s 25m **19M**; W twr, G top; 50°44'·44N 01°34'·05E.

Clearing brg 122·4° : Front, FG in a neon ▽ 4m 5M; 50°43'·71N 01°35'·66E. Rear, FR 44m 11M; intens 113°-133°; 560m from front.
Inner NE jetty ⚓ FR 11m 7M; 50°43'·91N 01°35'·24E. Inner SW jetty ⚓ FG 17m 5M; W col, G top; *Horn 30s;* 50°43'·90N 01°35'·11E.
Cap d'Alprech ☆ Fl (3) 15s 62m **23M**; W twr, B top; 50°41'·91N 01°33'·75E, 2·5M S of hbr ent.

LE TOUQUET/ÉTAPLES
Pointe de Lornel ⚓ VQ (9) 10s 6m 3M; 50°33'·24N 01°35'·12E.
Mérida wreck ⚓ 50°32'·85N 01°33'·44E.
Camiers lt ho ⚓ Oc (2) WRG 6s 17m W10M, R/G7M; 015°-G-090°-W-105°-R-141°; R pylon; 50°32'·86N 01°36'·28E.
Canche Est groyne ⚓ Fl R 4s 8m; 50°32'·57N 01°35'·66E.
Le Touquet ☆ Fl (2) 10s 54m **25M**; Or twr, brown band, W&G top; 50°31'·43N 01°35'·52E.

Pointe du Haut-Blanc ☆ Fl 5s 44m **23M**; W twr, R bands, G top; 50°23'·90N 01°33'·67E (Berck).

BAIE DE LA SOMME
ATSO ⚓ Mo (A) 12s; 50°14'·00N 01°28'·08E (shifts frequently).
Pte du Hourdel ⚓ Oc (3) WG 12s 19m, W12M, G9M; 053°-W-248°-G-323°; tidal sigs; *Horn (3) 30s;* W twr, G top; 50°12'·90N 01°33'·98E.
Cayeux-sur-Mer ☆ Fl R 5s 32m **22M**; W twr, R top; 50°11'·65N 01°30'·72E.
Le Crotoy ⚓ Oc (2) R 6s 19m 8M; 285°-135°; W pylon; 50°12'·91N 01°37'·40E. Marina ⚓ Fl R & Fl G 2s 4m 2M; 50°12'·98N 01°38'·20E.

ST VALÉRY-SUR-SOMME
Trng wall head, ⚓ Fl G 2.5s 2m 1M; 50°12'·25N 01°35'·85E.
Embankment head ⚓ Iso G 4s 9m 9M; 347°-222°; W pylon, G top; 50°12'·25N 01°36'·02E.
La Ferté môle ⚓ Fl R 4s 9m 9M; 000°-250°; W pylon, R top; 50°11'·18N 01°38'·14E (ent to marina inlet).

LE TRÉPORT
Ault ☆ Oc (3) WR 12s 95m **W15M**, R11M; 040°-W-175°-R-220°; W twr, R top; 50°06'·28N 01°27'·23E (4M NE of Le Tréport).
W jetty ☆ Fl (2) G 10s 15m **20M**; W twr, G top; *Horn (2) 30s;* 50°03'·88N 01°22'·14E.

DIEPPE
W jetty ⚓ Iso G 4s 11m 8M; W twr, G top; *Horn 30s;* 49°56'·27N 01°04'·97E.
Quai de la Marne ⚓ QR 12m 3M; 49°55'·93N 01°05'·20E, E quay.
Pointe d'Ailly ☆ Fl (3) 20s 95m **31M**; W □ twr, G top; *Horn (3) 60s;* 49°54'·96N 00°57'·50E.

DIEPPE TO LE HAVRE

SAINT VALÉRY-EN-CAUX
W jetty ⚓ Fl (2) G 6s 13m 11M; W twr, G top; 49°52'·40N 00°42'·54E. Paluel power station ⚓ Q; 49°52'·22N 00°38'·03E.

FÉCAMP
N jetty ☆ Fl (2) 10s 15m **16M**; Gy twr, R top; 49°45'·94N 00°21'·80E.

PORT D'ANTIFER
Cap d'Antifer ☆ Fl 20s 128m **29M**; 021°-222°; Gy 8-sided twr, G top, on 90m cliffs; 49°41'·01N 00°09'·93E.

A17 ⚓ Iso G 4s; 49°41'·53N 00°01·75E.

A18 ⚓ QR; 49°42'·02N 00°02'·18E. Cross the chan W of A17/18.

Ldg lts 127·5°, both Dir Oc 4s 113/135m **22M**; 127°-128°; by day F **33M** 126·5°-128·5° occas. **Front** ☆, 49°38'·32N 00°09'·12E.

LE HAVRE, APPROACH CHANNEL

Cap de la Hève ☆ Fl 5s 123m **24M**; 225°-196°; W 8-sided twr, R top; 49°30'·74N 00°04'·16E.

LHA ⌑ Mo (A) 12s 10m 6M; R&W; *Racon, 8-10M* (a series of 8 dots, or 8 groups of dots; distance between each dot or group represents 0·3M); 49°31'·38N 00°09'·86W. Reserve lt Mo (A).

Ldg lts 106·8°, both Dir F 36/78m **25M** (H24); intens 106°-108°; Gy twrs, G tops. Front, 49°28'·91N 00°06'·50E; rear, 0·73M from front.

LH3 ⚓ QG; 49°30'·84N 00°04'·02W. (LH1 & 2 buoys do not exist).

LH4 ⚓ QR; 49°31'·11N 00°03'·90W.

FVs and yachts <19.8m LOA may cross the appr chan west of LH 7/8 buoys, keeping clear of all other shipping, even if under sail.

LH7 ⚓ Iso G 4s; 49°30'·25N 00000'·82W.

LH8 ⚓ Fl (2) R 6s; 49°30'·44N 00°00'·70W.

Note the W-E longitude change. (LH9 buoy does not exist).

LH13 ⚓ Fl G 4s; 49°29'·32N 00°03'·62E (Ent to Port 2000).

LH14 ⚓ Fl R 4s; 49°29'·67N 00°03'·43E; 1m shoal depth close W.

LH16 ⚓ Fl (2) R 6s; 49°29'·45N 00°04'·28E.

LH 2000 ⚓ VQ (9) 10s; 49°29'·14N 00°04'·78E (Ent to Port 2000).

LE HAVRE

Digue N ☆ Fl R 5s 15m **21M**; IPTS; W ○ twr, R top; *Horn 15s;* 49°29'·19N 00°05'·44E.

Digue S ✦ VQ (3) G 2s 15m 11M; W twr, G top; 49°29'·05N 00°05'·38E.

Marina ent, W spur ✦ Fl (2) R 6s 3M; 49°29'·22N 00°05'·53E.

THE SEINE ESTUARY UP TO HONFLEUR

CHENAL DE ROUEN

Nord du Mouillage ⚓ Fl (4) Y 15s; 49°28'·80N 00°00'·22E.

Rade de la Carosse ⚓ Q (9) 15s; 49°28'·26N 00°00'·69E.

No. 2 ⚓ QR; *Racon T;* 49°27'·40N 00°01'·35E.

No. 4 ⚓ Fl R 2·5s; 49°26'·97N 00°02'·60E. Yachts keep N of chan.

Amfard SW ⚓ Fl (3) R 12s; 49°26'·30N 00°04'·82E.

No. 10 ⚓ QR; 49°26'·10N 00°06'·39E.

Digue du Ratier ⚓ VQ 10m 4M; 49°25'·94N 00°06'·59E.

Falaise des Fonds ✦ Fl(3) WRG 12s 15m, **W17M**, R/G13M; 040°-G-080°-R-084°-G-100°- W-109°-R-162°-G-260°; W twr, G top; 49°25'·47N 00°12'·85E.

No. 20 ⚓ QR; 49°25'·85N 00°13'·71E. (Cross here to Honfleur)

HONFLEUR

Digue Ouest ✦ QG 10m 6M; 49°25'·67N 00°13'·83E.

Digue Est ✦ Q 9m 8M; *Horn (5) 40s;* 49°25'·67N 00°13'·95E.

Inner E jetty, Oc (2) R 6s 12m 6M; W twr, R top; 49°25'·38N 00°14'·12E.

No. 22 ⚓ QR; 49°25'·85N 00°15'·38E.

TROUVILLE TO COURSEULLES

CHENAL DE ROUEN TO DEAUVILLE and TROUVILLE

Ratelets ⚓ Q (9) 15s; 49°25'·29N 00°01'·71E.

Semoy ⚓ VQ (3) 5s; 49°24'·15N 00°02'·35E, close to 148° ldg line.

Trouville SW ⚓ VQ (9) 10s; 49°22'·54N 00°02'·56E.

DEAUVILLE and TROUVILLE

Ldg lts 148°, both Oc R 4s 11/17m 12/10M: Front, East inner jetty (*estacade*); 330°-150°; W twr, R top; 49°22'·03N 00°04'·48E.

Rear, Pte de la Cahotte; synch; 120°-170°; 49°21'·93N 00°04'·58E.

W trng wall ✦ Fl WG 4s 10m W9M, G6M; 005°-W-176°-G-005°; B pylon, G top; 49°22'·37N 00°04'·11E. Also 4 unlit SHM bcns.

E trng wall ✦ Fl (4) WR 12s 8m W7M, R4M; 131°-W-175°-R-131°; W pylon, R top; 49°22'·22N 00°04'·33E. Also 3 unlit PHM bcns.

W outer bkwtr ✦ Iso G 4s 9m 5M; 49°22'·11N 00°04'·33E.

West inner jetty (*estacade*) ✦ QG 11m 9M; 49°22'·03N 00°04'·43E.

DIVES-SUR-MER *Note the E-W longitude change.*

Dir lt 159·5°, Oc (2+1) WRG 12s 6m, W12M, R/G9M; 125°-G-157°-W-162°-R-194°; brown hut; 49°17'·80N 00°05'·22W.

DI ⚓ L Fl 10s; 49°19'·18N 00°05'·85W.

No. 1 ⚐ 49°18'·50N 00°05'·67W. Buoys are moved to mark chan.

No. 2 ⚑ 49°18'·51N 00°05'·56W.

No. 3 ⚓ QG 7m 4M; W pylon, G top; 49°18'·30N 00°05'·50W.

No. 5 ⚓ Fl G 4s 8m 4M; W pylon, G top; 49°18'·09N 00°05'·50W.

Bcns 3 & 5, if damaged, may be temporarily replaced by buoys.

No. 7 ⚓ Fl G 4s; 49°17'·65N 00°05'·31W.

OUISTREHAM and CAEN

Merville ⚓ VQ; 49°19'·65N 00°13'·39W; spoil ground buoy.

Ouistreham ⚓ VQ (3) 5s; wreck buoy; 49°20'·42N 00°14'·81W.

Ldg lts 185°, both Dir Oc (3+1) R 12s 10/30m **17M**; intens 183·5°-186·5°, synch. **Front** ☆, E jetty, W mast, R top, 49°16'·99N 00°14'·81W. **Rear** ☆, 610m from front, tripod, R top.

No. 1 ⚓ QG; 49°19'·19N 00°14'·67W.

No. 2 ⚓ QR; 49°19'·17N 00°14'·43W.

Barnabé ✦ QG 7m 5M; W pylon, G top; 49°18'·02N 00°14'·76W.

St-Médard ✦ QR 7m 5M; 49°18'·02N 00°14'·62W.

Riva ✦ Fl G 4s 9m 3M; W pylon, G top; 49°17'·73N 00°14'·79W.

Quilbé ✦ Fl R 4s 9m 3M; W pylon, R top; 49°17'·72N 00°14'·67W.

Ouistreham lt ho ☆ Oc WR 4s 37m **W17M**, R13M; 115°-R-151°-W-115°; W twr, R top; 49°16'·79N 00°14'·87W.

COURSEULLES-SUR-MER

Courseulles ⚓ Iso 4s; 49°21'·28N 00°27'·68W.

W jetty ✦ Iso WG 4s 7m; W9M, G6M; 135°-W-235°-G-135°; brown pylon on dolphin, G top; 49°20'·41N 00°27'·37W.

E jetty ✦ Oc (2) R 6s 9m 7M; 49°20'·26N 00°27'·39W.

COURSEULLES TO ST VAAST

Ver ☆ Fl (3)15s 42m **26M**; obsc'd by cliffs of St Aubin when brg >275°; conspic lt ho, W twr, Gy top; 49°20'·41N 00°31'·13W.

ARROMANCHES

Ent buoys: ⚐ 49°21'·35N 00°37'·26W; ⚑ 49°21'·25N 00°37'·30W.

Bombardons ⚓ wreck buoys; 49°21'·66N 00°38'·97W.

PORT-EN-BESSIN

Ldg lts 204°, both Oc (3) 12s 25/42m 10/11M; synch. Front, 069°-339°, W pylon, G top; 49°20'·96N 00°45'·53W. Rear; 114°-294°, W and Gy ho; 93m from front.
E mole ☆ Oc R 4s 14m 7M, R pylon; 49°21'·12N 00°45'·38W.
W mole ☆ Fl WG 4s 14m, W10M, G7M; G065°-114·5°, W114·5°-065°; G pylon; 49°21'·17N 00°45'·43W.

COASTAL MARKS

Omaha Beach, 1M off : ⌀ 49°22'·66N 00°50'·28W; ⌀ 49°23'·17N 00°51'·93W; ⌀ 49°23'·66N 00°53'·74W.
Broadsword ⌀ Q (3) 10s, wreck buoy; 49°25'·34N 00°52'·96W.
Est du Cardonnet ⌀ VQ (3) 5s; 49°26'·83N 01°01'·10W.

GRANDCAMP

Les Roches de Grandcamp: No. 1 ⌀ 49°24'·72N 01°01'·75W; No. 3 ⌀ 49°24'·92N 01°03'·70W; No. 5 ⌀ 49°24'·78N 01°04'·98W.
Ldg lts 146°, both Dir Q 9/12m **15M**, 144·5°-147·5°. **Front** ☆, 49°23'·42N 01°02'·90W. **Rear** ☆,102m from front.
Jetée Est ☆ Oc (2) R 6s 9m 9M; *Horn Mo(N) 30s;* 49°23'·53N 01°02'·96W.
Jetée Ouest ☆ Fl G 4s 9m 6M; 49°23'·47N 01°02'·96W.

ISIGNY-SUR-MER

IS, small B/Y ⌀, no topmark (⌀ on AC 2135); 49°24'·28N 01°06'·37W.
Ldg lts 172·5°, both Dir Oc (2+1) 12s 7/19m **18M**; intens 170·5°-174·5°, synch. **Front** , W mast; 49°19'·55N 01°06'·78W. **Rear** , W pylon, B top; 625m from front.
Training wall heads ⌀ 49°21'·42N 01°07'·24W; ⌀ 49°21'·40N 01°07'·14W, off Pte du Grouin.

CARENTAN

C-I ⌀ Iso 4s; 49°25'·44N 01°07'·08W; 210°/1·76M to Nos 1 & 2 buoys.
No. 1 ⌀ Fl G 2·5s; 49°23'·93N 01°08'·52W.
No. 2 ⌀ Fl R 2·5s; 49°23'·88N 01°08'·37W.
Trng wall ⌀ Fl (4) G 15s; G △ on G bcn;49°21'·96N 01°09'·95W.
Trng wall ⌀ Fl (4) R 15s; R ☐ on R bcn;49°21'·93N 01°09'·878W.
Ldg lts 209·5°. **Front** ☆ Dir Oc (3) R 12s 6m **18M**; intens 208·2°-210·7°; W mast, R top; 49°20'·47N 01°11'·17W. Rear, Dir Oc (3) 12s 14m 10M; vis 120°-005°; W gantry, G top; 723m from front.

ÎLES SAINT-MARCOUF

Iles St-Marcouf ☆ VQ (3) 5s 18m 8M; ☐ Gy twr, G top; 49°29'·86N 01°08'·81W.
Ouest-Saint-Marcouf ⌀ Q (9) 15s; 49°29'·73N 01°11'·97W.
Saint Floxel ⌀ 49°30'·64N 01°13'·94W.
Quineville ⌀ Q (9) 10s, wreck buoy; 49°31'·79N 01°12'·38W.

ST VAAST TO POINTE DE BARFLEUR

ST VAAST-LA-HOUGUE

Ldg lts 267°: Front, La Hougue Oc 4s 9m 10M; W pylon, G top; 49°34'·25N 01°16'·37W. Rear, Morsalines Oc (4) WRG 12s 90m, W11M, R/G8M; 171°-W-316°-G-321°-R-342°-W-355°; W 8-sided twr, G top; 49°34'·16N 01°19'·10W, 1·8M from front.
Le Manquet ⌀ 49°34'·26N 01°15'·56W.
Le Bout du Roc ⌀ 49°34'·68N 01°15'·27W.
La Dent ⌀ 49°34'·57N 01°14'·20W.
Le Gavendest ⌀ Q (6) + L Fl 15s; 49°34'·36N 01°13'·89W.
Jetty ☆ Dir Oc(2) WRG 6s 12m W10M, R/G7M; 219°-R-237°-

G-310°-W-350°-R-040°; W 8-sided twr, R top; *Siren Mo(N) 30s;* 49°35'·17N 01°15'·41W.
Pte de Saire ☆ Oc (2+1) 10s 11m 10M; squat W twr, G top; 49°36'·36N 01°13'·78W.

BARFLEUR

Ldg lts 219·5°, both Oc (3) 12s 7/13m 10M; synch. Front, W ☐ twr;49°40'·18N 01°15'·61W. Rear, 085°-355°; Gy and W ☐ twr, G top; 288m from front.
La Grotte ⌀ 49°41'·06N 01°14'·86W.
Roche-à-l'Anglais ⌀ 49°40'·78N 01°14'·93W.
La Vimberge ⌀ 49°40'·54N 01°15'·25W.
W jetty ☆ Fl G 4s 8m 6M; 49°40'·32N 01°15'·57W.
E jetty ☆ Oc R 4s 5m 6M; 49°40'·31N 01°15'·47W.
La Jamette ⌀ 49°41'·87N 01°15'·59W.
Pte de Barfleur ☆ Fl (2) 10s 72m **29M**; obsc when brg less than 088°; Gy twr, B top; *Horn (2) 60s;* 49°41'·78N 01°15'·96W.

POINTE DE BARFLEUR TO CAP DE LA HAGUE

Les Équets ⌀ Q 8m 3M; 49°43'·62N 01°18'·36W.
Basse du Rénier ⌀ VQ 8m 4M; 49°44'·84N 01°22'·09W.
Les Trois Pierres ⌀ 49°42'·90N 01°21'·80W.
Anse de Vicq, 158° ldg lts; both Iso R 4s 8/14m 6M; front 49°42'·20N 01°23'·95W.
La Pierre Noire ⌀ Q (9) 15s 8m 4M;49°43'·54N 01°29'·07W.

PORT DU LÉVI

Cap Lévi ☆ Fl R 5s 36m **22M**; Gy ☐ twr; 49°41'·75N 01°28'·38W.
Port Lévi ☆ Oc (2) WRG 6s 7m 7M; 055°-G-083°-W-105°-R-163°; W & Gy hut, W lantern; 49°41'·24N 01°28'·34W.

PORT DU BECQUET

Ldg lts 186·5°, both intens 183°-190°; synch. Front, Oc (2+1) 12s 8m 10M; W 8-sided twr; 49°39'·22N 01°32'·85W. Rear, Oc (2+1) R 12s 13m 7M. W 8-sided twr, R top; 49m from front.

CHERBOURG, EASTERN ENTRANCES

Passe Collignon ☆ Fl (2) R 6s 5m 4M; 49°39'·59N 01°34'·24W.
Passe de l'Est, Jetée des Flamands ldg lts 189°, both Q 9/16m 13M. Front, 49°39'·33N 01°35'·94W . Rear, 516m from front.
Roches du Nord-Ouest ⌀ Fl R 2·5s; 49°40'·64N 01°35'·28W.
La Truite ⌀ Fl (4) R 15s; 49°40'·33N 01°35'·49W.
Fort d'Île Pelée ☆ Oc (2) WR 6s 19m; W10M, R7M; 055°-W-120°-R-055°; W & R pedestal; 49°40'·21N 01°35'·08W.
Fort de l'Est ☆ 49°40'·28N 01°35'·92W, Iso G 4s 19m 9M.
Fort Central ☆ VQ (6) + L Fl 10s 5m 4M; 322°-032°; 49°40'·40N 01°37'·04W.

CHERBOURG, PASSE DE L'OUEST

CH1 ⌀ L Fl 10s 8m 4M; 49°43'·24N 01°42'·09W.
Passe de l'Ouest outer ldg lts 141·2°. **Front,** Dir Q (2 horiz, 63m apart) 5m **17M**; intens 137·3°-143·3° & 139·2°-145·2°; W △ on bcn; 49°39'·55N 01°37'·95W. **Rear,** Dir Q 35m **19M**; intens 140°-142·5°; W △ on Gy pylon.
Fort de l'Ouest ☆ Fl (3) WR 15s 19m **W24M, R20M**; 122°-W-355°-R-122°; Gy twr, R top; 49°40'·45N 01°38'·87W.
Fort de l'Ouest ⌀ Fl R 4s; 49°40'·39N 01°38'·89W.
⌀ Q (6) + L Fl 15s; 49°40'·34N 01°38'·65W.

Digue de Querqueville ⚓ Fl (4) G 15s 8m 4M; W col, G top; 49°40'·30N 01°39'·80W.

Inner ldg lts 124·3°; both intens 114·3°-134·3°: Front, Digue du Homet head, FG 10m 8M; 49°39'·48N 01°36'·96W. Rear, Dir Iso G 4s 16m 13M; W col, B bands, 397m from front.

La Ténarde ⚓ VQ 8m 4M; 49°39'·74N 01°37'·75W.

CHERBOURG, PETITE RADE and MARINA

Entrance, W side, Digue du Homet ⚓ FG 10m 8M; intens 114·3°-134·3°; W pylon, G top; 49°39'·48N 01°36'·96W.

E side, ⚓ VQ R, off Jetée des Flamands; 49°39'·44N 01°36'·60W.

Marina ent, E side, ⚓ Fl (3) R 12s 6m 6M; W col, R lantern; 49°38'·91N 01°37'·08W.

W mole ⚓ Fl (3) G 12s 7m 6M; G pylon; 49°38'·87N 01°37'·15W.

E quay ⚓ Fl (4) R 15s 3m 3M; R bcn; 49°38'·79N 01°37'·12W.

Wavescreen pontoon, N end ⚓ Fl (4) G 15s 4m 2M; W post, G top.

Detached ♥ pontoon, F Vi; 49°38'·77N 01°37'·22W.

CHERBOURG TO CAP DE LA HAGUE

Raz de Bannes ⚓ 49°41'·32N 01°44'·53W.

Omonville Dir lt 257°: Iso WRG 4s13m; W10M, R/G7M; 180°-G-252°-W-262°-R-287°; W pylon, G top; 49°42'·24N 01°50'·15W.

L'Étonnard ⚓ 49°42'·33N 01°49'·84W.

Basse Bréfort ⚓ VQ 8m 4M; 49°43'·90N 01°51'·15W.

Jobourg Nuclear plant chimney, R lts; 49°40'·80N 01°52'·91W.

La Plate ⚓ Fl (2+1) WR 10s 11m; W9M, R6M; 115°-W-272°-R-115°; Y 8-sided twr, with B top; 49°43'·97N 01°55'·74W.

Cap de la Hague (Gros du Raz) ☆ Fl 5s 48m 23M; Gy twr, W top; *Horn 30s*; 49°43'·31N 01° 57'·26W.

La Foraine ⚓ VQ (9) 10s, 12m 6M; 49°42'·90N 01°58'·31W.

		1	2	3	4	5	6	7	8	9	10	11	12	13	14	15	16	17	18	19
1.	Dunkerque-Est	**1**																		
2.	Calais	28	**2**																	
3.	Boulogne	49	21	**3**																
4.	St Valéry-sur-Somme	86	58	37	**4**															
5.	Le Tréport	90	62	41	16	**5**														
6.	Dieppe	100	74	53	30	15	**6**													
7.	St Valéry-en-Caux	109	81	62	42	28	16	**7**												
8.	Fécamp	121	93	76	57	44	32	17	**8**											
9.	Le Havre	148	121	103	84	71	61	47	27	**9**										
10.	Honfleur	157	129	108	92	80	67	51	35	13	**10**									
11.	Deauville/Trouville	152	125	108	91	79	61	53	34	9	13	**11**								
12.	Dives-sur-Mer	155	129	110	94	83	66	55	38	16	19	9	**12**							
13.	Ouistreham	160	138	115	97	85	73	59	41	20	24	15	9	**13**						
14.	Courseulles	162	136	115	100	87	75	60	44	24	30	23	18	14	**14**					
15.	Grandcamp	177	150	130	118	104	94	80	62	47	52	45	41	37	27	**15**				
16.	Carentan	187	159	139	126	112	100	85	69	56	61	55	50	45	36	13	**16**			
17.	St Vaast	179	151	131	120	107	96	80	65	54	50	46	35			16	20	**17**		
18.	Barfleur	175	147	128	118	105	94	78	64	56	62	57	53	48	39	21	26	10	**18**	
19.	Cherbourg	188	160	142	131	120	108	94	80	71	77	73	69	66	57	40	44	28	21	**19**

DISTANCE TABLES

Approx distances in nautical miles are by the most direct route allowing for dangers and TSS.

AREA 15 *N Central France (Cap de la Hague to St Quay) & Channel Is*

SELECTED LIGHTS, BUOYS & WAYPOINTS

Positions are referenced to WGS84

CAP DE LA HAGUE TO ST MALO

GOURY

La Foraine ⚓ VQ (9) 10s 12m 6M; 49°42'·90 N 01°58'·32W.

Ldg lts 065·2°: Front, QR 5m 7M; R □ in W □ on pier, 49°42'·89N 01°56'·70W. Rear, 116m from front, Q 11m 7M; intens 056·2°-074·2°; W pylon on hut.

Hervieu ⚓ 49°42'·77N 01°56'·92W.

DIELETTE

W bkwtr Dir lt 140°, Iso WRG 4s 12m W10M, R/G7M; 070°-G-135°-W-145°-R-180°; W twr, G top ;49°33'·18N 01°51'·81W.

E bkwtr ⚓ Fl R 4s 6m 2M; 49°33'·21N 01°51'·78W.

Inner N jetty, Fl (2) R 6s. Inner S jetty, Fl (2) G 6s; both 6m 1M.

Banc des Dious ⚓ Q (9) 15s; 49°32'·58N 01°54'·02W.

CARTERET

Cap de Carteret ☆ Fl (2+1) 15s 81m **26M**; Gy twr, G top; 49°22'·40N 01°48'·41W.

W bkwtr ⚓ Oc R 4s 7m 7M; W post, R top; 49°22'·07N 01°47'·32W.

E training wall ⚓ Fl G 2·5s 4m 2M; W post, G top; 49°22'·17N 01°47'·30W.

Channel bend ⚓ Fl (2) R 6s 5m 1M; R pylon; 49°22'·58N 01°47'·23W. Inside the bend: ⚓ Fl (2) G 6s 5m 1M; G pylon; 49°22'·55N 01°47'·20W.

Marina entry sill: ⚓ Fl (3) R 12s and Fl (3) G 12s; R & G pylons.

PORTBAIL

PB ⚓ 49°18'·37N 01°44'·75W.

Ldg lts 042°: Front, Q 14m 10M; W pylon, R top; 49°19'·75N 01°42'·50W. Rear, 870m from front, Oc 4s 20m 10M; stubby ch spire.

⚓ 49°19'·32N 01°43'·16W.

▲ 49°19'·20N 01°43'·00W.

Training wall head ⚓ Q (2) R 5s 5m 1M; W mast, R top; 49°19'·43N 01°42'·99W.

REGNÉVILLE

La Catheue ⚓ Q (6) + L Fl 15s, 48°57'·67N 01°42'·23W.

Le Ronquet ⚓ Fl(2)WR 6s, W6M, R4M; 100°-R-293°-W-100°; 49°00'·11N 01°38'·07W.

Pte d'Agon ⚓ Oc (2) WR 6s 12m, W10M, R7M; 063°-R-110°-W-063°; W twr, R top, W dwelling; 49°00'·18N 01°34'·63W.

Dir lt 028°, Oc WRG 4s 9m, W12M, R/G9M; 024°-G-027°-W-029°-R-033°; house; 49°00'·63N 01°33'·36W.

PASSAGE DE LA DÉROUTE

Les Trois-Grunes ↙ Q (9) 15s, 49°21'·84N 01°55'·21W.
Écrévière ↙ Q (6) + L Fl 15s; *Bell;* 49°15'·27N 01°52'·16W.
Basse Jourdan ↙ Q (3) 10s; 49°06'·85N 01°43'·96W.
Le Boeuf ⚓ 49°06'·56N 01°47'·17W.
Les Boeuftins ↙ 49°07'·03N 01°45'·96W.
La Basse du Sénéquet ↙ 49°05'·96N 01°41'·11W.
Le Sénéquet ≼ Fl (3) WR 12s 18m W13M, R10M; 083·5°-R-116·5°-W-083·5°; W twr; 49°05'·48N 01°39'·73W.
Les Nattes ↙ 49°03'·46N 01°41'·81W.
International F ↙ 49°02'·16N 01°42'·98W.
International E ↙ 49°02'·08N 01°47'·21W.
Basse le Marié ↙ Q (9) 15s; 49°01'·79N 01°48'·57W.
NE Minquiers ↙ VQ (3) 5s; *Bell;* 49°00'·85N 01°55'·30W.
Les Ardentes ↙ Q (3) 10s; 48°57'·89N 01°51'·53W.
SE Minquiers ↙ Q (3) 10s; *Bell;* 48°53'·42N 02°00'·09W.
S Minquiers ↙ Q (6) + L Fl 15s; 48°53'·09N 02°10'·10W.

ÎLES CHAUSEY

La Pointue ↙ 48°54'·44N 01°50'·92W.
L'Enseigne, W twr, B top; 48°53'·67N 01°50'·37W.
L'Etat, BW ☐, 48°54'·67N 01°46'·21W.
Anvers wreck ↙ 48°53'·91N 01°41'·07W.
Le Founet ↳ Q (3) 10s; 48°53'·25N 01°42'·34W.
Le Pignon ↙ Fl (2) WR 6s 10m, W9M, R6M; 005°-R- 150°-W-005°; B twr, W band; 48°53'·49N 01°43'·36 W.
La Haute Foraine ⚓ 48°52'·89N 01°43'·66W.

Grande Île ☆ Fl 5s 39m **23M**; Gy ☐ twr, G top; *Horn 30s;* 48°52'·17N 01°49'·34W.
Channel ◣ Fl G 2s; 48°52'·07N 01°49'·08W.
La Crabière Est ↓ Dir Oc(3)WRG 12s 5m, W9M, R/G6M;079°-W-291°-G-329°-W-335°-R-079°; B beacon, Y top; 48°52'·46N 01°49'·39W.
La Cancalaise ↙ 48°51'·90N 01°51'·11W.

GRANVILLE

Le Videcoq ↙ VQ (9) 10s; 48°49'·66N 01°42'·06W.
La Fourchie ⚓ 48°50'·15N 01°37'·00W.
Pointe du Roc ☆ Fl (4) 15s 49m **23M**; 48°50'·06N 01°36'·78W.
Le Loup ↳ Fl (2) 6s 8m 11M; 48°49'·57N 01°36'·24W.
Avant Port, E jetty ≼ Fl G 2·5s 11m 4M; 48°49'·93N 01°36'·19W.
W jetty ≼ Fl R 2·5s 12m 4M; 48°49'·86N 01°36'·23W.
Marina S bkwtr ≼ Fl (2) R 6s 12m 5M; W post, R top; *Horn (2) 40s;* 48°49'·89N 01°35'·90W.
N bkwtr ≼ Fl (2) G 6s 4m 5M; 48°49'·93N 01°35'·90W.
Sill, E & W sides: Oc (2) G 6s & Oc (2) R 6s, G & R topped pylons.

CANCALE

La Fille ↙ 48°44'·16N 01°48'·46W.
Pierre-de-Herpin ☆ Oc (2) 6s 20m 13M; W twr, B top and base; 48°43'·77N 01°48'·92W.
Ruet ↙ *Bell;* 48°43'·44N 01°50'·11W.
Grande Bunouze ↙ 48°43'·17N 01°50'·95W.
Barbe Brûlée ↙ 48°42'·11N 01°50'·57W.
Jetty hd ≼ Oc (3) G 12s 9m 3M; W pylon B top; 48°40'·10N 01°51'·11W.

ST MALO AND RIVER RANCE

CHENAL DE LA BIGNE

Basse Rochefort (aka Basse aux Chiens) ↙ 48°42'·69N 01°57'·31W.
La Petite Bigne ↓ 48°41'·66N 01°58'·72W.
La Crolante ⌂; 48°41'·01N 01°59'·51W, off Pte de la Varde.

Les Létruns ▲; *Bell;* 48°40'·71N 02°00'·61W.
Roches-aux-Anglais ◣ Fl G 4s; 48°39'·65N 02°02'·27W.
Les Crapauds-du-Bey ⚐ Fl R 4s; 48°39'·37N 02°02'·57W.

CHENAL DES PETITS POINTUS

Dinard ch spire (74m) brg 203° to right of Le Petit Bé rks.
La Saint-Servantine ◣ Fl G 2·5s; *Bell;* 48°41'·93N 02°00'·94W.
Les Petits Pontus ↓ 48°41'·30N 02°00'·86W.

CHENAL DE LA GRANDE CONCHÉE

Villa Brisemoulin 181·5°, on with LH edge of Le Petit Bé rocks.
La Plate ↳ Q WRG 11m, W10M, R/G7M; 140°-W-203°-R-210°-W-225°-G-140°; 48°40'·78N 02°01'·91W.
Le Bouton ↙ 48°40'·59N 02°01'·85W.

CHENAL DU BUNEL

Dinard water twr lt 158·2° on with St Énogat lts.
St Énogat ldg lts 158·2°; both Iso 4s 3/85m 6/8M, synch. Front 48°38'·29N 02°04'·11W, vis 126°-236°. Rear, 1.4M from front, on water twr; vis 143°-210°.
Bunel ↙ Q (9) 15s; 48°40'·84N 02°05'·38W.

CHENAL DE LA PETITE PORTE

Outer ldg lts 129·7°: **Front, Le Grand Jardin** ☆ Fl (2) R 10s 24m **15M**, 48°40'·20N 02°04'·97W. Rear, **La Balue** ☆ FG 20m 22M; 3·1M from front; intens 128°-129·5°; Gy ☐ twr; 48°38'·16N 02°01'·30W.
Vieux-Banc E ↙ Q; 48°42'·38N 02°09'·12W.
Vieux-Banc W ↙ VQ (9) 10s; 48°41'·84N 02°10'·20W.
St Malo Atterrisage (Fairway) ↙ Iso 4s; 48°41'·39N 02°07'·28W.
Les Courtis ◣ Fl G 4s 14m 7M; 48°40'·46N 02°05'·80W.
Nearing Le Grand Jardin, jink stbd briefly onto Ch du Bunel 152·8° ldg lts to pick up:
Inner ldg lts 128·6°, both Dir FG 20/69m **22/25M**; H24. Front, **Les Bas Sablons** ☆, intens 127·2°-130·2°; W ☐ twr, B top; 48°38'·16N 02°01'·30W. Rear, **La Balue** ☆, 0·9M from front; intens 128°-129·5°; Gy ☐ twr; 48°37'·60N 02°00'·24W.
Basse du Nord No. 5 ◣ 48°39'·98N 02°05'·04W.
Les Pierres-Garnier No. 8 ⚐ 48°39'·98N 02°04'·41W.
Les Patouillets ◣ Fl (3) G 12s, 48°39'·68N 02°04'·30W.
Clef d'Aval No. 10 ⚐ 48°39'·72N 02°03'·91W.
Basse du Buron No. 12 ⚐ Fl (4) R 15s, 48°39'·42N 02°03'·51W.
Le Buron ◣ Fl (4) G 15s 15m 7M; G twr; 48°39'·32N 02°03'·66W.
Les Grelots ↙ VQ (6) + L Fl 10s; 48°39'·16N 02°03'·03W.

CHENAL DE LA GRANDE PORTE

Banchenou ↙ VQ, 48°40'·44N 02°11'·48W.
Outer ldg lts 089·1°: **Front, Le Grand Jardin** ☆ Fl (2) R 10s 24m **15M**, 48°40'·20N 02°04'·97W.
Rear, **Rochebonne** ☆ Dir FR 40m **24M**; intens 088·2°-089·7°; Gy ☐ twr, R top, 4·2M from front; 48°40'·26N 01°58'·71W.
Buharats W No. 2 ↙ Fl R 2·5s, 48°40'·22N 02°07'·50W.
Buharats E No. 4 ↙ *Bell;* 48°40'·24N 02°07'·20W.
Bas du Boujaron No. 1 ↙ Fl (2) G 6s, 48°40'·17N 02°05'·97W.
Le Sou ↙ VQ (3) 5s; 48°40'·11N 02°05'·30W.
Continue on inner 128·6° ldg line: see Chenal de la Petite Porte.

RADE DE ST MALO

Plateau Rance Nord ↙ VQ, 48°38'·64N 02°02'·35W.
Plateau Rance Sud ↙ Q (6) + L Fl 15s, 48°38'·43N 02°02'·28W.
Crapaud de la Cité ↙ QG, 48°38'·34N 02°02'·01W.

ST MALO

Môle des Noires hd ⚓ VQ R 11m 6M; W twr, R top; *Horn (2) 20s*; 48°38'·52N 02°01'·91W.

Écluse du Naye ldg lts 070·4°, both FR 7/23m 3/7M. Front, 48°38'·58N 02°01'·48W. Rear, 030°-120°.

Ferry jetty hd, ⚓ VQ G 6M; 48°38'·44N 02°01'·82W (also on 128·6° ldg line).

Ferry jetty, ⚓ Fl R 4s 3m 1M; 260°-080°; 48°38'·44N 02°01'·76W.

Bas-Sablons marina, mole head ⚓ Fl G 4s 7m 5M; Gy mast; 48°38'·42N 02°01'·70W.

LA RANCE BARRAGE

La Jument ⚓ Fl G 4s 6m 4M; G twr, 48°37'·44N 02°01'·76W.

ZI 12 ⚓ Fl R 4s, 48°37'·47N 02°01'·62W.

NE dolphin ⚓ Fl (2) R 6s 6m 5M; 040°-200°, 48°37'·09N 02°01'·71W.

Barrage lock, NW wall ⚓ Fl (2) G 6s 6m 5M,191°-291°; G pylon, 48°37'·06N 02°01'·73W.

Barrage lock, SW wall, ⚓ Fl (3) G 12s, 48°37'·00N 02°01'·70W.

SE dolphin ⚓ Fl (3) R 12s, 48°36'·97N 02°01'·66W.

ZI 24 ⚓ Fl (2) R 6s, 48°36'·63N 02°01'·33W.

ST MALO TO ST QUAY-PORTRIEUX

ST BRIAC

R. Frémur mouth. Dir lt 125° Iso WRG 4s 10m, W13M, R/G 11M; 121·5°-G-124·5°-W-125·5°-R-129·5°; W mast on hut, 48°37'·07N 02°08'·20W.

ST CAST

Les Bourdinots ⚓ 48°39'·01N 02°13'·48W.

St Cast môle ⚓ Iso WG 4s 12m, W9M, G6M; 180°-G-206°-W-217°-G-235°-W-245°-G-340°; G & W structure; 48°38'·41N 02°14'·61W.

Laplace ⚓, 48°39'·73N 2°16'·45W; wreck 6m, 5ca SE of Pte de la Latte.

Cap Fréhel ☆ Fl (2) 10s 85m **29M**; Gy ⬜ twr, G lantern; 48°41'·05N 02°19'·13W. Reserve lt range **15M**.

CHENAL and PORT D'ERQUY

Les Justières ⚓ Q (6) + L Fl 15s; 48°40'·56N 02°26'·48W.

Basses du Courant ⚓ VQ (6) + L Fl 10s; 48°39'·21N 02°29'·16W.

L'Evette ⚓ 48°38'·51N 02°31'·45W.

S môle ⚓ Fl (2) WRG 6s 11m W10M, R/G7M; 055°-R-081°-W-094°-G-111°-W-120°-R-134°; W twr; 48°38'·06N 02°28'·68W.

Inner jetty ⚓ Fl (3) R 12s 10m 3M; R/W twr; 48°38'·09N 02°28'·39W.

DAHOUET

Petit Bignon ⚓ 48°36'·82N 02°35'·06W.

Le Dahouet ⚓ 48°35'·15N 02°35'·43W.

La Petite Muette ⚓ Fl WRG 4s 10m W9M, R/G6M; 055°-G-114°-W-146°-R-196°; W twr, G band; 48°34'·82N 02°34'·29W.

Entry chan, Fl (2) G 6s 5m 1M; 156°-286°; 48°34'·71N 02°34'·19W.

BAIE DE ST BRIEUC

Grand Léjon ☆ Fl (5) WR 20s 17m **W18M**, R14M; 015°-R-058°-W-283°-R-350°-W-015°; R twr, W bands; 48°44'·91N 02°39'·87W.

Petit Léjon ⚓ ; 48°41'·80N 02°37'·55W.

Les Landas ⚓ Q, 48°41'·43N 02°31'·29W.

Le Rohein ⚓ Q (9) WRG 15s 13m, W8M, R/G5M; 072°-R-105°-W-180°-G-193°-W-237°-G-282°-W-301°-G-330°-W-072°; Y twr, B band; 48°38'·80N 02°37'·77W.

SAINT-BRIEUC LE LÉGUÉ

Tra-Hillion ⚓ 48°33'·38N 02°38'·50W.

Le Légué ⚓ Mo (A)10s; 48°34'·32N 02°41'·15W.

No. 1 ⚓ Fl G 2·5s; 48°32'·42N 02°42'·51W.

No. 2 ⚓ Fl R 2·5s; 48°32'·37N 02°42'·40W.

No. 3 ⚓ Fl (2) G 6s; 48°32'·27N 02°42'·78W.

No. 4 ⚓ Fl (2) R 6s; 48°32'·23N 02°42'·70W.

No. 5 ⚓ Fl (3) G 12s; 48°32'·18N 02°42'·92W.

No. 6 ⚓ Fl (3) R 12s; 48°32'·14N 02°42'·90W.

NE jetty ⚓ VQ R 4M; 48°32'·12N 02°42'·88W.

Pte à l'Aigle jetty ⚓ VQ G 13m 8M; 160°-070°; W twr, G top; 48°32'·12N 02°43'·11W.

No. 7 ⚓ Fl (4) G 15s; 48°32'·11N 02°43'·08W.

No. 8 ⚓ Fl R 2·5s; 48°32'·01N 02°43'·16W.

No. 9 ⚓ Fl (2) G 6s; 48°31'·96N 02°43'·29W.

No. 10 ⚓ Fl (2) R 6s; 48°31'·91N 02°43'·31W.

Custom House jetty ⚓ Iso G 4s 6m 2M; W cols, G top; 48°31'·90N 02°43'·43W.

No. 11 ⚓ Fl (3) G 12s; 48°31'·90N 02°43'·43W.

No. 13 ⚓ Fl (4) G 15s; 48°31'·76N 02°43'·56W.

No. 14 ⚓ Fl (4) R 15s; 48°31'·70N 02°43'·61W.

BINIC

N môle ⚓ Oc (3) 12s 12m 11M; unintens 020°-110°; W twr, G lantern; 48°36'·07N 02°48'·92W.

ST QUAY-PORTRIEUX

Les Hors ⚓ 48°39'·60N 02°44'·04W.

Caffa ⚓ Q (3) 10s; 48°37'·82N 02°43'·08W.

La Longue ⚓ 48°37'·88N 02°44'·68W.

La Roselière ⚓ VQ (6) + L Fl 10s; 48°37'·31N 02°46'·19W.

Herflux ⚓ Dir ⚓ 130°, Fl (2) WRG 6s 10m, W 8M, R/G 6M; 115°-G-125°-W-135°-R-145°; 48°39'·07N 02°47'·95W.

Île Harbour (Roches de Saint-Quay) ⚓ Fl WRG 4s 16m, W9M, R/G6M; 011°-R-133°-G-270°-R-306°-G-358°-W-011°; W twr & dwelling, R top; 48°39'·99N 02°48'·49W.

Madeux ⚓ 48°40'·41N 02°48'·81W.

Grandes Moulières de St Quay ⚓ 48°39'·76N 02°49'·91W.

Moulières de Portrieux ⚓ 48°39'·26N 02°49'·21W.

Les Noirs ⚓ 48°39'·09N 02°48·46W.

Marina, **NE mole elbow**, Dir lt 318·2°: Iso WRG 4s 16m **W15M**, R/G11M; W159°-179°, G179°-316°, W316°-320·5°, R320·5° -159°; Reserve lt ranges 11/8M; 48°38'·99N 02°49'·09W.

NE môle hd ⚓ Fl (3) G 12s 10m 2M; 48°38'·84N 02°48'·91W.

S môle hd ⚓ Fl (3) R 12s 10m 2M; 48°38'·83N 02°49'·03W.

Old hbr ent: N side, Fl G 2.5s 11m 2M; 48°38'·71N 02°49'·36W.

S side, Fl R 2.5s 8m 2M; 48°38'·67N 02°49'·35W.

MID-CHANNEL MARKS

CHANNEL LT VESSEL ⚓ Fl 15s 12m **15M**; R hull with lt twr amidships; *Horn (20s)*; ***Racon O, 15M***; 49°54'·46N 02°53'·74W.

E Channel ⚓ Fl Y 5s 6M; ***Racon T, 10M***; 49°58'·67N 02°29'·01W.

COTENTIN PENINSULA (NW COAST)

La Plate ⚓ Fl (2+1) WR 10s 11m; W9M, R6M; 115°-W- 272°-R-115°; Y 8-sided twr, with B top; 49°43'·98N 01°55'·76W.

Cap de la Hague (Gros du Raz) ☆ Fl 5s 48m **23M**; Gy twr, W top; *Horn 30s*; 49°43'·31N 01° 57'·27W.

La Foraine ⟂ VQ (9) 10s 12m 6M; 49°42'·90 N 01°58'·32W.
Cap de Carteret ☆ Fl (2+1) 15s 81m **26M**; Gy twr, G top; 49°22'·41N 01°48'·41W.

THE CASQUETS AND ALDERNEY

Casquets ☆ Fl (5) 30s 37m **24M**, H24; W twr, 2 R bands; NW'most of three; *Horn (2) 60s*; *Racon T, 25M*; 49°43'·32N 02°22'·63W.
Ortac rock, unlit; 49°43'·40N 02°17'·44W.
Pierre au Vraic, unmarked rk 1·2m ⊙; 49°41'·61N 02°16'·94W.
Quenard Pt (Alderney) ⚡ Fl (4) 15s 37m 12M; 085°-027°; W ○ twr, B band; 49°43'·75N 02°09'·86W.
Château à L'Étoc Pt ⚡ Iso WR 4s 20m W10M, R7M; 071·1°-R-111·1°-W-151·1°; 49°43'·94N 02°10'·63W.

BRAYE

Ldg bns 142° (to clear the submerged Adm'ty bkwtr). Front, W ⚓, 49°43'·90N 02°10'·97W. Rear, BW ⚓; 720m from front.
Ldg lts 215°: both Q 8/17m 9/12M, synch; 210°-220°; orange △s. Front, old pier elbow, 49°43'·40N 02°11'·91W. Rear, 215°/335m.
Admiralty bkwtr head ⚡ L Fl 10s 7m 5M; 49°43'·82N 02°11'·67W.
Fairway No. 1 ⚓ QG; 49°43'·72N 02°11'·72W.
No. 2 ⚑ QR; 49°43'·60N 02°11'·75W.
Inner fairway ⚓ Q (2) G 5s; 49°43'·58N 02°11'·98W.
Braye quay ⚡ 2 FR (vert) 8m 5M; 49°43'·53N 02°12'·00W.
Little Crabby hbr ent ⚡ FG & FR 5m 2M; 49°43'·45N 02°12'·12W.

GUERNSEY, NORTHERN APPROACHES

LITTLE RUSSEL CHANNEL

Grande Amfroque, two unlit bcn twrs: larger, BW-banded; smaller, white; 49°30'·57N 02°24'·62W.
Tautenay ⚡ Q (3) WR 6s 7m 7M, R6M; 050°-W-215°-R-050°; B & W striped bcn 49°30'·11N 02°26'·84W.
Platte Fougère ☆ Fl WR 10s 15m **16M**; 155°-W-085°-R-155°; W 8-sided twr, B band; *Horn 45s*; *Racon P;* 49°30'·83N 02°29'·14W.
Corbette d'Amont ⚓ Y bcn twr, topmark; 49°29'·64N 02°29'·38W.
Roustel ⚡ Q 8m 7M; BW chequered base, W framework col; 49°29'·23N 02°28'·79W.
Rousse, Y bcn twr, topmark ⊞; 49°28'·98N 02°28'·36W.
Platte, ⚡, Fl WR 3s 6m, W7M, R5M; 024°-R-219°-W-024°; G conical twr; 49°29'·08N 02°29'·57W.
Vivian bcn twr, BW bands, 49°28'·45N 02°30'·66W.
Brehon ⚡ Iso 4s 19m 9M; bcn on ○ twr, 49°28'·28N 02°29'·28W.
Demie Flieroque, Y bcn twr, topmark F; 49°28'·13N 02°31'·38W.

BIG RUSSEL

Noire Pute ⚡ Fl (2) WR 15s 8m 6M; 220°-W-040°-R-220°; on 2m high rock; 49°28'·21N 02°25'·02W.
Fourquies ⚓ Q; 49°27'·34N 02°26'·47W.
Lower Heads ⚓ Q (6) + L Fl 15s; *Bell;* 49°25'·85N 02°28'·55W.

GUERNSEY, HERM AND SARK

BEAUCETTE MARINA

Petite Canupe ⚓ Q (6) + L Fl 15s; 49°30'·20N 02°29'·14W.
Ldg lts 277°: Both FR. Front, W □, R stripe; 49°30'·19N 02°30'·23W. Rear, R □, W stripe; 185m from front.

Appr chan buoys: SWM L Fl 10s 49°30'·15N 02°29'·66W. SHM Fl G 5s, PHM Fl R 5s & Fl (3) R 5s. NCM perch Q 49°30'·165N 02°30'·06W. SHM perch Q (3) G 5s at ent; 49°30'·18N 02°30'·24W.

ST SAMPSON

Ldg lts 286°: Front, FR 3m 5M; 230°-340°; tfc sigs; 49°28'·90N 02°30'·74W. Rear, FG 13m; clock twr, 390m from front.
N Pier ⚡ FG 3m 5M; 230°-340°; 49°28'·92N 02°30'·71W.
Crocq pier ⚡ FR 11m 5M; 250°-340°; 49°28'·98N 02°31'·00W.

ST PETER PORT

Outer ldg lts 220°: **Front**, Castle bkwtr, Al WR 10s 14m **16M**; 187°-007°; dark ○ twr, W on NE side; *Horn 15s;* 49°27'·31N 02°31'·45W. **GY RDF beacon** 304·5kHz is synchronised with the co-located horn (15s) to give distance finding. After the 4 GY ident signals (— — · — · — —), a 27 sec long dash begins at the same time as the horn blast. Time the number of seconds from the start of the long dash until the horn is next heard, multiply by 0·18 = distance in M from the horn; several counts are advised.
Rear 220° ldg lt, Belvedere, Oc 10s 61m 14M; 179°-269°; intens 217°-223°; W □ on W twr; 980m from front.
Queen Elizabeth II marina, 270° Dir Oc ⚡ WRG 3s 5m 6M; 258°-G-268°-W-272°-R-282°; 49°27'·73N 02°31'·87W.
Reffée ⚓ Q (6) + L Fl 15s; 49°27'·74N 02°31'·27W.
Appr buoys: outer pair ⚓ QG; 49°27'·83N 02°31'·54W. ⚑ QR; 49°27'·71N 02°31'·52W. Inner pair: ⚓ QG; 49°27'·76N 02°31'·74W. ⚑ QR; 49°27'·72N 02°31'·74W.
The Pool ldg lts 265° (*not* into moorings): Front, Victoria marina, S Pier, ⚡ Oc R 5s 10m 14M; 49°27'·32N 02°32'·03W. Rear, ⚡ Iso R 2s 22m 3M; 260°-270°; on Woolworth's bldg, 160m from front.
White Rock pier ⚡ Oc G 5s 11m 14M; intens 174°-354°; ○ twr; tfc sigs; 49°27'·38N 02°31'·59W.
S Fairway ⚓ QG; 49°27'·30N 02°31'·76W; pontoon W of buoy.
⚑ Fl R; 49°27'·28N 02°31'·74W. 49°27'·27N 02°31'·80W. 49°27'·27N 02°31'·86W.

HAVELET BAY

Oyster Rock ⚓ Y bcn, topmark 'O'; 49°27'·09N 02°31'·46W.
Oyster Rock ⚓ QG; 49°27'·04N 02°31'·47W.
Moulinet ⚑ QR; 49°26'·97N 02°31'·54W.
Moulinet ⚓ Y bcn, topmark 'M'; 49°26'·95N 02°31'·58W.

GUERNSEY, SOUTH-EAST and SOUTH COASTS

Anfré, Y bcn, topmark 'A'; 49°26'·45N 02°31'·48W.
Longue Pierre, Y bcn, topmark 'LP'; 49°25'·36N 02°31'·48W.
St Martin's Pt ⚡ Fl (3) WR 10s 15m 14M; 185°-R-191°-W-011°-R-061·5°; flat-topped, W bldg. *Horn (3) 30s;* 49°25'·30N 02°31'·70W.

GUERNSEY, NORTH-WEST COAST

Les Hanois ☆ Fl (2) 13s 33m **20M**; 294°-237°; Gy ○ twr, B lantern, helicopter platform; *Horn (2) 60s.* 49°26'·10N 02°42'·15W.
4 FR on mast 1·3M ESE of Les Hanois lt ho.
Portelet Hbr, bkwtr bcn, 49°26'·16N 02°39'·84W.
Cobo Bay, Grosse Rock, B bcn 11m; 49°29'·02N 02°36'·19W.
Grand Havre, Rousse Point bkwtr, B bcn; 49°29'·92N 02°33'·05W.

HERM

Corbette de la Mare, white disc on Y pole, 49°28'·48N 02°28'·72W.

Petit Creux ☆ QR; red 'C' on red pole; 49°28'·09N 02°28'·72W.

Alligande ☆ Fl (3) G 5s; B pole, Or 'A'; 49°27'·86N 02°28'·78W.

Épec ☆ Fl G 3s; black 'E' on G mast; 49°27'·98N 02°27'·89W.

Vermerette ☆ Fl (2) Y 5s; Or 'V' on bcn; 49°28'·12N 02°27'·75W.

Gate Rock (Percée Pass) ⌁ Q (9) 15s; 49°27'·88N 02°27'·54W.

Hbr ldg lts 078°: White drums. ☆ 2F occas; 49°28'·25N 02°27'·11W.

Hbr pier, N end ☆ 2 FG; G □ on G bcn; 49°28'·21N 02°27'·26W.

SARK

Courbée du Nez ☆ Fl (4) WR 15s 14m 8M; 057°-W-230°-R-057°; W structure on rock; 49°27'·09N 02°22'·17W.

Point Robert ☆ Fl 15s 65m **20M**; vis 138°-353°; W 8-sided twr; *Horn (2) 30s*; 49°26'·19N 02°20'·75W.

Founiais ⌁, topmark 'F'; 49°26'·02N 02°20'·36W.

Blanchard ⌁ Q (3) 10s; *Bell*; 49°25'·36N 02°17'·42W.

Pilcher monument (070° appr brg); 49°25'·71N 02°22'·44W.

JERSEY, WEST AND SOUTH COASTS

Desormes ⌁ Q (9) 15s; 49°18'·94N 02°17'·98W.

Grosnez Point ☆ Fl (2) WR 15s 50m **W19M, R17M**; 081°-W-188°-R-241°; W hut; 49°15'·50N 02°14'·80W.

L a Rocco twr (conspic) 15m; 49°11'·90N 02°14'·05W.

La Frouquie ⌁ (seasonal); 49°11'·30N 02°15'·38W.

La Corbière ☆ Iso WR 10s 36m **W18M, R16M**; shore-W-294°-R-328°-W-148°-R-shore; W ○ twr; *Horn Mo (C) 60s*; 49°10'·79N 02°15'·01W.

Pt Corbière ☆ FR; R □, W stripe; 49°10'·87N 02°14'·38W.

WESTERN PASSAGE

Ldg lts 082°. Front, La Gréve d'Azette Oc 5s 23m 14M; 034°-129°; 49°10'·16N 02°05'·09W. Rear, Mont Ubé, Oc R 5s 46m 12M; 250°-095°; 1M from front.

Passage Rock ⌁ VQ; 49°09'·54N 02°12'·26W.

Les Fours ⌁ Q; 49°09'·59N 02°10'·16W.

Noirmont Pt ☆ Fl (4) 12s 18m 10M; B twr, W band; 49°09'·91N 02°10'·08W.

Pignonet ⌁ 49°09'·88N 02°09'·70W.

Ruaudière Rock ▲ Fl G 3s; *Bell*; 49°09'·74N 02°08'·62W.

ST AUBIN'S BAY and HARBOUR

Les Grunes du Port ⌁ 49°10'·02N 02°09'·14W.

Diamond Rock ⌁ Fl (2) R 6s; 49°10'·12N 02°08'·64W.

Castle pier ☆ Fl R 4s 8m 1M; 49°11'·13N 02°09'·634W.

North pier, Dir lt 254° ☆ F WRG 5m, 248°-G-253°-W-255°-R-260°; 49°11'·22N 02°10'·03W. Same col, Iso R 4s 12m 10M.

Beach Rock ⌁ 49°11'·29N 02°08'·42W, (Apr-Oct).

Rocquemin ⌁ 49°10'·64N 02°07'·95W.

Baleine ▲ 49°10'·41N 02°08'·23W.

ST HELIER

Elizabeth marina, west appr: Dir ☆ 106°: F WRG 4m 1M; 096°-G-104°-W-108°-R-119°; R dayglo □, B stripe; 49°10'·76N 02°07'·12W.

La Vrachiére ⌁ 49°10'·90N 02°07'·59W, Fl (2) 5s 1M.

Fort Charles North ⌁ 49°10'·81N 02°07'·50W.

Marina ent ☆ Oc G & Oc R, both 4s 2M; 49°10'·83N 02°07'·13W.

Red & Green Passage, ldg lts 022·7° on dayglo R dolphins: Front, Elizabeth E berth Dn ☆ Oc G 5s 10m 11M; 49°10'·63N 02°06'·94W. Rear, Albert Pier root ☆ Oc R 5s 18m 12M; synch; 230m SSW.

East Rock ▲ QG; 49°09'·96N 02°07'·28W.

Oyster Rocks, R/W bcn, topmark 'O'; 49°10'·10N 02°07'·49W.

Platte Rock ⌁ Fl R 1·5s 6m 5M; R col; 49°10'·16N 02°07'·34W.

Small Road No. 2 ⌁ QR; 49°10'·39N 02°07'·24W.

No. 4 ⌁ QR; 49°10'·53N 02°07'·12W.

Elizabeth marina, S appr: E1 ▲ Fl G 3s; 49°10'·59N 02°07'·09W.

E2 ⌁ Fl R 2s; 49°10'·58N 02°07'·13W.

E5 ▲ Fl G 5s; 49°10'·70N 02°07'·17W.

E6 ⌁ Fl R 2s; 49°10'·69N 02°07'·21W.

Fort Charles East ⌁ Q (3) 5s 2m 1M; 49°10'·74N 02°07'·26W.

La Collette basin

⌁ QR; 49°10'·54N 02°06'·91W. ⌁ 49°10'·52N 02°06'·90W. St Helier Hbr, ldg lts 078°, both FG on W cols. Front, 49°10'·62N 02°06'·66W. Rear, 80m from front.

Victoria pier hd, Port control twr; IPTS; 49°10'·57N 02°06'·88W.

JERSEY, SOUTH-EAST AND EAST COASTS

Hinguette ⌁ QR; 49°09'·33N 02°07'·32W.

Hettich ⌁ Fl Y 5s; 49°08'·10N 02°09'·00W.

South Pier Marine ⌁ Fl Y 5s; 49°09'·10N 02°06'·30W.

Demie de Pas ▲ Mo (D) WR 12s 11m, W14M, R10M; 130°-R-303°-W-130°; *Horn (3) 60s*; **Racon T, 10M**; B bn twr, Y top; 49°09'·01N 02°06'·15W. Icho Tower (conspic, 14m) 49°08'·89N 02°02'·90W.

Canger Rock ⌁ Q (9) 15s; 49°07'·35N 02°00'·38W.

La Conchière ⌁ Q (6) + L Fl 15s 2M; 49°08'·22N 02°00'·17W.

Frouquier Aubert ⌁ Q (6) + L Fl 15s; 49°06'·08N 01°58'·84W.

Violet ⌁ L Fl 10s; 49°07'·81N 01°57'·14W.

Petite Anquette, W bcn, topmark 'PA'; 49°08'·46N 01°56'·30W.

Grande Anquette, W bcn ⌁ 49°08'·32N 01°55'·20W.

Le Cochon ⌁ 49°09'·77N 01°58'·80W.

La Noire ⌁ 49°10'·13N 01°59'·23W. Le Giffard ⌁ 49°10'·59N 01°59'·00W.

GOREY

Pier Hd Dir lt 298°, ☆ WRG, 6m 8M; 293·5°-G-296·5°-W-299·5°-R-302·5°; ☆ Oc RG 5s 8m 12M; 304°-R-353°-G-304°; W twr on pierhead; 49°11'·80N 02°01'·34W.

Horn Rock ⌁, topmark 'H'; 49°10'·96N 01°59'·85W.

Les Burons, RW bcn, topmark 'B'; 49°11'·33N 02°00'·81W.

Fairway ▲ QG; 49°11'·50N 02°00'·34W.

Écureuil Rock ⌁ 49°11'·67N 02°00'·78W.

Equerrière Rk, bcn 'fishtail' topmark; 49°11'·80N 02°00'·67W.

Les Arch ⌁, BW bcn, 'A' topmark; 49°12'·02N 02°00'·60W.

ST CATHERINE BAY

St Catherine Bay, Le Fara ⌁ Q (3) 10s 3M; 49°12'·85N 02°00'·48W.

Archirondel Tower (conspic, 16m) 49°12'·72N 02°01'·42W.

Verclut bkwtr ⚡ Fl 1·5s 18m 13M; 49°13'·34N 02°00'·64W. In line 315° with unlit turret, 49°13'·96N 02°01'·57W, on La Coupe Pt.

JERSEY, NORTH COAST

Rozel Bay Dir lt 245°, F WRG 11m 5M; 240°-G-244°-W-246°-R-250°; W col; 49°14'·21N 02°02'·76W.
Bonne Nuit Bay ldg lts 223°: both FG 7/34m 6M. Front, Pier 49°15'·10N 02°07'·17W. Rear, 170m from front. Demie Rock ▲ 49°15'·56N 02°07'·36W.
Sorel Point ☆ L Fl WR 7·5s 50m **15M**; 095°-W-112°-R-173°-W-230°-R-269°-W-273°; W ○ twr, only 3m high; 49°15'·60N 02°09'·54W.

OFFLYING ISLANDS

LES ÉCREHOU
Écrevière ⚓ Q (6) + L Fl 15s; 49°15'·26N 01°52'·15W.
Mâitre Ile ⚓ 49°17'·08N 01°55'·60W.

PLATEAU DES MINQUIERS
N Minquiers ⚓ Q; 49°01'·64N 02°00'·58W.

NE Minquiers ⚓ VQ (3) 5s; *Bell;* 49°00'·85N 01°55'·30W.
SE Minquiers ⚓ Q (3) 10s; *Bell;* 48°53'·42N 02°00'·09W.
S Minquiers ⚓ Q (6) + L Fl 15s; 48°53'·09N 02°10'·10W.
SW Minquiers ⚓ Q (9) 15s 5M; *Whis;* 48°54'·35N 02°19'·41W.
NW Minquiers ⚓ Q 5M; *Bell;* 48°59'·63N 02°20'·59W.
Refuge ⚓; B/W bcn; 49°00'·13N 02°10'·16W.
Demie de Vascelin ▲ 49°00'·81N 02°05'·17W.
Grand Vascelin, BW bcn ⚓ 48°59'·97N 02°07'·26W.
Maitresse Ile, Puffin B&W bcn twr ⚓ 48°58'·33N 02°03'·65W.
Le Coq Reef, ⚓ Q (3) 10s 6m 3M; 48°57'·88N 02°01'·29W.

FRENCH MARKS NORTH OF ILE DE BRÉHAT

Roches Douvres ☆ Fl 5s 60m **24M**; pink twr on dwelling with G roof; 49°06'·30N 02°48'·87W (16M NNE of Ile de Bréhat).
Barnouic ⚓ VQ (3) 5s 15m 7M; 49°01'·64N 02°48'·41W.
Roche Gautier ⚓ VQ (9) 10s; 49°02'·013N 02°54'·36W.
Les Héaux de Bréhat ☆ Fl (4) WRG 15s 48m, **W15M**, R/G11M; 227°-R-247°-W-270°-G-302°-W-227°; Gy twr; 48°54'·50N 03°05'·18W (4·7M WNW of Ile de Bréhat).

DISTANCE TABLES
Approx distances in nautical miles are by the most direct route allowing for dangers and TSS.

	1	2	3	4	5	6	7	8	9	10	11	12	13	14	15	16	17
1 Cherbourg	**1**																
2 Omonville	10	**2**															
3 Braye (Alderney)	25	15	**3**														
4 St Peter Port	44	34	23	**4**													
5 Creux (Sark)	37	29	22	10	**5**												
6 St Helier	64	51	46	29	24	**6**											
7 Carteret	41	29	28	31	23	26	**7**										
8 Portbail	49	33	32	35	27	25	5	**8**									
9 Iles Chausey	69	61	58	48	43	25	33	30	**9**								
10 Granville	75	67	66	55	50	30	38	35	9	**10**							
11 Dinan	102	91	85	66	64	50	62	59	29	35	**11**						
12 St Malo	90	79	73	54	52	38	50	47	17	23	12	**12**					
13 Dahouet	88	80	72	54	52	41	60	59	37	45	41	29	**13**				
14 Le Légué/St Brieuc	96	86	76	57	56	46	69	69	41	49	45	33	8	**14**			
15 Binic	95	84	75	56	55	46	70	70	43	51	45	33	10	8	**15**		
16 St Quay-Portrieux	88	80	73	56	51	46	64	64	47	54	47	35	11	7	4	**16**	
17 Lézardrieux	88	80	68	48	38	47	68	71	53	54	61	49	33	32	30	21	**17**

AREA 16 *N & S Brittany – Paimpol to Lesconil*

SELECTED LIGHTS, BUOYS & WAYPOINTS

Positions are referenced to WGS84

OFFSHORE MARKS
Roches Douvres ☆ Fl 5s 60m **24M**; pink twr on dwelling with G roof; 49°06'·30N 02°48'·87W.
Barnouic ⚓ VQ (3) 5s 15m 7M; 49°01'·63N 02°48'·41W.
Roche Gautier ⚓ VQ (9) 10s; 49°02'·013N 02°54'·36W.

PAIMPOL TO ÎLE DE BRÉHAT

PAIMPOL
Les Calemarguiers ⚓ 48°46'·98N 02°54'·84W.
L'Ost Pic ⚡ Fl(4)WR 15s 20m, W9M, R6M; 105°-W-116°-R-221°-W-253°- R-291°-W-329°; obsc by islets near Bréhat when brg < 162°; W twr/turret, R top; 48°46'·77N 02°56'·42W.
Les Charpentiers ⚓ 48°47'·89N 02°56'·01W.
Pte de Porz-Don ☆ Oc (2) WR 6s 13m **W15M**, R11M; 269°-W-272°-R-279°; W house; 48°47'·48N 03°01'·55W.
El Bras ▲ Fl G 2·5s; 48°47'·21N 03°01'·50W.
⚓ Fl R 2·5s; 48°47'·17N 03°01'·49W.
Ldg lts 262·2°, both QR 5/12m 7/10M. Front, Kernoa jetty; W & R hut; 48°47'·09N 03°02'·44W. Rear, Dir QR, intens 260·2°-264·2°; W pylon, R top; 360m from front. ⚡ QG 48°47'·12N 03°02'·47W.

CHENAL DU FERLAS (277°-257°-271°)
Lel Ar Serive ⚓ 48°49'·98N 02°58'·76W.
Loguivy Dir lt 257°: Q WRG 12m 10/8M; 254°-G-257°-W-257·7°- R-260·7°; Gy twr; 48°49'·37N 03°03'·67W.
Les Piliers ⚓ 48°49'·77N 02°59'·99W.
Kermouster Dir ⚡ 271°: Fl WRG 2s 16m, W 10M, R/G 8M; 267°-G-270°-W-272°- R-274°; W col; 48°49'·55N 03°05'·19W (R. Trieux).

ÎLE DE BRÉHAT
Le Paon ⚡ Oc WRG 4s 22m W11M, R/G8M; 033°-W-078°-G-181°-W-196°- R-307°-W-316°-R-348°; Y twr; 48°51'·92N 02°59'·15W.
Roche Guarine ⚓ 48°51'·63N 02°57'·63W, Chenal de Bréhat.
Rosédo ☆ Fl 5s 29m **20M**; W twr; 48°51'·45N 03°00'·29W.
La Chambre ⚓ 48°50'·16N 02°59'·58W.
Men-Joliguet ⚓ Iso WRG 4s 6m W13M, R/G10M; 255°-R-279°-W-283°-G-175°; 48°50'·12N 03°00'·20W.

LÉZARDRIEUX TO TRÉGUIER
LE TRIEUX RIVER to LÉZARDRIEUX
Nord Horaine ⚓ 48°54'·54N 02°55'·23W.

La Horaine ⚓ Fl (3) 12s 13m 7M; Gy 8-sided twr on B hut; 48°53'·50N 02°55'·22W.

Men-Marc'h ⚓ 48°53'·17N 02°51'·82W.

Ldg lts 224·8°: Front, **La Croix** ☆ Q 15m **18M**; intens 215°-235°; two Gy ○ twrs joined, W on NE side, R tops; 48°50'·23N 03°03'·25W. Rear **Bodic** ☆ Dir Q 55m **22M**; intens 221°-229°; W ho with G gable; 2·1M from front.

Les Sirlots ⚓ *Whis*; 48°52'·95N 02°59'·58W.

Men-Grenn ⚓ Q (9) 15s 7m 7M; 48°51'·22N 03°03'·89W.

Coatmer ldg lts 218·7°. Front, Q RG 16m R/G7M; 200°-R-250°-G-053°; W gable; 48°48'·26N 03°05'·75W. Rear, QR 50m 7M; vis 197°-242°; W gable; 660m from front.

Les Perdrix ⚓ Fl (2) WG 6s 5m, W6M, G3M; 165°-G-197°-W-202·5°-G-040°; G twr; 48°47'·74N 03°05'·79W.

CHENAL DE LA MOISIE (339·4°); PASSE DE LA GAINE (241·5°)

La Vieille du Tréou ⚓ 48°52'·00N 03°01'·09W.

An Ogejou Bihan ⚓ 48°53'·37N 03°01'·91W.

La Moisie ⚓ 48°53'·83N 03°02'·22W.

Les Héaux de Bréhat ☆ Fl (4) WRG 15s 48m, **W15M**, R/G11M; 227°-R-247°-W-270°-G-302°-W-227°; Gy ○ twr; 48°54'·50N 03°05'·17W.

Basse des Héaux ⚓ 48°54'·07N 03°05'·28W.

Pont de la Gaine ⚓ 48°53'·12N 03°07'·40W.

JAUDY RIVER TO TRÉGUIER

La Jument des Héaux ⚓ VQ; 48°55'·36N 03°08'·04W.

Grande Passe ldg lts 137°. Front, Port de la Chaine, Oc 4s 12m 11M; 042°-232°; W house; 48°51'·55N 03°07'·89W. Rear, **St Antoine** ☆ Dir Oc R 4s 34m **15M**; intens 134°-140°; R & W house; 0·75M from front. (Both marks are hard to see by day.)

Basse Crublent ⚓ QR; *Whis*; 48°54'·29N 03°11'·16W.

Le Corbeau ⚓ Fl R 4s; 48°53'·35N 03°10'·26W.

Pierre à l'Anglais ⚓ Fl G 4s; 48°53'·21N 03°10'·46W.

Petit Pen ar Guézec ⚓ Fl (2) G 6s; 48°52'·52N 03°09'·44W.

La Corne ⚓ Fl (3) WRG 12s 14m W8M, R/G6M; 052°-W-059°-R-173°-G-213°-W-220°-R-052°; W twr, R base; 48°51'·35N 03°10'·62W.

TRÉGUIER TO TRÉBEURDEN

PORT BLANC

Le Voleur Dir ⚓ 150°: Fl WRG 4s 17m, W14M, R/G 11M; 140°-G- 148°-W-152°-R-160°; W twr; 48°50'·20N 03°18'·52W.

Basse Guazer ⚓ ; 48°51'·58N 03°20'·96W.

PERROS-GUIREC

Passe de l'Est, ldg lts 224·8°. Front, Le Colombier ⚓ Dir Q 28m 14M; intens 214·5°-234·5°; W house; 48°47'·87N 03°26'·66W. Rear, **Kerprigent** ☆, Dir Q 79m **21M**; intens 221°-228°; W twr, 1·5M from front.

Pierre du Chenal ⚓ 48°49'·29N 03°24'·67W.

Passe de l'Ouest. **Kerjean** ☆ Dir lt 143·6°, Oc (2+1) WRG 12s 78m, **W15M**, R/G12M; 133·7°-G-143·2°-W-144·8°-R-154·3°; W twr, B top; 48°47'·79N 03°23'·39W.

Les Couillons de Tomé ⚓ 48°50'·88N 03°25'·68W.

La Horaine ⚓ 48°49'·89N 03°27'·26W.

Roche Bernard ⚓ 48°49'·43N 03°25'·46W.

Gommonénou ⚓ VQ R 1M; 48°48'·27N 03°25'·83W.

Jetée du Linkin ⚓ Fl (2) G 6s 4m 6M; W pile, G top; 48°48'·20N 03°26'·31W.

PLOUMANAC'H

Mean-Ruz ⚓ Oc WR 4s 26m W12M, R9M; 226°-W- 242°-R-226°; obsc by Pte de Trégastel when brg <080°; partly

obsc by Les Sept-Îles 156°-207° and partly by Île Tomé 264°-278°; pink □ twr; 48°50'·25N 03°29'·00W.

LES SEPT ÎLES

Île-aux-Moines ☆ Fl (3) 20s 59m **24M**; obsc by Îliot Rouzic and E end of Île Bono 237°-241°, and in Baie de Lannion when brg <039°; Gy twr and dwelling; 48°52'·72N 03°29'·40W.

Les Dervinis ⚓ 48°52'·35N 03°27'·32W.

TRÉGASTEL-PLAGE

Île Dhu ⚓ 48°50'·37N 03°31'·24W.

Les Triagoz ⚓ Fl (2) WR 6s 31m W14M, R11M; 010°-W-339°-R-010°; obsc in places 258°-268° by Les Sept-Îles; Gy □ twr, R lantern; 48°52'·28N 03°38'·80W.

Bar-ar-Gall ⚓ VQ (9) 10s; 48°49'·79N 03°36'·22W.

Le Crapaud ⚓ Q (9) 15s; 48°46'·67N 03°40'·59W.

TRÉBEURDEN

Pte de Lan Kerellec ⚓ Iso WRG 4s; W8M, R/G5M; 058°-G-064°-W-069°-R-130°; Gy twr; 48°46'·74N 03°35'·06W.

Ar Gouredec ⚓ VQ (6) + L Fl 10s; 48°46'·41N 03°36'·59W.

An Ervennou ⚓ Fl (2) R 6s; 48°46'·48N 03°35'·96W.

NW bkwtr ☆ Fl G 2·5s 8m 2M; IPTS; 48°46'·33N 03°35'·21W.

TRÉBEURDEN TO MORLAIX

LÉGUER RIVER

Beg-Léguer ⚓ Oc (4) WRG 12s 60m W12M, R/G9M; 007°-G-084°-W-098°-R-129°; west face of W house, R lantern; 48°44'·31N 03°32'·91W.

Kinierbel ⚓; *Bell* 48°44'·15N 03°35'·18W.

LOCQUÉMEAU

Ldg lts 121°: Front, ⚓ QR 19m 6M; 068°-228°; W pylon, R top; 48°43'·41N 03°34'·44W. Rear, ⚓ QR 39m 7M; 016°-232°; W gabled house; 484m from front.

Locquémeau ⚓ *Whis*; 48°43'·86N 03°35'·93W.

LOCQUIREC

Gouliat ⚓ 48°42'·57N 03°38'·97W.

PRIMEL-TRÉGASTEL

Méloine ⚓ 48°45'·56N 03°50'·68W.

Ldg lts 152°, both ⚓ QR 35/56m 7M. Front, 134°-168°; W □, R stripe, on pylon; 48°42'·45N 03°49'·19W. Rear, R vert stripe on W wall; 172m from front.

W bkwtr ⚓ Fl G 4s 6m 7M; 48°42'·77N 03°49'·52W.

BAIE DE MORLAIX

Chenal de Tréguier ldg lts 190·5°: Front, ⚓ Île Noire Oc (2) WRG 6s 15m, W11M, R/G8M; 051°-G-135°-R-211°-W-051°; obsc in places; W □ twr, R top; 48°40'·35N 03°52'·54W. Common Rear, **La Lande** ☆ Fl 5s 85m **23M**; obsc by Pte Annelouesten when brg >204°; W □ twr, B top; 48°38'·20N 03°53'·14W.

La Pierre Noire ⚓ 48°42'·56N 03°52'·20W.

La Chambre ⚓ 48°40'·74N 03°52'·51W.

Grande Chenal ldg lts 176·4°: Front, **Île Louet** ☆ Oc (3) WG 12s 17m **W15M**, G10M; 305°-W (except where obsc by islands)-244°-G-305°; W □ twr, B top; 48°40'·41N 03°53'·34W. Common Rear, **La Lande** as above.

Pot de Fer ⚓ *Bell*; 48°44'·23N 03°54'·02W.

Stolvezen ⚓ 48°42'·64N 03°53'·41W.

Ricard ⚓ 48°41'·54N 03°53'·51W.

Vieille ⚓ 48°42'·60N 03°54'·11W. (Chenal Ouest de Ricard 188·8°)

La Noire ⚓ 48°41'·65N 03°54'·06W.

Corbeau ⚓ 48°40'·63N 03°53'·33W.

MORLAIX RIVER

Barre de-Flot No. 1 ⚓ 48°40'·18N 03°52'·95W.

No. 2 ⬦ Fl R 2s; 48°39'·88N 03°52'·53W.

No. 3 ⬦ Fl G 2s; 48°39'·25N 03°52'·32W.

No. 4 ⬦ Fl R 2s; 48°38'·62N 03°51'·62W.

No. 5 ⬦ Fl G 2s; 48°38'·04N 03°51'·34W.

No. 7 ⚓ 48°37'·68N 03°51'·03W.

PENZÉ RIVER

Cordonnier ⬦ 48°42'·93N 03°56'·59W.

Guerhéon ⬦ 48°42'·73N 03°57'·18W.

Trousken ⬦ 48°42'·26N 03°56'·54W.

Pte Fourche ⬦ 48°42'·14N 03°56'·76W.

Ar Tourtu ⬦ 48°41'·99N 03°56'·57W.

An Nehou (Caspari) ⬦ 48°41'·56N 03°56'·45W.

Le Figuier ⬦ 48°40'·46N 03°56'·16W.

ROSCOFF TO ÎLE VIERGE

BLOSCON/ROSCOFF

Astan ⬦ VQ (3) 5s 9m 6M; 48°44'·91N 03°57'·66W.

Le Menk ⬦ Q (9) WR 15s 6m W5M, R3M; 160°-W- 88°-R-160°; 48°43'·28N 03°56'·71W.

Basse de Bloscon ⬦ VQ; 48°43'·71N 03°57'·55W.

Bloscon pier ⬦ Fl WG 4s 9m W10M, G7M (in fog Fl 2s); 200°-W-210°-G-200°; W twr, G top; 48°43'·21N 03°57'·69W.
⬦ Fl (2) R 6s, 48°43'·11N 03°57'·92W.

Ar Pourven ⬦ Q; 48°43'·04N 03°57'·70W.

Ar-Chaden ⬦ Q (6) + L Fl WR 15s 14m, W8M, R6M; 262°-R-289·5°-W-293°-R-326°- W-110°; YB twr; 48°43'·94N 03°58'·26W.

Men-Guen-Bras ⬦ Q WRG 14m, W9M, R/ G6M; 068°-W-073°-R-197°-W-257°-G-068°; BY twr; 48°43'·76N 03°58'·07W.

Roscoff ldg lts 209°: Front, N môle ⬦ Oc (3) G 12s 7m 7M; synch; 078°-318°; W col, G top; 48°43'·56N 03°58'·67W. **Rear** ☆ Oc (3) 12s 24m **15M**; 062°-242°; Gy ☐ twr, W on NE side; 430m from front.

CANAL DE L'ÎLE DE BATZ

Roc'h Zu ⬦ 48°43'·88N 03°58'·59W.

Jetty hd (LW landing) ⬦ Q 5m 1M; BY col; 48°43'·92N 03°58'·97W.

Run Oan ⬦ 48°44'·10N 03°59'·30W.

Perroch ⬦ 48°44'·10N 03°59'·71W.

Tec'hit Bihan ⬦ 48°44'·02N 04°00'·88W.

La Croix ⬦ 48°44'·19N 04°01'·30W.

L'Oignon ⬦ 48°44'·04N 04°01'·35W.

Basse Plate ⬦ 48°44'·25N 04°02'·53W.

ÎLE DE BATZ

Île aux Moutons ⬦ VQ (6)+ L Fl 10s 3m 7M; 48°44'·25N 04°00'·52W; landing stage, S end and ent to hbr.

Malvoch ⬦ 48°44'·26N 04°00'·67W, W side of ent.

Lt ho ☆ Fl (4) 25s 69m **23M**; Gy twr; 48°44'·71N 04°01'·62W. Same twr, auxiliary lt, FR 65m 7M; 024°-059°.

MOGUÉRIEC

Ldg lts 162°: Front ⬦ Iso WG 4s 9m W11M, G6M; 158°-W-166°-G-158°; W twr, G top; jetty 48°41'·34N 04°04'·47W. Rear ⬦ Iso G 4s 22m 7M, synch; 142°-182°; W col, G top; 440m from front.

PONTUSVAL

Pointe de Pontusval ⬦ 48°41'·42N 04°19'·32W.

Ar Peich ⬦ 48°40'·90N 04°19'·16W.

Pte de Beg-Pol ⬦ Oc (3) WR 12s 16m W10M, R7M; Shore-W-056°-R-096°-W-shore; W twr, B top, W dwelling; 48°40'·67N 04°20'·76W. QY and FR lts on towers 2·4M S.

Aman-ar-Ross ⬦ Q 7M; 48°41'·88N 04°27'·03W.

Lizen Ven Ouest ⬦ VQ (9) 10s 5M; 48°40'·53N 04°33'·63W.

Île-Vierge ☆ Fl 5s 77m **27M**; 337°-325°; Gy twr; *Horn 60s*; 48°38'·33N 04°34'·05W.

ÎLE VIERGE TO L'ABER-ILDUT

L'ABER WRAC'H

Libenter ⬦ Q (9) 15s 6M; 48°37'·45N 04°38'·46W.

Outer ldg lts 100·1°: Front, Île Wrac'h ⬦ QR 20m 7M; W ☐ twr, Or top; 48°36'·88N 04°34'·56W. Rear, Lanvaon ⬦ Q 55m 12M; intens 090°-110°; W ☐ twr, Or △ on top; 1·63M from front.

Grand Pot de Beurre ⬦ 48°37'·21N 04°36'·48W.

Petit Pot de Beurre ⬦ 48°37'·12N 04°36'·23W.

Basse de la Croix ⬦ Fl G 2·5s; 48°36'·92N 04°35'·99W.

Breac'h Ver ⬦ Fl (2) G 6s 6m 3M; △ on twr; 48°36'·63N 04°35'·38W.

Dir ⬦ 128°, Oc (2) WRG 6s 5m W13M, R/G11M; 125·7°-G-127·2°-W-128·7°-R-130·2°; 48°35'·89N 04°33'·82W, root of W bkwtr .

Marina ent: QG 3m 2M; vis 186°-167° (341°); 48°35'·97N 04°33'·64W. QR 3m 2M; vis 244°-226° (342°).

L'ABER BENOÎT

Petite Fourche ⬦ 48°36'·99N 04°38'·75W.

Rusven Est ⬦ 48°36'·30N 04°38'·63W.

Rusven Ouest ⬦ Bell; 48°36'·07N 04°39'·43W.

Basse du Chenal ⬦ 48°35'·81N 04°38'·53W.

Poul Orvil ⬦ 48°35'·52N 04°38'·29W.

La Jument ⬦ 48°35'·10N 04°37'·41W.

Ar Gazel ⬦ 48°34'·90N 04°37'·27W.

Le Chien ⬦ 48°34'·67N 04°36'·88W.

ROCHES DE PORTSALL

Le Relec ⬦ 48°35'·99N 04°40'·84W.

Corn-Carhai ⬦ Fl (3) 12s 19m 9M; W 8-sided twr, B top; 48°35'·19N 04°43'·94W.

Grande Basse de Portsall ⬦ VQ (9) 10s 9m 4M; 48°36'·70N 04°46'·13W.

Basse Paupian ⬦ 48°35'·31N 04°46'·27W.

Bosven Aval ⬦ 48°33'·82N 04°44'·27W.

Men ar Pic ⬦ 48°33'·65N 04°44'·03W.

Portsall ⬦ Oc (4) WRG 12s 9m W13M, R/G10M; 058°-G-084°-W- 088°-R-058°; W col, R top; 48°33'·84N 04°42'·26W.

ARGENTON to L'ABER-ILDUT

Le Taureau ⬦ 48°31'·46N 04°47'·34W.

Argenton, Île Dolvez, front ldg bcn 086° ⬦ 48°31'·25N 04°46'·23W.

Le Four ☆ Fl (5) 15s 28m **18M**; Gy ○ twr; *Horn (3+2) 60s*; 48°31'·38N 04°48'·32W.

L'Aber-Ildut ☆ Dir Oc (2) WR 6s 12m **W25M, R20M**; 081°-W-085°-R-087°; W bldg; 48°28'·26N 04°45'·56W.

CHENAL DU FOUR AND CHENAL DE LA HELLE

Ldg lts 158·5°. Front, **Kermorvan** ☆ Fl 5s 20m **22M**; obsc'd by Pte de St Mathieu when brg <341°; W ☐ twr; *Horn 60s*; 48°21'·72N 04°47'·40W.

Rear, **Pte de St Mathieu** ☆ Fl 15s 56m **29M**; W twr, R top; 48°19'·79N 04°46'·26W. Same twr: Dir F 54m **28M**; intens 157·5°-159·5°.

⬦ Q WRG 26m, W14M, R/G11M; 085°-G-107°-W-116°-R-134°; W twr 54 m WNW of previous entry; 48°19'·80N 04°46'·30W.

Plâtresses N ⨪ Fl G 2·5s; 48°26'·61N 04°50'·73W.
Valbelle ⨪ Fl (2) R 6s 8m 5M; 48°26'·42N 04°50'·03W.
Plâtresses SE ⨪ Fl (2) G 6s; 48°25'·96N 04°50'·52W.
Tendoc ⌕ 48°25'·67N 04°49'·44W.
Saint Paul ⨪ Oc (2) R 6s; 48°24'·82N 04°49'·16W.
Pte de Corsen ⚡ Dir Q WRG 33m W12M, R/G8M;
008°-R-012°-W-015° (ldg sector)- G-021°; W hut; 48°24'·89N
04°47'·61W.
Taboga ⨪ 48°23'·77N 04°48'·08W.

CHENAL DE LA HELLE
Ldg lts 137·9°: Front, **Kermorvan** ☆ see above. Rear,
Lochrist ☆ Dir Oc (3) 12s 49m **22M**; intens 135°-140°;
W 8-sided twr, R top; 48°20'·55N 04°45'·82W.
Luronne ⨪; 48°26'·61N 04°53'·78W.
Ldg lts 293·5° astern (to join Ch du Four S of St Paul ⨪):
Front, Le Faix ⨪ VQ 16m 8M; 48°25'·73N 04°53'·91W.
Rear, **Le Stiff** ☆ (below at Ouessant); 6·9M from front.
Ldg line 142·5°, optional day only (to join Ch du Four
SE of St Pierre ⨪): Front, **Kermorvan** ☆ see above. Rear,
two W gables (Les Pignons de Kéravel, 48m) 48°20'·10N
04°45'·55W.
Pourceaux ⨪ Q; 48°24'·00N 04°51'·31W.
Saint-Pierre ⨪ 48°23'·09N 04°49'·09W.
Rouget ⨪ Fl G 4s; 48°22'·04N 04°48'·88W (Ch du Four).
Grande Vinotière ⨪ L Fl R 10s 15m 5M; R 8-sided twr;
48°21'·93N 04°48'·42W.
Le Conquet, Môle Ste Barbe ⚡ Oc G 4s 5m 6M; 48°21'·58N
04°46'·98W.
Les Renards ⨪ 48°21'·00N 04°47'·48W.
Tournant et Lochrist ⨪ 48°20'·64N 04°48'·12W, Iso R 4s.
Ar Christian Braz ⨪ 48°20'·68N 04°50'·14W, E of Ile de
Béniguet.
Ldg line 325°: Front, Grand Courleau ⨪; rear, La Faix
(above).
Ldg lts 007°: Front, **Kermorvan** ☆ above. Rear, **Trézien**
☆ Dir Oc (2) 6s 84m **20M**; intens 003°-011°; Gy twr, W
on S side; 48°25'·41N 04°46'·74W.
Les Vieux-Moines ⨪ Fl R 4s 15m 5M; 280°-133°; R 8-sided twr;
48°19'·33N 04°46'·63W, 5ca SSW of Pte de St Mathieu.
La Fourmi ⨪ 48°19'·25N 04°47'·97W.

OUESSANT AND ÎLE MOLÉNE

OFF USHANT TSS
Ouessant NE ⨪ L Fl 10s; *Whis*; *Racon B, 20M*; 48°59'·51N
05°24'·00W.
Ouessant SW ⌑ Fl 4s 7M; *Racon M, 10M*; 48°30'·00N
05°45'·00W.

ÎLE D'OUESSANT
Le Stiff ☆ Fl (2) R 20s 85m **24M**; two adjoining W twrs;
48°28'·47N 05°03'·41W. Radar twr, conspic, 340m NE, ⚡ Q
(day); ⚡ FR (night).
Port du Stiff, E môle ⚡ Dir Q WRG 11m W10M, R/G7M;
251°-G-254°-W-264°-R-267°; W twr, G top; 48°28'·12N
05°03'·25W.
Baie du Stiff: Gorle Vihan ⨪ 48°28'·32N 05°02'·60W.
Men-Korn ⨪ VQ (3) WR 5s 21m 8M; 145°-W-040°-R-145°;
BYB twr; 48°27'·96N 05°01'·32W.
Men ar Froud ⨪ 48°26'·62N 05°03'·67W.
La Jument ☆ Fl (3) R 15s 36m **22M**; 241°-199°; *Horn
(3) 60s*;
Gy 8-sided twr, R top; 48°25'·33N 05°08'·03W.
Nividic ⚡ VQ (9) 10s 28m 10M; 290°-225°; Gy 8-sided twr,
helicopter platform; 48°26'·74N 05°09'·06W.
Créac'h ☆ Fl (2) 10s 70m **32M**; obsc 247°-255°; *Horn (2)*

120s; Racon C (3cm), 20M, 030°-248°; W twr, B bands;
48°27'·55N 05°07'·76W.

ÎLE MOLÉNE and ARCHIPELAGO
Kéréon ☆ Oc (2+1) WR 24s 38m **W17M**, R7M; 019°-W-248°-
R-019°; Gy twr; *Horn (2+1) 120s*; 48°26'·24N 05°01'·55W.
Les Trois-Pierres ⚡ Iso WRG 4s 15m W9M, R/G6M;
070°-G-147°-W-185°-R-191°-G-197°-W-213°-R-070°;   W
col; 48°24'·70N 04°56'·84W.
Molène, Old môle Dir ⚡ 191°, Fl (3) WRG 12s 6m W9M, R/
G7M; 183°-G-190°-W-192°-R-203°; 48°23'·85N 04°57'·29W.
Same structure: Chenal des Laz , Dir ⚡ 261°: Fl (2) WRG 6s
9m W9M, R/G7M ; 252·5°-G-259·5°-W-262·5°-R-269·5°.
Pierres-Vertes ⨪ VQ (9) 10s 9m 5M; 48°22'·19N
05°04'·76W.
Pierres Noires ⨪; 48°18'·47N 04°58'·15W.
Les Pierres Noires ☆ Fl R 5s 27m **19M**; W twr, R top; *Horn
(2) 60s*; 48°18'·67N 04°54'·88W.

BREST AND APPROACHES
Basse Royale ⨪ Q (6) + L Fl 15s; 48°17'·45N 04°49'·61W.
Vandrée ⨪ VQ (9) 10s; *Whis*; 48°15'·21N 04°48'·24W.
Goëmant ⨪ ; 48°15'·12N 04°46'·34W.
La Parquette ⨪ Fl RG 4s 17m R6M, G6M; 244°-R-285°-G-244°;
W 8-sided twr, B diagonal stripes; 48°15'·90N 04°44'·29W.
Coq Iroise ⨪ 48°19'·07N 04°43'·99W.
Charles Martel ⨪ Fl (4) R 15s; 48°18'·95N 04°41'·92W.
Trépied ⨪ 48°16'·73N 04°41'·50W.
Swansea Vale ⨪ Fl (2) 6s; *Whis*; 48°18'·27N 04°38'·85W.

GOULET DE BREST
Le Chat ⨪ 48°20'·29N 04°41'·72W (Anse de Bertheaume).
Le Trez Hir ⨪ 48°20'·78N 04°41'·96W.
Pte du Petit-Minou ☆ Fl (2) WR 6s 32m **W19M, R15M**; Shore-R-
252°-W-260°-R-307°-W(unintens)-015°-W-065·5°;
70·5°-W-shore; Gy twr, R top; 48°20'·19N 04°36'·86W.
Ldg lts 068°, both Dir Q 30/54m **23/22M**. **Front, Pte du
Petit-Minou**, intens 067·3°-068·8°. **Rear, Pte du Portzic**
☆, Aux Dir Q 54m **22M**; intens 065°-071° (see below).
Fillettes ⨪ VQ (9) 10s; 48°19'·75N 04°35'·66W.
Kerviniou ⨪ Fl R 2·5s; 48°19'·77N 04°35'·25W.
Basse Goudron ⨪ Fl (2) R 6s; 48°20'·03N 04°34'·86W.
Mengam ⨪ Fl (3) WR 12s 10m W11M, R8M; 034°-R-054°-
W-034°; R twr, B bands; 48°20'·32N 04°34'·56W.
Pte du Portzic ☆ Oc (2) WR 12s 56m **W19M, R15M**;
219°-R-259°-W-338°-R-000°-W-065·5° (vis 041°-069° when
west of Goulet)-W-219°; Gy twr; 48°21'·49N 04°32'·05W.
Same lt ho, Aux Dir Q, rear 068° ldg lt. Aux ☆ Dir Q (6) + L
Fl 15s 54m **23M**; intens 045°-050°.

BREST
Pénoupèle ⨪ Fl (3) R 12s; 48°21'·45N 04°30'·53W.
S jetty ⚡ QR 10m 7M; 094°-048°; W/R twr; 48°22'·10N
04°29'·46W.
E jetty ⚡ QG 10m 7M; W/G twr; 48°22'·15N 04°29'·22W.
Ldg lts 344°: Front ⚡ Dir Q WRG 24m W9M, R/G6M;
334°-G-342°-W-346°-R-024°; 48°22'·79N 04°29'·63W. Rear
⚡ Dir Q 32m 9M; intens 342°-346°; 115m from front.
Le Château Marina, S Jetty hd ⚡ Fl G 2·5s 8m 4M;
48°22'·66N 04°29'·49W.
Le Château Marina, N Jetty hd, ⚡ Fl R 2·5s 8m 4M;
48°22'·67N 04°29'·45W.
Port de Commerce, E ent: N jetty ⚡ Oc (2) G 6s 8m 7M;
W/G pylon; 48°22'·76N 04°28'·53W. S jetty ⚡ Oc (2) R 6s
8m 5M; W pylon, R top; 48°22'·69N 04°28'·48W.
R2 ⨪ Fl (2) R 6s; 48°22'·01N 04°28'·75W.
R1 ⨪ Fl G 4s; 48°21'·83N 04°28'·29W.

R4 L Fl R 10s; 48°22'·22N 04°28'·06W.
R3 Q (6) + L Fl 15s; 48°22'·48N 04°27'·36W.

LE MOULIN BLANC MARINA
Moulin Blanc ↙ Fl (2) R 6s; 48°22'·79N 04°25'·99W.
MBA ↓ Q(3) 10s 3m 2M; pontoon elbow; 48°23'·54N 04°25'·74W.

CAMARET
N môle ↯ Iso WG 4s 7m W12M, G9M; 135°-W-182°-G-027°; W pylon, G top; 48°16'·85N 04°35'·31W.
Port Vauban wavebreak, S end, ↯ Fl (2) G 6s 2m 2M; 48°16'·74N 04° 35'·33W.
S môle ↯ Fl (2) R 6s 9m 5M; R pylon; 48°16'·63N 04°35'·33W.

POINTE DU TOULINGUET TO RAZ DE SEIN
Pte du Toulinguet ☆ Oc (3) WR 12s 49m **W15M**, R11M; Shore-W-028°-R-090°-W-shore; W □ twr; 48°16'·81N 04°37'·72W.
La Louve ⏚ 48°16'·76N 04°38'·03W.
Mendufa ⬧ 48°16'·05N 04°39'·43W.
Basse du Lis ↙ Q (6) + L Fl 15s 9m 6M; 48°12'·99N 04°44'·53W.
Le Chevreau ⬧ 48°13'·30N 04°36'·98W.
Le Bouc ↙ Q (9) 15s; 48°11'·51N 04°37'·37W.
Basse Vieille ↙ Fl (2) 6s 8m 7M; 48°08'·22N 04°35'·75W.

MORGAT
Pointe de Morgat ☆ Oc (4) WRG 12s 77m **W15M**, R11M, G10M; Shore-W-281°-G-301°-W-021°-R-043°; W □ twr, R top, W dwelling; 48°13'·17N 04°29'·80W. ↙ Fl R 4s; 48°13'·60N 04°29'·55W.

DOUARNENEZ to RAZ DE SEIN
Île Tristan ↯ Oc (3) WR 12s 35m, W13M, R10M; Shore-W-138°-R-153°-W-shore; Gy twr, W band, B top; 48°06'·14N 04°20'·24W.
Pointe du Millier ☆ Oc (2) WRG 6s 34m **W16M**, R12M, G11M; 080°-G-087°-W-113°-R-120°-W-129°-G-148°-W-251°-R-258°; W house; 48°05'·92N 04°27'·93W.
Basse Jaune ⬧ 48°04'·70N 04°42'·45W.

RAZ DE SEIN
Tévennec ↯ Q WR 28m W9M R6M; 090°-W-345°-R-090°; W □ twr and dwelling; 48°04'·28N 04°47'·73W. Same twr, Dir ↯ Fl 4s 24m 12M; intens 324°-332° (through Raz de Sein).
La Vieille ☆ Oc (2+1) WRG 12s 33m **W18M**, R13M, G14M; 290°-W-298°-R-325°-W-355°-G-017°-W-035°-G-105°-W-123°-R-158°-W-205°; Gy □ twr; Horn (2+1) 60s; 48°02'·44N 04°45'·40W.
La Plate ⏚ VQ (9) 10s 19m 8M; 48°02'·37N 04°45'·58W.
Le Chat ⏚ Fl (2) WRG 6s 27m, W9M, R/ G6M; 096°-G-215°-W-230°-R-271°-G-286°-R-096°; YB twr; 48°01'·43N 04°48'·86W.

CHAUSSÉE DE SEIN and ÎLE DE SEIN
Cornoc-An-Ar-Braden ↙ Fl G 4s; 48°03'·23N 04°50'·84W.

Men-Brial ↯ Oc (2) WRG 6s 16m, W12M, R9M, G7M; 149°-G-186°-W-192°-R-221°-W-227°-G-254°; G&W twr; 48°02'·28N 04°50'·97W.
Île de Sein Fl (4) 25s 49m **29M**; W twr, B top; 48°02'·62N 04°52'·02W. Same twr, Dir Q WRG, W8M, R/G 6M; 267°-G-269°-W-271°-R-275°.
Ar-Men Fl (3) 20s 29m **23M**; W twr, B top; 48°03'·01N 04°59'·87W.
Chaussée de Sein ↙ VQ (9) 10s 9m 6M; Whis; **Racon O (3cm), 10M**; 48°03'·74N 05°07'·75W.

AUDIERNE
Pointe de Lervily ↯ Fl (3) WR 12s 20m W14M, R11M; 236°-W-269°-R-294°-W-087°-R-109°; W twr, R top; 48°00'·04N 04°33'·94W. Gamelle W ↙, VQ (9) 10s; 47°59'·46N 04°32'·85W.
Jetée de Ste-Évette ↯ Oc (2) R 6s 2m 7M; R lantern; 090°-000° (270°); 48°00'·31N 04°33'·07W.
Passe de l'Est ldg lts 331°: Front, Jetée de Raoulic ↯ Fl (3) RG 12s 11m, R/G6M; 085°-R-034°-G-085°-R-085°; 48°00'·55N 04°32'·46W.
Kergadec ↯ 006°: Dir Q WRG 43m W12M, R/G9M; 000°-G-005·3°-W-006·7°-R-017°; W 8-sided twr, R top; 48°00'·95N 04°32'·79W.
Gamelle E ⬧; 47°59'·46N 04°32'·05W.

POINTE DE PENMARC'H
Eckmühl ☆ Fl 5s 60m **23M**; Gy 8-sided twr; Horn 60s; 47°47'·89N 04°22'·36W.
Men-Hir ↯ Fl (2) WG 6s 19m, W7M, G4M; G135°-315°, W315°-135°; W twr, B band; 47°47'·74N 04°23'·99W.
Cap Caval ↙ Q (9) 15s; 47°46'·47N 04°22'·68W.
Locarec ↯ Iso WRG 4s 11m, W9M, R/G6M; 063°-G-068°-R-271°-W-285°-R-298°-G-340°-R-063°; iron col on rk; 47°47'·29N 04°20'·31W.

LE GUILVINEC
Névez ↙ Fl G 2·5s; 47°45'·84N 04°20'·08W.
Ldg lts (triple Q) 053°, all synch: **Front**, ↯ Q 7m 8M; 233°-066°; W pylon; Môle de Léchiagat, spur; 47°47'·43N 04°17'·07W. Middle, ↯ Q WG 12m W14M, G11M; 006°-W-293°-G-006°; synch; R □ on R col; Rocher Le Faoutés, 210m from front. Rear, ↯ Q 26m 8M, 051·5°-054·5°, R □ on W twr; 0·58M from front.
Spineg ↙ Q (6) + L Fl 15s; 47°45'·19N 04°18'·90W.

LESCONIL
Karek Greis ↙ Q (3) 10s; 47°46'·03N 04°11'·36W.
Men-ar-Groas ↯ Fl (3) WRG 12s 14m, W10M, R/G7M; 268°-G-313°-W-333°-R-050°; W lt ho, G top; 47°47'·79N 04°12'·68W.

DISTANCE TABLES
Approx distances in nautical miles by the most direct route allowing for dangers and TSS.

1	Lézardrieux	1	12	16	18	24	42	43	45	72	97	100	105	124	Pornic 12
2	Tréguier	22	2	11	12	24	39	40	41	66	87	90	95	113	St Nazaire 11
3	Perros-Guirec	28	21	3	10	13	30	30	34	55	78	80	85	106	La Baule/Pornichet 10
4	Trébeurden	40	32	17	4	9	18	22	27	48	73	75	79	100	Le Croisic 9
5	Morlaix	60	46	36	23	5	8	28	36	57	78	80	84	105	Arzal/Camöel 8
6	Roscoff	54	41	28	17	12	6	7	16	37	58	60	64	85	Crouesty 7
7	L'Aberwrac'h	84	72	60	49	48	32	7	6	26	47	48	54	74	Le Palais (Belle Ile) 6
8	Le Conquet	106	98	83	72	68	55	29	8	5	32	33	38	61	Lorient 5
9	Brest (marina)	114	107	92	83	79	67	42	18	9	4	4	12	37	Concarneau 4
10	Morgat	126	118	103	92	88	75	49	20	24	10	3	12	36	Port-la-Forêt 3
11	Douarnenez	131	123	108	97	93	80	54	25	29	11	11	2	30	Loctudy 2
12	Audierne	135	128	113	102	98	86	55	30	34	27	30	12	1	Audierne 1

AREA 17 *South Biscay – River Loire to Bordeaux*

SELECTED LIGHTS, BUOYS & WAYPOINTS

Positions are referenced to WGS84

LOCTUDY TO CONCARNEAU

Rostolou ⚓ 47°46'·64N 04°07'·29W.
Boulanger ⚓ VQ (6) + L Fl 10s;47°47'·38N 04°09'·13W.
Chenal de Bénodet ⚓ 47°48'·53N 04°07'·04W.
Bilien ⚓ VQ (3) 5s; 47°49'·10N 04°08'·09W.

LOCTUDY

Pte de Langoz ☆ Fl (4) WRG 12s 12m, **W15M**, R/G11M; 115°-W-257°-G-284°-W-295°-R-318°-W-328°-R-025°; W twr, R top; 47°49'·88N 04°09'·55W.
Karek-Saoz ⚓ Fl R 2·5s 3m 1M; R twr; 47°50'·02N 04°09'·38W.
Men Audierne ⚓ 47°50'·34N 04°08'·94W.
No. 2 (Karek-Croisic) ⚓ Fl (2) R 6s; 47°50'·19N 04°09'·49W.
No. 1 ⚓ Fl (2) G 6s; 47°50'·22N 04°09'·73W.
No. 3 ⚓ Fl (3) G 12s; 47°50'·22N 04°09'·99W.
Groyne head ☆ Q 3m 10M; 47°50'·21N 04°10'·34W.
Le Blas ⚓ Fl (4) G 15s 5m 1M; truncated col; 47°50'·28N 04°10'·23W.

BENODET

Ldg lts 345·5°: Front, Pte du Coq ☆ Dir Oc (3) G 12s 11m 10M; intens 345°-347°; W ○ twr, G stripe; 47°52'·31N 04°06'·70W. Pyramide ☆ Oc (3) 12s 48m 14M; 338°-016°, synch; W twr, G top; common rear, 348m from front.
Lts in line 000·5°: Front, Pte de Combrit ☆ Oc (2) WR 6s 19m, W12M, R9M; 325°-W-017°-R-325°; W □ twr, Gy corners 47°51'·86N 04°06'·78W. Common rear, Pyramide; see above.
Rousse ⚓ 47°51'·55N 04°06'·47W. La Potée ⚓ 47°51'·78N 04°06'·55W.
Pte du Toulgoët ☆ Fl R 2·5s 2m 1M; 47°52'·30N 04°06'·86W.
Le Taro ⚓ 47°50'·51N 04°04'·83W.
La Voleuse ⚓ Q (6) + L Fl 15s; 47°48'·76N 04°02'·49W.

ILE AUX MOUTONS and LES POURCEAUX

Île-aux-Moutons ☆ Iso WRG 2s 18m, **W15M**, R/G11M; 035°-W-050°-G-063°-W-081°-R-141°-W-292°-R-035°; W □ twr and dwelling; 47°46'·48N 04°01'·66W.
Rouge de Glénan ⚓ VQ (9) 10s 8m 8M; 47°45'·48N 04°03'·95W.
Grand Pourceaux ⚓ Q; 47°45'·98N 04°00'·80W.

ÎLES DE GLÉNAN

Penfret ☆ Fl R 5s 36m **21M**; W □ twr, R top; 47°43'·26N 03°57'·18W. Same twr: auxiliary ☆ Dir Q 34m 12M; 295°-315°.
La Pie ⚓ Fl (2) 6s 9m 3M; 47°43'·75N 03°59'·76W.
Pte de la Baleine ⚓ VQ (3) 5s 2M; 47°43'·26N 03°59'·20W.
Les Bluiniers ⚓ 47°43'·35N 04°03'·81W.
Offlying marks, anticlockwise from the west:
Basse Pérennès ⚓ Q (9) 15s 8m 5M; 47°41'·06N 04°06'·14W.
Jument de Glénan ⚓ Q (6) + L Fl 15s 10m 4M; 47°38'·76N 04°01'·41W.
Laoennou ⚓ 47°39'·65N 03°54'·70W.
Jaune de Glénan ⚓ Q (3) 10s; 47°42'·56N 03°49'·83W.

PORT-LA-FORÊT

Linuen ⚓ Q (3) 10s; 47°50'·76N 03°57'·31W.
Laouen Pod ⚓ 47°51'·23N 03°58'·00W.

Cap Coz mole ☆ Fl (2) WRG 6s 5m, W7M, R/G5M; Shore-R-335°-G-340°-W-346°-R-shore; 47°53'·49N 03°58'·28W.
Le Scoré ⚓ 47°52'·75N 03°57'·56W.
Les Ormeaux ⚓ 47°53'·27N 03°58'·34W.
Entry channel ⚓ Fl G 2·5s; 47°53'·39N 03°58'·12W.
⚓ Fl R 2·5s; 47°53'·39N 03°58'·22W.
Kerleven mole ☆ Fl G 4s 8m 6M; 47°53'·60N 03°58'·37W.

CONCARNEAU

Ldg lts 028·5°: Front, La Croix ☆ Q 14m 13M; 006·5°-093°; R&W twr; 47°52'·16N 03°55'·08W. **Rear, Beuzec** ☆ Dir Q 87m **23M**; synch, intens 026·5°-030·5°; spire, 1·34M from front.
⚓ QR; 47°51'·40N 03°55'·75W.
Le Cochon ⚓ Fl (3) WRG 12s 5m W9M, R/G6M; 230°-R-352°-W-048°-G-207°-Obsc'd-230°; G twr; 47°51'·47N 03°55'·54W.
Basse du Chenal ⚓ Fl R 4s; 47°51'·54N 03°55'·66W.
Men Fall ⚓ Fl (2) G 6s; 47°51'·76N 03°55'·28W.
Kersos ⚓ 47°51'·80N 03°54'·93W (Anse de Kersos).
Lanriec ⚓ QG 13m 8M; 063°-078°; G window on W gable end; 47°52'·01N 03°54'·64W.
La Medée ⚓ Fl (3) R 12s 9m 4M; 47°52'·07N 03°54'·80W.
Ville-Close ⚓ Q WR, W9M, R6M; 209°-R-354°-W-007°-R-018°; R turret; 47°52'·27N 03°54'·76W.
No. 1 ☆ Fl (4) G 15s 4m 5M; G turret; 47°52'·16N 03°54'·72W.
Marina wavescreen ☆ Fl (4) R 15s 3m 1M; 47°52'·23N 03°54'·79W. No. 2 ☆ Fl R 4s 4m 5M; G turret; 47°52'·31N 03°54'·71W.
Ville-Close (NE end) ☆ Fl (2) R 6s; R twr; 47°52'·37N 03°54'·68W.
Ent to FV basin ☆ Fl (2) G 6s; G twr; 47°52'·36N 03°54'·63W.
Pouldohan ☆ Fl G 4s 6m 8M; 053°-065°; W □ twr, G top; 47°50'·97N 03°53'·69W.
Roché Tudy ⚓ 47°50'·52N 03°54'·49W.

CONCARNEAU TO ÎLE DE GROIX

PTE DE TRÉVIGNON TO PORT MANEC'H

Les Soldats ⚓ VQ (9) 10s; 47°47'·86N 03°53'·42W.
Trévignon mole ☆ Fl G 4s 5m 8M; 47°47'·70N 03°51'·30W.
Trévignon bkwtr root ☆ Oc (3+1) WRG 12s 11m, W14M, R/G11M; 004°-W-051°-G-085°-W-092°-R-127°; 322°-R-351°; W □ twr, G top; 47°47'·59N 03°51'·32W.
Men Du ⚓ 47°46'·41N 03°50'·50W.
Men an Tréas ⚓ 47°45'·77N 03°49'·66W.

PORT MANEC'H (Aven and Bélon rivers)

Port Manech ☆ Oc (4) WRG 12s 38m, W10M, R/G7M; obscd by Pte de Beg-Morg when brg <299°; 050°-W (unintens)-140°-W-296°-G-303°-W-311°-R (over Les Verrès)-328°-W-050°; W & R twr; 47°47'·99N 03°44'·34W.
Les Verrès ⚓ 47°46'·65N 03°42'·71W.

BRIGNEAU

Brigneau ⚓ 47°46'·11N 03°40'·10W.
W mole, ☆ Oc (2) WRG 6s 7m, W12M, R/G9M; R col, W top; 280°-G-329°-W-339°-R-034°; 47°46'·86N 03°40'·18W.

In line 331° with W ☐ daymark behind, Hard to see, rear beacon unlit.

MERRIEN
⚲ Dir QR 26m 7M; 004°-009°; W ☐ twr, R top; 47°47'·04N 03°38'·97W.
Ent, W side △. E side ⚓ 47°46'·45N 03°38'·89W.

DOËLAN
Ldg lts 013·8°: Front ⚲ Oc (3) WG 12s 20m, W13M, G10M; W shore-305°, G305°-314°, W314°-shore; W lt ho, G band and top; 47°46'·32N 03°36'·51W. Rear ⚲ Oc (3)R 12s 27m 9M; W lt ho, R band & top; 326m from front.

LE POULDU
Ent ⛊ 47°45'·74N 03°32'·25W.
Grand Cochon ⏚ 47°43'·03N 03°30'·81W.
Pte de Kerroc'h ⚲ Oc (2) WRG 6s 22m W11M, R/G8M; 096·5°-R-112°·5-G-132°-R-302°-W-096·5°; W twr, R top; 47°41'·97N 03°27'·66W.

ÎLE DE GROIX
Pen Men ☆ Fl (4) 25s 60m **29M**; 309°-275°; W ☐ twr, B top; 47°38'·84N 03°30'·56W.
Speerbrecker, ⏚ 47°39'·10N 03°26'·33W.
Port Tudy, N môle ⚲ Iso G 4s 12m 6M; W twr, G top; 47°38'·72N 03°26'·74W.
E môle ⚲ Fl (2) R 6s 11m 6M; 112°-226°; W twr R top; 47°38'·68N 03°26'·78W.
Basse Melité ⏚ 47°38'·84N 03°25'·54W.
Pte de la Croix ⚲ Oc WR 4s 16m, W12M, R9M; 169°-W-336°-R-345°-W-353°; W pedestal, R lantern; 47°38'·05N 03°25'·02W.
Edouard de Cougy ⏚ 47°37'·93N 03°23'·90W.
Pointe des Chats ☆ Fl R 5s 16m **19M**; W ☐ twr and dwelling; 47°37'·24N 03°25'·30W.
Les Chats ⏛ Q (6) + L Fl 15s; 47°35'·70N 03°23'·57W.

LORIENT AND RIVER ÉTEL
LORIENT, PASSE DE L'OUEST
Passe de l'Ouest ldg lts 057°: both Dir Q 11/22m 13/**18M**. Front, Les Sœurs; intens 042·5°-058·5°, 058·5°-042·5°, 4M range only; R twr, W bands; 47°42'·13N 03°21'·84W. Rear **Port Louis** ☆, 740m from front (see below).
Banc des Truies ⏛ Q (9) 15s; 47°40'·76N 03°24'·48W.
Loméner, Anse de Stole, Dir ⚲ 357·2°: Q WRG 13m, W10M, R/G8M; 349·2°-G-355·2°-W-359·2°-R-005·2°; W twr, R top; 47°42'·30N 03°25'·54W.
A2 ⏛ Fl R 2·5s; 47°40'·94N 03°24'·98W.
Les Trois Pierres ⏛ Q RG 11m R/G6M; 060°-G-196°-R-002°; B twr, W bands; 47°41'·53N 03°22'·47W.
A8 ⏛ Fl R 2·5s; 47°41'·90N 03°22'·52W.

PASSE DU SUD
Bastresses Sud ⏛ QG; 47°40'·77N 03°22'·09W.
Les Errants ⏛ Fl (2) R 6s; 47°41'·10N 03°22'·38W.
Bastresses Nord ⏛ Fl (2) G 6s; 47°41'·11N 03°22'·20W.
Locmalo ⏛ Fl (3) G 12s; 47°41'·67N 03°22'·13W.

SOUTH OF PORT LOUIS
La Paix ⚶ Fl G 2·5s; 47°41'·84N 03°21'·92W.
Île aux Souris ☆ Dir Q WG 6m, W3M, G2M; 041·5°-W-043·5°-G-041·5°; G twr; 47°42'·15N 03°21'·52W.
⚶ Fl G 2·5s; 47°42'·13N 03°21'·21W.
Ban-Gâvres FV/yacht hbr, W jetty ☆ Fl (2) G 6s 3M; 47°42'·06N 03°21'·11W. E jetty ☆ Fl (2) R 6s 3M; 47°42'·06N 03°21'·06W.

ENTRANCE CHANNEL
Ldg lts 016·5°, both Dir QG 8/14m 13M; intens 014·5°-017·5°; synch; W twrs, G tops. Front ☆, 47°43'·47N 03°21'·63W (Île St Michel). Rear ☆, 306m from front.
La Citadelle ⚶ Oc G 4s 6m 6M; 012°-192°; 47°42'·59N 03°21'·94W.
Secondary yacht chan, ⬒ RGR, 47°42'·49N 03°22'·12W.
La Petite Jument ⏛ Oc R 4s 5m 6M; 182°-024°; R twr; 47°42'·58N 03°22'·07W.
Le Cochon ⏛ Fl R 4s 5m 5M; RGR twr; 47°42'·80N 03°22'·00W.
No. 1 ⚶ 47°42'·80N 03°21'·84W.

PORT LOUIS (Port de la Pointe)
D 1 ⚶ 47°42'·76N 03°21'·52W.
Jetty ⚲ Fl G 2·5s 7m 6M; W twr, G top; 47°42'·71N 03°21'·37W.
Anse du Driasker Stage Head Fl R 2·5s 2M, metal mast.

KERNEVEL
Kéroman ldg lts 350°, both Dir Oc (2) R 6s 25/31m **15M**; synch; intens 349°-351°: **Front** ☆, 47°43'·60N 03°22'·02W, R ho, W bands. **Rear** ☆ R&W topmark on Gy pylon, R top; 91m from front.
Banc du Turc ⏛ Fl G 2·5s; 47°43'·33N 03°21'·85W.
Kernével marina, entrance: ⚲ QR 1M; 47°43'·39N 03°22'·10W.
Ldg lts 217°, both Dir QR 10/18m **15M**; intens 215°-219°; synch: **Front, Kernével** ☆ R&W twr; 47°43'·02N 03°22'·32W. **Rear** ☆ W ☐ twr, R top; 290m from front.
⏛ Q (3) 10s; marks wreck; 47°43'·49N 03°22'·05W.

NORTHERN PART OF LORIENT HARBOUR
Grand Bassin (FV hbr), E side of ent, ⚲ Fl RG 4s 7m 6M; 000°-G-235°-R-000°; W twr, G top; 47°43'·63N 03°21'·87W.
Ste Catherine marina ent ⚲ QG 5m 3M; 47°43'·52N 03°21'·12W.
N side of marina ent ⚲ QR 2m 2M 47°43'·53N 03°21'·10W.
Pengarne ⚶ Fl G 2·5s 3m 3M; G twr; 47°43'·88N 03°21'·23W.
No. 9 ⚶ Fl (2) G 6s; 47°43'·95N 03°21'·16W.
No. 11 ⚶ Fl (3) G 12s; 47°44'·04N 03°21'·01W.
Pen-Mané marina, bkwtr elbow ⚲ Fl (2) G 6s 4M; 47°44'·11N 03°20'·86W.
Blavet River, No. 1 ⚶ Fl (2+1)G 10s; 47°44'·20N 03°20'·78W.
No. 2 ⏛ Fl R 2·5s; 47°44'·26N 03°20'·74W.
Pointe de l'Espérance, Dir ⚲ 037°, Q WRG 8m W10M, R/G8M; 034·2°-G-036·7°-W-037·2°-R-047·2°; W twr, G top; 47°44'·51N 03°20'·66W.
Ro-Ro jetty ⚲ QR 7m 2M; 47°44'·42N 03°20'·96W.
No. 8 ⏛ Fl R 2·5s; 47°44'·56N 03°20'·98W, ent to Lorient marina.

RIVIÈRE D'ÉTEL
Roheu ⛊ 47°38'·54N 03°14'·70W.
Épi de Plouhinec ⚲ Fl R 2·5s 7m 2M; 47°38'·59N 03°12'·86W.
W side ent ⚲ Oc (2) WRG 6s 13m W9M, R/G6M; 022°-W-064°-R-123°-W-330°-G-022°; R twr; 47°38'·69N 03°12'·83W.
Conspic R/W radio mast (CROSS Étel), 47°39'·73N 03°12'·11W.
Les Pierres Noires ⛊ 47°35'·53N 03°13'·29W.

BELLE ÎLE AND QUIBERON BAY (W OF 2° 50'W)
PLATEAU DES BIRVIDEAUX (6M NNW of Belle Île)
⚶ Fl (2) 6s 24m 10M; BRB twr; 47°29'·15N 03°17'·46W.

BELLE ÎLE

Pte des Poulains ☆ Fl 5s 34m **23M**; 023°-291°; W ☐ twr and dwelling; 47°23'·31N 03°15'·11W.

Les Poulains *1* 47°23'·44N 03°16'·68W.

N Poulains *1* 47°23'·68N 03°14'·88W.

Sauzon, NW jetty ⚡ Fl G 4s 8m 8M; 47°22'·49N 03°13'·04W.

SE jetty ⚡ Fl R 4s 8m 8M; 315°-272°; W twr, R top; 47°22'·45N 03°13'·00W. Inner hbr, W jetty ⚡, QG 9m 5M; 194°-045°; W twr, G top; 47°22'·37N 03°13'·13W.

Le Palais, N jetty ⚡ QG 11m 7M; obsc 298°-170° by Ptes de Kerdonis and Taillefer; W twr, G top; 47°20'·84N 03°09'·04W.

No 1 ⬥ Fl (2) G 6s; 47°20'·82N 03°08'·96W;

No 2 ⬥ Fl R 4s; 47°20'·71N 03°08'·89W;

No 4 ⬥ Fl (2) R 6s; 47°20'·78N 03°09'·01W.

S jetty ⚡ QR 11m 7M; obsc'd 298°-170° (see N jetty); W twr, R lantern; 47°20'·82N 03°09'·07W.

Pointe de Kerdonis ☆ Fl (3) R 15s 35m **15M**; obsc'd 025°-129° by Pointes d'Arzic and de Taillefer; W ☐ twr, R top and W dwelling; 47°18'·60N 03°03'·58W.

Les Galères *1* 47°18'·77N 03°02'·76W.

SW coast of Belle Île: La Truie ⬥ 47°17'·11N 03°11'·79W.

Goulphar ☆ Fl (2) 10s 87m **27M**; Gy twr; 47°18'·65N 03°13'·63W.

PORT MARIA (Quiberon ferry port)

Light ho ⚡ Q WRG 28m W14M, R/ G10M; 246°-W-252°-W-297°-G-340°-W-017°-R-051°-W-081°-G-098°-W-143°; W twr, G lantern; 47°28'·78N 03°07'·45W.

Le Pouilloux *1* 47°27'·88N 03°08'·01W.

Ldg lts 006·5°, both Dir QG 5/13m **16/17M**; intens 005°-008°; W twrs, B bands: **Front**, 47°28'·63N 03°07'·18W. **Rear**, 230m north.

Les Deux Frères ⬥ Fl R 2·5s; 175°-047°;47°28'·34N 03°07'·29W.

S bkwtr ⚡ Oc (2) R 6s 9m 7M; W twr, R top; 47°28'·54N 03°07'·31W.

CHAUSSÉE and PASSAGE DE LA TEIGNOUSE

Le Four ⬥ 47°27'·78N 03°06'·54W.

Les Trois Pierres ⬥ 47°27'·46N 03°05'·24W.

Roc er Vy ⬥ 47°27'·70N 03°04'·40W; Chenal en Toull Bras.

Roc er Vy ⬥ 47°27'·86N 03°04'·35W.

Basse Cariou *1* 47°26'·94N 03°06'·38W.

Basse du Chenal *1* 47°26'·66N 03°05'·77W.

Goué Vaz S ⬥ Q (6) + L Fl 15s; 47°25'·76N 03°04'·93W.

La Teignouse ☆ Fl WR 4s 20m **W15M**, R11M; 033°-W-039°-R-033°; W ○ twr, R top; 47°27'·44N 03°02'·75W.

Basse du Milieu ⬥ Fl (2) G 6s 9m 2M; 47°25'·91N 03°04'·12W.

Goué Vaz E ⬥ Fl (3) R 12s; 47°26'·23N 03°04'·28W.

NE Teignouse ⬥ Fl (3) G 12s; 47°26'·55N 03°01'·87W.

Basse Nouvelle ⬥ Fl R 2·5s; 47°26'·98N 03°01'·99W.

CHAUSSÉE AND PASSAGE DU BÉNIGUET

Les Esclassiers ⬥ 47°25'·68N 03°03'·05W.

Le Grand Coin ⬥ 47°24'·45N 03°00'·26W.

Bonen Bras ⬥ 47°24'·26N 02°59'·88W.

ÎLE DE HOUAT

Le Rouleau ⬥ 47°23'·67N 03°00'·31W.

Port St-Gildas N môle ⚡ Fl (2) WG 6s 8m W9M, G6M;

168°-W-198°-G-210°-W-240°-G-168°; W twr, G top; 47°23'·57N 02°57'·34W.

Mussel beds, 1 -1.5M NNE of above ⚡ and in its G sector (198°-210°), marked by 2 ⬥ at S end, and ⬥ VQ (3) 5s & ⬥ VQ at N end.

Bcns SE and S of Houat: Men Groise ⬥ 47°22'·77N 02°55'·00W.

Er Spernec Bras ⬥ 47°22'·09N 02°55'·23W.

Men er Houteliguet ⬥ 47°22'·54N 02°56'·38W.

ÎLE DE HOËDIC

Les Sœurs ⬥ 47°21'·14N 02°54'·74W.

La Chèvre ⬥ 47°21'·08N 02°52'·55W.

Port de l'Argol bkwtr ⚡ Fl WG 4s 10m W9M, G6M; 143°-W-163°-G-183°-W-194°-G-143°; W twr, G top; 47°20'·66N 02°52'·48W.

Er Gurranic'h ⬥ 47°20'·51N 02°50'·44W.

Cohfournik ⬥ 47°19'·49N 02°49'·69W.

Grands Cardinaux ⚡ Fl (4) 15s 28m 13M; R and W twr; 47°19'·27N 02°50'·10W, 2·1M SE of Argol.

Le Chariot *1* 47°18'·87N 02°52'·95W.

Er Palaire ⬥ 47°20'·16N 02°55'·01W.

PORT HALIGUEN

Banc de Quiberon S ⬥ Q (6) + L Fl 15s; 47°28'·04N 03°02'·34W.

Banc de Quiberon N *1* 47°29'·65N 03°02'·58W.

E bkwtr hd ⚡ Oc (2) WR 6s 10m, W11M, R8M; 233°-W-240·5°-R-299°-W-306°-R-233°; W twr, R top; 47°29'·36N 03°05'·94W.

Port Haliguen *1* 47°29'·38N 03°05'·55W; marks 1·7m patch.

NW bkwtr hd ⚡ Fl G 2·5s 9m 6M; 47°29'·34N 03°06'·02W.

Bugalet wreck *1* 47°31'·19N 03°05'·45W.

Men er Roué ⬥ 47°32'·25N 03°06'·06W.

LA TRINITÉ-SUR-MER

Ldg lts 347°, both W twrs, G tops: Front, ⚡ Q WRG 11m W10M, R/G7M; 321°-G-345°-W-013·5°-R-080°; 47°34'·09N 03°00'·37W. **Rear** ☆ Dir Q 21m **15M**, intens 337°-357°; synch; 540m NNW.

Buissons de Méaban *1* 47°31'·66N 02°58'·49W.

Le Petit Buisson *1* 47°32'·14N 02°58'·57W.

Roche Révision *1* 47°32'·63N 02°59'·36W.

Petit Trého ⬥ Fl (4) R 15s; 47°33'·47N 03°00'·71W.

R. de Crac'h Dir ⚡ 347°: Oc WRG 4s 9m W13M, R/G 11M; 345°-G-346°-W-348°-R-349°; W twr; 47°35'·03N 03°00'·98W.

S pier ⚡ Oc (2) WR 6s 6m, W9M, R6M; 090°-R-293·5°-W-300·5°-R-329°; W twr, R top; 47°35'·09N 03°01'·50W.

Marina wavebreak/pier ⚡ Iso R 4s 8m 5M; 47°35'·28N 03°01'·46W.

GOLFE DU MORBIHAN

Méaban *1* 47°30'·77N 02°56'·23W.

Outer ldg marks 001°: Front, Petit Vezid ⬚; W obelisk; 47°34'·17N 02°55'·23W. Rear, Baden ch spire (83m), 47°37'·20N 02°55'·14W.

Pointe de Port-Navalo ☆ Oc (3) WRG 12s 32m, **W15M**, R/G11M; 155°-G-220°; 317°-G-359°-W-015°-R-105°; W twr and dwelling; 47°32'·87N 02°55'·11W.

Ldg marks 359°: Front, Grégan ⬥ Q (6) + L Fl 15s 3m 8M; 47°33'·91N 02°55'·05W. Rear, Baden ch spire (5 lines above).

Auray river: Catis ⬥ 47°36'·14N 02°57'·23W.

César ⚓ 47°38'·36N 02°58'·22W.

No. 13 ⚓ 47°39'·48N 02°58'·64W (last bcn before 14m bridge).

Morbihan: Grand Mouton ⚓ QG; 47°33'·71N 02°54'·85W.
Gavrinis ⚓ 47°34'·21N 02°54'·05W.
Jument ⚓ 47°34'·29N 02°53'·43W.
Creizic S ⚓ 47°34'·63N 02°52'·84W.
Creizic N ⚓ 47°34'·93N 02°52'·20W.
Les Rechauds, two ⚓ 47°36'·18N 02°51'·30W.
Truie d'Arradon ⚓ 47°36'·58N 02°50'·27W.
Logoden ⚓ 47°36'·70N 02°49'·91W.
Drenec ⚓ 47°36'·84N 02°48'·39W.
Bœdic ⚓ 47°36'·85N 02°47'·59W.
Roguédas ⚓ Fl G 2·5s 4m 4M; G twr; 47°37'·12N 02°47'·28W.

CROUESTY
Ldg lts 058°, both Dir Q 10/27m **19M**; intens 056·5°-059·5°:
Front ☆ R panel, W stripe; 47°32'·53N 02°53'·95W. **Rear** ☆, grey lt ho; 315m from front.
No. 1 ⚓ QG; 47°32'·26N 02°54'·76W.
No. 2 ⚓ 47°32'·26N 02°54'·76W.
N jetty ⚓ Fl R 4s 9m 7M; R&W ☐ twr; 47°32'·47N 02°54'·14W.
S jetty ⚓ Fl G 4s 9m 7M; G&W ☐ twr; 47°32'·45N 02°54'·10W.

PLATEAU DU GRAND MONT
Chimère ⚓ 47°28'·83N 02°53'·98W.
L'Epieu ⚓ 47°29'·51N 02°52'·91W.
St Gildas ⚓ 47°29'·78N 02°52'·87W.
Grand Mont ⚓ 47°28'·98N 02°51'·12W.

QUIBERON BAY (E OF 2° 50'W) TO PTE DU CROISIC
PLATEAU DE SAINT JACQUES
Le Bauzec ⚓ 47°28'·89N 02°49'·40W.
St Jacques ⚓ 47°28'·17N 02°47'·52W.
Port St Jacques, jetty ⚓ Oc (2) R 6s 5m 6M; W 8-sided twr, R top; 47°29'·24N 02°47'·41W.

PLATEAU DE LA RECHERCHE
Recherche ⚓ Q (9) 15s; 47°25'·56N 02°50'·39W.
Locmariaquer ⚓ 47°25'·82N 02°47'·36W.

PÉNERF
⚓ Fl (5) Y 20s; 47°27'·58N 02°39'·56W.
Penvins ⚓ 47°28'·93N 02°40'·09W. Borenis ⚓ 47°29'·21N 02°38'·35W.
Tour des Anglais ⚓ W bcn; 47°30'·21N 02°37'·94W; appr brg 031·4°.
Pignon ⚓ Fl (3) WR 12s 6m W9M, R6M; 028·5°-R-167°-W-175°-R-349·5°-W-028·5°; R twr; 47°30'·03N 02°38'·89W.

VILAINE RIVER
Pte de Penlan ☆ Oc (2) WRG 6s 26m, **W15M**, R/G11M; 292·5°-R-025°-G-052°-W-060°-R-138°-G-180°; W sector defines Passe de la Grande Accroche; W twr, R bands; 47°30'·97N 02°30'·11W.
Bertrand ⚓ Iso WG 4s 6m, W9M, G6M; 040°-W-054°-G-227°-W-234°-G-040°; G twr; 47°31'·06N 02°30'·72W.
Basse de Kervoyal ⚓ Dir Q WR W8M, R5M; 269°-W-271°-R-269°; W sector leads to/from Nos 1 & 2 buoys; 47°30'·37N 02°32'·62W.
No. 1 ⚓ Fl G 2·5s; 47°30'·32N 02°28'·73W.
No. 2 ⚓ Fl R 2·5s; 47°30'·41N 02°28'·71W.

Pointe du Scal ⚓ QG 8m 4M; 47°29'·67N 02°26'·87W.

ÎLE DUMET
Fort ⚓ Fl (3) WRG 15s 14m, W7M, R/G4M; 090°-G-272°-W-285°-R-335°-W-090°; W col, G top; 47°24'·69N 02°37'·21W.
Basse-Est Île Dumet ⚓ Q (3) 10s; 47°25'·20N 02°34'·93W.
Île Dumet ⚓ Q; 47°25'·90N 02°36'·05W.

MESQUER
Laronesse ⚓ 47°25'·96N 02°29'·50W.
Basse Normande ⚓ 47°25'·47N 02°29'·80W.
Jetty ⚓ Oc WRG 4s 7m W10M, R/G7M; 067°-W-072°-R-102°-W-118°-R-293°-W-325°-G-067°; W col & bldg; 47°25'·31N 02°28'·05W.

PIRIAC-SUR-MER
Grand Norven ⚓ Q; 47°23'·55N 02°32'·89W.
Inner mole ⚓ Oc (2) WRG 6s 8m, W10M, R/G7M; 066°-R-148°-G-194°-W-201°-R-221°; W col; 47°22'·93N 02°32'·71W. *Siren 120s (occas), 35m SW.* E bkwtr ⚓ Fl R 4s 4m 5M; W pylon, R top; 47°23'·00N 02°32'·67W.
Les Bayonnelles ⚓ Q (9) 15s; 47°22'·56N 02°35'·23W.

LA TURBALLE
Ldg lts 006·5°, both Dir Iso R 4s 11/19m 3M; intens 004°-009°: Front, 47°20'·70N 02°30'·87W. Rear, 275m N of the front lt.
Ouest Jetée de Garlahy ⚓ Fl (4) WR 12s 13m, W10M, R7M; 060°-R-315°-W-060°; W pylon, R top; 47°20'·70N 02°30'·93W.
Digue Tourlandroux ⚓ Fl G 4s 4m 2M; G post, E side of access chan; 47°20'·75N 02°30'·88W.

LE CROISIC
Basse Hergo ⚓ Fl G 2·5s 5m 3M; 47°18'·62N 02°31'·69W.
Jetée du Tréhic ⚓ Iso WG 4s 12m W14M, G11M; 042°-G-093°-W-137°-G-345°; Gy twr, G top; 47°18'·49N 02°31'·42W. F Bu fog det lt, 100m SE.
Outer ldg lts 155·5°, both Dir Q 10/14m 13M; intens 154°-158°: Front ☆ 47°17'·96N 02°30'·99W . Rear ☆, 116m from front.
Middle ldg lts 174°, both QG 5/8m 11M; 170·5°-177·5°: Front 47°18'·06N 02°31'·07W. Rear, 48m from front.
Le Grand Mabon ⚓ Fl (3) R 12s 6m 2M; 47°18'·05N 02°31'·03W.
Inner ldg lts 134·7°, both QR 6/10m 8M; intens 132·5°-143·5°; synch.
Basse Castouillet ⚓ Q (9) 15s; 47°18'·12N 02°34'·37W.
Basse Lovre ⚓ Q; 47°15'·87N 02°29'·58W, Chenal du Nord.

PLATEAU DU FOUR/BANC DE GUÉRANDE
Bonen du Four ⚓ Q; 47°18'·53N 02°39'·29W.
Le Four ☆ Fl 5s 23m **18M**; W twr, B diagonal stripes; 47°17'·87N 02°38'·05W.
Ouest Basse Capella ⚓ Q (9) 15s; *Whis;* 47°15'·66N 02°42'·78W.
Goué-Vas-du-Four ⚓ Q (6) + L Fl 15s; 47°14'·91N 02°38'·20W.
Sud Banc Guérande ⚓ VQ (6) + L Fl 10s; 47°08'·80N 02°42'·81W.

POINTE DU CROISIC TO POINTE DE ST GILDAS
PLATEAU DE LA BANCHE
NW Banche ⚓ Q 8m 4M; 47°12'·86N 02°31'·02W.
W Banche ⚓ VQ (9) 10s; 47°11'·64N 02°32'·41W.
La Banche ☆ Fl (2) WR 6s 22m **W15M**, R11M;

266°-R-280°-W-266°; B twr, W bands; 47°10'·62N 02°28'·08W.

SE Banche *Ɫ* 47°10'·40N 02°26'·10W.

PLATEAU DE LA LAMBARDE

NW Lambarde *Ɫ* 47°10'·84N 02°22'·93W.

SE Lambarde *Ɫ* Q (6) + L Fl 15s; 47°10'·04N 02°20·80W.

BAIE DU POULIGUEN (or Baie de la Baule)

Penchateau *Ɫ* Fl R 2·5s; 47°15'·24N 02°24'·35W.

Les Guérandaises *Ɫ* Fl G 2·5s; 47°15'·03N 02°24'·29W.

Ȧ 47°15'·24N 02°23'·50W.

Les Evens *Ɫ* 47°14'·32N 02°22'·55W.

Les Troves *Ɫ* 47°14'·23N 02°22'·41W.

NNW Pierre Percée *Ɫ* 47°13'·63N 02°20'·63W.

La Vieille *ȧ* 47°14'·03N 02°19'·51W.

Sud de la Vieille *Ɫ* 47°13'·75N 02°19'·54W.

Le Caillou *Ɫ* 47°13'·65N 02°19'·18W.

Le Petit Charpentier *Ɫ* 47°13'·34N 02°18'·95W.

Le Grand Charpentier ⚡ Q WRG 22m, W14M, R/G10M; 020°-G-049°-W-111°-R-310°-W-020°; Gy lt ho, G lantern; 47°12'·83N 02°19'·13W.

LE POULIGUEN

Basse Martineau *ȧ* 47°15'·54N 02°24'·34W.

Petits Impairs *Ȧ* Fl (2) G 6s 6m 2M; 47°15'·99N 02°24'·61W.

SW jetty ⚡ QR 13m 9M; 171°-081°; W col; 47°16'·39N 02°25'·39W.

PORNICHET (La Baule)

S bkwtr ⚡ Iso WRG 4s 11m, W10M, R/G7M; 303°-G-081°-W-084°-R-180°; W twr, G top; 47°15'·49N 02°21'·14W.

Ent,W side ⚡ QG 3m 1M; B perch, G top; 47°15'·51N 02°21'·12W.

E side ⚡ QR 4m 1M; B perch, R top; 47°15'·50N 02°21'·10W.

ST NAZAIRE APPROACH (Chenal du Sud)

S-N1 *Ɫ* L Fl 10s 8m 5M; *Racon Z (3cm), 3-8M;* 47°00'·07N 02°39'·84W.

S-N2 *Ɫ* Iso 4s 8m 5M; 47°02'·08N 02°33'·47W.

Les Chevaux *Ȧ* Fl G 2·5s; 47°03'·53N 02°26'·37W.

Thérèsia *Ɫ* Fl R 2·5s; 47°04'·84N 02°27'·27W.

La Couronnée *Ȧ* Fl (2) G 6s; *Racon T, 3-5M;* 47°07'·60N 02°20'·05W.

Lancastria *Ɫ* Fl (2) R 6s;47°08'·88N 02°20'·37W.

PASSE DES CHARPENTIERS

Portcé ☆ ldg lts 025·5°, both Dir Q 6/36m **22/24M: Front**, intens 024·7°-026·2°; synch; W col; 47°14'·57N 02°15'·44W. **Rear** ☆ (H24); intens 024°-027°; W ☐ twr, W stripe; 0·75M from front.

Wreck (anon)*Ɫ* Fl (3) R 12s; 47°09'·87N 02°19'·46W.

No. 1 *Ȧ* VQ G; 47°09'·94N 02°18'·40W.

No. 2 *Ɫ* VQ R; 47°10'·06N 02°18'·72W.

No. 6 *Ɫ* Fl (3) R 12s; 47°12'·05N 02°17'·31W.

No. 5 *Ȧ* Fl (4) G 15s; 47°12'·65N 02°16'·57W.

No. 8 *Ȧ* Fl (4) R 15s; 47°12'·75N 02°16'·86W.

No. 7 *Ȧ* VQ G; 47°13'·30N 02°16'·11W.

No. 10 *Ɫ* VQ R; 47°13'·62N 02°16'·16W. (Buoys 9 - 18 not listed).

Pointe d'Aiguillon ☆ Oc (3) WR 12s 27m, W13M, R10M; 207°-R-233°-W-293°; 297°-W-300°-R-327°-W-023°; 027°-R-089°; W lt ho, conspic; 47°14'·54N 02°15'·79W.

Ville-ès-Martin jetty ⚡ Fl (2) 6s 10m 10M; W twr, R top; 47°15'·33N 02°13'·65W.

Morées *ʀ* Fl (3) WR 12s 12m, W6M, R4M; W058°-224°, R300°-058°; G twr; 47°15'·00N 02°13'·02W.

SAINT NAZAIRE

W jetty ⚡ Oc (4) R 12s 11m 8M; W twr, R top; 47°15'·97N 02°12'·25W.

E jetty ⚡ Oc (4) G 12s 11m 11M; W twr, G top; 47°15'·99N 02°12'·14W. (Ent for big ships locking into Bassin St Nazaire)

No. 20 *Ɫ* QR; 47°16'·19N 02°11'·37W.

Sud Basse Nazaire *Ɫ* Q (6) + L Fl 15s; 47°16'·21N 02°11'·51W.

Basse Nazaire *Ȧ* Fl G 2·5s; 47°16'·24N 02°11'·63W.

SE Old mole *⚓* Fl R 2·5s; 47°16'·24N 02°11'·73W.

Old Môle ⚡ Q (3) 10s 18m 11M; 153·5°-063·5°; W twr, R top; weather signals; 47°16'·27N 02°11'·82W.

⅃ Fl (2) R 6s 5m 1M; R dolphin ; 47°16'·37N 02°11'·80W.

⚡ Fl (3) R 12s 9m 9M; R pylon; 47°16'·47N 02°11'·85W.

Ldg lts 280° (into E lock) 2 VQ Vi; front 47°16'·49N 02°11'·92W.

EAST SIDE OF RIVER, SOUTH TO PTE DE ST GILDAS

Le Pointeau, Digue S ⚡ Fl WG 4s 4m, W10M, G7M; 050°-G-074°-W-149°-G-345°-W-050°; G&W ○ hut; 47°14'·02N 02°10'·96W.

Port de Comberge La Truie *Ɫ* 47°12'·06N 00°13'·36W.

S jetty ⚡ Fl (2) WG 6s 7m W9M, G6M; 123°-W-140°-G-123°; W twr, G top; 47°10'·53N 02°10'·01W.

Port de la Gravette La Gravette *Ɫ* 47°09'·81N 02°13'·06W.

Bkwtr hd ⚡ Fl (3) WG 12s 7m, W8M, G5M; 183°-W-188°-G-124°-W-138°-G-183°; W structure, G top; 47°09'·64N 02°12'·70W.

Anse du Boucau bkwtr ⚡ Fl (2) G 6s 3M; 47°08'·41N 02°14'·80W.

Pte de Saint Gildas ⚡ Q WRG 20m, W14M, R/G10M; 264°-R-308°-G-078°-W-088°-R-174°-W-180°-G-264°; col on W house, G top; 47°08'·02N 02°14'·74W.

Nord Couronnée *Ɫ* Q; 47°07'·34N 02°17'·78W.

RIVER LOIRE TO NANTES

Well buoyed/lit to Île de Bois, thence G lts, S side; R lts N side.

No. 21 *Ȧ* VQ G; 47°16'·96N 02°10'·25W.

Suspension bridge, mid-span ⚡ Iso 4s 55m, vis up/down stream; 47°17'·10N 02°10'·24W; between 2 conspic R/W twrs.

MA *Ȧ* Fl (2) G 6s; 47°17'·50N 02°09'·22W.

MB *Ȧ* Fl (3) G 12s; 47°17'·95N 02°07'·53W.

Fernais-25 *Ȧ* Fl (4) G 15s; 47°18'·10N 02°06'·60W.

Paimboeuf, môle root ⚡ Oc (3) WG 12s 9m, W10M, G7M; Shore-G-123°-W-shore; W twr, G top; 47°17'·42N 02°01'·96W.

Île de Bois (upstream) Fl (2) G 6s; 47°12'·79N 01°48'·27W.

Ldg lts 064° Rear Dir VQ R; 47°12'·00N 01°34'·35W, Y-junction with Bras de la Madeleine.

POINTE DE SAINT GILDAS TO FROMENTINE

Pte de Saint Gildas ° Q WRG 20m, W14M, R/G10M; 264°-R-308°-G-078°-W-088°-R-174°-W-180°-G-264°;

47°08'·02N 02°14'·75W.Notre Dame ⚓ VQ (9) 10s 7m 3M; 47°05'·42N 02°08'·26W.

PORNIC
Marina ent, S side ⚡ Fl (2) R 6s 4m 2M; 47°06'·47N 02°06'·67W.
Pte de Noëveillard ⚡ Oc (4) WRG 12s 22m W13M, R/G9M; Shore-G-051°-W-079°-R-shore; W ☐ twr, G top, W dwelling; 47°06'·62N 02°06'·92W.

ÎLE DE NOIRMOUTIER anti-clockwise from the East
Pte des Dames ☆ Oc (3) WRG 12s 34m, **W19M, R/G15M**; 016·5°-G-057°-R-124°-G-165°-W-191°, R191°-267°-W-357°-R-016·5°; W ☐ twr; 47°00'·67N 02°13'·26W. La Chaise ⯑ 47°01'·21N 02°12'·64W.
L'Herbaudière, ldg lts 187·5°, both Q 5/21m 7M, Gy masts. Front, 47°01'·59N 02°17'·84W. Rear, 310m from front.
Martroger ⚓, Q WRG 11m W9M, R/G6M; 033°-G-055°-W-060°-R-095°-G-124°-W-153°-R-201°-W-240°-R-033°; 47°02'·61N 02°17'·11W.
W jetty ⚡ Oc (2+1) WG 12s 9m W10M, G7M; 187·5°-W-190°-G-187·5°; W col and hut, G top; 47°01'·63N 02°17'·84W.
E jetty ⚡ Fl (2) R 6s 8m 4M; 47°01'·61N 02°17'·81W.
Île du Pilier ☆ Fl (3) 20s 33m **29M**; Gy twr; 47°02'·55N 02°21'·60W. Same twr, auxiliary ⚡ QR 10m 11M, 321°-034°.
Passe de la Grise ⯑ Q (6) + L Fl 15s; 47°01'·66N 02°19'·97W.
Les Boeufs ⯑ VQ (9) 10s; 46°55'·04N 02°27'·99W.
Réaumur ⯑ Q (9) 15s; 46°57'·46N 02°24'·22W.
Le Bavard ⯑ VQ (6) + L Fl 10s; 46°56'·79N 02°23'·34W.
Pte du Devin (Morin) ⚡ Oc (4) WRG 12s 10m W11M, R/G8M; 314°-G-028°-W-035°-R-134°; W col & hut, G top; 46°59'·15N 02°17'·60W.

GOULET DE FROMENTINE
Fromentine ⚓ L Fl 10s; 46°53'·07N 02°11'·63W (buoyed chan).
Milieu ⚓ Fl (4) R 12s 6m 5M; 46°53'·59N 02°09'·63W.
Pte de Notre Dame-de-Monts ⚡ Dir Oc (2) WRG 6s 21m, W13M, R/G10M; 000°-G-043°-W-063°-R-073°-W-094°-G-113°-W-116°-R-175°-G-196°-R-230°; W twr, B top; 46°53'·33N 02°08'·54W.

ÎLE D'YEU TO BOURGENAY
ÎLE D'YEU
Petite Foule (main lt) ☆ Fl 5s 56m **24M**; W ☐ twr, G lantern; 46°43'·04N 02°22'·91W.
Les Chiens Perrins ⚓ Q (9) WG 15s 16m W7M, G4M; 330°-G-350°-W-200°; 46°43'·60N 02°24'·58W.
Pont d'Yeu ⯑ 46°45'·81N 02°13'·81W.
La Sablaire ⯑ Q (6) + L Fl 15s; 46°43'·62N 02°19'·49W.
Port Joinville ldg lts 219°, both QR 11/16m 6M, 169°-269°: Front, Quai du Canada 46°43'·61N 02°20'·94W. Rear, 85m from front.
NW jetty ⚡ Oc (3) WG 12s 7m, W11M, G8M; Shore-G-150°-W-232°-G-279°-W-285°-G-shore; W 8-sided twr, G top; 46°43'·77N 02°20'·82W. La Galiote ⚓ 46°43'·73N 02°20'·71W.
Pte des Corbeaux ☆ Fl (2+1) R 15s 25m **20M**; 083°-143° obsc by Île de Yeu; W ☐ twr, R top; 46°41'·41N 02°17'·08W.

Port de la Meule ⚡ Oc WRG 4s 9m, W9M, R/G6M; 007·5°-G-018°-W-027·5°-R-041·5°; Gy twr, R top; 46°41'·62N 02°20'·72W.

SAINT GILLES-CROIX-DE-VIE
Pte de Grosse Terre ☆ Fl (4) WR 12s 25m, **W18M, R15M**; 290°-R-339°-W-125°-R-145°; W truncated twr; 46°41'·54N 01°57'·92W.
Ldg lts 043·7°, both Q 7/28m **15M**; 033·5°-053·5°; synch; W ☐ twrs, R tops: Front, 46°41'·86N 01°56'·75W. Rear, 260m NE.
Pilours ⯑ Q (6) + L Fl 15s; *Bell*; 46°40'·99N 01°58'·09W.
Jetée de la Garenne ⚡ Fl G 4s 8m 6M; 46°41'·46N 01°57'·25W.
Jetée de Boisvinet ⚡ Fl R 4s 8m 6M; 46°41'·62N 01°57'·16W.

LES SABLES D'OLONNE
Les Barges ⚡ Fl (2) R 10s 25m 13M; Gy twr; 46°29'·70N 01°50'·50W.
Petite Barge ⯑ Q (6) + L Fl 15s 3M; *Whis*; 46°28'·90N 01°50'·61W.
L'Armandèche ☆ Fl (2+1) 15s 42m **24M**; 295°-130°; W 6-sided twr, R top; 46°29'·39N 01°48'·29W.
Nouch Sud ⯑ Q (6) + L Fl 15s; 46°28'·55N 01°47'·41W.
Nouch Nord ⯑ 46°28'·88N 01°47'·36W.
SW Pass, ldg lts 032·5°, both Iso 4s 12/33m **16M**, H24: **Front** ☆, 46°29'·42N 01°46'·37W; mast. **Rear** ☆, **La Potence**, W ☐ twr.
SE Pass, ldg lts 320°: Front, E jetty ⚡ QG 11m 8M; W twr, G top; 46°29'·44N 01°47'·51W. Rear, Tour d'Arundel ⚡ Q 33m 13M, synch; large Gy ☐ twr; 46°29'·63N 01°47'·74W.
Jetée St Nicolas (W jetty) ⚡ QR 16m 8M; 143°-094°; W twr, R top; 46°29'·23N 01°47'·52W.

BOURGENAY
Ldg lts 040°, both QG 9/19m 7M. Front, 020°-060°; on S bkwtr; 46°26'·34N 01°40'·62W. Rear, 010°-070°; 162m from front.
Landfall ⚓ L Fl 10s; 46°25'·26N 01°41'·93W.
Ent ⚡ Fl R 4s 8m 9M & ⚡ Iso G 4s 6m 5M; 46°26'·29N 01°40'·75W.

PLATEAU DE ROCHEBONNE (Shoal 32M offshore)
NW ⯑ Q (9) 15s; *Whis*; 46°12'·92N 02°31'·58W.
NE ⚓ Iso G 4s; 46°12'·73N 02°24'·83W.
SE ⯑ Q (3) 10s; *Bell*; 46°09'·20N 02°21'·13W.
SW ⯑ Fl (2) R 6s; 46°10'·11N 02°27'·04W.

PERTUIS BRETON
JARD-SUR-MER and LA TRANCHE-SUR-MER
Ldg marks 036°, two unlit W bcns; 46°24'·47N 01°34'·16W.
Pte du Grouin du Cou ☆ Fl WRG 5s 29m, **W20M, R/G16M**; 034°-R-061°-W-117°-G-138°-W-034°; W 8-sided twr, B top; 46°20'·67N 01°27'·83W.
La Tranche pier ⚡ Fl (2) R 6s 6m 6M; R col; 46°20'·55N 01°25'·63W.
Mussel farm, No entry, marked by: ⯑ Q, 46°17'·17N 01°22'·19W.
⯑ Q (3) 10s, 46°15'·73N 01°18'·42W. ⯑ Q (6) + L Fl 15s, 46°15'·16N 01°19'·98W. ⯑ Q (9) 15s, 46°16'·28N 01°22'·88W.

L'AIGUILLON and LA FAUTE-SUR-MER
Le Lay ⚓ Q (6) + L Fl 15s; 46°16'·10N 01°16'·53W.
No. 1 ⚓ 46°16'·65N 01°16'·25W. Many mussel beds.

ANSE DE L'AIGUILLON (for La Sèvre Niortaise & Marans)
ATT de L'Aiguillon ⚓ L Fl 10s; 46°15'·33N 01°11'·50W.
Inner fairway ⚓ 46°17'·19N 01°09'·65W.
Port du Pavé ⚡ Fl G 4s 9m 7M; W col, G top; 46°18'·15N 01°08'·01W.

ÎLE DE RÉ
Les Baleineaux ⚡ VQ 23m 7M; pink twr, R top; 46°15'·81N 01°35'·22W.
Les Baleines ☆ Fl (4) 15s 53m **27M**; conspic Gy 8-sided twr, R lantern; 46°14'·64N 01°33'·69W.

ARS-EN-RÉ
Dir ⚡ 268° Oc WRG 4s, W10M, R/G 7M, 275·5°-G-267·5°-W-268·5°-R-274·5°; W hut with W ☐ topmark; 46°14'·05N 01°28'·60W.
Les Islattes ⚓ Q 13m 3M; NCM bcn twr 46°14'·03N 01°23'·32W.
Bûcheron No 1 ⚓ Fl G 2·5s; 46°14'·21N 01°25'·98W.
Bûcheron No 3 ⚓ Fl (2) G 6s; 46°14'·14N 01°26'·94W.
Le Fier d'Ars, inner ldg lts 232·5°, both Q 5/13m 9/11M: Front ⚡ R/W frame on W col; 46°12'·75N 01°30'·59W. Rear ⚡ 142°-322°; B vert rectangle on W mast, 370m from front.

ST MARTIN DE RÉ
Lt ho, E of ent ⚡ Oc (2) WR 6s 18m W10M, R7M; Shore-W-245°-R-281°-W-shore; W twr, R top; 46°12'·44N 01°21'·89W.
W mole ⚡ Fl G 2·5s 10m 5M; obsc'd by Pte du Grouin when brg <124°; W post, G top; 46°12'·49N 01°21'·91W.

LA FLOTTE
N bkwtr ⚡ Fl WG 4s 10m W12M, G9M; 130°-G-205°-W-220°-G-257°; W ◯ twr, G top; 46°11'·33N 01°19'·30W.
Dir lt 212·5°, Moiré effect, is next to the main lt twr.
ÎLE DE RÉ (South coast, from the W, inc bridge)
Chanchardon ⚡ Fl WR 4s 15m W11M, R8M; 118°-R-290°-W-118°; B 8-sided twr, W base; 46°09'·71N 01°28'·41W.
Chauveau ☆ Oc (3) WR 12s 27m **W15M**, R11M; 057°-W-094°-R-104°-W-342°-R-057°; W ◯ twr, R top; 46°08'·03N 01°16'·42W.
Bridge span (30m cl'nce) for SE-bound vessels, ⚡ Iso 4s 34m 8M; 46°10'·18N 01°14'·75W . Span (30m cl'nce) for NW-bound vessels, ⚡ Iso 4s 34m 8M; 46°10'·26N 01°14'·52W.
La Pallice, W mole, ⚡ Fl G 4s 5m 6M; 46°09'·78N 01°14'·45W. S end, ⚡ Q (6) + L Fl 15s 6m 9M; 46°09'·36N 01°14'·52W.

LA ROCHELLE AND LA CHARENTE TO ROCHEFORT
LA ROCHELLE
PA ⚓ Iso 4s 8m 7M; *Whis*; 46°05'·62N 01°42'·45W.
Chauveau ⚓ VQ (6) + L Fl 10s; 46°06'·56N 01°16'·06W.
Roche du Sud ⚓ Q (9) 15s; 46°06'·37N 01°15'·22W.
La Rochelle ldg lts 059°, both Dir Q 15/25m 13/14M; synch; by day Fl 4s. Front; intens 056°-062°; R ◯ twr, W bands; 46°09'·35N 01°09'·16W. Rear, 044°-074°, obsc'd 061°-065°; W 8-sided twr, G top, 235m from front.

Lavardin ⚓ Fl (2) 6s 14m 7M; BRB IDM twr; 46°08'·09N 01°14'·52W.
Les Minimes ⚓ Q (9) 15s; 46°08'·01N 01°11'·60W.
Pte des Minimes ⚡ Fl (3) WG 12s 8m; W8M, G5M; 059°-W-213°; 313°-G-059°; 8-sided twr on piles; 46°08'·27N 01°10'·76W.
Chan buoy ⚓ QG; 46°08'·53N 01°10'·87W; marking hbr limit.
Tour Richelieu ⚓ Fl R 4s 10m 9M; R twr; 46°08'·90N 01°10'·34W.
Port des Minimes, W bkwtr ⚡ Fl (2) G 6s 9m 7M; 46°08'·82N 01°10'·15W.

LA CHARENTE
Fort Boyard twr ⚡ Q (9) 15s; 45°59'·96N 01°12'·85W.
Ldg lts 115°, both Dir QR 8/21m **19/20M**; intens 113°-117°; W ☐ twr, R top: **Front** ☆, 45°57'·96N 01°04'·38W. **Rear**, **Soumard** ☆. 600m from front. Same twr: ⚡ QR 21m 8M; vis 322°-067°.
Îled'Aix ☆ Fl WR 5s 24m **W24M, R20M**; 103°-R-118°-W-103°; two conspic W ◯ twrs, R top; 46°00'·60N 01°10'·67W.
Pte Ste Catherine, jetty hd ⚓ Q (6) + L Fl 15s 5m 4M; 45°59'·05N 01°07'·85W. Les Palles ⚓; 45°59'·54N 01°09'·56W.
Fouras, Port Sud bkwtr ⚡ Fl WR 4s 6m 9/6M; 115°-R-177°-W-115°; 45°58'·97N 01°05'·72W. Rear 75m from front.

ROCHEFORT Night passage by yachts is not advised.
⚡ Fl (2) G 6s; bcn 45°55'·21N 00°56'·98W, 1·4M S of Rochefort.

ÎLE D'OLÉRON
Pte de Chassiron ☆ Fl 10s 50m, **28M**; conspic W twr, B bands; 46°02'·80N 01°24'·62W, NW tip of island.
Antioche ⚓ Q 20m 11M; 46°03'·94N 01°23'·71W.

ST DENIS
Dir ⚡ 205°, Iso WRG 4s 14m, W11M, R/G8M; 190°-G-204°-W-206°-R-220°; 46°01'·61N 01°21'·92W.
E jetty ⚡ Fl (2) WG 6s 6m, W9M, G6M; 205°-G-277°-W-292°-G-165°; ☐ hut; 46°02'·10N 01°22'·06W.

PORT DU DOUHET and PASSAGE DE L'OUEST
Seaweed farm ⚓ VQ; 46°00'·65N 01°17'·38W.
N ent ⚓ 46°00'·10N 01°19'·20W.
Fishfarm ⚓ Q; 46°00'·24N 01°15'·34W. ⚓ Q (3) 10s; 45°59'·84N 01°14'·79W.

BOYARDVILLE
Mole ⚡ Fl (2) R 6s 8m 5M; obsc'd by Pte des Saumonards when brg <150°; W twr, R top; 45°58'·24N 01°13'·83W.

COUREAU D'OLÉRON and LE CHÂTEAU D'OLÉRON
Juliar ⚓ Q (3) WG 10s 12m, W11M; G8M; 147°-W-336°-G-147°; 45°54'·11N 01°09'·48W.
Chateau d'Oléron, ldg lts 318·5°, both QR 11/24m 7M; synch. Front, 191°-087°; R line on W twr; 45°53'·03N 01°11'·45W. Rear, W twr, R top; 240m from front.

LA SEUDRE RIVER
Pte du Mus de Loup ⚡ Oc G 4s 8m 6M; 118°-147°; 45°47'·70N 01°08'·60W.
Pertuis de Maumusson. Depths & buoys subject to change.
ATT Maumusson ⚓ L Fl 10s; 45°46'·16N 01°17'·92W.
La Barre ⚓ 45°46'·79N 01°15'·97W.
Tabouret ⚓ 45°46'·93N 01°16'·15W.

Mattes ⚓ 45°46'·93N 01°15'·29W.
Gatseau ⚓ 45°47'·36N 01°14'·70W.

LA COTINIÈRE (SW side of island)
Ent ldg lts 339°, both ⚡ Dir Oc (2) 6s 6/14m 13/12M; synch: Front, 329°-349°; W twr, R top; 45°54'·72N 01°19'·79W. Rear, intens 329°-349°; W twr, R bands; 425m from front on W bkwtr.
W bkwtr head, Fl R 4s 10m; 45°54'·63N 01°19'·70W.

GIRONDE APPROACHES AND TO BORDEAUX
GRANDE PASSE DE L'OUEST
Pte de la Coubre ☆ Fl (2) 10s 64m **28M**; W twr, R top; 45°41'·78N 01°13'·99W. Same twr, F RG 42m10M; 030°-R-043°-G-060°-R-110°.
BXA ⚓ Iso 4s 8m 7M; *Racon B*; 45°37'·53N 01°28'·69W.
Ldg lts 081·5°. **Front** ☆, Dir Iso 4s 21m **20M**; intens 080·5°-082·5°; W pylon on dolphin; 45°39'·56N 01°08'·78W, 1·1M from rear. Same structure, Q (2) 5s 10m 3M.
La Palmyre, common rear ☆ Dir Q 57m **27M**; intens 080·5°-082·5°; W radar twr; 45°39'·71N 01°07'·25W.
Same twr, Dir FR 57m **17M**; intens 325·5°-328·5°.
No. 1 ⚓ QG; 45°38'·03N 01°22'·69W
No. 6 ⚓ VQ (6) + L Fl 10s; 45°38'·28N 01°18'·68W.
No. 7a ⚓ Fl G 4s; 45°38'·96N 01°14'·85W.
No. 9 ⚓ Q; 45°39'·43N 01°12'·79W.
No. 11 ⚓ Iso G 4s; 45°39'·06N 01°10'·60W.
No. 11A ⚓ Fl G 2·5s; 45°38'·37N 01°07'·90W.
No. 13 ⚓ Fl (2) G 6s; 45°37'·33N 01°06'·41W.
No. 13A ⚓ Fl (3) G 12s; 45°35'·68N 01°04'·19W.
No. 13B ⚓ QG; 45°34'·67N 01°02'·98W.
Ldg lts 327° (down-river): Front, **Terre-Nègre** ☆, Oc (3) WRG 12s 39m **W18M**, R/G14M; 304°-R-319°-W-327°-G-000°-W-004°-G-097°-W-104°-R-116°; W twr, R top on W side; 45°38'·77N 01°06'·39W, 1·1M from rear (La Palmyre above).
Cordouan ☆ Oc (2+1) WRG 12s 60m, **W19M, R16M, G15M**; 014°-W-126°-G-178·5°-W-250°-W (unintens) -267°-R (unintens)-294·5°-R-014°; obsc'd in estuary when brg >285°; W twr, Gy band; 45°35'·18N 01°10'·40W.

PASSE SUD (or DE GRAVE)
Ldg lts 063°: **Front, St Nicolas** ☆ Dir QG 22m **16M**; intens 061·5°-064·5°; W ☐ twr; 45°33'·73N 01°05'·01W.
Rear, Pte de Grave ☆ Oc WRG 4s 26m, **W17M, R/G13M**; 033°-W(unintens)-054°-W-233·5°-R-303°-W-312°-G-

330°-W-341°- W(unintens)-025°; W ☐ twr, B corners and top, 0·84M from front.
G ⚓ 45°30'·33N 01°15'·55W. G3 ⚓ 45°32'·79N 01°07'·72W.
Ldg lts 041°, both Dir QR 33/61m **18M. Front, Le Chay** ☆ 45°37'·31N 01°02'·43W. **Rear, St Pierre** ☆, 0·97M from front.
G4 ⚓ 45°34'·70N 01°05'·80W. G6 ⚓ 45°34'·88N 01°04'·80W.

ROYAN
R1 ⚓ Iso G 4s; 45°36'·56N 01°01'·96W.
S jetty ⚡ Fl (2) R 10s 11m 12M; 199°-116°; 45°37'·00N 01°01'·81W.
Hbr ent, W jetty ⚡ Fl (3) R 12s 8m 6M; 45°37'·12N 01°01'·53W.

PORT BLOC and PORT-MÉDOC
Pte de Grave, jetty ⚓ Q 6m 2M; 45°34'·42N 01°03'·68W.
Port Bloc, ent N side ⚡ Fl G 4s 9m 3M; 45°34'·14N 01°03'·74W.
Port-Médoc, N bkwtr head ⚡ QG 4M; 45°33'·40N 01°03'·39W.

MESCHERS, MORTAGNE, PORT MAUBERT, PAUILLAC and BLAYE
Meschers ldg lts 349·5°: 2 FW (privately maintained). Front 45°33'·20N 00°56'·62W, on E bkwtr head. Rear, 130m from front.
Mortagne ent ⚓ VQ (9) 10s; 45°28'·24N 00°49'·02W.
Port Maubert, ldg lts 024·5°, both QR 5/9m 5M; 45°25'·56N 00°45'·47W.
Pauillac, No. 43 ⚓ Fl (2) G 6s; 45°12'·44N 00°44'·27W.
NE elbow ⚡ Fl G 4s 7m 5M; 45°11'·95N 00°44'·59W.
Ent E side ⚡ QG 7m 4M; 45°11'·83N 00°44'·59W.
Blaye, No. S9 ⚓ 45°09'·35N 00°40'·27W; 1·8M N of Blaye.
N quay ⚡ Q (3) R 5s 6m 3M; 45°07'·49N 00°39'·99W.
D6 ⚓ Fl (2) R 6s; 45°06'·91N 00°39'·93W, 0.6M S of Blaye.
Bec d'Ambés ⚓ QG 5m 5M; 45°02'·53N 00°36'·47W (here Rivers Dordogne and Garonne flow into River Gironde).

BORDEAUX
Pont d'Aquitaine ⚡ 4 F Vi; 44°52'·82N 00°32'·28W.
No 73 ⚓ Iso G 4s; 44°52'·72N 00°32'·24W.
Lormont Iso R 4s, S end of ❶ pontoon; 44°52'·62N 00°32'·12W.
Lock ent to Bassins Nos 1 and 2, 44°51'·72N 00°33'·07W.
Pont de Pierre, 44°50'·30N 00°33'·78W, Km 0.

1	Port Joinville	1														
2	St Gilles-C-de-Vie	18	2													
3	Sables d'Olonne	31	16	3												
4	Bourgenay	40	25	9	4											
5	St Martin (I de Ré)	55	44	27	20	5										
6	La Rochelle	66	51	36	29	12	6									
7	Rochefort	84	75	61	54	36	26	7								
8	R La Seudre	89	71	58	52	33	24	30	8							
9	Port St Denis	59	48	33	30	21	13	26	22	9						
10	Port Bloc/Royan	97	85	71	60	56	52	68	27	42	10					
11	Bordeaux	152	140	126	115	111	107	123	82	97	55	11				
12	Cap Ferret	138	130	113	110	102	98	114	75	88	68	123	12			
13	Capbreton	192	186	169	166	165	156	172	131	145	124	179	58	13		
14	Anglet/Bayonne	200	195	181	178	177	168	184	143	157	132	187	70	12	14	
15	Santander	212	210	204	204	206	202	218	184	192	180	235	133	106	103	15
16	Cabo Finisterre	377	395	393	394	406	407	423	399	397	401	456	376	370	373	274	16

DISTANCE TABLES
Approx distances in nautical miles are by the most direct route allowing for dangers and TSS.

Times are UT - add 1 hour in non-shaded months to convert to Summer Time

SUN RISE/SET LATITUDE 56°N – 2012

	Rise JANUARY	Set	Rise FEBRUARY	Set	Rise MARCH	Set	Rise APRIL	Set	Rise MAY	Set	Rise JUNE	Set
1	0831	1536	0756	1632	0651	1735	0530	1839	0415	1940	0322	2035
4	0830	1539	0750	1638	0643	1741	0522	1845	0409	1946	0319	2039
7	0829	1544	0744	1645	0635	1748	0514	1851	0402	1952	0316	2042
10	0827	1548	0738	1651	0628	1754	0506	1857	0356	1958	0315	2045
13	0824	1553	0731	1658	0620	1800	0459	1903	0350	2004	0313	2047
16	0821	1559	0724	1705	0612	1806	0451	1910	0345	2009	0313	2049
19	0817	1605	0717	1711	0604	1812	0444	1916	0340	2015	0313	2050
22	0813	1611	0710	1718	0556	1819	0436	1922	0335	2020	0313	2051
25	0808	1617	0703	1724	0548	1825	0429	1928	0330	2025	0315	2051
28	0803	1623	0656	1731	0540	1831	0422	1934	0326	2029	0316	2050
31	0758	1630			0532	1837			0323	2034		

	JULY		AUGUST		SEPTEMBER		OCTOBER		NOVEMBER		DECEMBER	
1	0319	2049	0405	2007	0505	1854	0604	1734	0708	1619	0807	1531
4	0321	2047	0410	2001	0511	1846	0610	1727	0714	1612	0812	1528
7	0325	2045	0416	1954	0517	1838	0616	1719	0720	1606	0816	1527
10	0328	2042	0422	1947	0522	1830	0622	1711	0727	1600	0820	1525
13	0332	2038	0428	1941	0528	1822	0628	1703	0733	1555	0824	1525
16	0337	2034	0434	1934	0534	1814	0634	1656	0739	1550	0826	1525
19	0342	2030	0439	1926	0540	1806	0640	1649	0745	1545	0829	1526
22	0347	2025	0445	1919	0546	1758	0647	1641	0751	1541	0830	1527
25	0352	2020	0451	1911	0552	1750	0653	1634	0757	1537	0831	1529
28	0357	2015	0457	1904	0558	1742	0659	1628	0802	1533	0832	1532
31	0403	2009	0503	1856			0706	1621			0831	1535

SUN RISE/SET LATITUDE 48°N – 2012

	Rise JANUARY	Set	Rise FEBRUARY	Set	Rise MARCH	Set	Rise APRIL	Set	Rise MAY	Set	Rise JUNE	Set
1	0750	1617	0729	1659	0640	1745	0538	1831	0441	1914	0405	1952
4	0750	1620	0725	1704	0635	1749	0532	1835	0437	1918	0403	1954
7	0749	1623	0720	1709	0629	1754	0526	1839	0432	1922	0402	1957
10	0748	1627	0716	1713	0623	1758	0520	1844	0428	1926	0401	1959
13	0747	1631	0711	1718	0617	1803	0514	1848	0424	1930	0400	2001
16	0745	1635	0706	1723	0611	1807	0508	1852	0420	1934	0400	2002
19	0742	1639	0701	1728	0604	1812	0503	1856	0416	1938	0400	2003
22	0740	1644	0655	1732	0558	1816	0457	1901	0413	1941	0401	2003
25	0737	1648	0650	1737	0552	1820	0452	1905	0410	1945	0402	2004
28	0734	1653	0644	1742	0546	1825	0446	1909	0407	1948	0403	2003
31	0730	1657			0540	1829			0405	1951		

	JULY		AUGUST		SEPTEMBER		OCTOBER		NOVEMBER		DECEMBER	
1	0405	2003	0437	1935	0518	1840	0600	1739	0645	1641	0729	1609
4	0407	2002	0440	1931	0522	1834	0604	1733	0650	1637	0733	1608
7	0409	2001	0444	1926	0527	1828	0608	1727	0655	1632	0736	1607
10	0412	1959	0448	1921	0531	1822	0612	1721	0659	1628	0739	1607
13	0414	1957	0452	1916	0535	1816	0617	1715	0704	1624	0742	1607
16	0418	1954	0457	1911	0539	1810	0621	1709	0708	1621	0744	1607
19	0421	1951	0501	1905	0543	1803	0626	1703	0713	1618	0746	1609
22	0424	1948	0505	1900	0547	1757	0630	1658	0717	1615	0748	1610
25	0428	1945	0509	1854	0551	1751	0635	1653	0721	1613	0749	1612
28	0431	1941	0513	1848	0555	1745	0639	1648	0725	1611	0750	1614
31	0435	1937	0517	1842			0644	1643			0750	1617

Times are UT - add 1 hour in non-shaded months to convert to Summer Time

SUN RISE/SET LATITUDE 40°N – 2012

	Rise JANUARY	Set	Rise FEBRUARY	Set	Rise MARCH	Set	Rise APRIL	Set	Rise MAY	Set	Rise JUNE	Set
1	0722	1645	0709	1718	0633	1752	0544	1825	0500	1855	0433	1923
4	0722	1648	0706	1722	0628	1755	0539	1828	0456	1858	0432	1925
7	0722	1650	0703	1726	0624	1759	0534	1831	0453	1901	0431	1927
10	0722	1653	0700	1729	0619	1802	0529	1834	0449	1904	0431	1928
13	0721	1656	0656	1733	0614	1805	0525	1837	0446	1907	0431	1930
16	0720	1700	0653	1736	0609	1808	0520	1840	0444	1910	0431	1931
19	0719	1703	0649	1740	0605	1811	0516	1843	0441	1912	0431	1932
22	0717	1706	0645	1743	0600	1814	0512	1846	0439	1915	0432	1933
25	0715	1710	0640	1747	0555	1817	0508	1849	0437	1918	0433	1933
28	0713	1714	0636	1750	0550	1821	0504	1852	0435	1920	0434	1933
31	0710	1717			0545	1824			0434	1922		

	JULY		AUGUST		SEPTEMBER		OCTOBER		NOVEMBER		DECEMBER	
1	0435	1933	0459	1913	0528	1831	0557	1742	0629	1657	0703	1635
4	0437	1932	0501	1910	0531	1826	0559	1737	0633	1654	0706	1635
7	0438	1931	0504	1907	0534	1821	0603	1732	0636	1651	0709	1635
10	0440	1930	0507	1903	0536	1817	0606	1728	0640	1648	0711	1635
13	0442	1929	0510	1859	0539	1812	0609	1723	0643	1645	0713	1635
16	0445	1927	0513	1855	0542	1807	0612	1719	0647	1643	0716	1636
19	0447	1925	0516	1851	0545	1802	0615	1714	0650	1641	0717	1637
22	0450	1923	0519	1846	0548	1757	0618	1710	0653	1639	0719	1639
25	0452	1920	0521	1842	0551	1752	0622	1706	0657	1637	0720	1640
28	0455	1917	0524	1837	0554	1747	0625	1702	0700	1636	0721	1642
31	0458	1914	0527	1833			0628	1658			0722	1645

MOON RISE/SET LATITUDE 56°N – 2012

	Rise JANUARY	Set	Rise FEBRUARY	Set	Rise MARCH	Set	Rise APRIL	Set	Rise MAY	Set	Rise JUNE	Set
1	1102	0022	1033	0242	0950	0229	1154	0259	1332	0204	1651	0124
4	1202	0352	1257	0529	1259	0434	1601	0402	1754	0300	2050	0314
7	1410	0653	1646	0701	1707	0542	2031	0501	2207	0438	2250	0654
10	1748	0836	2102	0755	2133	0638	****	0651	****	0800	2346	1054
13	2155	0932	****	0857	0025	0809	0154	1018	0107	1155	0016	1430
16	0045	1025	0346	1101	0320	1112	0301	1406	0153	1532	0117	1754
19	0450	1208	0550	1438	0438	1501	0346	1741	0248	1858	0315	2031
22	0721	1537	0648	1830	0524	1841	0443	2107	0429	2150	0631	2158
25	0826	1935	0732	2207	0615	2211	0631	2352	0728	2330	1020	2252
28	0909	2314	0835	0025	0747	0017	0939	0100	1114	0010	1427	2352
31	1005	0135			1040	0231			1523	0103		

	JULY		AUGUST		SEPTEMBER		OCTOBER		NOVEMBER		DECEMBER	
1	1829	0102	1915	0320	1836	0619	1735	0743	1738	0953	1815	1005
4	2049	0424	2014	0724	1930	1000	1859	1104	2024	1203	2143	1122
7	2152	0831	2104	1108	2100	1317	2131	1330	2358	1316	0013	1216
10	2240	1215	2223	1431	2344	1534	****	1453	0236	1412	0420	1325
13	2349	1542	****	1703	0209	1652	0342	1551	0654	1532	0813	1555
16	0109	1828	0315	1829	0612	1749	0802	1704	1032	1823	1018	1959
19	0418	2004	0712	1925	1028	1906	1151	1931	1216	2223	1119	2356
22	0808	2100	1122	2031	1359	2140	1349	2319	1312	0056	1213	0220
25	1212	2158	1509	2240	1545	0010	1448	0152	1407	0431	1336	0539
28	1613	2347	1716	0102	1642	0403	1540	0531	1537	0747	1607	0806
31	1846	0200	1819	0502			1659	0854			1932	0929

Times are UT - add 1 hour in non-shaded months to convert to Summer Time

MOON RISE/SET LATITUDE 48°N – 2012

	Rise Set JANUARY	Rise Set FEBRUARY	Rise Set MARCH	Rise Set APRIL	Rise Set MAY	Rise Set JUNE
1	1116 0011	1111 0206	1032 0147	1221 0231	1338 0155	1625 0144
4	1237 0319	1338 0448	1331 0401	1602 0356	1732 0316	2008 0355
7	1452 0610	1706 0639	1713 0532	2004 0521	2125 0517	2225 0724
10	1812 0809	2055 0758	2111 0654	2344 0733	2355 0834	2344 1059
13	2153 0929	**** 0925	**** 0848	0121 1049	0054 1206	0028 1414
16	0025 1048	0303 1144	0242 1148	0250 1414	0201 1520	0149 1718
19	0407 1252	0521 1506	0421 1515	0356 1727	0316 1826	0355 1952
22	0647 1609	0641 1833	0529 1832	0513 2033	0510 2109	0657 2137
25	0815 1942	0747 2148	0641 2141	0712 2312	0800 2304	1024 2253
28	0920 2259	0910 ****	0828 ****	1008 0030	1123 ****	1405 ****
31	1036 0105		1114 0156		1506 0114	

	JULY	AUGUST	SEPTEMBER	OCTOBER	NOVEMBER	DECEMBER
1	1748 0141	1851 0350	1838 0620	1756 0725	1816 0915	1849 0930
4	2020 0458	2012 0729	1954 0939	1936 1028	2056 1130	2157 1105
7	2147 0840	2124 1050	2139 1239	2206 1254	**** 1302	0012 1220
10	2256 1201	2300 1354	**** 1500	0011 1435	0231 1420	0354 1353
13	**** 1508	0033 1626	0230 1637	0342 1555	0624 1604	0734 1635
16	0149 1748	0339 1810	0608 1757	0736 1732	0954 1901	0955 2019
19	0447 1940	0713 1929	0959 1937	1111 2010	1157 2240	1119 2352
22	0814 2059	1058 2058	1319 2219	1325 2340	1314 0057	1233 0202
25	1153 2220	1428 2321	1523 0037	1446 0158	1429 0411	1413 0503
28	1533 ****	1649 0135	1642 0407	1559 0515	1614 0710	1642 0730
31	1815 0237	1815 0511		1734 0820		1949 0910

MOON RISE/SET LATITUDE 40°N – 2012

	Rise Set JANUARY	Rise Set FEBRUARY	Rise Set MARCH	Rise Set APRIL	Rise Set MAY	Rise Set JUNE
1	1127 0002	1136 0141	1100 0119	1240 0211	1342 0149	1607 0159
4	1301 0256	1405 0420	1352 0338	1603 0352	1717 0327	1939 0423
7	1521 0541	1720 0623	1717 0525	1946 0536	2057 0544	2208 0745
10	1829 0751	2049 0800	2056 0705	2316 0801	2335 0857	2343 1103
13	2152 0928	**** 0945	**** 0915	0058 1111	0044 1213	0037 1402
16	0011 1104	0234 1214	0216 1213	0242 1420	0207 1511	0211 1653
19	0339 1321	0500 1525	0409 1525	0403 1717	0335 1803	0423 1926
22	0623 1632	0636 1835	0533 1825	0534 2009	0537 2042	0716 2121
25	0807 1948	0757 2134	0659 2120	0740 2244	0821 2245	1026 2253
28	0928 2248	0934 ****	0855 ****	1028 0008	1129 ****	1349 ****
31	1059 0044		1137 0131		1453 0123	

	JULY	AUGUST	SEPTEMBER	OCTOBER	NOVEMBER	DECEMBER
1	1720 0208	1834 0411	1840 0621	1811 0712	1842 0850	1912 0906
4	2000 0522	2011 0733	2010 0924	2001 1004	2118 1107	2207 1053
7	2143 0847	2139 1038	2205 1213	2230 1229	**** 1251	0012 1223
10	2308 1151	2326 1330	**** 1436	0028 1421	0228 1425	0336 1412
13	0011 1444	0101 1600	0244 1626	0342 1558	0604 1626	0707 1701
16	0217 1721	0357 1756	0605 1803	0718 1752	0928 1926	0939 2034
19	0507 1923	0713 1931	0938 1959	1044 2037	1144 2251	1119 2349
22	0818 2058	1040 2117	1253 2246	1308 2355	1316 0058	1248 0149
25	1139 2235	1400 2348	1507 0056	1444 0203	1446 0356	1438 0439
28	1505 0001	1630 0157	1641 0410	1612 0504	1640 0644	1706 0705
31	1752 0302	1811 0517		1759 0756		2001 0856

SPEED, TIME AND DISTANCE (NAUTICAL MILES)

Speed in knots

Time in minutes	1	2	3	4	5	6	7	8	9	10	15	20
1	0·0	0·0	0·1	0·1	0·1	0·1	0·1	0·1	0·2	0·2	0·3	0·3
2	0·0	0·1	0·1	0·1	0·2	0·2	0·2	0·3	0·3	0·3	0·5	0·7
3	0·1	0·1	0·2	0·2	0·3	0·3	0·4	0·4	0·5	0·5	0·8	1·0
4	0·1	0·1	0·2	0·3	0·3	0·4	0·5	0·5	0·6	0·7	1·0	1·3
5	0·1	0·2	0·3	0·3	0·4	0·5	0·6	0·7	0·8	0·8	1·3	1·7
6	0·1	0·2	0·3	0·4	0·5	0·6	0·7	0·8	0·9	1·0	1·5	2·0
7	0·1	0·2	0·4	0·5	0·6	0·7	0·8	0·9	1·1	1·2	1·8	2·3
8	0·1	0·3	0·4	0·5	0·7	0·8	0·9	1·1	1·2	1·3	2·0	2·7
9	0·2	0·3	0·5	0·6	0·8	0·9	1·1	1·2	1·4	1·5	2·3	3·0
10	0·2	0·3	0·5	0·7	0·8	1·0	1·2	1·3	1·5	1·7	2·5	3·3
11	0·2	0·4	0·6	0·7	0·9	1·1	1·3	1·5	1·7	1·8	2·8	3·7
12	0·2	0·4	0·6	0·8	1·0	1·2	1·4	1·6	1·8	2·0	3·0	4·0
13	0·2	0·4	0·7	0·9	1·1	1·3	1·5	1·7	2·0	2·2	3·3	4·3
14	0·2	0·5	0·7	0·9	1·2	1·4	1·6	1·9	2·1	2·3	3·5	4·7
15	0·3	0·5	0·8	1·0	1·3	1·5	1·8	2·0	2·3	2·5	3·8	5·0
16	0·3	0·5	0·8	1·1	1·3	1·6	1·9	2·1	2·4	2·7	4·0	5·3
17	0·3	0·6	0·9	1·1	1·4	1·7	2·0	2·3	2·6	2·8	4·3	5·7
18	0·3	0·6	0·9	1·2	1·5	1·8	2·1	2·4	2·7	3·0	4·5	6·0
19	0·3	0·6	1·0	1·3	1·6	1·9	2·2	2·5	2·9	3·2	4·8	6·3
20	0·3	0·7	1·0	1·3	1·7	2·0	2·3	2·7	3·0	3·3	5·0	6·7
21	0·4	0·7	1·1	1·4	1·8	2·1	2·5	2·8	3·2	3·5	5·3	7·0
22	0·4	0·7	1·1	1·5	1·8	2·2	2·6	2·9	3·3	3·7	5·5	7·3
23	0·4	0·8	1·2	1·5	1·9	2·3	2·7	3·1	3·5	3·8	5·8	7·7
24	0·4	0·8	1·2	1·6	2·0	2·4	2·8	3·2	3·6	4·0	6·0	8·0
25	0·4	0·8	1·3	1·7	2·1	2·5	2·9	3·3	3·8	4·2	6·3	8·3
30	0·5	1·0	1·5	2·0	2·5	3·0	3·5	4·0	4·5	5·0	7·5	10·0
35	0·6	1·2	1·8	2·3	2·9	3·5	4·1	4·7	5·3	5·8	8·8	11·7
40	0·7	1·3	2·0	2·7	3·3	4·0	4·7	5·3	6·0	6·7	10·0	13·3
45	0·8	1·5	2·3	3·0	3·8	4·5	5·3	6·0	6·8	7·5	11·3	15·0
50	0·8	1·7	2·5	3·3	4·2	5·0	5·8	6·7	7·5	8·3	12·5	16·7

DISTANCE (NAUTICAL MILES) OFF RISING/DIPPING LIGHTS

Height of eye in feet

Height of light in metres	2	3	4	5	6	7	8	9	10	20	30	40	50
2	4·6	4·9	5·2	5·5	5·7	6·0	6·2	6·4	6·6	8·1	9·2	10·2	11·0
3	5·2	5·6	5·9	6·2	6·4	6·6	6·8	7·0	7·2	8·7	9·9	10·8	11·7
4	5·8	6·1	6·4	6·7	6·9	7·2	7·4	7·6	7·8	9·3	10·4	11·4	12·2
5	6·3	6·6	6·9	7·2	7·4	7·7	7·9	8·1	8·3	9·8	10·9	11·9	12·7
6	6·7	7·1	7·4	7·6	7·9	8·1	8·3	8·5	8·7	10·2	11·3	12·3	13·2
7	7·1	7·5	7·8	8·0	8·3	8·5	8·7	8·9	9·1	10·6	11·8	12·7	13·6
8	7·5	7·8	8·2	8·4	8·7	8·9	9·1	9·3	9·5	11·0	12·1	13·1	14·0
9	7·8	8·2	8·5	8·8	9·0	9·2	9·5	9·7	9·8	11·3	12·5	13·5	14·3
10	8·2	8·5	8·8	9·1	9·4	9·6	9·8	10·0	10·2	11·7	12·8	13·8	14·6
11	8·5	8·9	9·2	9·4	9·7	9·9	10·1	10·3	10·5	12·0	13·1	14·1	15·0
12	8·8	9·2	9·5	9·7	10·0	10·2	10·4	10·6	10·8	12·3	13·4	14·4	15·3
13	9·1	9·5	9·8	10·0	10·3	10·5	10·7	10·9	11·1	12·6	13·7	14·7	15·6
14	9·4	9·7	10·0	10·3	10·6	10·8	11·0	11·2	11·4	12·9	14·0	15·0	15·8
15	9·6	10·0	10·3	10·6	10·8	11·1	11·3	11·5	11·6	13·1	14·3	15·3	16·1
16	9·9	10·3	10·6	10·8	11·1	11·3	11·5	11·7	11·9	13·4	14·6	15·5	16·4
17	10·2	10·5	10·8	11·1	11·3	11·6	11·8	12·0	12·2	13·7	14·8	15·8	16·6
18	10·4	10·8	11·1	11·4	11·6	11·8	12·0	12·2	12·4	13·9	15·1	16·0	16·9
19	10·7	11·0	11·3	11·6	11·8	12·1	12·3	12·5	12·7	14·2	15·3	16·3	17·1
20	10·9	11·3	11·6	11·8	12·1	12·3	12·5	12·7	12·9	14·4	15·5	16·5	17·3
25	12·0	12·3	12·6	12·9	13·2	13·4	13·6	13·8	14·0	15·5	16·6	17·6	18·4
30	13·0	13·3	13·6	13·9	14·1	14·4	14·6	14·8	15·0	16·5	17·6	18·6	19·4
40	14·7	15·1	15·4	15·7	15·9	16·1	16·3	16·5	16·7	18·2	19·4	20·3	21·2
50	16·3	16·6	16·9	17·2	17·4	17·7	17·9	18·1	18·3	19·8	20·9	21·9	22·7
60	17·7	18·0	18·3	18·6	18·8	19·1	19·3	19·5	19·7	21·2	22·3	23·3	24·1

CONVERSION TABLE

Sq inches to sq millimetres *multiply by* **645.20**	**Sq millimetres to sq inches** *multiply by* **0.0016**
Inches to millimetres *multiply by* **25.40**	**Millimetres to inches** *multiply by* **0.0394**
Sq feet to square metres *multiply by* **0.093**	**Sq metres to sq feet** *multiply by* **10.7640**
Inches to centimetres *multiply by* **2.54**	**Centimetres to inches** *multiply by* **0.3937**
Feet to metres *multiply by* **0.305**	**Metres to feet** *multiply by* **3.2810**
Nautical miles to kilometres *multiply by* **1.852**	**Kilometres to nautical miles** *multiply by* **0.5400**
Statute miles to kilometres *multiply by* **1.609**	**Kilometres to statute miles** *multiply by* **0.6214**
Statute miles to nautical miles *multiply by* **0.8684**	**Nautical miles to statute miles** *multiply by* **1.1515**
HP to metric HP *multiply by* **1.014**	**Metric HP to HP** *multiply by* **0.9862**
Pounds per sq inch to **kg per sq centimetre** *multiply by* **0.0703**	**Kg per sq centimetre** **to pounds per sq inch** *multiply by* **14.2200**
HP to kilowatts *multiply by* **0.746**	**Kilowatts to HP** *multiply by* **1.341**
Cu inches to cu centimetres *multiply by* **16.39**	**Cu centimetres to cu inches** *multiply by* **0.0610**
Imperial gallons to litres *multiply by* **4.540**	**Litres to imperial gallons** *multiply by* **0.2200**
Pints to litres *multiply by* **0.5680**	**Litres to pints** *multiply by* **1.7600**
Pounds to kilogrammes *multiply by* **0.4536**	**Kilogrammes to pounds** *multiply by* **2.2050**

LIGHT CHARACTERISTICS

CLASS OF LIGHT	International abbreviations	National abbreviations	Illustration — Period shown
FIXED	F		
OCCULTING (total duration of light longer than dark)			
Single-occulting		Oc Occ	
Group-occulting	eg Oc(2)	Gp Occ(2)	
Composite group-occulting	eg Oc(2+3)	Gp Occ(2+3)	
ISOPHASE (light and dark equal)		Iso	
FLASHING (total duration of light shorter than dark)			
Single-flashing	Fl		
Long-flashing (flash 2s or longer)	L Fl		
Group-flashing	eg Fl(3)	Gp Fl(3)	
Composite group-flashing	eg Fl(2+1)	Gp Fl(2+1)	
QUICK (50 to 79, usually either 50 or 60, flashes per min.)			
Continuous quick	Q	Qk Fl	
Group quick	eg Q(3)	Qk Fl(3)	
Interrupted quick	IQ	Int Qk Fl	
VERY QUICK (80 to 159, usually either 100 or 120, flashes per min.)			
Continuous very quick	VQ	V Qk Fl	
Group very quick	eg VQ(3)	V Qk Fl(3)	
Interrupted very quick	IVQ	Int V Qk Fl	
ULTRA QUICK (160 or more, usually 240 to 300, flashes per min.)			
Continuous ultra quick	UQ		
Interrupted ultra quick	IUQ		
MORSE CODE	eg Mo(K)		
FIXED AND FLASHING	F Fl		
ALTERNATING	eg Al. WR	Alt. WR	

COLOUR	International abbreviations	NOMINAL RANGE in miles	International abbreviations
White	W (may be omitted)	Light with single range	eg 15M
Red	R	Light with two different ranges	eg 15/10M
Green	G	Light with three or more ranges	eg 15-7M
Blue	Bu		
Violet	Vi	PERIOD is given in seconds	eg 90s
Yellow	Y	DISPOSITION horizontally disposed	(hor)
Orange	Y		
Amber	Y	ELEVATION is given in metres (m) or feet (ft) above MHWS	

NAVIGATION

85

Chapter 2 – Weather

Beaufort scale

Force	Wind speed (knots)	(km/h)	(m/sec)	Description	State of sea	Probable wave ht(m)
0	0–1	0–2	0–0·5	Calm	Like a mirror	0
1	1–3	2–6	0·5–1·5	Light airs	Ripples like scales are formed	0
2	4–6	7–11	2–3	Light breeze	Small wavelets, still short but more pronounced, not breaking	0·1
3	7–10	13–19	4–5	Gentle breeze	Large wavelets, crests begin to break; a few white horses	0·4
4	11–16	20–30	6–8	Moderate breeze	Small waves growing longer; fairly frequent white horses	1
5	17–21	31–39	8–11	Fresh breeze	Moderate waves, taking more pronounced form; many white horses, perhaps some spray	2
6	22–27	41–50	11–14	Strong breeze	Large waves forming; white foam crests more extensive; probably some spray	3
7	28–33	52–61	14–17	Near gale	Sea heaps up; white foam from breaking waves begins to blow in streaks	4
8	34–40	63–74	17–21	Gale	Moderately high waves of greater length; edge of crests break into spindrift; foam blown in well-marked streaks	5·5

Terminology used in forecasts
Pressure systems' speed of movement

Slowly	< 15 knots
Steadily	15–25 knots
Rather quickly	25–35 knots
Rapidly	35–45 knots
Very rapidly	> 45 knots

Visibility

Good	> 5 miles
Moderate	2–5 miles
Poor	1000 metres–2 miles
Fog	< 1000 metres

Barometric pressure tendency

Rising/falling slowly: Change of 0·1 to 1·5 hPa/mb in the preceding 3 hours.
Rising/falling: Change of 1·6 to 3·5 hPa/mb in the preceding 3 hours.
Rising/falling quickly: Change of 3·6 to 6 hPa/mb in the preceding 3 hours.
Rising/falling very rapidly: Change of > 6 hPa/mb in the preceding 3 hours.
Now rising/falling: Pressure has been falling (rising) or steady in the preceding 3 hours, but was definitely rising (falling) at the time of observation.

Gale warnings

A *Gale* warning means that winds of at least F8 (34-40kn) or gusts up to 43-51kn are expected somewhere within the area, but not necessarily over the whole area

Severe Gale means winds of at least F9 (41-47kn) or gusts reaching 52-60kn

Storm means winds of F10 (48-55kn) or gusts of 61-68kn

Violent Storm means winds of F11 (56-63kn) or gusts of 69+ kn

Hurricane Force means winds of F12 (64+ kn)

Gale warnings remain in force until amended or cancelled. If a gale persists for >24 hours the warning is re-issued.

Timing of gale warnings from time of issue

Imminent	<6 hrs
Soon	6–12 hrs
Later	>12 hrs

Strong wind warnings

Issued, if possible 6 hrs in advance, when winds F6 or more are expected up to 5M offshore; valid for 12 hrs.

MAP OF UK SHIPPING FORECAST AREAS

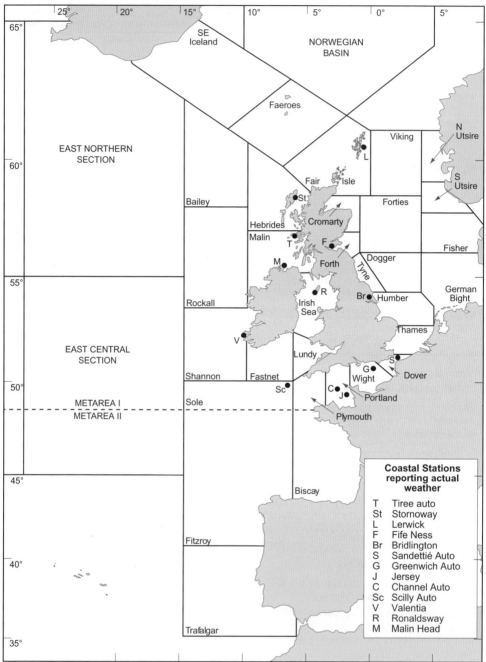

Coastal Stations reporting actual weather

T	Tiree auto
St	Stornoway
L	Lerwick
F	Fife Ness
Br	Bridlington
S	Sandettié Auto
G	Greenwich Auto
J	Jersey
C	Channel Auto
Sc	Scilly Auto
V	Valentia
R	Ronaldsway
M	Malin Head

SHIPPING FORECAST RECORD Time/Day/Date ....

GENERAL SYNOPSIS

at .... UT/BST

System position	Present position at	Movement	Forecast	

Gales	SEA AREA FORECAST	Wind (At first)	(Later)	Weather	Visibility
	VIKING				
	NORTH UTSIRE				
	SOUTH UTSIRE				
	FORTIES				
	CROMARTY				
	FORTH				
	TYNE				
	DOGGER				
	FISHER				
	GERMAN BIGHT				
	HUMBER				
	THAMES				
	DOVER				
	WIGHT				
	PORTLAND				
	PLYMOUTH				
	BISCAY				
	FITZROY				
	TRAFALGAR				
	SOLE				
	LUNDY				
	FASTNET				
	IRISH SEA				
	SHANNON				
	ROCKALL				
	MALIN				
	HEBRIDES				
	BAILEY				
	FAIR ISLE				
	FAEROES				
	S E ICELAND				

COASTAL REPORTS BST at .... UTC	Wind Direction	Force	Weather	Visibility	Pressure	Change	COASTAL REPORTS	Wind Direction	Force	Weather	Visibility	Pressure	Change
Tiree Auto (T)							Greenwich Lt V (G)						
Stornoway (St)							Jersey (J)						
Lerwick (L)							Channel Auto (C)						
Fife Ness (F)							Scilly Auto (Sc)						
Bridlington (Br)							Valentia (V)						
Sandettie Auto (S)							Ronaldsway (R)						
							Malin Head (M)						

WEATHER

SOURCES OF WEATHER INFORMATION IN THE UK

BBC Radio 4 Shipping forecasts
are broadcast at:

0048 LT[1]	LW, MW, FM
0520 LT[1]	LW, MW, FM
1201 LT	LW only
1754 LT	LW, FM (Sat/Sun)

[1] Includes weather reports from coastal stations

Frequencies

LW		198 kHz
MW	Tyneside	603 kHz
	London & N Ireland	720 kHz
	Redruth	756 kHz
	Plymouth & Enniskillen	774 kHz
	Aberdeen	1449 kHz
	Carlisle	1485 kHz
FM	England	92·4–94·6 MHz
	Scotland	91·3–96·1 MHz
		103·5–104·9 MHz
	Wales	92·8–96·1 MHz
		103·5–104·9 MHz
	N Ireland	93·2–96·0 MHz
		103·5–104·6 MHz
	Channel Islands	94·8 MHz

The Shipping forecast contains:
Time of issue; summary of gale warnings in force at that time; a general synopsis of weather systems and their expected development and movement over the next 24 hours; sea area forecasts for the same 24 hours, including wind direction/force, weather and visibility in each; and an outlook for the following 24 hours.

Gale warnings for all affected areas are broadcast at the earliest break in Radio 4 programmes after receipt, as well as after the next news bulletin.

Shipping forecasts cover large sea areas, and rarely include the detailed variations that may occur near land. The inshore waters forecast can be more helpful on coastal passages.

Weather reports from coastal stations follow the 0048 and 0520 shipping forecasts. They include wind direction and force, present weather, visibility, and sea-level pressure and tendency, if available. The stations are shown on the previous page.

BBC Radio 4 Inshore waters forecast
A forecast for inshore waters (up to 12M offshore) in 17 areas around the UK and N Ireland, valid for 24 hrs, is broadcast after the 0048 and 0520 coastal station reports.

It includes forecasts of wind direction and force, weather, visibility, sea state and an outlook for a further 24 hrs. It ends with a national inshore outlook for the next 3 days. The 17 inshore areas are defined by the following well-known places and headlands, clockwise around the UK: Cape Wrath, Orkney, Rattray Hd, Berwick-upon-Tweed, Whitby, Gibraltar Point, N Foreland, Selsey Bill, Lyme Regis, Land's End, St David's Head, Great Ormes Head, Isle of Man, Mull of Galloway, Carlingford Lough, Lough Foyle, Mull of Kintyre, Ardnamurchan Pt and Shetland.

Strong wind warnings are issued by the Met Office whenever winds of Force 6 or more are expected over coastal waters up to 5M offshore.

Reports of actual weather. The 0048 broadcast includes a set of coastal station reports. These include: Boulmer, *Bridlington*, Sheerness, St Catherine's Point*, *Scilly**, Milford Haven, Aberporth, Valley, Liverpool (Crosby), *Ronaldsway*, Larne, Machrihanish*, Greenock, *Stornoway*, *Lerwick*, Wick*, Aberdeen and Leuchars. Asterisk* denotes an automatic station. Stations in italics also feature in the 0520 coastal reports.

BBC general (land) forecasts
Land area forecasts may include an outlook up to 48 hours beyond the shipping forecast, plus more details of frontal systems and weather along the coasts. The most comprehensive land area forecasts are broadcast by Radio 4 on the frequencies above.

Land area forecasts – Wind strength
Wind descriptions used in land forecasts, with their Beaufort scale equivalents, are:

Calm	0	Fresh	5
Light	1–3	Strong	6–7
Moderate	4	Gale	8

Land area forecasts – Visibility
The following visibility definitions are used in land forecasts:

Mist	2000m–1000m
Fog	<1000m
Dense fog	< 50m

NAVTEX

Navtex is the prime method of disseminating MSI, with typical coverage out to 270 miles offshore. A dedicated aerial, receiver and LCD screen (or integrated printer) are required but receipt is free and no contract is required. The user selects which stations and categories are recorded for automatic display or printing.

Two frequencies are used: 518 kHz and *490 kHz*. 518 kHz messages are in English (occas. in the national language as well), with excellent coverage of Europe. Interference between stations is avoided by time sharing and by limiting the range of transmitters to about 300M. Navtex information applies only to the geographic area for which each station is responsible.

490 kHz (for clarity shown in italics throughout this chapter) is used abroad for transmissions in the national language. In the UK it is used for inshore waters forecasts in English. Identification letters for 490 kHz stations differ from 518 kHz stations.

Weather information accounts for about 75% of all messages and Navtex is particularly valuable when out of range of other sources, otherwise occupied or if there is a language problem.

Messages

Each message is prefixed by a four-character group:

The first character is the code letter of the transmitting station (eg E for Niton).

The second character is the message category, see below.

The third and fourth are message serial numbers, running from 01 to 99 and then re-starting at 01.

The serial number 00 denotes urgent messages which are always printed.

Messages which are corrupt or have already been printed are rejected. Weather messages, and certain other message types, are dated and timed.

Message categories

A*	Navigational warnings
B*	Meteorological warnings
C	Ice reports
D*	SAR info and piracy warnings
E	Weather forecasts
F	Pilot service
H	Loran-C
J	Satellite navigation
K	Other electronic navaids
L	Subfacts and Gunfacts (UK)
V	Amplifies Navwarnings initially sent under A; plus weekly oil/gas rig moves.
W-Y	Special service, trials
Z	No messages on hand at scheduled time

Missing category letters are unallocated.

*The receiver cannot reject these categories.

Navtex stations/areas – UK & W Europe

Navtex Stations

(L) Rogaland (518 kHz)

(O) Portpatrick (518 kHz)
(C) Portpatrick (490 kHz)

(Q) Malin Head (518 kHz)
(A) Malin Head (490 kHz)

(G) Cullercoats (518 kHz)
(U) Cullercoats (490 kHz)

(P) Netherlands CG (518 kHz)

(W) Valentia (518 kHz)

(M) Oostende (518 kHz)
(T) Oostende (518 kHz)

NAVAREA I (UK)

(E) Niton (518 kHz)
(K) Niton (518 kHz)
(I) Niton (490 kHz)
(T) Niton (490 kHz)

NAVAREA II (France)

(A) Corsen (518 kHz)
(E) Corsen (490 kHz)

(W) La Garde (518 kHz)
(S) La Garde (490 kHz)

(D) La Coruña (518 kHz)
(W) La Coruña (490 kHz)

NAVAREA III (Spain)

(R) Monsanto (518 kHz)
(G) Monsanto (490 kHz)

(T) Cagliari (518 kHz)
(X) Valencia (518 kHz)
(M) Valencia (490 kHz)

(G) Tarifa (518 kHz)
(T) Tarifa (490 kHz)

UK 518 kHz stations

The times (UT) of weather messages are in bold; the times of an extended outlook (a further 2 or 3 days beyond the shipping forecast period) are in italics.

G – **Cullercoats**	*0100*	0500	**0900**	1300	1700	**2100**

Fair Isle clockwise to Thames, excluding N & S Utsire, Fisher and German Bight.

O – **Portpatrick**	*0220*	**0620**	1020	1420	**1820**	2220

Lundy clockwise to SE Iceland.

E – **Niton**	*0040*	0440	**0840**	1240	1640	**2040**

Thames clockwise to Fastnet, excluding Trafalgar.

UK 490 kHz stations (in yellow) provide forecasts for UK inshore waters, a national 3 day outlook for inshore waters and, at times in bold, reports of actual weather at some or all of the places listed below. To receive these reports select message category 'V' on the receiver. Times (UT) are listed in chronological order. Reports include some or all of: Sea level pressure (hPa/mb), wind direction and speed (kn), weather, visibility (M), air and sea temperatures (°C), dewpoint temperature (°C) and mean wave height (m).

A – **Malin Head**	**0000**	**0400**	0800	**1200**	**1600**	2000

Lough Foyle to Carlingford Lough, Mull of Galloway to Cape Wrath, the Minch.
Note times of forecasts and actuals not known at time of going to press.

C – **Portpatrick** Land's End to Shetland	**0020**	**0420**	0820	**1220**	**1620**	2020

N Rona, Stornoway, S Uist, Lusa (Skye), Tiree, Macrihanish, Belfast, Malin Hd, Belmullet, St Bees Hd, Ronaldsway, Crosby, Valley, Aberporth, Roches Pt, Valentia, St Mawgan.

I – **Niton** The Wash to St David's Head	**0120**	0520	**0920**	1320	1720	**2120**

Sandettie Lt V, Greenwich Lt V, Solent, Hurn airport, Guernsey airport, Jersey airport, Portland, Channel Lt V, Plymouth, Culdrose, Seven Stones Lt V, St Mawgan & Roches Pt.

U – **Cullercoats** Cape Wrath to N Foreland	**0320**	0720	**1120**	**1520**	1920	**2320**

Sandettie Lt V, Manston, Shoeburyness, Weybourne, Donna Nook, Boulmer, Leuchars, Aberdeen, Lossiemouth, Wick, Kirkwall, Lerwick, Foula, K7 Met buoy, Sule Skerry.

Navtex coverage abroad: Selected Navtex stations in Metareas I and II, with identity codes and transmission times, are listed below. Times of weather messages are shown in **bold**. Gale warnings are usually transmitted 4 hourly.

METAREA I (Co-ordinator – UK)   **Transmission times (UT)**

K – **Niton** (Note 1)	0140	0540	0940	1340	1740	2140
L – Pinneberg, *Hamburg*	*0150*	*0550*	*0950*	*1350*	*1750*	*2150*
M – **Oostende,** Belgium (Note 2)	0200	0600	1000	1400	1800	2200
P – **Netherlands CG**, Den Helder	**0230**	0630	1030	**1430**	1830	2230
Q – **Malin Head**, Eire	0240	**0640**	**1040**	1440	**1840**	2240
S – **Pinneberg,** Hamburg	**0300**	**0700**	**1100**	**1500**	**1900**	2300
T – **Oostende,** Belgium (Note 3)	0310	**0710**	1110	1510	**1910**	2310
W – **Valentia,** Eire	0340	**0740**	**1140**	1540	**1940**	2340

Notes:
1 In English, no weather; only Nav warnings for waters from Cap Gris Nez to Île de Bréhat.
2 No weather information, only Nav warnings for NavArea Juliett.
3 Forecasts and strong wind warnings for Thames and Dover, plus Nav info for Belgium.

METAREA II (Co-ordinator – France)

A – **Corsen,** Le Stiff, France	**0000**	0400	0800	**1200**	1600	2000
E – Corsen, *Le Stiff, France (In French)*	*0040*	*0440*	*0840*	*1240*	*1640*	*2040*
D – **Coruña,** Spain	0030	0430	**0830**	1230	1630	2030
W – Coruña, *Spain (in Spanish)*	*0340*	*0740*	*1140*	*1540*	*1940*	*2340*
F – **Horta,** Açores, Portugal	**0050**	0450	**0850**	1250	1650	2050
G – **Tarifa,** Spain (English & Spanish)	0100	0500	**0900**	1300	1700	2100
R – **Monsanto,** Portugal	**0250**	**0650**	**1050**	**1450**	**1850**	**2250**

MARINECALL WEATHER BY TELEPHONE & FAX

Marinecall is a private company providing a wide range of inshore and offshore telephone and fax weather services, quality controlled by Met Office forecasters.

For further information contact:
Marinecall Customer Services
Buongiorno UK Ltd
Avalon House, 57-63 Scrutton Street
London EC2A 4PF
☎ 0845 610 1800 (M-F 0900-1700)
www.marinecall.co.uk
marinecall@itouch.co.uk

Inshore and Offshore forecasts start with a 48 hour inshore waters forecast for the coastal area and up to 12 miles offshore. This is followed by a 5-day sea area forecast based upon data from the Met Office Atmospheric Weather model relating to the lat/long for the area you have selected. Forecasts are updated three times daily at 0700/1200/1800 LT.

Operation

Dial the telephone or fax number shown for the required inshore, offshore or European weather forecast areas.

Listen to the spoken menu and select a location, or for faster (cheaper) operation, enter one of the 4-digit location codes (a full list of these is at www.marinecall.co.uk).

Inshore Areas

Cape Wrath to Rattray Head
☎ 09068 969 641   📠 09065 222 341
Rattray Head to Berwick
☎ 09068 969 642   📠 09065 222 342
Berwick to Whitby
☎ 09068 969 643   📠 09065 222 343
Whitby to Gibraltar Point
☎ 09068 969 644   📠 09065 222 344
Gibraltar Point to North Foreland
☎ 09068 969 645   📠 09065 222 345
North Foreland to Selsey Bill
☎ 09068 969 646   📠 09065 222 346
Selsey Bill to Lyme Regis
☎ 09068 969 647   📠 09065 222 347
Lyme Regis to Hartland Point
☎ 09068 969 648   📠 09065 222 348
Hartland Point to St David's Head
☎ 09068 969 649   📠 09065 222 349
St David's Head to Great Ormes Head
☎ 09068 969 650   📠 09065 222 350

Great Ormes Head to Mull of Galloway
☎ 09068 969 651   📠 09065 222 351
Mull of Galloway to Mull of Kintyre
☎ 09068 969 652   📠 09065 222 352
Mull of Kintyre to Ardnamurchan
☎ 09068 969 653   📠 09065 222 353
Ardnamurchan to Cape Wrath
☎ 09068 969 654   📠 09065 222 354
Lough Foyle to Carlingford Lough
☎ 09068 969 655   📠 09065 222 355

Offshore Areas

English Channel
☎ 09068 969 657   📠 09065 222 357
Southern North Sea
☎ 09068 969 658   📠 09065 222 358
Irish Sea
☎ 09068 969 659   📠 09065 222 359
Bay of Biscay
☎ 09068 969 660   📠 09065 222 360
North West Scotland
☎ 09068 969 661   📠 09065 222 361
Northern North Sea
☎ 09068 969 662   📠 09065 222 362

European Areas

North East France
☎ 09064 700 421   📠 09065 501 611
North France
☎ 09064 700 422   📠 09065 501 612
North Brittany
☎ 09064 700 423   📠 09065 501 613
South Brittany
☎ 09064 700 424   📠 09065 501 614

Marinecall Online

You may buy all weather forecasts online at www.marinecall.co.uk. Buying online gives unlimited access to all areas during the subscribed period. Subscriptions available for 24 hrs, 1 week, 1 month, 3 months, 6 months and 12 months.

Pricing

09068 / 09064 calls cost £0·60 / minute.
090655 calls cost £1 / minute.
090652 calls cost £1·50 / minute
Note: costs are from a UK landline and calls from mobile phones may be subject to network operator charges.

You can only access Marinecall from within the UK (including Channel Islands) from a landline or mobile network which receives a UK operator signal.

For information on how to use Marinecall from overseas, visit www.marinecall.co.uk and look up Marinecall Club.

WEATHER

93

INTERNET WEATHER SOURCES

The Internet provides a useful back-up for GMDSS services as well as information not available by conventional means.

www.metoffice.gov.uk/weather/marine/ has texts of all high seas, shipping and inshore waters forecasts, warnings, weather actuals from coastal stations, light vessels and data buoys. www.bbc.co.uk/weather/coast/ has texts of Navtex broadcasts.

National meteorological services provide the best forecasts for their own waters.

Other useful websites include:
www.franksweather.co.uk /
www.weatheronline.com/www.saildocs.com/
www.mailasail.com/www.grib.us/
www.passageweather.com/
www.windfinder.com/www.xcweather.co.uk/
www.windguru.com/www.theyr.com /
www.wetterzentrale.de/topkarten/tknf.html

Broadcasts of shipping and inshore waters forecasts by HM Coastguard

HM CG Centres routinely broadcast MSI every 3 hours at the local times below.

Each broadcast contains one of 3 different Groups of MSI:

Group A, the full broadcast, contains the Shipping forecast, a new Inshore waters forecast and 24 hrs outlook, Gale warnings, a 3 day forecast for Fishermen in the winter months*, Navigational (WZ) warnings and Subfacts & Gunfacts where relevant ‡. 'A' broadcast times are in bold type.

Group B contains a new Inshore waters forecast, plus the previous outlook, and Gale warnings. 'B' broadcast times are in plain type.

Group C is a repeat of the Inshore forecast and Gale warnings (as per the previous Group A or B) plus new Strong wind warnings. 'C' broadcast times are italicised.

Notes
*Fisherman's 3 day forecast (1 Oct-31 Mar).
‡ Subfacts & Gunfacts.

Coastguard	Shipping forecast areas	Inshore areas	B	C	A	C	B	C	A	C
South Coast			B	C	A	C	B	C	A	C
Falmouth‡	Portland, Plymouth, Sole, Shannon, Fastnet	8, 9	0110	*0410*	**0710**	*1010*	1310	*1610*	**1910**	*2210*
Brixham‡	Same as Falmouth CG	8, 9	0110	*0410*	**0710**	*1010*	1310	*1610*	**1910**	*2210*
Portland	Plymouth, Portland, Wight	6–8	0130	*0430*	**0730**	*1030*	1330	*1630*	**1930**	*2230*
Solent	Plymouth, Portland, Wight	6–8	0130	*0430*	**0730**	*1030*	1330	*1630*	**1930**	*2230*
Dover	Dover, Wight, Thames, Humber	5, 6	0110	*0410*	**0710**	*1010*	1310	*1610*	**1910**	*2210*
East Coast			B	C	A	C	B	C	A	C
Thames	Dover, Wight, Thames, Humber	5, 6	0110	*0410*	**0710**	*1010*	1310	*1610*	**1910**	*2210*
Yarmouth	Humber, German Bight, Dogger, Tyne	3–5	0150	*0450*	**0750**	*1050*	1350	*1650*	**1950**	*2250*
Humber	Same as Yarmouth CG	3–5	0150	*0450*	**0750**	*1050*	1350	*1650*	**1950**	*2250*
Forth	Tyne, Forth, Cromarty, Forties, Fair Isle	1, 2	0130	*0430*	**0730**	*1030*	1330	*1630*	**1930**	*2230*
Aberdeen‡	Same as Forth CG	1, 2	0130	*0430*	**0730**	*1030*	1330	*1630*	**1930**	*2230*
Shetland	Cromarty, Viking, Fair Isle, Faeroes	1, 16	0110	*0410*	**0710**	*1010*	1310	*1610*	**1910**	*2210*
West Coast			B	C	A	C	B	C	A	C
Stornoway‡	Rockall, Malin, Hebrides, Bailey, Fair Is, Faeroes, SE Iceland	16	0110	*0410*	**0710**	*1010*	1310	*1610*	**1910**	*2210*
Clyde‡	Rockall, Malin, Hebrides, Bailey	14, 15	0210	*0510*	**0810**	*1110*	1410	*1710*	**2010**	*2310*
Belfast‡	Irish Sea, Malin	12–14	0110	*0410*	**0710**	*1010*	1310	*1610*	**1910**	*2210*
Liverpool	Irish Sea	11, 12	0130	*0430*	**0730**	*1030*	1330	*1630*	**1930**	*2230*
Holyhead	Irish Sea	10, 11	0150	*0450*	**0750**	*1050*	1350	*1650*	**1950**	*2250*
Milford Hvn	Lundy, Fastnet, Irish Sea	9, 10	0150	*0450*	**0750**	*1050*	1350	*1650*	**1950**	*2250*
Swansea	Lundy, Fastnet, Irish Sea	9, 10	0150	*0450*	**0750**	*1050*	1350	*1650*	**1950**	*2250*

MSI broadcasts are transmitted via remote aerial sites geographically selected to give optimum coverage. The table below lists their positions and the VHF broadcast channel to be used. It will be one of channels 10, 23, 84 or 86 and is also specified in a prior announcement on Ch 16.

To minimise the risk of missing a broadcast, pre-select Ch 16 on Dual watch with the relevant (clearest) channel; and/or monitor the prior announcement to verify the working channel. **MF frequencies** (*kHz*), as quoted below, are also used for the broadcasts, primarily for fishermen.

Falmouth CG

Trevose Head	84	50°33'N 05°02'W
St Mary's (Scilly)	86	49°56'N 06°18'W
Lizard*	*1880kHz,* 23	49°58'N 05°12'W
Falmouth	84	50°09'N 05°03'W

Brixham CG

Fowey	10	50°20'N 04°38'W
Rame Head	86	50°19'N 04°13'W
East Prawle	84	50°13'N 03°42'W
Dartmouth	10	50°21'N 03°35'W
Berry Head	23	50°24'N 03°29'W

Portland CG

Beer Head	86	50°41'N 03°05'W
Grove Pt (Portland Bill)	84	50°33'N 02°25'W

Solent CG

Needles	86	50°39'N 01°35'W
Boniface (Ventnor, IoW)	23	50°36'N 01°12'W
Newhaven	86	50°47'N 00°03'E

Dover CG

Fairlight (Hastings)	84	50°52'N 00°39'E
Langdon (Dover)	86	51°08'N 01°21'E

Thames CG

Shoeburyness	23	51°31'N 00°47'E
Bradwell (R Blackwater)	86	51°44'N 00°53'E
Walton-on-the-Naze	23	51°51'N 01°17'E
Bawdsey (R Deben)	84	52°00'N 01°25'E

Yarmouth CG

Lowestoft	23	52°29'N 01°46'E
Great Yarmouth	86	52°36'N 01°43'E
Trimingham (Cromer)	23	52°54'N 01°21'E
Langham (Blakeney)	86	52°57'N 00°58'E
Guy's Head (Wisbech)	23	52°48'N 00°13'E

Humber CG

Easington (Spurn Hd)	86	53°39'N 00°06'E
Flamborough*	*1925kHz,* 23	54°07'N 00°05'W
Ravenscar	86	54°24'N 00°30'W
Hartlepool	23	54°42'N 01°10'W
Cullercoats (Blyth)	86	55°04'N 01°28'W
Newton	23	55°31'N 01°37'W

Forth CG

St Abbs/Cross Law	86	55°54'N 02°12'W
Craigkelly (Burntisland)	23	56°04'N 03°14'W
Fife Ness	84	56°17'N 02°35'W
Inverbervie	23	56°51'N 02°16'W

Aberdeen CG

Greg Ness*	*2226kHz,* 86	57°08'N 02°03'W

Windyheads Hill	23	57°39'N 02°14'W
Rosemarkie (Cromarty)	86	57°38'N 04°05'W
Noss Head (Wick)	84	58°29'N 03°03'W
Durness (Loch Eriboll)	23	58°34'N 04°44'W

Shetland CG

Wideford Hill (Kirkwall)	86	58°59'N 03°01'W
Fitful Head (Sumburgh)	23	59°54'N 01°23'W
Lerwick (Shetland)	84	60°10'N 01°08'W
Collafirth*	*2226kHz,* 86	60°32'N 01°23'W
Saxa Vord (Unst)	23	60°42'N 00°51'W

Stornoway CG

Butt of Lewis	*1743kHz,* 86	58°28'N 06°14'W
Portnaguran (Stornoway)	84	58°15'N 06°10'W
Forsnaval (W Lewis)	23	58°13'N 07°00'W
Melvaig (Loch Ewe)	23	57°50'N 05°47'W
Rodel (S Harris)	86	57°45'N 06°57'W
Clettreval (N Uist)	84	57°37'N 07°26'W
Skriag (Portree, Skye)	84	57°23'N 06°15'W
Drumfearn (SE Skye)	86	57°12'N 05°48'W
Barra	10	57°01'N 07°30'W
Arisaig (S of Mallaig)	23	56°55'N 06°50'W

Clyde CG

Glengorm (N Mull)	23	56°38'N 06°08'W
Tiree	*1883kHz,* 86	56°31'N 06°57'W
Torosay (E Mull)	10	56°27'N 05°43'W
Clyde CG (Greenock)	84	55°58'N 04°48'W
South Knapdale (Loch Fyne)	23	55°55'N 05°28'W
Kilchiaran (W Islay)	84	55°46'N 06°27'W
Lawhill (Ardrossan)	86	55°42'N 04°50'W
Rhu Staffnish (Kintyre)	10	55°22'N 05°32'W

Belfast CG

Navar (Lower L Erne)	86	54°28'N 07°54'W
Limvady (Lough Foyle)	84	55°06'N 06°53'W
West Torr (Fair Head)	86	55°12'N 06°06'W
Black Mountain (Belfast)	23	54°35'N 06°01'W
Orlock Point (Bangor)	84	54°40'N 05°35'W
Slievemartin (Rostrevor)	86	54°06'N 06°10'W

Liverpool CG

Caldbeck (Carlisle)	23	54°46'N 03°07'W
Snaefell (Isle of Man)	86	54°16'N 04°28'W
Langthwaite (Lancaster)	84	54°02'N 02°46'W
Moel-y-Parc (Anglesey)	23	53°13'N 04°28'W

Holyhead CG

Great Ormes Head	86	53°20'N 03°51'W
South Stack (Holyhead)	23	53°19'N 04°41'W

Continued overleaf

WEATHER

WEATHER

Milford Haven CG			Swansea CG		
Blaenplwyf			Mumbles	86	51°34'N 03°59'W
(Aberystwyth)	84	52°22'N 04°06'W	St Hilary (Barry)	23	51°27'N 03°25'W
Dinas Hd (Fishguard)	86	52°00'N 04°54'W	Severn Bridges	86	51°36'N 02°38'W
St Ann's Head	84	51°40'N 05°11'W	Combe Martin	23	51°12'N 04°03'W
Monkstone (Tenby)	84	51°42'N 04°41'W	Hartland Point	86	51°01'N 04°31'W

Inshore waters forecasts: Area boundaries used by the Coastguard

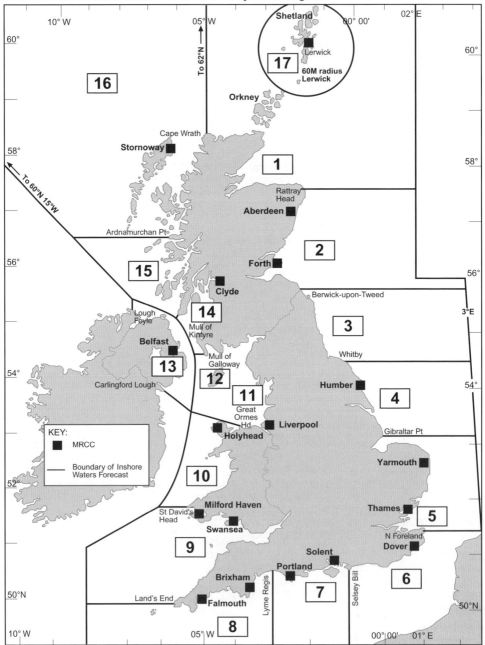

CHANNEL ISLANDS

Jersey Meteorological department

From the CI and UK call ☎ 0900 665 0022 for the Channel Islands recorded shipping forecast. From France call ☎ +44 1534 448787. For Guernsey only, call ☎ 06969 8800; it is chargeable. For more detailed info call ☎ +44 1534 448770, 🖷 448778.

Forecasts include: general situation, 24hr forecast for wind, weather, vis, sea state, swell, sea temperature, plus 2 & 4 day outlooks and St Helier tide times/heights. The area is bounded by 50°N, 03°W and the mainland from Cap de la Hague to Ile de Bréhat.

Weather broadcasts and bulletins

BBC Radio Guernsey 93·2 MHz, 1116 kHz
Bulletins for the waters around Guernsey, Herm and Sark are broadcast Mon-Fri at 0630, 0730 and 0830 LT; Sat/Sun at 0730 and 0830 LT. They contain forecast, synopsis, coastal forecast, storm warnings and wind strength.

In the summer coastal reports are included from: Portland, Chan lt V, Alderney, Guernsey, Jersey, Cherbourg, Cap de la Hague and Dinard. ☎ 01481 200600

BBC Radio Jersey 1026 kHz, 88·8 MHz.
Storm warnings on receipt. Wind info for Jersey waters: Mon-Fri 0725, 0825, 1325, 1725 LT; Sat/Sun 0725, 0825. ☎ 01534 870000

Shipping forecast for local waters: Mon-Fri @ H+00 (0600-1900, after the news) and 0625 & 1625 LT; Sat/Sun @ H+00 (0700-1300, after the news) and 0725 LT.

Jersey Coastguard Ch 25, 82. Gale warnings at 0307, 0907, 1507, 2107UT. Gale warnings, synopsis, 24h forecast, outlook for next 24 hrs, plus reports from observation stations, are broadcast on request and at 0645*, 0745*, 0845*, 1245, 1845, 2245 UT; *broadcast 1 hr earlier when DST in force. ☎ 01534 447705.

IRELAND

Met Éireann (Irish Met Office) is at Glasnevin Hill, Dublin 9, Ireland. ☎ 1 806 4200, 🖷 1 806 4247, www.met.ie. General forecasting division: ☎ 1 806 4255, 🖷 1 806 4275 (H24, charges may apply).

Coast radio stations

CRS and their VHF channels are listed below (anti-clockwise from Malin Head) and shown overleaf. Weather bulletins for 30M offshore and the Irish Sea are broadcast on VHF at 0103, 0403, 0703, 1003, 1303, 1603, 1903 and 2203UT after an announcement on Ch 16. Broadcasts are made 1 hour earlier when DST is in force. Bulletins include gale warnings, synopsis and a 24-hour forecast.

Malin Head	23	Bantry	23
Glen Head	24	Mizen Head	04
Donegal Bay	02	Cork	26
Belmullet	83	Mine Head	83
Clifden	26	Rosslare	23
Galway	04	Wicklow Head	02
Shannon	28	Dublin	83
Valentia	24	Carlingford	04

Gale warnings are broadcast on these VHF channels on receipt and at 0033, 0633, 1233 and 1833 UT, after an announcement Ch 16.

MF Valentia Radio broadcasts forecasts for sea areas Shannon and Fastnet on 1752 kHz at 0833 & 2033 UT, and on request.

Gale warnings are broadcast on 1752 kHz on receipt and at 0303, 0903, 1503 and 2103 (UT) after an announcement on 2182 kHz.

Malin Head does not broadcast weather information on 1677 kHz. At Dublin there is no MF transmitter.

Radio Telefís Éireann (RTE) Radio 1

RTE Radio 1 broadcasts weather bulletins daily at 0602, 1253 & 2355LT on 252kHz (LW) Summerhill (15M W ofDublin airport) and FM (88·2-95·2MHz).

Bulletins contain a situation, forecast and coastal reports. Forecasts include: wind, weather, vis, swell (if higher than 4m) and a 24 hrs outlook.

Gale warnings are included in hourly news bulletins on FM & MF.

Coastal reports include wind, weather, visibility, pressure and pressure tendency. The change over the last 3 hrs is described as:

Steady	=	0–0·4hPa
Rising/falling slowly	=	0·5–1·9
Rising/falling	=	2·0–3·4
Rising/falling rapidly	=	3·5–5·9
Rising/falling very rapidly	=	> 6·0

Weather by telephone

The latest sea area forecast and gale warnings are available as recorded messages H24 from Weatherdial.

Dial ☎ 1550 123 plus the suffixes below:

850	Munster
851	Leinster
852	Connaught
853	Ulster
854	Dublin (plus winds in Dublin Bay and HW times)
855	Coastal waters and Irish Sea.

Weather by fax

Similar information, plus isobaric, swell and wave charts and any small craft warnings (>F6 up to 10M offshore; Apr-Sep inc) is available H24 by Weatherdial Fax.

Dial ▦ 1550 131 838 (from within ROI only). From the menu below select the required 4-digit product code (see 0400 for full listing):

0015: Latest analysis chart
0016: Forecast valid for next 24 hrs

0017: Forecast valid for next 36 hrs
0018: Forecast valid for next 48 hrs
0021: Forecasts for coastal waters and Irish Sea
0031, 0032, 0033, 0034: Forecast (days 1-4) for sea/swell wave hts/periods

5-day forecasts (plain language, farming/national)
0001: Munster. 0002: Leinster. 0003: Connaught.
0004: Ulster. 0005: Dublin.

Sea Planners provide graphic forecasts for up to 5 days (updated at 0430 daily) of expected winds and waves at the following seven offshore positions:

	0041:	53°N 05°30'W
	0042:	51°N 06°W
	0043:	51°N 10°30'W
	0044:	53°N 11°W
	0045:	54°N 11°W
	0046:	55°N 10°W
	0047:	56°N 08°W

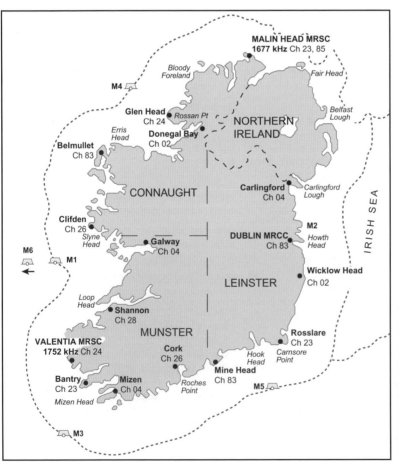

Provinces, headlands, sea areas and coastal stations referred to in weather broadcasts are shown here. Forecasts for coastal waters cover areas within 30M of the shore.

DENMARK

Gale warnings and forecasts are broadcast on receipt, on request and at 0133, 0533, 0933, 1333, 1733, 2133 UT in Danish/English by remote CRS, callsign *Lyngby Radio:*

Areas	VHF Channels
2 South Baltic	02, 04,
3 West Baltic	01, 02, 03, 04, 07, 28
4 The Belts & Sound	01, 02, 03, 04, 05, 07, 28, 65, 83
5 Kattegat	03, 04, 05, 07, 64, 65, 66, 83
6 Skagerrack	01, 02, 04, 64, 66
8 Fisher	01, 02, 23, 26
9 German Bight	02, 23

Forecast areas: see above. Skagen and Blåvand CRS broadcast on MF gale warnings for all areas on receipt.

Areas 2–5 are north of the Kiel Canal and east of 10°E.

MF: Blåvand 1734 kHz, Skagen 1758 kHz, Skamlebæk 1704 kHz and Rønne 2586 kHz broadcast gale warnings for all areas in Danish/**English** on receipt.

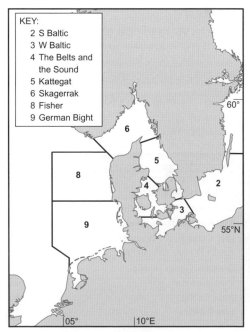

KEY:
2 S Baltic
3 W Baltic
4 The Belts and the Sound
5 Kattegat
6 Skagerrak
8 Fisher
9 German Bight

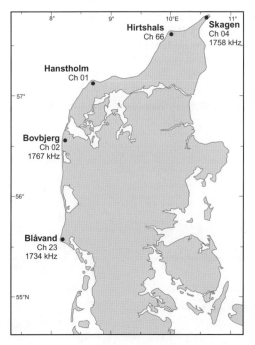

Hirtshals Ch 66
Skagen Ch 04 1758 kHz
Hanstholm Ch 01
Bovbjerg Ch 02 1767 kHz
Blåvand Ch 23 1734 kHz

Danmarks Radio, Programme 1

Kalundborg (55°44'N 11°E) broadcasts on MW 1062 kHz:
- Gale warnings, weather reports and forecast for areas 2-6, 8, 9 at 0545, 0845, 1145, 1745LT.
- A 5 day forecast for areas 2-6, 8 and 9 at 1145 & 1745LT.

Danmarks Meteorologiske Institut (DM)

provides marine forecasts in Danish, **English** and German on www.dmi.dk/dmi/index/

WEATHER

99

GERMANY

Deutsche Wetterdienst (DWD)

DWD (German weather service) provides Met info through a databank which is updated twice daily; more often for weather reports and text forecasts.

DWD ☎ + 49 (0) 40 6690 1851. 🖷 + 49 (0) 40 6690 1946. www.dwd.de seeschifffahrt@dwd.de.

Traffic Centres

Traffic Centres, below, broadcast local storm warnings, weather bulletins, visibility (and when appropriate ice reports) in German or **English** on request.

Traffic Centre	VHF Ch	Every
German Bight Traffic	80	H+00
Cuxhaven-Elbe Traffic	71 (outer Elbe)	H+35
Brunsbüttel-Elbe Traffic	68 (lower Elbe)	H+05
Kiel Kanal II (E-bound)	02	H+15 & H+45
Kiel Kanal III (W-bound)	03	H+20 & H+50
Bremerhaven-Weser Traffic	02, 04, 05, 07, 21, 22, 82	H+20
Bremen-Weser Traffic	19, 78, 81	H+30
Hunte Traffic	63	H+30
Jade Traffic	20, 63	H+10
Ems Traffic	15, 18, 20, 21	H+50

Coast Radio Stations

DP07 (Seefunk) has commercial CRS, below, at:

Nordfriesland (Sylt) Ch 26. **Elbe-Weser** Ch 01, 24. **Hamburg** (Control centre) Ch 83. **Bremen** Ch 25. **Borkum** Ch 28.

DP07 broadcasts (only in German): gale and strong wind warnings on receipt. At 0745⑩, 0945, 1245, 1645 and 1945⑩ UT for Fisher, German Bight and Humber, DP07 broadcasts: a synopsis, 12hr forecast, 24hrs outlook and coastal station reports. ⑩summer only. Also a 4–5 day outlook for the North Sea (and Baltic) at 0945 and 1645.

Radio broadcasting: Nord Deutscher Rundfunk (NDR)
NDR 1 Welle Nord (FM)

A summary, outlook and wind forecast for the German Bight are broadcast after the news at H (0600-2200LT) and at H +30 (0530-17300LT) by:

Sylt 90·9 MHz; **Helgoland** 88·9 MHz; **Hamburg**

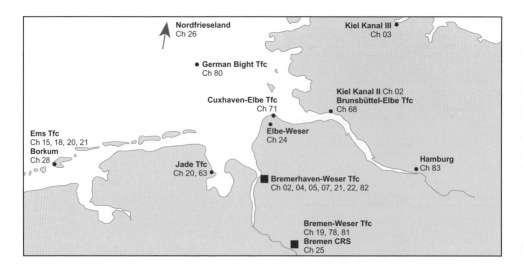

89·5 MHz; **Flensburg** 89·6 MHz; **Heide** 90·5 MHz; **Kiel** 91·3 MHz.

NDR Info (AM)

Synopsis, forecast and coastal station reports for the North Sea (and Baltic) are broadcast at 0005, 0830 and 2205 UT on 972 (Hamburg) & 702 (Flensburg) kHz.

Radio Bremen (MW and FM)

Warnings of extreme weather conditions in German Bight, with associated hazards, are broadcast after the news by: **Bremerhaven** 936 kHz; 89·3, 92·1, 95·4 & 100·8 MHz; and by **Bremen** 88·3, 93·8, 96·7 & 101·2 MHz.

Telephone forecasts (Marineweather)

For wind forecast and outlook (1 April – 30 Sept) call 0190 1160 (only within Germany) plus two digits for the following areas:

45	North Frisian Islands and Helgoland
46	R Elbe, Cuxhaven to Hamburg
47	Weser , Jade Bay and Helgoland
48	East Frisians and Ems Estuary
53	For pleasure craft

For year-round weather synopsis, forecast and outlook, call 0190 1169 plus two digits:

20	General information
21	North Sea and Baltic
22	German Bight, Fisher and SW North Sea
31	Reports for North Sea and Baltic

For the latest wind warnings (greater than F6) and storm warnings for individual areas of the North Sea coasts, call +49 40 66901209 (H24). If no warning is in force, a wind forecast for the German Bight, west and southern Baltic is given.

NETHERLANDS
VHF MSI broadcasts

Forecasts for 7 areas to 30M offshore and 3 inland waterways (IJsselmeer, Marken and Zierikzee) are broadcast in **English** and Dutch at 0805, 1305, 1905, 2305 LT on VHF as shown below, **without** prior announcement on Ch 16 or 70.

VHF Ch 23: Schiermonnikoog, Kornwerderzand, Wezep, Huisduinen (Den Helder), IJmuiden, Renesse, Woensdrecht.
VHF Ch 83: Appingedam, West Terschelling, Hoorn, Schoorl, Scheveningen, Westkapelle. All stations monitor Ch 16.

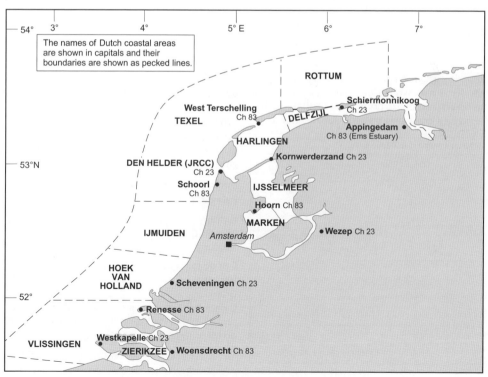

The names of Dutch coastal areas are shown in capitals and their boundaries are shown as pecked lines.

MF weather broadcasts

Forecasts for areas Dover, Thames, Humber, German Bight, Dogger, Fisher, Forties and Viking are broadcast by Scheveningen in **English** at 0940 & 2140 UT on 3673 kHz. Gale warnings for these areas are broadcast in **English** on receipt and at 0333, 0733, 1133, 1533, 1933 and 2333 UT.

Radio Noord-Holland (FM)

Coastal forecasts for northern areas, gale warnings and wind strength are broadcast in Dutch, Mon-Fri at 0730, 0838, 1005, 1230 and 1705LT; Sat/Sun 1005, by: **Haarlem** 97.6 MHz and **Wieringermeer** 93.9 MHz.

Omroep Zeeland (FM)

Coastal forecasts for southern areas, synopsis, gale warnings and wind strength are broadcast in Dutch, Mon-Fri at 0715, 0915, 1215 and 1715LT; Sat/Sun 1015, by:

Philippine 97.8 MHz and **Goes** 101.9 MHz.

BELGIUM, Coast radio stations

Oostende Radio, after prior notice on VHF 16, 24, DSC 70 and 2182kHz, broadcasts in **English** and Dutch on VHF 27, MF 2256, 2376 and 2761 kHz: Strong wind warnings on receipt and after the next 2 silent periods. Forecasts for Thames, Dover and the Belgian coast at 0720 LT and 0820, 1720 UT.

Antwerpen Radio broadcasts in **English** and Dutch on VHF Ch 24 for the Schelde estuary: Gale warnings on receipt and at every H+55. Also strong wind warnings (F6+) on receipt and at every H+55.

FRANCE

Le Guide Marine is a useful, free annual booklet which summarises the various means by which weather forecasts and warnings are broadcast or otherwise disseminated. It is available from marinas or Météo-France, 1 quai Branly, 75340 Paris. ☎ 01.45.56.74.36; 🖷 01.45.56.71.70. marine@meteo.fr www.meteo.fr

CROSS VHF and MF broadcasts

CROSS broadcasts Met bulletins in French, after an announcement on Ch 16. In the English Channel broadcasts can be given in English, on request Ch 16. Broadcasts include: Any gale warnings, general situation, 24 hrs forecast (actual weather, wind, sea state and vis) and further trends for coastal waters, which extend 20M offshore. VHF channels, remote stations and local times are shown below.

Gale warnings feature in Special Met Bulletins (*Bulletins Météorologique Spéciaux* or BMS). They are broadcast in French by all CROSS on VHF at H+03 and at other times on MF frequencies as shown below.

CROSS GRIS-NEZ Ch 79
Belgian border to Baie de la Somme

Dunkerque	0720, 1603, 1920
St Frieux	0710, 1545, 1910

Baie de la Somme to Cap de la Hague

L'Ailly	
0703, 1533, 1903	

Gale warnings for areas 12-13 are broadcast in French on MF 1650 & 2677 kHz at 0833 & 2033LT

CROSS JOBOURG Ch 80
Baie de la Somme to Cap de la Hague

Antifer	0803, 1633, 2003
Port-en-Bessin	0745, 1615, 1945
Jobourg	0733, 1603, 1933

Cap de la Hague to Pointe de Penmarc'h

Jobourg	0715, 1545, 1915
Granville	0703, 1533, 1903

Gale warnings for areas 13-14 in **English** on receipt and at H+20 and H+50. No gale warnings on MF.

French forecast areas

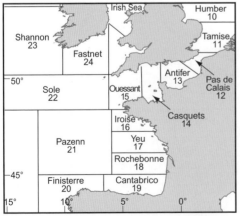

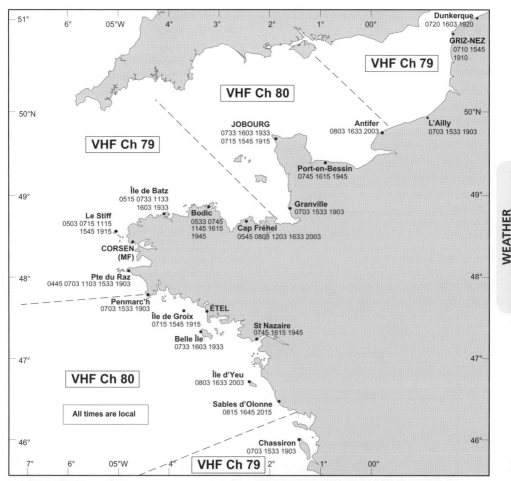

CROSS CORSEN Ch 79

Cap de la Hague to Pte de Penmarc'h   (Times in bold = 1 May to 30 Sep only).

Cap Fréhel   0545, 0803, **1203**, 1633, 2003 **Bodic** 0533, 0745, **1145**, 1615, 1945

Ile de Batz	0515, 0733, **1133**, 1603, 1933
Le Stiff	0503, 0715, **1115**, 1545, 1915
Pte du Raz	0445, 0703, **1103**, 1533, 1903

Corsen broadcasts gale warnings for areas 13-22 in French at 0815 and 2015LT on MF 1650 & 2677 kHz.

CROSS ÉTEL Ch 80

Pte de Penmarc'h to l'Anse de l'Aiguillon (46° 15'N 01°10'W). Étel has no MF freqs

Penmarc'h	0703, 1533, 1903
Ile de Groix	0715, 1545, 1915
Belle Ile	0733, 1603, 1933
Saint-Nazaire	0745, 1615, 1945
Ile d'Yeu	0803, 1633, 2003
Les Sables d'Olonne	0815, 1645, 2015

CROSS ÉTEL Ch 79

L'Anse de l'Aiguillon to Spanish border

Chassiron	0703, 1533, 1903

Commercial radio broadcasting
Radio France (Inter-Service-Mer)

Broadcasts in French on LW 162 kHz at 2003LT daily: gale warnings, synopsis, 24 hrs forecast and outlook for all areas.

MF broadcasts are made at 0640LT by:

Brest	1404 kHz
Rennes	711 kHz

Radio France Internationale (RFI)

RFI broadcasts gale warnings, synopsis, development and 24 hrs forecasts in French on HF at 1130 UT daily.

Frequencies and reception areas are:

6175 kHz: North Sea, English Channel, Bay of Biscay. 15300, 15515, 17570 and 21645 kHz: North Atlantic, E of 50°W.

See opposite for the High Seas forecast areas in the Eastern Atlantic.

Engineering bulletins giving any changes in frequency are transmitted between H+53 and H+00.

Local radio (FM)

Radio France Cherbourg broadcasts daily at 0829 LT:

Coastal forecast, gale warnings, visibility, wind strength, tidal information, small craft warnings, in French, for the Cherbourg peninsula on the following frequencies:

St Vaast-la-Hougue	85·0 MHz
Cherbourg	100·7 MHz
Cap de la Hague	99·8 MHz
Carteret	99·9 MHz

Forecasts by telephone

For recorded Inshore and Coastal forecasts. Dial 08·92·68·02·dd (dd is the number, as given, for the

département); press the * key then 1 to access the main menu. Follow instructions:

For Inshore (*rivage*) or Coastal (*côte*) bulletins, say 'STOP' as your choice is spoken.

Inshore bulletins contain 7 day forecasts, tide times, actual reports, sea temperature, surf conditions, etc.

Coastal bulletins contain strong wind/gale warnings, general synopsis, 24 hrs forecast and outlook. Five bulletins cover the N & W coasts, out to 20M offshore.

For Offshore bulletins (*large*), out to 200M offshore, dial ☎ 08·92·68·08·77. Select one of three offshore areas (English Channel & southern North Sea, Bay of Biscay or the N part of the western Mediterranean) by saying 'STOP' as it is named. Offshore bulletins contain strong wind/gale warnings, the general synopsis and forecast, and the outlook for up to 7 days.

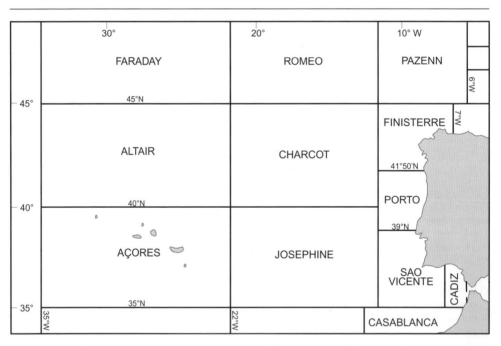

Forecast areas for the Eastern Atlantic and Coastal/Offshore Areas off France, Spain, Portugal and North West Africa

WEATHER VOCABULARY

English	German	French	Spanish	Dutch
Air mass	Luftmasse	Masse d'air	Massa de aire	Luchtmassa
Anticyclone	Antizyklonisch	Anticyclone	Anticiclón	Hogedrukgebied
Area	Gebiet	Zone	Zona	Gebied
Backing wind	Rückdrehender Wind	Vent reculant	Rolar el viento	Krimpende wind
Barometer	Barometer	Baromètre	Barómetro	Barometer
Breeze	Brise	Brise	Brisa	Bries
Calm	Flaute	Calme	Calma	Kalmte
Centre	Zentrum	Centre	Centro	Centum
Clouds	Wolken	Nuages	Nube	Wolken
Cold	Kalt	Froid	Frio	Koud
Cold front	Kaltfront	Front froid	Frente frio	Kou front
Cyclonic	Zyklonisch	Cyclonique	Ciclonica	Cycloonachtig
Decrease	Abnahme	Affaiblissement	Disminución	Afnemen
Deep	Tief	Profond	Profundo	Diep
Deepening	Vertiefend	Approfondissant	Ahondamiento	Verdiepend
Depression	Sturmtief	Dépression	Depresión	Depressie
Air mass	Luftmasse	Masse d'air	Massa de aire	Luchtmassa
Anticyclone	Antizyklonisch	Anticyclone	Anticiclón	Hogedrukgebied
Area	Gebiet	Zone	Zona	Gebied
Backing wind	Rückdrehender Wind	Vent reculant	Rolar el viento	Krimpende wind
Barometer	Barometer	Baromètre	Barómetro	Barometer
Breeze	Brise	Brise	Brisa	Bries
Calm	Flaute	Calme	Calma	Kalmte
Centre	Zentrum	Centre	Centro	Centum
Clouds	Wolken	Nuages	Nube	Wolken
Cold	Kalt	Froid	Frio	Koud
Cold front	Kaltfront	Front froid	Frente frio	Kou front
Cyclonic	Zyklonisch	Cyclonique	Ciclonica	Cycloonachtig
Decrease	Abnahme	Affaiblissement	Disminución	Afnemen
Deep	Tief	Profond	Profundo	Diep
Deepening	Vertiefend	Approfondissant	Ahondamiento	Verdiepend
Depression	Sturmtief	Dépression	Depresión	Depressie
Direction	Richtung	Direction	Direción	Richting
Dispersing	Auflösend	Se dispersant	Disipación	Oplossend
Disturbance	Störung	Perturbation	Perturbación	Verstoving
Drizzle	Niesel	Bruine	Lioviena	Motregen
East	Ost	Est	Este	Oosten
Extending	Ausdehnung	S'étendant	Extension	Uitstrekkend
Extensive	Ausgedehnt	Etendu	General	Uitgebreid
Falling	Fallend	Descendant	Bajando	Dalen
Filling	Auffüllend	Secomblant	Relleno	Vullend
Fog	Nebel	Brouillard	Niebla	Nevel
Fog bank	Nebelbank	Ligne de brouillard	Banco de niebla	Mist bank
Forecast	Vorhersage	Prévision	Previsión	Vooruitzicht
Frequent	Häufig	Fréquent	Frecuenta	Veelvuldig
Fresh	Frisch	Frais	Fresco	Fris
Front	Front	Front	Frente	Front
Gale	Sturm	Coup de vent	Temporal	Storm
Gale warning	Sturmwarnung	Avis de coup de vent	Aviso de temporal	Stormwaarschuwing
Good	Gut	Bon	Bueno	Goed
Gradient	Druckunterschied	Gradient	Gradiente	Gradiatie
Gust, squall	Bö	Rafalle	Ráfaga	Windvlaag
Hail	Hagel	Grêle	Granizo	Hagel
Haze	Diesig	Brume	Calina	Nevel
Heavy	Schwer	Abondant	Abunante	Zwaar
High	Hoch	Anticyclone	Alta presión	Hoog
Increasing	Zunehmend	Augmentant	Aumentar	Toenemend
Isobar	Isobar	Isobare	Isobara	Isobar
Isolated	Vereinzelt	Isolé	Aislado	Verspreid
Lightning	Blitze	Eclair de foudre	Relampago	Bliksem
Local	Örtlich	Locale	Local	Plaatselijk

English	German	French	Spanish	Dutch
Low	Tief	Dépression	Baja presión	Laag
Mist	Dunst	Brume légere	Nablina	Mist
Moderate	Mäßig	Modéré	Moderado	Matig
Moderating	Abnehmend	Se modérant	Medianente	Matigend
Moving	Bewegend	Se déplacant	Movimiento	Bewegend
North	Nord	Nord	Septentrional	Noorden
Occluded	Okklusion	Couvert	Okklusie	Bewolkt
Poor	Schlecht	Mauvais	Mal	Slecht
Precipitation	Niederschlag	Précipitation	Precipitación	Neerslag
Pressure	Druck	Pression	Presión	Druk
Rain	Regen	Pluie	lluvia	Regen
Ridge	Hochdruckbrücke	Crête	Cresta	Rug
Rising	Ansteigend	Montant	Subiendo	Stijgen
Rough	Rauh	Agitée	Bravo o alborotado	Ruw
Sea	See	Mer	Mar	Zee
Seaway	Seegang	Haute mer	Alta mar	Zee
Scattered	Vereinzelt	Sporadiques	Difuso	Verspreid
Shower	Schauer	Averse	Aguacero	Bui
Slight	Leicht	Un peu	Leicht	Licht
Slow	Langsam	Lent	Lent	Langzaam
Snow	Schnee	Neige	Nieve	Sneeuw
South	Süd	Sud	Sur	Zuiden
Storm	Sturm	Tempête	Temporal	Storm
Sun	Sonne	Soleil	Sol	Zon
Swell	Schwell	Houle	Mar de fondo	Deining
Thunder	Donner	Tonnerre	Tormenta	Donder
Thunderstorm	Gewitter	Orage	Tronada	Onweer
Trough	Trog, Tiefausläufer	Creux	Seno	Trog
Variable	Umlaufend	Variable	Variable	Veranderlijk
Veering	Rechtdrehend	Virement de vent	Dextrogiro	Ruimende wind
Warm front	Warmfront	Front chaud	Frente calido	Warm front
Weather	Wetter	Temps	Tiempo	Weer
Wind	Wind	Vent	Viento	Wind
Weather report	Wetterbericht	Météo	Previsión	Weer bericht meteorologica

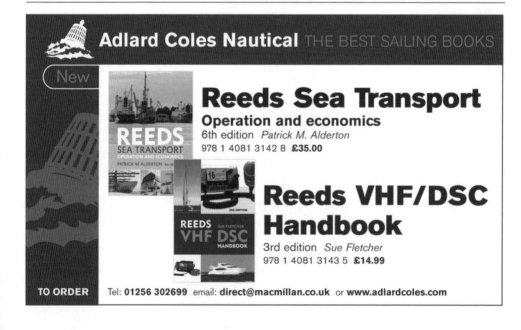

Chapter 3 – Communications

COMMUNICATIONS

RADIO OPERATION

Avoiding interference

Before transmitting, first listen on the VHF channel. If occupied, wait for a break before transmitting, or choose another channel. If you cause interference you must comply immediately with any request from a Coastguard or Coast radio station to stop transmitting.

Control of communications

Ship-to-Shore: Communications between ship and shore stations are controlled by the latter, except in distress, urgency or safety cases.

Intership: The ship *called* controls communication. If you call another ship, then it has control. If you are called by a ship, you assume control. If a shore-based station breaks in, both ships must comply with instructions given.

Radio confidentiality

Private conversations heard on the radio must not be reproduced, passed on or otherwise used.

Making yourself understood

Clear R/T speech is vital. If a message cannot be understood by the receiver it is useless. Messages which have to be written down at the receiving station should be spoken slowly. This gives time for it to be written down by the receiving operator. If the transmitting operator himself writes it down all should be well. The average reading speed is 250 words a minute, whilst average writing speed is only 20.

When speaking, consider the following:

- **What** to say, ie *voice Procedure*
- **How** to say it, ie *voice Technique*

Voice Procedure is discussed below and overleaf. It includes procedural words, callsigns, making contact etc.

Voice Technique depends on a few simple rules:

Hold the microphone a few inches in front of the mouth and speak directly into it at a normal level. Speak clearly so that there can be no confusion. The voice should be pitched up at a higher level than normal. Do not drop the voice pitch at the end of a phrase or sentence. Emphasise words with weak syllables; 'Tower', if badly pronounced, could sound like 'tar'. Non Anglophones, or people with strong regional accents must try to pronounce words as clearly as possible.

Difficult words may be spelled phonetically, preceded with 'I spell'. If the word can be pronounced, include it before and after it has been spelt. For example, the message 'I will berth on the yacht *Coila*' would be sent as: 'I will berth on the yacht *Coila* – I spell – Charlie Oscar India Lima Alfa – *Coila*'.

The phonetic alphabet

The syllables to emphasise are underlined

Letter	Morse	Phonetic	Spoken as
A	•–	Alfa	AL-fah
B	–•••	Bravo	BRAH-voh
C	–•–•	Charlie	CHAR-lee
D	–••	Delta	DELL-tah
E	•	Echo	ECK-oh
F	••–•	Foxtrot	FOKS-trot
G	––•	Golf	GOLF
H	••••	Hotel	hoh-TELL
I	••	India	IN-dee-ah
J	•–––	Juliett	JEW-lee-ett
K	–•–	Kilo	KEY-loh
L	•–••	Lima	LEE-mah
M	––	Mike	MIKE
N	–•	November	no-VEM-ber
O	–––	Oscar	OSS-car
P	•––•	Papa	pa-PAH
Q	––•–	Quebec	keh-BECK
R	•–•	Romeo	ROW-me-oh
S	•••	Sierra	see-AIR-rah
T	–	Tango	TANG-go
U	••–	Uniform	OO-nee-form
V	•••–	Victor	VIK-tah
W	•––	Whiskey	WISS-key
X	–••–	X-Ray	ECKS-ray
Y	–•––	Yankee	YANG-key
Z	––••	Zulu	ZOO-loo

Phonetic numerals

When numerals are transmitted, the following pronunciations make them easier to understand.

No	Morse	Spoken	No	Morse	Spoken
1	•––––	WUN	6	–••••	SIX
2	••–––	TOO	7	––•••	SEV-EN
3	•••––	TREE	8	–––••	AIT
4	••••–	FOW-ER	9	––––•	NIN-ER
5	•••••	FIFE	0	–––––	ZERO

Numerals are transmitted digit by digit except that multiples of thousands may be spoken as follows:

Numeral	Spoken as
44	FOW-ER FOW-ER
90	NIN-ER ZERO
136	WUN TREE SIX
500	FIFE ZERO ZERO
1478	WUN FOW-ER SEV-EN AIT
7000	SEV-EN THOU-SAND

Punctuation

Punctuation marks should be used only where their omission would cause confusion.

Mark	Word	Spoken as
.	Decimal	DAY-SEE-MAL
,	Comma	COMMA
.	Stop	STOP

Procedural words or 'prowords'

These are used to shorten transmissions

All after and **All before**. Used after proword *'say again'* to request repetition of a part of a message

Correct Reply to repeat of message that was preceded by prowords *'read back for check'* when it has been correctly repeated. Often said twice

Correction Cancel the last word or group of words. The correct word or group follows. Spoken when an error has been made in a transmission.

I say again I repeat the transmission or the part indicated (see 'All after' and 'All before').

I spell I shall spell the next word or group of letters phonetically

Out This is the end of working to you

Over Invitation to reply

Read back If the receiver is doubtful about accuracy of all or part of message he may repeat it back to the sending station, preceding the repetition with prowords *'I read back'*

Station calling Used when a station is uncertain of the calling station's identification/callsign

This is This transmission is from the station whose callsign or name immediately follows

Wait If a called station cannot accept traffic immediately, it will reply **'WAIT.......MINUTES'**, with reason if delay may exceed 10 minutes

Word after or Word before Used after the proword *'say again'* to request repetition

Wrong Reply to repetition of message preceded by prowords *'read back'* when it has been incorrectly repeated

Calls, calling and callsigns

Shore stations normally use a callsign of their geographic name followed by Coastguard or Radio, eg Solent Coastguard, Dublin Radio etc. Vessels usually identify themselves by the ship's name but the International callsign may be used in certain cases. If two yachts have the same or confusingly similar names, give your International callsign when starting communications, and thereafter use your ship's name as callsign.

'All ships' broadcast

Address used by Coastguard Radio where broadcast information is to be received or used by all who intercept it, eg gale warnings etc. No reply is needed.

Communicating with a coast radio station

Call initially on a working channel or very briefly on channel 16 to establish a working channel.

- Pause to check the working channel is clear before transmitting
- Use low power *(1 watt)* if close enough , ie up to 10 miles away. High power *(25 watts)* drains more from the battery
- The callsign of calling station up to three times only, and prowords 'This is'
- Say how many R/T calls you have to make
- Proword 'Over'

Using high power decreases battery state and the range your VHF will achieve. Continued calling also clutters up the channel and denies access to other users.

Aerial faults commonly reduce your transmitting range. Possibly the station aerial for the channel chosen is directionally orientated and you are on the wrong side. Try another channel or station. Call again when closer.

RADIO DATA

SHORT, MEDIUM and LONG RANGE RADIO COMMUNICATIONS

A suitable radio receiver on board will provide weather forecasts and time signals at scheduled times on a number of frequencies in various wavebands. With a maritime receiver you are not limited to the familiar BBC and commercial broadcasts. HM Coastguard transmit navigation warnings, storm warnings and weather messages for shipping in their respective sea areas.

Short range radiotelephony (RT) transmits and receives on VHF channels in the marine VHF (Very High Frequency) band. The equipment and procedures are simple, but range is normally limited to about 20 miles from ship to shore, rather less from ship to ship. Interconnection with national telephone systems is possible on certain VHF/RT channels when a yacht is within range of a Coast Radio Station, although there are now no such stations on the mainland of the UK, France or the Netherlands. Mobile telephones are now by far the most common form of ship to shore communication.

Medium range two-way communication operate in the marine MF (medium frequency) RT band, the 2MHz 'trawler band'. Single sideband techniques are employed on these medium frequencies and SSB equipment is essential. The effective range depends on the power of the transmitter and the sensitivity of the associated receiver; in general this might be up to 200 miles from certain (but not all) Coast Radio Stations.

THE MARINE VHF BAND

VHF is used by most vessels, Coast Radio Stations, CG centres and other rescue services. Its range is slightly better than the line of sight between the transmitting and receiving aerials. A good aerial, as high as possible, is most important.

In the Marine VHF band (156·00–174·00 MHz) the individual frequencies are separated from their neighbours by exactly 25kHz 'elbow-room' to eliminate mutual interference. Each frequency is given a channel number, not necessarily consecutive. Thus 55 channels are available, plus some with special purposes (see below).

VHF Channel Grouping

Channels are grouped for three main purposes, but some can be used for more than one purpose. They are listed below in their preferred order of usage:

• **Public correspondence** (ie link calls via CRS into the shore telephone system): Ch 26, 27, 25, 24, 23, 28, 04, 01, 03, 02, 07, 05, 84, 87, 86, 83, 85, 88, 61, 64, 65, 62, 66, 63, 60, 82, 78, 81.

• **Inter-ship:** Ch 06, 08, 10, 13, 09, 72, 73, 67, 69, 77, 15, 17. Remember these, so that if another vessel calls you, you can swiftly nominate a working channel from within this group.

• **Port Operations:** Ch 12, 14, 11, 13, 09, 68, 71, 74, 69, 73, 17, 15, 20, 22, 18, 19, 21, 05, 07, 02, 03, 01, 04, 78, 82, 79, 81, 80, 60, 63, 66, 62, 65, 64, 61, 84.

Special purposes. The following channels have one specific purpose only:

Ch 0 (156·00 MHz): SAR ops, not available to yachts.

Ch's 10 (156·500 MHz), **23** (161·750 MHz) **84** (161·825 MHz) and **86** (161·925 MHz): for MSI broadcasts by HMCG.

Ch 13 (156·650 MHz): Intership safety of navigation (sometimes referred to as bridge-to-bridge); a possible channel for calling a merchant ship if no contact on Ch 16.

Ch 16 (156·80 MHz): Distress, Safety and calling. *See Chapter 4 for Distress and Safety.* Ch 16 will be monitored by ships, CG centres (and, in some areas, any remaining Coast Radio Stations) for Distress and Safety until at least 2005, in parallel with DSC Ch 70. Yachts should monitor Ch 16. After an initial call, the stations concerned **must** switch to a working channel, except for Safety matters.

Ch 67 (156·375 MHz): the Small Craft Safety channel in the UK, accessed via Ch 16.

Ch 70 (156·525 MHz): exclusively for digital selective calling for Distress and Safety purposes.

Ch 80 (157·025 MHz): the primary working channel between yachts and UK marinas.

Ch M (157·85 MHz): the secondary working channel between yachts and UK marinas; previously known as Ch 37.

Ch M2 (161·425 MHz): for race control, with Ch M as stand-by. YCs may apply to use Ch M2.

SILENCE PERIODS

The periods are the 3 minutes immediately after the whole and half hours, ie H to H+03 and H+30 to H+33, when no transmissions should be made.

MEDIUM RANGE MF RADIO

Single sideband MF/RT provides communications in the offshore waters of the UK and Western Europe where small craft may be out of VHF contact. A receiver alone gives the ability to hear weather bulletins, storm and navigation warnings for local sea areas broadcast from CRS in the 1.6 to 4.0MHz maritime band, ie on frequencies from 1605 to 4200 kHz.

MF transmissions tend to follow the curvature of the earth, which makes them suitable for direction-finding. For this reason, and because of their good range, the marine Distress R/T frequency (2182 kHz) is in the MF band.

TRAFFIC LISTS

If a Coast Radio station has messages for a vessel, but is unable to contact her, that vessel's name will be added to the Traffic List broadcast at (usually) two hour intervals. This is not a system much used by yachts and small craft.

LONG RANGE HF RADIO

HF radios use short wave frequencies in the 4, 8, 12, 16 and 22 MHz bands, as chosen to suit propagation conditions. HF is more expensive than MF and requires more power, but can provide worldwide coverage. A good installation and skilled operating techniques are essential for satisfactory results.

GLOBAL COMMUNICATIONS

Once out of range of VHF/MF or wireless telephony/broadband service, the yachtsman's communications options are limited to MF/HF radio and satellite systems (Satcoms).

A yachtsman embarking on an extended offshore venture would usually choose a mix of equipment for sensible reasons of redundancy, this will allow a choice of listening and transmitting, via terrestrial and satellite radio systems, to meet his needs at various times and in different circumstances. A typical setup might include a fixed or handheld satcoms transceiver, a HF SSB transceiver and receiver. For data capability, these would be interfaced to an on-board PC.

HF/single sideband radio (HF-SSB)

HF SSB radios use frequencies in the 4, 8, 12, 16 and 22 MHz bands (short wave), provide worldwide coverage and usually include MF frequencies as well.

Despite rapid growth in marine satellite communications, HF SSB remains a popular choice amongst long-distance cruisers, providing a cost-free voice (and limited email) capability for cruisers, sometimes operating over vast distances. Operators have the Long Range Certificate (LRC) or General Operators Certificate (GOC). To use Amateur (ham) bands (giving more frequencies and higher power, therefore range) operators must take the ham examination.

Using HF SSB radio for email requires a radio modem, often proprietary to the supplier. Though slow and requiring some skill to operate effectively, the almost-nil operating costs appeal to many and SSB radio has a strong following amongst blue-water cruisers. Established suppliers include Sailmail and Globe Wireless.

HF SSB radio is also extensively used for receipt of weatherfax images, although a receive-only SSB radio (with an adequate, grounded antenna installation) may be used rather than a full transceiver. Though declining in popularity, several useful weatherfax transmitting stations remain, including Northwood, UK and Offenbach, Germany.

Satellite Communications (Satcoms)

Satellite communications systems operate over **Ultra High Frequency (UHF)** radio using digital technology that makes them simpler-to-operate and more reliable for voice (and data) communications than HF SSB radio; they operate with either a dedicated ship installation or a standalone handheld terminal. Apart from the equipment purchase (and installation if necessary), ongoing costs usually include a monthly service fee and usage charges that will be related to either the amount of satellite time used, or the volume of data transmitted and received.

For two-way voice communications, the 'Ship Station' (aka 'Mobile Earth Station') transmits to a visible satellite that is simultaneously in sight of a 'Land Earth Station', eg Goonhilly, Cornwall. From there, the call is routed to its destination through the normal terrestrial telephone network.

The satellite 'constellations' have different architectures. Inmarsat for example has four geostationary (GEO) satellites, one each positioned over the Pacific and Indian oceans and two over the Atlantic. Because they are comparatively high up 19,400M (36,000km), each satellite has a large signal 'footprint', overlapping the next one and thus world-wide coverage is provided (although not in the polar regions above about 70°N and 70°S).

Other systems employ many more Low Earth Orbit (LEO) satellites orbiting the Earth about 540M (1,000km) above the surface.

The smaller, low-data rate, handheld voice terminals incorporate an omni-directional antenna that works best with an unobstructed view of the satellite. Fixed installations use an external gyro-stabilised antenna (to keep it pointing at the satellite as the boat moves); more powerful systems that support higher data rates employ antenna radomes that are really too large for installation aboard a 10–15m yacht.

The GMDSS provides automatic distress, urgency and safety communications, with some satcom systems (eg Inmarsat C) providing a red button that alerts a Maritime Rescue Coordination Centre (MRCC) when pressed.

There are several service providers, each offering an array of capabilities. The table opposite provides a useful summary of systems that might be used aboard a 10–20m yacht.

This is a fast moving market place and you should check with manufacturers/retailers for up-to-date specifications and prices.

[1] typical, **if** in coverage area [2] using VOIP [3] Likely to be expensive	Wired Broadband	Wi-Fi	Cellular GSM	Cellular GPRS	Cellular 3G	Wi-Max
Range offshore[1] (NM)	0	0-1	0-15	0-15	0-15	0-30
Voice communication	Y [2]	Y [2]	Y	Y	Y	Y [2]
Text messages	Y	Y	Y	Y	Y	Y
Light email traffic	Y	Y	Y [3]	Y	Y	Y
Text weather forecasts	Y	Y	Y [3]	Y	Y	Y
Heavy email traffic	Y	Y	×	Y [3]	Y	Y
Graphical weather forecasts	Y	Y	×	Y [3]	Y	Y
Full web browsing	Y	Y	×	Y [3]	Y	Y

SATELLITE COMMUNICATION SERVICES

System	Antenna	Satellites	Coverage	GMDSS	Phone (voice)	Fax	SMS text	Position tracking	Data rate
INMARSAT C	Omni-directional	4 GEO	Global excepting polar regions	Yes	No	Yes	Yes	Yes (GPS)	Very low, uneconomic for email
INMARSAT Mini-M	Gyro-stabilised 40cms diameter	4 GEO	Global excepting polar regions	No	Yes	Yes	No	No	2.4kbps
INMARSAT D+	Omni-directional	4 GEO	Global excepting polar regions	No	No	No	No	Yes (GPS)	Very low, uneconomic for email
Fleet 33	Gyro-stabilised 40cms diameter	4 GEO	Global excepting polar regions	No	Yes	Yes	Yes	No	9.6kbps uncompressed
Iridium	Omni-directional	66 LEO	Global	No	Yes	Out only	Yes	No	Data kit required 2.4kbps, higher with compression
Globalstar	Omni-directional	40 LEO	Global excepting polar regions	No	Yes	Yes	Yes	To 10km	9.6kbps uncompressed, 38.6kbps compressed, 56k with data kit
Thuraya	Omni-directional	1 GEO	Europe, N Africa & Middle East, India	No	Yes	Yes	Yes	Yes (GPS)	9.6kbps (144kbps possible with land *DSL receiver)

*DSL (Digital Subscriber Line) allows broadband Internet access via normal copper telephone lines. It is used in the wireless/Satcoms arena to denote broadband-like speeds over the wireless link. This usually means data transfer speeds of 5 to 24mbps which is fast for Satcoms.

PORT and/or MARINA VHF channels and telephone details

In larger ports it is sensible to monitor the VTS channel (if any) or the primary port channel (in bold) before changing to a marina channel. Times are local, unless marked UT. Abbreviations are at the front of the book. Telephone codes are shown only once unless more than one applies.

ENGLAND – SOUTH COAST

ISLES OF SCILLY, St Mary's HM Ch 14 (0800-1700); ☎ 01720 422768. *Falmouth CG* covers Scilly and the TSS off Land's End on Ch 23. **Tresco** HM ☎ 07778 601237.

NEWLYN HM Ch 09, **12** (M-F: 0800-1700, Sat: 0800-1200). ☎ 01736 362523.

PENZANCE HM Ch 09, **12** (M-F: 0830-1730 and HW −2 to +1). ☎ 01736 366113.

FALMOUTH *Falmouth Hbr Radio* Ch 11, **12**, 14 (M-F 0800-1700). ☎ 01326 312285.
Ch 80: Falmouth ☎ 316620 and Port Pendennis marinas ☎ 311113. **Ch 12**: Visitors Yacht Haven ☎ 310991; St Mawes HM ☎ 270553. **Ch M** (HO): Mylor Yacht Hbr ☎ 372121.

TRURO HM *Carrick One* Ch 12. ☎ 01872 272130. **Ch M** (HO): Malpas Marine ☎ 271260.

MEVAGISSEY HM Ch 14 (Summer: 0900-2100, Winter: 0900-1700). ☎ 01726 843305.

CHARLESTOWN HM Ch 14, HW −2 to +1, only when a vessel is expected. ☎ 01726 70241.

FOWEY HM Ch 12 (0900-1700); also Hbr Patrol (0900-2000). ☎ 01726 832471. Water taxi: Ch 06.

LOOE. HM Ch 16, occas. ☎ 01503 262839.

PLYMOUTH *Long Room Port Control* Ch 14 H24, ☎ 01752 836528. **QAB** Ch 80, ☎ 671142. **Sutton Hbr lock**: Ch 12 H24, ☎ 204702. **Cattewater HM** Ch 14 (M-F 0900-1700), ☎ 836528. **Plymouth Yacht Haven**, Ch 80, M; ☎ 404231. **Mayflower marina**, Ch 80; ☎ 556633.

SALCOMBE HM & launch: Ch 14, May to mid-Sep: 7/7, 0600-2100; otherwise: M-F 0900-1600; ☎ 01548 843791. *Hbr Taxi* Ch 12. Fuel barge Ch 06, ☎ 07801 798862. *Egremont* (ICC) Ch M.

DARTMOUTH HM *Dartnav* Ch 11, 7/7 0730-dusk; ☎ 01803 832337. Darthaven marina Ch 80, ☎ 752545. Dart & Noss-on-Dart marinas Ch 80, ☎ 833351. Fuel barge Ch 06. Water taxi Ch 08.

TORBAY HBRS Brixham Marina Ch 80, ☎ 01803 882929; YC, ☎ 853332, & Water taxi *Shuttle* Ch M. Torquay Marina Ch 80, ☎ 200210. Fuel Ch M.

EXETER Exmouth Marina Ch 14, ☎ 01395 269314. **Retreat BY**: Ch M, ☎ 01392 874720. **Port of Exeter** HM Ch 12, M-F: 0730-1730 and when vessel due; ☎ 274306.

LYME REGIS HM Ch 14. Summer 0800-2000, winter 1000-1500. ☎ 01297 442137.

BRIDPORT HM Ch 11. ☎ 01308 423222.

PORTLAND PORT Port Control Ch 74 (H24). ☎ 01305 824044. **Sailing Academy** ☎ 866000.

WEYMOUTH HM & Town Bridge: Ch 12, M-F 0800-2000 summer & when vessel due; ☎ 01305 838423. **Marina** Ch 80, ☎ 767576. **Fuel** Ch 60.

POOLE
HM/bridge Ch 14 (H24); Code 01202 ☎ 440233. **Marinas Ch 80 M**: Salterns ☎ 709971. Parkstone YC ☎ 743610. Poole Quay ☎ 649488. Cobbs Quay ☎ 674299. **Poole Bay Fuels: Ch M** M-F: 0900-1730; Sat/Sun 0830-1800. ☎ 07768 71511.

YARMOUTH (IoW)
HM & Yar bridge **Ch 68** H24. ☎ 01983 760321. Water taxi **Ch 15**.

LYMINGTON
Marinas Ch 80, M: Yacht Haven ☎ 01590 677071. Berthon Marina ☎ 01590 673312.

COWES
Harbour Radio, Chain Ferry & Folly Inn Ch 69 Mon-Fri: 0800-1700. Marinas **Ch 80, M**. Tel code 01983: Yacht Haven ☎ 299975. Shepards ☎ 297821. East Cowes ☎ 293983. Island Hbr **Ch 80**, ☎ 822999. Water Taxi **Ch 06**.

NEWPORT HM & Yacht Hbr Ch 69 0800-1600. ☎ 01983 525994.

RYDE HM **Ch 80**. Summer 0900-2000, Winter HX. ☎ 01983 613879. Access HW±2.

BEMBRIDGE Marina **Ch 80**, ☎ 01983 872828. Hbr launch **Ch M**.

SOUTHAMPTON
Port Ops and VTS Ch 12 14. Marinas **Ch 80, M**. Tel code 02380: Hythe ☎ 207073. Ocean Village ☎ 229385. Shamrock Quay ☎ 229461. Kemp's ☎ 632323.

HAMBLE
Hbr Radio Ch 68 Apr-Sep daily 0600-2200; Oct-Mar 0700-1830. Marinas **Ch 80, M**. Tel code 02380: Hamble Pt ☎ 452464. Port Hamble ☎ 452741. Mercury ☎ 455994. Water Taxi **Ch 77**, ☎ 454512. Tel code 01489: Universal ☎ 574272. Swanwick ☎ 885000.

PORTSMOUTH
VTS **Ch 11** (& *QHM* if essential). Marinas **80**. Tel code 02392: Haslar ☎ 601201. Gosport ☎ 524811. Royal Clarence ☎ 523810. Port Solent ☎ 210765. THE CAMBER (Commercial Hbr): *Portsmouth Hbr Radio* **Ch 11** 14 (H24).

LANGSTONE HBR
HM **Ch 12**. Summer, daily 0830-1700; Winter, M-F 0830-1700; Sat/Sun 0830-1300. Southsea Marina **Ch 80, M, ☎** 02392 822719.

CHICHESTER
HM *Chichester Hbr Radio* **Ch 14**. 1 Apr-Sep: M-Fri: 0830-1700. Sat: 0900-1300. 1 Oct - 31 Mar: 0900-1300, 1400-1700. Marinas **Ch 80, M**. Sparkes ☎ 02392 463572. Tel code 01243: Northney ☎ 466321. Emsworth Yacht Hbr ☎ 377727. Thornham ☎ 375335. Birdham Pool ☎ 512310. Chichester ☎ 512731. Water taxi **Ch 08** 0900-1800, mobile 07970 378350

LITTLEHAMPTON
HM/Bridge **Ch 71** 0900-1700. Marina **Ch 80, M;** ☎ 01903 241663.

SHOREHAM
HM & lock *Shoreham Hbr Radio* **Ch 14** (H24). Marina ☎ 01273 593801.

BRIGHTON
Marina *Brighton Control* **Ch M 80;** ☎ 01273 819919.

NEWHAVEN
HM & Bridge *Newhaven Radio* **Ch 12**. Marina **Ch 80, M;** ☎ 01273 513881.

EASTBOURNE
Sovereign Hbr, inc lock/berthing: **Ch 17**. ☎ 01323 470099.

RYE
Hbr Radio, **Ch 14** 0900-1700 or when ship due. ☎ 01797 225225.

FOLKESTONE
Port Control **Ch 15** for entry; ☎ 01303 254597.

DOVER
Port Control **Ch 74** for entry. Marina Ch 80; ☎ 01304 241663.

RAMSGATE
Port Control **Ch 14**. Marina **Ch 80;** ☎ 01843 572110.

ENGLAND – EAST COAST

WHITSTABLE
Hbr Radio Ch 09 12, Mon-Fri: 0830-1700 and –3HW+1. ☎ 01227 274086.

MEDWAY
Medway VTS **Ch 74**. Kingsferry Bridge (W Swale) **Ch 10** H24. Marinas **Ch 80, M**. Tel code 01634: Gillingham ☎ 280022. Hoo ☎ 250311. Chatham ☎ 899200.

PORT OF LONDON
LONDON VTS: Ch 69 from sea to Sea Reach No 4 buoy. **Ch 68** Sea Reach No 4 to Crayford Ness. **Ch 14**, 22, W of Crayford Ness.
Thames Barrier Ch 14. ☎ 020 8855 0315.

RIVER THAMES
Patrol Launches *Thames Patrol* **Ch 06, 13, 14, 68**
King George V Dock lock *KG Control* **Ch 13.**
West India Dock lock **Ch 13**
Greenwich Yacht Club **Ch M**

Thames lock (Brentford) **Ch 74** Summer 0800-1800; Winter 0800-1630.
Cadogan Pier **Ch 14** 0900-1700.
Marinas Ch 80, M; Tel code 0207: Gallions Point ☎ 4767054. Poplar Dock ☎ 5151046. South Dock ☎ 2522244. Limehouse Basin ☎ 3089930. St Katherine Haven ☎ 2645312. Chelsea Hbr ☎ 2259100. Brentford Dock ☎ 0208 2328941.

RIVER ROACH
Havengore Bridge **Ch 72** *Shoe Bridge* HW±2. ☎ 01702 383436.

BURNHAM-ON-CROUCH
Ch 80: HM Launch 0900-1700. Yacht Hbr ☎ 01621 782150. Essex Marina ☎ 01702 258531.

RIVER BLACKWATER
Marinas **Ch 80, M**; Tel code 01621: Tollesbury ☎ 869202. Bradwell ☎ 776235. **Ch M:** Blackwater ☎ 740264. Heybridge Lock, **Ch 80** ☎ 853506.

RIVER COLNE
Brightlingsea Hbr Radio **Ch 68** 0800-2000. ☎ 01206 302200, mob 07952 734814.

WALTON BACKWATERS
Titchmarsh Marina **Ch 80**, ☎ 01255 672185.

RIVERS STOUR AND ORWELL
HARWICH VTS **Ch 71**, 11, 20, H24
SUNK VTS **Ch 14**, H24
Orwell Navigation Service **Ch 68**, H24
Marinas **Ch 80, M**. Tel code 01473: Shotley ☎ 788982. Suffolk Hbr ☎ 659240. Woolverstone ☎ 780206. Fox's ☎ 689111. Neptune ☎ 215204. Ipswich Haven ☎ 236644.

RIVER DEBEN
HM *Odd Times* **Ch 08**. Tidemill Yacht Hbr ☎ 01394 385745.

SOUTHWOLD
Port Radio **Ch 09 12**. HM ☎ 01502 724712.

LOWESTOFT
Hbr Control **Ch 11, 14**. HM ☎ 01502 572286. Royal Norfolk & Suffolk YC **Ch 80.** ☎ 566726. Haven Marina **Ch 80** ☎ 580300. **Mutford Bridge & Lock Ch 09, 14** ☎ 531778.

GREAT YARMOUTH
Yarmouth Radio **Ch 12**. HM ☎ 01493 335511. *Haven & Breydon bridges* **Ch 12**.

WELLS-NEXT-THE-SEA
Wells Hbr **Ch 12**, HJ, HW±2 and when vessel expected. HM ☎ 01328 711646.

WISBECH
Ch 09 HW–3 when vessel expected. HM 01945 588059. Sutton Bridge **Ch 09**

KING'S LYNN
Harbour Radio **Ch 14** 11 Mon-Fri: 0800-1700 and –3HW+1. HM ☎ 01553 773411.

BOSTON
Port Control **Ch 12** Mon-Fri 0800-1700 and HW HW -2½ to HW + 1½. HM ☎ 01205 362328.
Grand Sluice **Ch 74** only when lock operates. Marina ☎ 364420.

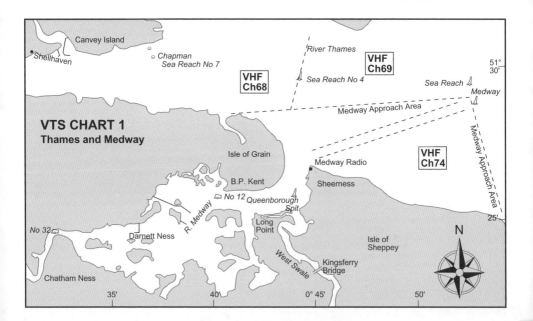

VTS CHART 1
Thames and Medway

Canvey Island
Shellhaven
Chapman
Sea Reach No 7
River Thames
VHF Ch69
VHF Ch68
Sea Reach No 4
Sea Reach
Medway
51° 30'
Medway Approach Area
Isle of Grain
Medway Radio
VHF Ch74
B.P. Kent
Sheerness
No 12 Queenborough Spit
R. Medway
Darnett Ness
Long Point
Medway Approach Area
25'
No 32
Chatham Ness
West Swale
Kingsferry Bridge
Isle of Sheppey
N
35'   40'   0° 45'   50'

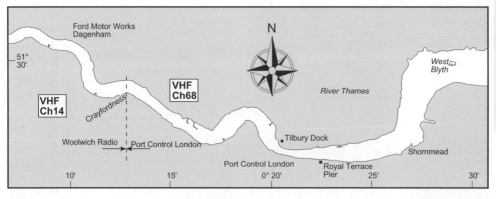

Ford Motor Works Dagenham
N
West Blyth
51° 30'
VHF Ch14
VHF Ch68
River Thames
Crayfordness
Woolwich Radio   Port Control London
Tilbury Dock
Shornmead
Port Control London
Royal Terrace Pier
10'   15'   0° 20'   25'   30'

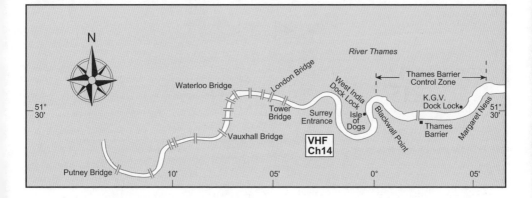

N
River Thames
Thames Barrier Control Zone
Waterloo Bridge
London Bridge
West India Dock Lock
K.G.V. Dock Lock
Margaret Ness
51° 30'
Tower Bridge
Surrey Entrance
Isle of Dogs
Blackwall Point
Thames Barrier
51° 30'
Vauxhall Bridge
VHF Ch14
Putney Bridge
10'   05'   0°   05'

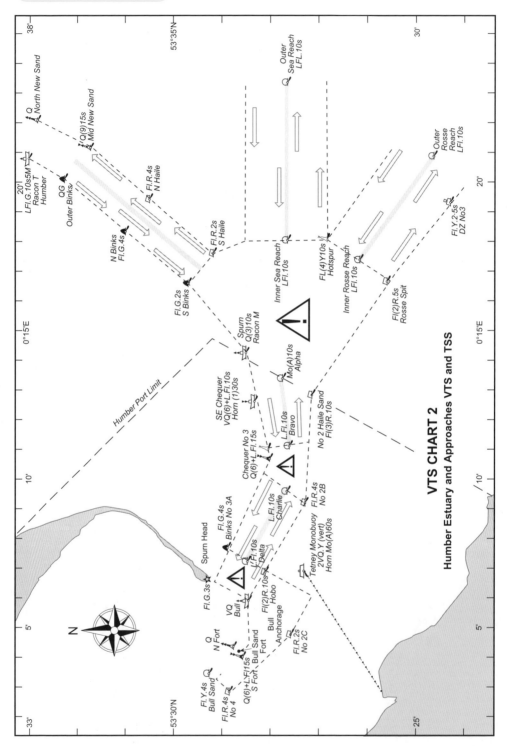

VTS CHART 2

Humber Estuary and Approaches VTS and TSS

RIVER HUMBER
VTS 1, Ch 14 to seaward of Clee Ness Lt F
VTS 2, Ch 12 Clee Ness–Gainsborough (R Trent) & Goole (R Ouse). MSI broadcasts Ch 12 & 14 every 2 hrs from 0103LT.
Grimsby Docks Radio Ch 74; 18 79 H24
Marinas: Grimsby, Meridian Quay Ch 74, ☎ 01472 268424. Hull, Ch 80, ☎ 01482 330508.
South Ferriby, Sluice Ch 74. Brough, Humber Yawl club ☎ 01482 667224. Goole Boathouse ☎ 01405 763985.

BRIDLINGTON
HM, call Ch 16; work Ch 12. ☎ 01262 670148.

SCARBOROUGH
HM *Scarborough Port Control* Ch 12 H24. ☎ 01723 373530.

WHITBY
HM, Bridge & Marina Ch 11, 12 H24. ☎ 01947 602354.

RIVER TEES and HARTLEPOOL
Monitor *Tees Port control* Ch 14, 08, 11, 12, 22.
Hartlepool Marina Ch 80, M H24. ☎ 01429 865744.

SEAHAM
HM Ch 12, M-F 0800-1700. ☎ 0191 5161700.

SUNDERLAND
Hbr Radio Ch 14 (H24). Marina Ch 80, M. ☎ 0191 5144721.

RIVER TYNE
Tyne VTS Ch 12, 08, 11, inc Info service.
Royal Quays Marina Ch 80. ☎ 0191 2728282.
St Peter's Marina Ch 80. ☎ 0191 2654472.

BLYTH
Port control Ch 12, 11. ☎ 01670 352066. Marina ☎ 01670 353636 (R Northumberland YC).

WARKWORTH HARBOUR (Amble)
HM Ch 16, work Ch 14. ☎ 01665 710306. Marina Ch 80, ☎ 01665 712168.

BERWICK-UPON-TWEED
HM Ch 12, M-F 0800-1700. ☎ 01289 307404.

SCOTLAND
EYEMOUTH HM Ch 12, 06 HO. ☎ 01890 750223.
FIRTH OF FORTH
Forth Navigation Ch 71; may work 12, 20.
PORT EDGAR Marina Ch 80, M. ☎ 0131 3313330.
GRANTON, Royal Forth YC, Call *Boswell* Ch M. ☎ 0131 5523006.
GRANGEMOUTH Docks Ch 14. ☎ 01324 498566.
FORTH & CLYDE CANAL *Carron Sea Lock* Ch 74. ☎ 01324 483034.
METHIL Docks Ch 14. ☎ 01324 498585.
ANSTRUTHER Ch 11. ☎ 01333 310836.
DUNDEE *Harbour Radio* Ch 12. ☎ 01382 224121.
Royal Tay YC Ch M. ☎ 01382 477516.

PERTH *Perth Harbour* Ch 09. ☎ 01738 624056.
ARBROATH *Port Control* Ch 11. ☎ 01241 872166.
MONTROSE *Port Control* Ch 12. ☎ 01674 672302.
STONEHAVEN HM Ch 11. ☎ 01569 762741.
ABERDEEN VTS Ch 12, ☎ 01224 597000.
PETERHEAD *Peterhead Hbrs* Ch 14 for cl'nce to enter/exit. Marina ☎ 01779 477868.
FRASERBURGH Ch 12 H24, ☎ 01346 515858.
MACDUFF Ch 12 H24, ☎ 01261 832236.
BANFF Ch 12, ☎ 01261 815544.
WHITEHILLS *Whitehills Hbr Radio* Ch 14, ☎ 01261 861291.
BUCKIE Ch 12, 16 (H24), ☎ 01542 831700.
LOSSIEMOUTH
HM Ch 12 0700-1700. Marina, ☎ 01343 813066.
HOPEMAN and BURGHEAD
Same HM: *Burghead Radio* Ch 14 HX, ☎ 01343 835337.
NAIRN HM/Marina ☎ 01667 454330. No VHF.
INVERNESS
HM Ch 12, M-Fri 0900-1700; Tel code 01463: ☎ 715715.
Clachnaharry Sealock Ch 74, ☎ 713896. HW ±4.
Inverness Marina Ch 12.
Seaport Marina ☎ 239745.
Caley Marina ☎ 236539.
HELMSDALE Ch 13, ☎ 01431 821692.
WICK Ch 14 HX, ☎ 01955 602030.
SCRABSTER
HM Ch 12 H24. Call on arr/dep, ☎ 01847 892779.
ORKNEY HARBOURS NAVIGATION SERVICE
Orkney Harbour Radio Ch 09 11 12
Stromness HM Ch 14 M-Fri 0900-1700; Tel code 01856: ☎ 850744. Marina, ☎ 465825.
Kirkwall *Hbr Radio* Ch 14, ☎ 872292. M-Fri, 0800-1700.
Westray Pier, *Pierowall Hbr* Ch 14 when vessel expected. ☎ 01857 677216.
SHETLAND
Lerwick Hbr Radio Ch 12 ☎ 01595 692991.
Scalloway Hbr Radio Ch 09, 12, M-F 0700-1800, Sat 0900-1230. Piermaster ☎ 01595 880574.
Sullom Voe VTS Ch 14 for tfc info, weather & radar assistance on request. ☎ 01806 242551.
Balta Sound Harbour Ch 16, 20 HO
OUTER HEBRIDES
STORNOWAY HM Ch 12 H24, ☎ 01851 702688.
Loch Maddy, N Uist Ch 12, ☎ 01876 500337.
St Kilda, *Kilda Radio* Ch 16, ☎ 01870 604406.
MAINLAND
Kinlochbervie Ch 14 HX, ☎ 01971 521235.
Loch Inver Ch 09 HX, ☎ 01571 844247.

COMMUNICATIONS

ULLAPOOL Ch 14, ☎ 01854 612724.

Loch Gairloch Hbr Ch 16, ☎ 01445 712140.

ISLE OF SKYE
Portree Ch 12 (occas), ☎ 01478 612926.

Kyle Akin Ch 11, ☎ 01599 534167.

KYLE OF LOCH ALSH Ch 11, ☎ 01599 534589.

Mallaig Ch 09 HO, ☎ 01687 462154.

Tiree, Gott Bay Pier, Ch 31, ☎ 01879 230337.

Coll, Arinagour Pier, Ch 31, ☎ 01879 230347.

L Sunart, Salen Bay, Ch 16, ☎ 01967 431333.

ISLAND OF MULL
Tobermory, Ch 12, M HJ, ☎ 01688 302017.

Loch Lathaich; Sound of Iona; Craignure Pier.

Corpach basin & lock/Caledonian Canal Ch 74, ☎ 01397 772249.

DUNSTAFFNAGE Marina, Ch M, ☎ 01631 566555.

Oban North Bay Ch 12. Marina, ☎ 01631 565333.

L Melfort, Kilmelford Haven, Ch M, ☎ 01852 200248.

L Shuna, Craobh Marina, Ch M, ☎ 01852 500222.

L Craignish, Ardfern Ch 80, M, ☎ 01852 500247.

CRINAN CANAL, Ch 74. BWB, ☎ 01546 603210.

Islay, Port Ellen, ☎ 01496 300301; no VHF.

Tarbert, Loch Fyne Ch 14, ☎ 01880 820344.

Portavadie Marina Ch 80, ☎ 01700 811075.

CAMPBELTOWN Ch 12, 13, ☎ 01586 552552.

ROTHESAY, Bute Ch 12, ☎ 01700 500630.

LARGS Yacht Haven Ch 80, M, ☎ 01475 675333.

KIP Marina Ch 80, M, ☎ 01475 521485.

HOLY LOCH Marina Ch 80, M, ☎ 01369 701800.

RHU Marina Ch 80, M, ☎ 01436 820238.

ARDROSSAN Marina Ch 80, M, ☎ 01294 607077.

IRVINE HM/Bridge Ch 12, ☎ 01292 487286.

TROON Ch 14. Marina Ch 80, M, ☎ 01294 315553.

GIRVAN HM Ch 12, ☎ 01465 713648.

KIRKCUDBRIGHT HM Ch 12, ☎ 01557 331135.

ENGLAND W COAST AND WALES

MARYPORT Marina Ch 80, ☎ 01900 814431.

WORKINGTON HM Ch 14, ☎ 01900 602301.

WHITEHAVEN Marina Ch 12, ☎ 01946 692435.

ISLE OF MAN (Tel code 01624) If unable to contact IoM hbrs below, call Douglas.

Douglas Hbr Control Ch 12 H24.

Port St Mary HM Ch 12 HJ, ☎ 833205.

Peel HM Ch 12 HJ, ☎ 842338.

Ramsey HM Ch 12 0800-1600. HO, ☎ 812245.

MAINLAND
GLASSON DOCK Marina Ch 69, ☎ 01524 751491.

FLEETWOOD Fleetwood Dock Radio (HW±2) Ch 12 for Marina, ☎ 01253 879062.

PRESTON Lock Riversway Ch 14. Marina Ch 80, ☎ 01772 733595.

LIVERPOOL Mersey Radio Ch 12. Info Ch 09. Radar Ch 18. Liverpool Marina (Brunswick Dock) Ch M, ☎ 0151 7076777. Albert Dock Ch M, ☎ 0151 7096558; access via Canning Dock lock.

CONWY HM Ch 14. Marinas, both Ch 80: Conwy, ☎ 01492 593000. Deganwy 576888.

MENAI STRAIT and ANGLESEY
Beaumaris/Menai HM Ch 69, ☎ 01248 712312.

Caernarfon, HM & Victoria Dock Ch 80, ☎ 01286 672118. Mon-Fri: 0900-1700 Sat: 0900-1200

HOLYHEAD Port Control Ch 14, ☎ 01407 606700. Marina 764242.

MAINLAND
PWLLHELI, HM Ch 12. Marina Ch 80, M, ☎ 01758 704081.

PORTHMADOG Hbr Ch 12, ☎ 01766 512927.

BARMOUTH HM Barmouth Hbr Ch 12, ☎ 01341 280671.

ABERDOVEY Aberdovey Hbr Ch 12, ☎ 01654 767626.

ABERYSTWYTH HM Ch 14. Marina Ch 80, ☎ 01970 611422.

FISHGUARD HM Ch 14, ☎ 01348 873369.

MILFORD HAVEN Monitor Port Control (and Patrol launch) Ch 12, whilst under way. Milford Docks Pierhead Ch 18. Milford Dock Marina Ch 14, ☎ 01646 696312. Neyland Yacht Haven Ch 80, M, ☎ 01646 601601.

Tenby Ch 80, ☎ 01834 842717.

Saundersfoot Ch 11

SWANSEA
Tawe Lock Ch 18. Marina Ch 80, ☎ 01792 470310.

BARRY Barry Radio Ch 11. HM ☎ 01446 732665.

CARDIFF Cardiff Radio Ch 14. Barrage control Ch 18. Penarth Marina Ch 80, ☎ 02920 705021.

NEWPORT HM Ch 71, ☎ 0870 6096699.

SHARPNESS Sharpness Radio Ch 13 for lock. Marina, ☎ 01453 811476. Canal Ch 74

BRISTOL Bristol VTS Ch 12 with intentions. City Docks Radio Ch 14 (low power) to confirm. Bristol Floating Hbr Ch 73. Bristol Marina Ch 80, ☎ 0117 9213198.

PORTISHEAD Marina Ch 80, ☎ 0198 4631264.

BURNHAM-ON-SEA HM Ch 08, ☎ 01938 822666.

WATCHET Marina Marina Ch 80, ☎ 01984 631264.

ILFRACOMBE HM **Ch 80**, ☎ 01271 862108.

APPLEDORE-BIDEFORD HM *Two Rivers* **Ch 12**, Appledore ☎ 01237 474569.

BUDE HM **Ch 12**, ☎ 01288 353111.

PADSTOW HM **Ch 12**, ☎ 01841 532239.

ST IVES HM **Ch 12**, ☎ 01736 795018.

IRELAND

ROSSAVEEL Ch 12, ☎ 091 572108.

GALWAY, HM **Ch 12**, ☎ 091 561874.

SHANNON ESTUARY *Shannon Ports Radio* **Ch 11** (HO), ☎ 087 2560427.

KILRUSH Marina **Ch 80**, ☎ 06590 52072.

LIMERICK HBR Ch 12 13, ☎ 061 315377.

MFENIT HM **Ch 14, M**, ☎ 066 7136231.

DINGLE HM **Ch 14** (no calls req'd), ☎ 066 9151629.

CAHERSIVEEN (Valentia) Marina **Ch 80**, ☎ 066 9472777.

BANTRY BAY, Lawrence Cove Marina **Ch M**, ☎ 027 75044.

CASTLETOWN BEARHAVEN ⚓, ☎ 027 70220.

CROOKHAVEN ⚓, ☎ 028 35319.

SCHULL ⚓, mobile ☎ 086 1039105.

BALTIMORE Ch 09, mobile 087 2351485.

GLANDORE HM **Ch 06**, ☎ 028 34737.

COURTMACSHERRY HM ☎ 08610 40812.

KINSALE HM **Ch 14** ☎ 021 4772503. Marinas **Ch M:** KYC ☎ 4772196. Castlepark ☎ 4774959.

CORK *Cork Hbr Radio* **Ch 12**, 14 H24. HM ☎ 021 4273125. Marinas **Ch M:** Crosshaven ☎ 4831161. Salve ☎ 4831145. Royal Cork YC ☎ 4831023. East Ferry ☎ 4813390.

YOUGHAL HM/Pilots **Ch 14** Mon-Fri 0900-1700 and when ships expected. ☎ 024 92577.

DUNMORE EAST HM/Pilots **Ch 14** ☎ 051 383166.

WATERFORD & NEW ROSS Ch 12, 14. ☎ 051 873501.

KILMORE QUAY Ch 09. Marina, ☎ 053 29955.

ROSSLARE HM **Ch 12** H24, ☎ 053 33114.

WEXFORD Hbr Boat club. **Ch 16**, ☎ 053 22039.

ARKLOW HM **Ch 12**, ☎ 0402 32466. Marina 39901.

WICKLOW HM **Ch 14** 12, ☎ 0404 67455.

DUN LAOGHAIRE HM **Ch 14**, ☎ 01 2801130. YCs & Marina **Ch M:** Marina 2020040. National 2805725. R. St George 2801811. R. Irish 2809452. DL Motor YC 2801371.

DUBLIN HM and VTS *Dublin VTS* **Ch 12**, 13. Poolbeg Marina **Ch M**, ☎ 01 6689983. Lifting bridge *Eastlink* **Ch 12, 13**. City moorings, ☎ 01 8183300.

HOWTH HM **Ch 11**. Marina **Ch M**, 80, ☎ 01 8392777.

MALAHIDE Marina **Ch 80, M**, ☎ 01 8454129.

CARLINGFORDFORD LOUGH
Carlingford Marina **Ch M**, ☎ 042 93730739.

Warrenpoint Ch 12, ☎ 028 41752878.

Kilkeel Ch 12, ☎ 028 41762287.

ARDGLASS (Phennick Cove) Marina **Ch M, 80**, ☎ 028 44842332.

STRANGFORD LOUGH
HM **Ch 12 14**, ☎ 028 44881637.

Portaferry Marina Ch 80, M, ☎ 07703 209780.

Donaghadee Copelands Marina, ☎ 028 91882184.

BELFAST VTS *Belfast Hbr Radio* **Ch 12**. **Marinas Ch 80, M:** Carrickfergus, ☎ 028 93366666. Bangor, ☎ 028 91453217.

LARNE *Port Control* **Ch 14**, 11.

Glenarm HM/Marina, mobile ☎ 07703 606763.

Ballycastle HM/Marina, mob ☎ 07803 505084.

PORTRUSH HM **Ch 12**, ☎ 028 70822307.

COLERAINE HM **Ch 12**. Marina, ☎ 028 70832086.

LONDONDERRY *Hbr radio* **Ch 14**, ☎ 028 71860555.

L SWILLY Fahan Marina, ☎ 074 9360008.

KILLYBEGS HM **Ch 14**, ☎ 07497 31032.

Burton Port HM **Ch 06, 12, 14**, ☎ 075 42155.

SLIGO HM **Ch 12, 14**, ☎ 071 9153819.

DENMARK

Skagen HM **Ch 12** 13 HX, ☎ 98 941346.

Hirtshals HM **Ch 12** 13 HX, ☎ 98 941422.

Torup Strand HM **Ch 12** 13 HX.

Hanstholm HM **Ch 12** 13 HX, ☎ 97 961833.

THYBORØN HM **Ch 12** 13 H24, ☎ 97 831188.

Thisted (Limfjord) Ch 12 13 HX, ☎ 97 911400.

Torsminde HM **Ch 12** 13, ☎ 24 233345.

Hvide Sande HM **Ch 12** HX, ☎ 97 311633.

ESBJERG *Hbr Control* **Ch 12** 13 14 H24, ☎ 75 124000. **Fanø** HM, ☎ 75 163100.

Rømø HM **Ch 10, 12, 13** HX, ☎ 74 755245.

GERMANY

HELGOLAND HM **Ch 67**, ☎ 04725 81593583.
May-Aug Mon-Thu 0700-1200, 1300-2000. Fri-Sun 0700-1200.
Sep-Apr Mon-Thu 0700-1200, 1300-1600. Fri 0700-1200.

COMMUNICATIONS

List HM **Ch 11,** ☎ 046 51870374.
Hörnum HM **67,** ☎ 046 51881027.
Wyk HM **Ch 11,** ☎ 046 81500430.
Pellworm HM **Ch 11,** ☎ 048 44726.
Husum HM **Ch 11,** ☎ 048 16670.
R. Eider sealock **Ch 14,** ☎ 04833 4535211.
Büsum HM **Ch 11,** ☎ 048 413607.

INNER DEUTSCHE BUCHT (GERMAN BIGHT)
VTS, Eastern part **Ch 80,** ☎ 04421 489282.
VTS, Western part **Ch 79**

BRUNSBÜTTEL WSA (hbr info) ☎ 04852 8850.

NORD-OSTSEE KANAL (KIEL CANAL)
VTS Canal I	**Ch 13,** ☎ 04852 885371.
VTS Canal II	**Ch 02,** ☎ 04852 885369.
VTS Canal III	**Ch 03,** ☎ 0431 3603456.
VTS Canal IV	**Ch 12,** ☎ 0431 3603465.

Brieholz, Ch 73
Ostermoor, Ch 73

RIVER ELBE
CUXHAVEN HM **Ch 69** HX, ☎ 04721 500150.
Cuxhaven Marina, ☎ 37363. YC Marina, ☎ 34111.
R. Stör **Lock Ch 09** Bridge opens on request.
Glückstadt HM **Ch 08,** ☎ 04124 913200.

HAMBURG Port HM **Ch 12,** ☎ 040 7411540.

VTS *Hamburg Port Traffic* **Ch 13, 14, 74.** Wedel
Yacht Hbr, ☎ 040 1034438. City Sporthafen, ☎
040 364297.

BREMERHAVEN *Weser VTS* **Ch 22. Port Ch 12,** ☎
0471 59613401. **Locks Ch 69, 70. Marinas** Weser YC,
☎ 23531. NYC, ☎ 77555. WVW, ☎ 73268.

BREMEN *Port Radio* **Ch 03,** ☎ 0421 3618504.

JADE VTS *Jade Traffic* **Ch 63, 20.**

WILHEMSHAVEN
Port **Ch 11,** ☎ 04421 154580. **Sealock Ch 13.**
Bridges **Ch 11. Marinas** Nassauhafen, ☎ 41439.
Wiking Sportsboothafen, ☎ 41301.

HOOKSIEL Ch 63. Alterhafen Marina.

WANGEROOGE HM **Ch 17,** ☎ 04469 1322. Marina,
☎ 942126.

SPIEKEROOG HM No VHF, ☎ 04976 9193133.

DORNUMER-ACCUMERSIEL HM No VHF, ☎ 04933
2510. YC ☎ 2240.

LANGEOOG HM **Ch 17,** ☎ 04972 301.

NORDERNEY HM **Ch 17,** ☎ 04932 82826.

NORDDEICH HM **Ch 17,** ☎ 04931 81317.

BORKUM HM **Ch 14,** ☎ 04922 81317.

EMS VTS *Ems Traffic* **Ch 15, 18, 20, 21**

EMDEN HM & locks **Ch 13,** ☎ 04921 897260.
YC Marina, ☎ 997147. Mariners' Club, ☎ 953795.
City Marina, ☎ 8907211.

NETHERLANDS

DELFZIJL/EEMSHAVEN VTS is not compulsory
for leisure craft. **Delfzijl Radar** Ch 03 gives radar
assistance when visibility falls below 2000m.
Eemshaven Radar Ch 01. **Port Control** Ch 66
broadcasts info every even H+10.

DELFZIJL HBR. HM Ch 14; ☎ 0596 640400. **Locks**
Ch 26, M-Sat H24, Sun & hols on request; ☎
693293. **Bridges:** Weiwerder Ch 11. Heemskes &
Handelshaven Ch 14. **Farmsumerhaven,** Ch 66,
☎ 640494.

EEMSHAVEN HM Ch 14; ☎ 516142. Radar Ch 19.

LAUWERSOOG. HM, *Havendienst,* Ch 09; ☎ 0519
39023. Mon 0000-1700; Tu-Wed 0800-1700; Th-Sat
0700-1500.

TERSCHELLING VTS Call/monitor *Brandaris* Ch 02;
☎ 0562 443100. **Marina,** Ch 31; ☎ 443337.

VLIELAND. HM Ch 12. **Marina,** Ch 31; ☎ 0562
451729.

HARLINGEN HM Ch 11 (not on Sun); ☎ 0517
413423. **Locks** Ch 22.

OUDESCHILD HM Ch 12; ☎ 0222 312710. **Marina,**
Ch 31; ☎ 0222 321227. See Den Helder VTS.

DEN HELDER VTS. Monitor *Tfc Centre* Ch 62, H24;
broadcasts info and gives radar surveillance. **PORT
CONTROL** Ch 14; ☎ 0223 62770. **Marina** ☎ 652645.
Bridge: Moormanbrug Ch 18. **Lock:** Koopvaarders
Ch 22.

IJSSELMEER Den Oever lock Ch 20, ☎ 0227
511383. **Port** Ch 11, ☎ 511303. Marina ☎ 511789.
Kornwerderzand lock Ch 18, ☎ 0517 57441.

ENKHUIZEN Naviduct (also Krabbersgat) Ch 22.

IJMUIDEN VTS. Traffic Centre Ch 07, Roads (W
of IJmuiden buoy). Thence **Port Control** Ch 61 to
Noordzeesluizen (locks).
Seaport Marina Ch 75, ☎ 0255 560300.

NORDZEEKANAAL VTS
Noordzeesluizen. *Sluis IJmuiden* Ch 22.
Noordzeekanaal. Ch 03, from locks to km 11·2.

AMSTERDAM
Port Control Ch 68 (Km 11·2 to Oranjesluisen).
Port Info Ch 14. Access to Standing Mast route:
Westerkeersluis Ch 22. **Haarlem hbr** Ch 18.
Marinas: Sixhaven, ☎ 020 6329429. **WV Aeolus,**
☎ 6360791. **Aquadam,** ☎ 6320616.
Access to Markermeer: **Oranjesluisen** Ch 18.

SCHEVENINGEN. Traffic Centre & Port Ch 21; ☎
070 3527711. **Marina** Ch 31; ☎ 070 3520017.

HOEK VAN HOLLAND ROADSTEAD
To cross the mouth of the Maas, call *Maas Entrance*
Ch 03, with vessel's name, position and course.
Follow a track close W of a line joining buoys MV,
MVN and Indusbank N. See VTS Chart No 4. Whilst
crossing, maintain continuous listening watch and
keep a very sharp lookout.

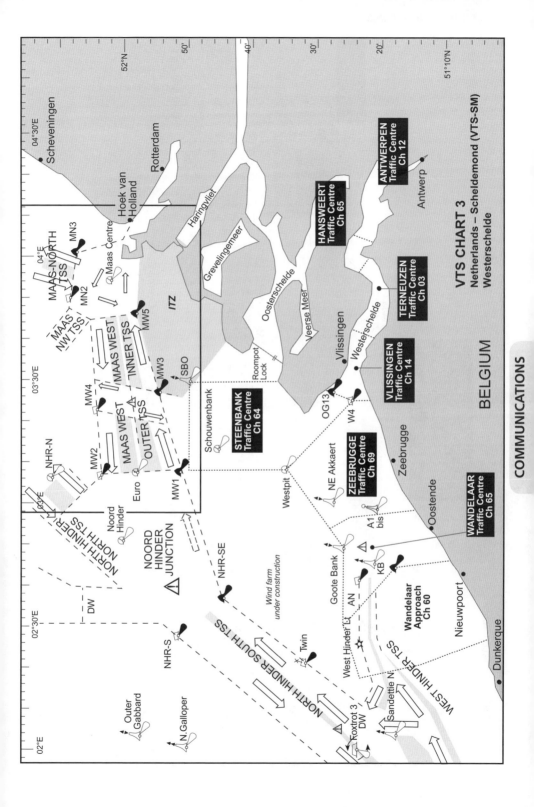

VTS CHART 3

Netherlands – Scheldemond (VTS-SM)
Westerschelde

BELGIUM

ANTWERPEN
Traffic Centre
Ch 12

HANSWEERT
Traffic Centre
Ch 65

TERNEUZEN
Traffic Centre
Ch 03

VLISSINGEN
Traffic Centre
Ch 14

STEENBANK
Traffic Centre
Ch 64

ZEEBRUGGE
Traffic Centre
Ch 69

WANDELAAR
Traffic Centre
Ch 65

Wandelaar
Approach
Ch 60

Scheveningen

Rotterdam

Hoek van
Holland

Maas Centre

MAAS-NORTH
TSS

MAAS
NW TSS

MAAS WEST
INNER TSS

MAAS WEST
OUTER TSS

Schouwenbank

NOORD
HINDER
JUNCTION

NOORD HINDER TSS

NORTH HINDER
NORTH TSS

Noord
Hinder

Outer
Gabbard

N. Galloper

NHR-S

NHR-N

NHR-SE

Euro

Harringvliet

Grevelingemeer

Oosterschelde

Veerse Meer

Roompot
Lock

ITZ

Vlissingen

Westerschelde

Antwerp

OG13

W4

Zeebrugge

Oostende

Nieuwpoort

Dunkerque

NE Akkaert

Westpit

A1
bis

Goote Bank

AN

KB

West Hinder Lt

Twin

Sandettie N

Foxtrot 3
DW

NORTH HINDER SOUTH TSS

WEST HINDER TSS

Wind farm
under construction

SBO

MW5

MW3

MW4

MW2

MW1

MN3

MN2

DW

COMMUNICATIONS

121

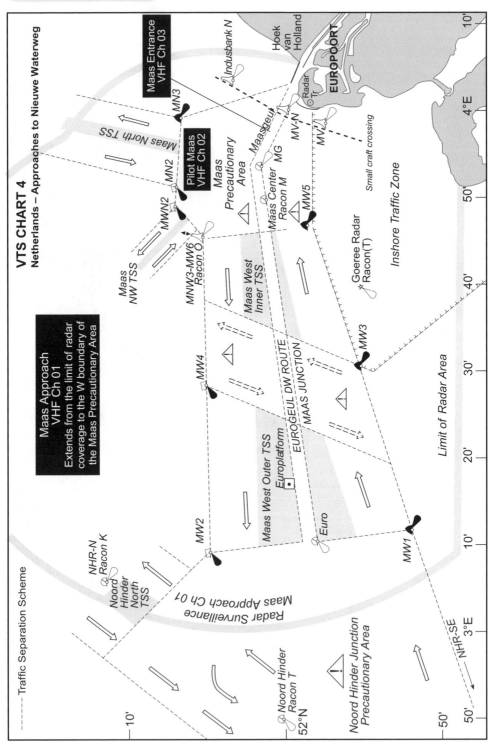

VTS CHART 4
Netherlands – Approaches to Nieuwe Waterweg

Maas Entrance
VHF Ch 03

Pilot Maas
VHF Ch 02

Maas Approach
VHF Ch 01

Extends from the limit of radar
coverage to the W boundary of
the Maas Precautionary Area

Maas North TSS

Maas
Precautionary
Area

Maas
NW TSS

Maas West
Inner TSS

Maas West Outer TSS

EUROGEUL DW ROUTE

MAAS JUNCTION

Europlatform

Euro

Goeree Radar
Racon(T)

Inshore Traffic Zone

Limit of Radar Area

Small craft crossing

Hoek
van
Holland

EUROPOORT

Indusbank N

Radar
Tr

Maasgeul

Maas Center
Racon M   MG

MV-N

MV-S

MW5

MW3

MW4

MW2

MW1

MN3

MN2

MWN2

MNW3-MW6
Racon O

NHR-N
Racon K

Noord
Hinder
North
TSS

Radar Surveillance
Maas Approach Ch 01

Noord Hinder
Racon T

52°N

Noord Hinder Junction
Precautionary Area

NHR-SE

Traffic Separation Scheme

10'

50'

3°E

4°E

10'

50'

40'

30'

20'

10'

NIEUWE WATERWEG VTS.
Outer areas as shown on VTS Charts 3 & 4:
Maas Approach Ch 01. **Pilot Maas** Ch 02. **Maas Entrance** Ch 03.
HCC *Central Traffic Control* Ch 14 19.
Report to/monitor continuously the relevant Tfc Centre, as listed from seaward to City Marina: Rozenburg Ch 65; Maassluis Ch 80; Botlek Ch 61; Eemhaven Ch 63; Waalhaven Ch 60; Maasbruggen Ch 81.

ROTTERDAM Rotterdam Tfc Centre Ch 11. **Hbr Coordination Centre** (HCC) Ch 19.
Marinas/Yacht hbrs: Vlaardingen ☎ 010 4746774; Lock Ch 20. **Spuihaven** ☎ 4667765. Coolhaven ☎ 4738614. **Veerhaven** ☎ 4365460. **City Marina** ☎ 0187 48540986, via Erasmus bridge Ch 18.

STELLENDAM Haringvliet lock & lifting bridge: *Goereese Sluis* Ch 20, ☎ 0187 497350. Opening hrs: M-F 0000-2200. 1 Nov - 1 Apr: Sat 0800-2200; Sun 0800-1000, 1600-1800. 1 Apr - 1 Nov: Sat & Sun 0800-2000. **Marina** Ch 31, ☎ 493769.

OOSTERSCHELDE
Lock *Roompotsluis* Ch 18, ☎ 0111 659265. Opening hours: Mon & Thu, 0000-2200; Tue & Sun, 0600-0000; Wed H24; Fri & Sat: 0600-2200. **Roompot Marina** Ch 31.

WESTERSCHELDE VTS
See VTS Chart No 3. Reporting is not compulsory for leisure craft, but they should monitor the VHF channel for the appropriate Traffic Area. Each Traffic Area is controlled by a Traffic Centre and bounded by buoys. *In emergency call the relevant Traffic Centre: Ch 67.*
Tfc Centre Steenbank & Radar Ch 64.
Tfc Centre Vlissingen Ch 14. **Radar** Ch 21. **Info broadcast** Ch 14 H+55.
Tfc Centre Terneuzen & Radar Ch 03. **Info broadcast** Ch 11 H+00.
Tfc Centre Hansweert Ch 65.
Antwerpen, Zeebrugge and Wandelaar Traffic Areas are listed under Belgium.

VLISSINGEN De Ruyter Marina no VHF, ☎ 0118 414498, mobile 06 5353 7181. *Flushing Port Control* Ch 09. **Sealocks & canal bridge** Ch 22. **VVW Schelde Marina** Ch 14, ☎ 465912.

BRESKENS Marina, Ch 31, ☎ 0117 381902.

TERNEUZEN Port control Ch 11. **Marina,** ☎ 0115 697089. **Oostsluis** (E lock, small craft) Ch 18.

BELGIUM
ANTWERPEN, Tfc Centre Zandvliet Ch 12. **Info broadcast** Ch 12 H+35.

ANTWERPEN PORT Calling and safety Ch 74. **Royerssluis** Ch 22. **Siberia & Londen bridges** Ch 62. **Willemdok Marina** Ch 23, ☎ 03 2315066. **Linkeroever Marina** Ch 09, ☎ 03 2190895.

ZEEBRUGGE Tfc Centre Zeebrugge Ch 69. **Info broadcasts** Ch 69 H+15.

ZEEBRUGGE Port Control Ch 71 H24, ☎ 050 546867/550801. **Marina** ☎ 544903. **E lock** Ch 68.

BLANKENBERGE Marinas: VNZ, ☎ 050 429150, & **SYCB,** ☎ 411420, Ch 31. **VVW** ☎ 417536, Ch 23.

WANDELAAR Tfc Centre Wandelaar Ch 65. **Wandelaar Approach** Ch 60.

OOSTENDE Port Control Ch 09 H24, ☎ 059 566313. **Mercator lock,** ☎ 321669, & **marina,** ☎ 705762: Ch 14 H24. **Marinas: RNSYC,** ☎ 505912. **RYCO,** ☎ 321452.

NIEUWPOORT Port HM Ch 60 H24, ☎ 058 233000. **Marinas: KYCN,** Ch 23, ☎ 234413. **WSKLM,** Ch 23, ☎ 5233641. **VVW-N,** Ch 08, ☎ 235232.

NORTH FRANCE
DUNKERQUE Port & VTS Ch 73, H24. The VTS does not affect leisure craft, but monitor Ch 73. **Marinas** Ch 09: Grande Large ☎ 03.28.63.23.00. YCMN ☎ 03.28.66.79.90. **Trystram lock** Ch 73.

GRAVELINES HM/Marina, Ch 09, ☎ 03.28.23.19.45.

CALAIS VTS, Port Control & Marina Ch 17 H24, ☎ 03.21.34.55.23.

BOULOGNE Boulogne Port, ☎ 03.21.31.52.43, Ch 12, H24. **Marina** Ch 09, ☎ 06.76.98.74.98.

LE TOUQUET/ÉTAPLES-SUR-MER Ch 09, 77. **Étaples Marina,** ☎ 03.21.84.54.03.

LE TRÉPORT Marina/lock Ch 12, 72, ☎ 02.35.50.63.06

DIEPPE Port HM Ch 12, HO. **Marina** Ch 09, ☎ 02.35.40.19.79.

ST VALÉRY-EN-CAUX Entry gate & marina Ch 09, ☎ 02.35.97.01.30.

FÉCAMP Port HM, Ch 10, **12,** ☎ 02.35.28.25.53. **Marina & Bérigny lock,** Ch 09, ☎ 02.35.28.13.58.

LE HAVRE Control Tower Ch **12,** 20. **Port Ops** Ch 67, 69. **Marina,** Ch 09, ☎ 02.35.21.23.95.

LA SEINE VTS Rouen Port Control Ch 73 (Estuary), 68 (River). **Honfleur radar** Ch 15, 19, **73.**

HONFLEUR HM Ch **17,** 73 HX, ☎ 02.31.14.61.09. **Lock,** ☎ 02.31.98.72.82, & **Bridge** Ch 17 H24.

ROUEN Port HM Ch **73,** 68 H24. **Halte Nautique,** ☎ 02.32.08.31.40.

ROUEN – PARIS, LOCKS Amfreville Ch 18. **Notre-Dame-de-la-Garenne** Ch 22. **Mericourt** Ch 18. **Andrésy** Ch 22. **Bougival** Ch 22. **Chatou** Ch 18. **Suresnes** Ch 22.

PARIS-ARSENAL Marina Ch 09, ☎ 01.43.41.39.32.

DEAUVILLE Port Deauville lock, ☎ 02.31.88.95.66; Marina ☎ 02.31.98.30.01, Ch 09 0800-1730. **Port Morny** gate ☎ 02.31.88.57.89; Marina, Ch 09, ☎ 02.31.98.50.40.

DIVES-SUR-MER. Marina Ch 09, ☎ 02.31.24.48.00.

COMMUNICATIONS

123

COMMUNICATIONS

OUISTREHAM Port 74; lock Ch 12, ☎ 02.31.36.22.00. Marina Ch 09, ☎ 02.31.96.91.37. Canal Ch 68. CAEN HM/Marina Ch 74, ☎ 02.31.95.24.47.

COURSEULLES-SUR-MER Marina Ch 09, ☎ 02.31.37.51.69.

PORT-EN-BESSIN HM, ☎ 02.31.21.70.49. Gate/bridge Ch 18, ☎ 02.31.21.71.77.

GRANDCAMP Marina Ch 09, ☎ 02.31.22.63.16.

CARENTAN Lock Ch 09, ☎ 02.33.71.10.85. Marina Ch 09, ☎ 02.33.42.24.44.

ST VAAST-LA-HOUGUE Marina Ch 09, ☎ 02.33.21.61.00.

BARFLEUR HM, ☎ 02.33.54.08.29. No VHF.

CHERBOURG VTS (yachts to monitor) Vigie du Homet Ch 12 H24. Marina Chantereyne Ch 09, ☎ 02.33.87.65.70. Gate (B du Commerce) Ch 06.

OMONVILLE-LA-ROGUE No VHF/Tel. 6 W ⚓s.

DIÉLETTE Marina Ch 09, ☎ 02.33.53.68.78.

CARTERET Marina Ch 09, ☎ 02.33.04.70.84.

PORTBAIL Yacht hbr Ch 09, ☎ 02.33.04.83.48.

GRANVILLE Port HM Ch 12. Marina Ch 09, ☎ 02.33.50.20.06.

ST MALO Port HM Ch 12 H24. Marinas Ch 09: Bas Sablons, ☎ 02.99.81.71.34. Bassin Vauban, ☎ 02.99.56.51.91. DINARD, ☎ 02.99.46.65.55.

R RANCE barrage lock Ch 13, ☎ 02.99.46.21.87. Chatelier lock Ch 14, ☎ 02.99.39.55.66.

ST CAST-LE-GUILDO Marina ☎ 02 96 81 04 43

DAHOUËT Marina Ch 09, ☎ 02.96.72.82.85.

LE LÉGUÉ HM/Marina Ch 12, ☎ 02.96.77.49.85.

BINIC Marina Ch 09, ☎ 02.96.73.61.86.

ST QUAY-PORTRIEUX Marina ☎ 02.96.70.81.30. Ch 09.

PAIMPOL Lock/Marina Ch 09, ☎ 02.96.20.47.65.

LÉZARDRIEUX Marina Ch 09, ☎ 02.96.20.14.22.

PONTRIEUX Lock/Marina Ch 12, ☎ 02.96.95.34.87.

TRÉGUIER Marina Ch 09, ☎ 02.96.92.42.37.

PERROS-GUIREC Marina Ch 09, ☎ 02.96.49.80.50.

PLOUMANAC'H Marina Ch 09, ☎ 02.96.91.44.31.

TRÉBEURDEN Marina Ch 09, ☎ 02.96.23.64.00.

MORLAIX Marina Ch 09, ☎ 02.98.62.13.14.

ROSCOFF HM/S Basin Ch 09, ☎ 02.98.69.76.37.

BLOSCON Ferry Port Ch 12, ☎ 02.98.61.27.84.

L'ABERWRACH Marina Ch 09, ☎ 02.98.04.91.62.

CHANNEL ISLANDS

ALDERNEY, Braye Hbr, Alderney Coastguard Ch 67, ☎ 01481 822620. Otherwise, try Guernsey Coastguard. Alderney Port Control Ch 74.

GUERNSEY Beaucette Marina, Ch 80, ☎ 01481 245000. St Sampson Ch 12 H24 via St Peter Port Control Ch 12 H24, ☎ 720229.

Victoria Marina Ch 80 HO, ☎ 720220. Guernsey Coastguard Ch 20 H24 (Ch 62 for emergecy link calls).

JERSEY St Helier Port Control Ch 14 H24; 8M max range. St Helier Marina, ☎ 01534 885508, has no VHF; call Ch 14 only if essential.

Gorey Ch 74, ☎ 853616.

WEST FRANCE

BREST VTS Brest Port Ch 08 H24. Marina Ch 09, ☎ 02.98.02.20.02.

CAMARET Marina Ch 09, ☎ 02.98.27.95.99.

MORGAT Marina Ch 09, ☎ 02.98.27.01.97.

DOUARNENEZ HM Ch 12. Marinas Ch 09: Tréboul ☎ 02.98.74.02.56; Port Rhu ☎ 02.98.92.00.67.

AUDIERNE No VHF. Marina ☎ 02.98.74.04.93. Ste Evette ☎ 02.98.70.00.28.

LOCTUDY Marina Ch 09, ☎ 02.98.87.51.36.

BENODÉT Marinas Ch 09: Penfoul ☎ 02.98.57.05.78. Ste Marine ☎ 02.98.56.38.72.

PORT-LA-FORÊT Marina Ch 09, ☎ 02.98.56.98.45.

CONCARNEAU Marina Ch 09, ☎ 02.98.97.57.96.

LORIENT Port Ch 12. Marinas Ch 09: Ban-Gâvres ☎ 02.97.65.48.25. Kernével ☎ 02.97.65.48.25. Port Louis ☎ 02.97.83.59.55. Locmiquélic ☎ 02.97.33.59.51. Lorient ☎ 02.97.21.10.14.

PORT TUDY Marina Ch 09, ☎ 02.97.86.54.62.

RIVER ÉTEL Marina Ch 13, ☎ 02.97.55.46.62.

BELLE ILE Sauzon HM Ch 09, ☎ 02.97.31.63.40. Le Palais HM Ch 09, ☎ 02.97.31.42.90.

PORT HALIGUEN Marina Ch 09, ☎ 02.97.50.20.56.

LA TRINITÉ Marina Ch 09, ☎ 02.97.55.71.49.

VANNES Marina Ch 09, ☎ 02.97.54.16.08.

CROUESTY Marina Ch 09, ☎ 02.97.53.73.33.

LA VILAINE Arzal Marina Ch 09, ☎ 02.97.45.02.97.

PIRIAC Marina Ch 09, ☎ 02.40.23.52.32.

LA TURBALLE Marina Ch 09, ☎ 02.40.23.41.65.

LE CROISIC Marina Ch 09, ☎ 09.81.12.75.92.

LE POULIGUEN Marina Ch 09, ☎ 02.40.11.97.97.

PORNICHET Marina Ch 09, ☎ 02.40.61.03.20.

ST-NAZAIRE VTS Loire Ports Control Ch 14. Port HM Ch 14, ☎ 02.40.91.03.17.

PORNIC Marina Ch 09, ☎ 02.40.82.05.40.

L'HERBAUDIÈRE Marina Ch 09, ☎ 02.51.39.05.05.

PORT JOINVILLE Marina Ch 09, ☎ 02.51.58.38.11.

ST GILLES-CROIX-DE-VIE Marina Ch 09, ☎ 02.51.55.30.83.

LES SABLES D'OLONNE Port HM Ch 12, ☎ 02.51.95.11.79. Marina Ch 09, ☎ 02.51.32.51.16.

BOURGENAY Marina Ch 09, ☎ 02.51.22.20.36.

ILE DE RÉ Ars-en-Ré Ch 09, ☎ 05.46.29.08.52.
St Martin Ch 09, ☎ 05.46.09.26.69.

LA ROCHELLE Marinas Ch 09: **Port des Minimes** ☎ 05.46.44.41.20. **Vieux Port** ☎ 05.46.41.32.05.

ROCHEFORT Marina Ch 09, ☎ 05.46.83.99.06.

ILE D'OLÉRON St Denis Ch 09, ☎ 05.46.47.97.97.
Boyardville Ch 09, ☎ 05.46.76.48.56.

LA GIRONDE VTS Ch 12 (yachts to monitor).
Radar *Bordeaux Port Control* Ch 12 on request.
Depths in Gironde broadcast Ch 17 every 5 mins.

ROYAN Marina Ch 09, ☎ 05.46.38.72.22.

COAST RADIO STATIONS

Coast Radio Stations (CRS) deal with public correspondence (and a few other things). They enable a yachtsman to be linked by radio into the public telephone system in order to converse with a subscriber ashore, ie he can make or receive a Link call.

However the mobile 'phone has to a great extent rendered Link calls obsolescent. Thus there are no longer any CRS in the UK, France and Netherlands. In Germany a limited service is provided by a commercial company (see below).

CRS still operate in the Channel Islands, Ireland*, Denmark, Belgium, Spain and Portugal; see below. But they too may gradually be withdrawn. *In Ireland CRS no longer handle commercial link calls, but Medico link calls are still available on both VHF and MF.

The CG does **not** handle Link calls, except in Denmark and Belgium where the functions of CG and CRS have always been co-located.

CHANNEL ISLANDS

GUERNSEY COASTGUARD 49°27'·00N 02°32'00W ☎ 01481 720672 📠 01534 714177 Emergency link calls on **Ch 62** only. Ch 20 is used for navigation, pilotage and ships' business

JERSEY COAST GUARD 49°10'·85N 02°14'30W ☎ 01534 447705 📠 01534 499089
Link calls on **Ch 25** only

REPUBLIC OF IRELAND

A Coast Radio service is provided by the Dept of the Marine, Leeson Lane, Dublin 2, Eire. ☎ +353 (0)1 662 0922; ext 670 for enquiries. Broadcasts are made on a working channel/frequency following a prior announcement on Ch 16 and 2182 kHz. Ch 67 is used for Safety messages only.
VHF calls to an Irish Coast Radio Station should be made on a working channel. Only use Ch 16 in case of difficulty or in emergency.

NW and SE Ireland

Weather broadcasts at 0103, 0403, 0703, 1003, 1303, 1603, 1903, 2203 UT and at 0033, 0633, 1233, 1833 UT on the VHF Channels below. Nav warnings are broadcast at 0033, 0433, 0833, 1233, 1633 and 2033 UT.

Clifden Radio	53°30'N 09°56'W	Ch 26
Belmullet Radio	54°16'N 10°03'W	Ch 83
Donegal Bay	54°22'N 08°31'W	Ch 02
Glen Head Radio	54°44'N 08°43'W	Ch 24
MALIN HD RADIO	55°22'N 07°21'W	Ch 23
MF 1677 kHz, ☎ +353 (0) 77 70103		
MMSI 002500100 DSC: 2187·5 kHz		
Carlingford Radio	54°05'N 06°19'W	Ch 04
DUBLIN RADIO	53°23'N 06°04'W	Ch 83
Wicklow Hd Radio	52°58'N 06°00'W	Ch 02
Rosslare Radio	52°15'N 06°20'W	Ch 23
Mine Hd Radio	52°00'N 07°35'W	Ch 83

SW Ireland

Weather is broadcast at 0103, 0403, 0703, 1003, 1303, 1603, 1903, 2203 and at 0033, 0633, 1233, 1833 UT on the VHF Channels listed.
Navwarnings are broadcast every 4 hrs from 0233.

Cork Radio	51°51'N 08°29'W	Ch 26
Mizen Radio	51°34'N 09°33'W	Ch 04
Bantry Radio	51°38'N 10°00'W	Ch 23
VALENTIA RADIO	51°56'N 10°21'W	Ch 24
MF 1752 kHz, ☎ + 353 (0) 66947 6109		
MMSI 002500200, DSC: 2187·5 kHz		
Shannon Radio	52°31'N 09°36'W	Ch 28
Galway Bay Radio	53°18'N 09°07'W	Ch 04

DENMARK

All VHF/MF CRS are remotely controlled from Lyngby Radio (55°50N 11°25'E) (MMSI 002191000). The callsign for all stations is Lyngby Radio. Call on working frequencies to help keep Ch 16 clear. The stations listed below monitor Ch 16 H24 and Ch 70 DSC. Traffic lists are broadcast on all VHF channels every odd H+05. All MF stations, except Skagen, keep watch H24 on 2182 kHz. Blåvand, Skagen and Lyngby also monitor MF 2187·5 kHz DSC. MF DSC Public correspondence facilities are available from Blåvand and Skagen on 1624·5 and 2177 kHz.

VHF & MF CRS		
Skagen	57°44'N 10°35'E	Ch 04
MF: Tx 1758, Rx 2045, 2102		
Hirtshals	57°31'N 09°57'E	Ch 66
Hanstholm	57°07'N 08°39'E	Ch 01
Bovbjerg	56°32'N 08°10'E	Ch 02
MF: Tx 1767, Rx 2045, 2111		
Blåvand	55°33'N 08°07'E	Ch 23
MF: Tx 1734, Rx 2045, 2078		

COMMUNICATIONS

GERMANY

CRS: DPO7 – Seefunk (Hamburg) *(MMSI 002113100)*. All stns monitor DSC Ch 70 and 16. Traffic lists are broadcast: 0745, 0945, 1245, 1645, 1945 and H & H+30 on request Ch 16.

Nordfriesland	54°31'N 08°41'E	Ch 26
Elbe-Weser	53°50'N 08°39'E	Ch 24
Hamburg	53°33'N 09°58'E	Ch 83
Bremen	53°05'N 08°48'E	Ch 25
Accumersiel	53°40'N 07°29'E	Ch 28
Borkum	53°35'N 06°40'E	Ch 61

SHAPES

◆	Towing vessel - length of tow > 200m	**Rule 24**
▼	Yacht under sail *and* power	**Rule 25**
✕	Vessel fishing or trawling	**Rule 26**
✕+▲	Vessel fishing with outlying gear >150m long	**Rule 26**
●◆●	Vessel restricted in her ability to manoeuvre	**Rule 27**
●●	Vessel not under command	**Rule 27**
▮	Vessel constrained by her draught	**Rule 28**
●	Vessel at anchor	**Rule 30**

SOUND SIGNALS
MANOEUVRING AND WARNING Rule 34

•	A short blast = about 1 second.
–	A prolonged blast = 4 – 6 seconds.
•	I am altering course to **Starboard**
••	I am altering course to **Port**
•••	My engines are going **Astern**
•••••	I do not understand your intentions/ actions

Note: The above sound signals may be supplemented by light signals flashed on an all-round white light with least range of 5 miles.

In a narrow channel

– –•	I intend to overtake on your starboard side.
– –••	I intend to overtake on your port side.
–•–•	I agree with your overtaking signal
–	Warning by vessel nearing a bend where other vessels may not be seen
–	Approaching vessel acknowledges.

VESSELS IN RESTRICTED VISIBILITY Rule 35

–	Power-driven vessel making way.
– –	Power-driven vessel underway, but stopped and not making way.
–••	**A sailing vessel**; vessels not under command; restricted in ability to manoeuvre; constrained by draught; engaged in fishing, towing or pushing.
–•••	Vessel being towed or, if more than one vessel is towed, the last vessel in the tow.

VESSELS AT ANCHOR

🔔	Bell, ring for 5 seconds every minute
🔔	Vessel >100m: Bell forward, ring for 5 seconds every minute; plus
⊙	Gong aft, for 5 seconds every minute.
• –•	Optional extra to warn any approaching vessel

Sailing vessels < 12m at ⚓ do not have to sound the above fog signals. But if they do not, they *must* make an efficient noise every 2 minutes.

INTERNATIONAL PORT TRAFFIC SIGNALS (IPTS)

IPTS are widely used on the Continent, but less so around the UK. They may also be used to control traffic at locks and bridges.

- The main movement signal is always 3 lights in a vertical column, to which no extra light shall be added. Thus it is always recognisable as IPTS, as distinct from some kind of navigational lights.

- Red lights ℝ indicate *Do not proceed.*

- Green lights Ⓖ indicate *Proceed, subject to the conditions stipulated*. To avoid confusion ℝ and Ⓖ lights are never displayed together.

- Signals may be omni-directional ie seen by all vessels simultaneously; or directional, ie seen only from outside or from inside the harbour.

- Some ports may only use signals 2 and 4, or only Signal 1 when necessary

- Signal 1 *Serious Emergency* must show at least 60 flashes/minute.

- All other signals may be fixed or slow occulting, eg every 10s (helpful when background glare poses a problem), but never a mixture of both.

- Signal 5 assumes that VHF, signal lamp, loud-hailer, auxiliary signal or other means of communication will specifically inform a vessel that she may proceed.

- Exemption signals. A single Ⓨ light, shown to the left of signals 2 or 5 and level with the upper light, means *Vessels which can safely navigate outside the main channel need not comply with the main message.* This signal is obviously important to small craft, which nevertheless have a clear duty to keep clear of manoeuvring vessels.

- Auxiliary signals (only Ⓦ and/or Ⓨ lights) may be locally authorised and displayed to the right of the main signal. Their meanings must be promulgated.

No	Lights		Main message
1	ℝ ℝ ℝ	Flashing	Serious emergency – all vessels to stop or divert according to instructions
2	ℝ ℝ ℝ		Vessels shall not proceed (*Note:* Some ports may use an exemption signal, as in 2a below)
3	Ⓖ Ⓖ Ⓖ	Fixed or Slow Occulting	Vessels may proceed. One-way traffic
4	Ⓖ Ⓖ Ⓦ		Vessels may proceed. Two-way traffic
5	Ⓖ Ⓦ Ⓖ		A vessel may proceed only when she has received specific orders to do so. (*Note:* Some ports may use an exemption signal, as in 5a below)
Exemption signals and messages			
2a	Ⓨ ℝ ℝ ℝ	Fixed or Slow Occulting	Vessels shall not proceed, except that vessels which navigate outside the main channel need not comply with the main message
5a	Ⓨ Ⓖ Ⓦ Ⓖ		A vessel may proceed when she has received specific orders to do so, except that vessels which navigate outside the main channel need not comply with the main message
Auxiliary signals and messages			
White and/or yellow lights, displayed with the main lights			

COMMUNICATIONS

127

Chapter 4 – Safety

CHOOSING SAFE WEATHER

On an offshore passage you and your boat must be prepared for anything the weather might throw at you. With a reliable long-term forecast it may be possible to take some sort of avoiding action, but it may not be easy.

Most of us, however, are more concerned about the weather during the next few hours, perhaps the next couple of days if contemplating a short passage. Weather forecasts are widely available from Navtex and VHF MSI broadcasts, radio and TV, the Internet, SMS, etc. The trick is to gather as much information as possible and then use your knowledge and experience to distil the data and make your own decisions.

Weather forecasting, which uses increasingly sophisticated techniques, is not an exact science, nor will it ever be. The area covered by a forecast is a significant factor in its usefulness for your purposes. The Shipping Forecast issued by the Met Office is often seen as the benchmark for all others, but any one forecast area covers a lot of sea and is inevitably short on detail. This may be fine for getting the general weather pattern in the southern North Sea, for example, but it is probably a bit too imprecise for a day sail in local waters. The Inshore Forecast is rather more detailed – up to 12 miles offshore – but even that may not give a good indication of conditions in, say, the Solent or other areas where the weather is greatly affected by local topography and tidal streams. For this, a local radio station may prove more useful.

Whatever your sources, there is absolutely no substitute for a 'look out of the window' and intelligent interpretation of what you see. Without any special training, most of us who go to sea can form an instinctive view on what the weather is going to be like in the immediate future. This 'gut feeling', backed up by a local forecast and some solid facts - actual wind speed and direction, barometric trends and cloud type/cover - will serve for most short inshore or coastal passages. Trends are important, so the more observations you make, the better your forecast.

Next we need to ask ourselves if the predicted conditions are suitable and safe for our planned trip. Two main factors are relevant: wind and sea state. It is the latter which causes more problems than the former. A well-found cruising yacht, properly handled, should be able to cope easily with a gale in sheltered waters, but even a Force 5 against a spring ebb tide over a shallow bank can raise distinctly dangerous seas which must be avoided at all costs. In some places the tidal stream alone can kick up a heavy and confused sea even in the most benign weather conditions.

Timing is also an important consideration. A beat into a Force 4 against the tidal stream may be hard work, uncomfortable and potentially hazardous. The same passage with the same wind could be a pleasant and fast sail once the tidal stream has turned in your favour. However, wind against tide can, in some areas, make a broad reach a nail-biting trial of strength, whereas a wait of a couple of hours to allow the tide to turn may make all the difference.

A change of wind with a change of tide is not just an old fishermen's tale, it really does happen – perhaps over an hour or so as the wind adjusts to a new water temperature and direction of flow.

In summary, a 'bad' weather forecast does not necessarily mean a cancelled trip, just as a 'good' forecast is no guarantee that conditions will be suitable in your specific area. There is no substitute for data, observation, knowledge, interpretation and a healthy dose of commonsense.

When the wind backs and the weather glass falls, then be on your guard against gales and squalls.

If clouds look as if scratched by a hen, get ready to reef your topsails then.

Good advice.

DISTRESS, URGENCY, SAFETY

MAYDAY (Distress) must only be used if a ship or person is in *grave and imminent danger and requires immediate assistance*. It may be appropriate for a man overboard if not quickly recovered.

PAN-PAN (Urgency) is appropriate for *a very urgent message concerning the safety of a vessel or person*.

SÉCURITÉ (Safety) is used typically by coast stations to announce navigational or weather warnings. May also be used by vessels to report a hazard.

DISTRESS CALL BY RADIO

A distress call may only be made with the skipper's authority, and only if the *boat or a person* is in *grave and imminent danger*. The initial call may be made by DSC or voice.

Distress alert by DSC
Depending on the particular layout of your radio, a distress alert is typically sent as follows:

> Briefly press the red, guarded Distress button. The set will automatically switch to Ch 70. Press *again* for 5 seconds to transmit a basic distress alert* with position and time. The set then reverts to Ch 16.
>
> *If time permits, select the nature of the distress from the menu (eg Collision, Fire, Flooding) then press the Distress button for 5 seconds to send a full distress alert.

A CG/CRS should automatically send a distress acknowledgement on Ch 70 before replying on Ch 16. Ships in range should reply directly on Ch 16. If a distress acknowledgement is not received from a CG/CRS, the distress alert will automatically be repeated by the radio every four minutes.

> When a DSC distress acknowledgement has been received, or after about 15 seconds, the vessel in distress should transmit a MAYDAY message by voice on Ch 16 (see below), including its MMSI.

False alerts
If a distress alert is inadvertently transmitted, an All Stations voice message on VHF Ch 16 cancelling the false alert must be sent at once: 'Cancel my Distress Alert of (date/time (GMT/UT)'.

MAYDAY call by voice
The MAYDAY message format below should be displayed near the radio. A MAYDAY call by voice should usually be sent on VHF Ch 16. A distress call has priority over all other transmissions. If you hear a MAYDAY call, immediately cease all transmissions that may interfere with the call, listen on the frequency concerned and note down the details.

Before making the call check that the radio is ON, and that HIGH POWER (25 watts) and Ch 16 are selected.

Press and hold down the transmit button, and say slowly and distinctly:

MAYDAY MAYDAY MAYDAY

THIS IS ....
(name of boat, spoken three times)

MAYDAY ....
(name of boat spoken once)

MY POSITION IS ....
(latitude and longitude or true bearing and distance *from* a known point)

Nature of distress ....
(sinking, on fire etc)

Help required ....
(immediate assistance)

Number of persons on board ....
Any other important, helpful information ..
(you are taking to the liferaft; distress rockets are being fired etc)

OVER

Release the transmit button and listen.

MAYDAY acknowledgement
An acknowledgement should be expected:

MAYDAY ....
(name of vessel sending the distress message, spoken three times)

THIS IS ....
(name of station acknowledging, spoken three times)

RECEIVED MAYDAY

If an acknowledgement is not received, check the set and repeat the distress call.

If you hear a distress message, write down the details and, if you can help, acknowledge accordingly but only after giving an opportunity for the nearest Coastguard station or more suitable vessel to do so.

MAYDAY relay
If you hear a distress message from a vessel which is not acknowledged, you should pass on the message as follows:

MAYDAY RELAY ....
(spoken three times)

THIS IS ....
(name of vessel re-transmitting the distress message, spoken three times), followed by the intercepted message.

HELICOPTER RESCUE

- **COMMUNICATE ON CHANNEL 16**
- Use flares or smoke when helicopter is seen or heard
- Helicopter may ask you to drop sails and motor on a specific course
- You may be asked to stream the casualty astern in the dinghy
- Brief your crew early (too noisy when helicopter is close)
- **MAINTAIN YOUR COURSE** and do not get distracted
- Weighted line lowered
- Let it touch boat or water first (to earth any static charge)
- Take in slack line only
- **PULL LINE IN AS DIRECTED**
- **DO NOT SECURE IT TO THE BOAT**
- **DO EXACTLY AS YOU ARE TOLD**

  Note: The text and sketch relate to a Hi-line transfer, one of several techniques which may be used

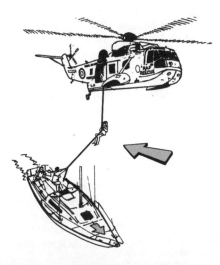

SAFETY

URGENT MEDICAL HELP - PAN PAN

- Send an **URGENCY call by DSC**, if possible, and/or...
- **Make a PAN PAN voice call:**
- **CHANNEL 16, HIGH POWER (25W)** (if necessary, turn off dual watch)
- **PAN PAN** .... (repeat 3 times)
- **ALL STATIONS** .... (repeat 3 times)
- **THIS IS** .... (vessel's name; repeat 3 times)
- **OVER**

  Next message should include:
  Yacht's name, callsign, nationality
  Yacht's position and nearest harbour
  Patient's details, symptoms and advice wanted
  The medication you have on board

FIRST AID

The objectives of First Aid at sea are to:

- **Preserve life** • **Prevent further damage**
- **Relieve pain and distress** • **Deliver a live casualty ashore**

With any casualty be calm, reassuring and methodical. But first ensure your own safety and that of the vessel. If in doubt call for advice and assistance.

MEDICAL ADVICE can be obtained almost anywhere in European waters by making an All Stations 'PAN PAN' call or a DSC Urgency Alert to the Coastguard or to a Coast Radio Station. You will then be connected to a doctor or to the nearest hospital.

The Urgency signal 'PAN PAN' is always advised, especially abroad, because it is internationally understood and eliminates most language problems; it is also free.

If you are not qualified to judge how serious the casualty's condition is, get the best possible advice and/or help as quickly as possible. **Urgent help needed** is shown against the more serious medical problems.

Be ready to describe the patient's symptoms, eg consciousness, pulse rate, breathing rate, temperature, skin colour, site and type of injury, any pain, amount of blood lost etc. If a doctor needs to come aboard, or a casualty has to be landed, the Coastguard will arrange.

If non-urgent, wait until in harbour. Consider calling the port authority before arrival so that a doctor or paramedic can meet you on arrival.

MEDICAL CARE ABROAD It is advisable for each person on board to carry the European Health Insurance Card (EHIC) which entitles you to medical treatment on a reciprocal basis, although it may not cover the full charge. See *www.dh.gov.uk* for full details.

EMERGENCY RESUSCITATION (ABC)

The immediate procedure for any collapsed or apparently unconscious person is: Assess whether or not the casualty is conscious. Carefully shake his/her shoulders and ask loudly 'What's happened?' or 'Are you all right?' or give a command such as 'Open your eyes'. An unconscious casualty will not respond.

A = Airway

Remove any visible obstruction from the casualty's mouth (leave well-fitting dentures in place). Listen at the mouth for breathing. Tilt the head backwards, using head tilt and chin lift to maintain a clear airway.

Look, listen and feel for *no more than 10 seconds* to determine if the casualty is breathing normally. If in any doubt, act as if it is *not* normal.

If breathing, place casualty in recovery position. Check the area is clear of danger.

B = Breathing and C = Circulation

If not breathing and the airway is clear, start chest compressions. This situation is called **cardiac arrest**. The casualty will be unconscious and may appear very pale, grey or bluish in colour. An artificial circulation will have to be provided by chest compression. If the circulation stops, the breathing will also stop. Casualties with cardiac arrest will need both rescue breathing and chest compression, a combination known as Cardio Pulmonary Resuscitation (**CPR**).

External chest compression

To start external chest compression, lay the casualty face up on a hard, flat surface. Kneel beside casualty. The point at which pressure will be applied is the centre of the chest.

Place the heel of your hand on top of the other hand and interlock your fingers.

Depress breastbone 5–6cm (2-2½in) then release.

With either one or two operators give 30 chest compressions and continue cycles of 2 breaths to 30 compressions. Use a compression rate of 100 per minute. Chest compression must always be combined with rescue breathing so after every 30 compressions, give 2 effective rescue breaths (the 2 breaths should not take more than 5 seconds). *Do not stop.*

Action plan for the resuscitation of adults

Casualty unconscious but is breathing normally:

- **Urgent help needed**
- Turn casualty into the recovery position
- Check for continued breathing

Casualty is unconscious and not breathing:

- **Urgent help needed**
- Start chest compressions
- After 30 chest compressions, give 2 rescue breaths

Continue with chest compressions and rescue breaths in a ratio of 30:2. Stop to re-check casualty only if he/she starts to show signs of regaining consciousness, such as coughing, opening eyes, speaking or moving purposefully *and* starts to breath normally. Otherwise, *do not interrupt resuscitation*.

If you are not trained to, or are unwilling to give rescue breaths, give chest compressions only.

If breathing restarts, place casualty in the recovery position.

BITES AND STINGS Injected poison from bites and stings usually only causes local swelling and discomfort, but some people may react severely. For insect stings, resuscitate if collapse occurs; otherwise give rest, painkillers, antihistamines (eg chlorpheniramine).

BLEEDING – OPEN WOUND Bleeding is often very dramatic, but is virtually always controllable.

• Apply firm continuous direct pressure; bandage on a large pad. If bleeding continues, bandage more pads on top of initial pads; then press directly over wound for at least 10 minutes (blood takes this long to clot).

• Elevate if wound is on a limb.

• Do *not* apply a tourniquet. This practice is out of date due to the danger of losing a limb.

BLEEDING – INTERNAL (CLOSED INJURY)
Follows fractured bones, crush injuries, or rupture of organs such as the liver or spleen. Treat for shock which may appear rapidly. ***Urgent help needed***.

BURNS AND SCALDS Move the victim into fresh air to avoid inhaling smoke.
ABC – Airway, Breathing, Circulation

• Stop further injury: dip the whole of the burnt part into cold water for 10–15 minutes. Seawater is excellent but may be very painful.

• Remove only loose clothing. Do not pull off clothing stuck to the skin.

• Cover with sterile dressing. If skin is broken or blistered, use sterile paraffin gauze beneath the dressing. Separate burnt fingers with paraffin gauze. Never use adhesive dressings.

• Do not prick blisters or apply ointments.

• Elevate burnt limb and immobilise.

• Give strong painkillers.

• Treat for shock: give frequent and copious drinks of water.

• Start giving antibiotics for major burns. If burns extensive or deep, ***urgent help needed***.

CHOKING If blockage by some object (eg a peanut) is suspected, turn the casualty on his side and give up to 5 sharp back slaps with the flat of the hand between the shoulder blades. Check mouth and remove any obstruction.

If unsuccessful, wrap both arms around the victim's waist from behind, and give 5 sharp upward thrusts with both fists into the abdomen above the navel but below the ribs so as to cause coughing. Clear object from mouth.

CUTS AND WOUNDS Often dramatic but only potentially serious if nerves, tendons or blood vessels are severed.

Clean thoroughly with antiseptic. Remove dirt or other foreign bodies. Small clean cuts can be closed using as many Steristrips as necessary to keep the skin edges together. Skin must be dry. Leave for 5 days at least. Larger deep cuts may require stitches; apply a dressing and seek help. Do not try amateur surgery at sea.

Ragged lacerations or very dirty wounds – do not attempt to close these. Clean as well as possible, sprinkle antibiotic powder in wound and apply a dressing. Seek help. If in doubt a wound is best left open and lightly covered to keep it clean and dry.

Fingers and toes Blood may collect under the nail following an injury. Release the blood by piercing the nail with a red hot needle or paper clip. It will not hurt!

DENTAL PAIN seems worse at sea; prevention is better than cure. Dentanurse is an emergency treatment pack which enables an amateur to make temporary repairs, eg replacing crowns, lost fillings. It contains zinc oxide and Eugenol.

Throbbing toothache made worse by hot or cold or when bitten on. Clean out any cavity and apply temporary filling. Take painkiller.

Dull toothache tender to bite on; gum swollen or red with possible discharge. Treat as above but also take an antibiotic.

Broken tooth or filling Cover exposed surfaces with zinc oxide paste. Teeth knocked out should be put in a clean container with milk or moist gauze for a dentist to re-implant asap. This can be attempted onboard - ideally within 1 hour

Bleeding gums Clean teeth more thoroughly. Use regular hot salt water rinses and antibiotics.

Pain round wisdom tooth Clean area with toothbrush; use hot salt water rinses; take antibiotics and painkillers.

Mouth ulcers Hot salt water rinses.

DIARRHOEA Can become serious, especially in young children if much fluid is lost. Stop food, give plenty of fluid. Plain water is usually sufficient, or add salt (1 teaspoonful/litre) and sugar (4–5 teaspoons/litre). Lomotil or Imodium tablets are very effective in adults.

DROWNING ABC Clear seaweed, dentures. If not breathing start mouth to mouth ventilation as soon as possible and in the water if practicable. If no pulse, start chest compression as soon as on board. Keep the head low so that vomit is not inhaled and water can drain.

If stomach is bulging, turn casualty on to side to empty water and avoid inhaling it. Prevent cooling. Remove wet clothes; wrap casualty in blankets to warm him/her.

Continue resuscitation until the casualty revives or death is certain. Hypothermia may mimic death. Do not abandon resuscitation until the casualty has been warmed or signs of death persist despite attempts at warming.

Once revived, put in the recovery position.

Any person rescued from drowning may collapse in the next 24 hours as the lungs react to inhaled water. *Urgent help needed.*

EYE INJURIES are potentially serious. Never put old or previously opened ointment or drops into an eye; serious infection could result.

Foreign object Flush with clean water, pull the lower lid out to inspect, remove object with a clean tissue. For objects under upper eyelid, ask casualty to grasp lashes and pull the upper lid over the lower lid. An eye-bath is very effective. Blinking under water may help. After removal of object, insert sterile antibiotic ointment inside pulled out lower lid. Cover with pad.

Corrosive fluid Flush continuously with water for 15 minutes. Give painkillers and chloramphenicol ointment; cover with pad. *Seek help asap.*

Conjunctivitis Sticky, weeping eye with yellow discharge. Chloramphenicol 4 times a day.

FISH HOOKS Push the hook round until the point and barb can be cut off; withdraw the hook. Dress the holes and give an antibiotic.

FRACTURES AND DISLOCATIONS Fracture is a broken bone. Dislocation is a displaced joint. Both produce pain (aggravated by attempted movement), localised swelling, abnormal shape, and a grating feeling on movement (if it is a fracture). Blood vessels or nerves around the fracture or dislocation may also be damaged causing a cold, pale, or numb limb below the site of the injury.

Fractures of large bones such as the femur (upper leg) will result in major internal bleeding and may cause shock. When complications occur *urgent help is needed*.

Early application of a splint and raising the injured limb where possible will reduce pain and complications. Treat for shock and pain.

Specific fractures and dislocations
Cheek Caused by a direct blow. Rarely serious but requires specialist care.

Jaw Beware of associated brain or spinal injury. Remove blood and teeth fragments; leave loose teeth in place; protect broken teeth. Ensure airway is clear. Start regular antiseptic mouth washes and antibiotics. Support jaw with bandage over top of the head. Give only fluids by mouth.

Neck May result from a direct blow, a fall or a whiplash type injury. If conscious, casualty may complain of pain, tingling, numbness or weakness in limbs below the injury. *Mishandling may damage the spinal cord, causing paralysis or death*. Avoid movement and support the head. Immobilise by wrapping a folded towel around the neck. If movement is necessary then lift the victim as one rigid piece, never allowing the neck to bend. *Urgent help needed.*

Nose Control bleeding by pinching.

Ribs Very painful. Strapping is not advised.

Spine Fracture of the spine below the neck, may cause *paralysis or death*. Mishandling of the victim may greatly worsen the damage. Avoid movement if possible. Lift the casualty without allowing the spine to sag. *Urgent help needed.*

Collar bone Support arm in sling.

Dislocated shoulder If this has happened before, the casualty may remedy the dislocation himself; otherwise do not attempt to remedy it in case a fracture exists.

Upper arm Support the arm with a collar and cuff inside the shirt, ie tie a clove hitch around the wrist and loop the ends behind the neck.

Forearm and wrist Splint (eg with battens or wood). Do not bandage tightly. Elevate or support in a sling.

Fingers Elevate hand and, unless badly crushed, leave unbandaged; keep moving. If very wobbly, bandage to adjacent finger.

Lower limb
Thigh Shock may be considerable. Strap to other leg with padding between. Gently straighten the lower leg. If necessary apply traction at the ankle to help straighten the leg. Do not bandage too tightly.

Knee Twisting injuries or falls damage the ligaments and cartilages of the knee. Very painful and swollen. Treat as for fracture.

Lower leg Pad very well. Splint using oar, broom handle or similar pieces of wood.

Ankle Fracture or severe sprain may be indistinguishable. Immobilise in neutral position with foot at right angles. Raise the limb.

HEART ATTACK Severe 'crushing' chest pain; may spread to shoulders, neck or arms. Sweating, then bluish lips, then collapse. Breathing and heart may stop. Give one 300mg aspirin tablet (to chew) *Urgent help needed*.

Rest, reassure. If unconscious: recovery position; observe breathing and pulse. If breathing stops or no pulse, start mouth to mouth ventilation and chest compression immediately; do not stop.

STROKE Symptoms: sudden unconsciousness, paralysis or weakness on one side of the body, slurring of speech, or if the victim has any difficulty smiling, speaking, raising both arms, sticking out tongue. Place in recovery position and check airway. *Urgent help needed* – specialist treatment within 3 hours can reverse the effects of a stroke. If you are more than 3 hours from help, and the casualty is conscious and able to swallow, give 300mg of asprin even if he/she is improving.

HEAT STROKE Cool casualty by spraying with cold water or wrap the casualty in a cold wet sheet until their temperature under the tongue falls to 38°C. Encourage drinking (1 teaspoon of salt/half litre of water). If casualty stops sweating, has a rapid pounding pulse and is becoming unconscious: *Urgent help needed*.

HYPOTHERMIA Symptoms include: unreasonable behaviour, apathy and confusion; unsteady gait, stumbling; slurring of speech; pale, cold skin; slow, weak pulse; slow breathing; shivering. It leads to collapse, unconsciousness and ultimately death.

ABC Put in recovery position. If not breathing, start mouth to mouth ventilation. Be prepared to use chest compressions.

Remove wet clothing. Avoid wind chill. Dry and wrap in blankets or sleeping bag plus warm hat and cover, if available, in foil survival bag. *Urgent help needed*.

Give hot sweet drinks if conscious. Do not give alcohol, rub the skin, or place very hot objects against skin.

SEASICKNESS is aggravated by anxiety, fatigue and boredom. Symptoms: lethargy, dizziness, headache and nausea/vomiting. Help prevent by taking anti-seasickness pills, avoiding rich foods and alcohol. Take frequent small amounts of fluid and food. Keep warm; keep busy. Prolonged seasickness may cause serious loss of fluid – seek advice.

SHOCK can result from almost any accident or medical emergency; it can lead to collapse.

Signs and symptoms Thirst, apathy, nausea, restlessness. Pale, cold, clammy skin, sweating. Rapid, weak pulse. Rapid, shallow breathing. Dull, sunken eyes, bluish lips.

ABC Control any bleeding. Lay the casualty flat or in recovery position; raise legs 20°. Splint any fractures; avoid movement. Avoid chilling, keep warm. Give pain killers. Reassure the casualty. Do not let the casualty eat, drink, smoke or move unnecessarily. If complaining of thirst, moisten the lips with a little water. Note: Fluids may be life saving in cases of dehydration (eg diarrhoea, vomiting, severe burns).

FIRST AID KIT

Stow the following items in a waterproof container, readily accessible and clearly marked:

Triangular bandage x 2 (doubles as a sling)
Crepe bandage 75mm x 2
Gauze bandage 50mm x 2
Elastoplast 75mm x 1
Band Aids (or similar) various shapes and sizes
Wound dressings, 1 large, 1 medium
Sterile non-adhesive dressing (Melolin) x 5
Steristrips x 5 packs
Cotton wool. Safety pins. Thermometer.
Scissors and forceps, good quality stainless steel
Disposable gloves
Antiseptic solution (eg Savlon)
Sunscreen with high protection factor
Antifungal powder or cream (athlete's foot)
Insect repellent (DEET, diethyltoluamide)
Individual choice of anti-seasick tablets
Antibiotic eye ointment (prescription only)

Additional items for extended cruising

Vaccinations – a course may need to start as much as 6 months before departure.
Syringes 2ml x 2 (if carrying injections)
Dental kit – see Dental pain.

DRUGS AND MEDICATION

Paracetamol, painkiller. 1-2 500mg tablets 4 hrly.
Asprin, blood thiner. 300mg single dose for heart attack or stroke.
Ibuprofen, anti-inflammatory. 400mg every 8 hours (avoid if history of asthma or stomach ulcer).
*Dihydrocodeine, strong painkiller. 1-2 30mg tablets 4 hourly.
Certirizine, antihistamine. 10mg once a day.
Aludrox, indigestion. 1-2 before meals.
Loperamide, diarrhoea. 2 x 2mg capsules initially, then 1 after each loose stool; max 8 day.
Senokot, constipation. 2-4 tablets per day.
*Amoxycillin, antibiotic. 2 x 250mg capsules 8 hourly (beware penicillin allergy)
*Erythromycin, antibiotic for penicillin-allergic adults. 4 x 250mg tablets daily.
Cinnarizine, seasickness. 2 x 15mg tablets before sailing, then 1 every 8 hours.
*Scopolamine patches, seasickness. 1 patch behind ear 5-6 hours before voyage; replace after 72 hrs if necessary.
*   Only available on prescription.

OBSERVATION FORM

The information recorded by you on this form will be invaluable in helping doctors and/or paramedics ashore to diagnose the problem and arrange the best possible treatment for your casualty.

This is particularly important if there may be a considerable time lapse between requesting medical help and the casualty reaching hospital.

- Keep photocopies of this form in your First Aid kit so as to preserve the original.
  Whilst awaiting help, record your careful observations by ticking or annotating the various boxes at 10 minute intervals. This will help doctors detect any improvement or deterioration in the casualty's condition.

- If within radio range of shore attempt to pass the observations via the Coastguard to a medical authority; or ask a ship to relay.

- Before the casualty is taken off the yacht ensure that this form and personal documents (money, passport, EHIC and mobile 'phone) are securely tied to him/her.

DATE .... CASUALTY'S NAME .... AGE .... M/F ....

Times of observations @ 10 minute intervals:		10	20	30	40	50	60
EYES Observe for reactions whilst testing other responses	Open spontaneously						
	Open when spoken to						
	Open to painful stimulus						
	Nil response						
MOVEMENT Apply painful stimulus: Pinch ear lobe or skin on back of hand	Obeys commands						
	Responds						
	Nil response						
SPEECH Speak clearly and directly, close to the casualty's ear	Responds sensibly to queries						
	Seems confused						
	Uses inappropriate words						
	Incomprehensible sounds						
	Nil response						
PULSE (Beats per minute) Take adult's pulse at wrist or neck. Note rate and whether beats are: weak (w); strong (s); regular (reg) or irregular (irreg)	Over 110						
	101-110						
	91-100						
	81-90						
	71-80						
	61-70						
	Below 61						
BREATHING (Breaths per minute) Note rate and whether breathing is: quiet (q); noisy (n); easy (e); or difficult (d)	Over 40						
	31-40						
	21-30						
	11-20						
	Below 11						

GMDSS

The Global Maritime Distress and Safety System (GMDSS) is a sophisticated, but complex, semi-automatic, third-generation communications system. Although not compulsory for yachts, its potential for saving life, particularly when far offshore and out of VHF range, is so great that every yachtsman should seriously consider it. Equipment costs continue to fall. Training courses, leading to the award of the Short Range Certificate (SRC) of Competence, are widely available. The Long Range Certificate covers MF, HF, SatCom, EPIRBs and SART.

Recommended reading:

- *ALRS, Vol 5* (UK Hydrographic Office)
- *GMDSS: a User's Handbook* (Bréhaut/ACN)
- *GMDSS for small craft* (Clemmetsen/Fernhurst)
- *Reeds VHF/DSC Handbook* (Fletcher/ACN)

Purpose

GMDSS enables a coordinated SAR operation to be mounted rapidly and reliably anywhere at sea. To this end, terrestrial and satellite communications and navigation equipment is used to alert SAR authorities ashore and ships in the vicinity to a Distress incident or Urgency situation. GMDSS also promulgates Maritime Safety Information.

Sea areas

For the purposes of GMDSS, the world's sea areas are divided into 4 categories (A1-4), defined mainly by the range of radio communications. These are:

A1	An area within R/T coverage of at least one VHF Coastguard or Coast radio station in which continuous VHF alerting is available via DSC. Range: 20–50M from the CG/CRS.
A2	An area, excluding sea area A1, within R/T coverage of at least one MF CG/CRS in which continuous DSC alerting is available. Range: approx 50–250M from the CG/CRS.
A3	An area between 76°N and 76°S, excluding sea areas A1 and A2, within coverage of HF or an Inmarsat satellite in which continuous alerting is available.
A4	An area outside sea areas A1, A2 and A3, ie the polar regions, within coverage of HF.

In each category of sea area certain types of radio equipment must be carried by GMDSS vessels: in A1 areas VHF DSC; A2 areas VHF and MF DSC; A3 areas VHF, MF and HF or SatCom; A4 VHF, MF and HF.

Most UK yachtsmen will operate in A1 areas (the English Channel, for example, is an A1 area) where a simple VHF radio and a Navtex receiver will initially meet GMDSS requirements. As equipment becomes more affordable, yachtsmen may decide to fit GMDSS. This will become increasingly necessary as the present system for sending and receiving Distress calls is run down. The CG will continue a loudspeaker watch on VHF Ch 16 until further notice.

Functions

Regardless of the sea areas in which they operate, vessels complying with GMDSS must be able to perform certain functions:

- transmit ship-to-shore Distress alerts by two independent means
- receive shore-to-ship Distress alerts
- transmit & receive ship-to-ship Distress alerts
- transmit signals for locating incidents
- transmit and receive communications for SAR co-ordination
- transmit/receive maritime safety info, eg navigation and weather warnings

Distress alerts

A Distress alert is simply a Distress call using DSC. It is transmitted on Ch 70 and is automatically repeated five times. Whenever possible, a Distress alert should always include the last known position and time in UT. The position is normally entered automatically from an interfaced GPS, but can be entered manually if required. The nature of the distress can also be selected from the receiver's menu. The vessel's identity (MMSI number) is automatically included.

GMDSS requires participating ships to be able to send Distress alerts by two out of three independent means. These are:

- Digital Selective Calling (DSC) using terrestrial communications, ie VHF Ch 70, MF 2187·5 kHz, or HF distress and alerting frequencies in the 4, 6, 8,12 and 16 MHz bands.
- Emergency Position Indicating Radio Beacons (EPIRBs). See below.
- Inmarsat, via ship terminals.

Digital Selective Calling

DSC is an essential component of GMDSS. It is so called because information is sent by a burst of digital code; selective because it can be addressed to a specific DSC-equipped vessel or to a selected group of vessels.

In all DSC messages every vessel and relevant shore station has a 9-digit identification number, or MMSI (Maritime Mobile Service Identity), which is in effect an automatic, electronic callsign.

DSC is used to transmit Distress alerts from ships, to receive Distress acknowledgements from ships or shore stations; to send Urgency and Safety alerts; to relay Distress alerts; and for routine calling & answering. A thorough working knowledge is needed.

Maritime Safety Information (MSI)

MSI consists of the vital navigational, weather and safety messages which traditionally were sent to vessels at sea by CRS in Morse, but by R/T on VHF and MF in more recent years – and now by GMDSS. For navigation and weather warnings see this and chapter 2 respectively.

GMDSS transmits MSI in English by two independent but complementary means, Navtex and SafetyNet.

- Navtex on MF (518 kHz and 490 kHz) which can be received out to about 300 miles offshore, see Chapter 2.
- SafetyNet uses Inmarsat-C satellites to cover beyond MF range, except Area A4. Enhanced Group Calling (EGC) is a part of SafetyNet which enables MSI to be sent to selected groups of users in any of the four oceans.

Emergency Position Indicating Radio Beacons (EPIRB) may be hand-held or float-free, they transmit on 406 MHz. (Note that 121·5 MHz, 243·0 MHz and L-band EPIRBS are no longer used.) Most EPIRBs have a built in GPS and about 48 hours of battery life. They communicate via the Cospas-Sarsat (C/S) network of geostationary and polar orbit satellites. Although C/S will relay an EPIRB signal to earth with no delay, the position of a non-GPS EPIRB may take several hours to determine. The cost of an EPIRB ranges from less than £300 to more than £1000 for float-free, GPS models.

An EPIRB transmits data which is uniquely coded to identify the individual beacon and, because it may be transmitting from anywhere in the world, it must be registered. The UK registration centre is:

The EPIRB Registry, The Maritime and Coastguard Agency, MRCC Falmouth, Pendennis Point, Castle Drive, Falmouth, Cornwall TR11 4WZ; n 01326 211569; email: epirb@mcga.gov.uk.

It is just as important that any changes are immediately notified. False alerts caused by inadvertent or incorrect use of EPIRBs put a significant burden on SAR Centres and may coincide with an actual distress situation.

All crew members should be aware of the proper use of the particular EPIRB onboard. Make sure that testing is adequately supervised; that the EPIRB is correctly installed and maintained; and that it is not activated if assistance is already available. If an EPIRB is activated accidentally, make every effort to advise the nearest MRCC of the false alert as soon as possible.

Personal Locator Beacons (PLB) operate on the same principle. They must also be registered but they do not have a vessel-specific MMSI. A PLB with GPS costs about £250.

Search And Rescue Transponders (SART) are radar transceivers which operate on 9 GHz and respond to 3 cm (X-band) radars, like a small portable Racon (see Chapter 3). They are primarily intended for use in liferafts to help searching ships and aircraft find survivors. The transmitted signal shows on a radar screen as 12 dots radiating out from the SART's position. A SART costs about £500.

HM COASTGUARD - MRCC CONTACT DETAILS

EASTERN REGION
PORTLAND COASTGUARD
50°36'N 02°27'W. DSC MMSI 002320012
Custom House Quay, Weymouth DT4 8BE.
☎ 01305 760439. 📠 01305 760451.
Area: Topsham to Chewton Bunney (50°44'N 01°42'W).

SOLENT COASTGUARD
50°48'N 01°12'W. DSC MMSI 002320011
44A Marine Parade West, Lee-on-Solent, PO13 9NR. ☎ 02392 552100. 📠 02392 554131. Area: Chewton Bunney to Beachy Hd. Call on Ch 67 to keep Ch 16 clear.

DOVER COASTGUARD
50°08'N 01°20'E. DSC MMSI 002320010
Langdon Battery, Dover CT15 5NA.
☎ 01304 210008. 📠 01304 225762.
Area: Beachy Head to Reculver Towers (51°23'N 01°12'E). Operates Channel Navigation Information Service.

THAMES COASTGUARD

51°51'N 01°17'E. MMSI 002320009
East Terrace, Walton-on-the-Naze CO14 8PY. ☎
01255 675518. 🕿 01255 679415.
Area: Reculver Towers to Southwold.

LONDON COASTGUARD

51°30'N 00°03'E. MMSI 002320063
Thames Barrier Navigation Centre, Unit 28,
34 Bowater Rd, Woolwich, London SE18 5TF.
☎ 0208 312 7380. 🕿 0208 309 8196.
Area: River Thames from Shell Haven Pt (N bank)
& Egypt Bay (S bank) up-river to Teddington Lock.

YARMOUTH COASTGUARD

52°37'N 01°43'E. MMSI 002320008
Haven Bridge House, North Quay, Great
Yarmouth NR30 1HZ.
☎ 01493 851338. 🕿 01493 331975.
Area: Southwold to Haile Sand Fort.

†HUMBER COASTGUARD

54°06'N 00°11'W. MMSI 002320007
Lime Kiln Lane, Bridlington, N Humberside YO15
2LX.
☎ 01262 672317. 🕿 01262 400779.
Area: Haile Sand Fort to Scottish border.

SCOTLAND & NORTHERN IRELAND

FORTH COASTGUARD

56°17'N 02°35'W. MMSI 002320005
Fifeness, Crail, Fife KY10 3XN.
☎ 01333 450666. 🕿 01333 450703.
Area: English border to Doonies Pt (57°01'N
02°10'W).

†ABERDEEN COASTGUARD

57°08'N 02°05'W. MMSI 002320004
Marine House, Blaikies Quay, Aberdeen AB11 5PB.
☎ 01224 592334. 🕿 01224 575920.
Area: Doonies Pt to Cape Wrath, incl Pentland Firth.

†SHETLAND COASTGUARD

60°09'N 01°08'W. MMSI 002320001
Knab Road, Lerwick ZE1 0AX.
☎ 01595 692976. 🕿 01595 693634.
Area: Orkney, Fair Isle and Shetland.

†*STORNOWAY COASTGUARD

58°12'N 06°22'W. MMSI 002320024
Battery Pt, Stornoway, Isle of Lewis H51 2RT.
☎ 01851 702013. 🕿 01851 706796.
Area: Cape Wrath to Ardnamurchan Pt, Western
Isles and St Kilda.

†*CLYDE COASTGUARD

55°58'N 04°48'W. MMSI 002320022
Navy Bldgs, Eldon St, Greenock PA16 7QY.

☎ 01475 729988. 🕿 01475 888095.
Area: Ardnamurchan Pt to Mull of Galloway inc
islands.

*BELFAST COASTGUARD

54°40'N 05°40'W. MMSI 002320021
Bregenz House, Quay St, Bangor, Co Down BT20
5ED.
☎ 02891 463933. 🕿 02891 469854.
Area: Carlingford Lough to Lough Foyle.

WESTERN REGION

LIVERPOOL COASTGUARD

53°30'N 03°03'W. MMSI 002320019
Hall Rd West, Crosby, Liverpool L23 8SY.
☎ 0151 9313341. 🕿 0151 9320978
Area: Mull of Galloway to Queensferry (near
Chester).

†HOLYHEAD COASTGUARD

53°19'N 04°38'W. MMSI 002320018
Prince of Wales Rd, Holyhead, Anglesey LL65
1ET.
☎ 01407 762051. 🕿 01407 761613
Area: Queensferry to Friog (1·6M S of
Barmouth).

†MILFORD HAVEN COASTGUARD

51°42'N 05°03'W. MMSI 002320017
Gorsewood Drive, Hakin, Milford Haven, SA73
2HD.
☎ 01646 690909. 🕿 01646 697287.
Area: Friog to River Towy (11M N of Worms
Head).

SWANSEA COASTGUARD

51°34'N 03°58'W. MMSI 002320016
Tutt Head, Mumbles, Swansea SA3 4EX.
☎ 01792 366534. 🕿 01792 368371.
Area: River Towy to Marsland Mouth (near
Bude).

†*FALMOUTH COASTGUARD

50°09'N 05°03'W. MMSI 002320014
Pendennis Point, Castle Drive, Falmouth TR11
4WZ.
☎ 01326 317575. 🕿 01326 315610.
Area: Marsland Mouth (near Bude) to Dodman
Point.

*BRIXHAM COASTGUARD

50°24'N 03°31'W. DSC MMSI 002320013
King's Quay, Brixham TQ5 9TW.
☎ 01803 882704. 🕿 01803 859562.
Area: Dodman Point to Topsham (R. Exe).

NOTES: †Monitors DSC MF 2187.5 kHz.
*Broadcasts Gunfacts/Subfacts.

NATIONAL COASTWATCH INSTITUTION

The NCI is a charitable organisation keeping a visual watch along the UK's shores to assist in the preservation and protection of life at sea. It works closely with HM Coastguard, the RNLI and other SAR services.

Since 1994 the NCI has re-introduced visual watch stations, often by re-opening old CG lookouts. 40 stations are operational (2011) manned by over 1700 volunteers.

All stations monitor VHF Ch 16, and many are equipped with radar (® = Radar equipped).

All passing small boats are logged to assist in the search for missing craft.

NCI stations will provide actual weather and sea states on request.

For more information, and for news of stations being developed, visit: www.nci.org.uk.

Area 1

Gwennap Head ®	01736 871351
Penzance	01736 367063
Bass Point (Lizard) ®	01326 290212
Nare Point (Helford River)	01326 231113
Portscatho (w/ends only)	01872 580180
Charlestown ®	01726 817068
Polruan (Fowey) ®	01726 870291
Rame Head (Plymouth) ®	01752 823706
Prawle Point (Salcombe) ®	01548 511259
Froward Pt (Dartmouth) ®	07976 505649
Torbay	01803 411145
Teignmouth	01626 772377
Exmouth	01395 222492
Portland Bill ®	01305 860178
St Alban's Head ®	01929 439220

Area 2

Peveril Pt (Swanage) ®	01929 422596

Calshot	023 8089 3562
Lee on Solent	023 9255 6758
Gosport	023 9276 5194

Area 3

Shoreham	07530 041733
Newhaven	01273 516464
Folkestone (Copt Pt)	01303 227132

Area 4

Herne Bay (w/ends only)	01227 743208
Whitstable (w/ends only)	07932 968707
Holehaven (Canvey Is)	01268 696971
Southend (w/ends only)	07815 945210
Felixstowe	01394 670808
Gorleston (Gt Yarmouth) ®	01493 440384
Mundesley (Norfolk) ®	01263 722399
Wells-next-the-Sea ®	01328 710587
Skegness ®	01754 610900
Mablethorpe	07958 038564
Hartlepool ®	01429 274931
Sunderland Life Brigade ®	01915 672579
Berwick (w/e; limited hrs)	07950 149865

Area 8

Rossall Point (Fleetwood)	01253 681378
Porth Dinllean	07814 823430
Wooltack Point	07817 871549
Worms Head (Gower)	01792 390167

Area 9

Nells Point (Barry)	01446 420746
Boscastle (N Cornwall) ®	01840 250965
Stepper Point (Padstow) ®	07810 898041
St Agnes Head	01872 552073
St Ives ®	01736 799398
Cape Cornwall ®	01736 787890

Royal National Lifeboat Institution

The RNLI is a registered charity which saves life at sea. It provides, on call H24, a lifeboat service up to 50M off the UK and Irish coasts.

There are over 230 lifeboat stations, 130 all-weather and 191 inshore LBs from 4·9 to 17·0m LOA, plus 3 hovercraft. There are 131 LBs in the reserve fleet. All new LBs are capable of at least 25 knots.

When launched on service, lifeboats >10m keep watch on VHF and MF DSC as well as VHF Ch 16. They can also use alternative frequencies to contact other vessels, SAR aircraft, HM CG, Coast radio stations or other SAR agencies. All lifeboats show a quick-flashing blue light when on operational service.

The RNLI also actively promotes safety at sea by providing a free comprehensive safety service to members and the general public including advice, publications and demonstrations. The RNLI aims to save lives and prevent accidents by helping people be prepared through water safety awareness.

A useful A5 size, ring-bound RNLI Handbook covers emergencies, first aid, seamanship, weather, navigation and engines. It is recommended.

For more details of how the RNLI can help you to be safer at sea, to support the work of the RNLI by becoming a Shoreline Member, Offshore Member or a Governor call the RNLI on 0845 122 6999, or visit www.rnli.org.uk.

The headquarters are at: RNLI, West Quay Road, Poole, Dorset BH15 1HZ.

THE CHANNEL ISLANDS

Guernsey and Jersey Coastguard stations direct SAR operations in the North and South of the CI area respectively, they also provide communications on VHF and DSC.

Close liaison is maintained with adjacent French SAR authorities. A distress situation may be controlled by the Channel Islands or France, whichever is more appropriate. For example a British yacht in difficulty in French waters may be handled by St Peter Port or Jersey so as to avoid language problems; and vice versa for a French yacht.

GUERNSEY CG 49°27'·00N 02°32'00W. DSC MMSI 002320064. ☎ 01481 720672. ℻ 714177. Area: Channel Islands North.

JERSEY CG 49°10'·85N 02°14'30W. DSC MMSI 002320060. ☎: 01534 741121. ℻: 499089. Area: Channel Islands South.

SEARCH AND RESCUE ABROAD
THE IRISH REPUBLIC

The Irish CG co-ordinates SAR operations around the coast of Ireland via Dublin MRCC, Malin Head and Valentia MRSCs and remote sites. It may liaise with the UK and France during any rescue operation within 100M of the Irish coast.

It is part of the Dept of Marine, Leeson Lane, Dublin 2. ☎ (01) 6620922; ℻ (01) 6620795. The Irish EPIRB Registry is co-located; ☎ (01) 6199280; ℻ (01) 6621571.

The MRCC/MRSCs are co-located with the Coast radio stations of the same name and manned by the same staff. All stations keep watch H24 on VHF Ch 16 and DSC Ch 70. If ashore dial 999 or 112 in an emergency and ask for Marine Rescue.

Details of the MRCC/MRSCs are as follows:

DUBLIN (MRCC)
53°20'N 06°15W. DSC MMSI 002500300 (+2187·5 kHz).
☎ +353 1 662 0922/3; ℻ +353 1 662 0795. Area: Carlingford Lough to Youghal.

VALENTIA (MRSC)
51°56'N 10°21'W. DSC MMSI 002500200 (+2187·5 kHz).
☎ +353 669 476 109; ℻ +353 669 476 289. Area: Youghal to Slyne Head.

MALIN HEAD (MRSC)
55°22'N 07°20W. DSC MMSI 002500100 (+2187·5 kHz).
☎ +353 77 70103; ℻ +353 77 70221. Area: Slyne Head to Lough Foyle.

SAR resources

The Irish CG provides some 50 units around the coast and is on call H24. The RNLI maintains 4 stations around the coast and operates 42 lifeboats; six community-run inshore rescue boats are also available.

Sikorsky S-61 helicopters, based at Dublin, Waterford, Shannon and Sligo, can respond within 15 to 45 minutes and operate to a radius of 200M. They are equipped with infrared search equipment and can uplift 30 survivors.

Military and civilian aircraft and vessels, together with the Garda and lighthouse service, can also be called upon.

Some stations provide specialist cliff climbing services. They are manned by volunteers, who are trained in first aid and equipped with inflatables, breeches buoys, cliff ladders, etc. Their ☎ numbers (the Leader's residence) are given, where appropriate, under each port.

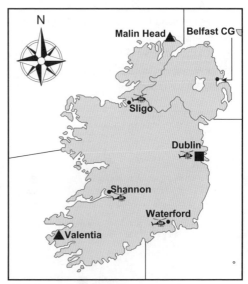

Irish Coastguard centres

DENMARK

The national SAR agency is: Ministry of Defence, 42 Holmens Kanal, DK-1060 København K.
☎ +45 339 23320; ℻ +45 333 20655.

The SAR coordinator for Denmark is MRCC Århus, ☎ +45 894 33099 ext 3203; ℻ +45 894 33230; mas@sok.dk. Århus has no direct communications with vessels in distress, but operates via two MRSCs and several Coast radio stations (CRS). MRSC Kattegat, ☎ +45 992 22255; ℻ +45 992 22838, deals with the W coast of Denmark.

Lyngby Radio

This is the main Danish CRS and is DSC VHF/MF/HF equipped (☎ +45 452 89800; 🖷 +45 458 82485, lyngby-radio@tdc.dk MMSI 002191000).

It operates through remote sites at Skagen, Hirtshals, Hantsholm, Bovbjerg and Blavand, all of which guard Ch 16 H24 and use callsign *Lyngby Radio*. Their VHF and MF frequencies are shown in the chartlet below.

There are at least 12 lifeboats stationed at the major harbours along the west coast. They are designed to double up as Pilot boats.

Firing practice areas

There are 4 such areas on the W coast as in the chartlet and listed below. Firing times are broadcast daily by Danmarks Radio 1 after the weather at 1645UT. Times can also be obtained from the Range office Ch 16 or ☎.

Ⓐ Tranum & Blokhus ☎ 982 35088 or call *Tranum*.

Ⓑ Nymindegab ☎ 752 89355 or call *Nymindegab*.

Ⓒ Oksbøl ☎ 765 41213 or call *Oksbøl*.

Ⓓ Rømø E ☎ 747 55219; Rømø W ☎ 745 41340 – or call *Fly Rømø*.

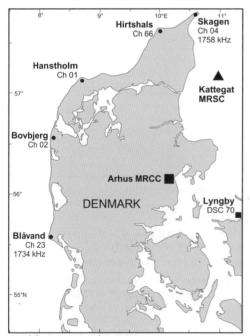

Danish Coastguard centres

GERMANY

The national SAR agency is: *Deutsche Gesellschaft zur Rettung Schiffbrüchiger* (DGzRS), the German Sea Rescue Service. Werderstrasse 2, Hermann-Helms-Haus, D-28199 Bremen. mail@mrcc-bremen.de. ☎ 421 537 070; 🖷 421 537 0714.

DGzRS is responsible for coordinating SAR operations, supported by ships and SAR helicopters of the German Navy.

Bremen MRCC (☎ 421 536870; 🖷 421 5368714; MMSI 002111240), using callsign *Bremen Rescue Radio,* maintains an H24 watch on Ch 16 and DSC Ch 70 via remote Coast radio stations at:

Blumenthal / Borkum / Cuxhaven / Helgoland / kampen / Norderney / Stade / Wangerooge / Westerhever.

There are 21 offshore lifeboats, LOA 23–44m, and 21 smaller <10m lifeboats, based at List, Amrum, Helgoland, Cuxhaven, Bremerhaven, Wilhelmshaven, Langeoog, Norderney and Borkum. There are also many inshore lifeboats.

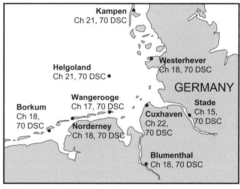

German Coastguard stations

THE NETHERLANDS

The national SAR agency is: SAR Commission, Directorate Transport Safety (DGG), PO Box 20904, 2500 EX The Hague, Netherlands.

The Netherlands CG at Den Helder, co-located with the Navy HQ, coordinates SAR operations as the Dutch JRCC for A1 and A2 Sea Areas. (JRCC = Joint Rescue Coordination Centre – marine & aeronautical.) Callsign is *Netherlands Coastguard*, but *Den Helder Rescue* during SAR operations.

The JRCC keeps a listening watch H24 on DSC Ch 70, and MF DSC 2187·5 kHz (but not on 2182 kHz); MMSI 002442000.

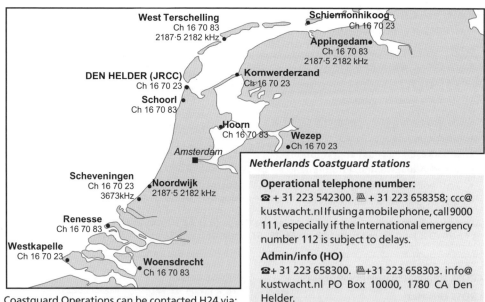

Netherlands Coastguard stations

Operational telephone number:
☎ + 31 223 542300. 🖷 + 31 223 658358; ccc@kustwacht.nl If using a mobile phone, call 9000 111, especially if the International emergency number 112 is subject to delays.

Admin/info (HO)
☎+ 31 223 658300. 🖷+31 223 658303. info@kustwacht.nl PO Box 10000, 1780 CA Den Helder.

Remote CG stations are shown above. Working channels are VHF 23 and 83.

Coastguard Operations can be contacted H24 via:

In emergency:
☎ + 31 9000 111 or dial 112.

BELGIUM

The Belgian CG coordinates SAR operations from Oostende MRCC, callsign *Coastguard Oostende*. The MRCC and *Oostende Radio* (Coast radio rtation) both keep listening watch H24 on Ch 16, 67, 2182 kHz and DSC Ch 70 and 2187·5 kHz.

Coastguard stations

MRCC OOSTENDE
☎ +32 59 701000; 🖷 +32 59 703605. MMSI 002059981.

MRSC Nieuwpoort
☎ +32 58 230000; 🖷 +32 58 231575.

MRSC Zeebrugge
☎ +32 50 550801; 🖷 +32 50 547400.

RCC Brussels (COSPAS/SARSAT agency)
☎ +32 2 7200338; 🖷 +32 2 7524201.

Coast Radio Stations

OOSTENDE Radio
☎ 50 558241; 🖷 50 558748.
Ch 16, DSC Ch 70 and MF DSC 2187·5 kHz. MMSI 002050480.

Antwerpen Radio (remotely controlled by Oostende CRS) MMSI 002050485. Ch 16, DSC Ch 70.

Resources

Offshore and inshore lifeboats are based at Nieuwpoort, Oostende and Zeebrugge.

The Belgian Air Force provides helicopters from Koksijde near the French border. The Belgian Navy also participates in SAR operations as required.

SAFETY

FRANCE – CROSS

Four CROSS (Centres Régionaux Opérationnels de Surveillance et de Sauvetage, ie an MRCC) provide a permanent, H24, all weather operational presence along the N and W coasts and liaise with foreign CGs.

CROSS' main functions include:

- Co-ordinating SAR operations.
- Navigational surveillance.
- Broadcasting navigational warnings.
- Broadcasting weather information.
- Anti-pollution control.
- Marine and fishery surveillance.

All centres keep watch on VHF Ch 16 as well as Ch 70 (DSC) and co-ordinate SAR on Ch 15, 67, 68, 73. They also broadcast gale warnings, weather forecasts and local navigational warnings.

CROSSA Étel specialises in medical advice and responds to alerts from Cospas/Sarsat satellites.

CROSS can be contacted by R/T, by ☎, through Coast Radio Stations, via the National Gendarmerie or Affaires Maritimes, or via a Semaphore station. Call *Semaphore* stations on Ch 16 (working Ch 10) or by ☎ as listed later in this section.

CROSS also monitor TSS in the Dover Strait, off Casquets and off Ouessant using, for example, the callsign *Corsen Traffic*.

For medical advice call CROSS which will contact a doctor or SAMU (Service d'Aide Médicale Urgente). In harbour/marina SAMU responds faster to a medical emergency than calling a doctor. Simply dial 15.

CROSS stations (Emergency ☎ 1616).

CROSS Gris-Nez
50°52'N 01°35'E   MMSI 002275100
☎ 03 21 87 21 87; ☒ 03 21 87 78 55
Belgian border to Cap d'Antifer.

NavWarnings Ch 79 at every H+10 via Dunkerque, Saint-Frieux and L'Ailly.

CROSS Jobourg
49°41'N 01°54'W   MMSI 002275200
☎ 02 33 52 72 13; ☒ 02 33 52 71 72
Cap de la Hague to Mont St Michel

NavWarnings Ch 80 every H+20 and H+50 via Antifer, Ver-sur-Mer, Gatteville, Jobourg, Granville and Roche Douvres.

CROSS Corsen
48°24'N 04°47'W   MMSI 002275300
☎ 02 98 89 31 31; ☒ 02 98 89 65 75
Mont St Michel to Pointe de Penmarc'h.

NavWarnings Ch 79 every H+10 and H+40 via Cap Fréhel, Bodic, Ile de Batz, Le Stiff and Pte du Raz.

CROSS Étel
47°39'N 03°12'W   MMSI 002275000
☎ 02 97 55 35 35; ☒ 02 97 55 49 34
Pte de Penmarc'h to the Spanish border

NavWarnings Ch 79 for Landes range activity via Chassiron 1903.

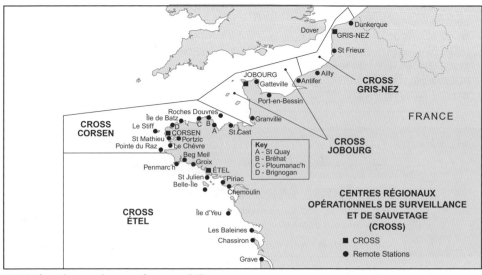

CROSS locations and areas of responsibility

Semaphore stations keep visual, radar and radio watch (Ch 16); are equipped with VHF DF; relay emergency calls to CROSS; show gale warning signals, repeat forecasts and offer local weather reports. Hours sunrise-sunset, but * H24.

*	Dunkerque	03·28·66·86·18
	Boulogne	03·21·31·32·10
	Ault	03·22·60·47·33
	Dieppe	02·35·84·23·82
*	Fécamp	02·35·28·00·91
*	La Hève	02·35·46·07·81
*	Le Havre	02·35·21·74·39
	Villerville	02·31·88·11·13
*	Port-en-Bessin	02·31·21·81·51
	St-Vaast	02·33·54·44·50
*	Barfleur	02·33·54·04·37
	Lévy	02·33·54·31·17
*	Le Homet	02·33·92·60·08
	La Hague	02·33·52·71·07
	Carteret	02·33·53·85·08
	Barneville Le Roc	02·33·50·05·85
	St-Cast	02·96·41·85·30
*	St Quay-Portrieux	02·96.70.42.18
	Bréhat	02·96·20·00·12
*	Ploumanac'h	02·96·91·46·51
	Batz	02·98·61·76·06
*	Brignogan	02·98·83·50·84
*	Ouessant Stiff	02·98·48·81·50
*	St-Mathieu	02·98·89·01·59
*	Portzic (Ch 08)	02·98·22·21·47
	Toulinguet	02·98·27·90·02
	Cap-de-la-Chèvre	02·98·27·09·55
*	Pointe-du-Raz	02·98·70·66·57
*	Penmarc'h	02·98·58·61·00
	Beg Meil	02·98·94·98·92
*	Port-Louis	02·97·82·52·10
	Étel Mât Fenoux	02·97·55·35·35
	Beg Melen (Groix)	02·97·86·80·13
	Talut (Belle-Île)	02·97·31·85·07
	St-Julien	02·97·50·09·35
	Piriac-sur-Mer	02·40·23·59·87
*	Chemoulin	02·40·91·99·00
	St-Sauveur (Yeu)	02·51·58·31·01
	Les Baleines (Ré)	05·46·29·42·06
	Chassiron (Oléron)	05·46·47·85·43

Lifeboats

The lifeboat service Société National de Sauvetage en Mer (SNSM) comes under CROSS, but ashore it is best to contact local lifeboat stations direct. A hefty charge may be levied if a SNSM lifeboat attends a vessel not in distress.

Navigation warnings

Long-range warnings are broadcast by SafetyNet for Navarea II, which includes the W coast of France. The N coast is in Navarea I.

Avurnavs (AVis URgents aux NAVigateurs) are regional, coastal and local warnings issued by Cherbourg and Brest and broadcast by Niton and Brest Navtex and on MF. Warnings are prefixed by 'Sécurité Avurnav'.

EMERGENCY VHF DF SERVICE

A yacht in emergency can call CROSS on VHF Ch 16, 11 or 67 to obtain a true bearing of the yacht *from* the DF station. These monitor Ch 16 and other continuously scanned frequencies, which include Ch 1-29, 36, 39, 48, 50, 52, 55, 56 and 60-88. The Semaphore stations overleaf are also equipped with VHF DF.

HJ = Day service only.

VHF DF stations, are listed below geographically from NE to W then S:

Station	Lat/Long	Hrs
Dunkerque	51°03'.40N 02°20'.40E	H24
*Gris-Nez	50°52'.20N 01°35'.01E	H24
Boulogne	50°44'.00N 01°36'.00E	HJ
Ault	50°06'.50N 01°27'.50E	HJ
Dieppe	49°56'.00N 01°05'.20E	HJ
Fécamp	49°46'.10N 00°22'.20E	H24
La Hève	49°30'.60N 00°04'.20E	H24
Villerville	49°23'.20N 00°06'.50E	HJ
Port-en-Bessin	49°21'.10N 00°46'.30W	H24
Saint-Vaast	49°34'.50N 01°16'.50W	HJ
Barfleur	49°41'.90N 01°15'.90W	H24
Levy	49°41'.70N 01°28'.20W	HJ
†Homet	49°39'.50N 01°37'.90W	H24
*Jobourg	49°41'.50N 01°54'.50W	H24
La Hague	49°43'.60N 01°56'.30W	HJ
Carteret	49°22'.40N 01°48'.30W	HJ
Le Roc	48°50'.10N 01°36'.90W	HJ
Grouin/Cancale	48°42'.60N 01°50'.60W	HJ
Saint-Cast	48°38'.60N 02°14'.70W	HJ
St-Quay-Port'x	48°39'.30N 02°49'.50W	H24
Bréhat	48°51'.30N 03°00'.10W	HJ
Ploumanac'h	48°49'.50N 03°28'.20W	H24
Batz	48°44'.80N 04°00'.60W	HJ
Brignogan	48°40'.60N 04°19'.70W	H24
Creac'h (Ushant)	48°27'.60N 05°07'.70W	HJ
*Creac'h	48°27'.60N 05°07'.80W	H24
†Saint-Mathieu	48°19'.80N 04°46'.20W	H24
Toulinguet	48°16'.80N 04°37'.50W	HJ
Cap de la Chèvre	48°10'.20N 04°33'.00W	HJ
Pointe du Raz	48°02'.30N 04°43'.80W	H24
Penmarc'h	47°47'.90N 04°22'.40W	H24
Beg-Meil	47°51'.30N 03°58'.40W	HJ
Beg Melen	47°39'.20N 03°30'.10W	HJ
†Port-Louis	47°42'.60N 03°21'.80W	H24
*Etel	47°39'.80N 03°12'.00W	H24
Saint-Julien	47°29'.70N 03°07'.50W	HJ
Taillefer	47°21'.80N 03°09'.00W	HJ
Le Talut	47°17'.70N 03°13'.00W	HJ
Piriac	47°22'.50N 02°33'.40W	HJ
Chemoulin	47°14'.10N 02°17'.80W	H24
Saint-Sauveur	46°41'.70N 02°18'.80W	HJ
Les Baleines	46°14'.60N 01°33'.70W	HJ
Chassiron	46°02'.80N 01°24'.50W	HJ

Chapter 5 – Tides

2012 TIDAL COEFFICIENTS

Date	Jan am	Jan pm	Feb am	Feb pm	Mar am	Mar pm	Apr am	Apr pm	May am	May pm	June am	June pm	July am	July pm	Aug am	Aug pm	Sept am	Sept pm	Oct am	Oct pm	Nov am	Nov pm	Dec am	Dec pm
1	46	42	32	30	35	31	32	35	45	49	67	73	70	75	85	90	97	98	92	91	80	77	76	74
2	38	36	30		29		40	46	55	62	78	84	80	85	94	97	97	96	89	87	75	71	72	70
3	35		33	38	30	33	54	62	70	77	89	94	89	93	98	99	93	90	84	80	68	64	67	64
4	36	39	43	50	39	46	71	79	85	91	97	100	96	98	98	97	86	81	76	71	59	55	61	58
5	42	46	56	63	54	62	87	95	97	102	102	102	99	99	94	90	76	71	66	60	51	46	54	51
6	51	56	70	77	70	79	101	106	106	108	101	100	97	95	86	81	65	58	55	49	42	39	49	47
7	61	66	83	88	86	93	110	113	109	108	97	93	92	88	75	69	52	46	44	38	37	37	47	47
8	71	75	93	98	99	105	114	113	106	103	88	83	83	77	63	57	40	34	34	31	39			
9	79	83	101	103	108	111	110	106	98	92	78	72	72	66	50	44	30		30		43	48	53	58
10	86	88	104	104	112	112	101	94	86	79	66	60	60	54	39	34	28	29	32	36	55	62	64	70
11	90	91	102	99	110	106	86	78	72	66	56	51	49	44	32		32	37	42	49	69	77	76	83
12	91	90	95	90	101	94	70	62	60	54	48		41		31	33	44	51	57	65	84	90	89	94
13	89	87	84	77	87	79	55	49	50		46	44	38	37	36	41	59	66	73	80	96	101	98	102
14	84	80	70	62	70	61	46		48	47	45	46	38	40	47	53	73	80	87	94	104	106	104	105
15	76	71	56	50	54	47	45	47	48	50	48	51	44	48	59	66	87	92	99	104	107	107	104	103
16	66	61	46		44		50	54	52	55	54	57	52	57	72	77	97	101	107	109	104	101	100	96
17	57	54	46	49	44	46	59	64	59	62	60	63	61	66	83	87	104	106	109	108	97	91	91	86
18	53		53	59	51	57	68	72	65	68	66	69	70	74	91	95	106	105	105	101	85	78	80	74
19	53	56	66	72	63	69	76	79	70	72	72	74	78	81	97	98	103	99	95	89	72	65	67	61
20	60	65	78	84	75	80	81	83	74	76	76	77	84	86	99	98	94	88	81	74	59	55	55	51
21	71	77	88	91	84	87	84	84	77	77	78	79	87	88	97	94	81	73	66	59	51	49	47	44
22	82	87	94	95	89	91	84	83	77	77	79	79	88	88	90	85	65	58	53	49	49		43	
23	91	93	96	95	92	91	82	80	76	75	78	76	86	84	79	73	51	47	48		50	52	44	46
24	95	96	94	91	90	89	78	76	74	72	75	73	81	78	66	60	46		48	51	55	58	48	52
25	96	95	88	85	87	84	72	69	69	67	70	68	74	70	54		48	52	55	60	62	65	55	59
26	92	89	80	76	80	77	65	61	64	61	65	62	65	61	50	48	57	64	64	69	68	71	62	66
27	86	81	70	65	72	67	56	52	58	55	60	58	57		49	53	69	75	73	77	73	75	69	72
28	76	71	59	53	62	57	48	44	53	52	57		54	53	58	65	80	85	80	82	76	77	74	76
29	65	59	46	41	51	46	42	41	51		57	59	54	57	71	78	88	91	83	84	77	78	78	79
30	53	47			40	36	42		52	54	61	65	62	68	83	88	92	93	85	84	77	77	80	80
31	41	36			33				57	62			73	79	92	95			83	82			80	79

Tidal coefficients indicate the magnitude of the tide on any particular day without having to look up and calculate the range, and thus determine whether it is springs, neaps or somewhere in between. This table is valid for all areas covered by this Almanac. Typical values are:

120	Very big spring tide
95	**Mean spring tide**
70	Average tide
45	**Mean neap tide**
20	Very small neap tide

TIDES

TIDAL CALCULATIONS

Find the height at a given time (STANDARD PORT)

1. On Standard Curve diagram, plot heights of HW and LW occuring either side of required time and join by sloping line.
2. Enter HW Time and sufficient others to bracket required time.
3. From required time, proceed vertically to curves, using heights plotted in (1) to help interpolation between Spring and Neaps. Do NOT extrapolate.
4. Proceed horizontally to sloping line, thence vertically to Height scale.
5. Read off height.

EXAMPLE:

Find the height of tide at ULLAPOOL at 1900 on 6th January

From tables	JANUARY	
ULLAPOOL	6 0420 1033 1641 F 2308	4.6 1.6 4.6 1.2

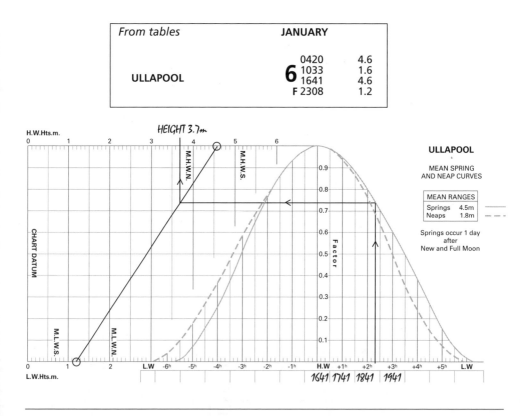

Find the time for a given height (STANDARD PORT)

1. On Standard Curve diagram, plot heights of HW and LW occurring either side of required event and join by sloping line.
2. Enter HW time and those for half-tidal cycle covering required event.
3. From required height, proceed vertically to sloping line, thence horizontally to curves, using heights plotted in (1) to assist interpolation between Spring and Neaps. Do NOT extrapolate.
4. Proceed vertically to Time scale.
5. Read off time.

EXAMPLE:

Find the time at which the afternoon tide at ULLAPOOL falls to 3.7m on 6 January

From tables	JANUARY	
ULLAPOOL	**6** 0420 1033 1641 F 2308	4.6 1.6 4.6 1.2

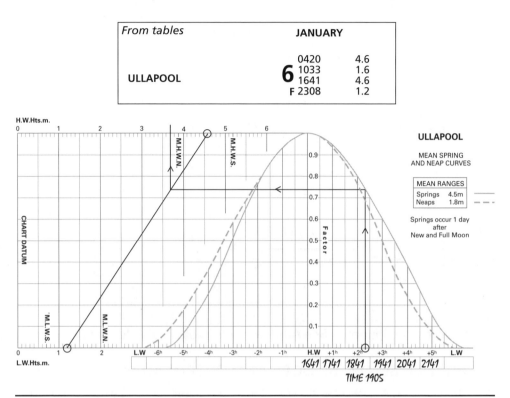

H.W.Hts.m.

CHART DATUM

M.L.W.S. M.L.W.N. M.H.W.N. M.H.W.S.

L.W.Hts.m.

ULLAPOOL

MEAN SPRING
AND NEAP CURVES

MEAN RANGES
Springs 4.5m
Neaps 1.8m

Springs occur 1 day
after
New and Full Moon

L.W -6ʰ -5ʰ -4ʰ -3ʰ -2ʰ -1ʰ H.W +1ʰ +2ʰ +3ʰ +4ʰ +5ʰ L.W

1641 1741 1841 1941 2041 2141

TIME 1905

Find the time and height of HW and LW at a Secondary Port

EXAMPLE:

Find the time and height of the afternoon HW and LW at ST MARY's (Isles of Scilly) on 14th July (BST)

Note: *The data used in this example do not refer to the year of these tables.*

From tables	JULY	
PLYMOUTH (DEVONPORT)	**14** 0309 0927 1532 SA 2149	1.0 5.3 1.1 5.0

From tables

Location	Lat	Long	High Water		Low Water		MHWS	MHWN	MLWN	MLWS
DEVONPORT *Standard port*	50°22'N	4°11'W	0000 and 1200	0600 and 1800	0000 and 1200	0600 and 1800	5.5	4.4	2.2	0.8
St Mary's, *Scilly*	49° 55'N	6°19'W	−0035	−0100	−0040	−0025	+0.2	−0.1	−0.2	−0.1

TIDES

TIDAL PREDICTION FORM (NP 204)

STANDARD PORT _Devonport_   TIME/HEIGHT REQUIRED _pm_

SECONDARY PORT _St Mary's_   DATE _14 July_ TIME ZONE _B.S.T_

	TIME		HEIGHT		
	HW	LW	HW	LW	RANGE
STANDARD PORT	1 2149	2 1532	3 5·0	4 1·1	5 3·9
Seasonal change	Standard Ports -		6 0·0	6 0·0	
DIFFERENCES	7* -0044	8 -0032	9 0·1	10 -0·1	
Seasonal change *	Secondary Ports +		11 0·0	11 0·0	
SECONDARY PORT	12 2105	13 1500	14 5·1	15 1·0	
Duration	16 0605		LW 1500 UT = 1600 BST		
			HW 2105 UT = 2205 BST		

* The seasonal changes are generally less than – 0.1m and for most purposes can be ignored. See Admiraly Tide Tables Vol 1. for details

CLEARANCE BELOW BRIDGES AND OVERHEAD POWER LINES

Vertical clearance heights are above the level of HAT (Highest Astronomical Tide) instead of MHWS as in the past. HAT is always a higher level than MHWS, as shown in the diagram on the back cover flap. It helps to draw such a diagram and insert the relevant dimensions when calculating overhead clearances. The Height of HAT above Chart Datum is stated at the foot of each page of Standard port tide tables. New editions of Admiralty charts are referenced to HAT; earlier editions to MHWS. Check the title block under **Height**s.

INTERMEDIATE TIMES/HEIGHTS (SECONDARY PORT)

These are the same as the appropriate calculations for a Standard Port except that the Standard Curve diagram for the Standard Port must be entered with HW and LW heights and times for the Secondary Port obtained on Form N.P. 204. When interpolating between the Spring and Neap curves the Range at the Standard Port must be used.

EXAMPLE:
Find the height of the tide at PADSTOW at 1100 on 28th February. Find the time at which the morning tide at PADSTOW falls to 4.9m on 28th February.

Note: The data in these examples do not refer to the year of these tables.

From tables	FEBRUARY	
MILFORD HAVEN		
	28 0315	1.1
	0922	6.6
	1538	1.3
	TU 2145	6.3

From tables

Location	Lat	Long	High Water		Low Water		MHWS	MHWN	MLWN	MLWS
			0100 and 1300	0700 and 1900	0100 and 1300	0700 and 1900				
MILFORD HAVEN *Standard port*	51°42′N	5°03′W					7.0	5.2	2.5	0.7
River Camel										
Padstow	50°33′N	4°56′W	−0055	−0050	−0040	−0050	+0.3	+0.4	+0.1	+0.1
Wadebridge	50°31′N	4°50′W	−0052	−0052	+0235	+0245	−3.8	−3.8	−2.5	−0.4

TIDAL PREDICTION FORM (NP 204)

STANDARD PORT ___Milford Haven___ TIME/HEIGHT REQUIRED ___1100 : 4.9___

SECONDARY PORT ___Padstow___ DATE ___28 Feb___ TIME ZONE ___UT___

	TIME		HEIGHT		
STANDARD PORT	HW	LW	HW	LW	RANGE
	¹ 0922	² 1538	³ 6·6	⁴ 1·3	⁵ 5·3
Seasonal change	Standard Ports +		⁶ 0·0	⁶ 0·0	
DIFFERENCES	⁷* −0052	⁸ –	⁹ +0·3	¹⁰ +0·1	
Seasonal change *	Secondary Ports -		¹¹ 0·0	¹¹ 0·0	
SECONDARY PORT	¹² 0830	¹³ –	¹⁴ 6·9	¹⁵ 1·4	
Duration	¹⁶ –				

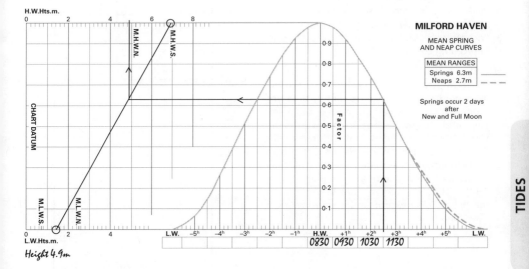

H.W.Hts.m.

CHART DATUM

M.H.W.N. M.H.W.S. M.L.W.N. M.L.W.S.

L.W.Hts.m.

Height 4.9m

MILFORD HAVEN

MEAN SPRING AND NEAP CURVES

MEAN RANGES
Springs 6.3m
Neaps 2.7m

Springs occur 2 days after New and Full Moon

Factor

L.W. −5ʰ −4ʰ −3ʰ −2ʰ −1ʰ H.W. +1ʰ +2ʰ +3ʰ +4ʰ +5ʰ L.W.

| 0830 | 0930 | 1030 | 1130 |

TIDES

SPECIAL INSTRUCTIONS FOR PLACES BETWEEN BOURNEMOUTH AND SELSEY BILL

• Owing to the rapid change of tidal characteristics and distortion of the tidal curve in this area, curves are shown for individual ports. It is a characteristic of the tide here that Low Water is more sharply defined than High Water and these curves have therefore been drawn with their times relative to that of Low Water.

• Apart from differences caused by referring the times to Low Water the procedure for obtaining intermediate heights at places whose curves are shown is identical to that used for normal Secondary Ports.

• The **height** differences for ports between Bournemouth and Yarmouth always refer to the higher High Water, i.e. that which is shown as reaching a factor of 1.0 on the curves. Note that the **time** differences, which are not required for this calculation, also refer to the higher High Water.

• The tide at ports between Bournemouth and Christchurch shows considerable change of shape and duration between Springs and Neaps and it is not practical to define the tide with only two curves. A third curve has therefore been drawn for the range at Portsmouth at which the two High Waters are equal at the port concerned – this range being marked on the body of the graph. Interpolation here should be between this 'critical' curve and either the Spring or Neap curve as appropriate.

Note that while the critical curve extends throughout the tidal cycle the Spring and Neap curves stop at the higher High Water. Thus for a range at Portsmouth of 3.5m the factor for 7 hours after LW at Bournemouth should be referred to the following Low Water, whereas had the range at Portsmouth been 2.5, it should be referred to the preceding Low Water.

NOTES

1. NEWPORT. Owing to the constriction of the River Medina, Newport requires slightly different treatment since the harbour dries out at 1.4m. The calculation should be performed using the Low Water Time and Height Differences for Cowes and the High Water Height Differences for Newport. Any calculated heights which fall below 1.4m should be treated as 1.4m

2. CHRISTCHURCH (Tuckton). Low Waters do not fall below 0.7m except under very low river flow conditions.

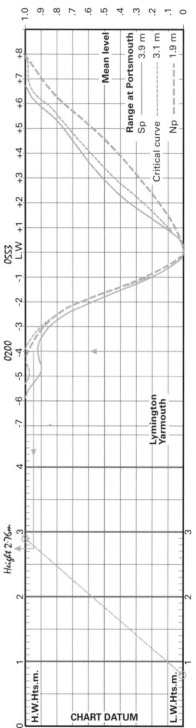

To find the Height of tide at a given time at any Secondary Port between Bournemouth and Selsey Bill

1. Complete top section of N.P. 204 (as below). Omit HW time column (Boxes 1,7,12)
2. On Standard Curve diagram (previous page), plot Secondary Port HW and LW heights and join by sloping line.
3. From the time required, using Secondary Port LW time, proceed vertically to curve, interpolating as necessary using Range at Portsmouth. Do NOT extrapolate.
4. Proceed horizontally to sloping line, thence vertically to Height Scale.
5. Read off height.

EXAMPLE:
Find the height of tide at LYMINGTON at 0200 UT on 18th November

From tables	NOVEMBER	
	0110	4.6
PORTSMOUTH	**18** 0613	1.1
	1318	4.6
	SA 1833	1.0

From tables Location	Lat	Long	High Water		Low Water		MHWS	MHWN	MLWN	MLWS
			0000	0600	0500	1100				
PORTSMOUTH	50°48′N	1°07′W	and	and	and	and	4.7	3.8	1.9	0.8
Standard port			1200	1800	1700	2300				
Lymington	50°46′N	1°32′W	−0110	+0005	−0020	−0020	−1.7	−1.2	−0.5	−0.1

STANDARD PORT ..... *Portsmouth* ..... TIME/HEIGHT REQUIRED 0200

SECONDARY PORT ..... *Lymington* ..... DATE *18 Nov* ..... TIME ZONE ..... UT

	TIME		HEIGHT		
	HW	LW	HW	LW	RANGE
STANDARD PORT	1 —	2 0613	3 4·6	4 1·1	5 3·5
Seasonal change	Standard Ports -		6 0·0	6 0·0	
DIFFERENCES	7* —	8 −0020	9 −1·7	10 −0·2	
Seasonal change *	Secondary Ports +		11 0·0	11 0·0	
SECONDARY PORT	12 —	13 0553	14 2·9	15 0·9	
Duration	16 —				

* The Seasonal changes are generally less than ± 0.1m and for most purposes can be ignored. See Admiralty Tide Tables Vol 1 for full details.

TIDAL CURVES -
BOURNEMOUTH TO FRESHWATER

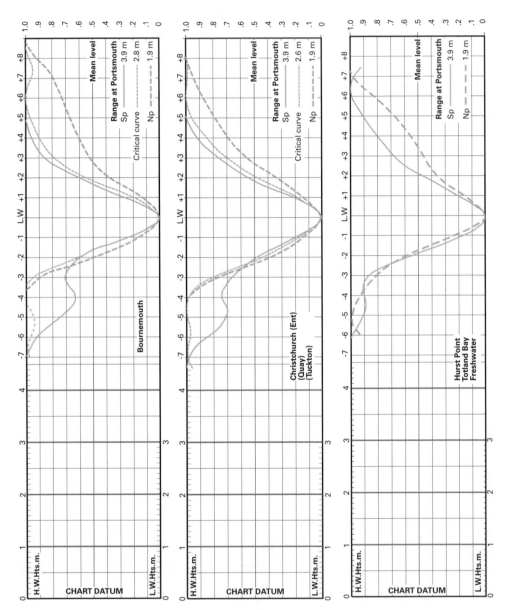

Note: The curves for Lymington and Yarmouth are on page 136, together with a worked example.

TIDAL CURVES -
BUCKLERS HARD TO SELSEY BILL

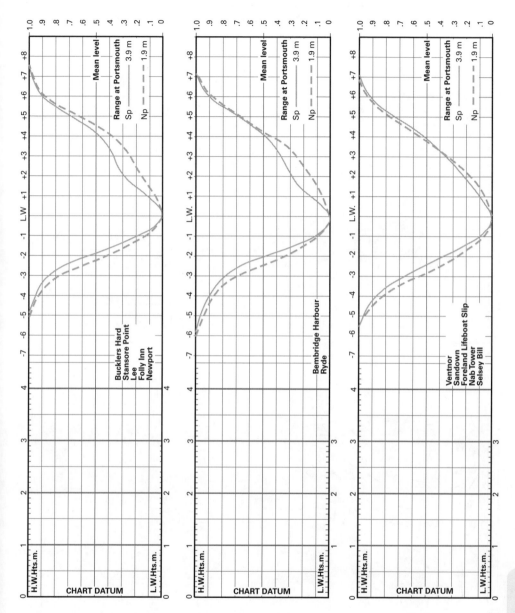

ENGLISH CHANNEL AND SOUTH BRITTANY

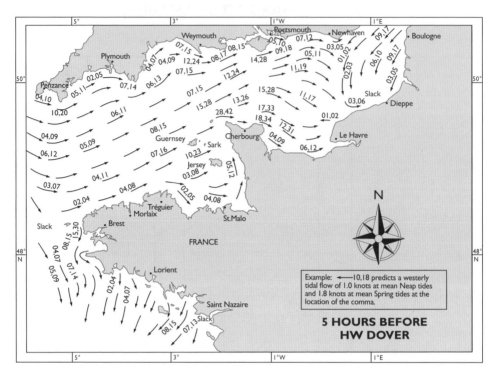

Example: ←—10,18 predicts a westerly tidal flow of 1.0 knots at mean Neap tides and 1.8 knots at mean Spring tides at the location of the comma.

5 HOURS BEFORE HW DOVER

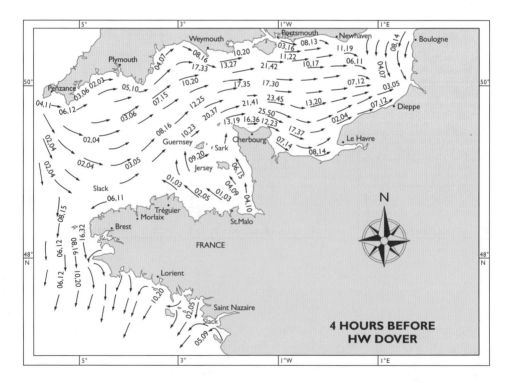

4 HOURS BEFORE HW DOVER

ENGLISH CHANNEL AND SOUTH BRITTANY

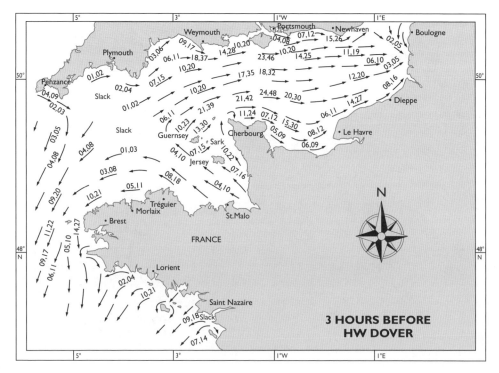

3 HOURS BEFORE HW DOVER

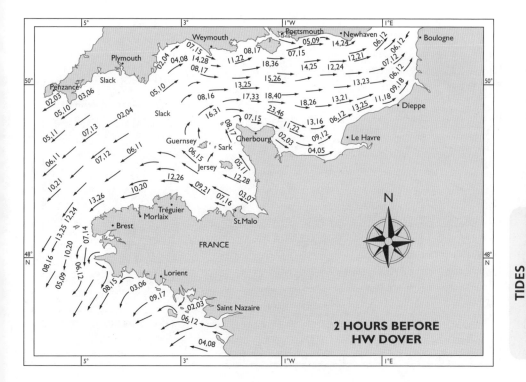

2 HOURS BEFORE HW DOVER

ENGLISH CHANNEL AND SOUTH BRITTANY

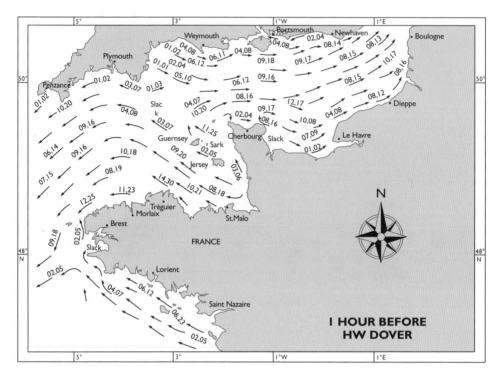

1 HOUR BEFORE HW DOVER

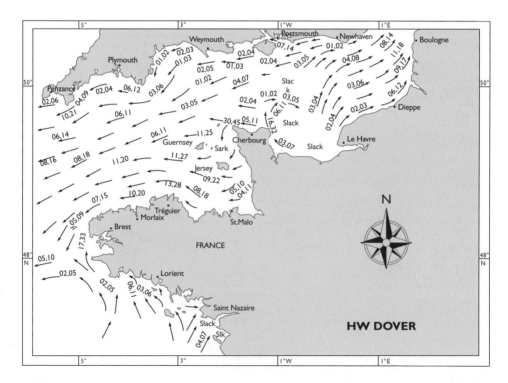

HW DOVER

ENGLISH CHANNEL AND SOUTH BRITTANY

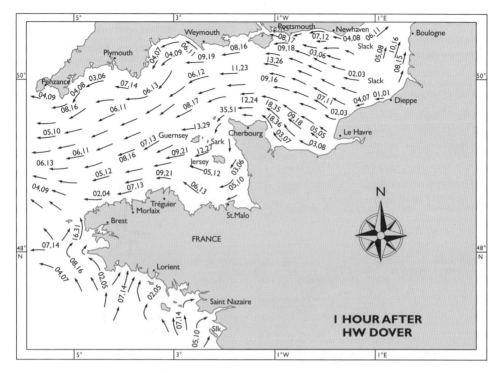

1 HOUR AFTER
HW DOVER

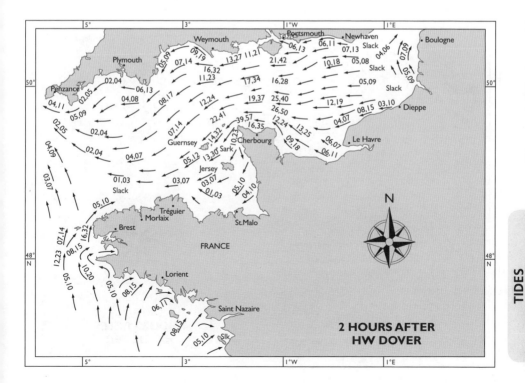

2 HOURS AFTER
HW DOVER

ENGLISH CHANNEL AND SOUTH BRITTANY

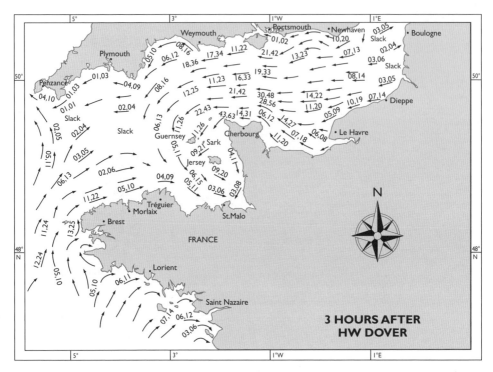

3 HOURS AFTER HW DOVER

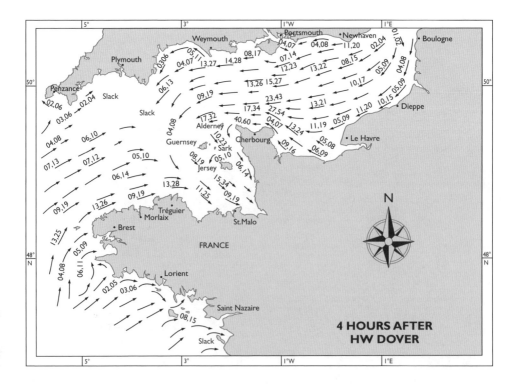

4 HOURS AFTER HW DOVER

ENGLISH CHANNEL AND SOUTH BRITTANY

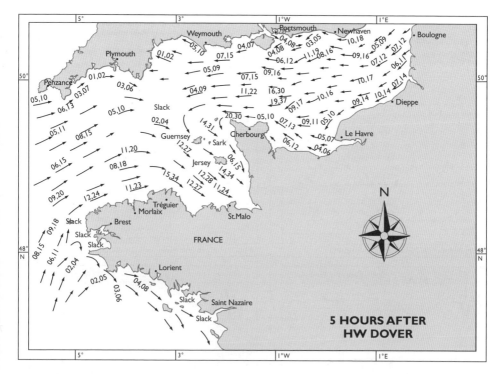

5 HOURS AFTER HW DOVER

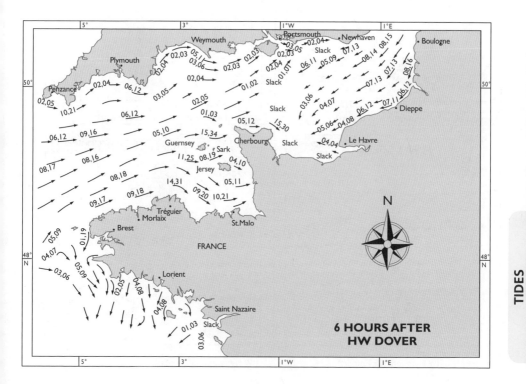

6 HOURS AFTER HW DOVER

PORTLAND

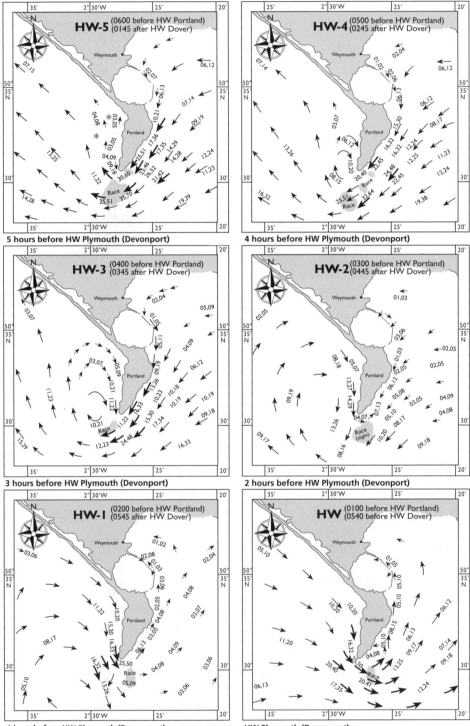

5 hours before HW Plymouth (Devonport)

4 hours before HW Plymouth (Devonport)

3 hours before HW Plymouth (Devonport)

2 hours before HW Plymouth (Devonport)

1 hour before HW Plymouth (Devonport)

HW Plymouth (Devonport)

PORTLAND

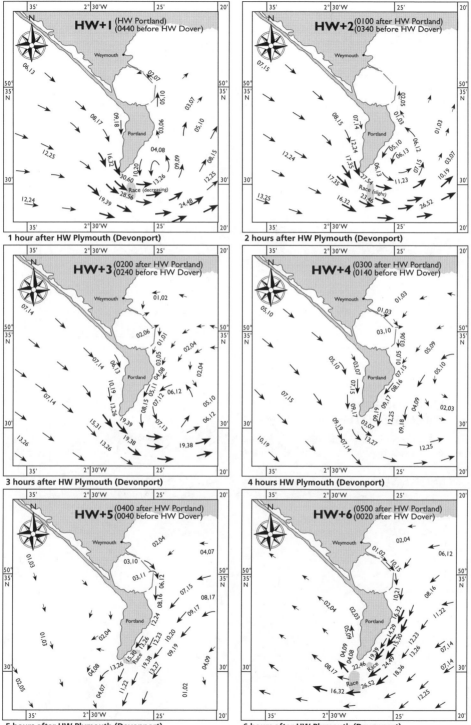

HW+1 (HW Portland)
(0440 before HW Dover)

1 hour after HW Plymouth (Devonport)

HW+2 (0100 after HW Portland)
(0340 before HW Dover)

2 hours after HW Plymouth (Devonport)

HW+3 (0200 after HW Portland)
(0240 before HW Dover)

3 hours after HW Plymouth (Devonport)

HW+4 (0300 after HW Portland)
(0140 before HW Dover)

4 hours HW Plymouth (Devonport)

HW+5 (0400 after HW Portland)
(0040 before HW Dover)

5 hours after HW Plymouth (Devonport)

HW+6 (0500 after HW Portland)
(0020 after HW Dover)

6 hours after HW Plymouth (Devonport)

TIDES

163

ISLE OF WIGHT

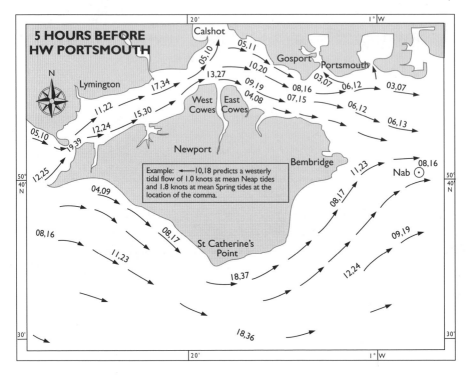

5 HOURS BEFORE HW PORTSMOUTH

Example: ←—10,18 predicts a westerly tidal flow of 1.0 knots at mean Neap tides and 1.8 knots at mean Spring tides at the location of the comma.

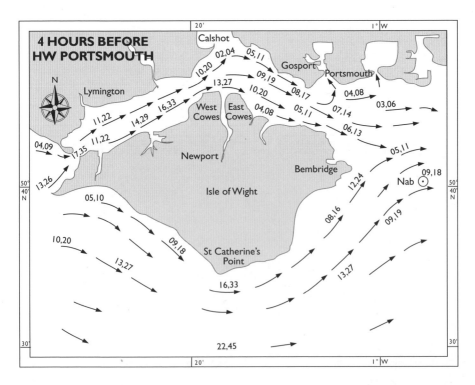

4 HOURS BEFORE HW PORTSMOUTH

ISLE OF WIGHT

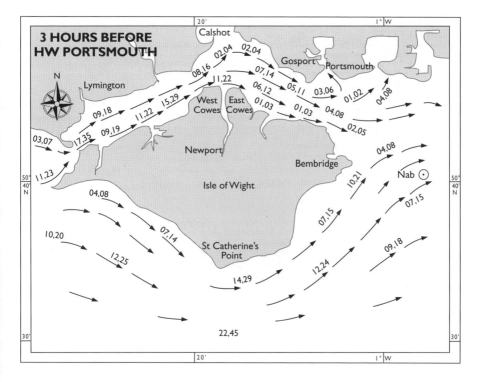

3 HOURS BEFORE HW PORTSMOUTH

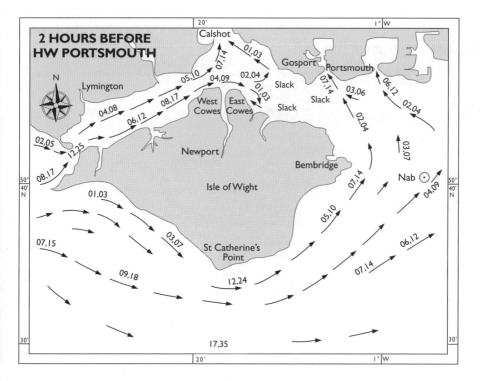

2 HOURS BEFORE HW PORTSMOUTH

ISLE OF WIGHT

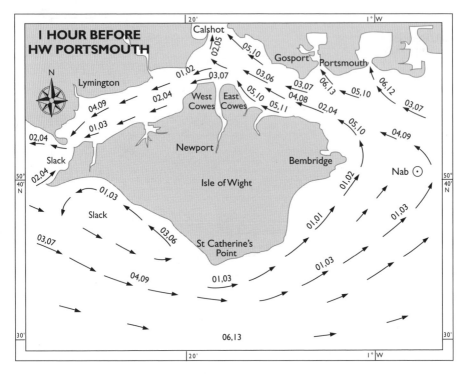

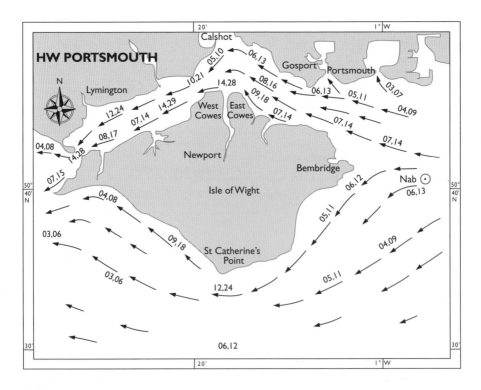

ISLE OF WIGHT

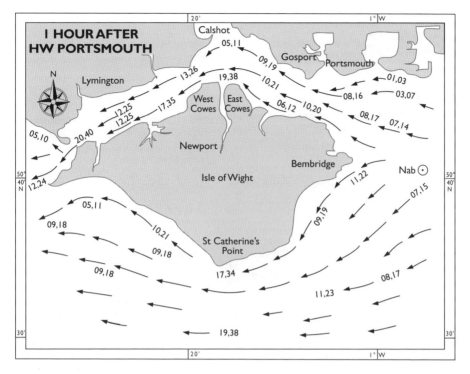

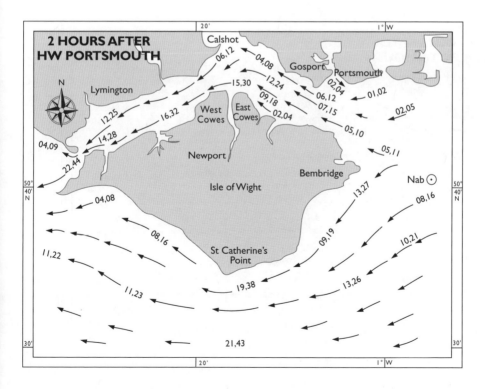

ISLE OF WIGHT

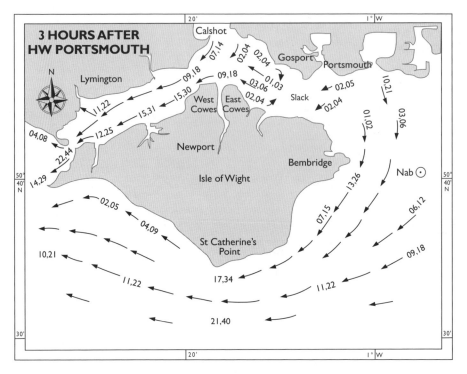

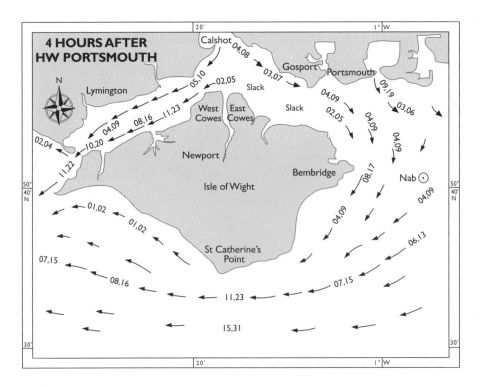

ISLE OF WIGHT

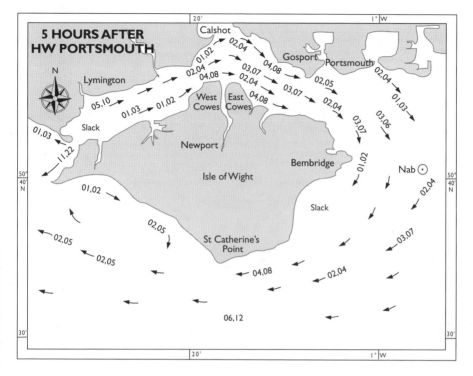

5 HOURS AFTER HW PORTSMOUTH

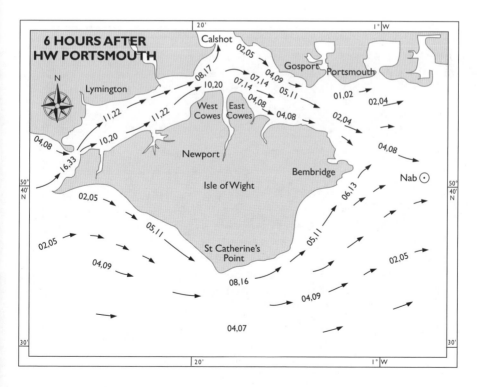

6 HOURS AFTER HW PORTSMOUTH

CHANNEL ISLANDS

Example: ←—10,18 predicts a westerly tidal flow of 1.0 knots at mean Neap tides and 1.8 knots at mean Spring tides at the location of the comma.

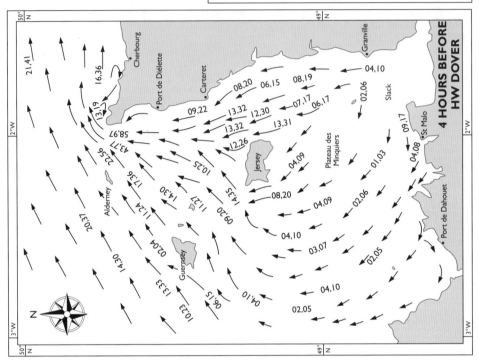

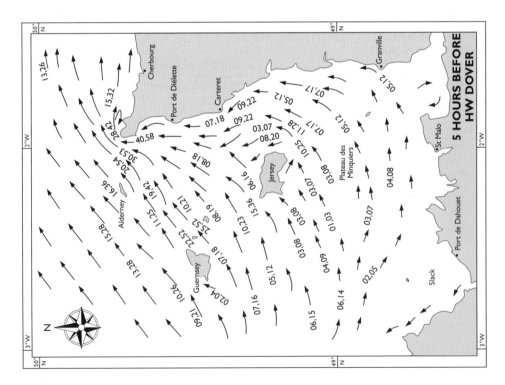

CHANNEL ISLANDS

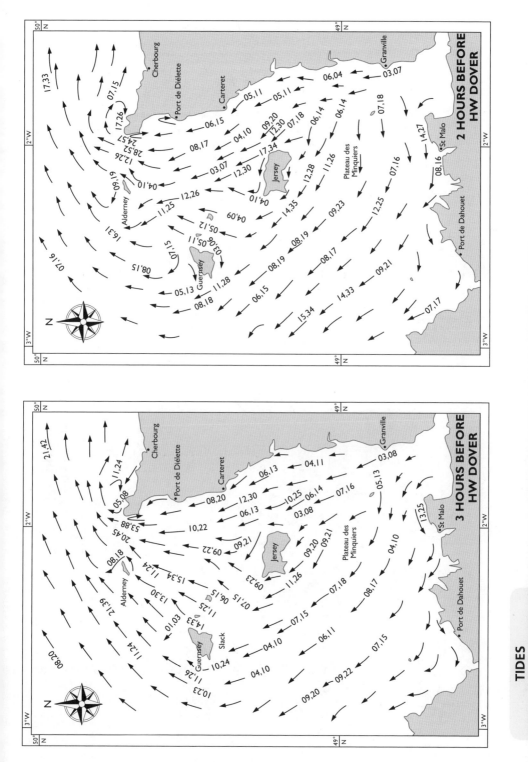

TIDES

171

CHANNEL ISLANDS

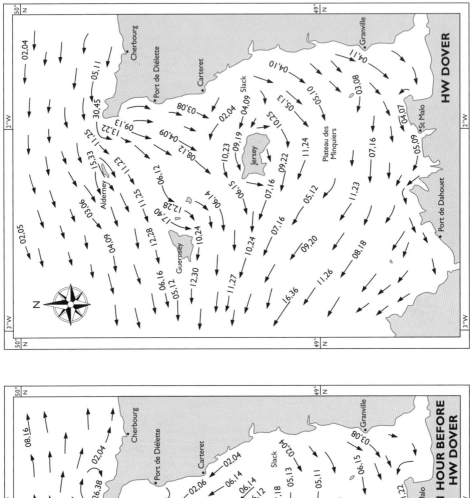

HW DOVER

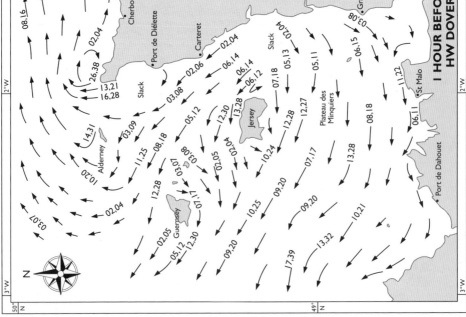

1 HOUR BEFORE HW DOVER

CHANNEL ISLANDS

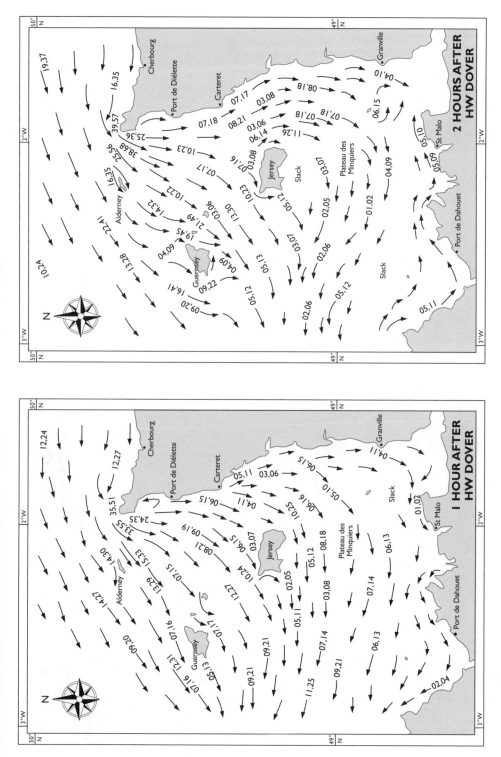

CHANNEL ISLANDS

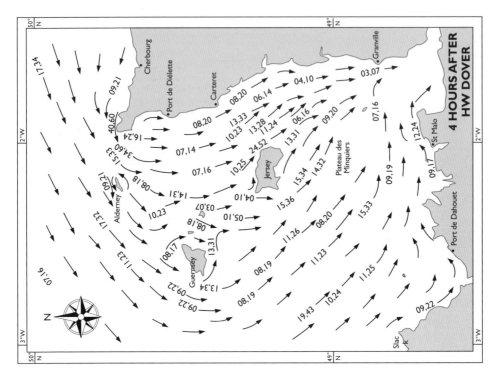

4 HOURS AFTER HW DOVER

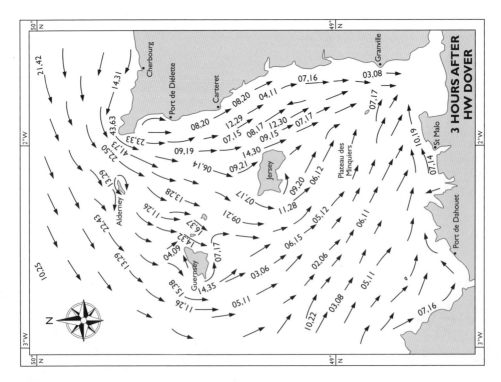

3 HOURS AFTER HW DOVER

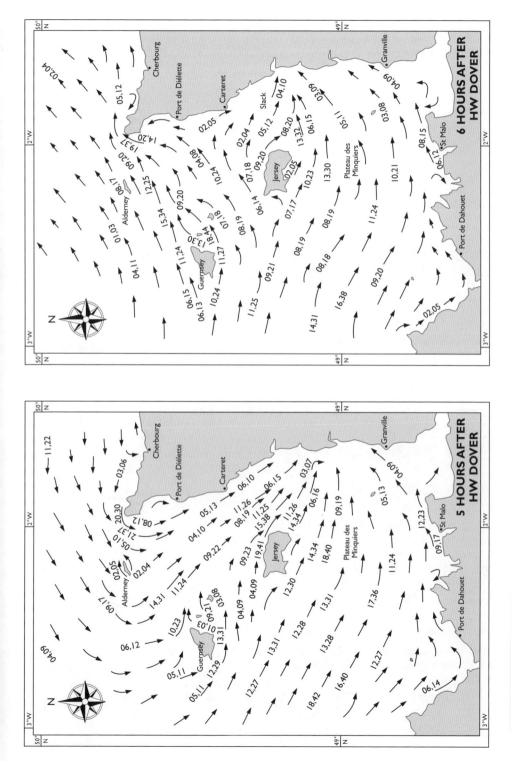

NORTH SEA

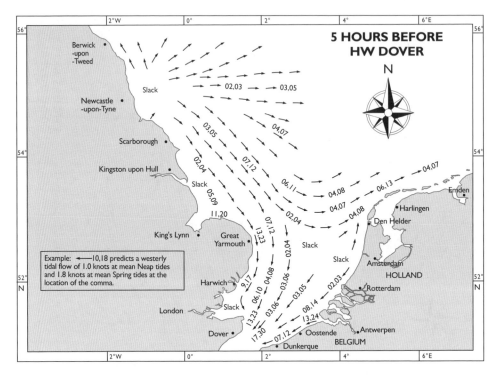

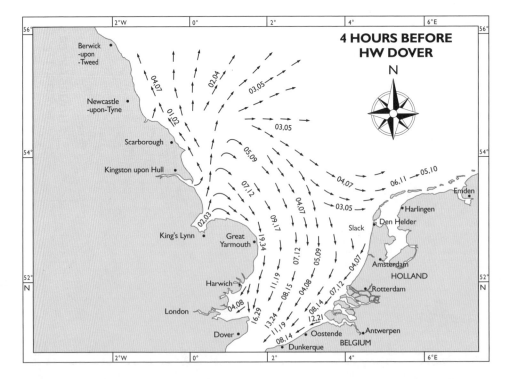

NORTH SEA

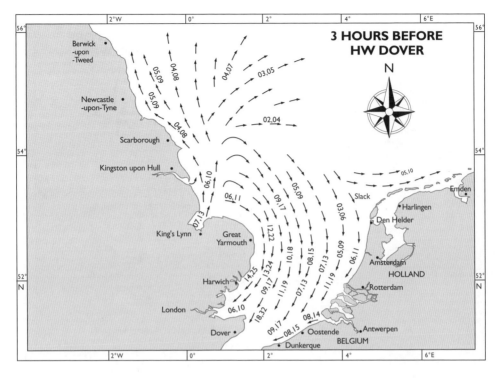

3 HOURS BEFORE HW DOVER

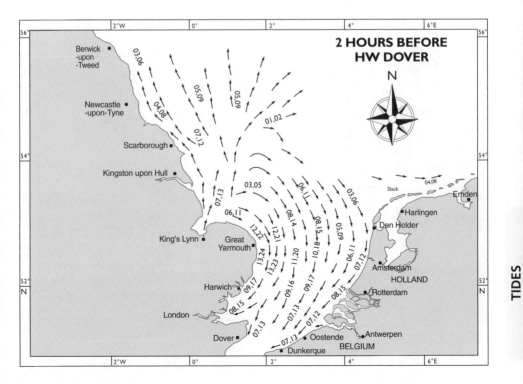

2 HOURS BEFORE HW DOVER

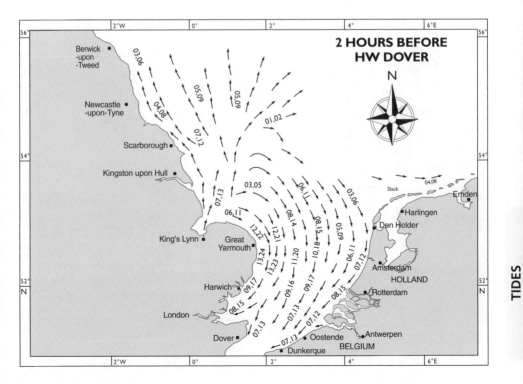

NORTH SEA

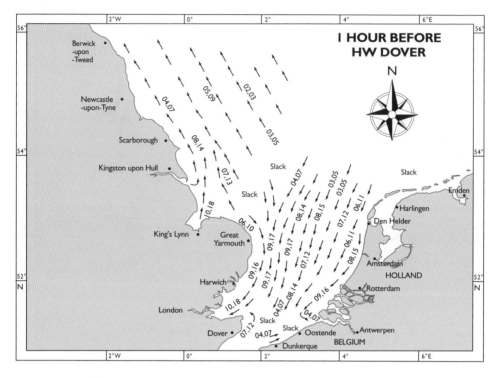

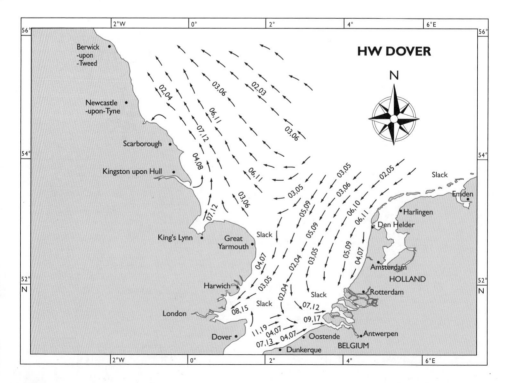

NORTH SEA

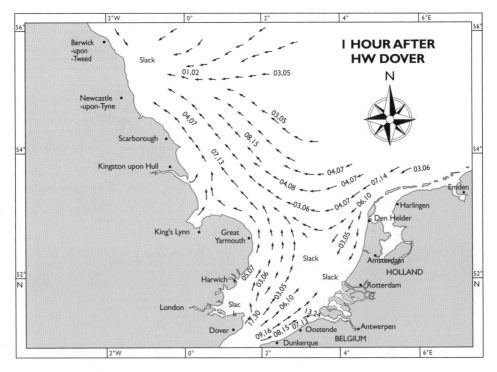

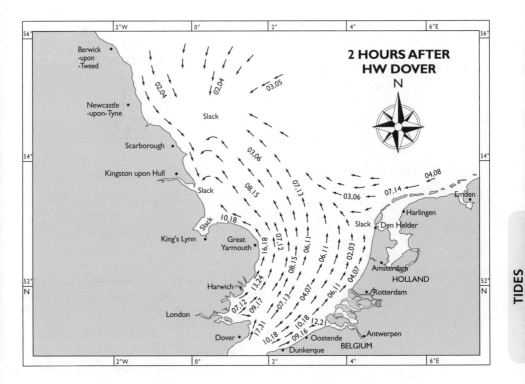

NORTH SEA

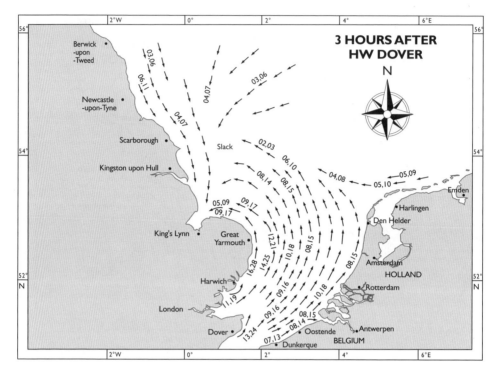

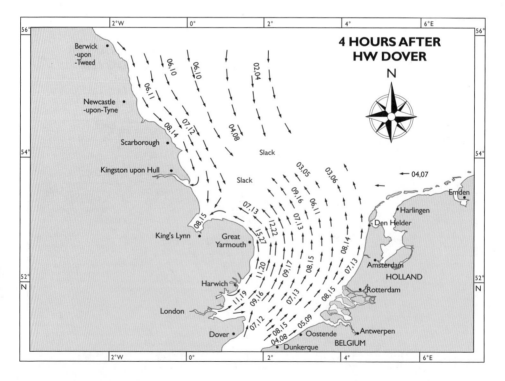

NORTH SEA

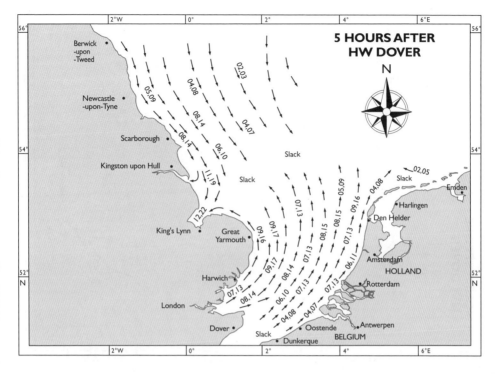

5 HOURS AFTER HW DOVER

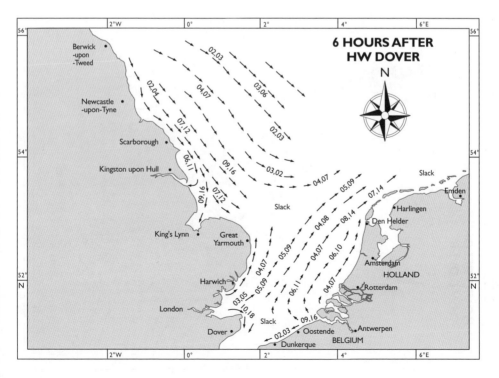

6 HOURS AFTER HW DOVER

SCOTLAND

Example: ◄——10,18 predicts a westerly tidal flow of 1.0 knots at mean
Neap tides and 1.8 knots at mean Spring tides at the location of the comma.

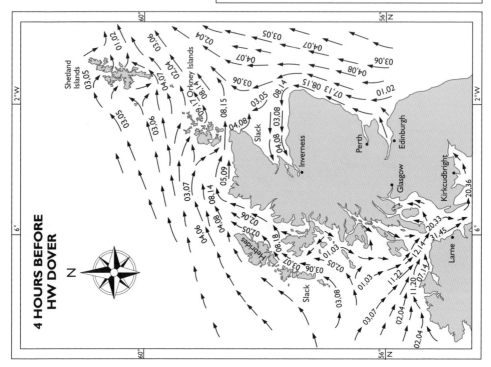

4 HOURS BEFORE HW DOVER

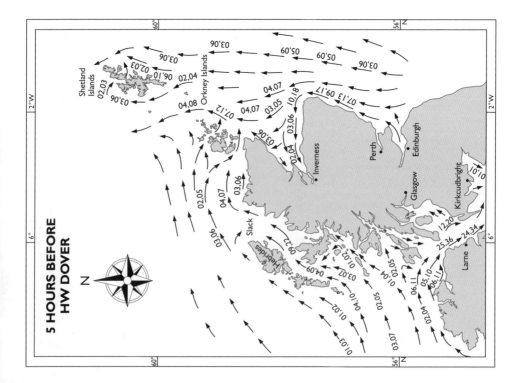

5 HOURS BEFORE HW DOVER

SCOTLAND

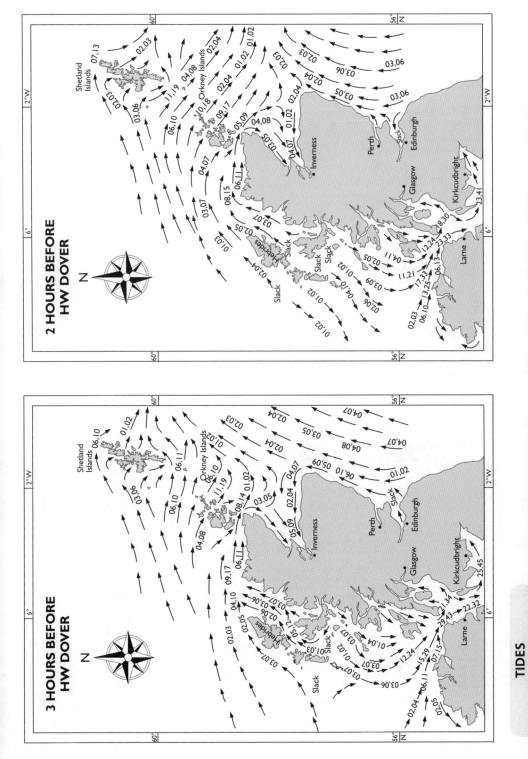

SCOTLAND

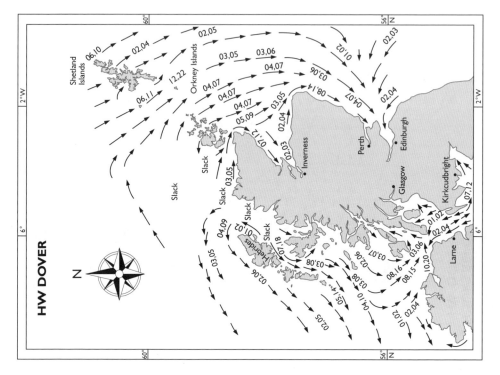

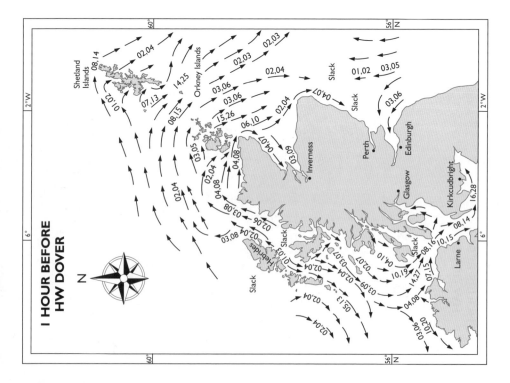

SCOTLAND

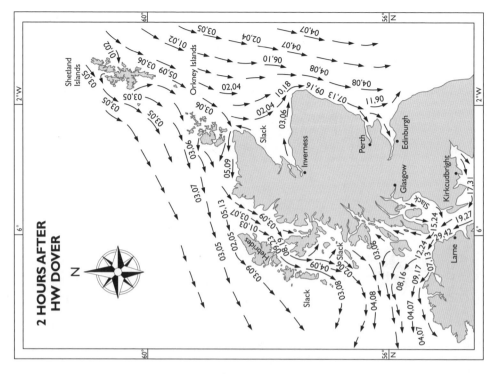

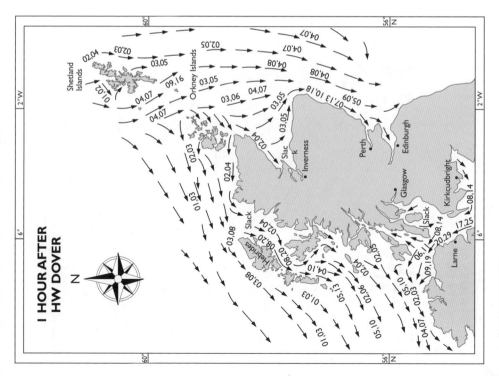

SCOTLAND

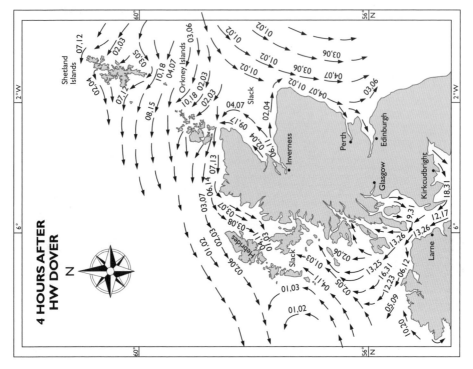

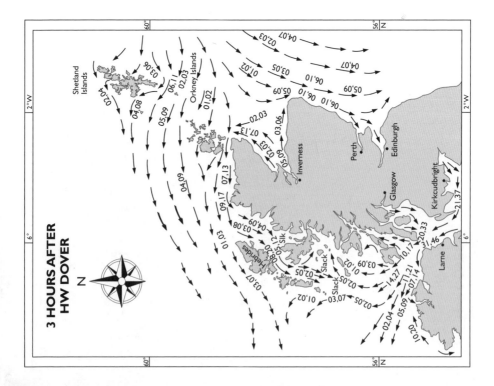

SCOTLAND

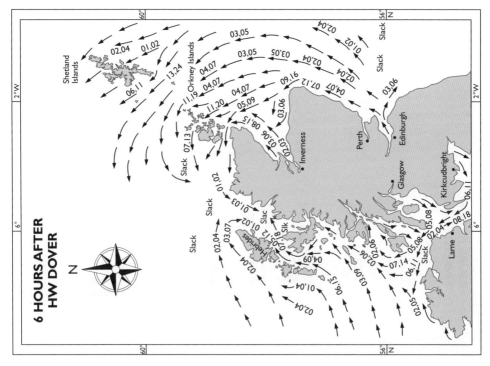

6 HOURS AFTER HW DOVER

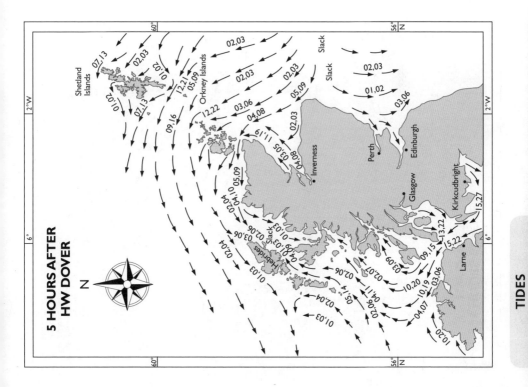

5 HOURS AFTER HW DOVER

WEST UK AND IRELAND

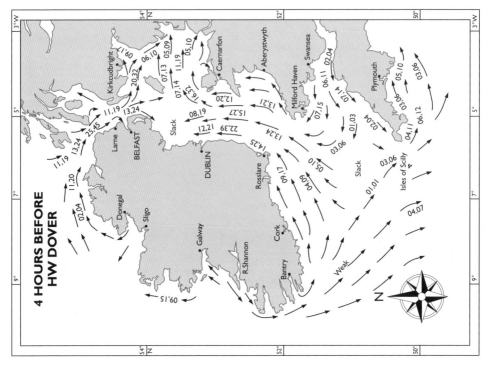

4 HOURS BEFORE HW DOVER

Kirkcudbright · Caernarfon · Aberystwyth · Swansea · Milford Haven · Plymouth
Larne · BELFAST · Slack · Isles of Scilly
Donegal · Sligo · DUBLIN · Rosslare · Slack
Galway · R.Shannon · Cork · Bantry · Weak

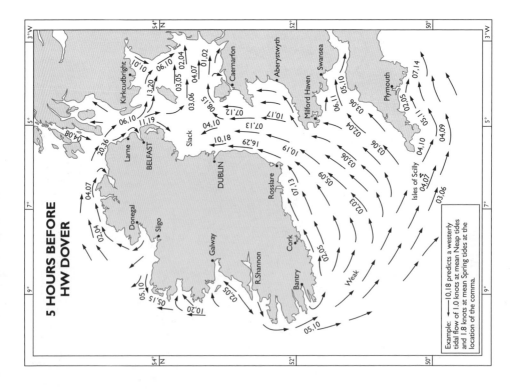

5 HOURS BEFORE HW DOVER

Kirkcudbright · Caernarfon · Aberystwyth · Swansea · Milford Haven · Plymouth
Larne · BELFAST · Slack · Isles of Scilly
Donegal · Sligo · DUBLIN · Rosslare
Galway · R.Shannon · Cork · Bantry · Weak

Example: ——— 10,18 predicts a westerly
tidal flow of 1.0 knots at mean Neap tides
and 1.8 knots at mean Spring tides at the
location of the comma.

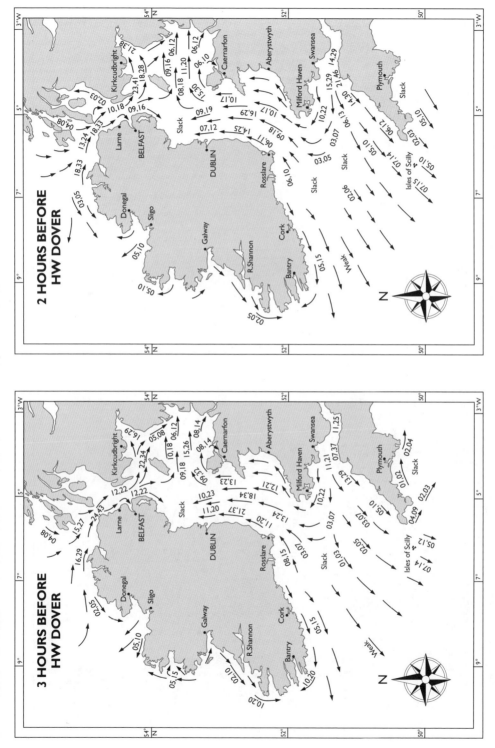

2 HOURS BEFORE HW DOVER

3 HOURS BEFORE HW DOVER

WEST UK AND IRELAND

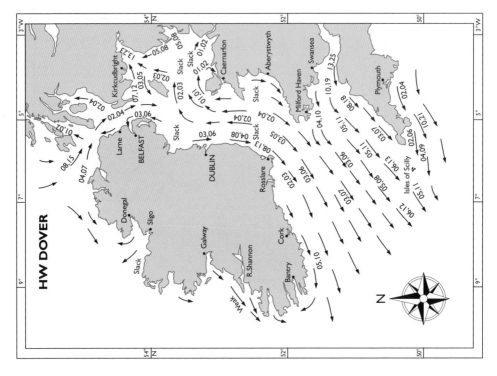

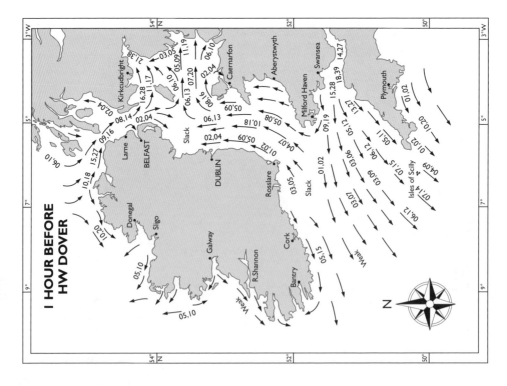

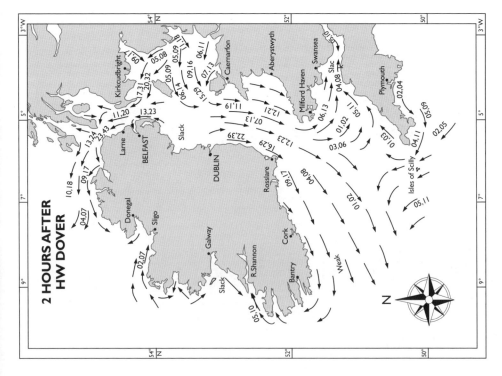

2 HOURS AFTER HW DOVER

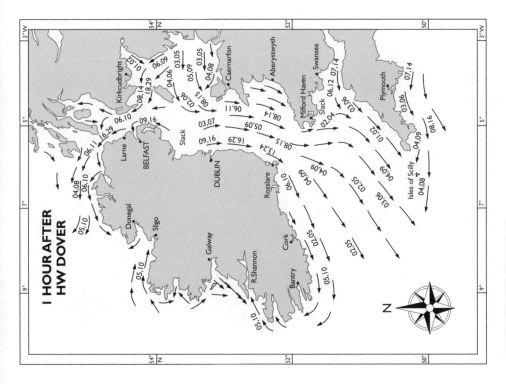

1 HOUR AFTER HW DOVER

WEST UK AND IRELAND

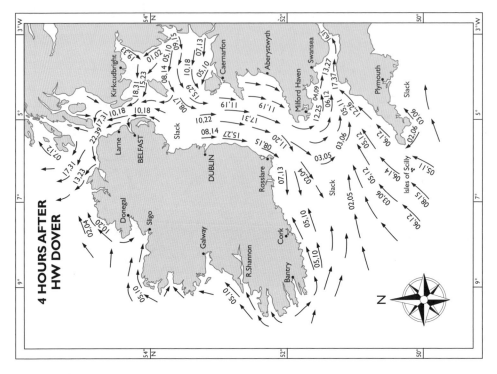

4 HOURS AFTER HW DOVER

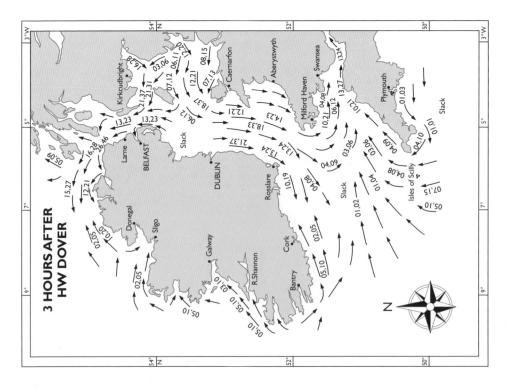

3 HOURS AFTER HW DOVER

WEST UK AND IRELAND

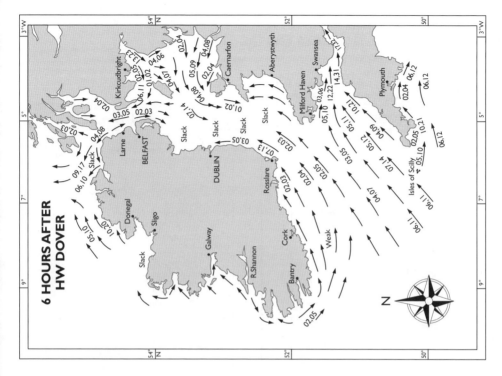

6 HOURS AFTER HW DOVER

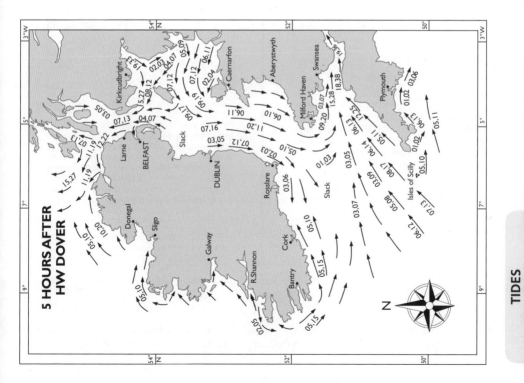

5 HOURS AFTER HW DOVER

TIDAL GATES – SOUTHERN ENGLAND

A guide to the time of tide turn at tidal gates, the approximate maximum strength of the tidal flow (spring rates shown - neaps are approximately 60% of these), and the position and timing of races, counter tides, etc.

LAND'S END (AC 1148)

Tidal streams set hard north/south round Land's End, and east/west around Gwennap and Pendeen. But the inshore currents run counter to the tidal streams. By staying close inshore, this tidal gate favours a N-bound passage. With careful timing nearly 9½hrs of fair tide can be carried, from HWD–3 to HWD+5. The chartlets, referenced to HW Dover, depict both tidal streams and inshore currents.

FLOOD	EBB
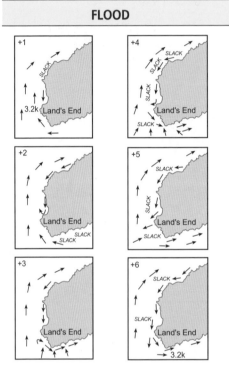	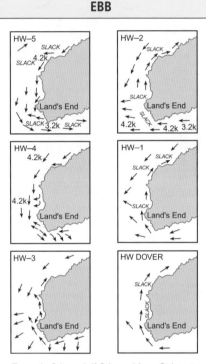

Example N-bound: At HWD+1 the N-going flood starts off Gwennap and does not turn NE along the N Cornish coast until HWD+3. But as early as HWD–3 an inshore current is beginning to set north. Utilise this by arriving off Runnel Stone at HWD–2 and then keeping within ¼M of the shore. If abeam the Brisons at HWD, the tide and current should serve for the next 6 or 7 hours to make good St Ives, or even Newquay and Padstow.

Example S-bound: If S-bound from St Ives to Newlyn, aim to reach the Runnel Stone by HWD+5, ie with 2hrs of E-going tide in hand for the remaining 9M to Newlyn. To achieve this 20M passage, leave St Ives 5 hours earlier, ie at HWD. Buck a foul tide for the first 3 hours, then use the S-going inshore current, keeping as close inshore as is prudent, only moving seaward to clear the Wra and the Brisons. This timing would also suit a passage from S Wales or the Bristol Channel, going inshore of Longships if conditions allow.

From Ireland, ie Cork or further W, the inshore passage would not benefit. But aim to be off the Runnel Stone at HWD+5 if bound for Newlyn; or at HWD+3 if bound for Helford/Falmouth, with the W-going stream slackening and 5hrs of fair tide to cover the remaining 20M past the Lizard.

With acknowledgements to the Royal Cruising Club Pilotage Foundation for their kind permission to use the tide stream chartlets and text written by Hugh Davies, as first published in Yachting Monthly *magazine.*

TIDAL GATES – SOUTHERN ENGLAND

A guide to the time of tide turn at tidal gates, the approximate maximum strength of the tidal flow (spring rates shown - neaps are approximately 60% of these), and the position and timing of races, counter tides, etc.

FLOOD	EBB

THE LIZARD (AC 777, 2345)

Drying rocks lie approx 5 cables S of the Lizard lt ho and extend westwards. 49°57'N is about as far N as yachts may safely pass inshore of the Race, which extends 2-3M to seaward of these rocks. Race conditions may also exist SE of the Lizard with short, heavy seas in westerlies. If passing S of the Race, route via 49°55'N 05°13'W to clear the worst of the Race.

Inshore the E-going Channel flood, 2kn max @ springs, begins at HW Dover +0145; and outside the Race at approx HWD +0300.	Inshore the W-going Channel ebb, 3kn max @ springs, begins at HW Dover –0345; and outside the Race at HWD –0240.

START POINT (AC 1634)

Start Pt, and to a lesser extent Prawle Pt (3.3M WSW), can be slow to round when W-bound with a fair tide against a W'ly wind raising a bad sea. Drying rocks extend 3 cables SSE of the lt ho and a Race may extend up to 1.7M ESE and 1.0M S of the lt ho. It is safe to pass between the Race and the rocks, but in bad weather wiser to go outside the Race. The Skerries Bank (least depth 2.1m) lies 8 cables NE of Start Pt. On both the flood and the ebb back eddies form between Start Pt and Hallsands, 1M NW.

The NE-going Channel flood, 3.1kn max @ springs, begins at HW Dover +0430.	The SW-going Channel ebb, 2.2kn max @ springs, begins at HW Dover –0140, but an hour earlier it is possible to round Start Pt close inshore using the back eddy.

PORTLAND (AC 2255)

Tidal streams off Portland Bill run very strongly. The notorious Portland Race is caused by the almost constant strong southerly flow down both sides of the Bill meeting the main E and W-going streams in the English Channel. The violence of the race is increased by the sudden decrease in depth on Portland Ledge. The tidal stream chartlets on Pages 158–159 show that the race shifts to the E on the flood, and to the W on the ebb. Even in calm weather the race can be dangerous for small craft; in heavy weather or with wind against tide the whole area should be given a wide berth. In such conditions, pass at least 3 miles S of the Bill and do not pass between Portland and The Shambles bank.

In settled weather, with winds <F4/5, but not at springs nor with wind against tide, passage may be made very close S of the Bill in the narrow stretch of relatively smooth water N of the race. Night passage should not be attempted due to numerous fishing floats which may be semi-submerged.

Seaward of the race the Channel flood sets east from HW Plymouth -1 to HW +5; the ebb sets west from HW Plymouth +5 to HW -1.

Inshore passage

E-bound across Lyme Bay timing is critical to be close inshore about 2M north of the Bill by HW Plymouth –2 to achieve passage around the Bill between HW Plymouth –2 to HW+1.	W-bound timing is easier if starting from Portland Hbr, Weymouth or Lulworth Cove. Aim to be close inshore about 2M north of the Bill at HW Plymouth +4, and make the passage between HW Plymouth +5 and HW–5.

When using the inshore passage be particularly wary of being set S into the race itself.

ST ALBAN'S HEAD (AC 2610)

A sometimes vicious Race forms over St Alban's Ledge, a rocky dorsal ridge (least depth 8.5m) which extends approx 4M SW from St Alban's Head. Three yellow naval target buoys (DZ A, B and C) straddle the middle and outer sections, but are only occasionally used. In settled weather and at neaps the Race can be barely perceptible in which case it can be crossed with impunity. Avoid it either by keeping to seaward via 50°31'.40N 02°07'.80W; or by using the narrow inshore passage at the foot of St Alban's Head.

Based on a position 1M S of St Alban's Head, the tidal stream windows are:

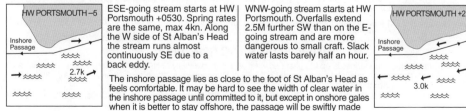

ESE-going stream starts at HW Portsmouth +0530. Spring rates are the same, max 4kn. Along the W side of St Alban's Head the stream runs almost continuously SE due to a back eddy.	WNW-going stream starts at HW Portsmouth. Overfalls extend 2.5M further SW than on the E-going stream and are more dangerous to small craft. Slack water lasts barely half an hour.

The inshore passage lies as close to the foot of St Alban's Head as feels comfortable. It may be hard to see the width of clear water in the inshore passage until committed to it, but except in onshore gales when it is better to stay offshore, the passage will be swiftly made with only a few, if any, overfalls. The NCI station on the Head (☎ 01929 439220) may advise on conditions.

TIDES

TIDAL GATES – SOUTHERN ENGLAND

A guide to the time of tide turn at tidal gates, the approximate maximum strength of the tidal flow (spring rates shown - neaps are approximately 60% of these), and the position and timing of races, counter tides, etc.

FLOOD	EBB

THE NEEDLES CHANNEL (AC 2035)

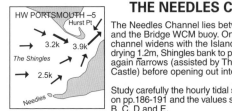

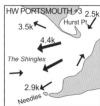

The Needles Channel lies between the SW Shingles PHM buoy and the Bridge WCM buoy. Once through this narrow section the channel widens with the Island shore to starboard and the long, drying 1.2m, Shingles bank to port. Abeam Hurst Castle the channel again narrows (assisted by The Trap, a shoal spit south of Hurst Castle) before opening out into the west Solent.

Study carefully the hourly tidal stream chartlets for the Isle of Wight on pp.186-191 and the values shown on AC 2035 at tidal diamonds B, C, D and E.

The ENE-going flood runs from HW Portsmouth +5 until HW P −1½, at springs reaching 3.1kn at The Bridge and 3.9kn at Hurst.	The WSW-going ebb runs from HW P −1 until HW P +4½, reaching 4.4kn at Hurst and 3.4kn at The Bridge, both spring rates. The ebb sets strongly WSW across the Shingles which with adequate rise is routinely crossed by racing yachts; but cruisers should stay clear even in calm conditions when any swell causes the sea to break heavily.

Prevailing W/SW winds, even if only F4, against the ebb raise dangerous breaking seas in the Needles Channel and at The Bridge, a shallow ridge extending 9 cables west from the Needles light. Worst conditions are often found just after LW slack. In such conditions it is safer to go via the North Channel to Hurst. In W/SW gales avoid the Needles altogether by sheltering at Poole or going east-about via Nab Tower.

ON PASSAGE UP CHANNEL

The following 3 tidal gates (Looe Channel, Beachy Head and Dungeness) are components in the tidal conveyor belt which, if stepped onto at the outset, can enable a fastish yacht to carry a fair tide for 88M from Selsey Bill to Dover. Go through the Looe at slackish water, HW Portsmouth +4½ (HW Dover +5). Based on a mean SOG of 7 knots, Beachy Head will be passed at HW D −1, Dungeness at HW D +3 and Dover at HW +5½, only bucking the first of the ebb in the last hour. A faster boat could make Ramsgate. The down-Channel passage is less rewarding and many yachts will pause at Brighton.

LOOE CHANNEL (AC 2045, 1652)

This channel is little shorter than the detour south of the Owers, but is much used by yachts on passage from/to points east of the Solent. Although adequately lit, it is best not attempted at night due to many lobster floats; nor in onshore gales as searoom is limited by extensive shoals on which the sea breaks.

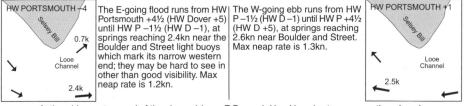

The E-going flood runs from HW Portsmouth +4½ (HW Dover +5) until HW P −1½ (HW D −1), at springs reaching 2.4kn near the Boulder and Street light buoys which mark its narrow western end; they may be hard to see in other than good visibility. Max neap rate is 1.2kn.	The W-going ebb runs from HW P −1½ (HW D −1) until HW P +4½ (HW D +5), at springs reaching 2.6kn near Boulder and Street. Max neap rate is 1.3kn.

At the wider eastern end of the channel (near E Borough Head buoy) rates are greatly reduced.

BEACHY HEAD (AC 1652, 536)

Stay at least 5 cables to seaward of the towering chalk cliffs to avoid isolated boulders and rocky, part-drying ridges such as Head Ledge. The lt ho stands on a drying rock ledge. Close inshore many fishing floats are a trap for the unwary. In bad weather stay 2M offshore to avoid overfalls caused by a ridge of uneven ground which extends 1M SSE from Beachy Head.

2M south of Beachy Head the E-going flood starts at HW Dover +0530, max spring rate 2.6kn.	The W-going ebb starts at HW Dover +0030, max spring rate 2.0kn.

Between 5M and 7M east of Beachy Head avoid breakers and eddies caused by the Horse of Willingdon, Royal Sovereign and other shoals.

DUNGENESS (AC 536, 1892)

Tidal stream atlases: Dungeness is on the east and west edges respectively of NP 250 (English Channel) and NP 233 (Dover Strait). The nearest tidal stream diamond (2.2M SE of Dungeness) is 'H' on AC 536 and 'B' on AC 1892; their positions and values are the same.

The NE-going flood starts at HW Dover −0100, max spring rate 1.9kn.	The SW-going ebb starts at HW Dover +0430, max spring rate 2.1kn.

TIDAL GATES – NORTH EAST SCOTLAND

A guide to the time of tide turn at tidal gates, and in straits and estuaries, showing the approximate strength of the tidal flow (spring rates shown - neaps are approximately 60% of these), and the position and timing of races, counter tides etc.

FLOOD	EBB

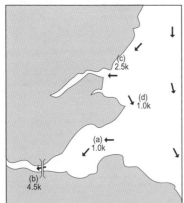 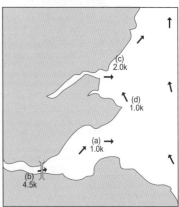

FIRTHS of FORTH (AC 175) & TAY (AC 1481)

Tidal streams are quite weak in the outer part of the Firth, increasing as the narrows at islands and the bridges are approached.

Apart from the stream of the Tay, which attains 5 knots in most places, the coastwise tidal streams between Fife Ness and Arbroath are weak.

(a) Dover –0225 to Dover +0330
(b) Dover –0200 to Dover +0400
(c) Dover –0210 to Dover +0420
(d) Dover –0110 to Dover +0520

(a) Dover +0330 to Dover –0225
(b) Dover +0400 to Dover –0200
(c) Dover +0420 to Dover –0210
(d) Dover +0520 to Dover –0110

PASSAGES FROM FORTH & TAY

Northbound. Leave before HW (Dover +0400) to be at N Carr at Dover +0600. Bound from Forth to Tay aim to arrive at Abertay By at LW slack (Dover –0200).

Southbound. Leave before LW (Dover -0200) to be at Bass Rk at HW Dover. Similar timings if bound from Tay to Forth, leave late in ebb to pick up early flood off St Andrews to N Carr and into Forth.

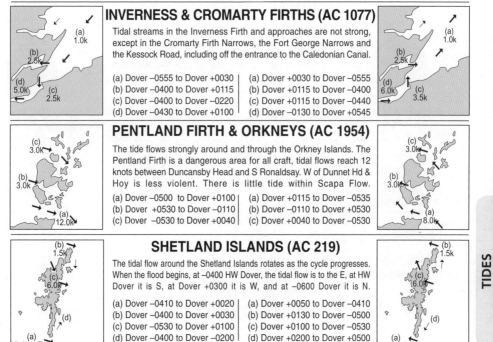

INVERNESS & CROMARTY FIRTHS (AC 1077)

Tidal streams in the Inverness Firth and approaches are not strong, except in the Cromarty Firth Narrows, the Fort George Narrows and the Kessock Road, including off the entrance to the Caledonian Canal.

(a) Dover –0555 to Dover +0030	(a) Dover +0030 to Dover –0555
(b) Dover –0400 to Dover +0115	(b) Dover +0115 to Dover –0400
(c) Dover –0400 to Dover –0220	(c) Dover +0115 to Dover –0440
(d) Dover –0430 to Dover +0100	(d) Dover –0130 to Dover +0545

PENTLAND FIRTH & ORKNEYS (AC 1954)

The tide flows strongly around and through the Orkney Islands. The Pentland Firth is a dangerous area for all craft, tidal flows reach 12 knots between Duncansby Head and S Ronaldsay. W of Dunnet Hd & Hoy is less violent. There is little tide within Scapa Flow.

(a) Dover –0500 to Dover +0100	(a) Dover +0115 to Dover –0535
(b) Dover +0530 to Dover –0110	(b) Dover –0110 to Dover +0530
(c) Dover –0530 to Dover +0040	(c) Dover +0040 to Dover –0530

SHETLAND ISLANDS (AC 219)

The tidal flow around the Shetland Islands rotates as the cycle progresses. When the flood begins, at –0400 HW Dover, the tidal flow is to the E, at HW Dover it is S, at Dover +0300 it is W, and at –0600 it is N.

(a) Dover –0410 to Dover +0020	(a) Dover +0050 to Dover –0410
(b) Dover –0400 to Dover +0030	(b) Dover +0130 to Dover –0500
(c) Dover –0530 to Dover +0100	(c) Dover +0100 to Dover –0530
(d) Dover –0400 to Dover –0200	(d) Dover +0200 to Dover +0500

TIDAL GATES – NORTH WEST SCOTLAND

A guide to the time of tide turn at tidal gates, the approximate maximum strength of the tidal flow (spring rates shown – neaps are approximately 60% of these), and the position and timing of races, counter tides, etc.

FLOOD	EBB

SOUND OF HARRIS (AC 2642)

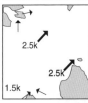

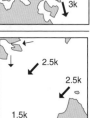

The behaviour of tidal streams in the Sd of Harris varies from day to night, springs to neaps, and winter to summer. The following data applies to daylight, in summer at spring tides in the Cope Channel. Further information can be sought in the Admiralty West of Scotland Pilot.
HW Dover - HW D +0200: SE stream.
HW D +0300 - HW D +0600: Incoming stream from both ends.
HW D –0600 - HW D –0500: NW stream.
HW D –0500 - HW Dover: Outgoing stream from both ends.
At neaps in summer the stream will run SE for most of the day.
Tide rates shown are the maxima likely to be encountered at any time.

THE LITTLE MINCH (AC 1795)

The N going stream on both shores begins at HW Dover +0430 (HW Ullapool -0345), with the strongest flow from mid channel to the Skye coast. There is a W going counter tide E of Vaternish Point.

The S going stream on both shores begins at HW Dover –0130 (HW Ullapool +0240), with the strongest flow from mid channel to the Skye coast. The E going stream in Sound of Scalpay runs at up to 2k.The E going flood and W going ebb in Sound of Scalpay run at up to 2k.

KYLE OF LOCHALSH & KYLERHEA (AC 2540)
NOTE: THESE STREAMS ARE SUBJECT TO VARIATION

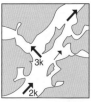

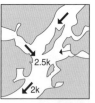

N going stream in Kyle Rhea begins HW Dover +0140 (HW Ullapool +0555) and runs for 6 hours. The E going stream in Kyle Akin begins (Sp) HW Dover +0350 (HW Ullapool –0415). (Nps) HW Dover –0415 (HW Ullapool).

S going stream in Kyle Rhea begins HW Dover -0415 (HW Ullapool) and runs for 6 hours. The W going stream in Kyle Akin begins (Sp) HW Dover –0015 (HW Ullapool +0400). (Nps) HW Dover +0140 (HW Ullapool +0555).

ARDNAMURCHAN POINT (AC 2171)

The N going stream off Ardnamurchan begins at HW Dover +0130 (HW Oban –0525). The E going stream in the Sound of Mull begins at HW Dover +0555 (HW Oban –0100).

The S going stream off Ardnamurchan begins at HW Dover –0430 (HW Oban +0100). The W going stream in the Sound of Mull begins at HW Dover –0130 (HW Oban +0400).

SOUND OF MULL – EAST (AC 2171)

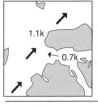

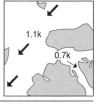

The N going stream in the Firth of Lorne begins at HW Dover –0100 (HW Oban +0430). The W going stream in the Sound of Mull begins at HW Dover +0105 (HW Oban –0550). The ingoing tides at Lochs Feochan, Etive and Creran begin at HW Dover +0300, –0100 & +0030.

The S going stream in the Firth of Lorne begins at HW Dover +0500 (HW Oban –0155). The E going stream in the Sound of Mull begins at HW Dover +0555 (HW Oban –0025). The outgoing tides at Lochs Feochan, Etive and Creran begin at HW Dover –0500, –0520 & –0505.

SOUND OF LUING & DORUS MOR (AC 2343)

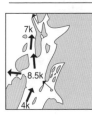

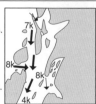

The N or W going stream begins as follows:
Dorus Mor: HW Dover –0200 (HW Oban +0330). Springs: 8 knots.
Corryvreckan: HW D –0120 (HW O +0410). Sp: 8.5 knots.
Cuan Sound: HW D –0110 (HW O +0420). Sp: 6 knots.
Sound of Jura: HW D –0130 (HW O +0400). Sp: 4 knots.
Sound of Luing: HW D –0100 (HW O +0430). Sp: 7 knots.
The S or E going stream begins as follows:
Dorus Mor: HW Dover +0440 (HW Oban –0215). Springs: 8 knots.
Corryvreckan: HW D +0445 (HW O –0210). Sp: 8.5 knots.
Cuan Sound: HW D +0455 (HW O –0200). Sp: 6 knots.
Sound of Jura: HW D +0450 (HW O –0205). Sp: 4 knots.
Sound of Luing: HW D +0500 (HW O –0155). Sp: 7 knots.

TIDAL GATES – SOUTH WEST SCOTLAND

A guide to the time of tide turn at tidal gates, the approximate maximum strength of the tidal flow (spring rates shown - neaps are approximately 60% of these), and the position and timing of races, counter tides, etc.

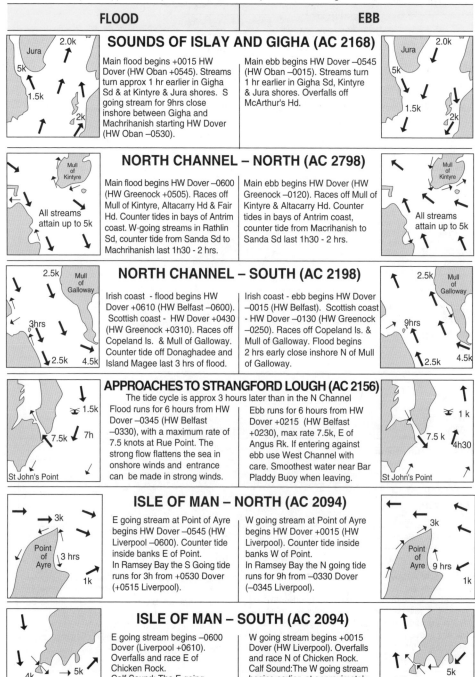

FLOOD	EBB

SOUNDS OF ISLAY AND GIGHA (AC 2168)

FLOOD: Main flood begins +0015 HW Dover (HW Oban +0545). Streams turn approx 1 hr earlier in Gigha Sd & at Kintyre & Jura shores. S going stream for 9hrs close inshore between Gigha and Machrihanish starting HW Dover (HW Oban –0530).

EBB: Main ebb begins HW Dover –0545 (HW Oban –0015). Streams turn 1 hr earlier in Gigha Sd, Kintyre & Jura shores. Overfalls off McArthur's Hd.

NORTH CHANNEL – NORTH (AC 2798)

FLOOD: Main flood begins HW Dover –0600 (HW Greenock +0505). Races off Mull of Kintyre, Altacarry Hd & Fair Hd. Counter tides in bays of Antrim coast. W-going streams in Rathlin Sd, counter tide from Sanda Sd to Machrihanish last 1h30 - 2 hrs.

EBB: Main ebb begins HW Dover (HW Greenock –0120). Races off Mull of Kintyre & Altacarry Hd. Counter tides in bays of Antrim coast, counter tide from Macrihanish to Sanda Sd last 1h30 - 2 hrs.

NORTH CHANNEL – SOUTH (AC 2198)

FLOOD: Irish coast - flood begins HW Dover +0610 (HW Belfast –0600). Scottish coast - HW Dover +0430 (HW Greenock +0310). Races off Copeland Is. & Mull of Galloway. Counter tide off Donaghadee and Island Magee last 3 hrs of flood.

EBB: Irish coast - ebb begins HW Dover –0015 (HW Belfast). Scottish coast - HW Dover –0130 (HW Greenock –0250). Races off Copeland Is. & Mull of Galloway. Flood begins 2 hrs early close inshore N of Mull of Galloway.

APPROACHES TO STRANGFORD LOUGH (AC 2156)

The tide cycle is approx 3 hours later than in the N Channel

FLOOD: Flood runs for 6 hours from HW Dover –0345 (HW Belfast –0330), with a maximum rate of 7.5 knots at Rue Point. The strong flow flattens the sea in onshore winds and entrance can be made in strong winds.

EBB: Ebb runs for 6 hours from HW Dover +0215 (HW Belfast +0230), max rate 7.5, E of Angus Rk. If entering against ebb use West Channel with care. Smoothest water near Bar Pladdy Buoy when leaving.

ISLE OF MAN – NORTH (AC 2094)

FLOOD: E going stream at Point of Ayre begins HW Dover –0545 (HW Liverpool –0600). Counter tide inside banks E of Point. In Ramsey Bay the S Going tide runs for 3h from +0530 Dover (+0515 Liverpool).

EBB: W going stream at Point of Ayre begins HW Dover +0015 (HW Liverpool). Counter tide inside banks W of Point. In Ramsey Bay the N going tide runs for 9h from –0330 Dover (–0345 Liverpool).

ISLE OF MAN – SOUTH (AC 2094)

FLOOD: E going stream begins –0600 Dover (Liverpool +0610). Overfalls and race E of Chicken Rock. Calf Sound: The E going stream begins earlier, at approximately Dover +0400 (Liverpool +0345).

EBB: W going stream begins +0015 Dover (HW Liverpool). Overfalls and race N of Chicken Rock. Calf Sound:The W going stream begins earlier, at approximately –0130 Dover (–0145 Liverpool). Note: all times may vary due to weather conditions.

MENAI STRAIT (AC 1464) – TIDAL GATES

FLOOD

(T) : turning → : < 2k ⟹ : 2-4k ⟫ : 4k +

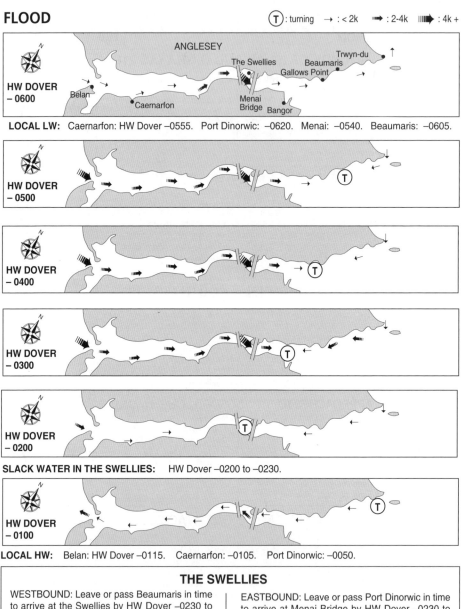

HW DOVER – 0600

ANGLESEY

Belan · Caernarfon · The Swellies · Menai Bridge · Bangor · Gallows Point · Beaumaris · Trwyn-du

LOCAL LW: Caernarfon: HW Dover –0555. Port Dinorwic: –0620. Menai: –0540. Beaumaris: –0605.

HW DOVER – 0500

HW DOVER – 0400

HW DOVER – 0300

HW DOVER – 0200

SLACK WATER IN THE SWELLIES: HW Dover –0200 to –0230.

HW DOVER – 0100

LOCAL HW: Belan: HW Dover –0115. Caernarfon: –0105. Port Dinorwic: –0050.

THE SWELLIES

WESTBOUND: Leave or pass Beaumaris in time to arrive at the Swellies by HW Dover –0230 to –0200. If in doubt about passage speed, leave early; the adverse tide will check your progress. For a first time passage this is useful, as the yacht's speed over the ground is reduced. Late arrival will mean a faster passage, but with perhaps less control.

EASTBOUND: Leave or pass Port Dinorwic in time to arrive at Menai Bridge by HW Dover –0230 to –0200. Progress towards the Swellies should be closely monitored, as you are travelling with the last of the flood. Early arrival will mean a fast, perhaps dangerous passage, being late may make it impossible.

MENAI STRAIT (AC 1464) – TIDAL GATES *contd*

EBB

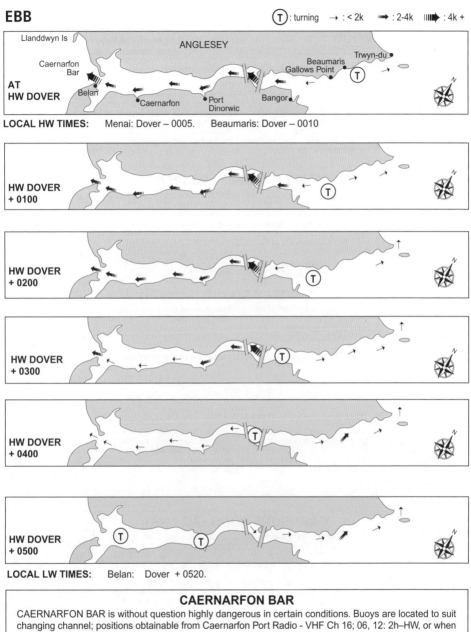

LOCAL HW TIMES: Menai: Dover – 0005.   Beaumaris: Dover – 0010

LOCAL LW TIMES: Belan: Dover + 0520.

CAERNARFON BAR

CAERNARFON BAR is without question highly dangerous in certain conditions. Buoys are located to suit changing channel; positions obtainable from Caernarfon Port Radio - VHF Ch 16; 06, 12: 2h–HW, or when vessel expected. Beware cross track tides near high water. Bar impassable during or after fresh or strong onshore weather. Keep strictly in channel.

OUTWARD BOUND: Do not leave Belan Narrows after half tide, better as soon as possible after the ebb commences, which gives maximum depth and duration of fair tide if bound S & W.

INWARD BOUND: Locating the bar buoys may be difficult; head for Llanddwyn I. until they are located. Only cross after half tide (HW Dover –0400), which inevitably limits onward passage to max of 3 hours.

TIDES

201

TIDAL GATES – IRISH SEA

A guide to the time of tide turn at tidal gates, the approximate strength of the tidal flow (spring rates shown – neaps are approximately 60% of these), and the position and timing of races, counter tides, etc.

FLOOD	EBB

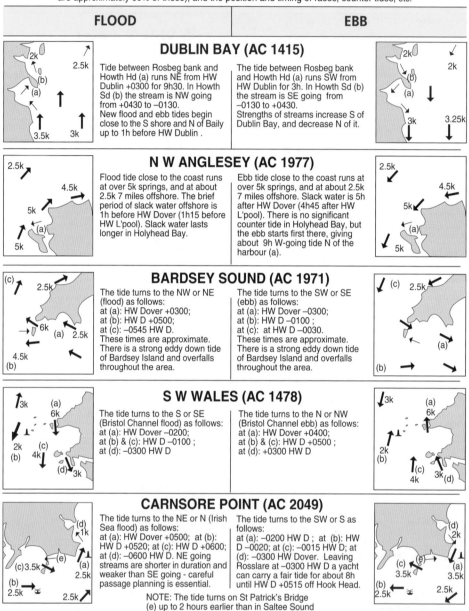

DUBLIN BAY (AC 1415)

Tide between Rosbeg bank and Howth Hd (a) runs NE from HW Dublin +0300 for 9h30. In Howth Sd (b) the stream is NW going from +0430 to –0130.
New flood and ebb tides begin close to the S shore and N of Baily up to 1h before HW Dublin .

The tide between Rosbeg bank and Howth Hd (a) runs SW from HW Dublin for 3h. In Howth Sd (b) the stream is SE going from –0130 to +0430.
Strengths of streams increase S of Dublin Bay, and decrease N of it.

N W ANGLESEY (AC 1977)

Flood tide close to the coast runs at over 5k springs, and at about 2.5k 7 miles offshore. The brief period of slack water offshore is 1h before HW Dover (1h15 before HW L'pool). Slack water lasts longer in Holyhead Bay.

Ebb tide close to the coast runs at over 5k springs, and at about 2.5k 7 miles offshore. Slack water is 5h after HW Dover (4h45 after HW L'pool). There is no significant counter tide in Holyhead Bay, but the ebb starts first there, giving about 9h W-going tide N of the harbour (a).

BARDSEY SOUND (AC 1971)

The tide turns to the NW or NE (flood) as follows:
at (a): HW Dover +0300;
at (b): HW D +0500 ;
at (c): –0545 HW D.
These times are approximate.
There is a strong eddy down tide of Bardsey Island and overfalls throughout the area.

The tide turns to the SW or SE (ebb) as follows:
at (a): HW Dover –0300;
at (b): HW D –0100 ;
at (c): at HW D –0030.
These times are approximate.
There is a strong eddy down tide of Bardsey Island and overfalls throughout the area.

S W WALES (AC 1478)

The tide turns to the S or SE (Bristol Channel flood) as follows:
at (a): HW Dover –0200;
at (b) & (c): HW D –0100 ;
at (d): –0300 HW D

The tide turns to the N or NW (Bristol Channel ebb) as follows:
at (a): HW Dover +0400;
at (b) & (c): HW D +0500 ;
at (d): +0300 HW D

CARNSORE POINT (AC 2049)

The tide turns to the NE or N (Irish Sea flood) as follows:
at (a): HW Dover +0500; at (b): HW D +0520; at (c): HW D +0600; at (d): –0600 HW D. NE going streams are shorter in duration and weaker than SE going - careful passage planning is essential.

The tide turns to the SW or S as follows:
at (a): –0200 HW D ; at (b): HW D –0020; at (c): –0015 HW D; at (d): –0300 HW Dover. Leaving Rosslare at –0300 HW D a yacht can carry a fair tide for about 8h until HW D +0515 off Hook Head.

NOTE: The tide turns on St Patrick's Bridge (e) up to 2 hours earlier than in Saltee Sound

CORK COAST (AC 2049)

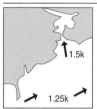

The tide, which flows coastwise, turns to the NE at HW Dover +0045. There is an eddy 5 miles ESE of Old Head of Kinsale at HW Dover +0400. The ingoing Cork Harbour tide begins at HW Dover +0055.

The tide turns SW at HW Dover +0500. The outgoing Cork Harbour tide begins at HW Dover –0540.

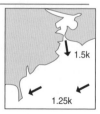

SECONDARY PORTS: TIME & HEIGHT DIFFERENCES
SOUTH COAST OF ENGLAND *Time zone UT*

Location	Lat	Long	High Water		Low Water		MHWS	MHWN	MLWN	MLWS
			0000	0600	0000	0600				
PLYMOUTH (DEVONPORT)	50 22N	4 11W	and	and	and	and	5.5	4.4	2.2	0.8
Standard port			1200	1800	1200	1800				
Isles of Scilly, St Mary's	49 55N	6 19W	−0035	−0100	−0040	−0025	+0.2	−0.1	−0.2	−0.1
Penzance & Newlyn	50 06N	5 33W	−0040	−0110	−0035	−0025	+0.1	0.0	−0.2	0.0
Porthleven	50 05N	5 19W	−0045	−0105	−0030	−0025	0.0	−0.1	−0.2	0.0
Lizard Point	49 57N	5 12W	−0045	−0100	−0030	−0030	−0.2	−0.2	−0.3	−0.2
Coverack	50 01N	5 05W	−0030	−0050	−0020	−0015	−0.2	−0.2	−0.3	−0.2
Helford River Entrance	50 05N	5 05W	−0030	−0035	−0015	−0010	−0.2	−0.2	−0.3	−0.2
FALMOUTH	50 09N	5 03W	*Standard port (no Secondaries)*							
River Fal, Truro	50 16N	5 03W	−0020	−0025	*Dries*	*Dries*	−2.0	−2.0	*Dries*	
Mevagissey	50 16N	4 47W	−0015	−0020	−0010	−0005	−0.1	−0.1	−0.2	−0.1
Par	50 21N	4 42W	−0010	−0015	−0010	−0005	−0.4	−0.4	−0.4	−0.2
River Fowey, Fowey	50 20N	4 38W	−0010	−0015	−0010	−0005	−0.1	−0.1	−0.2	−0.2
Lostwithiel	50 24N	4 40W	+0005	−0010	*Dries*	*Dries*	−4.1	−4.1	*Dries*	
Looe	50 21N	4 27W	−0010	−0010	−0005	−0005	−0.1	−0.2	−0.2	−0.2
Whitsand Bay	50 20N	4 15W	0000	0000	0000	0000	0.0	+0.1	−0.1	+0.2
River Tamar										
Saltash	50 24N	4 12W	0000	+0010	0000	−0005	+0.1	+0.1	+0.1	+0.1
Cargreen	50 26N	4 12W	0000	+0010	+0020	+0020	0.0	0.0	−0.1	0.0
Cotehele Quay	50 29N	4 13W	0000	+0020	+0045	+0045	−0.9	−0.9	−0.8	−0.4
River Tavy, Lopwell	50 28N	4 09W	*No data*	*No data*	*Dries*	*Dries*	−2.6	−2.7	*Dries*	
River Lynher, Jupiter Point	50 23N	4 14W	+0010	+0005	0000	−0005	0.0	0.0	+0.1	0.0
St Germans	50 23N	4 18W	0000	0000	+0020	+0020	−0.3	−0.1	0.0	+0.2
Turnchapel	50 22N	4 07W	0000	0000	+0010	−0015	0.0	+0.1	+0.2	+0.1
Bovisand Pier	50 20N	4 08W	0000	−0020	0000	−0010	−0.2	−0.1	0.0	+0.1
River Yealm, Entrance	50 18N	4 04W	+0006	+0006	+0002	+0002	−0.1	−0.1	−0.1	−0.1
			0100	0600	0100	0600				
PLYMOUTH (DEVONPORT)	50 22N	4 11W	and	and	and	and	5.5	4.4	2.2	0.8
Standard port			1300	1800	1300	1800				
Salcombe	50 13N	3 47W	0000	+0010	+0005	−0005	−0.2	−0.3	−0.1	−0.1
Start Point	50 13N	3 39W	+0015	+0015	+0005	+0010	−0.1	−0.2	+0.1	+0.2
River Dart										
DARTMOUTH	50 21N	3 34W	*Standard port (no Secondaries)*							
Greenway Quay	50 23N	3 35W	+0030	+0045	+0025	+0005	−0.6	−0.6	−0.2	−0.2
Totnes	50 26N	3 41W	+0030	+0040	+0115	+0030	−2.0	−2.1	*Dries*	
Torquay	50 28N	3 31W	+0025	+0045	+0010	0000	−0.6	−0.7	−0.2	−0.1
Teignmouth, Approaches	50 33N	3 29W	+0020	+0050	+0025	0000	−0.9	−0.8	−0.2	−0.1
Teignmouth, New Quay	50 33N	3 30W	+0025	+0055	+0040	+0005	−0.8	−0.8	−0.2	+0.1
Exmouth Approaches	50 36N	3 23W	+0030	+0050	+0015	+0005	−0.9	−1.0	−0.5	−0.3
River Exe										
Exmouth Dock	50 37N	3 25W	+0035	+0055	+0050	+0020	−1.5	−1.6	−0.9	−0.6
Starcross	50 38N	3 27W	+0040	+0100	+0055	+0025	−1.4	−1.5	−0.8	−0.1
Turf Lock	50 40N	3 28W	+0045	+0100	+0034	*No data*	− 1.6	−1.6	−1.2	*No data*
Topsham	50 41N	3 28W	+0045	+0105	*No data*	*No data*	− 1.5	−1.6	*No data*	
Lyme Regis	50 43N	2 56W	+0040	+0100	+0005	−0005	−1.2	−1.3	−0.5	−0.2
Bridport (West Bay)	50 42N	2 45W	+0025	+0040	0000	0000	−1.4	−1.4	−0.6	−0.2
Chesil Beach	50 37N	2 33W	+0040	+0055	−0005	+0010	−1.6	−1.5	−0.5	0.0
Chesil Cove	50 34N	2 28W	+0035	+0050	−0010	+0005	−1.5	−1.6	−0.5	−0.2
			0100	0700	0100	0700				
PORTLAND	50 34N	2 26W	and	and	and	and	2.1	1.4	0.8	0.1
Standard port			1300	1900	1300	1900				
Lulworth Cove, Mupe Bay	50 37N	2 14W	+0005	+0015	−0005	0000	+0.1	+0.1	+0.2	+0.1
			—	—	0500	1100				
POOLE HARBOUR	50 42N	1 59W			and	and	2.2	1.7	1.2	0.6
Standard port			—	—	1700	2300				
Swanage	50 37N	1 57W	—	—	−0045	+0055	−0.2	−0.1	0.0	−0.1
Poole Harbour Entrance	50 41N	1 57W	—	—	−0025	−0010	0.0	0.0	0.0	0.0
Ro-Ro terminal	50 42N	1 59W	*Standard port*							
Pottery Pier	50 42N	1 59W	—	—	−0010	0000	−0.2	0.0	+0.1	+0.2
Wareham, River Frome	50 41N	2 06W	—	—	+0130	+0145	0.0	0.0	0.0	+0.3
Cleavel Point	50 40N	2 00W	—	—	−0005	−0005	−0.1	−0.2	0.0	*No data*
			0000	0600	0500	1100				
PORTSMOUTH	50 48N	1 07W	and	and	and	and	4.7	3.8	1.9	0.8
Standard port			1200	1800	1700	2300				
Bournemouth	50 43N	1 52W	−0240	+0055	−0050	−0030	−2.7	−2.2	−0.8	−0.3
Christchurch Entrance	50 43N	1 45W	−0230	+0030	−0035	−0035	−2.9	−2.4	−1.2	−0.2

Location	Lat	Long	High Water		Low Water		MHWS	MHWN	MLWN	MLWS
Christchurch Quay	50 44N	1 47W	−0210	+0100	+0105	+0055	−2.9	−2.4	−1.0	0.0
Christchurch, Tuckton	50 44N	1 47W	−0205	+0110	+0110	+0105	−3.0	−2.5	−1.0	+0.1
Hurst Point	50 42N	1 33W	−0115	−0005	−0030	−0025	−2.0	−1.5	−0.5	−0.1
Lymington	50 46N	1 32W	−0110	+0005	−0020	−0020	−1.7	−1.2	−0.5	−0.1
Bucklers Hard	50 48N	1 25W	−0040	−0010	+0010	−0010	−1.0	−0.8	−0.2	−0.3
Stansore Point	50 47N	1 20W	−0050	−0010	−0005	−0010	−0.8	−0.5	−0.3	−0.1
Isle of Wight										
Yarmouth	50 42N	1 30W	−0105	+0005	−0025	−0030	−1.7	−1.2	−0.3	0.0
Totland Bay	50 41N	1 33W	−0130	−0045	−0035	−0045	−2.2	−1.7	−0.4	−0.1
Freshwater	50 40N	1 31W	−0210	+0025	−0040	−0020	−2.1	−1.5	−0.4	0.0
Ventnor	50 36N	1 12W	−0025	−0030	−0025	−0030	−0.8	−0.6	−0.2	+0.2
Sandown	50 39N	1 09W	0000	+0005	+0010	+0025	−0.6	−0.5	−0.2	0.0
Foreland Lifeboat Slip	50 41N	1 04W	−0005	0000	+0005	+0010	+0.1	+0.1	0.0	+0.1
Bembridge Harbour	50 42N	1 07W	+0020	0000	+0100	+0020	−1.5	−1.4	−1.3	−1.0
Ryde	50 44N	1 10W	−0010	+0010	−0005	−0005	−0.1	0.0	0.0	0.0
Medina River										
Cowes	50 46N	1 18W	−0015	+0015	0000	−0020	−0.5	−0.3	−0.1	0.0
Folly Inn	50 44N	1 17W	−0015	+0015	0000	−0020	−0.6	−0.4	−0.1	+0.2
Newport	50 42N	1 17W	No data	No data	No data	No data	−0.6	−0.4	+0.1	+0.8
			0400	**1100**	**0000**	**0600**				
SOUTHAMPTON	50 53N	1 24W	and	and	and	and	4.5	3.7	1.8	0.5
Standard port			**1600**	**2300**	**1200**	**1800**				
Calshot Castle	50 49N	1 18W	0000	+0025	0000	0000	0.0	0.0	+0.2	+0.3
Redbridge	50 55N	1 28W	−0020	+0005	0000	−0005	−0.1	−0.1	−0.1	−0.1
River Hamble										
Warsash	50 51N	1 18W	+0020	+0010	+0010	0000	0.0	+0.1	+0.1	+0.3
Bursledon	50 53N	1 18W	+0020	+0020	+0010	+0010	+0.1	+0.2	+0.2	+0.2
			0500	**1000**	**0000**	**0600**				
PORTSMOUTH	50 48N	1 07W	and	and	and	and	4.7	3.8	1.9	0.8
Standard port			**1700**	**2200**	**1200**	**1800**				
Lee-on-the-Solent	50 48N	1 12W	−0005	+0005	−0015	−0010	−0.2	−0.1	+0.1	+0.2
Chichester Harbour Entrance	50 47N	0 56W	−0010	+0005	+0015	+0020	+0.2	+0.2	0.0	+0.1
Northney	50 50N	0 58W	+0010	+0015	+0015	+0025	+0.2	0.0	−0.2	−0.3
Bosham	50 50N	0 52W	0000	+0010	No data	No data	+0.2	+0.1	No data	
Itchenor	50 48N	0 52W	−0005	+0005	+0005	+0025	+0.1	0.0	−0.2	−0.2
Dell Quay	50 49N	0 49W	+0005	+0015	no data	No data	+0.2	+0.1	No data	
Selsey Bill	50 43N	0 47W	+0010	−0010	+0035	+0020	+0.5	+0.3	−0.1	−0.2
Nab Tower	50 40N	0 57W	+0015	0000	+0015	+0015	−0.2	0.0	+0.2	0.0
			0500	**1000**	**0000**	**0600**				
SHOREHAM	50 50N	0 15W	and	and	and	and	6.3	4.8	1.9	0.6
Standard port			**1700**	**2200**	**1200**	**1800**				
Pagham	50 46N	0 43W	+0015	0000	−0015	−0025	−0.7	−0.5	−0.1	−0.1
Bognor Regis	50 47N	0 40W	+0010	−0005	−0005	−0020	−0.6	−0.5	−0.2	−0.1
River Arun										
Littlehampton Entrance	50 48N	0 33W	+0010	0000	−0005	−0010	−0.4	−0.4	−0.2	−0.2
Littlehampton UMA wharf	50 49N	0 33W	+0015	+0005	0000	+0045	−0.7	−0.7	−0.3	+0.2
Arundel	50 51N	0 33W	No data	+0120	No data	No data	−3.1	−2.8	No data	
Worthing	50 48N	0 22W	+0010	0000	−0005	−0010	−0.1	−0.2	0.0	0.0
Brighton	50 49N	0 08W	0000	−0005	0000	0000	+0.3	+0.2	+0.1	0.0
Newhaven	50 47N	0 04E	−0015	−0010	0000	0000	+0.2	+0.1	−0.1	−0.2
Eastbourne	50 46N	0 17E	−0010	−0005	+0015	+0020	+1.1	+0.6	+0.2	+0.1
			0000	**0600**	**0100**	**0700**				
DOVER	51 07N	1 19E	and	and	and	and	6.8	5.3	2.1	0.8
Standard port			**1200**	**1800**	**1300**	**1900**				
Hastings	50 51N	0 36E	0000	−0010	−0030	−0030	+0.8	+0.5	+0.1	−0.1
Rye Approaches	50 55N	0 47E	+0005	−0010	No data	No data	+1.0	+0.7	No data	
Rye Harbour	50 56N	0 48E	+0005	−0010	Dries	Dries	−1.4	−1.7	Dries	
Dungeness	50 55N	0 58E	−0010	−0015	−0020	−0010	+1.0	+0.6	+0.4	+0.1
Folkestone	51 05N	1 12E	−0020	−0005	−0010	−0010	+0.4	+0.4	0.0	−0.1
Deal	51 13N	1 25E	+0010	+0020	+0010	+0005	−0.6	−0.3	0.0	0.0
Richborough	51 18N	1 21E	+0015	+0015	+0030	+0030	−3.4	−2.6	−1.7	−0.7
Ramsgate	51 20N	1 25E	+0030	+0030	+0017	+0007	−1.6	−1.3	−0.7	−0.2

EAST COAST ENGLAND *Time Zone UT*

Location	Lat	Long	High Water		Low Water		MHWS	MHWN	MLWN	MLWS
			0100	**0700**	**0100**	**0700**				
MARGATE	51 23N	1 23E	and	and	and	and	4.8	3.9	1.4	0.5
Standard port			**1300**	**1900**	**1300**	**1900**				
Herne Bay	51 23N	1 07E	+0034	+0022	+0015	+0032	+0.6	+0.4	+0.1	0.0
Whitstable approaches	51 22N	1 02E	+0042	+0029	+0025	+0050	+0.6	+0.6	+0.1	0.0

Location	Lat	Long	High Water		Low Water		MHWS	MHWN	MLWN	MLWS
SHEERNESS	51 27N	0 45E	0200	0800	0200	0700	**5.8**	**4.7**	**1.5**	**0.6**
Standard port			and	and	and	and				
River Swale			1400	2000	1400	1900				
Grovehurst Jetty	51 22N	0 46E	−0007	0000	0000	+0016	0.0	0.0	0.0	−0.1
Faversham	51 19N	0 54E	No data	No data	No data	No data	−0.2	−0.2	No data	
River Medway										
Bee Ness	51 25N	0 39E	+0002	+0002	0000	+0005	+0.2	+0.1	0.0	0.0
Bartlett Creek	51 23N	0 38E	+0016	+0008	No data	No data	+0.1	0.0	No data	
Darnett Ness	51 24N	0 36E	+0004	+0004	0000	+0010	+0.2	+0.1	0.0	−0.1
Chatham, Lock approaches	51 24N	0 33E	+0010	+0012	+0012	+0018	+0.3	+0.1	−0.1	−0.2
Upnor	51 25N	0 32E	+0015	+0015	+0015	+0025	+0.2	+0.2	−0.1	−0.1
Rochester, Strood Pier	51 24N	0 30E	+0018	+0018	+0018	+0028	+0.2	+0.2	−0.2	−0.3
Wouldham	51 21N	0 27E	+0030	+0025	+0035	+0120	−0.2	−0.3	−1.0	−0.3
New Hythe	51 19N	0 28E	+0035	+0035	+0220	+0240	−1.6	−1.7	−1.2	−0.3
Allington Lock	51 17N	0 30E	+0050	+0035	No data	No data	−2.1	−2.2	−1.3	−0.4
River Thames										
Southend−on−Sea	51 31N	0 43E	−0005	−0005	−0005	−0005	0.0	0.0	−0.1	−0.1
Coryton	51 30N	0 31E	+0005	+0010	+0010	+0010	+0.4	+0.3	0.0	0.0
LONDON BRIDGE	51 30N	0 05W	0300	0900	0400	1100	**7.1**	**5.9**	**1.3**	**0.5**
Standard port			and	and	and	and				
			1500	2100	1600	2300				
Tilbury	51 27N	0 22E	−0055	−0040	−0050	−0115	−0.7	−0.5	+0.1	0.0
North Woolwich	51 30N	0 05E	−0020	−0020	−0035	−0045	−0.1	0.0	+0.2	0.0
Albert bridge	51 29N	0 10W	+0025	+0020	+0105	+0110	−0.9	−0.8	−0.7	−0.4
Hammersmith bridge	51 29N	0 14W	+0040	+0035	+0205	+0155	−1.4	−1.3	−1.0	−0.5
Kew bridge	51 29N	0 17W	+0055	+0050	+0255	+0235	−1.8	−1.8	−1.2	−0.5
Richmond lock	51 28N	0 19W	+0105	+0055	+0325	+0305	−2.2	−2.2	−1.3	−0.5
SHEERNESS	51 27N	0 45E	0200	0700	0100	0700	**5.8**	**4.7**	**1.5**	**0.6**
Standard port			and	and	and	and				
Thames Estuary Shivering Sand	51 30N	1 05E	1400	1900	1300	1900				
			−0025	−0019	−0008	−0026	−0.6	−0.6	−0.1	−0.1
WALTON-ON-THE-NAZE	51 51N	1 17E	0000	0600	0500	1100	**4.2**	**3.4**	**1.1**	**0.4**
Standard port			and	and	and	and				
			1200	1800	1700	2300				
Whitaker Beacon	51 40N	1 06E	+0022	+0024	+0033	+0027	+0.6	+0.5	+0.2	+0.1
Holliwell Point	51 38N	0 56E	+0034	+0037	+0100	+0037	+1.1	+0.9	+0.3	+0.1
River Roach Rochford	51 35N	0 43E	+0050	+0040	Dries	Dries	−0.8	−1.1	Dries	
River Crouch										
Burnham-on-Crouch	51 37N	0 48E	+0050	+0035	+0115	+0050	+1.0	+0.8	−0.1	−0.2
North Fambridge	51 38N	0 41E	+0115	+0050	+0130	+0100	+1.1	+0.8	0.0	−0.1
Hullbridge	51 38N	0 38E	+0115	+0050	+0135	+0105	+1.1	+0.8	0.0	−0.1
Battlesbridge	51 37N	0 34E	+0120	+0110	Dries	Dries	−1.8	−2.0	Dries	
River Blackwater										
Bradwell Waterside	51 45N	0 54E	+0035	+0023	+0047	+0004	+1.0	+0.8	+0.2	0.0
Osea Island	51 43N	0 46E	+0057	+0045	+0050	+0007	+1.1	+0.9	+0.1	0.0
Maldon	51 44N	0 42E	+0107	+0055	No data	No data	−1.3	−1.1	No data	
West Mersea	51 47N	0 54E	+0035	+0015	+0055	+0010	+0.9	+0.4	+0.1	+0.1
River Colne										
Brightlingsea	51 48N	1 00E	+0025	+0021	+0046	+0004	+0.8	+0.4	+0.1	0.0
Colchester	51 53N	0 56E	+0035	+0025	Dries	Dries	0.0	−0.3	Dries	
Clacton−on−Sea	51 47N	1 10E	+0012	+0010	+0025	+0008	+0.3	+0.1	+0.1	+0.1
Bramble Creek	51 53N	1 14E	+0010	−0007	−0005	+0010	+0.3	+0.3	+0.3	+0.3
Sunk Head	51 47N	1 30E	0000	+0002	−0002	+0002	−0.3	−0.3	−0.1	−0.1
Harwich	51 57N	1 17E	+0007	+0002	−0010	−0012	−0.2	0.0	0.0	0.0
Mistley	51 57N	1 05E	+0032	+0027	−0010	−0012	0.0	0.0	−0.1	−0.1
Ipswich	52 03N	1 10E	+0022	+0027	0000	−0012	0.0	0.0	−0.1	−0.1
WALTON−ON−THE−NAZE	51 51N	1 17E	0100	0700	0100	0700	**4.2**	**3.4**	**1.1**	**0.4**
Standard port			and	and	and	and				
			1300	1900	1300	1900				
Felixstowe Pier	51 57N	1 21E	−0005	−0007	−0018	−0020	−0.5	−0.4	0.0	0.0
River Deben										
Woodbridge Haven	51 59N	1 24E	0000	−0005	−0020	−0025	−0.5	−0.5	−0.1	+0.1
Woodbridge	52 05N	1 19E	+0045	+0025	+0025	−0020	−0.2	−0.3	−0.2	0.0
Bawdsey	52 01N	1 26E	−0016	−0020	−0030	−0032	−0.8	−0.6	−0.1	−0.1
Orford Haven										
Bar	52 02N	1 28E	−0026	−0030	−0036	−0038	−1.0	−0.8	−0.1	0.0
Orford Quay	52 05N	1 32E	+0040	+0040	+0055	+0055	−1.4	−1.1	0.0	+0.2
Slaughden Quay	52 08N	1 36E	+0105	+0105	+0125	+0125	−1.3	−0.8	−0.1	+0.2
Iken Cliffs	52 09N	1 31E	+0130	+0130	+0155	+0155	−1.3	−1.0	0.0	+0.2

TIDES

Location	Lat	Long	High Water		Low Water		MHWS	MHWN	MLWN	MLWS
			0300	0900	0200	0800				
LOWESTOFT	52 28N	1 45E	and	and	and	and	2.4	2.1	1.0	0.5
Standard port			1500	2100	1400	2000				
Orford Ness	52 05N	1 35E	+0135	+0135	+0135	+0125	+0.4	+0.6	−0.1	0.0
Aldeburgh	52 09N	1 36E	+0130	+0130	+0115	+0120	+0.3	+0.2	−0.1	−0.2
Minsmere Sluice	52 14N	1 38E	+0110	+0110	+0110	+0110	0.0	−0.1	−0.2	−0.2
Southwold	52 19N	1 40E	+0105	+0105	+0055	+0055	0.0	0.0	−0.1	0.0
Great Yarmouth										
Gorleston-on-Sea	52 34N	1 44E	−0035	−0035	−0030	−0030	0.0	0.0	0.0	0.0
Britannia Pier	52 36N	1 45E	−0105	−0100	−0040	−0055	+0.1	+0.1	0.0	0.0
Caister-on-Sea	52 39N	1 44E	−0120	−0120	−0100	−0100	0.0	−0.1	0.0	0.0
Winterton-on-Sea	52 43N	1 42E	−0225	−0215	−0135	−0135	+0.8	+0.5	+0.2	+0.1
			0100	0700	0100	0700				
IMMINGHAM	53 38N	0 11W	and	and	and	and	7.3	5.8	2.6	0.9
Standard port			1300	1900	1300	1900				
Cromer	52 56N	1 18E	+0050	+0030	+0050	+0130	−2.1	−1.7	−0.5	−0.1
Blakeney Bar	52 59N	0 59E	+0035	+0025	+0030	+0040	−1.6	−1.3	No data	
Blakeney	52 57N	1 01E	+0115	+0055	No data	No data	−3.9	−3.8	No data	
Wells Bar	52 59N	0 49E	+0020	+0020	+0020	+0020	−1.3	−1.0	No data	
Wells	52 57N	0 51E	+0035	+0045	+0340	+0310	−3.8	−3.8	Not below CD	
Burnham Overy Staithe	52 58N	0 48E	+0045	+0055	No data	No data	−5.0	−4.9	No data	
The Wash										
Hunstanton	52 56N	0 29E	+0010	+0020	+0105	+0025	+0.1	−0.2	−0.1	0.0
West Stones	52 50N	0 21E	+0025	+0025	+0115	+0040	−0.3	−0.4	−0.3	+0.2
King's Lynn	52 45N	0 24E	+0030	+0030	+0305	+0140	−0.5	−0.8	−0.8	+0.1
Outer Westmark Knock	52 53N	0 13E	+0010	+0015	+0040	+0020	−0.2	−0.5	−0.6	−0.4
Wisbech Cut	52 48N	0 13E	+0020	+0010	+0120	+0055	−0.3	−0.7	−0.4 No data	
Port Sutton bridge	52 46N	0 12E	+0030	+0020	+0130	+0105	−0.3	−0.6	−0.6	+0.3
Wisbech	52 40N	0 09E	+0055	+0040	Dries	Dries	−0.2	−0.6	Dries	Dries
Lawyer's Creek	52 53N	0 05E	+0010	+0020	No data	No data	−0.3	−0.6	No data	
Tabs Head	52 56N	0 05E	0000	+0005	+0125	+0020	+0.2	−0.2	−0.2	−0.2
Boston	52 58N	0 01W	0000	+0010	+0140	+0050	−0.5	−1.0	−0.9	−0.5
Skegness	53 09N	0 21E	+0010	+0015	+0030	+0020	−0.4	−0.5	−0.1	0.0
Inner Dowsing Light Tower	53 19N	0 35E	0000	0000	+0010	+0010	−0.9	−0.7	−0.1	+0.3
River Humber										
Bull Sand Fort	53 34N	0 04E	−0020	−0030	−0035	−0015	−0.4	−0.3	+0.1	+0.2
Grimsby	53 35N	0 04W	−0012	−0012	−0015	−0015	−0.2	−0.1	0.0	+0.2
Hull, King George Dock	53 44N	0 16W	+0010	+0010	+0021	+0017	+0.3	+0.2	−0.1	−0.2
Hull, Albert Dock	53 44N	0 21W	+0019	+0019	+0033	+0027	+0.3	+0.1	−0.1	−0.2
Humber Bridge	53 43N	0 27W	+0027	+0022	+0049	+0039	−0.1	−0.4	−0.7	−0.6
River Trent										
Burton Stather	53 39N	0 42W	+0105	+0045	+0335	+0305	−2.1	−2.3	−2.3	Dries
Flixborough Wharf	53 37N	0 42W	+0120	+0100	+0400	+0340	−2.3	−2.6	Dries	
Keadby	53 36N	0 44W	+0135	+0120	+0425	+0410	−2.5	−2.8	Dries	
Owston Ferry	53 29N	0 46W	+0155	+0145	Dries	Dries	−3.5	−3.9	Dries	
River Ouse										
Blacktoft	53 42N	0 43W	+0100	+0055	+0325	+0255	−1.6	−1.8	−2.2	−1.1
Goole	53 42N	0 52W	+0130	+0115	+0355	+0350	−1.6	−2.1	−1.9	−0.6
			0000	0600	0000	0600				
R TEES ENTRANCE	54 38N	1 09W	and	and	and	and	5.5	4.3	2.0	0.9
Standard port			1200	1800	1200	1800				
Bridlington	54 05N	0 11W	+0100	+0050	+0055	+0050	+0.6	+0.4	+0.3	+0.2
Filey Bay	54 13N	0 16W	+0042	+0042	+0047	+0034	+0.3	+0.6	+0.4	+0.1
Scarborough	54 17N	0 23W	+0040	+0040	+0030	+0030	+0.2	+0.3	+0.3	0.0
Whitby	54 29N	0 37W	+0015	+0030	+0020	+0005	+0.1	0.0	−0.1	−0.1
Middlesbrough Dock ent	54 35N	1 13W	0000	+0002	0000	−0003	+0.1	+0.2	+0.1	−0.1
Tees (Newport) Bridge	54 34N	1 16W	−0002	+0004	+0005	−0003	+0.1	+0.2	0.0	−0.1
Hartlepool	54 42N	1 12W	−0004	−0004	−0006	−0006	−0.1	−0.1	−0.2	−0.1
Seaham	54 50N	1 19W	−0015	−0015	−0015	−0015	−0.3	−0.2	0.0	−0.2
Sunderland	54 55N	1 22W	−0017	−0017	−0016	−0016	−0.2	−0.1	0.0	0.0
			0200	0800	0100	0800				
R TYNE, NORTH SHIELDS	55 00N	1 26W	and	and	and	and	5.0	3.9	1.8	0.7
Standard port			1400	2000	1300	2000				
Newcastle-upon-Tyne	54 58N	1 36W	+0003	+0003	+0008	+0008	+0.3	+0.2	+0.1	+0.1
Blyth	55 07N	1 29W	+0005	−0007	−0001	+0009	0.0	0.0	−0.1	+0.1
Coquet Island	55 20N	1 32W	−0010	−0010	−0020	−0020	+0.1	+0.1	0.0	+0.1
Amble	55 20N	1 34W	−0013	−0013	−0016	−0020	0.0	0.0	+0.1	+0.1

Location	Lat	Long	High Water		Low Water		MHWS	MHWN	MLWN	MLWS
North Sunderland	55 35N	1 39W	−0048	−0044	−0058	−0102	−0.2	−0.2	−0.2	0.0
Holy Island	55 40N	1 48W	−0043	−0039	−0105	−0110	−0.2	−0.2	−0.3	−0.1
Berwick	55 46N	1 59W	−0053	−0053	−0109	−0109	−0.3	−0.1	−0.5	−0.1

SCOTLAND *Time Zone UT*

Location	Lat	Long	High Water		Low Water		MHWS	MHWN	MLWN	MLWS
			0300	0900	0300	0900				
LEITH	55 59N	3 11W	and	and	and	and	5.6	4.4	2.0	0.8
Standard port			1500	2100	1500	2100				
Eyemouth	55 52N	2 05W	−0005	+0007	+0012	+0008	−0.4	−0.3	0.0	+0.1
Dunbar	56 00N	2 31W	−0005	+0003	+0003	−0003	−0.3	−0.3	0.0	+0.1
Fidra	56 04N	2 47W	−0001	0000	−0002	+0001	−0.2	−0.2	0.0	0.0
Cockenzie	55 58N	2 57W	−0007	−0015	−0013	−0005	−0.2	0.0	*No data*	
Granton	55 59N	3 13W	0000	0000	0000	0000	0.0	0.0	0.0	0.0
River Forth Grangemouth	56 02N	3 41W	+0015	+0010	−0050	−0045	0.0	−0.1	−0.2	−0.2
Kincardine	56 04N	3 43W	+0015	+0030	−0030	−0030	0.0	−0.2	−0.5	−0.3
Alloa	56 06N	3 48W	+0040	+0040	+0025	+0025	−0.2	−0.5	*No data*	−0.7
Stirling	56 07N	3 56W	+0100	+0100	*No data*		−2.9	−3.1	−2.3	−0.7
Firth of Forth										
Burntisland	56 03N	3 14W	+0013	+0004	−0002	+0007	+0.1	0.0	+0.1	+0.2
Kirkcaldy	56 09N	3 09W	+0005	0000	−0004	−0001	−0.3	−0.3	−0.2	−0.2
Methil	56 11N	3 00W	−0005	−0001	−0001	−0001	−0.1	−0.1	−0.1	−0.1
Anstruther Easter	56 13N	2 42W	−0018	−0012	−0006	−0008	−0.3	−0.2	0.0	0.0
			0000	0600	0100	0700				
ABERDEEN	57 09N	2 04W	and	and	and	and	4.3	3.4	1.6	0.6
Standard port			1200	1800	1300	1900				
River Tay										
Bar	56 28N	2 38W	+0100	+0100	+0050	+0110	+0.9	+0.8	+0.3	+0.1
Dundee	56 27N	2 58W	+0140	+0120	+0055	+0145	+1.3	+0.9	+0.4	+0.2
Newburgh	56 21N	3 14W	+0215	+0200	+0250	+0335	−0.2	−0.4	−1.1	−0.5
Perth	56 24N	3 25W	+0220	+0225	+0510	+0530	−0.9	−1.4	−1.2	−0.3
Arbroath	56 33N	2 35W	+0056	+0037	+0034	+0055	+1.0	+0.8	+0.4	+0.2
Montrose	56 42N	2 28W	+0055	+0055	+0030	+0040	+0.5	+0.4	+0.2	0.0
Stonehaven	56 58N	2 12W	+0013	+0008	+0013	+0009	+0.2	+0.2	+0.1	0.0
Peterhead	57 30N	1 46W	−0035	−0045	−0035	−0040	−0.4	−0.3	+0.1	+0.1
Fraserburgh	57 41N	2 00W	−0105	−0115	−0120	−0110	−0.6	−0.5	−0.2	0.0
			0200	0900	0400	0900				
ABERDEEN	57 09N	2 04W	and	and	and	and	4.3	3.4	1.6	0.6
Standard port			1400	2100	1600	2100				
Banff	57 40N	2 31W	−0100	−0150	−0150	−0050	−0.4	−0.2	−0.1	+0.2
Whitehills	57 41N	2 35W	−0122	−0137	−0117	−0127	−0.4	−0.3	+0.1	+0.1
Buckie	57 41N	2 57W	−0130	−0145	−0125	−0140	−0.2	−0.2	0.0	+0.1
Lossiemouth	57 43N	3 18W	−0125	−0200	−0130	−0130	−0.2	−0.2	0.0	0.0
Burghead	57 42N	3 29W	−0120	−0150	−0135	−0120	−0.2	−0.2	0.0	0.0
Nairn	57 36N	3 52W	−0120	−0150	−0135	−0130	0.0	−0.1	0.0	+0.1
McDermott Base	57 36N	3 59W	−0110	−0140	−0120	−0115	−0.1	−0.1	+0.1	+0.3
			0300	1000	0000	0700				
ABERDEEN	57 09N	2 04W	and	and	and	and	4.3	3.4	1.6	0.6
Standard port			1500	2200	1200	1900				
Inverness Firth										
Fortrose	57 35N	4 08W	−0125	−0125	−0125	−0125	0.0	0.0	*No data*	
Inverness	57 30N	4 15W	−0050	−0150	−0200	−0150	+0.5	+0.3	+0.2	+0.1
Cromarty Firth										
Cromarty	57 42N	4 03W	−0120	−0155	−0155	−0120	0.0	0.0	+0.1	+0.2
Invergordon	57 41N	4 10W	−0105	−0200	−0200	−0110	+0.1	+0.1	+0.1	+0.1
Dingwall	57 36N	4 25W	−0045	−0145	*No data*	*No data*	+0.1	+0.2	*No data*	
			0300	0800	0200	0800				
ABERDEEN	57 09N	2 04W	and	and	and	and	4.3	3.4	1.6	0.6
Standard port			1500	2000	1400	2000				
Dornoch Firth										
Portmahomack	57 50N	3 50W	−0120	−0210	−0140	−0110	−0.2	−0.1	+0.1	+0.1
Meikle Ferry	57 51N	4 08W	−0100	−0140	−0120	−0055	+0.1	0.0	−0.1	0.0
Golspie	57 58N	3 59W	−0130	−0215	−0155	−0130	−0.3	−0.3	−0.1	0.0
			0000	0700	0200	0700				
WICK	58 26N	3 05W	and	and	and	and	3.5	2.8	1.4	0.7
Standard port			1200	1900	1400	1900				
Helmsdale	58 07N	3 39W	+0025	+0015	+0035	+0030	+0.4	+0.3	+0.1	0.0
Duncansby Head	58 39N	3 02W	−0115	−0115	−0110	−0110	−0.4	−0.4	*No data*	
Orkney Islands										
Muckle Skerry	58 41N	2 55W	−0025	−0025	−0020	−0020	−0.9	−0.8	−0.4	−0.3

Location	Lat	Long	High Water		Low Water		MHWS	MHWN	MLWN	MLWS
Burray Ness	58 51N	2 52W	+0005	+0005	+0015	+0015	−0.2	−0.3	−0.1	−0.1
Deer Sound	58 58N	2 50W	−0040	−0040	−0035	−0035	−0.3	−0.3	−0.1	−0.1
Kirkwall	58 59N	2 58W	−0042	−0042	−0041	−0041	−0.5	−0.4	−0.1	−0.1
Egilsay	59 09N	2 57W	−0125	−0125	−0125	−0125	−0.1	0.0	+0.2	+0.1
Whitehall	58 09N	2 36W	−0030	−0030	−0025	−0030	−0.1	0.0	+0.2	+0.2
Loth	59 11N	2 42W	−0045	−0045	−00558	−0105	−0.4	−0.3	+0.1	+0.2
Kettletoft Pier	59 14N	2 36W	−0030	−0025	−0025	−0025	0.0	0.0	+0.2	+0.2
Rapness	59 15N	2 52W	−0205	−0205	−0205	−0205	+0.1	0.0	+0.2	0.0
Pierowall	59 19N	2 59W	−0150	−0150	−0145	−0145	+0.2	0.0	0.0	−0.1
Tingwall	59 05N	3 03W	−0200	−0125	−0145	−0125	−0.4	−0.4	−0.1	−0.1
Stromness	58 58N	3 18W	−0225	−0135	−0205	−0205	+0.1	−0.1	0.0	0.0
St Mary's	58 54N	2 55W	−0140	−0140	−0140	−0140	−0.2	−0.2	0.0	−0.1
Widewall Bay	58 49N	3 01W	−0155	−0155	−0150	−0150	+0.1	−0.1	−0.1	−0.3
Bur Wick	58 44N	2 58W	−0100	−0100	−0150	−0150	−0.1	−0.1	+0.2	+0.1
			0000	**0600**	**0100**	**0800**				
LERWICK	60 09N	1 08W	and	and	and	and	**2.1**	**1.7**	**0.9**	**0.5**
Standard port			**1200**	**1800**	**1300**	**2000**				
Fair Isle	59 32N	1 36W	−0006	−0015	−0031	−0037	+0.1	0.0	+0.1	+0.1
Shetland Islands										
Sumburgh (Grutness Voe)	59 53N	1 17W	+0006	+0008	+0004	−0002	−0.3	−0.3	−0.2	−0.1
Dury Voe	60 21N	1 10W	−0015	−0015	−0010	−0010	0.0	−0.1	0.0	−0.2
Out Skerries	60 25N	0 45W	−0025	−0025	−0010	−0010	+0.1	0.0	0.0	−0.1
Toft Pier	60 28N	1 12W	−0105	−0100	−0125	−0115	+0.2	+0.1	−0.1	−0.1
Burra Voe (Yell Sound)	60 30N	1 03W	−0025	−0025	−0025	−0025	+0.2	+0.1	0.0	−0.1
Mid Yell	60 36N	1 03W	−0030	−0020	−0035	−0025	+0.3	+0.2	+0.2	+0.1
Balta Sound	60 46N	0 50W	−0055	−0055	−0045	−0045	+0.2	+0.1	0.0	−0.1
Burra Firth	60 48N	0 52W	−0110	−0110	−0115	−0115	+0.4	+0.2	0.0	0.0
Bluemull Sound	60 42N	1 00W	−0135	−0135	−0155	−0155	+0.5	+0.2	+0.1	0.0
Sullom Voe	60 27N	1 18W	−0135	−0125	−0135	−0120	0.0	0.0	−0.2	−0.2
Hillswick	60 29N	1 29W	−0220	−0220	−0200	−0200	−0.1	−0.1	−0.1	−0.1
Scalloway	60 08N	1 16W	−0150	−0150	−0150	−0150	−0.5	−0.4	−0.3	0.0
Bay of Quendale	59 54N	1 21W	−0025	−0025	−0030	−0030	−0.4	−0.3	0.0	+0.1
Foula	60 07N	2 03W	−0140	−0130	−0140	−0120	−0.1	−0.1	0.0	0.0
			0200	**0700**	**0100**	**0700**				
WICK	58 26N	3 05W	and	and	and	and	**3.5**	**2.8**	**1.4**	**0.7**
Standard port			**1400**	**1900**	**1300**	**1900**				
Stroma	58 40N	3 08W	−0115	−0115	−0110	−0110	−0.4	−0.5	−0.1	−0.2
Gills Bay	58 38N	3 10W	−0150	−0150	−0202	−0202	+0.7	+0.7	+0.6	+0.3
Scrabster	58 37N	3 33W	−0255	−0225	−0240	−0230	+1.5	+1.2	+0.8	+0.3
Sule Skerry	59 05N	4 24W	−0320	−0255	−0315	−0250	+0.4	+0.3	+0.2	+0.1
Loch Eriboll Portnancon	58 30N	4 42W	−0340	−0255	−0315	−0255	+1.6	+1.3	+0.8	+0.4
Kyle of Durness	58 36N	4 47W	−0350	−0350	−0315	−0315	+1.1	+0.7	+0.4	−0.1
Rona	59 08N	5 49W	−0410	−0345	−0330	−0340	−0.1	−0.2	−0.2	−0.1
			0100	**0700**	**0300**	**0900**				
STORNOWAY	58 12N	6 23W	and	and	and	and	**4.8**	**3.7**	**2.0**	**0.7**
Standard port			**1300**	**1900**	**1500**	**2100**				
Outer Hebrides										
Loch Shell	58 00N	6 25W	−0013	0000	0000	−0017	0.0	−0.1	−0.1	0.0
E Loch Tarbert	57 54N	6 48W	−0025	−0010	−0010	−0020	+0.2	0.0	+0.1	+0.1
Leverburgh	57 46N	7 02W	−0041	−0020	−0015	−0025	−0.2	−0.2	−0.2	−0.1
Bays Loch	57 43N	7 10W	−0038	−0013	−0014	−0027	−0.1	−0.2	−0.2	−0.1
Loch Maddy	57 36N	7 09W	−0044	−0014	−0016	−0030	0.0	−0.1	−0.1	0.0
Loch Carnan	57 22N	7 16W	−0050	−0010	−0020	−0040	−0.3	−0.5	−0.1	−0.1
Loch Skiport	57 20N	7 16W	−0100	−0025	−0024	−0024	−0.2	−0.4	−0.3	−0.2
Loch Boisdale	57 09N	7 16W	−0055	−0030	−0020	−0040	−0.7	−0.7	−0.3	−0.2
Barra (North Bay)	57 00N	7 24W	−0103	−0031	−0034	−0048	−0.6	−0.5	−0.2	−0.1
Castle Bay	56 57N	7 29W	−0115	−0040	−0045	−0100	−0.5	−0.6	−0.3	−0.1
Barra Head	56 47N	7 38W	−0115	−0040	−0045	−0055	−0.8	−0.7	−0.2	+0.1
Shillay	57 32N	7 42W	−0103	−0043	−0047	−0107	−0.6	−0.7	−0.7	−0.3
Balivanich	57 29N	7 23W	−0103	−0017	−0031	−0045	−0.7	−0.6	−0.5	−0.2
Scolpaig	57 39N	7 29W	−0033	−0033	−0040	−0040	−1.0	−0.9	−0.5	0.0
W Loch Tarbert	57 55N	6 55W	−0015	−0015	−0046	−0046	−1.1	−0.9	−0.5	0.0
Little Bernera	58 16N	6 52W	−0021	−0011	−0017	−0027	−0.5	−0.6	−0.4	−0.2
Carloway	58 17N	6 47W	−0040	+0020	−0035	−0015	−0.6	−0.5	−0.4	−0.1
St Kilda Village Bay	57 48N	8 34W	−0040	−0040	−0045	−0045	−1.4	−1.2	−0.8	−0.3
Flannan Isles	58 17N	7 35W	−0026	−0016	−0016	−0026	−0.9	−0.7	−0.6	−0.2
Rockall	57 36N	13 41W	−0055	−0055	−0105	−0105	−1.8	−1.5	−0.9	−0.2

Location	Lat	Long	High Water		Low Water		MHWS	MHWN	MLWN	MLWS
			0000	0600	0300	0900				
ULLAPOOL	57 54N	5 09W	and	and	and	and	5.2	3.9	2.1	0.7
Standard port			1200	1800	1500	2100				
Loch Bervie	58 27N	5 03W	+0020	+0010	+0010	+0020	−0.4	−0.3	−0.2	−0.1
Loch Laxford	58 24N	5 05W	+0015	+0015	+0005	+0005	−0.3	−0.4	−0.2	0.0
Eddrachillis Bay										
Badcall Bay	58 19N	5 08W	+0005	+0005	+0005	+0005	−0.7	−0.5	−0.5	+0.2
Loch Nedd	58 14N	5 10W	0000	0000	0000	0000	−0.3	−0.2	−0.2	0.0
Loch Inver	58 09N	5 18W	−0005	−0005	−0005	−0005	−0.2	0.0	0.0	+0.1
Summer Isles Tanera Mor	58 01N	5 24W	−0005	−0005	−0010	−0010	−0.1	+0.1	0.0	+0.1
Loch Ewe Mellon Charles	57 51N	5 38W	−0010	−0010	−0010	−0010	−0.1	−0.1	−0.1	0.0
Loch Gairloch Gairloch	57 43N	5 41W	−0020	−0020	−0010	−0010	0.0	+0.1	−0.3	−0.1
Loch Torridon Shieldaig	57 31N	5 39W	−0020	−0020	−0015	−0015	+0.4	+0.3	+0.1	0.0
Inner Sound Applecross	57 26N	5 49W	−0010	−0015	−0010	−0010	0.0	0.0	0.0	+0.1
Loch Carron Plockton	57 21N	5 39W	+0005	−0025	−0005	−0010	+0.5	+0.5	+0.5	+0.2
Rona Loch a' Bhraige	57 35N	5 58W	−0020	0000	−0010	0000	−0.1	−0.1	−0.1	−0.2
Skye										
Broadford Bay	57 15N	5 54W	−0015	−0015	−0010	−0015	+0.2	+0.1	+0.1	0.0
Portree	57 24N	6 11W	−0025	−0025	−0025	−0025	+0.1	−0.2	−0.2	0.0
Loch Snizort (Uig Bay)	57 35N	6 22W	−0045	−0020	−0005	−0025	+0.1	−0.4	−0.2	0.0
Loch Dunvegan	57 27N	6 38W	−0105	−0030	−0020	−0040	0.0	−0.1	0.0	0.0
Loch Harport	57 20N	6 25W	−0115	−0035	−0020	−0100	−0.1	−0.1	0.0	+0.1
Soay Camus nan Gall	57 09N	6 13W	−0055	−0025	−0025	−0045	−0.4	−0.2	*No data*	
Loch Alsh										
Kyle of Lochalsh	57 17N	5 43W	−0040	−0020	−0005	−0025	+0.1	0.0	0.0	−0.1
Dornie Bridge	57 17N	5 31W	−0040	−0010	−0005	−0020	+0.1	−0.1	0.0	0.0
Kyle Rhea Glenelg Bay	57 13N	5 38W	−0105	−0035	−0035	−0055	−0.4	−0.4	−0.9	−0.1
Loch Hourn	57 06N	5 34W	−0125	−0050	−0040	−0110	−0.2	−0.1	−0.1	+0.1
			0000	0600	0100	0700				
OBAN	56 25N	5 29W	and	and	and	and	4.0	2.9	1.8	0.7
Standard port			1200	1800	1300	1900				
Loch Nevis										
Inverie Bay	57 02N	5 41W	+0030	+0020	+0035	+0020	+1.0	+0.9	+0.2	0.0
Mallaig	57 00N	5 50W	+0017	+0017	+0017	+0017	+1.0	+0.7	+0.3	+0.1
Eigg Bay of Laig	56 55N	6 10W	+0015	+0030	+0040	+0005	+0.7	+0.6	−0.2	− 0.2
Loch Moidart	56 47N	5 53W	+0015	+0015	+0040	+0020	+0.8	+0.6	− 0.2	−0.2
Coll Loch Eatharna	56 37N	6 31W	+0025	+0010	+0015	+0025	+0.4	+0.3	*No data*	
Tiree Gott Bay	56 31N	6 48W	0000	+0010	+0005	+0010	0.0	+0.1	0.0	0.0
			0100	0700	0100	0800				
OBAN	56 25N	5 29W	and	and	and	and	4.0	2.9	1.8	0.7
Standard port			1300	1900	1300	2000				
Mull										
Carsaig Bay	56 19N	5 58W	−0015	−0005	−0030	+0020	+0.1	+0.2	0.0	−0.1
Iona	56 20N	6 23W	−0010	−0005	−0020	+0015	0.0	+0.1	−0.3	−0.2
Bunessan	56 19N	6 14W	−0015	−0015	−0010	−0015	+0.3	+0.1	0.0	−0.1
Ulva Sound	56 29N	6 08W	−0010	−0015	0000	−0005	+0.4	+0.3	0.0	−0.1
Loch Sunart Salen	56 43N	5 47W	−0015	+0015	+0010	+0005	+0.6	+0.5	−0.1	−0.1
Sound of Mull										
Tobermory	56 37N	6 04W	+0025	+0010	+0015	+0025	+0.4	+0.4	0.0	0.0
Salen	56 31N	5 57W	+0045	+0015	+0020	+0030	+0.2	+0.2	−0.1	0.0
Loch Aline	56 32N	5 46W	+0012	+0012	*No data*	*No data*	+0.5	+0.3	*No data*	
Craignure	56 28N	5 42W	+0030	+0005	+0010	+0015	0.0	+0.1	−0.1	−0.1
Loch Linnhe										
Corran	56 43N	5 14W	+0007	+0007	+0004	+0004	+0.4	+0.4	−0.1	0.0
Corpach	56 51N	5 07W	0000	+0020	+0040	0000	0.0	0.0	−0.2	−0.2
Loch Eil Head	56 51N	5 20W	+0025	+0045	+0105	+0025	*No data*		*No data*	
Loch Leven Head	56 43N	5 00W	+0045	+0045	+0045	+0045	*No data*		*No data*	
Loch Linnhe Port Appin	56 33N	5 25W	−0005	−0005	−0030	0000	+0.2	+0.2	+0.1	+0.1
Loch Creran										
Barcaldine Pier	56 32N	5 19W	+0010	+0020	+0040	+0015	+0.1	+0.1	0.0	+0.1
Loch Creran Head	56 33N	5 16W	+0015	+0025	+0120	+0020	−0.3	−0.3	−0.4	−0.3
Loch Etive										
Dunstaffnage Bay	56 27N	5 26W	+0005	0000	0000	+0005	+0.1	+0.1	+0.1	+0.1
Connel	56 27N	5 24W	+0020	+0005	+0010	+0015	−0.3	−0.2	−0.1	+0.1
Bonawe	56 27N	5 13W	+0150	+0205	+0240	+0210	−2.0	−1.7	−1.3	−0.5
Seil Sound	56 18N	5 35W	−0035	−0015	−0040	−0015	−1.3	−0.9	−0.7	−0.3
Colonsay Scalasaig	56 04N	6 11W	−0020	−0005	−0015	+0005	−0.1	−0.2	−0.2	−0.2
Jura Glengarrisdale Bay	56 07N	5 47W	−0020	0000	−0010	0000	−0.4	−0.2	0.0	−0.2

Location	Lat	Long	High Water		Low Water		MHWS	MHWN	MLWN	MLWS
Islay										
Rubha A'Mhail	55 56N	6 07W	−0020	0000	+0005	−0015	−0.3	−0.1	−0.3	−0.1
Ardnave Point	55 52N	6 20W	−0035	+0010	0000	−0025	−0.4	−0.2	−0.3	−0.1
Orsay	55 41N	6 31W	−0110	−0110	−0040	−0040	−1.4	−0.6	−0.5	−0.2
Bruichladdich	55 46N	6 22W	−0105	−0035	−0110	−0110	−1.8	−1.3	−0.4	+0.1
Port Ellen	55 38N	6 11W	−0530	−0050	−0045	−0530	−3.1	−2.1	−1.3	−0.4
Port Askaig	55 51N	6 06W	−0110	−0030	−0020	−0020	−1.9	−1.4	−0.8	−0.3
Sound of Jura										
Craighouse	55 50N	5 57W	−0230	−0250	−0150	−0230	−3.0	−2.4	−1.3	−0.6
Loch Melfort	56 15N	5 29W	−0055	−0025	−0040	−0035	−1.2	−0.8	−0.5	−0.1
Loch Beag	56 09N	5 36W	−0110	−0045	−0035	−0045	−1.6	−1.2	−0.8	−0.4
Carsaig Bay	56 02N	5 38W	−0105	−0040	−0050	−0050	−2.1	−1.6	−1.0	−0.4
Sound of Gigha	55 41N	5 44W	−0450	−0210	−0130	−0410	−2.5	−1.6	−1.0	−0.1
Machrihanish	55 25N	5 45W	−0520	−0350	−0340	−0540	*Mean range 0.5 metres*			
			0000	**0600**	**0000**	**0600**				
GREENOCK	55 57N	4 46W	and	and	and	and	**3.4**	**2.8**	**1.0**	**0.3**
Standard port			**1200**	**1800**	**1200**	**1800**				
Firth of Clyde										
Southend, Kintyre	55 19N	5 38W	−0030	−0010	+0005	+0035	−1.3	−1.2	−0.5	−0.2
Campbeltown	55 25N	5 36W	−0025	−0005	−0015	+0005	−0.5	−0.3	+0.1	+0.2
Carradale	55 36N	5 28W	−0015	−0005	−0005	+0005	−0.3	−0.2	+0.1	+0.1
Loch Ranza	55 43N	5 18W	−0015	−0005	−0010	−0005	−0.4	−0.3	−0.1	0.0
Loch Fyne										
East Loch Tarbert	55 52N	5 24W	−0005	−0005	0000	−0005	+0.2	+0.1	0.0	0.0
Inveraray	56 14N	5 04W	+0011	+0011	+0034	+0034	−0.1	+0.1	−0.5	−0.2
Kyles of Bute										
Rubha a'Bhodaich	55 55N	5 09W	−0020	−0010	−0007	−0007	−0.2	−0.1	+0.2	+0.2
Tighnabruich	55 55N	5 13W	+0007	−0010	−0002	−0015	0.0	+0.2	+0.4	+0.5
Firth of Clyde – continued										
Millport	55 45N	4 56W	−0005	−0025	−0025	−0005	0.0	−0.1	0.0	+0.1
Rothesay Bay	55 50N	5 03W	−0020	−0015	−0010	−0002	+0.2	+0.2	+0.2	+0.2
Wemyss Bay	55 53N	4 53W	−0005	−0005	−0005	−0005	0.0	0.0	+0.1	+0.1
Loch Long										
Coulport	56 03N	4 53W	−0011	−0011	−0008	−0008	0.0	0.0	0.0	0.0
Lochgoilhead	56 10N	4 54W	+0015	0000	−0005	−0005	−0.2	−0.3	−0.3	−0.3
Arrochar	56 12N	4 45W	−0005	−0005	−0005	−0005	0.0	0.0	−0.1	−0.1
Gare Loch										
Rhu Marina	56 01N	4 46W	−0007	−0007	−0007	−0007	−0.1	−0.1	−0.1	−0.2
Faslane	56 04N	4 49W	−0010	−0010	−0010	−0010	0.0	0.0	−0.1	−0.2
Garelochhead	56 05N	4 50W	0000	0000	0000	0000	0.0	0.0	0.0	−0.1
River Clyde										
Helensburgh	56 00N	4 44W	0000	0000	0000	0000	0.0	0.0	0.0	0.0
Port Glasgow	55 56N	4 41W	+0010	+0005	+0010	+0020	+0.2	+0.1	0.0	0.0
Bowling	55 56N	4 29W	+0020	+0010	+0030	+0055	+0.6	+0.5	+0.3	+0.1
Clydebank (Rothesay Dock)	55 54N	4 24W	+0025	+0015	+0035	+0100	+1.1	+0.9	+0.6	+0.3
Glasgow	55 51N	4 16W	+0025	+0015	+0035	+0105	+1.3	+1.1	+0.7	+0.4
Firth of Clyde – continued										
Brodick Bay	55 35N	5 08W	−0013	−0013	−0008	−0008	−0.2	−0.1	0.0	+0.1
Lamlash	55 32N	5 07W	−0016	−0036	−0024	−0004	−0.2	−0.2	*No data*	
Ardrossan	55 38N	4 49W	−0020	−0010	−0010	−0010	−0.2	−0.2	+0.1	+0.1
Irvine	55 36N	4 42W	−0020	−0020	−0030	−0010	−0.3	−0.3	−0.1	0.0
Troon	55 33N	4 41W	−0025	−0025	−0020	−0020	−0.2	−0.2	0.0	0.0
Ayr	55 28N	4 39W	−0025	−0025	−0030	−0015	−0.4	−0.3	+0.1	+0.1
Girvan	55 15N	4 52W	−0025	−0040	−0035	−0010	−0.3	−0.3	−0.1	0.0
Loch Ryan Stranraer	54 55N	5 02W	−0030	−0025	−0010	−0010	−0.2	−0.1	0.0	+0.1
			0000	**0600**	**0200**	**0800**				
LIVERPOOL	53 27N	3 01W	and	and	and	and	**9.4**	**7.5**	**3.2**	**1.1**
Standard port			**1200**	**1800**	**1400**	**2000**				
Portpatrick	54 51N	5 07W	+0022	+0030	−0003	−0032	−5.6	−4.5	−2.3	−0.8
Luce Bay										
Drummore	54 42N	4 53W	+0035	+0045	+0010	+0015	−3.5	−2.6	−1.2	−0.5
Port William	54 46N	4 35W	+0035	+0035	+0020	−0005	−3.0	−2.3	−1.1	*No data*
Wigtown Bay										
Isle of Whithorn	54 42N	4 22W	+0025	+0030	+0020	0000	−2.5	−2.1	−1.1	−0.4
Garlieston	54 47N	4 22W	+0030	+0040	+0025	0000	−2.4	−1.8	−0.8	*No data*
Solway Firth										
Kirkcudbright Bay	54 48N	4 04W	+0020	+0020	+0005	−0005	−1.9	−1.6	−0.8	−0.3
Hestan Islet	54 50N	3 48W	+0030	+0030	+0015	+0020	−1.1	−1.2	−0.8	−0.2
Southerness Point	54 52N	3 36W	+0035	+0035	+0025	+0005	−0.8	−0.8	*No data*	

Location	Lat	Long	High Water		Low Water		MHWS	MHWN	MLWN	MLWS
Annan Waterfoot	54 58N	3 16W	+0055	+0110	+0215	+0305	−2.3	−2.7	−3.0	
Torduff Point	54 58N	3 09W	+0110	+0145	+0515	+0405	−4.2	−5.0		
Redkirk	54 59N	3 06W	+0115	+0220	+0710	+0440	−5.6	−6.3		
WEST COAST OF ENGLAND										
Silloth	54 52N	3 24W	+0035	+0045	+0040	+0050	−0.2	−0.4	−0.9	−0.3
Maryport	54 43N	3 30W	+0021	+0036	+0017	+0002	−0.8	−0.9	−0.7	−0.2
Workington	54 39N	3 34W	+0025	+0025	+0015	+0005	−1.3	−1.2	−0.6	−0.2
Whitehaven	54 33N	3 36W	+0010	+0020	+0005	0000	−1.4	−1.2	−0.8	−0.1
Tarn Point	54 17N	3 25W	+0010	+0010	+0005	−0005	−1.1	−1.1	−0.7	−0.2
Duddon Bar	54 09N	3 20W	+0007	+0007	+0005	−0001	−0.9	−0.9	−0.6	−0.2
			0000	**0600**	**0200**	**0700**				
LIVERPOOL	53 27N	3 01W	and	and	and	and	**9.4**	**7.5**	**3.2**	**2.1**
Standard port			**1200**	**1800**	**1400**	**1900**				
Barrow-in-Furness	54 06N	3 12W	+0020	+0020	+0010	+0010	+0.1	−0.2	−0.2	0.0
Ulverston	54 11N	3 04W	+0025	+0045	*No data*	*no data*	−0.1	−0.2	*No data*	
Arnside	54 12N	2 51W	+0105	+0140	*No data*	*no data*	+0.4	+0.1	*No data*	
Morecambe	54 04N	2 53W	+0010	+0015	+0025	+0010	+0.1	−0.1	−0.3	0.0
Heysham	54 02N	2 55W	+0010	+0010	+0010	−0005	+0.2	−0.1	−0.2	0.0
River Lune Glasson Dock	54 00N	2 51W	+0025	+0035	+0215	+0235	−2.8	−3.1	*No data*	
Lancaster	54 03N	2 49W	+0115	+0035	*Dries*	*Dries*	−5.1	−5.0	*Dries*	
River Wyre										
Wyre Lighthouse	53 57N	3 02W	−0005	−0005	0000	−0005	−0.2	−0.2	*No data*	
Fleetwood	53 56N	3 00W	−0004	−0004	−0006	−0006	−0.2	−0.2	−0.2	+0.1
Blackpool	53 49N	3 04W	−0010	0000	−0010	−0020	−0.5	−0.5	−0.4	−0.1
River Ribble Preston	53 45N	2 45W	+0015	+0015	+0330	+0305	−4.1	−4.2	−3.1	−1.0
Liverpool Bay										
Southport	53 39N	3 01W	−0015	−0005	*No data*	*No data*	−0.4	−0.4	*No data*	
Formby	53 32N	3 07W	−0010	−0005	−0025	−0025	−0.4	−0.2	−0.3	−0.1
River Mersey										
Alfred Dock	53 24N	3 01W	+0007	+0007	0000	0000	−0.1	−0.1	−0.3	−0.2
Eastham	53 19N	2 57W	+0014	+0014	+0006	+0006	+0.2	0.0	−0.4	−0.5
Hale Head	53 19N	2 48W	+0035	+0030	*No data*	*No data*	−2.5	−2.6	*No data*	
Widnes	53 21N	2 44W	+0045	+0050	+0355	+0340	−4.3	−4.5	−2.8	−0.6
Fiddler's Ferry	53 22N	2 40W	+0105	+0120	+0535	+0445	−6.0	−6.4	−2.7	−0.6
River Dee										
Hilbre Island	53 23N	3 14W	−0011	−0006	−0013	−0018	−0.4	−0.3	−0.1	+0.2
Chester	53 12N	2 54W	+0110	+0110	+0455	+0455	−5.4	−5.5	*Dries*	
Connah's Quay (Wales)	53 13N	3 03W	+0005	+0020	+0350	+0335	−4.7	−4.5	*Dries*	
Mostyn Docks (Wales)	53 19N	3 16W	−0015	−0010	−0025	−0025	−0.9	−0.8	*No data*	
Isle of Man Peel	54 14N	4 42W	+0010	+0010	−0020	−0030	−4.2	−3.2	−1.7	−0.7
Ramsey	54 19N	4 22W	+0010	+0020	−0010	−0020	−2.0	−1.6	−0.9	−0.2
Douglas	54 09N	4 28W	+0010	+0020	−0020	−0030	−2.5	−2.1	−0.6	−0.3
Port St Mary	54 04N	4 44W	+0010	+0020	−0015	−0035	−3.5	−2.7	−1.6	−0.6
Calf Sound	54 04N	4 48W	+0010	+0010	−0020	−0030	−3.3	−2.7	−1.2	−0.5
Port Erin	54 05N	4 46W	0000	+0020	−0015	−0055	−4.2	−3.3	−1.6	−0.7

WALES

Location	Lat	Long	High Water		Low Water		MHWS	MHWN	MLWN	MLWS
Colwyn Bay	53 18N	3 43W	−0020	−0020	*No data*	*No data*	−1.5	−1.3	*No data*	
Llandudno	53 20N	3 50W	−0020	−0020	−0035	−0040	−1.7	−1.4	−0.7	−0.3
			0000	**0600**	**0500**	**1100**				
HOLYHEAD	53 19N	4 37W	and	and	and	and	**5.6**	**4.4**	**2.0**	**0.7**
Standard port			**1200**	**1800**	**1700**	**2300**				
Conwy	53 17N	3 50W	+0025	+0035	+0120	+0105	+2.3	+1.8	+0.6	+0.4
Menai Strait										
Beaumaris	53 16N	4 05W	+0025	+0010	+0055	+0035	+2.0	+1.6	+0.5	+0.1
Menai Bridge	53 13N	4 10W	+0030	+0010	+0100	+0035	+1.7	+1.4	+0.3	0.0
Port Dinorwic	53 11N	4 13W	−0015	−0025	+0030	0000	0.0	0.0	0.0	+0.1
Caernarfon	53 09N	4 16W	−0030	−0030	+0015	−0005	−0.4	−0.4	−0.1	−0.1
Fort Belan	53 07N	4 20W	−0040	−0015	−0025	−0005	−1.0	−0.9	−0.2	−0.1
Trwyn Dinmor	53 19N	4 03W	+0025	+0015	+0050	+0035	+1.9	+1.5	+0.5	+0.2
Moelfre	53 20N	4 14W	+0025	+0020	+0050	+0035	+1.9	+1.4	+0.5	+0.2
Amlwch	53 25N	4 20W	+0020	+0010	+0035	+0025	+1.6	+ 1.3	+0.5	+0.2
Cemaes Bay	53 25N	4 27W	+0020	+0025	+0040	+0035	+1.0	+0.7	+0.3	+0.1
Trearddur Bay	53 16N	4 37W	−0045	−0025	−0015	−0015	−0.4	−0.4	0.0	+0.1
Porth Trecastell	53 12N	4 30W	−0045	−0025	−0005	−0015	−0.6	−0.6	0.0	0.0
Llanddwyn Island	53 08N	4 25W	−0115	−0055	−0030	−0020	−0.7	−0.5	−0.1	0.0
Trefor	53 00N	4 25W	−0115	−0100	−0030	−0020	−0.8	−0.9	−0.2	−0.1
Porth Dinllaen	52 57N	4 34W	−0120	−0105	−0035	−0025	−1.0	−1.0	−0.2	−0.2
Porth Ysgaden	52 54N	4 39W	−0125	−0110	−0040	−0035	−1.1	−1.0	−0.1	−0.1
Bardsey Island	52 46N	4 47W	−0220	−0240	−0145	−0140	−1.2	−1.2	−0.5	−0.1

Location	Lat	Long	High Water		Low Water		MHWS	MHWN	MLWN	MLWS
			0100	0800	0100	0700				
MILFORD HAVEN	51 42N	5 03W	and	and	and	and	7.0	5.2	2.5	0.7
Standard port			1300	2000	1300	1900				
Cardigan Bay										
Aberdaron	52 48N	4 43W	+0210	+0200	+0240	+0310	−2.4	−1.9	−0.6	−0.2
St Tudwal's Roads	52 49N	4 29W	+0155	+0145	+0240	+0310	−2.2	−1.9	−0.7	−0.2
Pwllheli	52 53N	4 24W	+0210	+0150	+0245	+0320	−2.0	− 1.8	−0.6	−0.2
Criccieth	52 55N	4 14W	+0210	+0155	+0255	+0320	−2.0	−1.8	−0.7	−0.3
Porthmadog	52 55N	4 08W	+0235	+0210	No data	No data	−1.9	−1.8	No data	
Barmouth	52 43N	4 03W	+0215	+0205	+0310	+0320	−2.0	−1.7	−0.7	0.0
Aberdovey	52 33N	4 03W	+0215	+0200	+0230	+0305	−2.0	−1.7	−0.5	0.0
Aberystwyth	52 24N	4 05W	+0145	+0130	+0210	+0245	−2.0	−1.7	−0.7	0.0
New Quay	52 13N	4 21W	+0150	+0125	+0155	+0230	−2.1	−1.8	−0.6	−0.1
Aberporth	52 08N	4 33W	+0135	+0120	+0150	+0220	−2.1	−1.8	−0.6	−0.1
Port Cardigan	52 07N	4 41W	+0140	+0120	+0220	+0130	−2.3	−1.8	−0.5	0.0
Cardigan (Town)	52 05N	4 40W	+0220	+0150	No data	No data	−2.2	−1.6	No data	
Fishguard	52 01N	4 59W	+0115	+0100	+0110	+0135	−2.2	−1.8	−0.5	+0.1
Porthgain	51 57N	5 11W	+0055	+0045	+0045	+0100	−2.5	−1.8	−0.6	0.0
Ramsey Sound	51 53N	5 19W	+0030	+0030	+0030	+0030	−1.9	−1.3	−0.3	0.0
Solva	51 52N	5 12W	+0015	+0010	+0035	+0015	−1.5	−1.0	−0.2	0.0
Little Haven	51 46N	5 07W	+0010	+0010	+0025	+0015	−1.1	−0.8	−0.2	0.0
Martin's Haven	51 44N	5 15W	+0010	+0010	+0015	+0015	−0.8	−0.5	+0.1	+0.1
Skomer Island	51 44N	5 17W	−0005	−0005	+0005	+0005	−0.4	−0.1	0.0	0.0
Dale Roads	51 42N	5 09W	−0005	−0005	−0008	−0008	0.0	0.0	0.0	−0.1
Cleddau River										
Neyland	51 42N	4 57W	+0002	+0010	0000	0000	0.0	0.0	0.0	0.0
Black Tar	51 45N	4 54W	+0010	+0020	+0005	0000	+0.1	+0.1	0.0	−0.1
Haverfordwest	51 48N	4 58W	+0010	+0025	Dries	Dries	−4.8	−4.9	Dries	
Stackpole Quay	51 37N	4 54W	−0005	+0025	−0010	−0010	+0.9	+0.7	+0.2	+0.3
Tenby	51 40N	4 42W	−0015	−0010	−0015	−0020	+1.4	+1.1	+0.5	+0.2
Towy River										
Ferryside	51 46N	4 22W	0000	−0010	+0220	0000	−0.3	−0.7	−1.7	−0.6
Carmarthen	51 51N	4 18W	+0010	0000	Dries	Dries	−4.4	−4.8	Dries	
Burry Inlet										
Burry Port	51 41N	4 15W	+0003	+0003	+0007	+0007	+1.6	+1.4	+0.5	+0.4
Llanelli	51 40N	4 10W	−0003	−0003	+0150	+0020	+0.8	+0.6	No data	
Mumbles	51 34N	3 58W	+0005	+0010	−0020	−0015	+2.3	+1.7	+0.6	+0.2
River Neath Entrance	51 37N	3 51W	+0002	+0011	Dries	Dries	+2.7	+2.2	Dries	
Port Talbot	51 35N	3 49W	+0003	+0005	−0010	−0005	+2.8	+2.2	+1.0	+0.5
Porthcawl	51 28N	3 42W	+0005	+0010	−0010	−0005	+2.9	+2.3	+0.8	+0.3
			0600	1100	0300	0800				
BRISTOL, AVONMOUTH	51 30N	2 44W	and	and	and	and	13.2	9.8	3.8	1.0
Standard port			1800	2300	1500	2000				
Barry	51 23N	3 16W	−0025	−0025	−0130	−0045	−1.7	−1.0	−0.2	0.0
Flat Holm	51 23N	3 07W	−0015	−0015	−0035	−0035	−1.4	−1.0	−0.5	0.0
Steep Holm	51 20N	3 06W	−0020	−0020	−0040	−0040	−1.7	−1.1	−0.5	−0.4
Cardiff	51 27N	3 10W	−0015	−0015	−0100	−0030	−1.0	−0.5	0.0	0.0
Newport	51 33N	2 59W	−0020	−0010	0000	−0020	−1.1	−0.9	−0.6	−0.6
River Wye Chepstow	51 39N	2 40W	+0020	+0020	No data	No data	No data		No data	
			0000	0600	0000	0700				
BRISTOL, AVONMOUTH	51 30N	2 44W	and	and	and	and	13.2	9.8	3.8	1.0
Standard port			1200	1800	1200	1900				

WEST COAST OF ENGLAND

Location	Lat	Long	High Water		Low Water		MHWS	MHWN	MLWN	MLWS
River Severn										
Sudbrook	51 35N	2 43W	+0010	+0010	+0025	+0015	+0.2	+0.1	−0.1	+0.1
Beachley (Aust)	51 36N	2 38W	+0010	+0015	+0040	+0025	−0.2	−0.2	−0.5	−0.3
Inward Rocks	51 39N	2 37W	+0020	+0020	+0105	+0045	−1.0	−1.1	−1.4	−0.6
Narlwood Rocks	51 39N	2 36W	+0025	+0025	+0120	+0100	−1.9	−2.0	−2.3	−0.8
White House	51 40N	2 33W	+0025	+0025	+0145	+0120	−3.0	−3.1	−3.6	−1.0
Berkeley	51 42N	2 30W	+0030	+0045	+0245	+0220	−3.8	−3.9	−3.4	−0.5
Sharpness Dock	51 43N	2 29W	+0035	+0050	+0305	+0245	−3.9	−4.2	−3.3	−0.4
Wellhouse Rock	51 44N	2 29W	+0040	+0055	+0320	+0305	−4.1	−4.4	−3.1	−0.2
Epney	51 42N	2 24W	+0130	No data	No data	No data	−9.4	No data	No data	
Minsterworth	51 50N	2 23W	+0140	No data	No data	No data	−10.1	No data	No data	
Llanthony	51 51N	2 21W	+0215	No data	No data	No data	−10.7	No data	No data	
			0200	0800	0300	0800				
BRISTOL, AVONMOUTH	51 30N	2 44W	and	and	and	and	13.2	9.8	3.8	1.0
Standard port			1400	2000	1500	2000				
River Avon										
Shirehampton	51 29N	2 41W	0000	0000	+0035	+0010	−0.7	−0.7	−0.8	0.0
Sea Mills	51 29N	2 39W	+0005	+0005	+0105	+0030	−1.4	−1.5	−1.7	−0.1
Cumberland Basin Entrance	51 27N	2 37W	+0010	+0010	Dries	Dries	−2.9	−3.0	Dries	
Portishead	51 30N	2 45W	−0002	0000	No data	No data	−0.1	−0.1	No data	

Location	Lat	Long	High Water		Low Water		MHWS	MHWN	MLWN	MLWS
Clevedon	51 27N	2 52W	−0010	−0020	−0025	−0015	−0.4	−0.2	+0.2	0.0
St Thomas Head	51 24N	2 56W	0000	0000	−0030	−0030	−0.4	−0.2	+0.1	+0.1
English & Welsh Grounds	51 28N	2 59W	−0008	−0008	−0030	−0030	−0.5	−0.8	−0.3	0.0
Weston-super-Mare	51 21N	2 59W	−0020	−0030	−0130	−0030	−1.2	−1.0	−0.8	−0.2
River Parrett										
Burnham-on-Sea	51 14N	3 00W	−0020	−0025	−0030	0000	−2.3	−1.9	−1.4	−1.1
Bridgwater	51 08N	3 00W	−0015	−0030	+0305	+0455	−8.6	−8.1	*Dries*	
Hinkley Point	51 13N	3 08W	−0020	−0025	−0100	−0040	−1.7	−1.4	−0.2	−0.2
Watchet	51 11N	3 20W	−0035	−0050	−0145	−0040	−1.9	−1.5	+0.1	+0.1
Minehead	51 13N	3 28W	−0037	−0052	−0155	−0045	−2.6	−1.9	−0.2	0.0
Porlock Bay	51 13N	3 38W	−0045	−0055	−0205	−0050	−3.0	−2.2	−0.1	−0.1
Lynmouth	51 14N	3 50W	−0055	−0115	*No data*	*No data*	−3.6	−2.7	*No data*	
			0100	**0700**	**0100**	**0700**				
MILFORD HAVEN	51 42N	5 03W	and	and	and	and	**7.0**	**5.2**	**2.5**	**0.7**
Standard port			**1300**	**1900**	**1300**	**1900**				
Ilfracombe	51 13N	4 07W	−0016	−0016	−0041	−0031	+2.3	+1.8	+0.6	+0.3
Rivers Taw & Torridge										
Appledore	51 03N	4 12W	−0020	−0025	+0015	−0045	+0.5	0.0	−0.9	−0.5
Yelland Marsh	51 04N	4 10W	−0010	−0015	+0100	−0015	+0.1	−0.4	−1.2	−0.6
Fremington	51 05N	4 07W	−0010	−0015	+0030	−0030	−1.1	−1.8	−2.2	−0.5
Barnstaple	51 05N	4 04W	0000	−0015	−0155	−0245	−2.9	−3.8	−2.2	−0.4
Bideford	51 01N	4 12W	−0020	−0025	0000	0000	−1.1	−1.6	−2.5	−0.7
Clovelly	51 00N	4 24W	−0030	−0030	−0020	−0040	+1.3	+1.1	+0.2	+0.2
Lundy	51 10N	4 39W	−0025	−0025	−0020	−0035	+0.9	+0.7	+0.3	+0.1
Bude	50 50N	4 33W	−0040	−0040	−0035	−0045	+0.7	+0.6	*No data*	
Boscastle	50 41N	4 42W	−0045	−0010	−0110	−0100	+0.3	+0.4	+0.2	+0.2
Port Isaac	50 35N	4 50W	−0100	−0100	−0100	−0100	+0.5	+0.6	0.0	+0.2
River Camel										
Padstow	50 33N	4 56W	−0055	−0050	−0040	−0050	+0.3	+0.4	+0.1	+0.1
Wadebridge	50 31N	4 50W	−0052	−0052	+0235	+0245	−3.8	−3.8	−2.5	−0.4
Newquay	50 25N	5 05W	−0100	−0110	−0105	−0050	0.0	+0.1	0.0	−0.1
Perranporth	50 21N	5 09W	−0100	−0110	−0110	−0050	−0.1	0.0	0.0	+0.1
St Ives	50 13N	5 29W	−0050	−0115	−0105	−0040	−0.4	−0.3	−0.1	+0.1
Cape Cornwall	50 08N	5 42 W	−0130	−0145	−0120	−0120	−1.0	−0.9	−0.5	−0.1
Sennen Cove	50 05N	5 42W	−0130	−0145	−0125	−0125	−0.9	−0.4	*No data*	

IRELAND

			0000	**0700**	**0000**	**0500**				
DUBLIN, NORTH WALL	53 21N	6 13W	and	and	and	and	**4.1**	**3.4**	**1.5**	**0.7**
Standard port			**1200**	**1900**	**1200**	**1700**				
Courtown	52 39N	6 13W	−0328	−0242	−0158	−0138	−2.8	−2.4	−0.5	0.0
Arklow	52 48N	6 08W	−0315	−0201	−0140	−0134	−2.7	−2.2	−0.6	−0.1
Wicklow	52 59N	6 02W	−0019	−0019	−0024	−0026	−1.4	−1.1	−0.4	0.0
Greystones	53 09N	6 04W	−0008	−0008	−0008	−0008	−0.5	−0.4	*No data*	
Dun Laoghaire	53 18N	6 08W	−0006	−0001	−0002	−0003	0.0	0.0	0.0	+0.1
Dublin Bar	53 21N	6 09W	−0006	−0001	−0002	−0003	0.0	0.0	0.0	+0.1
Howth	53 23N	6 04W	−0007	−0005	+0001	+0005	0.0	−0.1	−0.2	−0.2
Malahide	53 27N	6 09W	+0002	+0003	+0009	+0009	+0.1	−0.2	−0.4	−0.2
Balbriggan	53 37N	6 11W	−0021	−0015	+0010	+0002	+0.3	+0.2	*No data*	
River Boyne Bar	53 43N	6 14W	−0005	0000	+0020	+0030	+0.4	+0.3	−0.1	−0.2
Dunany Point	53 52N	6 14W	−0028	−0018	−0008	−0006	+0.7	+0.9	*No data*	
Dundalk Soldiers Point	54 00N	6 21W	−0010	−0010	0000	+0045	+1.0	+0.8	+0.1	−0.1

NORTHERN IRELAND

Carlingford Lough

Cranfield Point	54 01N	6 04W	−0027	−0011	+0005	−0010	+0.7	+0.9	+0.3	+0.2
Warrenpoint	54 06N	6 15W	−0020	−0010	+0025	+0035	+1.0	+0.7	+0.2	+0.0
Newry (Victoria Lock)	54 09N	6 19W	+0005	+0015	+0045	*Dries*	+1.2	+0.9	+0.1	*Dries*

			0100	**0700**	**0000**	**0600**				
BELFAST	54 36N	5 55W	and	and	and	and	**3.5**	**3.0**	**1.1**	**0.4**
Standard port			**1300**	**1900**	**1200**	**1800**				
Kilkeel	54 03N	5 59W	+0040	+0030	+0010	+0010	+1.2	+1.1	+0.4	+0.4
Newcastle	54 12N	5 53W	+0025	+0035	+0020	+0040	+1.6	+1.1	+0.4	+0.1
Killough Harbour	54 15N	5 38W	0000	+0020	*No data*	*No data*	+1.8	+1.6	*No data*	
Ardglass	54 16N	5 36W	+0010	+0015	+0005	+0010	+1.7	+1.2	+0.6	+0.3
Strangford Lough										
Killard Point	54 19N	5 31W	+0011	+0021	+0005	+0025	+1.0	+0.8	+0.1	+0.1
Strangford	54 22N	5 33W	+0147	+0157	+0148	+0208	+0.1	+0.1	−0.2	0.0
Quoile Barrier	54 22N	5 41W	+0150	+0200	+0150	+0300	+0.2	+0.2	−0.3	−0.1
Killyleagh	54 24N	5 39W	+0157	+0207	+0211	+0231	+0.3	+0.3	*No data*	
South Rock	54 24N	5 25W	+0023	+0023	+0025	+0025	+1.0	+0.8	+0.1	+0.1
Portavogie	54 27N	5 26W	+0010	+0020	+0010	+0020	+1.2	+0.9	+0.3	+0.2
Donaghadee	54 39N	5 32W	+0020	+0020	+0023	+0023	+0.5	+0.4	0.0	+0.1
Carrickfergus	54 43N	5 48W	+0005	+0005	+0005	+0005	−0.3	−0.3	−0.2	−0.1
Larne	54 51N	5 48W	+0005	0000	+0010	−0005	−0.7	−0.5	−0.3	0.0

TIDES

213

Location	Lat	Long	High Water		Low Water		MHWS	MHWN	MLWN	MLWS
Red Bay	55 04N	6 03W	+0022	−0010	+0007	−0017	−1.9	−1.5	−0.8	−0.2
Cushendun	55 08N	6 02W	+0010	−0030	0000	−0025	−1.7	−1.5	−0.6	−0.2
Portrush	55 12N	6 40W	−0433	−0433	−0433	−0433	−1.6	−1.6	−0.3	0.0
Coleraine	55 08N	6 40W	−0403	−0403	−0403	−0403	−1.3	−1.2	−0.2	0.0
			0200	**0900**	**0200**	**0800**				
GALWAY	53 16N	9 03W	and	and	and	and	**5.1**	**3.9**	**2.0**	**0.6**
Standard port			**1400**	**2100**	**1400**	**2000**				
Londonderry	55 00N	7 19W	+0254	+0319	+0322	+0321	−2.4	−1.8	−0.8	−0.1

IRELAND

Location	Lat	Long	High Water		Low Water		MHWS	MHWN	MLWN	MLWS
Inishtrahull	55 26N	7 14W	+0100	+0100	+0115	+0200	−1.8	−1.4	−0.4	−0.2
Bulbinbeg	55 22N	7 20W	+0120	+0120	+0135	+0135	−1.3	−1.1	−0.4	−0.1
Trawbreaga Bay	55 19N	7 23W	+0115	+0059	+0109	+0125	−1.1	−0.8	No data	
Lough Swilly										
Rathmullan	55 06N	7 32W	+0125	+0050	+0126	+0118	−0.8	−0.7	−0.1	−0.1
Fanad Head	55 17N	7 38W	+0115	+0040	+0125	+0120	−1.1	−0.9	−0.5	−0.1
Mulroy Bay Bar	55 15N	7 46W	+0108	+0052	+0102	+0118	−1.2	−1.0	No data	
Fanny's Bay	55 12N	7 49W	+0145	+0129	+0151	+0207	−2.2	−1.7	No data	
Seamount Bay	55 11N	7 44W	+0210	+0154	+0226	+0242	−3.1	−2.3	No data	
Cranford Bay	55 09N	7 42W	+0329	+0313	+0351	+0407	−3.7	−2.8		
No data										
Sheephaven Downies Bay	55 11N	7 50W	+0057	+0043	+0053	+0107	−1.1	−0.9	No data	
Inishbofin Bay	55 10N	8 10W	+0040	+0026	+0032	+0046	−1.2	−0.9	No data	
			0600	**1100**	**0000**	**0700**				
GALWAY	53 16N	9 03W	and	and	and	and	**5.1**	**3.9**	**2.0**	**0.6**
Standard port			**1800**	**2300**	**1200**	**1900**				
Gweedore Harbour	55 04N	8 19W	+0048	+0100	+0055	+0107	−1.3	−1.0	−0.5	−0.1
Burtonport	54 59N	8 26W	+0042	+0055	+0115	+0055	−1.2	−1.0	−0.6	−0.1
Loughros More Bay	54 47N	8 30W	+0042	+0054	+0046	+0058	−1.1	−0.9	No data	
Donegal Bay										
Killybegs	54 38N	8 26W	+0040	+0050	+0055	+0035	−1.0	−0.9	−0.5	0.0
Donegal Hbr, Salt Hill Quay	54 38N	8 12W	+0038	+0050	+0052	+0104	−1.2	−0.9	No data	
Mullaghmore	54 28N	8 27W	+0036	+0048	+0047	+0059	−1.4	−1.0	−0.4	−0.2
Sligo Hbr (Oyster Island)	54 18N	8 34W	+0043	+0055	+0042	+0054	−1.0	−0.9	−0.5	−0.1
Ballysadare Bay, Culleenamore	54 16N	8 36W	+0059	+0111	+0111	+0123	−1.2	−0.9	No data	
Killala Bay (Inishcrone)	54 13N	9 06W	+0035	+0055	+0030	+0050	−1.3	−1.2	−0.7	−0.2
Broadhaven	54 16N	9 53W	+0040	+0050	+0040	+0050	−1.4	−1.1	−0.4	−0.1
Blacksod Bay										
Blacksod Quay	54 06N	10 04W	+0025	+0035	+0040	+0040	−1.2	−1.0	−0.6	−0.2
Inishbiggle	54 00N	9 53W	+0055	+0100	+0125	+0110	−1.3	− 0.9	−0.5	0.0
Clare Island	53 48N	9 57W	+0015	+0021	+0039	+0027	−0.6	−0.4	−0.1	+0.2
Clew Bay Inishgort	53 50N	9 40W	+0035	+0045	+0115	+0100	−0.7	−0.5	−0.2	+0.2
Killary Harbour	53 38N	9 53W	+0021	+0015	+0035	+0029	−1.0	−0.8	−0.4	−0.1
Inishbofin Bofin Harbour	53 37N	10 12W	+0013	+0009	+0021	+0017	−1.0	−0.8	−0.4	−0.1
Clifden Bay	53 29N	10 04W	+0005	+0005	+0016	+0016	−0.7	−0.5	No data	
Slyne Head	53 24N	10 14W	+0002	+0002	+0010	+0010	−0.7	−0.5	No data	
Roundstone Bay	53 23N	9 55W	+0003	+0003	+0008	+0008	−0.7	−0.5	−0.3	−0.1
Kilkieran Cove	53 19N	9 44W	+0005	+0005	+0016	+0016	−0.3	−0.2	−0.1	0.0
Aran Islands Killeany Bay	53 07N	9 40W	−0008	−0008	+0003	+0003	−0.4	−0.3	−0.2	−0.1
Liscannor	52 56N	9 23W	−0003	−0007	+0006	+0002	−0.4	−0.3	No data	
Seafield Point	52 48N	9 30W	−0006	−0014	+0004	−0004	−0.5	−0.4	No data	
Kilrush	52 38N	9 30W	−0006	+0027	+0057	−0016	−0.1	−0.2	−0.3	−0.1
Limerick Dock	52 40N	8 38W	+0135	+0141	+0141	+0219	+1.0	+0.7	−0.8	−0.2
			0500	**1100**	**0500**	**1100**				
COBH	51 51N	8 18 W	and	and	and	and	**4.1**	**3.2**	**1.3**	**0.4**
Standard port			**1700**	**2300**	**1700**	**2300**				
Tralee Bay Fenit Pier	52 16N	9 52W	−0057	−0017	−0029	−0109	+0.5	+0.2	+0.3	+0.1
Smerwick Harbour	52 12N	10 24W	−0107	−0027	−0041	−0121	−0.3	−0.4	No data	
Dingle Harbour	52 07N	10 15W	−0111	−0041	−0049	−0119	−0.1	0.0	+0.3	+0.4
Castlemaine Hbr Cromane Pt	52 08N	9 54W	−0026	−0006	−0017	−0037	+0.4	+0.2	+0.4	+0.2
Valentia Harbour										
Knights Town	51 56N	10 18W	−0118	−0038	−0056	−0136	−0.6	−0.4	−0.1	0.0
Ballinskelligs Bay Castle	51 49N	10 16W	−0119	−0039	−0054	−0134	−0.5	−0.5	−0.1	0.0
Kenmare River										
West Cove	51 46N	10 03W	−0113	−0033	−0049	−0129	−0.6	−0.5	−0.1	0.0
Dunkerron Harbour	51 52N	9 39W	−0117	−0027	−0050	−0140	−0.2	−0.3	+0.1	0.0
Coulagh Bay										
Ballycrovane Hbr	51 43N	9 57W	−0116	−0036	−0053	−0133	−0.6	−0.5	−0.1	0.0
Black Ball Harbour	51 36N	10 02W	−0115	−0035	−0047	−0127	−0.7	−0.6	−0.1	+0.1
Bantry Bay										
Castletown Bearhaven	51 39N	9 54W	−0048	−0012	−0025	−0101	−0.9	−0.6	−0.1	0.0
Bantry	51 41N	9 28W	−0045	−0025	−0040	−0105	−0.7	−0.6	−0.2	+0.1

Location	Lat	Long	High Water		Low Water		MHWS	MHWN	MLWN	MLWS
Dunmanus Bay										
Dunbeacon Harbour	51 37N	9 33W	−0057	−0025	−0032	−0104	−0.8	−0.7	−0.3	−0.1
Dunmanus Harbour	51 32N	9 40W	−0107	−0031	−0044	−0120	−0.7	−0.6	−0.2	0.0
Crookhaven	51 28N	9 44W	−0057	−0033	−0048	−0112	−0.8	−0.6	−0.4	−0.1
Skull	51 31N	9 32W	−0040	−0015	−0015	−0110	−0.9	−0.6	−0.2	0.0
Baltimore	51 29N	9 23W	−0025	−0005	−0010	−0050	−0.6	−0.3	+0.1	+0.2
Castletownshend	51 32N	9 10W	−0020	−0030	−0020	−0050	−0.4	−0.2	+0.1	+0.3
Clonakilty Bay	51 35N	8 50W	−0033	−0011	−0019	−0041	−0.3	−0.2	No data	
Courtmacsherry	51 38N	8 43W	−0025	−0008	−0008	−0015	−0.1	−0.1	−0.0	+0.1
Kinsale	51 42N	8 31W	−0019	−0005	−0009	−0023	−0.2	0.0	+0.1	+0.2
Roberts Cove	51 45N	8 19W	−0005	−0005	−0005	−0005	−0.1	0.0	0.0	+0.1
Cork Harbour										
Ringaskiddy	51 50N	8 19W	+0005	+0020	+0007	+0013	+0.1	+0.1	+0.1	+0.1
Marino Point	51 53N	8 20W	0000	+0010	0000	+0010	+0.1	+0.1	0.0	0.0
Cork City	51 54N	8 27W	+0005	+0010	+0020	+0010	+0.4	+0.4	+0.3	+0.2
Ballycotton	51 50N	8 01W	−0011	+0001	+0003	−0009	0.0	0.0	−0.1	0.0
Youghal	51 57N	7 51W	0000	+0010	+0010	0000	−0.2	−0.1	−0.1	−0.1
Dungarvan Harbour	52 05N	7 34W	+0004	+0012	+0007	−0001	0.0	+0.1	−0.2	0.0
Waterford Harbour										
Dunmore East	52 09N	6 59W	+0008	+0003	0000	0000	+0.1	0.0	+0.1	+0.2
Cheekpoint	52 16N	7 00W	+0022	+0020	+0020	+0020	+0.3	+0.2	+0.2	+0.1
Kilmokea Point	52 17N	7 00W	+0026	+0022	+0020	+0020	+0.2	+0.1	+0.1	+0.1
Waterford	52 16N	7 07W	+0057	+0057	+0046	+0046	+0.4	+0.3	−0.1	+0.1
New Ross	52 24N	6 57W	+0100	+0030	+0055	+0130	+0.3	+0.4	+0.3	+0.4
Baginbun Head	52 10N	6 50W	+0003	+0003	−0008	−0008	−0.2	−0.1	+0.2	+0.2
Great Saltee	52 07N	6 37W	+0019	+0009	−0004	+0006	−0.3	−0.4	No data	
Carnsore Point	52 10N	6 22W	+0029	+0019	−0002	+0008	−1.1	−1.0	No data	
Rosslare Europoort	52 15N	6 21W	+0045	+0035	+0015	−0005	−2.2	−1.8	−0.5	−0.1
Wexford Harbour	52 20N	6 27W	+0126	+0126	+0118	+0108	−2.1	−1.7	−0.3	+0.1

DENMARK *Time zone −0100*

			0300	0700	0100	0800				
ESBJERG	55 28N	8 27E	and	and	and	and	1.9	1.5	0.5	0.1
Standard port			1500	1900	1300	2000				
Hirtshals	57 36N	9 58E	+0055	+0320	+0340	+0100	−1.6	−1.3	−0.4	−0.1
Hanstholm	57 08N	8 36E	+0100	+0340	+0340	+0130	−1.6	−1.2	−0.4	−0.1
Thyborøn	56 42N	8 14E	+0120	+0230	+0410	+0210	−1.5	−1.2	−0.4	−0.1
Torsminde	56 22N	8 07E	+0045	+0050	+0040	+0010	−1.3	−1.0	−0.4	−0.1
Hvide Sande	56 00N	8 08E	0000	+0010	−0015	−0025	−1.1	−0.8	−0.3	−0.1
Blavands Huk	55 33N	8 05E	−0120	−0110	−0050	−0100	−0.1	−0.1	−0.2	−0.1
Esbjerg, Gradyb Bar	55 26N	8 15E	−0130	−0115	No data	No data	−0.4	−0.3	−0.2	−0.1
Havneby (Rømø)	55 05N	8 34E	−0040	−0005	0000	−0020	0.0	+0.1	−0.2	−0.2
Hojer	54 58N	8 40E	−0020	+0015	No data	No data	+0.5	+0.6	−0.1	−0.1

GERMANY *Time zone −0100*

			0100	0600	0100	0800				
HELGOLAND	54 11N	7 53E	and	and	and	and	2.7	2.4	0.5	0.0
Standard port			1300	1800	1300	2000				
Lister Tief, List	55 01N	8 26E	+0252	+0240	+0201	+0210	−0.7	−0.6	−0.3	0.0
Hörnum	54 45N	8 18E	+0223	+0218	+0131	+0137	−0.4	−0.3	−0.2	0.0
Amrum - Hafen	54 38N	8 23E	+0138	+0137	+0128	+0134	+0.2	+0.2	−0.1	0.0
Dagebüll	54 44N	8 41E	+0226	+0217	+0211	+0225	+0.5	+0.5	−0.2	0.0
Suderoogsand	54 25N	8 30E	+0116	+0102	+0038	+0122	+0.5	+0.4	0.0	0.0
River Hever, Husum	54 28N	9 01E	+0205	+0152	+0118	+0200	+1.1	+1.0	−0.1	0.0
Suederhoeft	54 16N	8 42E	+0103	+0056	+0051	+0112	+0.7	+0.6	−0.2	0.0
Eidersperrwerk	54 16N	8 51E	+0120	+0115	+0130	+0155	+0.7	+0.6	−0.1	0.0
Linnenplate	54 13N	8 40E	+0047	+0046	+0034	+0046	+0.7	+0.6	−0.1	−0.1
Büsum	54 07N	8 52E	+0054	+0049	−0001	+0027	+0.9	+0.8	−0.1	0.0

			0200	0800	0200	0900				
CUXHAVEN	53 52N	8 43E	and	and	and	and	3.8	3.4	0.9	0.5
Standard port			1400	2000	1400	2100				
River Elbe Großer Vogelsand	54 00N	8 29E	−0044	−0046	−0101	−0103	0.0	0.0	+0.1	−0.1
Scharhörn	53 58N	8 28E	−0045	−0047	−0101	−0103	0.0	0.0	0.0	−0.1
Otterndorf	53 50N	8 52E	+0029	+0029	+0027	+0027	−0.1	−0.1	−0.1	0.0
Brunsbüttel	53 53N	9 08E	+0057	+0105	+0121	+0112	−0.3	−0.2	−0.1	0.0
Glückstadt	53 47N	9 25E	+0205	+0214	+0220	+0213	−0.2	−0.1	−0.1	0.0
Stadersand	53 38N	9 32E	+0241	+0245	+0300	+0254	−0.1	0.0	−0.2	0.0
Schulau	53 34N	9 42E	+0304	+0315	+0337	+0321	+0.1	+0.2	−0.3	−0.1
Seemannshoeft	53 32N	9 53E	+0324	+0332	+0403	+0347	+0.3	+0.3	−0.4	−0.2
Hamburg	53 33N	9 58E	+0338	+0346	+0422	+0406	+0.3	+0.4	−0.4	−0.3

TIDES

TIDES

Location	Lat	Long	High Water		Low Water		MHWS	MHWN	MLWN	MLWS
			0200	0800	0200	0900				
WILHELMSHAVEN	53 31N	8 09E	and	and	and	and	4.8	4.2	1.1	0.5
Standard port			1400	2000	1400	2100				
River Weser										
Alter Weser lt ho	53 32N	8 08E	−0055	−0048	−0015	−0029	−1.0	−0.9	−0.1	0.0
Dwarsgat	53 43N	8 18E	−0015	+0002	−0006	−0001	−0.5	−0.4	−0.1	0.0
Bremerhaven	53 33N	8 34E	+0029	+0046	+0033	+0038	−0.1	0.0	−0.1	0.0
Nordenham	53 28N	8 29E	+0051	+0109	+0055	+0058	0.0	+0.1	−0.2	−0.1
Brake	53 19N	8 29E	+0120	+0119	+0143	+0155	−0.2	−0.1	−0.4	−0.2
Elsfleth	53 16N	8 29E	+0137	+0137	+0206	+0216	−0.2	−0.1	−0.3	0.0
Vegesack	53 10N	8 37E	+0208	+0204	+0250	+0254	−0.2	−0.1	−0.5	−0.2
Bremen	53 07N	8 43E	+0216	+0211	+0311	+0314	0.0	0.0	−0.6	−0.3
River Jade										
Wangerooge East	53 46N	7 59E	−0058	−0053	−0024	−0034	−1.0	−0.8	−0.1	0.0
Wangerooge West	53 47N	7 52E	−0101	−0058	−0035	−0045	−1.0	−0.9	−0.1	0.0
Schillig	53 42N	8 03E	−0031	−0025	−0006	−0014	−0.7	−0.6	−0.1	0.0
Hooksiel	53 39N	8 05E	−0023	−0022	−0008	−0012	−0.5	−0.4	−0.1	0.0
			0200	0700	0200	0800				
HELGOLAND	54 11N	7 53E	and	and	and	and	2.7	2.4	0.5	0.0
Standard port			1400	1900	1400	2000				
East Frisian Islands and coast										
Spiekeroog	53 45N	7 41E	+0003	−0003	−0031	−0012	+0.4	+0.3	−0.1	0.0
Neuharlingersiel	53 42N	7 42E	+0014	+0008	−0024	−0013	+0.5	+0.4	−0.1	−0.1
Langeoog	53 43N	7 30E	+0003	−0001	−0034	−0018	+0.3	+0.3	0.0	0.0
Norderney (Riffgat)	53 42N	7 09E	−0024	−0030	−0056	−0045	+0.1	+0.1	0.0	0.0
Norddeich Hafen	53 39N	7 09E	−0018	−0017	−0029	−0012	+0.1	+0.1	−0.1	−0.1
Juist	53 40N	7 00E	−0026	−0032	−0019	−0008	+0.6	+0.5	+0.4	+0.4
River Ems										
Memmert	53 38N	6 54E	−0032	−0038	−0114	−0103	+0.5	+0.5	+0.3	+0.4
Borkum (Fischerbalje)	53 33N	6 45E	−0048	−0052	−0124	−0105	+0.4	+0.4	+0.3	+0.4
Emshorn	53 30N	6 50E	−0037	−0041	−0108	−0047	+0.5	+0.5	+0.4	+0.4
Knock	53 20N	7 02E	+0018	+0005	−0028	+0004	+1.1	+1.0	+0.4	+0.5
Emden	53 20N	7 11E	+0041	+0028	−0011	+0022	+1.3	+1.2	+0.4	+0.4

NETHERLANDS *Time zone −0100*

Location	Lat	Long	High Water		Low Water		MHWS	MHWN	MLWN	MLWS
			0200	0700	0200	0800				
HELGOLAND	54 11N	7 53E	and	and	and	and	2.7	2.4	0.5	0.0
Standard port			1400	1900	1400	2000				
Delfzijl	53 20N	6 56E	+0020	−0005	−0040	0000	+1.0	+1.0	+0.3	+0.4
Eemshaven	53 26N	6 52E	−0025	−0045	−0115	−0045	+0.5	+0.5	+0.3	+0.4
Huibergat	53 35N	6 24E	−0150	−0150	−0210	−0210	0.0	0.0	+0.2	+0.3
Schiermonnikoog	53 28N	6 12E	−0120	−0130	−0240	−0220	+0.2	+0.1	+0.2	+0.3
Waddenzee										
Lauwersoog	53 25N	6 12E	−0130	−0145	−0235	−0220	+0.2	+0.2	+0.2	+0.5
Nes	53 26N	5 47E	−0135	−0150	−0245	−0225	+0.2	+0.2	+0.2	+0.5
West Terschelling	53 22N	5 13E	−0220	−0250	−0335	−0310	−0.3	−0.2	+0.1	+0.3
Vlieland-Haven	53 18N	5 06E	−0250	−0320	−0355	−0330	−0.3	−0.2	+0.1	+0.4
Harlingen	53 10N	5 25E	−0155	−0245	−0210	−0130	−0.3	−0.3	0.0	+0.4
Kornwerderzand	53 04N	5 20E	−0210	−0315	−0300	−0215	−0.5	−0.4	0.0	+0.3
Den Oever	52 56N	5 02E	−0245	−0410	−0400	−0305	−0.7	−0.6	−0.1	+0.3
Oudeschild	53 02N	4 51E	−0310	−0420	−0445	−0400	−0.8	−0.7	0.0	+0.3
Den Helder	52 58N	4 45E	−0410	−0520	−0520	−0430	−0.8	−0.7	+0.1	+0.2
Noordwinning (Platform K13–A)	53 13N	3 13E	−0420	−0430	−0520	−0530	−0.9	−0.9	+0.2	+0.3
			0300	0900	0400	1000				
VLISSINGEN	51 27N	3 36E	and	and	and	and	5.0	4.1	1.1	0.5
Standard port			1500	2100	1600	2200				
IJmuiden	52 28N	4 35E	+0145	+0140	+0305	+0325	−2.8	−2.3	−0.7	−0.2
Scheveningen	52 06N	4 16E	+0105	+0100	+0220	+0245	−2.7	−2.2	−0.7	−0.2
Europlatform	52 00N	3 17E	+0005	−0005	−0030	−0055	−2.7	−2.2	−0.6	−0.1
Nieuwe Waterweg										
HOEK VAN HOLLAND			*Standard port, no Secondaries*							
Maassluis	51 55N	4 15E	+0155	+0115	+0100	+0310	−2.9	−2.3	−0.8	−0.2
Nieuwe Maas, Vlaardingen	51 54N	4 21E	+0150	+0120	+0130	+0330	−2.9	−2.3	−0.8	−0.2
Haringvlietsluizen	51 50N	4 02E	+0015	+0015	+0015	−0020	−2.0	−1.9	−0.7	−0.2
Ooster Schelde										
Roompot Buiten	51 37N	3 40E	−0015	+0005	+0005	−0020	−1.3	−1.1	−0.4	−0.1
Walcheren, Westkapelle	51 31N	3 27E	−0025	−0015	−0010	−0025	−0.6	−0.6	−0.2	−0.1
Westerschelde										
Terneuzen	51 20N	3 50E	+0020	+0020	+0020	+0030	+0.3	+0.4	0.0	+0.1
Hansweert	51 27N	4 00E	+0100	+0050	+0040	+0100	+0.6	+0.7	0.0	0.0
Bath	51 24N	4 13E	+0125	+0115	+0115	+0140	+1.1	+1.0	+0.1	+0.1

Location	Lat	Long	High Water		Low Water		MHWS	MHWN	MLWN	MLWS
BELGIUM *Time zone –0100*										
Antwerpen	51 21N	4 14E	+0128	+0116	+0121	+0144	+1.2	+1.0	+0.1	+0.1
Blankenberge	51 19N	3 07E	–0040	–0040	–0040	–0040	–0.3	0.0	+0.3	+0.2
			0300	0900	0300	0900				
ZEEBRUGGE	51 21N	3 12E	and	and	and	and	4.8	4.0	1.1	0.5
Standard port			1500	2100	1500	2100				
Oostende	51 14N	2 56E	–0019	–0019	–0008	–0008	+0.4	+0.3	+0.2	+0.1
Nieuwpoort	51 09N	2 43E	–0031	–0031	–0010	–0010	+0.7	+0.5	+0.3	+0.1
FRANCE *Time zone –0100*										
			0200	0800	0200	0900				
DUNKERQUE	51 03N	2 22E	and	and	and	and	6.0	5.0	1.5	0.6
Standard port			1400	2000	1400	2100				
Gravelines	51 01N	2 06E	–0010	–0015	–0010	–0005	+0.5	+0.3	0.0	0.0
Sandettie Bank	51 09N	1 47E	–0015	–0025	–0020	–0005	+0.1	–0.1	–0.1	–0.1
Calais	51 58N	1 51E	–0020	–0030	–0015	–0005	+1.2	+0.9	+0.6	+0.3
Wissant	50 53N	1 40E	–0035	–0050	–0030	–0010	+1.9	+1.5	+0.8	+0.4
BOULOGNE			*Standard port, no Secondaries*							
			0100	0600	0100	0700				
DIEPPE	49 56N	1 05E	and	and	and	and	9.3	7.4	2.5	0.8
Standard port			1300	1800	1300	1900				
Le Touquet, Étaples	50 31N	1 35E	+0005	+0015	+0030	+0030	+0.2	+0.3	+0.4	+0.4
Berck	50 24N	1 34E	+0005	+0015	+0030	+0030	+0.5	+0.5	+0.4	+0.4
La Somme										
Le Hourdel	50 13N	1 34E	+0020	+0020	*No data*	*No data*	+0.8	+0.6	*No data*	
St Valéry	50 11N	1 37E	+0035	+0035	*No data*	*No data*	+0.9	+0.7	*No data*	
Cayeux	50 11N	1 29E	0000	+0005	+0015	+0010	+0.5	+0.6	+0.4	+0.4
Le Tréport	50 04N	1 22E	+0005	0000	+0007	+0007	+0.1	+0.1	0.0	+0.1
St Valéry–en–Caux	49 52N	0 42E	–0005	–0005	–0015	–0020	–0.5	–0.4	–0.1	–0.1
Fécamp	49 46N	0 22E	–0015	–0010	–0030	–0040	–1.0	–0.6	+0.3	+0.4
Etretat	49 42N	0 12E	–0020	–0020	–0045	–0050	–1.2	–0.8	+0.3	+0.4
			0000	0500	0000	0700				
LE HAVRE	49 29N	0 07E	and	and	and	and	7.9	6.6	2.8	1.2
Standard port			1200	1700	1200	1900				
Antifer (Le Havre)	49 39N	0 09E	+0025	+0015	+0005	–0005	+0.1	0.0	0.0	0.0
La Seine										
Chenal du Rouen	49 26N	0 07E	0000	0000	0000	+0015	0.0	–0.1	0.0	–0.1
Honfleur	49 25N	0 14E	–0150	–0135	+0025	+0040	0.0	0.0	+0.1	+0.4
Tancarville	49 28N	0 28E	–0135	–0120	+0030	+0145	+0.1	+0.1	+0.1	+0.3
Quilleboeuf	49 28N	0 32E	–0055	–0110	+0105	+0210	+0.1	+0.1	+0.5	+1.4
Vatteville	49 29N	0 40E	+0015	–0040	+0205	+0240	–0.1	–0.1	+0.9	+2.2
Caudebec	49 32N	0 44E	–0005	–0030	+0220	+0300	–0.1	–0.1	+1.0	+2.3
Heurteauville	49 27N	0 49E	+0055	+0005	+0250	+0330	–0.2	–0.1	+1.2	+2.6
Duclair	49 29N	0 53E	+0210	+0125	+0350	+0410	–0.2	0.0	+1.5	+3.2
Rouen	49 27N	1 06E	+0305	+0240	+0505	+0515	–0.1	+0.2	+1.6	+3.3
Trouville	49 22N	0 05E	–0100	–0010	0000	+0005	+0.4	+0.3	+0.3	+0.1
Dives	49 18N	0 05W	–0100	–0010	0000	0000	+0.3	+0.2	+0.2	+0.1
Ouistreham	49 17N	0 15W	–0045	–0010	–0005	0000	–0.3	–0.3	–0.2	–0.3
Courseulles-sur-Mer	49 20N	0 27W	–0045	–0015	–0020	–0025	–0.5	–0.5	–0.1	–0.1
Arromanches	49 21N	0 37W	–0055	–0025	–0025	–0035	–0.6	–0.6	–0.2	–0.2
Port-en-Bessin	49 21N	0 45W	–0055	–0030	–0030	–0035	–0.7	–0.7	–0.2	–0.1
Alpha-Baie de Seine	49 49N	0 20W	+0030	+0020	–0005	–0020	–1.0	–0.9	–0.4	–0.2
			0300	1000	0400	1000				
CHERBOURG	49 39N	1 38W	and	and	and	and	6.4	5.0	2.5	1.1
Standard port			1500	2200	1600	2200				
Rade de la Capelle	49 25N	1 05W	+0115	+0050	+0130	+0115	+0.8	+0.9	+0.1	+0.1
Iles Saint Marcouf	49 30N	1 08W	+0115	+0050	+0125	+0110	+0.6	+0.7	+0.1	+0.1
St Vaast-la-Hougue	49 34N	1 16W	+0120	+0050	+0120	+0115	+0.3	+0.5	0.0	–0.1
Barfleur	49 40N	1 15W	+0110	+0055	+0050	+0050	+0.1	+0.3	0.0	0.0
Omonville	49 42N	1 50W	–0010	–0010	–0015	–0015	–0.1	–0.1	0.0	0.0
Goury	49 43N	1 57W	–0100	–0040	–0105	–0120	+1.7	+1.6	+1.0	+0.3
CHANNEL ISLANDS *Time zone UT*										
			0300	0900	0200	0900				
ST HELIER	49 11N	2 07W	and	and	and	and	11.0	8.1	4.0	1.4
Standard port			1500	2100	1400	2100				
Alderney, Braye	49 43N	2 12W	+0050	+0040	+0025	+0105	–4.8	–3.4	–1.5	–0.5
Sark, Maseline Pier	49 26N	2 21W	+0005	+0015	+0005	+0010	–2.1	–1.5	–0.6	–0.3
Guernsey, ST PETER PORT	49 27N	2 31W	*Standard port (no Secondaries)*							

Location	Lat	Long	High Water		Low Water		MHWS	MHWN	MLWN	MLWS
Jersey										
St Catherine Bay	49 13N	2 01W	0000	+0010	+0010	+0010	0.0	−0.1	0.0	+0.1
Bouley Bay	49 14N	2 05W	+0002	+0002	+0004	+0004	−0.3	−0.3	−0.1	−0.1
Les Ecrehou	49 17N	1 56W	+0005	+0009	+0011	+0009	−0.2	+0.1	−0.2	0.0
Les Minquiers	48 57N	2 08W	−0014	−0018	−0001	−0008	+0.5	+0.6	+0.1	+0.1

FRANCE *Time zone −0100*

Location	Lat	Long	High Water		Low Water		MHWS	MHWN	MLWN	MLWS
			0100	0800	0300	0800				
ST MALO	48 38N	2 02W	and	and	and	and	12.2	9.3	4.2	1.5
Standard port			1300	2000	1500	2000				
Les Ardentes	48 58N	1 52W	+0010	+0010	+0020	+0010	0.0	−0.1	0.0	−0.1
Iles Chausey	48 52N	1 49W	+0005	+0005	+0015	+0015	+0.8	+0.7	+0.6	+0.4
Diélette	49 33N	1 52W	+0045	+0035	+0020	+0035	−2.5	−1.9	−0.7	−0.3
Carteret	49 22N	1 47W	+0030	+0020	+0015	+0030	−1.6	−1.2	−0.5	−0.2
Portbail	49 18N	1 45W	+0030	+0025	+0025	+0030	−0.8	−0.6	−0.2	−0.1
St Germain sur Ay	49 14N	1 36W	+0025	+0025	+0035	+0035	−0.7	−0.5	0.0	+0.1
Le Sénéquet	49 05N	1 40W	+0015	+0015	+0025	+0025	−0.3	−0.3	+0.1	+0.1
Regnéville sur Mer	49 01N	1 33W	+0010	+0010	+0030	+0020	+0.5	+0.4	+0.2	0.0
Granville	48 50N	1 36W	+0005	+0005	+0020	+0010	+0.7	+0.5	+0.3	+0.1
Cancale	48 40N	1 51W	0000	0000	+0010	+0010	+0.8	+0.6	+0.3	+0.1
Ile des Hebihens	48 37N	2 11W	0000	0000	−0005	−0005	−0.2	−0.2	−0.1	−0.1
St Cast	48 38N	2 15W	0000	0000	−0005	−0005	−0.2	−0.2	−0.1	−0.1
Erquy	48 38N	2 28W	−0010	−0005	−0025	−0015	−0.6	−0.5	0.0	0.0
Dahouët	48 35N	2 34W	−0010	−0010	−0025	−0020	−0.9	−0.7	−0.2	−0.2
Le Légué (Buoy)	48 34N	2 41W	−0010	−0005	−0020	−0015	−0.8	−0.5	−0.2	−0.1
Binic	48 36N	2 49W	−0010	−0010	−0030	−0015	−0.8	−0.7	−0.2	−0.2
St Quay-Portrieux	48 38N	2 49W	−0010	−0005	−0025	−0020	−0.9	−0.7	−0.2	−0.1
Paimpol	48 47N	3 02W	−0010	−0005	−0035	−0025	−1.4	−1.0	−0.4	−0.2
Ile de Bréhat	48 51N	3 00W	−0015	−0015	−0045	−0035	−1.9	−1.4	−0.6	−0.3
Les Héaux de Bréhat	48 55N	3 05W	−0020	−0020	−0055	−0045	−2.4	−1.7	−0.7	−0.3
Lézardrieux	48 47N	3 06W	−0020	−0015	−0055	−0045	−1.7	−1.3	−0.5	−0.2
Port-Béni	48 51N	3 10W	−0025	−0025	−0105	−0050	−2.4	−1.7	−0.6	−0.2
Tréguier	48 47N	3 13W	−0020	−0020	−0100	−0045	−2.3	−1.6	−0.6	−0.2
Perros-Guirec	48 49N	3 28W	−0040	−0045	−0120	−0105	−2.9	−2.0	−0.8	−0.3
Ploumanac'h	48 50N	3 29W	−0035	−0040	−0120	−0100	−2.9	−2.0	−0.7	−0.2
			0000	0600	0000	0600				
BREST	48 23N	4 30W	and	and	and	and	7.0	5.5	2.7	1.1
Standard port			1200	1800	1200	1800				
Trébeurden	48 46N	3 35W	+0100	+0110	+0120	+0100	+2.2	+1.8	+0.8	+0.3
Locquirec	48 42N	3 38W	+0100	+0110	+0120	+0100	+2.1	+1.7	+0.7	+0.2
Anse de Primel	48 43N	3 50W	+0100	+0110	+0120	+0100	+2.0	+1.6	+0.7	+0.2
Chateau du Taureau (Morlaix)	48 41N	3 53W	+0055	+0105	+0115	+0055	+1.9	+1.6	+0.7	+0.2
Roscoff	48 43N	3 58W	+0055	+0105	+0115	+0055	+1.8	+1.5	+0.7	+0.2
Ile de Batz	48 44N	4 00W	+0045	+0100	+0105	+0055	+1.9	+1.5	+0.8	+0.3
Brignogan	48 40N	4 19W	+0040	+0045	+0100	+0040	+1.4	+1.1	+0.5	+0.1
L'Aber Wrac'h	48 36N	4 34W	+0030	+0030	+0040	+0035	+0.7	+0.6	+0.1	−0.1
Aber Benoit	48 35N	4 37W	+0022	+0025	+0035	+0020	+0.9	+0.8	+0.3	+0.1
Portsall	48 34N	4 43W	+0015	+0020	+0025	+0015	+0.5	+0.4	0.0	−0.1
L'Aber-Ildut	48 28N	4 45W	+0010	+0010	+0023	+0010	+0.3	+0.2	−0.1	−0.1
Ouessant, Baie de Lampaul	48 27N	5 06W	+0010	+0010	0000	+0005	−0.1	−0.1	−0.1	−0.1
Molene	48 24N	4 58W	+0015	+0010	+0020	+0020	+0.3	+0.3	+0.1	+0.1
Le Conquet	48 22N	4 47W	0000	0000	+0005	+0005	−0.2	−0.2	−0.1	0.0
Le Trez Hir	48 21N	4 42W	−0005	−0005	−0015	−0010	−0.4	−0.4	−0.2	−0.1
Camaret	48 17N	4 35W	−0010	−0010	−0015	−0010	−0.4	−0.4	−0.3	−0.1
Morgat	48 13N	4 30W	−0005	−0010	−0020	−0005	−0.5	−0.4	−0.2	0.0
Douarnenez	48 06N	4 19W	−0010	−0010	−0020	−0010	−0.4	−0.4	−0.2	−0.1
Ile de Sein	48 02N	4 51W	−0005	−0005	−0015	−0010	−0.9	−0.8	−0.4	−0.2
Anse de Feunteun Aod	48 02N	4 42W	−0030	−0040	−0035	−0025	−1.4	−1.2	−0.6	−0.2
Audierne	48 01N	4 33W	−0035	−0030	−0035	−0030	−1.8	−1.4	−0.7	−0.3
Le Guilvinec	47 48N	4 17W	−0010	−0025	−0025	−0015	−1.9	−1.5	−0.7	−0.2
Lesconil	47 48N	4 13W	−0010	−0030	−0030	−0020	−2.0	−1.5	−0.7	−0.2
Pont l'Abbe River, Loctudy	47 50N	4 10W	−0010	−0030	−0030	−0020	−2.1	−1.7	−0.8	−0.4
Odet River										
Bénodet	47 53N	4 07W	0000	−0020	−0025	−0015	−1.8	−1.4	−0.6	−0.2
Corniguel	47 58N	4 06W	+0015	+0010	−0015	−0010	−2.1	−1.7	−1.1	−0.8

Location	Lat	Long	High Water		Low Water		MHWS	MHWN	MLWN	MLWS
Concarneau	47 52N	3 55W	−0010	−0030	−0030	−0020	−2.0	−1.6	−0.8	−0.3
Iles de Glenan, Ile de Penfret	47 44N	3 57W	−0005	−0030	−0030	−0020	−2.0	−1.6	−0.8	−0.3
Port Louis	47 42N	3 21W	+0005	−0020	−0020	−0010	−1.9	−1.5	−0.7	−0.2
Lorient	47 45N	3 21W	+0005	−0020	−0020	−0010	−1.9	−1.5	−0.7	−0.3
Hennebont	47 48N	3 17W	+0015	−0015	+0005	+0003	−2.0	−1.6	−0.9	−0.3
Ile de Groix, Port Tudy	47 39N	3 27W	0000	−0025	−0025	−0015	−1.9	−1.5	−0.7	−0.2
Port d'Etel	47 39N	3 12W	+0020	−0010	+0030	+0010	−2.1	−1.4	−0.5	+0.4
Port Haliguen	47 29N	3 06W	+0010	−0020	−0015	−0010	−1.7	−1.3	−0.7	−0.3
Port Maria	47 29N	3 08W	+0010	−0025	−0025	−0015	−1.7	−1.4	−0.7	−0.2
Belle Ile, Le Palais	47 21N	3 09W	+0005	−0025	−0025	−0010	−1.9	−1.4	−0.8	−0.3
Crac'h River, La Trinité	47 35N	3 01W	+0025	−0020	−0015	−0010	−1.7	−1.2	−0.6	−0.3
Golfe du Morbihan										
Port Navalo	47 33N	2 55W	+0030	−0005	−0010	−0005	−2.1	−1.6	−0.9	−0.4
Auray	47 40N	2 59W	+0035	0000	+0015	−0005	−2.3	−1.9	−1.2	−0.5
Arradon	47 37N	2 50W	+0135	+0145	+0140	+0115	−3.9	−3.1	−1.9	−0.8
Vannes	47 39N	2 46W	+0200	+0150	+0140	+0120	−3.8	−3.0	−2.1	−0.9
St Armel (Le Passage)	47 36N	2 43W	+0200	+0200	+0210	+0135	−3.8	−3.0	−2.0	−0.9
Le Logeo	47 33N	2 51W	+0140	+0140	+0145	+0115	−4.1	−3.2	−2.1	−0.9
Port du Crouesty	47 32N	2 54W	+0010	−0025	−0025	−0030	−1.7	−1.3	−0.7	−0.4
Ile de Houat	47 24N	2 57W	+0005	−0025	−0025	−0010	−1.8	−1.4	−0.7	−0.4
Ile de Hoëdic	47 20N	2 52W	+0010	−0035	−0025	−0020	−1.9	−1.5	−0.8	−0.4
Pénerf	47 31N	2 37W	+0015	−0025	−0015	−0015	−1.6	−1.2	−0.7	−0.4
Tréhiguier	47 30N	2 27W	+0035	−0020	−0005	−0010	−1.5	−1.1	−0.6	−0.4
Le Croisic	47 18N	2 31W	+0015	−0040	−0020	−0015	−1.6	−1.2	−0.7	−0.4
Le Pouliguen	47 17N	2 25W	+0020	−0025	−0020	−0025	−1.6	−1.2	−0.7	−0.4
Le Grand-Charpentier	47 13N	2 19W	+0015	−0045	−0025	−0020	−1.6	−1.2	−0.7	−0.4
Pornichet	47 16N	2 21W	+0020	−0045	−0022	−0022	−1.5	−1.1	−0.6	−0.3
La Loire										
St Nazaire	47 16N	2 12W	+0030	−0040	−0010	−0010	−1.2	−0.9	−0.5	−0.3
Donges	47 18N	2 05W	+0035	−0035	+0005	+0005	−1.1	−0.8	−0.6	−0.5
Cordemais	47 17N	1 54W	+0055	−0005	+0105	+0030	−0.8	−0.6	−0.8	−0.5
Le Pellerin	47 12N	1 46W	+0110	+0010	+0145	+0100	−0.8	−0.6	−1.0	−0.5
Nantes (Chantenay)	47 12N	1 35W	+0135	+0055	+0215	+0125	−0.7	−0.4	−0.9	−0.2
			0500	**1100**	**0500**	**1100**				
BREST	48 23N	4 30W	and	and	and	and	**7.0**	**5.5**	**2.7**	**1.1**
Standard port			**1700**	**2300**	**1700**	**2300**				
Pointe de Saint–Gildas	47 08N	2 15W	−0045	+0025	−0020	−0020	−1.4	−1.1	−0.6	−0.3
Pornic	47 06N	2 07W	−0050	+0030	−0010	−0010	−1.2	−0.9	−0.5	−0.3
Ile de Noirmoutier, L'Herbaudière	47 02N	2 18W	−0045	+0025	−0020	−0020	−1.5	−1.1	−0.6	−0.3
Fromentine	46 54N	2 10W	−0045	+0020	−0015	+0005	−1.8	−1.4	−0.9	−0.2
Ile de Yeu, Port Joinville	46 44N	2 21W	−0040	+0015	−0030	−0035	−2.0	−1.5	−0.8	−0.4
St Gilles-Croix-de-Vie	46 41N	1 56W	−0030	+0015	−0030	−0030	−1.9	−1.4	−0.7	−0.4
Les Sables d'Olonne	46 30N	1 48W	−0030	+0015	−0035	−0035	−1.8	−1.4	−0.7	−0.4
			0000	**0600**	**0000**	**0500**				
POINTE DE GRAVE	45 34N	1 04W	and	and	and	and	**5.4**	**4.4**	**2.1**	**1.0**
Standard port			**1200**	**1800**	**1200**	**1700**				
Ile de Ré, St Martin	46 12N	1 22W	+0005	−0030	−0025	−0030	+0.5	+0.3	+0.2	−0.1
La Pallice	46 10N	1 13W	+0015	−0030	−0020	−0025	+0.6	+0.5	+0.3	−0.1
La Rochelle	46 09N	1 09W	+0015	−0030	−0020	−0025	+0.6	+0.5	+0.3	−0.1
Ile d'Aix	46 01N	1 10W	+0015	−0040	−0025	−0030	+0.7	+0.5	+0.3	−0.1
La Charente, Rochefort	45 57N	0 58W	+0035	−0010	+0125	+0030	+1.1	+0.9	+0.1	−0.2
Le Chapus	45 51N	1 11W	+0015	−0040	−0015	−0025	+0.6	+0.6	+0.4	+0.2
La Cayenne	45 47N	1 08W	+0030	−0015	−0005	−0010	+0.2	+0.2	+0.3	0.0
Pointe de Gatseau	45 48N	1 14W	+0055	0000	−0020	−0015	−0.1	−0.1	+0.2	+0.1
Cordouan	45 35N	1 10W	−0010	−0010	−0025	−0015	−0.5	−0.4	−0.1	−0.2
La Gironde										
Royan	45 37N	1 01W	0000	−0005	0000	0000	−0.2	−0.1	0.0	0.0
Richard	45 27N	0 56W	+0020	+0020	+0035	+0030	−0.1	−0.1	−0.4	−0.5
Lamena	45 20N	0 48W	+0035	+0045	+0125	+0100	+0.2	+0.1	−0.5	−0.3
Pauillac	45 12N	0 45W	+0100	+0100	+0205	+0135	+0.1	0.0	−1.0	−0.5
La Reuille	45 03N	0 36W	+0135	+0145	+0230	+0305	−0.2	−0.3	−1.3	−0.7
La Garonne										
Le Marquis	45 00N	0 33W	+0145	+0150	+0320	+0245	−0.3	−0.4	− 1.5	−0.9
Bordeaux	44 52N	0 33W	+0200	+0225	+0405	+0330	−0.1	−0.2	−1.7	−1.0

TIDES

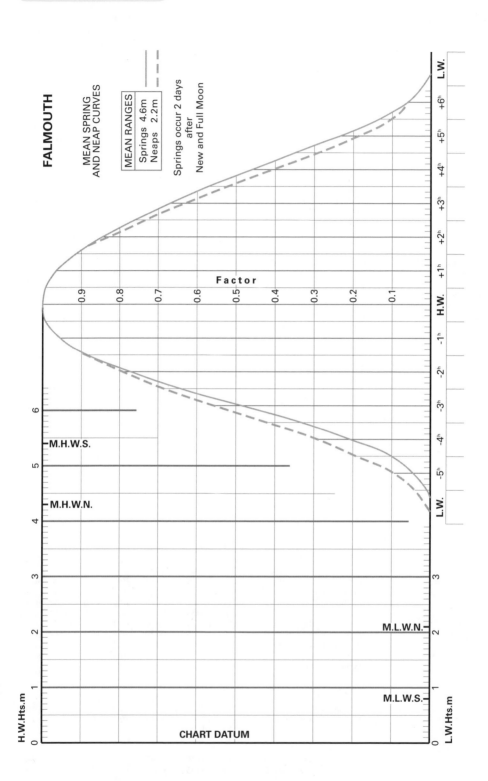

FALMOUTH

MEAN SPRING
AND NEAP CURVES

MEAN RANGES	
Springs	4.6m
Neaps	2.2m

Springs occur 2 days
after
New and Full Moon

Factor

0.9 0.8 0.7 0.6 0.5 0.4 0.3 0.2 0.1

L.W. +6ʰ +5ʰ +4ʰ +3ʰ +2ʰ +1ʰ H.W. -1ʰ -2ʰ -3ʰ -4ʰ -5ʰ L.W.

H.W.Hts.m

M.H.W.S.

M.H.W.N.

M.L.W.N.

M.L.W.S.

L.W.Hts.m

CHART DATUM

FALMOUTH

LAT 50°09'N   LONG 5°03'W

TIMES AND HEIGHTS OF HIGH AND LOW WATERS

2012

JANUARY

Day	Time	m	Time	m	Time	m	Time	m
1 SU	0414	1.5	0957	4.4	1642	1.6	) 2232	4.1
16 M	0356	1.1	0952	4.7	1629	1.2	) 2224	4.3
2 M	0504	1.8	1049	4.2	1736	1.8	2333	4.0
17 TU	0453	1.3	1055	4.4	1732	1.4	2337	4.2
3 TU	0607	1.9	1153	4.0	1843	1.9		
18 W	0604	1.5	1212	4.2	1849	1.5		
4 W	0047	4.0	0717	1.9	1311	4.0	1950	1.8
19 TH	0101	4.2	0728	1.5	1337	4.2	2016	1.4
5 TH	0204	4.1	0824	1.7	1427	4.2	2051	1.6
20 F	0220	4.4	0858	1.3	1452	4.4	2132	1.2
6 F	0302	4.4	0921	1.5	1523	4.4	2143	1.3
21 SA	0323	4.6	1007	1.0	1551	4.6	2233	0.9
7 SA	0349	4.6	1011	1.2	1608	4.6	2229	1.1
22 SU	0415	4.9	1104	0.7	1642	4.8	2326	0.6
8 SU	0429	4.8	1056	1.0	1649	4.7	2312	0.9
23 M	0501	5.1	1153	0.4	1727	4.8		
9 M	0507	5.0	1139	0.8	1728	4.8	O 2354	0.8
24 TU	0012	0.4	0543	5.2	1238	0.3	1807	5.0
10 TU	0545	5.1	1219	0.7	1807	4.9		
25 W	0054	0.4	0623	5.3	1316	0.3	1845	5.0
11 W	0034	0.7	0622	5.2	1259	0.6	1845	4.9
26 TH	0130	0.4	0700	5.3	1350	0.4	1920	4.9
12 TH	0113	0.6	0700	5.2	1337	0.5	1923	4.9
27 F	0201	0.6	0735	5.2	1420	0.6	1954	4.8
13 F	0150	0.6	0739	5.1	1416	0.6	2000	4.8
28 SA	0230	0.8	0807	5.0	1447	0.9	2027	4.7
14 SA	0228	0.7	0819	5.1	1455	0.7	2039	4.7
29 SU	0256	1.1	0839	4.8	1511	1.2	2101	4.5
15 SU	0309	0.9	0902	4.9	1538	0.9	2125	4.5
30 M	0321	1.3	0914	4.5	1538	1.4	2140	4.3
31 TU	0352	1.6	0958	4.2	1617	1.7	) 2231	4.0

FEBRUARY

Day	Time	m	Time	m	Time	m	Time	m
1 W	0443	1.9	1055	4.0	1721	1.9	2337	3.9
16 TH	0535	1.6	1150	4.0	1819	1.7		
2 TH	0610	2.1	1205	3.9	1852	2.0		
17 F	0042	4.0	0709	1.7	1328	4.0	2004	1.6
3 F	0056	3.9	0736	2.0	1330	3.9	2009	1.8
18 SA	0208	4.2	0854	1.4	1445	4.2	2126	1.3
4 SA	0223	4.2	0845	1.7	1451	4.2	2111	1.5
19 SU	0310	4.5	1000	1.0	1541	4.4	2224	0.9
5 SU	0320	4.5	0942	1.3	1543	4.4	2203	1.2
20 M	0400	4.8	1052	0.7	1627	4.7	2312	0.6
6 M	0403	4.8	1032	1.0	1625	4.7	2252	0.9
21 TU	0443	5.0	1137	0.4	1707	4.9	● 2355	0.4
7 TU	0442	5.0	1119	0.7	1706	4.8	O 2337	0.6
22 W	0523	5.2	1217	0.3	1744	5.0		
8 W	0522	5.2	1202	0.5	1747	5.0		
23 TH	0033	0.3	0600	5.2	1254	0.3	1819	5.0
9 TH	0019	0.4	0602	5.3	1244	0.3	1827	5.0
24 F	0106	0.4	0636	5.2	1324	0.4	1854	5.0
10 F	0059	0.3	0643	5.3	1323	0.2	1906	5.1
25 SA	0135	0.5	0709	5.1	1350	0.6	1927	4.9
11 SA	0137	0.3	0723	5.3	1400	0.3	1942	5.0
26 SU	0159	0.7	0740	5.0	1411	0.8	1957	4.8
12 SU	0214	0.4	0801	5.2	1437	0.5	2018	4.9
27 M	0219	0.8	0808	4.8	1429	1.0	2025	4.6
13 M	0251	0.6	0840	5.0	1516	0.7	2057	4.7
28 TU	0239	1.2	0837	4.5	1452	1.3	2054	4.4
14 TU	0334	0.9	0924	4.6	1601	1.1	) 2149	4.4
29 W	0307	1.4	0913	4.3	1525	1.6	2139	4.2
15 W	0426	1.3	1024	4.3	1700	1.5	2303	4.1

MARCH

Day	Time	m	Time	m	Time	m	Time	m
1 TH	0349	1.7	1009	4.0	1614	1.9	) 2244	4.0
16 F	0519	1.6	1140	3.9	1759	1.8		
2 F	0459	2.0	1120	3.8	1746	2.1	2359	3.9
17 SA	0027	4.0	0659	1.7	1319	3.9	1952	1.7
3 SA	0647	2.0	1239	3.8	1926	2.0		
18 SU	0151	4.2	0842	1.4	1431	4.1	2111	1.3
4 SU	0121	4.1	0808	1.7	1405	4.1	2037	1.6
19 M	0251	4.5	0942	1.0	1523	4.4	2204	1.0
5 M	0236	4.4	0911	1.3	1509	4.4	2136	1.2
20 TU	0339	4.7	1030	0.7	1605	4.6	2250	0.7
6 TU	0328	4.7	1005	0.9	1555	4.7	2227	0.8
21 W	0420	4.9	1113	0.5	1642	4.8	2330	0.5
7 W	0412	5.0	1055	0.6	1638	4.9	2315	0.5
22 TH	0458	5.1	1151	0.4	1717	5.0		
8 TH	0455	5.2	1140	0.3	1721	5.1	O	
23 F	0006	0.4	0534	5.1	1225	0.4	1752	5.0
9 F	0000	0.4	0539	5.4	1224	0.1	1803	5.2
24 SA	0038	0.5	0610	5.1	1254	0.5	1827	5.0
10 SA	0042	0.1	0623	5.4	1304	0.1	1845	5.2
25 SU	0106	0.6	0643	5.0	1318	0.7	1859	5.0
11 SU	0120	0.1	0705	5.4	1342	0.1	1923	5.2
26 M	0129	0.7	0714	4.9	1338	0.8	1928	4.8
12 M	0158	0.2	0745	5.2	1419	0.3	2000	5.0
27 TU	0148	0.9	0741	4.7	1357	1.0	1953	4.7
13 TU	0235	0.5	0824	4.9	1457	0.7	2039	4.8
28 W	0210	1.1	0807	4.5	1422	1.2	2019	4.5
14 W	0317	0.8	0907	4.6	1541	1.1	2128	4.5
29 TH	0240	1.3	0839	4.3	1455	1.5	2058	4.3
15 TH	0409	1.2	1006	4.2	1639	1.5	) 2241	4.1
30 F	0320	1.6	0933	4.1	1540	1.8	) 2204	4.1
31 SA	0421	1.8	1046	3.9	1657	2.0	2318	4.0

APRIL

Day	Time	m	Time	m	Time	m	Time	m
1 SU	0601	1.9	1201	3.9	1841	1.9		
16 M	0123	4.2	0809	1.4	1404	4.1	2037	1.3
2 M	0033	4.1	0727	1.7	1318	4.1	1959	1.6
17 TU	0223	4.4	0910	1.1	1455	4.3	2133	1.1
3 TU	0146	4.4	0836	1.3	1426	4.4	2102	1.2
18 W	0311	4.6	0958	0.9	1536	4.6	2218	0.9
4 W	0247	4.7	0933	0.9	1519	4.7	2158	0.8
19 TH	0352	4.8	1040	0.7	1613	4.8	2258	0.7
5 TH	0338	5.0	1026	0.5	1607	5.0	2249	0.5
20 F	0430	4.9	1118	0.6	1649	4.9	2334	0.6
6 F	0427	5.2	1115	0.3	1653	5.2	O 2336	0.2
21 SA	0508	4.9	1151	0.6	1726	5.0	●	
7 SA	0515	5.4	1201	0.1	1739	5.3		
22 SU	0008	0.6	0544	4.9	1222	0.7	1801	5.0
8 SU	0021	0.1	0602	5.4	1244	0.0	1823	5.3
23 M	0038	0.7	0618	4.9	1248	0.8	1834	4.9
9 M	0104	0.0	0648	5.3	1325	0.1	1906	5.3
24 TU	0103	0.8	0650	4.8	1311	0.9	1903	4.8
10 TU	0144	0.2	0731	5.1	1404	0.4	1946	5.1
25 W	0125	0.9	0718	4.6	1335	1.0	1929	4.7
11 W	0224	0.4	0814	4.9	1444	0.7	2028	4.9
26 TH	0151	1.1	0747	4.5	1403	1.2	1958	4.6
12 TH	0308	0.8	0859	4.5	1530	1.1	2118	4.6
27 F	0224	1.2	0821	4.3	1438	1.4	2037	4.4
13 F	0401	1.2	0959	4.1	1628	1.5	) 2226	4.2
28 SA	0305	1.4	0910	4.2	1523	1.6	2135	4.3
14 SA	0508	1.5	1129	3.9	1742	1.7		
29 SU	0403	1.6	1016	4.0	1631	1.8	2244	4.2
15 SU	0003	4.1	0635	1.6	1258	3.9	1915	1.7
30 M	0525	1.7	1127	4.0	1759	1.8	2354	4.3

Chart Datum: 2·99 metres below Ordnance Datum (Newlyn)
HAT is 5·8 metres above Chart Datum

TIDES

221

TIDES

TIME ZONE (UT)	FALMOUTH	Dates in amber are SPRINGS
For Summer Time add ONE hour in **non-shaded areas**	LAT 50°09'N LONG 5°03'W	Dates in yellow are NEAPS
	TIMES AND HEIGHTS OF HIGH AND LOW WATERS	**2012**

MAY

Day	Time m		Day	Time m	
1 TU	0646 1.5 / 1237 4.2 / 1917 1.6		**16** W	0144 4.2 / 0818 1.3 / 1417 4.2 / 2043 1.4	
2 W	0104 4.4 / 0755 1.2 / 1345 4.4 / 2024 1.2		**17** TH	0236 4.4 / 0913 1.2 / 1502 4.4 / 2135 1.2	
3 TH	0209 4.7 / 0858 0.9 / 1443 4.7 / 2124 0.9		**18** F	0321 4.5 / 0959 1.0 / 1542 4.7 / 2219 1.0	
4 F	0307 5.0 / 0955 0.6 / 1536 5.0 / 2220 0.6		**19** SA	0402 4.6 / 1039 0.9 / 1621 4.8 / 2259 0.9	
5 SA	0401 5.1 / 1048 0.4 / 1627 5.2 / 2313 0.3		**20** SU	0442 4.7 / 1116 0.9 / 1659 4.8 / 2336 0.9 ●	
6 SU	0453 5.2 / 1138 0.2 / 1717 5.3 ○		**21** M	0520 4.7 / 1150 0.9 / 1736 4.9	
7 M	0002 0.2 / 0544 5.3 / 1226 0.2 / 1805 5.3		**22** TU	0010 0.9 / 0556 4.7 / 1222 0.9 / 1810 4.9	
8 TU	0050 0.1 / 0634 5.2 / 1311 0.2 / 1851 5.3		**23** W	0040 0.9 / 0629 4.7 / 1251 0.8 / 1841 4.8	
9 W	0134 0.2 / 0721 5.1 / 1354 0.4 / 1936 5.2		**24** TH	0109 0.9 / 0701 4.6 / 1320 1.0 / 1911 4.8	
10 TH	0218 0.4 / 0806 4.8 / 1438 0.7 / 2020 5.0		**25** F	0140 1.0 / 0733 4.5 / 1353 1.1 / 1944 4.7	
11 F	0303 0.7 / 0853 4.5 / 1524 1.1 / 2108 4.7		**26** SA	0216 1.1 / 0809 4.4 / 1430 1.2 / 2023 4.6	
12 SA	0354 1.0 / 0947 4.2 / 1617 1.3 / 2206 4.4 ◑		**27** SU	0258 1.2 / 0852 4.3 / 1515 1.4 / 2113 4.5	
13 SU	0452 1.3 / 1058 4.0 / 1717 1.5 / 2322 4.3		**28** M	0350 1.3 / 0949 4.2 / 1613 1.5 / 2214 4.4 ◑	
14 M	0557 1.5 / 1217 4.0 / 1825 1.6		**29** TU	0455 1.4 / 1053 4.2 / 1722 1.5 / 2320 4.4	
15 TU	0040 4.2 / 0709 1.5 / 1324 4.1 / 1937 1.5		**30** W	0606 1.4 / 1200 4.3 / 1835 1.4	
			31 TH	0027 4.5 / 0715 1.2 / 1308 4.4 / 1944 1.2	

JUNE

Day	Time m		Day	Time m	
1 F	0136 4.6 / 0822 1.0 / 1413 4.6 / 2051 1.1		**16** SA	0247 4.3 / 0910 1.4 / 1512 4.5 / 2137 1.3	
2 SA	0240 4.8 / 0925 0.8 / 1512 4.9 / 2154 0.7		**17** SU	0334 4.4 / 0959 1.2 / 1555 4.6 / 2224 1.2	
3 SU	0340 5.0 / 1025 0.6 / 1607 5.1 / 2253 0.5		**18** M	0417 4.6 / 1042 1.1 / 1636 4.8 / 2306 1.0	
4 M	0436 5.1 / 1120 0.4 / 1700 5.2 / 2348 0.3 ○		**19** TU	0457 4.6 / 1122 1.0 / 1714 4.9 / 2345 1.0 ●	
5 TU	0530 5.1 / 1213 0.3 / 1751 5.3		**20** W	0535 4.7 / 1159 1.0 / 1750 4.9	
6 W	0039 0.2 / 0622 5.1 / 1302 0.3 / 1839 5.3		**21** TH	0021 0.9 / 0611 4.7 / 1235 0.9 / 1823 4.9	
7 TH	0127 0.2 / 0710 5.0 / 1347 0.4 / 1925 5.2		**22** F	0056 0.9 / 0647 4.7 / 1309 0.9 / 1856 4.9	
8 F	0212 0.4 / 0755 4.9 / 1430 0.6 / 2008 5.1		**23** SA	0132 0.9 / 0721 4.7 / 1345 1.0 / 1931 4.9	
9 SA	0255 0.6 / 0838 4.7 / 1512 0.8 / 2051 4.9		**24** SU	0209 0.9 / 0756 4.6 / 1423 1.0 / 2009 4.9	
10 SU	0339 0.8 / 0922 4.4 / 1557 1.1 / 2136 4.6		**25** M	0249 1.0 / 0835 4.6 / 1504 1.1 / 2053 4.8	
11 M	0425 1.1 / 1012 4.2 / 1646 1.4 / 2229 4.4 ◑		**26** TU	0334 1.1 / 0922 4.5 / 1553 1.2 / 2145 4.7	
12 TU	0516 1.4 / 1111 4.1 / 1740 1.6 / 2332 4.2		**27** W	0427 1.2 / 1020 4.4 / 1651 1.3 / 2247 4.6 ◑	
13 W	0613 1.6 / 1220 4.0 / 1840 1.7		**28** TH	0529 1.3 / 1126 4.4 / 1758 1.4 / 2355 4.5	
14 TH	0045 4.1 / 0713 1.6 / 1327 4.1 / 1942 1.6		**29** F	0638 1.3 / 1237 4.4 / 1910 1.3	
15 F	0152 4.2 / 0815 1.5 / 1424 4.3 / 2043 1.5		**30** SA	0109 4.5 / 0750 1.2 / 1351 4.5 / 2025 1.2	

JULY

Day	Time m		Day	Time m	
1 SU	0223 4.6 / 0902 1.1 / 1457 4.7 / 2137 1.0		**16** M	0308 4.3 / 0922 1.5 / 1532 4.5 / 2151 1.4	
2 M	0328 4.8 / 1009 0.8 / 1555 5.0 / 2242 0.7		**17** TU	0354 4.5 / 1012 1.3 / 1614 4.7 / 2239 1.2	
3 TU	0426 4.9 / 1109 0.6 / 1648 5.2 / 2339 0.5 ○		**18** W	0436 4.6 / 1057 1.1 / 1652 4.9 / 2323 1.0	
4 W	0519 5.0 / 1203 0.4 / 1739 5.3		**19** TH	0515 4.7 / 1139 0.9 / 1728 5.0 ●	
5 TH	0031 0.3 / 0609 5.0 / 1252 0.3 / 1825 5.3		**20** F	0003 0.8 / 0552 4.8 / 1219 0.8 / 1804 5.1	
6 F	0118 0.2 / 0655 5.0 / 1336 0.4 / 1909 5.3		**21** SA	0042 0.7 / 0630 4.9 / 1257 0.7 / 1840 5.1	
7 SA	0200 0.3 / 0736 5.0 / 1415 0.5 / 1948 5.2		**22** SU	0119 0.7 / 0706 4.9 / 1333 0.7 / 1917 5.1	
8 SU	0238 0.5 / 0814 4.8 / 1452 0.7 / 2026 5.0		**23** M	0156 0.6 / 0742 4.9 / 1410 0.7 / 1954 5.1	
9 M	0315 0.7 / 0850 4.7 / 1529 1.0 / 2102 4.8		**24** TU	0234 0.7 / 0817 4.8 / 1449 0.8 / 2033 5.0	
10 TU	0351 1.1 / 0929 4.5 / 1608 1.3 / 2142 4.5		**25** W	0315 0.9 / 0857 4.7 / 1532 1.0 / 2119 4.8	
11 W	0432 1.4 / 1013 4.3 / 1653 1.6 / 2228 4.3 ◑		**26** TH	0401 1.1 / 0949 4.5 / 1623 1.2 / 2218 4.6 ◑	
12 TH	0519 1.6 / 1107 4.1 / 1748 1.8 / 2326 4.1		**27** F	0458 1.3 / 1056 4.4 / 1727 1.4 / 2330 4.4	
13 F	0617 1.8 / 1215 4.0 / 1851 1.9		**28** SA	0607 1.5 / 1216 4.3 / 1845 1.5	
14 SA	0042 4.0 / 0722 1.8 / 1338 4.1 / 1957 1.8		**29** SU	0055 4.3 / 0728 1.5 / 1340 4.4 / 2012 1.4	
15 SU	0208 4.1 / 0825 1.7 / 1442 4.3 / 2058 1.6		**30** M	0217 4.4 / 0853 1.3 / 1450 4.7 / 2132 1.1	
			31 TU	0323 4.6 / 1003 1.0 / 1547 4.9 / 2236 0.8	

AUGUST

Day	Time m		Day	Time m	
1 W	0418 4.8 / 1101 0.7 / 1637 5.2 / 2331 0.5		**16** TH	0412 4.7 / 1033 1.1 / 1627 5.0 / 2259 0.9	
2 TH	0507 5.0 / 1152 0.5 / 1724 5.3 ○		**17** F	0451 4.9 / 1118 0.8 / 1703 5.2 / 2342 0.7 ●	
3 F	0019 0.3 / 0551 5.1 / 1238 0.3 / 1806 5.4		**18** SA	0529 5.0 / 1200 0.7 / 1741 5.3	
4 SA	0102 0.2 / 0632 5.1 / 1318 0.3 / 1846 5.4		**19** SU	0023 0.5 / 0608 5.1 / 1240 0.5 / 1820 5.3	
5 SU	0140 0.3 / 0709 5.1 / 1353 0.5 / 1923 5.3		**20** M	0102 0.4 / 0647 5.1 / 1318 0.5 / 1859 5.3	
6 M	0213 0.5 / 0744 5.0 / 1425 0.7 / 1956 5.1		**21** TU	0139 0.4 / 0724 5.0 / 1354 0.5 / 1938 5.2	
7 TU	0243 0.8 / 0817 4.8 / 1456 1.0 / 2028 4.9		**22** W	0216 0.6 / 0759 5.0 / 1431 0.7 / 2016 5.1	
8 W	0312 1.0 / 0850 4.6 / 1525 1.3 / 2101 4.6		**23** TH	0254 0.8 / 0838 4.8 / 1512 0.9 / 2100 4.8	
9 TH	0341 1.4 / 0927 4.4 / 1557 1.6 / 2141 4.3 ◑		**24** F	0338 1.1 / 0927 4.6 / 1601 1.3 / 2157 4.5 ◑	
10 F	0417 1.7 / 1014 4.2 / 1643 1.9 / 2234 4.1		**25** SA	0432 1.4 / 1044 4.3 / 1706 1.6 / 2317 4.2	
11 SA	0513 2.0 / 1114 4.0 / 1757 2.1 / 2340 3.9		**26** SU	0545 1.7 / 1205 4.2 / 1832 1.7	
12 SU	0631 2.1 / 1232 4.0 / 1916 2.1		**27** M	0053 4.1 / 0718 1.7 / 1334 4.2 / 2015 1.5	
13 M	0111 3.9 / 0745 1.9 / 1408 4.2 / 2024 1.8		**28** TU	0216 4.3 / 0852 1.4 / 1443 4.6 / 2130 1.2	
14 TU	0241 4.2 / 0849 1.7 / 1506 4.5 / 2123 1.5		**29** W	0317 4.5 / 0956 1.0 / 1537 4.9 / 2227 0.8	
15 W	0331 4.4 / 0944 1.4 / 1549 4.8 / 2213 1.2		**30** TH	0406 4.8 / 1049 0.7 / 1622 5.2 / 2315 0.5	
			31 F	0449 5.0 / 1135 0.5 / 1704 5.3 / 2359 0.7 ○	

Chart Datum: 2·99 metres below Ordnance Datum (Newlyn)
HAT is 5·8 metres above Chart Datum

FALMOUTH

LAT 50°09′N   LONG 5°03′W

TIMES AND HEIGHTS OF HIGH AND LOW WATERS

Dates in amber are **SPRINGS**
Dates in yellow are **NEAPS**

2012

SEPTEMBER

Day	Time	m	Time	m	Time	m	Time	m	Moon
1 SA	0529	5.1	1217	0.4	1743	5.4			
2 SU	0038	0.3	0605	5.2	1254	0.4	1820	5.3	
3 M	0113	0.4	0640	5.1	1326	0.5	1854	5.2	
4 TU	0143	0.6	0713	5.1	1355	0.7	1926	5.1	
5 W	0208	0.9	0745	5.0	1420	1.0	1956	4.9	
6 TH	0230	1.1	0816	4.8	1441	1.3	2026	4.7	
7 F	0251	1.4	0849	4.6	1503	1.6	2103	4.4	
8 SA	0318	1.7	0931	4.3	1538	1.9	2155	4.1	◑
9 SU	0402	2.0	1029	4.1	1647	2.1	2301	3.9	
10 M	0532	2.2	1140	4.0	1831	2.2			
11 TU	0020	3.9	0706	2.1	1307	4.2	1950	1.9	
12 W	0201	4.1	0817	1.8	1428	4.5	2052	1.5	
13 TH	0300	4.4	0915	1.4	1516	4.8	2145	1.2	
14 F	0342	4.7	1006	1.1	1555	5.1	2232	0.8	
15 SA	0421	5.0	1053	0.8	1635	5.3	2318	0.6	
16 SU	0501	5.1	1137	0.5	1716	5.4			●
17 M	0000	0.4	0542	5.3	1759	5.5			
18 TU	0042	0.3	0624	5.3	1300	0.3	1841	5.4	
19 W	0121	0.3	0704	5.3	1338	0.4	1922	5.3	
20 TH	0158	0.5	0743	5.2	1416	0.6	2003	5.1	
21 F	0237	0.8	0824	5.0	1457	0.9	2048	4.7	
22 SA	0320	1.1	0914	4.7	1547	1.3	2147	4.4	◑
23 SU	0416	1.5	1022	4.4	1654	1.6	2313	4.1	
24 M	0531	1.8	1156	4.2	1827	1.8			
25 TU	0051	4.0	0712	1.8	1322	4.3	2010	1.5	
26 W	0207	4.2	0841	1.5	1428	4.6	2116	1.1	
27 TH	0304	4.5	0939	1.1	1519	4.9	2207	0.8	
28 F	0348	4.8	1028	0.8	1602	5.1	2252	0.6	
29 SA	0426	5.0	1111	0.6	1640	5.2	2333	0.4	
30 SU	0502	5.1	1150	0.5	1717	5.2			○

OCTOBER

Day	Time	m	Time	m	Time	m	Time	m	Moon
1 M	0009	0.5	0536	5.2	1225	0.5	1752	5.2	
2 TU	0042	0.6	0611	5.2	1256	0.6	1826	5.1	
3 W	0110	0.7	0644	5.1	1324	0.8	1858	5.0	
4 TH	0134	0.9	0716	5.0	1347	1.0	1928	4.8	
5 F	0154	1.2	0746	4.9	1407	1.3	1958	4.6	
6 SA	0215	1.4	0817	4.7	1430	1.5	2034	4.4	
7 SU	0243	1.6	0857	4.4	1506	1.8	2124	4.2	
8 M	0324	1.9	0953	4.2	1602	2.0	2229	4.0	◑
9 TU	0436	2.2	1100	4.1	1741	2.1	2343	3.9	
10 W	0620	2.2	1214	4.2	1908	1.9			
11 TH	0102	4.1	0738	1.9	1329	4.4	2015	1.6	
12 F	0213	4.4	0817	1.5	1431	4.7	2112	1.2	
13 SA	0304	4.7	0935	1.1	1520	5.0	2202	0.8	
14 SU	0348	5.0	1025	0.7	1605	5.3	2250	0.5	
15 M	0432	5.2	1113	0.5	1651	5.4	2336	0.3	●
16 TU	0517	5.4	1158	0.3	1738	5.5			
17 W	0020	0.3	0602	5.4	1242	0.2	1824	5.4	
18 TH	0103	0.3	0646	5.4	1323	0.3	1909	5.3	
19 F	0143	0.5	0730	5.3	1405	0.5	1954	5.0	
20 SA	0224	0.8	0814	5.1	1448	0.8	2042	4.7	
21 SU	0310	1.1	0904	4.8	1540	1.2	2141	4.3	
22 M	0405	1.5	1008	4.5	1645	1.5	2303	4.1	◑
23 TU	0516	1.7	1134	4.3	1809	1.7			
24 W	0033	4.0	0644	1.8	1247	4.3	1940	1.5	
25 TH	0144	4.2	0810	1.5	1402	4.5	2047	1.2	
26 F	0238	4.5	0910	1.2	1453	4.7	2138	1.0	
27 SA	0322	4.7	0959	1.0	1536	4.9	2222	0.8	
28 SU	0359	4.9	1041	0.8	1614	5.0	2301	0.7	
29 M	0434	5.0	1119	0.7	1651	5.0	2337	0.7	○
30 TU	0509	5.1	1155	0.7	1727	5.0	2336	0.3	
31 W	0010	0.7	0544	5.1	1228	0.8	1801	5.0	

NOVEMBER

Day	Time	m	Time	m	Time	m	Time	m	Moon
1 TH	0039	0.8	0619	5.1	1257	0.9	1834	4.9	
2 F	0105	1.0	0651	5.0	1322	1.0	1905	4.8	
3 SA	0128	1.1	0722	4.9	1345	1.2	1937	4.6	
4 SU	0153	1.3	0753	4.7	1412	1.4	2013	4.4	
5 M	0225	1.5	0831	4.6	1449	1.6	2058	4.3	
6 TU	0305	1.7	0922	4.4	1539	1.8	2159	4.1	
7 W	0404	1.9	1025	4.3	1655	1.9	2307	4.0	◑
8 TH	0529	2.0	1132	4.3	1820	1.8			
9 F	0016	4.2	0651	1.8	1241	4.4	1932	1.5	
10 SA	0124	4.4	0801	1.5	1346	4.7	2035	1.2	
11 SU	0224	4.7	0901	1.2	1444	4.9	2131	0.9	
12 M	0316	5.0	0957	0.8	1538	5.1	2223	0.6	
13 TU	0406	5.2	1049	0.5	1629	5.3	2313	0.4	●
14 W	0455	5.3	1139	0.3	1719	5.3			
15 TH	0002	0.3	0543	5.4	1227	0.2	1809	5.3	
16 F	0048	0.3	0631	5.4	1313	0.3	1858	5.2	
17 SA	0133	0.4	0718	5.4	1358	0.4	1945	5.0	
18 SU	0216	0.7	0803	5.2	1443	0.7	2033	4.7	
19 M	0302	0.9	0851	4.9	1532	1.0	2126	4.4	
20 TU	0353	1.3	0946	4.7	1628	1.3	2232	4.2	◐
21 W	0452	1.5	1054	4.4	1733	1.5	2351	4.1	
22 TH	0559	1.7	1211	4.3	1846	1.5			
23 F	0102	4.1	0713	1.7	1321	4.3	1958	1.4	
24 SA	0201	4.3	0824	1.5	1418	4.4	2057	1.3	
25 SU	0249	4.5	0920	1.3	1505	4.6	2145	1.1	
26 M	0329	4.7	1006	1.1	1547	4.7	2226	1.0	
27 TU	0408	4.8	1047	0.9	1626	4.8	2305	0.9	
28 W	0445	5.0	1125	0.9	1704	4.9	2340	0.9	○
29 TH	0523	5.0	1201	0.9	1741	4.9			
30 F	0012	0.9	0558	5.0	1233	0.9	1816	4.8	

DECEMBER

Day	Time	m	Time	m	Time	m	Time	m	Moon
1 SA	0042	1.0	0632	5.0	1302	1.0	1849	4.8	
2 SU	0110	1.0	0704	4.9	1330	1.1	1922	4.7	
3 M	0140	1.2	0736	4.8	1401	1.2	1956	4.5	
4 TU	0213	1.3	0811	4.7	1437	1.3	2035	4.4	
5 W	0252	1.4	0854	4.6	1521	1.4	2125	4.3	
6 TH	0340	1.6	0948	4.5	1618	1.6	2227	4.2	◑
7 F	0444	1.7	1052	4.4	1729	1.6	2333	4.2	
8 SA	0600	1.7	1158	4.4	1844	1.6			
9 SU	0040	4.3	0715	1.6	1306	4.5	1955	1.3	
10 M	0147	4.5	0826	1.3	1413	4.7	2100	1.0	
11 TU	0249	4.8	0929	1.0	1514	4.9	2159	0.8	
12 W	0345	5.0	1028	0.7	1611	5.1	2255	0.5	
13 TH	0438	5.2	1124	0.4	1705	5.2	2348	0.4	●
14 F	0529	5.4	1216	0.3	1757	5.2			
15 SA	0037	0.3	0618	5.4	1305	0.2	1846	5.1	
16 SU	0124	0.3	0705	5.4	1351	0.3	1932	5.0	
17 M	0208	0.5	0749	5.3	1434	0.4	2016	4.8	
18 TU	0250	0.7	0832	5.1	1517	0.7	2059	4.6	
19 W	0333	1.0	0916	4.8	1602	1.0	2146	4.4	
20 TH	0420	1.3	1005	4.5	1651	1.3	2241	4.4	◐
21 F	0513	1.5	1102	4.3	1747	1.6	2348	4.0	
22 SA	0613	1.7	1213	4.1	1851	1.7			
23 SU	0104	4.1	0720	1.7	1329	4.1	1958	1.6	
24 M	0209	4.2	0828	1.6	1431	4.2	2100	1.4	
25 TU	0300	4.4	0926	1.4	1521	4.4	2150	1.2	
26 W	0344	4.6	1015	1.2	1605	4.6	2234	1.1	
27 TH	0425	4.8	1058	1.0	1645	4.7	2313	1.0	
28 F	0504	4.9	1137	0.9	1724	4.8	2350	0.9	○
29 SA	0542	5.0	1213	0.9	1801	4.8			
30 SU	0023	0.9	0616	5.0	1246	0.8	1835	4.8	
31 M	0056	0.9	0648	5.0	1317	0.8	1908	4.7	

Chart Datum: 2·99 metres below Ordnance Datum (Newlyn)
HAT is 5·8 metres above Chart Datum

TIDES

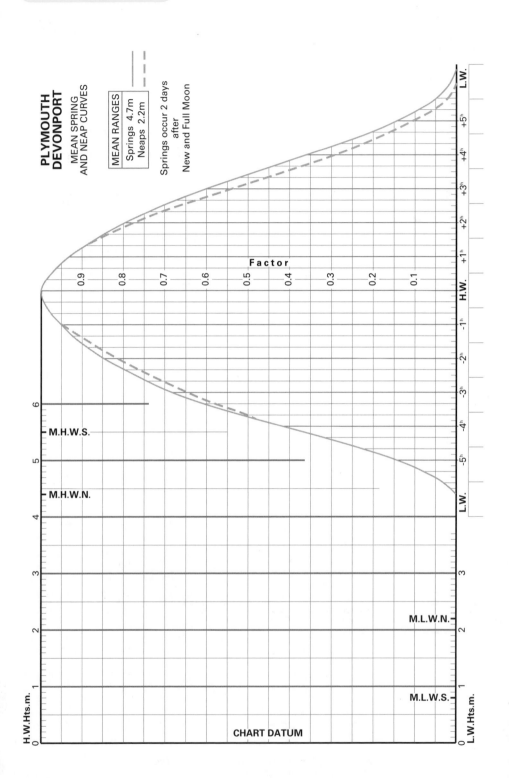

PLYMOUTH
DEVONPORT

MEAN SPRING
AND NEAP CURVES

MEAN RANGES
Springs 4.7m
Neaps 2.2m

Springs occur 2 days
after
New and Full Moon

Factor

0.9 0.8 0.7 0.6 0.5 0.4 0.3 0.2 0.1

M.H.W.S.
M.H.W.N.
M.L.W.N.
M.L.W.S.

H.W.Hts.m.
L.W.Hts.m.

CHART DATUM

L.W. +5ʰ +4ʰ +3ʰ +2ʰ +1ʰ H.W. -1ʰ -2ʰ -3ʰ -4ʰ -5ʰ L.W.

TIME ZONE (UT)
For Summer Time add ONE hour in non-shaded areas

PLYMOUTH (DEVONPORT)
LAT 50°22'N   LONG 4°11'W
TIMES AND HEIGHTS OF HIGH AND LOW WATERS

Dates in amber are SPRINGS
Dates in yellow are NEAPS

2012

JANUARY

Time	m	Time	m
1 0420	2.0	**16** 0405	1.5
1020	4.8	1024	5.0
SU 1649	2.0	M 1635	1.6
☾ 2249	4.5	☽ 2254	4.8
2 0507	2.2	**17** 0459	1.8
1109	4.5	1122	4.8
M 1740	2.2	TU 1735	1.8
2346	4.4		
3 0608	2.4	**18** 0001	4.6
1213	4.4	0610	2.0
TU 1843	2.3	W 1237	4.6
		1857	2.0
4 0059	4.4	**19** 0123	4.6
0718	2.4	0744	2.0
W 1335	4.4	TH 1400	4.6
1950	2.2	2029	1.9
5 0217	4.5	**20** 0241	4.8
0828	2.2	0910	1.8
TH 1448	4.5	F 1516	4.7
2054	2.0	2143	1.6
6 0319	4.7	**21** 0348	5.0
0929	2.0	1017	1.4
F 1546	4.7	SA 1620	4.9
2150	1.8	2242	1.3
7 0410	5.0	**22** 0445	5.3
1021	1.7	1111	1.1
SA 1636	4.9	SU 1715	5.1
2239	1.5	2333	1.0
8 0456	5.2	**23** 0534	5.5
1107	1.4	1159	0.8
SU 1721	5.0	M 1803	5.3
2324	1.3		
9 0538	5.3	**24** 0018	0.8
1151	1.2	0619	5.6
M 1804	5.1	TU 1244	0.6
○		1845	5.3
10 0006	1.2	**25** 0100	0.7
0619	5.4	0700	5.6
TU 1233	1.0	W 1324	0.6
1845	5.2	1924	5.3
11 0047	1.0	**26** 0138	0.7
0658	5.5	0736	5.6
W 1313	1.0	TH 1400	0.7
1924	5.2	1956	5.2
12 0126	1.0	**27** 0211	0.9
0736	5.5	0808	5.4
TH 1351	0.9	F 1432	0.9
2002	5.2	2025	5.1
13 0204	1.0	**28** 0241	1.1
0815	5.5	0837	5.3
F 1429	1.0	SA 1501	1.2
2039	5.2	2053	5.0
14 0241	1.1	**29** 0308	1.4
0854	5.4	0906	5.1
SA 1507	1.1	SU 1527	1.5
2118	5.1	2124	4.8
15 0321	1.2	**30** 0335	1.7
0936	5.2	0939	4.8
SU 1548	1.3	M 1555	1.8
2202	4.9	2200	4.6
		31 0405	2.0
		1018	4.6
		TU 1630	2.1
		☾ 2245	4.4

FEBRUARY

Time	m	Time	m
1 0453	2.3	**16** 0543	2.0
1109	4.3	1216	4.4
W 1733	2.3	TH 1825	2.1
2347	4.3		
2 0617	2.4	**17** 0102	4.4
1222	4.2	0724	2.1
TH 1856	2.4	F 1350	4.3
		2016	2.1
3 0112	4.3	**18** 0228	4.6
0738	2.4	0904	1.9
F 1404	4.2	SA 1509	4.5
2010	2.2	2135	1.7
4 0241	4.5	**19** 0336	4.9
0850	2.1	1008	1.4
SA 1518	4.5	SU 1612	4.8
2116	1.9	2232	1.3
5 0343	4.8	**20** 0431	5.2
0952	1.7	1059	1.0
SU 1613	4.7	M 1703	5.0
2214	1.6	2319	1.0
6 0432	5.1	**21** 0518	5.4
1045	1.3	1144	0.7
M 1701	5.0	TU 1746	5.2
2304	1.2	●	
7 0517	5.3	**22** 0001	0.7
1133	1.0	0559	5.5
TU 1745	5.1	W 1225	0.6
○ 2350	1.0	1823	5.3
8 0600	5.5	**23** 0040	0.6
1217	0.8	0636	5.6
W 1828	5.3	TH 1302	0.5
		1856	5.3
9 0033	0.8	**24** 0115	0.6
0641	5.6	0709	5.6
TH 1259	0.6	F 1335	0.6
1908	5.4	1925	5.3
10 0114	0.6	**25** 0145	0.8
0722	5.6	0739	5.4
F 1338	0.5	SA 1403	0.8
1947	5.4	1952	5.2
11 0152	0.6	**26** 0211	1.0
0802	5.6	0807	5.3
SA 1416	0.6	SU 1427	1.1
2024	5.4	2020	5.1
12 0229	0.7	**27** 0234	1.2
0841	5.4	0835	5.1
SU 1452	0.8	M 1447	1.4
2101	5.3	2049	4.9
13 0306	0.9	**28** 0253	1.5
0920	5.2	0905	4.8
M 1529	1.1	TU 1507	1.6
2140	5.1	2120	4.7
14 0347	1.2	**29** 0316	1.8
1004	5.0	0939	4.6
TU 1612	1.5	W 1533	1.9
☽ 2227	4.8	2159	4.5
15 0436	1.6		
1058	4.7		
W 1706	1.9		
2331	4.5		

MARCH

Time	m	Time	m
1 0351	2.1	**16** 0528	2.0
1025	4.3	1208	4.3
TH 1618	2.2	F 1807	2.2
2254	4.3		
2 0503	2.3	**17** 0047	4.4
1131	4.1	0712	2.1
F 1801	2.4	SA 1341	4.2
		2002	2.2
3 0009	4.2	**18** 0212	4.5
0656	2.4	0850	1.8
SA 1307	4.1	SU 1456	4.5
1931	2.3	2118	1.8
4 0152	4.3	**19** 0317	4.8
0814	2.1	0949	1.4
SU 1446	4.3	M 1554	4.7
2044	2.0	2211	1.3
5 0309	4.7	**20** 0410	5.1
0921	1.7	1037	1.0
M 1546	4.7	TU 1640	5.0
2146	1.5	2256	1.0
6 0403	5.0	**21** 0454	5.3
1018	1.2	1120	0.8
TU 1635	4.9	W 1720	5.2
2240	1.1	2337	0.8
7 0450	5.3	**22** 0533	5.4
1109	0.8	1159	0.6
W 1720	5.2	TH 1755	5.3
2329	0.8	●	
8 0535	5.6	**23** 0014	0.7
1155	0.6	0608	5.4
TH 1803	5.4	F 1234	0.6
○		1825	5.3
9 0013	0.5	**24** 0048	0.7
0619	5.6	0640	5.4
F 1239	0.4	SA 1305	0.7
1845	5.5	1854	5.3
10 0056	0.4	**25** 0117	0.8
0702	5.7	0710	5.3
SA 1319	0.4	SU 1332	0.9
1925	5.6	1922	5.3
11 0135	0.3	**26** 0141	1.0
0744	5.7	0739	5.2
SU 1358	0.4	M 1354	1.1
2004	5.5	1951	5.2
12 0213	0.5	**27** 0202	1.2
0825	5.5	0808	5.0
M 1435	0.6	TU 1414	1.3
2042	5.4	2020	5.0
13 0251	0.7	**28** 0222	1.4
0905	5.3	0837	4.8
TU 1513	1.0	W 1434	1.5
2121	5.2	2049	4.8
14 0332	1.1	**29** 0246	1.6
0949	4.9	0910	4.6
W 1555	1.4	TH 1502	1.8
2206	4.8	2125	4.6
15 0421	1.6	**30** 0322	1.9
1043	4.5	0955	4.3
TH 1649	1.9	F 1545	2.1
☽ 2310	4.5	☽ 2217	4.4
		31 0421	2.2
		1058	4.1
		SA 1705	2.3
		2326	4.3

APRIL

Time	m	Time	m
1 0615	2.2	**16** 0145	4.5
1219	4.1	0816	1.8
SU 1853	2.3	M 1427	4.5
		2044	1.9
2 0051	4.4	**17** 0247	4.7
0738	2.0	0917	1.5
M 1401	4.3	TU 1521	4.7
2009	2.0	2139	1.5
3 0223	4.6	**18** 0338	4.9
0847	1.6	1006	1.2
TU 1509	4.6	W 1607	4.9
2114	1.5	2226	1.2
4 0326	5.0	**19** 0422	5.1
0947	1.2	1048	1.0
W 1602	5.0	TH 1647	5.1
2211	1.1	2307	1.0
5 0418	5.3	**20** 0502	5.2
1040	0.8	1127	0.9
TH 1649	5.2	F 1722	5.2
2302	0.7	2344	0.9
6 0507	5.5	**21** 0538	5.2
1129	0.5	1202	0.9
F 1735	5.4	SA 1754	5.3
○ 2350	0.4	●	
7 0554	5.6	**22** 0018	0.9
1214	0.3	0611	5.2
SA 1820	5.6	SU 1234	0.9
		1825	5.3
8 0034	0.3	**23** 0047	1.0
0640	5.7	0644	5.2
SU 1258	0.3	M 1301	1.0
1903	5.7	1856	5.3
9 0117	0.3	**24** 0114	1.1
0725	5.6	0716	5.1
M 1339	0.4	TU 1325	1.2
1945	5.6	1927	5.2
10 0158	0.4	**25** 0138	1.2
0809	5.5	0747	5.0
TU 1420	0.6	W 1349	1.3
2025	5.5	1957	5.1
11 0239	0.7	**26** 0202	1.4
0853	5.2	0818	4.8
W 1500	1.0	TH 1414	1.5
2107	5.2	2027	4.9
12 0323	1.0	**27** 0231	1.5
0940	4.9	0852	4.6
TH 1545	1.4	F 1446	1.7
2152	4.9	2104	4.8
13 0413	1.5	**28** 0309	1.7
1037	4.5	0937	4.4
F 1639	1.8	SA 1531	1.9
☽ 2256	4.6	2153	4.6
14 0517	1.9	**29** 0406	1.9
1158	4.3	1034	4.3
SA 1750	2.1	SU 1638	2.1
		☽ 2255	4.5
15 0027	4.4	**30** 0533	2.0
0645	2.0	1145	4.3
SU 1320	4.3	M 1811	2.1
1927	2.1		

Chart Datum: 3·22 metres below Ordnance Datum (Newlyn)
HAT is 5·9 metres above Chart Datum

TIDES

TIME ZONE (UT)	PLYMOUTH (DEVONPORT)	Dates in amber are SPRINGS
For Summer Time add ONE hour in **non-shaded** areas	LAT 50°22'N LONG 4°11'W	Dates in yellow are NEAPS
	TIMES AND HEIGHTS OF HIGH AND LOW WATERS	**2012**

MAY

Time m	Time m
1 0008 4.5 / 0658 1.9 / TU 1308 4.4 / 1930 1.9	**16** 0205 4.6 / 0829 1.7 / W 1439 4.6 / 2055 1.8
2 0130 4.7 / 0809 1.6 / W 1423 4.7 / 2039 1.6	**17** 0259 4.7 / 0923 1.5 / TH 1527 4.8 / 2146 1.6
3 0243 4.9 / 0912 1.2 / TH 1523 5.0 / 2139 1.2	**18** 0346 4.9 / 1010 1.4 / F 1609 4.9 / 2231 1.4
4 0344 5.2 / 1009 0.9 / F 1617 5.2 / 2234 0.8	**19** 0428 5.0 / 1051 1.2 / SA 1648 5.1 / 2311 1.2
5 0438 5.4 / 1102 0.6 / SA 1707 5.5 / 2326 0.6	**20** 0508 5.0 / 1129 1.2 / SU 1725 5.2 / ● 2347 1.2
6 0530 5.5 / 1151 0.5 / SU 1755 5.6 / ○	**21** 0546 5.1 / 1202 1.1 / M 1801 5.2
7 0014 0.4 / 0620 5.6 / M 1238 0.4 / 1842 5.7	**22** 0020 1.1 / 0623 5.1 / TU 1234 1.0 / 1835 5.2
8 0100 0.4 / 0709 5.5 / TU 1323 0.5 / 1927 5.6	**23** 0051 1.2 / 0659 5.0 / W 1304 1.2 / 1909 5.2
9 0145 0.5 / 0757 5.4 / W 1407 0.7 / 2012 5.5	**24** 0121 1.2 / 0733 4.9 / TH 1334 1.3 / 1941 5.1
10 0230 0.7 / 0844 5.2 / TH 1451 1.0 / 2056 5.3	**25** 0152 1.3 / 0807 4.8 / F 1405 1.4 / 2014 5.0
11 0315 1.0 / 0933 4.9 / F 1536 1.3 / 2143 5.0	**26** 0225 1.4 / 0842 4.7 / SA 1441 1.6 / 2051 4.9
12 0404 1.4 / 1028 4.6 / SA 1626 1.7 / ◑ 2239 4.8	**27** 0305 1.5 / 0924 4.6 / SU 1524 1.7 / 2136 4.8
13 0500 1.7 / 1133 4.4 / SU 1725 1.9 / 2352 4.6	**28** 0355 1.6 / 1015 4.5 / M 1619 1.8 / ◑ 2231 4.7
14 0605 1.9 / 1242 4.4 / M 1835 2.1	**29** 0458 1.7 / 1116 4.5 / TU 1729 1.9 / 2335 4.7
15 0103 4.5 / 0720 1.9 / TU 1345 4.4 / 1951 2.0	**30** 0614 1.7 / 1226 4.5 / W 1848 1.8
	31 0048 4.7 / 0729 1.6 / TH 1340 4.7 / 2001 1.6

JUNE

Time m	Time m
1 0204 4.9 / 0837 1.4 / F 1447 4.9 / 2108 1.3	**16** 0306 4.6 / 0922 1.7 / SA 1531 4.8 / 2150 1.7
2 0312 5.1 / 0940 1.1 / SA 1547 5.2 / 2209 1.0	**17** 0355 4.7 / 1011 1.6 / SU 1617 4.9 / 2236 1.5
3 0413 5.2 / 1038 0.9 / SU 1643 5.4 / 2305 0.8	**18** 0441 4.9 / 1054 1.4 / M 1659 5.1 / 2318 1.4
4 0510 5.4 / 1131 0.7 / M 1735 5.5 / ○ 2357 0.6	**19** 0524 5.0 / 1134 1.3 / TU 1740 5.2 / ● 2356 1.2
5 0604 5.4 / 1222 0.6 / TU 1825 5.6	**20** 0605 5.0 / 1211 1.2 / W 1818 5.2
6 0047 0.5 / 0655 5.4 / W 1310 0.6 / 1913 5.6	**21** 0033 1.2 / 0645 5.0 / TH 1248 1.2 / 1855 5.2
7 0135 0.5 / 0745 5.3 / TH 1356 0.7 / 1959 5.6	**22** 0109 1.1 / 0723 5.0 / F 1323 1.2 / 1930 5.2
8 0220 0.6 / 0834 5.2 / F 1439 0.9 / 2044 5.4	**23** 0144 1.1 / 0759 4.9 / SA 1358 1.2 / 2004 5.2
9 0304 0.9 / 0919 5.0 / SA 1522 1.2 / 2127 5.2	**24** 0220 1.2 / 0835 4.9 / SU 1434 1.3 / 2041 5.1
10 0348 1.2 / 1004 4.8 / SU 1605 1.5 / 2209 4.9	**25** 0257 1.2 / 0913 4.8 / M 1514 1.4 / 2122 5.0
11 0433 1.5 / 1051 4.6 / M 1652 1.7 / ◑ 2257 4.7	**26** 0340 1.4 / 0957 4.7 / TU 1600 1.5 / 2210 4.9
12 0522 1.7 / 1145 4.4 / TU 1744 2.0 / 2358 4.5	**27** 0430 1.5 / 1050 4.7 / W 1655 1.7 / ◑ 2307 4.8
13 0618 1.9 / 1245 4.4 / W 1845 2.1	**28** 0532 1.6 / 1152 4.6 / TH 1805 1.8
14 0107 4.4 / 0720 2.0 / TH 1346 4.4 / 1952 2.1	**29** 0016 4.7 / 0648 1.7 / F 1305 4.7 / 1925 1.7
15 0210 4.5 / 0825 1.9 / F 1441 4.6 / 2055 1.9	**30** 0134 4.7 / 0806 1.6 / SA 1419 4.8 / 2042 1.6

JULY

Time m	Time m
1 0250 4.8 / 0918 1.4 / SU 1525 5.0 / 2151 1.3	**16** 0326 4.5 / 0931 1.8 / M 1549 4.8 / 2202 1.7
2 0356 5.0 / 1021 1.1 / M 1625 5.3 / 2251 1.0	**17** 0417 4.7 / 1023 1.6 / TU 1636 5.0 / 2251 1.4
3 0456 5.2 / 1118 0.9 / TU 1719 5.5 / ○ 2346 0.7	**18** 0503 4.9 / 1109 1.3 / W 1719 5.2 / 2335 1.2
4 0551 5.3 / 1210 0.7 / W 1810 5.6	**19** 0547 5.0 / 1152 1.2 / TH 1800 5.3 / ●
5 0036 0.5 / 0642 5.3 / TH 1258 0.6 / 1858 5.6	**20** 0016 1.1 / 0628 5.1 / F 1232 1.1 / 1839 5.3
6 0123 0.5 / 0731 5.3 / F 1342 0.6 / 1943 5.6	**21** 0055 1.0 / 0708 5.1 / SA 1310 1.0 / 1917 5.4
7 0206 0.6 / 0815 5.2 / SA 1424 0.8 / 2024 5.5	**22** 0132 0.9 / 0746 5.1 / SU 1347 1.0 / 1953 5.4
8 0246 0.7 / 0854 5.1 / SU 1501 1.0 / 2059 5.3	**23** 0208 0.9 / 0822 5.1 / M 1423 1.0 / 2030 5.3
9 0323 1.0 / 0927 4.9 / M 1537 1.3 / 2131 5.0	**24** 0244 1.0 / 0858 5.0 / TU 1459 1.1 / 2108 5.2
10 0359 1.3 / 0959 4.7 / TU 1614 1.6 / 2204 4.8	**25** 0322 1.1 / 0933 4.8 / W 1540 1.3 / 2152 5.0
11 0437 1.7 / 1036 4.6 / W 1656 1.9 / ◑ 2244 4.6	**26** 0405 1.4 / 1025 4.8 / TH 1629 1.6 / ◑ 2243 4.8
12 0522 1.9 / 1125 4.4 / TH 1748 2.1 / 2339 4.4	**27** 0459 1.6 / 1124 4.6 / F 1732 1.8 / 2350 4.6
13 0619 2.1 / 1231 4.3 / F 1852 2.2	**28** 0612 1.8 / 1239 4.6 / SA 1858 1.9
14 0101 4.3 / 0724 2.1 / SA 1350 4.4 / 2000 2.2	**29** 0115 4.5 / 0743 1.9 / SU 1401 4.7 / 2027 1.8
15 0224 4.4 / 0830 2.0 / SU 1456 4.6 / 2106 2.0	**30** 0239 4.6 / 0906 1.6 / M 1513 4.9 / 2142 1.4
	31 0348 4.8 / 1012 1.3 / TU 1614 5.2 / 2243 1.1

AUGUST

Time m	Time m
1 0447 5.1 / 1108 1.0 / W 1707 5.4 / 2335 0.7	**16** 0441 4.9 / 1045 1.3 / TH 1656 5.2 / 2312 1.1
2 0539 5.2 / 1157 0.7 / TH 1755 5.6 / ○	**17** 0525 5.1 / 1131 1.1 / F 1739 5.4 / ● 2355 0.9
3 0022 0.5 / 0626 5.3 / F 1242 0.6 / 1839 5.6	**18** 0607 5.2 / 1213 0.9 / SA 1819 5.5
4 0106 0.4 / 0709 5.4 / SA 1323 0.6 / 1920 5.6	**19** 0036 0.7 / 0647 5.3 / SU 1253 0.8 / 1859 5.5
5 0145 0.5 / 0746 5.3 / SU 1400 0.7 / 1955 5.5	**20** 0115 0.7 / 0726 5.3 / M 1330 0.7 / 1937 5.5
6 0220 0.7 / 0818 5.2 / M 1433 0.9 / 2025 5.3	**21** 0151 0.7 / 0803 5.3 / TU 1407 0.8 / 2015 5.5
7 0252 1.0 / 0845 5.0 / TU 1503 1.2 / 2053 5.1	**22** 0227 0.8 / 0839 5.3 / W 1443 0.9 / 2053 5.3
8 0320 1.3 / 0914 4.9 / W 1533 1.5 / 2122 4.9	**23** 0303 1.0 / 0918 5.1 / TH 1522 1.2 / 2134 5.1
9 0349 1.7 / 0947 4.7 / TH 1604 1.9 / ◑ 2158 4.6	**24** 0344 1.4 / 1002 4.9 / F 1609 1.6 / ◑ 2224 4.7
10 0424 2.0 / 1029 4.5 / F 1649 2.2 / 2244 4.4	**25** 0435 1.7 / 1100 4.6 / SA 1711 1.9 / 2332 4.5
11 0519 2.2 / 1126 4.3 / SA 1800 2.4 / 2350 4.2	**26** 0549 2.1 / 1222 4.5 / SU 1842 2.1
12 0635 2.4 / 1248 4.3 / SU 1917 2.4	**27** 0108 4.4 / 0734 2.1 / M 1352 4.6 / 2024 1.9
13 0139 4.2 / 0749 2.2 / M 1421 4.4 / 2028 2.1	**28** 0236 4.5 / 0901 1.8 / TU 1505 4.9 / 2136 1.5
14 0259 4.4 / 0856 2.0 / TU 1523 4.7 / 2131 1.8	**29** 0344 4.8 / 1003 1.4 / W 1602 5.3 / 2231 1.1
15 0354 4.7 / 0955 1.6 / W 1612 5.0 / 2224 1.4	**30** 0437 5.1 / 1054 1.0 / TH 1652 5.4 / 2319 0.7
	31 0523 5.3 / 1139 0.7 / F 1736 5.6 / ○

Chart Datum: 3·22 metres below Ordnance Datum (Newlyn)
HAT is 5·9 metres above Chart Datum

PLYMOUTH (DEVONPORT)

LAT 50°22'N LONG 4°11'W

TIMES AND HEIGHTS OF HIGH AND LOW WATERS

Dates in amber are **SPRINGS**
Dates in yellow are **NEAPS**

2012

SEPTEMBER

Day	Time m	Day	Time m
1 SA	0002 0.5 / 0603 5.4 / 1221 0.6 / 1816 5.6	**16**	0541 5.4 / 1149 0.7 / 1755 5.6 ●
2 SU	0042 0.5 / 0640 5.4 / 1259 0.6 / 1852 5.6	**17** M	0012 0.6 / 0622 5.5 / 1231 0.6 / 1836 5.7
3 M	0118 0.6 / 0712 5.4 / 1332 0.7 / 1923 5.5	**18** TU	0053 0.5 / 0702 5.5 / 1311 0.6 / 1917 5.7
4 TU	0149 0.8 / 0740 5.3 / 1402 0.9 / 1951 5.3	**19** W	0132 0.6 / 0741 5.5 / 1349 0.6 / 1958 5.6
5 W	0216 1.1 / 0807 5.2 / 1428 1.2 / 2018 5.1	**20** TH	0209 0.8 / 0820 5.4 / 1427 0.9 / 2038 5.4
6 TH	0240 1.4 / 0836 5.0 / 1451 1.5 / 2048 4.9	**21** F	0247 1.1 / 0900 5.3 / 1508 1.2 / 2121 5.1
7 F	0301 1.7 / 0909 4.8 / 1512 1.8 / 2122 4.6	**22** SA	0329 1.4 / 0945 5.0 / 1556 1.6 / 2212 4.7 ◐
8 SA	0323 2.0 / 0948 4.6 / 1542 2.2 / 2205 4.4 ◐	**23** SU	0421 1.9 / 1044 4.7 / 1700 2.0 / 2325 4.4
9 SU	0402 2.3 / 1039 4.4 / 1655 2.4 / 2306 4.2	**24** M	0536 2.2 / 1211 4.5 / 1835 2.2
10 M	0544 2.5 / 1150 4.3 / 1838 2.5	**25** TU	0105 4.3 / 0726 2.2 / 1341 4.6 / 2014 1.9
11 TU	0039 4.1 / 0712 2.4 / 1335 4.4 / 1954 2.2	**26** W	0228 4.5 / 0847 1.9 / 1450 4.9 / 2119 1.5
12 W	0229 4.3 / 0824 2.1 / 1451 4.7 / 2100 1.8	**27** TH	0329 4.8 / 0944 1.4 / 1545 5.2 / 2211 1.1
13 TH	0327 4.7 / 0925 1.7 / 1543 5.0 / 2155 1.4	**28** F	0418 5.1 / 1032 1.1 / 1631 5.4 / 2256 0.9
14 F	0414 5.0 / 1018 1.3 / 1629 5.3 / 2244 1.0	**29** SA	0459 5.4 / 1115 0.8 / 1712 5.5 / 2337 0.7
15 SA	0458 5.2 / 1105 1.0 / 1712 5.5 / 2329 0.8	**30** SU	0536 5.4 / 1155 0.7 / 1749 5.5 ○

OCTOBER

Day	Time m	Day	Time m
1 M	0014 0.7 / 0609 5.4 / 1231 0.7 / 1822 5.5	**16** TU	0555 5.6 / 1208 0.6 / 1814 5.7
2 TU	0048 0.8 / 0639 5.4 / 1303 0.9 / 1852 5.4	**17** W	0030 0.5 / 0638 5.7 / 1252 0.5 / 1858 5.7
3 W	0117 1.0 / 0707 5.4 / 1330 1.1 / 1921 5.3	**18** TH	0113 0.6 / 0721 5.7 / 1334 0.6 / 1942 5.6
4 TH	0142 1.2 / 0736 5.3 / 1354 1.3 / 1950 5.1	**19** F	0153 0.8 / 0803 5.6 / 1416 0.8 / 2026 5.4
5 F	0203 1.4 / 0806 5.1 / 1415 1.6 / 2021 4.9	**20** SA	0235 1.1 / 0847 5.4 / 1500 1.2 / 2113 5.1
6 SA	0222 1.7 / 0838 4.9 / 1436 1.8 / 2054 4.7	**21** SU	0319 1.5 / 0934 5.1 / 1550 1.6 / 2206 4.7
7 SU	0245 1.9 / 0915 4.7 / 1506 2.1 / 2136 4.4	**22** M	0412 1.9 / 1034 4.8 / 1652 1.9 / 2320 4.5 ◐
8 M	0322 2.2 / 1004 4.5 / 1557 2.3 / 2234 4.2 ◐	**23** TU	0522 2.2 / 1155 4.6 / 1816 2.1
9 TU	0432 2.5 / 1108 4.4 / 1753 2.6 / 2350 4.2	**24** W	0048 4.4 / 0657 2.2 / 1316 4.7 / 1945 2.0
10 W	0631 2.5 / 1230 4.4 / 1917 2.3	**25** TH	0202 4.6 / 0817 2.0 / 1422 4.8 / 2050 1.7
11 TH	0140 4.3 / 0748 2.2 / 1404 4.6 / 2024 1.9	**26** F	0301 4.8 / 0918 1.7 / 1517 5.1 / 2142 1.4
12 F	0250 4.7 / 0851 1.8 / 1506 5.0 / 2121 1.4	**27** SA	0349 5.0 / 1004 1.3 / 1603 5.2 / 2227 1.1
13 SA	0341 5.0 / 0946 1.4 / 1556 5.3 / 2213 1.1	**28** SU	0430 5.2 / 1047 1.1 / 1644 5.3 / 2307 1.0
14 SU	0427 5.4 / 1037 1.0 / 1643 5.5 / 2301 0.8	**29** M	0507 5.4 / 1126 1.0 / 1721 5.4 / 2344 1.0 ○
15 M	0512 5.5 / 1124 0.7 / 1729 5.6 / 2347 0.6 ●	**30** TU	0540 5.4 / 1202 1.0 / 1755 5.4
		31 W	0017 1.0 / 0610 5.4 / 1234 1.1 / 1827 5.3

NOVEMBER

Day	Time m	Day	Time m
1 TH	0047 1.1 / 0641 5.4 / 1303 1.2 / 1858 5.2	**16** F	0057 0.7 / 0704 5.8 / 1322 0.6 / 1930 5.6
2 F	0112 1.3 / 0713 5.3 / 1328 1.4 / 1930 5.1	**17** SA	0142 0.8 / 0751 5.7 / 1407 0.8 / 2018 5.4
3 SA	0136 1.5 / 0744 5.2 / 1353 1.6 / 2002 4.9	**18** SU	0226 1.0 / 0837 5.5 / 1454 1.1 / 2107 5.1
4 SU	0200 1.7 / 0816 5.1 / 1418 1.7 / 2035 4.8	**19** M	0312 1.4 / 0926 5.3 / 1542 1.4 / 2159 4.9
5 M	0228 1.9 / 0852 4.9 / 1451 1.9 / 2115 4.6	**20** TU	0401 1.7 / 1020 5.0 / 1636 1.7 / 2300 4.6 ◐
6 TU	0305 2.1 / 0937 4.7 / 1538 2.1 / 2208 4.4	**21** W	0458 2.0 / 1125 4.8 / 1739 1.9
7 W	0402 2.3 / 1034 4.6 / 1657 2.3 / 2314 4.3	**22** TH	0011 4.5 / 0608 2.2 / 1237 4.7 / 1854 2.0
8 TH	0534 2.4 / 1143 4.6 / 1829 2.4	**23** F	0120 4.5 / 0727 2.1 / 1342 4.7 / 2005 1.9
9 F	0034 4.4 / 0702 2.2 / 1301 4.7 / 1942 1.9	**24** SA	0219 4.7 / 0835 2.0 / 1439 4.8 / 2104 1.7
10 SA	0157 4.6 / 0812 1.9 / 1417 4.9 / 2045 1.6	**25** SU	0311 4.9 / 0930 1.7 / 1529 5.0 / 2153 1.6
11 SU	0300 4.9 / 0913 1.5 / 1518 5.2 / 2142 1.4	**26** M	0356 5.1 / 1016 1.5 / 1614 5.1 / 2236 1.4
12 M	0353 5.2 / 1008 1.2 / 1613 5.4 / 2234 0.9	**27** TU	0437 5.2 / 1058 1.4 / 1654 5.2 / 2315 1.3
13 TU	0443 5.5 / 1059 0.9 / 1704 5.6 / 2323 0.7 ●	**28** W	0513 5.3 / 1135 1.3 / 1732 5.2 / 2349 1.3 ○
14 W	0531 5.7 / 1148 0.7 / 1754 5.7	**29** TH	0548 5.4 / 1209 1.3 / 1808 5.2
15 TH	0011 0.6 / 0618 5.8 / 1236 0.6 / 1842 5.7	**30** F	0021 1.3 / 0622 5.4 / 1241 1.3 / 1843 5.2

DECEMBER

Day	Time m	Day	Time m
1 SA	0051 1.3 / 0657 5.4 / 1313 1.4 / 1917 5.1	**16** SU	0132 0.7 / 0739 5.8 / 1359 0.6 / 2009 5.4
2 SU	0119 1.4 / 0730 5.3 / 1340 1.5 / 1951 5.0	**17** M	0217 0.8 / 0826 5.7 / 1444 0.8 / 2055 5.3
3 M	0148 1.5 / 0803 5.2 / 1410 1.6 / 2024 4.9	**18** TU	0300 1.1 / 0911 5.5 / 1527 1.1 / 2140 5.0
4 TU	0220 1.7 / 0837 5.0 / 1444 1.7 / 2101 4.7	**19** W	0343 1.4 / 0956 5.2 / 1611 1.4 / 2225 4.8
5 W	0257 1.8 / 0917 4.9 / 1525 1.8 / 2146 4.6	**20** TH	0427 1.7 / 1043 4.9 / 1658 1.8 / 2316 4.6 ◐
6 TH	0343 2.0 / 1007 4.8 / 1619 2.0 / 2241 4.5 ◐	**21** F	0517 2.0 / 1138 4.7 / 1752 2.0
7 F	0444 2.1 / 1106 4.7 / 1731 2.0 / 2347 4.5	**22** SA	0017 4.5 / 0618 2.2 / 1245 4.6 / 1856 2.2
8 SA	0605 2.1 / 1214 4.7 / 1853 2.0	**23** SU	0125 4.5 / 0731 2.3 / 1352 4.5 / 2008 2.1
9 SU	0101 4.6 / 0727 2.0 / 1329 4.8 / 2006 1.7	**24** M	0227 4.6 / 0844 2.1 / 1451 4.6 / 2111 2.0
10 M	0216 4.8 / 0839 1.7 / 1441 5.0 / 2111 1.4	**25** TU	0321 4.8 / 0942 1.9 / 1543 4.8 / 2203 1.7
11 TU	0320 5.1 / 0942 1.4 / 1546 5.2 / 2210 1.2	**26** W	0408 5.0 / 1030 1.7 / 1629 4.9 / 2246 1.5
12 W	0418 5.4 / 1039 1.0 / 1644 5.4 / 2305 0.9	**27** TH	0450 5.2 / 1111 1.5 / 1712 5.1 / 2325 1.3
13 TH	0511 5.6 / 1133 0.8 / 1738 5.5 / 2356 0.7 ●	**28** F	0529 5.3 / 1149 1.3 / 1752 5.1 ○
14 F	0602 5.8 / 1223 0.6 / 1830 5.6	**29** SA	0001 1.3 / 0607 5.4 / 1225 1.3 / 1830 5.1
15 SA	0045 0.7 / 0651 5.8 / 1313 0.6 / 1920 5.5	**30** SU	0035 1.3 / 0644 5.4 / 1258 1.2 / 1907 5.1
		31 M	0108 1.3 / 0720 5.3 / 1330 1.3 / 1942 5.1

Chart Datum: 3·22 metres below Ordnance Datum (Newlyn)
HAT is 5·9 metres above Chart Datum

TIDES

TIDES

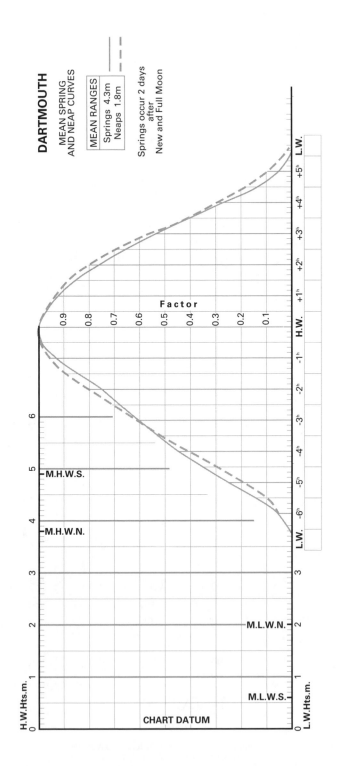

228

DARTMOUTH

LAT 50°21′N   LONG 3°34′W

TIMES AND HEIGHTS OF HIGH AND LOW WATERS

2012

JANUARY

Day	Time m		Day	Time m	
1 SU	0417 1.8 / 1039 4.2 / 1645 1.8 / ◗2307 3.9		**16** M	0402 1.3 / 1043 4.4 / 1631 1.4 / 2312 4.2	
2 M	0503 2.0 / 1127 3.9 / 1735 2.0		**17** TU	0455 1.6 / 1139 4.2 / 1730 1.6	
3 TU	0002 3.8 / 0603 2.2 / 1229 3.8 / 1839 2.1		**18** W	0017 4.0 / 0605 1.8 / 1252 4.0 / 1853 1.8	
4 W	0114 3.8 / 0714 2.0 / 1351 3.8 / 1946 2.0		**19** TH	0139 4.0 / 0740 1.8 / 1417 4.0 / 2025 1.7	
5 TH	0235 3.9 / 0824 2.0 / 1507 3.9 / 2051 1.8		**20** F	0259 4.2 / 0907 1.6 / 1536 4.1 / 2141 1.4	
6 F	0339 4.1 / 0926 1.8 / 1607 4.1 / 2148 1.6		**21** SA	0409 4.4 / 1015 1.2 / 1642 4.3 / 2241 1.1	
7 SA	0431 4.4 / 1019 1.5 / 1658 4.4 / 2238 1.3		**22** SU	0508 4.7 / 1110 0.9 / 1739 4.5 / 2332 0.8	
8 SU	0519 4.6 / 1106 1.2 / 1745 4.4 / 2323 1.1		**23** M	0558 4.9 / 1158 0.6 / 1828 4.7 ●	
9 M	0602 4.7 / 1150 1.0 / 1829 4.5 ○		**24** TU	0017 0.6 / 0644 5.0 / 1244 0.4 / 1909 4.7	
10 TU	0005 1.0 / 0644 4.6 / 1233 0.8 / 1909 4.6		**25** W	0100 0.5 / 0724 5.0 / 1324 0.4 / 1947 4.7	
11 W	0047 0.8 / 0722 4.6 / 1313 0.8 / 1947 4.6		**26** TH	0137 0.5 / 0759 5.0 / 1359 0.5 / 2018 4.6	
12 TH	0126 0.8 / 0759 4.9 / 1350 0.7 / 2024 4.6		**27** F	0210 0.7 / 0830 4.8 / 1430 0.7 / 2047 4.5	
13 F	0203 0.8 / 0837 4.9 / 1428 0.8 / 2100 4.6		**28** SA	0239 0.9 / 0858 4.7 / 1459 1.0 / 2114 4.4	
14 SA	0239 0.9 / 0915 4.8 / 1505 0.9 / 2138 4.5		**29** SU	0306 1.2 / 0927 4.5 / 1525 1.3 / 2144 4.2	
15 SU	0319 1.0 / 0956 4.6 / 1545 1.1 / 2221 4.3		**30** M	0332 1.5 / 0959 4.2 / 1552 1.6 / 2219 4.0	
			31 TU	0402 1.8 / 1037 4.0 / 1626 1.9 / ◗2303 3.8	

FEBRUARY

Day	Time m		Day	Time m	
1 W	0449 2.1 / 1127 3.7 / 1728 2.1		**16** TH	0538 1.8 / 1232 3.8 / 1820 1.9	
2 TH	0003 3.7 / 0612 2.2 / 1238 3.6 / 1852 2.2		**17** F	0117 3.8 / 0720 1.9 / 1407 3.7 / 2012 1.9	
3 F	0127 3.7 / 0734 2.2 / 1421 3.6 / 2006 2.0		**18** SA	0246 4.0 / 0901 1.7 / 1528 3.9 / 2133 1.5	
4 SA	0259 3.9 / 0847 1.9 / 1538 3.9 / 2113 1.7		**19** SU	0356 4.3 / 1006 1.2 / 1633 4.2 / 2231 1.1	
5 SU	0403 4.2 / 0950 1.5 / 1634 4.1 / 2212 1.4		**20** M	0453 4.6 / 1058 0.8 / 1726 4.4 / 2318 0.8	
6 M	0454 4.5 / 1044 1.1 / 1724 4.4 / 2303 1.0		**21** TU	0542 4.8 / 1143 0.5 / 1811 4.6 ●	
7 TU	0541 4.7 / 1132 0.8 / 1810 4.5 / ○2349 0.8		**22** W	0000 0.4 / 0624 4.9 / 1224 0.4 / 1848 4.7	
8 W	0625 4.9 / 1216 0.6 / 1853 4.7		**23** TH	0040 0.4 / 0700 5.0 / 1302 0.3 / 1920 4.7	
9 TH	0033 0.6 / 0705 5.0 / 1259 0.4 / 1932 4.8		**24** F	0115 0.4 / 0733 4.9 / 1334 0.4 / 1948 4.7	
10 F	0114 0.4 / 0745 5.0 / 1337 0.3 / 2009 4.8		**25** SA	0144 0.6 / 0802 4.8 / 1402 0.6 / 2014 4.6	
11 SA	0151 0.4 / 0824 5.0 / 1415 0.4 / 2046 4.8		**26** SU	0210 0.8 / 0829 4.7 / 1426 0.9 / 2042 4.5	
12 SU	0228 0.5 / 0902 4.9 / 1450 0.6 / 2122 4.7		**27** M	0232 1.0 / 0856 4.5 / 1445 1.2 / 2110 4.3	
13 M	0304 0.7 / 0940 4.7 / 1527 0.9 / 2200 4.5		**28** TU	0251 1.3 / 0926 4.2 / 1505 1.4 / 2140 4.1	
14 TU	0344 1.0 / 1023 4.4 / 1609 1.3 / ◗2246 4.2		**29** W	0314 1.6 / 0959 4.0 / 1530 1.7 / 2218 3.9	
15 W	0432 1.4 / 1116 4.1 / 1702 1.7 / 2348 3.9				

MARCH

Day	Time m		Day	Time m	
1 TH	0348 1.9 / 1044 3.7 / 1615 2.0 / ◗2312 3.7		**16** F	0524 1.8 / 1224 3.7 / 1802 2.0	
2 F	0459 2.1 / 1148 3.5 / 1756 2.2		**17** SA	0102 3.8 / 0708 1.9 / 1357 3.6 / 1958 2.0	
3 SA	0025 3.6 / 0652 2.2 / 1322 3.5 / 1927 2.1		**18** SU	0229 3.9 / 0847 1.6 / 1515 3.9 / 2115 1.6	
4 SU	0209 3.7 / 0810 1.9 / 1505 3.7 / 2041 1.8		**19** M	0337 4.2 / 0947 1.2 / 1615 4.1 / 2209 1.1	
5 M	0328 4.1 / 0918 1.5 / 1607 4.1 / 2144 1.3		**20** TU	0431 4.5 / 1036 0.8 / 1702 4.4 / 2255 0.8	
6 TU	0424 4.4 / 1016 1.0 / 1657 4.3 / 2239 0.9		**21** W	0517 4.7 / 1119 0.6 / 1744 4.6 / 2336 0.6	
7 W	0513 4.7 / 1108 0.6 / 1744 4.6 / 2328 0.6		**22** TH	0557 4.8 / 1158 0.4 / 1820 4.7 ●	
8 TH	0559 4.9 / 1154 0.4 / 1828 4.8 ○		**23** F	0013 0.6 / 0633 4.8 / 1234 0.4 / 1850 4.7	
9 F	0012 0.3 / 0644 5.0 / 1239 0.2 / 1909 4.9		**24** SA	0048 0.6 / 0704 4.8 / 1305 0.5 / 1918 4.7	
10 SA	0056 0.2 / 0726 5.1 / 1319 0.1 / 1948 5.0		**25** SU	0117 0.6 / 0734 4.7 / 1331 0.7 / 1945 4.7	
11 SU	0134 0.1 / 0807 5.1 / 1357 0.2 / 2026 4.9		**26** M	0140 0.8 / 0802 4.6 / 1353 0.9 / 2013 4.6	
12 M	0212 0.3 / 0847 4.9 / 1433 0.4 / 2103 4.8		**27** TU	0201 1.0 / 0830 4.4 / 1413 1.1 / 2042 4.4	
13 TU	0249 0.5 / 0926 4.6 / 1511 0.8 / 2141 4.6		**28** W	0221 1.2 / 0858 4.2 / 1432 1.3 / 2110 4.2	
14 W	0329 0.9 / 1008 4.3 / 1552 1.2 / 2225 4.2		**29** TH	0244 1.4 / 0931 4.0 / 1500 1.6 / 2145 4.0	
15 TH	0418 1.4 / 1101 3.9 / 1645 1.7 / ◗2328 3.9		**30** F	0320 1.7 / 1014 3.7 / 1542 1.9 / ◗2236 3.8	
			31 SA	0418 2.0 / 1116 3.5 / 1701 2.1 / 2343 3.7	

APRIL

Day	Time m		Day	Time m	
1 SU	0610 2.0 / 1235 3.5 / 1849 2.1		**16** M	0202 3.9 / 0812 1.6 / 1445 3.9 / 2041 1.7	
2 M	0106 3.8 / 0734 1.8 / 1418 3.7 / 2005 1.8		**17** TU	0306 4.1 / 0914 1.3 / 1541 4.1 / 2137 1.3	
3 TU	0241 4.0 / 0844 1.4 / 1528 4.0 / 2111 1.3		**18** W	0358 4.3 / 1004 1.0 / 1628 4.3 / 2224 1.0	
4 W	0346 4.4 / 0945 1.0 / 1623 4.4 / 2209 0.9		**19** TH	0444 4.5 / 1047 0.8 / 1710 4.5 / 2306 0.8	
5 TH	0440 4.7 / 1039 0.6 / 1712 4.6 / 2301 0.5		**20** F	0525 4.6 / 1126 0.7 / 1746 4.6 / 2343 0.7	
6 F	0530 4.9 / 1128 0.3 / 1759 4.8 / ○2349 0.2		**21** SA	0602 4.6 / 1201 0.7 / 1819 4.7 ●	
7 SA	0619 5.0 / 1213 0.1 / 1845 5.0		**22** SU	0017 0.7 / 0636 4.6 / 1234 0.7 / 1850 4.7	
8 SU	0034 0.1 / 0704 5.1 / 1258 0.1 / 1927 5.1		**23** M	0047 0.6 / 0708 4.6 / 1301 0.8 / 1920 4.7	
9 M	0117 0.1 / 0748 5.0 / 1338 0.2 / 2007 5.0		**24** TU	0114 0.9 / 0739 4.5 / 1325 1.0 / 1950 4.6	
10 TU	0157 0.2 / 0831 4.9 / 1419 0.4 / 2047 4.9		**25** W	0137 1.0 / 0809 4.4 / 1348 1.1 / 2019 4.5	
11 W	0237 0.5 / 0914 4.6 / 1458 0.8 / 2128 4.6		**26** TH	0201 1.2 / 0840 4.2 / 1413 1.3 / 2049 4.3	
12 TH	0321 0.9 / 0959 4.3 / 1542 1.2 / 2211 4.3		**27** F	0229 1.3 / 0913 4.0 / 1444 1.5 / 2125 4.2	
13 F	0410 1.3 / 1055 3.9 / 1635 1.6 / ◗2314 4.0		**28** SA	0307 1.5 / 0957 3.8 / 1528 1.7 / 2212 4.0	
14 SA	0513 1.7 / 1214 3.7 / 1745 1.9		**29** SU	0403 1.7 / 1052 3.7 / 1634 1.9 / ◗2313 3.9	
15 SU	0043 3.8 / 0641 1.8 / 1336 3.7 / 1923 1.9		**30** M	0528 1.8 / 1201 3.7 / 1806 1.9	

TIDES

Chart Datum: 2·62 metres below Ordnance Datum (Newlyn)
HAT is 5·3 metres above Chart Datum

TIDES

DARTMOUTH
LAT 50°21'N   LONG 3°34'W
TIMES AND HEIGHTS OF HIGH AND LOW WATERS

Dates in amber are **SPRINGS**
Dates in yellow are **NEAPS**

2012

MAY

Day	Time	m	Time	m	Time	m	Time	m
1 TU	0024	3.9	0654	1.7	1323	3.8	1926	1.7
2 W	0146	4.1	0805	1.4	1441	4.1	2036	1.4
3 TH	0301	4.3	0909	1.0	1543	4.4	2137	1.0
4 F	0404	4.6	1007	0.7	1639	4.6	2233	0.6
5 SA	0500	4.8	1101	0.4	1730	4.9	2325	0.4
6 SU ○	0554	4.9	1150	0.3	1820	5.0		
7 M	0013	0.2	0645	5.0	1238	0.2	1906	5.1
8 TU	0100	0.2	0733	4.9	1323	0.3	1950	4.6
9 W	0144	0.3	0819	4.8	1406	0.5	2034	4.9
10 TH	0228	0.5	0905	4.6	1449	0.8	2117	4.7
11 F	0313	0.8	0953	4.3	1533	1.1	2203	4.4
12 SA ◑	0401	1.2	1047	4.0	1623	1.5	2257	4.2
13 SU	0456	1.5	1150	3.8	1721	1.7		
14 M	0008	4.0	0600	1.7	1257	3.8	1831	1.9
15 TU	0118	3.9	0716	1.7	1402	3.8	1947	1.8
16 W	0222	4.0	0825	1.5	1457	4.0	2052	1.6
17 TH	0318	4.1	0920	1.3	1547	4.2	2144	1.4
18 F	0407	4.3	1008	1.2	1630	4.3	2230	1.2
19 SA	0450	4.4	1050	1.0	1711	4.4	2310	1.0
20 SU ●	0531	4.4	1128	1.0	1749	4.6	2346	1.0
21 M	0611	4.5	1201	0.9	1826	4.6		
22 TU	0019	0.9	0648	4.5	1234	1.0	1859	4.6
23 W	0051	1.0	0723	4.4	1304	1.0	1933	4.6
24 TH	0121	1.0	0756	4.3	1333	1.1	2004	4.5
25 F	0151	1.1	0829	4.2	1404	1.2	2036	4.4
26 SA	0224	1.2	0903	4.1	1439	1.4	2112	4.3
27 SU	0303	1.3	0944	4.0	1522	1.5	2156	4.2
28 M ◑	0352	1.4	1034	3.9	1616	1.6	2249	4.1
29 TU	0454	1.5	1133	3.9	1725	1.7	2352	4.1
30 W	0609	1.5	1242	3.9	1844	1.6		
31 TH	0103	4.1	0725	1.4	1356	4.1	1957	1.8

JUNE

Day	Time	m	Time	m	Time	m	Time	m
1 F	0221	4.3	0834	1.2	1506	4.4	2105	1.1
2 SA	0331	4.5	0938	0.9	1608	4.6	2207	0.8
3 SU	0434	4.6	1037	0.7	1705	4.8	2304	0.6
4 M ○	0533	4.8	1130	0.5	1759	4.9	2356	0.4
5 TU	0629	4.8	1210	0.4	1850	5.0		
6 W	0047	0.3	0719	4.8	1310	0.4	1937	5.0
7 TH	0134	0.3	0807	4.7	1355	0.5	2021	4.9
8 F	0219	0.4	0855	4.6	1437	0.7	2105	4.8
9 SA	0302	0.7	0939	4.4	1520	1.0	2147	4.6
10 SU	0345	1.0	1023	4.2	1602	1.3	2228	4.3
11 M ◑	0429	1.3	1109	4.0	1648	1.5	2315	4.1
12 TU	0518	1.5	1201	3.8	1739	1.8		
13 W	0014	3.9	0613	1.7	1300	3.8	1841	1.9
14 TH	0122	3.8	0716	1.8	1403	3.8	1948	1.9
15 F	0227	3.9	0821	1.7	1459	4.0	2052	1.7
16 SA	0325	4.0	0919	1.5	1551	4.2	2148	1.5
17 SU	0416	4.1	1009	1.4	1639	4.3	2235	1.3
18 M	0503	4.3	1053	1.2	1722	4.5	2317	1.2
19 TU ●	0548	4.4	1133	1.1	1804	4.6	2355	1.0
20 W	0630	4.4	1210	1.0	1843	4.6		
21 TH	0033	1.0	0709	4.4	1248	1.0	1919	4.6
22 F	0109	0.9	0746	4.2	1323	1.0	1953	4.6
23 SA	0143	0.9	0821	4.3	1357	1.0	2026	4.6
24 SU	0219	1.0	0856	4.3	1432	1.1	2102	4.5
25 M	0255	1.0	0934	4.2	1512	1.2	2142	4.4
26 TU	0337	1.2	1016	4.1	1557	1.3	2229	4.3
27 W ◑	0426	1.3	1108	4.1	1651	1.5	2325	4.2
28 TH	0527	1.4	1208	4.0	1800	1.6		
29 F	0032	4.1	0644	1.5	1320	4.1	1921	1.5
30 SA	0150	4.1	0802	1.4	1437	4.2	2039	1.4

JULY

Day	Time	m	Time	m	Time	m	Time	m
1 SU	0309	4.2	0915	1.2	1545	4.4	2149	1.1
2 M	0417	4.4	1019	0.9	1647	4.7	2250	0.8
3 TU ○	0519	4.6	1117	0.7	1743	4.9	2345	0.5
4 W	0616	4.7	1209	0.5	1835	5.0		
5 TH	0036	0.3	0706	4.7	1258	0.4	1922	5.0
6 F	0123	0.3	0754	4.7	1341	0.4	2006	5.0
7 SA	0205	0.4	0837	4.6	1422	0.6	2046	4.9
8 SU	0244	0.5	0915	4.5	1459	0.8	2120	4.7
9 M	0321	0.8	0947	4.3	1534	1.1	2151	4.4
10 TU	0356	1.1	1018	4.1	1611	1.4	2223	4.2
11 W ◑	0433	1.5	1054	4.0	1652	1.7	2302	4.0
12 TH	0518	1.7	1142	3.8	1743	1.9	2356	3.8
13 F	0614	1.9	1246	3.7	1848	2.0		
14 SA	0116	3.7	0720	1.9	1407	3.8	1956	2.0
15 SU	0242	3.8	0827	1.8	1515	4.0	2103	1.8
16 M	0346	3.9	0929	1.6	1610	4.2	2200	1.5
17 TU	0439	4.1	1021	1.4	1658	4.4	2250	1.2
18 W	0526	4.3	1108	1.1	1743	4.6	2334	1.0
19 TH ●	0612	4.4	1151	1.0	1825	4.7		
20 F	0015	0.9	0653	4.5	1232	0.9	1903	4.7
21 SA	0055	0.8	0732	4.5	1310	0.8	1940	4.8
22 SU	0131	0.7	0808	4.5	1346	0.8	2015	4.8
23 M	0207	0.7	0844	4.5	1422	0.8	2051	4.7
24 TU	0242	0.8	0919	4.4	1457	0.9	2129	4.6
25 W	0320	0.9	0958	4.3	1537	1.1	2211	4.4
26 TH ◑	0402	1.2	1044	4.2	1626	1.4	2301	4.2
27 F	0455	1.4	1141	4.0	1727	1.6		
28 SA	0006	4.0	0607	1.6	1254	4.0	1854	1.7
29 SU	0131	3.9	0739	1.7	1418	4.1	2023	1.6
30 M	0257	4.0	0903	1.4	1532	4.3	2140	1.2
31 TU	0409	4.2	1010	1.1	1635	4.6	2242	0.7

AUGUST

Day	Time	m	Time	m	Time	m	Time	m
1 W	0510	4.5	1107	0.8	1730	4.8	2334	0.5
2 TH ○	0603	4.6	1156	0.5	1820	5.0		
3 F	0021	0.3	0651	4.7	1242	0.4	1903	5.0
4 SA	0106	0.2	0733	4.8	1323	0.4	1943	5.0
5 SU	0144	0.3	0808	4.7	1359	0.5	2017	4.9
6 M	0219	0.5	0840	4.6	1431	0.7	2047	4.7
7 TU	0250	0.8	0906	4.4	1501	1.0	2114	4.5
8 W	0318	1.1	0935	4.3	1530	1.3	2142	4.3
9 TH	0346	1.5	1006	4.1	1601	1.7	2217	4.0
10 F	0421	1.8	1048	3.9	1645	2.0	2302	3.8
11 SA	0515	2.0	1143	3.7	1755	2.2		
12 SU	0006	3.6	0631	2.2	1303	3.7	1913	2.2
13 M	0155	3.6	0745	2.0	1439	3.8	2024	1.9
14 TU	0318	3.8	0853	1.8	1543	4.1	2129	1.6
15 W	0415	4.1	0953	1.4	1633	4.4	2222	1.2
16 TH	0503	4.3	1044	1.1	1719	4.6	2311	0.9
17 F ●	0549	4.5	1130	0.9	1803	4.8	2354	0.7
18 SA	0632	4.6	1212	0.7	1844	4.9		
19 SU	0036	0.5	0709	4.7	1253	0.6	1923	4.9
20 M	0115	0.5	0749	4.7	1329	0.5	2000	4.9
21 TU	0150	0.5	0825	4.7	1406	0.6	2037	4.9
22 W	0226	0.6	0900	4.7	1441	0.7	2114	4.7
23 TH	0301	0.8	0938	4.5	1520	1.0	2154	4.5
24 F ◑	0341	1.2	1021	4.3	1606	1.4	2243	4.2
25 SA	0431	1.5	1118	4.0	1707	1.7	2349	3.9
26 SU	0544	1.9	1238	3.9	1838	1.9		
27 M	0123	3.8	0730	1.9	1409	4.0	2020	1.7
28 TU	0254	3.9	0858	1.6	1524	4.3	2134	1.3
29 W	0404	4.2	1001	1.2	1624	4.6	2230	0.9
30 TH	0459	4.5	1053	0.8	1715	4.8	2318	0.5
31 F ○	0547	4.7	1138	0.5	1800	5.0		

Chart Datum: 2·62 metres below Ordnance Datum (Newlyn)
HAT is 5·3 metres above Chart Datum

TIME ZONE (UT)
For Summer Time add ONE hour in non-shaded areas

DARTMOUTH
LAT 50°21'N LONG 3°34'W
TIMES AND HEIGHTS OF HIGH AND LOW WATERS

Dates in amber are SPRINGS
Dates in yellow are NEAPS

2012

SEPTEMBER

Time m / Time m

	Time m		Time m
1 SA	0001 0.3 / 0628 4.8 / 1220 0.4 / 1841 5.0	**16** SU ●	0605 4.8 / 1148 0.5 / 1820 5.0
2 SU	0042 0.3 / 0704 4.8 / 1259 0.4 / 1916 5.0	**17** M	0011 0.4 / 0647 4.9 / 1231 0.4 / 1900 5.1
3 M	0118 0.4 / 0736 4.8 / 1331 0.5 / 1946 4.9	**18** TU	0053 0.3 / 0726 4.9 / 1311 0.4 / 1940 5.1
4 TU	0148 0.6 / 0803 4.7 / 1401 0.7 / 2013 4.7	**19** W	0131 0.4 / 0804 4.9 / 1348 0.4 / 2020 5.0
5 W	0215 0.9 / 0829 4.6 / 1427 1.0 / 2040 4.5	**20** TH	0208 0.6 / 0842 4.8 / 1426 0.7 / 2059 4.8
6 TH	0238 1.2 / 0857 4.4 / 1449 1.3 / 2109 4.3	**21** F	0245 0.9 / 0921 4.7 / 1506 1.0 / 2141 4.5
7 F	0259 1.5 / 0930 4.2 / 1510 1.6 / 2142 4.0	**22** SA ◗	0327 1.2 / 1004 4.4 / 1553 1.4 / 2231 4.1
8 SA ◗	0321 1.8 / 1007 4.0 / 1539 2.0 / 2224 3.8	**23** SU	0418 1.7 / 1102 4.1 / 1656 1.8 / 2342 3.8
9 SU	0359 2.1 / 1057 3.8 / 1651 2.2 / 2324 3.6	**24** M	0531 2.0 / 1227 3.9 / 1831 2.0
10 M	0539 2.3 / 1206 3.7 / 1834 2.3	**25** TU	0120 3.7 / 0722 2.0 / 1357 4.0 / 2010 1.7
11 TU	0054 3.5 / 0708 2.2 / 1351 3.8 / 1950 2.0	**26** W	0246 3.9 / 0844 1.7 / 1509 4.3 / 2116 1.3
12 W	0247 3.7 / 0820 1.9 / 1510 4.1 / 2057 1.6	**27** TH	0349 4.2 / 0942 1.2 / 1606 4.6 / 2209 0.9
13 TH	0347 4.1 / 0922 1.5 / 1603 4.4 / 2153 1.2	**28** F	0440 4.5 / 1031 0.9 / 1653 4.8 / 2255 0.7
14 F	0435 4.4 / 1016 1.1 / 1651 4.7 / 2243 0.8	**29** SA	0522 4.7 / 1114 0.6 / 1735 4.9 / 2336 0.5
15 SA	0521 4.6 / 1104 0.8 / 1735 4.9 / 2328 0.6	**30** SU ○	0600 4.8 / 1154 0.5 / 1814 4.9

OCTOBER

	Time m		Time m
1 M	0013 0.5 / 0634 4.8 / 1231 0.5 / 1847 4.9	**16** TU	0620 5.0 / 1207 0.4 / 1839 5.1
2 TU	0048 0.6 / 0703 4.8 / 1303 0.7 / 1916 4.8	**17** W	0030 0.3 / 0702 5.1 / 1252 0.3 / 1922 5.1
3 W	0117 0.8 / 0731 4.8 / 1329 0.9 / 1944 4.7	**18** TH	0113 0.4 / 0744 5.1 / 1333 0.4 / 2005 5.0
4 TH	0141 1.0 / 0759 4.7 / 1353 1.1 / 2012 4.5	**19** F	0152 0.6 / 0825 5.0 / 1415 0.6 / 2048 4.8
5 F	0202 1.2 / 0828 4.5 / 1414 1.4 / 2043 4.3	**20** SA	0233 0.9 / 0908 4.8 / 1458 1.0 / 2134 4.5
6 SA	0221 1.5 / 0859 4.3 / 1434 1.6 / 2115 4.1	**21** SU	0317 1.3 / 0954 4.5 / 1547 1.4 / 2225 4.1
7 SU	0243 1.7 / 0935 4.1 / 1504 1.9 / 2156 3.8	**22** M	0409 1.7 / 1052 4.2 / 1648 1.7 / 2337 3.9
8 M	0320 2.0 / 1023 3.9 / 1544 2.1 / 2252 3.6	**23** TU	0518 2.0 / 1211 4.0 / 1811 1.9
9 TU	0428 2.3 / 1126 3.8 / 1748 2.3	**24** W	0103 3.8 / 0653 2.0 / 1332 4.1 / 1941 1.8
10 W	0006 3.6 / 0627 2.3 / 1245 3.8 / 1913 2.1	**25** TH	0219 4.0 / 0813 1.8 / 1440 4.2 / 2047 1.5
11 TH	0156 3.7 / 0744 2.0 / 1421 4.0 / 2020 1.7	**26** F	0320 4.2 / 0913 1.5 / 1537 4.5 / 2140 1.2
12 F	0309 4.1 / 0848 1.6 / 1525 4.4 / 2118 1.2	**27** SA	0410 4.4 / 1002 1.1 / 1624 4.6 / 2225 0.9
13 SA	0401 4.4 / 0944 1.2 / 1617 4.7 / 2211 0.9	**28** SU	0452 4.6 / 1046 0.9 / 1706 4.7 / 2306 0.8
14 SU	0449 4.7 / 1036 0.8 / 1705 4.9 / 2300 0.6	**29** M ○	0530 4.8 / 1125 0.8 / 1745 4.8 / 2343 0.8
15 M ●	0535 4.9 / 1123 0.5 / 1753 5.0 / 2346 0.4	**30** TU	0604 4.8 / 1201 0.8 / 1820 4.8
		31 W	0016 0.8 / 0635 4.8 / 1234 0.9 / 1852 4.7

NOVEMBER

	Time m		Time m
1 TH	0047 0.9 / 0705 4.8 / 1303 1.0 / 1922 4.6	**16** F	0057 0.5 / 0728 5.2 / 1322 0.4 / 1953 5.0
2 F	0112 1.1 / 0737 4.7 / 1328 1.2 / 1953 4.5	**17** SA	0141 0.6 / 0813 5.1 / 1406 0.6 / 2040 4.8
3 SA	0135 1.3 / 0807 4.6 / 1352 1.4 / 2024 4.3	**18** SU	0225 0.8 / 0858 4.9 / 1452 0.9 / 2128 4.5
4 SU	0159 1.5 / 0838 4.5 / 1417 1.5 / 2056 4.2	**19** M	0310 1.2 / 0946 4.7 / 1539 1.2 / 2218 4.3
5 M	0227 1.7 / 0913 4.3 / 1449 1.7 / 2135 4.0	**20** TU ◗	0358 1.5 / 1039 4.4 / 1632 1.5 / 2318 4.0
6 TU	0303 1.9 / 0957 4.1 / 1535 1.9 / 2227 3.8	**21** W	0454 1.8 / 1142 4.2 / 1734 1.7
7 W	0359 2.1 / 1052 4.0 / 1653 2.1 / 2332 3.7	**22** TH	0027 3.9 / 0603 2.0 / 1252 4.1 / 1850 1.8
8 TH	0529 2.2 / 1200 4.0 / 1824 2.0	**23** F	0136 3.9 / 0723 1.9 / 1358 4.1 / 2001 1.7
9 F	0049 3.8 / 0658 2.0 / 1316 4.1 / 1938 1.7	**24** SA	0237 4.1 / 0832 1.8 / 1457 4.2 / 2101 1.5
10 SA	0214 4.0 / 0808 1.7 / 1435 4.3 / 2042 1.4	**25** SU	0330 4.3 / 0928 1.5 / 1549 4.4 / 2151 1.4
11 SU	0319 4.3 / 0910 1.3 / 1538 4.6 / 2140 1.0	**26** M	0417 4.5 / 1014 1.3 / 1635 4.5 / 2235 1.2
12 M	0414 4.6 / 1006 1.0 / 1634 4.8 / 2233 0.7	**27** TU	0459 4.6 / 1057 1.2 / 1717 4.6 / 2314 1.1
13 TU ●	0505 4.9 / 1058 0.7 / 1727 5.0 / 2322 0.5	**28** W ○	0536 4.7 / 1134 1.1 / 1756 4.6 / 2348 1.1
14 W	0555 5.1 / 1147 0.5 / 1819 5.1	**29** TH	0613 4.8 / 1208 1.1 / 1833 4.6
15 TH	0010 0.4 / 0643 5.2 / 1236 0.4 / 1906 5.1	**30** F	0020 1.1 / 0647 4.8 / 1241 1.1 / 1907 4.6

DECEMBER

	Time m		Time m
1 SA	0051 1.1 / 0721 4.8 / 1311 1.2 / 1940 4.5	**16** SU	0131 0.5 / 0802 5.2 / 1358 0.4 / 2031 4.8
2 SU	0119 1.2 / 0753 4.7 / 1339 1.3 / 2013 4.4	**17** M	0216 0.8 / 0848 5.1 / 1442 0.6 / 2116 4.7
3 M	0147 1.3 / 0825 4.6 / 1409 1.4 / 2046 4.3	**18** TU	0258 0.9 / 0932 4.9 / 1525 0.9 / 2200 4.4
4 TU	0219 1.5 / 0858 4.4 / 1442 1.5 / 2122 4.1	**19** W	0340 1.2 / 1015 4.6 / 1608 1.2 / 2244 4.2
5 W	0255 1.6 / 0937 4.3 / 1523 1.6 / 2205 4.0	**20** TH ◗	0424 1.5 / 1101 4.3 / 1654 1.6 / 2333 4.0
6 TH	0340 1.8 / 1026 4.2 / 1616 1.8 / 2259 3.9	**21** F	0513 1.8 / 1155 4.1 / 1747 1.8
7 F	0440 1.9 / 1124 4.1 / 1726 1.8	**22** SA	0033 3.9 / 0613 2.0 / 1300 4.0 / 1852 2.0
8 SA	0003 3.9 / 0600 1.9 / 1230 4.1 / 1849 1.8	**23** SU	0141 3.9 / 0727 2.1 / 1409 3.9 / 2004 1.9
9 SU	0116 4.0 / 0723 1.8 / 1345 4.2 / 2002 1.5	**24** M	0245 4.0 / 0841 1.9 / 1510 4.0 / 2108 1.8
10 M	0234 4.2 / 0836 1.5 / 1459 4.4 / 2108 1.2	**25** TU	0341 4.2 / 0940 1.7 / 1603 4.2 / 2201 1.5
11 TU	0340 4.5 / 0940 1.2 / 1607 4.6 / 2208 1.0	**26** W	0429 4.4 / 1029 1.5 / 1651 4.3 / 2245 1.3
12 W	0440 4.8 / 1038 0.8 / 1706 4.8 / 2304 0.7	**27** TH	0513 4.6 / 1110 1.3 / 1735 4.5 / 2324 1.2
13 TH ●	0534 5.0 / 1132 0.6 / 1802 4.9 / 2355 0.5	**28** F ○	0553 4.7 / 1148 1.1 / 1817 4.5
14 F	0627 5.2 / 1224 0.5 / 1854 5.0	**29** SA	0000 1.1 / 0632 4.8 / 1224 1.1 / 1854 4.5
15 SA	0045 0.5 / 0715 5.2 / 1313 0.4 / 1943 4.9	**30** SU	0035 1.1 / 0708 4.8 / 1258 1.0 / 1931 4.5
		31 M	0108 1.1 / 0743 4.7 / 1329 1.1 / 2005 4.5

Chart Datum: 2·62 metres below Ordnance Datum (Newlyn)
HAT is 5·3 metres above Chart Datum

TIDES

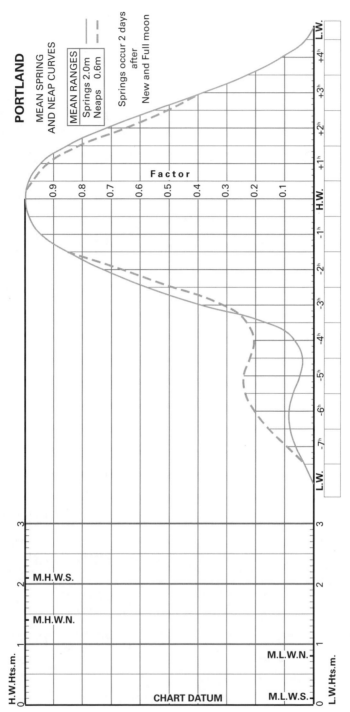

PORTLAND

MEAN SPRING
AND NEAP CURVES

MEAN RANGES
Springs 2.0m
Neaps 0.6m

Springs occur 2 days
after
New and Full moon

Factor

0.9 0.8 0.7 0.6 0.5 0.4 0.3 0.2 0.1

H.W. -1ʰ -2ʰ -3ʰ -4ʰ -5ʰ -6ʰ -7ʰ L.W.

+4ʰ +3ʰ +2ʰ +1ʰ H.W. L.W.

H.W.Hts.m.

3   2   1   0

M.H.W.S.

M.H.W.N.

M.L.W.N.

M.L.W.S.

CHART DATUM

L.W.Hts.m.

Note - Double LWs occur at Portland. The predictions
are for the first LW. The second LW occurs from 3
to 4 Hrs later and may, at Springs, on occasions be
lower than the first.

PORTLAND

LAT 50°34'N   LONG 2°26'W

TIMES AND HEIGHTS OF HIGH AND LOW WATERS

Dates in amber are **SPRINGS**
Dates in yellow are **NEAPS**

2012

JANUARY

Day	Time m	Time m	Time m	Time m
1 SU	0352 0.7	1054 1.5	1639 0.6	◐2328 1.4
16 M	0356 0.5	1100 1.7	1632 0.4	◑2334 1.6
2 M	0433 0.8	1138 1.4	1731 0.7	
17 TU	0452 0.6	1152 1.6	1737 0.5	
3 TU	0023 1.4	0545 0.8	1239 1.4	1839 0.7
18 W	0038 1.5	0607 0.7	1302 1.5	1854 0.6
4 W	0134 1.4	0719 0.8	1356 1.4	1947 0.7
19 TH	0205 1.5	0739 0.7	1436 1.6	2018 0.6
5 TH	0251 1.5	0832 0.8	1516 1.4	2046 0.6
20 F	0335 1.6	0906 0.7	1609 1.6	2131 0.5
6 F	0357 1.6	0928 0.7	1623 1.5	2138 0.5
21 SA	0447 1.8	1011 0.5	1721 1.7	2228 0.4
7 SA	0452 1.8	1015 0.6	1720 1.7	2226 0.4
22 SU	0547 2.0	1102 0.4	1819 1.9	2316 0.3
8 SU	0542 1.9	1058 0.5	1813 1.8	2310 0.3
23 M	0638 2.1	1147 0.3	1909 2.0	●2359 0.2
9 M	0630 2.0	1139 0.4	1902 1.9	○2353 0.3
24 TU	0724 2.2	1228 0.2	1952 2.0	
10 TU	0716 2.1	1218 0.3	1947 1.9	
25 W	0039 0.2	0804 2.2	1307 0.1	2028 2.0
11 W	0034 0.2	0757 2.1	1258 0.2	2026 1.9
26 TH	0117 0.1	0838 2.2	1344 0.1	2058 1.9
12 TH	0115 0.2	0835 2.1	1337 0.2	2102 1.9
27 F	0152 0.2	0905 2.1	1419 0.1	2122 1.8
13 F	0154 0.2	0909 2.0	1416 0.2	2134 1.8
28 SA	0224 0.2	0929 1.9	1450 0.2	2144 1.7
14 SA	0232 0.2	0942 2.0	1457 0.2	2207 1.8
29 SU	0251 0.3	0953 1.7	1514 0.3	2210 1.6
15 SU	0312 0.3	1018 1.8	1541 0.3	2245 1.7
30 M	0311 0.5	1020 1.5	1531 0.4	2240 1.5
31 TU	0334 0.6	1049 1.4	1558 0.5	◐2318 1.4

FEBRUARY

Day	Time m	Time m	Time m	Time m
1 W	0413 0.7	1130 1.3	1646 0.6	
16 TH	0006 1.5	0540 0.7	1237 1.4	1829 0.7
2 TH	0019 1.3	0523 0.8	1248 1.2	1814 0.7
17 F	0134 1.4	0727 0.7	1423 1.4	2007 0.7
3 F	0146 1.3	0742 0.8	1430 1.3	2004 0.7
18 SA	0320 1.5	0905 0.6	1607 1.5	2123 0.6
4 SA	0314 1.5	0903 0.7	1557 1.4	2113 0.6
19 SU	0436 1.7	1004 0.5	1715 1.6	2217 0.5
5 SU	0424 1.7	0955 0.5	1702 1.4	2205 0.4
20 M	0534 1.9	1050 0.3	1808 1.8	2301 0.3
6 M	0522 1.8	1039 0.4	1759 1.7	2252 0.3
21 TU	0623 2.1	1130 0.2	1852 1.9	●2341 0.2
7 TU	0615 2.0	1120 0.3	1849 1.9	○2336 0.2
22 W	0706 2.2	1207 0.1	1931 2.0	
8 W	0703 2.1	1201 0.2	1934 2.0	
23 TH	0018 0.1	0743 2.2	1245 0.0	2005 2.0
9 TH	0018 0.1	0746 2.2	1242 0.0	2014 2.1
24 F	0055 0.0	0814 2.1	1320 0.0	2032 2.0
10 F	0100 0.0	0825 2.2	1322 0.0	2049 2.1
25 SA	0129 0.0	0840 2.0	1352 0.0	2054 1.9
11 SA	0139 0.0	0900 2.2	1402 0.0	2121 2.0
26 SU	0200 0.1	0903 1.9	1420 0.1	2116 1.8
12 SU	0217 0.1	0933 2.1	1441 0.1	2153 1.9
27 M	0223 0.2	0927 1.7	1436 0.2	2138 1.6
13 M	0256 0.2	1007 1.9	1522 0.2	2227 1.7
28 TU	0239 0.3	0951 1.5	1449 0.3	2201 1.5
14 TU	0337 0.3	1044 1.7	1607 0.4	◑2310 1.6
29 W	0259 0.4	1013 1.4	1512 0.4	2228 1.4
15 W	0427 0.5	1131 1.5	1706 0.5	

MARCH

Day	Time m	Time m	Time m	Time m
1 TH	0331 0.5	1044 1.3	1551 0.5	◐2315 1.3
16 F	0527 0.7	1230 1.4	1808 0.7	
2 F	0426 0.7	1147 1.2	1702 0.7	
17 SA	0120 1.4	0723 0.7	1425 1.3	1953 0.7
3 SA	0035 1.3	0624 0.8	1345 1.2	1918 0.7
18 SU	0304 1.5	0855 0.6	1556 1.5	2106 0.6
4 SU	0226 1.4	0833 0.7	1531 1.3	2046 0.6
19 M	0415 1.7	0947 0.5	1655 1.6	2155 0.5
5 M	0352 1.6	0929 0.5	1642 1.5	2142 0.4
20 TU	0510 1.8	1027 0.3	1743 1.8	2236 0.4
6 TU	0457 1.8	1014 0.3	1738 1.7	2229 0.2
21 W	0557 2.0	1104 0.2	1825 1.9	2315 0.2
7 W	0552 2.0	1057 0.1	1827 1.9	2314 0.1
22 TH	0639 2.1	1140 0.1	1903 2.0	●2352 0.1
8 TH	0641 2.2	1139 0.0	1912 2.1	○2357 0.0
23 F	0715 2.1	1216 0.0	1936 2.0	
9 F	0726 2.3	1221 -0.1	1953 2.2	
24 SA	0029 0.1	0746 2.1	1252 0.0	2002 2.0
10 SA	0038 -0.1	0806 2.3	1302 -0.1	2029 2.2
25 SU	0104 0.1	0813 2.0	1324 0.1	2026 1.9
11 SU	0119 -0.1	0843 2.2	1343 -0.1	2104 2.1
26 M	0135 0.1	0838 1.9	1350 0.1	2049 1.8
12 M	0159 0.0	0918 2.1	1422 0.0	2137 2.0
27 TU	0157 0.2	0903 1.7	1405 0.2	2111 1.7
13 TU	0238 0.1	0954 1.9	1502 0.2	2212 1.8
28 W	0213 0.3	0927 1.6	1420 0.3	2131 1.6
14 W	0320 0.3	1032 1.7	1547 0.4	2254 1.6
29 TH	0234 0.4	0949 1.4	1443 0.4	2156 1.5
15 TH	0412 0.5	1120 1.5	1644 0.6	◑2350 1.5
30 F	0305 0.5	1021 1.4	1518 0.5	2237 1.4
31 SA	0355 0.6	1119 1.2	1621 0.7	2346 1.3

APRIL

Day	Time m	Time m	Time m	Time m
1 SU	0537 0.7	1305 1.2	1834 0.7	
16 M	0234 1.5	0824 0.6	1526 1.5	2034 0.7
2 M	0131 1.4	0747 0.6	1458 1.3	2011 0.6
17 TU	0341 1.6	0914 0.5	1622 1.6	2123 0.6
3 TU	0311 1.5	0854 0.5	1610 1.5	2112 0.5
18 W	0435 1.7	0953 0.4	1709 1.7	2204 0.5
4 W	0422 1.7	0943 0.3	1707 1.8	2201 0.3
19 TH	0522 1.8	1030 0.3	1750 1.9	2244 0.3
5 TH	0521 2.0	1029 0.1	1757 2.0	2248 0.1
20 F	0604 1.9	1108 0.2	1828 1.9	2323 0.2
6 F	0613 2.1	1113 0.0	1844 2.1	○2332 0.0
21 SA	0642 1.9	1146 0.1	1902 2.0	●
7 SA	0701 2.2	1157 -0.1	1927 2.2	
22 SU	0002 0.2	0715 2.0	1223 0.1	1931 2.0
8 SU	0016 -0.1	0744 2.3	1240 -0.1	2007 2.3
23 M	0039 0.2	0746 1.9	1256 0.2	1959 2.0
9 M	0059 -0.1	0825 2.2	1322 -0.1	2046 2.2
24 TU	0111 0.2	0815 1.8	1323 0.2	2025 1.9
10 TU	0141 0.0	0904 2.1	1404 0.1	2124 2.1
25 W	0135 0.3	0844 1.7	1343 0.3	2050 1.8
11 W	0223 0.1	0944 1.9	1446 0.3	2202 1.9
26 TH	0156 0.3	0911 1.6	1403 0.4	2112 1.7
12 TH	0309 0.3	1026 1.7	1531 0.5	2245 1.7
27 F	0220 0.4	0937 1.5	1429 0.5	2139 1.6
13 F	0403 0.5	1107 1.5	1627 0.6	◑2342 1.6
28 SA	0254 0.4	1012 1.4	1506 0.6	2217 1.5
14 SA	0514 0.6	1233 1.4	1743 0.8	
29 SU	0344 0.5	1107 1.3	1608 0.7	◑2317 1.4
15 SU	0105 1.5	0656 0.7	1411 1.4	1918 0.8
30 M	0506 0.6	1233 1.3	1753 0.7	

Chart Datum: 0·93 metres below Ordnance Datum (Newlyn)
HAT is 2·5 metres above Chart Datum

TIDES

PORTLAND

LAT 50°34'N LONG 2°26'W

TIMES AND HEIGHTS OF HIGH AND LOW WATERS

TIME ZONE (UT)
For Summer Time add ONE hour in **non-shaded areas**

Dates in amber are **SPRINGS**
Dates in yellow are **NEAPS**

2012

MAY

Time	m	Time	m	Time	m	Time	m
1 0044	1.4	**16** 0253	1.5				
0649	0.6	0823	0.5				
TU 1414	1.4	W 1538	1.6				
1927	0.7	2039	0.7				
2 0223	1.5	**17** 0349	1.6				
0808	0.5	0909	0.5				
W 1530	1.6	TH 1626	1.7				
2035	0.5	2127	0.6				
3 0341	1.7	**18** 0439	1.7				
0907	0.3	0952	0.4				
TH 1630	1.8	F 1709	1.8				
2130	0.4	2211	0.5				
4 0445	1.9	**19** 0524	1.7				
0958	0.2	1033	0.3				
F 1725	2.0	SA 1749	1.9				
2221	0.2	2254	0.4				
5 0543	2.0	**20** 0606	1.8				
1047	0.1	1114	0.3				
SA 1815	2.1	SU 1826	1.9				
2309	0.1	●2335	0.3				
6 0636	2.2	**21** 0645	1.8				
1134	0.0	1154	0.3				
SU 1903	2.3	M 1902	2.0				
○2356	0.0						
7 0725	2.2	**22** 0014	0.3				
1220	0.0	0722	1.8				
M 1948	2.3	TU 1231	0.3				
		1936	2.0				
8 0041	0.0	**23** 0049	0.3				
0810	2.2	0758	1.8				
TU 1306	0.1	W 1303	0.3				
2031	2.3	2009	1.9				
9 0127	0.1	**24** 0118	0.3				
0855	2.1	0832	1.8				
W 1349	0.2	TH 1331	0.4				
2113	2.1	2038	1.9				
10 0212	0.2	**25** 0146	0.3				
0938	1.9	0904	1.7				
TH 1433	0.3	F 1359	0.4				
2155	2.0	2105	1.8				
11 0259	0.3	**26** 0216	0.4				
1024	1.8	0934	1.6				
F 1518	0.5	SA 1431	0.5				
2239	1.8	2134	1.7				
12 0351	0.4	**27** 0252	0.4				
1114	1.6	1009	1.5				
SA 1609	0.6	SU 1510	0.5				
◑2329	1.7	2211	1.6				
13 0451	0.6	**28** 0339	0.4				
1216	1.5	1057	1.4				
SU 1710	0.6	M 1604	0.6				
		◑2301	1.5				
14 0031	1.5	**29** 0442	0.5				
0603	0.6	1202	1.4				
M 1331	1.4	TU 1718	0.7				
1824	0.8						
15 0145	1.5	**30** 0009	1.5				
0722	0.6	0601	0.5				
TU 1441	1.5	W 1323	1.4				
1939	0.8	1840	0.7				
		31 0133	1.5				
		0719	0.5				
		TH 1443	1.6				
		1955	0.6				

JUNE

Time	m	Time	m
1 0257	1.6	**16** 0345	1.5
0829	0.4	0912	0.5
F 1552	1.7	SA 1623	1.7
2100	0.5	2140	0.6
2 0411	1.8	**17** 0441	1.6
0930	0.3	1000	0.5
SA 1654	1.9	SU 1710	1.8
2158	0.4	2227	0.5
3 0516	1.9	**18** 0532	1.7
1025	0.2	1045	0.4
SU 1751	2.1	M 1755	1.9
2252	0.3	2311	0.4
4 0616	2.0	**19** 0620	1.7
1118	0.2	1129	0.4
M 1844	2.2	TU 1838	2.0
○2343	0.2	●2352	0.4
5 0710	2.1	**20** 0705	1.8
1207	0.1	1209	0.3
TU 1934	2.3	W 1920	2.0
6 0031	0.1	**21** 0029	0.3
0800	2.1	0747	1.8
W 1254	0.2	TH 1247	0.3
2020	2.3	1958	2.0
7 0118	0.1	**22** 0104	0.3
0847	2.1	0825	1.8
TH 1339	0.2	F 1322	0.3
2104	2.2	2033	2.0
8 0203	0.2	**23** 0138	0.3
0932	2.0	0900	1.8
F 1421	0.3	SA 1356	0.3
2146	2.1	2105	1.9
9 0248	0.3	**24** 0212	0.3
1014	1.8	0932	1.7
SA 1503	0.4	SU 1431	0.4
2225	1.9	2135	1.8
10 0332	0.4	**25** 0249	0.3
1054	1.7	1004	1.6
SU 1546	0.5	M 1509	0.4
2302	1.7	2209	1.7
11 0420	0.5	**26** 0331	0.3
1136	1.5	1043	1.6
M 1635	0.7	TU 1553	0.5
◑2341	1.6	2250	1.6
12 0514	0.6	**27** 0421	0.4
1224	1.4	1132	1.5
TU 1732	0.8	W 1649	0.6
		◑2342	1.6
13 0028	1.5	**28** 0525	0.5
0614	0.6	1237	1.5
W 1324	1.4	TH 1800	0.7
1839	0.8		
14 0129	1.4	**29** 0050	1.5
0719	0.6	0639	0.5
TH 1431	1.4	F 1356	1.5
1947	0.8	1918	0.6
15 0240	1.4	**30** 0215	1.6
0819	0.6	0757	0.5
F 1532	1.5	SA 1518	1.7
2048	0.7	2036	0.6

JULY

Time	m	Time	m
1 0342	1.6	**16** 0404	1.4
0910	0.4	0931	0.6
SU 1631	1.8	M 1637	1.7
2144	0.5	2204	0.6
2 0458	1.8	**17** 0505	1.6
1014	0.4	1020	0.5
M 1734	2.0	TU 1729	1.8
2243	0.4	2248	0.5
3 0604	1.9	**18** 0559	1.7
1109	0.3	1105	0.4
TU 1831	2.2	W 1819	1.9
○2336	0.3	2330	0.4
4 0701	2.0	**19** 0649	1.8
1158	0.2	1148	0.3
W 1923	2.3	TH 1905	2.0
●		●	
5 0023	0.2	**20** 0009	0.3
0752	2.1	0734	1.9
TH 1244	0.2	F 1228	0.2
2009	2.3	1947	2.1
6 0108	0.1	**21** 0047	0.2
0837	2.1	0814	1.9
F 1326	0.2	SA 1307	0.2
2051	2.3	2026	2.1
7 0150	0.1	**22** 0124	0.2
0917	2.0	0850	1.9
SA 1405	0.2	SU 1344	0.2
2129	2.2	2059	2.0
8 0230	0.2	**23** 0201	0.2
0952	1.9	0922	1.9
SU 1443	0.3	M 1420	0.2
2201	2.0	2130	2.0
9 0308	0.2	**24** 0238	0.2
1022	1.7	0951	1.8
M 1520	0.4	TU 1457	0.3
2228	1.8	2201	1.8
10 0347	0.4	**25** 0317	0.2
1049	1.6	1025	1.7
TU 1557	0.5	W 1537	0.4
2256	1.6	2237	1.7
11 0426	0.5	**26** 0402	0.3
1122	1.5	1107	1.6
W 1639	0.7	TH 1625	0.5
◑2331	1.4	◑2321	1.6
12 0510	0.6	**27** 0457	0.5
1207	1.4	1202	1.5
TH 1734	0.8	F 1730	0.6
13 0018	1.3	**28** 0021	1.5
0609	0.7	0611	0.6
F 1308	1.4	SA 1320	1.5
1851	0.8	1855	0.7
14 0125	1.3	**29** 0146	1.5
0724	0.7	0740	0.6
SA 1423	1.4	SU 1456	1.6
2009	0.8	2027	0.7
15 0248	1.3	**30** 0329	1.5
0833	0.6	0904	0.6
SU 1537	1.5	M 1618	1.7
2113	0.7	2141	0.6
		31 0452	1.7
		1008	0.4
		TU 1724	1.9
		2238	0.4

AUGUST

Time	m	Time	m
1 0557	1.8	**16** 0539	1.7
1100	0.3	1041	0.3
W 1820	2.1	TH 1757	2.0
2326	0.3	2305	0.3
2 0651	2.0	**17** 0629	1.9
1145	0.2	1123	0.2
TH 1909	2.3	F 1845	2.1
○		●2345	0.2
3 0010	0.1	**18** 0714	2.0
0737	2.1	1204	0.1
F 1228	0.1	SA 1929	2.2
1953	2.3		
4 0051	0.1	**19** 0024	0.1
0818	2.1	0755	2.1
SA 1307	0.1	SU 1244	0.1
2031	2.3	2008	2.2
5 0130	0.0	**20** 0104	0.0
0853	2.1	0831	2.1
SU 1344	0.1	M 1323	0.0
2104	2.2	2044	2.2
6 0206	0.1	**21** 0142	0.1
0921	1.9	0903	2.0
M 1418	0.2	TU 1401	0.1
2130	2.0	2115	2.1
7 0240	0.2	**22** 0220	0.1
0944	1.8	0933	1.9
TU 1451	0.3	W 1438	0.2
2153	1.8	2147	1.9
8 0311	0.3	**23** 0259	0.2
1006	1.6	1006	1.8
W 1519	0.4	TH 1518	0.3
2217	1.6	2222	1.8
9 0335	0.4	**24** 0342	0.4
1034	1.5	1046	1.7
TH 1542	0.6	F 1606	0.5
◑2244	1.4	◑2305	1.6
10 0354	0.6	**25** 0436	0.5
1109	1.4	1138	1.6
F 1611	0.7	SA 1714	0.7
2319	1.3		
11 0430	0.7	**26** 0004	1.5
1201	1.3	0554	0.7
SA 1717	0.8	SU 1258	1.5
		1849	0.7
12 0020	1.2	**27** 0140	1.4
0550	0.7	0736	0.7
SU 1320	1.3	M 1447	1.6
1931	0.8	2030	0.7
13 0200	1.2	**28** 0333	1.5
0756	0.7	0900	0.6
M 1452	1.4	TU 1609	1.7
2048	0.7	2136	0.6
14 0336	1.3	**29** 0448	1.7
0905	0.6	0958	0.5
TU 1607	1.6	W 1711	1.9
2141	0.6	2226	0.4
15 0444	1.5	**30** 0544	1.8
0956	0.5	1044	0.4
W 1705	1.8	TH 1802	2.1
2224	0.5	2308	0.2
		31 0632	2.0
		1125	0.2
		F 1848	2.2
		○2348	0.1

Chart Datum: 0·93 metres below Ordnance Datum (Newlyn)
HAT is 2·5 metres above Chart Datum

| TIME ZONE (UT) |
| For Summer Time add ONE hour in **non-shaded areas** |

PORTLAND

LAT 50°34'N LONG 2°26'W

TIMES AND HEIGHTS OF HIGH AND LOW WATERS

Dates in amber are **SPRINGS**
Dates in yellow are **NEAPS**

2012

SEPTEMBER		OCTOBER		NOVEMBER		DECEMBER	
Time m	Time m	Time m	Time m	Time m	Time m	Time m	Time m
1 0714 2.1 / 1204 0.1 / SA 1929 2.3	**16** 0647 2.1 / 1137 0.1 / SU 1903 2.2 / ● 2357 0.0	**1** 0718 2.1 / 1213 0.2 / M 1932 2.1	**16** 0659 2.3 / 1151 0.1 / TU 1918 2.3	**1** 0034 0.3 / 0737 2.1 / TH 1257 0.4 / 1955 1.9	**16** 0035 0.2 / 0802 2.4 / F 1302 0.2 / 2027 2.1	**1** 0043 0.4 / 0746 2.1 / SA 1307 0.4 / 2010 1.8	**16** 0110 0.2 / 0837 2.3 / SU 1340 0.2 / 2105 2.1
2 0026 0.1 / 0750 2.1 / SU 1242 0.1 / 2004 2.2	**17** 0728 2.2 / 1218 0.0 / M 1944 2.3	**2** 0031 0.1 / 0746 2.1 / TU 1249 0.2 / 1959 2.1	**17** 0012 0.0 / 0740 2.3 / W 1234 0.1 / 1959 2.3	**2** 0105 0.3 / 0803 2.0 / F 1326 0.4 / 2024 1.8	**17** 0120 0.3 / 0845 2.3 / SA 1349 0.3 / 2112 2.0	**2** 0112 0.4 / 0817 2.0 / SU 1333 0.4 / 2043 1.7	**17** 0153 0.3 / 0920 2.2 / M 1426 0.3 / 2148 1.9
3 0103 0.0 / 0822 2.1 / M 1317 0.1 / 2033 2.1	**18** 0038 0.0 / 0806 2.2 / TU 1259 0.0 / 2021 2.2	**3** 0106 0.2 / 0809 2.0 / W 1323 0.2 / 2023 1.9	**18** 0054 0.1 / 0819 2.3 / TH 1317 0.2 / 2039 2.2	**3** 0127 0.4 / 0829 1.9 / SA 1346 0.5 / 2051 1.7	**18** 0205 0.4 / 0928 2.1 / SU 1438 0.4 / 2158 1.9	**3** 0138 0.5 / 0845 1.9 / M 1359 0.5 / 2112 1.6	**18** 0236 0.4 / 1001 2.1 / TU 1511 0.4 / 2229 1.8
4 0137 0.1 / 0846 2.0 / TU 1351 0.2 / 2057 1.9	**19** 0118 0.0 / 0840 2.2 / W 1338 0.1 / 2056 2.1	**4** 0135 0.3 / 0831 1.9 / TH 1351 0.3 / 2047 1.8	**19** 0136 0.2 / 0857 2.2 / F 1401 0.3 / 2119 2.0	**4** 0144 0.5 / 0853 1.8 / SU 1405 0.5 / 2117 1.5	**19** 0250 0.5 / 1013 2.0 / M 1531 0.5 / 2247 1.7	**4** 0205 0.5 / 0912 1.8 / TU 1429 0.5 / 2143 1.5	**19** 0319 0.5 / 1040 1.9 / W 1559 0.5 / 2310 1.6
5 0208 0.2 / 0906 1.9 / W 1420 0.3 / 2118 1.8	**20** 0158 0.1 / 0913 2.1 / TH 1418 0.2 / 2131 2.0	**5** 0155 0.4 / 0854 1.8 / F 1408 0.4 / 2111 1.6	**20** 0219 0.4 / 0936 2.0 / SA 1448 0.4 / 2201 1.8	**5** 0205 0.6 / 0917 1.7 / M 1433 0.6 / 2148 1.4	**20** 0341 0.7 / 1103 1.8 / TU 1631 0.6 / ☾ 2348 1.5	**5** 0236 0.6 / 0944 1.7 / W 1508 0.5 / 2223 1.5	**20** 0405 0.7 / 1119 1.7 / TH 1652 0.6 / ☾ 2354 1.5
6 0232 0.3 / 0927 1.7 / TH 1441 0.4 / 2141 1.6	**21** 0238 0.3 / 0948 1.9 / F 1501 0.4 / 2208 1.8	**6** 0206 0.5 / 0915 1.7 / SA 1423 0.5 / 2133 1.5	**21** 0304 0.5 / 1019 1.9 / SU 1544 0.6 / 2252 1.6	**6** 0234 0.7 / 0951 1.6 / TU 1516 0.7 / 2235 1.3	**21** 0441 0.8 / 1204 1.7 / W 1742 0.7	**6** 0318 0.7 / 1027 1.6 / TH 1603 0.6 / ☾ 2319 1.4	**21** 0500 0.8 / 1204 1.6 / F 1750 0.7
7 0245 0.4 / 0950 1.6 / F 1455 0.5 / 2204 1.4	**22** 0322 0.5 / 1029 1.8 / SA 1553 0.6 / ☾ 2254 1.6	**7** 0223 0.6 / 0938 1.6 / SU 1448 0.6 / 2200 1.3	**22** 0400 0.7 / 1115 1.7 / M 1656 0.7 / ☾	**7** 0321 0.8 / 1043 1.5 / W 1633 0.7 / ☾ 2353 1.3	**22** 0103 1.5 / 0554 0.9 / TH 1321 1.6 / 1856 0.7	**7** 0422 0.8 / 1127 1.5 / F 1721 0.6	**22** 0051 1.4 / 0607 0.9 / SA 1302 1.5 / 1853 0.7
8 0300 0.5 / 1016 1.6 / SA 1520 0.7 / ☾ 2228 1.3	**23** 0417 0.7 / 1123 1.6 / SU 1707 0.7	**8** 0250 0.7 / 1014 1.5 / M 1532 0.7 / ☾ 2250 1.2	**23** 0005 1.5 / 0515 0.9 / TU 1239 1.6 / 1829 0.8	**8** 0500 0.9 / 1203 1.5 / TH 1823 0.7	**23** 0220 1.5 / 0717 0.9 / F 1433 1.6 / 1959 0.7	**8** 0038 1.4 / 0552 0.8 / SA 1247 1.5 / 1842 0.6	**23** 0206 1.5 / 0721 0.9 / SU 1418 1.4 / 1954 0.7
9 0330 0.7 / 1057 1.4 / SU 1609 0.8 / 2320 1.2	**24** 0000 1.5 / 0539 0.8 / M 1251 1.5 / 1849 0.8	**9** 0339 0.8 / 1116 1.4 / TU 1720 0.8	**24** 0147 1.5 / 0653 0.9 / W 1412 1.6 / 1955 0.7	**9** 0144 1.4 / 0658 0.8 / F 1349 1.5 / 1941 0.6	**24** 0320 1.6 / 0824 0.8 / SA 1531 1.6 / 2047 0.6	**9** 0208 1.5 / 0718 0.7 / SU 1418 1.6 / 1953 0.5	**24** 0314 1.5 / 0830 0.8 / M 1528 1.5 / 2049 0.6
10 0430 0.8 / 1212 1.3 / M 1843 0.9	**25** 0156 1.4 / 0727 0.8 / TU 1439 1.6 / 2023 0.7	**10** 0033 1.2 / 0601 0.9 / W 1301 1.4 / 1936 0.8	**25** 0307 1.6 / 0818 0.8 / TH 1520 1.7 / 2050 0.6	**10** 0306 1.6 / 0811 0.7 / SA 1512 1.7 / 2038 0.5	**25** 0409 1.7 / 0913 0.7 / SU 1621 1.7 / 2129 0.5	**10** 0322 1.7 / 0828 0.6 / M 1537 1.7 / 2055 0.4	**25** 0406 1.7 / 0925 0.7 / TU 1624 1.6 / 2138 0.5
11 0116 1.2 / 0712 0.8 / TU 1403 1.4 / 2020 0.7	**26** 0331 1.5 / 0847 0.7 / W 1551 1.8 / 2120 0.6	**11** 0237 1.3 / 0757 0.8 / TH 1447 1.6 / 2034 0.6	**26** 0402 1.7 / 0910 0.7 / F 1614 1.8 / 2131 0.5	**11** 0405 1.8 / 0906 0.6 / SU 1616 1.9 / 2128 0.3	**26** 0451 1.8 / 0956 0.6 / M 1705 1.8 / 2210 0.4	**11** 0424 1.9 / 0928 0.5 / TU 1643 1.9 / 2151 0.3	**26** 0452 1.8 / 1012 0.6 / W 1713 1.7 / 2224 0.5
12 0312 1.3 / 0836 0.8 / W 1532 1.6 / 2113 0.6	**27** 0432 1.7 / 0939 0.6 / TH 1647 1.9 / 2203 0.4	**12** 0349 1.6 / 0854 0.6 / F 1557 1.8 / 2120 0.4	**27** 0448 1.9 / 0950 0.6 / SA 1701 1.9 / 2208 0.4	**12** 0457 2.0 / 0955 0.4 / M 1712 2.0 / 2216 0.2	**27** 0529 1.9 / 1037 0.5 / TU 1746 1.8 / 2251 0.4	**12** 0520 2.1 / 1023 0.4 / W 1744 2.0 / 2245 0.3	**27** 0535 1.9 / 1056 0.5 / TH 1759 1.7 / 2307 0.4
13 0421 1.5 / 0928 0.5 / TH 1635 1.8 / 2155 0.4	**28** 0520 1.9 / 1020 0.5 / F 1735 2.0 / 2242 0.3	**13** 0442 1.8 / 0944 0.5 / SA 1654 2.0 / 2203 0.3	**28** 0529 2.0 / 1028 0.5 / SU 1744 2.0 / 2245 0.3	**13** 0546 2.2 / 1042 0.3 / TU 1805 2.2 / ● 2303 0.1	**28** 0605 2.0 / 1118 0.5 / W 1824 1.9 / ○ 2331 0.4	**13** 0613 2.2 / 1115 0.3 / TH 1840 2.1 / ● 2335 0.3	**28** 0617 2.0 / 1137 0.4 / F 1844 1.8 / ○ 2349 0.4
14 0514 1.7 / 1013 0.4 / F 1728 2.0 / 2236 0.3	**29** 0603 2.0 / 1059 0.3 / SA 1819 2.1 / 2319 0.2	**14** 0530 2.0 / 1025 0.3 / SU 1745 2.1 / 2246 0.1	**29** 0607 2.0 / 1106 0.4 / M 1822 2.0 / ○ 2322 0.3	**14** 0633 2.3 / 1129 0.2 / W 1855 2.2 / 2349 0.1	**29** 0639 2.1 / 1158 0.4 / TH 1901 1.9	**14** 0704 2.3 / 1205 0.2 / F 1932 2.2	**29** 0657 2.1 / 1216 0.4 / SA 1925 1.8
15 0602 1.9 / 1055 0.2 / SA 1818 2.1 / 2317 0.1	**30** 0643 2.1 / 1136 0.2 / SU 1858 2.2 / ○ 2355 0.1	**15** 0616 2.2 / 1108 0.2 / M 1833 2.2 / ● 2329 0.1	**30** 0641 2.1 / 1144 0.3 / TU 1856 2.0 / 2359 0.2	**15** 0719 2.4 / 1215 0.2 / TH 1942 2.2	**30** 0009 0.4 / 0713 2.1 / F 1235 0.4 / 1936 1.9	**15** 0023 0.2 / 0751 2.4 / SA 1253 0.2 / 2020 2.1	**30** 0027 0.3 / 0736 2.1 / SU 1252 0.3 / 2004 1.8
			31 0710 2.1 / 1222 0.3 / W 1927 2.0				**31** 0102 0.3 / 0812 2.0 / M 1323 0.3 / 2039 1.8

Chart Datum: 0·93 metres below Ordnance Datum (Newlyn)
HAT is 2·5 metres above Chart Datum

TIDES

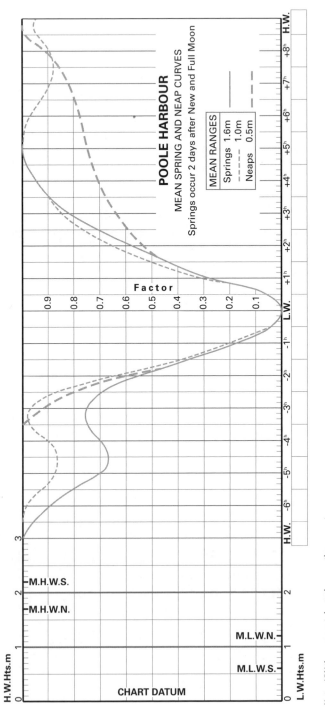

POOLE HARBOUR

MEAN SPRING AND NEAP CURVES

Springs occur 2 days after New and Full Moon

MEAN RANGES	
Springs	1.6m
	1.0m
Neaps	0.5m

Factor

Note - HW times are not shown because they cannot be predicted with reasonable accuracy. Approximate times can be gained using LW times and the Tidal Curves at the start of this section.

POOLE HARBOUR

LAT 50°42'N   LONG 1°59'W

2012

TIMES AND HEIGHTS OF HIGH AND LOW WATERS

JANUARY

Time	m	Time	m
1 0924 / SU / ◐ 2142	1.9 1.2 1.8 1.2	**16** 0908 / M / ◑ 2134	2.1 0.9 1.9 0.9
2 1023 / M / 2243	1.9 1.3 1.7 1.3	**17** 1012 / TU / 2241	2.0 0.9 1.9 0.9
3 1133 / TU / 2355	1.8 1.3 1.6 1.3	**18** 1129 / W	1.9 1.1 1.8
4 1243 / W	1.8 1.3 1.7	**19** 0000 / TH 1251	1.1 1.9 1.1 1.9
5 0104 / TH 1342	1.3 1.9 1.2 1.8	**20** 0120 / F 1403	1.0 2.0 0.9 2.0
6 0201 / F 1431	1.2 1.9 1.0 1.9	**21** 0227 / SA 1502	0.9 2.1 0.8 2.1
7 0249 / SA 1514	1.0 2.0 0.9 2.0	**22** 0323 / SU 1553	0.8 2.1 0.7 2.1
8 0331 / SU 1555	0.9 2.1 0.8 2.1	**23** 0411 / M 1638 / ●	0.7 2.2 0.6 2.2
9 0411 / M 1634 / ○	0.8 2.1 0.7 2.1	**24** 0455 / TU 1719	0.7 2.2 0.5
10 0449 / TU 1711	0.8 2.1 0.7	**25** 0535 / W 1757	2.3 0.6 2.2 0.5
11 0526 / W 1748	2.1 0.7 2.1 0.6	**26** 0613 / TH 1832	2.2 0.7 2.1 0.6
12 0604 / TH 1827	2.2 0.7 2.1 0.6	**27** 0648 / F 1904	2.2 0.7 2.1 0.7
13 0645 / F 1908	2.2 0.7 2.1 0.6	**28** 0721 / SA 1936	2.1 0.8 2.0 0.8
14 0728 / SA 1951	2.2 0.7 2.1 0.7	**29** 0753 / SU 2008	2.0 0.9 1.9 0.9
15 0814 / SU 2038	2.1 0.8 2.0 0.8	**30** 0828 / M 2044	2.0 1.0 1.8 1.0
		31 0910 / TU / ◑ 2131	1.9 1.2 1.7 1.2

FEBRUARY

Time	m	Time	m
1 1011 / W / 2244	1.8 1.3 1.6 1.3	**16** 1107 / TH / 2346	1.8 1.1 1.8 1.2
2 1145 / TH	1.7 1.3 1.6	**17** 1239 / F	1.8 1.1 1.8
3 0022 / F 1306	1.3 1.7 1.0 1.7	**18** 0114 / SA 1355	1.1 1.9 1.0 1.9
4 0134 / SA 1405	1.3 1.8 1.1 1.8	**19** 0223 / SU 1453	1.0 2.0 0.8 2.0
5 0227 / SU 1452	1.1 1.9 0.9 2.0	**20** 0316 / M 1540	0.8 2.1 0.7 2.1
6 0312 / M 1535	0.9 2.0 0.8 2.0	**21** 0400 / TU 1621 / ●	0.7 2.1 0.6 2.2
7 0352 / TU 1615 / ○	0.8 2.1 0.6 2.1	**22** 0439 / W 1658	0.6 2.1 0.6 0.5
8 0431 / W 1654	0.7 2.1 0.5 2.2	**23** 0515 / TH / 1733	2.2 0.6 2.1 0.5
9 0510 / TH 1733	0.6 2.2 0.4	**24** 0549 / F / 1805	2.2 0.6 2.1 0.6
10 0549 / F 1812	2.3 0.5 2.2 0.4	**25** 0619 / SA 1834	2.1 0.6 2.0 0.6
11 0629 / SA 1852	2.3 0.5 2.2 0.4	**26** 0647 / SU 1902	2.1 0.7 2.0 0.7
12 0711 / SU 1933	2.3 0.6 2.2 0.6	**27** 0715 / M 1929	2.1 0.8 2.0 0.8
13 0755 / M 2018	2.2 0.7 2.1 0.7	**28** 0744 / TU 2001	2.0 0.9 1.9 1.0
14 0844 / TU / ◑ 2111	2.1 0.8 2.0 0.9	**29** 0820 / W 2042	1.9 1.0 1.8 1.2
15 0946 / W 2219	1.9 1.0 1.8 1.0		

MARCH

Time	m	Time	m
1 0908 / TH / ◐ 2142	1.8 1.2 1.6 1.3	**16** 1050 / F / 2335	1.8 1.1 1.8 1.2
2 1027 / F / 2332	1.6 1.3 1.6 1.4	**17** 1222 / SA	1.7 1.1 1.8
3 1224 / SA	1.6 1.3 1.6	**18** 0103 / SU 1338	1.1 1.8 1.0 1.9
4 0104 / SU 1334	1.3 1.7 1.1 1.8	**19** 0210 / M 1433	1.0 1.9 0.8 2.0
5 0202 / M 1424	1.1 1.8 0.9 1.9	**20** 0259 / TU 1517	0.8 2.0 0.7 2.1
6 0247 / TU 1508	0.9 2.0 0.7 2.1	**21** 0339 / W 1556	0.7 2.1 0.6 2.1
7 0329 / W 1550	0.7 2.1 0.6 2.1	**22** 0416 / TH 1631 / ●	0.6 2.1 0.6 2.1
8 0409 / TH 1630 / ○	0.6 2.1 0.4 2.3	**23** 0450 / F 1705	0.6 2.1 0.6
9 0449 / F 1711	0.6 2.3 0.4	**24** 0521 / SA / 1736	2.2 0.6 2.1 0.6
10 0529 / SA 1752	2.3 0.4 2.3 0.4	**25** 0551 / SU / 1805	2.1 0.6 2.1 0.7
11 0610 / SU 1833	2.3 0.4 2.3 0.4	**26** 0617 / M / 1832	2.1 0.7 2.1 0.7
12 0653 / M 1915	2.3 0.4 2.3 0.5	**27** 0643 / TU / 1900	2.1 0.7 2.0 0.8
13 0737 / TU 2001	2.2 0.6 2.1 0.7	**28** 0712 / W / ◑ 1931	2.0 0.8 1.9 0.9
14 0826 / W 2055	2.1 0.8 2.0 0.9	**29** 0747 / TH 2011	1.9 0.9 1.8 1.1
15 0927 / TH / ◑ 2205	1.9 0.9 1.8 1.1	**30** 0834 / F / ◑ 2107	1.8 1.1 1.7 1.3
		31 0940 / SA 2235	1.6 1.2 1.6 1.3

APRIL

Time	m	Time	m
1 1125 / SU	1.6 1.2 1.7	**16** 0036 / M 1306	1.1 1.8 1.0 1.9
2 0019 / M 1251	1.3 1.6 1.1 1.8	**17** 0141 / TU 1401	1.0 1.9 0.9 2.0
3 0125 / TU 1347	1.1 1.8 0.9 2.0	**18** 0230 / W 1445	0.9 1.9 0.8 2.1
4 0214 / W 1434	0.9 1.9 0.7 2.1	**19** 0310 / TH 1524	0.8 2.0 0.7 2.1
5 0259 / TH 1519	0.7 2.1 0.6 2.2	**20** 0347 / F 1600	0.7 2.0 0.7 2.1
6 0342 / F 1603 / ○	0.5 2.2 0.4 2.3	**21** 0421 / SA 1635 / ●	0.7 2.0 0.7 2.1
7 0425 / SA 1646	0.4 2.3 0.4 2.3	**22** 0454 / SU 1709	0.6 2.1 0.7
8 0508 / SU 1730	0.3 2.3 0.4	**23** 0524 / M / 1739	2.1 0.7 2.1 0.7
9 0552 / M 1814	0.3 2.4 0.4	**24** 0552 / TU / 1808	0.7 2.3 2.1 0.7
10 0636 / TU 1859	2.3 0.4 2.2 0.6	**25** 0620 / W / 1837	2.0 0.7 2.0 0.8
11 0723 / W 1948	2.2 0.6 2.1 0.7	**26** 0650 / TH / 1911	2.0 0.8 1.9 0.9
12 0813 / TH 2043	2.1 0.7 2.0 0.9	**27** 0727 / F / 1952	1.9 0.9 1.9 1.0
13 0913 / F / ◑ 2151	1.9 0.9 1.9 1.0	**28** 0813 / SA / 2045	1.8 1.0 1.8 1.2
14 1029 / SA 2313	1.8 1.0 1.8 1.2	**29** 0913 / SU / ◑ 2156	1.8 1.0 1.8 1.2
15 1153 / SU	1.7 1.0 1.9	**30** 1032 / M 2320	1.9 1.1 1.8 1.2

TIDES

Chart Datum: 1·40 metres below Ordnance Datum (Newlyn)
HAT is 2·6 metres above Chart Datum

TIME ZONE (UT)	POOLE HARBOUR	Dates in amber are SPRINGS
For Summer Time add ONE hour in non-shaded areas	LAT 50°42'N LONG 1°59'W	Dates in yellow are NEAPS
	TIMES AND HEIGHTS OF HIGH AND LOW WATERS	2012

MAY

Date	Time	m		Date	Time	m
1 TU	1154	1.7 / 1.0 / 1.9		16 W	0057 / 1317	1.1, 1.8 / 1.0, 1.9
2 W	0034 / 1301	1.0 / 1.8, 2.0		17 TH	0150 / 1406	1.0, 1.8 / 0.9, 2.0
3 TH	0134 / 1356	0.9, 1.9 / 0.7, 2.1		18 F	0235 / 1448	0.9, 1.9 / 0.9, 2.0
4 F	0225 / 1446	0.7 / 2.1, 0.6, 2.2		19 SA	0314 / 1528	0.8, 2.0 / 0.8, 2.0
5 SA	0314 / 1535	0.6, 2.2 / 0.5, 2.3		20 SU	0351 / 1606 ●	0.8, 2.0 / 0.8, 2.1
6 SU	0402 / 1623 ○	0.4, 2.3 / 0.4, 2.4		21 M	0427 / 1643	0.7, 2.0 / 0.8, 2.1
7 M	0450 / 1711	0.7, 2.3 / 0.4, 0.4		22 TU	0501 / 1717	0.7, 2.1 / 0.8
8 TU	0536 / 1758	2.4, 0.4, 2.3 / 0.5		23 W	0532 / 1748	2.1, 0.7 / 0.8
9 W	0624 / 1846	2.3, 0.4 / 0.6		24 TH	0603 / 1821	2.0, 0.7 / 0.8
10 TH	0712 / 1936	2.2, 0.6 / 0.7		25 F	0636 / 1856	2.0, 0.8 / 0.9
11 F	0801 / 2029	2.1, 2.1 / 0.9		26 SA	0714 / 1938	2.0, 0.8 / 0.9
12 SA	0856 / ◑ 2129	1.9, 0.8, 2.0 / 1.0		27 SU	0759 / 2027	1.9, 0.9 / 1.0
13 SU	0959 / 2238	1.8, 1.0, 1.9 / 1.1		28 M	0852 / ◑ 2126	1.9, 0.9 / 1.0
14 M	1109 / 2351	1.8, 1.9 / 1.1		29 TU	0956 / 2235	1.8, 1.0 / 1.1
15 TU	1219	1.8, 1.0, 1.9		30 W	1106 / 2346	1.8, 1.0 / 1.9
				31 TH	1216	1.9, 0.9, 2.0

JUNE

Date	Time	m		Date	Time	m
1 F	0054 / 1320	0.9, 1.9 / 0.8, 2.1		16 SA	0156 / 1413	1.0, 1.8 / 1.0, 1.9
2 SA	0155 / 1418	0.8, 2.0 / 0.7, 2.2		17 SU	0242 / 1458	0.9, 1.9 / 1.0, 2.0
3 SU	0251 / 1513	0.7, 2.1 / 0.6, 2.3		18 M	0324 / 1540	0.9, 2.0 / 0.9, 2.0
4 M	0345 / 1606 ○	0.6, 2.2 / 0.6, 2.3		19 TU	0404 / 1620 ●	0.8, 2.0 / 0.8, 2.1
5 TU	0436 / 1657	0.4, 2.3 / 0.6		20 W	0441 / 1657	0.7, 2.3 / 0.8, 2.1
6 W	0525 / 1746	2.3, 0.4 / 0.6		21 TH	0516 / 1732	0.7, 2.3 / 0.8
7 TH	0613 / 1834	2.3, 0.4 / 0.6		22 F	0550 / 1807	0.7, 2.1 / 0.8
8 F	0700 / 1921	2.2, 0.6 / 2.3, 0.7		23 SA	0625 / 1843	0.7, 2.1 / 0.8
9 SA	0746 / 2009	2.1, 0.7 / 0.8		24 SU	0702 / 1924	0.7, 2.0 / 0.9
10 SU	0832 / 2059	2.0, 0.8 / 0.9		25 M	0744 / 2009	0.8, 2.0 / 0.9
11 M	0922 / ◑ 2154	1.9, 0.9 / 1.0		26 TU	0832 / 2101	0.8, 2.0 / 0.9
12 TU	1018 / 2257	1.8, 1.0 / 1.2		27 W	0927 / ◑ 2201	0.9, 2.0 / 1.0
13 W	1120	1.7, 1.1, 1.8		28 TH	1030 / 2310	0.9, 2.0 / 1.0
14 TH	0002 / 1224	1.2 / 1.7, 1.2, 1.9		29 F	1140	0.9, 2.0
15 F	0104 / 1322	1.1 / 1.8, 1.1, 1.9		30 SA	0024 / 1253	0.9 / 1.9, 0.9, 2.0

JULY

Date	Time	m		Date	Time	m
1 SU	0136 / 1401	0.9, 2.0 / 0.8, 2.1		16 M	0214 / 1433	1.0, 1.9 / 1.1, 1.9
2 M	0239 / 1501	0.7, 2.1 / 0.8, 2.2		17 TU	0300 / 1518	0.9, 2.0 / 0.9, 2.0
3 TU	0335 / 1556 ○	0.6, 2.2 / 0.7, 2.3		18 W	0342 / 1559	0.8, 2.0 / 0.9, 2.0
4 W	0427 / 1646	0.5, 2.3 / 0.6, 2.3		19 TH	0421 / 1637 ●	0.7, 2.1 / 0.8, 2.1
5 TH	0515 / 1734	0.4, 2.3 / 0.6		20 F	0458 / 1714	0.7, 2.1 / 0.7
6 F	0600 / 1819	2.3, 0.4 / 0.6		21 SA	0534 / 1750	0.6, 2.1 / 0.7
7 SA	0642 / 1901	2.2, 0.5 / 2.3, 0.7		22 SU	0610 / 1827	0.6, 2.1 / 0.7
8 SU	0722 / 1943	0.6, 2.2 / 0.8		23 M	0647 / 1907	0.6, 2.1 / 0.7
9 M	0801 / 2024	0.7, 2.0 / 0.9		24 TU	0727 / 1950	0.7, 2.1 / 0.7
10 TU	0841 / 2108	0.9, 1.9 / 1.0		25 W	0811 / 2038	0.7, 2.0 / 0.8
11 W	0925 / ◑ 2159	1.0, 1.8 / 1.1		26 TH	0901 / ◑ 2135	0.8, 2.0 / 0.9
12 TH	1020 / 2303	1.2, 1.7 / 1.2		27 F	1002 / 2245	1.0, 1.9 / 1.0
13 F	1128	1.3, 1.6, 1.8		28 SA	1118	1.0, 1.8, 1.9
14 SA	0014 / 1240	1.2 / 1.6, 1.3, 1.8		29 SU	0007 / 1240	1.0 / 1.0, 1.8, 2.0
15 SU	0120 / 1342	1.2 / 1.8, 1.2, 1.9		30 M	0127 / 1354	0.9 / 0.9, 1.0, 1.9
				31 TU	0232 / 1455	0.8, 2.0 / 0.8, 2.1

AUGUST

Date	Time	m		Date	Time	m
1 W	0327 / 1547	0.7, 2.2 / 0.7, 2.2		16 TH	0319 / 1537	0.8, 2.0 / 0.8, 2.1
2 TH	0415 / 1634 ○	0.6, 2.3 / 0.6, 2.3		17 F	0358 / 1615 ●	0.7, 2.1 / 0.7, 2.1
3 F	0500 / 1718	0.5, 2.3 / 0.6		18 SA	0436 / 1652	0.6, 2.2 / 0.6, 2.1
4 SA	0540 / 1758	2.2, 0.4 / 2.3, 0.6		19 SU	0513 / 1730	0.6, 2.2 / 0.6
5 SU	0618 / 1836	2.2, 0.5 / 2.3, 0.6		20 M	0550 / 1807	0.5, 2.2 / 0.6
6 M	0653 / 1911	2.1, 0.6 / 0.7		21 TU	0628 / 1847	0.5, 2.2 / 0.6
7 TU	0726 / 1945	2.1, 0.6 / 0.8		22 W	0707 / 1929	2.2, 0.7 / 0.7
8 W	0759 / 2020	2.0, 0.6 / 0.9		23 TH	0750 / 2017	2.1, 0.7 / 0.8
9 TH	0835 / ◑ 2101	1.9, 1.0 / 1.1		24 F	0841 / ◑ 2113	0.9, 2.0 / 0.9
10 F	0921 / 2158	1.8, 1.2 / 1.2		25 SA	0944 / 2228	1.0, 1.9 / 1.1
11 SA	1029 / 2323	1.6, 1.3 / 1.3		26 SU	1106 / 2358	1.2, 1.8 / 1.1
12 SU	1201	1.6, 1.4, 1.7		27 M	1236	1.2, 1.8, 1.9
13 M	0046 / 1316	1.3 / 1.3, 1.7, 1.8		28 TU	0121 / 1350	1.0 / 1.0, 1.9, 2.0
14 TU	0148 / 1411	1.1 / 1.1, 1.2, 1.9		29 W	0224 / 1447	0.8 / 0.8, 0.9, 2.1
15 W	0236 / 1456	1.0, 2.0 / 1.0, 2.0		30 TH	0315 / 1535	0.7, 2.2 / 0.7, 2.2
				31 F	0358 / 1617 ○	0.6, 2.3 / 0.6, 2.2

Chart Datum: 1·40 metres below Ordnance Datum (Newlyn)
HAT is 2·6 metres above Chart Datum

TIME ZONE (UT)		
For Summer Time add ONE hour in **non-shaded areas**		

POOLE HARBOUR

LAT 50°42′N LONG 1°59′W

TIMES AND HEIGHTS OF HIGH AND LOW WATERS

Dates in amber are **SPRINGS**
Dates in yellow are **NEAPS**

2012

SEPTEMBER

Time	m		Time	m
1 0439 SA 1656	0.5 2.3 0.6 2.2	**16** 0408 SU 1626 ●	0.6 2.3 0.6 2.3
2 0516 SU 1733	0.5 2.3 0.6	**17** 0447 M 1705	0.5 2.3 0.5
3 0550 M 1806	2.2 0.6 2.3 0.6	**18** 0526 TU 1745	2.3 0.4 2.3 0.5
4 0621 TU 1837	2.1 0.6 2.2 0.7	**19** 0606 W 1826	2.3 0.5 2.3 0.6
5 0651 W 1906	2.1 0.7 2.1 0.8	**20** 0648 TH 1910	2.3 0.6 2.3 0.6
6 0720 TH 1937	2.0 0.9 2.0 0.9	**21** 0733 F 1959	2.2 0.7 2.1 0.8
7 0752 F 2013	1.9 1.0 1.9 1.0	**22** 0826 SA 2058 ◐	2.0 0.9 2.0 0.9
8 0833 SA 2100 ◐	1.8 1.2 1.8 1.2	**23** 0933 SU 2215	1.9 1.1 1.9
9 0933 SU 2220	1.7 1.4 1.7 1.3	**24** 1058 M 2345	1.8 1.2 1.2
10 1120 M	1.6 1.4 1.6	**25** 1227 TU	1.9 1.2 1.9
11 0009 TU 1247	1.3 1.7 1.4 1.7	**26** 0107 W 1338	1.0 1.8 1.0 2.0
12 0118 W 1344	1.2 1.8 1.2 1.9	**27** 0207 TH 1431	0.9 2.0 0.9 2.1
13 0208 TH 1429	1.0 2.0 1.0 2.0	**28** 0254 F 1515	0.8 2.2 0.8 2.1
14 0250 F 1509	0.8 2.1 0.8 2.1	**29** 0335 SA 1554	0.7 2.3 0.7 2.2
15 0330 SA 1547	0.7 2.2 0.7 2.2	**30** 0412 SU 1630 ○	0.6 2.3 0.6 2.2

OCTOBER

Time	m		Time	m
1 0447 M 1704	0.6 2.3 0.6	**16** 0420 TU 1641	0.5 2.4 0.5 2.4
2 0520 TU 1735	2.2 0.6 2.2 0.7	**17** 0502 W 1724	0.5 2.4 0.5
3 0551 W 1805	2.1 0.7 2.2 0.7	**18** 0546 TH 1809	2.4 0.5 2.3 0.5
4 0620 TH 1833	2.1 0.8 2.1 0.8	**19** 0632 F 1856	2.3 0.6 2.3 0.6
5 0648 F 1902	2.1 0.9 2.0 0.9	**20** 0721 SA 1947	2.3 0.7 2.1 0.8
6 0719 SA 1936	2.0 1.0 1.9 1.0	**21** 0816 SU 2045	2.1 0.9 2.0 0.9
7 0758 SU 2021	1.9 1.2 1.8 1.2	**22** 0922 M 2157 ◐	2.0 1.1 1.9 1.0
8 0852 M 2125 ◐	1.8 1.3 1.7 1.3	**23** 1040 TU 2319	1.9 1.2 1.8 1.1
9 1021 TU 2310	1.7 1.4 1.6 1.3	**24** 1202 W	1.9 1.2 1.9
10 1202 W	1.7 1.4 1.7	**25** 0037 TH 1312	1.1 2.0 1.1 1.9
11 0033 TH 1306	1.2 1.8 1.2 1.8	**26** 0138 F 1405	1.0 2.1 0.9 2.0
12 0129 F 1353	1.0 2.0 1.0 2.0	**27** 0225 SA 1448	0.9 2.2 0.8 2.1
13 0215 SA 1436	0.9 2.1 0.8 2.1	**28** 0305 SU 1526	0.8 2.2 0.8 2.1
14 0256 SU 1517	0.7 2.2 0.7 2.2	**29** 0343 M 1602 ○	0.7 2.2 0.7 2.1
15 0338 M 1558 ●	0.6 2.3 0.6 2.3	**30** 0418 TU 1636	0.7 2.2 0.7 2.1
			31 0452 W 1709	0.7 2.2 0.7

NOVEMBER

Time	m		Time	m
1 0524 TH 1739	2.1 0.8 2.1 0.8	**16** 0530 F 1756	2.4 0.6 2.4 0.5
2 0554 F 1808	2.1 0.8 2.1 0.8	**17** 0619 SA 1845	2.4 0.6 2.3 0.6
3 0624 SA 1837	2.1 0.9 2.0 0.9	**18** 0710 SU 1936	2.3 0.7 2.2 0.7
4 0655 SU 1912	2.0 1.0 2.0 1.0	**19** 0803 M 2030	2.2 0.9 2.0 0.8
5 0734 M 1954	2.0 1.2 1.9 1.1	**20** 0903 TU 2131 ◑	2.1 1.0 1.9 1.0
6 0823 TU 2049	1.9 1.3 1.8 1.2	**21** 1010 W 2239	2.0 1.1 1.8 1.1
7 0930 W 2204 ◑	1.8 1.3 1.7 1.3	**22** 1123 TH 2350	1.9 1.2 1.8 1.1
8 1054 TH 2327	1.8 1.3 1.8	**23** 1232 F	2.0 1.2 1.9
9 1210 F	1.9 1.2 1.8	**24** 0055 SA 1330	1.1 2.0 1.1 1.9
10 0036 SA 1309	1.1 2.0 1.1 2.0	**25** 0148 SU 1417	1.0 2.1 1.0 2.0
11 0132 SU 1400	0.9 2.1 0.9 2.1	**26** 0233 M 1458	0.9 2.1 0.9 2.0
12 0221 M 1447	0.8 2.2 0.7 2.2	**27** 0313 TU 1536	0.9 2.1 0.8 2.1
13 0308 TU 1534 ●	0.7 2.3 0.6 2.3	**28** 0351 W 1613 ○	0.8 2.1 0.7 2.1
14 0355 W 1621	0.6 2.4 0.5 2.4	**29** 0428 TH 1648	0.8 2.1 0.8 2.1
15 0443 TH 1709	0.6 2.4 0.5	**30** 0503 F 1721	0.8 2.1 0.8

DECEMBER

Time	m		Time	m
1 0535 SA 1751	2.1 0.9 2.1 0.8	**16** 0608 SU 1835	2.4 0.6 2.3 0.5
2 0606 SU 1822	2.1 0.9 2.1 0.8	**17** 0657 M 1922	2.3 0.6 2.2 0.6
3 0638 M 1855	2.1 1.0 2.1 0.9	**18** 0745 TU 2009	2.3 0.8 2.1 0.7
4 0715 TU 1935	2.1 1.0 2.0 0.9	**19** 0836 W 2058	2.1 0.9 2.0 0.9
5 0759 W 2022	2.0 1.1 1.9 1.0	**20** 0930 TH 2152 ◑	2.0 1.0 1.9 1.0
6 0853 TH 2120 ◑	1.9 1.2 1.8 1.1	**21** 1032 F 2253	1.9 1.1 1.8 1.2
7 0959 F 2229	1.9 1.2 1.8 1.1	**22** 1139 SA	1.9 1.2 1.7
8 1112 SA 2341	1.9 1.2 1.8 1.0	**23** 0000 SU 1246	1.1 1.9 1.2 1.8
9 1223 SU	2.0 1.0 1.9	**24** 0105 M 1343	1.2 1.9 1.1 1.8
10 0049 M 1327	1.0 2.1 0.9 2.0	**25** 0159 TU 1431	1.1 2.0 1.0 1.9
11 0150 TU 1424	0.9 2.2 0.8 2.1	**26** 0246 W 1513	1.0 2.0 0.9 2.0
12 0246 W 1517	0.7 2.3 0.7 2.3	**27** 0328 TH 1552	0.9 2.1 0.8 2.0
13 0339 TH 1609 ●	0.7 2.4 0.6 2.3	**28** 0408 F 1630 ○	0.9 2.1 0.9 2.1
14 0430 F 1659	0.6 2.4 0.5 2.4	**29** 0444 SA 1705	0.8 2.1 0.7
15 0519 SA 1747	2.4 0.6 2.4 0.4	**30** 0518 SU 1738	2.1 0.8 2.1 0.7
			31 0551 M 1809	2.1 0.8 2.1 0.7

TIDES

Chart Datum: 1·40 metres below Ordnance Datum (Newlyn)
HAT is 2·6 metres above Chart Datum

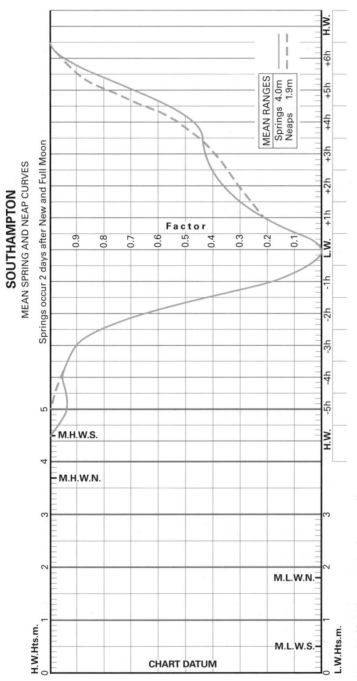

SOUTHAMPTON
MEAN SPRING AND NEAP CURVES
Springs occur 2 days after New and Full Moon

MEAN RANGES	
Springs	4.0m
Neaps	1.9m

Factor

0.9 0.8 0.7 0.6 0.5 0.4 0.3 0.2 0.1

H.W. +6h +5h +4h +3h +2h +1h L.W. -1h -2h -3h -4h -5h H.W.

H.W.Hts.m.   L.W.Hts.m.

M.H.W.S.
M.H.W.N.

M.L.W.N.
M.L.W.S.

CHART DATUM

Note - Double HWs occur at Southampton. The predictions are for the first HW.

SOUTHAMPTON
LAT 50°54'N LONG 1°24'W
TIMES AND HEIGHTS OF HIGH AND LOW WATERS

2012

JANUARY

	Time	m		Time	m
1 SU	0334	4.1	**16** M	0315	4.3
	0925	1.8		0908	1.3
☽	1551	3.9	☽	1535	4.2
	2140	1.8		2133	1.3
2 M	0426	3.9	**17** TU	0415	4.2
	1022	2.0		1010	1.5
	1648	3.7		1640	4.0
	2242	2.0		2240	1.5
3 TU	0529	3.8	**18** W	0525	4.1
	1133	2.1		1127	1.7
	1800	3.7		1758	3.9
	2356	2.1			
4 W	0640	3.9	**19** TH	0000	1.6
	1244	2.0		0643	4.1
	1917	3.7		1250	1.6
				1920	3.9
5 TH	0105	2.0	**20** F	0120	1.6
	0746	4.0		0757	4.2
	1345	1.8		1403	1.4
	2020	3.9		2033	4.1
6 F	0202	1.8	**21** SA	0228	1.3
	0840	4.1		0900	4.4
	1435	1.6		1504	1.1
	2108	4.1		2132	4.3
7 SA	0251	1.6	**22** SU	0326	1.1
	0923	4.3		0953	4.5
	1519	1.3		1556	0.8
	2148	4.2		2222	4.5
8 SU	0334	1.3	**23** M	0416	0.9
	1002	4.4		1039	4.6
	1600	1.1	●	1643	0.6
	2225	4.4		2305	4.6
9 M	0415	1.1	**24** TU	0501	0.7
	1038	4.5		1121	4.6
○	1639	0.9		1725	0.5
	2301	4.4		2346	4.6
10 TU	0454	1.0	**25** W	0542	0.6
	1115	4.6		1159	4.6
	1718	0.7		1803	0.5
	2338	4.5			
11 W	0533	0.9	**26** TH	0023	4.6
	1152	4.6		0620	0.7
	1755	0.7		1236	4.5
				1838	0.5
12 TH	0016	4.5	**27** F	0059	4.5
	0611	0.8		0655	0.8
	1231	4.6		1312	4.4
	1833	0.7		1910	0.7
13 F	0057	4.5	**28** SA	0134	4.4
	0650	0.9		0727	1.0
	1312	4.6		1347	4.3
	1912	0.7		1939	1.0
14 SA	0139	4.5	**29** SU	0209	4.3
	0731	1.0		0757	1.2
	1354	4.5		1423	4.1
	1953	0.9		2009	1.3
15 SU	0224	4.4	**30** M	0246	4.1
	0816	1.1		0831	1.5
	1441	4.3		1503	3.9
	2039	1.1		2044	1.6
			31 TU	0328	3.9
				0913	1.8
			☽	1550	3.7
				2132	1.9

FEBRUARY

	Time	m		Time	m
1 W	0420	3.8	**16** TH	0456	3.9
	1013	2.0		1102	1.7
	1653	3.6		1739	3.8
	2244	2.1		2343	1.8
2 TH	0531	3.6	**17** F	0626	3.8
	1142	2.1		1236	1.7
	1818	3.6		1914	3.8
3 F	0018	2.2	**18** SA	0113	1.7
	0655	3.7		0750	4.0
	1306	2.0		1356	1.5
	1941	3.7		2030	4.0
4 SA	0132	2.0	**19** SU	0224	1.4
	0807	3.9		0855	4.2
	1407	1.7		1456	1.1
	2041	3.9		2126	4.2
5 SU	0227	1.7	**20** M	0318	1.1
	0858	4.1		0945	4.4
	1455	1.4		1544	0.8
	2125	4.1		2211	4.4
6 M	0313	1.3	**21** TU	0403	0.8
	0940	4.3		1027	4.5
	1539	1.0	●	1626	0.6
	2204	4.3		2250	4.5
7 TU	0356	1.0	**22** W	0444	0.6
	1018	4.4		1104	4.5
	1620	0.7		1704	0.4
○	2241	4.5		2325	4.5
8 W	0437	0.7	**23** TH	0521	0.5
	1056	4.6		1138	4.5
	1700	0.5		1740	0.4
	2318	4.6		2357	4.5
9 TH	0517	0.6	**24** F	0556	0.5
	1133	4.7		1210	4.5
	1739	0.4		1812	0.5
	2356	4.7			
10 F	0556	0.5	**25** SA	0028	4.5
	1212	4.7		0627	0.6
	1818	0.3		1242	4.4
				1840	0.6
11 SA	0036	4.7	**26** SU	0100	4.4
	0616	0.5		0654	0.8
	1253	4.7		1315	4.3
	1856	0.4		1906	0.9
12 SU	0117	4.6	**27** M	0132	4.3
	0714	0.6		0728	1.0
	1335	4.6		1349	4.2
	1935	0.6		1932	1.2
13 M	0201	4.5	**28** TU	0205	4.1
	0756	0.8		0748	1.3
	1420	4.4		1424	4.0
	2018	0.9		2002	1.5
14 TU	0249	4.3	**29** W	0241	3.9
	0844	1.1		0823	1.6
	1511	4.2		1506	3.8
☽	2109	1.2		2042	1.8
15 W	0345	4.1			
	0943	1.4			
	1614	3.9			
	2214	1.6			

MARCH

	Time	m		Time	m
1 TH	0326	3.7	**16** F	0438	3.8
	0911	1.9		1045	1.7
☽	1601	3.6		1731	3.7
	2142	2.1		2332	1.8
2 F	0430	3.6	**17** SA	0613	3.7
	1029	2.1		1221	1.7
	1721	3.5		1907	3.8
	2322	2.2			
3 SA	0558	3.5	**18** SU	0104	1.7
	1216	2.0		0739	3.9
	1854	3.6		1340	1.5
				2018	4.0
4 SU	0056	2.0	**19** M	0211	1.5
	0724	3.7		0841	4.1
	1331	1.7		1437	1.2
	2005	3.8		2110	4.2
5 M	0158	1.7	**20** TU	0300	1.2
	0825	3.9		0928	4.3
	1425	1.4		1521	0.9
	2054	4.1		2152	4.4
6 TU	0247	1.3	**21** W	0342	0.9
	0912	4.2		1007	4.4
	1512	1.0		1601	0.7
	2136	4.3		2227	4.5
7 W	0331	0.9	**22** TH	0420	0.7
	0952	4.4		1041	4.4
	1555	0.6		1637	0.5
	2215	4.5		2259	4.5
8 TH	0414	0.6	**23** F	0455	0.5
	1032	4.6		1112	4.4
	1637	0.3		1711	0.5
○	2254	4.7		2329	4.5
9 F	0455	0.3	**24** SA	0528	0.5
	1111	4.7		1143	4.4
	1718	0.2		1743	0.6
	2333	4.8		2358	4.4
10 SA	0536	0.2	**25** SU	0558	0.6
	1152	4.8		1213	4.4
	1758	0.2		1811	0.7
11 SU	0014	4.8	**26** M	0028	4.4
	0616	0.2		0624	0.7
	1234	4.8		1246	4.3
	1837	0.3		1836	0.9
12 M	0056	4.7	**27** TU	0100	4.3
	0657	0.3		0649	0.9
	1317	4.7		1319	4.2
	1918	0.5		1901	1.2
13 TU	0140	4.6	**28** W	0132	4.1
	0739	0.6		0716	1.2
	1403	4.4		1354	4.1
	2001	0.8		1931	1.4
14 W	0228	4.3	**29** TH	0207	4.0
	0826	1.0		0750	1.4
	1455	4.2		1434	3.9
	2052	1.3		2010	1.7
15 TH	0325	4.0	**30** F	0248	3.8
	0924	1.4		0835	1.7
	1602	3.9		1526	3.7
☽	2200	1.6		2105	2.0
			31 SA	0346	3.6
				0941	1.9
				1639	3.6
				2230	2.1

APRIL

	Time	m		Time	m
1 SU	0508	3.5	**16** M	0038	1.8
	1119	1.9		0712	3.8
	1806	3.6		1308	1.5
				1950	4.0
2 M	0009	2.0	**17** TU	0142	1.5
	0635	3.6		0813	4.0
	1245	1.7		1404	1.3
	1920	3.8		2042	4.2
3 TU	0119	1.6	**18** W	0231	1.3
	0744	3.9		0901	4.1
	1347	1.3		1448	1.1
	2016	4.1		2123	4.3
4 W	0213	1.2	**19** TH	0312	1.0
	0837	4.2		0941	4.2
	1438	0.9		1528	0.9
	2103	4.4		2159	4.4
5 TH	0301	0.8	**20** F	0349	0.9
	0922	4.4		1015	4.3
	1525	0.6		1605	0.8
	2146	4.6		2231	4.4
6 F	0347	0.5	**21** SA	0425	0.7
	1005	4.6		1046	4.3
	1610	0.3	●	1640	0.7
○	2228	4.8		2300	4.4
7 SA	0431	0.2	**22** SU	0458	0.7
	1048	4.8		1116	4.3
	1654	0.2		1713	0.8
	2310	4.9		2330	4.4
8 SU	0515	0.1	**23** M	0529	0.7
	1132	4.8		1148	4.3
	1737	0.2		1743	0.9
	2353	4.9			
9 M	0558	0.1	**24** TU	0001	4.3
	1216	4.8		0558	0.8
	1820	0.3		1221	4.3
				1811	1.0
10 TU	0038	4.8	**25** W	0033	4.3
	0641	0.3		0625	0.9
	1303	4.6		1256	4.2
	1903	0.5		1839	1.2
11 W	0125	4.6	**26** TH	0107	4.2
	0725	0.6		0655	1.1
	1352	4.4		1332	4.1
	1949	0.9		1911	1.4
12 TH	0215	4.3	**27** F	0144	4.0
	0814	0.9		0730	1.3
	1448	4.2		1413	4.0
	2042	1.3		1951	1.6
13 F	0312	4.0	**28** SA	0226	3.9
	0911	1.3		0814	1.5
☽	1555	3.9		1503	3.9
	2149	1.6		2044	1.8
14 SA	0424	3.8	**29** SU	0320	3.8
	1026	1.6		0914	1.7
	1719	3.8		1608	3.8
	2314	1.8	☽	2155	1.9
15 SU	0551	3.7	**30** M	0430	3.7
	1153	1.7		1032	1.7
	1844	3.9		1723	3.8
				2320	1.8

Chart Datum: 2·74 metres below Ordnance Datum (Newlyn)
HAT is 5·0 metres above Chart Datum

TIDES

SOUTHAMPTON

LAT 50°54'N   LONG 1°24'W

TIMES AND HEIGHTS OF HIGH AND LOW WATERS

TIME ZONE (UT)
For Summer Time add ONE hour in **non-shaded areas**

Dates in amber are **SPRINGS**
Dates in yellow are **NEAPS**

2012

MAY

Day	Time	m	Time	m		Day	Time	m	Time	m
1 TU	0549 1154	3.7 1.6	1836	4.0		**16** W	0058 0733	1.7 3.8	1318 2003	1.5 4.1
2 W	0034 0700	1.6 3.9	1303 1937	1.3 4.2		**17** TH	0152 0826	1.5 4.0	1408 2049	1.4 4.2
3 TH	0135 0800	1.2 4.2	1400 2029	1.0 4.4		**18** F	0236 0910	1.3 4.1	1451 2127	1.2 4.3
4 F	0229 0852	0.9 4.4	1453 2118	0.7 4.6		**19** SA	0317 0948	1.1 4.1	1532 2202	1.1 4.3
5 SA	0319 0940	0.6 4.6	1543 2204	0.5 4.8		**20** SU	0355 1022	1.0 4.2	1610 ● 2234	1.0 4.3
6 SU	0408 1028	0.3 4.7	1631 ○ 2250	0.4 4.8		**21** M	0431 1054	0.9 4.2	1646 2306	1.0 4.3
7 M	0455 1115	0.2 4.7	1718 2337	0.3 4.8		**22** TU	0505 1127	0.9 4.1	1720 2339	1.0 4.3
8 TU	0542 1203	0.2 4.7	1805	0.4		**23** W	0537 1201	0.9 4.3	1753	1.1
9 W	0024 0628	4.7 0.3	1253 1851	4.6 0.7		**24** TH	0013 0608	4.3 0.9	1238 1824	4.2 1.2
10 TH	0113 0714	4.6 0.6	1345 1939	4.4 0.9		**25** F	0050 0641	4.2 1.0	1316 1859	4.2 1.3
11 F	0204 0803	4.3 0.9	1440 2032	4.3 1.2		**26** SA	0128 0717	4.1 1.1	1358 1940	4.1 1.4
12 SA	0300 0856	4.1 1.2	1541 ◑ 2132	4.1 1.5		**27** SU	0210 0801	4.0 1.3	1445 2028	4.0 1.6
13 SU	0402 0959	3.9 1.6	1650 2242	3.9 1.7		**28** M	0300 0853	4.0 1.4	1541 ◐ 2128	4.0 1.7
14 M	0514 1110	3.8 1.6	1803 2354	3.9 1.8		**29** TU	0400 0957	3.9 1.6	1646 2238	4.0 1.7
15 TU	0629 1219	3.7 1.6	1909	4.0		**30** W	0509 1109	3.9 1.5	1754 2350	4.1 1.5
						31 TH	0620 1220	4.0 1.4	1859	4.2

JUNE

Day	Time	m	Time	m		Day	Time	m	Time	m
1 F	0057 0726	1.3 4.1	1325 1958	1.2 4.4		**16** SA	0159 0838	1.6 3.9	1416 2055	1.6 4.1
2 SA	0158 0825	1.0 4.3	1424 2053	0.9 4.6		**17** SU	0245 0922	1.4 4.0	1502 2135	1.4 4.2
3 SU	0255 0920	0.8 4.5	1520 2145	0.8 4.7		**18** M	0327 1001	1.2 4.1	1544 2211	1.3 4.3
4 M	0349 1013	0.6 4.6	1613 ○ 2235	0.6 4.7		**19** TU	0407 1036	1.0 4.2	1624 ● 2246	1.2 4.3
5 TU	0441 1104	0.4 4.6	1704 2324	0.6 4.7		**20** W	0444 1110	0.9 4.3	1702 2320	1.1 4.3
6 W	0530 1154	0.4 4.6	1754	0.6		**21** TH	0520 1145	0.9 4.3	1738 2356	1.1 4.3
7 TH	0013 0617	4.7 0.4	1244 1841	4.6 0.7		**22** F	0555 1221	0.9 4.3	1813	1.1
8 F	0102 0703	4.5 0.5	1334 1928	4.5 0.9		**23** SA	0033 0630	4.3 0.9	1300 1849	4.3 1.1
9 SA	0150 0748	4.4 0.8	1423 2016	4.4 1.1		**24** SU	0112 0706	4.3 0.9	1340 1928	4.3 1.2
10 SU	0239 0834	4.2 1.0	1515 2105	4.2 1.4		**25** M	0153 0747	4.2 1.0	1424 2012	4.2 1.3
11 M	0331 0923	4.0 1.3	1609 ◑ 2200	4.1 1.6		**26** TU	0239 0833	4.2 1.2	1514 2103	4.2 1.4
12 TU	0427 1019	3.8 1.6	1708 2301	3.9 1.8		**27** W	0332 0927	4.1 1.3	1611 ◑ 2204	4.1 1.5
13 W	0532 1121	3.7 1.7	1812	3.9		**28** TH	0434 1031	4.0 1.4	1717 2313	4.1 1.5
14 TH	0005 0640	1.8 3.7	1226 1914	1.8 3.9		**29** F	0545 1143	4.0 1.5	1826	4.2
15 F	0106 0745	1.7 3.8	1325 2009	1.7 4.0		**30** SA	0026 0658	1.4 4.0	1257 1933	1.4 4.3

JULY

Day	Time	m	Time	m		Day	Time	m	Time	m
1 SU	0137 0807	1.2 4.2	1405 2036	1.2 4.4		**16** M	0217 0859	1.6 3.9	1437 2111	1.7 4.1
2 M	0240 0909	1.0 4.3	1506 2132	1.0 4.5		**17** TU	0303 0941	1.4 4.1	1523 2150	1.5 4.2
3 TU	0338 1004	0.7 4.5	1603 ○ 2225	0.8 4.6		**18** W	0345 1017	1.1 4.2	1604 2226	1.2 4.3
4 W	0431 1056	0.5 4.6	1655 2314	0.7 4.6		**19** TH	0425 1052	0.9 4.3	1644 ● 2301	1.1 4.4
5 TH	0520 1144	0.4 4.6	1744	0.6		**20** F	0503 1126	0.8 4.4	1722 2337	0.9 4.4
6 F	0000 0605	4.6 0.4	1231 1829	4.6 0.6		**21** SA	0540 1202	0.7 4.4	1759	0.9
7 SA	0045 0648	4.6 0.5	1315 1911	4.6 0.8		**22** SU	0014 0616	4.5 0.7	1240 1835	4.5 0.9
8 SU	0128 0728	4.4 0.6	1357 1952	4.5 1.0		**23** M	0052 0652	4.5 0.7	1319 1913	4.5 0.9
9 M	0210 0805	4.3 0.9	1439 2031	4.3 1.2		**24** TU	0133 0731	4.4 0.8	1401 1954	4.4 1.0
10 TU	0253 0844	4.1 1.2	1523 2113	4.1 1.5		**25** W	0216 0813	4.3 1.0	1447 2040	4.3 1.2
11 W	0339 0926	3.9 1.5	1610 ◑ 2203	4.0 1.8		**26** TH	0306 0903	4.2 1.1	1541 ◑ 2136	4.2 1.4
12 TH	0432 1020	3.7 1.8	1706 2305	3.8 1.9		**27** F	0405 1002	4.0 1.5	1645 2245	4.1 1.6
13 F	0539 1128	3.6 2.0	1814	3.8		**28** SA	0519 1117	3.9 1.6	1801	4.1
14 SA	0017 0657	2.0 3.6	1242 1925	2.0 3.8		**29** SU	0006 0641	1.6 3.9	1241 1919	1.6 4.1
15 SU	0123 0806	1.8 3.8	1345 2024	1.9 4.0		**30** M	0127 0800	1.4 4.0	1357 2028	1.5 4.3
						31 TU	0234 0905	1.2 4.2	1501 2126	1.2 4.4

AUGUST

Day	Time	m	Time	m		Day	Time	m	Time	m
1 W	0331 0959	0.9 4.4	1556 2216	0.9 4.6		**16** TH	0322 0953	1.2 4.3	1542 2202	1.2 4.4
2 TH	0421 1047	0.6 4.6	1644 ○ 2301	0.7 4.6		**17** F	0403 1027	0.9 4.4	1622 ● 2238	1.0 4.5
3 F	0507 1130	0.4 4.6	1729 2343	0.6 4.6		**18** SA	0442 1102	0.6 4.5	1701 2314	0.8 4.6
4 SA	0548 1210	0.4 4.6	1810	0.6		**19** SU	0520 1138	0.5 4.6	1739 2351	0.6 4.6
5 SU	0022 0626	4.6 0.4	1248 1847	4.6 0.7		**20** M	0558 1216	0.5 4.6	1817	0.6
6 M	0100 0701	4.5 0.6	1325 1922	4.5 0.9		**21** TU	0030 0634	4.6 0.5	1256 1854	4.6 0.7
7 TU	0136 0733	4.3 0.9	1400 1954	4.3 1.1		**22** W	0111 0713	4.6 0.7	1337 1935	4.6 0.9
8 W	0214 0803	4.2 1.2	1437 2026	4.2 1.4		**23** TH	0155 0754	4.5 0.9	1423 2020	4.4 1.1
9 TH	0253 0837	4.0 1.5	1517 ◑ 2105	4.0 1.7		**24** F	0244 0841	4.3 1.2	1517 ◑ 2114	4.2 1.4
10 F	0339 0920	3.8 1.9	1606 2159	3.8 2.0		**25** SA	0344 0942	4.0 1.6	1623 2226	4.0 1.7
11 SA	0440 1025	3.6 2.2	1711 2320	3.7 2.1		**26** SU	0504 1104	3.8 1.8	1747 2357	3.9 1.7
12 SU	0603 1157	3.6 2.3	1835	3.7		**27** M	0638 1237	3.8 1.8	1914	4.0
13 M	0046 0729	2.1 3.7	1316 1950	2.1 3.8		**28** TU	0122 0759	1.6 4.0	1354 2024	1.6 4.2
14 TU	0150 0831	1.8 3.9	1414 2044	1.8 4.0		**29** W	0228 0900	1.2 4.3	1454 2118	1.3 4.4
15 W	0239 0915	1.5 4.1	1500 2125	1.5 4.2		**30** TH	0320 0949	0.9 4.5	1543 2204	1.0 4.5
						31 F	0405 1032	0.6 4.6	1627 ○ 2244	0.7 4.6

Chart Datum: 2·74 metres below Ordnance Datum (Newlyn)
HAT is 5·0 metres above Chart Datum

SOUTHAMPTON

LAT 50°54'N   LONG 1°24'W

TIMES AND HEIGHTS OF HIGH AND LOW WATERS

Dates in amber are **SPRINGS**
Dates in yellow are **NEAPS**

2012

SEPTEMBER

Day	Time m	Time m	Time m	Time m	Day	Time m	Time m	Time m	Time m
1 SA	0446 0.5	1109 4.6	1707 0.6	2320 4.6	**16** SU	0416 0.6	1034 4.7	1636 0.6	● 2249 4.7
2 SU	0524 0.4	1144 4.6	1744 0.6	2354 4.6	**17** M	0456 0.4	1112 4.8	1716 0.5	2328 4.8
3 M	0559 0.5	1217 4.6	1818 0.7		**18** TU	0535 0.4	1151 4.8	1756 0.5	
4 TU	0028 4.5	0630 0.7	1250 4.5	1848 0.9	**19** W	0008 4.8	0614 0.6	1233 4.8	1835 0.6
5 W	0102 4.4	0658 0.9	1322 4.4	1915 1.1	**20** TH	0051 4.7	0654 0.6	1317 4.7	1917 0.8
6 TH	0136 4.2	0728 1.2	1356 4.2	1943 1.4	**21** F	0137 4.5	0738 0.9	1404 4.5	2004 1.1
7 F	0213 4.1	0754 1.5	1432 4.0	2016 1.7	**22** SA	0229 4.3	0827 1.3	1500 4.2	☽ 2100 1.4
8 SA	0255 3.9	0832 1.9	1516 3.8	☽ 2102 2.0	**23** SU	0333 4.0	0931 1.7	1610 4.0	2214 1.7
9 SU	0350 3.7	0929 2.2	1617 3.7	2216 2.2	**24** M	0458 3.9	1057 1.9	1739 3.9	2348 1.8
10 M	0509 3.6	1105 2.4	1742 3.6		**25** TU	0633 3.9	1230 1.9	1906 4.0	
11 TU	0000 2.2	0642 3.2	1241 2.2	1908 3.7	**26** W	0110 1.6	0749 4.1	1343 1.6	2012 4.2
12 W	0115 1.9	0753 3.9	1343 1.9	2009 4.0	**27** TH	0212 1.3	0845 4.4	1437 1.3	2103 4.4
13 TH	0208 1.5	0841 4.1	1431 1.5	2054 4.2	**28** F	0259 1.0	0930 4.5	1522 1.1	2145 4.5
14 F	0253 1.2	0921 4.4	1514 1.2	2133 4.4	**29** SA	0341 0.8	1009 4.6	1602 0.8	2221 4.6
15 SA	0335 0.8	0958 4.6	1555 0.9	2211 4.6	**30** SU	0419 0.7	1044 4.6	1639 0.7	○ 2255 4.6

OCTOBER

Day	Time m	Time m	Time m	Time m	Day	Time m	Time m	Time m	Time m
1 M	0454 0.6	1115 4.6	1714 0.7	2326 4.5	**16** TU	0429 0.5	1047 4.9	1652 0.4	2306 4.9
2 TU	0528 0.7	1145 4.5	1747 0.8	2358 4.5	**17** W	0512 0.4	1130 4.9	1735 0.4	2350 4.9
3 W	0559 0.8	1216 4.5	1816 0.9		**18** TH	0555 0.5	1213 4.9	1818 0.5	
4 TH	0030 4.4	0626 1.0	1248 4.4	1842 1.1	**19** F	0036 4.8	0639 0.7	1300 4.7	1903 0.7
5 F	0105 4.3	0652 1.3	1321 4.2	1909 1.3	**20** SA	0125 4.6	0725 1.0	1350 4.5	1951 1.0
6 SA	0141 4.2	0722 1.6	1357 4.1	1941 1.6	**21** SU	0220 4.4	0818 1.3	1448 4.3	2048 1.3
7 SU	0222 4.0	0759 1.8	1439 3.9	2023 1.9	**22** M	0326 4.1	0922 1.7	1557 4.0	☽ 2158 1.6
8 M	0313 3.8	0851 2.1	1535 3.7	☽ 2126 2.1	**23** TU	0447 4.0	1043 1.9	1720 3.9	2322 1.8
9 TU	0424 3.7	1013 2.3	1652 3.7	2300 2.1	**24** W	0612 4.0	1207 1.9	1841 4.0	
10 W	0549 3.7	1152 2.2	1817 3.7		**25** TH	0040 1.7	0723 4.2	1316 1.7	1946 4.1
11 TH	0027 2.0	0704 3.9	1302 1.9	1925 4.0	**26** F	0140 1.5	0819 4.4	1410 1.5	2038 4.3
12 F	0128 1.6	0800 4.2	1355 1.6	2017 4.2	**27** SA	0228 1.3	0904 4.5	1454 1.2	2120 4.5
13 SA	0217 1.2	0845 4.4	1441 1.2	2101 4.5	**28** SU	0309 1.1	0942 4.6	1533 1.1	2157 4.5
14 SU	0302 0.9	0926 4.6	1525 0.8	2143 4.7	**29** M	0347 1.0	1016 4.6	1610 0.9	○ 2230 4.5
15 M	0346 0.6	1006 4.8	1609 0.6	● 2224 4.8	**30** TU	0423 0.9	1047 4.6	1644 0.9	2301 4.5
					31 W	0457 0.9	1117 4.5	1717 0.9	2332 4.5

NOVEMBER

Day	Time m	Time m	Time m	Time m	Day	Time m	Time m	Time m	Time m
1 TH	0530 1.0	1148 4.5	1748 1.0		**16** F	0539 0.6	1159 4.9	1805 0.5	
2 F	0005 4.4	0559 1.1	1221 4.4	1816 1.1	**17** SA	0025 4.8	0626 0.7	1248 4.8	1851 0.7
3 SA	0041 4.4	0628 1.3	1255 4.3	1844 1.3	**18** SU	0117 4.7	0715 1.0	1339 4.6	1940 0.9
4 SU	0118 4.3	0659 1.5	1332 4.2	1917 1.5	**19** M	0211 4.5	0807 1.2	1434 4.3	2033 1.2
5 M	0159 4.1	0737 1.8	1413 4.0	1958 1.7	**20** TU	0311 4.3	0905 1.5	1535 4.1	☽ 2132 1.5
6 TU	0247 4.0	0825 2.0	1503 3.9	2052 1.9	**21** W	0419 4.1	1012 1.8	1644 4.0	2241 1.7
7 W	0347 3.9	0931 2.1	1609 3.8	2205 2.0	**22** TH	0532 4.1	1125 1.9	1758 3.9	2352 1.7
8 TH	0500 3.9	1055 2.1	1725 3.8	2328 1.9	**23**	0642 4.1	1234 1.8	1907 4.0	
9 F	0612 4.0	1211 1.9	1837 4.0		**24** SA	0055 1.7	0741 4.2	1332 1.7	2005 4.1
10 SA	0038 1.7	0715 4.2	1313 1.6	1937 4.2	**25** SU	0149 1.6	0831 4.3	1421 1.5	2052 4.2
11 SU	0136 1.3	0808 4.5	1406 1.2	2029 4.4	**26** M	0234 1.4	0913 4.4	1503 1.3	2132 4.3
12 M	0228 1.0	0855 4.7	1456 0.9	2117 4.7	**27** TU	0315 1.3	0949 4.5	1541 1.1	2208 4.4
13 TU	0317 0.8	0941 4.8	1544 0.7	● 2203 4.8	**28** W	0354 1.2	1022 4.5	1618 1.0	○ 2241 4.4
14 W	0404 0.6	1026 4.9	1631 0.5	2249 4.9	**29** TH	0431 1.1	1054 4.5	1654 1.0	2314 4.4
15 TH	0452 0.5	1112 5.0	1718 0.4	2337 4.9	**30** F	0506 1.1	1127 4.5	1727 1.0	2347 4.4

DECEMBER

Day	Time m	Time m	Time m	Time m	Day	Time m	Time m	Time m	Time m
1 SA	0540 1.2	1200 4.5	1758 1.0		**16** SU	0016 4.8	0615 0.7	1236 4.8	1840 0.5
2 SU	0023 4.4	0611 1.3	1236 4.4	1829 1.1	**17** M	0106 4.7	0703 0.8	1324 4.6	1926 0.7
3 M	0100 4.3	0644 1.4	1313 4.3	1902 1.3	**18** TU	0155 4.6	0750 1.0	1413 4.4	2011 0.9
4 TU	0140 4.3	0720 1.5	1352 4.2	1940 1.4	**19** W	0246 4.4	0839 1.3	1503 4.2	2059 1.2
5 W	0223 4.2	0804 1.7	1437 4.1	2026 1.6	**20** TH	0339 4.2	0932 1.6	1558 4.0	☽ 2152 1.5
6 TH	0314 4.1	0857 1.8	1531 4.0	2123 1.7	**21** F	0438 4.1	1032 1.8	1700 3.9	2254 1.8
7 F	0414 4.1	1003 1.9	1636 3.9	2232 1.7	**22**	0544 4.0	1140 1.9	1812 3.8	
8 SA	0522 4.1	1117 1.8	1748 4.0	2347 1.7	**23** SU	0002 1.9	0651 4.0	1247 1.9	1922 3.8
9 SU	0630 4.2	1229 1.6	1857 4.1		**24** M	0106 1.9	0753 4.1	1346 1.7	2022 4.0
10 M	0055 1.5	0732 4.4	1332 1.4	1959 4.3	**25** TU	0201 1.7	0844 4.2	1435 1.5	2110 4.1
11 TU	0156 1.2	0828 4.6	1430 1.1	2055 4.5	**26** W	0249 1.5	0926 4.3	1517 1.3	2150 4.2
12 W	0252 1.0	0920 4.7	1524 0.8	2147 4.7	**27** TH	0331 1.4	1003 4.4	1557 1.1	2225 4.3
13 TH	0346 0.8	1010 4.8	1616 0.6	● 2237 4.8	**28** F	0411 1.2	1037 4.5	1635 1.0	○ 2259 4.4
14 F	0437 0.7	1059 4.9	1706 0.5	2327 4.8	**29** SA	0448 1.1	1110 4.5	1710 0.9	2332 4.4
15 SA	0527 0.6	1148 4.9	1754 0.4		**30** SU	0524 1.1	1144 4.5	1744 0.9	
					31 M	0006 4.8	0557 1.1	1219 4.5	1816 0.9

Chart Datum: 2·74 metres below Ordnance Datum (Newlyn)
HAT is 5·0 metres above Chart Datum

TIDES

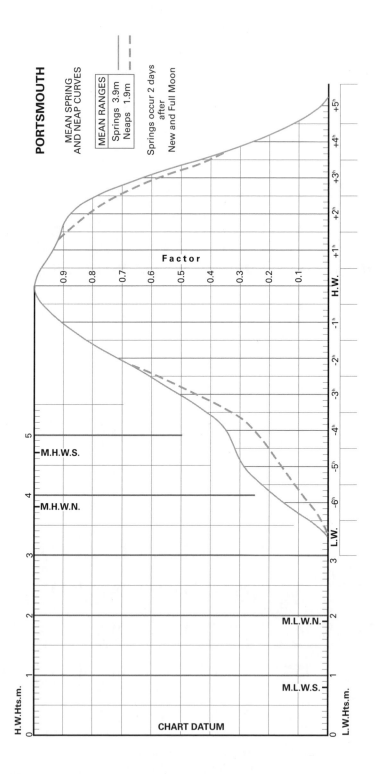

PORTSMOUTH

MEAN SPRING
AND NEAP CURVES

MEAN RANGES
Springs 3.9m
Neaps 1.9m

Springs occur 2 days
after
New and Full Moon

Factor

0.9 0.8 0.7 0.6 0.5 0.4 0.3 0.2 0.1

H.W.Hts.m.

M.H.W.S.

M.H.W.N.

CHART DATUM

L.W.Hts.m.

M.L.W.N.

M.L.W.S.

H.W.

L.W.

PORTSMOUTH

LAT 50°48'N   LONG 1°07'W

2012

TIMES AND HEIGHTS OF HIGH AND LOW WATERS

JANUARY

Day	Time m	Day	Time m
1	0408 4.2 / 0939 1.8 / SU 1620 3.9 / ☽ 2157 1.8	**16**	0349 4.5 / 0923 1.3 / M 1607 4.2 / ☽ 2149 1.3
2	0456 4.1 / 1038 2.0 / M 1714 3.8 / 2258 2.0	**17**	0446 4.3 / 1027 1.5 / TU 1712 4.1 / 2256 1.5
3	0554 4.0 / 1148 2.1 / TU 1821 3.7	**18**	0555 4.2 / 1144 1.7 / W 1830 4.0
4	0010 2.0 / 0701 4.0 / W 1258 2.0 / 1936 3.8	**19**	0015 1.7 / 0712 4.2 / TH 1306 1.6 / 1954 4.1
5	0119 2.0 / 0806 4.1 / TH 1357 1.8 / 2042 3.9	**20**	0135 1.6 / 0826 4.3 / F 1418 1.4 / 2108 4.3
6	0216 1.8 / 0901 4.2 / F 1446 1.6 / 2134 4.1	**21**	0242 1.4 / 0930 4.5 / SA 1517 1.1 / 2208 4.5
7	0304 1.6 / 0948 4.4 / SA 1529 1.4 / 2218 4.3	**22**	0338 1.2 / 1024 4.6 / SU 1608 0.9 / 2259 4.6
8	0346 1.4 / 1029 4.5 / SU 1610 1.1 / 2258 4.5	**23**	0426 1.0 / 1112 4.7 / M 1653 0.7 / ● 2345 4.7
9	0426 1.2 / 1108 4.6 / M 1649 1.0 / ○ 2337 4.6	**24**	0510 0.9 / 1156 4.7 / TU 1734 0.6
10	0504 1.1 / 1146 4.6 / TU 1726 0.9	**25**	0027 4.8 / 0550 0.8 / W 1237 4.7 / 1812 0.6
11	0015 4.6 / 0541 1.0 / W 1225 4.6 / 1803 0.8	**26**	0106 4.7 / 0628 0.9 / TH 1314 4.6 / 1847 0.7
12	0055 4.7 / 0619 1.0 / TH 1304 4.6 / 1842 0.8	**27**	0140 4.7 / 0703 0.9 / F 1349 4.5 / 1919 0.9
13	0135 4.7 / 0700 1.0 / F 1345 4.6 / 1923 0.8	**28**	0213 4.6 / 0736 1.1 / SA 1423 4.4 / 1951 1.1
14	0216 4.7 / 0743 1.0 / SA 1428 4.5 / 2006 0.9	**29**	0246 4.4 / 0808 1.3 / SU 1458 4.2 / 2023 1.3
15	0300 4.6 / 0829 1.2 / SU 1514 4.4 / 2053 1.1	**30**	0321 4.3 / 0843 1.6 / M 1536 4.0 / 2059 1.6
		31	0401 4.1 / 0925 1.8 / TU 1622 3.8 / ☽ 2146 1.9

FEBRUARY

Day	Time m	Day	Time m
1	0451 3.9 / 1026 2.0 / W 1722 3.7 / 2259 2.1	**16**	0526 4.0 / 1122 1.7 / TH 1816 3.9
2	0557 3.8 / 1200 2.1 / TH 1842 3.6	**17**	0001 1.8 / 0653 3.9 / F 1254 1.7 / 1949 3.9
3	0037 2.1 / 0716 3.8 / F 1321 2.0 / 2005 3.8	**18**	0129 1.7 / 0818 4.1 / SA 1410 1.5 / 2104 4.2
4	0149 2.0 / 0827 4.0 / SA 1420 1.7 / 2108 4.0	**19**	0238 1.5 / 0923 4.3 / SU 1508 1.2 / 2200 4.4
5	0242 1.7 / 0922 4.2 / SU 1507 1.4 / 2156 4.3	**20**	0331 1.2 / 1015 4.5 / M 1555 0.9 / 2247 4.6
6	0327 1.4 / 1007 4.4 / M 1550 1.1 / 2238 4.4	**21**	0415 0.9 / 1059 4.6 / TU 1636 0.7 / ● 2329 4.7
7	0407 1.1 / 1048 4.5 / TU 1630 0.8 / ○ 2318 4.6	**22**	0454 0.8 / 1139 4.6 / W 1713 0.6
8	0446 0.9 / 1129 4.6 / W 1709 0.6 / 2357 4.7	**23**	0006 4.7 / 0530 0.7 / TH 1216 4.6 / 1748 0.6
9	0525 0.7 / 1209 4.7 / TH 1748 0.5	**24**	0039 4.7 / 0604 0.7 / F 1249 4.6 / 1820 0.7
10	0036 4.8 / 0604 0.6 / F 1250 4.7 / 1827 0.5	**25**	0109 4.6 / 0634 0.8 / SA 1321 4.5 / 1849 0.8
11	0117 4.8 / 0644 0.6 / SA 1332 4.7 / 1907 0.5	**26**	0139 4.6 / 0702 0.9 / SU 1354 4.4 / 1917 1.0
12	0157 4.8 / 0726 0.7 / SU 1414 4.7 / 1948 0.7	**27**	0209 4.5 / 0730 1.1 / M 1427 4.3 / 1944 1.2
13	0239 4.7 / 0810 0.9 / M 1459 4.5 / 2033 0.9	**28**	0241 4.3 / 0759 1.3 / TU 1502 4.1 / 2016 1.5
14	0324 4.5 / 0859 1.1 / TU 1550 4.3 / ☽ 2126 1.3	**29**	0316 4.1 / 0835 1.6 / W 1543 3.9 / 2057 1.8
15	0418 4.2 / 1001 1.5 / W 1652 4.0 / 2234 1.6		

MARCH

Day	Time m	Day	Time m
1	0359 3.9 / 0923 1.8 / TH 1638 3.7 / ☽ 2157 2.1	**16**	0507 3.9 / 1105 1.7 / F 1809 3.9 / 2350 1.8
2	0502 3.7 / 1042 2.1 / F 1756 3.6 / 2347 2.2	**17**	0641 3.8 / 1237 1.7 / SA 1940 4.0
3	0625 3.6 / 1239 2.0 / SA 1924 3.7	**18**	0118 1.7 / 0806 3.9 / SU 1353 1.3 / 2049 4.2
4	0119 2.0 / 0748 3.8 / SU 1349 1.7 / 2035 4.0	**19**	0225 1.5 / 0909 4.2 / M 1448 1.2 / 2142 4.4
5	0217 1.7 / 0851 4.0 / M 1439 1.3 / 2127 4.2	**20**	0314 1.2 / 0953 4.5 / TU 1532 1.0 / 2226 4.6
6	0302 1.3 / 0940 4.3 / TU 1523 1.0 / 2211 4.5	**21**	0354 1.0 / 1039 4.5 / W 1611 0.8 / 2304 4.6
7	0344 1.0 / 1023 4.5 / W 1605 0.7 / 2252 4.6	**22**	0431 0.8 / 1117 4.5 / TH 1646 0.7 / ● 2338 4.6
8	0424 0.7 / 1106 4.6 / TH 1645 0.5 / ○ 2333 4.8	**23**	0505 0.7 / 1150 4.5 / F 1720 0.7
9	0504 0.5 / 1149 4.8 / F 1726 0.4	**24**	0008 4.6 / 0536 0.7 / SA 1222 4.5 / 1751 0.7
10	0014 4.9 / 0544 0.4 / SA 1233 4.8 / 1807 0.4	**25**	0038 4.6 / 0606 0.8 / SU 1254 4.5 / 1820 0.9
11	0056 4.9 / 0625 0.4 / SU 1316 4.8 / 1848 0.4	**26**	0107 4.5 / 0632 0.9 / M 1326 4.4 / 1847 1.0
12	0137 4.9 / 0708 0.5 / M 1400 4.8 / 1930 0.6	**27**	0137 4.5 / 0658 1.0 / TU 1400 4.4 / 1915 1.2
13	0219 4.7 / 0752 0.7 / TU 1447 4.6 / 2016 0.9	**28**	0208 4.3 / 0727 1.2 / W 1435 4.2 / 1946 1.4
14	0304 4.5 / 0841 1.0 / W 1538 4.3 / 2110 1.3	**29**	0241 4.1 / 0802 1.4 / TH 1514 4.0 / 2026 1.7
15	0357 4.2 / 0942 1.4 / TH 1643 4.0 / ☽ 2220 1.7	**30**	0321 3.9 / 0849 1.7 / F 1606 3.8 / ☽ 2122 2.0
		31	0419 3.7 / 0955 1.9 / SA 1717 3.7 / 2250 2.1

APRIL

Day	Time m	Day	Time m
1	0538 3.6 / 1140 1.9 / SU 1840 3.8	**16**	0051 1.7 / 0740 3.9 / M 1321 1.5 / 2020 4.2
2	0034 2.0 / 0701 3.7 / M 1306 1.7 / 1952 4.0	**17**	0156 1.5 / 0842 4.1 / TU 1416 1.3 / 2112 4.4
3	0140 1.7 / 0810 4.0 / TU 1402 1.3 / 2049 4.3	**18**	0245 1.3 / 0930 4.2 / W 1500 1.1 / 2156 4.5
4	0229 1.3 / 0905 4.2 / W 1449 1.0 / 2137 4.5	**19**	0325 1.1 / 1012 4.3 / TH 1539 1.0 / 2233 4.5
5	0314 0.9 / 0953 4.5 / TH 1534 0.7 / 2222 4.7	**20**	0402 0.9 / 1049 4.4 / F 1615 0.9 / 2307 4.6
6	0357 0.6 / 1040 4.7 / F 1618 0.5 / ○ 2306 4.9	**21**	0436 0.9 / 1123 4.4 / SA 1650 0.9 / ● 2337 4.6
7	0440 0.4 / 1127 4.8 / SA 1701 0.4 / 2350 4.9	**22**	0509 0.8 / 1155 4.5 / SU 1724 0.9
8	0523 0.3 / 1213 4.8 / SU 1745 0.4	**23**	0007 4.5 / 0539 0.9 / M 1228 4.5 / 1754 1.0
9	0034 5.0 / 0607 0.3 / M 1301 4.9 / 1829 0.5	**24**	0039 4.5 / 0607 0.9 / TU 1302 4.5 / 1823 1.1
10	0119 4.9 / 0651 0.4 / TU 1348 4.8 / 1914 0.7	**25**	0111 4.4 / 0635 1.0 / W 1336 4.4 / 1852 1.2
11	0204 4.7 / 0738 0.7 / W 1437 4.6 / 2003 1.0	**26**	0143 4.3 / 0705 1.2 / TH 1413 4.3 / 1926 1.4
12	0251 4.5 / 0828 1.0 / TH 1531 4.4 / 2058 1.3	**27**	0217 4.2 / 0742 1.3 / F 1453 4.1 / 2007 1.6
13	0345 4.2 / 0928 1.3 / F 1635 4.1 / ☽ 2206 1.6	**28**	0257 4.0 / 0828 1.5 / SA 1542 4.0 / 2100 1.8
14	0453 3.9 / 1044 1.6 / SA 1755 4.0 / 2328 1.8	**29**	0350 3.9 / 0928 1.7 / SU 1645 3.9 / ☽ 2211 1.9
15	0620 3.8 / 1208 1.6 / SU 1915 4.1	**30**	0459 3.8 / 1047 1.7 / M 1757 3.9 / 2335 1.9

TIDES

Chart Datum: 2·73 metres below Ordnance Datum (Newlyn)
HAT is 5·1 metres above Chart Datum

PORTSMOUTH

LAT 50°48'N   LONG 1°07'W

TIMES AND HEIGHTS OF HIGH AND LOW WATERS

2012

TIME ZONE (UT)
For Summer Time add ONE hour in **non-shaded areas**

Dates in amber are **SPRINGS**
Dates in yellow are **NEAPS**

MAY

Time	m		Time	m
1 TU 0615	3.8	**16** W	0112	1.7
1209	1.6		0801	3.9
1908	4.1		1332	1.5
			2032	4.2
2 W 0049	1.6	**17** TH	0205	1.5
0726	4.0		0854	4.0
1316	1.3		1421	1.4
2008	4.3		2118	4.3
3 TH 0149	1.3	**18** F	0250	1.3
0827	4.2		0939	4.2
1411	1.2		1503	1.3
2102	4.5		2158	4.4
4 F 0240	1.0	**19** SA	0329	1.2
0922	4.5		1018	4.3
1501	0.8		1543	1.2
2152	4.7		2234	4.4
5 SA 0329	0.7	**20** SU	0406	1.1
1015	4.7		1055	4.3
1550	0.6		1621	1.1
2241	4.9		● 2308	4.5
6 SU 0417	0.5	**21** M	0442	1.0
1106	4.8		1129	4.4
1638	0.5		1658	1.1
○ 2329	5.0		2341	4.5
7 M 0505	0.4	**22** TU	0516	1.0
1157	4.9		1204	4.5
1726	0.5		1732	1.1
8 TU 0017	5.0	**23** W	0015	4.5
0551	0.4		0547	1.0
1247	4.9		1241	4.5
1813	0.6		1803	1.2
9 W 0104	4.9	**24** TH	0049	4.4
0639	0.5		0618	1.0
1337	4.8		1317	4.4
1901	0.7		1836	1.2
10 TH 0151	4.7	**25** F	0123	4.4
0727	0.7		0651	1.1
1428	4.7		1355	4.4
1951	1.0		1911	1.3
11 F 0240	4.5	**26** SA	0159	4.3
0816	0.9		0729	1.2
1522	4.5		1435	4.3
2044	1.3		1953	1.4
12 SA 0333	4.2	**27** SU	0240	4.2
0911	1.2		0811	1.3
1620	4.3		1521	4.2
◐ 2144	1.5		2042	1.6
13 SU 0433	4.0	**28** M	0328	4.1
1014	1.5		0907	1.4
1726	4.1		1616	4.1
2253	1.7		◐ 2141	1.6
14 M 0544	3.9	**29** TU	0427	4.0
1124	1.6		1011	1.5
1835	4.1		1718	4.1
			2250	1.7
15 TU 0006	1.7	**30** W	0535	4.0
0657	3.9		1121	1.5
1234	1.6		1825	4.2
1938	4.2			
		31 TH	0001	1.5
			0645	4.1
			1231	1.4
			1930	4.3

JUNE

Time	m		Time	m
1 F 0109	1.3	**16** SA	0211	1.6
0753	4.2		0903	4.0
1335	1.2		1428	1.6
2030	4.5		2121	4.2
2 SA 0210	1.1	**17** SU	0257	1.4
0856	4.4		0949	4.1
1433	1.0		1513	1.5
2127	4.7		2203	4.3
3 SU 0306	0.9	**18** M	0339	1.3
0954	4.6		1029	4.3
1528	0.8		1555	1.3
2220	4.8		2241	4.4
4 M 0400	0.7	**19** TU	0419	1.1
1050	4.7		1108	4.4
1621	0.7		1635	1.2
○ 2312	4.9		● 2318	4.5
5 TU 0451	0.5	**20** W	0456	1.0
1144	4.8		1145	4.5
1712	0.7		1712	1.2
			2354	4.5
6 W 0002	4.9	**21** TH	0531	1.0
0540	0.5		1222	4.5
1236	4.9		1747	1.1
1801	0.7			
7 TH 0051	4.8	**22** F	0030	4.5
0628	0.5		0605	1.0
1327	4.8		1300	4.5
1849	0.8		1822	1.1
8 F 0139	4.7	**23** SA	0106	4.4
0715	0.7		0640	1.0
1416	4.8		1338	4.5
1936	0.9		1858	1.2
9 SA 0227	4.5	**24** SU	0144	4.4
0801	0.9		0717	1.0
1505	4.6		1418	4.5
2024	1.2		1939	1.2
10 SU 0314	4.3	**25** M	0224	4.4
0847	1.1		0759	1.1
1554	4.4		1500	4.4
2114	1.4		2024	1.3
11 M 0403	4.1	**26** TU	0309	4.3
0937	1.3		0847	1.2
1645	4.3		1548	4.4
◐ 2209	1.6		2116	1.4
12 TU 0456	3.9	**27** W	0401	4.2
1033	1.6		0942	1.3
1740	4.1		1643	4.3
2312	1.8		◐ 2216	1.5
13 W 0557	3.8	**28** TH	0502	4.1
1135	1.7		1045	1.4
1840	4.0		1747	4.3
			2325	1.5
14 TH 0017	1.8	**29** F	0613	4.1
0704	3.8		1155	1.4
1239	1.8		1857	4.3
1939	4.1			
15 F 0119	1.7	**30** SA	0039	1.4
0808	3.9		0728	4.2
1337	1.7		1308	1.4
2034	4.1		2005	4.4

JULY

Time	m		Time	m
1 SU 0151	1.3	**16** M	0229	1.6
0839	4.3		0922	4.1
1416	1.2		1448	1.7
2108	4.6		2135	4.2
2 M 0254	1.0	**17** TU	0315	1.4
0943	4.5		1008	4.3
1516	1.1		1533	1.4
2205	4.7		2217	4.4
3 TU 0350	0.8	**18** W	0357	1.2
1041	4.7		1048	4.4
1611	0.9		1614	1.3
○ 2259	4.8		2256	4.4
4 W 0442	0.6	**19** TH	0436	1.0
1135	4.8		1126	4.5
1701	0.8		1652	1.1
2349	4.8		● 2334	4.5
5 TH 0530	0.5	**20** F	0513	0.9
1225	4.9		1204	4.6
1749	0.7		1729	1.0
6 F 0037	4.8	**21** SA	0011	4.5
0615	0.5		0549	0.8
1313	4.9		1242	4.6
1834	0.8		1805	1.0
7 SA 0127	4.7	**22** SU	0049	4.6
0657	0.6		0625	0.8
1357	4.8		1319	4.7
1916	0.9		1842	0.9
8 SU 0205	4.6	**23** M	0127	4.6
0737	0.8		0702	0.8
1438	4.7		1358	4.7
1958	1.1		1922	1.0
9 M 0246	4.4	**24** TU	0207	4.5
0816	1.0		0742	0.9
1517	4.5		1438	4.6
2039	1.3		2005	1.0
10 TU 0326	4.2	**25** W	0250	4.4
0856	1.3		0826	1.0
1557	4.3		1522	4.5
2123	1.5		2053	1.2
11 W 0408	4.0	**26** TH	0338	4.3
0940	1.5		0916	1.2
1640	4.1		1613	4.4
◐ 2214	1.7		◐ 2150	1.4
12 TH 0457	3.8	**27** F	0436	4.2
1035	1.8		1017	1.5
1731	4.0		1714	4.2
2318	1.9		2300	1.6
13 F 0558	3.7	**28** SA	0549	4.0
1143	2.0		1133	1.6
1834	3.9		1830	4.2
14 SA 0029	1.9	**29** SU	0022	1.6
0713	3.7		0714	4.0
1255	2.0		1255	1.6
1943	4.0		1948	4.3
15 SU 0135	1.8	**30** M	0142	1.4
0826	3.9		0833	4.2
1357	1.9		1409	1.5
2045	4.1		2058	4.4
		31 TU	0247	1.2
			0939	4.4
			1510	1.2
			2156	4.6

AUGUST

Time	m		Time	m
1 W 0342	0.9	**16** TH	0334	1.1
1034	4.7		1025	4.4
1602	1.0		1552	1.2
2248	4.7		2233	4.5
2 TH 0430	0.7	**17** F	0413	0.9
1124	4.8		1103	4.6
1649	0.8		1630	1.0
○ 2335	4.8		● 2311	4.6
3 F 0515	0.6	**18** SA	0451	0.8
1209	4.9		1141	4.7
1733	0.8		1707	0.9
			2349	4.6
4 SA 0019	4.7	**19** SU	0528	0.7
0555	0.5		1218	4.7
1252	4.8		1745	0.8
1813	0.8			
5 SU 0100	4.7	**20** M	0028	4.7
0633	0.6		0605	0.6
1330	4.8		1256	4.8
1851	0.8		1822	0.7
6 M 0137	4.6	**21** TU	0108	4.7
0708	0.8		0643	0.6
1404	4.7		1335	4.8
1926	1.0		1902	0.8
7 TU 0213	4.5	**22** W	0149	4.7
0741	1.0		0722	0.6
1437	4.5		1415	4.7
2000	1.2		1944	0.9
8 W 0248	4.3	**23** TH	0232	4.6
0814	1.2		0805	1.0
1511	4.4		1458	4.6
2035	1.4		2032	1.1
9 TH 0325	4.1	**24** F	0320	4.4
0850	1.5		0856	1.3
1549	4.2		1548	4.4
◐ 2116	1.7		◐ 2128	1.4
10 F 0409	3.9	**25** SA	0419	4.1
0936	1.9		0959	1.6
1634	4.0		1641	4.2
2213	1.9		2243	1.7
11 SA 0506	3.7	**26** SU	0537	4.0
1044	2.1		1121	1.8
1735	3.8		1813	4.0
2338	2.1			
12 SU 0622	3.7	**27** M	0013	1.7
1216	2.2		0710	4.0
1853	3.8		1251	1.8
			1941	4.1
13 M 0101	2.0	**28** TU	0136	1.5
0751	3.8		0831	4.2
1331	2.0		1405	1.6
2011	3.9		2052	4.3
14 TU 0203	1.7	**29** W	0239	1.2
0857	4.0		0932	4.5
1426	1.8		1502	1.3
2108	4.1		2148	4.5
15 W 0251	1.4	**30** TH	0330	0.9
0944	4.3		1023	4.9
1511	1.5		1550	1.0
2153	4.3		2235	4.7
		31 F	0413	0.7
			1107	4.8
			1632	0.8
			○ 2317	4.7

Chart Datum: 2·73 metres below Ordnance Datum (Newlyn)
HAT is 5·1 metres above Chart Datum

PORTSMOUTH

LAT 50°48'N   LONG 1°07'W

TIMES AND HEIGHTS OF HIGH AND LOW WATERS

Dates in amber are **SPRINGS**
Dates in yellow are **NEAPS**

2012

SEPTEMBER

Day	Time m	Time m	Time m	Time m
1 SA	0454 0.6	1147 4.8	1711 0.8	2356 4.7
2 SU	0531 0.6	1224 4.8	1748 0.8	
3 M	0032 4.7	0605 0.7	1257 4.8	1821 0.8
4 TU	0106 4.6	0636 0.8	1328 4.7	1852 1.0
5 W	0139 4.5	0706 1.0	1359 4.6	1921 1.2
6 TH	0213 4.4	0735 1.3	1431 4.4	1952 1.4
7 F	0249 4.2	0807 1.6	1506 4.2	2028 1.6
8 SA	0330 4.0	0848 1.9	1548 4.0	◑ 2115 1.9
9 SU	0423 3.8	0948 2.2	1646 3.8	2235 2.1
10 M	0538 3.7	1135 2.3	1805 3.7	
11 TU	0024 2.1	0703 3.8	1302 2.2	1931 3.8
12 W	0133 1.8	0822 4.0	1359 1.9	2036 4.1
13 TH	0223 1.5	0913 4.3	1444 1.5	2123 4.3
14 F	0305 1.2	0954 4.5	1524 1.2	2205 4.5
15 SA	0345 0.9	1033 4.7	1602 0.9	2244 4.7
16 SU	0423 0.7	1112 4.8	1641 0.7	● 2324 4.8
17 M	0502 0.6	1151 4.9	1720 0.6	
18 TU	0006 4.9	0541 0.5	1232 4.9	1800 0.6
19 W	0048 4.9	0621 0.6	1312 4.9	1841 0.7
20 TH	0132 4.8	0703 0.7	1354 4.8	1925 0.8
21 F	0217 4.7	0748 1.0	1439 4.6	2014 1.1
22 SA	0308 4.4	0841 1.3	1530 4.4	◑ 2113 1.4
23 SU	0409 4.2	0948 1.7	1635 4.1	2230 1.7
24 M	0531 4.0	1113 1.9	1803 4.0	
25 TU	0000 1.8	0704 4.1	1242 1.8	1933 4.1
26 W	0122 1.6	0819 4.3	1353 1.6	2040 4.3
27 TH	0222 1.3	0916 4.6	1446 1.3	2132 4.5
28 F	0309 1.1	1002 4.7	1530 1.1	2216 4.6
29 SA	0350 0.9	1043 4.8	1609 0.9	2255 4.7
30 SU	0427 0.8	1120 4.8	1645 0.8	○ 2331 4.7

OCTOBER

Day	Time m	Time m	Time m	Time m
1 M	0502 0.8	1153 4.8	1719 0.8	
2 TU	0004 4.7	0535 0.8	1224 4.7	1750 0.9
3 W	0036 4.6	0606 0.9	1254 4.7	1820 1.0
4 TH	0109 4.6	0635 1.1	1324 4.6	1848 1.2
5 F	0142 4.5	0703 1.3	1357 4.4	1917 1.4
6 SA	0218 4.3	0734 1.6	1431 4.2	1951 1.6
7 SU	0258 4.1	0813 1.9	1510 4.0	2036 1.9
8 M	0348 3.9	0907 2.1	1604 3.8	◑ 2140 2.1
9 TU	0456 3.8	1036 2.3	1717 3.7	2325 2.1
10 W	0619 3.8	1217 2.2	1841 3.8	
11 TH	0048 1.9	0735 4.0	1321 1.9	1952 4.0
12 F	0144 1.6	0831 4.3	1408 1.5	2046 4.3
13 SA	0230 1.3	0917 4.5	1451 1.2	2131 4.5
14 SU	0311 1.0	1000 4.7	1532 0.9	2215 4.7
15 M	0353 0.7	1042 4.9	1613 0.7	● 2259 4.9
16 TU	0435 0.6	1125 5.0	1656 0.6	2344 5.0
17 W	0517 0.6	1208 5.0	1739 0.6	
18 TH	0030 5.0	0601 0.6	1252 5.0	1824 0.6
19 F	0117 4.9	0647 0.8	1337 4.8	1911 0.8
20 SA	0206 4.8	0736 1.0	1425 4.6	2002 1.1
21 SU	0259 4.5	0831 1.4	1518 4.4	2100 1.4
22 M	0402 4.3	0937 1.7	1624 4.1	◑ 2212 1.6
23 TU	0520 4.2	1055 1.9	1747 4.0	2334 1.7
24 W	0643 4.2	1217 1.8	1911 4.1	
25 TH	0052 1.7	0753 4.3	1327 1.7	2016 4.2
26 F	0153 1.5	0848 4.5	1420 1.4	2108 4.4
27 SA	0240 1.3	0934 4.7	1503 1.2	2152 4.5
28 SU	0320 1.1	1015 4.7	1541 1.1	2231 4.6
29 M	0358 1.0	1050 4.7	1617 1.0	○ 2305 4.6
30 TU	0433 1.0	1122 4.7	1651 1.0	2338 4.6
31 W	0507 1.0	1153 4.7	1724 1.0	

NOVEMBER

Day	Time m	Time m	Time m	Time m
1 TH	0010 4.6	0539 1.1	1224 4.6	1754 1.1
2 F	0043 4.6	0609 1.2	1256 4.6	1823 1.2
3 SA	0118 4.5	0639 1.4	1329 4.4	1852 1.3
4 SU	0154 4.4	0710 1.6	1403 4.3	1927 1.5
5 M	0233 4.3	0749 1.8	1441 4.1	2009 1.7
6 TU	0319 4.1	0838 2.0	1529 4.0	2104 1.9
7 W	0418 4.0	0945 2.1	1632 3.8	◐ 2219 2.0
8 TH	0529 4.0	1109 2.1	1747 3.9	2342 1.9
9 F	0642 4.1	1225 1.9	1901 4.0	
10 SA	0051 1.7	0745 4.3	1324 1.6	2003 4.3
11 SU	0147 1.4	0838 4.6	1415 1.3	2058 4.5
12 M	0236 1.1	0927 4.8	1502 1.0	2148 4.7
13 TU	0323 0.9	1015 4.9	1549 0.8	● 2238 4.9
14 W	0410 0.7	1102 5.0	1636 0.6	2327 5.0
15 TH	0458 0.7	1149 5.1	1724 0.6	
16 F	0017 5.0	0545 0.7	1237 5.0	1811 0.6
17 SA	0107 5.0	0634 0.8	1325 4.9	1900 0.7
18 SU	0158 4.8	0725 1.0	1414 4.7	1951 1.0
19 M	0251 4.7	0818 1.3	1507 4.4	2045 1.2
20 TU	0350 4.5	0918 1.5	1606 4.2	◐ 2146 1.5
21 W	0455 4.3	1025 1.8	1715 4.0	2254 1.7
22 TH	0606 4.2	1138 1.8	1830 4.0	
23 F	0005 1.7	0712 4.3	1247 1.8	1938 4.1
24 SA	0110 1.7	0811 4.4	1345 1.7	2036 4.2
25 SU	0203 1.6	0901 4.5	1432 1.5	2124 4.3
26 M	0248 1.4	0943 4.5	1513 1.3	2205 4.4
27 TU	0328 1.3	1020 4.6	1551 1.2	2242 4.5
28 W	0406 1.2	1054 4.6	1628 1.1	○ 2315 4.5
29 TH	0443 1.2	1126 4.6	1703 1.1	2349 4.6
30 F	0518 1.2	1159 4.6	1736 1.1	

DECEMBER

Day	Time m	Time m	Time m	Time m
1 SA	0023 4.6	0550 1.3	1233 4.6	1806 1.1
2 SU	0058 4.6	0621 1.4	1307 4.5	1837 1.2
3 M	0135 4.5	0653 1.5	1342 4.4	1910 1.3
4 TU	0213 4.4	0730 1.6	1419 4.3	1950 1.4
5 W	0255 4.3	0814 1.7	1502 4.1	2037 1.6
6 TH	0345 4.2	0908 1.8	1555 4.0	◐ 2135 1.7
7 F	0444 4.2	1014 1.9	1659 4.0	2244 1.7
8 SA	0551 4.2	1127 1.8	1811 4.0	2356 1.6
9 SU	0659 4.3	1238 1.6	1923 4.1	
10 M	0104 1.5	0802 4.5	1342 1.4	2028 4.4
11 TU	0205 1.3	0859 4.7	1439 1.1	2127 4.6
12 W	0301 1.0	0953 4.9	1532 0.9	2222 4.8
13 TH	0354 0.9	1044 5.0	1624 0.7	● 2315 4.9
14 F	0445 0.8	1134 5.0	1714 0.6	
15 SA	0007 5.0	0534 0.7	1224 5.0	1802 0.5
16 SU	0058 5.0	0623 0.8	1313 4.9	1850 0.6
17 M	0148 4.9	0712 0.9	1402 4.7	1937 0.8
18 TU	0237 4.8	0800 1.1	1450 4.5	2024 1.0
19 W	0327 4.6	0851 1.4	1539 4.3	2113 1.3
20 TH	0418 4.4	0945 1.6	1632 4.1	◐ 2207 1.5
21 F	0513 4.2	1047 1.8	1732 3.9	2308 1.8
22 SA	0615 4.1	1154 1.9	1841 3.8	
23 SU	0015 1.9	0719 4.1	1301 1.9	1952 3.9
24 M	0120 1.8	0819 4.2	1358 1.7	2052 4.0
25 TU	0214 1.7	0910 4.3	1446 1.6	2140 4.2
26 W	0301 1.6	0952 4.4	1528 1.4	2221 4.3
27 TH	0343 1.4	1030 4.5	1607 1.2	2257 4.4
28 F	0423 1.3	1105 4.5	1645 1.1	○ 2332 4.5
29 SA	0459 1.2	1140 4.6	1720 1.0	
30 SU	0006 4.5	0533 1.2	1215 4.5	1753 1.0
31 M	0042 4.6	0606 1.2	1250 4.5	1824 1.0

Chart Datum: 2·73 metres below Ordnance Datum (Newlyn)
HAT is 5·1 metres above Chart Datum

TIDES

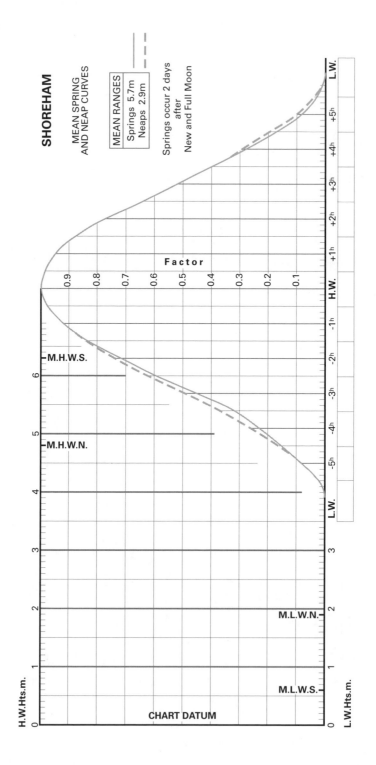

SHOREHAM

MEAN SPRING
AND NEAP CURVES

MEAN RANGES	
Springs	5.7m
Neaps	2.9m

Springs occur 2 days
after
New and Full Moon

Factor

0.9 0.8 0.7 0.6 0.5 0.4 0.3 0.2 0.1

M.H.W.S.

M.H.W.N.

M.L.W.N.

M.L.W.S.

CHART DATUM

H.W.Hts.m.

L.W.Hts.m.

L.W. +5ʰ +4ʰ +3ʰ +2ʰ +1ʰ H.W. -1ʰ -2ʰ -3ʰ -4ʰ -5ʰ L.W.

TIME ZONE (UT)
For Summer Time add ONE hour in **non-shaded areas**

SHOREHAM

LAT 50°50′N LONG 0°15′W

TIMES AND HEIGHTS OF HIGH AND LOW WATERS

Dates in amber are **SPRINGS**
Dates in yellow are **NEAPS**

2012

JANUARY

Date	Day	Time	m	Time	m	Time	m	Time	m
1	SU	0403	5.4	1009	1.7	1625	5.0	◐ 2231	1.8
2	M	0454	5.1	1102	1.9	1722	4.8	2328	2.0
3	TU	0553	4.9	1207	2.1	1825	4.7		
4	W	0037	2.1	0656	4.9	1330	2.0	1930	4.8
5	TH	0200	2.0	0758	5.0	1437	1.8	2032	5.0
6	F	0300	1.8	0853	5.3	1527	1.5	2124	5.3
7	SA	0347	1.6	0940	5.6	1609	1.3	2209	5.6
8	SU	0427	1.3	1022	5.8	1649	1.1	2250	5.9
9	M	0505	1.2	1101	6.0	1727	0.9	○ 2328	6.1
10	TU	0542	1.0	1139	6.1	1804	0.8		
11	W	0006	6.2	0618	0.9	1217	6.2	1840	0.7
12	TH	0044	6.2	0655	0.9	1255	6.2	1917	0.7
13	F	0122	6.3	0734	0.9	1335	6.2	1957	0.7
14	SA	0202	6.2	0817	0.9	1417	6.1	2039	0.9
15	SU	0246	6.1	0903	1.0	1504	5.9	2127	1.0
16	M	0335	5.8	0957	1.3	1557	5.6	◑ 2223	1.3
17	TU	0433	5.6	1102	1.5	1703	5.3	2333	1.6
18	W	0546	5.3	1220	1.6	1827	5.1		
19	TH	0056	1.7	0709	5.3	1339	1.6	1954	5.2
20	F	0212	1.6	0827	5.5	1448	1.3	2107	5.5
21	SA	0315	1.3	0931	5.8	1545	1.0	2206	5.8
22	SU	0409	1.0	1025	6.0	1635	0.8	2256	6.1
23	M	0457	0.8	1112	6.2	1721	0.6	● 2342	6.3
24	TU	0541	0.7	1156	6.3	1804	0.5		
25	W	0023	6.4	0622	0.7	1237	6.3	1843	0.6
26	TH	0102	6.4	0700	0.8	1314	6.2	1920	0.7
27	F	0137	6.2	0735	0.9	1348	6.0	1954	0.8
28	SA	0209	6.1	0809	1.0	1418	5.8	2027	1.0
29	SU	0237	5.8	0844	1.2	1448	5.5	2103	1.3
30	M	0305	5.5	0922	1.5	1522	5.2	2143	1.6
31	TU	0340	5.2	1008	1.8	1609	4.9	◐ 2231	1.9

FEBRUARY

Date	Day	Time	m	Time	m	Time	m	Time	m
1	W	0434	4.9	1105	2.0	1725	4.6	2335	2.2
2	TH	0601	4.7	1217	2.2	1844	4.6		
3	F	0057	2.3	0715	4.7	1351	2.0	1953	4.8
4	SA	0227	2.0	0819	5.0	1459	1.7	2054	5.1
5	SU	0322	1.7	0914	5.4	1546	1.3	2145	5.5
6	M	0405	1.3	0959	5.7	1626	1.0	2228	5.9
7	TU	0444	1.0	1041	6.0	1705	0.8	○ 2309	6.1
8	W	0522	0.8	1122	6.2	1743	0.6	2348	6.3
9	TH	0600	0.7	1201	6.4	1821	0.5		
10	F	0027	6.5	0638	0.6	1241	6.4	1900	0.4
11	SA	0106	6.5	0718	0.5	1320	6.4	1940	0.4
12	SU	0145	6.5	0800	0.6	1401	6.3	2022	0.6
13	M	0226	6.3	0844	0.8	1445	6.0	2107	0.9
14	TU	0312	6.0	0934	1.1	1536	5.6	◑ 2200	1.2
15	W	0407	5.5	1035	1.4	1640	5.2	2309	1.6
16	TH	0519	5.1	1157	1.7	1808	4.9		
17	F	0040	1.8	0651	5.0	1327	1.7	1946	4.9
18	SA	0203	1.7	0820	5.2	1438	1.4	2102	5.3
19	SU	0307	1.4	0925	5.5	1535	1.1	2158	5.7
20	M	0358	1.1	1016	5.9	1622	0.8	2244	6.1
21	TU	0443	0.8	1100	6.1	1704	0.6	● 2325	6.3
22	W	0523	0.7	1141	6.2	1743	0.5		
23	TH	0004	6.4	0600	0.6	1218	6.2	1819	0.5
24	F	0039	6.3	0635	0.7	1251	6.2	1852	0.6
25	SA	0110	6.2	0707	0.7	1319	6.0	1924	0.7
26	SU	0134	6.1	0737	0.9	1343	5.9	1955	0.9
27	M	0154	5.9	0809	1.0	1408	5.7	2026	1.1
28	TU	0219	5.7	0842	1.3	1438	5.4	2100	1.4
29	W	0252	5.3	0919	1.6	1516	5.1	2141	1.8

MARCH

Date	Day	Time	m	Time	m	Time	m	Time	m
1	TH	0335	5.0	1009	1.9	1610	4.7	◐ 2241	2.1
2	F	0439	4.6	1122	2.2	1758	4.5		
3	SA	0007	2.3	0634	4.5	1254	2.1	1917	4.6
4	SU	0144	2.1	0746	4.8	1422	1.8	2022	5.0
5	M	0252	1.7	0845	5.2	1515	1.4	2116	5.5
6	TU	0337	1.3	0934	5.7	1558	1.0	2202	5.9
7	W	0417	0.9	1018	6.1	1637	0.7	2245	6.3
8	TH	0456	0.6	1101	6.3	1717	0.4	○ 2326	6.5
9	F	0536	0.4	1142	6.5	1757	0.3		
10	SA	0006	6.6	0617	0.3	1224	6.6	1838	0.2
11	SU	0047	6.7	0659	0.3	1305	6.6	1921	0.3
12	M	0127	6.6	0742	0.4	1347	6.4	2005	0.5
13	TU	0208	6.3	0828	0.6	1431	6.1	2052	0.8
14	W	0254	5.9	0917	1.0	1523	5.6	2145	1.2
15	TH	0350	5.5	1017	1.4	1629	5.2	◑ 2255	1.7
16	F	0502	5.0	1140	1.7	1755	4.8		
17	SA	0028	1.9	0636	4.8	1313	1.7	1934	4.9
18	SU	0150	1.7	0808	5.0	1422	1.5	2047	5.3
19	M	0251	1.4	0910	5.4	1516	1.1	2139	5.7
20	TU	0340	1.1	0958	5.7	1601	0.9	2222	6.0
21	W	0422	0.9	1040	6.0	1641	0.7	2302	6.2
22	TH	0500	0.7	1119	6.1	1717	0.6	● 2338	6.2
23	F	0535	0.7	1154	6.1	1752	0.6		
24	SA	0011	6.2	0608	0.7	1225	6.1	1824	0.7
25	SU	0038	6.1	0639	0.7	1250	6.0	1855	0.8
26	M	0059	6.0	0709	0.8	1314	5.9	1926	0.9
27	TU	0121	5.9	0740	0.9	1340	5.8	1956	1.1
28	W	0148	5.7	0810	1.2	1410	5.5	2028	1.4
29	TH	0220	5.4	0844	1.4	1447	5.2	2107	1.7
30	F	0301	5.1	0930	1.7	1536	4.9	◐ 2202	2.0
31	SA	0358	4.7	1035	2.0	1702	4.6	2322	2.2

APRIL

Date	Day	Time	m	Time	m	Time	m	Time	m
1	SU	0547	4.5	1202	2.0	1840	4.7		
2	M	0054	2.1	0709	4.7	1332	1.8	1947	5.1
3	TU	0210	1.7	0811	5.2	1435	1.4	2043	5.5
4	W	0302	1.2	0904	5.6	1523	1.0	2132	6.0
5	TH	0346	0.8	0951	6.0	1606	0.6	2217	6.3
6	F	0428	0.5	1037	6.3	1649	0.4	○ 2301	6.6
7	SA	0511	0.3	1121	6.5	1733	0.3	2344	6.7
8	SU	0555	0.2	1206	6.6	1818	0.2		
9	M	0027	6.7	0640	0.2	1250	6.6	1903	0.3
10	TU	0110	6.6	0726	0.3	1335	6.4	1950	0.5
11	W	0154	6.3	0814	0.6	1423	6.1	2039	0.8
12	TH	0242	5.9	0905	0.9	1517	5.7	2134	1.3
13	F	0339	5.4	1004	1.3	1620	5.3	◑ 2242	1.6
14	SA	0448	5.0	1123	1.6	1736	5.0		
15	SU	0009	1.8	0612	4.8	1249	1.7	1905	5.0
16	M	0126	1.7	0740	4.9	1355	1.5	2016	5.3
17	TU	0225	1.5	0842	5.2	1448	1.3	2109	5.6
18	W	0313	1.2	0931	5.5	1533	1.1	2153	5.8
19	TH	0355	1.0	1013	5.7	1612	0.9	2232	6.0
20	F	0432	0.9	1051	5.9	1649	0.9	2308	6.0
21	SA	0508	0.8	1126	5.9	1724	0.8	● 2340	6.0
22	SU	0541	0.8	1156	5.9	1758	0.9		
23	M	0006	6.0	0614	0.8	1224	5.9	1830	0.9
24	TU	0030	5.9	0646	0.9	1250	5.9	1902	1.0
25	W	0056	5.8	0717	1.0	1319	5.8	1933	1.1
26	TH	0125	5.7	0748	1.1	1351	5.6	2006	1.3
27	F	0200	5.5	0823	1.3	1429	5.4	2046	1.6
28	SA	0241	5.2	0907	1.5	1517	5.1	2138	1.8
29	SU	0334	4.9	1005	1.7	1622	4.9	◐ 2246	1.9
30	M	0450	4.8	1118	1.8	1753	4.9		

Chart Datum: 3·27 metres below Ordnance Datum (Newlyn)
HAT is 6·9 metres above Chart Datum

TIME ZONE (UT)
For Summer Time add ONE hour in **non-shaded areas**

SHOREHAM
LAT 50°50'N   LONG 0°15'W

Dates in amber are **SPRINGS**
Dates in yellow are **NEAPS**

2012

TIMES AND HEIGHTS OF HIGH AND LOW WATERS

MAY

Day	Time m	Time m	Time m	Time m
1 TU	0007 1.9 / 0626 4.9 / 1240 1.7 / 1906 5.3		16 W	0149 1.6 / 0801 5.0 / 1411 1.5 / 2028 5.3
2 W	0122 1.6 / 0734 5.2 / 1349 1.4 / 2006 5.6		17 TH	0239 1.4 / 0855 5.2 / 1459 1.3 / 2116 5.5
3 TH	0222 1.2 / 0831 5.6 / 1445 1.0 / 2059 6.0		18 F	0324 1.2 / 0940 5.4 / 1542 1.2 / 2158 5.7
4 F	0313 0.8 / 0923 6.0 / 1535 0.7 / 2148 6.3		19 SA	0404 1.1 / 1020 5.6 / 1621 1.1 / 2235 5.8
5 SA	0401 0.5 / 1012 6.3 / 1623 0.5 / 2236 6.5		20 SU	0441 1.0 / 1056 5.7 / 1658 1.1 / 2307 5.8 ●
6 SU	0448 0.3 / 1101 6.5 / 1711 0.4 / 2323 6.6 ○		21 M	0517 0.9 / 1128 5.8 / 1734 1.0 / 2337 5.9
7 M	0536 0.2 / 1150 6.5 / 1759 0.3		22 TU	0552 0.9 / 1200 5.9 / 1809 1.0
8 TU	0010 6.6 / 0624 0.2 / 1239 6.5 / 1847 0.4		23 W	0006 5.9 / 0626 0.9 / 1231 5.9 / 1843 1.1
9 W	0057 6.5 / 0712 0.4 / 1327 6.4 / 1936 0.6		24 TH	0037 5.8 / 0700 1.0 / 1303 5.8 / 1916 1.1
10 TH	0144 6.2 / 0801 0.6 / 1417 6.2 / 2027 0.9		25 F	0110 5.7 / 0732 1.1 / 1337 5.7 / 1950 1.2
11 F	0234 5.9 / 0853 0.9 / 1509 5.9 / 2121 1.2		26 SA	0146 5.6 / 0807 1.2 / 1416 5.6 / 2030 1.4
12 SA	0328 5.5 / 0949 1.2 / 1605 5.5 / 2223 1.5 ◐		27 SU	0227 5.5 / 0850 1.3 / 1501 5.5 / 2118 1.5
13 SU	0427 5.2 / 1056 1.6 / 1706 5.3 / 2337 1.7		28 M	0317 5.3 / 0942 1.4 / 1556 5.3 / 2217 1.6 ◑
14 M	0535 4.9 / 1210 1.6 / 1817 5.1		29 TU	0417 5.1 / 1043 1.6 / 1703 5.3 / 2326 1.6
15 TU	0048 1.7 / 0652 4.9 / 1316 1.6 / 1929 5.2		30 W	0533 5.1 / 1155 1.5 / 1819 5.3
			31 TH	0039 1.5 / 0650 5.2 / 1308 1.4 / 1927 5.6

JUNE

Day	Time m	Time m	Time m	Time m
1 F	0146 1.2 / 0757 5.5 / 1413 1.1 / 2027 5.9		16 SA	0251 1.5 / 0900 5.1 / 1512 1.5 / 2118 5.4
2 SA	0245 0.9 / 0856 5.8 / 1510 0.9 / 2123 6.1		17 SU	0336 1.4 / 0946 5.4 / 1555 1.4 / 2159 5.6
3 SU	0339 0.7 / 0952 6.1 / 1603 0.7 / 2216 6.4		18 M	0417 1.2 / 1025 5.6 / 1635 1.2 / 2237 5.7
4 M	0430 0.5 / 1046 6.3 / 1655 0.5 / 2307 6.5 ○		19 TU	0455 1.1 / 1103 5.7 / 1713 1.1 / 2312 5.8 ●
5 TU	0521 0.4 / 1138 6.4 / 1745 0.5 / 2357 6.5		20 W	0533 1.0 / 1138 5.8 / 1751 1.1 / 2346 5.9
6 W	0611 0.3 / 1229 6.5 / 1835 0.5		21 TH	0609 0.9 / 1213 5.9 / 1827 1.1
7 TH	0046 6.4 / 0700 0.4 / 1318 6.4 / 1924 0.6		22 F	0021 5.9 / 0644 0.9 / 1248 5.9 / 1901 1.1
8 F	0134 6.2 / 0748 0.6 / 1406 6.3 / 2012 0.8		23 SA	0056 5.9 / 0718 0.9 / 1323 5.9 / 1936 1.1
9 SA	0222 6.0 / 0837 0.8 / 1453 6.0 / 2101 1.1		24 SU	0133 5.8 / 0753 1.0 / 1401 5.9 / 2014 1.1
10 SU	0309 5.7 / 0925 1.0 / 1540 5.8 / 2152 1.3		25 M	0213 5.8 / 0833 1.0 / 1444 5.8 / 2058 1.2
11 M	0359 5.4 / 1016 1.3 / 1630 5.5 / 2249 1.6 ◐		26 TU	0259 5.6 / 0920 1.1 / 1532 5.7 / 2150 1.3
12 TU	0453 5.1 / 1113 1.6 / 1724 5.2 / 2354 1.7		27 W	0351 5.5 / 1014 1.3 / 1628 5.6 / 2252 1.4 ◑
13 W	0551 4.9 / 1219 1.7 / 1822 5.1		28 TH	0453 5.3 / 1119 1.4 / 1735 5.4
14 TH	0101 1.8 / 0655 4.8 / 1326 1.8 / 1926 5.1		29 F	0004 1.4 / 0609 5.2 / 1235 1.4 / 1850 5.5
15 F	0200 1.7 / 0803 4.9 / 1422 1.7 / 2027 5.2		30 SA	0118 1.4 / 0728 5.3 / 1349 1.3 / 2002 5.6

JULY

Day	Time m	Time m	Time m	Time m
1 SU	0225 1.1 / 0839 5.6 / 1454 1.1 / 2106 5.9		16 M	0311 1.6 / 0911 5.2 / 1532 1.6 / 2127 5.4
2 M	0324 0.9 / 0941 5.9 / 1551 0.9 / 2204 6.1		17 TU	0355 1.3 / 0958 5.5 / 1614 1.4 / 2210 5.6
3 TU	0419 0.6 / 1038 6.1 / 1644 0.7 / 2258 6.3 ○		18 W	0434 1.1 / 1039 5.7 / 1653 1.2 / 2249 5.8
4 W	0510 0.5 / 1130 6.3 / 1734 0.6 / 2348 6.4		19 TH	0512 1.0 / 1117 5.9 / 1731 1.1 / 2327 6.0 ●
5 TH	0559 0.4 / 1219 6.5 / 1822 0.6		20 F	0549 0.8 / 1154 6.0 / 1807 0.9
6 F	0035 6.4 / 0645 0.4 / 1306 6.5 / 1907 0.6		21 SA	0003 6.0 / 0625 0.8 / 1230 6.1 / 1843 0.9
7 SA	0121 6.3 / 0730 0.5 / 1349 6.4 / 1952 0.8		22 SU	0040 6.1 / 0700 0.8 / 1306 6.2 / 1919 0.9
8 SU	0203 6.1 / 0813 0.7 / 1430 6.2 / 2034 0.9		23 M	0117 6.1 / 0736 0.7 / 1344 6.2 / 1957 0.9
9 M	0244 5.8 / 0853 0.9 / 1510 5.9 / 2114 1.2		24 TU	0156 6.0 / 0815 0.8 / 1424 6.1 / 2039 0.9
10 TU	0325 5.5 / 0932 1.2 / 1551 5.6 / 2156 1.5		25 W	0239 5.9 / 0859 0.9 / 1508 5.9 / 2127 1.1
11 W	0409 5.2 / 1015 1.5 / 1636 5.3 / 2243 1.7 ◐		26 TH	0327 5.7 / 0950 1.2 / 1600 5.7 / 2224 1.3 ◑
12 TH	0501 4.9 / 1106 1.8 / 1728 5.0 / 2341 1.9		27 F	0426 5.4 / 1052 1.4 / 1705 5.4 / 2336 1.5
13 F	0600 4.7 / 1209 2.0 / 1829 4.9		28 SA	0543 5.1 / 1212 1.6 / 1826 5.3
14 SA	0101 2.0 / 0704 4.7 / 1335 2.0 / 1933 4.9		29 SU	0058 1.6 / 0713 5.1 / 1335 1.6 / 1949 5.4
15 SU	0217 1.8 / 0812 4.9 / 1442 1.8 / 2035 5.1		30 M	0214 1.4 / 0833 5.4 / 1445 1.3 / 2100 5.7
			31 TU	0317 1.0 / 0937 5.8 / 1543 1.0 / 2159 6.0

AUGUST

Day	Time m	Time m	Time m	Time m
1 W	0410 0.8 / 1032 6.1 / 1634 0.8 / 2251 6.2		16 TH	0410 1.1 / 1013 5.8 / 1629 1.1 / 2226 5.9
2 TH	0458 0.6 / 1120 6.4 / 1720 0.6 / 2337 6.4 ○		17 F	0448 0.9 / 1052 6.1 / 1707 0.9 / 2305 6.1 ●
3 F	0543 0.5 / 1205 6.5 / 1804 0.6		18 SA	0525 0.7 / 1130 6.3 / 1744 0.8 / 2343 6.3
4 SA	0021 6.4 / 0625 0.5 / 1247 6.5 / 1846 0.6		19 SU	0602 0.6 / 1207 6.4 / 1820 0.7
5 SU	0102 6.3 / 0705 0.6 / 1325 6.4 / 1924 0.7		20 M	0020 6.3 / 0638 0.6 / 1245 6.4 / 1858 0.6
6 M	0138 6.1 / 0742 0.7 / 1400 6.2 / 2000 0.9		21 TU	0059 6.3 / 0716 0.6 / 1323 6.4 / 1937 0.7
7 TU	0212 5.9 / 0816 0.9 / 1433 6.0 / 2034 1.1		22 W	0138 6.2 / 0756 0.7 / 1403 6.3 / 2020 0.8
8 W	0245 5.6 / 0850 1.2 / 1505 5.7 / 2111 1.4		23 TH	0220 6.1 / 0840 0.9 / 1447 6.0 / 2107 1.0
9 TH	0320 5.3 / 0929 1.5 / 1540 5.3 / 2153 1.7 ◐		24 F	0308 5.8 / 0931 1.2 / 1538 5.7 / 2204 1.4 ◑
10 F	0405 5.0 / 1015 1.8 / 1629 5.0 / 2246 2.0		25 SA	0407 5.3 / 1035 1.6 / 1644 5.3 / 2318 1.7
11 SA	0510 4.7 / 1115 2.1 / 1740 4.7 / 2354 2.2		26 SU	0531 5.0 / 1159 1.8 / 1813 5.1
12 SU	0623 4.6 / 1232 2.2 / 1852 4.7		27 M	0048 1.7 / 0708 5.0 / 1328 1.8 / 1944 5.2
13 M	0130 2.1 / 0733 4.7 / 1411 2.1 / 2000 4.9		28 TU	0207 1.5 / 0830 5.3 / 1438 1.5 / 2056 5.5
14 TU	0243 1.8 / 0838 5.1 / 1508 1.7 / 2058 5.3		29 W	0308 1.1 / 0931 5.8 / 1533 1.1 / 2151 5.9
15 W	0330 1.4 / 0930 5.5 / 1551 1.4 / 2145 5.6		30 TH	0358 0.8 / 1020 6.1 / 1620 0.8 / 2238 6.2
			31 F	0441 0.6 / 1104 6.4 / 1702 0.7 / 2321 6.3 ○

Chart Datum: 3·27 metres below Ordnance Datum (Newlyn)
HAT is 6·9 metres above Chart Datum

SHOREHAM

LAT 50°50'N   LONG 0°15'W

TIMES AND HEIGHTS OF HIGH AND LOW WATERS

Dates in amber are **SPRINGS**
Dates in yellow are **NEAPS**

2012

SEPTEMBER

Day	Time m	Time m	Time m	Time m
1 SA	0522 0.5	1144 6.5	1742 0.6	
16 SU	0456 0.7	1103 6.4	1716 0.6	● 2320 6.5
2 SU	0000 6.4	0600 0.6	1222 6.5	1819 0.7
17 M	0534 0.5	1143 6.6	1755 0.5	2359 6.5
3 M	0037 6.3	0636 0.7	1256 6.4	1854 0.8
18 TU	0614 0.5	1222 6.6	1836 0.5	
4 TU	0109 6.1	0709 0.8	1327 6.2	1926 0.9
19 W	0039 6.5	0654 0.5	1302 6.6	1918 0.6
5 W	0137 6.0	0740 1.0	1352 6.0	1958 1.1
20 TH	0120 6.4	0738 0.6	1343 6.4	2003 0.7
6 TH	0203 5.7	0813 1.2	1415 5.7	2032 1.3
21 F	0204 6.2	0825 0.9	1429 6.1	2052 1.0
7 F	0231 5.5	0849 1.5	1445 5.4	2111 1.6
22 SA	0254 5.8	0918 1.3	1522 5.6	◑ 2150 1.4
8 SA	0308 5.1	0932 1.8	1526 5.0	◐ 2200 2.0
23 SU	0359 5.3	1024 1.7	1633 5.2	2305 1.7
9 SU	0404 4.8	1030 2.2	1637 4.7	2307 2.2
24 M	0524 5.0	1151 1.9	1804 5.0	
10 M	0543 4.6	1148 2.4	1815 4.6	
25 TU	0038 1.8	0659 5.0	1318 1.8	1935 5.1
11 TU	0034 2.2	0658 4.7	1327 2.2	1926 4.8
26 W	0154 1.6	0817 5.4	1424 1.5	2043 5.5
12 W	0207 1.9	0804 5.0	1437 1.8	2027 5.2
27 TH	0252 1.2	0913 5.8	1516 1.2	2134 5.9
13 TH	0300 1.5	0859 5.5	1522 1.4	2116 5.6
28 F	0339 1.0	0959 6.1	1600 0.9	2218 6.1
14 F	0341 1.1	0943 5.9	1601 1.1	2159 6.0
29 SA	0420 0.8	1040 6.3	1639 0.8	2258 6.3
15 SA	0419 0.9	1024 6.2	1638 0.8	2240 6.3
30 SU	0458 0.7	1118 6.4	1717 0.7	○ 2336 6.3

OCTOBER

Day	Time m	Time m	Time m	Time m
1 M	0533 0.7	1153 6.4	1752 0.8	
16 TU	0508 0.5	1117 6.7	1731 0.4	2339 6.6
2 TU	0009 6.2	0607 0.8	1225 6.3	1824 0.8
17 W	0551 0.5	1159 6.7	1815 0.4	
3 W	0039 6.1	0638 0.9	1250 6.1	1856 0.9
18 TH	0022 6.6	0636 0.5	1243 6.6	1900 0.5
4 TH	0104 6.0	0710 1.0	1313 5.9	1927 1.1
19 F	0107 6.5	0722 0.7	1327 6.4	1948 0.7
5 F	0129 5.8	0742 1.2	1338 5.7	2000 1.3
20 SA	0154 6.2	0812 0.9	1416 6.1	2040 1.0
6 SA	0158 5.6	0817 1.5	1409 5.5	2036 1.6
21 SU	0248 5.9	0907 1.3	1513 5.6	2138 1.4
7 SU	0233 5.3	0857 1.8	1448 5.1	2121 1.9
22 M	0353 5.5	1012 1.6	1622 5.2	◑ 2251 1.7
8 M	0320 5.0	0951 2.1	1543 4.8	◐ 2223 2.2
23 TU	0509 5.3	1135 1.9	1744 5.0	
9 TU	0451 4.7	1106 2.3	1733 4.6	2345 2.2
24 W	0016 1.8	0634 5.2	1255 1.8	1909 5.1
10 W	0620 4.7	1233 2.2	1850 4.8	
25 TH	0128 1.6	0748 5.4	1359 1.6	2016 5.4
11 TH	0113 2.0	0726 5.1	1352 1.9	1951 5.2
26 F	0225 1.4	0844 5.7	1451 1.3	2108 5.7
12 F	0218 1.6	0822 5.5	1444 1.5	2043 5.6
27 SA	0312 1.2	0930 6.0	1534 1.1	2152 5.9
13 SA	0305 1.2	0910 6.0	1527 1.1	2129 6.0
28 SU	0354 1.0	1011 6.1	1614 0.9	2232 6.1
14 SU	0346 0.9	0953 6.3	1607 0.8	2213 6.3
29 M	0432 1.0	1049 6.2	1651 0.9	○ 2311 6.1
15 M	0426 0.7	1035 6.6	1648 0.6	● 2256 6.6
30 TU	0507 0.9	1123 6.2	1726 0.9	2342 6.2
31 W	0541 1.0	1152 6.1	1800 0.9	

NOVEMBER

Day	Time m	Time m	Time m	Time m
1 TH	0010 6.1	0614 1.0	1219 6.1	1832 1.0
16 F	0009 6.6	0620 0.6	1228 6.6	1846 0.5
2 F	0038 6.0	0646 1.1	1244 5.9	1904 1.1
17 SA	0058 6.5	0709 0.7	1317 6.4	1936 0.6
3 SA	0106 5.9	0719 1.3	1313 5.8	1937 1.3
18 SU	0149 6.4	0800 0.9	1407 6.1	2028 0.9
4 SU	0136 5.7	0753 1.5	1345 5.6	2011 1.5
19 M	0241 6.1	0854 1.2	1502 5.8	2123 1.2
5 M	0211 5.5	0832 1.7	1424 5.3	2052 1.7
20 TU	0339 5.8	0954 1.5	1603 5.4	◑ 2227 1.5
6 TU	0254 5.2	0920 1.9	1513 5.0	2146 1.9
21 W	0441 5.5	1105 1.7	1710 5.2	2339 1.7
7 W	0354 5.0	1024 2.1	1623 4.8	◐ 2255 2.1
22 TH	0551 5.3	1219 1.8	1825 5.1	
8 TH	0528 4.6	1141 2.1	1803 4.8	
23 F	0049 1.7	0702 5.3	1324 1.7	1936 5.2
9 F	0014 2.0	0642 5.1	1257 1.9	1911 5.1
24 SA	0149 1.6	0805 5.5	1418 1.5	2034 5.3
10 SA	0126 1.7	0743 5.5	1359 1.5	2008 5.5
25 SU	0240 1.5	0856 5.6	1506 1.3	2123 5.6
11 SU	0223 1.4	0835 5.9	1451 1.1	2059 5.9
26 M	0326 1.4	0940 5.8	1549 1.2	2205 5.8
12 M	0312 1.0	0923 6.3	1537 0.8	2147 6.3
27 TU	0407 1.2	1019 5.9	1628 1.1	2243 5.9
13 TU	0359 0.8	1009 6.5	1623 0.6	● 2234 6.5
28 W	0445 1.2	1054 6.0	1704 1.0	○ 2317 6.0
14 W	0445 0.6	1055 6.7	1710 0.4	2321 6.6
29 TH	0520 1.1	1125 6.0	1740 1.0	2348 6.0
15 TH	0532 0.5	1141 6.7	1758 0.4	
30 F	0555 1.1	1154 6.0	1814 1.0	

DECEMBER

Day	Time m	Time m	Time m	Time m
1 SA	0018 6.0	0628 1.2	1224 5.9	1848 1.1
16 SU	0051 6.6	0657 0.6	1308 6.5	1924 0.5
2 SU	0049 5.9	0702 1.2	1255 5.8	1921 1.2
17 M	0140 6.2	0746 0.8	1356 6.3	2013 0.7
3 M	0120 5.9	0735 1.3	1329 5.7	1953 1.3
18 TU	0228 6.3	0836 1.0	1445 6.0	2102 0.9
4 TU	0154 5.7	0811 1.5	1406 5.6	2030 1.5
19 W	0316 6.0	0927 1.2	1535 5.7	2153 1.2
5 W	0234 5.6	0853 1.6	1450 5.4	2115 1.6
20 TH	0406 5.7	1022 1.5	1628 5.3	◑ 2248 1.5
6 TH	0323 5.4	0946 1.8	1544 5.2	◐ 2211 1.7
21 F	0500 5.4	1125 1.7	1726 5.1	2353 1.8
7 F	0423 5.2	1051 1.9	1652 5.1	2319 1.8
22 SA	0559 5.2	1236 1.9	1832 4.9	
8 SA	0541 5.2	1205 1.8	1817 5.1	
23 SU	0103 1.9	0705 5.1	1341 1.8	1945 4.9
9 SU	0034 1.7	0657 5.4	1315 1.6	1929 5.4
24 M	0205 1.8	0812 5.2	1436 1.7	2048 5.1
10 M	0144 1.5	0800 5.7	1418 1.3	2029 5.7
25 TU	0258 1.7	0907 5.4	1525 1.5	2137 5.4
11 TU	0244 1.2	0856 6.1	1513 0.9	2125 6.1
26 W	0344 1.5	0951 5.6	1607 1.3	2219 5.6
12 W	0338 0.9	0948 6.4	1605 0.7	2218 6.3
27 TH	0425 1.3	1029 5.8	1646 1.1	2255 5.8
13 TH	0429 0.7	1039 6.5	1656 0.5	● 2310 6.5
28 F	0502 1.2	1103 5.9	1723 1.0	○ 2329 5.9
14 F	0519 0.6	1129 6.8	1746 0.4	
29 SA	0538 1.0	1135 6.0	1758 1.0	
15 SA	0001 6.6	0608 0.6	1219 6.6	1835 0.4
30 SU	0001 6.0	0612 1.1	1208 6.0	1833 1.0
31 M	0032 6.0	0646 1.1	1240 6.0	1906 1.0

Chart Datum: 3·27 metres below Ordnance Datum (Newlyn)
HAT is 6·9 metres above Chart Datum

TIDES

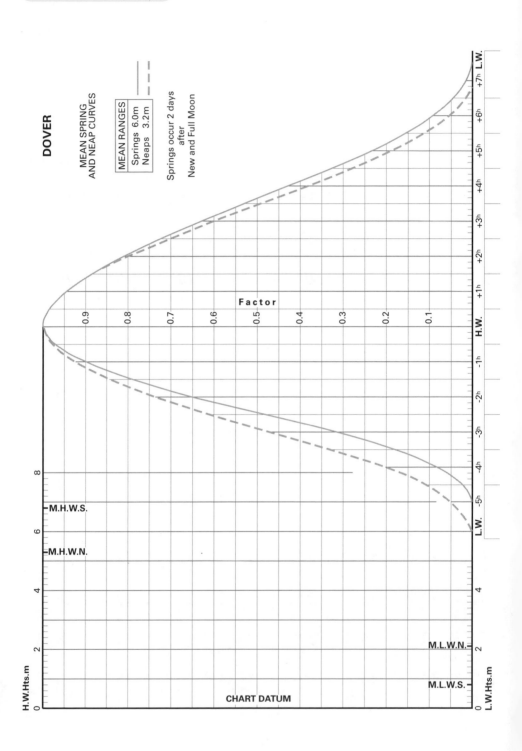

DOVER

MEAN SPRING
AND NEAP CURVES

MEAN RANGES	
Springs	6.0m
Neaps	3.2m

Springs occur 2 days
after
New and Full Moon

DOVER

LAT 51°07′N   LONG 1°19′E

TIMES AND HEIGHTS OF HIGH AND LOW WATERS

2012

JANUARY

Day	Time m	Day	Time m
1 SU	0350 5.9 / 1102 1.8 / 1627 5.5 / ◐ 2308 2.1	**16** M	0323 6.4 / 1046 1.3 / 1549 6.0 / ◑ 2304 1.6
2 M	0444 5.6 / 1151 2.1 / 1728 5.3	**17** TU	0423 6.1 / 1143 1.6 / 1700 5.7
3 TU	0007 2.3 / 0547 5.4 / 1255 2.2 / 1835 5.2	**18** W	0009 1.9 / 0538 5.8 / 1253 1.8 / 1831 5.5
4 W	0124 2.4 / 0655 5.4 / 1402 2.2 / 1940 5.3	**19** TH	0126 2.0 / 0706 5.7 / 1408 1.8 / 1952 5.6
5 TH	0234 2.2 / 0758 5.5 / 1504 2.0 / 2035 5.6	**20** F	0244 1.9 / 0824 5.9 / 1525 1.7 / 2100 5.9
6 F	0334 2.0 / 0850 5.7 / 1559 1.7 / 2121 5.8	**21** SA	0404 1.6 / 0931 6.1 / 1648 1.4 / 2156 6.2
7 SA	0425 1.7 / 0934 5.9 / 1648 1.5 / 2201 6.1	**22** SU	0518 1.2 / 1026 6.3 / 1751 1.1 / 2244 6.5
8 SU	0511 1.4 / 1014 6.1 / 1733 1.3 / 2238 6.3	**23** M	0615 1.0 / 1111 6.5 / 1841 1.0 / ● 2325 6.7
9 M	0555 1.2 / 1052 6.3 / 1816 1.2 / ○ 2314 6.5	**24** TU	0703 0.8 / 1150 6.6 / 1924 0.9
10 TU	0637 1.1 / 1129 6.4 / 1857 1.1 / 2350 6.6	**25** W	0003 6.8 / 0745 0.7 / 1227 6.6 / 2000 0.9
11 W	0719 1.0 / 1205 6.5 / 1937 1.1	**26** TH	0042 6.8 / 0821 0.8 / 1302 6.5 / 2031 1.0
12 TH	0027 6.7 / 0800 0.9 / 1243 6.6 / 2015 1.1	**27** F	0118 6.8 / 0852 0.9 / 1338 6.4 / 2057 1.1
13 F	0106 6.8 / 0840 0.9 / 1322 6.6 / 2052 1.1	**28** SA	0154 6.6 / 0918 1.1 / 1413 6.2 / 2118 1.3
14 SA	0147 6.8 / 0918 1.0 / 1405 6.5 / 2130 1.2	**29** SU	0226 6.4 / 0941 1.3 / 1448 5.9 / 2143 1.5
15 SU	0232 6.6 / 0959 1.1 / 1453 6.3 / 2213 1.4	**30** M	0258 6.1 / 1008 1.6 / 1525 5.6 / 2217 1.8
		31 TU	0337 5.7 / 1045 1.9 / 1617 5.3 / ◐ 2301 2.1

FEBRUARY

Day	Time m	Day	Time m
1 W	0436 5.4 / 1138 2.2 / 1736 5.1	**16** TH	0515 5.6 / 1228 2.0 / 1807 5.3
2 TH	0007 2.4 / 0600 5.2 / 1305 2.4 / 1852 5.1	**17** F	0104 2.1 / 0654 5.4 / 1350 2.1 / 1939 5.4
3 F	0143 2.4 / 0716 5.2 / 1424 2.2 / 1957 5.3	**18** SA	0230 2.0 / 0825 5.6 / 1520 1.9 / 2053 5.7
4 SA	0256 2.1 / 0818 5.4 / 1528 1.9 / 2051 5.6	**19** SU	0405 1.7 / 0933 5.9 / 1647 1.5 / 2149 6.1
5 SU	0355 1.8 / 0908 5.8 / 1623 1.6 / 2136 6.0	**20** M	0515 1.2 / 1023 6.2 / 1744 1.2 / 2233 6.4
6 M	0447 1.4 / 0952 6.1 / 1712 1.3 / 2215 6.3	**21** TU	0606 0.9 / 1102 6.4 / 1828 0.9 / ● 2311 6.6
7 TU	0535 1.1 / 1032 6.4 / 1759 1.1 / ○ 2253 6.6	**22** W	0650 0.7 / 1135 6.5 / 1906 0.9 / 2346 6.8
8 W	0621 0.9 / 1111 6.6 / 1843 1.0 / 2331 6.8	**23** TH	0726 0.7 / 1207 6.6 / 1938 0.9
9 TH	0706 0.8 / 1148 6.7 / 1924 0.8	**24** F	0021 6.8 / 0756 0.8 / 1240 6.5 / 2003 0.9
10 F	0009 6.9 / 0747 0.6 / 1226 6.8 / 2002 0.8	**25** SA	0055 6.7 / 0821 0.9 / 1311 6.4 / 2023 1.0
11 SA	0048 7.0 / 0826 0.6 / 1305 6.8 / 2038 0.8	**26** SU	0124 6.6 / 0841 1.0 / 1339 6.3 / 2043 1.1
12 SU	0129 7.0 / 0903 0.7 / 1346 6.7 / 2115 0.9	**27** M	0147 6.4 / 0901 1.2 / 1401 6.1 / 2108 1.3
13 M	0212 6.8 / 0942 0.9 / 1432 6.5 / 2156 1.1	**28** TU	0209 6.2 / 0928 1.4 / 1425 5.9 / 2141 1.6
14 TU	0301 6.5 / 1025 1.2 / 1526 6.1 / ◑ 2243 1.5	**29** W	0239 5.9 / 1002 1.7 / 1500 5.6 / 2220 1.9
15 W	0359 6.1 / 1118 1.6 / 1634 5.6 / 2345 1.9		

MARCH

Day	Time m	Day	Time m
1 TH	0322 5.5 / 1046 2.1 / 1555 5.2 / ◐ 2313 2.3	**16** F	0500 5.5 / 1213 2.1 / 1744 5.3
2 F	0454 5.1 / 1154 2.4 / 1806 5.0	**17** SA	0051 2.1 / 0642 5.3 / 1338 2.1 / 1920 5.4
3 SA	0048 2.5 / 0639 5.1 / 1344 2.4 / 1919 5.2	**18** SU	0221 2.0 / 0819 5.5 / 1512 1.9 / 2037 5.7
4 SU	0220 2.2 / 0747 5.3 / 1456 2.0 / 2018 5.5	**19** M	0356 1.6 / 0921 5.8 / 1629 1.5 / 2131 6.0
5 M	0324 1.8 / 0841 5.7 / 1555 1.7 / 2107 6.0	**20** TU	0458 1.2 / 1006 6.1 / 1721 1.2 / 2212 6.4
6 TU	0419 1.4 / 0927 6.1 / 1647 1.3 / 2149 6.4	**21** W	0546 0.9 / 1041 6.3 / 1803 1.0 / 2249 6.6
7 W	0511 1.0 / 1009 6.5 / 1736 1.0 / 2229 6.7	**22** TH	0626 0.8 / 1113 6.5 / 1839 0.9 / ● 2324 6.7
8 TH	0600 0.8 / 1048 6.7 / 1822 0.8 / ○ 2308 6.9	**23** F	0659 0.6 / 1143 6.5 / 1908 0.9 / 2358 6.7
9 F	0647 0.6 / 1127 6.9 / 1905 0.7 / 2348 7.1	**24** SA	0726 0.9 / 1214 6.5 / 1931 1.0
10 SA	0730 0.4 / 1205 7.0 / 1944 0.6	**25** SU	0029 6.6 / 0746 1.0 / 1244 6.4 / 1950 1.0
11 SU	0028 7.2 / 0809 0.4 / 1246 7.0 / 2021 0.6	**26** M	0055 6.5 / 0806 1.1 / 1308 6.3 / 2013 1.1
12 M	0109 7.1 / 0846 0.5 / 1329 6.8 / 2100 0.7	**27** TU	0112 6.3 / 0829 1.2 / 1326 6.2 / 2041 1.2
13 TU	0154 6.9 / 0925 0.8 / 1416 6.5 / 2141 1.0	**28** W	0133 6.2 / 0858 1.4 / 1350 6.1 / 2114 1.5
14 W	0243 6.5 / 1008 1.2 / 1511 6.1 / 2228 1.4	**29** TH	0204 6.0 / 0932 1.7 / 1426 5.8 / 2153 1.8
15 TH	0343 6.0 / 1101 1.7 / 1619 5.7 / ◑ 2330 1.9	**30** F	0246 5.6 / 1014 2.0 / 1516 5.4 / ◑ 2241 2.1
		31 SA	0348 5.2 / 1109 2.3 / 1711 5.1 / 2356 2.3

APRIL

Day	Time m	Day	Time m
1 SU	0603 5.1 / 1255 2.4 / 1839 5.2	**16** M	0201 1.9 / 0753 5.5 / 1439 1.9 / 2005 5.7
2 M	0139 2.2 / 0714 5.3 / 1420 2.1 / 1942 5.6	**17** TU	0321 1.6 / 0853 5.7 / 1549 1.6 / 2100 6.0
3 TU	0248 1.8 / 0811 5.7 / 1521 1.7 / 2033 6.0	**18** W	0424 1.3 / 0936 6.0 / 1643 1.4 / 2144 6.2
4 W	0346 1.4 / 0859 6.1 / 1615 1.3 / 2119 6.4	**19** TH	0512 1.1 / 1012 6.2 / 1727 1.2 / 2222 6.4
5 TH	0440 1.0 / 0942 6.5 / 1706 1.0 / 2202 6.8	**20** F	0552 1.0 / 1044 6.3 / 1803 1.1 / 2258 6.5
6 F	0533 0.7 / 1023 6.8 / 1756 0.8 / ○ 2244 7.0	**21** SA	0623 1.0 / 1116 6.4 / 1832 1.1 / ● 2332 6.5
7 SA	0623 0.5 / 1104 6.9 / 1842 0.6 / 2325 7.1	**22** SU	0649 1.1 / 1148 6.4 / 1857 1.1
8 SU	0709 0.4 / 1145 7.0 / 1925 0.5	**23** M	0002 6.4 / 0712 1.1 / 1218 6.4 / 1922 1.1
9 M	0008 7.2 / 0751 0.4 / 1229 7.0 / 2006 0.5	**24** TU	0028 6.3 / 0737 1.1 / 1243 6.3 / 1950 1.1
10 TU	0052 7.0 / 0831 0.6 / 1314 6.8 / 2047 0.7	**25** W	0047 6.2 / 0806 1.2 / 1303 6.3 / 2021 1.2
11 W	0139 6.8 / 0912 0.8 / 1404 6.6 / 2131 1.0	**26** TH	0111 6.2 / 0837 1.4 / 1331 6.2 / 2056 1.4
12 TH	0232 6.4 / 0957 1.2 / 1501 6.3 / 2221 1.4	**27** F	0144 6.0 / 0912 1.6 / 1409 6.0 / 2134 1.7
13 F	0333 6.0 / 1051 1.7 / 1604 5.8 / ◑ 2323 1.8	**28** SA	0227 5.8 / 0953 1.8 / 1459 5.7 / 2221 1.9
14 SA	0444 5.5 / 1201 2.0 / 1717 5.5	**29** SU	0325 5.5 / 1044 2.1 / 1614 5.4 / ◑ 2325 2.1
15 SU	0040 2.0 / 0617 5.3 / 1320 2.1 / 1845 5.5	**30** M	0511 5.3 / 1200 2.2 / 1749 5.4

Chart Datum: 3·67 metres below Ordnance Datum (Newlyn)
HAT is 7·4 metres above Chart Datum

TIDES

DOVER
LAT 51°07′N   LONG 1°19′E

TIME ZONE (UT)
For Summer Time add ONE hour in **non-shaded areas**

Dates in amber are **SPRINGS**
Dates in yellow are **NEAPS**

2012

TIMES AND HEIGHTS OF HIGH AND LOW WATERS

MAY

Day	Time m	Time m	Time m	Time m	Day	Time m	Time m	Time m	Time m
1 TU	0055 2.0	0634 5.4	1334 1.6	1859 5.7	**16** W	0230 1.7	0807 5.6	1456 1.8	2018 5.8
2 W	0208 1.7	0735 5.8	1440 1.7	1956 6.0	**17** TH	0331 1.6	0856 5.8	1553 1.6	2108 6.0
3 TH	0308 1.4	0827 6.1	1538 1.4	2047 6.4	**18** F	0423 1.4	0937 6.0	1642 1.4	2151 6.1
4 F	0406 1.0	0914 6.4	1633 1.1	2134 6.7	**19** SA	0506 1.3	1014 6.1	1722 1.3	2229 6.2
5 SA	0503 0.8	0959 6.6	1728 0.9	2220 6.9	**20** SU	0542 1.3	1049 6.2	1756 1.2	2304 6.3
6 SU	0559 0.6	1044 6.8	1820 0.7	2306 7.0	**21** M	0614 1.2	1122 6.3	1827 1.2	2336 6.3
7 M	0650 0.5	1129 6.9	1909 0.6	2352 7.0	**22** TU	0645 1.2	1154 6.3	1859 1.2	
8 TU	0738 0.5	1215 6.9	1955 0.6		**23** W	0004 6.2	0716 1.2	1223 6.3	1933 1.2
9 W	0039 6.9	0822 0.7	1304 6.8	2041 0.7	**24** TH	0031 6.2	0749 1.3	1250 6.3	2008 1.2
10 TH	0130 6.7	0906 0.9	1354 6.6	2127 0.9	**25** F	0059 6.1	0824 1.4	1321 6.2	2045 1.3
11 F	0223 6.4	0952 1.2	1448 6.4	2218 1.2	**26** SA	0133 6.1	0900 1.5	1359 6.2	2124 1.5
12 SA	0320 6.0	1043 1.5	1544 6.1	2314 1.5	**27** SU	0215 6.0	0939 1.6	1447 6.0	2208 1.5
13 SU	0422 5.7	1143 1.8	1645 5.8		**28** M	0308 5.8	1026 1.8	1545 5.9	2303 1.7
14 M	0018 1.7	0534 5.4	1248 2.0	1756 5.6	**29** TU	0415 5.6	1126 1.9	1656 5.8	
15 TU	0125 1.8	0701 5.4	1354 2.0	1914 5.6	**30** W	0012 1.7	0539 5.6	1244 1.9	1810 5.8
					31 TH	0125 1.6	0653 5.8	1357 1.7	1917 6.0

JUNE

Day	Time m	Time m	Time m	Time m	Day	Time m	Time m	Time m	Time m
1 F	0230 1.4	0754 6.0	1500 1.5	2016 6.3	**16** SA	0329 1.7	0859 5.7	1555 1.7	2116 5.8
2 SA	0332 1.2	0849 6.3	1602 1.2	2111 6.5	**17** SU	0419 1.6	0943 5.9	1643 1.5	2159 6.0
3 SU	0435 1.0	0941 6.5	1704 1.0	2203 6.7	**18** M	0503 1.5	1021 6.1	1724 1.4	2236 6.1
4 M	0539 0.8	1031 6.7	1803 0.8	2255 6.8	**19** TU	0543 1.3	1057 6.2	1802 1.2	2310 6.2
5 TU	0637 0.7	1120 6.8	1858 0.7	2344 6.8	**20** W	0622 1.3	1130 6.3	1841 1.2	2343 6.2
6 W	0729 0.7	1207 6.8	1949 0.6		**21** TH	0700 1.2	1203 6.4	1919 1.1	
7 TH	0033 6.8	0816 0.7	1255 6.8	2037 0.7	**22** F	0015 6.4	0737 1.2	1235 6.4	1958 1.1
8 F	0121 6.6	0901 0.9	1342 6.7	2123 0.8	**23** SA	0047 6.2	0814 1.3	1309 6.4	2036 1.2
9 SA	0210 6.4	0943 1.1	1430 6.5	2207 1.0	**24** SU	0122 6.2	0850 1.3	1347 6.4	2114 1.2
10 SU	0300 6.1	1026 1.4	1520 6.3	2254 1.3	**25** M	0202 6.2	0928 1.4	1430 6.4	2155 1.3
11 M	0353 5.9	1112 1.6	1612 6.0	2343 1.6	**26** TU	0248 6.1	1009 1.5	1520 6.2	2241 1.4
12 TU	0450 5.6	1204 1.9	1709 5.8		**27** W	0343 5.9	1059 1.6	1618 6.1	2337 1.5
13 W	0038 1.8	0555 5.4	1302 2.0	1814 5.6	**28** TH	0449 5.8	1202 1.8	1727 5.9	
14 TH	0136 1.9	0705 5.4	1403 2.0	1924 5.6	**29** F	0046 1.6	0611 5.7	1317 1.8	1843 5.9
15 F	0234 1.8	0807 5.5	1501 1.9	2025 5.7	**30** SA	0157 1.6	0729 5.8	1429 1.7	1955 6.1

JULY

Day	Time m	Time m	Time m	Time m	Day	Time m	Time m	Time m	Time m
1 SU	0305 1.4	0834 6.0	1538 1.4	2100 6.2	**16** M	0342 1.8	0911 5.7	1609 1.7	2128 5.8
2 M	0416 1.2	0933 6.3	1648 1.2	2200 6.4	**17** TU	0432 1.6	0954 6.0	1656 1.5	2208 6.0
3 TU	0527 1.0	1026 6.5	1754 0.9	2254 6.6	**18** W	0518 1.4	1031 6.2	1740 1.3	2245 6.2
4 W	0629 0.9	1114 6.7	1851 0.7	2342 6.7	**19** TH	0601 1.3	1106 6.4	1822 1.1	2320 6.3
5 TH	0721 0.8	1159 6.8	1943 0.6		**20** F	0643 1.2	1140 6.5	1904 1.0	2355 6.4
6 F	0027 6.7	0807 0.8	1243 6.9	2028 0.6	**21** SA	0723 1.1	1215 6.6	1945 1.0	
7 SA	0109 6.6	0847 0.8	1326 6.8	2108 0.7	**22** SU	0029 6.5	0800 1.1	1251 6.7	2023 0.9
8 SU	0152 6.5	0924 1.0	1408 6.7	2146 0.9	**23** M	0105 6.6	0836 1.1	1328 6.7	2100 1.0
9 M	0234 6.2	0957 1.2	1451 6.5	2221 1.2	**24** TU	0143 6.5	0912 1.1	1409 6.7	2137 1.1
10 TU	0319 6.0	1030 1.5	1536 6.2	2258 1.5	**25** W	0226 6.4	0950 1.3	1455 6.5	2219 1.2
11 W	0408 5.7	1105 1.8	1625 5.9	2340 1.8	**26** TH	0317 6.1	1035 1.5	1549 6.2	2309 1.5
12 TH	0503 5.5	1154 2.1	1722 5.6		**27** F	0418 5.8	1132 1.7	1657 5.9	
13 F	0036 2.1	0607 5.3	1303 2.2	1828 5.4	**28** SA	0014 1.7	0542 5.6	1248 1.9	1822 5.7
14 SA	0142 2.1	0716 5.3	1413 2.2	1937 5.4	**29** SU	0132 1.8	0715 5.6	1408 1.9	1948 5.8
15 SU	0245 2.0	0819 5.5	1515 2.0	2039 5.6	**30** M	0249 1.7	0828 5.8	1525 1.6	2101 6.0
					31 TU	0410 1.5	0929 6.1	1644 1.3	2202 6.2

AUGUST

Day	Time m	Time m	Time m	Time m	Day	Time m	Time m	Time m	Time m
1 W	0524 1.2	1021 6.5	1750 0.9	2252 6.5	**16** TH	0455 1.4	1002 6.3	1716 1.2	2218 6.3
2 TH	0621 0.9	1106 6.7	1844 0.7	2335 6.7	**17** F	0540 1.2	1039 6.5	1801 1.0	2255 6.5
3 F	0709 0.8	1146 6.9	1930 0.6		**18** SA	0623 1.1	1115 6.7	1845 0.9	2331 6.6
4 SA	0013 6.7	0749 0.8	1226 6.9	2010 0.6	**19** SU	0703 1.0	1151 6.9	1926 0.8	
5 SU	0050 6.6	0824 0.8	1305 6.9	2044 0.7	**20** M	0006 6.7	0741 0.9	1228 6.9	2004 0.8
6 M	0126 6.5	0854 1.0	1342 6.8	2114 0.9	**21** TU	0043 6.8	0817 0.9	1306 7.0	2040 0.8
7 TU	0203 6.3	0919 1.2	1419 6.5	2140 1.2	**22** W	0122 6.7	0853 1.0	1347 6.9	2117 0.9
8 W	0241 6.1	0941 1.4	1456 6.2	2204 1.5	**23** TH	0205 6.5	0931 1.1	1433 6.6	2157 1.2
9 TH	0323 5.8	1008 1.7	1537 5.9	2235 1.8	**24** F	0255 6.2	1015 1.4	1528 6.2	2246 1.6
10 F	0414 5.5	1047 2.0	1632 5.5	2322 2.2	**25** SA	0359 5.8	1111 1.8	1639 5.8	2351 1.9
11 SA	0520 5.2	1147 2.4	1743 5.2		**26** SU	0529 5.5	1227 2.1	1814 5.6	
12 SU	0044 2.4	0632 5.2	1324 2.4	1856 5.2	**27** M	0116 2.1	0704 5.5	1356 2.1	1947 5.6
13 M	0206 2.3	0740 5.3	1439 2.2	2003 5.4	**28** TU	0244 1.9	0821 5.8	1525 1.7	2102 6.0
14 TU	0311 2.0	0838 5.6	1539 1.9	2057 5.7	**29** W	0412 1.6	0921 6.1	1644 1.3	2158 6.3
15 W	0406 1.7	0924 6.0	1630 1.5	2140 6.0	**30** TH	0516 1.2	1009 6.5	1741 0.9	2242 6.5
					31 F	0606 1.0	1050 6.8	1828 0.7	2318 6.7

Chart Datum: 3·67 metres below Ordnance Datum (Newlyn)
HAT is 7·4 metres above Chart Datum

DOVER

LAT 51°07'N   LONG 1°19'E

TIMES AND HEIGHTS OF HIGH AND LOW WATERS

2012

SEPTEMBER

Day	Time m	Day	Time m
1 SA	0648 0.9 / 1127 6.9 / 1909 0.7 / 2351 6.7	**16** SU	0557 1.0 / 1047 6.9 / ● 2304 6.8
2 SU	0724 0.9 / 1204 6.9 / 1944 0.7	**17** M	0639 0.9 / 1124 7.1 / 1903 0.7 / 2341 6.9
3 M	0024 6.7 / 0753 0.9 / 1240 6.9 / 2012 0.9	**18** TU	0718 0.8 / 1203 7.1 / 1942 0.7
4 TU	0058 6.6 / 0818 1.1 / 1314 6.7 / 2035 1.1	**19** W	0020 7.0 / 0755 0.8 / 1243 7.1 / 2019 0.7
5 W	0131 6.4 / 0837 1.2 / 1345 6.5 / 2054 1.3	**20** TH	0101 6.9 / 0834 0.9 / 1326 6.9 / 2057 0.9
6 TH	0201 6.2 / 0858 1.4 / 1411 6.2 / 2116 1.5	**21** F	0147 6.7 / 0914 1.1 / 1415 6.6 / 2139 1.3
7 F	0230 5.9 / 0928 1.7 / 1440 5.9 / 2148 1.8	**22** SA	0240 6.3 / 1000 1.5 / 1514 6.2 / ● 2229 1.7
8 SA	0304 5.6 / 1005 2.0 / 1524 5.5 / ◐ 2229 2.2	**23** SU	0348 5.9 / 1058 1.9 / 1630 5.7 / 2337 2.1
9 SU	0427 5.3 / 1055 2.3 / 1701 5.2 / 2330 2.5	**24** M	0514 5.6 / 1217 2.1 / 1806 5.5
10 M	0551 5.1 / 1223 2.6 / 1821 5.1	**25** TU	0106 2.2 / 0646 5.5 / 1349 2.1 / 1941 5.6
11 TU	0124 2.5 / 0702 5.3 / 1402 2.4 / 1929 5.3	**26** W	0240 2.0 / 0805 5.8 / 1522 1.7 / 2051 5.9
12 W	0202 2.2 / 0802 5.6 / 1507 2.0 / 2025 5.7	**27** TH	0359 1.6 / 0903 6.2 / 1629 1.3 / 2142 6.3
13 TH	0337 1.8 / 0850 6.0 / 1600 1.6 / 2110 6.1	**28** F	0455 1.3 / 0948 6.5 / 1721 1.0 / 2221 6.5
14 F	0427 1.5 / 0930 6.4 / 1649 1.2 / 2150 6.4	**29** SA	0541 1.1 / 1027 6.7 / 1804 0.8 / 2254 6.6
15 SA	0513 1.2 / 1009 6.7 / 1735 1.0 / 2227 6.7	**30** SU	0619 1.0 / 1103 6.8 / 1841 0.8 / ○ 2325 6.7

OCTOBER

Day	Time m	Day	Time m
1 M	0652 1.0 / 1139 6.9 / 1911 0.9 / 2357 6.7	**16** TU	0613 0.9 / 1058 7.2 / 1838 0.7 / 2318 7.1
2 TU	0719 1.1 / 1213 6.8 / 1935 1.1	**17** W	0656 0.8 / 1140 7.2 / 1921 0.7
3 W	0029 6.6 / 0740 1.2 / 1244 6.6 / 1955 1.2	**18** TH	0000 7.1 / 0737 0.8 / 1223 7.1 / 2001 0.8
4 TH	0059 6.5 / 0801 1.3 / 1310 6.4 / 2015 1.4	**19** F	0045 7.0 / 0819 0.9 / 1310 6.9 / 2043 1.0
5 F	0124 6.3 / 0827 1.4 / 1329 6.2 / 2042 1.5	**20** SA	0134 6.7 / 0904 1.1 / 1402 6.6 / 2127 1.3
6 SA	0144 6.1 / 0858 1.6 / 1355 6.0 / 2115 1.8	**21** SU	0230 6.4 / 0953 1.4 / 1504 6.2 / 2220 1.7
7 SU	0215 5.8 / 0936 1.9 / 1434 5.6 / 2155 2.1	**22** M	0336 6.0 / 1052 1.8 / 1618 5.8 / ◐ 2327 2.1
8 M	0302 5.5 / 1022 2.2 / 1541 5.3 / 2247 2.4	**23** TU	0449 5.7 / 1208 2.0 / 1745 5.6
9 TU	0504 5.2 / 1129 2.5 / 1745 5.2	**24** W	0049 2.2 / 0613 5.6 / 1332 2.0 / 1917 5.6
10 W	0021 2.6 / 0620 5.3 / 1316 2.4 / 1854 5.4	**25** TH	0212 2.1 / 0733 5.8 / 1453 1.7 / 2025 5.9
11 TH	0159 2.4 / 0721 5.6 / 1428 2.0 / 1950 5.7	**26** F	0325 1.8 / 0833 6.1 / 1559 1.4 / 2114 6.1
12 F	0302 2.0 / 0812 6.0 / 1525 1.6 / 2037 6.1	**27** SA	0421 1.5 / 0920 6.4 / 1650 1.2 / 2153 6.3
13 SA	0354 1.6 / 0856 6.4 / 1616 1.2 / 2119 6.5	**28** SU	0507 1.3 / 1000 6.6 / 1732 1.1 / 2226 6.5
14 SU	0442 1.3 / 0937 6.8 / 1705 1.0 / 2159 6.8	**29** M	0545 1.2 / 1037 6.7 / 1806 1.1 / ○ 2258 6.6
15 M	0528 1.0 / 1018 7.0 / 1753 0.8 / ● 2238 7.0	**30** TU	0618 1.2 / 1113 6.7 / 1835 1.2 / 2331 6.6
		31 W	0645 1.2 / 1146 6.6 / 1859 1.1

NOVEMBER

Day	Time m	Day	Time m
1 TH	0003 6.6 / 0709 1.2 / 1217 6.5 / 1922 1.3	**16** F	0726 0.8 / 1209 7.0 / 1951 0.8
2 F	0033 6.5 / 0735 1.3 / 1241 6.4 / 1949 1.4	**17** SA	0034 7.0 / 0813 0.8 / 1259 6.9 / 2036 1.0
3 SA	0057 6.4 / 0805 1.4 / 1303 6.2 / 2019 1.5	**18** SU	0125 6.8 / 0900 1.0 / 1352 6.6 / 2123 1.2
4 SU	0119 6.2 / 0838 1.6 / 1330 6.0 / 2053 1.7	**19** M	0219 6.6 / 0951 1.2 / 1451 6.2 / 2213 1.6
5 M	0151 6.1 / 0916 1.8 / 1408 5.8 / 2132 2.0	**20** TU	0317 6.3 / 1046 1.5 / 1555 5.9 / ◐ 2311 1.9
6 TU	0236 5.8 / 1000 2.0 / 1500 5.5 / 2219 2.2	**21** W	0419 6.0 / 1148 1.8 / 1707 5.6
7 W	0343 5.5 / 1056 2.2 / 1645 5.3 / 2322 2.4	**22** TH	0017 2.1 / 0527 5.8 / 1256 1.9 / 1828 5.6
8 TH	0523 5.4 / 1219 2.2 / 1811 5.4	**23** F	0126 2.1 / 0644 5.8 / 1404 1.8 / 1940 5.6
9 F	0101 2.4 / 0634 5.6 / 1341 2.0 / 1911 5.7	**24** SA	0233 2.0 / 0752 5.9 / 1510 1.7 / 2035 5.8
10 SA	0215 2.1 / 0731 6.0 / 1444 1.7 / 2003 6.0	**25** SU	0334 1.8 / 0846 6.1 / 1606 1.5 / 2119 6.0
11 SU	0314 1.7 / 0821 6.3 / 1540 1.3 / 2048 6.4	**26** M	0426 1.6 / 0931 6.2 / 1651 1.4 / 2157 6.2
12 M	0408 1.4 / 0907 6.7 / 1634 1.0 / 2132 6.7	**27** TU	0509 1.4 / 1011 6.3 / 1728 1.2 / 2233 6.4
13 TU	0459 1.1 / 0951 6.9 / 1726 0.8 / ● 2215 6.9	**28** W	0544 1.3 / 1048 6.4 / 1800 1.3 / ○ 2307 6.5
14 W	0549 0.9 / 1036 7.1 / 1817 0.7 / 2300 7.0	**29** TH	0615 1.3 / 1121 6.4 / 1829 1.3 / 2340 6.3
15 TH	0638 0.8 / 1122 7.1 / 1905 0.7 / 2346 7.1	**30** F	0645 1.3 / 1153 6.4 / 1859 1.3

DECEMBER

Day	Time m	Day	Time m
1 SA	0011 6.5 / 0717 1.3 / 1221 6.3 / 1931 1.4	**16** SU	0026 7.0 / 0811 0.7 / 1251 6.8 / 2034 0.9
2 SU	0039 6.4 / 0750 1.3 / 1247 6.2 / 2004 1.5	**17** M	0114 6.9 / 0858 0.8 / 1341 6.6 / 2118 1.0
3 M	0105 6.4 / 0826 1.4 / 1316 6.1 / 2039 1.6	**18** TU	0203 6.8 / 0944 1.0 / 1432 6.4 / 2200 1.3
4 TU	0137 6.3 / 0903 1.6 / 1351 6.0 / 2116 1.7	**19** W	0253 6.5 / 1029 1.2 / 1525 6.1 / 2244 1.6
5 W	0218 6.1 / 0944 1.7 / 1436 5.9 / 2158 1.9	**20** TH	0345 6.2 / 1117 1.5 / 1622 5.8 / ◐ 2334 1.9
6 TH	0308 6.0 / 1031 1.8 / 1533 5.7 / ◐ 2249 2.1	**21** F	0442 5.9 / 1210 1.8 / 1726 5.5
7 F	0413 5.8 / 1131 1.9 / 1652 5.5 / 2356 2.2	**22** SA	0031 2.1 / 0546 5.7 / 1309 2.0 / 1836 5.4
8 SA	0532 5.7 / 1246 1.9 / 1820 5.6	**23** SU	0136 2.2 / 0658 5.6 / 1411 2.0 / 1945 5.5
9 SU	0119 2.1 / 0646 5.9 / 1359 1.7 / 1925 5.9	**24** M	0240 2.1 / 0805 5.7 / 1511 1.9 / 2042 5.7
10 M	0231 1.8 / 0747 6.2 / 1503 1.5 / 2021 6.2	**25** TU	0340 1.9 / 0901 5.8 / 1606 1.7 / 2130 5.9
11 TU	0334 1.5 / 0842 6.5 / 1604 1.2 / 2112 6.5	**26** W	0431 1.7 / 0946 6.0 / 1651 1.6 / 2210 6.1
12 W	0434 1.2 / 0935 6.7 / 1704 1.0 / 2202 6.7	**27** TH	0513 1.5 / 1025 6.1 / 1731 1.4 / 2246 6.3
13 TH	0532 1.0 / 1024 6.9 / 1803 0.8 / ● 2251 6.9	**28** F	0551 1.3 / 1059 6.2 / 1807 1.3 / ○ 2319 6.4
14 F	0628 0.8 / 1114 6.9 / 1857 0.8 / 2339 6.7	**29** SA	0626 1.2 / 1131 6.3 / 1842 1.3 / 2350 6.5
15 SA	0721 0.7 / 1202 6.9 / 1948 0.8	**30** SU	0702 1.2 / 1202 6.3 / 1918 1.3
		31 M	0020 6.5 / 0739 1.2 / 1232 6.3 / 1953 1.3

Chart Datum: 3·67 metres below Ordnance Datum (Newlyn)
HAT is 7·4 metres above Chart Datum

TIDES

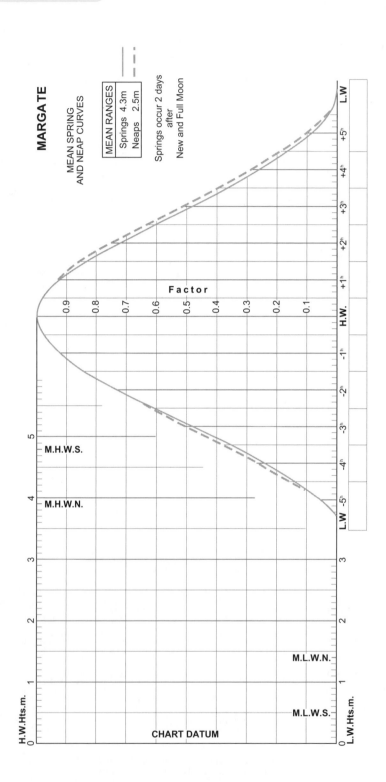

MARGATE

MEAN SPRING
AND NEAP CURVES

MEAN RANGES
Springs 4.3m
Neaps   2.5m

Springs occur 2 days
after
New and Full Moon

TIME ZONE (UT)
For Summer Time add ONE hour in **non-shaded areas**

MARGATE

LAT 51°23'N   LONG 1°23'E

Dates in amber are **SPRINGS**
Dates in yellow are **NEAPS**

2012

TIMES AND HEIGHTS OF HIGH AND LOW WATERS

JANUARY

Day	Time m	Day	Time m
1 SU	0434 4.3 / 1104 1.0 / 1719 4.0 / ◐ 2309 1.5	**16** M	0418 4.6 / 1049 0.7 / 1657 4.3 / 2302 1.1
2 M	0527 4.1 / 1158 1.2 / 1824 3.9	**17** TU	0513 4.4 / 1146 0.8 / 1757 4.2
3 TU	0012 1.6 / 0637 3.9 / 1308 1.3 / 1932 3.9	**18** W	0009 1.2 / 0621 4.3 / 1300 1.0 / 1916 4.1
4 W	0146 1.6 / 0749 3.9 / 1418 1.3 / 2034 3.9	**19** TH	0133 1.3 / 0746 4.2 / 1417 1.1 / 2035 4.1
5 TH	0256 1.4 / 0853 3.9 / 1517 1.3 / 2130 4.1	**20** F	0255 1.2 / 0907 4.3 / 1528 1.0 / 2146 4.3
6 F	0353 1.2 / 0951 4.1 / 1609 1.2 / 2220 4.2	**21** SA	0411 1.0 / 1021 4.4 / 1631 1.0 / 2248 4.4
7 SA	0443 1.0 / 1040 4.2 / 1654 1.1 / 2303 4.4	**22** SU	0517 0.7 / 1120 4.6 / 1725 0.9 / 2338 4.6
8 SU	0527 0.9 / 1123 4.4 / 1734 1.0 / 2341 4.5	**23** M	0610 0.6 / 1209 4.7 / 1810 0.9
9 M	0607 0.7 / 1201 4.5 / 1809 0.9 ○	**24** TU	0021 4.7 / 0654 0.5 / 1253 4.7 / 1850 0.8
10 TU	0017 4.6 / 0644 0.6 / 1241 4.6 / 1843 0.9	**25** W	0100 4.8 / 0733 0.4 / 1333 4.7 / 1927 0.8
11 W	0054 4.7 / 0721 0.5 / 1322 4.6 / 1920 0.8	**26** TH	0137 4.8 / 0808 0.5 / 1410 4.6 / 2002 0.9
12 TH	0133 4.8 / 0800 0.4 / 1405 4.7 / 2000 0.8	**27** F	0212 4.8 / 0839 0.5 / 1444 4.5 / 2035 0.9
13 F	0213 4.8 / 0839 0.4 / 1447 4.7 / 2041 0.8	**28** SA	0246 4.7 / 0908 0.6 / 1515 4.4 / 2108 1.0
14 SA	0252 4.7 / 0919 0.5 / 1528 4.5 / 2124 0.9	**29** SU	0320 4.6 / 0938 0.8 / 1546 4.3 / 2142 1.1
15 SU	0333 4.6 / 1001 0.6 / 1609 4.4 / 2210 1.0	**30** M	0354 4.6 / 1012 0.9 / 1622 4.1 / 2222 1.3
		31 TU	0434 4.2 / 1053 1.1 / 1705 3.9 / ◐ 2312 1.5

FEBRUARY

Day	Time m	Day	Time m
1 W	0524 4.0 / 1148 1.4 / 1804 3.8	**16** TH	0604 4.2 / 1234 1.2 / 1852 3.9
2 TH	0019 1.6 / 0633 3.8 / 1307 1.5 / 1934 3.7	**17** F	0116 1.3 / 0735 4.1 / 1401 1.3 / 2020 4.0
3 F	0201 1.6 / 0802 3.7 / 1434 1.5 / 2050 3.9	**18** SA	0249 1.2 / 0906 4.2 / 1521 1.2 / 2138 4.2
4 SA	0315 1.3 / 0917 3.9 / 1538 1.3 / 2151 4.1	**19** SU	0414 0.9 / 1021 4.4 / 1627 1.1 / 2241 4.4
5 SU	0413 1.1 / 1017 4.1 / 1630 1.2 / 2241 4.3	**20** M	0515 0.7 / 1116 4.5 / 1718 1.0 / 2330 4.5
6 M	0502 0.9 / 1104 4.3 / 1713 1.0 / 2323 4.5	**21** TU	0601 0.5 / 1201 4.6 / 1757 0.9 ●
7 TU	0546 0.7 / 1145 4.5 / 1751 0.9 ○	**22** W	0009 4.7 / 0638 0.5 / 1239 4.6 / 1831 0.8
8 W	0000 4.6 / 0625 0.5 / 1225 4.7 / 1828 0.8	**23** TH	0042 4.7 / 0709 0.5 / 1311 4.6 / 1905 0.8
9 TH	0037 4.8 / 0703 0.4 / 1306 4.8 / 1905 0.7	**24** F	0114 4.8 / 0737 0.5 / 1341 4.6 / 1938 0.8
10 F	0116 4.9 / 0741 0.3 / 1347 4.8 / 1945 0.7	**25** SA	0146 4.8 / 0804 0.5 / 1411 4.6 / 2010 0.8
11 SA	0155 4.9 / 0819 0.3 / 1428 4.8 / 2024 0.7	**26** SU	0219 4.7 / 0832 0.6 / 1440 4.5 / 2040 0.9
12 SU	0235 4.9 / 0856 0.4 / 1507 4.6 / 2105 0.8	**27** M	0251 4.6 / 0859 0.7 / 1510 4.4 / 2111 1.0
13 M	0315 4.8 / 0935 0.5 / 1546 4.5 / 2148 0.9	**28** TU	0322 4.4 / 0929 0.8 / 1542 4.2 / 2145 1.1
14 TU	0400 4.7 / 1019 0.5 / 1631 4.3 / ◐ 2239 1.0	**29** W	0358 4.2 / 1005 1.1 / 1621 4.0 / 2228 1.3
15 W	0453 4.5 / 1116 0.9 / 1729 4.1 / 2346 1.2		

MARCH

Day	Time m	Day	Time m
1 TH	0443 4.0 / 1053 1.3 / 1710 3.8 / ◐ 2328 1.4	**16** F	0556 4.1 / 1217 1.3 / 1835 3.9
2 F	0542 3.8 / 1202 1.6 / 1819 3.7	**17** SA	0107 1.2 / 0729 4.0 / 1349 1.4 / 2003 4.0
3 SA	0057 1.5 / 0704 3.7 / 1339 1.6 / 1958 3.7	**18** SU	0244 1.0 / 0859 4.2 / 1510 1.3 / 2121 4.1
4 SU	0231 1.4 / 0837 3.8 / 1502 1.4 / 2114 4.0	**19** M	0403 0.8 / 1008 4.4 / 1613 1.1 / 2223 4.4
5 M	0338 1.1 / 0946 4.1 / 1600 1.2 / 2210 4.2	**20** TU	0458 0.6 / 1100 4.5 / 1700 1.0 / 2310 4.5
6 TU	0432 0.8 / 1038 4.4 / 1647 1.0 / 2256 4.5	**21** W	0540 0.6 / 1142 4.5 / 1736 0.9 / 2346 4.6
7 W	0518 0.6 / 1122 4.6 / 1728 0.9 / 2336 4.6	**22** TH	0612 0.5 / 1215 4.5 / 1808 0.8 ●
8 TH	0600 0.4 / 1203 4.7 / 1807 0.7 ○	**23** F	0016 4.7 / 0636 0.5 / 1242 4.6 / 1841 0.7
9 F	0014 4.8 / 0639 0.3 / 1244 4.8 / 1847 0.6	**24** SA	0046 4.7 / 0702 0.5 / 1308 4.6 / 1914 0.7
10 SA	0054 4.9 / 0717 0.2 / 1325 4.8 / 1927 0.6	**25** SU	0119 4.7 / 0730 0.5 / 1338 4.6 / 1946 0.7
11 SU	0136 5.0 / 0754 0.3 / 1406 4.8 / 2008 0.6	**26** M	0153 4.7 / 0759 0.6 / 1410 4.5 / 2016 0.8
12 M	0218 5.0 / 0832 0.3 / 1445 4.7 / 2049 0.6	**27** TU	0226 4.6 / 0826 0.7 / 1441 4.4 / 2046 0.8
13 TU	0301 4.9 / 0911 0.5 / 1525 4.5 / 2133 0.7	**28** W	0258 4.4 / 0856 0.9 / 1512 4.3 / 2119 0.9
14 W	0348 4.7 / 0956 0.8 / 1612 4.3 / 2225 0.9	**29** TH	0332 4.2 / 0930 1.0 / 1547 4.1 / 2159 1.1
15 TH	0443 4.4 / 1054 1.1 / 1711 4.1 / ◐ 2336 1.1	**30** F	0414 4.1 / 1015 1.3 / 1634 3.9 / ◐ 2253 1.2
		31 SA	0510 3.9 / 1118 1.5 / 1736 3.8

APRIL

Day	Time m	Day	Time m
1 SU	0013 1.3 / 0622 3.8 / 1245 1.5 / 1859 3.8	**16** M	0220 0.9 / 0834 4.2 / 1442 1.3 / 2048 4.1
2 M	0145 1.2 / 0751 3.8 / 1416 1.4 / 2027 3.9	**17** TU	0332 0.8 / 0939 4.3 / 1543 1.2 / 2149 4.3
3 TU	0258 1.0 / 0907 4.1 / 1522 1.2 / 2130 4.2	**18** W	0426 0.7 / 1031 4.4 / 1630 1.0 / 2237 4.4
4 W	0356 0.7 / 1004 4.4 / 1614 1.0 / 2220 4.5	**19** TH	0505 0.7 / 1112 4.4 / 1708 0.9 / 2314 4.5
5 TH	0445 0.5 / 1052 4.6 / 1700 0.8 / 2305 4.7	**20** F	0533 0.7 / 1143 4.5 / 1743 0.8 / 2346 4.6
6 F	0529 0.4 / 1135 4.7 / 1743 0.7 / ○ 2347 4.8	**21** SA	0601 0.6 / 1209 4.5 / 1818 0.7 ●
7 SA	0611 0.3 / 1217 4.8 / 1827 0.6	**22** SU	0018 4.6 / 0630 0.6 / 1237 4.5 / 1852 0.7
8 SU	0031 5.0 / 0651 0.3 / 1301 4.8 / 1910 0.5	**23** M	0053 4.7 / 0700 0.6 / 1310 4.6 / 1925 0.7
9 M	0117 5.0 / 0731 0.3 / 1344 4.8 / 1954 0.5	**24** TU	0128 4.6 / 0730 0.7 / 1344 4.5 / 1956 0.7
10 TU	0204 5.0 / 0811 0.6 / 1426 4.7 / 2039 0.5	**25** W	0204 4.5 / 0800 0.8 / 1418 4.4 / 2028 0.7
11 W	0252 4.9 / 0853 0.6 / 1510 4.5 / 2125 0.6	**26** TH	0239 4.4 / 0832 0.9 / 1451 4.3 / 2102 0.8
12 TH	0341 4.7 / 0941 0.9 / 1558 4.4 / 2221 0.8	**27** F	0315 4.3 / 0908 1.0 / 1527 4.2 / 2143 0.9
13 F	0437 4.6 / 1040 1.1 / 1656 4.1 / ◐ 2331 0.9	**28** SA	0357 4.1 / 0952 1.2 / 1611 4.1 / 2234 1.0
14 SA	0549 4.1 / 1158 1.3 / 1816 4.0	**29** SU	0448 4.0 / 1050 1.3 / 1707 4.0 / ◐ 2343 1.1
15 SU	0054 1.0 / 0715 4.1 / 1326 1.4 / 1937 4.0	**30** M	0551 3.9 / 1204 1.4 / 1814 3.9

Chart Datum: 2·50 metres below Ordnance Datum (Newlyn)
HAT is 5·2 metres above Chart Datum

TIDES

TIME ZONE (UT)
For Summer Time add ONE hour in **non-shaded areas**

MARGATE
LAT 51°23'N   LONG 1°23'E
TIMES AND HEIGHTS OF HIGH AND LOW WATERS

Dates in amber are **SPRINGS**
Dates in yellow are NEAPS

2012

MAY

Time	m		Time	m
1 0102 / 0708 / TU 1327 / 1935	1.0 / 4.0 / 1.3 / 4.0	**16** 0243 / 0855 / W 1502 / 2103		0.9 / 4.2 / 1.2 / 4.2
2 0216 / 0825 / W 1441 / 2045	0.9 / 4.1 / 1.1 / 4.2	**17** 0335 / 0948 / TH 1554 / 2154		0.9 / 4.2 / 1.1 / 4.3
3 0318 / 0926 / TH 1539 / 2142	0.6 / 4.4 / 0.9 / 4.5	**18** 0418 / 1032 / F 1638 / 2239		0.8 / 4.3 / 1.0 / 4.4
4 0410 / 1019 / F 1631 / 2233	0.5 / 4.5 / 0.8 / 4.7	**19** 0454 / 1108 / SA 1718 / 2317		0.8 / 4.4 / 0.8 / 4.4
5 0458 / 1107 / SA 1719 / 2322	0.4 / 4.6 / 0.6 / 4.8	**20** 0529 / 1139 / SU 1756 / ● 2353		0.8 / 4.4 / 0.7 / 4.5
6 0544 / 1152 / SU 1808 / ○	0.4 / 4.7 / 0.5	**21** 0604 / 1211 / M 1832		0.7 / 4.5 / 0.7
7 0011 / 0628 / M 1239 / 1857	4.9 / 0.4 / 4.8 / 0.5	**22** 0029 / 0636 / TU 1246 / 1906		4.5 / 0.7 / 4.5 / 0.6
8 0103 / 0713 / TU 1325 / 1946	5.0 / 0.4 / 4.8 / 0.4	**23** 0106 / 0707 / W 1322 / 1940		4.5 / 0.8 / 4.5 / 0.6
9 0154 / 0758 / W 1411 / 2035	5.0 / 0.5 / 4.7 / 0.4	**24** 0144 / 0740 / TH 1359 / 2014		4.5 / 0.8 / 4.5 / 0.6
10 0244 / 0842 / TH 1457 / 2124	4.8 / 0.7 / 4.6 / 0.5	**25** 0223 / 0815 / F 1436 / 2051		4.4 / 0.8 / 4.4 / 0.7
11 0334 / 0929 / F 1545 / 2217	4.7 / 0.9 / 4.5 / 0.6	**26** 0303 / 0854 / SA 1513 / 2133		4.4 / 0.9 / 4.3 / 0.7
12 0428 / 1023 / SA 1640 / ◑ 2318	4.4 / 1.1 / 4.3 / 0.8	**27** 0344 / 1032 / SU 1555 / 2221		4.2 / 1.0 / 4.3 / 0.8
13 0533 / 1129 / SU 1749	4.2 / 1.3 / 4.2	**28** 0430 / 1029 / M 1643 / ◑ 2318		4.2 / 1.1 / 4.2 / 0.8
14 0028 / 0645 / M 1248 / 1900	0.9 / 4.1 / 1.4 / 4.1	**29** 0524 / 1131 / TU 1740		4.1 / 1.2 / 4.2
15 0140 / 0753 / TU 1402 / 2004	0.9 / 4.1 / 1.3 / 4.1	**30** 0024 / 0628 / W 1243 / 1848		0.8 / 4.1 / 1.2 / 4.2
		31 0134 / 0742 / TH 1359 / 2002		0.8 / 4.2 / 1.1 / 4.3

JUNE

Time	m		Time	m
1 0240 / 0850 / F 1506 / 2108	0.7 / 4.3 / 1.0 / 4.5	**16** 0335 / 0951 / SA 1606 / 2206		1.0 / 4.2 / 1.1 / 4.2
2 0338 / 0949 / SA 1605 / 2207	0.6 / 4.4 / 0.8 / 4.6	**17** 0421 / 1036 / SU 1653 / 2252		1.0 / 4.3 / 0.9 / 4.3
3 0432 / 1043 / SU 1700 / 2304	0.5 / 4.6 / 0.7 / 4.8	**18** 0504 / 1115 / M 1736 / 2332		0.9 / 4.4 / 0.8 / 4.4
4 0523 / 1134 / M 1755 / ○ 2359	0.5 / 4.6 / 0.5 / 4.9	**19** 0542 / 1150 / TU 1815 / ●		0.9 / 4.5 / 0.7
5 0612 / 1222 / TU 1849	0.5 / 4.7 / 0.4	**20** 0009 / 0616 / W 1226 / 1850		4.5 / 0.9 / 4.5 / 0.6
6 0052 / 0700 / W 1311 / 1940	4.9 / 0.6 / 4.7 / 0.4	**21** 0047 / 0649 / TH 1303 / 1926		4.5 / 0.8 / 4.6 / 0.6
7 0144 / 0747 / TH 1358 / 2030	4.9 / 0.7 / 4.7 / 0.4	**22** 0127 / 0724 / F 1341 / 2002		4.6 / 0.8 / 4.6 / 0.5
8 0234 / 0831 / F 1444 / 2117	4.8 / 0.8 / 4.7 / 0.4	**23** 0208 / 0801 / SA 1420 / 2040		4.6 / 0.8 / 4.6 / 0.5
9 0323 / 0915 / SA 1530 / 2203	4.7 / 0.9 / 4.6 / 0.5	**24** 0249 / 0841 / SU 1459 / 2121		4.5 / 0.8 / 4.5 / 0.6
10 0412 / 1000 / SU 1617 / 2252	4.5 / 1.1 / 4.5 / 0.7	**25** 0329 / 0923 / M 1538 / 2204		4.4 / 0.9 / 4.5 / 0.6
11 0505 / 1050 / M 1711 / ◑ 2346	4.3 / 1.2 / 4.3 / 0.8	**26** 0411 / 1009 / TU 1620 / 2251		4.3 / 1.0 / 4.4 / 0.7
12 0605 / 1152 / TU 1815	4.1 / 1.3 / 4.2	**27** 0457 / 1102 / W 1711 / ◑ 2348		4.2 / 1.1 / 4.4 / 0.8
13 0048 / 0705 / W 1308 / 1917	1.0 / 4.0 / 1.4 / 4.1	**28** 0552 / 1205 / TH 1811		4.2 / 1.2 / 4.3
14 0149 / 0804 / TH 1417 / 2017	1.0 / 4.0 / 1.3 / 4.1	**29** 0055 / 0702 / F 1322 / 1926		0.8 / 4.2 / 1.2 / 4.3
15 0245 / 0900 / F 1515 / 2113	1.0 / 4.1 / 1.2 / 4.2	**30** 0206 / 0819 / SA 1438 / 2042		0.9 / 4.2 / 1.1 / 4.4

JULY

Time	m		Time	m
1 0313 / 0926 / SU 1545 / 2152	0.8 / 4.3 / 0.9 / 4.5	**16** 0353 / 1007 / M 1628 / 2229		1.2 / 4.2 / 1.0 / 4.2
2 0413 / 1027 / M 1648 / 2255	0.7 / 4.5 / 0.7 / 4.7	**17** 0441 / 1053 / TU 1714 / 2314		1.1 / 4.3 / 0.9 / 4.4
3 0509 / 1122 / TU 1748 / ○ 2352	0.7 / 4.6 / 0.6 / 4.8	**18** 0523 / 1132 / W 1755 / 2352		1.0 / 4.5 / 0.7 / 4.5
4 0600 / 1212 / W 1843	0.7 / 4.7 / 0.4	**19** 0600 / 1207 / TH 1833 / ●		0.9 / 4.6 / 0.6
5 0044 / 0648 / TH 1259 / 1932	4.8 / 0.7 / 4.8 / 0.4	**20** 0029 / 0633 / F 1244 / 1909		4.6 / 0.9 / 4.7 / 0.5
6 0134 / 0733 / F 1345 / 2017	4.8 / 0.7 / 4.8 / 0.4	**21** 0108 / 0708 / SA 1322 / 1945		4.7 / 0.8 / 4.7 / 0.5
7 0220 / 0814 / SA 1428 / 2059	4.8 / 0.8 / 4.8 / 0.4	**22** 0149 / 0746 / SU 1401 / 2023		4.7 / 0.8 / 4.8 / 0.4
8 0304 / 0853 / SU 1508 / 2136	4.7 / 0.9 / 4.7 / 0.5	**23** 0230 / 0825 / M 1439 / 2101		4.6 / 0.8 / 4.7 / 0.5
9 0345 / 0930 / M 1547 / 2213	4.5 / 1.0 / 4.6 / 0.7	**24** 0310 / 0905 / TU 1517 / 2140		4.6 / 0.9 / 4.7 / 0.6
10 0425 / 1010 / TU 1628 / 2253	4.3 / 1.1 / 4.4 / 0.9	**25** 0348 / 0948 / W 1557 / 2222		4.4 / 0.9 / 4.6 / 0.7
11 0509 / 1056 / W 1716 / ◑ 2342	4.1 / 1.3 / 4.3 / 1.1	**26** 0430 / 1035 / TH 1645 / ◑ 2313		4.3 / 1.0 / 4.5 / 0.8
12 0605 / 1154 / TH 1818	4.0 / 1.4 / 4.1	**27** 0521 / 1134 / F 1745		4.2 / 1.2 / 4.4
13 0046 / 0710 / F 1320 / 1927	1.2 / 3.9 / 1.5 / 4.0	**28** 0021 / 0631 / SA 1254 / 1903		1.0 / 4.1 / 1.2 / 4.3
14 0156 / 0813 / SA 1433 / 2033	1.3 / 3.9 / 1.4 / 4.0	**29** 0141 / 0755 / SU 1419 / 2028		1.0 / 4.1 / 1.2 / 4.3
15 0258 / 0913 / SU 1534 / 2135	1.3 / 4.1 / 1.2 / 4.1	**30** 0256 / 0912 / M 1536 / 2147		1.0 / 4.2 / 1.0 / 4.4
		31 0402 / 1019 / TU 1646 / 2253		1.0 / 4.4 / 0.8 / 4.6

AUGUST

Time	m		Time	m
1 0500 / 1115 / W 1745 / 2347	0.9 / 4.6 / 0.6 / 4.7	**16** 0501 / 1110 / TH 1731 / 2331		1.1 / 4.5 / 0.7 / 4.5
2 0549 / 1203 / TH 1834 / ○	0.8 / 4.7 / 0.4	**17** 0539 / 1146 / F 1810 / ●		1.0 / 4.6 / 0.7
3 0035 / 0632 / F 1246 / 1916	4.8 / 0.8 / 4.8 / 0.4	**18** 0007 / 0614 / SA 1222 / 1846		4.6 / 0.9 / 4.7 / 0.5
4 0118 / 0713 / SA 1325 / 1955	4.8 / 0.8 / 4.9 / 0.4	**19** 0046 / 0650 / SU 1259 / 1922		4.7 / 0.8 / 4.8 / 0.4
5 0158 / 0751 / SU 1403 / 2029	4.7 / 0.8 / 4.9 / 0.5	**20** 0126 / 0727 / M 1337 / 1959		4.8 / 0.7 / 4.9 / 0.4
6 0235 / 0826 / M 1439 / 2059	4.6 / 0.9 / 4.8 / 0.6	**21** 0206 / 0806 / TU 1416 / 2035		4.8 / 0.7 / 4.9 / 0.5
7 0308 / 0900 / TU 1513 / 2129	4.5 / 0.9 / 4.7 / 0.7	**22** 0245 / 0846 / W 1455 / 2112		4.7 / 0.8 / 4.8 / 0.6
8 0339 / 0934 / W 1547 / 2202	4.4 / 1.1 / 4.5 / 0.9	**23** 0322 / 0927 / TH 1537 / 2154		4.5 / 0.9 / 4.7 / 0.7
9 0412 / 1012 / TH 1626 / ◑ 2241	4.2 / 1.2 / 4.3 / 1.1	**24** 0404 / 1014 / F 1626 / ◑ 2245		4.4 / 1.0 / 4.6 / 1.0
10 0454 / 1059 / F 1714 / 2334	4.0 / 1.4 / 4.1 / 1.4	**25** 0457 / 1114 / SA 1729 / 2357		4.2 / 1.1 / 4.4 / 1.2
11 0551 / 1205 / SA 1820	3.9 / 1.5 / 3.9	**26** 0610 / 1239 / SU 1853		4.0 / 1.2 / 4.2
12 0053 / 0718 / SU 1343 / 1947	1.5 / 3.8 / 1.5 / 3.8	**27** 0125 / 0741 / M 1410 / 2025		1.3 / 4.0 / 1.2 / 4.2
13 0219 / 0834 / M 1458 / 2103	1.5 / 3.9 / 1.4 / 4.0	**28** 0247 / 0902 / TU 1535 / 2148		1.2 / 4.2 / 1.0 / 4.4
14 0324 / 0936 / TU 1558 / 2204	1.4 / 4.1 / 1.1 / 4.2	**29** 0356 / 1011 / W 1644 / 2249		1.0 / 4.4 / 0.7 / 4.6
15 0417 / 1027 / W 1648 / 2252	1.2 / 4.3 / 0.9 / 4.4	**30** 0451 / 1105 / TH 1736 / 2338		1.0 / 4.6 / 0.6 / 4.7
		31 0535 / 1149 / F 1817 / ○		0.9 / 4.7 / 0.5

Chart Datum: 2·50 metres below Ordnance Datum (Newlyn)
HAT is 5·2 metres above Chart Datum

MARGATE
LAT 51°23'N LONG 1°23'E
TIMES AND HEIGHTS OF HIGH AND LOW WATERS

Dates in amber are **SPRINGS**
Dates in yellow are **NEAPS**

2012

SEPTEMBER

Day	Time m	Time m	Time m	Time m
1 SA	0019 4.8	0613 0.8	1225 4.8	1852 0.5
2 SU	0055 4.8	0649 0.8	1259 4.9	1923 0.5
3 M	0128 4.7	0725 0.8	1333 4.9	1952 0.6
4 TU	0158 4.7	0759 0.8	1407 4.8	2021 0.7
5 W	0228 4.6	0831 0.9	1441 4.7	2049 0.8
6 TH	0258 4.4	0903 1.0	1514 4.5	2119 1.0
7 F	0331 4.3	0936 1.1	1549 4.3	2154 1.2
8 SA ◑	0409 4.1	1017 1.3	1633 4.1	2240 1.4
9 SU	0457 3.9	1113 1.5	1730 3.9	2345 1.7
10 M	0603 3.8	1240 1.6	1848 3.8	
11 TU	0124 1.7	0742 3.8	1414 1.4	2021 3.9
12 W	0249 1.5	0857 4.0	1521 1.2	2130 4.2
13 TH	0346 1.3	0953 4.3	1614 0.9	2220 4.4
14 F	0432 1.1	1038 4.5	1700 0.7	2302 4.6
15 SA	0512 0.9	1117 4.7	1740 0.6	2340 4.7
16 SU ●	0550 0.8	1153 4.8	1818 0.5	
17 M	0018 4.8	0628 0.7	1231 4.9	1855 0.4
18 TU	0058 4.9	0707 0.7	1311 5.0	1931 0.4
19 W	0138 4.8	0747 0.7	1353 5.0	2008 0.5
20 TH	0217 4.7	0828 0.7	1436 4.9	2047 0.6
21 F	0258 4.6	0911 0.8	1522 4.8	2131 0.9
22 SA ◐	0344 4.4	1000 0.9	1615 4.6	2225 1.1
23 SU	0439 4.2	1105 1.1	1722 4.3	2341 1.4
24 M	0555 4.0	1232 1.2	1849 4.2	
25 TU	0113 1.4	0726 4.0	1404 1.1	2022 4.3
26 W	0236 1.4	0847 4.2	1526 0.9	2137 4.5
27 TH	0343 1.2	0954 4.4	1628 0.7	2234 4.6
28 F	0435 1.0	1045 4.6	1715 0.6	2320 4.7
29 SA	0515 0.9	1126 4.7	1751 0.6	2356 4.7
30 SU ○	0550 0.8	1158 4.8	1820 0.6	

OCTOBER

Day	Time m	Time m	Time m	Time m
1 M	0025 4.7	0624 0.8	1229 4.8	1847 0.6
2 TU	0052 4.7	0700 0.7	1303 4.8	1916 0.7
3 W	0121 4.7	0734 0.8	1338 4.8	1946 0.7
4 TH	0153 4.6	0806 0.8	1412 4.7	2014 0.9
5 F	0225 4.5	0836 0.9	1446 4.5	2043 1.0
6 SA	0257 4.4	0908 1.0	1521 4.3	2117 1.2
7 SU	0333 4.2	0946 1.1	1603 4.1	2159 1.4
8 M ◑	0417 4.0	1037 1.3	1655 4.0	2258 1.6
9 TU	0515 3.8	1149 1.4	1801 3.8	
10 W	0019 1.7	0632 3.8	1321 1.4	1927 3.9
11 TH	0155 1.6	0805 3.9	1437 1.2	2045 4.1
12 F	0305 1.4	0914 4.5	1535 0.9	2141 4.4
13 SA	0356 1.1	0959 4.3	1623 0.7	2228 4.6
14 SU	0441 0.9	1042 4.7	1707 0.6	2309 4.8
15 M ●	0523 0.8	1122 4.8	1747 0.5	2349 4.9
16 TU	0605 0.7	1203 5.0	1827 0.4	
17 W	0029 4.9	0647 0.6	1248 5.0	1906 0.5
18 TH	0111 4.9	0731 0.6	1335 5.0	1946 0.6
19 F	0154 4.8	0815 0.6	1424 4.9	2028 0.7
20 SA	0240 4.7	0902 0.7	1514 4.8	2115 0.8
21 SU	0328 4.5	0955 0.8	1609 4.6	2211 0.9
22 M ◐	0425 4.3	1101 0.9	1716 4.3	2324 1.4
23 TU	0539 4.1	1221 1.0	1840 4.2	
24 W	0051 1.5	0704 4.1	1345 1.0	2001 4.3
25 TH	0211 1.4	0818 4.2	1458 0.9	2111 4.4
26 F	0317 1.3	0922 4.4	1558 0.8	2207 4.5
27 SA	0409 1.1	1014 4.5	1643 0.7	2252 4.6
28 SU	0456 1.0	1056 4.6	1717 0.7	2326 4.6
29 M ○	0527 0.9	1129 4.6	1745 0.7	2353 4.6
30 TU ●	0603 0.7	1201 4.7	1815 0.5	2349 4.9
31 W	0019 4.7	0638 0.7	1236 4.7	1846 0.7

NOVEMBER

Day	Time m	Time m	Time m	Time m
1 TH	0051 4.7	0713 0.7	1312 4.7	1917 0.8
2 F	0125 4.6	0745 0.7	1348 4.6	1946 0.9
3 SA	0159 4.6	0816 0.8	1424 4.5	2016 1.0
4 SU	0233 4.4	0848 0.9	1500 4.3	2051 1.2
5 M ◐	0307 4.3	0926 1.0	1540 4.2	2132 1.3
6 TU	0348 4.2	1013 1.1	1627 4.1	2225 1.5
7 W ◑	0440 4.0	1113 1.2	1724 4.0	2332 1.6
8 TH	0542 3.9	1228 1.2	1834 4.0	
9 F	0052 1.6	0658 4.0	1345 1.1	1953 4.1
10 SA	0212 1.4	0816 4.2	1450 0.9	2058 4.4
11 SU	0316 1.1	0916 4.4	1545 0.7	2152 4.6
12 M	0408 0.9	1007 4.6	1633 0.6	2239 4.7
13 TU ●	0457 0.8	1055 4.8	1718 0.5	2323 4.8
14 W	0545 0.7	1143 4.9	1803 0.5	
15 TH	0007 4.9	0632 0.6	1233 5.0	1847 0.6
16 F	0052 4.9	0721 0.5	1325 5.0	1932 0.6
17 SA	0139 4.8	0810 0.5	1416 4.9	2017 0.8
18 SU	0227 4.7	0859 0.5	1508 4.8	2105 1.0
19 M	0316 4.6	0952 0.6	1602 4.6	2157 1.2
20 TU ◐	0410 4.4	1051 0.8	1703 4.4	2258 1.3
21 W	0515 4.3	1158 0.9	1814 4.2	
22 TH	0014 1.5	0630 4.2	1309 0.9	1925 4.2
23 F	0132 1.5	0737 4.2	1416 0.9	2029 4.3
24 SA	0238 1.4	0839 4.3	1513 0.9	2127 4.3
25 SU	0335 1.2	0935 4.3	1601 0.9	2216 4.4
26 M	0422 1.1	1023 4.4	1639 0.9	2254 4.5
27 TU	0504 0.9	1103 4.5	1715 0.9	2326 4.5
28 W ○	0543 0.8	1140 4.5	1750 0.9	2355 4.6
29 TH	0620 0.7	1214 4.6	1823 0.9	
30 F	0028 4.6	0655 0.7	1251 4.6	1854 0.9

DECEMBER

Day	Time m	Time m	Time m	Time m
1 SA	0103 4.6	0727 0.7	1327 4.6	1925 0.9
2 SU	0139 4.6	0800 0.7	1405 4.5	1957 1.0
3 M	0215 4.5	0834 0.7	1444 4.4	2033 1.2
4 TU	0251 4.4	0912 0.8	1523 4.3	2114 1.2
5 W	0328 4.3	0954 0.9	1604 4.2	2200 1.3
6 TH ◐	0412 4.2	1044 0.9	1652 4.1	2255 1.4
7 F	0504 4.2	1144 1.0	1748 4.1	
8 SA	0001 1.4	0604 4.1	1252 1.0	1858 4.1
9 SU	0118 1.4	0719 4.2	1403 0.9	2014 4.3
10 M	0234 1.2	0834 4.3	1507 0.8	2118 4.4
11 TU	0337 1.0	0938 4.5	1603 0.7	2214 4.6
12 W	0435 0.8	1036 4.7	1656 0.6	2305 4.7
13 TH ●	0529 0.6	1131 4.8	1746 0.6	
14 F	0623 0.5	1225 4.9	1835 0.7	
15 SA	0041 4.9	0715 0.6	1318 5.0	1923 0.7
16 SU	0130 4.9	0806 0.4	1409 4.9	2008 0.8
17 M	0217 4.8	0854 0.4	1459 4.8	2052 0.9
18 TU	0304 4.7	0941 0.5	1548 4.6	2137 1.1
19 W	0351 4.6	1028 0.8	1639 4.4	2224 1.2
20 TH ◐	0443 4.4	1119 0.8	1736 4.2	2321 1.4
21 F	0545 4.3	1218 0.9	1838 4.1	
22 SA	0034 1.5	0651 4.1	1322 1.1	1940 4.1
23 SU	0150 1.5	0754 4.1	1422 1.1	2039 4.1
24 M	0255 1.4	0855 4.1	1517 1.1	2135 4.2
25 TU	0352 1.2	0952 4.2	1606 1.1	2224 4.3
26 W	0442 1.0	1042 4.3	1650 1.1	2304 4.4
27 TH	0525 0.9	1123 4.4	1730 1.1	2338 4.5
28 F ○	0604 0.8	1158 4.5	1806 1.0	
29 SA	0011 4.5	0639 0.7	1233 4.5	1837 0.9
30 SU	0045 4.6	0712 0.6	1309 4.6	1908 0.9
31 M	0121 4.7	0744 0.6	1348 4.6	1942 0.9

Chart Datum: 2·50 metres below Ordnance Datum (Newlyn)
HAT is 5·2 metres above Chart Datum

TIDES

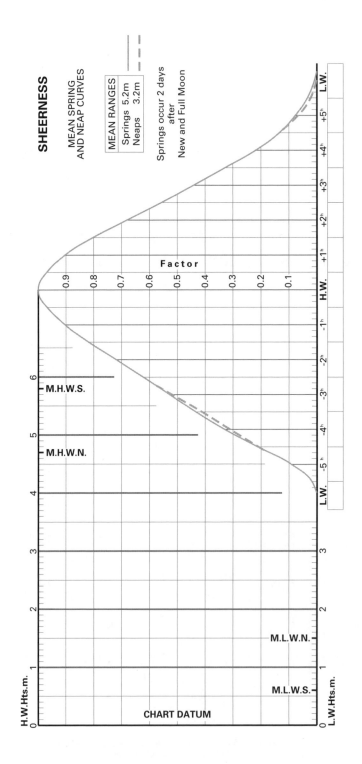

SHEERNESS

MEAN SPRING AND NEAP CURVES

MEAN RANGES	
Springs	5.2m
Neaps	3.2m

Springs occur 2 days after New and Full Moon

SHEERNESS
LAT 51°27'N   LONG 0°45'E
TIMES AND HEIGHTS OF HIGH AND LOW WATERS

2012

JANUARY

Day	Time m	Time m	Time m	Time m
1 SU	0510 5.1	1117 1.2	1751 4.9	☾2325 1.6
16 M	0451 5.5	1109 0.8	1732 5.3	2316 1.2
2 M	0559 4.9	1204 1.4	1843 4.7	
17 TU	0545 5.3	1159 1.0	1832 5.1	
3 TU	0023 1.7	0658 4.7	1313 1.1	1943 4.6
18 W	0017 1.3	0653 5.1	1311 1.2	1943 5.0
4 W	0142 1.8	0808 4.6	1431 1.5	2050 4.7
19 TH	0139 1.4	0813 5.0	1437 1.3	2058 5.0
5 TH	0259 1.6	0918 4.7	1535 1.4	2153 4.9
20 F	0309 1.3	0933 5.1	1555 1.2	2210 5.2
6 F	0401 1.4	1020 4.9	1628 1.3	2247 5.1
21 SA	0432 1.1	1045 5.4	1704 1.1	2313 5.4
7 SA	0455 1.2	1111 5.2	1715 1.2	2333 5.3
22 SU	0543 0.8	1144 5.6	1801 1.0	
8 SU	0542 1.0	1156 5.4	1757 1.1	
23 M	0006 5.5	0638 0.6	1236 5.6	●1847 0.9
9 M	0015 5.5	0626 0.9	1237 5.5	○1836 1.0
24 TU	0052 5.7	0725 0.5	1320 5.8	1927 0.8
10 TU	0054 5.6	0709 0.7	1316 5.7	1916 0.9
25 W	0133 5.7	0806 0.5	1401 5.8	2003 0.8
11 W	0131 5.7	0752 0.6	1355 5.8	1956 0.8
26 TH	0211 5.8	0842 0.5	1439 5.8	2037 0.8
12 TH	0208 5.7	0836 0.5	1434 5.8	2037 0.8
27 F	0247 5.7	0914 0.6	1515 5.7	2107 0.9
13 F	0245 5.7	0917 0.5	1514 5.8	2115 0.9
28 SA	0320 5.6	0940 0.7	1549 5.5	2135 1.0
14 SA	0324 5.7	0955 0.6	1556 5.7	2151 1.0
29 SU	0353 5.5	1004 0.9	1623 5.3	2204 1.2
15 SU	0405 5.6	1031 0.7	1641 5.5	2229 1.1
30 M	0428 5.3	1031 1.0	1659 5.1	2238 1.3
31 TU	0507 5.0	1107 1.3	1741 4.8	☾2323 1.5

FEBRUARY

Day	Time m	Time m	Time m	Time m
1 W	0556 4.7	1157 1.5	1835 4.6	
16 TH	0633 5.1	1244 1.3	1917 4.8	
2 TH	0024 1.7	0702 4.5	1313 1.7	1946 4.5
17 F	0121 1.4	0759 4.9	1418 1.5	2040 4.8
3 F	0159 1.7	0824 4.5	1447 1.7	2105 4.6
18 SA	0304 1.3	0926 5.0	1542 1.4	2159 5.0
4 SA	0323 1.5	0942 4.7	1555 1.5	2213 4.9
19 SU	0432 1.1	1040 5.3	1655 1.2	2303 5.3
5 SU	0426 1.2	1044 5.0	1649 1.3	2308 5.2
20 M	0539 0.8	1137 5.6	1749 1.0	2354 5.5
6 M	0520 1.0	1134 5.3	1736 1.1	2353 5.5
21 TU	0628 0.6	1223 5.7	1831 0.9 ●	
7 TU	0609 0.8	1217 5.5	1820 0.9 ○	
22 W	0036 5.6	0708 0.5	1304 5.8	1907 0.8
8 W	0034 5.6	0655 0.6	1258 5.8	1901 0.8
23 TH	0114 5.7	0743 0.5	1340 5.8	1941 0.8
9 TH	0113 5.8	0739 0.4	1337 5.9	1943 0.7
24 F	0148 5.8	0815 0.5	1413 5.8	2012 0.7
10 F	0150 5.9	0822 0.3	1416 6.0	2024 0.6
25 SA	0220 5.8	0843 0.6	1444 5.7	2041 0.8
11 SA	0228 5.9	0902 0.3	1456 6.0	2102 0.7
26 SU	0250 5.7	0908 0.7	1514 5.6	2108 0.9
12 SU	0306 5.9	0939 0.4	1536 5.8	2136 0.8
27 M	0321 5.6	0930 0.8	1544 5.4	2133 1.0
13 M	0346 5.8	1013 0.6	1619 5.6	2211 0.9
28 TU	0353 5.4	0954 1.0	1615 5.2	2202 1.2
14 TU	0431 5.6	1047 0.8	1706 5.3	☽2255 1.0
29 W	0428 5.1	1025 1.2	1652 5.0	2240 1.3
15 W	0524 5.4	1134 1.0	1804 5.0	2353 1.2

MARCH

Day	Time m	Time m	Time m	Time m
1 TH	0511 4.9	1107 1.5	1739 4.7	2333 1.5
16 F	0623 5.1	1227 1.5	1858 4.8	
2 F	0609 4.6	1210 1.7	1846 4.5	
17 SA	0118 1.3	0749 4.9	1402 1.6	2023 4.8
3 SA	0053 1.7	0730 4.4	1352 1.8	2015 4.5
18 SU	0258 1.2	0915 5.1	1525 1.4	2142 5.0
4 SU	0241 1.6	0900 4.6	1517 1.6	2135 4.8
19 M	0421 1.0	1025 5.4	1636 1.2	2245 5.3
5 M	0353 1.2	1011 5.0	1618 1.3	2236 5.2
20 TU	0521 0.7	1119 5.6	1727 1.0	2333 5.5
6 TU	0453 0.9	1105 5.4	1710 1.1	2325 5.5
21 W	0606 0.6	1203 5.7	1807 0.9	
7 W	0546 0.7	1151 5.7	1757 0.9	
22 TH	0014 5.6	0641 0.6	1241 5.7	●1841 0.8
8 TH	0008 5.7	0633 0.5	1234 5.9	○1841 0.7
23 F	0049 5.7	0713 0.6	1313 5.7	1914 0.7
9 F	0048 5.9	0718 0.3	1314 6.0	1925 0.6
24 SA	0121 5.7	0742 0.6	1344 5.7	1946 0.7
10 SA	0127 6.0	0801 0.2	1354 6.1	2007 0.5
25 SU	0152 5.7	0809 0.6	1413 5.7	2016 0.7
11 SU	0206 6.1	0842 0.2	1434 6.0	2046 0.5
26 M	0222 5.7	0836 0.7	1441 5.6	2044 0.8
12 M	0247 6.1	0919 0.3	1515 5.9	2123 0.6
27 TU	0253 5.6	0900 0.8	1510 5.5	2109 0.9
13 TU	0329 6.0	0954 0.6	1557 5.7	2200 0.8
28 W	0325 5.4	0925 1.0	1541 5.3	2137 1.0
14 W	0416 5.7	1030 0.8	1645 5.4	2244 0.9
29 TH	0400 5.2	0954 1.2	1616 5.1	2211 1.2
15 TH	0512 5.4	1117 1.2	1743 5.0	☽2344 1.2
30 F	0441 5.0	1033 1.4	1701 4.9	2300 1.4
31 SA	0535 4.8	1131 1.7	1801 4.6	

APRIL

Day	Time m	Time m	Time m	Time m
1 SU	0012 1.5	0647 4.6	1258 1.8	1925 4.5
16 M	0238 1.1	0850 5.1	1455 1.5	2113 5.0
2 M	0153 1.5	0815 4.7	1433 1.6	2051 4.8
17 TU	0351 0.9	0958 5.3	1601 1.3	2215 5.2
3 TU	0314 1.2	0931 5.1	1540 1.3	2157 5.1
18 W	0449 0.8	1051 5.5	1654 1.1	2305 5.4
4 W	0417 0.9	1031 5.4	1636 1.1	2251 5.5
19 TH	0533 0.8	1135 5.6	1736 1.0	2346 5.5
5 TH	0514 0.7	1121 5.7	1728 0.9	2337 5.7
20 F	0607 0.8	1212 5.6	1812 0.9	
6 F	0606 0.5	1206 5.9	1817 0.7 ○	
21 SA	0021 5.6	0637 0.8	1245 5.6	●1846 0.8
7 SA	0020 5.9	0653 0.3	1249 6.1	1904 0.6
22 SU	0054 5.6	0707 0.7	1314 5.6	1919 0.7
8 SU	0103 6.1	0737 0.3	1331 6.1	1949 0.5
23 M	0126 5.6	0737 0.7	1343 5.6	1952 0.7
9 M	0146 6.2	0819 0.3	1413 6.1	2032 0.4
24 TU	0157 5.6	0806 0.8	1412 5.6	2022 0.8
10 TU	0230 6.2	0859 0.4	1455 5.9	2113 0.5
25 W	0230 5.6	0835 0.9	1443 5.5	2052 0.9
11 W	0316 6.0	0937 0.6	1539 5.7	2155 0.7
26 TH	0303 5.5	0904 1.0	1515 5.4	2123 1.0
12 TH	0407 5.7	1017 0.9	1628 5.4	2241 0.9
27 F	0340 5.3	0935 1.2	1552 5.2	2158 1.1
13 F	0505 5.4	1105 1.2	1727 5.1	☽2342 1.1
28 SA	0422 5.1	1014 1.4	1636 5.0	2244 1.2
14 SA	0614 5.1	1211 1.5	1839 4.9	
29 SU	0513 5.0	1107 1.5	1732 4.8	☽2347 1.3
15 SU	0110 1.2	0732 5.0	1337 1.6	1958 4.8
30 M	0618 4.9	1219 1.6	1844 4.8	

Chart Datum: 2·90 metres below Ordnance Datum (Newlyn)
HAT is 6·3 metres above Chart Datum

TIDES

TIME ZONE (UT)
For Summer Time add ONE hour in **non-shaded areas**

SHEERNESS
LAT 51°27'N LONG 0°45'E
TIMES AND HEIGHTS OF HIGH AND LOW WATERS

Dates in amber are **SPRINGS**
Dates in yellow are **NEAPS**

2012

MAY

Day	Times & heights (m)	Day	Times & heights (m)
1 TU	0109 1.3 / 0735 4.9 / 1344 1.5 / 2004 4.9	16 W	0305 1.1 / 0918 5.2 / 1515 1.4 / 2136 5.1
2 W	0231 1.1 / 0850 5.2 / 1456 1.3 / 2115 5.2	17 TH	0402 1.0 / 1015 5.3 / 1611 1.2 / 2230 5.2
3 TH	0337 0.9 / 0953 5.5 / 1558 1.1 / 2214 5.5	18 F	0448 1.0 / 1101 5.4 / 1659 1.1 / 2314 5.3
4 F	0438 0.7 / 1048 5.7 / 1655 0.9 / 2306 5.7	19 SA	0527 0.9 / 1141 5.5 / 1741 1.0 / 2354 5.4
5 SA	0535 0.5 / 1138 5.9 / 1751 0.7 / 2355 5.9	20 SU	0602 0.9 / 1215 5.5 / 1819 0.9 / ●
6 SU	0627 0.4 / 1224 6.0 / 1844 0.6 / ○	21 M	0029 5.5 / 0635 0.9 / 1248 5.6 / 1855 0.8
7 M	0042 6.1 / 0714 0.4 / 1310 6.0 / 1934 0.4	22 TU	0104 5.5 / 0708 0.9 / 1319 5.6 / 1931 0.8
8 TU	0130 6.2 / 0759 0.4 / 1354 6.0 / 2021 0.4	23 W	0138 5.6 / 0741 0.9 / 1351 5.6 / 2006 0.8
9 W	0218 6.1 / 0842 0.5 / 1436 5.9 / 2107 0.4	24 TH	0212 5.5 / 0814 0.9 / 1424 5.5 / 2041 0.8
10 TH	0307 6.0 / 0923 0.7 / 1526 5.7 / 2152 0.6	25 F	0248 5.5 / 0849 1.0 / 1459 5.4 / 2117 0.9
11 F	0359 5.8 / 1004 1.0 / 1615 5.5 / 2240 0.7	26 SA	0326 5.4 / 0924 1.1 / 1536 5.3 / 2155 0.9
12 SA	0455 5.5 / 1050 1.2 / 1711 5.2 / ○ 2336 0.9	27 SU	0409 5.3 / 1003 1.2 / 1619 5.2 / 2238 1.0
13 SU	0556 5.3 / 1147 1.4 / 1814 5.0	28 M	0457 5.2 / 1050 1.3 / 1709 5.1 / ◑ 2329 1.1
14 M	0046 1.1 / 0702 5.1 / 1259 1.5 / 1922 4.9	29 TU	0553 5.1 / 1147 1.4 / 1810 5.0
15 TU	0159 1.1 / 0812 5.1 / 1411 1.5 / 2033 5.0	30 W	0032 1.1 / 0659 5.1 / 1257 1.4 / 1921 5.0
		31 TH	0147 1.0 / 0811 5.2 / 1412 1.3 / 2034 5.2

JUNE

Day	Times & heights (m)	Day	Times & heights (m)
1 F	0258 0.9 / 0918 5.4 / 1521 1.2 / 2139 5.4	16 SA	0400 1.2 / 1022 5.1 / 1621 1.3 / 2242 5.1
2 SA	0404 0.8 / 1018 5.6 / 1626 1.0 / 2239 5.6	17 SU	0447 1.1 / 1108 5.3 / 1711 1.1 / 2327 5.3
3 SU	0506 0.7 / 1113 5.7 / 1730 0.8 / 2335 5.8	18 M	0530 1.1 / 1148 5.4 / 1755 1.0
4 M	0604 0.6 / 1205 5.8 / 1829 0.6 / ○	19 TU	0008 5.4 / 0608 1.0 / 1226 5.5 / ● 1835 0.9
5 TU	0028 6.0 / 0655 0.6 / 1254 5.9 / 1923 0.5	20 W	0046 5.5 / 0644 1.0 / 1301 5.6 / 1914 0.8
6 W	0119 6.1 / 0743 0.6 / 1341 5.9 / 2014 0.4	21 TH	0122 5.5 / 0721 0.9 / 1336 5.6 / 1953 0.7
7 TH	0209 6.1 / 0827 0.7 / 1427 5.9 / 2101 0.4	22 F	0158 5.6 / 0759 0.9 / 1411 5.6 / 2033 0.7
8 F	0258 6.0 / 0909 0.8 / 1513 5.7 / 2147 0.5	23 SA	0235 5.6 / 0837 0.9 / 1446 5.6 / 2113 0.7
9 SA	0347 5.8 / 0949 1.0 / 1600 5.6 / 2230 0.6	24 SU	0314 5.6 / 0915 1.0 / 1524 5.5 / 2152 0.7
10 SU	0437 5.6 / 1030 1.2 / 1648 5.4 / 2315 0.8	25 M	0355 5.5 / 0953 1.1 / 1604 5.4 / 2230 0.8
11 M	0528 5.4 / 1119 1.3 / 1740 5.2 / ◑	26 TU	0439 5.4 / 1032 1.2 / 1648 5.4 / 2311 0.9
12 TU	0005 1.0 / 0623 5.2 / 1210 1.5 / 1837 5.0	27 W	0529 5.3 / 1119 1.3 / 1741 5.3 / ◐
13 W	0105 1.1 / 0723 5.0 / 1316 1.6 / 1941 4.9	28 TH	0000 1.0 / 0627 5.2 / 1217 1.3 / 1844 5.2
14 TH	0208 1.2 / 0826 4.9 / 1424 1.5 / 2047 4.9	29 F	0105 1.0 / 0735 5.2 / 1331 1.4 / 1959 5.2
15 F	0307 1.2 / 0928 5.0 / 1526 1.4 / 2148 5.0	30 SA	0224 1.0 / 0846 5.2 / 1451 1.3 / 2112 5.3

JULY

Day	Times & heights (m)	Day	Times & heights (m)
1 SU	0338 1.0 / 0953 5.4 / 1606 1.1 / 2221 5.5	16 M	0413 1.3 / 1035 5.1 / 1643 1.2 / 2302 5.1
2 M	0446 0.9 / 1055 5.5 / 1718 0.9 / 2324 5.7	17 TU	0503 1.2 / 1123 5.3 / 1733 1.0 / 2347 5.3
3 TU	0548 0.8 / 1151 5.7 / 1822 0.6 / ○	18 W	0546 1.1 / 1205 5.5 / 1818 0.9
4 W	0020 5.9 / 0641 0.8 / 1243 5.8 / 1917 0.5	19 TH	0027 5.5 / 0625 1.0 / 1243 5.6 / ● 1859 0.8
5 TH	0112 6.0 / 0729 0.7 / 1330 5.9 / 2006 0.4	20 F	0105 5.6 / 0704 0.9 / 1320 5.7 / 1940 0.6
6 F	0159 6.0 / 0812 0.8 / 1414 5.9 / 2051 0.4	21 SA	0142 5.7 / 0744 0.9 / 1355 5.7 / 2022 0.6
7 SA	0245 6.0 / 0852 0.9 / 1457 5.8 / 2132 0.4	22 SU	0219 5.8 / 0824 0.8 / 1431 5.8 / 2102 0.5
8 SU	0328 5.8 / 0929 0.9 / 1538 5.7 / 2209 0.6	23 M	0257 5.7 / 0903 0.9 / 1507 5.7 / 2141 0.6
9 M	0411 5.7 / 1003 1.1 / 1618 5.6 / 2242 0.8	24 TU	0336 5.7 / 0938 1.0 / 1545 5.7 / 2216 0.7
10 TU	0453 5.4 / 1038 1.2 / 1700 5.4 / 2316 1.0	25 W	0418 5.6 / 1013 1.1 / 1627 5.6 / 2250 0.8
11 W	0538 5.2 / 1119 1.4 / 1747 5.1 / ◐ 2357 1.2	26 TH	0504 5.4 / 1053 1.2 / 1715 5.4 / ◑ 2332 1.0
12 TH	0627 4.9 / 1210 1.6 / 1842 4.9 / ◐	27 F	0558 5.2 / 1146 1.3 / 1816 5.2
13 F	0054 1.4 / 0724 4.8 / 1322 1.7 / 1948 4.7	28 SA	0032 1.2 / 0705 5.1 / 1300 1.4 / 1933 5.1
14 SA	0209 1.5 / 0830 4.7 / 1440 1.6 / 2100 4.7	29 SU	0158 1.3 / 0821 5.1 / 1434 1.4 / 2056 5.2
15 SU	0315 1.5 / 0937 4.9 / 1546 1.4 / 2207 4.9	30 M	0321 1.2 / 0936 5.2 / 1558 1.2 / 2213 5.4
		31 TU	0433 1.1 / 1044 5.4 / 1715 0.9 / 2318 5.6

AUGUST

Day	Times & heights (m)	Day	Times & heights (m)
1 W	0537 1.0 / 1142 5.6 / 1817 0.6	16 TH	0523 1.2 / 1140 5.5 / 1756 0.9
2 TH	0013 5.8 / 0629 0.9 / 1232 5.8 / ○ 1907 0.5	17 F	0003 5.6 / 0604 1.0 / 1220 5.7 / ● 1839 0.7
3 F	0101 5.8 / 0713 0.8 / 1315 5.9 / 1951 0.4	18 SA	0043 5.8 / 0645 0.9 / 1257 5.8 / 1921 0.6
4 SA	0144 6.0 / 0753 0.8 / 1356 5.9 / 2031 0.4	19 SU	0121 5.9 / 0726 0.8 / 1333 5.9 / 2003 0.5
5 SU	0225 6.0 / 0830 0.8 / 1434 5.9 / 2106 0.5	20 M	0158 6.0 / 0807 0.8 / 1409 6.0 / 2043 0.5
6 M	0303 5.8 / 0903 0.9 / 1510 5.8 / 2137 0.6	21 TU	0236 6.0 / 0845 0.8 / 1446 6.0 / 2121 0.5
7 TU	0339 5.7 / 0933 1.0 / 1545 5.7 / 2204 0.8	22 W	0315 5.9 / 0921 0.9 / 1525 5.9 / 2156 0.7
8 W	0414 5.5 / 1002 1.2 / 1620 5.5 / 2229 1.0	23 TH	0355 5.7 / 0955 1.0 / 1607 5.7 / 2229 0.9
9 TH	0449 5.2 / 1034 1.3 / 1658 5.2 / ◑ 2301 1.2	24 F	0439 5.5 / 1034 1.1 / 1656 5.5 / ◑ 2310 1.1
10 F	0530 5.0 / 1115 1.5 / 1745 4.9 / 2347 1.5	25 SA	0532 5.2 / 1127 1.3 / 1759 5.2
11 SA	0621 4.7 / 1212 1.7 / 1848 4.6	26 SU	0011 1.3 / 0640 5.0 / 1246 1.4 / 1920 5.0
12 SU	0056 1.7 / 0729 4.6 / 1343 1.8 / 2008 4.5	27 M	0142 1.5 / 0802 4.9 / 1429 1.4 / 2048 5.1
13 M	0230 1.7 / 0848 4.7 / 1510 1.6 / 2128 4.7	28 TU	0309 1.4 / 0924 5.1 / 1558 1.1 / 2208 5.4
14 TU	0340 1.6 / 0959 5.0 / 1615 1.3 / 2232 5.0	29 W	0424 1.2 / 1034 5.4 / 1711 0.8 / 2311 5.7
15 W	0435 1.3 / 1054 5.3 / 1709 1.1 / 2321 5.4	30 TH	0525 1.1 / 1129 5.6 / 1806 0.6
		31 F	0001 5.9 / 0612 0.9 / 1215 5.8 / ○ 1850 0.5

Chart Datum: 2·90 metres below Ordnance Datum (Newlyn)
HAT is 6·3 metres above Chart Datum

TIME ZONE (UT)
For Summer Time add ONE hour in **non-shaded areas**

SHEERNESS

LAT 51°27′N LONG 0°45′E

TIMES AND HEIGHTS OF HIGH AND LOW WATERS

Dates in amber are **SPRINGS**
Dates in yellow are **NEAPS**

2012

SEPTEMBER

Date	Day	Time	m	Time	m	Time	m	Time	m
1	SA	0045	5.9	0652	0.9	1255	5.9	1928	0.5
2	SU	0123	5.9	0728	0.8	1332	5.9	2002	0.5
3	M	0159	5.9	0802	0.8	1406	5.9	2033	0.6
4	TU	0232	5.8	0834	0.9	1439	5.8	2101	0.7
5	W	0304	5.7	0903	1.0	1511	5.7	2125	0.9
6	TH	0334	5.5	0929	1.1	1544	5.5	2148	1.1
7	F	0405	5.3	0956	1.3	1619	5.3	2217	1.3
8	SA	0441	5.1	1031	1.4	1701	5.0	◑ 2257	1.6
9	SU	0526	4.8	1121	1.6	1756	4.7	2356	1.8
10	M	0629	4.6	1237	1.8	1913	4.5		
11	TU	0130	1.9	0755	4.6	1426	1.7	2042	4.6
12	W	0301	1.7	0917	4.8	1540	1.4	2154	5.0
13	TH	0402	1.4	1018	5.2	1637	1.1	2248	5.4
14	F	0452	1.2	1107	5.5	1727	0.8	2333	5.7
15	SA	0538	1.0	1150	5.7	1812	0.7		
16	SU	0014	5.9	0620	0.9	1229	5.9	● 1856	0.5
17	M	0054	6.0	0703	0.8	1307	6.0	1938	0.4
18	TU	0133	6.1	0745	0.7	1345	6.1	2019	0.4
19	W	0212	6.1	0826	0.7	1425	6.1	2058	0.5
20	TH	0252	6.0	0904	0.8	1506	6.0	2134	0.7
21	F	0333	5.8	0941	0.9	1552	5.8	2210	0.9
22	SA	0419	5.5	1023	1.1	1644	5.5	◐ 2254	1.2
23	SU	0513	5.2	1119	1.3	1750	5.2	2357	1.5
24	M	0623	5.0	1243	1.4	1912	5.1		
25	TU	0127	1.6	0746	4.9	1424	1.3	2038	5.2
26	W	0252	1.5	0908	5.1	1548	1.1	2154	5.4
27	TH	0405	1.3	1015	5.4	1655	0.8	2253	5.7
28	F	0503	1.1	1109	5.6	1745	0.7	2341	5.8
29	SA	0548	1.0	1152	5.8	1824	0.7		
30	SU	0021	5.9	0625	0.9	1231	5.8	○ 1858	0.7

OCTOBER

Date	Day	Time	m	Time	m	Time	m	Time	m
1	M	0057	5.9	0659	0.9	1305	5.9	1928	0.7
2	TU	0130	5.8	0733	0.8	1338	5.9	1957	0.7
3	W	0200	5.8	0805	0.8	1410	5.8	2024	0.8
4	TH	0229	5.7	0834	0.9	1441	5.7	2049	1.0
5	F	0258	5.6	0900	1.1	1514	5.5	2113	1.1
6	SA	0329	5.4	0926	1.2	1548	5.3	2142	1.3
7	SU	0403	5.2	0959	1.3	1628	5.1	2220	1.6
8	M	0445	5.0	1046	1.5	1719	4.8	◑ 2313	1.8
9	TU	0541	4.7	1151	1.7	1826	4.6		
10	W	0031	1.9	0659	4.6	1328	1.7	1951	4.7
11	TH	0207	1.8	0827	4.8	1454	1.4	2108	5.0
12	F	0318	1.5	0934	5.1	1556	1.1	2208	5.4
13	SA	0414	1.3	1028	5.5	1650	0.8	2258	5.7
14	SU	0504	1.1	1115	5.7	1740	0.7	2343	5.9
15	M	0551	0.9	1158	5.9	1827	0.6	●	
16	TU	0026	6.1	0638	0.8	1241	6.1	1911	0.5
17	W	0108	6.1	0724	0.7	1323	6.2	1954	0.5
18	TH	0149	6.1	0808	0.6	1407	6.2	2035	0.6
19	F	0231	6.0	0852	0.7	1452	6.1	2115	0.8
20	SA	0315	5.8	0934	0.8	1541	5.9	2155	1.0
21	SU	0403	5.5	1020	1.0	1637	5.6	2241	1.3
22	M	0458	5.3	1118	1.1	1742	5.3	◐ 2342	1.5
23	TU	0606	5.0	1238	1.3	1858	5.2		
24	W	0102	1.7	0724	5.0	1405	1.2	2015	5.2
25	TH	0223	1.6	0840	5.1	1521	1.0	2127	5.4
26	F	0332	1.4	0947	5.3	1624	0.9	2226	5.6
27	SA	0430	1.2	1041	5.5	1713	0.8	2313	5.7
28	SU	0516	1.1	1125	5.6	1751	0.9	2354	5.7
29	M	0555	1.0	1204	5.7	1822	0.9	○	
30	TU	0029	5.7	0630	0.9	1239	5.7	1851	0.9
31	W	0101	5.7	0704	0.8	1312	5.7	1921	0.9

NOVEMBER

Date	Day	Time	m	Time	m	Time	m	Time	m
1	TH	0130	5.7	0737	0.8	1345	5.7	1950	0.9
2	F	0200	5.7	0808	0.9	1417	5.6	2018	1.0
3	SA	0230	5.6	0837	1.0	1450	5.5	2047	1.1
4	SU	0301	5.5	0907	1.1	1526	5.4	2118	1.3
5	M	0336	5.3	0941	1.2	1606	5.2	2155	1.5
6	TU	0417	5.1	1024	1.3	1653	5.0	2242	1.6
7	W	0507	4.9	1120	1.4	1751	4.9	◑ 2346	1.8
8	TH	0612	4.8	1233	1.5	1903	4.9		
9	F	0105	1.8	0731	4.8	1358	1.3	2018	5.0
10	SA	0225	1.6	0845	5.1	1509	1.1	2125	5.3
11	SU	0330	1.3	0947	5.4	1609	0.9	2222	5.6
12	M	0427	1.1	1041	5.7	1705	0.7	2312	5.9
13	TU	0522	0.9	1130	5.9	1757	0.6	●	
14	W	0000	6.0	0615	0.8	1218	6.1	1846	0.6
15	TH	0046	6.1	0706	0.6	1306	6.2	1932	0.6
16	F	0130	6.1	0756	0.5	1353	6.2	2017	0.6
17	SA	0215	6.0	0843	0.5	1442	6.1	2059	0.8
18	SU	0301	5.8	0930	0.6	1533	5.9	2142	1.0
19	M	0350	5.6	1018	0.8	1627	5.7	2227	1.2
20	TU	0443	5.4	1111	0.9	1727	5.4	◐ 2320	1.4
21	W	0544	5.2	1215	1.1	1831	5.2		
22	TH	0025	1.6	0651	5.1	1328	1.2	1940	5.2
23	F	0139	1.6	0801	5.1	1437	1.2	2048	5.2
24	SA	0247	1.5	0908	5.1	1538	1.1	2149	5.3
25	SU	0347	1.4	1007	5.3	1630	1.1	2241	5.4
26	M	0439	1.2	1056	5.4	1711	1.1	2324	5.5
27	TU	0524	1.1	1139	5.5	1746	1.0		
28	W	0002	5.6	0603	1.0	1217	5.5	○ 1819	1.0
29	TH	0036	5.6	0640	0.9	1252	5.6	1851	1.0
30	F	0107	5.6	0715	0.8	1325	5.6	1923	1.0

DECEMBER

Date	Day	Time	m	Time	m	Time	m	Time	m
1	SA	0138	5.6	0749	0.8	1359	5.6	1955	1.0
2	SU	0210	5.6	0822	0.9	1433	5.5	2028	1.0
3	M	0243	5.5	0857	0.9	1509	5.5	2102	1.1
4	TU	0318	5.4	0933	1.0	1548	5.4	2138	1.3
5	W	0357	5.3	1012	1.1	1632	5.2	2219	1.4
6	TH	0442	5.1	1056	1.2	1722	5.1	◑ 2309	1.5
7	F	0535	5.0	1151	1.2	1822	5.0		
8	SA	0011	1.6	0640	5.0	1300	1.2	1931	5.1
9	SU	0127	1.5	0755	5.1	1418	1.1	2042	5.2
10	M	0244	1.4	0906	5.3	1530	1.0	2147	5.4
11	TU	0353	1.2	1010	5.5	1633	0.8	2245	5.7
12	W	0457	1.0	1108	5.8	1732	0.7	2338	5.8
13	TH	0558	0.8	1202	5.9	1827	0.7	●	
14	F	0028	5.9	0655	0.6	1254	6.1	1916	0.6
15	SA	0116	6.0	0748	0.4	1344	6.1	2003	0.7
16	SU	0203	5.9	0837	0.4	1433	6.1	2046	0.8
17	M	0249	5.9	0924	0.4	1522	6.0	2128	0.9
18	TU	0336	5.7	1008	0.6	1611	5.8	2208	1.1
19	W	0423	5.6	1052	0.8	1702	5.5	2250	1.3
20	TH	0513	5.4	1138	1.0	1756	5.3	◐ 2339	1.4
21	F	0609	5.2	1232	1.2	1854	5.1		
22	SA	0040	1.6	0711	5.0	1337	1.3	1957	4.9
23	SU	0152	1.6	0819	4.9	1441	1.4	2103	4.9
24	M	0300	1.5	0926	4.9	1540	1.3	2203	5.0
25	TU	0401	1.4	1025	5.1	1631	1.3	2254	5.2
26	W	0455	1.2	1115	5.2	1715	1.2	2336	5.4
27	TH	0541	1.0	1157	5.4	1754	1.1		
28	F	0014	5.5	0621	0.9	1235	5.5	○ 1829	1.0
29	SA	0049	5.5	0658	0.8	1310	5.5	1903	1.0
30	SU	0122	5.6	0735	0.8	1344	5.6	1938	0.9
31	M	0155	5.6	0812	0.7	1418	5.6	2014	0.9

Chart Datum: 2·90 metres below Ordnance Datum (Newlyn)
HAT is 6·3 metres above Chart Datum

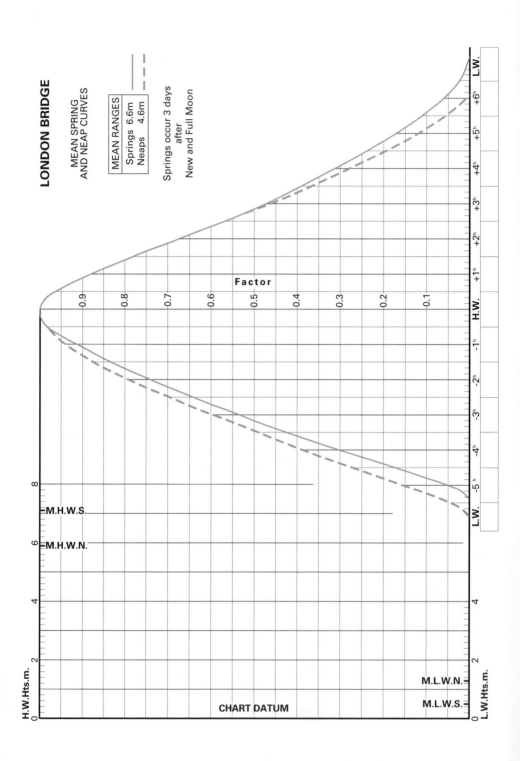

LONDON BRIDGE

MEAN SPRING
AND NEAP CURVES

MEAN RANGES
Springs 6.6m
Neaps 4.6m

Springs occur 3 days
after
New and Full Moon

Factor

0.9
0.8
0.7
0.6
0.5
0.4
0.3
0.2
0.1

H.W.
L.W.

+6ʰ +5ʰ +4ʰ +3ʰ +2ʰ +1ʰ H.W. -1ʰ -2ʰ -3ʰ -4ʰ -5ʰ L.W.

H.W.Hts.m.

M.H.W.S.
M.H.W.N.

CHART DATUM

M.L.W.N.
M.L.W.S.

L.W.Hts.m.

LONDON BRIDGE

LAT 51°30′N   LONG 0°05′W

TIMES AND HEIGHTS OF HIGH AND LOW WATERS

Dates in amber are **SPRINGS**
Dates in yellow are **NEAPS**

2012

JANUARY

	Time m		Time m
1 SU ☾	0018 1.4 / 0625 6.2 / 1244 1.0 / 1900 6.1	**16** M	0018 1.1 / 0612 6.6 / 1242 0.7 / 1848 6.5
2 M	0057 1.6 / 0713 6.0 / 1421 1.3 / 1952 5.8	**17** TU	0102 1.3 / 0705 6.5 / 1328 1.0 / 1948 6.2
3 TU	0146 1.8 / 0818 5.8 / 1421 1.5 / 2055 5.7	**18** W	0159 1.5 / 0812 6.3 / 1438 1.2 / 2100 6.1
4 W	0259 1.9 / 0929 5.7 / 1544 1.6 / 2200 5.8	**19** TH	0320 1.6 / 0934 6.2 / 1601 1.3 / 2215 6.1
5 TH	0427 1.7 / 1035 5.9 / 1653 1.5 / 2306 6.0	**20** F	0447 1.4 / 1051 6.3 / 1723 1.3 / 2332 6.2
6 F	0532 1.4 / 1137 6.2 / 1752 1.3	**21** SA	0615 1.1 / 1204 6.5 / 1843 1.1
7 SA	0006 6.2 / 0630 1.1 / 1230 6.4 / 1847 1.2	**22** SU	0039 6.5 / 0725 0.7 / 1305 6.8 / 1944 0.9
8 SU	0056 6.5 / 0724 0.9 / 1315 6.7 / 1938 1.1	**23** M ●	0133 6.7 / 0822 0.5 / 1356 7.0 / 2035 0.9
9 M ○	0140 6.6 / 0815 0.7 / 1356 6.8 / 2023 1.1	**24** TU	0219 6.8 / 0911 0.3 / 1441 7.1 / 2120 0.8
10 TU	0220 6.7 / 0901 0.6 / 1436 7.0 / 2106 1.0	**25** W	0301 6.9 / 0954 0.3 / 1523 7.1 / 2158 0.9
11 W	0259 6.8 / 0945 0.5 / 1515 7.1 / 2148 0.9	**26** TH	0338 7.0 / 1030 0.4 / 1601 7.1 / 2230 1.0
12 TH	0336 6.9 / 1027 0.4 / 1555 7.2 / 2227 0.9	**27** F	0412 7.0 / 1058 0.5 / 1635 6.9 / 2255 1.0
13 F	0412 6.9 / 1104 0.3 / 1634 7.1 / 2304 0.9	**28** SA	0444 6.8 / 1116 0.6 / 1706 6.7 / 2318 1.1
14 SA	0449 6.9 / 1136 0.4 / 1715 6.9 / 2340 1.0	**29** SU	0516 6.7 / 1136 0.7 / 1736 6.4 / 2346 1.2
15 SU	0529 6.8 / 1206 0.6 / 1759 6.7	**30** M	0547 6.4 / 1202 0.9 / 1809 6.2
		31 TU ☾	0017 1.3 / 0623 6.2 / 1232 1.1 / 1848 5.9

FEBRUARY

	Time m		Time m
1 W	0054 1.5 / 0708 5.9 / 1310 1.4 / 1941 5.7	**16** TH	0134 1.4 / 0749 6.2 / 1407 1.4 / 2031 5.9
2 TH	0143 1.8 / 0815 5.6 / 1405 1.7 / 2100 5.5	**17** F	0253 1.5 / 0914 6.0 / 1537 1.6 / 2156 5.8
3 F	0308 1.9 / 0944 5.6 / 1556 1.8 / 2221 5.6	**18** SA	0426 1.5 / 1040 6.1 / 1708 1.5 / 2324 6.0
4 SA	0450 1.6 / 1058 5.9 / 1714 1.6 / 2333 6.0	**19** SU	0607 1.1 / 1158 6.4 / 1831 1.2
5 SU	0557 1.2 / 1200 6.3 / 1818 1.3	**20** M	0030 6.4 / 0715 0.6 / 1257 6.8 / 1928 0.9
6 M	0031 6.4 / 0658 0.9 / 1252 6.6 / 1917 1.2	**21** TU ●	0122 6.7 / 0807 0.4 / 1345 7.0 / 2017 0.8
7 TU ○	0119 6.6 / 0755 0.7 / 1336 6.9 / 2010 1.1	**22** W	0204 6.8 / 0852 0.4 / 1426 7.0 / 2059 0.8
8 W	0201 6.8 / 0846 0.5 / 1418 7.1 / 2058 1.0	**23** TH	0241 6.4 / 0930 0.4 / 1502 7.0 / 2136 0.9
9 TH	0241 7.0 / 0932 0.3 / 1459 7.2 / 2142 0.8	**24** F	0314 7.0 / 1001 0.5 / 1535 7.0 / 2206 0.9
10 F	0319 7.1 / 1014 0.2 / 1538 7.3 / 2223 0.7	**25** SA	0345 7.1 / 1024 0.6 / 1604 6.9 / 2230 0.9
11 SA	0356 7.2 / 1041 0.6 / 1618 7.2 / 2259 0.7	**26** SU	0415 7.0 / 1041 0.6 / 1631 6.7 / 2253 0.9
12 SU	0433 7.1 / 1104 0.3 / 1657 7.0 / 2332 0.8	**27** M	0445 6.8 / 1102 0.7 / 1700 6.5 / 2319 1.0
13 M	0511 7.0 / 1151 0.5 / 1738 6.7	**28** TU	0515 6.6 / 1126 0.8 / 1730 6.3 / 2345 1.1
14 TU ☾	0005 1.0 / 0554 6.8 / 1222 0.7 / 1823 6.4	**29** W	0548 6.3 / 1152 1.0 / 1805 6.0
15 W	0044 1.0 / 0644 6.5 / 1302 1.0 / 1919 6.1		

MARCH

	Time m		Time m
1 TH ☾	0014 1.3 / 0627 6.0 / 1224 1.3 / 1849 5.7	**16** F	0116 1.2 / 0735 6.2 / 1347 1.5 / 2010 5.8
2 F	0053 1.5 / 0719 5.7 / 1309 1.6 / 1951 5.5	**17** SA	0233 1.4 / 0900 6.0 / 1516 1.7 / 2139 5.8
3 SA	0152 1.7 / 0838 5.5 / 1423 1.9 / 2129 5.4	**18** SU	0407 1.4 / 1026 6.1 / 1647 1.6 / 2305 6.0
4 SU	0359 1.7 / 1014 5.7 / 1629 1.7 / 2254 5.8	**19** M	0551 1.0 / 1142 6.5 / 1808 1.2
5 M	0518 1.3 / 1124 6.2 / 1741 1.4 / 2358 6.3	**20** TU	0011 6.4 / 0654 0.6 / 1239 6.8 / 1904 0.9
6 TU	0626 0.9 / 1221 6.6 / 1848 1.2	**21** W	0100 6.7 / 0742 0.5 / 1324 6.9 / 1951 0.9
7 W	0049 6.6 / 0729 0.6 / 1309 6.9 / 1948 1.0	**22** TH ●	0140 6.8 / 0822 0.5 / 1402 6.9 / 2031 0.8
8 TH ○	0134 6.9 / 0823 0.4 / 1354 7.1 / 2040 0.9	**23** F	0215 6.9 / 0856 0.6 / 1435 6.9 / 2106 0.8
9 F	0215 7.1 / 0911 0.2 / 1436 7.3 / 2126 0.7	**24** SA	0246 7.0 / 0924 0.6 / 1504 6.9 / 2137 0.8
10 SA	0255 7.3 / 0954 0.1 / 1517 7.3 / 2208 0.6	**25** SU	0316 7.1 / 0946 0.6 / 1531 6.9 / 2203 0.7
11 SU	0334 7.4 / 1032 0.1 / 1557 7.2 / 2246 0.6	**26** M	0346 7.1 / 1006 0.6 / 1559 6.8 / 2228 0.8
12 M	0414 7.4 / 1104 0.3 / 1637 7.0 / 2319 0.6	**27** TU	0416 6.9 / 1030 0.7 / 1628 6.6 / 2254 0.9
13 TU	0454 7.2 / 1131 0.5 / 1718 6.7 / 2350 0.8	**28** W	0447 6.7 / 1055 0.8 / 1659 6.4 / 2319 1.0
14 W	0538 6.9 / 1201 0.8 / 1803 6.4	**29** TH	0520 6.4 / 1121 1.0 / 1733 6.1 / 2344 1.1
15 TH ☾	0027 1.0 / 0629 6.6 / 1243 1.2 / 1857 6.0	**30** F ○	0559 6.2 / 1152 1.2 / 1815 5.9
		31 SA ☾	0019 1.2 / 0647 5.9 / 1235 1.4 / 1910 5.6

APRIL

	Time m		Time m
1 SU	0113 1.4 / 0753 5.7 / 1339 1.7 / 2033 5.5	**16** M	0340 1.2 / 0958 6.2 / 1612 1.5 / 2232 6.1
2 M	0250 1.6 / 0927 5.8 / 1538 1.7 / 2207 5.8	**17** TU	0507 1.0 / 1112 6.4 / 1729 1.2 / 2338 6.4
3 TU	0434 1.2 / 1043 6.2 / 1658 1.4 / 2317 6.2	**18** W	0617 0.8 / 1210 6.6 / 1829 1.0
4 W	0543 0.8 / 1144 6.6 / 1807 1.1	**19** TH	0029 6.6 / 0704 0.7 / 1256 6.7 / 1916 0.9
5 TH	0012 6.7 / 0651 0.6 / 1238 6.9 / 1916 1.0	**20** F	0110 6.7 / 0742 0.7 / 1333 6.7 / 1957 0.8
6 F ○	0102 7.0 / 0752 0.4 / 1325 7.1 / 2014 0.8	**21** SA ●	0145 6.8 / 0814 0.7 / 1405 6.8 / 2034 0.8
7 SA	0146 7.2 / 0843 0.3 / 1410 7.2 / 2104 0.6	**22** SU	0217 7.0 / 0843 0.7 / 1434 6.8 / 2107 0.7
8 SU	0230 7.4 / 0928 0.2 / 1454 7.3 / 2149 0.5	**23** M	0248 7.0 / 0910 0.7 / 1502 6.8 / 2137 0.7
9 M	0313 7.5 / 1008 0.3 / 1537 7.2 / 2229 0.4	**24** TU	0319 7.0 / 0936 0.7 / 1532 6.8 / 2206 0.7
10 TU	0355 7.5 / 1042 0.4 / 1619 7.0 / 2305 0.5	**25** W	0351 6.9 / 1003 0.8 / 1603 6.6 / 2234 0.7
11 W	0439 7.3 / 1112 0.6 / 1702 6.7 / 2337 0.6	**26** TH	0424 6.7 / 1031 0.9 / 1636 6.4 / 2300 0.8
12 TH	0526 7.0 / 1145 0.9 / 1749 6.4	**27** F	0500 6.6 / 1100 1.0 / 1712 6.2 / 2327 0.9
13 F ☾	0014 0.8 / 0620 6.6 / 1229 1.2 / 1843 6.1	**28** SA	0540 6.4 / 1134 1.1 / 1754 6.0
14 SA	0103 1.0 / 0725 6.3 / 1331 1.5 / 1953 5.9	**29** SU ☾	0003 1.0 / 0627 6.2 / 1218 1.3 / 1847 5.9
15 SU	0216 1.2 / 0841 6.1 / 1451 1.6 / 2114 5.9	**30** M	0053 1.2 / 0728 6.0 / 1318 1.5 / 1956 5.8

Chart Datum: 3·20 metres below Ordnance Datum (Newlyn)
HAT is 7·6 metres above Chart Datum

TIDES

TIME ZONE (UT)
For Summer Time add ONE hour in **non-shaded areas**

LONDON BRIDGE
LAT 51°30′N   LONG 0°05′W
TIMES AND HEIGHTS OF HIGH AND LOW WATERS

Dates in amber are **SPRINGS**
Dates in yellow are **NEAPS**

2012

MAY

Day	Time m	Time m	Time m	Time m
1 TU	0209 1.2	0848 6.0	1453 1.6	2122 5.9
2 W	0350 1.1	1004 6.3	1617 1.3	2235 6.3
3 TH	0500 0.8	1108 6.6	1729 1.1	2336 6.7
4 F	0608 0.6	1205 6.9	1842 0.9	
5 SA	0030 7.0	0716 0.5	1258 7.1	1947 0.7
6 SU ○	0120 7.3	0814 0.4	1347 7.1	2041 0.6
7 M	0207 7.4	0903 0.4	1434 7.2	2130 0.4
8 TU	0254 7.5	0946 0.4	1520 7.1	2214 0.3
9 W	0341 7.5	1025 0.6	1605 7.0	2253 0.3
10 TH	0428 7.3	1059 0.7	1651 6.7	2330 0.5
11 F	0518 7.0	1135 0.9	1738 6.5	
12 SA ◐	0007 0.6	0610 6.7	1217 1.2	1830 6.3
13 SU	0053 0.8	0710 6.4	1311 1.4	1931 6.1
14 M	0154 1.0	0814 6.2	1419 1.5	2039 6.0
15 TU	0303 1.1	0920 6.2	1530 1.4	2147 6.1
16 W	0408 1.0	1028 6.2	1638 1.3	2253 6.2
17 TH	0509 1.0	1130 6.4	1740 1.1	2349 6.4
18 F	0605 0.9	1219 6.5	1834 1.0	
19 SA	0035 6.6	0651 0.9	1301 6.6	1921 0.8
20 SU ●	0115 6.8	0733 0.8	1336 6.6	2002 0.7
21 M	0151 6.9	0810 0.8	1409 6.7	2041 0.7
22 TU	0225 6.9	0843 0.8	1441 6.7	2117 0.6
23 W	0258 6.9	0913 0.8	1513 6.7	2150 0.6
24 TH	0332 6.9	0943 0.8	1547 6.6	2222 0.6
25 F	0408 6.8	1016 0.9	1622 6.5	2252 0.7
26 SA	0446 6.7	1050 0.9	1700 6.4	2323 0.7
27 SU	0527 6.6	1128 1.0	1741 6.3	2358 0.8
28 M ◐	0613 6.4	1211 1.2	1830 6.2	
29 TU	0044 0.9	0708 6.3	1306 1.3	1929 6.1
30 W	0146 1.0	0816 6.2	1419 1.4	2043 6.1
31 TH	0308 0.9	0929 6.4	1540 1.3	2158 6.4

JUNE

Day	Time m	Time m	Time m	Time m
1 F	0423 0.8	1035 6.5	1657 1.1	2303 6.7
2 SA	0531 0.7	1137 6.7	1812 0.9	
3 SU	0003 7.0	0643 0.6	1235 6.9	1923 0.7
4 M ○	0059 7.2	0748 0.6	1328 7.0	2022 0.5
5 TU	0150 7.4	0842 0.6	1418 7.0	2115 0.3
6 W	0241 7.4	0930 0.6	1507 7.1	2203 0.2
7 TH	0330 7.4	1013 0.7	1554 7.0	2246 0.2
8 F	0419 7.3	1051 0.8	1640 6.9	2325 0.3
9 SA	0507 7.1	1127 0.9	1725 6.7	
10 SU	0001 0.5	0555 6.8	1204 1.1	1811 6.5
11 M ◐	0039 0.7	0645 6.6	1247 1.2	1901 6.3
12 TU	0123 0.8	0738 6.3	1337 1.4	1958 6.2
13 W	0217 1.0	0835 6.1	1439 1.5	2059 6.1
14 TH	0316 1.1	0934 6.0	1547 1.4	2201 6.1
15 F	0415 1.1	1036 6.1	1650 1.3	2302 6.2
16 SA	0512 1.1	1136 6.2	1750 1.1	2358 6.4
17 SU	0608 1.0	1226 6.4	1845 0.9	
18 M	0045 6.6	0659 1.0	1310 6.6	1934 0.7
19 TU ●	0128 6.8	0745 1.0	1349 6.7	2019 0.6
20 W	0206 6.8	0826 1.0	1426 6.7	2101 0.6
21 TH	0243 6.9	0902 1.0	1502 6.7	2140 0.5
22 F	0319 6.9	0937 0.9	1537 6.7	2218 0.5
23 SA	0355 7.0	1013 0.9	1612 6.7	2254 0.5
24 SU	0433 6.9	1050 0.9	1649 6.6	2326 0.5
25 M	0513 6.8	1128 1.0	1728 6.5	2358 0.6
26 TU	0557 6.6	1207 1.1	1812 6.4	
27 W ◐	0035 0.7	0646 6.5	1254 1.2	1903 6.3
28 TH	0123 0.8	0745 6.3	1351 1.3	2007 6.3
29 F	0229 0.9	0856 6.3	1507 1.4	2124 6.4
30 SA	0349 1.0	1005 6.3	1629 1.2	2236 6.5

JULY

Day	Time m	Time m	Time m	Time m
1 SU	0503 0.9	1113 6.5	1749 1.0	2343 6.8
2 M	0619 0.8	1218 6.6	1905 0.7	
3 TU ○	0044 7.0	0730 0.7	1316 6.8	2009 0.4
4 W	0140 7.2	0827 0.7	1408 7.0	2104 0.2
5 TH	0232 7.3	0918 0.7	1456 7.1	2153 0.1
6 F	0320 7.4	1002 0.7	1541 7.1	2237 0.1
7 SA	0406 7.3	1041 0.8	1624 7.1	2314 0.2
8 SU	0449 7.1	1115 0.9	1704 6.9	2345 0.4
9 M	0531 6.9	1145 1.0	1743 6.7	
10 TU	0012 0.6	0611 6.6	1227 1.1	1823 6.5
11 W ◐	0042 0.8	0654 6.3	1252 1.3	1909 6.2
12 TH	0118 1.0	0742 6.0	1338 1.5	2005 6.0
13 F	0209 1.3	0838 5.8	1443 1.6	2110 5.9
14 SA	0321 1.4	0941 5.8	1602 1.5	2216 5.9
15 SU	0430 1.4	1048 5.9	1710 1.3	2321 6.2
16 M	0533 1.3	1153 6.2	1811 1.0	
17 TU	0017 6.4	0631 1.1	1245 6.5	1908 0.8
18 W	0106 6.7	0725 1.0	1330 6.7	1959 0.6
19 TH ●	0148 6.8	0812 1.0	1410 6.8	2046 0.5
20 F	0226 6.9	0855 1.0	1447 6.8	2129 0.4
21 SA	0304 7.0	0935 0.9	1523 6.9	2210 0.3
22 SU	0340 7.1	1014 0.8	1558 6.9	2248 0.3
23 M	0418 7.1	1051 0.8	1633 6.9	2322 0.3
24 TU	0456 6.9	1125 0.9	1710 6.8	2350 0.5
25 W	0536 6.7	1159 1.0	1751 6.7	
26 TH ◐	0019 0.7	0621 6.5	1238 1.2	1837 6.5
27 F	0058 0.9	0714 6.2	1326 1.3	1937 6.3
28 SA	0154 1.1	0823 6.1	1437 1.5	2055 6.2
29 SU	0320 1.3	0939 6.1	1607 1.4	2216 6.3
30 M	0443 1.2	1056 6.2	1733 1.1	2331 6.6
31 TU	0606 1.0	1209 6.5	1856 0.7	

AUGUST

Day	Time m	Time m	Time m	Time m
1 W	0038 6.9	0718 0.8	1309 6.7	1959 0.3
2 TH ○	0134 7.1	0814 0.7	1359 6.9	2052 0.1
3 F	0222 7.3	0903 0.7	1443 7.1	2138 0.1
4 SA	0306 7.3	0946 0.7	1523 7.2	2218 0.1
5 SU	0346 7.3	1024 0.7	1600 7.2	2252 0.3
6 M	0424 7.1	1055 0.8	1636 7.1	2317 0.5
7 TU	0459 6.9	1119 0.9	1709 6.9	2336 0.6
8 W	0531 6.6	1143 1.1	1743 6.6	2357 0.8
9 TH ◗	0604 6.3	1212 1.2	1820 6.3	
10 F	0024 1.1	0641 6.0	1247 1.4	1904 6.0
11 SA	0101 1.4	0732 5.7	1335 1.7	2008 5.7
12 SU	0155 1.7	0845 5.5	1459 1.8	2129 5.6
13 M	0341 1.8	1004 5.6	1631 1.5	2243 5.9
14 TU	0459 1.6	1118 6.0	1738 1.1	2347 6.3
15 W	0603 1.0	1216 6.4	1839 0.8	
16 TH	0039 6.6	0701 1.1	1304 6.7	1935 0.6
17 F ●	0123 6.9	0753 1.0	1346 6.8	2025 0.5
18 SA	0203 7.0	0840 1.0	1424 7.0	2111 0.4
19 SU	0242 7.1	0923 0.9	1501 7.1	2153 0.3
20 M	0319 7.2	1004 0.8	1537 7.2	2232 0.2
21 TU	0357 7.2	1042 0.7	1612 7.1	2306 0.3
22 W	0434 7.0	1115 0.8	1649 7.0	2333 0.5
23 TH	0513 6.7	1146 1.1	1730 6.8	2359 0.8
24 F ◗	0556 6.4	1220 1.1	1816 6.4	
25 SA	0034 1.0	0646 6.1	1306 1.3	1914 6.3
26 SU	0129 1.3	0754 5.9	1415 1.5	2036 6.1
27 M	0300 1.6	0919 5.9	1550 1.4	2203 6.2
28 TU	0428 1.4	1045 6.1	1725 1.1	2323 6.5
29 W	0556 1.1	1200 6.3	1847 0.6	
30 TH	0029 6.9	0703 0.9	1257 6.8	1944 0.3
31 F ○	0122 7.1	0756 0.7	1343 7.0	2032 0.2

Chart Datum: 3·20 metres below Ordnance Datum (Newlyn)
HAT is 7·6 metres above Chart Datum

LONDON BRIDGE

LAT 51°30'N   LONG 0°05'W

Dates in amber are **SPRINGS**
Dates in yellow are **NEAPS**

2012

TIMES AND HEIGHTS OF HIGH AND LOW WATERS

SEPTEMBER

Day	Time m / Time m / Time m / Time m	Day	Time m / Time m / Time m / Time m
1 SA	0206 7.2 / 0842 0.7 / 1423 7.1 / 2114 0.2	16 SU	0133 7.1 / 0816 1.0 / 1354 7.1 / ● 2045 0.4
2 SU	0245 7.2 / 0923 0.7 / 1458 7.2 / 2150 0.3	17 M	0214 7.2 / 0903 0.8 / 1433 7.2 / 2129 0.3
3 M	0320 7.2 / 0958 0.8 / 1531 7.2 / 2219 0.5	18 TU	0254 7.3 / 0946 0.7 / 1512 7.3 / 2209 0.3
4 TU	0352 7.0 / 1027 0.8 / 1603 7.1 / 2239 0.6	19 W	0333 7.2 / 1026 0.7 / 1550 7.4 / 2243 0.4
5 W	0422 6.9 / 1049 0.9 / 1635 7.0 / 2255 0.7	20 TH	0412 7.0 / 1101 0.7 / 1630 7.2 / 2311 0.6
6 TH	0451 6.6 / 1112 1.0 / 1706 6.7 / 2317 0.9	21 F	0452 6.7 / 1132 0.9 / 1712 7.0 / 2339 0.9
7 F	0520 6.3 / 1137 1.2 / 1739 6.4 / 2342 1.1	22 SA	0535 6.4 / 1206 1.0 / 1801 6.7 / ◐
8 SA	0552 6.0 / 1206 1.3 / 1817 6.0 / ◐	23 SU	0016 1.2 / 0626 6.1 / 1251 1.2 / 1901 6.1
9 SU	0011 1.4 / 0633 5.7 / 1531 1.6 / 1905 5.7	24 M	0114 1.5 / 0734 5.9 / 1402 1.4 / 2024 6.1
10 M	0053 1.7 / 0731 5.5 / 1338 1.8 / 2023 5.5	25 TU	0244 1.7 / 0903 5.8 / 1534 1.3 / 2149 6.2
11 TU	0203 2.0 / 0910 5.4 / 1543 1.8 / 2157 5.7	26 W	0411 1.5 / 1028 6.1 / 1710 1.0 / 2308 6.5
12 W	0414 1.9 / 1035 5.7 / 1700 1.3 / 2308 6.1	27 TH	0535 1.2 / 1140 6.3 / 1826 0.6
13 TH	0525 1.5 / 1140 6.2 / 1803 0.9	28 F	0011 6.9 / 0639 0.9 / 1236 6.8 / 1919 0.4
14 F	0003 6.6 / 0627 1.2 / 1231 6.6 / 1903 0.7	29 SA	0102 7.1 / 0731 0.8 / 1320 6.9 / 2004 0.4
15 SA	0051 6.9 / 0724 1.1 / 1314 6.9 / 1957 0.5	30 SU	0143 7.1 / 0815 0.8 / 1357 7.0 / ○ 2041 0.5

OCTOBER

Day	Time m / Time m / Time m / Time m	Day	Time m / Time m / Time m / Time m
1 M	0219 7.0 / 0854 0.8 / 1430 7.1 / 2113 0.6	16 TU	0146 7.2 / 0838 0.8 / 1405 7.4 / 2101 0.4
2 TU	0250 7.0 / 0927 0.8 / 1501 7.2 / 2138 0.7	17 W	0229 7.3 / 0925 0.7 / 1448 7.5 / 2144 0.5
3 W	0319 7.0 / 0955 0.8 / 1532 7.2 / 2157 0.7	18 TH	0312 7.2 / 1008 0.6 / 1531 7.5 / 2221 0.6
4 TH	0347 6.9 / 1019 0.8 / 1604 7.0 / 2218 0.8	19 F	0354 7.1 / 1046 0.6 / 1614 7.3 / 2253 0.7
5 F	0416 6.7 / 1043 0.9 / 1635 6.8 / 2242 1.0	20 SA	0436 6.8 / 1121 0.7 / 1700 7.1 / 2325 1.0
6 SA	0445 6.4 / 1108 1.1 / 1707 6.5 / 2308 1.2	21 SU	0521 6.5 / 1156 0.8 / 1752 6.8
7 SU	0516 6.2 / 1133 1.2 / 1744 6.2 / 2335 1.3	22 M	0006 1.3 / 0613 6.2 / 1242 1.0 / ◐ 1854 6.4
8 M	0555 5.9 / 1203 1.3 / 1829 5.9 / ◐	23 TU	0104 1.5 / 0721 6.0 / 1350 1.2 / 2010 6.3
9 TU	0013 1.6 / 0645 5.6 / 1249 1.5 / 1928 5.7	24 W	0222 1.7 / 0841 6.0 / 1513 1.2 / 2125 6.3
10 W	0110 1.9 / 0757 5.5 / 1410 1.7 / 2059 5.7	25 TH	0343 1.5 / 0959 6.1 / 1632 1.0 / 2239 6.5
11 TH	0304 2.0 / 0941 5.6 / 1612 1.4 / 2219 6.1	26 F	0459 1.3 / 1109 6.4 / 1748 0.8 / 2343 6.7
12 F	0435 1.6 / 1105 6.2 / 1718 1.0 / 2320 6.5	27 SA	0606 1.1 / 1205 6.6 / 1844 0.7
13 SA	0541 1.3 / 1149 6.6 / 1820 0.7	28 SU	0034 6.9 / 0658 0.9 / 1250 6.8 / 1926 0.7
14 SU	0013 6.9 / 0646 1.1 / 1238 6.9 / 1920 0.5	29 M	0116 6.9 / 0742 0.8 / 1328 6.9 / ○ 2002 0.8
15 M	0101 7.1 / 0746 0.9 / 1322 7.2 / ● 2014 0.5	30 TU	0150 6.9 / 0821 0.8 / 1401 7.0 / 2032 0.8
		31 W	0221 6.9 / 0856 0.8 / 1433 7.1 / 2059 0.8

NOVEMBER

Day	Time m / Time m / Time m / Time m	Day	Time m / Time m / Time m / Time m
1 TH	0249 6.9 / 0926 0.7 / 1505 7.1 / 2122 0.9	16 F	0254 7.2 / 0952 0.4 / 1516 7.5 / 2205 0.7
2 F	0318 6.9 / 0954 0.8 / 1537 7.0 / 2148 0.9	17 SA	0340 7.1 / 1035 0.4 / 1604 7.4 / 2242 0.8
3 SA	0348 6.7 / 1021 0.8 / 1610 6.8 / 2216 1.0	18 SU	0426 6.9 / 1114 0.5 / 1653 7.2 / 2319 1.0
4 SU	0420 6.5 / 1047 0.9 / 1644 6.6 / 2244 1.1	19 M	0513 6.7 / 1153 0.6 / 1745 6.9 / 2359 1.2
5 M	0453 6.3 / 1113 1.0 / 1721 6.4 / 2315 1.3 / ◐	20 TU	0604 6.4 / 1236 0.8 / 1843 6.6
6 TU	0531 6.1 / 1144 1.1 / 1805 6.2 / 2353 1.4	21 W	0049 1.4 / 0703 6.2 / 1333 1.0 / 1946 6.4
7 W	0618 5.9 / 1226 1.2 / 1858 6.0 / ◐	22 TH	0153 1.5 / 0810 6.1 / 1439 1.0 / 2051 6.3
8 TH	0045 1.6 / 0717 5.8 / 1327 1.4 / 2008 6.0	23 F	0304 1.6 / 0919 6.1 / 1544 1.0 / 2158 6.3
9 F	0201 1.8 / 0839 5.8 / 1509 1.3 / 2130 6.1	24 SA	0413 1.6 / 1026 6.2 / 1647 1.0 / 2304 6.4
10 SA	0340 1.7 / 1002 6.1 / 1629 1.0 / 2237 6.5	25 SU	0519 1.3 / 1127 6.4 / 1747 1.0
11 SU	0456 1.4 / 1106 6.5 / 1734 0.8 / 2336 6.8	26 M	0000 6.5 / 0617 1.1 / 1217 6.6 / 1837 1.0
12 M	0606 1.1 / 1202 6.9 / 1838 0.6	27 TU	0045 6.6 / 0707 0.9 / 1259 6.7 / 1919 0.9
13 TU	0030 7.0 / 0714 0.9 / 1253 7.2 / ● 1941 0.6	28 W	0123 6.7 / 0749 0.8 / 1336 6.8 / ○ 1957 0.9
14 W	0120 7.2 / 0813 0.7 / 1342 7.4 / 2035 0.6	29 TH	0156 6.7 / 0828 0.7 / 1411 6.9 / 2031 1.0
15 TH	0208 7.2 / 0905 0.5 / 1429 7.5 / 2122 0.6	30 F	0227 6.8 / 0904 0.7 / 1444 6.9 / 2100 1.0

DECEMBER

Day	Time m / Time m / Time m / Time m	Day	Time m / Time m / Time m / Time m
1 SA	0259 6.8 / 0936 0.7 / 1517 6.9 / 2128 1.0	16 SU	0330 7.1 / 1028 0.2 / 1555 7.5 / 2236 0.8
2 SU	0331 6.7 / 1007 0.7 / 1551 6.9 / 2159 1.0	17 M	0416 7.1 / 1110 0.3 / 1643 7.3 / 2314 0.9
3 M	0404 6.6 / 1037 0.8 / 1627 6.8 / 2232 1.1	18 TU	0502 6.9 / 1148 0.4 / 1731 7.0 / 2350 1.0
4 TU	0439 6.5 / 1106 0.8 / 1705 6.7 / 2306 1.2	19 W	0548 6.7 / 1224 0.6 / 1821 6.7
5 W	0517 6.4 / 1136 0.9 / 1747 6.5 / 2344 1.3	20 TH	0029 1.2 / 0635 6.5 / 1305 0.8 / ◐ 1913 6.5
6 TH	0559 6.2 / 1214 1.0 / 1835 6.4	21 F	0115 1.4 / 0730 6.3 / 1353 1.0 / 2009 6.2
7 F	0030 1.4 / 0650 6.1 / 1304 1.1 / 1932 6.2	22 SA	0212 1.6 / 0831 6.1 / 1451 1.2 / 2107 6.1
8 SA	0129 1.6 / 0753 6.0 / 1409 1.1 / 2045 6.2	23 SU	0320 1.6 / 0935 6.0 / 1552 1.3 / 2211 6.0
9 SU	0247 1.6 / 0914 6.1 / 1538 1.1 / 2158 6.4	24 M	0427 1.5 / 1039 6.1 / 1651 1.3 / 2316 6.1
10 M	0414 1.5 / 1028 6.4 / 1653 0.9 / 2303 6.6	25 TU	0531 1.3 / 1140 6.3 / 1750 1.2
11 TU	0533 1.2 / 1132 6.8 / 1803 0.8	26 W	0011 6.3 / 0629 1.1 / 1231 6.5 / 1844 1.1
12 W	0004 6.8 / 0647 0.9 / 1230 7.1 / 1913 0.7	27 TH	0057 6.5 / 0720 0.9 / 1315 6.7 / 1932 1.1
13 TH	0100 7.0 / 0753 0.7 / 1324 7.3 / ● 2014 0.7	28 F	0137 6.6 / 0805 0.7 / 1353 6.8 / ○ 2014 1.1
14 F	0152 7.1 / 0850 0.4 / 1415 7.4 / 2107 0.7	29 SA	0213 6.7 / 0846 0.7 / 1429 6.8 / 2050 1.1
15 SA	0242 7.1 / 0941 0.3 / 1506 7.5 / 2154 0.7	30 SU	0247 6.7 / 0924 0.7 / 1503 6.9 / 2122 1.1
		31 M	0319 6.8 / 1000 0.6 / 1536 6.9 / 2155 1.0

Chart Datum: 3·20 metres below Ordnance Datum (Newlyn)
HAT is 7·6 metres above Chart Datum

TIDES

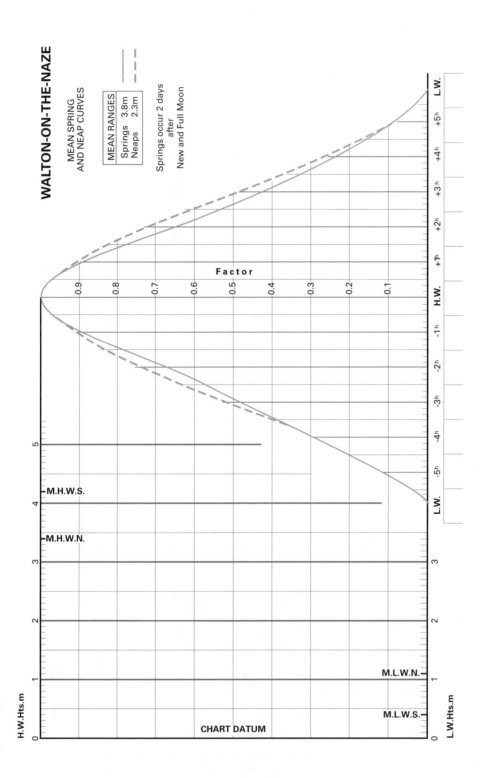

WALTON-ON-THE-NAZE

MEAN SPRING
AND NEAP CURVES

MEAN RANGES	
Springs	3.8m
Neaps	2.3m

Springs occur 2 days
after
New and Full Moon

Factor

0.9 0.8 0.7 0.6 0.5 0.4 0.3 0.2 0.1

H.W.Hts.m

M.H.W.S.
M.H.W.N.

CHART DATUM

H.W. -1ʰ -2ʰ -3ʰ -4ʰ -5ʰ L.W.
+1ʰ +2ʰ +3ʰ +4ʰ +5ʰ L.W.

M.L.W.N.
M.L.W.S.

L.W.Hts.m

WALTON-ON-THE-NAZE

LAT 51°51'N   LONG 1°17'E

TIMES AND HEIGHTS OF HIGH AND LOW WATERS

2012

JANUARY

#	Time	m	Time	m	#	Time	m	Time	m
1	0423	3.8	1037	0.7	16	0404	4.1	1025	0.5
SU	1704	3.6	☽ 2243	1.3	M	1638	3.9	☽ 2239	1.0
2	0515	3.6	1131	0.9	17	0457	3.9	1126	0.6
M	1758	3.4	2351	1.4	TU	1738	3.7	2348	1.0
3	0614	3.5	1237	1.0	18	0604	3.8	1236	0.7
TU	1858	3.4			W	1850	3.6		
4	0113	1.3	0718	3.4	19	0107	1.0	0726	3.7
W	1344	1.1	2003	3.4	TH	1348	0.8	2011	3.6
5	0223	1.2	0826	3.5	20	0226	0.9	0846	3.8
TH	1447	1.1	2106	3.6	F	1459	0.9	2127	3.7
6	0324	1.0	0924	3.6	21	0340	0.7	0952	4.0
F	1544	1.0	2157	3.7	SA	1604	0.8	2227	3.9
7	0415	0.7	1013	3.8	22	0446	0.5	1048	4.1
SA	1630	0.9	2242	3.9	SU	1659	0.8	2317	4.1
8	0458	0.7	1057	3.9	23	0539	0.4	1136	4.2
SU	1707	0.9	2322	4.0	M	1746	0.7 ●		
9	0536	0.5	1138	4.0	24	0001	4.2	0624	0.3
M	1740	0.8 ○			TU	1221	4.3	1827	0.7
10	0002	4.1	0613	0.4	25	0043	4.3	0705	0.2
TU	1218	4.2	1814	0.7	W	1302	4.2	1905	0.7
11	0042	4.2	0651	0.3	26	0121	4.3	0741	0.3
W	1258	4.3	1850	0.7	TH	1342	4.2	1940	0.8
12	0122	4.3	0731	0.3	27	0157	4.2	0814	0.3
TH	1338	4.3	1929	0.7	F	1420	4.1	2012	0.8
13	0201	4.3	0811	0.2	28	0230	4.2	0843	0.4
F	1419	4.2	2011	0.7	SA	1456	3.9	2042	0.8
14	0239	4.2	0851	0.3	29	0304	4.2	0912	0.5
SA	1502	4.1	2054	0.8	SU	1531	3.8	2114	0.9
15	0319	4.1	0935	0.4	30	0340	3.9	0943	0.7
SU	1547	4.0	2143	0.9	M	1609	3.6	2153	1.0
					31	0422	3.7	1023	0.9
					TU	1655	3.4	☽ 2243	1.2

FEBRUARY

#	Time	m	Time	m	#	Time	m	Time	m
1	0515	3.5	1120	1.1	16	0543	3.7	1211	0.9
W	1754	3.3	2358	1.3	TH	1827	3.4		
2	0622	3.3	1248	1.2	17	0048	1.0	0713	3.6
TH	1904	3.3			F	1331	1.0	1959	3.4
3	0132	1.3	0739	3.3	18	0219	0.9	0840	3.7
F	1408	1.2	2019	3.4	SA	1451	1.0	2119	3.6
4	0246	1.1	0851	3.4	19	0342	0.7	0948	3.9
SA	1514	1.1	2125	3.6	SU	1559	0.9	2218	3.9
5	0346	0.9	0949	3.6	20	0442	0.5	1042	4.0
SU	1606	1.0	2217	3.8	M	1650	0.9	2306	4.0
6	0433	0.7	1036	3.8	21	0529	0.3	1126	4.1
M	1646	0.9	2301	4.0	TU	1730	0.8 ●	2346	4.2
7	0514	0.5	1119	4.0	22	0607	0.3	1205	4.2
TU	1722	0.8	○ 2343	4.1	W	1807	0.7		
8	0553	0.3	1200	4.2	23	0023	4.2	0641	0.3
W	1758	0.7			TH	1242	4.2	1841	0.7
9	0023	4.3	0632	0.2	24	0057	4.3	0711	0.3
TH	1241	4.4	1835	0.6	F	1317	4.1	1915	0.6
10	0103	4.4	0712	0.1	25	0129	4.3	0740	0.3
F	1318	4.4	1914	0.6	SA	1350	4.1	1945	0.7
11	0142	4.4	0751	0.1	26	0159	4.2	0807	0.4
SA	1402	4.3	1955	0.6	SU	1422	4.0	2013	0.7
12	0221	4.4	0829	0.2	27	0231	4.1	0831	0.5
SU	1444	4.2	2037	0.6	M	1452	3.8	2042	0.8
13	0301	4.3	0910	0.3	28	0304	3.9	0858	0.7
M	1527	4.0	2123	0.7	TU	1524	3.7	2116	0.9
14	0344	4.2	0957	0.5	29	0340	3.8	0932	0.8
TU	1615	3.8	☽ 2217	0.8	W	1602	3.5	☽ 2159	1.0
15	0435	4.0	1057	0.7					
W	1713	3.6	2324	0.9					

MARCH

#	Time	m	Time	m	#	Time	m	Time	m
1	0423	3.5	1018	1.1	16	0533	3.7	1151	1.1
TH	1653	3.3	☽ 2257	1.2	F	1812	3.4		
2	0522	3.3	1129	1.3	17	0037	0.9	0704	3.5
F	1806	3.2			SA	1316	1.2	1943	3.4
3	0035	1.2	0647	3.2	18	0213	0.8	0829	3.7
SA	1324	1.3	1930	3.2	SU	1439	1.1	2102	3.6
4	0204	1.1	0814	3.3	19	0332	0.6	0935	3.9
SU	1438	1.2	2047	3.4	M	1544	1.0	2159	3.8
5	0309	0.8	0919	3.6	20	0427	0.5	1026	4.0
M	1534	1.0	2145	3.7	TU	1631	0.9	2245	4.0
6	0401	0.6	1010	3.8	21	0508	0.4	1107	4.1
TU	1617	0.6	2233	3.9	W	1708	0.8	2323	4.1
7	0446	0.4	1054	4.1	22	0541	0.4	1143	4.1
W	1657	0.7	2316	4.1	TH	1742	0.7 ●	2357	4.2
8	0527	0.2	1136	4.2	23	0610	0.3	1216	4.1
TH	1736	0.6	○ 2357	4.3	F	1816	0.6		
9	0608	0.1	1218	4.4	24	0028	4.2	0638	0.4
F	1816	0.5			SA	1249	4.1	1849	0.6
10	0038	4.5	0648	0.0	25	0059	4.2	0706	0.4
SA	1300	4.4	1857	0.5	SU	1320	4.1	1920	0.6
11	0119	4.6	0726	0.1	26	0130	4.2	0732	0.5
SU	1342	4.4	1938	0.5	M	1350	4.0	1948	0.6
12	0200	4.5	0805	0.2	27	0202	4.1	0755	0.6
M	1424	4.2	2021	0.5	TU	1419	3.9	2016	0.6
13	0242	4.4	0846	0.4	28	0234	4.0	0822	0.7
TU	1508	4.0	2107	0.6	W	1451	3.8	☽ 2049	0.7
14	0327	4.2	0934	0.6	29	0309	3.8	0856	0.8
W	1556	3.8	2201	0.7	TH	1527	3.6	2128	0.8
15	0421	3.9	1036	0.9	30	0349	3.6	0939	1.0
TH	1654	3.6	☽ 2309	0.8	F	1613	3.5	☽ 2219	1.0
					31	0442	3.4	1040	1.2
					SA	1717	3.3	2341	1.1

APRIL

#	Time	m	Time	m	#	Time	m	Time	m
1	0554	3.3	1224	1.3	16	0151	0.7	0803	3.7
SU	1841	3.3			M	1410	1.1	2031	3.6
2	0120	1.0	0728	3.4	17	0306	0.6	0908	3.8
M	1354	1.2	2002	3.4	TU	1516	1.0	2129	3.8
3	0229	0.8	0840	3.6	18	0359	0.5	0959	3.9
TU	1454	1.0	2106	3.7	W	1604	0.9	2215	3.9
4	0324	0.5	0936	3.9	19	0439	0.5	1040	4.0
W	1543	0.8	2159	3.9	TH	1642	0.8	2253	4.0
5	0413	0.3	1024	4.1	20	0509	0.5	1116	4.0
TH	1628	0.7	2245	4.2	F	1717	0.7	2327	4.1
6	0458	0.2	1109	4.2	21	0537	0.5	1149	4.0
F	1712	0.6	○ 2329	4.4	SA	1751	0.5	● 2358	4.1
7	0541	0.1	1153	4.4	22	0606	0.5	1220	4.1
SA	1756	0.5			SU	1825	0.5		
8	0012	4.5	0622	0.1	23	0030	4.2	0635	0.5
SU	1237	4.4	1840	0.4	M	1252	4.1	1857	0.5
9	0056	4.6	0703	0.2	24	0104	4.2	0702	0.6
M	1322	4.4	1924	0.4	TU	1323	4.0	1927	0.5
10	0140	4.6	0745	0.3	25	0137	4.1	0727	0.6
TU	1406	4.2	2009	0.4	W	1354	3.9	1957	0.6
11	0226	4.4	0829	0.5	26	0211	4.0	0757	0.7
W	1452	4.0	2057	0.5	TH	1428	3.8	2030	0.6
12	0314	4.2	0919	0.7	27	0247	3.9	0832	0.8
TH	1542	3.8	2152	0.6	F	1505	3.7	2109	0.7
13	0411	3.9	1019	1.0	28	0328	3.7	0916	1.0
F	1641	3.6	☽ 2259	0.7	SA	1550	3.6	2158	0.8
14	0523	3.7	1130	1.1	29	0418	3.6	1014	1.1
SA	1754	3.5			SU	1648	3.5	☽ 2308	0.9
15	0024	0.8	0645	3.6	30	0521	3.5	1136	1.2
SU	1252	1.2	1915	3.5	M	1800	3.4		

Chart Datum: 2·16 metres below Ordnance Datum (Newlyn)
HAT is 4·7 metres above Chart Datum

TIDES

TIDES

TIME ZONE (UT)
For Summer Time add ONE hour in **non-shaded areas**

WALTON-ON-THE-NAZE
LAT 51°51′N   LONG 1°17′E
TIMES AND HEIGHTS OF HIGH AND LOW WATERS

Dates in amber are **SPRINGS**
Dates in yellow are **NEAPS**

2012

MAY

Day	Time	m	Time	m	Time	m	Time	m
1	0036	0.8	0640	3.5	TU 1305	1.2	1916	3.5
2	0148	0.7	0756	3.7	W 1412	1.0	2024	3.7
3	0246	0.5	0859	3.9	TH 1508	0.8	2123	4.0
4	0339	0.3	0953	4.1	F 1600	0.7	2214	4.2
5	0428	0.2	1042	4.2	SA 1649	0.5	2302	4.4
6	0515	0.2	1130	4.3	SU 1739	0.4	○ 2349	4.5
7	0602	0.2	1217	4.3	M 1828	0.3		
8	0036	4.6	0647	0.3	TU 1304	4.3	1916	0.3
9	0124	4.6	0732	0.5	W 1351	4.2	2004	0.3
10	0213	4.4	0818	0.6	TH 1439	4.1	2054	0.3
11	0304	4.2	0906	0.8	F 1529	3.9	2146	0.4
12	0401	4.0	1000	1.0	SA 1626	3.8	◗ 2247	0.5
13	0505	3.8	1102	1.1	SU 1729	3.7	2357	0.6
14	0614	3.7	1214	1.2	M 1837	3.6		
15	0109	0.7	0724	3.7	TU 1328	1.2	1947	3.6
16	0220	0.7	0829	3.7	W 1434	1.1	2048	3.7
17	0318	0.7	0923	3.8	TH 1529	1.0	2138	3.8
18	0400	0.7	1008	3.9	F 1613	0.8	2220	3.9
19	0434	0.7	1046	3.9	SA 1652	0.7	2256	4.0
20	0506	0.7	1121	4.0	SU 1729	0.6	● 2331	4.1
21	0540	0.6	1155	4.0	M 1805	0.5		
22	0006	4.1	0611	0.7	TU 1230	4.0	1838	0.5
23	0043	4.1	0640	0.7	W 1304	4.0	1911	0.5
24	0118	4.1	0708	0.7	TH 1338	4.0	1944	0.5
25	0154	4.0	0741	0.8	F 1414	3.9	2021	0.6
26	0232	4.0	0819	0.8	SA 1452	3.8	2101	0.6
27	0313	3.9	0904	0.9	SU 1536	3.8	2147	0.6
28	0401	3.8	0957	1.0	M 1626	3.7	◗ 2246	0.7
29	0457	3.7	1103	1.1	TU 1727	3.7	2356	0.7
30	0604	3.7	1219	1.1	W 1834	3.7		
31	0107	0.6	0715	3.8	TH 1333	1.0	1944	3.8

JUNE

Day	Time	m	Time	m	Time	m	Time	m
1	0210	0.5	0823	3.9	F 1437	0.8	2050	4.0
2	0308	0.4	0925	4.0	SA 1535	0.7	2148	4.2
3	0403	0.4	1021	4.1	SU 1631	0.5	2242	4.4
4	0455	0.4	1112	4.2	M 1726	0.4	○ 2332	4.5
5	0546	0.4	1202	4.3	TU 1820	0.3		
6	0022	4.5	0635	0.5	W 1251	4.3	1911	0.2
7	0112	4.5	0722	0.6	TH 1339	4.3	2000	0.2
8	0201	4.4	0807	0.7	F 1426	4.2	2048	0.3
9	0251	4.3	0851	0.8	SA 1514	4.1	2135	0.4
10	0343	4.1	0937	0.9	SU 1603	4.0	2223	0.5
11	0437	3.9	1027	1.1	M 1655	3.8	◗ 2316	0.6
12	0535	3.7	1126	1.2	TU 1751	3.7		
13	0014	0.7	0634	3.6	W 1235	1.2	1852	3.6
14	0116	0.8	0738	3.6	TH 1343	1.2	1956	3.6
15	0217	0.9	0839	3.6	F 1447	1.1	2054	3.7
16	0312	0.9	0932	3.7	SA 1542	0.9	2144	3.8
17	0400	0.9	1016	3.8	SU 1629	0.8	2228	3.9
18	0442	0.8	1056	3.9	M 1710	0.6	2308	4.0
19	0519	0.8	1134	4.0	TU 1747	0.6	● 2347	4.1
20	0553	0.8	1211	4.1	W 1822	0.5		
21	0025	4.1	0623	0.8	TH 1249	4.1	1856	0.4
22	0103	4.1	0655	0.7	F 1326	4.1	1933	0.4
23	0141	4.1	0730	0.7	SA 1403	4.1	2011	0.4
24	0219	4.1	0809	0.8	SU 1441	4.0	2050	0.5
25	0259	4.0	0852	0.9	M 1520	4.0	2133	0.5
26	0343	3.9	0939	0.9	TU 1605	3.9	2221	0.6
27	0434	3.9	1034	1.0	W 1657	3.9	◗ 2321	0.6
28	0533	3.8	1142	1.1	TH 1759	3.9		
29	0029	0.6	0640	3.7	F 1258	1.0	1910	3.8
30	0138	0.6	0753	3.8	SA 1410	0.9	2024	3.9

JULY

Day	Time	m	Time	m	Time	m	Time	m
1	0243	0.6	0904	3.9	SU 1517	0.8	2130	4.1
2	0344	0.6	1007	4.0	M 1620	0.6	2229	4.2
3	0443	0.6	1102	4.1	TU 1720	0.4	○ 2322	4.4
4	0536	0.6	1152	4.2	W 1814	0.3		
5	0012	4.5	0624	0.6	TH 1240	4.3	1904	0.2
6	0100	4.5	0709	0.7	F 1325	4.4	1950	0.2
7	0147	4.4	0751	0.7	SA 1409	4.3	2032	0.3
8	0232	4.3	0831	0.8	SU 1451	4.2	2110	0.4
9	0317	4.1	0909	0.9	M 1532	4.1	2147	0.5
10	0402	3.9	0948	1.0	TU 1615	4.0	2227	0.6
11	0450	3.7	1034	1.1	W 1702	3.8	◗ 2315	0.8
12	0541	3.6	1133	1.2	TH 1757	3.6		
13	0014	1.0	0638	3.5	F 1247	1.3	1859	3.5
14	0121	1.1	0744	3.5	SA 1400	1.2	2008	3.5
15	0229	1.1	0850	3.6	SU 1508	1.0	2110	3.7
16	0331	1.0	0946	3.7	M 1605	0.9	2202	3.8
17	0421	1.0	1032	3.9	TU 1650	0.7	2247	3.9
18	0502	0.9	1113	4.0	W 1728	0.6	2328	4.0
19	0536	0.8	1152	4.1	TH 1804	0.5	●	
20	0007	4.1	0607	0.8	F 1231	4.2	1839	0.4
21	0046	4.2	0640	0.7	SA 1309	4.3	1916	0.3
22	0124	4.3	0716	0.7	SU 1347	4.3	1954	0.3
23	0203	4.2	0755	0.7	M 1423	4.2	2032	0.4
24	0242	4.2	0835	0.8	TU 1501	4.2	2111	0.4
25	0324	4.0	0919	0.9	W 1542	4.1	2154	0.5
26	0410	3.9	1009	1.0	TH 1630	4.0	◗ 2249	0.7
27	0505	3.8	1113	1.0	F 1729	3.9	2359	0.8
28	0611	3.7	1230	1.0	SA 1845	3.8		
29	0114	0.9	0730	3.6	SU 1351	1.0	2008	3.8
30	0226	0.9	0852	3.7	M 1507	0.8	2122	4.0
31	0334	0.9	1000	3.9	TU 1617	0.6	2223	4.2

AUGUST

Day	Time	m	Time	m	Time	m	Time	m
1	0435	0.8	1054	4.1	W 1716	0.4	2315	4.3
2	0525	0.7	1142	4.3	TH 1805	0.3	○	
3	0001	4.4	0609	0.7	F 1226	4.4	1849	0.2
4	0045	4.4	0650	0.7	SA 1306	4.4	1929	0.2
5	0127	4.4	0729	0.7	SU 1345	4.4	2004	0.3
6	0207	4.2	0805	0.8	M 1421	4.3	2037	0.4
7	0245	4.1	0838	0.8	TU 1456	4.2	2106	0.6
8	0323	3.9	0910	0.9	W 1533	4.0	2137	0.7
9	0402	3.7	0947	1.0	TH 1614	3.8	◗ 2215	0.9
10	0446	3.6	1035	1.1	F 1705	3.6	2310	1.1
11	0542	3.4	1144	1.3	SA 1809	3.5		
12	0030	1.3	0648	3.3	SU 1312	1.3	1924	3.4
13	0151	1.3	0804	3.4	M 1430	1.1	2037	3.5
14	0301	1.2	0912	3.6	TU 1534	0.9	2136	3.7
15	0357	1.1	1004	3.8	W 1623	0.7	2223	3.9
16	0438	0.9	1048	4.0	TH 1703	0.6	2305	4.1
17	0513	0.9	1127	4.1	F 1739	0.5	● 2344	4.2
18	0546	0.8	1206	4.3	SA 1816	0.4		
19	0023	4.3	0620	0.7	SU 1245	4.4	1853	0.3
20	0102	4.4	0657	0.6	M 1323	4.4	1930	0.3
21	0142	4.3	0736	0.7	TU 1401	4.4	2007	0.3
22	0221	4.2	0816	0.7	W 1439	4.4	2044	0.5
23	0302	4.1	0859	0.8	TH 1519	4.3	2128	0.6
24	0347	3.9	0949	0.8	F 1607	4.1	◗ 2223	0.8
25	0440	3.7	1052	1.0	SA 1708	3.9	2336	1.0
26	0549	3.5	1213	1.0	SU 1831	3.7		
27	0058	1.1	0717	3.5	M 1341	0.9	2002	3.8
28	0216	1.1	0844	3.7	TU 1504	0.8	2117	4.0
29	0327	1.0	0950	3.9	W 1614	0.6	2215	4.2
30	0425	0.9	1042	4.1	TH 1705	0.4	2303	4.3
31	0510	0.8	1126	4.3	F 1748	0.3	○ 2345	4.3

Chart Datum: 2·16 metres below Ordnance Datum (Newlyn)
HAT is 4·7 metres above Chart Datum

TIME ZONE (UT)
For Summer Time add ONE hour in **non-shaded areas**

WALTON-ON-THE-NAZE

LAT 51°51'N   LONG 1°17'E

TIMES AND HEIGHTS OF HIGH AND LOW WATERS

Dates in amber are **SPRINGS**
Dates in yellow are **NEAPS**

2012

SEPTEMBER

Day	Time m	Time m	Time m	Time m
1 SA	0549 0.7	1205 4.4	1825 0.3	
2 SU	0024 4.3	0626 0.7	1241 4.4	1859 0.3
3 M	0101 4.3	0703 0.7	1315 4.4	1930 0.4
4 TU	0137 4.2	0737 0.7	1348 4.3	1959 0.5
5 W	0210 4.1	0808 0.8	1420 4.2	2025 0.7
6 TH	0242 4.0	0837 0.8	1454 4.1	2050 0.8
7 F	0315 3.8	0910 0.9	1531 3.9	2122 1.0
8 SA	0352 3.6	0951 1.1	1615 3.6	◗ 2206 1.2
9 SU	0441 3.4	1047 1.2	1714 3.4	2317 1.4
10 M	0553 3.3	1218 1.3	1837 3.3	
11 TU	0108 1.5	0714 3.3	1346 1.2	1958 3.4
12 W	0225 1.3	0829 3.5	1454 1.0	2102 3.7
13 TH	0322 1.1	0927 3.7	1546 0.7	2152 3.9
14 F	0406 1.0	1014 4.0	1629 0.6	2236 4.1
15 SA	0443 0.8	1056 4.2	1709 0.4	2316 4.3
16 SU	0520 0.7	1136 4.3	1747 0.3	● 2356 4.4
17 M	0558 0.6	1216 4.5	1825 0.3	
18 TU	0037 4.4	0636 0.6	1256 4.6	1902 0.3
19 W	0118 4.4	0717 0.6	1336 4.6	1940 0.4
20 TH	0159 4.3	0758 0.6	1417 4.5	2019 0.5
21 F	0242 4.2	0843 0.7	1501 4.3	2106 0.7
22 SA	0327 3.9	0935 0.8	1551 4.1	◗ 2205 1.0
23 SU	0422 3.7	1040 0.9	1657 3.8	2319 1.2
24 M	0535 3.5	1203 0.9	1825 3.7	
25 TU	0042 1.2	0705 3.5	1332 0.9	1952 3.8
26 W	0202 1.2	0828 3.7	1454 0.7	2104 4.0
27 TH	0313 1.1	0931 3.9	1558 0.5	2159 4.2
28 F	0406 0.9	1021 4.1	1645 0.5	2244 4.3
29 SA	0448 0.8	1102 4.2	1723 0.4	2323 4.3
30 SU	0525 0.7	1139 4.3	1755 0.4	○ 2358 4.3

OCTOBER

Day	Time m	Time m	Time m	Time m
1 M	0601 0.7	1212 4.3	1825 0.5	
2 TU	0032 4.3	0637 0.6	1244 4.3	1854 0.5
3 W	0105 4.2	0711 0.6	1315 4.3	1922 0.6
4 TH	0136 4.1	0742 0.7	1348 4.2	1947 0.7
5 F	0206 4.0	0810 0.7	1421 4.1	2011 0.9
6 SA	0237 3.9	0840 0.8	1456 3.9	2043 1.0
7 SU	0311 3.7	0918 0.9	1536 3.7	2123 1.2
8 M	0354 3.5	1006 1.0	1625 3.5	◗ 2219 1.4
9 TU	0454 3.4	1120 1.2	1735 3.4	2356 1.5
10 W	0618 3.3	1257 1.1	1908 3.4	
11 TH	0137 1.4	0738 3.4	1408 0.9	2018 3.7
12 F	0238 1.2	0842 3.7	1504 0.7	2113 3.9
13 SA	0327 1.0	0935 3.9	1551 0.5	2201 4.1
14 SU	0410 0.8	1021 4.2	1634 0.4	2245 4.3
15 M	0452 0.7	1104 4.4	1716 0.3	● 2328 4.4
16 TU	0534 0.6	1147 4.5	1757 0.3	
17 W	0011 4.5	0617 0.5	1231 4.6	1837 0.3
18 TH	0056 4.5	0701 0.5	1315 4.6	1918 0.4
19 F	0140 4.4	0746 0.5	1400 4.5	2002 0.6
20 SA	0225 4.2	0834 0.5	1448 4.4	2051 0.8
21 SU	0313 4.0	0928 0.6	1542 4.1	2150 1.0
22 M	0410 3.8	1033 0.7	1649 3.9	◗ 2300 1.2
23 TU	0521 3.6	1152 0.8	1810 3.8	
24 W	0018 1.3	0641 3.6	1313 0.7	1929 3.8
25 TH	0136 1.2	0759 3.7	1429 0.7	2038 3.9
26 F	0245 1.1	0902 3.9	1531 0.6	2134 4.1
27 SA	0340 1.0	0953 4.0	1617 0.6	2219 4.1
28 SU	0424 0.9	1034 4.1	1653 0.6	2257 4.2
29 M	0501 0.8	1110 4.2	1723 0.6	○ 2332 4.2
30 TU	0538 0.7	1142 4.2	1753 0.6	
31 W	0004 4.2	0613 0.6	1215 4.3	1823 0.6

NOVEMBER

Day	Time m	Time m	Time m	Time m
1 TH	0036 4.2	0647 0.6	1248 4.2	1852 0.7
2 F	0107 4.1	0719 0.6	1322 4.2	1917 0.8
3 SA	0138 4.1	0748 0.6	1356 4.1	1943 0.9
4 SU	0210 4.0	0819 0.7	1431 3.9	2016 1.0
5 M	0245 3.8	0850 0.8	1510 3.8	2056 1.1
6 TU	0326 3.7	0940 0.9	1556 3.7	2147 1.3
7 W	0417 3.6	1041 1.0	1653 3.6	◗ 2257 1.4
8 TH	0524 3.5	1202 1.0	1807 3.5	
9 F	0029 1.4	0641 3.5	1319 0.8	1924 3.7
10 SA	0147 1.2	0753 3.7	1419 0.7	2029 3.9
11 SU	0246 1.0	0853 3.9	1512 0.5	2125 4.1
12 M	0337 0.8	0947 4.2	1601 0.4	2215 4.3
13 TU	0426 0.7	1036 4.4	1648 0.4	● 2303 4.4
14 W	0515 0.5	1123 4.5	1734 0.4	2350 4.4
15 TH	0603 0.4	1210 4.6	1820 0.4	
16 F	0037 4.4	0652 0.4	1258 4.6	1905 0.5
17 SA	0125 4.4	0741 0.3	1347 4.6	1952 0.7
18 SU	0213 4.3	0831 0.4	1437 4.4	2041 0.9
19 M	0302 4.1	0923 0.4	1532 4.2	2135 1.0
20 TU	0356 3.9	1022 0.5	1634 3.9	◗ 2234 1.2
21 W	0458 3.8	1128 0.6	1742 3.8	2343 1.3
22 TH	0607 3.7	1237 0.7	1853 3.8	
23 F	0056 1.3	0718 3.7	1347 0.7	2001 3.8
24 SA	0206 1.2	0824 3.8	1451 0.8	2100 3.9
25 SU	0307 1.1	0918 3.9	1541 0.8	2148 4.0
26 M	0357 0.9	1003 3.9	1620 0.8	2230 4.0
27 TU	0439 0.8	1042 4.0	1653 0.8	2306 4.1
28 W	0517 0.7	1117 4.1	1727 0.7	○ 2340 4.1
29 TH	0553 0.6	1151 4.1	1759 0.8	
30 F	0013 4.1	0627 0.5	1227 4.1	1829 0.8

DECEMBER

Day	Time m	Time m	Time m	Time m
1 SA	0047 4.1	0700 0.5	1302 4.1	1856 0.8
2 SU	0120 4.1	0732 0.5	1337 4.1	1925 0.8
3 M	0154 4.0	0805 0.6	1413 4.0	2000 0.9
4 TU	0229 3.9	0842 0.6	1451 3.9	2039 1.0
5 W	0308 3.9	0922 0.7	1534 3.8	2125 1.1
6 TH	0353 3.8	1011 0.7	1624 3.8	◗ 2221 1.2
7 F	0447 3.7	1113 0.8	1724 3.7	2332 1.3
8 SA	0552 3.7	1226 0.8	1834 3.7	
9 SU	0053 1.2	0703 3.7	1335 0.7	1945 3.8
10 M	0206 1.0	0814 3.9	1436 0.6	2052 4.0
11 TU	0308 0.8	0917 4.1	1532 0.5	2151 4.1
12 W	0405 0.7	1014 4.3	1626 0.5	2245 4.2
13 TH	0500 0.5	1106 4.3	1718 0.5	● 2335 4.3
14 F	0554 0.3	1156 4.6	1809 0.5	
15 SA	0025 4.4	0646 0.2	1246 4.6	1857 0.6
16 SU	0113 4.4	0736 0.2	1336 4.5	1943 0.7
17 M	0201 4.4	0825 0.2	1425 4.4	2028 0.8
18 TU	0248 4.3	0912 0.3	1516 4.3	2114 0.9
19 W	0336 4.1	1000 0.4	1609 4.0	2203 1.0
20 TH	0427 3.9	1051 0.5	1706 3.8	◗ 2258 1.2
21 F	0523 3.8	1147 0.7	1806 3.7	
22 SA	0003 1.2	0625 3.6	1248 0.8	1910 3.6
23 SU	0114 1.3	0733 3.6	1351 0.9	2016 3.6
24 M	0224 1.2	0837 3.6	1453 1.0	2114 3.7
25 TU	0327 1.0	0930 3.7	1546 0.9	2202 3.8
26 W	0417 0.8	1015 3.8	1629 0.9	2243 3.9
27 TH	0459 0.7	1055 3.9	1708 0.9	2320 4.0
28 F	0536 0.6	1133 4.0	1742 0.8	○ 2356 4.1
29 SA	0610 0.5	1210 4.1	1812 0.8	
30 SU	0031 4.1	0642 0.5	1246 4.1	1841 0.8
31 M	0107 4.2	0716 0.4	1322 4.1	1912 0.8

Chart Datum: 2·16 metres below Ordnance Datum (Newlyn)
HAT is 4·7 metres above Chart Datum

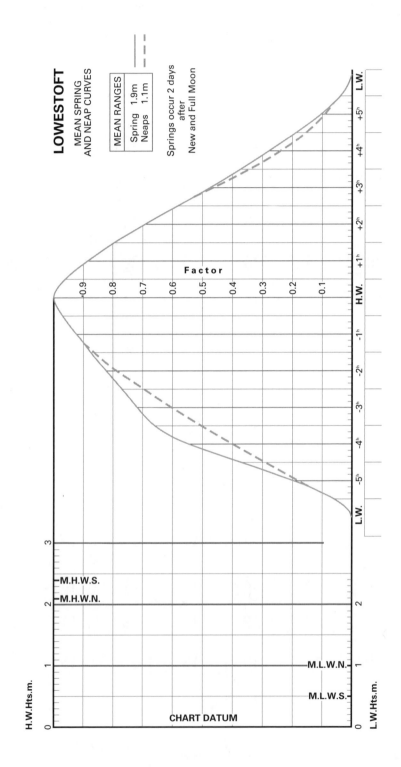

LOWESTOFT
MEAN SPRING
AND NEAP CURVES

MEAN RANGES

Spring 1.9m
Neaps 1.1m

Springs occur 2 days
after
New and Full Moon

LOWESTOFT

LAT 52°28'N   LONG 1°45'E

TIMES AND HEIGHTS OF HIGH AND LOW WATERS

Dates in amber are **SPRINGS**
Dates in yellow are **NEAPS**

2012

JANUARY

Day	Time	m	Day	Time	m
1 SU	0158 / 0843 / 1531 / ☽2021	2.4 / 0.9 / 2.1 / 1.3	**16** M	0141 / 0818 / 1427 / 2014	2.6 / 0.7 / 2.2 / 1.1
2 M	0249 / 0944 / 1634 / 2121	2.3 / 1.0 / 2.1 / 1.4	**17** TU	0234 / 0917 / 1542 / 2118	2.5 / 0.8 / 2.2 / 1.1
3 TU	0356 / 1054 / 1729 / 2306	2.2 / 1.1 / 2.1 / 1.4	**18** W	0347 / 1032 / 1704 / 2251	2.4 / 0.9 / 2.2 / 1.1
4 W	0510 / 1151 / 1820	2.2 / 1.1 / 2.2	**19** TH	0514 / 1145 / 1805	2.4 / 0.9 / 2.2
5 TH	0014 / 0613 / 1239 / 1906	1.3 / 2.2 / 1.1 / 2.3	**20** F	0014 / 0627 / 1250 / 1900	1.0 / 2.4 / 0.9 / 2.3
6 F	0105 / 0713 / 1321 / 1946	1.2 / 2.2 / 1.1 / 2.3	**21** SA	0124 / 0738 / 1350 / 1954	0.8 / 2.4 / 0.9 / 2.4
7 SA	0150 / 0807 / 1400 / 2022	1.0 / 2.2 / 1.0 / 2.4	**22** SU	0227 / 0840 / 1444 / 2042	0.7 / 2.4 / 0.9 / 2.5
8 SU	0233 / 0851 / 1438 / 2058	0.9 / 2.3 / 0.9 / 2.5	**23** M	0320 / 0929 / 1531 / 2127	0.5 / 2.5 / 0.8 / 2.6
9 M	0315 / 0930 / 1518 / ○2135	0.8 / 2.3 / 0.9 / 2.5	**24** TU	0406 / 1013 / 1612 / 2209	0.4 / 2.5 / 0.8 / 2.6
10 TU	0359 / 1009 / 1559 / 2213	0.6 / 2.4 / 0.8 / 2.6	**25** W	0448 / 1054 / 1648 / 2250	0.4 / 2.4 / 0.8 / 2.7
11 W	0442 / 1047 / 1641 / 2252	0.6 / 2.4 / 0.8 / 2.6	**26** TH	0527 / 1133 / 1722 / 2328	0.4 / 2.4 / 0.8 / 2.6
12 TH	0524 / 1127 / 1721 / 2331	0.5 / 2.4 / 0.8 / 2.6	**27** F	0604 / 1211 / 1754	0.5 / 2.3 / 0.9
13 F	0606 / 1207 / 1800	0.5 / 2.4 / 0.9	**28** SA	0005 / 0638 / 1247 / 1825	2.6 / 0.6 / 2.2 / 0.9
14 SA	0012 / 0647 / 1249 / 1839	2.6 / 0.5 / 2.3 / 0.9	**29** SU	0042 / 0711 / 1322 / 1859	2.5 / 0.7 / 2.2 / 1.0
15 SU	0054 / 0730 / 1334 / 1923	2.6 / 0.6 / 2.3 / 1.0	**30** M	0122 / 0746 / 1402 / 1940	2.4 / 0.9 / 2.1 / 1.0
			31 TU	0207 / 0826 / 1453 / ☽2029	2.3 / 1.0 / 2.1 / 1.2

FEBRUARY

Day	Time	m	Day	Time	m
1 W	0304 / 0920 / 1613 / 2138	2.2 / 1.2 / 2.1 / 1.3	**16** TH	0342 / 1007 / 1629 / 2243	2.3 / 1.0 / 2.1 / 1.0
2 TH	0429 / 1057 / 1721 / 2331	2.1 / 1.2 / 2.1 / 1.2	**17** F	0517 / 1133 / 1740	2.3 / 1.1 / 2.2
3 F	0546 / 1204 / 1818	2.1 / 1.2 / 2.2	**18** SA	0008 / 0637 / 1244 / 1843	0.9 / 2.3 / 1.1 / 2.3
4 SA	0033 / 0654 / 1254 / 1909	1.1 / 2.1 / 1.1 / 2.2	**19** SU	0119 / 0748 / 1346 / 1941	0.7 / 2.3 / 1.0 / 2.4
5 SU	0124 / 0753 / 1337 / 1954	1.0 / 2.2 / 1.1 / 2.3	**20** M	0219 / 0838 / 1436 / 2028	0.6 / 2.4 / 0.9 / 2.4
6 M	0210 / 0836 / 1420 / 2034	0.8 / 2.3 / 1.0 / 2.4	**21** TU	0307 / 0918 / 1517 / ●2110	0.5 / 2.4 / 0.9 / 2.4
7 TU	0256 / 0913 / 1502 / ○2113	0.7 / 2.3 / 0.8 / 2.5	**22** W	0348 / 0955 / 1554 / 2149	0.4 / 2.4 / 0.8 / 2.6
8 W	0340 / 0950 / 1545 / 2152	0.5 / 2.4 / 0.8 / 2.6	**23** TH	0426 / 1031 / 1627 / 2227	0.4 / 2.4 / 0.7 / 2.6
9 TH	0424 / 1027 / 1628 / 2231	0.4 / 2.4 / 0.7 / 2.7	**24** F	0501 / 1105 / 1658 / 2303	0.4 / 2.4 / 0.7 / 2.6
10 F	0506 / 1105 / 1706 / 2311	0.3 / 2.5 / 0.7 / 2.7	**25** SA	0533 / 1136 / 1728 / 2338	0.5 / 2.3 / 0.8 / 2.5
11 SA	0546 / 1144 / 1744 / 2351	0.3 / 2.4 / 0.7 / 2.7	**26** SU	0602 / 1207 / 1757	0.6 / 2.3 / 0.8
12 SU	0626 / 1224 / 1823	0.4 / 2.4 / 0.8	**27** M	0013 / 0630 / 1239 / 1830	2.5 / 0.7 / 2.2 / 0.9
13 M	0034 / 0706 / 1308 / 1905	2.7 / 0.5 / 2.3 / 0.8	**28** TU	0051 / 0700 / 1315 / 1908	2.4 / 0.9 / 2.2 / 0.9
14 TU	0121 / 0751 / 1357 / ☽1956	2.6 / 0.7 / 2.2 / 0.9	**29** W	0134 / 0735 / 1359 / 1954	2.2 / 1.0 / 2.1 / 1.1
15 W	0218 / 0846 / 1501 / 2101	2.4 / 0.9 / 2.1 / 1.0			

MARCH

Day	Time	m	Day	Time	m
1 TH	0226 / 0820 / 1454 / ☽2053	2.1 / 1.2 / 2.1 / 1.2	**16** F	0353 / 0946 / 1556 / 2239	2.2 / 1.2 / 2.1 / 0.9
2 F	0345 / 0922 / 1615 / 2238	2.0 / 1.3 / 2.1 / 1.2	**17** SA	0520 / 1121 / 1713 / 2356	2.2 / 1.2 / 2.2 / 0.8
3 SA	0522 / 1121 / 1731 / 2359	2.0 / 1.3 / 2.1 / 1.1	**18** SU	0639 / 1232 / 1822	2.3 / 1.2 / 2.2
4 SU	0631 / 1224 / 1830	2.1 / 1.2 / 2.2	**19** M	0103 / 0741 / 1332 / 1922	0.7 / 2.3 / 1.1 / 2.3
5 M	0053 / 0727 / 1312 / 1920	0.9 / 2.2 / 1.1 / 2.3	**20** TU	0200 / 0824 / 1419 / 2009	0.6 / 2.3 / 1.0 / 2.4
6 TU	0142 / 0811 / 1357 / 2004	0.7 / 2.3 / 1.0 / 2.4	**21** W	0244 / 0900 / 1457 / 2048	0.5 / 2.3 / 0.9 / 2.4
7 W	0229 / 0849 / 1441 / 2045	0.6 / 2.4 / 0.8 / 2.5	**22** TH	0323 / 0933 / 1531 / ●2126	0.5 / 2.4 / 0.8 / 2.5
8 TH	0315 / 0925 / 1524 / ○2126	0.4 / 2.4 / 0.7 / 2.6	**23** F	0358 / 1004 / 1603 / 2203	0.5 / 2.4 / 0.7 / 2.5
9 F	0359 / 1003 / 1607 / 2207	0.3 / 2.5 / 0.6 / 2.7	**24** SA	0430 / 1035 / 1634 / 2238	0.5 / 2.4 / 0.7 / 2.5
10 SA	0442 / 1041 / 1648 / 2249	0.2 / 2.5 / 0.6 / 2.8	**25** SU	0459 / 1104 / 1703 / 2313	0.6 / 2.4 / 0.7 / 2.4
11 SU	0523 / 1123 / 1728 / 2332	0.3 / 2.3 / 0.6 / 2.7	**26** M	0527 / 1133 / 1733 / 2348	0.7 / 2.3 / 0.7 / 2.4
12 M	0603 / 1201 / 1810	0.4 / 2.4 / 0.6	**27** TU	0553 / 1205 / 1806	0.8 / 2.3 / 0.8
13 TU	0018 / 0644 / 1245 / 1854	2.6 / 0.5 / 2.3 / 0.7	**28** W	0025 / 0622 / 1241 / 1843	2.3 / 0.9 / 2.3 / 0.9
14 W	0110 / 0729 / 1334 / 1947	2.5 / 0.8 / 2.3 / 0.8	**29** TH	0107 / 0658 / 1323 / 1928	2.2 / 1.0 / 2.2 / 0.9
15 TH	0215 / 0822 / 1435 / ☽2058	2.3 / 1.0 / 2.2 / 0.9	**30** F	0156 / 0742 / 1413 / ☽2024	2.1 / 1.1 / 2.1 / 1.0
			31 SA	0303 / 0838 / 1515 / 2147	2.0 / 1.3 / 2.1 / 1.0

APRIL

Day	Time	m	Day	Time	m
1 SU	0454 / 1005 / 1637 / 2319	2.0 / 1.3 / 2.1 / 1.0	**16** M	0621 / 1204 / 1751	2.3 / 1.2 / 2.2
2 M	0601 / 1143 / 1747	2.1 / 1.2 / 2.1	**17** TU	0034 / 0718 / 1304 / 1852	0.6 / 2.3 / 1.1 / 2.2
3 TU	0017 / 0655 / 1239 / 1841	0.8 / 2.2 / 1.1 / 2.2	**18** W	0129 / 0801 / 1351 / 1942	0.6 / 2.3 / 1.1 / 2.3
4 W	0109 / 0740 / 1327 / 1929	0.7 / 2.3 / 1.0 / 2.4	**19** TH	0213 / 0837 / 1430 / 2024	0.6 / 2.3 / 0.9 / 2.3
5 TH	0158 / 0820 / 1414 / 2014	0.5 / 2.4 / 0.8 / 2.5	**20** F	0251 / 0908 / 1505 / 2102	0.6 / 2.3 / 0.8 / 2.4
6 F	0246 / 0858 / 1500 / ○2059	0.4 / 2.4 / 0.7 / 2.6	**21** SA	0326 / 0937 / 1538 / ●2139	0.6 / 2.4 / 0.7 / 2.4
7 SA	0332 / 0937 / 1546 / 2144	0.3 / 2.5 / 0.6 / 2.7	**22** SU	0357 / 1006 / 1610 / 2216	0.6 / 2.4 / 0.7 / 2.4
8 SU	0416 / 1017 / 1630 / 2230	0.3 / 2.5 / 0.5 / 2.7	**23** M	0425 / 1034 / 1641 / 2251	0.7 / 2.4 / 0.7 / 2.3
9 M	0459 / 1058 / 1714 / 2317	0.3 / 2.5 / 0.5 / 2.7	**24** TU	0453 / 1104 / 1713 / 2327	0.8 / 2.4 / 0.7 / 2.3
10 TU	0542 / 1141 / 1800	0.4 / 2.5 / 0.5	**25** W	0522 / 1138 / 1748	0.8 / 2.4 / 0.7
11 W	0008 / 0624 / 1227 / 1848	2.6 / 0.6 / 2.4 / 0.5	**26** TH	0004 / 0553 / 1215 / 1826	2.2 / 0.9 / 2.3 / 0.8
12 TH	0106 / 0710 / 1317 / 1944	2.4 / 0.9 / 2.3 / 0.6	**27** F	0046 / 0631 / 1256 / 1910	2.2 / 1.0 / 2.3 / 0.8
13 F	0219 / 0804 / 1415 / ☽2056	2.3 / 1.1 / 2.3 / 0.7	**28** SA	0133 / 0716 / 1344 / 2003	2.1 / 1.1 / 2.2 / 0.9
14 SA	0352 / 0921 / 1526 / 2222	1.2 / 1.2 / 2.2 / 0.7	**29** SU	0232 / 0809 / 1438 / ☽2112	2.1 / 1.2 / 2.2 / 0.9
15 SU	0509 / 1054 / 1642 / 2332	2.2 / 1.3 / 2.2 / 0.7	**30** M	0413 / 0917 / 1543 / 2235	2.1 / 1.3 / 2.2 / 0.8

Chart Datum: 1·50 metres below Ordnance Datum (Newlyn)
HAT is 3·0 metres above Chart Datum

TIDES

TIME ZONE (UT)	LOWESTOFT	Dates in amber are SPRINGS
For Summer Time add ONE hour in non-shaded areas	LAT 52°28'N LONG 1°45'E	Dates in yellow are NEAPS
	TIMES AND HEIGHTS OF HIGH AND LOW WATERS	2012

MAY

Day	Time	m	Day	Time	m
1 TU	0525 / 1048 / 1658 / 2339	2.1 / 1.2 / 2.2 / 1.2	16 W	0645 / 1224 / 1815	2.2 / 1.2 / 2.2
2 W	0619 / 1158 / 1802	2.2 / 1.1 / 2.3	17 TH	0051 / 0732 / 1317 / 1910	0.7 / 2.3 / 1.1 / 2.2
3 TH	0033 / 0706 / 1253 / 1855	0.6 / 2.3 / 1.0 / 2.4	18 F	0137 / 0810 / 1400 / 1958	0.8 / 2.3 / 1.0 / 2.2
4 F	0126 / 0749 / 1345 / 1945	0.5 / 2.4 / 0.8 / 2.5	19 SA	0217 / 0842 / 1438 / 2041	0.8 / 2.3 / 0.9 / 2.3
5 SA	0216 / 0831 / 1436 / 2035	0.4 / 2.4 / 0.7 / 2.6	20 SU	0252 / 0911 / 1514 / 2120	0.8 / 2.4 / 0.8 / 2.3
6 SU	0305 / 0912 / 1527 / 2125	0.4 / 2.5 / 0.5 / 2.6	21 M	0324 / 0939 / 1548 / 2157	0.8 / 2.4 / 0.7 / 2.3
7 M	0353 / 0955 / 1616 / 2216	0.4 / 2.5 / 0.4 / 2.6	22 TU	0354 / 1008 / 1622 / 2234	0.8 / 2.4 / 0.7 / 2.3
8 TU	0438 / 1039 / 1704 / 2309	0.4 / 2.6 / 0.4 / 2.6	23 W	0425 / 1041 / 1658 / 2311	0.8 / 2.4 / 0.7 / 2.3
9 W	0523 / 1124 / 1752	0.6 / 2.5 / 0.4	24 TH	0458 / 1116 / 1735 / 2349	0.9 / 2.4 / 0.7 / 2.2
10 TH	0003 / 0607 / 1211 / 1842	2.5 / 0.7 / 2.5 / 0.4	25 F	0534 / 1154 / 1815	0.9 / 2.4 / 0.7
11 F	0103 / 0653 / 1301 / 1937	2.4 / 0.9 / 2.4 / 0.5	26 SA	0029 / 0612 / 1236 / 1858	2.2 / 1.0 / 2.4 / 0.7
12 SA	0212 / 0743 / 1355 / 2041	2.3 / 1.1 / 2.4 / 0.6	27 SU	0114 / 0656 / 1320 / 1947	2.2 / 1.1 / 2.3 / 0.7
13 SU	0332 / 0845 / 1455 / 2153	2.2 / 1.2 / 2.3 / 0.6	28 M	0205 / 0745 / 1409 / 2044	2.1 / 1.1 / 2.3 / 0.8
14 M	0443 / 1009 / 1605 / 2259	2.2 / 1.3 / 2.2 / 0.7	29 TU	0310 / 0843 / 1504 / 2152	2.1 / 1.2 / 2.3 / 0.7
15 TU	0547 / 1123 / 1713 / 2358	2.2 / 1.3 / 2.2 / 0.7	30 W	0442 / 0954 / 1610 / 2301	2.1 / 1.2 / 2.3 / 0.7
			31 TH	0542 / 1114 / 1723	2.2 / 1.1 / 2.3

JUNE

Day	Time	m	Day	Time	m
1 F	0000 / 0632 / 1221 / 1824	0.6 / 2.3 / 1.0 / 2.4	16 SA	0100 / 0738 / 1329 / 1934	0.9 / 2.3 / 1.1 / 2.2
2 SA	0056 / 0720 / 1320 / 1921	0.6 / 2.4 / 0.9 / 2.5	17 SU	0143 / 0814 / 1412 / 2025	0.9 / 2.3 / 0.9 / 2.2
3 SU	0150 / 0805 / 1417 / 2017	0.5 / 2.4 / 0.7 / 2.5	18 M	0220 / 0845 / 1451 / 2106	0.9 / 2.4 / 0.8 / 2.2
4 M	0243 / 0851 / 1512 / 2113	0.5 / 2.5 / 0.5 / 2.6	19 TU	0254 / 0914 / 1528 / 2143	0.9 / 2.4 / 0.8 / 2.3
5 TU	0334 / 0936 / 1605 / 2209	0.5 / 2.6 / 0.4 / 2.6	20 W	0328 / 0946 / 1606 / 2219	0.9 / 2.5 / 0.7 / 2.3
6 W	0422 / 1023 / 1655 / 2302	0.6 / 2.6 / 0.3 / 2.5	21 TH	0403 / 1021 / 1645 / 2256	0.9 / 2.5 / 0.6 / 2.3
7 TH	0507 / 1109 / 1744 / 2355	0.7 / 2.6 / 0.3 / 2.5	22 F	0441 / 1059 / 1724 / 2333	0.9 / 2.5 / 0.6 / 2.3
8 F	0551 / 1155 / 1832	0.8 / 2.6 / 0.3	23 SA	0519 / 1137 / 1805	0.9 / 2.5 / 0.6
9 SA	0049 / 0634 / 1242 / 1921	2.4 / 0.9 / 2.6 / 0.4	24 SU	0012 / 0557 / 1216 / 1845	2.3 / 0.9 / 2.5 / 0.6
10 SU	0147 / 0718 / 1330 / 2014	2.3 / 1.0 / 2.5 / 0.5	25 M	0053 / 0638 / 1258 / 1928	2.2 / 1.0 / 2.5 / 0.6
11 M	0256 / 0805 / 1421 / 2114	2.2 / 1.0 / 2.4 / 0.7	26 TU	0138 / 0723 / 1342 / 2017	2.2 / 1.0 / 2.5 / 0.7
12 TU	0405 / 0903 / 1520 / 2218	2.2 / 1.3 / 2.3 / 0.8	27 W	0230 / 0814 / 1432 / 2114	2.2 / 1.1 / 2.4 / 0.7
13 W	0505 / 1026 / 1629 / 2318	2.2 / 1.3 / 2.2 / 0.8	28 TH	0342 / 0914 / 1533 / 2223	2.2 / 1.1 / 2.4 / 0.7
14 TH	0602 / 1139 / 1734	2.2 / 1.3 / 2.2	29 F	0503 / 1033 / 1652 / 2331	2.2 / 1.1 / 2.4 / 0.7
15 F	0012 / 0654 / 1239 / 1835	0.9 / 2.2 / 1.2 / 2.2	30 SA	0601 / 1154 / 1803	2.3 / 1.0 / 2.4

JULY

Day	Time	m	Day	Time	m
1 SU	0032 / 0653 / 1301 / 1906	0.7 / 2.3 / 0.9 / 2.4	16 M	0112 / 0739 / 1346 / 2011	1.1 / 2.3 / 1.0 / 2.2
2 M	0131 / 0744 / 1405 / 2010	0.7 / 2.4 / 0.7 / 2.5	17 TU	0153 / 0816 / 1428 / 2052	1.1 / 2.4 / 0.9 / 2.2
3 TU	0227 / 0833 / 1504 / 2110	0.7 / 2.5 / 0.5 / 2.5	18 W	0230 / 0850 / 1508 / 2127	1.0 / 2.4 / 0.8 / 2.3
4 W	0320 / 0921 / 1557 / 2203	0.7 / 2.6 / 0.4 / 2.5	19 TH	0307 / 0925 / 1548 / 2201	0.9 / 2.5 / 0.7 / 2.3
5 TH	0408 / 1007 / 1645 / 2252	0.7 / 2.7 / 0.3 / 2.5	20 F	0346 / 1001 / 1628 / 2236	0.9 / 2.6 / 0.6 / 2.4
6 F	0452 / 1052 / 1730 / 2339	0.7 / 2.7 / 0.3 / 2.5	21 SA	0425 / 1038 / 1708 / 2312	0.8 / 2.6 / 0.5 / 2.4
7 SA	0532 / 1136 / 1814	0.8 / 2.7 / 0.3	22 SU	0504 / 1116 / 1748 / 2350	0.8 / 2.6 / 0.5 / 2.4
8 SU	0025 / 0611 / 1219 / 1856	2.4 / 0.9 / 2.6 / 0.4	23 M	0542 / 1154 / 1827	0.9 / 2.6 / 0.5
9 M	0112 / 0648 / 1301 / 1939	2.3 / 1.0 / 2.6 / 0.6	24 TU	0028 / 0620 / 1235 / 1906	2.3 / 0.9 / 2.6 / 0.6
10 TU	0203 / 0727 / 1345 / 2025	2.2 / 1.1 / 2.5 / 0.7	25 W	0111 / 0702 / 1318 / 1949	2.3 / 1.0 / 2.6 / 0.6
11 W	0305 / 0811 / 1435 / 2120	2.1 / 1.2 / 2.3 / 0.9	26 TH	0158 / 0801 / 1407 / 2040	2.3 / 1.1 / 2.5 / 0.7
12 TH	0410 / 0907 / 1538 / 2228	2.1 / 1.3 / 2.2 / 1.0	27 F	0257 / 0846 / 1509 / 2147	2.2 / 1.1 / 2.4 / 0.9
13 F	0508 / 1043 / 1654 / 2332	2.1 / 1.3 / 2.2 / 1.1	28 SA	0421 / 1005 / 1636 / 2308	2.2 / 1.1 / 2.4 / 0.9
14 SA	0602 / 1200 / 1802	2.2 / 1.2 / 2.1	29 SU	0531 / 1139 / 1755	2.3 / 1.0 / 2.4
15 SU	0026 / 0654 / 1257 / 1912	1.1 / 2.2 / 1.1 / 2.1	30 M	0017 / 0629 / 1252 / 1907	1.0 / 2.3 / 0.9 / 2.4
			31 TU	0120 / 0725 / 1358 / 2013	0.9 / 2.4 / 0.7 / 2.4

AUGUST

Day	Time	m	Day	Time	m
1 W	0218 / 0817 / 1456 / 2107	0.9 / 2.5 / 0.5 / 2.5	16 TH	0207 / 0820 / 1443 / 2103	1.0 / 2.5 / 0.8 / 2.3
2 TH	0309 / 0905 / 1546 / 2152	0.9 / 2.6 / 0.4 / 2.5	17 F	0246 / 0858 / 1524 / 2137	1.0 / 2.6 / 0.6 / 2.4
3 F	0354 / 0949 / 1629 / 2234	0.8 / 2.7 / 0.3 / 2.5	18 SA	0326 / 0935 / 1605 / 2211	0.9 / 2.7 / 0.5 / 2.5
4 SA	0433 / 1032 / 1710 / 2315	0.8 / 2.8 / 0.3 / 2.5	19 SU	0407 / 1013 / 1646 / 2247	0.8 / 2.7 / 0.4 / 2.5
5 SU	0510 / 1113 / 1749 / 2355	0.8 / 2.7 / 0.4 / 2.4	20 M	0446 / 1052 / 1725 / 2324	0.8 / 2.8 / 0.4 / 2.5
6 M	0545 / 1152 / 1825	0.8 / 2.7 / 0.5	21 TU	0525 / 1131 / 1804	0.8 / 2.8 / 0.5
7 TU	0033 / 0618 / 1231 / 1900	2.3 / 0.9 / 2.6 / 0.7	22 W	0003 / 0603 / 1213 / 1842	2.5 / 0.8 / 2.7 / 0.6
8 W	0111 / 0653 / 1311 / 1936	2.3 / 1.0 / 2.5 / 0.8	23 TH	0045 / 0644 / 1257 / 1924	2.4 / 0.9 / 2.6 / 0.7
9 TH	0151 / 0732 / 1356 / 2015	2.2 / 1.1 / 2.4 / 1.0	24 F	0131 / 0731 / 1349 / 2013	2.3 / 0.9 / 2.5 / 0.9
10 F	0241 / 0819 / 1452 / 2104	2.2 / 1.2 / 2.2 / 1.2	25 SA	0227 / 0830 / 1459 / 2118	2.3 / 1.0 / 2.4 / 1.0
11 SA	0353 / 0926 / 1616 / 2237	2.2 / 1.3 / 2.1 / 1.3	26 SU	0343 / 0958 / 1638 / 2252	2.3 / 1.1 / 2.3 / 1.1
12 SU	0501 / 1121 / 1735 / 2353	2.2 / 1.3 / 2.1 / 1.3	27 M	0503 / 1132 / 1800	2.3 / 1.0 / 2.4
13 M	0600 / 1225 / 1847	2.2 / 1.2 / 2.2	28 TU	0007 / 0607 / 1244 / 1914	1.1 / 2.4 / 0.8 / 2.4
14 TU	0044 / 0654 / 1316 / 1948	1.2 / 2.3 / 1.0 / 2.2	29 W	0112 / 0707 / 1349 / 2012	1.1 / 2.4 / 0.7 / 2.5
15 W	0128 / 0741 / 1401 / 2029	1.2 / 2.4 / 0.9 / 2.3	30 TH	0209 / 0800 / 1442 / 2056	1.0 / 2.5 / 0.5 / 2.5
			31 F	0255 / 0845 / 1527 / 2134	0.9 / 2.6 / 0.4 / 2.5

Chart Datum: 1·50 metres below Ordnance Datum (Newlyn)
HAT is 3·0 metres above Chart Datum

TIME ZONE (UT)
For Summer Time add ONE hour in **non-shaded areas**

LOWESTOFT
LAT 52°28'N   LONG 1°45'E

Dates in amber are **SPRINGS**
Dates in yellow are **NEAPS**

2012

TIMES AND HEIGHTS OF HIGH AND LOW WATERS

SEPTEMBER

Day	Time	m	Day	Time	m
1 SA	0335 / 0927 / 1607 / 2212	0.9 / 2.7 / 0.4 / 2.5	**16** SU	0302 / 0906 / 1536 / ●2143	0.9 / 2.7 / 0.5 / 2.5
2 SU	0411 / 1008 / 1644 / 2248	0.8 / 2.8 / 0.4 / 2.5	**17** M	0344 / 0946 / 1618 / 2220	0.8 / 2.8 / 0.4 / 2.5
3 M	0446 / 1047 / 1719 / 2323	0.8 / 2.7 / 0.5 / 2.4	**18** TU	0426 / 1027 / 1659 / 2259	0.7 / 2.8 / 0.4 / 2.6
4 TU	0518 / 1125 / 1751 / 2356	0.8 / 2.7 / 0.6 / 2.4	**19** W	0507 / 1109 / 1739 / 2339	0.7 / 2.8 / 0.5 / 2.6
5 W	0550 / 1202 / 1821	0.9 / 2.6 / 0.8	**20** TH	0548 / 1154 / 1819	0.7 / 2.7 / 0.6
6 TH	0028 / 0623 / 1240 / 1850	2.4 / 1.0 / 2.5 / 0.9	**21** F	0021 / 0632 / 1243 / 1902	2.5 / 0.8 / 2.6 / 0.8
7 F	0104 / 0700 / 1322 / 1924	2.3 / 1.0 / 2.3 / 1.1	**22** SA	0109 / 0722 / 1342 / ◐1952	2.4 / 0.8 / 2.5 / 1.0
8 SA	0147 / 0744 / 1414 / ◐2005	2.3 / 1.1 / 2.2 / 1.2	**23** SU	0204 / 0826 / 1504 / 2058	2.4 / 0.9 / 2.4 / 1.2
9 SU	0239 / 0841 / 1535 / 2101	2.2 / 1.2 / 2.1 / 1.4	**24** M	0315 / 0958 / 1643 / 2237	2.3 / 0.9 / 2.3 / 1.3
10 M	0353 / 1025 / 1708 / 2302	2.2 / 1.3 / 2.1 / 1.4	**25** TU	0436 / 1121 / 1800 / 2352	2.3 / 0.9 / 2.4 / 1.3
11 TU	0510 / 1149 / 1817	2.2 / 1.1 / 2.2	**26** W	0544 / 1228 / 1909	2.4 / 0.8 / 2.4
12 W	0010 / 0609 / 1241 / 1914	1.3 / 2.3 / 1.0 / 2.3	**27** TH	0056 / 0645 / 1329 / 1959	1.2 / 2.4 / 0.7 / 2.5
13 TH	0057 / 0701 / 1326 / 1957	1.2 / 2.4 / 0.9 / 2.3	**28** F	0150 / 0738 / 1420 / 2038	1.1 / 2.5 / 0.6 / 2.5
14 F	0138 / 0745 / 1410 / 2033	1.1 / 2.5 / 0.7 / 2.4	**29** SA	0234 / 0823 / 1502 / 2112	1.0 / 2.6 / 0.6 / 2.5
15 SA	0220 / 0826 / 1454 / 2108	1.1 / 2.6 / 0.6 / 2.5	**30** SU	0311 / 0904 / 1539 / ○2146	0.9 / 2.7 / 0.5 / 2.5

OCTOBER

Day	Time	m	Day	Time	m
1 M	0347 / 0944 / 1614 / 2219	0.8 / 2.7 / 0.6 / 2.5	**16** TU	0320 / 0920 / 1550 / 2154	0.7 / 2.8 / 0.4 / 2.6
2 TU	0420 / 1022 / 1645 / 2250	0.8 / 2.6 / 0.7 / 2.5	**17** W	0406 / 1005 / 1634 / 2235	0.7 / 2.8 / 0.4 / 2.6
3 W	0453 / 1059 / 1715 / 2321	0.8 / 2.6 / 0.8 / 2.5	**18** TH	0451 / 1052 / 1717 / 2317	0.6 / 2.8 / 0.5 / 2.6
4 TH	0524 / 1135 / 1742 / 2353	0.9 / 2.5 / 0.9 / 2.5	**19** F	0537 / 1141 / 1800	0.6 / 2.7 / 0.7
5 F	0557 / 1212 / 1810	0.9 / 2.4 / 1.0	**20** SA	0002 / 0625 / 1236 / 1844	2.6 / 0.6 / 2.6 / 0.9
6 SA	0028 / 0633 / 1254 / 1843	2.4 / 1.0 / 2.3 / 1.1	**21** SU	0051 / 0718 / 1341 / 1935	2.5 / 0.7 / 2.4 / 1.1
7 SU	0109 / 0716 / 1343 / 1925	2.4 / 1.0 / 2.2 / 1.2	**22** M	0146 / 0823 / 1508 / ●2038	2.5 / 0.8 / 2.4 / 1.3
8 M	0158 / 0809 / 1448 / ◐2017	2.3 / 1.1 / 2.1 / 1.4	**23** TU	0251 / 0945 / 1634 / 2209	2.4 / 0.8 / 2.3 / 1.4
9 TU	0256 / 0925 / 1635 / 2126	2.3 / 1.2 / 2.1 / 1.4	**24** W	0406 / 1059 / 1744 / 2325	2.4 / 0.8 / 2.4 / 1.3
10 W	0412 / 1102 / 1741 / 2316	2.3 / 1.1 / 2.2 / 1.4	**25** TH	0516 / 1202 / 1847	2.4 / 0.7 / 2.4
11 TH	0524 / 1159 / 1836	2.3 / 1.0 / 2.3	**26** F	0028 / 0618 / 1300 / 1936	1.3 / 2.4 / 0.7 / 2.4
12 F	0015 / 0609 / 1248 / 1920	1.3 / 2.4 / 0.8 / 2.4	**27** SA	0122 / 0712 / 1350 / 2015	1.2 / 2.5 / 0.7 / 2.4
13 SA	0103 / 0700 / 1335 / 2000	1.1 / 2.5 / 0.7 / 2.5	**28** SU	0207 / 0759 / 1431 / 2048	1.0 / 2.5 / 0.7 / 2.5
14 SU	0149 / 0752 / 1420 / 2037	1.0 / 2.6 / 0.5 / 2.5	**29** M	0246 / 0841 / 1508 / ○2120	0.9 / 2.6 / 0.7 / 2.5
15 M	0234 / 0835 / 1506 / ●2115	0.9 / 2.7 / 0.5 / 2.6	**30** TU	0322 / 0921 / 1541 / 2151	0.9 / 2.5 / 0.7 / 2.5
			31 W	0357 / 1000 / 1612 / 2220	0.8 / 2.5 / 0.8 / 2.5

NOVEMBER

Day	Time	m	Day	Time	m
1 TH	0430 / 1037 / 1640 / 2251	0.8 / 2.5 / 0.9 / 2.5	**16** F	0439 / 1041 / 1658 / 2259	0.5 / 2.7 / 0.6 / 2.7
2 F	0502 / 1113 / 1708 / 2323	0.8 / 2.4 / 0.9 / 2.5	**17** SA	0528 / 1134 / 1743 / 2346	0.5 / 2.6 / 0.8 / 2.7
3 SA	0536 / 1150 / 1738 / 2359	0.9 / 2.4 / 1.0 / 2.5	**18** SU	0619 / 1231 / 1829	0.5 / 2.5 / 0.9
4 SU	0613 / 1231 / 1814	0.9 / 2.3 / 1.1	**19** M	0034 / 0711 / 1333 / 1917	2.6 / 0.6 / 2.4 / 1.1
5 M	0039 / 0655 / 1316 / 1856	2.4 / 0.9 / 2.2 / 1.2	**20** TU	0127 / 0811 / 1450 / ◑2012	2.5 / 0.6 / 2.3 / 1.2
6 TU	0126 / 0744 / 1410 / 1945	2.4 / 1.0 / 2.2 / 1.3	**21** W	0224 / 0919 / 1609 / 2123	2.5 / 0.7 / 2.3 / 1.3
7 W	0218 / 0846 / 1535 / ◑2045	2.3 / 1.0 / 2.1 / 1.4	**22** TH	0331 / 1028 / 1715 / 2244	2.4 / 0.8 / 2.3 / 1.4
8 TH	0317 / 1005 / 1700 / 2204	2.3 / 1.0 / 2.2 / 1.4	**23** F	0443 / 1130 / 1815 / 2351	2.4 / 0.8 / 2.3 / 1.3
9 F	0429 / 1114 / 1755 / 2326	2.3 / 0.9 / 2.3 / 1.3	**24** SA	0547 / 1225 / 1907	2.4 / 0.8 / 2.4
10 SA	0536 / 1209 / 1843	2.4 / 0.8 / 2.4	**25** SU	0049 / 0645 / 1316 / 1949	1.2 / 2.4 / 0.8 / 2.4
11 SU	0025 / 0630 / 1300 / 1926	1.2 / 2.5 / 0.7 / 2.4	**26** M	0139 / 0737 / 1359 / 2024	1.1 / 2.4 / 0.9 / 2.4
12 M	0118 / 0720 / 1349 / 2007	1.0 / 2.6 / 0.6 / 2.5	**27** TU	0221 / 0823 / 1437 / 2056	1.0 / 2.4 / 0.9 / 2.5
13 TU	0208 / 0809 / 1437 / ●2048	0.9 / 2.7 / 0.5 / 2.6	**28** W	0300 / 0905 / 1510 / ○2125	0.9 / 2.4 / 0.9 / 2.5
14 W	0259 / 0858 / 1525 / 2130	0.7 / 2.7 / 0.5 / 2.6	**29** TH	0336 / 0944 / 1541 / 2154	0.8 / 2.4 / 0.9 / 2.5
15 TH	0349 / 0949 / 1612 / 2214	0.6 / 2.7 / 0.5 / 2.7	**30** F	0411 / 1021 / 1611 / 2226	0.8 / 2.4 / 0.9 / 2.6

DECEMBER

Day	Time	m	Day	Time	m
1 SA	0445 / 1056 / 1641 / 2300	0.8 / 2.4 / 0.9 / 2.6	**16** SU	0520 / 1126 / 1728 / 2330	0.4 / 2.6 / 0.8 / 2.7
2 SU	0521 / 1133 / 1715 / 2337	0.8 / 2.3 / 1.0 / 2.5	**17** M	0609 / 1218 / 1812	0.4 / 2.5 / 0.9
3 M	0559 / 1211 / 1753	0.8 / 2.3 / 1.0	**18** TU	0017 / 0657 / 1312 / 1855	2.7 / 0.4 / 2.4 / 1.0
4 TU	0017 / 0639 / 1253 / 1833	2.5 / 0.8 / 2.2 / 1.1	**19** W	0105 / 0747 / 1414 / 1941	2.6 / 0.5 / 2.3 / 1.1
5 W	0059 / 0723 / 1338 / 1919	2.5 / 0.9 / 2.2 / 1.2	**20** TH	0155 / 0843 / 1529 / ◑2032	2.5 / 0.7 / 2.2 / 1.2
6 TH	0145 / 0814 / 1432 / ◑2012	2.4 / 0.9 / 2.2 / 1.2	**21** F	0252 / 0946 / 1635 / 2143	2.4 / 0.8 / 2.2 / 1.3
7 F	0236 / 0916 / 1553 / 2114	2.4 / 0.9 / 2.2 / 1.3	**22** SA	0402 / 1051 / 1734 / 2307	2.3 / 0.9 / 2.2 / 1.3
8 SA	0336 / 1026 / 1712 / 2232	2.4 / 0.8 / 2.2 / 1.3	**23** SU	0513 / 1150 / 1830	2.3 / 1.0 / 2.2
9 SU	0451 / 1131 / 1806 / 2348	2.4 / 0.8 / 2.3 / 1.2	**24** M	0014 / 0616 / 1243 / 1919	1.2 / 2.2 / 1.0 / 2.3
10 M	0558 / 1228 / 1854	2.4 / 0.7 / 2.4	**25** TU	0110 / 0720 / 1329 / 1959	1.1 / 2.2 / 1.0 / 2.4
11 TU	0049 / 0654 / 1322 / 1940	1.0 / 2.5 / 0.7 / 2.5	**26** W	0158 / 0814 / 1409 / 2033	1.0 / 2.3 / 1.0 / 2.4
12 W	0147 / 0749 / 1414 / 2025	0.9 / 2.6 / 0.6 / 2.6	**27** TH	0240 / 0857 / 1445 / 2103	0.9 / 2.3 / 1.0 / 2.5
13 TH	0243 / 0845 / 1506 / ●2111	0.7 / 2.6 / 0.6 / 2.6	**28** F	0318 / 0934 / 1517 / ○2133	0.8 / 2.3 / 1.0 / 2.5
14 F	0338 / 0940 / 1556 / 2157	0.5 / 2.7 / 0.6 / 2.7	**29** SA	0354 / 1007 / 1549 / 2206	0.7 / 2.3 / 0.9 / 2.4
15 SA	0430 / 1034 / 1643 / 2244	0.4 / 2.6 / 0.7 / 2.7	**30** SU	0430 / 1041 / 1623 / 2242	0.7 / 2.3 / 0.9 / 2.6
			31 M	0507 / 1115 / 1659 / 2319	0.7 / 2.3 / 0.9 / 2.6

Chart Datum: 1·50 metres below Ordnance Datum (Newlyn)
HAT is 3·0 metres above Chart Datum

TIDES

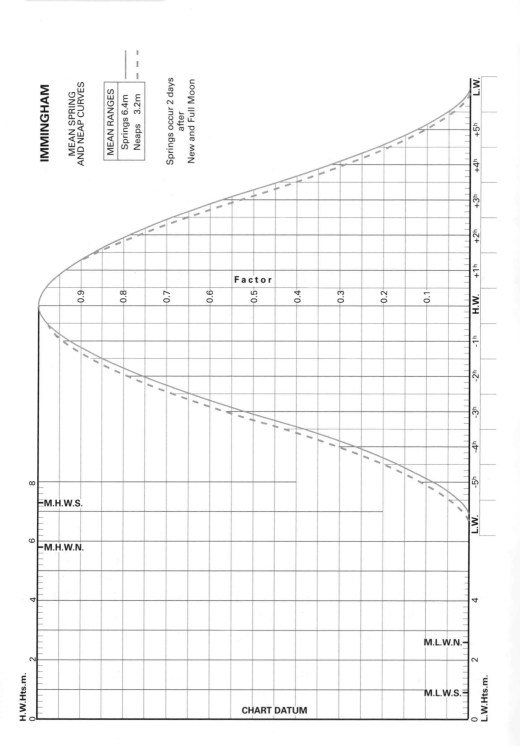

IMMINGHAM

MEAN SPRING
AND NEAP CURVES

MEAN RANGES
Springs 6.4m
Neaps 3.2m

Springs occur 2 days
after
New and Full Moon

Factor

0.9
0.8
0.7
0.6
0.5
0.4
0.3
0.2
0.1

L.W.
+5ʰ
+4ʰ
+3ʰ
+2ʰ
+1ʰ
H.W.
-1ʰ
-2ʰ
-3ʰ
-4ʰ
-5ʰ
L.W.

H.W.Hts.m.

M.H.W.S.
M.H.W.N.

M.L.W.N.
M.L.W.S.

CHART DATUM

L.W.Hts.m.

IMMINGHAM

LAT 53°38'N   LONG 0°11'W

TIMES AND HEIGHTS OF HIGH AND LOW WATERS

Dates in amber are **SPRINGS**
Dates in yellow are **NEAPS**

2012

JANUARY

Day	Time	m	Time	m	Time	m	Time	m
1 SU	0446	2.1	1107	5.9	1653	2.6	☽ 2310	6.1
16 M	0437	1.6	1041	6.3	1645	2.0	○ 2253	6.6
2 M	0534	2.4	1205	5.7	1749	2.8		
17 TU	0534	1.9	1145	6.1	1750	2.3		
3 TU	0015	5.8	0631	2.6	1855	2.9		
18 W	0004	6.3	0644	2.1	1302	6.0	1911	2.4
4 W	0125	5.7	0737	2.6	1415	5.7	2010	2.8
19 TH	0130	6.1	0803	2.2	1418	6.1	2038	2.3
5 TH	0232	5.8	0844	2.5	1512	6.0	2122	2.5
20 F	0254	6.2	0916	2.1	1526	6.3	2153	1.9
6 F	0330	6.0	0943	2.2	1602	6.3	2218	2.1
21 SA	0407	6.5	1018	1.8	1624	6.7	2255	1.5
7 SA	0419	6.3	1033	2.0	1644	6.5	2306	1.8
22 SU	0508	6.7	1112	1.6	1714	7.0	2348	1.1
8 SU	0504	6.5	1118	1.8	1724	6.8	2351	1.6
23 M	0559	6.9	1201	1.4	● 1759	7.2		
9 M	0547	6.7	1200	1.6	○ 1802	7.0		
24 TU	0036	0.9	0642	7.0	1245	1.2	1840	7.4
10 TU	0034	1.3	0628	6.8	1240	1.5	1839	7.1
25 W	0120	0.8	0721	7.0	1325	1.2	1919	7.4
11 W	0115	1.2	0709	6.8	1317	1.4	1915	7.2
26 TH	0158	0.9	0757	7.0	1401	1.4	1955	7.3
12 TH	0154	1.1	0747	7.0	1355	1.4	1951	7.3
27 F	0232	1.0	0829	6.8	1433	1.5	2029	7.2
13 F	0231	1.0	0826	6.9	1432	1.4	2028	7.3
28 SA	0302	1.3	0858	6.6	1502	1.7	2100	6.9
14 SA	0309	1.1	0905	6.8	1511	1.5	2109	7.1
29 SU	0330	1.6	0926	6.4	1532	1.9	2134	6.6
15 SU	0350	1.3	0949	6.6	1554	1.7	2156	6.9
30 M	0400	1.9	1000	6.1	1607	2.2	2213	6.2
31 TU	0439	2.3	1044	5.8	1653	2.5	☾ 2305	5.8

FEBRUARY

Day	Time	m	Time	m	Time	m	Time	m
1 W	0531	2.6	1147	5.5	1755	2.8		
16 TH	0617	2.4	1229	5.8	1851	2.5		
2 TH	0020	5.5	0637	2.8	1314	5.5	1909	2.9
17 F	0122	5.8	0745	2.5	1355	5.8	2031	2.4
3 F	0148	5.5	0752	2.8	1430	5.7	2031	2.7
18 SA	0256	5.9	0905	2.4	1510	6.1	2147	1.9
4 SA	0301	5.7	0905	2.5	1530	6.0	2148	2.3
19 SU	0410	6.3	1007	2.0	1611	6.5	2245	1.5
5 SU	0358	6.1	1006	2.2	1619	6.4	2244	1.9
20 M	0505	6.6	1058	1.7	1659	6.9	2334	1.1
6 M	0446	6.4	1056	1.9	1701	6.7	2332	1.4
21 TU	0549	6.9	1144	1.4	● 1742	7.1		
7 TU	0530	6.7	1141	1.6	○ 1741	7.0		
22 W	0018	0.9	0625	7.0	1226	1.2	1821	7.3
8 W	0017	1.1	0611	7.0	1223	1.3	1819	7.3
23 TH	0058	0.8	0658	7.0	1304	1.1	1857	7.3
9 TH	0059	0.9	0651	7.1	1303	1.2	1857	7.5
24 F	0133	0.9	0729	6.9	1338	1.2	1931	7.3
10 F	0139	0.7	0729	7.2	1342	1.0	1934	7.6
25 SA	0204	1.0	0756	6.9	1407	1.3	2001	7.2
11 SA	0216	0.7	0806	7.2	1419	1.0	2013	7.6
26 SU	0230	1.3	0820	6.7	1434	1.4	2030	6.9
12 SU	0253	0.8	0843	7.1	1457	1.2	2053	7.4
27 M	0255	1.5	0845	6.6	1501	1.7	2059	6.6
13 M	0331	1.1	0924	6.8	1537	1.4	2139	7.1
28 TU	0321	1.8	0915	6.3	1531	2.0	2133	6.3
14 TU	0412	1.5	1011	6.5	1623	1.8	☾ 2233	6.6
29 W	0352	2.1	0952	6.0	1610	2.3	2215	5.9
15 W	0504	2.0	1110	6.1	1724	2.2	2345	6.1

MARCH

Day	Time	m	Time	m	Time	m	Time	m
1 TH	0437	2.5	1041	5.6	1708	2.6	☽ 2318	5.5
16 F	0557	2.6	1206	5.8	1843	2.4		
2 F	0543	2.8	1202	5.4	1825	2.8		
17 SA	0122	5.7	0729	2.7	1335	5.8	2021	2.2
3 SA	0103	5.3	0704	2.9	1346	5.5	1947	2.7
18 SU	0252	5.9	0848	2.5	1451	6.1	2131	1.8
4 SU	0232	5.6	0826	2.7	1456	5.8	2112	2.3
19 M	0401	6.2	0948	2.1	1550	6.4	2224	1.4
5 M	0334	6.0	0936	2.3	1548	6.2	2216	1.8
20 TU	0449	6.6	1038	1.7	1637	6.8	2310	1.2
6 TU	0424	6.4	1030	1.9	1633	6.7	2306	1.3
21 W	0527	6.8	1121	1.4	1718	7.0	2351	1.0
7 W	0507	6.8	1117	1.5	1715	7.1	2352	0.9
22 TH	0559	6.9	1201	1.2	● 1757	7.1		
8 TH	0549	7.1	1201	1.2	○ 1755	7.4		
23 F	0029	1.0	0629	6.9	1239	1.2	1832	7.2
9 F	0036	0.6	0628	7.3	1244	0.9	1835	7.6
24 SA	0103	1.0	0658	6.9	1312	1.2	1905	7.1
10 SA	0117	0.5	0706	7.4	1325	0.8	1915	7.8
25 SU	0133	1.1	0723	6.9	1342	1.2	1935	7.0
11 SU	0156	0.5	0743	7.4	1404	0.7	1956	7.7
26 M	0159	1.3	0747	6.8	1409	1.4	2004	6.8
12 M	0234	0.7	0821	7.3	1443	0.9	2039	7.5
27 TU	0224	1.5	0813	6.7	1435	1.6	2033	6.6
13 TU	0311	1.0	0901	7.0	1524	1.2	2125	7.0
28 W	0249	1.7	0842	6.5	1505	1.8	2105	6.3
14 W	0352	1.5	0948	6.6	1610	1.6	2221	6.4
29 TH	0318	2.0	0916	6.2	1542	2.1	2144	5.9
15 TH	0443	2.1	1046	6.1	1712	2.1	☾ 2339	5.9
30 F	0359	2.4	0959	5.8	1636	2.4	☾ 2240	5.6
31 SA	0501	2.7	1104	5.5	1750	2.6		

APRIL

Day	Time	m	Time	m	Time	m	Time	m
1 SU	0016	5.4	0621	2.9	1250	5.5	1910	2.5
16 M	0227	5.9	0819	2.5	1421	6.1	2101	1.8
2 M	0157	5.6	0744	2.7	1413	5.8	2029	2.2
17 TU	0331	6.2	0919	2.2	1520	6.3	2153	1.4
3 TU	0303	6.0	0857	2.3	1510	6.2	2137	1.7
18 W	0418	6.4	1008	1.8	1608	6.6	2237	1.4
4 W	0355	6.4	0956	1.9	1559	6.7	2232	1.2
19 TH	0455	6.6	1052	1.6	1651	6.8	2318	1.3
5 TH	0440	6.8	1047	1.4	1644	7.1	2321	0.8
20 F	0528	6.7	1133	1.4	1729	6.9	2355	1.2
6 F	0522	7.1	1135	1.1	○ 1729	7.4		
21 SA	0559	6.8	1211	1.3	● 1805	6.9		
7 SA	0008	0.6	0602	7.3	1222	0.8	1813	7.7
22 SU	0030	1.2	0627	6.8	1246	1.3	1838	6.9
8 SU	0052	0.4	0642	7.5	1306	0.6	1857	7.7
23 M	0102	1.3	0654	6.9	1318	1.3	1911	6.8
9 M	0134	0.5	0721	7.5	1349	0.6	1942	7.7
24 TU	0131	1.4	0721	6.8	1348	1.4	1943	6.7
10 TU	0214	0.7	0801	7.4	1432	0.8	2028	7.4
25 W	0158	1.6	0750	6.7	1416	1.5	2015	6.5
11 W	0255	1.1	0843	7.1	1516	1.1	2118	6.9
26 TH	0225	1.7	0820	6.6	1448	1.7	2049	6.3
12 TH	0338	1.6	0930	6.7	1605	1.5	2217	6.4
27 F	0257	2.0	0853	6.3	1526	1.9	2129	6.0
13 F	0429	2.1	1028	6.2	1709	1.9	☾ 2339	5.9
28 SA	0338	2.2	0936	6.1	1618	2.1	2223	5.7
14 SA	0538	2.6	1145	5.9	1831	2.2		
29 SU	0433	2.5	1033	5.8	1724	2.2	☾ 2339	5.6
15 SU	0108	5.7	0702	2.7	1310	5.9	1955	2.1
30 M	0545	2.7	1152	5.7	1837	2.2		

Chart Datum: 3·90 metres below Ordnance Datum (Newlyn)
HAT is 8·0 metres above Chart Datum

TIDES

TIME ZONE (UT)	IMMINGHAM	Dates in amber are **SPRINGS**
For Summer Time add ONE hour in **non-shaded areas**	**LAT 53°38'N LONG 0°11'W**	Dates in yellow are **NEAPS**
	TIMES AND HEIGHTS OF HIGH AND LOW WATERS	**2012**

MAY

Time m	Time m	Time m	Time m
1 0113 5.7 / 0702 2.6 / TU 1320 5.9 / 1949 1.6	**16** 0244 6.0 / 0840 2.4 / W 1442 6.2 / 2112 1.9		
2 0224 6.0 / 0815 2.3 / W 1427 6.3 / 2056 1.6	**17** 0335 6.2 / 0934 2.1 / TH 1534 6.3 / 2159 1.7		
3 0320 6.4 / 0919 1.9 / TH 1523 6.4 / 2156 1.2	**18** 0417 6.4 / 1021 1.8 / F 1620 6.5 / 2241 1.6		
4 0409 6.8 / 1016 1.5 / F 1615 7.1 / 2250 0.9	**19** 0454 6.5 / 1104 1.6 / SA 1701 6.6 / 2321 1.5		
5 0455 7.1 / 1109 1.6 / SA 1705 7.3 / 2340 0.7	**20** 0527 6.7 / 1144 1.5 / SU 1739 6.6 / ● 2359 1.5		
6 0538 7.3 / 1200 0.8 / SU 1755 7.5 / ○	**21** 0559 6.8 / 1222 1.4 / M 1815 6.6		
7 0028 0.6 / 0621 7.4 / M 1249 0.6 / 1844 7.6	**22** 0034 1.5 / 0629 6.8 / TU 1258 1.4 / 1851 6.6		
8 0114 0.6 / 0703 7.5 / TU 1337 0.6 / 1933 7.5	**23** 0108 1.5 / 0702 6.8 / W 1332 1.4 / 1927 6.6		
9 0158 0.8 / 0746 7.4 / W 1423 0.7 / 2022 7.2	**24** 0138 1.6 / 0734 6.8 / TH 1405 1.5 / 2003 6.5		
10 0241 1.1 / 0830 7.2 / TH 1511 0.9 / 2114 6.8	**25** 0209 1.7 / 0806 6.7 / F 1439 1.6 / 2040 6.4		
11 0325 1.6 / 0918 6.8 / F 1601 1.3 / 2213 6.4	**26** 0243 1.8 / 0840 6.5 / SA 1518 1.7 / 2121 6.2		
12 0414 2.0 / 1013 6.4 / SA 1659 1.7 / ◑ 2325 6.0	**27** 0324 2.0 / 0921 6.4 / SU 1605 1.8 / 2209 6.0		
13 0513 2.4 / 1121 6.1 / SU 1805 1.9	**28** 0413 2.2 / 1013 6.2 / M 1702 1.9 / ◑ 2311 5.9		
14 0037 5.8 / 0622 2.6 / M 1235 6.0 / 1914 2.0	**29** 0514 2.4 / 1117 6.1 / TU 1806 1.9		
15 0144 5.8 / 0735 2.6 / TU 1342 6.0 / 2018 2.0	**30** 0026 5.9 / 0624 2.4 / W 1232 6.2 / 1912 1.8		
	31 0140 6.1 / 0736 2.2 / TH 1345 6.4 / 2019 1.6		

JUNE

Time m	Time m
1 0243 6.3 / 0845 2.0 / F 1451 6.6 / 2123 1.4	**16** 0336 6.1 / 0947 2.2 / SA 1548 6.1 / 2204 2.0
2 0339 6.6 / 0949 1.6 / SA 1551 6.9 / 2222 1.2	**17** 0420 6.3 / 1035 1.9 / SU 1634 6.3 / 2249 1.8
3 0430 6.9 / 1048 1.2 / SU 1649 7.1 / 2317 1.0	**18** 0458 6.5 / 1119 1.7 / M 1716 6.4 / 2332 1.7
4 0519 7.2 / 1144 0.9 / M 1744 7.3 / ○	**19** 0534 6.7 / 1201 1.5 / TU 1755 6.5 / ●
5 0009 0.9 / 0605 7.3 / TU 1237 0.7 / 1837 7.3	**20** 0011 1.6 / 0609 6.8 / W 1242 1.4 / 1834 6.6
6 0058 0.9 / 0650 7.4 / W 1328 0.6 / 1929 7.3	**21** 0049 1.6 / 0645 6.9 / TH 1321 1.3 / 1913 6.7
7 0144 1.0 / 0735 7.4 / TH 1416 0.6 / 2018 7.1	**22** 0124 1.6 / 0721 6.9 / F 1357 1.3 / 1952 6.7
8 0228 1.2 / 0819 7.3 / F 1503 0.8 / 2107 6.9	**23** 0157 1.6 / 0755 6.9 / SA 1433 1.3 / 2030 6.6
9 0311 1.5 / 0904 7.0 / SA 1549 1.1 / 2158 6.5	**24** 0232 1.7 / 0830 6.8 / SU 1510 1.4 / 2109 6.5
10 0354 1.8 / 0953 6.7 / SU 1636 1.4 / 2253 6.2	**25** 0311 1.8 / 0908 6.7 / M 1551 1.4 / 2152 6.4
11 0441 2.2 / 1048 6.4 / M 1727 1.8 / ◑ 2351 5.9	**26** 0355 1.9 / 0954 6.6 / TU 1639 1.6 / 2243 6.2
12 0534 2.5 / 1150 6.1 / TU 1821 2.1	**27** 0447 2.1 / 1049 6.5 / W 1735 1.7 / ◑ 2345 6.1
13 0050 5.8 / 0635 2.6 / W 1255 6.0 / 1920 2.2	**28** 0550 2.2 / 1156 6.3 / TH 1839 1.8
14 0150 5.8 / 0745 2.6 / TH 1357 5.9 / 2020 2.2	**29** 0057 6.1 / 0702 2.2 / F 1312 6.3 / 1949 1.8
15 0246 5.9 / 0851 2.4 / F 1456 6.0 / 2115 2.1	**30** 0209 6.2 / 0818 2.1 / SA 1429 6.4 / 2059 1.7

JULY

Time m	Time m
1 0314 6.4 / 0930 1.8 / SU 1539 6.6 / 2203 1.5	**16** 0346 6.1 / 1008 2.2 / M 1610 6.1 / 2222 2.1
2 0412 6.7 / 1035 1.4 / M 1643 6.8 / 2301 1.3	**17** 0431 6.4 / 1057 1.8 / TU 1655 6.3 / 2309 1.9
3 0504 7.0 / 1134 1.1 / TU 1741 7.0 / ○ 2355 1.2	**18** 0511 6.7 / 1143 1.5 / W 1737 6.5 / 2352 1.7
4 0553 7.2 / 1228 0.8 / W 1835 7.2	**19** 0550 6.9 / 1226 1.3 / TH 1818 6.7 / ●
5 0044 1.1 / 0638 7.4 / TH 1318 0.6 / 1923 7.2	**20** 0032 1.6 / 0627 7.0 / F 1307 1.2 / 1857 6.8
6 0130 1.0 / 0722 7.5 / F 1405 0.6 / 2008 7.1	**21** 0109 1.5 / 0704 7.1 / SA 1345 1.1 / 1936 6.9
7 0212 1.1 / 0804 7.4 / SA 1447 0.7 / 2050 6.9	**22** 0145 1.4 / 0740 7.2 / SU 1421 1.0 / 2013 6.9
8 0251 1.4 / 0845 7.2 / SU 1527 1.0 / 2130 6.7	**23** 0220 1.4 / 0815 7.2 / M 1457 1.1 / 2050 6.8
9 0328 1.6 / 0926 6.9 / M 1604 1.4 / 2211 6.4	**24** 0256 1.5 / 0852 7.1 / TU 1534 1.2 / 2129 6.7
10 0405 2.0 / 1010 6.6 / TU 1642 1.8 / 2256 6.1	**25** 0336 1.6 / 0935 6.9 / W 1615 1.4 / 2215 6.5
11 0445 2.3 / 1059 6.2 / W 1723 2.1 / ◑ 2347 5.8	**26** 0422 1.9 / 1026 6.7 / TH 1706 1.7 / ◑ 2311 6.2
12 0534 2.6 / 1159 5.9 / TH 1814 2.4	**27** 0520 2.1 / 1130 6.4 / F 1810 2.0
13 0048 5.7 / 0634 2.7 / F 1307 5.7 / 1915 2.5	**28** 0022 6.0 / 0635 2.3 / SA 1252 6.1 / 1926 2.2
14 0152 5.7 / 0749 2.7 / SA 1415 5.7 / 2025 2.5	**29** 0142 6.0 / 0801 2.3 / SU 1420 6.1 / 2043 2.1
15 0254 5.9 / 0909 2.5 / SU 1517 5.9 / 2129 2.3	**30** 0255 6.3 / 0922 2.0 / M 1538 6.4 / 2152 1.9
	31 0358 6.6 / 1029 1.5 / TU 1644 6.7 / 2250 1.6

AUGUST

Time m	Time m
1 0452 7.0 / 1126 1.1 / W 1740 7.0 / 2342 1.3	**16** 0446 6.7 / 1121 1.5 / TH 1717 6.6 / 2331 1.7
2 0540 7.2 / 1217 0.8 / TH 1827 7.1 / ○	**17** 0526 7.0 / 1204 1.2 / F 1757 6.9 / ●
3 0029 1.1 / 0623 7.4 / F 1304 0.6 / 1909 7.0	**18** 0011 1.5 / 0604 7.2 / SA 1246 1.0 / 1836 7.0
4 0112 1.1 / 0704 7.5 / SA 1346 0.6 / 1947 7.1	**19** 0050 1.3 / 0641 7.4 / SU 1325 0.8 / 1913 7.2
5 0151 1.1 / 0743 7.5 / SU 1424 0.8 / 2021 7.0	**20** 0127 1.2 / 0718 7.5 / M 1402 0.8 / 1950 7.2
6 0227 1.3 / 0820 7.3 / M 1457 1.1 / 2054 6.8	**21** 0203 1.2 / 0755 7.5 / TU 1437 0.9 / 2026 7.1
7 0258 1.5 / 0855 7.1 / TU 1527 1.4 / 2124 6.5	**22** 0240 1.2 / 0834 7.4 / W 1512 1.1 / 2104 6.9
8 0328 1.8 / 0930 6.7 / W 1556 1.8 / 2156 6.2	**23** 0318 1.4 / 0917 7.1 / TH 1551 1.4 / 2148 6.6
9 0402 2.1 / 1009 6.3 / TH 1631 2.2 / ◑ 2236 5.9	**24** 0402 1.7 / 1008 6.7 / F 1639 1.9 / ◑ 2242 6.3
10 0444 2.5 / 1100 5.9 / F 1717 2.5 / 2336 5.7	**25** 0459 2.1 / 1114 6.2 / SA 1745 2.3 / 2354 6.0
11 0541 2.7 / 1212 5.6 / SA 1819 2.8	**26** 0619 2.4 / 1246 5.9 / SU 1911 2.5
12 0057 5.6 / 0652 2.9 / SU 1335 5.5 / 1933 2.8	**27** 0122 5.9 / 0755 2.4 / M 1422 6.0 / 2034 2.4
13 0213 5.7 / 0820 2.7 / M 1448 5.7 / 2054 2.6	**28** 0241 6.2 / 0918 2.0 / TU 1541 6.3 / 2141 2.1
14 0315 6.0 / 0941 2.3 / TU 1547 6.0 / 2157 2.3	**29** 0345 6.6 / 1020 1.5 / W 1641 6.7 / 2236 1.7
15 0404 6.4 / 1035 1.9 / W 1634 6.3 / 2247 2.0	**30** 0436 7.0 / 1112 1.1 / TH 1729 7.0 / 2324 1.4
	31 0521 7.3 / 1158 0.8 / F 1809 7.1 / ○

Chart Datum: 3·90 metres below Ordnance Datum (Newlyn)
HAT is 8·0 metres above Chart Datum

IMMINGHAM

LAT 53°38'N   LONG 0°11'W

TIMES AND HEIGHTS OF HIGH AND LOW WATERS

Dates in amber are **SPRINGS**
Dates in yellow are **NEAPS**

2012

SEPTEMBER

Date	Time m	Time m	Time m	Time m
1 SA	0008 1.2	0601 7.4	1241 0.7	1844 7.2
2 SU	0049 1.1	0640 7.5	1319 0.8	1917 7.1
3 M	0126 1.1	0717 7.4	1353 0.9	1948 7.0
4 TU	0159 1.3	0751 7.3	1423 1.2	2015 6.9
5 W	0227 1.5	0823 7.1	1449 1.5	2040 6.7
6 TH	0254 1.7	0853 6.8	1514 1.8	2108 6.4
7 F	0324 2.0	0928 6.4	1544 2.2	2143 6.1
8 SA	0402 2.3	1011 5.9	1626 2.6	◖ 2232 5.8
9 SU	0456 2.7	1118 5.5	1727 2.9	2355 5.5
10 M	0610 2.9	1255 5.4	1846 3.0	
11 TU	0131 5.6	0734 2.8	1417 5.6	2012 2.8
12 W	0239 5.9	0904 2.4	1519 6.0	2126 2.5
13 TH	0332 6.3	1004 1.9	1608 6.4	2218 2.1
14 F	0416 6.7	1051 1.5	1651 6.8	2302 1.7
15 SA	0456 7.1	1135 1.1	1731 7.0	2344 1.4
16 SU	0536 7.4	1217 0.8	1810 7.2 ●	
17 M	0025 1.2	0615 7.6	1258 0.7	1847 7.4
18 TU	0105 1.0	0655 7.7	1336 0.7	1924 7.4
19 W	0144 1.0	0735 7.7	1414 0.8	2001 7.3
20 TH	0223 1.1	0817 7.5	1451 1.1	2040 7.1
21 F	0303 1.3	0902 7.1	1530 1.5	2124 6.8
22 SA	0349 1.7	0956 6.6	1619 2.0	◗ 2219 6.4
23 SU	0448 2.1	1107 6.1	1726 2.5	2333 6.0
24 M	0611 2.4	1246 5.9	1855 2.7	
25 TU	0103 5.9	0747 2.3	1417 6.0	2018 2.6
26 W	0221 6.2	0903 1.9	1530 6.3	2123 2.2
27 TH	0324 6.6	1000 1.5	1624 6.7	2215 1.8
28 F	0414 6.9	1048 1.2	1706 6.9	2301 1.5
29 SA	0457 7.2	1131 1.0	1741 7.1	2343 1.3
30 SU	0537 7.3	1211 1.0	1814 7.1 ○	

OCTOBER

Date	Time m	Time m	Time m	Time m
1 M	0022 1.2	0614 7.3	1248 1.0	1845 7.1
2 TU	0059 1.2	0650 7.3	1320 1.2	1914 7.1
3 W	0130 1.3	0723 7.2	1348 1.4	1940 7.0
4 TH	0158 1.5	0754 7.0	1414 1.6	2005 6.8
5 F	0225 1.7	0824 6.7	1439 1.8	2033 6.6
6 SA	0255 1.9	0857 6.4	1507 2.1	2105 6.3
7 SU	0331 2.2	0937 6.0	1545 2.5	2147 6.0
8 M	0421 2.5	1034 5.6	1641 2.9	◖ 2251 5.7
9 TU	0532 2.8	1209 5.4	1758 3.1	
10 W	0036 5.6	0651 2.7	1338 5.6	1922 3.0
11 TH	0155 5.8	0812 2.4	1443 6.0	2038 2.6
12 F	0252 6.3	0919 1.9	1535 6.4	2137 2.2
13 SA	0340 6.7	1012 1.5	1620 6.8	2227 1.7
14 SU	0424 7.1	1059 1.1	1701 7.1	2313 1.4
15 M	0506 7.4	1145 0.9	1741 7.3	● 2358 1.1
16 TU	0550 7.6	1228 0.7	1821 7.5	
17 W	0042 0.9	0633 7.7	1311 0.7	1900 7.5
18 TH	0126 0.8	0718 7.7	1351 0.8	1939 7.5
19 F	0209 0.9	0803 7.5	1432 1.1	2021 7.3
20 SA	0253 1.2	0852 7.1	1514 1.6	2107 6.9
21 SU	0342 1.5	0949 6.6	1604 2.1	2201 6.5
22 M	0442 1.9	1103 6.1	1708 2.6	◗ 2313 6.2
23 TU	0600 2.2	1233 5.9	1829 2.8	
24 W	0037 6.1	0723 2.2	1352 6.0	1948 2.7
25 TH	0151 6.2	0834 1.9	1500 6.3	2053 2.4
26 F	0253 6.5	0930 1.7	1553 6.5	2146 2.0
27 SA	0345 6.8	1017 1.4	1634 6.8	2233 1.7
28 SU	0430 7.0	1059 1.3	1710 6.9	2315 1.5
29 M	0510 7.1	1138 1.3	1743 7.0	○ 2355 1.4
30 TU	0548 7.1	1214 1.3	1814 7.0	
31 W	0031 1.3	0624 7.1	1247 1.4	1843 7.0

NOVEMBER

Date	Time m	Time m	Time m	Time m
1 TH	0105 1.4	0658 7.0	1317 1.5	1911 7.0
2 F	0135 1.5	0730 6.9	1344 1.6	1939 6.9
3 SA	0203 1.6	0803 6.7	1411 1.8	2008 6.7
4 SU	0234 1.8	0837 6.4	1441 2.1	2040 6.5
5 M	0309 2.0	0916 6.1	1518 2.3	2118 6.2
6 TU	0355 2.3	1006 5.8	1607 2.6	2210 5.9
7 W	0457 2.5	1118 5.7	1713 2.9	◖ 2324 5.8
8 TH	0610 2.5	1247 5.7	1830 2.9	
9 F	0054 5.9	0721 2.3	1357 6.0	1945 2.6
10 SA	0203 6.2	0829 1.9	1455 6.3	2051 2.3
11 SU	0300 6.6	0929 1.6	1545 6.7	2149 1.8
12 M	0351 7.0	1023 1.2	1631 7.0	2243 1.4
13 TU	0440 7.3	1113 1.0	1715 7.3	● 2333 1.1
14 W	0528 7.5	1201 0.9	1758 7.5	2355 1.4
15 TH	0023 0.9	0617 7.6	1248 0.8	1840 7.6
16 F	0111 0.8	0706 7.6	1333 0.9	1923 7.6
17 SA	0158 0.8	0755 7.4	1417 1.2	2007 7.4
18 SU	0246 1.0	0846 7.1	1501 1.5	2053 7.1
19 M	0335 1.3	0942 6.7	1548 2.0	2145 6.8
20 TU	0431 1.6	1049 6.3	1644 2.4	◗ 2248 6.4
21 W	0535 1.9	1202 6.1	1750 2.7	
22 TH	0001 6.2	0644 2.1	1310 6.0	1904 2.7
23 F	0112 6.2	0752 2.1	1413 6.1	2014 2.6
24 SA	0216 6.3	0850 2.0	1509 6.2	2113 2.3
25 SU	0312 6.4	0940 1.9	1556 6.5	2203 2.0
26 M	0401 6.6	1024 1.7	1636 6.7	2247 1.8
27 TU	0445 6.7	1105 1.6	1713 6.8	2329 1.6
28 W	0525 6.8	1142 1.6	1746 6.9 ○	
29 TH	0007 1.6	0601 6.8	1219 1.6	1818 7.0
30 F	0044 1.6	0637 6.8	1252 1.6	1849 7.0

DECEMBER

Date	Time m	Time m	Time m	Time m
1 SA	0117 1.5	0712 6.8	1322 1.7	1921 7.0
2 SU	0149 1.6	0747 6.7	1352 1.8	1952 6.8
3 M	0221 1.7	0823 6.5	1423 1.9	2023 6.7
4 TU	0255 1.8	0900 6.3	1459 2.1	2059 6.5
5 W	0336 1.9	0943 6.1	1542 2.3	2143 6.3
6 TH	0427 2.1	1036 6.0	1636 2.5	◖ 2239 6.2
7 F	0528 2.2	1145 5.9	1742 2.6	2349 6.1
8 SA	0635 2.1	1303 6.0	1856 2.6	
9 SU	0107 6.2	0744 2.0	1411 6.2	2008 2.3
10 M	0219 6.5	0850 1.7	1510 6.5	2116 2.0
11 TU	0322 6.8	0951 1.5	1603 6.8	2218 1.6
12 W	0420 7.1	1047 1.2	1653 7.1	2315 1.2
13 TH	0515 7.3	1140 1.1	1740 7.4 ●	
14 F	0009 0.9	0608 7.4	1231 1.0	1826 7.6
15 SA	0101 0.7	0700 7.5	1318 1.0	1911 7.6
16 SU	0150 0.6	0750 7.4	1403 1.1	1955 7.6
17 M	0237 0.8	0838 7.2	1447 1.3	2040 7.4
18 TU	0323 1.0	0928 6.8	1530 1.7	2126 7.1
19 W	0410 1.4	1021 6.5	1614 2.1	2218 6.7
20 TH	0458 1.7	1118 6.2	1703 2.4	◗ 2318 6.4
21 F	0552 2.1	1218 5.9	1802 2.7	
22 SA	0024 6.1	0653 2.3	1319 5.8	1913 2.8
23 SU	0131 6.0	0758 2.4	1419 5.9	2029 2.6
24 M	0235 6.0	0858 2.3	1515 6.1	2131 2.4
25 TU	0332 6.2	0949 2.2	1603 6.4	2221 2.1
26 W	0421 6.3	1034 2.0	1645 6.6	2306 1.8
27 TH	0504 6.5	1116 1.8	1723 6.8	2347 1.6
28 F	0543 6.6	1155 1.7	1758 6.9 ○	
29 SA	0027 1.5	0619 6.7	1233 1.6	1832 7.0
30 SU	0104 1.4	0656 6.7	1306 1.6	1906 7.0
31 M	0139 1.4	0732 6.7	1337 1.6	1938 7.0

Chart Datum: 3·90 metres below Ordnance Datum (Newlyn)
HAT is 8·0 metres above Chart Datum

TIDES

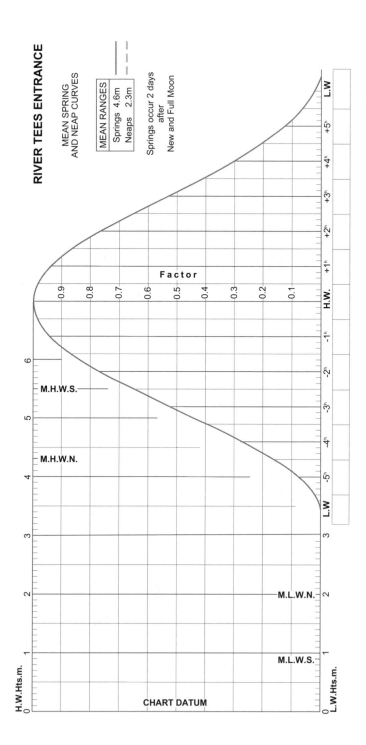

RIVER TEES ENTRANCE

MEAN SPRING
AND NEAP CURVES

MEAN RANGES
Springs 4.6m
Neaps 2.3m

Springs occur 2 days
after
New and Full Moon

Factor

0.9 0.8 0.7 0.6 0.5 0.4 0.3 0.2 0.1

H.W.

L.W.

M.H.W.S.

M.H.W.N.

M.L.W.N.

M.L.W.S.

CHART DATUM

H.W.Hts.m.

L.W.Hts.m.

RIVER TEES

LAT 54°38'N   LONG 0°90'W

Dates in amber are **SPRINGS**
Dates in yellow are **NEAPS**

2012

TIMES AND HEIGHTS OF HIGH AND LOW WATERS

JANUARY

Day	Time m	Time m	Day	Time m	Time m
1	0239 1.7	0858 4.4	**16**	0221 1.2	0834 4.7
	SU 1453 2.1	☽ 2103 4.6		M 1432 1.7	○ 2046 4.9
2	0332 1.9	0953 4.2	**17**	0320 1.4	0935 4.6
	M 1557 2.3	2205 4.4		TU 1540 1.9	2156 4.7
3	0437 2.1	1056 4.2	**18**	0430 1.6	1043 4.5
	TU 1710 2.3	2312 4.3		W 1701 1.9	2313 4.6
4	0548 2.1	1200 4.3	**19**	0548 1.7	1155 4.5
	W 1820 2.2			TH 1826 1.8	
5	0019 4.3	0650 2.0	**20**	0033 4.7	0703 1.6
	TH 1259 4.5	1918 2.0		F 1307 4.7	1941 1.5
6	0119 4.4	0741 1.8	**21**	0145 4.9	0806 1.4
	F 1348 4.7	2006 1.7		SA 1407 5.0	2040 1.1
7	0209 4.6	0824 1.7	**22**	0243 5.1	0858 1.3
	SA 1430 4.9	2050 1.4		SU 1458 5.2	2131 0.9
8	0253 4.8	0904 1.5	**23**	0332 5.2	0944 1.1
	SU 1508 5.1	2130 1.2		M 1542 5.4	● 2215 0.7
9	0332 5.0	0941 1.3	**24**	0415 5.3	1025 1.1
	M 1544 5.2	○ 2209 1.0		TU 1621 5.5	2255 0.6
10	0410 5.1	1018 1.2	**25**	0455 5.3	1103 1.1
	TU 1619 5.3	2247 0.8		W 1658 5.5	2332 0.6
11	0448 5.2	1056 1.2	**26**	0533 5.2	1138 1.1
	W 1656 5.4	2326 0.7		TH 1734 5.5	
12	0527 5.2	1133 1.2	**27**	0006 0.8	0609 5.1
	TH 1733 5.5			F 1212 1.2	1810 5.4
13	0005 0.7	0608 5.3	**28**	0039 1.0	0645 4.9
	F 1212 1.2	1812 5.4		SA 1244 1.4	1848 5.2
14	0047 0.8	0652 5.1	**29**	0111 1.3	0722 4.7
	SA 1253 1.3	1856 5.3		SU 1317 1.6	1928 4.9
15	0131 0.9	0740 4.9	**30**	0145 1.5	0803 4.5
	SU 1338 1.5	1947 5.1		M 1355 1.9	2014 4.6
			31	0224 1.8	0851 4.3
				TU 1445 2.1	☽ 2108 4.3

FEBRUARY

Day	Time m	Time m	Day	Time m	Time m
1	0317 2.1	0949 4.1	**16**	0404 1.8	1017 4.3
	W 1558 2.3	2216 4.1		TH 1644 1.9	2302 4.4
2	0436 2.3	1059 4.1	**17**	0534 2.0	1139 4.4
	TH 1727 2.3	2332 4.1		F 1825 1.8	
3	0605 2.2	1212 4.2	**18**	0034 4.5	0657 1.8
	F 1844 2.1			SA 1300 4.6	1940 1.4
4	0045 4.2	0711 2.0	**19**	0145 4.7	0759 1.6
	SA 1315 4.4	1941 1.8		SU 1400 4.9	2035 1.1
5	0144 4.5	0802 1.8	**20**	0237 4.9	0847 1.4
	SU 1404 4.8	2029 1.4		M 1447 5.2	2120 0.8
6	0231 4.8	0845 1.5	**21**	0320 5.1	0928 1.2
	M 1445 5.0	2111 1.1		TU 1527 5.3	● 2159 0.7
7	0312 5.0	0924 1.3	**22**	0358 5.2	1005 1.0
	TU 1523 5.3	○ 2151 0.8		W 1603 5.5	2233 0.6
8	0350 5.2	1002 1.1	**23**	0433 5.2	1039 1.0
	W 1559 5.5	2230 0.6		TH 1636 5.5	2305 0.7
9	0428 5.4	1040 0.9	**24**	0505 5.2	1111 1.0
	TH 1636 5.6	2308 0.4		F 1708 5.4	2335 0.8
10	0506 5.4	1117 0.8	**25**	0536 5.1	1140 1.1
	F 1713 5.7	2346 0.4		SA 1741 5.3	
11	0546 5.4	1154 0.9	**26**	0003 1.0	0607 5.0
	SA 1753 5.7			SU 1211 1.2	1815 5.2
12	0026 0.5	0628 5.3	**27**	0031 1.2	0640 4.8
	SU 1234 1.0	1836 5.5		M 1242 1.4	1852 4.9
13	0108 0.7	0713 5.1	**28**	0102 1.4	0717 4.6
	M 1317 1.2	1926 5.2		TU 1317 1.6	1935 4.6
14	0155 1.1	0804 4.8	**29**	0138 1.7	0801 4.4
	TU 1407 1.5	☽ 2025 4.9		W 1400 1.9	2025 4.3
15	0251 1.6	0905 4.5			
	W 1514 1.8	2137 4.6			

MARCH

Day	Time m	Time m	Day	Time m	Time m
1	0224 2.1	0856 4.2	**16**	0346 2.0	0955 4.3
	TH 1459 2.2	☽ 2127 4.1		F 1636 1.8	2256 4.3
2	0332 2.3	1004 4.0	**17**	0521 2.1	1123 4.3
	F 1631 2.3	2245 4.0		SA 1818 1.6	
3	0514 2.4	1122 4.1	**18**	0027 4.4	0643 1.9
	SA 1804 2.1			SU 1244 4.5	1926 1.3
4	0006 4.1	0637 2.1	**19**	0132 4.6	0741 1.7
	SU 1234 4.3	1910 1.7		M 1342 4.8	2017 1.1
5	0112 4.4	0733 1.8	**20**	0219 4.8	0828 1.4
	M 1329 4.6	2000 1.3		TU 1427 5.1	2059 0.9
6	0202 4.7	0818 1.5	**21**	0259 5.0	0905 1.2
	TU 1414 5.0	2045 0.9		W 1505 5.2	2134 0.8
7	0244 5.0	0859 1.2	**22**	0334 5.1	0940 1.1
	W 1454 5.3	2126 0.6		TH 1539 5.3	2205 0.8
8	0324 5.3	0939 0.9	**23**	0406 5.2	1012 1.0
	TH 1533 5.6	○ 2206 0.3		F 1611 5.3	2234 0.8
9	0403 5.5	1018 0.7	**24**	0435 5.2	1042 0.9
	SA 1612 5.8	2245 0.2		SA 1641 5.3	2302 0.9
10	0442 5.6	1057 0.6	**25**	0503 5.1	1112 1.0
	SA 1652 5.8	2325 0.2		SU 1713 5.2	2329 1.0
11	0523 5.5	1135 0.6	**26**	0532 5.0	1142 1.1
	SU 1735 5.8			M 1746 5.1	2357 1.2
12	0005 0.4	0604 5.4	**27**	0605 4.9	1214 1.2
	M 1216 0.7	1821 5.5		TU 1823 4.9	
13	0047 0.7	0650 5.2	**28**	0029 1.4	0641 4.7
	TU 1301 1.0	1913 5.2		W 1250 1.5	1904 4.6
14	0134 1.1	0740 4.9	**29**	0106 1.7	0724 4.5
	W 1353 1.3	2013 4.8		TH 1332 1.7	1953 4.4
15	0230 1.6	0841 4.5	**30**	0150 2.0	0816 4.3
	TH 1502 1.6	☽ 2127 4.4		F 1426 1.9	☽ 2052 4.1
			31	0250 2.2	0920 4.1
				SA 1544 2.1	2204 4.0

APRIL

Day	Time m	Time m	Day	Time m	Time m
1	0424 2.3	1034 4.1	**16**	0002 4.3	0612 2.0
	SU 1715 1.9	2322 4.1		M 1214 4.5	1857 1.4
2	0551 2.2	1146 4.3	**17**	0104 4.5	0711 1.8
	M 1827 1.6			TU 1312 4.7	1947 1.2
3	0031 4.4	0653 1.8	**18**	0151 4.7	0757 1.5
	TU 1247 4.6	1923 1.2		W 1358 4.9	2027 1.1
4	0125 4.7	0743 1.5	**19**	0231 4.9	0836 1.3
	W 1337 5.0	2011 0.8		TH 1437 5.0	2102 1.0
5	0211 5.1	0828 1.1	**20**	0305 5.0	0911 1.2
	TH 1422 5.3	2055 0.5		F 1512 5.1	2133 1.0
6	0253 5.3	0912 0.8	**21**	0336 5.1	0944 1.0
	F 1505 5.6	○ 2139 0.3		SA 1545 5.1	● 2203 1.0
7	0335 5.5	0954 0.6	**22**	0405 5.1	1016 1.0
	SA 1549 5.8	2221 0.2		SU 1617 5.1	2231 1.0
8	0417 5.6	1036 0.4	**23**	0433 5.1	1048 1.0
	SU 1634 5.8	2303 0.2		M 1649 5.1	2300 1.1
9	0500 5.6	1119 0.4	**24**	0503 5.0	1119 1.1
	M 1721 5.7	2346 0.5		TU 1723 5.0	2330 1.2
10	0544 5.5	1203 0.6	**25**	0537 5.0	1153 1.2
	TU 1811 5.5			W 1801 4.8	
11	0030 0.8	0630 5.2	**26**	0004 1.4	0614 4.8
	W 1251 0.8	1905 5.1		TH 1231 1.3	1842 4.7
12	0119 1.2	0722 4.9	**27**	0042 1.6	0656 4.6
	TH 1347 1.1	2007 4.7		F 1313 1.5	1930 4.5
13	0216 1.7	0822 4.6	**28**	0126 1.9	0746 4.4
	F 1456 1.4	☽ 2118 4.4		SA 1406 1.7	2027 4.3
14	0330 2.0	0935 4.4	**29**	0222 2.1	0845 4.2
	SA 1621 1.6	2240 4.3		SU 1513 1.8	☽ 2132 4.2
15	0455 2.0	1056 4.4	**30**	0340 2.2	0952 4.3
	SU 1750 1.5			M 1630 1.7	2241 4.3

TIDES

TIME ZONE (UT)
For Summer Time add ONE hour in **non-shaded areas**

RIVER TEES

LAT 54°38′N   LONG 0°90′W

TIMES AND HEIGHTS OF HIGH AND LOW WATERS

Dates in amber are **SPRINGS**
Dates in yellow are **NEAPS**

2012

MAY

Time	m		Time	m
1 TU 0503	2.1	**16** W 0022	4.4
1101	4.4	0629	1.9
1740	1.5	1231	4.6
2347	4.5	1905	1.4
2 W 0609	1.8	**17** TH 0114	4.6
1204	4.7	0720	1.7
1841	1.2	1322	4.7
		1950	1.4
3 TH 0045	4.7	**18** F 0157	4.7
0705	1.5	0804	1.5
1300	5.0	1406	4.8
1934	0.9	2028	1.3
4 F 0137	5.0	**19** SA 0234	4.8
0756	1.1	0842	1.3
1351	5.3	1445	4.9
2024	0.6	2102	1.2
5 SA 0224	5.3	**20** SU 0308	5.0
0845	0.8	0919	1.2
1441	5.5	1522	4.9
2113	0.4	● 2135	1.2
6 SU 0310	5.5	**21** M 0339	5.0
0932	0.6	0954	1.1
1530	5.7	1557	5.0
○ 2159	0.4	2206	1.2
7 M 0355	5.6	**22** TU 0410	5.1
1019	0.4	1028	1.1
1620	5.7	1631	5.0
2245	0.4	2237	1.2
8 TU 0441	5.6	**23** W 0442	5.1
1107	0.4	1102	1.1
1711	5.6	1706	4.9
2331	0.6	2311	1.3
9 W 0527	5.5	**24** TH 0516	5.0
1155	0.5	1138	1.1
1803	5.4	1744	4.9
		2347	1.4
10 TH 0018	0.9	**25** F 0554	4.9
0615	5.3	1217	1.2
1246	0.7	1826	4.8
1858	5.1		
11 F 0107	1.3	**26** SA 0026	1.5
0706	5.1	0635	4.8
1341	1.0	1300	1.3
1956	4.8	1912	4.6
12 SA 0202	1.6	**27** SU 0109	1.7
0803	4.8	0721	4.7
1442	1.2	1349	1.4
◐ 2059	4.5	2004	4.5
13 SU 0305	1.9	**28** M 0200	1.9
0908	4.6	0814	4.6
1551	1.4	1447	1.6
2208	4.3	◑ 2102	4.4
14 M 0416	2.1	**29** TU 0304	2.0
1019	4.5	0915	4.6
1705	1.5	1551	1.5
2319	4.3	2205	4.4
15 TU 0528	2.0	**30** W 0417	1.9
1129	4.5	1021	4.6
1812	1.5	1658	1.4
		2309	4.5
		31 TH 0526	1.8
		1127	4.8
		1801	1.2

JUNE

Time	m		Time	m
1 F 0010	4.7	**16** SA 0119	4.5
0628	1.5	0731	1.7
1229	5.0	1335	4.6
1901	1.4	1954	1.6
2 SA 0107	5.0	**17** SU 0203	4.7
0727	1.2	0816	1.5
1328	5.2	1420	4.7
1958	0.8	2035	1.5
3 SU 0200	5.2	**18** M 0242	4.8
0823	0.9	0856	1.3
1424	5.4	1501	4.8
2052	0.7	2112	1.4
4 M 0250	5.4	**19** TU 0317	5.0
0917	0.7	0935	1.2
1518	5.5	1539	4.9
○ 2143	0.6	● 2147	1.3
5 TU 0339	5.5	**20** W 0351	5.1
1009	0.5	1011	1.1
1611	5.5	1615	5.0
2232	0.7	2221	1.3
6 W 0427	5.5	**21** TH 0425	5.1
1059	0.4	1048	1.0
1703	5.5	1652	5.1
2320	0.8	2257	1.3
7 TH 0514	5.5	**22** F 0459	5.1
1148	0.5	1125	1.0
1754	5.4	1729	5.0
		2334	1.3
8 F 0006	1.0	**23** SA 0536	5.1
0600	5.4	1204	1.0
1237	0.6	1809	5.0
1844	5.2		
9 SA 0053	1.2	**24** SU 0012	1.4
0649	5.2	0614	5.1
1324	0.8	1246	1.0
1936	4.9	1852	4.9
10 SU 0141	1.5	**25** M 0053	1.5
0739	5.0	0657	5.0
1417	1.1	1331	1.1
2029	4.7	1940	4.8
11 M 0232	1.8	**26** TU 0139	1.6
0834	4.8	0746	4.9
1512	1.4	1421	1.2
◑ 2126	4.4	2033	4.7
12 TU 0331	2.0	**27** W 0232	1.7
0934	4.6	0842	4.8
1612	1.6	1518	1.3
2226	4.3	◐ 2132	4.6
13 W 0435	2.1	**28** TH 0337	1.8
1038	4.4	0947	4.7
1716	1.7	1622	1.4
2328	4.3	2235	4.6
14 TH 0541	2.0	**29** F 0449	1.8
1143	4.4	1057	4.8
1817	1.8	1730	1.4
		2340	4.6
15 F 0027	4.4	**30** SA 0600	1.6
0640	1.9	1207	4.8
1243	4.5	1837	1.3
1909	1.7		

JULY

Time	m		Time	m
1 SU 0043	4.8	**16** M 0133	4.6
0708	1.4	0751	1.7
1314	5.0	1357	4.6
1941	1.2	2010	1.7
2 M 0143	5.0	**17** TU 0218	4.8
0811	1.1	0836	1.4
1416	5.2	1442	4.8
2040	1.0	2052	1.5
3 TU 0238	5.3	**18** W 0257	5.0
0909	0.8	0916	1.2
1512	5.4	1521	4.9
○ 2133	0.9	2130	1.4
4 W 0328	5.4	**19** TH 0332	5.1
1002	0.6	0955	1.0
1604	5.5	1558	5.1
2221	0.8	● 2206	1.2
5 TH 0415	5.6	**20** F 0407	5.2
1050	0.5	1032	0.9
1653	5.5	1634	5.2
2307	0.9	2242	1.2
6 F 0500	5.6	**21** SA 0441	5.3
1136	0.4	1109	0.8
1739	5.4	1710	5.2
2349	1.0	2319	1.1
7 SA 0543	5.5	**22** SU 0516	5.4
1219	0.6	1147	0.7
1823	5.2	1749	5.2
		2355	1.1
8 SU 0030	1.1	**23** M 0553	5.4
0625	5.4	1226	0.8
1301	0.8	1830	5.1
1907	5.0		
9 M 0111	1.3	**24** TU 0034	1.2
0709	5.2	0633	5.3
1343	1.1	1308	0.9
1952	4.8	1914	5.0
10 TU 0153	1.6	**25** W 0116	1.4
0756	4.9	0720	5.2
1427	1.4	1355	1.1
2039	4.5	2004	4.8
11 W 0240	1.9	**26** TH 0204	1.5
0847	4.7	0815	5.0
1516	1.7	1448	1.3
◑ 2131	4.3	◐ 2100	4.7
12 TH 0337	2.1	**27** F 0305	1.7
0941	4.4	0921	4.8
1615	2.0	1553	1.6
2230	4.2	2205	4.5
13 F 0446	2.2	**28** SA 0421	1.8
1054	4.3	1037	4.6
1723	2.1	1707	1.7
2335	4.2	2316	4.5
14 SA 0558	2.1	**29** SU 0544	1.7
1202	4.3	1156	4.7
1829	2.0	1824	1.6
15 SU 0038	4.4	**30** M 0029	4.7
0659	1.9	0703	1.5
1305	4.4	1312	4.9
1924	1.9	1933	1.5
		31 TU 0135	4.9
		0809	1.1
		1414	5.1
		2032	1.2

AUGUST

Time	m		Time	m
1 W 0230	5.2	**16** TH 0231	5.0
0904	0.8	0854	1.2
1507	5.3	1458	5.0
2122	1.1	2108	1.4
2 TH 0318	5.4	**17** F 0308	5.2
0953	0.6	0933	0.9
1553	5.4	1534	5.2
○ 2207	0.9	● 2146	1.2
3 F 0401	5.6	**18** SA 0343	5.4
1036	0.5	1010	0.7
1636	5.5	1610	5.4
2248	0.9	2222	1.0
4 SA 0441	5.6	**19** SU 0418	5.5
1116	0.5	1047	0.6
1716	5.4	1646	5.4
2326	0.9	2258	0.9
5 SU 0519	5.6	**20** M 0453	5.6
1153	0.6	1124	0.5
1755	5.3	1724	5.4
		2335	0.9
6 M 0002	1.1	**21** TU 0530	5.6
0556	5.5	1203	0.6
1229	0.8	1805	5.4
1832	5.1		
7 TU 0037	1.2	**22** W 0013	1.0
0635	5.3	0611	5.5
1303	1.1	1245	0.8
1910	4.9	1848	5.2
8 W 0111	1.5	**23** TH 0054	1.1
0716	5.0	0659	5.3
1338	1.5	1330	1.1
1950	4.7	1936	5.0
9 TH 0150	1.7	**24** F 0142	1.4
0802	4.7	0755	5.0
1417	1.8	1423	1.4
◑ 2036	4.4	◑ 2033	4.7
10 F 0238	2.0	**25** SA 0243	1.7
0857	4.4	0904	4.7
1509	2.1	1530	1.8
2132	4.2	2141	4.5
11 SA 0347	2.2	**26** SU 0407	1.8
1004	4.2	1027	4.5
1623	2.3	1654	2.0
2241	4.1	2300	4.5
12 SU 0513	2.2	**27** M 0542	1.8
1121	4.1	1156	4.5
1748	2.3	1819	1.9
2355	4.2		
13 M 0628	2.1	**28** TU 0021	4.6
1234	4.3	0703	1.5
1855	2.1	1313	4.8
		1927	1.6
14 TU 0100	4.4	**29** W 0128	4.9
0725	1.8	0804	1.1
1332	4.5	1409	5.1
1946	1.8	2020	1.4
15 W 0150	4.7	**30** TH 0220	5.2
0813	1.5	0853	0.6
1418	4.8	1455	5.3
2029	1.6	2106	1.2
		31 F 0304	5.5
		0936	0.7
		1536	5.4
		○ 2146	1.0

TIME ZONE (UT)
For Summer Time add ONE hour in **non-shaded areas**

RIVER TEES
LAT 54°38'N   LONG 0°90'W
TIMES AND HEIGHTS OF HIGH AND LOW WATERS

Dates in amber are **SPRINGS**
Dates in yellow are **NEAPS**

2012

SEPTEMBER

Time	m		Time	m
1 0342	5.6	**16** 0314	5.5
1014	0.6	0943	0.6
SA 1614	5.4	SU 1542	5.5
2223	0.9	● 2157	0.9
2 0418	5.6	**17** 0351	5.7
1049	0.6	1022	0.4
SU 1649	5.4	M 1620	5.6
2257	1.0	2235	0.7
3 0452	5.6	**18** 0429	5.8
1121	0.8	1100	0.4
M 1722	5.3	TU 1659	5.6
2330	1.0	2314	0.7
4 0527	5.5	**19** 0510	5.8
1152	1.0	1140	0.5
TU 1755	5.2	W 1740	5.5
		2354	0.8
5 0002	1.2	**20** 0555	5.6
0602	5.3	1222	0.8
W 1222	1.2	TH 1824	5.3
1828	5.0		
6 0034	1.4	**21** 0037	1.0
0640	5.0	0645	5.3
TH 1252	1.5	F 1308	1.2
1905	4.8	1913	5.1
7 0109	1.6	**22** 0128	1.3
0723	4.7	0744	5.0
F 1328	1.8	SA 1403	1.6
1948	4.5	◗ 2011	4.8
8 0151	1.9	**23** 0233	1.6
0813	4.4	0856	4.6
SA 1413	2.1	SU 1515	2.0
◗ 2041	4.3	2122	4.6
9 0251	2.2	**24** 0401	1.8
0917	4.2	1022	4.4
SU 1522	2.4	M 1643	2.1
2148	4.1	2245	4.5
10 0424	2.3	**25** 0538	1.7
1036	4.1	1153	4.5
M 1702	2.4	TU 1808	2.0
2306	4.2		
11 0552	2.1	**26** 0008	4.6
1157	4.2	0653	1.4
TU 1821	2.2	W 1303	4.8
		1911	1.7
12 0020	4.4	**27** 0113	4.9
0654	1.8	0748	1.1
W 1301	4.5	TH 1354	5.0
1916	1.9	2001	1.5
13 0115	4.7	**28** 0202	5.2
0743	1.5	0834	0.9
TH 1348	4.8	F 1436	5.2
2000	1.6	2044	1.3
14 0159	5.0	**29** 0243	5.4
0826	1.1	0912	0.8
F 1428	5.1	SA 1514	5.3
2041	1.3	2121	1.1
15 0237	5.3	**30** 0319	5.5
0905	0.8	0947	0.8
SA 1505	5.3	SU 1548	5.4
2119	1.1	○ 2156	1.0

OCTOBER

Time	m		Time	m
1 0353	5.5	**16** 0326	5.8
1018	0.8	0956	0.4
M 1619	5.3	TU 1554	5.7
2229	1.0	2213	0.6
2 0426	5.4	**17** 0409	5.8
1048	1.0	1037	0.4
TU 1649	5.3	W 1635	5.7
2300	1.0	2256	0.6
3 0458	5.3	**18** 0455	5.8
1116	1.1	1120	0.6
W 1719	5.2	TH 1719	5.6
2332	1.2	2340	0.7
4 0533	5.2	**19** 0544	5.6
1144	1.3	1204	0.9
TH 1752	5.1	F 1806	5.4
5 0004	1.3	**20** 0027	0.9
0609	5.0	0637	5.3
F 1216	1.5	SA 1253	1.2
1828	4.9	1856	5.2
6 0039	1.5	**21** 0121	1.1
0651	4.7	0738	5.0
SA 1252	1.8	SU 1349	1.7
1911	4.7	1954	4.9
7 0120	1.8	**22** 0227	1.4
0739	4.5	0848	4.6
SU 1336	2.1	M 1459	2.0
2001	4.4	◗ 2103	4.7
8 0213	2.0	**23** 0348	1.6
0838	4.2	1008	4.5
M 1435	2.4	TU 1621	2.2
◗ 2103	4.3	2221	4.6
9 0332	2.2	**24** 0516	1.6
0950	4.1	1131	4.5
TU 1607	2.5	W 1741	2.1
2215	4.2	2340	4.7
10 0502	2.1	**25** 0628	1.4
1109	4.2	1238	4.7
W 1734	2.3	TH 1845	1.6
2328	4.4		
11 0612	1.8	**26** 0045	4.8
1216	4.5	0722	1.3
TH 1836	2.0	F 1329	4.9
		1935	1.6
12 0029	4.6	**27** 0136	5.0
0705	1.4	0806	1.1
F 1308	4.8	SA 1411	5.1
1924	1.7	2017	1.4
13 0119	5.0	**28** 0218	5.2
0750	1.1	0844	1.1
SA 1352	5.1	SU 1448	5.2
2008	1.4	2055	1.3
14 0203	5.3	**29** 0255	5.3
0833	0.8	0917	1.1
SU 1433	5.4	M 1521	5.3
2050	1.0	○ 2130	1.2
15 0244	5.6	**30** 0329	5.3
0914	0.5	0948	1.1
M 1513	5.6	TU 1552	5.3
● 2131	0.8	2203	1.1
		31 0403	5.3
		1018	1.2
		W 1621	5.3
		2236	1.1

NOVEMBER

Time	m		Time	m
1 0436	5.2	**16** 0445	5.7
1046	1.3	1105	0.7
TH 1650	5.2	F 1703	5.7
2309	1.2	2332	0.6
2 0510	5.1	**17** 0537	5.6
1116	1.4	1152	0.9
F 1723	5.1	SA 1751	5.6
2342	1.3		
3 0547	4.9	**18** 0022	0.7
1148	1.5	0631	5.3
SA 1800	5.0	SU 1242	1.3
		1841	5.4
4 0018	1.4	**19** 0115	0.9
0627	4.8	0728	5.0
SU 1226	1.8	M 1336	1.6
1842	4.8	1936	5.1
5 0059	1.6	**20** 0214	1.2
0714	4.6	0831	4.7
M 1308	2.0	TU 1437	1.9
1929	4.6	◑ 2038	4.9
6 0147	1.8	**21** 0321	1.4
0807	4.4	0939	4.5
TU 1401	2.2	W 1546	2.1
2024	4.5	2146	4.9
7 0250	1.9	**22** 0434	1.6
0910	4.3	1050	4.5
W 1513	2.4	TH 1659	2.1
◗ 2128	4.4	2257	4.6
8 0406	1.9	**23** 0546	1.6
1019	4.3	1158	4.6
TH 1637	2.3	F 1807	2.0
2236	4.5		
9 0517	1.7	**24** 0005	4.7
1125	4.5	0645	1.5
F 1746	2.1	SA 1255	4.7
2340	4.7	1902	1.9
10 0618	1.5	**25** 0102	4.8
1223	4.8	0733	1.5
SA 1843	1.8	SU 1341	4.8
		1949	1.6
11 0037	5.0	**26** 0150	4.9
0711	1.2	0813	1.4
SU 1315	5.1	M 1420	5.0
1933	1.4	2030	1.5
12 0129	5.3	**27** 0231	5.0
0800	0.9	0849	1.4
M 1401	5.3	TU 1456	5.1
2022	1.1	2107	1.3
13 0218	5.5	**28** 0309	5.0
0847	0.7	0922	1.3
TU 1447	5.5	W 1528	5.2
● 2109	0.8	○ 2143	1.2
14 0306	5.7	**29** 0345	5.1
0933	0.6	0954	1.3
W 1531	5.7	TH 1559	5.2
2156	0.6	2217	1.2
15 0355	5.8	**30** 0419	5.1
1019	0.6	1024	1.4
TH 1617	5.7	F 1630	5.2
2243	0.5	2251	1.2

DECEMBER

Time	m		Time	m
1 0454	5.0	**16** 0529	5.5
1056	1.4	1142	0.9
SA 1703	5.2	SU 1738	5.7
2326	1.2		
2 0530	5.0	**17** 0013	0.5
1130	1.5	0619	5.4
SU 1739	5.1	M 1229	1.1
		1825	5.5
3 0002	1.3	**18** 0102	0.7
0608	4.9	0710	5.1
M 1207	1.6	TU 1316	1.4
1818	5.0	1914	5.3
4 0042	1.4	**19** 0151	1.0
0651	4.7	0803	4.9
TU 1248	1.8	W 1406	1.7
1901	4.8	2006	5.0
5 0126	1.5	**20** 0244	1.3
0740	4.6	0859	4.6
W 1334	2.0	TH 1502	2.0
1950	4.7	◑ 2104	4.8
6 0217	1.6	**21** 0343	1.6
0835	4.5	0959	4.4
TH 1430	2.1	F 1606	2.1
◑ 2046	4.6	2208	4.6
7 0318	1.7	**22** 0450	1.8
0935	4.5	1104	4.4
F 1539	2.2	SA 1717	2.1
2148	4.6	2315	4.5
8 0425	1.6	**23** 0558	1.9
1039	4.5	1208	4.4
SA 1653	2.1	SU 1824	2.1
2254	4.7		
9 0532	1.5	**24** 0022	4.5
1141	4.7	0656	1.9
SU 1800	1.9	M 1305	4.6
2359	4.9	1920	1.9
10 0634	1.3	**25** 0120	4.6
1240	4.9	0744	1.8
M 1901	1.6	TU 1352	4.7
		2006	1.7
11 0100	5.1	**26** 0209	4.7
0732	1.1	0825	1.6
TU 1334	5.2	W 1433	4.9
1958	1.2	2048	1.5
12 0158	5.3	**27** 0251	4.8
0826	0.9	0902	1.5
W 1426	5.4	TH 1509	5.1
2053	0.9	2126	1.3
13 0253	5.5	**28** 0330	4.9
0918	0.8	0936	1.4
TH 1515	5.6	F 1542	5.2
● 2145	0.7	○ 2202	1.2
14 0346	5.6	**29** 0405	5.0
1007	0.8	1009	1.4
F 1603	5.7	SA 1614	5.2
2236	0.5	2237	1.1
15 0438	5.6	**30** 0439	5.0
1055	0.8	1042	1.3
SA 1650	5.7	SU 1646	5.2
2325	0.4	2312	1.0
		31 0514	5.0
		1116	1.4
		M 1720	5.2
		2347	1.0

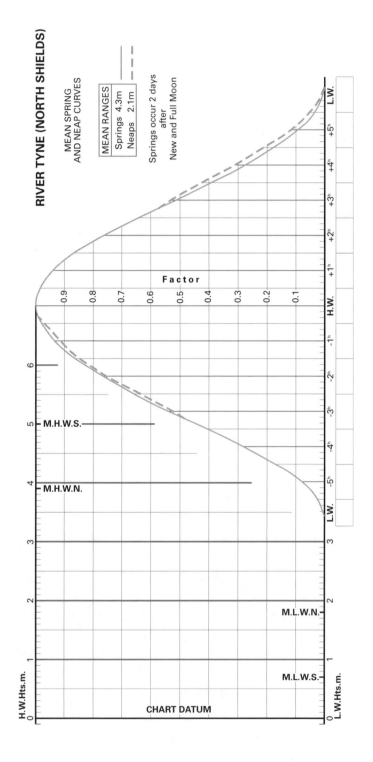

RIVER TYNE (NORTH SHIELDS)

MEAN SPRING
AND NEAP CURVES

MEAN RANGES
Springs 4.3m
Neaps 2.1m

Springs occur 2 days
after
New and Full Moon

NORTH SHIELDS

LAT 55°01′N   LONG 1°26′W

TIMES AND HEIGHTS OF HIGH AND LOW WATERS

JANUARY

Day	Time m	Time m	Time m	Time m	Day	Time m	Time m	Time m	Time m
1 SU	0226 1.6	0845 4.1	1434 2.0	◑2050 4.3	16 M	0208 1.1	0816 4.5	1415 1.6	2030 4.7
2 M	0320 1.8	0941 4.0	1540 2.2	2152 4.1	17 TU	0308 1.3	0919 4.3	1525 1.8	2141 4.5
3 TU	0424 2.0	1045 4.0	1656 2.2	2302 4.0	18 W	0419 1.5	1030 4.3	1650 1.8	2302 4.4
4 W	0532 2.0	1153 4.0	1809 2.1		19 TH	0537 1.6	1146 4.3	1814 1.7	
5 TH	0013 4.1	0636 1.9	1253 4.2	1910 1.9	20 F	0024 4.5	0651 1.5	1255 4.5	1928 1.4
6 F	0114 4.2	0729 1.8	1341 4.4	1959 1.6	21 SA	0133 4.6	0754 1.4	1352 4.8	2027 1.1
7 SA	0202 4.4	0813 1.6	1421 4.6	2041 1.4	22 SU	0229 4.8	0846 1.2	1441 5.0	2118 0.8
8 SU	0242 4.6	0853 1.4	1458 4.8	2120 1.2	23 M	0317 5.0	0931 1.1	1524 5.1	2202 0.8
9 M	0320 4.7	0930 1.3	1532 4.9	○2158 1.0	24 TU	0400 5.0	1011 1.0	1603 5.2	2243 0.6
10 TU	0357 4.9	1006 1.2	1606 5.1	2236 0.8	25 W	0439 5.0	1048 1.0	1641 5.2	2320 0.6
11 W	0434 5.0	1043 1.1	1641 5.1	2315 0.7	26 TH	0517 4.9	1122 1.1	1718 5.2	2354 0.8
12 TH	0512 5.0	1120 1.1	1718 5.2	2354 0.7	27 F	0554 4.8	1154 1.2	1755 5.0	
13 F	0552 4.9	1157 1.1	1758 5.1		28 SA	0026 1.0	0629 4.6	1227 1.3	1831 4.9
14 SA	0035 0.8	0634 4.8	1238 1.3	1841 5.1	29 SU	0059 1.2	0707 4.4	1301 1.6	1912 4.6
15 SU	0119 0.9	0721 4.7	1322 1.4	1931 4.9	30 M	0134 1.5	0748 4.2	1341 1.8	1957 4.4
					31 TU	0217 1.7	0837 4.0	1433 2.0	◑2053 4.1

FEBRUARY

Day	Time m	Time m	Time m	Time m	Day	Time m	Time m	Time m	Time m
1 W	0313 2.0	0937 3.9	1546 2.2	2202 3.9	16 TH	0355 1.7	1005 4.1	1635 1.8	2254 4.2
2 TH	0429 2.2	1051 3.8	1715 2.2	2324 3.8	17 F	0524 1.8	1129 4.2	1810 1.6	
3 F	0552 2.1	1209 4.0	1835 2.0		18 SA	0022 4.3	0645 1.7	1246 4.4	1925 1.3
4 SA	0041 4.0	0700 1.9	1310 4.2	1933 1.7	19 SU	0131 4.5	0747 1.5	1344 4.6	2021 1.0
5 SU	0137 4.2	0752 1.7	1356 4.4	2019 1.4	20 M	0223 4.7	0835 1.3	1431 4.9	2107 0.8
6 M	0221 4.5	0834 1.4	1435 4.7	2100 1.1	21 TU	0306 4.8	0916 1.1	1510 5.0	●2146 0.6
7 TU	0259 4.7	0912 1.2	1510 5.0	○2139 0.8	22 W	0343 4.9	0952 1.0	1546 5.1	2221 0.6
8 W	0336 4.9	0949 1.0	1545 5.2	2217 0.5	23 TH	0417 4.9	1025 0.9	1620 5.2	2253 0.6
9 TH	0413 4.9	1026 0.8	1621 5.3	2256 0.4	24 F	0449 4.9	1056 0.9	1653 5.1	2323 0.7
10 F	0451 5.1	1103 0.8	1658 5.4	2335 0.4	25 SA	0521 4.8	1126 1.0	1726 5.0	2351 0.9
11 SA	0530 5.1	1140 0.8	1738 5.4		26 SU	0552 4.7	1156 1.1	1800 4.9	
12 SU	0015 0.5	0611 5.0	1219 0.9	1822 5.2	27 M	0020 1.1	0625 4.5	1228 1.3	1836 4.6
13 M	0057 0.7	0656 4.8	1302 1.1	1911 5.0	28 TU	0052 1.4	0701 4.3	1304 1.5	1917 4.4
14 TU	0143 1.1	0747 4.6	1354 1.4	◑2011 4.7	29 W	0128 1.7	0744 4.1	1348 1.8	2008 4.1
15 W	0240 1.4	0849 4.3	1502 1.6	2125 4.4					

MARCH

Day	Time m	Time m	Time m	Time m	Day	Time m	Time m	Time m	Time m
1 TH	0215 1.9	0838 3.9	1450 2.0	◑2113 3.8	16 F	0340 1.9	0945 4.1	1628 1.6	2248 4.1
2 F	0326 2.2	0950 3.8	1619 2.1	2235 3.7	17 SA	0512 2.0	1112 4.1	1802 1.5	
3 SA	0503 2.2	1115 3.8	1751 2.0		18 SU	0014 4.2	0633 1.8	1230 4.3	1913 1.3
4 SU	0001 3.9	0626 2.0	1230 4.0	1859 1.7	19 M	0119 4.4	0731 1.6	1328 4.5	2005 1.0
5 M	0105 4.1	0723 1.7	1323 4.3	1950 1.3	20 TU	0207 4.6	0817 1.3	1412 4.7	2046 0.8
6 TU	0152 4.5	0808 1.4	1405 4.7	2033 0.9	21 W	0245 4.7	0854 1.1	1450 4.9	2121 0.7
7 W	0233 4.8	0847 1.1	1443 5.0	2113 0.6	22 TH	0319 4.8	0928 1.0	1523 5.0	●2153 0.7
8 TH	0311 5.0	0926 0.8	1519 5.2	○2153 0.3	23 F	0350 4.9	1000 0.9	1556 5.0	2222 0.7
9 F	0348 5.2	1004 0.6	1557 5.4	2233 0.2	24 SA	0420 4.9	1030 0.9	1628 5.0	2251 0.8
10 SA	0427 5.2	1043 0.5	1637 5.5	2313 0.2	25 SU	0450 4.8	1100 0.9	1700 4.9	2319 0.9
11 SU	0506 5.2	1122 0.6	1720 5.4	2354 0.4	26 M	0520 4.7	1131 1.0	1734 4.8	2347 1.1
12 M	0548 5.1	1203 0.7	1807 5.2		27 TU	0552 4.6	1202 1.2	1810 4.6	
13 TU	0036 0.7	0633 4.9	1249 0.9	1859 4.9	28 W	0018 1.3	0626 4.4	1238 1.4	1849 4.3
14 W	0123 1.1	0725 4.6	1343 1.2	2002 4.6	29 TH	0053 1.6	0706 4.2	1321 1.6	1937 4.1
15 TH	0221 1.5	0828 4.3	1454 1.5	◑2119 4.2	30 F	0136 1.9	0755 4.0	1417 1.8	◑2038 3.9
					31 SA	0239 2.1	0901 3.9	1534 1.9	2154 3.8

APRIL

Day	Time m	Time m	Time m	Time m	Day	Time m	Time m	Time m	Time m
1 SU	0411 2.2	1022 3.8	1702 1.8	2315 3.9	16 M	0605 1.8	1201 4.3	1845 1.3	
2 M	0540 2.0	1139 4.0	1815 1.5		17 TU	0051 4.3	0703 1.6	1300 4.4	1936 1.1
3 TU	0024 4.1	0644 1.7	1240 4.3	1911 1.2	18 W	0139 4.5	0749 1.4	1345 4.6	2016 1.0
4 W	0117 4.5	0733 1.4	1328 4.7	1959 0.8	19 TH	0217 4.6	0827 1.2	1424 4.7	2050 0.9
5 TH	0201 4.8	0817 1.1	1411 5.0	2043 0.5	20 F	0251 4.7	0902 1.1	1459 4.8	2121 0.9
6 F	0242 5.0	0859 0.8	1452 5.3	○2126 0.3	21 SA	0322 4.8	0935 1.0	1532 4.8	●2152 0.9
7 SA	0321 5.2	0941 0.5	1534 5.4	2209 0.2	22 SU	0353 4.8	1007 0.9	1605 4.8	2221 0.9
8 SU	0402 5.3	1023 0.4	1619 5.5	2251 0.3	23 M	0423 4.8	1038 0.9	1638 4.8	2251 1.0
9 M	0444 5.3	1107 0.4	1706 5.4	2335 0.5	24 TU	0454 4.7	1110 1.0	1713 4.7	2321 1.2
10 TU	0528 5.1	1152 0.6	1756 5.2		25 W	0526 4.7	1144 1.1	1750 4.5	2353 1.3
11 W	0019 0.8	0615 4.9	1241 0.8	1852 4.8	26 TH	0600 4.5	1221 1.2	1830 4.4	
12 TH	0108 1.2	0708 4.7	1338 1.1	1957 4.5	27 F	0029 1.6	0639 4.4	1304 1.4	1916 4.2
13 F	0207 1.6	0811 4.4	1449 1.3	◑2111 4.2	28 SA	0112 1.8	0727 4.2	1356 1.5	2012 4.0
14 SA	0323 1.9	0925 4.2	1614 1.4	2231 4.1	29 SU	0209 1.9	0825 4.1	1501 1.6	◑2119 4.0
15 SU	0449 2.0	1046 4.2	1738 1.4	2349 4.1	30 M	0325 2.0	0936 4.0	1617 1.6	2232 4.0

TIDES

Chart Datum: 2·60 metres below Ordnance Datum (Newlyn)
HAT is 5·7 metres above Chart Datum

TIME ZONE (UT)		
For Summer Time add ONE hour in **non-shaded areas**		

NORTH SHIELDS
LAT 55°01′N   LONG 1°26′W
TIMES AND HEIGHTS OF HIGH AND LOW WATERS

Dates in amber are **SPRINGS**
Dates in yellow are NEAPS

2012

MAY

Time	m		Time	m
1 TU 0449 / 1048 / 1729 / 2340	2.0 / 4.1 / 1.4 / 4.2	**16** W	0010 / 0623 / 1221 / 1855	4.2 / 1.8 / 4.3 / 1.4
2 W 0558 / 1153 / 1830	1.7 / 4.4 / 1.1	**17** TH	0102 / 0714 / 1312 / 1939	4.3 / 1.6 / 4.4 / 1.3
3 TH 0038 / 0654 / 1250 / 1923	4.5 / 1.4 / 4.7 / 0.8	**18** F	0145 / 0756 / 1355 / 2016	4.4 / 1.4 / 4.5 / 1.2
4 F 0128 / 0745 / 1340 / 2013	4.8 / 1.1 / 5.0 / 0.6	**19** SA	0222 / 0835 / 1434 / 2051	4.6 / 1.2 / 4.6 / 1.1
5 SA 0213 / 0833 / 1428 / 2100	5.0 / 0.8 / 5.2 / 0.4	**20**	0256 / 0911 / 1511 / ●2124	4.7 / 1.0 / 4.6 / 1.1
6 SU 0257 / 0920 / 1516 / ○2147	5.2 / 0.6 / 5.3 / 0.4	**21** M	0329 / 0946 / 1546 / 2156	4.7 / 1.0 / 4.7 / 1.1
7 M 0340 / 1007 / 1605 / 2233	5.3 / 0.4 / 5.4 / 0.5	**22** TU	0400 / 1020 / 1621 / 2228	4.8 / 1.0 / 4.7 / 1.1
8 TU 0425 / 1055 / 1655 / 2319	5.1 / 0.4 / 5.3 / 0.6	**23** W	0432 / 1054 / 1657 / 2301	4.8 / 1.0 / 4.6 / 1.2
9 W 0511 / 1144 / 1749	5.2 / 0.5 / 5.1	**24** TH	0506 / 1130 / 1734 / 2336	4.7 / 1.0 / 4.6 / 1.3
10 TH 0005 / 0600 / 1236 / 1845	0.9 / 5.0 / 0.6 / 4.8	**25** F	0541 / 1208 / 1814	4.7 / 1.1 / 4.5
11 F 0055 / 0653 / 1331 / 1946	1.3 / 4.8 / 0.9 / 4.5	**26** SA	0013 / 0620 / 1250 / 1857	1.4 / 4.6 / 1.2 / 4.3
12 SA 0150 / 0753 / 1434 / ◑2051	1.6 / 4.5 / 1.1 / 4.3	**27** SU	0055 / 0704 / 1338 / 1948	1.6 / 4.5 / 1.3 / 4.2
13 SU 0255 / 0858 / 1545 / 2158	1.8 / 4.4 / 1.3 / 4.1	**28** M	0145 / 0756 / 1433 / ◑2047	1.7 / 4.4 / 1.3 / 4.2
14 M 0409 / 1008 / 1656 / 2307	1.9 / 4.2 / 1.4 / 4.1	**29** TU	0246 / 0857 / 1537 / 2151	1.8 / 4.3 / 1.4 / 4.2
15 TU 0521 / 1118 / 1802	1.9 / 4.2 / 1.4	**30** W	0359 / 1004 / 1646 / 2257	1.8 / 4.3 / 1.3 / 4.3
		31 TH	0512 / 1112 / 1751	1.7 / 4.4 / 1.1

JUNE

Time	m		Time	m
1 F 0000 / 0617 / 1217 / 1850	4.5 / 1.5 / 4.4 / 0.9	**16** SA	0109 / 0724 / 1326 / 1943	4.3 / 1.6 / 4.3 / 1.5
2 SA 0057 / 0716 / 1316 / 1946	4.7 / 1.2 / 4.6 / 0.8	**17** SU	0153 / 0809 / 1411 / 2023	4.4 / 1.4 / 4.4 / 1.4
3 SU 0149 / 0812 / 1411 / 2040	4.9 / 0.9 / 5.1 / 0.7	**18** M	0232 / 0849 / 1451 / 2101	4.6 / 1.3 / 4.5 / 1.3
4 M 0237 / 0905 / 1504 / ○2130	5.1 / 0.6 / 5.2 / 0.6	**19** TU	0307 / 0927 / 1528 / ●2136	4.7 / 1.0 / 4.6 / 1.2
5 TU 0323 / 0957 / 1556 / 2218	5.2 / 0.5 / 5.2 / 0.7	**20** W	0341 / 1003 / 1604 / 2210	4.8 / 1.0 / 4.7 / 1.2
6 W 0410 / 1047 / 1647 / 2305	5.2 / 0.4 / 5.2 / 0.8	**21** TH	0414 / 1039 / 1640 / 2245	4.8 / 0.9 / 4.7 / 1.2
7 TH 0457 / 1136 / 1740 / 2351	5.2 / 0.4 / 5.0 / 1.0	**22** F	0448 / 1116 / 1717 / 2321	4.9 / 0.9 / 4.7 / 1.2
8 F 0545 / 1225 / 1832	5.1 / 0.5 / 4.9	**23** SA	0523 / 1154 / 1756 / 2358	4.8 / 0.9 / 4.6 / 1.3
9 SA 0037 / 0635 / 1315 / 1925	1.2 / 4.9 / 0.8 / 4.6	**24** SU	0601 / 1234 / 1837	4.8 / 0.9 / 4.6
10 SU 0125 / 0727 / 1407 / 2019	1.4 / 4.7 / 1.0 / 4.4	**25** M	0037 / 0642 / 1318 / 1923	1.4 / 4.7 / 1.0 / 4.5
11 M 0217 / 0824 / 1502 / ◑2116	1.7 / 4.5 / 1.3 / 4.2	**26** TU	0122 / 0729 / 1406 / 2015	1.5 / 4.7 / 1.1 / 4.4
12 TU 0317 / 0923 / 1602 / ◑2216	1.8 / 4.3 / 1.5 / 4.1	**27** W	0214 / 0825 / 1503 / ◑2115	1.6 / 4.6 / 1.2 / 4.3
13 W 0424 / 1027 / 1704 / 2319	1.9 / 4.2 / 1.6 / 4.1	**28** TH	0318 / 0929 / 1609 / 2220	1.7 / 4.5 / 1.3 / 4.3
14 TH 0531 / 1133 / 1804	1.9 / 4.1 / 1.6	**29** F	0433 / 1040 / 1718 / 2328	1.7 / 4.5 / 1.3 / 4.4
15 F 0018 / 0632 / 1234 / 1857	4.1 / 1.8 / 4.2 / 1.6	**30** SA	0548 / 1153 / 1826	1.5 / 4.5 / 1.2

JULY

Time	m		Time	m
1 SU 0033 / 0657 / 1303 / 1929	4.6 / 1.3 / 4.7 / 1.1	**16** M	0125 / 0745 / 1349 / 2000	4.3 / 1.6 / 4.3 / 1.5
2 M 0132 / 0801 / 1403 / 2027	4.8 / 1.0 / 4.9 / 1.0	**17** TU	0208 / 0829 / 1431 / 2040	4.5 / 1.3 / 4.4 / 1.4
3 TU 0224 / 0858 / 1458 / ○2118	5.0 / 0.7 / 5.0 / 0.9	**18** W	0246 / 0908 / 1509 / 2117	4.7 / 1.1 / 4.6 / 1.3
4 W 0311 / 0949 / 1548 / 2206	5.2 / 0.5 / 5.1 / 0.8	**19** TH	0320 / 0945 / 1545 / ●2153	4.8 / 0.9 / 4.7 / 1.1
5 TH 0357 / 1038 / 1637 / 2250	5.3 / 0.4 / 5.1 / 0.8	**20** F	0354 / 1021 / 1620 / 2228	5.0 / 0.8 / 4.8 / 1.0
6 F 0442 / 1123 / 1723 / 2332	5.3 / 0.4 / 5.0 / 0.9	**21** SA	0427 / 1058 / 1656 / 2304	5.0 / 0.7 / 4.9 / 1.0
7 SA 0526 / 1207 / 1809	5.2 / 0.5 / 4.9	**22** SU	0502 / 1136 / 1734 / 2340	5.1 / 0.6 / 4.9 / 1.0
8 SU 0013 / 0610 / 1256 / 1853	1.1 / 5.1 / 0.7 / 4.7	**23** M	0539 / 1214 / 1813	5.1 / 0.7 / 4.8
9 M 0053 / 0655 / 1330 / 1939	1.3 / 4.9 / 1.0 / 4.4	**24** TU	0017 / 0619 / 1255 / 1856	1.1 / 5.0 / 0.8 / 4.7
10 TU 0134 / 0743 / 1412 / 2027	1.5 / 4.6 / 1.3 / 4.2	**25** W	0059 / 0705 / 1340 / 1945	1.2 / 4.9 / 1.0 / 4.6
11 W 0221 / 0835 / 1501 / ◑2121	1.7 / 4.4 / 1.6 / 4.1	**26** TH	0147 / 0758 / 1433 / ◑2043	1.4 / 4.7 / 1.2 / 4.4
12 TH 0320 / 0933 / 1600 / 2221	1.9 / 4.2 / 1.8 / 4.0	**27** F	0248 / 0903 / 1538 / 2150	1.6 / 4.5 / 1.4 / 4.3
13 F 0431 / 1039 / 1707 / 2327	2.0 / 4.0 / 1.9 / 4.0	**28** SA	0406 / 1020 / 1655 / 2305	1.7 / 4.4 / 1.5 / 4.3
14 SA 0546 / 1152 / 1814	2.0 / 4.0 / 1.9	**29** SU	0532 / 1144 / 1812	1.6 / 4.4 / 1.5
15 SU 0031 / 0652 / 1257 / 1912	4.1 / 1.8 / 4.1 / 1.8	**30** M	0018 / 0651 / 1259 / 1921	4.5 / 1.4 / 4.6 / 1.4
		31 TU	0122 / 0757 / 1401 / 2018	4.7 / 1.0 / 4.8 / 1.2

AUGUST

Time	m		Time	m
1 W 0214 / 0852 / 1452 / 2108	4.9 / 0.7 / 5.0 / 1.0	**16** TH	0220 / 0844 / 1445 / 2055	4.7 / 1.1 / 4.7 / 1.3
2 TH 0300 / 0940 / 1538 / ○2151	5.2 / 0.5 / 5.1 / 0.9	**17** F	0255 / 0922 / 1520 / ●2131	4.9 / 0.8 / 4.9 / 1.1
3 F 0343 / 1023 / 1620 / 2231	5.3 / 0.4 / 5.1 / 0.8	**18** SA	0329 / 0958 / 1555 / 2207	5.1 / 0.6 / 5.0 / 0.9
4 SA 0423 / 1103 / 1700 / 2308	5.3 / 0.4 / 5.0 / 0.9	**19** SU	0403 / 1036 / 1631 / 2242	5.3 / 0.5 / 5.1 / 0.8
5 SU 0502 / 1140 / 1739 / 2344	5.3 / 0.5 / 4.9 / 1.0	**20** M	0438 / 1113 / 1708 / 2319	5.3 / 0.4 / 5.1 / 0.8
6 M 0541 / 1215 / 1817	5.1 / 0.7 / 4.7	**21** TU	0516 / 1152 / 1748 / 2357	5.3 / 0.5 / 5.0 / 0.9
7 TU 0018 / 0620 / 1249 / 1855	1.2 / 4.9 / 1.0 / 4.5	**22** W	0558 / 1231 / 1830	5.2 / 0.7 / 4.9
8 W 0053 / 0701 / 1324 / 1936	1.4 / 4.7 / 1.3 / 4.3	**23** TH	0038 / 0645 / 1316 / 1918	1.1 / 5.0 / 1.0 / 4.7
9 TH 0133 / 0747 / 1404 / ◑2024	1.6 / 4.4 / 1.6 / 4.1	**24** F	0128 / 0740 / 1408 / ◑2016	1.3 / 4.8 / 1.3 / 4.5
10 F 0223 / 0842 / 1457 / 2122	1.9 / 4.1 / 1.9 / 4.0	**25** SA	0230 / 0849 / 1517 / 2127	1.5 / 4.5 / 1.6 / 4.3
11 SA 0331 / 0948 / 1608 / 2232	2.1 / 3.9 / 2.1 / 3.9	**26** SU	0354 / 1014 / 1642 / 2249	1.7 / 4.3 / 1.8 / 4.3
12 SU 0456 / 1107 / 1730 / 2348	2.1 / 3.9 / 2.1 / 4.0	**27** M	0528 / 1143 / 1807	1.6 / 4.3 / 1.7
13 M 0617 / 1225 / 1843	2.0 / 4.0 / 2.0	**28** TU	0009 / 0649 / 1258 / 1915	4.4 / 1.3 / 4.5 / 1.5
14 TU 0052 / 0718 / 1323 / 1936	4.2 / 1.7 / 4.2 / 1.7	**29** W	0113 / 0751 / 1355 / 2008	4.7 / 1.0 / 4.8 / 1.3
15 W 0141 / 0805 / 1407 / 2018	4.4 / 1.4 / 4.4 / 1.5	**30** TH	0203 / 0841 / 1441 / 2052	4.9 / 0.6 / 4.9 / 1.1
		31 F	0246 / 0923 / 1521 / ○2132	5.1 / 0.6 / 5.0 / 0.9

Chart Datum: 2·60 metres below Ordnance Datum (Newlyn)
HAT is 5·7 metres above Chart Datum

NORTH SHIELDS

LAT 55°01′N   LONG 1°26′W

TIMES AND HEIGHTS OF HIGH AND LOW WATERS

Dates in amber are **SPRINGS**
Dates in yellow are **NEAPS**

2012

SEPTEMBER

Day	Time m	Time m	Time m	Time m
1 SA	0324 5.3	1001 0.5	1557 5.1	2208 0.9
2 SU	0400 5.3	1036 0.5	1632 5.0	2241 0.9
3 M	0436 5.3	1108 0.7	1705 5.0	2314 1.0
4 TU	0511 5.1	1138 0.9	1739 4.8	2345 1.1
5 W	0547 4.9	1208 1.1	1813 4.7	
6 TH	0018 1.3	0624 4.7	1240 1.4	1849 4.5
7 F	0055 1.5	0707 4.4	1316 1.7	1933 4.3
8 SA	0140 1.8	0758 4.2	1403 2.0	2027 4.1 ◑
9 SU	0241 2.0	0903 3.9	1510 2.2	2137 3.9
10 M	0405 2.1	1022 3.8	1643 2.3	2258 3.9
11 TU	0535 2.0	1145 3.9	1807 2.1	
12 W	0012 4.1	0643 1.7	1249 4.2	1905 1.8
13 TH	0106 4.4	0733 1.4	1336 4.5	1949 1.5
14 F	0148 4.7	0814 1.0	1415 4.8	2028 1.3
15 SA	0224 5.0	0853 0.7	1452 5.0	2105 1.0
16 SU	0300 5.2	0931 0.5	● 2142 0.8	
17 M	0336 5.4	1009 0.4	1604 5.3	2220 0.7
18 TU	0414 5.5	1048 0.3	1642 5.3	2259 0.7
19 W	0455 5.5	1128 0.5	1723 5.2	2339 0.8
20 TH	0540 5.3	1210 0.7	1807 5.0	
21 F	0024 1.0	0630 5.1	1256 1.1	1856 4.8
22 SA	0116 1.2	0730 4.7	1350 1.5	◑ 1956 4.6
23 SU	0223 1.5	0844 4.4	1503 1.8	2110 4.3
24 M	0350 1.6	1010 4.2	1633 2.0	2234 4.3
25 TU	0523 1.5	1137 4.3	1756 1.9	2354 4.4
26 W	0639 1.3	1247 4.5	1901 1.6	
27 TH	0057 4.7	0736 1.0	1340 4.7	1950 1.4
28 F	0146 4.9	0821 0.9	1422 4.9	2032 1.2
29 SA	0227 5.1	0900 0.8	1458 5.0	2109 1.0
30 SU	0302 5.2	0934 0.7	1531 5.0	○ 2142 1.0

OCTOBER

Day	Time m	Time m	Time m	Time m
1 M	0336 5.2	1005 0.8	1603 5.0	2215 0.9
2 TU	0410 5.2	1035 0.8	1634 5.0	2246 1.0
3 W	0444 5.1	1104 1.0	1705 4.9	2318 1.1
4 TH	0519 4.9	1133 1.2	1737 4.8	2350 1.3
5 F	0556 4.7	1204 1.4	1813 4.6	
6 SA	0026 1.5	0636 4.5	1239 1.7	1853 4.4
7 SU	0109 1.7	0725 4.2	1321 2.0	1942 4.2
8 M	0204 1.9	0825 4.0	1421 2.2	◑ 2047 4.0
9 TU	0318 2.0	0938 3.9	1548 2.3	2204 4.0
10 W	0444 2.0	1057 4.0	1718 2.2	2319 4.1
11 TH	0557 1.7	1205 4.2	1824 1.9	
12 F	0021 4.4	0652 1.4	1258 4.5	1913 1.6
13 SA	0109 4.7	0738 1.0	1341 4.8	1955 1.3
14 SU	0151 5.0	0820 0.7	1421 5.1	2036 1.0
15 M	0230 5.3	0902 0.5	1459 5.3	● 2117 0.8
16 TU	0311 5.5	0943 0.4	1538 5.4	2158 0.6
17 W	0353 5.6	1025 0.4	1619 5.4	2241 0.6
18 TH	0439 5.5	1108 0.6	1702 5.3	2327 0.7
19 F	0528 5.3	1152 0.9	1748 5.1	
20 SA	0015 0.9	0622 5.0	1241 1.2	1839 4.9
21 SU	0111 1.1	0725 4.7	1337 1.6	1940 4.7
22 M	0218 1.3	0838 4.4	1448 1.9	● 2052 4.5
23 TU	0340 1.5	0956 4.3	1613 2.0	2212 4.4
24 W	0503 1.5	1116 4.3	1732 2.0	2329 4.5
25 TH	0615 1.4	1223 4.5	1835 1.8	
26 F	0032 4.6	0701 1.2	1315 4.6	1926 1.6
27 SA	0122 4.8	0755 1.1	1357 4.8	2007 1.4
28 SU	0204 4.9	0832 1.0	1433 4.9	2044 1.2
29 M	0240 5.0	0905 1.0	1505 5.0	○ 2118 1.1
30 TU	0315 5.0	0936 1.0	1537 5.0	2152 1.1
31 W	0349 5.0	1006 1.1	1607 5.0	2224 1.1

NOVEMBER

Day	Time m	Time m	Time m	Time m
1 TH	0423 4.9	1035 1.2	1638 4.9	2256 1.1
2 F	0458 4.8	1105 1.3	1711 4.9	2330 1.2
3 SA	0535 4.7	1137 1.5	1745 4.7	
4 SU	0006 1.4	0614 4.5	1212 1.7	1823 4.6
5 M	0048 1.5	0659 4.4	1253 1.9	1909 4.4
6 TU	0137 1.7	0752 4.1	1345 2.1	2004 4.2
7 W	0239 1.8	0856 4.0	1455 2.2	◑ 2111 4.2
8 TH	0352 1.8	1007 4.1	1619 2.2	2223 4.2
9 F	0504 1.7	1115 4.2	1732 2.0	2329 4.4
10 SA	0606 1.4	1214 4.5	1831 1.7	
11 SU	0026 4.7	0659 1.1	1306 4.8	1921 1.4
12 M	0118 5.0	0748 0.9	1351 5.0	2008 1.1
13 TU	0205 5.2	0835 0.7	1434 5.3	● 2055 0.8
14 W	0251 5.4	0921 0.6	1516 5.4	2142 0.6
15 TH	0339 5.5	1007 0.6	1600 5.4	2230 0.6
16 F	0428 5.5	1053 0.7	1645 5.4	2319 0.6
17 SA	0520 5.3	1139 1.0	1733 5.3	
18 SU	0009 0.7	0615 5.1	1229 1.3	1824 5.1
19 M	0104 0.9	0715 4.8	1322 1.6	1922 4.8
20 TU	0205 1.2	0820 4.5	1424 1.8	● 2028 4.6
21 W	0314 1.4	0928 4.3	1536 2.0	2138 4.5
22 TH	0426 1.5	1037 4.3	1650 2.0	2249 4.4
23 F	0535 1.5	1144 4.3	1758 1.9	2356 4.5
24 SA	0635 1.5	1241 4.4	1854 1.8	
25 SU	0052 4.5	0722 1.4	1328 4.6	1941 1.6
26 M	0139 4.6	0802 1.4	1407 4.7	2021 1.4
27 TU	0220 4.7	0837 1.3	1442 4.8	2058 1.3
28 W	0257 4.8	0910 1.3	1515 4.9	○ 2133 1.2
29 TH	0332 4.8	0943 1.3	1547 5.0	2207 1.1
30 F	0407 4.8	1014 1.3	1619 5.0	2241 1.1

DECEMBER

Day	Time m	Time m	Time m	Time m
1 SA	0442 4.8	1046 1.3	1651 4.9	2315 1.1
2 SU	0518 4.7	1119 1.4	1725 4.8	2351 1.2
3 M	0556 4.6	1154 1.6	1802 4.7	
4 TU	0030 1.3	0636 4.5	1232 1.7	1842 4.6
5 W	0115 1.4	0722 4.4	1317 1.9	1929 4.5
6 TH	0205 1.5	0816 4.2	1411 2.0	◑ 2025 4.4
7 F	0305 1.6	0918 4.2	1520 2.1	2130 4.4
8 SA	0413 1.6	1025 4.3	1637 2.0	2239 4.4
9 SU	0520 1.5	1130 4.4	1747 1.8	2347 4.6
10 M	0623 1.3	1231 4.7	1850 1.5	
11 TU	0049 4.8	0720 1.1	1325 4.9	1946 1.2
12 W	0146 5.1	0814 0.9	1414 5.1	2040 0.9
13 TH	0239 5.3	0905 0.8	1500 5.3	● 2132 0.7
14 F	0330 5.4	0954 0.8	1546 5.4	2222 0.5
15 SA	0421 5.4	1041 0.8	1632 5.4	2312 0.5
16 SU	0512 5.3	1127 1.0	1719 5.4	
17 M	0001 0.5	0603 5.1	1213 1.2	1808 5.2
18 TU	0050 0.7	0656 4.8	1300 1.4	1859 5.0
19 W	0141 1.0	0751 4.6	1350 1.7	1955 4.8
20 TH	0235 1.3	0848 4.4	1447 1.9	◑ 2055 4.5
21 F	0335 1.6	0948 4.2	1554 2.0	2200 4.3
22 SA	0440 1.7	1053 4.1	1706 2.1	2309 4.2
23 SU	0545 1.8	1158 4.2	1815 2.0	
24 M	0016 4.3	0644 1.8	1255 4.3	1912 1.8
25 TU	0114 4.4	0733 1.7	1342 4.5	1959 1.6
26 W	0201 4.5	0814 1.6	1422 4.7	2040 1.4
27 TH	0242 4.6	0851 1.5	1458 4.8	2117 1.3
28 F	0318 4.7	0926 1.4	1531 4.9	○ 2152 1.1
29 SA	0353 4.7	0959 1.3	1603 5.0	2226 1.0
30 SU	0427 4.8	1031 1.3	1634 5.0	2301 1.0
31 M	0501 4.8	1104 1.3	1707 5.0	2336 1.0

Chart Datum: 2·60 metres below Ordnance Datum (Newlyn)
HAT is 5·7 metres above Chart Datum

TIDES

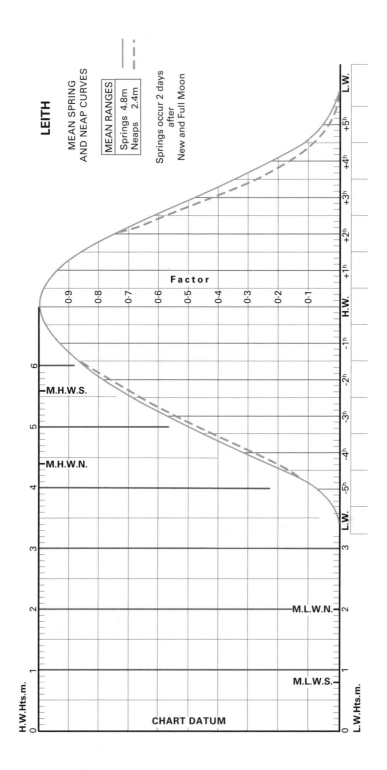

LEITH

MEAN SPRING
AND NEAP CURVES

MEAN RANGES	
Springs	4.8m
Neaps	2.4m

Springs occur 2 days
after
New and Full Moon

Factor

SCOTLAND – LEITH

LAT 55°59'N   LONG 3°11'W

TIMES AND HEIGHTS OF HIGH AND LOW WATERS

Dates in amber are **SPRINGS**
Dates in yellow are **NEAPS**

2012

JANUARY

Day	Time m	Time m	Time m	Time m
1 SU	0044 1.7	0754 4.6	1302 2.1	◑ 2011 4.6
2 M	0136 2.0	0847 4.4	1412 2.3	2108 4.5
3 TU	0250 2.2	0943 4.4	1540 2.4	2208 4.4
4 W	0418 2.2	1043 4.4	1654 2.2	2311 4.4
5 TH	0523 2.1	1145 4.6	1752 2.0	
6 F	0014 4.6	0611 1.9	1243 4.8	1839 1.7
7 SA	0107 4.8	0653 1.7	1339 5.0	1922 1.5
8 SU	0151 5.0	0732 1.5	1410 5.2	2002 1.2
9 M	0230 5.2	0811 1.3	1447 5.4	○ 2043 1.0
10 TU	0307 5.4	0850 1.2	1522 5.5	2124 0.8
11 W	0344 5.5	0930 1.1	1557 5.6	2205 0.7
12 TH	0422 5.5	1009 1.1	1634 5.6	2246 0.7
13 F	0502 5.5	1045 1.2	1713 5.5	2326 0.8
14 SA	0544 5.4	1118 1.3	1756 5.4	
15 SU	0004 1.0	0630 5.2	1153 1.5	1843 5.3
16 M	0045 1.2	0721 5.0	◑ 1939 5.1	
17 TU	0139 1.5	0821 4.8	1357 1.9	2051 4.9
18 W	0258 1.7	0934 4.7	1535 2.0	2212 4.8
19 TH	0427 1.8	1048 4.8	1703 1.8	2328 4.9
20 F	0543 1.7	1157 4.9	1820 1.5	
21 SA	0035 5.1	0646 1.5	1257 5.2	1924 1.2
22 SU	0133 5.3	0738 1.3	1348 5.4	2016 0.9
23 M	0221 5.5	0824 1.1	1433 5.5	● 2101 0.6
24 TU	0305 5.6	0904 1.0	1516 5.7	2142 0.6
25 W	0347 5.5	0941 0.9	1557 5.7	2218 0.6
26 TH	0427 5.4	1012 1.0	1637 5.6	2247 0.7
27 F	0505 5.3	1037 1.1	1715 5.4	2307 1.0
28 SA	0543 5.1	1059 1.3	1753 5.2	2324 1.3
29 SU	0621 4.9	1128 1.6	1832 5.0	2353 1.5
30 M	0703 4.6	1205 1.8	1917 4.7	
31 TU	0033 1.8	0750 4.4	1258 2.1	◑ 2010 4.4

FEBRUARY

Day	Time m	Time m	Time m	Time m
1 W	0130 2.2	0845 4.3	1418 2.4	2112 4.3
2 TH	0257 2.4	0948 4.2	1606 2.4	2219 4.2
3 F	0443 2.3	1057 4.3	1724 2.1	2331 4.4
4 SA	0548 2.1	1207 4.6	1820 1.8	
5 SU	0038 4.6	0635 1.8	1304 4.9	1905 1.5
6 M	0128 4.9	0716 1.5	1348 5.1	1948 1.1
7 TU	0209 5.2	0756 1.3	1426 5.4	○ 2029 0.9
8 W	0246 5.4	0836 1.0	1502 5.6	2110 0.5
9 TH	0323 5.6	0916 0.8	1537 5.7	2151 0.4
10 F	0401 5.7	0956 0.7	1614 5.8	2231 0.4
11 SA	0440 5.7	1032 0.8	1654 5.8	2310 0.5
12 SU	0522 5.5	1107 1.0	1737 5.6	2345 0.8
13 M	0606 5.3	1134 1.2	1825 5.4	
14 TU	0020 1.2	0655 5.0	1218 1.5	◑ 1920 5.1
15 W	0109 1.6	0753 4.7	1329 1.8	2033 4.8
16 TH	0232 1.9	0909 4.6	1522 2.0	2159 4.4
17 F	0416 2.0	1031 4.6	1707 1.8	2321 4.7
18 SA	0538 1.9	1147 4.8	1826 1.5	
19 SU	0033 4.9	0639 1.6	1250 5.0	1922 1.1
20 M	0128 5.2	0727 1.4	1339 5.3	2007 0.8
21 TU	0212 5.3	0807 1.1	1421 5.5	● 2045 0.7
22 W	0250 5.4	0843 0.9	1459 5.6	2120 0.6
23 TH	0326 5.4	0916 0.8	1536 5.6	2150 0.6
24 F	0401 5.4	0946 0.9	1611 5.5	2214 0.7
25 SA	0434 5.3	1010 1.0	1646 5.4	2231 0.8
26 SU	0508 5.1	1032 1.1	1720 5.2	2248 1.2
27 M	0543 4.9	1054 1.3	1756 5.0	2312 1.4
28 TU	0620 4.7	1123 1.6	1837 4.7	2343 1.7
29 W	0702 4.5	1203 1.9	1924 4.5	

MARCH

Day	Time m	Time m	Time m	Time m
1 TH	0028 2.1	0754 4.3	1310 2.2	◑ 2022 4.3
2 F	0149 2.4	0858 4.2	1457 2.4	2132 4.2
3 SA	0355 2.5	1011 4.2	1651 2.2	2247 4.3
4 SU	0519 2.2	1127 4.4	1754 1.8	
5 M	0001 4.5	0610 1.9	1231 4.7	1842 1.4
6 TU	0057 4.9	0654 1.5	1319 5.1	1925 1.0
7 W	0141 5.2	0734 1.2	1359 5.4	2007 0.6
8 TH	0220 5.5	0815 0.8	1436 5.7	○ 2049 0.3
9 F	0258 5.7	0856 0.6	1513 5.9	2131 0.2
10 SA	0336 5.8	0937 0.5	1553 6.0	2212 0.2
11 SU	0417 5.8	1017 0.5	1635 5.9	2251 0.4
12 M	0459 5.6	1054 0.7	1721 5.7	2328 0.8
13 TU	0544 5.4	1128 1.0	1811 5.4	
14 W	0005 1.2	0634 5.1	1214 1.3	1909 5.0
15 TH	0057 1.7	0734 4.7	1330 1.7	◑ 2025 4.7
16 F	0222 2.1	0853 4.5	1526 1.9	2149 4.5
17 SA	0405 2.1	1016 4.5	1706 1.7	2310 4.6
18 SU	0523 2.0	1132 4.7	1816 1.4	
19 M	0020 4.8	0621 1.7	1234 5.0	1907 1.1
20 TU	0113 5.1	0705 1.4	1322 5.2	1947 0.9
21 W	0154 5.2	0742 1.2	1402 5.3	2020 0.8
22 TH	0229 5.3	0816 1.0	1438 5.4	● 2050 0.7
23 F	0301 5.3	0848 0.8	1512 5.4	2117 0.7
24 SA	0333 5.3	0919 0.8	1546 5.4	2140 0.8
25 SU	0405 5.2	0946 0.9	1619 5.3	2159 1.0
26 M	0436 5.1	1009 1.0	1653 5.2	2218 1.2
27 TU	0510 5.0	1030 1.2	1728 5.0	2239 1.4
28 W	0545 4.8	1056 1.4	1807 4.8	2307 1.7
29 TH	0625 4.6	1133 1.7	1852 4.5	2345 2.0
30 F	0712 4.4	1231 2.0	1946 4.3	◑
31 SA	0056 2.3	0812 4.2	1404 2.1	2051 4.2

APRIL

Day	Time m	Time m	Time m	Time m
1 SU	0257 2.4	0926 4.2	1559 2.1	2205 4.3
2 M	0437 2.2	1043 4.4	1714 1.7	2318 4.5
3 TU	0534 1.9	1149 4.7	1806 1.3	
4 W	0019 4.9	0620 1.5	1242 5.1	1853 0.9
5 TH	0108 5.2	0703 1.1	1326 5.4	1938 0.6
6 F	0150 5.5	0747 0.8	1407 5.7	○ 2023 0.3
7 SA	0231 5.7	0832 0.5	1449 5.9	2107 0.2
8 SU	0312 5.8	0918 0.4	1532 6.0	2151 0.3
9 M	0354 5.8	1003 0.4	1619 5.9	2233 0.5
10 TU	0439 5.7	1048 0.6	1708 5.7	2315 0.9
11 W	0527 5.4	1133 0.9	1801 5.4	2358 1.3
12 TH	0619 5.1	1225 1.2	1903 5.0	
13 F	0051 1.8	0722 4.8	1337 1.5	◑ 2015 4.7
14 SA	0209 2.1	0838 4.6	1516 1.7	2130 4.6
15 SU	0338 2.1	0954 4.6	1642 1.6	2245 4.6
16 M	0450 2.0	1105 4.7	1748 1.4	2352 4.7
17 TU	0547 1.8	1206 4.9	1838 1.3	
18 W	0045 4.9	0631 1.5	1255 5.0	1916 1.1
19 TH	0127 5.1	0709 1.3	1337 5.1	1947 1.0
20 F	0203 5.2	0745 1.1	1414 5.2	2014 1.0
21 SA	0235 5.2	0820 1.0	1448 5.3	● 2041 0.9
22 SU	0306 5.2	0853 0.9	1522 5.2	2106 1.0
23 M	0337 5.2	0923 0.9	1555 5.2	2132 1.1
24 TU	0409 5.2	0952 1.0	1630 5.1	2156 1.2
25 W	0443 5.1	1018 1.2	1706 5.0	2221 1.4
26 TH	0519 4.9	1048 1.3	1745 4.8	2249 1.7
27 F	0558 4.8	1125 1.5	1828 4.7	2327 1.9
28 SA	0642 4.6	1219 1.7	1918 4.5	
29 SU	0030 2.1	0735 4.4	1333 1.9	2017 4.4
30 M	0210 2.3	0842 4.4	1502 1.8	2126 4.5

Chart Datum: 2·90 metres below Ordnance Datum (Newlyn)
HAT is 6·3 metres above Chart Datum

TIDES

TIME ZONE (UT)
For Summer Time add ONE hour in **non-shaded areas**

SCOTLAND – LEITH

LAT 55°59′N   LONG 3°11′W

TIMES AND HEIGHTS OF HIGH AND LOW WATERS

Dates in amber are **SPRINGS**
Dates in yellow are **NEAPS**

2012

MAY

#	Time	m		#	Time	m
1 TU	0343	2.1		**16** W	0501	1.9
	0958	4.5			1127	4.7
	1623	1.6			1754	1.5
	2237	4.6				
2 W	0449	1.8		**17** TH	0007	4.7
	1106	4.8			0550	1.7
	1723	1.3			1222	4.8
	2340	4.9			1833	1.4
3 TH	0542	1.5		**18** F	0054	4.9
	1203	5.1			0634	1.5
	1815	1.0			1308	4.9
					1904	1.3
4 F	0033	5.2		**19** SA	0133	5.0
	0630	1.1			0714	1.3
	1254	5.4			1348	5.0
	1905	0.7			1935	1.3
5 SA	0120	5.5		**20** SU	0208	5.1
	0719	0.8			0752	1.1
	1341	5.7			1425	5.1
	1955	0.5			2006	1.2 ●
6 SU	0205	5.7		**21** M	0241	5.2
	0811	0.6			0828	1.0
	1428	5.9			1500	5.1
	2044	0.4 ○			2037	1.2
7 M	0249	5.8		**22** TU	0314	5.2
	0903	0.4			0903	1.0
	1516	5.9			1534	5.1
	2132	0.4			2109	1.2
8 TU	0335	5.8		**23** W	0347	5.2
	0954	0.4			0936	1.0
	1606	5.9			1610	5.1
	2218	0.7			2142	1.3
9 W	0423	5.7		**24** TH	0422	5.1
	1043	0.5			1011	1.1
	1657	5.7			1647	5.1
	2303	1.0			2214	1.4
10 TH	0513	5.5		**25** F	0458	5.0
	1132	0.7			1046	1.2
	1752	5.4			1725	5.0
	2348	1.3			2246	1.5
11 F	0607	5.2		**26** SA	0536	4.9
	1224	1.0			1125	1.3
	1852	5.1			1808	4.9
					2323	1.7
12 SA	0038	1.7		**27** SU	0619	4.8
	0708	5.0			1211	1.4
	1326	1.3			1855	4.8
	1956	4.8 ◐				
13 SU	0141	2.0		**28** M	0014	1.9
	0816	4.8			0707	4.7
	1443	1.5			1308	1.5
	2101	4.6			1948	4.7 ◐
14 M	0255	2.1		**29** TU	0127	2.0
	0922	4.7			0804	4.7
	1558	1.6			1417	1.6
	2206	4.6			2050	4.7
15 TU	0403	2.0		**30** W	0250	2.0
	1027	4.7			0914	4.7
	1703	1.6			1532	1.5
	2310	4.6			2158	4.8
				31 TH	0403	1.8
					1025	4.8
					1640	1.3
					2303	4.9

JUNE

#	Time	m		#	Time	m
1 F	0505	1.6		**16** SA	0012	4.7
	1130	5.1			0601	1.7
	1740	1.1			1235	4.7
					1823	1.7
2 SA	0002	5.2		**17** SU	0101	4.8
	0601	1.3			0646	1.5
	1228	5.3			1322	4.8
	1836	0.9			1901	1.5
3 SU	0055	5.4		**18** M	0142	5.0
	0658	0.9			0728	1.3
	1321	5.6			1402	4.9
	1933	0.8			1938	1.4
4 M	0144	5.6		**19** TU	0219	5.1
	0757	0.7			0806	1.2
	1413	5.8			1439	5.1
	2027	0.7 ○			2014	1.3 ●
5 TU	0232	5.7		**20** W	0254	5.2
	0854	0.5			0844	1.0
	1504	5.8			1515	5.2
	2117	0.7			2051	1.2
6 W	0320	5.8		**21** TH	0329	5.3
	0946	0.4			0922	0.9
	1554	5.8			1551	5.2
	2204	0.8			2129	1.2
7 TH	0409	5.7		**22** F	0404	5.3
	1036	0.4			1001	0.9
	1646	5.7			1628	5.2
	2249	1.0			2206	1.2
8 F	0459	5.6		**23** SA	0440	5.2
	1123	0.6			1040	0.9
	1738	5.4			1706	5.2
	2331	1.2			2242	1.3
9 SA	0551	5.4		**24** SU	0517	5.2
	1209	0.9			1120	1.0
	1832	5.2			1747	5.1
					2317	1.4
10 SU	0012	1.5		**25** M	0558	5.1
	0646	5.2			1200	1.1
	1256	1.2			1831	5.0
	1926	4.9			2355	1.6
11 M	0057	1.8		**26** TU	0642	5.0
	0744	4.9			1244	1.2
	1347	1.5			1921	4.9
	2023	4.7 ◐				
12 TU	0154	2.0		**27** W	0046	1.7
	0842	4.7			0734	4.9
	1450	1.7			1339	1.4
	2120	4.5			2017	4.8 ◐
13 W	0303	2.1		**28** TH	0158	1.8
	0941	4.6			0837	4.9
	1555	1.8			1447	1.5
	2218	4.5			2123	4.8
14 TH	0411	2.1		**29** F	0319	1.8
	1040	4.5			0952	4.9
	1653	1.6			1604	1.5
	2317	4.5			2232	4.9
15 F	0509	1.9		**30** SA	0436	1.7
	1140	4.6			1104	5.0
	1742	1.8			1716	1.4
					2337	5.0

JULY

#	Time	m		#	Time	m
1 SU	0545	1.4		**16** M	0024	4.7
	1210	5.2			0624	1.7
	1820	1.2			1254	4.7
					1837	1.7
2 M	0036	5.2		**17** TU	0115	4.9
	0650	1.1			0708	1.4
	1309	5.4			1340	4.9
	1919	1.0			1917	1.5
3 TU	0129	5.5		**18** W	0157	5.1
	0752	0.8			0748	1.2
	1403	5.6			1419	5.1
	2013	0.9 ○			1956	1.3
4 W	0219	5.6		**19** TH	0235	5.3
	0847	0.5			0828	1.0
	1453	5.7			1455	5.2
	2103	0.8			2034	1.2 ●
5 TH	0307	5.7		**20** F	0310	5.4
	0937	0.3			0908	0.8
	1542	5.7			1531	5.4
	2148	0.8			2114	1.0
6 F	0355	5.7		**21** SA	0345	5.5
	1023	0.3			0948	0.7
	1629	5.6			1607	5.4
	2229	0.9			2153	1.0
7 SA	0442	5.7		**22** SU	0420	5.5
	1105	0.5			1027	0.6
	1713	5.4			1645	5.4
	2306	1.1			2230	1.0
8 SU	0528	5.5		**23** M	0456	5.5
	1142	0.8			1106	0.7
	1803	5.2			1724	5.4
	2337	1.3			2302	1.2
9 M	0616	5.3		**24** TU	0536	5.4
	1212	1.1			1143	0.8
	1850	5.0			1807	5.3
					2333	1.3
10 TU	0007	1.6		**25** W	0620	5.3
	0704	5.0			1219	1.1
	1239	1.4			1854	5.1
	1938	4.7				
11 W	0050	1.8		**26** TH	0014	1.5
	0755	4.8			0709	5.1
	1320	1.7			1305	1.3
	2028	4.5 ◐			1947	4.9 ◐
12 TH	0150	2.1		**27** F	0118	1.7
	0850	4.5			0811	4.9
	1422	2.0			1413	1.6
	2122	4.4			2053	4.8
13 F	0311	2.2		**28** SA	0248	1.8
	0948	4.4			0930	4.8
	1547	2.1			1542	1.7
	2220	4.4			2208	4.7
14 SA	0430	2.1		**29** SU	0424	1.8
	1050	4.4			1050	4.8
	1658	2.1			1705	1.7
	2323	4.5			2320	4.9
15 SU	0533	1.9		**30** M	0543	1.5
	1156	4.5			1202	5.0
	1752	1.9			1813	1.5
				31 TU	0025	5.1
					0652	1.1
					1304	5.3
					1910	1.2

AUGUST

#	Time	m		#	Time	m
1 W	0120	5.4		**16** TH	0131	5.1
	0750	0.8			0730	1.2
	1356	5.5			1354	5.1
	2000	1.0			1937	1.3
2 TH	0208	5.6		**17** F	0210	5.3
	0839	0.5			0809	0.9
	1442	5.6			1431	5.4
	2045	0.8 ○			2015	1.1 ●
3 F	0253	5.7		**18** SA	0246	5.5
	0923	0.4			0849	0.6
	1525	5.7			1506	5.5
	2126	0.8			2054	0.9
4 SA	0336	5.8		**19** SU	0321	5.7
	1003	0.4			0929	0.4
	1608	5.6			1542	5.6
	2204	0.8			2134	0.8
5 SU	0419	5.7		**20** M	0356	5.8
	1038	0.5			1008	0.4
	1649	5.4			1620	5.6
	2235	1.0			2211	0.8
6 M	0500	5.5		**21** TU	0434	5.8
	1106	0.8			1046	0.5
	1729	5.2			1700	5.6
	2259	1.2			2244	0.9
7 TU	0541	5.3		**22** W	0515	5.7
	1124	1.1			1122	0.7
	1809	5.0			1742	5.4
	2323	1.4			2314	1.1
8 W	0623	5.1		**23** TH	0600	5.5
	1145	1.4			1157	1.1
	1851	4.8			1829	5.2
	2358	1.7			2353	1.4
9 TH	0708	4.8		**24** F	0652	5.2
	1221	1.7			1241	1.4
	1938	4.6 ◐			1923	4.9 ◐
10 F	0047	2.0		**25** SA	0059	1.7
	0759	4.5			0756	4.9
	1314	2.1			1355	1.8
	2030	4.4			2031	4.7
11 SA	0202	2.3		**26** SU	0241	1.9
	0857	4.3			0919	4.7
	1434	2.3			1534	2.0
	2130	4.3			2153	4.7
12 SU	0347	2.3		**27** M	0427	1.8
	1001	4.2			1043	4.7
	1620	2.3			1700	1.9
	2235	4.4			2310	4.9
13 M	0508	2.1		**28** TU	0549	1.5
	1112	4.3			1157	5.0
	1728	2.1			1806	1.6
	2345	4.6				
14 TU	0604	1.8		**29** W	0016	5.1
	1221	4.6			0651	1.1
	1817	1.9			1258	5.2
					1858	1.4
15 W	0045	4.8		**30** TH	0110	5.4
	0649	1.5			0741	0.8
	1313	4.9			1345	5.4
	1858	1.6			1942	1.1
				31 F	0154	5.6
					0823	0.6
					1426	5.5
					2023	0.9 ○

Chart Datum: 2·90 metres below Ordnance Datum (Newlyn)
HAT is 6·3 metres above Chart Datum

SCOTLAND – LEITH

LAT 55°59'N   LONG 3°11'W

TIMES AND HEIGHTS OF HIGH AND LOW WATERS

2012

SEPTEMBER

#	Time m	#	Time m
1 SA	0235 5.7 / 0900 0.5 / 1504 5.6 / 2100 0.8	**16** SU	0217 5.7 / 0823 0.5 / 1438 5.7 / ● 2030 0.8
2 SU	0314 5.7 / 0935 0.5 / 1542 5.5 / 2134 0.8	**17** M	0253 5.9 / 0904 0.3 / 1515 5.8 / 2111 0.6
3 M	0353 5.7 / 1004 0.6 / 1619 5.4 / 2203 0.9	**18** TU	0331 6.0 / 0945 0.3 / 1554 5.8 / 2151 0.6
4 TU	0430 5.5 / 1025 0.9 / 1654 5.2 / 2225 1.1	**19** W	0412 5.9 / 1025 0.5 / 1636 5.7 / 2230 0.8
5 W	0507 5.3 / 1039 1.1 / 1731 5.1 / 2246 1.3	**20** TH	0456 5.8 / 1103 0.8 / 1720 5.5 / 2308 1.0
6 TH	0545 5.1 / 1100 1.4 / 1809 4.9 / 2315 1.6	**21** F	0544 5.5 / 1142 1.2 / 1808 5.3 / 2354 1.3
7 F	0627 4.8 / 1132 1.7 / 1852 4.6 / 2357 1.9	**22** SA	0640 5.2 / 1232 1.6 / 1904 5.0 / ●
8 SA	0715 4.5 / 1217 2.1 / 1943 4.4 / ◐	**23** SU	0105 1.7 / 0749 4.9 / 1349 2.0 / 2017 4.7
9 SU	0102 2.2 / 0812 4.3 / 1334 2.4 / 2044 4.3	**24** M	0246 1.8 / 0913 4.7 / 1526 2.2 / 2141 4.7
10 M	0244 2.4 / 0917 4.2 / 1533 2.5 / 2152 4.3	**25** TU	0427 1.7 / 1033 4.7 / 1648 2.0 / 2257 4.9
11 TU	0439 2.2 / 1027 4.3 / 1700 2.3 / 2304 4.5	**26** W	0542 1.4 / 1146 5.0 / 1749 1.5
12 W	0539 1.9 / 1140 4.5 / 1752 2.0	**27** TH	0001 5.1 / 0638 1.1 / 1244 5.2 / 1838 1.5
13 TH	0009 4.8 / 0624 1.5 / 1238 4.9 / 1833 1.6	**28** F	0053 5.2 / 0722 0.9 / 1328 5.4 / 1919 1.2
14 F	0059 5.1 / 0705 1.1 / 1322 5.2 / 1912 1.3	**29** SA	0136 5.2 / 0759 0.8 / 1406 5.5 / 1956 1.0
15 SA	0140 5.4 / 0744 0.8 / 1401 5.5 / 1950 1.0	**30** SU	0214 5.6 / 0832 0.7 / 1441 5.5 / ○ 2031 0.9

OCTOBER

#	Time m	#	Time m
1 M	0251 5.6 / 0901 0.7 / 1515 5.5 / 2104 0.9	**16** TU	0226 5.9 / 0837 0.4 / 1449 5.9 / 2049 0.6
2 TU	0327 5.5 / 0926 0.9 / 1549 5.4 / 2133 1.0	**17** W	0309 6.1 / 0921 0.4 / 1530 5.9 / 2135 0.6
3 W	0403 5.4 / 0946 1.0 / 1622 5.3 / 2157 1.1	**18** TH	0353 6.0 / 1006 0.6 / 1614 5.8 / 2222 0.7
4 TH	0438 5.3 / 1003 1.2 / 1656 5.1 / 2220 1.3	**19** F	0441 5.9 / 1049 0.9 / 1700 5.6 / 2310 0.9
5 F	0515 5.1 / 1026 1.5 / 1732 5.0 / 2247 1.5	**20** SA	0533 5.6 / 1135 1.3 / 1751 5.4
6 SA	0555 4.9 / 1055 1.7 / 1813 4.8 / 2324 1.8	**21** SU	0003 1.2 / 0631 5.2 / 1228 1.7 / 1850 5.1
7 SU	0640 4.6 / 1134 2.1 / 1901 4.6	**22** M	0110 1.5 / 0741 4.9 / 1338 2.1 / ◑ 2005 4.9
8 M	0022 2.1 / 0733 4.4 / 1240 2.4 / ◑ 1958 4.6	**23** TU	0239 1.7 / 0858 4.8 / 1504 2.2 / 2123 4.8
9 TU	0148 2.3 / 0835 4.3 / 1430 2.6 / 2108 4.4	**24** W	0407 1.6 / 1012 4.8 / 1619 2.1 / 2234 4.9
10 W	0343 2.2 / 0945 4.4 / 1616 2.4 / 2220 4.5	**25** TH	0518 1.5 / 1121 4.9 / 1720 1.9 / 2336 5.1
11 TH	0458 1.9 / 1055 4.6 / 1715 2.1 / 2326 4.8	**26** F	0613 1.3 / 1218 5.1 / 1810 1.7
12 F	0548 1.5 / 1156 4.9 / 1800 1.7	**27** SA	0029 5.2 / 0655 1.2 / 1304 5.2 / 1850 1.4
13 SA	0020 5.1 / 0630 1.2 / 1246 5.3 / 1841 1.4	**28** SU	0114 5.3 / 0729 1.1 / 1342 5.3 / 1927 1.2
14 SU	0105 5.4 / 0712 0.8 / 1329 5.6 / 1921 1.0	**29** M	0153 5.4 / 0758 1.1 / 1417 5.4 / ○ 2003 1.0
15 M	0146 5.7 / 0754 0.6 / 1409 5.8 / ● 2004 0.8	**30** TU	0230 5.4 / 0824 1.1 / 1450 5.4 / 2037 1.0
		31 W	0305 5.4 / 0849 1.1 / 1522 5.4 / 2108 1.1

NOVEMBER

#	Time m	#	Time m
1 TH	0339 5.3 / 0914 1.2 / 1554 5.3 / 2136 1.2	**16** F	0339 6.0 / 0951 0.7 / 1557 5.9 / 2218 0.6
2 F	0414 5.2 / 0939 1.3 / 1628 5.2 / 2204 1.3	**17** SA	0430 5.9 / 1038 1.0 / 1645 5.7 / 2308 0.8
3 SA	0451 5.1 / 1005 1.5 / 1703 5.1 / 2234 1.5	**18** SU	0523 5.6 / 1125 1.3 / 1738 5.5
4 SU	0530 4.9 / 1035 1.7 / 1742 4.9 / 2310 1.7	**19** M	0000 1.0 / 0621 5.3 / 1215 1.7 / 1836 5.3
5 M	0613 4.8 / 1110 2.0 / 1826 4.7 / 2359 1.9	**20** TU	0059 1.3 / 0725 5.0 / 1312 2.0 / ◐ 1945 5.0
6 TU	0701 4.6 / 1202 2.3 / 1918 4.6	**21** W	0210 1.6 / 0833 4.8 / 1423 2.2 / 2055 4.9
7 W	0107 2.0 / 0757 4.5 / 1332 2.4 / ◑ 2020 4.5	**22** TH	0327 1.7 / 0939 4.8 / 1535 2.2 / 2200 4.9
8 TH	0232 2.1 / 0902 4.5 / 1511 2.4 / 2132 4.6	**23** F	0437 1.7 / 1044 4.8 / 1639 2.1 / 2302 4.9
9 F	0358 1.9 / 1011 4.7 / 1625 2.1 / 2240 4.8	**24** SA	0536 1.7 / 1143 4.9 / 1734 1.9 / 2359 5.0
10 SA	0500 1.6 / 1114 4.9 / 1720 1.8 / 2339 5.1	**25** SU	0621 1.6 / 1234 5.0 / 1820 1.7
11 SU	0551 1.3 / 1209 5.2 / 1807 1.5	**26** M	0049 5.1 / 0654 1.5 / 1317 5.2 / 1901 1.5
12 M	0031 5.4 / 0638 1.0 / 1258 5.5 / 1853 1.1	**27** TU	0132 5.1 / 0722 1.4 / 1354 5.3 / 1939 1.3
13 TU	0119 5.7 / 0725 0.7 / 1343 5.8 / ● 1942 0.8	**28** W	0211 5.2 / 0751 1.3 / 1428 5.3 / ○ 2014 1.2
14 W	0204 5.9 / 0814 0.6 / 1426 5.9 / 2034 0.6	**29** TH	0246 5.2 / 0821 1.3 / 1501 5.4 / 2048 1.1
15 TH	0251 6.0 / 0903 0.6 / 1511 6.0 / 2126 0.5	**30** F	0320 5.3 / 0852 1.3 / 1533 5.3 / 2121 1.1

DECEMBER

#	Time m	#	Time m
1 SA	0355 5.2 / 0923 1.4 / 1607 5.3 / 2153 1.2	**16** SU	0419 5.9 / 1026 0.9 / 1632 5.8 / 2300 0.5
2 SU	0431 5.2 / 0955 1.5 / 1642 5.2 / 2227 1.3	**17** M	0510 5.9 / 1110 1.1 / 1723 5.7 / 2347 0.8
3 M	0508 5.1 / 1026 1.6 / 1719 5.1 / 2303 1.4	**18** TU	0603 5.4 / 1152 1.4 / 1817 5.4
4 TU	0549 5.0 / 1058 1.8 / 1759 5.0 / 2344 1.6	**19** W	0033 1.1 / 0658 5.1 / 1234 1.7 / 1915 5.2
5 W	0633 4.8 / 1137 2.0 / 1844 4.8	**20** TH	0122 1.5 / 0757 4.9 / 1324 2.0 / ◐ 2017 4.9
6 TH	0033 1.7 / 0722 4.7 / 1234 2.2 / ◑ 1936 4.8	**21** F	0220 1.8 / 0856 4.7 / 1431 2.2 / 2118 4.8
7 F	0137 1.8 / 0820 4.7 / 1400 2.2 / 2039 4.7	**22** SA	0331 2.0 / 0956 4.6 / 1546 2.2 / 2219 4.7
8 SA	0253 1.8 / 0926 4.7 / 1526 2.2 / 2153 4.8	**23** SU	0439 2.0 / 1057 4.6 / 1653 2.1 / 2322 4.6
9 SU	0408 1.6 / 1034 4.9 / 1637 1.9 / 2301 5.0	**24** M	0534 2.0 / 1157 4.7 / 1751 1.9
10 M	0512 1.4 / 1135 5.1 / 1736 1.6	**25** TU	0021 4.7 / 0616 1.9 / 1250 4.9 / 1838 1.7
11 TU	0002 5.3 / 0609 1.2 / 1231 5.4 / 1832 1.3	**26** W	0111 4.9 / 0652 1.7 / 1333 5.1 / 1919 1.5
12 W	0057 5.5 / 0705 1.0 / 1321 5.6 / 1930 1.0	**27** TH	0153 5.0 / 0727 1.6 / 1410 5.2 / 1956 1.3
13 TH	0149 5.8 / 0759 0.8 / 1408 5.8 / ● 2027 0.7	**28** F	0230 5.1 / 0801 1.4 / 1445 5.3 / ○ 2032 1.2
14 F	0239 5.9 / 0850 0.8 / 1456 5.9 / 2121 0.5	**29** SA	0304 5.2 / 0836 1.3 / 1518 5.4 / 2107 1.1
15 SA	0328 6.0 / 0939 0.8 / 1543 5.9 / 2212 0.4	**30** SU	0337 5.3 / 0911 1.3 / 1551 5.4 / 2143 1.0
		31 M	0412 5.3 / 0945 1.3 / 1625 5.3 / 2219 1.0

Chart Datum: 2·90 metres below Ordnance Datum (Newlyn)
HAT is 6·3 metres above Chart Datum

TIDES

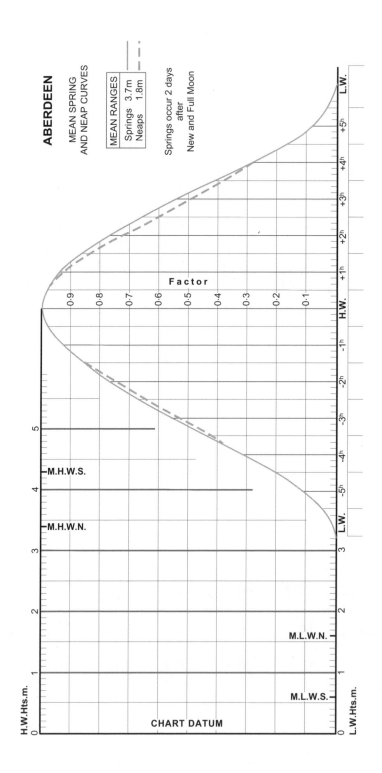

ABERDEEN

MEAN SPRING
AND NEAP CURVES

MEAN RANGES	
Springs	3.7m
Neaps	1.8m

Springs occur 2 days
after
New and Full Moon

TIME ZONE (UT)
For Summer Time add ONE hour in **non-shaded areas**

SCOTLAND – ABERDEEN
LAT 57°09′N   LONG 2°05′W
TIMES AND HEIGHTS OF HIGH AND LOW WATERS

Dates in amber are **SPRINGS**
Dates in yellow are **NEAPS**

2012

JANUARY

Day	Time	m	Day	Time	m
1 SU ◐	0007 / 0642 / 1218 / 1845	1.4 / 3.5 / 1.8 / 3.6	**16** M	0612 / 1156 / 1826	3.8 / 1.5 / 4.0
2 M	0100 / 0737 / 1323 / 1946	1.6 / 3.4 / 2.0 / 3.5	**17** TU	0046 / 0714 / 1307 / 1936	1.2 / 3.7 / 1.6 / 3.8
3 TU	0202 / 0841 / 1436 / 2055	1.8 / 3.4 / 2.0 / 3.4	**18** W	0156 / 0824 / 1428 / 2055	1.4 / 3.6 / 1.6 / 3.8
4 W	0314 / 0948 / 1555 / 2207	1.8 / 3.5 / 1.9 / 3.5	**19** TH	0315 / 0939 / 1556 / 2217	1.5 / 3.7 / 1.5 / 3.8
5 TH	0422 / 1046 / 1654 / 2306	1.7 / 3.6 / 1.7 / 3.6	**20** F	0432 / 1048 / 1708 / 2326	1.4 / 3.9 / 1.3 / 4.0
6 F	0512 / 1133 / 1740 / 2354	1.6 / 3.8 / 1.5 / 3.7	**21** SA	0532 / 1145 / 1804	1.3 / 4.1 / 1.0
7 SA	0552 / 1213 / 1819	1.5 / 3.9 / 1.3	**22** SU	0023 / 0621 / 1234 / 1852	4.1 / 1.2 / 4.2 / 0.8
8 SU	0035 / 0629 / 1250 / 1855	3.9 / 1.4 / 4.1 / 1.1	**23** M ●	0111 / 0705 / 1317 / 1936	4.2 / 1.0 / 4.4 / 0.6
9 M ○	0114 / 0705 / 1325 / 1933	4.0 / 1.2 / 4.2 / 0.9	**24** TU	0154 / 0744 / 1357 / 2016	4.3 / 1.0 / 4.5 / 0.6
10 TU	0151 / 0741 / 1359 / 2010	4.1 / 1.1 / 4.3 / 0.8	**25** W	0234 / 0821 / 1435 / 2053	4.2 / 0.9 / 4.5 / 0.6
11 W	0228 / 0818 / 1434 / 2049	4.2 / 1.0 / 4.4 / 0.7	**26** TH	0312 / 0856 / 1512 / 2128	4.2 / 1.0 / 4.4 / 0.7
12 TH	0306 / 0855 / 1511 / 2128	4.2 / 1.0 / 4.4 / 0.7	**27** F	0348 / 0930 / 1549 / 2202	4.0 / 1.1 / 4.3 / 0.9
13 F	0346 / 0933 / 1551 / 2209	4.2 / 1.1 / 4.4 / 0.7	**28** SA	0425 / 1004 / 1626 / 2235	3.9 / 1.2 / 4.1 / 1.1
14 SA	0429 / 1014 / 1635 / 2254	4.1 / 1.2 / 4.3 / 0.9	**29** SU	0503 / 1040 / 1706 / 2312	3.7 / 1.4 / 3.9 / 1.3
15 SU	0517 / 1100 / 1725 / 2345	3.9 / 1.3 / 4.1 / 1.0	**30** M	0545 / 1121 / 1752 / 2356	3.6 / 1.6 / 3.7 / 1.6
			31 TU ◐	0635 / 1215 / 1849	3.4 / 1.8 / 3.5

FEBRUARY

Day	Time	m	Day	Time	m
1 W	0052 / 0734 / 1329 / 1956	1.8 / 3.3 / 2.0 / 3.3	**16** TH	0133 / 0759 / 1413 / 2047	1.6 / 3.5 / 1.6 / 3.6
2 TH	0207 / 0845 / 1457 / 2117	1.9 / 3.3 / 2.0 / 3.3	**17** F	0302 / 0921 / 1553 / 2217	1.7 / 3.5 / 1.5 / 3.6
3 F	0334 / 1002 / 1622 / 2235	1.9 / 3.4 / 1.8 / 3.4	**18** SA	0426 / 1038 / 1704 / 2326	1.6 / 3.7 / 1.2 / 3.8
4 SA	0444 / 1103 / 1715 / 2331	1.8 / 3.6 / 1.5 / 3.6	**19** SU	0524 / 1137 / 1757	1.4 / 3.9 / 1.0
5 SU	0530 / 1149 / 1757	1.6 / 3.8 / 1.3	**20** M	0017 / 0610 / 1223 / 1840	4.0 / 1.2 / 4.1 / 0.8
6 M	0015 / 0609 / 1228 / 1835	3.8 / 1.3 / 4.0 / 1.0	**21** TU ●	0100 / 0650 / 1303 / 1919	4.1 / 1.0 / 4.3 / 0.6
7 TU ○	0054 / 0646 / 1304 / 1913	4.0 / 1.1 / 4.2 / 0.7	**22** W	0137 / 0726 / 1339 / 1954	4.1 / 0.9 / 4.4 / 0.6
8 W	0131 / 0723 / 1339 / 1951	4.2 / 0.9 / 4.4 / 0.5	**23** TH	0210 / 0759 / 1413 / 2027	4.1 / 0.8 / 4.4 / 0.6
9 TH	0208 / 0800 / 1415 / 2030	4.3 / 0.8 / 4.5 / 0.4	**24** F	0243 / 0831 / 1446 / 2057	4.1 / 0.8 / 4.3 / 0.7
10 F	0245 / 0837 / 1453 / 2108	4.3 / 0.7 / 4.5 / 0.4	**25** SA	0315 / 0902 / 1519 / 2126	4.0 / 0.9 / 4.2 / 0.8
11 SA	0324 / 0914 / 1533 / 2148	4.3 / 0.8 / 4.5 / 0.5	**26** SU	0346 / 0932 / 1553 / 2156	3.9 / 1.0 / 4.1 / 1.0
12 SU	0405 / 0954 / 1616 / 2231	4.2 / 1.0 / 4.4 / 0.7	**27** M	0419 / 1005 / 1630 / 2228	3.8 / 1.2 / 3.9 / 1.3
13 M	0450 / 1039 / 1706 / 2320	4.0 / 1.0 / 4.2 / 1.0	**28** TU	0455 / 1041 / 1712 / 2305	3.6 / 1.4 / 3.7 / 1.5
14 TU ◐	0542 / 1133 / 1807	3.8 / 1.3 / 3.9	**29** W	0540 / 1127 / 1804 / 2353	3.5 / 1.6 / 3.4 / 1.7
15 W	0019 / 0645 / 1244 / 1921	1.3 / 3.6 / 1.5 / 3.7			

MARCH

Day	Time	m	Day	Time	m
1 TH ◐	0637 / 1231 / 1911	3.3 / 1.8 / 3.3	**16** F	0117 / 0739 / 1407 / 2042	1.7 / 3.5 / 1.5 / 3.5
2 F	0105 / 0748 / 1400 / 2029	1.9 / 3.2 / 1.9 / 3.2	**17** SA	0251 / 0904 / 1544 / 2211	1.8 / 3.5 / 1.3 / 3.5
3 SA	0240 / 0908 / 1536 / 2155	2.0 / 3.3 / 1.8 / 3.3	**18** SU	0413 / 1023 / 1651 / 2314	1.6 / 3.6 / 1.1 / 3.7
4 SU	0409 / 1024 / 1642 / 2300	1.8 / 3.4 / 1.5 / 3.5	**19** M	0508 / 1120 / 1740	1.4 / 3.8 / 0.9
5 M	0502 / 1117 / 1728 / 2347	1.6 / 3.7 / 1.2 / 3.7	**20** TU	0001 / 0551 / 1205 / 1820	3.8 / 1.2 / 4.0 / 0.8
6 TU	0544 / 1159 / 1808	1.3 / 3.9 / 0.9	**21** W	0039 / 0629 / 1243 / 1855	4.0 / 1.0 / 4.1 / 0.7
7 W	0027 / 0622 / 1237 / 1847	4.0 / 1.0 / 4.2 / 0.6	**22** TH ●	0113 / 0703 / 1316 / 1927	4.0 / 0.9 / 4.2 / 0.7
8 TH ○	0105 / 0700 / 1314 / 1926	4.2 / 0.8 / 4.4 / 0.3	**23** F	0143 / 0735 / 1349 / 1957	4.1 / 0.8 / 4.2 / 0.7
9 F	0143 / 0738 / 1352 / 2006	4.4 / 0.6 / 4.6 / 0.2	**24** SA	0213 / 0806 / 1421 / 2026	4.1 / 0.8 / 4.2 / 0.8
10 SA	0221 / 0816 / 1432 / 2046	4.4 / 0.5 / 4.6 / 0.3	**25** SU	0243 / 0836 / 1453 / 2054	4.0 / 0.8 / 4.1 / 0.9
11 SU	0300 / 0855 / 1515 / 2127	4.4 / 0.5 / 4.6 / 0.4	**26** M	0313 / 0906 / 1527 / 2123	4.0 / 0.9 / 4.0 / 1.0
12 M	0342 / 0937 / 1601 / 2210	4.3 / 0.7 / 4.4 / 0.7	**27** TU	0344 / 0938 / 1603 / 2154	3.9 / 1.1 / 3.8 / 1.2
13 TU	0427 / 1024 / 1654 / 2300	4.1 / 0.9 / 4.2 / 1.0	**28** W	0418 / 1014 / 1644 / 2229	3.7 / 1.2 / 3.6 / 1.4
14 W	0519 / 1121 / 1758	3.8 / 1.1 / 3.8	**29** TH	0459 / 1057 / 1734 / 2314	3.6 / 1.4 / 3.4 / 1.7
15 TH ◐	0000 / 0623 / 1235 / 1914	1.4 / 3.6 / 1.3 / 3.6	**30** F	0551 / 1155 / 1838	3.4 / 1.6 / 3.3
			31 SA	0019 / 0700 / 1315 / 1950	1.9 / 3.3 / 1.7 / 3.2

APRIL

Day	Time	m	Day	Time	m
1 SU	0151 / 0816 / 1443 / 2108	1.9 / 3.2 / 1.6 / 3.3	**16** M	0344 / 0955 / 1624 / 2248	1.6 / 3.6 / 1.1 / 3.6
2 M	0320 / 0932 / 1557 / 2220	1.8 / 3.4 / 1.4 / 3.5	**17** TU	0441 / 1053 / 1712 / 2334	1.5 / 3.7 / 1.0 / 3.7
3 TU	0424 / 1035 / 1651 / 2312	1.6 / 3.6 / 1.1 / 3.7	**18** W	0525 / 1139 / 1752	1.3 / 3.8 / 0.9
4 W	0511 / 1123 / 1736 / 2356	1.3 / 3.9 / 0.8 / 4.0	**19** TH	0011 / 0603 / 1217 / 1826	3.8 / 1.1 / 3.9 / 0.9
5 TH	0554 / 1206 / 1818	1.0 / 4.2 / 0.5	**20** F	0045 / 0638 / 1252 / 1858	3.9 / 1.0 / 4.0 / 0.8
6 F ○	0036 / 0634 / 1248 / 1900	4.2 / 0.7 / 4.4 / 0.3	**21** SA ●	0116 / 0711 / 1325 / 1928	4.0 / 0.9 / 4.0 / 0.8
7 SA	0116 / 0715 / 1330 / 1941	4.4 / 0.5 / 4.6 / 0.2	**22** SU	0146 / 0743 / 1358 / 1958	4.0 / 0.8 / 4.0 / 0.9
8 SU	0156 / 0757 / 1414 / 2024	4.4 / 0.4 / 4.6 / 0.3	**23** M	0215 / 0815 / 1432 / 2027	4.0 / 0.9 / 4.0 / 1.0
9 M	0237 / 0840 / 1500 / 2108	4.4 / 0.4 / 4.5 / 0.5	**24** TU	0246 / 0846 / 1506 / 2057	4.0 / 0.9 / 3.9 / 1.1
10 TU	0321 / 0926 / 1551 / 2154	4.3 / 0.5 / 4.3 / 0.8	**25** W	0317 / 0920 / 1543 / 2130	3.9 / 1.0 / 3.8 / 1.2
11 W	0408 / 1017 / 1648 / 2245	4.1 / 0.7 / 4.1 / 1.1	**26** TH	0352 / 0957 / 1624 / 2206	3.8 / 1.1 / 3.6 / 1.4
12 TH	0502 / 1116 / 1754 / 2346	3.9 / 0.9 / 3.8 / 1.4	**27** F	0432 / 1040 / 1712 / 2251	3.7 / 1.2 / 3.5 / 1.6
13 F ◐	0607 / 1228 / 1906	3.7 / 1.2 / 3.6	**28** SA	0520 / 1133 / 1811 / 2349	3.5 / 1.4 / 3.4 / 1.7
14 SA	0100 / 0719 / 1352 / 2026	1.7 / 3.5 / 1.3 / 3.4	**29** SU ◐	0623 / 1240 / 1917	3.4 / 1.4 / 3.3
15 SU	0226 / 0838 / 1519 / 2147	1.8 / 3.5 / 1.2 / 3.5	**30** M	0732 / 1356 / 2025	3.4 / 1.4 / 3.4

Chart Datum: 2·25 metres below Ordnance Datum (Newlyn)
HAT is 4·9 metres above Chart Datum

TIDES

TIME ZONE (UT) For Summer Time add ONE hour in **non-shaded areas**	**SCOTLAND – ABERDEEN** LAT 57°09′N LONG 2°05′W TIMES AND HEIGHTS OF HIGH AND LOW WATERS	Dates in amber are **SPRINGS** Dates in yellow are **NEAPS** **2012**

MAY

Time	m	Time	m
1 0229	1.7	**16** 0403	1.6
0841	3.4	1016	3.6
TU 1507	1.1	W 1636	1.2
2133	3.5	2258	3.6
2 0337	1.5	**17** 0453	1.4
0947	3.6	1106	3.7
W 1608	1.0	TH 1718	1.1
2233	3.7	2339	3.7
3 0434	1.3	**18** 0536	1.2
1045	3.9	1149	3.7
TH 1701	0.7	F 1755	1.1
2323	4.0		
4 0523	1.0	**19** 0015	3.8
1136	4.1	0613	1.1
F 1749	0.5	SA 1228	3.8
		1829	1.0
5 0007	4.2	**20** 0049	3.9
0609	0.7	0649	1.0
SA 1224	4.3	SU 1304	3.9
1835	0.4	● 1902	1.0
6 0051	4.4	**21** 0121	4.0
0655	0.5	0723	0.9
SU 1311	4.5	M 1340	3.9
○ 1920	0.4	1934	1.0
7 0134	4.4	**22** 0153	4.0
0741	0.4	0757	0.9
M 1359	4.5	TU 1415	3.9
2006	0.5	2006	1.1
8 0218	4.4	**23** 0225	4.0
0829	0.4	0831	0.9
TU 1450	4.4	W 1450	3.9
2052	0.6	2038	1.1
9 0304	4.3	**24** 0258	4.0
0918	0.4	0906	0.9
W 1544	4.3	TH 1528	3.8
2141	0.9	2113	1.2
10 0353	4.2	**25** 0333	3.9
1011	0.6	0944	1.0
TH 1642	4.0	F 1608	3.7
2232	1.1	2151	1.3
11 0448	4.0	**26** 0412	3.8
1108	0.8	1026	1.0
F 1743	3.8	SA 1654	3.6
2329	1.4	2234	1.4
12 0549	3.8	**27** 0457	3.7
1212	1.0	1114	1.1
SA 1847	3.6	SU 1746	3.5
◐		2325	1.5
13 0033	1.6	**28** 0552	3.6
0653	3.6	1211	1.2
SU 1321	1.2	M 1845	3.5
1954	3.5	◑	
14 0145	1.7	**29** 0029	1.6
0801	3.5	0654	3.6
M 1435	1.3	TU 1317	1.2
2105	3.4	1947	3.5
15 0259	1.7	**30** 0142	1.6
0913	3.5	0759	3.6
TU 1543	1.3	W 1423	1.1
2208	3.5	2051	3.6
		31 0252	1.5
		0906	3.7
		TH 1528	1.0
		2154	3.7

JUNE

Time	m	Time	m
1 0357	1.3	**16** 0507	1.4
1011	3.9	1120	3.6
F 1629	0.9	SA 1725	1.3
2252	3.9	2346	3.7
2 0456	1.1	**17** 0550	1.3
1111	4.1	1205	3.7
SA 1725	0.7	SU 1804	1.3
2343	4.1		
3 0551	0.8	**18** 0024	3.8
1206	4.2	0628	1.1
SU 1816	0.6	M 1245	3.8
		1839	1.2
4 0030	4.3	**19** 0100	3.9
0641	0.6	0705	1.0
M 1259	4.4	TU 1323	3.8
○ 1905	0.6	● 1914	1.1
5 0117	4.4	**20** 0134	4.0
0731	0.4	0740	0.9
TU 1350	4.4	W 1359	3.9
1953	0.6	1948	1.1
6 0203	4.4	**21** 0207	4.1
0821	0.4	0816	0.8
W 1442	4.4	TH 1435	3.9
2040	0.7	2023	1.1
7 0250	4.4	**22** 0241	4.1
0910	0.4	0852	0.8
TH 1535	4.2	F 1512	3.9
2126	0.9	2058	1.1
8 0339	4.3	**23** 0316	4.1
1000	0.5	0930	0.8
F 1628	4.1	SA 1551	3.9
2213	1.1	2135	1.1
9 0430	4.1	**24** 0354	4.0
1051	0.7	1010	0.8
SA 1724	3.9	SU 1633	3.8
2303	1.3	2215	1.2
10 0524	4.0	**25** 0436	4.0
1144	0.9	1054	0.9
SU 1815	3.7	M 1720	3.7
2356	1.5	2301	1.3
11 0619	3.8	**26** 0524	3.9
1239	1.1	1143	1.0
M 1912	3.5	TU 1813	3.7
◐		2355	1.4
12 0055	1.6	**27** 0621	3.8
0718	3.6	1241	1.1
TU 1338	1.2	W 1912	3.6
2012	3.4	◑	
13 0201	1.7	**28** 0101	1.5
0821	3.5	0725	3.7
W 1443	1.4	TH 1346	1.1
2116	3.4	2015	3.6
14 0312	1.7	**29** 0214	1.5
0929	3.5	0835	3.7
TH 1548	1.5	F 1455	1.1
2214	3.5	2122	3.7
15 0417	1.6	**30** 0328	1.4
1029	3.5	0948	3.8
F 1642	1.4	SA 1605	1.1
2304	3.6	2227	3.8

JULY

Time	m	Time	m
1 0439	1.2	**16** 0528	1.4
1057	3.9	1142	3.6
SU 1709	1.0	M 1741	1.5
2325	4.0		
2 0541	0.9	**17** 0001	3.8
1158	4.1	0608	1.2
M 1805	0.9	TU 1226	3.7
		1819	1.3
3 0017	4.2	**18** 0039	3.9
0634	0.7	0645	1.0
TU 1253	4.2	W 1304	3.9
○ 1854	0.8	1854	1.2
4 0105	4.3	**19** 0114	4.1
0724	0.5	0721	0.8
W 1343	4.3	TH 1340	4.0
1941	0.8	● 1929	1.1
5 0151	4.4	**20** 0148	4.2
0811	0.4	0757	0.7
TH 1432	4.3	F 1416	4.0
2025	0.8	2005	1.0
6 0236	4.4	**21** 0222	4.2
0857	0.4	0834	0.6
F 1519	4.2	SA 1452	4.1
2107	0.9	2040	0.9
7 0321	4.4	**22** 0257	4.2
0941	0.5	0911	0.6
SA 1604	4.1	SU 1529	4.1
2148	1.0	2116	0.9
8 0405	4.3	**23** 0334	4.3
1024	0.6	0949	0.6
SU 1650	3.9	M 1609	4.0
2230	1.2	2154	1.0
9 0451	4.1	**24** 0414	4.2
1107	0.9	1030	0.7
M 1736	3.7	TU 1652	3.9
2314	1.3	2236	1.1
10 0539	3.9	**25** 0500	4.1
1151	1.1	1116	0.9
TU 1825	3.6	W 1742	3.8
		2327	1.3
11 0004	1.5	**26** 0555	4.0
0630	3.7	1211	1.1
W 1241	1.4	TH 1840	3.7
◐ 1917	3.4	◐	
12 0103	1.7	**27** 0030	1.4
0728	3.5	0700	3.8
TH 1339	1.6	F 1317	1.3
2016	3.4	1946	3.6
13 0212	1.8	**28** 0148	1.5
0834	3.4	0816	3.7
F 1447	1.7	SA 1432	1.4
2123	3.4	2058	3.6
14 0332	1.8	**29** 0313	1.6
0947	3.4	0937	3.7
SA 1601	1.7	SU 1553	1.4
2225	3.5	2211	3.8
15 0439	1.6	**30** 0434	1.2
1051	3.4	1054	3.9
SU 1657	1.6	M 1702	1.2
2317	3.6	2315	4.0
		31 0536	0.9
		1155	4.0
		TU 1757	1.1

AUGUST

Time	m	Time	m
1 0008	4.2	**16** 0013	4.0
0628	0.7	0621	1.0
W 1247	4.2	TH 1240	3.9
1843	0.9	1831	1.2
2 0054	4.3	**17** 0049	4.1
0714	0.5	0657	0.8
TH 1333	4.3	F 1316	4.1
○ 1926	0.8	● 1907	1.0
3 0137	4.5	**18** 0124	4.3
0757	0.4	0733	0.6
F 1415	4.3	SA 1351	4.2
2005	0.8	1942	0.8
4 0217	4.5	**19** 0158	4.4
0837	0.4	0810	0.5
SA 1455	4.2	SU 1427	4.3
2043	0.8	2018	0.8
5 0257	4.4	**20** 0234	4.5
0914	0.5	0847	0.4
SU 1534	4.1	M 1504	4.3
2119	0.9	2054	0.8
6 0336	4.3	**21** 0312	4.5
0950	0.7	0926	0.5
M 1612	4.0	TU 1543	4.2
2155	1.1	2133	0.9
7 0415	4.1	**22** 0353	4.4
1025	0.9	1006	0.7
TU 1652	3.8	W 1625	4.1
2232	1.3	2215	1.0
8 0457	3.9	**23** 0440	4.2
1102	1.2	1051	0.9
W 1734	3.6	TH 1714	3.9
2314	1.5	2306	1.2
9 0543	3.7	**24** 0537	4.0
1144	1.5	1147	1.2
TH 1822	3.5	F 1813	3.7
◐		◐	
10 0006	1.7	**25** 0011	1.4
0638	3.5	0647	3.8
F 1238	1.7	SA 1257	1.5
1919	3.4	1923	3.6
11 0115	1.8	**26** 0135	1.5
0743	3.3	0808	3.6
SA 1348	1.9	SU 1420	1.6
2026	3.3	2042	3.6
12 0240	1.9	**27** 0311	1.5
0901	3.3	0937	3.7
SU 1514	1.9	M 1549	1.6
2142	3.4	2201	3.8
13 0408	1.7	**28** 0432	1.2
1019	3.4	1053	3.8
M 1629	1.8	TU 1655	1.4
2245	3.6	2306	4.0
14 0503	1.5	**29** 0529	0.9
1117	3.5	1150	4.0
TU 1717	1.6	W 1745	1.2
2334	3.8	2356	4.2
15 0545	1.2	**30** 0617	0.7
1202	3.7	1235	4.1
W 1756	1.4	TH 1828	1.0
		31 0039	4.3
		0658	0.6
		F 1316	4.2
		○ 1906	0.9

Chart Datum: 2·25 metres below Ordnance Datum (Newlyn)
HAT is 4·9 metres above Chart Datum

SCOTLAND – ABERDEEN

LAT 57°09'N   LONG 2°05'W

TIMES AND HEIGHTS OF HIGH AND LOW WATERS

Dates in amber are **SPRINGS**
Dates in yellow are **NEAPS**

2012

SEPTEMBER

Time	m	Time	m
1 0118	4.4	**16** 0055	4.4
0735	0.5	0705	0.5
SA 1352	4.3	SU 1323	4.4
1942	0.8	○ 1917	0.8
2 0154	4.5	**17** 0132	4.6
0810	0.5	0743	0.4
SU 1426	4.2	M 1359	4.6
2016	0.8	1954	0.7
3 0230	4.4	**18** 0210	4.6
0843	0.6	0822	0.4
M 1500	4.2	TU 1437	4.6
2049	0.9	2033	0.7
4 0305	4.3	**19** 0251	4.6
0914	0.8	0902	0.5
TU 1533	4.0	W 1518	4.4
2122	1.0	2114	0.7
5 0341	4.2	**20** 0336	4.5
0944	1.0	0944	0.7
W 1608	3.9	TH 1601	4.2
2155	1.2	2159	0.9
6 0419	3.9	**21** 0426	4.3
1017	1.3	1032	1.0
TH 1645	3.8	F 1651	4.0
2233	1.4	2254	1.1
7 0502	3.7	**22** 0527	4.0
1054	1.5	1129	1.4
F 1729	3.6	SA 1753	3.8
2319	1.6	☾	
8 0555	3.5	**23** 0004	1.3
1142	1.8	0641	3.7
SA 1826	3.4	SU 1243	1.6
☽		1906	3.4
9 0023	1.8	**24** 0130	1.5
0700	3.3	0804	3.6
SU 1251	2.0	M 1411	1.8
1934	3.3	2027	3.7
10 0148	1.9	**25** 0306	1.4
0816	3.3	0934	3.7
M 1422	2.0	TU 1537	1.7
2050	3.4	2148	3.8
11 0323	1.8	**26** 0420	1.2
0939	3.5	1044	3.8
TU 1552	1.9	W 1640	1.5
2205	3.5	2251	4.0
12 0429	1.5	**27** 0514	1.0
1045	3.5	1135	4.0
W 1647	1.7	TH 1727	1.3
2300	3.7	2339	4.2
13 0514	1.3	**28** 0558	0.8
1132	3.8	1216	4.1
TH 1728	1.4	F 1808	1.1
2342	4.0		
14 0552	1.0	**29** 0019	4.3
1210	4.0	0635	0.7
F 1805	1.2	SA 1253	4.2
		1844	1.0
15 0019	4.2	**30** 0056	4.4
0628	0.7	0709	0.7
SA 1247	4.2	SU 1325	4.2
1840	0.9	○ 1918	0.9

OCTOBER

Time	m	Time	m
1 0130	4.4	**16** 0107	4.6
0741	0.7	0717	0.4
M 1357	4.2	TU 1333	4.6
1951	0.9	1933	0.6
2 0204	4.3	**17** 0150	4.7
0811	0.8	0759	0.4
TU 1428	4.2	W 1414	4.6
2023	0.9	2016	0.6
3 0238	4.3	**18** 0235	4.7
0840	1.0	0842	0.6
W 1459	4.1	TH 1456	4.5
2054	1.0	2101	0.7
4 0313	4.1	**19** 0323	4.5
0909	1.1	0927	0.8
TH 1531	4.0	F 1542	4.4
2127	1.2	2151	0.8
5 0350	3.9	**20** 0418	4.3
0941	1.3	1017	1.1
F 1606	3.9	SA 1634	4.2
2203	1.3	2248	1.0
6 0431	3.8	**21** 0523	4.0
1016	1.5	1116	1.5
SA 1646	3.7	SU 1737	3.9
2247	1.5	2358	1.2
7 0521	3.6	**22** 0635	3.8
1100	1.8	1228	1.7
SU 1738	3.6	M 1849	3.8
2343	1.7	☾	
8 0624	3.4	**23** 0118	1.4
1201	2.0	0751	3.7
M 1846	3.4	TU 1349	1.8
☽		2004	3.7
9 0100	1.8	**24** 0243	1.4
0735	3.3	0913	3.7
TU 1329	2.1	W 1510	1.8
1958	3.4	2122	3.8
10 0226	1.8	**25** 0356	1.2
0850	3.4	1020	3.8
W 1458	2.0	TH 1614	1.6
2112	3.5	2226	3.9
11 0340	1.6	**26** 0449	1.1
1001	3.6	1111	3.9
TH 1604	1.8	F 1703	1.4
2215	3.7	2316	4.0
12 0433	1.3	**27** 0532	1.0
1045	3.8	1144	4.0
F 1652	1.5	SA 1744	1.3
2304	4.0	2357	4.1
13 0516	1.0	**28** 0609	1.0
1136	4.1	1227	4.1
SA 1733	1.2	SU 1821	1.1
2345	4.2		
14 0557	0.7	**29** 0033	4.2
1215	4.3	0641	1.0
SU 1813	1.0	M 1259	4.2
		○ 1855	1.0
15 0026	4.5	**30** 0108	4.2
0636	0.5	0713	1.0
M 1254	4.5	TU 1330	4.2
● 1852	0.7	1929	1.0
		31 0143	4.2
		0743	1.0
		W 1401	4.2
		2001	1.0

NOVEMBER

Time	m	Time	m
1 0217	4.2	**16** 0223	4.6
0813	1.1	0827	0.7
TH 1431	4.2	F 1439	4.6
2033	1.1	2053	0.6
2 0251	4.1	**17** 0315	4.5
0843	1.2	0914	0.9
F 1503	4.1	SA 1526	4.5
2107	1.2	2144	0.7
3 0328	3.9	**18** 0411	4.3
0915	1.4	1004	1.2
SA 1537	4.0	SU 1619	4.3
2143	1.3	2241	0.9
4 0408	3.8	**19** 0512	4.1
0950	1.5	1100	1.4
SU 1616	3.9	M 1719	4.1
2225	1.4	2343	1.1
5 0455	3.7	**20** 0616	3.9
1032	1.7	1202	1.7
M 1702	3.7	TU 1824	3.9
2315	1.5	☾	
6 0551	3.5	**21** 0050	1.3
1125	1.9	0723	3.7
TU 1801	3.6	W 1312	1.8
		1931	3.8
7 0018	1.6	**22** 0202	1.4
0655	3.4	0834	3.6
W 1237	2.0	TH 1426	1.8
☽ 1909	3.5	2043	3.8
8 0132	1.6	**23** 0315	1.4
0801	3.5	0943	3.7
TH 1359	2.0	F 1537	1.8
2017	3.6	2151	3.8
9 0242	1.5	**24** 0415	1.4
0908	3.6	1038	3.8
F 1510	1.8	SA 1634	1.6
2122	3.7	2247	3.9
10 0344	1.3	**25** 0502	1.3
1009	3.8	1122	3.9
SA 1609	1.6	SU 1719	1.5
2221	4.0	2333	3.9
11 0437	1.1	**26** 0541	1.3
1100	4.1	1200	4.0
SU 1700	1.3	M 1759	1.3
2312	4.2		
12 0525	0.8	**27** 0013	4.0
1145	4.3	0616	1.2
M 1746	1.0	TU 1235	4.1
		1836	1.2
13 0000	4.4	**28** 0050	4.1
0610	0.7	0649	1.2
TU 1228	4.5	W 1308	4.2
● 1831	0.8	○ 1911	1.1
14 0047	4.6	**29** 0126	4.1
0655	0.6	0721	1.2
W 1311	4.6	TH 1340	4.2
1917	0.6	1944	1.1
15 0134	4.7	**30** 0201	4.1
0741	0.6	0752	1.2
TH 1354	4.6	F 1411	4.2
2004	0.6	2017	1.1

DECEMBER

Time	m	Time	m
1 0235	4.0	**16** 0307	4.5
0824	1.3	0901	0.9
SA 1443	4.2	SU 1513	4.6
2052	1.1	2135	0.5
2 0311	4.0	**17** 0359	4.3
0857	1.3	0948	1.1
SU 1517	4.1	M 1603	4.4
2128	1.1	2225	0.7
3 0350	3.9	**18** 0452	4.1
0932	1.4	1036	1.3
M 1554	4.0	TU 1655	4.3
2207	1.2	2317	0.9
4 0432	3.8	**19** 0547	3.9
1011	1.6	1128	1.5
TU 1635	3.9	W 1752	4.1
2251	1.3		
5 0520	3.7	**20** 0012	1.2
1056	1.7	0643	3.7
W 1724	3.8	TH 1226	1.7
2342	1.4	☽ 1850	3.9
6 0615	3.6	**21** 0111	1.4
1152	1.8	0744	3.6
TH 1823	3.7	F 1330	1.8
		1955	3.7
7 0043	1.5	**22** 0216	1.6
0716	3.6	0851	3.5
F 1303	1.9	SA 1443	1.9
1927	3.7	2105	3.6
8 0150	1.4	**23** 0327	1.6
0819	3.6	0955	3.6
SA 1416	1.8	SU 1558	1.8
2034	3.8	2212	3.6
9 0256	1.3	**24** 0428	1.6
0924	3.8	1050	3.7
SU 1525	1.6	M 1654	1.7
2141	3.9	2307	3.7
10 0359	1.2	**25** 0514	1.5
1025	4.0	1135	3.8
M 1628	1.4	TU 1739	1.5
2244	4.1	2354	3.8
11 0458	1.0	**26** 0554	1.5
1118	4.2	1214	4.0
TU 1725	1.1	W 1819	1.3
2341	4.3		
12 0551	0.9	**27** 0034	3.9
1207	4.4	0629	1.4
W 1817	0.9	TH 1250	4.1
		1854	1.2
13 0033	4.5	**28** 0112	4.0
0640	0.8	0703	1.3
TH 1254	4.5	F 1323	4.2
● 1907	0.7	○ 1929	1.1
14 0125	4.6	**29** 0146	4.0
0728	0.8	0735	1.2
F 1339	4.6	SA 1355	4.2
1956	0.5	2003	1.0
15 0215	4.6	**30** 0220	4.0
0815	0.8	0808	1.2
SA 1425	4.6	SU 1427	4.2
2045	0.5	2037	0.9
		31 0255	4.0
		0841	1.2
		M 1500	4.2
		2112	0.9

Chart Datum: 2·25 metres below Ordnance Datum (Newlyn)
HAT is 4·9 metres above Chart Datum

TIDES

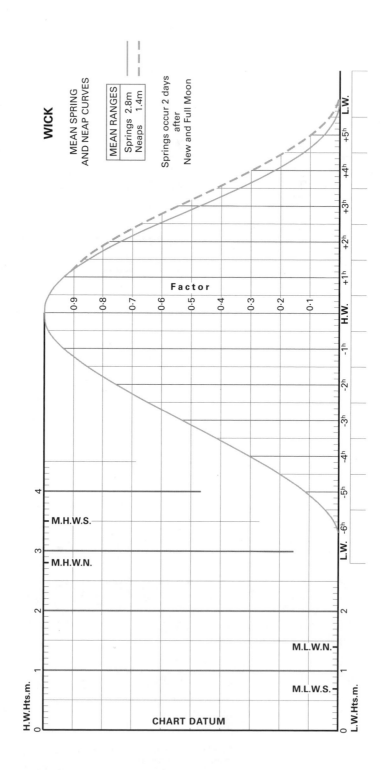

WICK

MEAN SPRING
AND NEAP CURVES

MEAN RANGES

Springs 2.8m
Neaps 1.4m

Springs occur 2 days
after
New and Full Moon

Factor

0·9 0·8 0·7 0·6 0·5 0·4 0·3 0·2 0·1

H.W. -1ʰ -2ʰ -3ʰ -4ʰ -5ʰ -6ʰ L.W.
+5ʰ +4ʰ +3ʰ +2ʰ +1ʰ H.W.

L.W.

M.H.W.S.

M.H.W.N.

M.L.W.N.

M.L.W.S.

CHART DATUM

H.W.Hts.m.

L.W.Hts.m.

4 3 2 1 0

2 1 0

SCOTLAND – WICK
LAT 58°26′N   LONG 3°05′W
TIMES AND HEIGHTS OF HIGH AND LOW WATERS

Dates in amber are **SPRINGS**
Dates in yellow are **NEAPS**

2012

JANUARY

Day	Time m	Time m	Time m	Time m
1 SU	0427 2.8	0953 1.6	1633 3.0	☽ 2247 1.4
2 M	0524 2.8	1103 1.7	1733 2.9	2353 1.5
3 TU	0626 2.8	1224 1.7	1839 2.8	
4 W	0106 1.5	0730 2.8	1346 1.6	1946 2.8
5 TH	0210 1.5	0831 2.9	1445 1.5	2049 2.9
6 F	0259 1.4	0920 3.1	1530 1.3	2140 3.0
7 SA	0339 1.3	1002 3.2	1610 1.1	2223 3.1
8 SU	0415 1.2	1040 3.4	1646 1.0	2303 3.3
9 M	0449 1.1	1117 3.5	1721 0.8	○ 2342 3.3
10 TU	0524 1.0	1154 3.6	1758 0.7	
11 W	0021 3.4	0600 1.0	1232 3.6	1835 0.6
12 TH	0100 3.4	0637 0.9	1310 3.6	1914 0.6
13 F	0141 3.4	0716 1.0	1350 3.6	1956 0.7
14 SA	0223 3.3	0757 1.0	1432 3.5	2041 0.8
15 SU	0308 3.2	0841 1.2	1519 3.4	2132 0.9
16 M	0359 3.1	0934 1.3	1615 3.3	◑ 2237 1.1
17 TU	0500 3.0	1049 1.4	1724 3.1	2351 1.2
18 W	0609 3.0	1220 1.4	1842 3.0	
19 TH	0111 1.3	0722 3.0	1350 1.3	2003 3.1
20 F	0224 1.2	0834 3.1	1500 1.1	2117 3.2
21 SA	0321 1.2	0935 3.3	1554 0.9	2215 3.3
22 SU	0408 1.1	1026 3.5	1641 0.7	2303 3.4
23 M	0449 1.0	1111 3.6	1722 0.6	● 2347 3.5
24 TU	0527 0.9	1153 3.7	1801 0.6	
25 W	0027 3.4	0603 0.9	1232 3.7	1837 0.6
26 TH	0105 3.4	0638 0.9	1309 3.6	1912 0.7
27 F	0141 3.3	0712 1.0	1345 3.5	1945 0.8
28 SA	0216 3.1	0744 1.1	1421 3.4	2018 1.0
29 SU	0252 3.0	0818 1.2	1458 3.2	2053 1.2
30 M	0331 2.8	0858 1.4	1539 3.0	2135 1.3
31 TU	0418 2.8	0951 1.5	1631 2.8	◑ 2236 1.5

FEBRUARY

Day	Time m	Time m	Time m	Time m
1 W	0518 2.7	1117 1.7	1739 2.7	2356 1.6
2 TH	0629 2.7	1254 1.6	1858 2.7	
3 F	0125 1.6	0742 2.8	1416 1.5	2015 2.7
4 SA	0233 1.5	0845 2.9	1508 1.3	2115 2.9
5 SU	0319 1.3	0934 3.1	1549 1.1	2202 3.1
6 M	0357 1.2	1016 3.3	1626 0.9	2243 3.2
7 TU	0431 1.0	1055 3.5	1702 0.7	○ 2323 3.4
8 W	0507 0.9	1134 3.6	1738 0.5	
9 TH	0002 3.5	0542 0.7	1213 3.7	1815 0.4
10 F	0041 3.5	0620 0.7	1252 3.8	1854 0.4
11 SA	0121 3.5	0658 0.7	1332 3.7	1934 0.5
12 SU	0201 3.4	0738 0.8	1414 3.6	2016 0.6
13 M	0244 3.3	0820 1.0	1501 3.4	2104 0.9
14 TU	0331 3.1	0910 1.1	1556 3.2	◑ 2205 1.1
15 W	0429 3.0	1025 1.3	1707 3.0	2326 1.3
16 TH	0542 2.9	1209 1.4	1833 2.9	
17 F	0059 1.4	0702 2.9	1351 1.2	2004 2.9
18 SA	0219 1.3	0822 3.0	1459 1.0	2115 3.0
19 SU	0314 1.2	0924 3.2	1548 0.8	2207 3.2
20 M	0357 1.1	1013 3.4	1629 0.7	2250 3.3
21 TU	0433 0.9	1056 3.5	1705 0.6	● 2329 3.3
22 W	0507 0.8	1134 3.6	1738 0.5	
23 TH	0004 3.4	0540 0.7	1211 3.6	1809 0.5
24 F	0038 3.3	0612 0.8	1244 3.6	1840 0.6
25 SA	0109 3.3	0644 0.8	1317 3.5	1910 0.7
26 SU	0140 3.2	0715 0.9	1349 3.3	1939 0.9
27 M	0211 3.1	0746 1.0	1422 3.2	2009 1.1
28 TU	0245 3.0	0820 1.2	1500 3.0	2042 1.3
29 W	0324 2.8	0903 1.4	1546 2.8	◑ 2127 1.5

MARCH

Day	Time m	Time m	Time m	Time m
1 TH	0415 2.7	1012 1.5	1647 2.6	☽ 2248 1.6
2 F	0526 2.6	1200 1.6	1811 2.5	
3 SA	0031 1.6	0647 2.6	1335 1.4	1934 2.6
4 SU	0158 1.5	0801 2.8	1436 1.2	2043 2.8
5 M	0251 1.3	0859 3.0	1520 1.0	2134 3.0
6 TU	0331 1.1	0946 3.2	1559 0.7	2217 3.2
7 W	0407 0.9	1028 3.4	1636 0.5	2258 3.4
8 TH	0444 0.7	1109 3.6	1713 0.3	○ 2338 3.5
9 F	0521 0.6	1150 3.7	1752 0.2	
10 SA	0018 3.6	0600 0.5	1232 3.8	1831 0.2
11 SU	0058 3.5	0639 0.6	1315 3.7	1912 0.4
12 M	0139 3.4	0721 0.6	1359 3.4	1954 0.6
13 TU	0221 3.3	0805 0.8	1448 3.3	2042 0.9
14 W	0309 3.1	0859 1.0	1546 3.1	2143 1.2
15 TH	0406 2.9	1021 1.2	1700 2.8	◑ 2309 1.4
16 F	0521 2.8	1207 1.2	1828 2.7	
17 SA	0047 1.5	0643 2.8	1343 1.1	1957 2.8
18 SU	0206 1.4	0804 2.9	1445 0.9	2101 2.9
19 M	0258 1.2	0906 3.1	1531 0.8	2149 3.1
20 TU	0338 1.1	0953 3.3	1608 0.7	2229 3.2
21 W	0412 0.9	1034 3.4	1639 0.6	2305 3.2
22 TH	0444 0.8	1111 3.4	1710 0.6	● 2338 3.3
23 F	0516 0.7	1145 3.4	1740 0.6	
24 SA	0009 3.3	0548 0.7	1218 3.4	1809 0.6
25 SU	0039 3.3	0619 0.7	1250 3.3	1837 0.7
26 M	0108 3.2	0650 0.8	1321 3.2	1906 0.9
27 TU	0137 3.1	0721 0.9	1354 3.1	1935 1.0
28 W	0210 3.0	0755 1.0	1432 2.9	2007 1.2
29 TH	0248 2.9	0835 1.2	1516 2.7	2047 1.4
30 F	0334 2.7	0934 1.3	1613 2.6	◑ 2150 1.5
31 SA	0435 2.6	1114 1.4	1729 2.5	2341 1.6

APRIL

Day	Time m	Time m	Time m	Time m
1 SU	0556 2.6	1242 1.3	1852 2.6	
2 M	0108 1.5	0711 2.7	1352 1.1	2002 2.7
3 TU	0211 1.3	0815 2.9	1443 0.9	2058 3.0
4 W	0258 1.1	0909 3.1	1526 0.6	2146 3.2
5 TH	0338 0.8	0957 3.4	1606 0.4	2229 3.4
6 F	0418 0.6	1042 3.6	1646 0.3	○ 2311 3.5
7 SA	0459 0.5	1127 3.7	1728 0.2	2353 3.6
8 SU	0541 0.4	1213 3.7	1809 0.3	
9 M	0035 3.6	0623 0.4	1259 3.7	1852 0.4
10 TU	0118 3.5	0708 0.5	1347 3.5	1936 0.6
11 W	0202 3.3	0758 0.6	1439 3.2	2026 1.0
12 TH	0251 3.2	0859 0.8	1539 3.0	2128 1.3
13 F	0349 3.0	1020 1.0	1652 2.8	◑ 2249 1.4
14 SA	0501 2.9	1152 1.0	1812 2.7	
15 SU	0018 1.5	0617 2.8	1318 1.0	1931 2.7
16 M	0137 1.4	0733 2.9	1418 0.9	2034 2.8
17 TU	0231 1.2	0836 3.0	1503 0.8	2121 3.0
18 W	0312 1.1	0926 3.1	1538 0.6	2201 3.1
19 TH	0347 0.9	1007 3.2	1610 0.7	2236 3.1
20 F	0420 0.8	1045 3.2	1640 0.7	2309 3.2
21 SA	0453 0.7	1120 3.2	1710 0.7	● 2340 3.2
22 SU	0526 0.7	1153 3.2	1740 0.7	
23 M	0010 3.2	0558 0.7	1226 3.2	1809 0.8
24 TU	0041 3.2	0630 0.8	1259 3.1	1839 0.9
25 W	0111 3.1	0703 0.8	1334 3.0	1909 1.0
26 TH	0145 3.1	0739 0.9	1412 2.9	1944 1.2
27 F	0222 3.0	0820 1.0	1456 2.8	2025 1.3
28 SA	0307 2.8	0915 1.1	1549 2.7	◑ 2121 1.4
29 SU	0402 2.7	1036 1.2	1656 2.6	◐ 2253 1.5
30 M	0512 2.7	1155 1.1	1810 2.6	

TIDES

Chart Datum: 1·71 metres below Ordnance Datum (Newlyn)
HAT is 4·0 metres above Chart Datum

TIME ZONE (UT)
For Summer Time add ONE hour in **non-shaded areas**

SCOTLAND – WICK
LAT 58°26'N   LONG 3°05'W
TIMES AND HEIGHTS OF HIGH AND LOW WATERS

Dates in amber are **SPRINGS**
Dates in yellow are **NEAPS**

2012

MAY

Day	Time m	Time m	Time m	Time m
1 TU	0017 1.4	0625 2.8	1303 1.0	1918 2.8
2 W	0125 1.3	0731 2.9	1401 0.8	2018 2.9
3 TH	0221 1.1	0830 3.1	1451 0.6	2111 3.1
4 F	0309 0.8	0925 3.3	1537 0.4	2200 3.3
5 SA	0354 0.6	1017 3.5	1622 0.3	2246 3.5
6 SU ○	0440 0.5	1108 3.6	1706 0.3	2331 3.6
7 M	0526 0.4	1157 3.6	1751 0.4	
8 TU	0015 3.6	0613 0.3	1247 3.6	1836 0.6
9 W	0101 3.5	0702 0.4	1338 3.4	1923 0.8
10 TH	0147 3.4	0755 0.5	1431 3.2	2012 1.0
11 F	0237 3.2	0856 0.7	1529 2.9	2110 1.2
12 SA ◑	0333 3.1	1004 0.8	1633 2.8	2217 1.4
13 SU	0436 2.9	1117 1.0	1739 2.7	2331 1.4
14 M	0543 2.9	1233 1.0	1847 2.7	
15 TU	0049 1.4	0650 2.8	1337 1.0	1951 2.8
16 W	0152 1.3	0755 2.9	1426 1.0	2044 2.8
17 TH	0240 1.2	0851 2.9	1505 0.9	2128 3.0
18 F	0320 1.1	0937 3.0	1539 0.9	2206 3.1
19 SA	0357 0.9	1018 3.0	1612 0.9	2241 3.1
20 SU ●	0433 0.8	1056 3.1	1644 0.9	2314 3.2
21 M	0508 0.8	1131 3.1	1716 0.9	2346 3.2
22 TU	0542 0.8	1206 3.1	1747 0.9	
23 W	0018 3.2	0616 0.8	1242 3.1	1819 1.0
24 TH	0052 3.2	0651 0.8	1318 3.0	1853 1.0
25 F	0127 3.1	0728 0.8	1357 2.9	1930 1.1
26 SA	0205 3.1	0810 0.9	1440 2.9	2011 1.2
27 SU	0248 3.0	0859 0.9	1529 2.8	2101 1.3
28 M ◐	0337 2.9	1002 1.0	1626 2.7	2209 1.3
29 TU	0437 2.9	1112 1.0	1732 2.7	2329 1.3
30 W	0544 2.9	1219 0.9	1838 2.8	
31 TH	0040 1.3	0652 3.0	1322 0.8	1940 2.9

JUNE

Day	Time m	Time m	Time m	Time m
1 F	0145 1.1	0757 3.1	1420 0.7	2039 3.1
2 SA	0243 0.9	0900 3.2	1513 0.6	2134 3.3
3 SU	0336 0.7	0959 3.4	1602 0.6	2225 3.4
4 M ○	0427 0.5	1054 3.5	1650 0.5	2313 3.5
5 TU	0517 0.4	1147 3.5	1737 0.6	
6 W	0000 3.6	0606 0.3	1238 3.5	1823 0.7
7 TH	0047 3.6	0656 0.4	1328 3.4	1908 0.8
8 F	0133 3.5	0747 0.5	1417 3.2	1954 1.0
9 SA	0221 3.4	0839 0.6	1508 3.0	2042 1.1
10 SU	0311 3.2	0932 0.8	1601 2.9	2135 1.3
11 M ◑	0404 3.1	1026 0.8	1657 2.7	2236 1.4
12 TU	0503 2.9	1131 1.1	1756 2.7	2345 1.4
13 W	0604 2.8	1237 1.2	1857 2.7	
14 TH	0100 1.4	0707 2.8	1338 1.2	1958 2.8
15 F	0204 1.3	0810 2.8	1428 1.1	2051 2.9
16 SA	0254 1.2	0906 2.8	1510 1.1	2136 3.0
17 SU	0337 1.1	0953 2.9	1548 1.1	2215 3.1
18 M	0416 1.0	1034 3.0	1623 1.0	2251 3.2
19 TU ●	0453 0.9	1112 3.0	1657 1.0	2326 3.2
20 W	0528 0.8	1149 3.1	1730 1.0	
21 TH	0000 3.3	0602 0.7	1226 3.1	1803 0.9
22 F	0036 3.3	0638 0.7	1303 3.1	1839 0.9
23 SA	0112 3.3	0715 0.7	1342 3.1	1916 1.0
24 SU	0149 3.3	0755 0.7	1422 3.0	1956 1.0
25 M	0230 3.2	0839 0.8	1507 3.0	2040 1.1
26 TU	0315 3.1	0930 0.8	1558 2.9	2133 1.2
27 W ◑	0408 3.1	1033 0.9	1656 2.9	2244 1.3
28 TH	0511 3.0	1141 0.9	1801 2.9	
29 F	0002 1.4	0621 3.0	1250 0.9	1907 2.9
30 SA	0119 1.2	0733 3.0	1357 0.9	2012 3.1

JULY

Day	Time m	Time m	Time m	Time m
1 SU	0229 1.0	0845 3.1	1458 0.9	2114 3.2
2 M	0329 0.8	0950 3.3	1551 0.8	2210 3.4
3 TU ○	0422 0.6	1047 3.4	1639 0.7	2300 3.5
4 W	0511 0.4	1138 3.4	1725 0.7	2347 3.6
5 TH	0558 0.3	1226 3.4	1808 0.7	
6 F	0032 3.6	0643 0.3	1312 3.4	1849 0.8
7 SA	0116 3.6	0727 0.4	1356 3.3	1929 0.9
8 SU	0159 3.5	0809 0.6	1439 3.1	2009 1.0
9 M	0242 3.3	0851 0.8	1522 2.9	2050 1.2
10 TU	0327 3.1	0935 1.0	1609 2.8	2139 1.3
11 W ◑	0416 3.0	1026 1.2	1702 2.7	2242 1.4
12 TH	0513 2.8	1126 1.3	1801 2.7	2358 1.5
13 F	0617 2.7	1237 1.4	1905 2.7	
14 SA	0123 1.4	0726 2.7	1349 1.4	2009 2.8
15 SU	0229 1.3	0834 2.7	1444 1.3	2104 2.9
16 M	0318 1.2	0929 2.8	1527 1.2	2149 3.1
17 TU	0359 1.0	1013 2.9	1604 1.1	2228 3.2
18 W	0436 0.9	1053 3.1	1639 1.0	2305 3.3
19 TH ●	0511 0.7	1130 3.1	1712 1.0	2341 3.4
20 F	0545 0.6	1207 3.2	1747 0.9	
21 SA	0017 3.5	0620 0.5	1245 3.3	1822 0.8
22 SU	0054 3.5	0657 0.5	1323 3.2	1859 0.8
23 M	0131 3.5	0735 0.5	1402 3.2	1937 0.9
24 TU	0211 3.4	0816 0.6	1444 3.1	2018 1.0
25 W	0254 3.3	0901 0.8	1530 3.0	2105 1.1
26 TH ◑	0344 3.2	0958 0.9	1625 3.0	2209 1.2
27 F	0446 3.0	1109 1.1	1730 2.9	2337 1.3
28 SA	0601 2.9	1227 1.2	1842 2.9	
29 SU	0108 1.2	0722 2.9	1347 1.1	1955 3.0
30 M	0228 1.0	0843 3.0	1452 1.1	2103 3.2
31 TU	0328 0.8	0947 3.2	1544 1.0	2159 3.4

AUGUST

Day	Time m	Time m	Time m	Time m
1 W	0417 0.6	1040 3.3	1628 0.9	2248 3.5
2 TH ○	0501 0.5	1126 3.4	1709 0.8	2333 3.6
3 F	0542 0.4	1209 3.4	1747 0.7	
4 SA	0014 3.7	0621 0.4	1249 3.4	1824 0.7
5 SU	0054 3.6	0658 0.5	1327 3.3	1900 0.8
6 M	0132 3.5	0733 0.6	1404 3.2	1935 0.9
7 TU	0210 3.4	0807 0.8	1440 3.0	2010 1.1
8 W	0248 3.2	0842 1.0	1519 2.9	2049 1.2
9 TH ◑	0330 3.0	0922 1.2	1605 2.8	2141 1.4
10 F	0420 2.8	1017 1.4	1701 2.7	2302 1.5
11 SA	0526 2.6	1134 1.5	1810 2.7	
12 SU	0037 1.5	0642 2.6	1303 1.5	1922 2.7
13 M	0201 1.4	0800 2.7	1416 1.5	2028 2.9
14 TU	0255 1.2	0903 2.8	1504 1.3	2119 3.0
15 W	0336 1.0	0949 3.0	1543 1.2	2201 3.2
16 TH	0412 0.8	1029 3.1	1617 1.0	2240 3.4
17 F ●	0447 0.7	1107 3.3	1650 0.9	2317 3.5
18 SA	0521 0.5	1144 3.4	1725 0.8	2354 3.6
19 SU	0556 0.4	1222 3.4	1801 0.7	
20 M	0032 3.7	0633 0.4	1300 3.4	1838 0.7
21 TU	0111 3.6	0711 0.4	1339 3.4	1916 0.7
22 W	0152 3.6	0751 0.6	1420 3.3	1957 0.9
23 TH	0236 3.4	0835 0.8	1505 3.2	2045 1.1
24 F ◗	0327 3.2	0930 1.0	1559 3.0	2150 1.2
25 SA	0432 3.0	1047 1.3	1706 2.9	2329 1.3
26 SU	0554 2.9	1216 1.4	1824 2.9	
27 M	0111 1.2	0723 2.9	1343 1.3	1943 3.0
28 TU	0227 1.0	0842 3.0	1445 1.2	2052 3.2
29 W	0323 0.8	0940 3.2	1533 1.1	2146 3.4
30 TH	0406 0.6	1027 3.3	1612 0.9	2232 3.5
31 F ○	0444 0.5	1108 3.4	1649 0.8	2313 3.6

Chart Datum: 1·71 metres below Ordnance Datum (Newlyn)
HAT is 4·0 metres above Chart Datum

TIME ZONE (UT)	SCOTLAND – WICK	Dates in amber are SPRINGS
For Summer Time add ONE hour in non-shaded areas	LAT 58°26′N LONG 3°05′W	Dates in yellow are NEAPS
	TIMES AND HEIGHTS OF HIGH AND LOW WATERS	2012

SEPTEMBER

Time	m	Time	m
1 SA	0519 0.5 / 1146 3.4 / 1723 0.7 / 2352 3.7	**16** SU ●	0453 0.5 / 1117 3.5 / 1701 0.7 / 2328 3.7
2 SU	0553 0.5 / 1222 3.4 / 1758 0.7	**17** M	0530 0.4 / 1156 3.6 / 1738 0.6
3 M	0028 3.6 / 0625 0.6 / 1256 3.4 / 1831 0.8	**18** TU	0009 3.8 / 0608 0.3 / 1235 3.6 / 1817 0.6
4 TU	0103 3.5 / 0656 0.7 / 1328 3.3 / 1903 0.9	**19** W	0051 3.8 / 0647 0.4 / 1315 3.6 / 1858 0.7
5 W	0137 3.4 / 0726 0.9 / 1400 3.2 / 1936 1.0	**20** TH	0134 3.6 / 0729 0.6 / 1357 3.4 / 1942 0.8
6 TH	0212 3.2 / 0757 1.1 / 1434 3.0 / 2012 1.2	**21** F	0222 3.5 / 0814 0.9 / 1444 3.3 / 2033 1.0
7 F	0250 3.0 / 0830 1.3 / 1514 2.9 / 2055 1.4	**22** SA ☽	0317 3.2 / 0910 1.2 / 1538 3.1 / 2147 1.2
8 SA ☽	0336 2.8 / 0914 1.5 / 1604 2.8 / 2207 1.5	**23** SU	0426 3.0 / 1032 1.4 / 1648 3.0 / 2330 1.2
9 SU	0437 2.7 / 1031 1.6 / 1713 2.7 / 2349 1.6	**24** M	0551 2.9 / 1206 1.5 / 1808 3.0
10 M	0558 2.6 / 1212 1.7 / 1832 2.7	**25** TU	0106 1.2 / 0719 2.9 / 1331 1.4 / 1927 3.1
11 TU	0121 1.4 / 0720 2.6 / 1340 1.6 / 1943 2.8	**26** W	0216 1.0 / 0831 3.0 / 1431 1.3 / 2035 3.2
12 W	0222 1.2 / 0828 2.8 / 1434 1.4 / 2041 3.0	**27** TH	0307 0.8 / 0924 3.2 / 1515 1.1 / 2127 3.4
13 TH	0305 1.0 / 0918 3.0 / 1514 1.2 / 2127 3.2	**28** F	0346 0.7 / 1006 3.3 / 1552 1.0 / 2211 3.5
14 F	0342 0.8 / 0959 3.2 / 1550 1.0 / 2209 3.4	**29** SA	0420 0.7 / 1045 3.4 / 1626 0.9 / 2251 3.6
15 SA	0417 0.6 / 1038 3.4 / 1625 0.8 / 2249 3.6	**30** SU ○	0452 0.6 / 1120 3.4 / 1659 0.8 / 2327 3.6

OCTOBER

Time	m	Time	m
1 M	0523 0.7 / 1152 3.4 / 1732 0.8	**16** TU ●	0504 0.4 / 1130 3.7 / 1717 0.6 / 2348 3.8
2 TU	0001 3.5 / 0553 0.7 / 1224 3.4 / 1805 0.8	**17** W	0545 0.4 / 1211 3.7 / 1800 0.6
3 W	0035 3.5 / 0623 0.8 / 1255 3.4 / 1837 0.9	**18** TH	0033 3.8 / 0626 0.6 / 1254 3.7 / 1844 0.6
4 TH	0108 3.3 / 0652 1.0 / 1325 3.3 / 1910 1.0	**19** F	0121 3.7 / 0711 0.8 / 1338 3.6 / 1933 0.7
5 F	0142 3.2 / 0721 1.1 / 1358 3.2 / 1944 1.2	**20** SA	0212 3.5 / 0759 1.0 / 1427 3.4 / 2030 0.9
6 SA	0220 3.0 / 0754 1.3 / 1436 3.0 / 2026 1.3	**21** SU	0310 3.2 / 0857 1.3 / 1522 3.2 / 2148 1.1
7 SU	0304 2.9 / 0833 1.5 / 1522 2.9 / 2125 1.5	**22** M ☽	0420 3.0 / 1015 1.5 / 1631 3.1 / 2317 1.2
8 M	0400 2.7 / 0933 1.6 / 1621 2.8 / 2301 1.5	**23** TU ☽	0538 2.9 / 1141 1.6 / 1746 3.1
9 TU	0514 2.6 / 1119 1.7 / 1739 2.8	**24** W	0044 1.1 / 0656 2.9 / 1304 1.5 / 1900 3.1
10 W	0027 1.4 / 0634 2.7 / 1247 1.7 / 1852 2.8	**25** TH	0152 1.0 / 0805 3.0 / 1405 1.4 / 2007 3.2
11 TH	0136 1.3 / 0743 2.8 / 1352 1.5 / 1954 3.0	**26** F	0242 1.0 / 0857 3.1 / 1451 1.3 / 2102 3.3
12 F	0226 1.1 / 0838 3.0 / 1439 1.3 / 2047 3.2	**27** SA	0320 0.9 / 0940 3.3 / 1529 1.1 / 2147 3.4
13 SA	0307 0.8 / 0924 3.2 / 1519 1.1 / 2134 3.4	**28** SU	0353 0.9 / 1018 3.3 / 1603 1.0 / 2226 3.4
14 SU	0346 0.6 / 1007 3.4 / 1557 0.9 / 2219 3.6	**29** M ○	0424 0.9 / 1052 3.4 / 1637 0.9 / 2303 3.5
15 M	0424 0.5 / 1048 3.6 / 1636 0.7 / 2303 3.8	**30** TU	0454 0.9 / 1125 3.5 / 1711 0.9 / 2337 3.4
31 W	0525 0.9 / 1156 3.5 / 1745 0.9		

NOVEMBER

Time	m	Time	m
1 TH	0011 3.4 / 0555 1.0 / 1227 3.4 / 1817 0.9	**16** F	0021 3.8 / 0611 0.7 / 1237 3.8 / 1837 0.6
2 F	0045 3.3 / 0625 1.1 / 1258 3.4 / 1851 1.0	**17** SA	0112 3.7 / 0657 0.9 / 1323 3.7 / 1929 0.7
3 SA	0120 3.2 / 0655 1.2 / 1331 3.3 / 1926 1.1	**18** SU	0204 3.5 / 0746 1.1 / 1412 3.6 / 2027 0.8
4 SU	0157 3.1 / 0729 1.3 / 1408 3.2 / 2007 1.2	**19** M	0300 3.3 / 0840 1.3 / 1506 3.4 / 2133 1.0
5 M	0240 3.0 / 0808 1.5 / 1451 3.1 / 2058 1.3	**20** TU	0403 3.1 / 0944 1.5 / 1608 3.3 / 2246 1.1
6 TU	0330 2.8 / 0858 1.6 / 1543 3.0 / 2212 1.4	**21** W	0509 3.0 / 1058 1.6 / 1715 3.1
7 W	0433 2.8 / 1018 1.7 / 1648 2.9 / 2332 1.4	**22** TH	0002 1.2 / 0616 2.9 / 1217 1.6 / 1822 3.1
8 TH	0546 2.8 / 1149 1.7 / 1801 2.9	**23** F	0113 1.2 / 0724 3.0 / 1328 1.5 / 1929 3.1
9 F	0041 1.3 / 0653 2.9 / 1300 1.6 / 1906 3.0	**24** SA	0208 1.2 / 0822 3.1 / 1422 1.4 / 2029 3.2
10 SA	0140 1.1 / 0753 3.1 / 1358 1.4 / 2005 3.2	**25** SU	0250 1.1 / 0910 3.2 / 1505 1.3 / 2120 3.2
11 SU	0229 0.9 / 0847 3.3 / 1446 1.2 / 2100 3.4	**26** M	0326 1.1 / 0950 3.3 / 1544 1.2 / 2203 3.3
12 M	0315 0.7 / 0935 3.5 / 1532 0.9 / 2152 3.6	**27** TU	0359 1.1 / 1027 3.4 / 1620 1.1 / 2241 3.3
13 TU ●	0358 0.6 / 1021 3.6 / 1616 0.7 / 2242 3.8	**28** W	0431 1.1 / 1101 3.4 / 1655 1.0 / 2318 3.3
14 W	0442 0.6 / 1106 3.8 / 1702 0.6 / 2331 3.8	**29** TH	0503 1.1 / 1134 3.5 / 1730 1.0 / 2353 3.3
15 TH	0526 0.6 / 1151 3.8 / 1748 0.6	**30** F	0534 1.1 / 1206 3.5 / 1804 1.0

DECEMBER

Time	m	Time	m
1 SA	0027 3.3 / 0605 1.1 / 1238 3.4 / 1837 1.0	**16** SU	0102 3.7 / 0644 0.9 / 1310 3.8 / 1921 0.6
2 SU	0103 3.2 / 0638 1.2 / 1312 3.4 / 1913 1.0	**17** M	0151 3.5 / 0729 1.0 / 1357 3.7 / 2011 0.7
3 M	0140 3.2 / 0712 1.3 / 1348 3.3 / 1952 1.1	**18** TU	0242 3.3 / 0816 1.2 / 1446 3.6 / 2105 0.9
4 TU	0220 3.1 / 0750 1.4 / 1428 3.2 / 2035 1.2	**19** W	0334 3.1 / 0906 1.4 / 1539 3.4 / 2201 1.1
5 W	0305 3.0 / 0833 1.5 / 1513 3.1 / 2129 1.2	**20** TH ☾	0429 3.0 / 1004 1.5 / 1636 3.2 / 2303 1.2
6 TH	0357 2.9 / 0928 1.6 / 1607 3.1 / 2238 1.3	**21** F	0528 2.9 / 1113 1.6 / 1738 3.1
7 F	0459 2.9 / 1046 1.6 / 1711 3.0 / 2348 1.4	**22** SA	0012 1.4 / 0630 2.9 / 1233 1.6 / 1843 3.0
8 SA	0606 2.9 / 1206 1.6 / 1820 3.1	**23** SU	0121 1.4 / 0736 2.9 / 1347 1.5 / 1951 3.0
9 SU	0053 1.1 / 0709 3.1 / 1315 1.4 / 1927 3.2	**24** M	0217 1.4 / 0835 3.0 / 1443 1.4 / 2052 3.0
10 M	0153 1.0 / 0810 3.2 / 1417 1.2 / 2030 3.3	**25** TU	0300 1.3 / 0923 3.2 / 1527 1.3 / 2141 3.1
11 TU	0248 0.9 / 0907 3.4 / 1512 1.0 / 2131 3.5	**26** W	0338 1.3 / 1004 3.3 / 1606 1.2 / 2223 3.2
12 W	0338 0.8 / 0959 3.6 / 1603 0.8 / 2228 3.7	**27** TH	0413 1.2 / 1041 3.4 / 1642 1.1 / 2301 3.2
13 TH ●	0426 0.7 / 1048 3.7 / 1653 0.6 / 2320 3.7	**28** F ○	0446 1.2 / 1115 3.4 / 1717 1.0 / 2337 3.3
14 F	0513 0.7 / 1136 3.8 / 1742 0.5	**29** SA	0518 1.1 / 1149 3.5 / 1751 0.9
15 SA	0011 3.7 / 0558 0.8 / 1224 3.8 / 1831 0.5	**30** SU	0011 3.3 / 0550 1.1 / 1222 3.5 / 1824 0.9
		31 M	0047 3.3 / 0622 1.1 / 1256 3.5 / 1858 0.9

Chart Datum: 1·71 metres below Ordnance Datum (Newlyn)
HAT is 4·0 metres above Chart Datum

TIDES

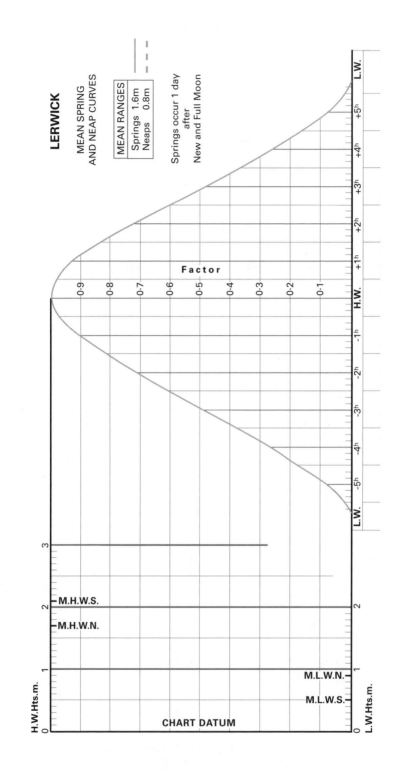

LERWICK

MEAN SPRING
AND NEAP CURVES

MEAN RANGES
Springs 1.6m
Neaps 0.8m

Springs occur 1 day
after
New and Full Moon

Factor

TIME ZONE (UT)
For Summer Time add ONE hour in **non-shaded areas**

SCOTLAND – LERWICK
LAT 60°09′N   LONG 1°08′W

TIMES AND HEIGHTS OF HIGH AND LOW WATERS

Dates in amber are **SPRINGS**
Dates in yellow are **NEAPS**

2012

JANUARY

Time	m		Time	m
1 0359	1.8	**16** 0340	1.9
0949	1.1	0928	0.9
SU 1604	1.9	M 1555	2.0
☽ 2236	1.0	2216	0.8
2 0454	1.7	**17** 0440	1.8
1100	1.1	1036	1.0
M 1702	1.8	TU 1704	1.9
2343	1.0	2332	0.9
3 0604	1.7	**18** 0550	1.8
1222	1.1	1212	1.0
TU 1822	1.7	W 1827	1.9
4 0051	1.1	**19** 0055	0.9
0714	1.8	0706	1.9
W 1333	1.1	TH 1337	0.9
1935	1.8	1949	1.9
5 0150	1.0	**20** 0204	0.9
0808	1.9	0814	2.0
TH 1427	1.0	F 1442	1.0
2030	1.8	2058	2.0
6 0238	1.0	**21** 0301	0.8
0854	2.0	0913	2.1
F 1511	0.9	SA 1536	0.6
2117	1.9	2156	2.1
7 0319	0.9	**22** 0349	0.8
0935	2.0	1004	2.2
SA 1550	0.8	SU 1622	0.5
2200	2.0	2245	2.1
8 0357	0.9	**23** 0433	0.7
1013	2.1	1051	2.3
SU 1627	0.7	M 1704	0.4
2240	2.0	● 2329	2.2
9 0435	0.8	**24** 0513	0.6
1051	2.2	1133	2.3
M 1704	0.6	TU 1744	0.4
○ 2320	2.1		
10 0511	0.8	**25** 0009	2.2
1129	2.3	0550	0.6
TU 1742	0.5	W 1212	2.3
2359	2.1	1821	0.4
11 0548	0.7	**26** 0046	2.1
1206	2.3	0627	0.6
W 1821	0.5	TH 1249	2.3
		1858	0.5
12 0039	2.1	**27** 0121	2.0
0626	0.7	0703	0.7
TH 1245	2.3	F 1324	2.2
1900	0.4	1934	0.6
13 0120	2.1	**28** 0155	2.0
0705	0.7	0738	0.8
F 1325	2.3	SA 1359	2.1
1942	0.5	2009	0.7
14 0202	2.0	**29** 0230	1.9
0748	0.7	0813	0.8
SA 1408	2.2	SU 1435	2.0
2027	0.5	2044	0.8
15 0249	2.0	**30** 0307	1.8
0834	0.8	0853	0.9
SU 1458	2.1	M 1515	1.9
2117	0.7	2126	0.9
		31 0350	1.7
		0947	1.1
		TU 1604	1.7
		☽ 2223	1.1

FEBRUARY

Time	m		Time	m
1 0443	1.7	**16** 0520	1.8
1115	1.1	1204	0.9
W 1705	1.6	TH 1819	1.7
2350	1.1		
2 0600	1.7	**17** 0044	1.0
1245	1.1	0649	1.8
TH 1844	1.6	F 1334	0.8
		1949	1.8
3 0107	1.1	**18** 0157	0.9
0729	1.7	0805	1.9
F 1355	1.0	SA 1439	0.7
2002	1.7	2056	1.9
4 0210	1.0	**19** 0253	0.8
0825	1.8	0904	2.0
SA 1446	0.9	SU 1529	0.6
2054	1.8	2147	2.0
5 0258	0.9	**20** 0338	0.7
0910	1.9	0953	2.1
SU 1529	0.7	M 1610	0.5
2138	1.9	2230	2.0
6 0339	0.8	**21** 0417	0.6
0951	2.1	1036	2.2
M 1607	0.6	TU 1647	0.4
2220	2.0	● 2309	2.1
7 0417	0.7	**22** 0454	0.6
1031	2.2	1114	2.2
TU 1645	0.4	W 1722	0.4
○ 2300	2.1	2344	2.1
8 0453	0.6	**23** 0528	0.5
1110	2.3	1149	2.2
W 1722	0.3	TH 1755	0.4
2340	2.1		
9 0530	0.5	**24** 0017	2.1
1149	2.3	0601	0.5
TH 1800	0.3	F 1223	2.2
		1827	0.4
10 0019	2.2	**25** 0048	2.0
0608	0.5	0634	0.6
F 1228	2.4	SA 1254	2.1
1839	0.3	1858	0.5
11 0059	2.1	**26** 0118	2.0
0647	0.5	0706	0.6
SA 1308	2.3	SU 1325	2.0
1920	0.3	1928	0.6
12 0139	2.1	**27** 0148	1.9
0729	0.6	0738	0.7
SU 1351	2.2	M 1359	1.9
2003	0.5	1959	0.8
13 0222	2.0	**28** 0221	1.8
0814	0.7	0815	0.8
M 1439	2.1	TU 1436	1.8
2051	0.6	2034	0.9
14 0311	1.9	**29** 0300	1.7
0906	0.8	0901	0.9
TU 1537	2.0	W 1523	1.7
☽ 2147	0.8	2119	1.0
15 0408	1.8		
1015	0.9		
W 1647	1.8		
2305	0.9		

MARCH

Time	m		Time	m
1 0349	1.7	**16** 0456	1.7
1009	1.0	1159	0.8
TH 1621	1.6	F 1815	1.6
☽ 2233	1.1		
2 0450	1.7	**17** 0030	1.0
1156	1.0	0630	1.7
F 1736	1.5	SA 1322	0.7
		1940	1.7
3 0026	1.1	**18** 0142	0.9
0619	1.6	0748	1.8
SA 1313	0.9	SU 1424	0.6
1926	1.6	2040	1.8
4 0137	1.0	**19** 0236	0.8
0748	1.7	0845	1.9
SU 1412	0.8	M 1511	0.5
2025	1.7	2126	1.8
5 0230	0.9	**20** 0319	0.7
0839	1.8	0933	2.0
M 1458	0.6	TU 1549	0.4
2111	1.8	2206	1.9
6 0313	0.8	**21** 0357	0.6
0923	2.0	1013	2.1
TU 1539	0.5	W 1623	0.4
2153	2.0	2242	2.0
7 0352	0.6	**22** 0431	0.5
1004	2.1	1050	2.1
W 1618	0.3	TH 1655	0.4
2234	2.1	● 2315	2.0
8 0430	0.5	**23** 0504	0.5
1045	2.2	1123	2.1
TH 1657	0.2	F 1726	0.4
○ 2314	2.1	2345	2.0
9 0509	0.4	**24** 0536	0.5
1126	2.3	1155	2.1
F 1736	0.1	SA 1755	0.4
2354	2.2		
10 0548	0.3	**25** 0014	2.0
1207	2.3	0607	0.5
SA 1816	0.2	SU 1226	2.0
		1824	0.5
11 0034	2.2	**26** 0043	2.0
0628	0.3	0638	0.5
SU 1251	2.3	M 1257	2.0
1857	0.3	1853	0.6
12 0115	2.1	**27** 0111	1.9
0711	0.4	0712	0.6
M 1337	2.2	TU 1330	1.9
1941	0.4	1924	0.7
13 0157	2.0	**28** 0143	1.8
0758	0.5	0749	0.7
TU 1428	2.0	W 1407	1.8
2028	0.6	1958	0.8
14 0246	1.9	**29** 0220	1.8
0853	0.6	0833	0.8
W 1528	1.9	TH 1454	1.6
2125	0.8	2040	0.9
15 0343	1.8	**30** 0307	1.7
1008	0.7	0932	0.9
TH 1640	1.7	F 1551	1.5
☽ 2249	1.0	☽ 2140	1.0
		31 0408	1.6
		1102	0.9
		SA 1700	1.5
		2335	1.0

APRIL

Time	m		Time	m
1 0521	1.6	**16** 0114	0.9
1227	0.8	0717	1.7
SU 1832	1.5	M 1356	0.6
		2009	1.7
2 0057	1.0	**17** 0209	0.8
0653	1.6	0815	1.8
M 1330	0.7	TU 1442	0.5
1946	1.6	2055	1.7
3 0154	0.8	**18** 0254	0.7
0759	1.7	0903	1.8
TU 1421	0.5	W 1521	0.5
2036	1.8	2135	1.8
4 0241	0.7	**19** 0332	0.6
0849	1.9	0945	1.9
W 1506	0.4	TH 1555	0.5
2121	1.9	2210	1.9
5 0324	0.5	**20** 0407	0.5
0934	2.1	1022	1.9
TH 1549	0.2	F 1626	0.5
2204	2.0	2243	1.9
6 0405	0.4	**21** 0440	0.5
1018	2.2	1056	1.9
F 1630	0.1	SA 1655	0.5
○ 2246	2.1	● 2314	2.0
7 0446	0.3	**22** 0512	0.5
1103	2.3	1129	1.9
SA 1712	0.1	SU 1725	0.5
2328	2.2	2344	2.0
8 0528	0.2	**23** 0544	0.5
1148	2.3	1201	1.9
SU 1754	0.2	M 1755	0.6
9 0009	2.2	**24** 0013	2.0
0611	0.2	0616	0.5
M 1236	2.2	TU 1234	1.9
1837	0.3	1825	0.6
10 0053	2.1	**25** 0043	1.9
0658	0.3	0652	0.5
TU 1321	2.1	W 1309	1.8
1922	0.5	1857	0.7
11 0138	2.0	**26** 0115	1.9
0748	0.4	0730	0.6
W 1422	1.9	TH 1348	1.7
2012	0.7	1934	0.8
12 0228	1.9	**27** 0153	1.8
0846	0.5	0815	0.7
TH 1521	1.8	F 1434	1.6
2110	0.9	2017	0.9
13 0326	1.8	**28** 0239	1.7
1003	0.6	0909	0.7
F 1630	1.6	SA 1529	1.6
☽ 2231	0.9	2114	0.9
14 0435	1.7	**29** 0337	1.6
1138	0.6	1017	0.7
SA 1755	1.6	SU 1632	1.5
		☽ 2232	1.0
15 0002	0.9	**30** 0444	1.6
0601	1.7	1137	0.7
SU 1255	0.6	M 1745	1.5
1912	1.6		

TIDES

Chart Datum: 1·22 metres below Ordnance Datum (Local)
HAT is 2·5 metres above Chart Datum

TIDES

TIME ZONE (UT)	SCOTLAND – LERWICK	Dates in amber are SPRINGS
For Summer Time add ONE hour in non-shaded areas	LAT 60°09'N LONG 1°08'W	Dates in yellow are NEAPS
	TIMES AND HEIGHTS OF HIGH AND LOW WATERS	2012

MAY

Day	Time m	Day	Time m
1 TU	0007 0.9 / 0600 1.6 / 1245 0.6 / 1859 1.6	16 W	0134 0.8 / 0736 1.7 / 1406 0.6 / 2015 1.7
2 W	0113 0.8 / 0714 1.7 / 1342 0.5 / 1958 1.7	17 TH	0224 0.7 / 0828 1.7 / 1448 0.6 / 2058 1.8
3 TH	0206 0.7 / 0813 1.8 / 1432 0.4 / 2047 1.9	18 F	0307 0.7 / 0913 1.8 / 1524 0.6 / 2137 1.8
4 F	0254 0.5 / 0904 2.0 / 1519 0.3 / 2134 2.0	19 SA	0344 0.6 / 0953 1.8 / 1556 0.6 / 2212 1.9
5 SA	0340 0.4 / 0953 2.1 / 1605 0.2 / 2219 2.1	20 SU	0418 0.5 / 1031 1.8 / 1628 0.6 / 2246 1.9
6 SU	0426 0.3 / 1043 2.2 / 1649 0.2 / 2304 2.2	21 M	0451 0.5 / 1107 1.9 / 1659 0.6 / 2318 2.0
7 M	0512 0.2 / 1134 2.2 / 1734 0.3 / 2349 2.2	22 TU	0525 0.5 / 1142 1.9 / 1732 0.6 / 2350 2.0
8 TU	0559 0.2 / 1226 2.1 / 1820 0.4	23 W	0600 0.5 / 1217 1.8 / 1805 0.7
9 W	0035 2.1 / 0647 0.2 / 1320 2.0 / 1907 0.5	24 TH	0023 1.9 / 0636 0.5 / 1254 1.8 / 1840 0.7
10 TH	0124 2.1 / 0740 0.3 / 1414 1.9 / 1957 0.7	25 F	0058 1.9 / 0716 0.5 / 1334 1.7 / 1918 0.8
11 F	0215 2.0 / 0837 0.4 / 1509 1.8 / 2053 0.8	26 SA	0136 1.9 / 0759 0.5 / 1418 1.7 / 2002 0.8
12 SA	0310 1.9 / 0944 0.5 / 1609 1.6 / 2200 0.9	27 SU	0221 1.8 / 0848 0.6 / 1508 1.6 / 2053 0.8
13 SU	0410 1.7 / 1100 0.6 / 1716 1.6 / 2318 0.9	28 M	0314 1.7 / 0944 0.6 / 1605 1.6 / 2154 0.9
14 M	0521 1.7 / 1213 0.6 / 1826 1.6	29 TU	0414 1.7 / 1049 0.6 / 1708 1.6 / 2309 0.9
15 TU	0032 0.9 / 0635 1.7 / 1316 0.6 / 1925 1.6	30 W	0521 1.7 / 1159 0.6 / 1816 1.6
		31 TH	0027 0.8 / 0633 1.7 / 1304 0.5 / 1920 1.7

JUNE

Day	Time m	Day	Time m
1 F	0132 0.7 / 0740 1.8 / 1401 0.5 / 2016 1.9	16 SA	0240 0.8 / 0842 1.7 / 1453 0.7 / 2105 1.8
2 SA	0229 0.6 / 0839 1.9 / 1454 0.4 / 2108 2.0	17 SU	0321 0.7 / 0927 1.7 / 1530 0.7 / 2145 1.9
3 SU	0321 0.4 / 0935 2.0 / 1544 0.4 / 2157 2.1	18 M	0358 0.6 / 1009 1.8 / 1605 0.7 / 2222 1.9
4 M	0411 0.3 / 1030 2.1 / 1632 0.4 / 2246 2.1	19 TU	0434 0.6 / 1048 1.8 / 1640 0.7 / 2258 2.0
5 TU	0500 0.2 / 1125 2.1 / 1719 0.4 / 2334 2.2	20 W	0509 0.5 / 1126 1.9 / 1715 0.7 / 2333 2.0
6 W	0549 0.2 / 1219 2.1 / 1806 0.5	21 TH	0545 0.5 / 1203 1.9 / 1750 0.6
7 TH	0023 2.2 / 0637 0.2 / 1310 2.0 / 1852 0.5	22 F	0008 2.0 / 0622 0.4 / 1240 1.9 / 1826 0.6
8 F	0112 2.1 / 0727 0.3 / 1359 1.9 / 1940 0.6	23 SA	0044 2.0 / 0700 0.4 / 1319 1.8 / 1904 0.7
9 SA	0200 2.0 / 0818 0.4 / 1447 1.8 / 2029 0.7	24 SU	0122 2.0 / 0741 0.4 / 1400 1.8 / 1946 0.7
10 SU	0248 1.9 / 0912 0.5 / 1536 1.7 / 2122 0.8	25 M	0204 1.9 / 0826 0.5 / 1446 1.8 / 2032 0.7
11 M	0339 1.8 / 1011 0.6 / 1630 1.6 / 2224 0.9	26 TU	0252 1.9 / 0915 0.5 / 1537 1.7 / 2124 0.8
12 TU	0435 1.7 / 1115 0.7 / 1730 1.6 / 2336 0.9	27 W	0347 1.8 / 1011 0.6 / 1635 1.7 / 2227 0.8
13 W	0542 1.6 / 1221 0.8 / 1835 1.6	28 TH	0450 1.8 / 1118 0.6 / 1739 1.7 / 2347 0.8
14 TH	0049 0.9 / 0651 1.6 / 1321 0.8 / 1932 1.6	29 F	0602 1.8 / 1231 0.6 / 1848 1.8
15 F	0151 0.8 / 0751 1.6 / 1411 0.8 / 2021 1.7	30 SA	0106 0.8 / 0717 1.8 / 1338 0.6 / 1951 1.8

JULY

Day	Time m	Day	Time m
1 SU	0212 0.6 / 0825 1.9 / 1437 0.6 / 2049 2.0	16 M	0259 0.8 / 0904 1.7 / 1507 0.8 / 2120 1.9
2 M	0310 0.5 / 0927 2.0 / 1531 0.6 / 2143 2.1	17 TU	0339 0.7 / 0948 1.8 / 1546 0.8 / 2200 2.0
3 TU	0403 0.4 / 1025 2.0 / 1620 0.5 / 2234 2.2	18 W	0415 0.6 / 1028 1.9 / 1622 0.7 / 2238 2.0
4 W	0452 0.3 / 1118 2.1 / 1707 0.5 / 2324 2.2	19 TH	0451 0.5 / 1107 1.9 / 1658 0.7 / 2315 2.1
5 TH	0538 0.2 / 1207 2.1 / 1751 0.5	20 F	0527 0.4 / 1144 2.0 / 1733 0.6 / 2351 2.1
6 F	0010 2.2 / 0623 0.2 / 1253 2.0 / 1834 0.5	21 SA	0603 0.4 / 1221 2.0 / 1809 0.6
7 SA	0055 2.2 / 0707 0.3 / 1336 2.0 / 1916 0.6	22 SU	0027 2.1 / 0640 0.3 / 1259 2.0 / 1846 0.6
8 SU	0138 2.1 / 0751 0.4 / 1417 1.9 / 1958 0.7	23 M	0105 2.1 / 0719 0.4 / 1339 1.9 / 1926 0.6
9 M	0220 2.0 / 0834 0.5 / 1458 1.8 / 2042 0.8	24 TU	0145 2.1 / 0801 0.4 / 1421 1.9 / 2010 0.7
10 TU	0303 1.9 / 0920 0.7 / 1542 1.7 / 2131 0.9	25 W	0230 2.0 / 0848 0.5 / 1509 1.8 / 2059 0.7
11 W	0349 1.8 / 1011 0.8 / 1631 1.6 / 2235 0.9	26 TH	0323 1.9 / 0940 0.6 / 1603 1.8 / 2159 0.8
12 TH	0442 1.7 / 1115 0.9 / 1732 1.6 / 2355 1.0	27 F	0426 1.8 / 1045 0.7 / 1707 1.7 / 2320 0.8
13 F	0554 1.6 / 1221 0.9 / 1845 1.6	28 SA	0542 1.8 / 1208 0.8 / 1822 1.8
14 SA	0111 0.9 / 0713 1.6 / 1330 0.9 / 1946 1.7	29 SU	0055 0.8 / 0707 1.8 / 1326 0.8 / 1936 1.8
15 SU	0212 0.9 / 0814 1.6 / 1423 0.9 / 2036 1.8	30 M	0208 0.7 / 0822 1.9 / 1430 0.8 / 2039 2.0
		31 TU	0306 0.5 / 0925 1.9 / 1523 0.7 / 2135 2.1

AUGUST

Day	Time m	Day	Time m
1 W	0356 0.4 / 1019 2.0 / 1609 0.6 / 2225 2.2	16 TH	0351 0.6 / 1004 1.9 / 1600 0.7 / 2214 2.1
2 TH	0441 0.3 / 1106 2.1 / 1652 0.5 / 2311 2.3	17 F	0427 0.5 / 1042 2.0 / 1636 0.6 / 2252 2.2
3 F	0522 0.2 / 1149 2.1 / 1732 0.5 / 2353 2.3	18 SA	0503 0.4 / 1120 2.1 / 1712 0.5 / 2329 2.2
4 SA	0602 0.3 / 1229 2.1 / 1811 0.5	19 SU	0540 0.3 / 1157 2.1 / 1748 0.5
5 SU	0032 2.3 / 0640 0.3 / 1306 2.0 / 1848 0.5	20 M	0006 2.3 / 0617 0.3 / 1235 2.1 / 1826 0.5
6 M	0110 2.2 / 0718 0.4 / 1342 1.9 / 1925 0.6	21 TU	0045 2.3 / 0656 0.3 / 1314 2.1 / 1906 0.5
7 TU	0147 2.1 / 0754 0.6 / 1417 1.9 / 2003 0.7	22 W	0126 2.2 / 0737 0.4 / 1355 2.0 / 1950 0.6
8 W	0225 1.9 / 0831 0.7 / 1455 1.8 / 2044 0.8	23 TH	0212 2.1 / 0823 0.6 / 1441 1.9 / 2040 0.7
9 TH	0306 1.8 / 0912 0.9 / 1536 1.7 / 2137 0.9	24 F	0307 2.0 / 0915 0.7 / 1536 1.9 / 2142 0.8
10 F	0353 1.7 / 1005 1.0 / 1627 1.7 / 2258 1.0	25 SA	0413 1.8 / 1022 0.9 / 1642 1.8 / 2314 0.9
11 SA	0452 1.6 / 1127 1.0 / 1736 1.6	26 SU	0535 1.7 / 1159 0.9 / 1804 1.8
12 SU	0028 1.0 / 0626 1.6 / 1249 1.1 / 1908 1.7	27 M	0055 0.8 / 0709 1.8 / 1321 0.9 / 1927 1.9
13 M	0140 0.9 / 0747 1.6 / 1354 1.0 / 2008 1.8	28 TU	0205 0.7 / 0822 1.8 / 1423 0.8 / 2031 2.0
14 TU	0232 0.8 / 0840 1.7 / 1443 0.9 / 2054 1.9	29 W	0300 0.5 / 0918 1.9 / 1512 0.7 / 2124 2.1
15 W	0314 0.7 / 0924 1.8 / 1523 0.8 / 2135 2.0	30 TH	0344 0.4 / 1005 2.0 / 1554 0.6 / 2210 2.2
		31 F	0424 0.4 / 1047 2.1 / 1632 0.6 / 2252 2.3

Chart Datum: 1·22 metres below Ordnance Datum (Local)
HAT is 2·5 metres above Chart Datum

TIME ZONE (UT)	SCOTLAND – LERWICK	Dates in amber are SPRINGS
For Summer Time add ONE hour in non-shaded areas	LAT 60°09'N LONG 1°08'W	Dates in yellow are NEAPS
		2012

TIMES AND HEIGHTS OF HIGH AND LOW WATERS

SEPTEMBER

Time	m		Time	m
1 0501	0.3	**16** 0436	0.3
1125	2.1	1051	2.2
SA 1709	0.5	SU 1647	0.5
2330	2.3	● 2303	2.3
2 0536	0.3	**17** 0513	0.3
1159	2.1	1130	2.2
SU 1745	0.5	M 1726	0.4
		2343	2.4
3 0005	2.3	**18** 0552	0.3
0610	0.4	1209	2.2
M 1233	2.1	TU 1806	0.4
1819	0.5		
4 0040	2.2	**19** 0024	2.3
0643	0.5	0632	0.3
TU 1304	2.0	W 1249	2.2
1854	0.6	1848	0.5
5 0113	2.1	**20** 0109	2.3
0715	0.6	0715	0.5
W 1336	2.0	TH 1331	2.1
1928	0.7	1934	0.6
6 0148	2.0	**21** 0200	2.1
0747	0.8	0802	0.7
TH 1410	1.9	F 1419	2.0
2006	0.8	2027	0.7
7 0227	1.9	**22** 0259	2.0
0822	0.9	0856	0.8
F 1449	1.8	SA 1515	1.9
2053	0.9	◐ 2133	0.8
8 0313	1.7	**23** 0407	1.8
0906	1.0	1008	1.0
SA 1537	1.7	SU 1624	1.8
◑ 2203	1.0	2318	0.8
9 0409	1.6	**24** 0533	1.7
1021	1.1	1152	1.0
SU 1636	1.7	M 1750	1.8
2344	1.0		
10 0523	1.6	**25** 0047	0.8
1209	1.1	0704	1.8
M 1802	1.7	TU 1309	1.0
		1913	1.9
11 0059	1.0	**26** 0153	0.7
0713	1.6	0809	1.9
TU 1320	1.1	W 1407	0.9
1932	1.7	2015	2.0
12 0156	0.9	**27** 0244	0.6
0811	1.7	0900	1.9
W 1412	1.0	TH 1454	0.8
2023	1.9	2106	2.1
13 0241	0.7	**28** 0325	0.5
0854	1.8	0943	2.0
TH 1455	0.8	F 1534	0.7
2105	2.0	2150	2.2
14 0321	0.6	**29** 0402	0.5
0934	1.9	1021	2.1
F 1533	0.7	SA 1611	0.6
2144	2.1	2229	2.2
15 0358	0.4	**30** 0436	0.5
1012	2.1	1056	2.1
SA 1610	0.6	SU 1646	0.6
2224	2.2	○ 2304	2.2

OCTOBER

Time	m		Time	m
1 0508	0.5	**16** 0448	0.3
1128	2.1	1103	2.3
M 1720	0.6	TU 1705	0.4
2338	2.2	2322	2.4
2 0540	0.5	**17** 0529	0.3
1159	2.1	1144	2.3
TU 1753	0.6	W 1748	0.4
3 0010	2.2	**18** 0009	2.4
0610	0.6	0612	0.4
W 1229	2.1	TH 1227	2.3
1826	0.7	1833	0.4
4 0044	2.1	**19** 0059	2.3
0640	0.7	0657	0.6
TH 1259	2.1	F 1312	2.2
1900	0.7	1923	0.5
5 0118	2.0	**20** 0154	2.1
0711	0.8	0746	0.8
F 1332	2.0	SA 1403	2.1
1937	0.8	2019	0.6
6 0156	1.9	**21** 0254	2.0
0744	1.0	0841	0.9
SA 1409	1.9	SU 1501	2.0
2022	0.9	2128	0.7
7 0242	1.8	**22** 0400	1.9
0826	1.1	0953	1.1
SU 1456	1.8	M 1608	1.9
2121	1.0	◐ 2303	0.8
8 0337	1.7	**23** 0518	1.8
0926	1.2	1127	1.1
M 1554	1.7	TU 1727	1.8
◑ 2253	1.0		
9 0443	1.6	**24** 0024	0.8
1120	1.2	0639	1.8
TU 1703	1.7	W 1243	1.0
		1847	1.9
10 0013	1.0	**25** 0129	0.7
0611	1.6	0742	1.8
W 1239	1.1	TH 1343	1.0
1833	1.7	1949	2.0
11 0113	0.9	**26** 0220	0.7
0728	1.7	0831	1.9
TH 1335	1.0	F 1431	0.9
1941	1.9	2040	2.1
12 0203	0.7	**27** 0301	0.7
0817	1.9	0914	2.0
F 1421	0.9	SA 1512	0.8
2029	2.0	2124	2.1
13 0240	0.6	**28** 0337	0.6
0900	2.0	0952	2.1
SA 1503	0.7	SU 1550	0.7
2112	2.2	2204	2.2
14 0327	0.5	**29** 0410	0.6
0941	2.1	1026	2.1
SU 1543	0.6	M 1625	0.7
2155	2.3	○ 2240	2.2
15 0407	0.4	**30** 0441	0.6
1022	2.1	1059	2.2
M 1623	0.5	TU 1658	0.6
● 2238	2.4	2314	2.1
		31 0511	0.7
		1130	2.2
		W 1731	0.7
		2347	2.1

NOVEMBER

Time	m		Time	m
1 0542	0.7	**16** 0556	0.5
1200	2.2	1211	2.4
TH 1804	0.7	F 1823	0.4
2 0021	2.1	**17** 0053	2.3
0612	0.8	0643	0.7
F 1231	2.1	SA 1300	2.3
1839	0.7	1914	0.5
3 0056	2.0	**18** 0148	2.2
0644	0.9	0732	0.8
SA 1304	2.1	SU 1351	2.2
1917	0.8	2009	0.6
4 0134	1.9	**19** 0243	2.0
0718	1.0	0826	0.9
SU 1341	2.0	M 1446	2.1
2000	0.9	2112	0.7
5 0218	1.8	**20** 0341	1.9
0759	1.1	0927	1.0
M 1425	1.9	TU 1546	2.0
2052	0.9	◐ 2227	0.8
6 0310	1.8	**21** 0446	1.8
0853	1.1	1043	1.1
TU 1519	1.8	W 1652	1.9
2158	1.0	2345	0.8
7 0410	1.7	**22** 0557	1.8
1006	1.2	1203	1.1
W 1623	1.8	TH 1807	1.9
◑ 2318	0.9		
8 0518	1.7	**23** 0053	0.8
1143	1.1	0701	1.8
TH 1734	1.8	F 1311	1.0
		1913	1.9
9 0025	0.9	**24** 0148	0.8
0633	1.8	0755	1.9
F 1251	1.1	SA 1405	0.9
1849	1.9	2009	2.0
10 0121	0.8	**25** 0233	0.8
0735	1.9	0842	2.0
SA 1345	0.9	SU 1451	0.9
1949	2.0	2057	2.0
11 0211	0.6	**26** 0311	0.8
0824	2.0	0922	2.1
SU 1432	0.8	M 1531	0.8
2041	2.1	2139	2.0
12 0257	0.5	**27** 0346	0.8
0910	2.2	0959	2.1
M 1518	0.7	TU 1607	0.8
2129	2.3	2218	2.1
13 0341	0.5	**28** 0418	0.8
0955	2.3	1034	2.2
TU 1603	0.5	W 1641	0.7
● 2218	2.4	○ 2255	2.1
14 0426	0.4	**29** 0449	0.8
1039	2.4	1107	2.2
W 1648	0.4	TH 1715	0.7
2307	2.4	2330	2.1
15 0511	0.5	**30** 0521	0.8
1124	2.4	1140	2.2
TH 1735	0.4	F 1749	0.7
2359	2.4		

DECEMBER

Time	m		Time	m
1 0005	2.1	**16** 0045	2.3
0552	0.9	0629	0.7
SA 1212	2.2	SU 1249	2.4
1824	0.7	1903	0.4
2 0041	2.0	**17** 0135	2.2
0626	0.9	0716	0.7
SU 1245	2.1	M 1338	2.3
1901	0.7	1953	0.5
3 0118	2.0	**18** 0224	2.1
0701	0.9	0804	0.8
M 1321	2.1	TU 1427	2.2
1941	0.8	2045	0.6
4 0158	1.8	**19** 0313	1.9
0741	1.0	0854	0.9
TU 1402	2.0	W 1517	2.1
2026	0.8	2142	0.8
5 0245	1.8	**20** 0404	1.8
0827	1.0	0952	1.0
W 1450	2.0	TH 1611	2.0
2118	0.8	◐ 2248	0.9
6 0337	1.8	**21** 0503	1.8
0922	1.1	1105	1.1
TH 1547	1.9	F 1716	1.9
◑ 2219	0.9		
7 0437	1.8	**22** 0001	0.9
1031	1.1	0610	1.8
F 1650	1.9	SA 1228	1.1
2330	0.9	1828	1.8
8 0543	1.8	**23** 0107	1.0
1155	1.1	0713	1.8
SA 1801	1.9	SU 1336	1.0
		1934	1.8
9 0038	0.8	**24** 0202	1.0
0651	1.9	0808	1.9
SU 1307	1.0	M 1430	1.0
1911	2.0	2030	1.9
10 0137	0.7	**25** 0247	1.0
0751	2.0	0855	2.0
M 1405	0.9	TU 1515	0.9
2013	2.1	2118	1.9
11 0231	0.7	**26** 0325	0.9
0844	2.1	0936	2.1
TU 1458	0.7	W 1553	0.8
2110	2.2	2200	2.0
12 0321	0.6	**27** 0400	0.9
0933	2.3	1014	2.1
W 1548	0.6	TH 1628	0.7
2204	2.3	2239	2.0
13 0409	0.6	**28** 0433	0.9
1022	2.4	1050	2.2
TH 1637	0.4	F 1701	0.7
● 2259	2.3	○ 2315	2.0
14 0457	0.6	**29** 0505	0.9
1111	2.4	1124	2.2
F 1726	0.4	SA 1735	0.6
2353	2.3	2351	2.1
15 0543	0.6	**30** 0538	0.8
1200	2.4	1157	2.2
SA 1814	0.3	SU 1809	0.6
		31 0025	2.0
		0611	0.8
		M 1231	2.2
		1844	0.6

TIDES

Chart Datum: 1·22 metres below Ordnance Datum (Local)
HAT is 2·5 metres above Chart Datum

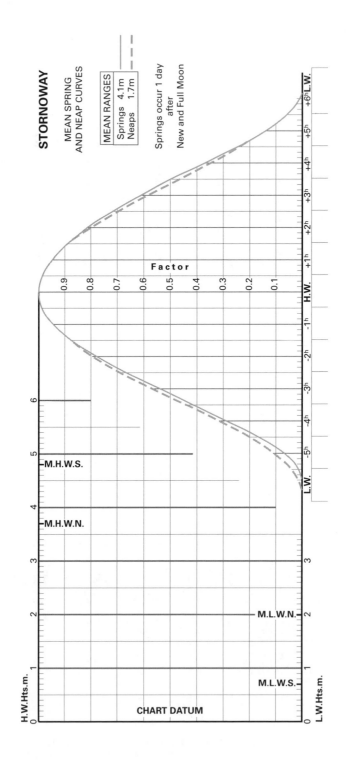

STORNOWAY

MEAN SPRING
AND NEAP CURVES

| MEAN RANGES |
| Springs 4.1m |
| Neaps 1.7m |

Springs occur 1 day
after
New and Full Moon

SCOTLAND – STORNOWAY

LAT 58°12'N   LONG 6°23'W

TIMES AND HEIGHTS OF HIGH AND LOW WATERS

Dates in amber are **SPRINGS**
Dates in yellow are **NEAPS**

2012

JANUARY

Day	Time m	Day	Time m
1 SU	0555 2.0 / 1216 3.9 / 1828 1.9 ●	16 M	0529 1.4 / 1153 4.1 / 1819 1.3 ◑
2 M	0111 3.5 / 0657 2.1 / 1326 3.9 / 1929 2.0	17 TU	0045 3.8 / 0632 1.6 / 1312 3.9 / 1927 1.5
3 TU	0233 3.5 / 0814 2.2 / 1440 3.7 / 2043 2.1	18 W	0201 3.8 / 0751 1.7 / 1431 3.9 / 2047 1.6
4 W	0337 3.6 / 0932 2.1 / 1546 3.7 / 2153 2.0	19 TH	0313 3.9 / 0922 1.7 / 1547 3.9 / 2206 1.5
5 TH	0427 3.8 / 1032 2.0 / 1638 3.8 / 2246 1.8	20 F	0418 4.1 / 1040 1.5 / 1651 4.1 / 2309 1.3
6 F	0508 4.0 / 1121 1.7 / 1722 3.9 / 2330 1.6	21 SA	0512 4.4 / 1140 1.2 / 1744 4.2 / 2359 1.1
7 SA	0543 4.2 / 1203 1.5 / 1800 4.1	22 SU	0559 4.6 / 1230 0.8 / 1828 4.4
8 SU	0009 1.4 / 0614 4.4 / 1242 1.2 / 1835 4.3	23 M	0044 0.9 / 0640 4.9 / 1314 0.7 / 1907 4.5
9 M	0046 1.1 / 0646 4.6 / 1319 1.0 / 1910 4.4 ○	24 TU	0125 0.7 / 0719 5.0 / 1353 0.6 / 1943 4.5
10 TU	0123 1.0 / 0719 4.7 / 1356 0.8 / 1945 4.5	25 W	0202 0.7 / 0755 5.0 / 1430 0.6 / 2017 4.5
11 W	0159 0.8 / 0753 4.8 / 1433 0.7 / 2021 4.5	26 TH	0239 0.7 / 0830 4.9 / 1505 0.7 / 2050 4.3
12 TH	0235 0.8 / 0828 4.8 / 1511 0.6 / 2059 4.4	27 F	0314 0.9 / 0904 4.7 / 1540 0.8 / 2123 4.2
13 F	0312 0.8 / 0906 4.7 / 1551 0.7 / 2140 4.3	28 SA	0350 1.3 / 0941 4.5 / 1615 1.1 / 2158 3.9
14 SA	0352 0.9 / 0950 4.5 / 1634 0.9 / 2230 4.1	29 SU	0427 1.4 / 1021 4.2 / 1652 1.4 / 2241 3.7
15 SU	0437 1.2 / 1044 4.3 / 1723 1.1 / 2332 3.9	30 M	0508 1.7 / 1111 3.9 / 1733 1.7 / 2337 3.5
		31 TU	0557 2.0 / 1212 3.6 / 1822 1.9 ◑

FEBRUARY

Day	Time m	Day	Time m
1 W	0054 3.4 / 0658 2.2 / 1331 3.5 / 1925 2.1	16 TH	0141 3.7 / 0731 1.8 / 1426 3.6 / 2030 1.8
2 TH	0241 3.4 / 0830 2.3 / 1504 3.4 / 2057 2.1	17 F	0300 3.8 / 0922 1.7 / 1547 3.7 / 2201 1.7
3 F	0352 3.6 / 1002 2.1 / 1611 3.6 / 2216 2.0	18 SA	0409 4.0 / 1041 1.5 / 1650 3.9 / 2302 1.4
4 SA	0442 3.8 / 1059 1.8 / 1700 3.8 / 2308 1.7	19 SU	0504 4.3 / 1136 1.1 / 1738 4.1 / 2349 1.1
5 SU	0521 4.1 / 1115 1.5 / 1741 4.0 / 2349 1.4	20 M	0548 4.5 / 1220 0.9 / 1816 4.2
6 M	0555 4.3 / 1222 1.1 / 1817 4.3	21 TU	0030 1.0 / 0625 4.7 / 1258 0.7 / 1849 4.4 ●
7 TU	0027 1.1 / 0627 4.6 / 1300 0.8 / 1851 4.5 ○	22 W	0108 0.7 / 0659 4.9 / 1333 0.5 / 1919 4.5
8 W	0044 0.9 / 0700 4.9 / 1336 0.5 / 1925 4.7	23 TH	0142 0.6 / 0730 4.9 / 1405 0.5 / 1948 4.5
9 TH	0141 0.6 / 0734 5.0 / 1412 0.3 / 1959 4.6	24 F	0216 0.6 / 0801 4.8 / 1436 0.6 / 2016 4.4
10 F	0217 0.4 / 0808 5.0 / 1449 0.3 / 2035 4.7	25 SA	0248 0.7 / 0831 4.7 / 1507 0.8 / 2045 4.3
11 SA	0254 0.4 / 0845 4.9 / 1528 0.4 / 2114 4.6	26 SU	0321 0.9 / 0903 4.4 / 1538 1.0 / 2116 4.1
12 SU	0333 0.6 / 0927 4.7 / 1609 0.6 / 2159 4.3	27 M	0354 1.2 / 0939 4.1 / 1612 1.3 / 2152 3.8
13 M	0416 0.8 / 1018 4.4 / 1654 0.9 / 2256 4.0	28 TU	0431 1.5 / 1023 3.8 / 1650 1.6 / 2238 3.6
14 TU	0504 1.2 / 1127 4.0 / 1747 1.3 ◑	29 W	0514 1.8 / 1122 3.6 / 1734 1.9 / 2348 3.4
15 W	0015 3.8 / 0604 1.5 / 1257 3.7 / 1855 1.6		

MARCH

Day	Time m	Day	Time m
1 TH	0607 2.1 / 1239 3.4 / 1831 2.1 ●	16 F	0125 3.7 / 0725 1.8 / 1421 3.5 / 2016 2.0
2 F	0116 3.4 / 0724 2.2 / 1414 3.3 / 1952 2.2	17 SA	0245 3.8 / 0916 1.7 / 1542 3.6 / 2147 1.8
3 SA	0257 3.4 / 0918 2.1 / 1537 3.5 / 2136 2.1	18 SU	0355 4.0 / 1030 1.4 / 1643 3.8 / 2246 1.5
4 SU	0403 3.7 / 1029 1.8 / 1631 3.7 / 2237 1.8	19 M	0448 4.2 / 1120 1.2 / 1726 4.0 / 2331 1.2
5 M	0449 4.0 / 1115 1.4 / 1714 4.1 / 2322 1.4	20 TU	0530 4.4 / 1200 0.9 / 1759 4.2
6 TU	0527 4.4 / 1155 1.0 / 1751 4.4	21 W	0009 1.0 / 0604 4.6 / 1235 0.8 / 1827 4.3
7 W	0002 1.1 / 0602 4.7 / 1233 0.6 / 1826 4.7	22 TH	0046 0.8 / 0635 4.7 / 1306 0.7 / 1854 4.4 ●
8 TH	0041 0.7 / 0637 5.0 / 1310 0.3 / 1901 4.9 ○	23 F	0119 0.7 / 0705 4.7 / 1337 0.6 / 1920 4.5
9 F	0118 0.4 / 0712 5.2 / 1348 0.1 / 1936 5.0	24 SA	0152 0.7 / 0733 4.7 / 1406 0.7 / 1947 4.5
10 SA	0156 0.3 / 0748 5.2 / 1425 0.1 / 2012 5.0	25 SU	0223 0.8 / 0802 4.5 / 1435 0.8 / 2015 4.4
11 SU	0235 0.3 / 0827 5.1 / 1504 0.3 / 2052 4.8	26 M	0254 0.9 / 0834 4.4 / 1506 1.0 / 2045 4.2
12 M	0315 0.4 / 0910 4.9 / 1545 0.6 / 2137 4.5	27 TU	0327 1.1 / 0910 4.1 / 1539 1.2 / 2120 4.0
13 TU	0358 0.7 / 1003 4.4 / 1630 1.0 / 2236 4.2	28 W	0402 1.4 / 0951 3.8 / 1615 1.5 / 2201 3.8
14 W	0448 1.1 / 1117 4.0 / 1723 1.4 / 2359 3.9	29 TH	0443 1.7 / 1049 3.6 / 1656 1.8 / 2304 3.6
15 TH	0550 1.5 / 1252 3.7 / 1833 1.8 ◑	30 F	0533 1.9 / 1206 3.4 / 1750 2.1 ◑
		31 SA	0029 3.5 / 0644 2.1 / 1331 3.4 / 1905 2.2

APRIL

Day	Time m	Day	Time m
1 SU	0154 3.5 / 0820 2.0 / 1452 3.5 / 2040 2.1	16 M	0328 4.0 / 1000 1.5 / 1623 3.8 / 2216 1.7
2 M	0310 3.7 / 0943 1.8 / 1553 3.8 / 2154 1.9	17 TU	0423 4.1 / 1050 1.3 / 1704 3.9 / 2303 1.4
3 TU	0407 4.0 / 1037 1.4 / 1640 4.1 / 2245 1.5	18 W	0505 4.3 / 1130 1.1 / 1736 4.1 / 2343 1.2
4 W	0452 4.4 / 1121 1.0 / 1721 4.5 / 2330 1.1	19 TH	0540 4.4 / 1205 1.0 / 1803 4.2
5 TH	0533 4.8 / 1202 0.6 / 1759 4.8	20 F	0020 1.0 / 0611 4.4 / 1238 0.9 / 1830 4.4
6 F	0012 0.8 / 0611 5.0 / 1243 0.3 / 1836 5.0 ○	21 SA	0055 0.9 / 0641 4.5 / 1308 0.9 / 1856 4.5 ●
7 SA	0054 0.5 / 0650 5.2 / 1322 0.2 / 1914 5.1	22 SU	0128 0.9 / 0710 4.5 / 1338 0.9 / 1923 4.5
8 SU	0135 0.3 / 0730 5.2 / 1402 0.2 / 1953 5.1	23 M	0200 0.9 / 0740 4.4 / 1408 0.9 / 1952 4.4
9 M	0217 0.3 / 0813 5.1 / 1443 0.4 / 2036 4.9	24 TU	0232 1.0 / 0814 4.2 / 1439 1.0 / 2024 4.3
10 TU	0301 0.5 / 0901 4.8 / 1526 0.7 / 2125 4.7	25 W	0306 1.2 / 0851 4.1 / 1512 1.2 / 2100 4.1
11 W	0347 0.8 / 0958 4.4 / 1612 1.1 / 2226 4.3	26 TH	0342 1.3 / 0935 3.8 / 1548 1.5 / 2141 3.9
12 TH	0440 1.2 / 1115 4.0 / 1705 1.5 / 2345 4.1	27 F	0423 1.5 / 1030 3.6 / 1629 1.7 / 2239 3.7
13 F	0546 1.5 / 1240 3.7 / 1817 1.9 ◑	28 SA	0513 1.7 / 1140 3.5 / 1721 1.9 / 2354 3.6
14 SA	0104 3.9 / 0713 1.7 / 1403 3.6 / 1950 2.0	29 SU	0618 1.8 / 1253 3.5 / 1830 2.1 ◑
15 SU	0220 3.9 / 0848 1.7 / 1523 3.6 / 2115 1.9	30 M	0108 3.7 / 0734 1.8 / 1405 3.6 / 1950 2.0

Chart Datum: 2·71 metres below Ordnance Datum (Local)
HAT is 5·5 metres above Chart Datum

TIDES

TIDES

TIME ZONE (UT)
For Summer Time add ONE hour in **non-shaded areas**

SCOTLAND – STORNOWAY
LAT 58°12'N   LONG 6°23'W

Dates in amber are **SPRINGS**
Dates in yellow are **NEAPS**

2012

TIMES AND HEIGHTS OF HIGH AND LOW WATERS

MAY

Day	Time	m	Day	Time	m
1 TU	0218 / 0849 / 1510 / 2104	3.8 / 1.6 / 3.8 / 1.8	**16** W	0347 / 1009 / 1634 / 2228	4.0 / 1.5 / 3.8 / 1.7
2 W	0321 / 0952 / 1603 / 2204	4.1 / 1.3 / 4.1 / 1.5	**17** TH	0434 / 1054 / 1709 / 2313	4.0 / 1.4 / 4.0 / 1.5
3 TH	0415 / 1044 / 1649 / 2256	4.4 / 1.0 / 4.5 / 1.2	**18** F	0514 / 1133 / 1740 / 2354	4.1 / 1.3 / 4.1 / 1.3
4 F	0503 / 1131 / 1732 / 2344	4.7 / 0.7 / 4.8 / 0.9	**19** SA	0549 / 1209 / 1809	4.2 / 1.2 / 4.3
5 SA	0548 / 1215 / 1813	4.9 / 0.5 / 5.0	**20** SU	0031 / 0621 / 1243 / 1836	1.2 / 4.2 / 1.1 / 4.4
6 SU	0031 / 0632 / 1300 / 1855	0.7 / 5.0 / 0.4 / 5.1	**21** M	0107 / 0653 / 1315 / 1905	1.1 / 4.2 / 1.0 / 4.4
7 M	0118 / 0717 / 1343 / 1938	0.5 / 5.0 / 0.4 / 5.1	**22** TU	0142 / 0726 / 1346 / 1936	1.1 / 4.2 / 1.0 / 4.4
8 TU	0204 / 0805 / 1427 / 2025	0.5 / 4.9 / 0.6 / 5.0	**23** W	0216 / 0802 / 1419 / 2010	1.1 / 4.2 / 1.1 / 4.3
9 W	0252 / 0856 / 1511 / 2116	0.6 / 4.7 / 0.8 / 4.8	**24** TH	0251 / 0840 / 1453 / 2047	1.1 / 4.0 / 1.2 / 4.1
10 TH	0341 / 0954 / 1558 / 2215	0.8 / 4.3 / 1.2 / 4.5	**25** F	0328 / 0923 / 1530 / 2127	1.2 / 3.9 / 1.3 / 4.1
11 F	0435 / 1100 / 1651 / 2323	1.1 / 4.0 / 1.5 / 4.3	**26** SA	0410 / 1013 / 1610 / 2216	1.3 / 3.8 / 1.5 / 3.9
12 SA	0536 / 1213 / 1755	1.4 / 3.8 / 1.8	**27** SU	0457 / 1112 / 1658 / 2319	1.4 / 3.6 / 1.7 / 3.8
13 SU	0033 / 0645 / 1329 / 1911	4.1 / 1.6 / 3.6 / 2.0	**28** M	0552 / 1216 / 1758	1.5 / 3.6 / 1.8
14 M	0142 / 0800 / 1444 / 2029	4.0 / 1.7 / 3.6 / 2.0	**29** TU	0027 / 0655 / 1322 / 1906	3.8 / 1.5 / 3.7 / 1.8
15 TU	0249 / 0912 / 1548 / 2135	3.9 / 1.6 / 3.7 / 1.9	**30** W	0134 / 0802 / 1426 / 2017	3.9 / 1.5 / 3.8 / 1.7
			31 TH	0239 / 0908 / 1525 / 2124	4.0 / 1.3 / 4.0 / 1.6

JUNE

Day	Time	m	Day	Time	m
1 F	0340 / 1008 / 1619 / 2225	4.2 / 1.1 / 4.3 / 1.3	**16** SA	0449 / 1102 / 1717 / 2330	3.8 / 1.6 / 4.0 / 1.6
2 SA	0437 / 1103 / 1708 / 2321	4.5 / 0.9 / 4.6 / 1.1	**17** SU	0529 / 1143 / 1750	3.9 / 1.4 / 4.1
3 SU	0529 / 1154 / 1755	4.6 / 0.8 / 4.8	**18** M	0011 / 0606 / 1221 / 1821	1.4 / 4.0 / 1.3 / 4.3
4 M	0015 / 0619 / 1243 / 1840	0.8 / 4.8 / 0.7 / 5.0	**19** TU	0050 / 0641 / 1256 / 1851	1.2 / 4.0 / 1.2 / 4.4
5 TU	0107 / 0709 / 1330 / 1927	0.7 / 4.8 / 0.6 / 5.1	**20** W	0126 / 0716 / 1330 / 1923	1.1 / 4.1 / 1.1 / 4.4
6 W	0157 / 0758 / 1415 / 2013	0.6 / 4.7 / 0.7 / 5.0	**21** TH	0201 / 0751 / 1404 / 1956	1.0 / 4.2 / 1.1 / 4.4
7 TH	0245 / 0847 / 1459 / 2102	0.6 / 4.6 / 0.8 / 4.9	**22** F	0236 / 0827 / 1438 / 2031	0.9 / 4.1 / 1.0 / 4.4
8 F	0333 / 0938 / 1545 / 2153	0.7 / 4.4 / 1.1 / 4.7	**23** SA	0313 / 0906 / 1514 / 2108	0.9 / 4.1 / 1.1 / 4.3
9 SA	0421 / 1032 / 1632 / 2249	0.9 / 4.1 / 1.4 / 4.5	**24** SU	0353 / 0949 / 1552 / 2150	1.0 / 4.0 / 1.2 / 4.2
10 SU	0511 / 1132 / 1725 / 2350	1.2 / 3.8 / 1.6 / 4.2	**25** M	0436 / 1038 / 1636 / 2242	1.1 / 3.9 / 1.4 / 4.1
11 M	0606 / 1239 / 1825	1.4 / 3.6 / 1.9	**26** TU	0524 / 1137 / 1727 / 2347	1.2 / 3.8 / 1.5 / 4.0
12 TU	0055 / 0705 / 1351 / 1934	4.0 / 1.6 / 3.5 / 2.0	**27** W	0619 / 1241 / 1828	1.3 / 3.7 / 1.6
13 W	0202 / 0812 / 1500 / 2047	3.8 / 1.8 / 3.5 / 2.0	**28** TH	0056 / 0721 / 1348 / 1937	3.9 / 1.3 / 3.8 / 1.7
14 TH	0306 / 0918 / 1556 / 2151	3.8 / 1.8 / 3.7 / 1.9	**29** F	0207 / 0829 / 1454 / 2052	3.9 / 1.4 / 3.9 / 1.6
15 F	0402 / 1015 / 1640 / 2244	3.8 / 1.7 / 3.8 / 1.7	**30** SA	0317 / 0940 / 1556 / 2205	4.0 / 1.3 / 4.1 / 1.4

JULY

Day	Time	m	Day	Time	m
1 SU	0422 / 1045 / 1651 / 2310	4.2 / 1.2 / 4.4 / 1.2	**16** M	0511 / 1120 / 1732 / 2352	3.7 / 1.6 / 4.0 / 1.5
2 M	0520 / 1142 / 1742	4.3 / 1.0 / 4.7	**17** TU	0551 / 1201 / 1805	3.9 / 1.4 / 4.2
3 TU	0008 / 0613 / 1233 / 1829	0.9 / 4.5 / 0.8 / 4.9	**18** W	0031 / 0626 / 1238 / 1835	1.3 / 4.1 / 1.2 / 4.4
4 W	0101 / 0701 / 1319 / 1914	0.7 / 4.6 / 0.7 / 5.0	**19** TH	0107 / 0700 / 1312 / 1906	1.0 / 4.2 / 1.0 / 4.6
5 TH	0148 / 0746 / 1403 / 1957	0.5 / 4.6 / 0.7 / 5.1	**20** F	0142 / 0733 / 1346 / 1937	0.8 / 4.3 / 0.9 / 4.6
6 F	0233 / 0830 / 1445 / 2040	0.5 / 4.5 / 0.7 / 5.0	**21** SA	0217 / 0808 / 1420 / 2010	0.7 / 4.4 / 0.8 / 4.7
7 SA	0315 / 0912 / 1525 / 2123	0.6 / 4.4 / 0.9 / 4.8	**22** SU	0252 / 0843 / 1455 / 2044	0.6 / 4.4 / 0.8 / 4.6
8 SU	0356 / 0955 / 1607 / 2208	0.8 / 4.2 / 1.1 / 4.5	**23** M	0330 / 0921 / 1532 / 2123	0.6 / 4.3 / 0.9 / 4.5
9 M	0438 / 1042 / 1650 / 2259	1.0 / 3.9 / 1.4 / 4.2	**24** TU	0410 / 1005 / 1613 / 2210	0.7 / 4.1 / 1.1 / 4.3
10 TU	0522 / 1136 / 1738 / 2357	1.3 / 3.7 / 1.7 / 3.9	**25** W	0454 / 1100 / 1700 / 2313	0.9 / 3.9 / 1.3 / 4.1
11 W	0609 / 1245 / 1835	1.6 / 3.5 / 2.0	**26** TH	0545 / 1207 / 1756	1.2 / 3.8 / 1.5
12 TH	0106 / 0704 / 1405 / 1947	3.7 / 1.8 / 3.5 / 2.1	**27** F	0030 / 0646 / 1320 / 1906	3.9 / 1.4 / 3.8 / 1.7
13 F	0221 / 0816 / 1516 / 2110	3.6 / 2.0 / 3.5 / 2.1	**28** SA	0150 / 0800 / 1433 / 2036	3.8 / 1.5 / 3.8 / 1.7
14 SA	0329 / 0933 / 1611 / 2217	3.6 / 2.0 / 3.7 / 2.0	**29** SU	0309 / 0926 / 1542 / 2203	3.8 / 1.5 / 4.0 / 1.5
15 SU	0425 / 1033 / 1655 / 2309	3.6 / 1.8 / 3.8 / 1.7	**30** M	0419 / 1038 / 1642 / 2310	4.0 / 1.4 / 4.3 / 1.2
			31 TU	0517 / 1135 / 1733	4.2 / 1.1 / 4.6

AUGUST

Day	Time	m	Day	Time	m
1 W	0004 / 0606 / 1224 / 1817	0.9 / 4.4 / 0.9 / 4.9	**16** TH	0008 / 0603 / 1215 / 1812	1.3 / 4.2 / 1.3 / 4.5
2 TH	0051 / 0649 / 1307 / 1858	0.7 / 4.5 / 0.7 / 5.0	**17** F	0043 / 0637 / 1249 / 1843	1.0 / 4.4 / 1.0 / 4.8
3 F	0133 / 0728 / 1346 / 1936	0.5 / 4.6 / 0.7 / 5.1	**18** SA	0117 / 0710 / 1324 / 1914	0.7 / 4.6 / 0.8 / 4.9
4 SA	0212 / 0805 / 1424 / 2013	0.5 / 4.6 / 0.7 / 5.0	**19** SU	0151 / 0743 / 1358 / 1947	0.5 / 4.7 / 0.6 / 5.0
5 SU	0249 / 0840 / 1501 / 2049	0.5 / 4.5 / 0.8 / 4.8	**20** M	0227 / 0817 / 1434 / 2021	0.4 / 4.7 / 0.6 / 4.9
6 M	0325 / 0915 / 1537 / 2127	0.5 / 4.3 / 1.0 / 4.6	**21** TU	0304 / 0854 / 1511 / 2100	0.4 / 4.6 / 0.7 / 4.7
7 TU	0401 / 0953 / 1615 / 2208	1.0 / 4.1 / 1.3 / 4.2	**22** W	0343 / 0937 / 1551 / 2147	0.6 / 4.4 / 0.9 / 4.5
8 W	0438 / 1035 / 1655 / 2257	1.3 / 3.8 / 1.6 / 3.9	**23** TH	0427 / 1031 / 1637 / 2251	0.9 / 4.2 / 1.2 / 4.1
9 TH	0518 / 1130 / 1743	1.6 / 3.6 / 1.9	**24** F	0516 / 1143 / 1733	1.3 / 3.9 / 1.5
10 F	0002 / 0605 / 1249 / 1843	3.6 / 1.9 / 3.5 / 2.2	**25** SA	0019 / 0618 / 1304 / 1849	3.8 / 1.6 / 3.8 / 1.8
11 SA	0128 / 0704 / 1427 / 2018	3.5 / 2.1 / 3.5 / 2.3	**26** SU	0148 / 0744 / 1422 / 2039	3.7 / 1.8 / 3.9 / 1.8
12 SU	0254 / 0838 / 1536 / 2151	3.4 / 2.2 / 3.6 / 2.1	**27** M	0310 / 0923 / 1534 / 2208	3.8 / 1.8 / 4.1 / 1.5
13 M	0359 / 1003 / 1627 / 2247	3.5 / 2.1 / 3.8 / 1.9	**28** TU	0419 / 1033 / 1634 / 2307	3.9 / 1.5 / 4.3 / 1.2
14 TU	0448 / 1056 / 1707 / 2330	3.7 / 1.8 / 4.0 / 1.6	**29** W	0513 / 1125 / 1722 / 2354	4.1 / 1.2 / 4.6 / 0.9
15 W	0528 / 1137 / 1741	4.0 / 1.6 / 4.3	**30** TH	0556 / 1208 / 1803	4.4 / 1.0 / 4.8
			31 F	0035 / 0632 / 1248 / 1839	0.7 / 4.5 / 0.8 / 5.0

Chart Datum: 2·71 metres below Ordnance Datum (Local)
HAT is 5·5 metres above Chart Datum

SCOTLAND – STORNOWAY
LAT 58°12'N   LONG 6°23'W
TIMES AND HEIGHTS OF HIGH AND LOW WATERS

Dates in amber are **SPRINGS**
Dates in yellow are **NEAPS**

2012

SEPTEMBER

Time m	Time m
1 0112 0.6 / 0705 4.6 / SA 1325 0.7 / 1912 4.6	**16** 0048 0.6 / 0643 4.9 / SU 1257 0.8 / ● 1850 5.2
2 0146 0.6 / 0737 4.6 / SU 1400 0.7 / 1945 5.0	**17** 0124 0.4 / 0717 5.0 / M 1334 0.6 / 1925 5.2
3 0219 0.6 / 0807 4.6 / M 1434 0.8 / 2016 4.8	**18** 0201 0.3 / 0753 5.0 / TU 1412 0.5 / 2002 5.2
4 0251 0.8 / 0837 4.6 / TU 1507 1.0 / 2049 4.6	**19** 0239 0.4 / 0831 4.9 / W 1451 0.6 / 2043 4.9
5 0323 1.0 / 0910 4.2 / W 1542 1.3 / 2125 4.3	**20** 0319 0.7 / 0916 4.7 / TH 1534 0.9 / 2133 4.6
6 0357 1.3 / 0947 4.0 / TH 1619 1.6 / 2210 3.9	**21** 0403 1.0 / 1013 4.4 / F 1622 1.2 / 2244 4.2
7 0435 1.7 / 1036 3.8 / F 1702 1.9 / 2311 3.6	**22** 0454 1.4 / 1130 4.1 / SA 1721 1.6 / ☾
8 0519 2.0 / 1146 3.6 / SA 1756 2.2 / ☽	**23** 0018 3.9 / 0559 1.8 / SU 1252 4.0 / 1847 1.9
9 0035 3.5 / 0614 2.2 / SU 1316 3.5 / 1914 2.4	**24** 0145 3.7 / 0735 2.0 / M 1410 4.0 / 2038 1.8
10 0210 3.4 / 0733 2.4 / M 1448 3.6 / 2114 2.3	**25** 0306 3.8 / 0914 1.9 / TU 1522 4.2 / 2200 1.6
11 0324 3.6 / 0923 2.3 / TU 1549 3.8 / 2217 2.0	**26** 0413 4.0 / 1018 1.7 / W 1621 4.4 / 2253 1.3
12 0417 3.8 / 1023 2.0 / W 1634 4.1 / 2300 1.6	**27** 0502 4.2 / 1107 1.4 / TH 1707 4.6 / 2335 1.1
13 0459 4.1 / 1106 1.7 / TH 1711 4.4 / 2337 1.3	**28** 0540 4.4 / 1148 1.2 / F 1744 4.8
14 0535 4.4 / 1144 1.3 / F 1744 4.7	**29** 0011 0.9 / 0611 4.5 / SA 1226 1.0 / 1817 4.9
15 0012 0.9 / 0609 4.7 / SA 1221 1.0 / 1817 5.0	**30** 0045 0.8 / 0640 4.6 / SU 1301 0.9 / ○ 1848 4.9

OCTOBER

Time m	Time m
1 0117 0.8 / 0709 4.7 / M 1335 0.9 / 1918 4.9	**16** 0057 0.5 / 0653 5.2 / TU 1312 0.6 / 1906 5.3
2 0148 0.8 / 0736 4.6 / TU 1408 1.0 / 1947 4.7	**17** 0137 0.5 / 0732 5.3 / W 1353 0.6 / 1948 5.2
3 0218 1.0 / 0805 4.5 / W 1440 1.1 / 2019 4.5	**18** 0217 0.6 / 0814 5.1 / TH 1436 0.7 / 2034 5.0
4 0249 1.2 / 0836 4.4 / TH 1514 1.3 / 2054 4.3	**19** 0300 0.8 / 0903 4.9 / F 1522 0.9 / 2129 4.6
5 0323 1.4 / 0912 4.2 / F 1550 1.6 / 2137 4.0	**20** 0345 1.2 / 1002 4.6 / SA 1614 1.2 / 2242 4.2
6 0359 1.7 / 0958 4.0 / SA 1631 1.9 / 2237 3.7	**21** 0438 1.6 / 1117 4.4 / SU 1716 1.6
7 0442 2.0 / 1104 3.8 / SU 1722 2.2 / 2356 3.5	**22** 0008 4.0 / 0544 1.9 / M 1234 4.2 / ☽ 1838 1.8
8 0535 2.2 / 1223 3.7 / M 1831 2.3	**23** 0128 3.8 / 0714 2.1 / TU 1347 4.2 / 2012 1.8
9 0120 3.5 / 0647 2.4 / TU 1342 3.7 / 2005 2.3	**24** 0247 3.8 / 0844 2.1 / W 1458 4.2 / 2131 1.7
10 0237 3.6 / 0819 2.4 / W 1454 3.9 / 2128 2.0	**25** 0354 4.0 / 0951 1.8 / TH 1557 4.3 / 2226 1.5
11 0337 3.9 / 0936 2.1 / TH 1549 4.1 / 2218 1.7	**26** 0443 4.1 / 1041 1.6 / F 1641 4.5 / 2308 1.3
12 0422 4.2 / 1026 1.8 / F 1633 4.4 / 2259 1.3	**27** 0519 4.3 / 1123 1.4 / SA 1722 4.6 / 2344 1.2
13 0502 4.5 / 1109 1.4 / SA 1712 4.8 / 2338 1.0	**28** 0549 4.4 / 1201 1.2 / SU 1756 4.6
14 0540 4.8 / 1150 1.1 / SU 1750 5.1	**29** 0017 1.1 / 0617 4.6 / M 1238 1.1 / ○ 1826 4.7
15 0017 0.7 / 0616 5.1 / M 1231 0.8 / ● 1827 5.3	**30** 0049 1.1 / 0649 4.6 / TU 1312 1.1 / 1856 4.6
	31 0120 1.1 / 0712 4.7 / W 1345 1.1 / 1926 4.6

NOVEMBER

Time m	Time m
1 0151 1.1 / 0741 4.6 / TH 1419 1.2 / 1959 4.4	**16** 0201 0.7 / 0802 5.2 / F 1427 0.7 / 2029 4.9
2 0223 1.2 / 0813 4.5 / F 1453 1.3 / 2036 4.3	**17** 0246 0.9 / 0853 5.1 / SA 1516 0.9 / 2125 4.6
3 0256 1.4 / 0850 4.3 / SA 1529 1.5 / 2118 4.0	**18** 0333 1.2 / 0949 4.8 / SU 1608 1.1 / 2229 4.3
4 0333 1.6 / 0933 4.1 / SU 1610 1.7 / 2213 3.8	**19** 0424 1.5 / 1055 4.6 / M 1706 1.4 / 2341 4.0
5 0414 1.9 / 1030 3.9 / M 1658 1.9 / 2322 3.7	**20** 0524 1.8 / 1204 4.4 / TU 1812 1.6 / ☽
6 0504 2.1 / 1140 3.8 / TU 1758 2.1	**21** 0055 3.8 / 0637 2.0 / W 1313 4.2 / 1926 1.8
7 0034 3.6 / 0608 2.3 / W 1250 3.8 / ☽ 1909 2.1	**22** 0210 3.8 / 0757 2.1 / TH 1421 4.1 / 2042 1.9
8 0144 3.7 / 0724 2.3 / TH 1356 3.9 / 2023 1.9	**23** 0320 3.8 / 0910 2.0 / F 1524 4.2 / 2145 1.7
9 0247 3.9 / 0838 2.1 / F 1457 4.1 / 2127 1.7	**24** 0413 4.0 / 1008 1.7 / SA 1616 4.2 / 2234 1.6
10 0341 4.2 / 0940 1.9 / SA 1552 4.4 / 2219 1.4	**25** 0454 4.1 / 1056 1.6 / SU 1659 4.3 / 2314 1.5
11 0427 4.5 / 1032 1.5 / SU 1640 4.7 / 2305 1.1	**26** 0527 4.3 / 1138 1.5 / M 1736 4.3 / 2351 1.4
12 0510 4.8 / 1118 1.2 / M 1724 4.9 / 2349 0.8	**27** 0558 4.4 / 1217 1.3 / TU 1809 4.4
13 0552 5.1 / 1207 0.9 / TU 1808 5.1 ●	**28** 0026 1.3 / 0627 4.5 / W 1254 1.2 / ○ 1841 4.4
14 0033 0.7 / 0633 5.2 / W 1254 0.8 / 1853 5.2	**29** 0059 1.2 / 0657 4.6 / TH 1329 1.2 / 1913 4.4
15 0117 0.6 / 0717 5.3 / TH 1340 0.7 / 1939 5.1	**30** 0131 1.2 / 0727 4.6 / F 1403 1.2 / 1947 4.3

DECEMBER

Time m	Time m
1 0204 1.2 / 0759 4.5 / SA 1438 1.2 / 2023 4.2	**16** 0235 0.8 / 0839 5.2 / SU 1508 0.7 / 2110 4.7
2 0238 1.3 / 0834 4.4 / SU 1514 1.3 / 2103 4.1	**17** 0320 1.0 / 0929 5.0 / M 1555 0.8 / 2202 4.4
3 0314 1.4 / 0912 4.3 / M 1553 1.4 / 2149 4.0	**18** 0407 1.2 / 1022 4.8 / TU 1644 1.1 / 2300 4.1
4 0353 1.6 / 0957 4.1 / TU 1636 1.6 / 2244 3.8	**19** 0457 1.4 / 1122 4.5 / W 1736 1.4
5 0438 1.8 / 1053 4.0 / W 1727 1.7 / 2348 3.7	**20** 0006 3.8 / 0553 1.8 / TH 1227 4.2 / ☽ 1834 1.7
6 0532 1.9 / 1158 3.9 / TH 1826 1.7	**21** 0119 3.7 / 0700 2.0 / F 1335 4.0 / 1940 1.9
7 0053 3.7 / 0635 2.0 / F 1304 3.9 / 1930 1.7	**22** 0232 3.6 / 0816 2.1 / SA 1443 3.9 / 2051 1.9
8 0157 3.9 / 0745 2.0 / SA 1409 4.0 / 2036 1.6	**23** 0336 3.7 / 0929 2.0 / SU 1544 3.9 / 2155 1.8
9 0258 4.1 / 0854 1.8 / SU 1512 4.2 / 2139 1.4	**24** 0426 3.9 / 1029 1.9 / M 1635 3.9 / 2246 1.7
10 0354 4.3 / 0958 1.6 / M 1611 4.4 / 2236 1.2	**25** 0507 4.0 / 1117 1.7 / TU 1718 4.0 / 2329 1.5
11 0444 4.6 / 1056 1.3 / TU 1705 4.7 / 2328 1.0	**26** 0542 4.2 / 1200 1.5 / W 1756 4.1
12 0532 4.9 / 1151 1.0 / W 1756 4.8	**27** 0007 1.4 / 0615 4.4 / TH 1240 1.3 / 1830 4.2
13 0017 0.8 / 0619 5.1 / TH 1243 0.8 / ● 1845 4.9	**28** 0043 1.2 / 0646 4.5 / F 1315 1.2 / ○ 1903 4.3
14 0105 0.7 / 0705 5.2 / F 1333 0.6 / 1933 4.9	**29** 0117 1.1 / 0715 4.6 / SA 1349 1.0 / 1936 4.3
15 0150 0.7 / 0752 5.3 / SA 1421 0.6 / 2021 4.8	**30** 0150 1.0 / 0746 4.6 / SU 1423 1.0 / 2009 4.3
	31 0223 1.0 / 0817 4.5 / M 1458 1.0 / 2044 4.2

Chart Datum: 2·71 metres below Ordnance Datum (Local)
HAT is 5·5 metres above Chart Datum

TIDES

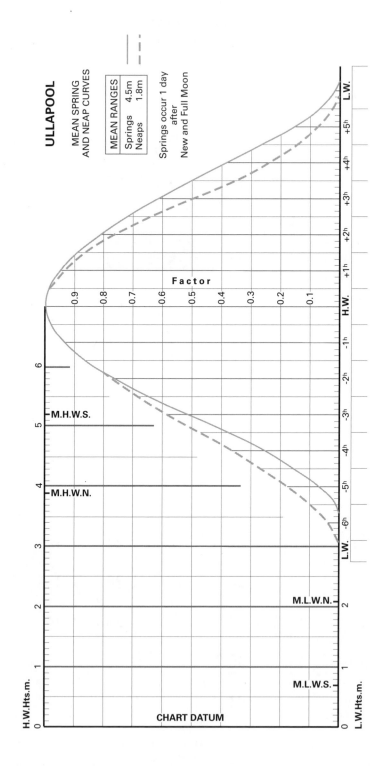

ULLAPOOL

MEAN SPRING
AND NEAP CURVES

MEAN RANGES
Springs 4.5m
Neaps 1.8m

Springs occur 1 day
after
New and Full Moon

Factor

0.9
0.8
0.7
0.6
0.5
0.4
0.3
0.2
0.1

CHART DATUM

M.H.W.S.
M.H.W.N.
M.L.W.N.
M.L.W.S.

H.W.Hts.m.
L.W.Hts.m.

SCOTLAND – ULLAPOOL

LAT 57°54'N LONG 5°10'W

TIMES AND HEIGHTS OF HIGH AND LOW WATERS

Dates in amber are **SPRINGS**
Dates in yellow are **NEAPS**

2012

JANUARY

Day	Time m	Time m	Time m	Time m		Day	Time m	Time m	Time m	Time m
1 SU	0603 2.2	1219 4.2	1833 2.1			16 M	0539 1.7	1154 4.6	1822 1.7	
2 M	0109 3.9	0704 2.4	1331 4.1	1934 2.3		17 TU	0050 4.4	0642 1.9	1313 4.4	1932 1.9
3 TU	0228 3.9	0821 2.5	1445 4.0	2049 2.3		18 W	0206 4.3	0802 2.1	1436 4.3	2056 2.0
4 W	0337 4.0	0939 2.4	1551 4.1	2159 2.2		19 TH	0321 4.4	0930 2.0	1558 4.4	2215 1.8
5 TH	0431 4.2	1040 2.2	1644 4.2	2254 2.1		20 F	0429 4.6	1046 1.8	1704 4.6	2318 1.6
6 F	0514 4.4	1128 2.0	1729 4.4	2338 1.8		21 SA	0523 4.9	1146 1.4	1756 4.8	
7 SA	0549 4.7	1209 1.7	1807 4.6			22 SU	0009 1.3	0608 5.2	1236 1.1	1839 5.0
8 SU	0017 1.6	0621 4.9	1248 1.5	1842 4.8		23 M	0054 1.1	0649 5.4	1320 0.9	1918 5.1
9 M	0055 1.4	0653 5.1	1325 1.2	1916 5.0		24 TU	0135 1.0	0727 5.5	1400 0.8	1954 5.1
10 TU	0131 1.2	0725 5.2	1402 1.1	1952 5.1		25 W	0213 0.9	0802 5.5	1437 0.8	2027 5.0
11 W	0207 1.1	0759 5.3	1438 0.9	2029 5.1		26 TH	0249 1.0	0837 5.4	1512 0.9	2100 4.9
12 TH	0244 1.0	0835 5.2	1516 0.9	2108 5.0		27 F	0324 1.1	0911 5.2	1546 1.1	2132 4.7
13 F	0322 1.1	0915 5.0	1555 1.0	2151 4.9		28 SA	0359 1.3	0945 4.9	1620 1.3	2205 4.5
14 SA	0402 1.2	0958 5.1	1637 1.1	2241 4.7		29 SU	0435 1.6	1023 4.6	1656 1.6	2244 4.2
15 SU	0447 1.4	1050 4.9	1725 1.4	2340 4.5		30 M	0513 1.9	1108 4.3	1736 1.9	2337 4.0
						31 TU	0600 2.2	1215 4.0	1824 2.2	

FEBRUARY

Day	Time m	Time m	Time m	Time m		Day	Time m	Time m	Time m	Time m
1 W	0103 3.8	0703 2.5	1342 3.9	1931 2.4		16 TH	0144 4.2	0740 2.1	1430 4.1	2038 2.2
2 TH	0235 3.8	0839 2.6	1506 3.9	2107 2.5		17 F	0309 4.2	0925 2.1	1559 4.2	2209 2.0
3 F	0352 4.0	1008 2.4	1616 4.0	2224 2.3		18 SA	0421 4.5	1045 1.8	1703 4.4	2311 1.7
4 SA	0447 4.2	1105 2.1	1707 4.2	2315 2.0		19 SU	0515 4.7	1141 1.4	1750 4.7	2359 1.4
5 SU	0527 4.5	1149 1.7	1747 4.5	2357 1.6		20 M	0557 5.0	1225 1.1	1827 4.9	
6 M	0601 4.8	1228 1.4	1823 4.8			21 TU	0040 1.1	0633 5.2	1305 0.9	1900 5.0
7 TU	0036 1.3	0632 5.1	1306 1.0	1856 5.0		22 W	0118 0.9	0707 5.3	1340 0.7	1930 5.1
8 W	0113 1.0	0705 5.3	1347 0.7	1931 5.2		23 TH	0152 0.8	0738 5.4	1412 0.7	1958 5.0
9 TH	0149 0.8	0739 5.5	1418 0.6	2007 5.3		24 F	0225 0.8	0809 5.3	1443 0.8	2026 4.9
10 F	0226 0.7	0815 5.6	1455 0.5	2045 5.3		25 SA	0257 1.0	0839 5.1	1514 0.9	2054 4.8
11 SA	0303 0.7	0854 5.5	1533 0.6	2126 5.1		26 SU	0328 1.1	0910 4.9	1544 1.2	2123 4.6
12 SU	0343 0.8	0927 5.3	1614 0.9	2212 4.9		27 M	0400 1.4	0944 4.6	1617 1.4	2156 4.4
13 M	0426 1.1	1027 4.9	1659 1.2	2308 4.6		28 TU	0435 1.7	1024 4.3	1652 1.7	2237 4.1
14 TU	0515 1.5	1131 4.6	1752 1.6			29 W	0515 2.0	1118 4.0	1733 2.1	2338 3.9
15 W	0021 4.3	0616 1.8	1257 4.2	1901 2.0						

MARCH

Day	Time m	Time m	Time m	Time m		Day	Time m	Time m	Time m	Time m
1 TH	0607 2.3	1245 3.8	1828 2.4			16 F	0128 4.1	0731 2.0	1427 3.9	2024 2.2
2 F	0126 3.7	0731 2.5	1418 3.7	2002 2.5		17 SA	0253 4.1	0918 2.0	1551 4.0	2155 2.0
3 SA	0259 3.8	0927 2.4	1538 3.8	2147 2.3		18 SU	0405 4.3	1033 1.7	1650 4.3	2255 1.7
4 SU	0408 4.0	1035 2.0	1637 4.0	2247 2.0		19 M	0457 4.6	1123 1.4	1733 4.5	2340 1.4
5 M	0454 4.3	1122 1.6	1720 4.4	2331 1.6		20 TU	0537 4.8	1204 1.1	1807 4.7	
6 TU	0531 4.7	1201 1.2	1756 4.8			21 W	0019 1.1	0611 5.0	1241 0.9	1836 4.9
7 W	0010 1.2	0605 5.1	1240 0.8	1830 5.1		22 TH	0055 0.9	0643 5.1	1314 0.8	1904 4.9
8 TH	0049 0.6	0639 5.4	1317 0.5	1905 5.3		23 F	0128 0.9	0713 5.1	1344 0.8	1931 5.0
9 F	0126 0.5	0715 5.6	1354 0.3	1942 5.5		24 SA	0200 0.8	0742 5.1	1414 0.8	1957 4.9
10 SA	0205 0.4	0753 5.6	1432 0.3	2021 5.4		25 SU	0230 0.9	0812 4.9	1443 0.9	2023 4.8
11 SU	0244 0.4	0835 5.5	1511 0.4	2102 5.2		26 M	0301 1.1	0843 4.8	1513 1.1	2052 4.6
12 M	0325 0.6	0917 5.2	1552 0.7	2150 5.0		27 TU	0332 1.3	0917 4.5	1544 1.3	2124 4.4
13 TU	0409 0.9	1014 4.8	1637 1.2	2247 4.6		28 W	0406 1.5	0957 4.3	1618 1.6	2203 4.2
14 W	0459 1.3	1125 4.4	1730 1.6			29 TH	0445 1.8	1049 4.0	1657 1.9	2256 3.9
15 TH	0003 4.3	0601 1.7	1254 4.1	1842 2.0		30 F	0533 2.1	1207 3.8	1748 2.2	
						31 SA	0025 3.8	0644 2.3	1335 3.7	1908 2.4

APRIL

Day	Time m	Time m	Time m	Time m		Day	Time m	Time m	Time m	Time m
1 SU	0202 3.8	0832 2.2	1453 3.8	2057 2.3		16 M	0337 4.2	1002 1.7	1625 4.1	2225 1.8
2 M	0316 3.9	0952 1.9	1557 4.0	2207 2.0		17 TU	0430 4.4	1053 1.4	1708 4.3	2312 1.5
3 TU	0411 4.2	1044 1.5	1644 4.4	2257 1.5		18 W	0511 4.6	1135 1.2	1742 4.6	2353 1.3
4 W	0455 4.6	1128 1.1	1725 4.8	2340 1.1		19 TH	0547 4.7	1211 1.1	1812 4.7	
5 TH	0534 5.0	1208 0.7	1802 5.1			20 F	0029 1.1	0618 4.8	1245 1.0	1839 4.8
6 F	0021 0.7	0612 5.3	1249 0.4	1839 5.4		21 SA	0104 1.0	0649 4.8	1316 0.9	1906 4.8
7 SA	0102 0.4	0652 5.5	1329 0.2	1918 5.5		22 SU	0136 1.0	0720 4.8	1346 0.9	1932 4.8
8 SU	0143 0.3	0734 5.5	1409 0.2	2000 5.5		23 M	0207 1.0	0751 4.7	1416 1.0	2000 4.8
9 M	0226 0.3	0820 5.4	1451 0.4	2044 5.3		24 TU	0238 1.1	0824 4.6	1446 1.1	2030 4.6
10 TU	0310 0.5	0910 5.1	1534 0.7	2134 5.0		25 W	0311 1.2	0900 4.4	1519 1.3	2103 4.5
11 W	0357 0.8	1011 4.7	1621 1.2	2235 4.6		26 TH	0346 1.4	0942 4.2	1554 1.5	2144 4.3
12 TH	0450 1.2	1125 4.3	1716 1.6	2349 4.3		27 F	0425 1.6	1034 4.0	1634 1.8	2235 4.1
13 F	0554 1.6	1245 4.0	1827 2.0			28 SA	0513 1.8	1141 3.9	1724 2.0	2346 3.9
14 SA	0108 4.2	0717 1.8	1409 3.9	1959 2.1		29 SU	0615 2.0	1256 3.8	1833 2.2	
15 SU	0228 4.1	0850 1.8	1528 4.0	2124 2.0		30 M	0111 3.9	0738 2.0	1408 3.9	2002 2.1

Chart Datum: 2·75 metres below Ordnance Datum (Newlyn)
HAT is 5·9 metres above Chart Datum

TIDES

TIME ZONE (UT)
For Summer Time add ONE hour in **non-shaded areas**

SCOTLAND – ULLAPOOL
LAT 57°54'N   LONG 5°10'W
TIMES AND HEIGHTS OF HIGH AND LOW WATERS

Dates in amber are **SPRINGS**
Dates in yellow are **NEAPS**

2012

MAY

Day	Time	m	Time	m	Day	Time	m	Time	m
1 TU	0224	4.0			16 W	0355	4.2		
	0859	1.8				1012	1.6		
	1512	4.1				1636	4.2		
	2119	1.9				2238	1.7		
2 W	0325	4.2			17 TH	0441	4.3		
	1000	1.4				1059	1.5		
	1606	4.4				1714	4.3		
	2217	1.5				2323	1.5		
3 TH	0417	4.6			18 F	0520	4.4		
	1051	1.1				1139	1.4		
	1652	4.7				1747	4.5		
	2307	1.2							
4 F	0504	4.9			19 SA	0003	1.4		
	1137	0.7				0556	4.5		
	1735	5.0				1215	1.2		
	2354	0.8				1817	4.6		
5 SA	0549	5.2			20 SU	0040	1.2		
	1222	0.5				0630	4.6		
	1817	5.3				1249	1.2		
					●	1846	4.7		
6 SU	0039	0.5			21 M	0114	1.2		
	0634	5.3				0703	4.6		
	1306	0.4				1322	1.1		
○	1859	5.4				1914	4.7		
7 M	0125	0.4			22 TU	0148	1.1		
	0721	5.3				0736	4.6		
	1350	0.4				1354	1.1		
	1944	5.4				1944	4.7		
8 TU	0212	0.4			23 W	0221	1.1		
	0811	5.2				0811	4.5		
	1435	0.5				1427	1.2		
	2031	5.3				2015	4.7		
9 W	0259	0.5			24 TH	0256	1.2		
	0906	4.9				0849	4.4		
	1521	0.8				1501	1.3		
	2124	5.0				2050	4.6		
10 TH	0349	0.8			25 F	0332	1.3		
	1006	4.6				0930	4.3		
	1610	1.2				1537	1.4		
	2223	4.7				2131	4.5		
11 F	0442	1.1			26 SA	0411	1.4		
	1112	4.3				1018	4.2		
	1703	1.5				1618	1.6		
	2328	4.5				2219	4.3		
12 SA	0541	1.4			27 SU	0456	1.5		
	1221	4.0				1115	4.1		
	1806	1.8				1705	1.7		
◐						2317	4.2		
13 SU	0038	4.3			28 M	0550	1.6		
	0649	1.6				1219	4.0		
	1335	3.9				1804	1.9		
	1920	2.0			◑				
14 M	0150	4.1			29 TU	0027	4.1		
	0803	1.8				0655	1.7		
	1448	3.9				1326	4.0		
	2038	2.0				1916	1.9		
15 TU	0258	4.1			30 W	0138	4.1		
	0914	1.7				0808	1.6		
	1549	4.0				1430	4.1		
	2145	1.9				2031	1.8		
					31 TH	0244	4.3		
						0916	1.5		
						1530	4.3		
						2138	1.6		

JUNE

Day	Time	m			Day	Time	m		
1 F	0344	4.5			16 SA	0454	4.2		
	1016	1.2				1106	1.7		
	1623	4.6				1722	4.3		
	2237	1.3				2338	1.6		
2 SA	0440	4.7			17 SU	0536	4.3		
	1111	1.0				1148	1.5		
	1713	4.9				1757	4.5		
	2332	1.0							
3 SU	0533	4.9			18 M	0018	1.5		
	1201	0.8				0613	4.4		
	1800	5.2				1226	1.3		
						1829	4.6		
4 M	0023	0.7			19 TU	0056	1.3		
	0624	5.1				0649	4.5		
	1250	0.6				1302	1.3		
○	1846	5.3			●	1859	4.7		
5 TU	0113	0.5			20 W	0132	1.2		
	0714	5.1				0723	4.6		
	1337	0.6				1337	1.2		
	1932	5.4				1930	4.8		
6 W	0202	0.5			21 TH	0207	1.1		
	0805	5.1				0758	4.6		
	1423	0.7				1411	1.2		
	2020	5.3				2002	4.8		
7 TH	0251	0.5			22 F	0242	1.1		
	0857	4.9				0834	4.6		
	1509	0.8				1446	1.2		
	2110	5.1				2037	4.8		
8 F	0338	0.7			23 SA	0318	1.1		
	0950	4.7				0913	4.5		
	1556	1.1				1522	1.2		
	2201	4.9				2115	4.7		
9 SA	0427	0.9			24 SU	0356	1.1		
	1044	4.4				0956	4.5		
	1644	1.4				1602	1.3		
	2257	4.6				2158	4.6		
10 SU	0517	1.2			25 M	0437	1.2		
	1142	4.1				1045	4.3		
	1736	1.6				1646	1.5		
	2356	4.4				2248	4.5		
11 M	0610	1.5			26 TU	0524	1.3		
	1245	4.0				1142	4.2		
	1835	1.8				1737	1.6		
◑						2349	4.4		
12 TU	0101	4.1			27 W	0619	1.5		
	0708	1.7				1247	4.2		
	1353	3.9				1839	1.8		
	1941	2.0			◐				
13 W	0208	4.0			28 TH	0100	4.3		
	0813	1.9				0724	1.6		
	1500	3.9				1355	4.2		
	2053	2.1				1950	1.8		
14 TH	0311	4.0			29 F	0212	4.3		
	0920	1.9				0837	1.6		
	1557	4.0				1500	4.3		
	2158	2.0				2106	1.7		
15 F	0407	4.1			30 SA	0322	4.3		
	1018	1.8				0949	1.5		
	1643	4.1				1602	4.5		
	2252	1.8				2217	1.5		

JULY

Day	Time	m			Day	Time	m		
1 SU	0429	4.5			16 M	0516	4.2		
	1053	1.3				1124	1.8		
	1659	4.8				1737	4.4		
	2319	1.2				2358	1.6		
2 M	0529	4.7			17 TU	0557	4.3		
	1149	1.1				1205	1.6		
	1750	5.0				1811	4.6		
3 TU	0015	0.9			18 W	0037	1.4		
	0621	4.9				0632	4.5		
	1240	0.9				1243	1.4		
○	1836	5.3				1841	4.8		
4 W	0106	0.7			19 TH	0114	1.2		
	0709	5.0				0705	4.7		
	1327	0.8				1319	1.2		
	1921	5.4			●	1912	4.9		
5 TH	0154	0.5			20 F	0149	1.0		
	0754	5.0				0738	4.8		
	1411	0.7				1354	1.0		
	2005	5.4				1944	5.0		
6 F	0238	0.5			21 SA	0224	0.8		
	0838	4.9				0813	4.9		
	1454	0.8				1429	1.0		
	2048	5.3				2017	5.1		
7 SA	0321	0.6			22 SU	0259	0.8		
	0921	4.8				0849	4.8		
	1536	1.0				1505	1.0		
	2131	5.0				2054	5.0		
8 SU	0402	0.8			23 M	0335	0.8		
	1004	4.5				0929	4.8		
	1617	1.2				1543	1.0		
	2216	4.8				2134	4.9		
9 M	0444	1.1			24 TU	0414	0.9		
	1050	4.3				1014	4.6		
	1701	1.5				1624	1.2		
	2305	4.5				2221	4.7		
10 TU	0526	1.4			25 W	0458	1.1		
	1143	4.0				1108	4.5		
	1748	1.8				1711	1.4		
						2318	4.5		
11 W	0003	4.2			26 TH	0548	1.4		
	0612	1.7				1214	4.3		
	1248	3.9				1808	1.7		
◑	1843	2.1			◐				
12 TH	0110	4.0			27 F	0032	4.3		
	0708	2.0				0650	1.7		
	1400	3.8				1327	4.2		
	1953	2.2				1920	1.9		
13 F	0222	3.9			28 SA	0155	4.2		
	0817	2.1				0809	1.8		
	1512	3.9				1441	4.2		
	2113	2.2				2046	1.9		
14 SA	0331	3.9			29 SU	0317	4.2		
	0933	2.1				0934	1.8		
	1611	4.0				1552	4.4		
	2222	2.1				2210	1.7		
15 SU	0429	4.0			30 M	0431	4.4		
	1036	2.0				1046	1.6		
	1658	4.2				1653	4.7		
	2315	1.9				2316	1.4		
					31 TU	0529	4.6		
						1142	1.3		
						1743	5.0		

AUGUST

Day	Time	m			Day	Time	m		
1 W	0010	1.0			16 TH	0014	1.4		
	0616	4.8				0608	4.6		
	1231	1.0				1221	1.4		
	1826	5.2				1817	4.9		
2 TH	0058	0.7			17 F	0050	1.1		
	0657	5.0				0641	4.8		
	1314	0.8				1257	1.1		
○	1906	5.4			●	1848	5.1		
3 F	0140	0.6			18 SA	0125	0.8		
	0735	5.1				0713	5.0		
	1355	0.7				1332	0.9		
	1944	5.4				1919	5.3		
4 SA	0219	0.5			19 SU	0200	0.6		
	0812	5.0				0747	5.2		
	1433	0.7				1407	0.7		
	2021	5.3				1953	5.4		
5 SU	0256	0.6			20 M	0235	0.5		
	0846	4.9				0822	5.2		
	1510	0.9				1443	0.7		
	2057	5.1				2030	5.3		
6 M	0332	0.8			21 TU	0311	0.6		
	0921	4.7				0901	5.1		
	1547	1.1				1521	0.8		
	2134	4.8				2111	5.2		
7 TU	0407	1.1			22 W	0350	0.8		
	0956	4.4				0945	4.9		
	1624	1.4				1603	1.0		
	2213	4.5				2158	4.9		
8 W	0443	1.4			23 TH	0433	1.1		
	1036	4.2				1038	4.6		
	1704	1.7				1650	1.3		
	2300	4.2				2258	4.6		
9 TH	0523	1.7			24 F	0522	1.4		
	1130	4.0				1148	4.4		
	1750	2.0				1746	1.7		
◑					◐				
10 F	0007	3.9			25 SA	0021	4.2		
	0608	2.0				0624	1.8		
	1252	3.8				1309	4.2		
	1850	2.3				1902	2.0		
11 SA	0130	3.8			26 SU	0152	4.1		
	0711	2.3				0752	2.1		
	1418	3.8				1430	4.2		
	2021	2.4				2041	2.0		
12 SU	0251	3.8			27 M	0320	4.1		
	0842	2.4				0929	2.0		
	1534	3.9				1546	4.4		
	2151	2.3				2210	1.7		
13 M	0401	3.9			28 TU	0432	4.3		
	1005	2.2				1040	1.7		
	1630	4.1				1645	4.7		
	2251	2.0				2312	1.4		
14 TU	0453	4.1			29 W	0524	4.6		
	1100	2.0				1132	1.4		
	1712	4.3				1731	5.0		
	2336	1.7							
15 W	0534	4.3			30 TH	0000	1.1		
	1142	1.7				0604	4.8		
	1746	4.6				1217	1.1		
						1810	5.2		
					31 F	0042	0.8		
						0639	5.0		
						1256	0.9		
					○	1846	5.4		

Chart Datum: 2·75 metres below Ordnance Datum (Newlyn)
HAT is 5·9 metres above Chart Datum

SCOTLAND – ULLAPOOL

LAT 57°54'N LONG 5°10'W

TIMES AND HEIGHTS OF HIGH AND LOW WATERS

Dates in amber are **SPRINGS**
Dates in yellow are **NEAPS**

2012

SEPTEMBER

Day	Time	m	Time	m		Day	Time	m	Time	m
1 SA	0119/0712	0.6/5.1	1333/1919	0.8/5.4		**16** SU ●	0057/0645	0.7/5.3	1306/1853	0.7/5.5
2 SU	0154/0742	0.6/5.1	1408/1952	0.8/5.3		**17** M	0133/0720	0.5/5.4	1343/1929	0.6/5.6
3 M	0227/0812	0.7/5.0	1442/2024	0.9/5.1		**18** TU	0209/0757	0.4/5.4	1421/2009	0.6/5.5
4 TU	0259/0841	0.9/4.8	1515/2057	1.1/4.9		**19** W	0247/0837	0.5/5.3	1501/2052	0.7/5.3
5 W	0331/0912	1.1/4.6	1549/2132	1.4/4.6		**20** TH	0328/0922	0.7/5.1	1545/2143	0.9/4.9
6 TH	0404/0945	1.4/4.4	1626/2213	1.7/4.3		**21** F	0411/1017	1.1/4.8	1634/2251	1.3/4.5
7 F	0440/1027	1.7/4.1	1707/2311	2.0/4.0		**22** SA ☽	0502/1131	1.6/4.5	1733	1.7
8 SA ☽	0521/1133	2.0/3.9	1759	2.3		**23** SU	0020/0608	4.2/2.0	1256/1854	4.3/2.0
9 SU	0041/0615	3.8/2.3	1320/1923	3.8/2.5		**24** M	0150/0743	4.1/2.2	1419/2037	4.3/2.0
10 M	0209/0744	3.7/2.5	1448/2113	3.8/2.4		**25** TU	0317/0919	4.1/2.1	1533/2200	4.4/1.7
11 TU	0325/0929	3.8/2.4	1553/2221	4.0/2.1		**26** W	0422/1025	4.3/1.8	1630/2256	4.7/1.4
12 W	0422/1030	4.1/2.1	1639/2306	4.3/1.7		**27** TH	0509/1114	4.6/1.5	1714/2340	4.9/1.2
13 TH	0504/1114	4.4/1.7	1715/2344	4.6/1.3		**28** F	0546/1156	4.8/1.2	1751	5.1
14 F	0540/1152	4.7/1.4	1748	5.0		**29** SA	0019/0617	1.0/5.0	1235/1824	1.0/5.2
15 SA	0020/0612	1.0/5.0	1229/1819	1.0/5.3		**30** SU ○	0054/0647	0.8/5.1	1310/1855	0.9/5.3

OCTOBER

Day	Time	m	Time	m		Day	Time	m	Time	m
1 M	0126/0715	0.8/5.1	1343/1926	0.9/5.2		**16** TU	0106/0655	0.5/5.6	1320/1909	0.6/5.6
2 TU	0157/0742	0.9/5.0	1415/1956	1.0/5.1		**17** W	0145/0735	0.4/5.6	1402/1953	0.5/5.5
3 W	0228/0810	1.0/4.9	1447/2028	1.2/4.9		**18** TH	0226/0818	0.5/5.5	1445/2041	0.6/5.3
4 TH	0259/0838	1.2/4.8	1520/2103	1.4/4.6		**19** F	0310/0906	0.8/5.2	1532/2138	0.9/4.9
5 F	0331/0909	1.4/4.6	1555/2143	1.6/4.3		**20** SA	0356/1004	1.2/4.9	1624/2250	1.3/4.5
6 SA	0405/0949	1.7/4.3	1635/2236	1.9/4.1		**21** SU	0449/1117	1.6/4.6	1726	1.6
7 SU	0445/1042	2.0/4.1	1723/2356	2.2/3.8		**22** M ☽	0012/0556	4.3/2.0	1238/1843	4.4/1.9
8 M ☽	0535/1215	2.3/3.9	1833	2.4		**23** TU	0135/0722	4.1/2.2	1357/2014	4.4/1.9
9 TU	0122/0650	3.8/2.5	1351/2016	3.9/2.4		**24** W	0256/0850	4.2/2.1	1509/2132	4.5/1.8
10 W	0239/0836	3.9/2.5	1503/2135	4.0/2.1		**25** TH	0400/0958	4.3/1.9	1607/2229	4.6/1.6
11 TH	0341/0948	4.1/2.2	1556/2226	4.3/1.7		**26** F	0447/1049	4.5/1.7	1652/2313	4.8/1.4
12 F	0428/1037	4.4/1.8	1638/2308	4.7/1.4		**27** SA	0524/1132	4.7/1.5	1729/2352	4.9/1.2
13 SA	0507/1119	4.8/1.4	1715/2348	5.0/1.0		**28** SU	0556/1211	4.9/1.3	1803	5.0
14 SU	0542/1159	5.1/1.0	1751	5.3		**29** M ○	0027/0624	1.1/5.0	1247/1834	1.2/5.1
15 M ●	0026/0618	0.7/5.4	1239/1829	0.7/5.5		**30** TU	0100/0652	1.1/5.1	1320/1905	1.2/5.0
						31 W	0131/0719	1.1/5.0	1353/1937	1.2/5.0

NOVEMBER

Day	Time	m	Time	m		Day	Time	m	Time	m
1 TH	0202/0747	1.2/5.0	1425/2009	1.3/4.8		**16** F	0211/0806	0.7/5.6	1435/2036	0.7/5.3
2 F	0233/0816	1.3/4.9	1458/2045	1.4/4.6		**17** SA	0257/0856	0.9/5.4	1524/2133	0.9/5.0
3 SA	0305/0849	1.5/4.7	1533/2125	1.6/4.4		**18** SU	0345/0952	1.2/5.1	1616/2237	1.1/4.7
4 SU	0340/0927	1.7/4.5	1612/2214	1.8/4.2		**19** M	0437/1056	1.6/4.9	1713/2347	1.5/4.4
5 M	0419/1014	2.0/4.3	1657/2317	2.0/4.0		**20** TU ◑	0537/1206	1.9/4.6	1818	1.7
6 TU	0506/1120	2.2/4.1	1755	2.2		**21** W	0101/0647	4.2/2.1	1320/1931	4.4/1.9
7 W ☽	0033/0608	3.9/2.4	1248/1913	4.1/2.2		**22** TH	0219/0805	4.1/2.2	1432/2046	4.4/1.9
8 TH	0147/0732	4.0/2.4	1404/2035	4.1/2.1		**23** F	0326/0917	4.2/2.1	1535/2150	4.4/1.9
9 F	0252/0853	4.2/2.2	1506/2138	4.3/1.8		**24** SA	0419/1017	4.4/2.0	1625/2241	4.5/1.7
10 SA	0346/0954	4.4/1.9	1557/2229	4.6/1.5		**25** SU	0500/1106	4.6/1.8	1707/2324	4.7/1.6
11 SU	0432/1044	4.8/1.6	1643/2315	5.0/1.1		**26** M	0535/1148	4.7/1.6	1744	4.8
12 M	0514/1131	5.1/1.2	1727/2359	5.2/0.8		**27** TU	0001/0606	1.5/4.9	1227/1818	1.5/4.8
13 TU ●	0555/1216	5.4/0.9	1811	5.5		**28** W ○	0036/0636	1.4/5.0	1302/1851	1.4/4.9
14 W	0042/0636	0.7/5.6	1301/1856	0.7/5.5		**29** TH	0110/0704	1.4/5.0	1336/1924	1.3/4.9
15 TH	0126/0719	0.6/5.7	1347/1944	0.6/5.5		**30** F	0142/0733	1.4/5.0	1409/1957	1.4/4.8

DECEMBER

Day	Time	m	Time	m		Day	Time	m	Time	m
1 SA	0214/0803	1.4/5.0	1443/2032	1.4/4.7		**16** SU	0246/0844	0.9/5.6	1514/2119	0.7/5.1
2 SU	0247/0835	1.5/4.9	1518/2110	1.5/4.6		**17** M	0332/0933	1.1/5.4	1602/2211	0.9/4.8
3 M	0322/0911	1.6/4.8	1555/2152	1.6/4.5		**18** TU	0419/1026	1.3/5.1	1651/2308	1.2/4.5
4 TU	0359/0953	1.8/4.6	1636/2242	1.8/4.3		**19** W	0509/1125	1.7/4.8	1743	1.6
5 W	0442/1044	1.9/4.4	1724/2344	1.9/4.2		**20** TH ◑	0011/0604	4.3/2.0	1231/1839	4.5/1.9
6 TH ☽	0534/1148	2.1/4.3	1823	2.0		**21** F	0123/0709	4.1/2.2	1342/1945	4.3/2.1
7 F	0053/0639	4.1/2.2	1305/1933	4.3/2.0		**22** SA	0238/0824	4.1/2.3	1452/2057	4.2/2.1
8 SA	0202/0755	4.2/2.2	1415/2045	4.4/1.9		**23** SU	0343/0938	4.2/2.3	1554/2203	4.3/2.1
9 SU	0304/0908	4.4/2.0	1518/2150	4.6/1.7		**24** M	0434/1038	4.3/2.1	1645/2255	4.4/1.9
10 M	0400/1011	4.7/1.7	1616/2246	4.8/1.4		**25** TU	0516/1127	4.5/1.9	1728/2339	4.5/1.8
11 TU	0451/1107	5.0/1.4	1710/2337	5.1/1.1		**26** W	0551/1209	4.7/1.7	1806	4.6
12 W	0538/1159	5.3/1.1	1801	5.3		**27** TH	0017/0623	1.6/4.8	1247/1840	1.5/4.8
13 TH ●	0026/0624	0.9/5.5	1250/1850	0.8/5.4		**28** F ○	0053/0653	1.5/5.0	1322/1913	1.4/4.8
14 F	0114/0709	0.8/5.7	1338/1939	0.7/5.4		**29** SA	0126/0722	1.4/5.0	1356/1945	1.3/4.9
15 SA	0200/0756	0.8/5.7	1427/2029	0.6/5.3		**30** SU	0159/0751	1.3/5.1	1429/2017	1.3/4.9
						31 M	0232/0821	1.3/5.1	1502/2051	1.3/4.8

Chart Datum: 2·75 metres below Ordnance Datum (Newlyn)
HAT is 5·9 metres above Chart Datum

TIDES

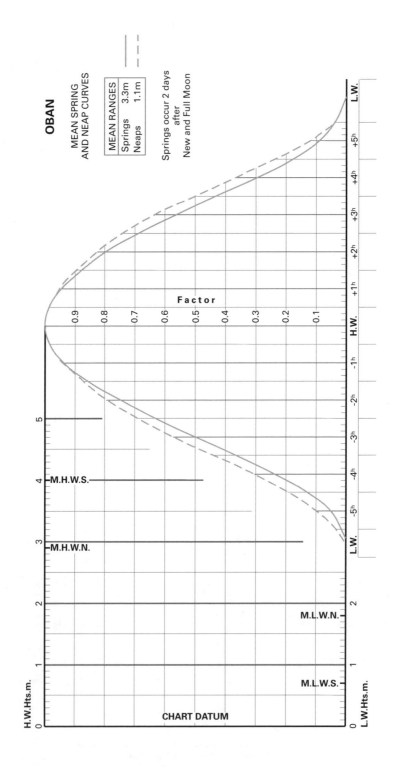

OBAN

MEAN SPRING
AND NEAP CURVES

MEAN RANGES
Springs 3.3m
Neaps 1.1m

Springs occur 2 days
after
New and Full Moon

SCOTLAND – OBAN
LAT 56°25'N LONG 5°29'W
TIMES AND HEIGHTS OF HIGH AND LOW WATERS

Dates in amber are **SPRINGS**
Dates in yellow are **NEAPS**

2012

JANUARY

Day	Time	m	Time	m	Time	m	Time	m
1 SU	0440	1.6	1036	3.3	1717	1.9	☽2236	3.0
2 M	0531	1.8	1140	3.1	1813	2.0	2346	2.9
3 TU	0631	2.0	1314	3.1	1917	2.0		
4 W	0128	3.0	0743	2.0	1436	3.1	2022	1.9
5 TH	0244	3.1	0917	1.9	1529	3.3	2121	1.7
6 F	0337	3.3	1018	1.8	1613	3.5	2210	1.5
7 SA	0422	3.5	1058	1.6	1653	3.6	2252	1.3
8 SU	0502	3.7	1135	1.4	1732	3.8	2330	1.1
9 M ○	0541	3.8	1210	1.3	1809	3.9		
10 TU	0007	0.9	0616	3.9	1247	1.1	1841	3.9
11 W	0044	0.8	0649	4.0	1322	1.1	1912	3.9
12 TH	0121	0.7	0722	4.0	1356	1.1	1944	3.8
13 F	0159	0.8	0758	4.0	1432	1.1	2021	3.7
14 SA	0240	0.8	0838	3.8	1513	1.4	2103	3.5
15 SU	0326	1.0	0922	3.7	1601	1.4	2151	3.3
16 M	0419	1.2	1015	3.4	1703	1.6	2251	3.2
17 TU	0524	1.3	1125	3.2	1818	1.7		
18 W	0017	3.1	0639	1.5	1311	3.1	1938	1.7
19 TH	0209	3.2	0759	1.5	1452	3.2	2055	1.5
20 F	0325	3.4	0918	1.4	1600	3.4	2159	1.3
21 SA	0419	3.6	1025	1.2	1647	3.6	2250	1.1
22 SU	0501	3.9	1117	1.0	1725	3.7	2335	0.9
23 M ●	0540	4.1	1202	0.9	1759	3.8		
24 TU	0017	0.8	0617	4.2	1244	0.9	1832	3.9
25 W	0057	0.7	0653	4.2	1322	0.9	1904	3.9
26 TH	0134	0.7	0727	4.1	1358	1.0	1935	3.8
27 F	0210	0.9	0800	4.0	1432	1.2	2005	3.7
28 SA	0243	1.1	0833	3.8	1506	1.3	2035	3.6
29 SU	0318	1.3	0906	3.6	1543	1.5	2108	3.4
30 M	0355	1.5	0943	3.4	1627	1.7	2145	3.2
31 TU	0439	1.8	1026	3.1	1720	1.9	☽2232	3.0

FEBRUARY

Day	Time	m	Time	m	Time	m	Time	m
1 W	0535	2.0	1136	2.9	1823	2.0	2345	2.9
2 TH	0645	2.1	1402	2.9	1933	2.0		
3 F	0206	2.9	0819	2.1	1518	3.1	2044	1.8
4 SA	0320	3.1	1008	1.8	1603	3.3	2145	1.6
5 SU	0407	3.3	1047	1.6	1641	3.5	2231	1.3
6 M	0447	3.6	1122	1.3	1718	3.7	2310	1.0
7 TU	0525	3.8	1156	1.0	1753	3.8	○2347	0.7
8 W	0600	4.0	1229	0.8	1824	3.9		
9 TH	0024	0.6	0633	4.1	1303	0.7	1853	4.0
10 F	0102	0.4	0706	4.1	1337	0.7	1924	3.9
11 SA	0142	0.4	0740	4.1	1412	0.8	2000	3.8
12 SU	0223	0.5	0818	3.9	1452	0.9	2040	3.7
13 M	0309	0.7	0900	3.7	1538	1.1	2125	3.4
14 TU	0401	1.0	0948	3.3	1635	1.4	☽2222	3.2
15 W	0504	1.3	1053	3.0	1748	1.6	2348	3.0
16 TH	0621	1.5	1301	2.8	1913	1.7		
17 F	0157	3.0	0747	1.6	1506	2.9	2042	1.5
18 SA	0319	3.2	0919	1.4	1612	3.2	2151	1.3
19 SU	0411	3.5	1023	1.2	1649	3.4	2241	1.1
20 M	0450	3.8	1120	0.9	1715	3.6	2322	0.8
21 TU	0524	4.0	1148	0.9	1743	3.7		
22 W	0001	0.7	0558	4.1	1224	0.8	1812	3.9
23 TH ○	0038	0.6	0631	4.1	1257	0.8	1842	3.9
24 F	0112	0.7	0702	4.1	1330	0.9	1909	3.9
25 SA	0144	0.8	0732	4.0	1401	1.0	1937	3.8
26 SU	0214	1.0	0802	3.8	1432	1.2	2005	3.7
27 M	0243	1.3	0831	3.6	1505	1.4	2035	3.5
28 TU	0315	1.5	0902	3.4	1543	1.6	2109	3.3
29 W	0350	1.8	0936	3.1	1632	1.8	2149	3.1

MARCH

Day	Time	m	Time	m	Time	m	Time	m
1 TH	0444	2.0	1024	2.9	1736	1.9	☽2244	2.9
2 F	0605	2.1	1320	2.7	1849	2.0		
3 SA	0112	2.8	0743	2.1	1456	2.9	2003	1.8
4 SU	0255	3.0	0938	1.8	1542	3.1	2110	1.5
5 M	0344	3.3	1020	1.5	1620	3.4	2201	1.2
6 TU	0424	3.6	1056	1.1	1655	3.6	2243	0.8
7 W	0501	3.8	1130	0.8	1728	3.8	2322	0.5
8 TH ○	0536	4.1	1204	0.6	1759	4.0		
9 F	0002	0.3	0610	4.2	1239	0.5	1829	4.0
10 SA	0042	0.2	0645	4.2	1314	0.4	1903	4.0
11 SU	0124	0.2	0721	4.1	1352	0.5	1940	3.9
12 M	0208	0.3	0759	3.9	1433	0.7	2021	3.7
13 TU	0255	0.6	0841	3.6	1521	0.9	2107	3.5
14 W	0349	0.9	0929	3.2	1617	1.2	2204	3.2
15 TH	0452	1.2	1034	2.8	1727	1.5	☽2333	2.9
16 F	0607	1.5	1301	2.7	1851	1.6		
17 SA	0142	3.0	0739	1.6	1510	2.8	2025	1.5
18 SU	0302	3.1	0913	1.4	1607	3.0	2133	1.3
19 M	0351	3.4	1009	1.2	1633	3.2	2222	1.0
20 TU	0426	3.6	1049	1.1	1650	3.4	2302	0.9
21 W	0500	3.8	1124	0.9	1717	3.6	2339	0.7
22 TH	0533	3.9	1156	0.8	1746	3.8		
23 F ○	0014	0.7	0604	4.0	1228	0.8	1814	3.9
24 SA	0047	0.8	0635	4.0	1259	0.8	1842	3.9
25 SU	0117	0.9	0705	3.9	1330	0.9	1910	3.9
26 M	0146	1.1	0734	3.8	1401	1.1	1938	3.8
27 TU	0214	1.3	0803	3.6	1432	1.3	2008	3.6
28 W	0240	1.5	0832	3.3	1505	1.5	2041	3.4
29 TH	0306	1.7	0905	3.1	1549	1.7	2120	3.2
30 F	0347	1.9	0952	2.9	1650	1.8	☽2212	3.0
31 SA	0530	2.1	1120	2.7	1803	1.9	2342	2.8

APRIL

Day	Time	m	Time	m	Time	m	Time	m
1 SU	0710	2.0	1417	2.8	1917	1.8		
2 M	0207	3.0	0844	1.8	1509	3.0	2024	1.5
3 TU	0307	3.3	0939	1.4	1549	3.3	2122	1.1
4 W	0350	3.6	1021	1.1	1625	3.5	2210	0.8
5 TH	0430	3.8	1059	0.8	1658	3.8	2255	0.5
6 F ○	0508	4.1	1135	0.5	1731	4.0	2339	0.2
7 SA	0546	4.2	1212	0.4	1806	4.1		
8 SU	0022	0.1	0624	4.2	1251	0.3	1843	4.1
9 M	0108	0.2	0703	4.0	1333	0.4	1924	4.0
10 TU	0155	0.3	0744	3.8	1417	0.6	2007	3.8
11 W	0244	0.6	0827	3.5	1506	0.8	2055	3.5
12 TH	0339	0.9	0917	3.1	1602	1.1	2154	3.2
13 F	0440	1.2	1023	2.8	1707	1.3	☽2318	3.0
14 SA	0552	1.5	1241	2.6	1825	1.5		
15 SU	0113	3.0	0721	1.5	1439	2.7	1953	1.4
16 M	0230	3.1	0846	1.5	1537	2.9	2103	1.3
17 TU	0320	3.3	0940	1.3	1555	3.1	2154	1.1
18 W	0356	3.4	1019	1.2	1616	3.3	2236	1.0
19 TH	0430	3.6	1053	1.1	1645	3.5	2313	0.9
20 F	0504	3.7	1124	1.0	1716	3.7	2347	0.9
21 SA ●	0537	3.8	1156	0.9	1747	3.8		
22 SU	0019	0.9	0609	3.8	1229	0.9	1816	3.8
23 M	0051	1.0	0641	3.8	1301	1.0	1847	3.8
24 TU	0122	1.2	0712	3.7	1334	1.1	1918	3.7
25 W	0152	1.3	0743	3.5	1405	1.2	1949	3.6
26 TH	0220	1.5	0815	3.3	1439	1.4	2023	3.4
27 F	0249	1.7	0851	3.1	1519	1.5	2103	3.3
28 SA	0333	1.8	0939	2.9	1612	1.6	2154	3.1
29 SU	0456	1.9	1048	2.8	1718	1.7	☽2306	3.0
30 M	0629	1.9	1308	2.8	1828	1.6		

Chart Datum: 2·10 metres below Ordnance Datum (Newlyn)
HAT is 4·5 metres above Chart Datum

TIDES

TIME ZONE (UT)	SCOTLAND – OBAN	Dates in amber are SPRINGS
For Summer Time add ONE hour in non-shaded areas	LAT 56°25′N LONG 5°29′W	Dates in yellow are NEAPS

TIMES AND HEIGHTS OF HIGH AND LOW WATERS — 2012

MAY

Time	m	Time	m
1 TU 0050 / 0750 / 1423 / 1936	3.1 / 1.7 / 3.0 / 1.4	**16** W 0239 / 0856 / 1504 / 2119	3.1 / 1.5 / 3.0 / 1.4
2 W 0215 / 0853 / 1510 / 2040	3.3 / 1.4 / 3.0 / 1.2	**17** TH 0322 / 0941 / 1538 / 2206	3.3 / 1.4 / 3.2 / 1.3
3 TH 0311 / 0942 / 1550 / 2137	3.5 / 1.1 / 3.5 / 0.8	**18** F 0359 / 1018 / 1613 / 2246	3.4 / 1.3 / 3.4 / 1.2
4 F 0358 / 1026 / 1627 / 2229	3.8 / 0.8 / 3.7 / 0.6	**19** SA 0435 / 1052 / 1647 / 2321	3.5 / 1.2 / 3.5 / 1.2
5 SA 0441 / 1108 / 1706 / 2318	4.0 / 0.6 / 3.9 / 0.4	**20** SU 0512 / 1126 / 1722 / ●2354	3.6 / 1.1 / 3.7 / 1.2
6 SU 0524 / 1150 / 1747 / ○	4.1 / 0.4 / 4.0	**21** M 0548 / 1201 / 1756	3.7 / 1.0 / 3.7
7 M 0006 / 0606 / 1233 / 1829	0.3 / 4.0 / 0.4 / 4.1	**22** TU 0028 / 0623 / 1237 / 1830	1.2 / 3.7 / 1.0 / 3.8
8 TU 0055 / 0649 / 1317 / 1912	0.3 / 3.9 / 0.4 / 4.0	**23** W 0103 / 0658 / 1312 / 1903	1.3 / 3.6 / 1.1 / 3.7
9 W 0144 / 0733 / 1403 / 1958	0.4 / 3.7 / 0.6 / 3.8	**24** TH 0138 / 0732 / 1345 / 1937	1.3 / 3.5 / 1.1 / 3.6
10 TH 0234 / 0819 / 1452 / 2047	0.7 / 3.4 / 0.8 / 3.6	**25** F 0212 / 0805 / 1419 / 2012	1.4 / 3.4 / 1.2 / 3.5
11 F 0327 / 0908 / 1545 / 2142	0.9 / 3.1 / 1.0 / 3.3	**26** SA 0244 / 0843 / 1458 / 2051	1.5 / 3.2 / 1.3 / 3.4
12 SA 0425 / 1008 / 1643 / ◐2250	1.2 / 2.9 / 1.2 / 3.1	**27** SU 0326 / 0927 / 1545 / 2139	1.6 / 3.1 / 1.4 / 3.3
13 SU 0529 / 1142 / 1749	1.4 / 2.7 / 1.4	**28** M 0424 / 1022 / 1641 / ◐2238	1.7 / 3.0 / 1.5 / 3.3
14 M 0023 / 0641 / 1323 / 1905	3.0 / 1.6 / 2.7 / 1.5	**29** TU 0540 / 1133 / 1745 / 2351	1.7 / 2.9 / 1.5 / 3.2
15 TU 0143 / 0757 / 1425 / 2020	3.0 / 1.6 / 2.8 / 1.5	**30** W 0657 / 1305 / 1854	1.6 / 3.0 / 1.4
		31 TH 0118 / 0806 / 1422 / 2002	3.3 / 1.4 / 3.2 / 1.2

JUNE

Time	m	Time	m
1 F 0232 / 0906 / 1517 / 2108	3.5 / 1.2 / 3.4 / 1.0	**16** SA 0330 / 0940 / 1543 / 2220	3.2 / 1.5 / 3.2 / 1.5
2 SA 0331 / 0958 / 1605 / 2208	3.6 / 1.0 / 3.4 / 0.8	**17** SU 0412 / 1022 / 1624 / 2300	3.3 / 1.3 / 3.4 / 1.4
3 SU 0422 / 1047 / 1650 / 2303	3.8 / 0.8 / 3.9 / 0.6	**18** M 0453 / 1101 / 1703 / 2336	3.5 / 1.2 / 3.6 / 1.4
4 M 0510 / 1133 / 1735 / ○2355	3.9 / 0.6 / 4.0 / 0.5	**19** TU 0533 / 1139 / 1742 / ●	3.6 / 1.1 / 3.7
5 TU 0556 / 1219 / 1820	3.9 / 0.5 / 4.1	**20** W 0012 / 0612 / 1217 / 1818	1.3 / 3.7 / 1.0 / 3.7
6 W 0045 / 0641 / 1305 / 1904	0.5 / 3.8 / 0.5 / 4.0	**21** TH 0050 / 0648 / 1252 / 1852	1.2 / 3.7 / 1.0 / 3.8
7 TH 0135 / 0725 / 1351 / 1949	0.6 / 3.7 / 0.6 / 3.9	**22** F 0127 / 0722 / 1327 / 1926	1.2 / 3.6 / 1.0 / 3.8
8 F 0223 / 0809 / 1437 / 2035	0.7 / 3.5 / 0.7 / 3.7	**23** SA 0202 / 0753 / 1401 / 2000	1.2 / 3.5 / 1.0 / 3.7
9 SA 0312 / 0853 / 1524 / 2122	1.0 / 3.3 / 0.9 / 3.5	**24** SU 0235 / 0828 / 1439 / 2037	1.3 / 3.4 / 1.0 / 3.6
10 SU 0401 / 0940 / 1614 / 2213	1.2 / 3.1 / 1.2 / 3.3	**25** M 0311 / 0908 / 1522 / 2120	1.4 / 3.3 / 1.1 / 3.5
11 M 0453 / 1023 / 1706 / ◐2312	1.4 / 2.9 / 1.4 / 3.1	**26** TU 0357 / 0955 / 1612 / 2211	1.4 / 3.2 / 1.2 / 3.4
12 TU 0549 / 1144 / 1804	1.6 / 2.8 / 1.5	**27** W 0457 / 1053 / 1712 / ◐2314	1.5 / 3.1 / 1.3 / 3.3
13 W 0028 / 0650 / 1306 / 1910	3.0 / 1.7 / 2.8 / 1.7	**28** TH 0611 / 1208 / 1821	1.6 / 3.0 / 1.4
14 TH 0144 / 0753 / 1409 / 2026	3.0 / 1.7 / 2.9 / 1.7	**29** F 0035 / 0727 / 1343 / 1934	3.2 / 1.5 / 3.1 / 1.3
15 F 0242 / 0851 / 1459 / 2132	3.1 / 1.6 / 3.0 / 1.6	**30** SA 0206 / 0838 / 1459 / 2048	3.3 / 1.4 / 3.3 / 1.2

JULY

Time	m	Time	m
1 SU 0318 / 0940 / 1557 / 2155	3.4 / 1.2 / 3.6 / 1.0	**16** M 0357 / 0958 / 1608 / 2249	3.2 / 1.5 / 3.3 / 1.6
2 M 0417 / 1034 / 1646 / 2255	3.6 / 0.9 / 3.8 / 0.8	**17** TU 0440 / 1042 / 1650 / 2325	3.4 / 1.3 / 3.5 / 1.4
3 TU 0507 / 1124 / 1731 / ○2348	3.7 / 0.7 / 4.0 / 0.7	**18** W 0521 / 1121 / 1729	3.6 / 1.1 / 3.7
4 W 0552 / 1210 / 1814	3.8 / 0.6 / 4.1	**19** TH 0000 / 0559 / 1158 / ●1805	1.2 / 3.7 / 0.9 / 3.8
5 TH 0037 / 0634 / 1255 / 1855	0.6 / 3.8 / 0.5 / 4.1	**20** F 0035 / 0634 / 1233 / 1839	1.1 / 3.8 / 0.8 / 3.9
6 F 0123 / 0714 / 1338 / 1936	0.7 / 3.7 / 0.6 / 4.1	**21** SA 0110 / 0706 / 1307 / 1911	1.0 / 3.8 / 0.7 / 3.9
7 SA 0207 / 0752 / 1419 / 2015	0.8 / 3.6 / 0.7 / 3.9	**22** SU 0144 / 0734 / 1342 / 1943	1.0 / 3.7 / 0.7 / 3.9
8 SU 0249 / 0829 / 1500 / 2054	0.9 / 3.5 / 0.9 / 3.7	**23** M 0216 / 0806 / 1419 / 2018	1.0 / 3.6 / 0.7 / 3.8
9 M 0330 / 0904 / 1540 / 2133	1.2 / 3.3 / 1.1 / 3.5	**24** TU 0251 / 0843 / 1501 / 2058	1.1 / 3.5 / 0.9 / 3.7
10 TU 0412 / 0941 / 1623 / 2216	1.4 / 3.1 / 1.4 / 3.2	**25** W 0333 / 0927 / 1549 / 2144	1.2 / 3.3 / 1.0 / 3.5
11 W 0458 / 1025 / 1710 / ◐2309	1.6 / 3.0 / 1.6 / 3.0	**26** TH 0428 / 1021 / 1648 / ◐2243	1.4 / 3.2 / 1.2 / 3.2
12 TH 0551 / 1125 / 1804	1.7 / 2.9 / 1.8	**27** F 0539 / 1135 / 1759	1.5 / 3.0 / 1.4
13 F 0024 / 0651 / 1301 / 1909	2.9 / 1.8 / 2.8 / 1.9	**28** SA 0007 / 0700 / 1330 / 1917	3.1 / 1.6 / 3.0 / 1.4
14 SA 0159 / 0758 / 1423 / 2037	2.9 / 1.8 / 2.9 / 1.9	**29** SU 0202 / 0820 / 1459 / 2038	3.1 / 1.5 / 3.3 / 1.4
15 SU 0308 / 0903 / 1521 / 2205	3.0 / 1.6 / 3.1 / 1.8	**30** M 0328 / 0931 / 1558 / 2152	3.2 / 1.3 / 3.5 / 1.2
		31 TU 0426 / 1027 / 1645 / 2251	3.4 / 1.0 / 3.8 / 1.0

AUGUST

Time	m	Time	m
1 W 0510 / 1115 / 1725 / 2340	3.6 / 0.8 / 4.0 / 0.8	**16** TH 0503 / 1100 / 1711 / 2340	3.6 / 1.0 / 3.8 / 1.1
2 TH 0547 / 1159 / 1803 / ○	3.7 / 0.6 / 4.1	**17** F 0539 / 1135 / 1746 / ●	3.7 / 0.8 / 3.9
3 F 0023 / 0621 / 1240 / 1839	0.7 / 3.8 / 0.5 / 4.2	**18** SA 0013 / 0612 / 1210 / 1818	0.9 / 3.9 / 0.6 / 4.1
4 SA 0104 / 0655 / 1319 / 1914	0.7 / 3.8 / 0.5 / 4.1	**19** SU 0047 / 0641 / 1245 / 1849	0.8 / 3.9 / 0.5 / 4.1
5 SU 0142 / 0727 / 1357 / 1948	0.8 / 3.8 / 0.7 / 4.0	**20** M 0119 / 0709 / 1321 / 1921	0.7 / 3.9 / 0.5 / 4.1
6 M 0219 / 0757 / 1432 / 2021	0.9 / 3.7 / 0.9 / 3.8	**21** TU 0153 / 0741 / 1400 / 1956	0.7 / 3.8 / 0.5 / 3.9
7 TU 0254 / 0827 / 1506 / 2054	1.1 / 3.5 / 1.1 / 3.6	**22** W 0230 / 0819 / 1443 / 2035	0.9 / 3.7 / 0.7 / 3.7
8 W 0331 / 0858 / 1543 / 2129	1.3 / 3.4 / 1.4 / 3.3	**23** TH 0313 / 0903 / 1533 / 2120	1.0 / 3.5 / 0.9 / 3.4
9 TH 0414 / 0935 / 1626 / 2210	1.5 / 3.2 / 1.7 / 3.1	**24** F 0407 / 0957 / 1633 / ◐2218	1.3 / 3.2 / 1.2 / 3.1
10 F 0505 / 1022 / 1719 / 2311	1.7 / 3.0 / 1.9 / 2.9	**25** SA 0518 / 1115 / 1746 / 2354	1.5 / 3.0 / 1.5 / 2.9
11 SA 0606 / 1139 / 1825	1.9 / 2.8 / 2.1	**26** SU 0641 / 1334 / 1909	1.6 / 3.0 / 1.6
12 SU 0120 / 0715 / 1356 / 1951	2.8 / 1.9 / 2.8 / 2.1	**27** M 0217 / 0809 / 1455 / 2038	2.9 / 1.5 / 3.3 / 1.5
13 M 0257 / 0831 / 1508 / 2156	2.9 / 1.8 / 3.0 / 1.9	**28** TU 0337 / 0923 / 1550 / 2152	3.1 / 1.3 / 3.5 / 1.3
14 TU 0345 / 0934 / 1554 / 2235	3.1 / 1.5 / 3.3 / 1.6	**29** W 0425 / 1017 / 1632 / 2243	3.3 / 1.0 / 3.8 / 1.0
15 W 0425 / 1021 / 1633 / 2308	3.4 / 1.5 / 3.5 / 1.3	**30** TH 0459 / 1101 / 1708 / 2324	3.5 / 0.8 / 4.0 / 0.9
		31 F 0528 / 1142 / 1742 / ○	3.7 / 0.6 / 4.1

Chart Datum: 2·10 metres below Ordnance Datum (Newlyn)
HAT is 4·5 metres above Chart Datum

SCOTLAND – OBAN

LAT 56°25'N   LONG 5°29'W

TIMES AND HEIGHTS OF HIGH AND LOW WATERS

2012

SEPTEMBER

Time	m		Time	m
1 0002	0.8	**16** 0543	3.9	
0558	3.9	1143	0.5	
SA 1220	0.6	SU 1752	4.2	
1814	4.2	●		
2 0038	0.7	**17** 0018	0.6	
0628	3.9	0612	4.0	
SU 1256	0.6	M 1221	0.4	
1846	4.2	1824	4.2	
3 0112	0.8	**18** 0052	0.5	
0657	3.9	0643	4.0	
M 1330	0.7	TU 1301	0.3	
1917	4.1	1858	4.2	
4 0146	0.9	**19** 0129	0.6	
0725	3.9	0718	4.0	
TU 1402	1.0	W 1343	0.4	
1947	3.9	1935	4.0	
5 0219	1.1	**20** 0209	0.7	
0753	3.7	0758	3.8	
W 1433	1.2	TH 1429	0.7	
2018	3.7	2015	3.7	
6 0254	1.3	**21** 0256	0.9	
0824	3.6	0844	3.6	
TH 1507	1.5	F 1522	1.0	
2050	3.4	2102	3.4	
7 0335	1.5	**22** 0351	1.2	
0859	3.3	0940	3.3	
F 1548	1.8	SA 1624	1.3	
2125	3.2	◑ 2201	3.0	
8 0425	1.7	**23** 0500	1.4	
0941	3.1	1106	3.1	
SA 1642	2.0	SU 1737	1.5	
◐ 2212	2.9	2358	2.8	
9 0526	1.9	**24** 0622	1.6	
1042	2.9	1324	3.1	
SU 1754	2.2	M 1902	1.6	
10 0043	2.8	**25** 0221	2.8	
0637	1.9	0752	1.5	
M 1329	2.8	TU 1440	3.3	
1927	2.2	2036	1.5	
11 0237	2.9	**26** 0333	3.1	
0753	1.8	0906	1.3	
TU 1451	3.0	W 1532	3.5	
2130	1.9	2140	1.3	
12 0325	3.1	**27** 0411	3.3	
0901	1.6	0958	1.1	
W 1533	3.3	TH 1610	3.8	
2206	1.6	2224	1.1	
13 0403	3.4	**28** 0434	3.5	
0950	1.3	1041	0.9	
TH 1609	3.6	F 1643	3.9	
2239	1.3	2301	1.0	
14 0438	3.6	**29** 0500	3.7	
1030	1.0	1120	0.8	
F 1644	3.9	SA 1715	4.1	
2312	1.0	2335	0.9	
15 0512	3.8	**30** 0529	3.8	
1107	0.7	1156	0.7	
SA 1719	4.1	SU 1746	4.1	
2345	0.8	○		

OCTOBER

Time	m		Time	m
1 0008	0.9	**16** 0545	4.1	
0558	4.0	1159	0.4	
M 1231	0.8	TU 1800	4.3	
1816	4.1			
2 0041	0.9	**17** 0027	0.5	
0627	4.0	0621	4.1	
TU 1303	0.9	W 1243	0.4	
1847	4.1	1837	4.2	
3 0114	1.0	**18** 0108	0.5	
0655	4.0	0700	4.1	
W 1334	1.1	TH 1329	0.5	
1917	3.9	1918	4.0	
4 0147	1.1	**19** 0152	0.7	
0725	3.9	0743	3.9	
TH 1404	1.4	F 1418	0.7	
1948	3.7	2001	3.7	
5 0222	1.3	**20** 0240	0.9	
0757	3.7	0832	3.7	
F 1437	1.6	SA 1512	1.0	
2020	3.5	2049	3.4	
6 0300	1.5	**21** 0335	1.1	
0832	3.5	0929	3.4	
SA 1516	1.9	SU 1613	1.3	
2054	3.2	2149	3.0	
7 0346	1.7	**22** 0439	1.4	
0912	3.3	1053	3.2	
SU 1609	2.1	M 1723	1.6	
2138	3.0	◑ 2338	2.8	
8 0444	1.9	**23** 0556	1.5	
1007	3.1	1258	3.2	
M 1726	2.2	TU 1846	1.7	
◑ 2305	2.8			
9 0553	2.0	**24** 0156	2.8	
1200	2.9	0721	1.5	
TU 1858	2.2	W 1413	3.3	
		2013	1.4	
10 0201	2.9	**25** 0310	3.0	
0705	1.9	0836	1.4	
W 1411	3.1	TH 1505	3.5	
2031	2.0	2114	1.5	
11 0253	3.1	**26** 0343	3.2	
0813	1.7	0932	1.2	
TH 1458	3.4	F 1542	3.6	
2124	1.7	2157	1.3	
12 0333	3.3	**27** 0401	3.4	
0908	1.4	1016	1.1	
F 1536	3.6	SA 1615	3.8	
2203	1.3	2232	1.2	
13 0408	3.6	**28** 0429	3.6	
0954	1.1	1056	1.0	
SA 1613	3.9	SU 1647	3.9	
2239	1.0	2305	1.1	
14 0441	3.8	**29** 0500	3.8	
1035	0.8	1132	1.0	
SU 1648	4.1	M 1718	4.0	
2314	0.8	○ 2337	1.0	
15 0513	4.0	**30** 0531	3.9	
1117	0.5	1206	1.1	
M 1724	4.3	TU 1750	4.0	
● 2349	0.6			
		31 0011	1.0	
		0601	4.0	
		W 1238	1.2	
		1822	4.0	

NOVEMBER

Time	m		Time	m
1 0046	1.1	**16** 0051	0.6	
0633	4.0	0649	4.2	
TH 1311	1.3	F 1318	0.6	
1855	3.9	1906	4.0	
2 0121	1.2	**17** 0138	0.6	
0705	3.9	0734	4.1	
F 1343	1.5	SA 1408	0.8	
1928	3.8	1951	3.7	
3 0156	1.3	**18** 0226	0.8	
0738	3.8	0823	3.9	
SA 1417	1.7	SU 1501	1.0	
2001	3.6	2038	3.4	
4 0232	1.5	**19** 0319	1.0	
0813	3.6	0917	3.6	
SU 1453	1.9	M 1557	1.3	
2037	3.3	2132	3.1	
5 0311	1.7	**20** 0416	1.3	
0852	3.4	1024	3.4	
M 1540	2.1	TU 1659	1.5	
2120	3.1	◑ 2244	2.9	
6 0400	1.8	**21** 0521	1.4	
0941	3.3	1204	3.3	
TU 1649	2.2	W 1809	1.7	
2220	3.0			
7 0500	1.9	**22** 0040	2.8	
1048	3.2	0635	1.6	
W 1811	2.2	TH 1329	3.3	
◐		1924	1.7	
8 0036	2.9	**23** 0203	2.9	
0607	1.9	0753	1.6	
TH 1238	3.2	F 1428	3.3	
1930	2.0	2031	1.7	
9 0206	3.0	**24** 0250	3.1	
0715	1.7	0859	1.5	
F 1404	3.4	SA 1512	3.5	
2032	1.7	2120	1.6	
10 0254	3.3	**25** 0324	3.3	
0818	1.5	0950	1.4	
SA 1455	3.6	SU 1548	3.6	
2121	1.4	2200	1.5	
11 0333	3.5	**26** 0358	3.5	
0914	1.2	1033	1.4	
SU 1539	3.9	M 1622	3.7	
2204	1.2	2235	1.3	
12 0409	3.8	**27** 0433	3.7	
1005	0.9	1111	1.3	
M 1620	4.1	TU 1656	3.8	
2244	0.9	2310	1.2	
13 0446	4.0	**28** 0508	3.8	
1054	0.7	1146	1.3	
TU 1700	4.2	W 1731	3.9	
● 2325	0.7	○ 2346	1.2	
14 0525	4.1	**29** 0543	3.9	
1141	0.5	1219	1.4	
W 1742	4.2	TH 1806	3.9	
15 0007	0.6	**30** 0023	1.1	
0606	4.2	0617	4.0	
TH 1230	0.5	F 1254	1.4	
1823	4.2	1841	3.9	

DECEMBER

Time	m		Time	m
1 0059	1.2	**16** 0126	0.6	
0651	3.9	0726	4.2	
SA 1329	1.5	SU 1358	0.8	
1916	3.8	1941	3.8	
2 0135	1.3	**17** 0213	0.7	
0725	3.9	0811	4.0	
SU 1404	1.6	M 1446	1.0	
1949	3.6	2024	3.6	
3 0208	1.4	**18** 0300	0.9	
0759	3.8	0858	3.8	
M 1437	1.8	TU 1535	1.2	
2023	3.5	2108	3.4	
4 0243	1.5	**19** 0349	1.1	
0835	3.6	0948	3.6	
TU 1512	1.9	W 1625	1.5	
2102	3.3	2156	3.1	
5 0324	1.6	**20** 0442	1.4	
0916	3.5	1047	3.3	
W 1559	2.0	TH 1720	1.7	
2149	3.2	◑ 2256	3.0	
6 0413	1.7	**21** 0541	1.6	
1008	3.4	1207	3.2	
TH 1706	2.0	F 1820	1.8	
◐ 2249	3.1			
7 0513	1.7	**22** 0023	2.9	
1115	3.3	0649	1.7	
F 1823	2.0	SA 1336	3.1	
		1925	1.9	
8 0010	3.0	**23** 0145	3.0	
0621	1.7	0811	1.6	
SA 1243	3.4	SU 1439	3.2	
1934	1.8	2030	1.8	
9 0152	3.2	**24** 0243	3.1	
0731	1.6	0923	1.7	
SU 1408	3.5	M 1525	3.3	
2037	1.6	2124	1.7	
10 0255	3.4	**25** 0330	3.3	
0839	1.4	1017	1.7	
M 1508	3.7	TU 1604	3.5	
2131	1.3	2209	1.5	
11 0344	3.7	**26** 0412	3.5	
0941	1.1	1059	1.6	
TU 1559	3.9	W 1641	3.6	
2221	1.1	2249	1.4	
12 0429	3.9	**27** 0451	3.7	
1038	0.9	1135	1.5	
W 1646	4.0	TH 1719	3.8	
2308	0.8	2327	1.2	
13 0513	4.1	**28** 0529	3.8	
1130	0.7	1208	1.4	
TH 1731	4.1	F 1756	3.9	
● 2354	0.7	○		
14 0557	4.2	**29** 0005	1.1	
1221	0.6	0606	3.9	
F 1815	4.1	SA 1242	1.4	
		1832	3.9	
15 0040	0.6	**30** 0041	1.1	
0641	4.3	0640	3.9	
SA 1310	0.7	SU 1316	1.4	
1858	4.0	1905	3.9	
		31 0115	1.1	
		0713	3.9	
		M 1350	1.4	
		1936	3.8	

TIDES

Chart Datum: 2·10 metres below Ordnance Datum (Newlyn)
HAT is 4·5 metres above Chart Datum

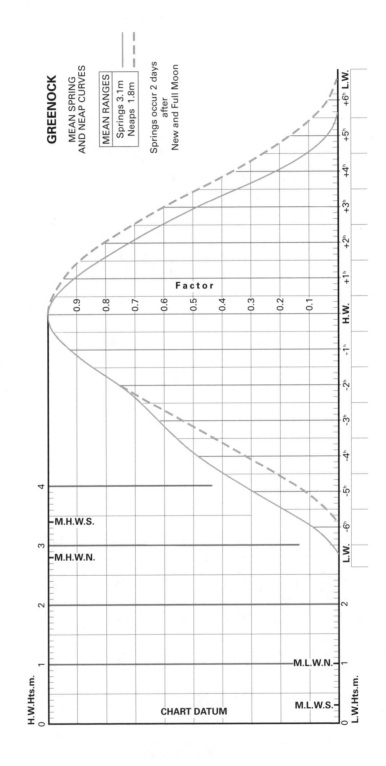

GREENOCK

MEAN SPRING
AND NEAP CURVES

MEAN RANGES
Springs 3.1m
Neaps 1.8m

Springs occur 2 days
after
New and Full Moon

TIME ZONE (UT)	SCOTLAND – GREENOCK	Dates in amber are SPRINGS
For Summer Time add ONE hour in **non-shaded areas**	LAT 55°57'N LONG 4°46'W	Dates in yellow are NEAPS
	TIMES AND HEIGHTS OF HIGH AND LOW WATERS	**2012**

JANUARY

Time m / Time m

1 SU 0516 3.1 / 1046 1.0 / 1732 3.3 / ☽2337 0.9
16 M 0457 3.2 / 1042 0.7 / 1704 3.6 / 2305 0.6

2 M 0603 3.0 / 1143 1.2 / 1823 3.1
17 TU 0546 3.1 / 1144 0.8 / 1758 3.4

3 TU 0042 1.0 / 0656 3.0 / 1254 1.3 / 1923 3.0
18 W 0010 0.7 / 0649 3.0 / 1257 0.9 / 1905 3.2

4 W 0149 1.0 / 0759 3.0 / 1413 1.3 / 2036 2.9
19 TH 0125 0.9 / 0826 3.0 / 1417 0.9 / 2043 3.1

5 TH 0248 1.0 / 0911 3.0 / 1515 1.1 / 2151 3.0
20 F 0241 0.9 / 0951 3.1 / 1527 0.7 / 2212 3.1

6 F 0339 0.9 / 1014 3.2 / 1604 1.0 / 2250 3.1
21 SA 0346 0.7 / 1051 3.3 / 1623 0.4 / 2316 3.2

7 SA 0424 0.8 / 1103 3.4 / 1645 0.8 / 2337 3.2
22 SU 0440 0.6 / 1141 3.5 / 1711 0.2

8 SU 0504 0.7 / 1144 3.5 / 1721 0.7
23 M 0009 3.3 / 0526 0.5 / 1227 3.6 / ●1754 0.1

9 M 0019 3.2 / 0540 0.7 / 1220 3.6 / ○1754 0.6
24 TU 0057 3.3 / 0609 0.5 / 1310 3.7 / 1835 0.1

10 TU 0058 3.3 / 0615 0.6 / 1255 3.7 / 1828 0.5
25 W 0139 3.3 / 0648 0.5 / 1349 3.7 / 1913 0.2

11 W 0136 3.3 / 0651 0.6 / 1332 3.8 / 1904 0.4
26 TH 0216 3.3 / 0725 0.5 / 1427 3.7 / 1949 0.2

12 TH 0214 3.3 / 0730 0.5 / 1411 3.8 / 1945 0.3
27 F 0250 3.3 / 0801 0.5 / 1502 3.7 / 2027 0.3

13 F 0253 3.5 / 0813 0.5 / 1452 3.8 / 2029 0.3
28 SA 0324 3.3 / 0838 0.6 / 1538 3.6 / 2107 0.5

14 SA 0333 3.4 / 0859 0.6 / 1534 3.8 / 2116 0.3
29 SU 0400 3.3 / 0916 0.6 / 1614 3.4 / 2150 0.6

15 SU 0414 3.3 / 0948 0.6 / 1617 3.7 / 2208 0.4
30 M 0437 3.2 / 0958 0.8 / 1653 3.3 / 2238 0.8

31 TU 0517 3.1 / 1044 1.0 / 1736 3.1 / ☽2335 1.0

FEBRUARY

Time m / Time m

1 W 0602 3.0 / 1142 1.2 / 1828 2.9
16 TH 0610 3.0 / 1239 0.8 / 1835 3.0

2 TH 0046 1.1 / 0657 2.9 / 1301 1.3 / 1934 2.7
17 F 0110 1.0 / 0754 2.8 / 1407 0.8 / 2042 2.8

3 F 0207 1.1 / 0810 2.9 / 1435 1.2 / 2107 2.7
18 SA 0235 1.0 / 0940 3.0 / 1518 0.6 / 2217 2.9

4 SA 0311 1.0 / 0936 3.0 / 1537 1.0 / 2228 2.9
19 SU 0340 0.8 / 1040 3.2 / 1613 0.3 / 2313 3.1

5 SU 0401 0.8 / 1037 3.2 / 1622 0.8 / 2320 3.0
20 M 0432 0.6 / 1128 3.4 / 1659 0.2

6 M 0442 0.7 / 1121 3.3 / 1659 0.6
21 TU 0000 3.2 / 0515 0.5 / 1213 3.6 / ●1739 0.1

7 TU 0003 3.2 / 0519 0.5 / 1159 3.5 / ○1733 0.4
22 W 0042 3.3 / 0554 0.4 / 1253 3.6 / 1816 0.1

8 W 0043 3.4 / 0554 0.4 / 1237 3.6 / 1807 0.3
23 TH 0119 3.3 / 0629 0.4 / 1331 3.6 / 1849 0.2

9 TH 0121 3.3 / 0630 0.3 / 1315 3.7 / 1844 0.2
24 F 0150 3.3 / 0700 0.4 / 1405 3.6 / 1921 0.2

10 F 0158 3.3 / 0709 0.3 / 1356 3.8 / 1924 0.1
25 SA 0221 3.3 / 0731 0.4 / 1438 3.5 / 1954 0.3

11 SA 0235 3.4 / 0751 0.2 / 1437 3.8 / 2007 0.1
26 SU 0252 3.3 / 0803 0.4 / 1510 3.5 / 2030 0.4

12 SU 0313 3.4 / 0836 0.2 / 1518 3.8 / 2053 0.2
27 M 0326 3.4 / 0839 0.5 / 1544 3.4 / 2108 0.3

13 M 0351 3.4 / 0925 0.3 / 1600 3.7 / 2143 0.3
28 TU 0400 3.3 / 0917 0.6 / 1620 3.2 / 2149 0.7

14 TU 0431 3.3 / 1018 0.5 / 1645 3.5 / ☽2239 0.6
29 W 0436 3.2 / 1000 0.7 / 1701 3.0 / 2238 0.9

15 W 0515 3.2 / 1120 0.6 / 1734 3.2 / 2345 0.8

MARCH

Time m / Time m

1 TH 0517 3.0 / 1052 1.0 / 1750 2.8 / ☽2341 1.1
16 F 0548 2.9 / 1231 0.6 / 1822 2.8

2 F 0608 2.9 / 1159 1.1 / 1853 2.6
17 SA 0059 1.0 / 0733 2.8 / 1354 0.6 / 2051 2.7

3 SA 0108 1.2 / 0714 2.8 / 1336 1.1 / 2022 2.6
18 SU 0221 1.0 / 0920 2.9 / 1459 0.4 / 2205 2.9

4 SU 0234 1.1 / 0842 2.8 / 1459 0.9 / 2202 2.8
19 M 0324 0.8 / 1019 3.2 / 1553 0.3 / 2256 3.0

5 M 0330 0.9 / 1000 3.0 / 1549 0.6 / 2256 3.0
20 TU 0414 0.6 / 1107 3.4 / 1638 0.1 / 2339 3.1

6 TU 0414 0.6 / 1050 3.2 / 1629 0.4 / 2339 3.1
21 W 0457 0.4 / 1150 3.5 / 1717 0.1

7 W 0452 0.4 / 1132 3.4 / 1705 0.2
22 TH 0017 3.2 / 0533 0.4 / 1231 3.5 / ●1751 0.1

8 TH 0019 3.2 / 0528 0.3 / 1214 3.5 / ○1741 0.0
23 F 0050 3.2 / 0605 0.4 / 1307 3.5 / 1822 0.2

9 F 0058 3.3 / 0606 0.1 / 1256 3.6 / 1820 -0.1
24 SA 0120 3.3 / 0633 0.4 / 1340 3.4 / 1852 0.3

10 SA 0136 3.4 / 0647 0.0 / 1338 3.7 / 1901 -0.1
25 SU 0149 3.3 / 0701 0.3 / 1411 3.4 / 1923 0.3

11 SU 0213 3.4 / 0730 0.0 / 1421 3.8 / 1946 0.0
26 M 0221 3.4 / 0732 0.3 / 1443 3.3 / 1957 0.4

12 M 0251 3.5 / 0816 0.0 / 1503 3.7 / 2033 0.1
27 TU 0253 3.4 / 0807 0.4 / 1516 3.3 / 2034 0.5

13 TU 0329 3.5 / 0905 0.1 / 1546 3.6 / 2123 0.3
28 W 0326 3.4 / 0845 0.4 / 1552 3.2 / 2115 0.7

14 W 0409 3.4 / 1000 0.3 / 1630 3.4 / 2220 0.6
29 TH 0400 3.3 / 0929 0.6 / 1633 3.0 / 2202 0.8

15 TH 0453 3.2 / 1106 0.5 / 1719 3.1 / ☽2330 0.9
30 F 0439 3.1 / 1020 0.8 / 1721 2.8 / ☽2300 1.0

31 SA 0526 2.9 / 1123 0.9 / 1822 2.6

APRIL

Time m / Time m

1 SU 0012 1.1 / 0628 2.8 / 1242 0.9 / 1942 2.6
16 M 0152 1.0 / 0846 2.9 / 1431 0.4 / 2135 2.8

2 M 0138 1.1 / 0748 2.8 / 1405 0.8 / 2122 2.7
17 TU 0256 0.8 / 0948 3.1 / 1524 0.3 / 2225 3.0

3 TU 0247 0.9 / 0912 2.9 / 1505 0.5 / 2222 2.9
18 W 0348 0.6 / 1038 3.3 / 1609 0.2 / 2307 3.1

4 W 0338 0.6 / 1012 3.2 / 1551 0.2 / 2308 3.1
19 TH 0431 0.5 / 1122 3.3 / 1649 0.2 / 2344 3.2

5 TH 0421 0.4 / 1100 3.3 / 1633 0.0 / 2349 3.2
20 F 0509 0.4 / 1202 3.3 / 1724 0.2

6 F 0502 0.1 / 1147 3.5 / 1714 -0.1 / ○
21 SA 0017 3.2 / 0540 0.4 / 1239 3.3 / ●1755 0.3

7 SA 0030 3.3 / 0543 0.0 / 1233 3.6 / 1756 -0.1
22 SU 0048 3.3 / 0608 0.4 / 1313 3.3 / 1825 0.4

8 SU 0111 3.4 / 0626 -0.1 / 1320 3.7 / 1841 -0.1
23 M 0119 3.4 / 0636 0.4 / 1344 3.2 / 1857 0.4

9 M 0150 3.5 / 0711 -0.1 / 1405 3.7 / 1927 0.0
24 TU 0151 3.5 / 0707 0.4 / 1417 3.2 / 1932 0.5

10 TU 0230 3.6 / 0758 -0.1 / 1450 3.6 / 2016 0.2
25 W 0223 3.5 / 0742 0.4 / 1452 3.2 / 2010 0.5

11 W 0310 3.5 / 0849 0.0 / 1535 3.5 / 2109 0.4
26 TH 0256 3.5 / 0821 0.4 / 1529 3.1 / 2052 0.6

12 TH 0352 3.4 / 0947 0.2 / 1622 3.2 / 2207 0.6
27 F 0331 3.4 / 0906 0.5 / 1611 3.0 / 2140 0.8

13 F 0439 3.2 / 1056 0.4 / 1715 3.0 / ☽2317 0.9
28 SA 0409 3.2 / 0958 0.6 / 1658 2.9 / 2235 0.9

14 SA 0537 3.0 / 1216 0.5 / 1827 2.7
29 SU 0453 3.1 / 1058 0.7 / 1755 2.7 / ☽2338 1.0

15 SU 0037 1.0 / 0710 2.8 / 1329 0.5 / 2024 2.7
30 M 0551 2.9 / 1206 0.7 / 1905 2.7

Chart Datum: 1·62 metres below Ordnance Datum (Newlyn)
HAT is 3·9 metres above Chart Datum

TIDES

SCOTLAND – GREENOCK
LAT 55°57'N   LONG 4°46'W
TIMES AND HEIGHTS OF HIGH AND LOW WATERS

TIME ZONE (UT)
For Summer Time add ONE hour in **non-shaded areas**

Dates in amber are **SPRINGS**
Dates in yellow are **NEAPS**

2012

MAY

Time	m		Time	m
1 0048	1.0		**16** 0217	0.9
0703	2.9		0907	3.0
TU 1316	0.6		W 1448	0.4
2028	2.8		2138	2.9
2 0158	0.8		**17** 0313	0.8
0824	3.0		1002	3.1
W 1420	0.4		TH 1535	0.3
2138	2.9		2225	3.0
3 0258	0.6		**18** 0401	0.6
0932	3.2		1049	3.2
TH 1514	0.2		F 1617	0.3
2231	3.1		2306	3.1
4 0350	0.3		**19** 0441	0.5
1029	3.3		1132	3.2
F 1603	0.0		SA 1655	0.4
2318	3.2		2344	3.2
5 0437	0.1		**20** 0516	0.5
1121	3.5		1207	3.2
SA 1649	0.0		SU 1730	0.5 ●
6 0003	3.4		**21** 0018	3.3
0522	-0.1		0547	0.5
SU 1212	3.5		M 1246	3.1
○ 1735	-0.1		1804	0.5
7 0047	3.5		**22** 0052	3.4
0608	-0.1		0617	0.4
M 1302	3.6		TU 1320	3.1
1823	0.0		1837	0.5
8 0130	3.6		**23** 0124	3.5
0655	-0.2		0648	0.4
TU 1351	3.5		W 1354	3.1
1912	0.1		1913	0.5
9 0213	3.6		**24** 0157	3.5
0744	-0.1		0723	0.4
W 1440	3.5		TH 1430	3.1
2003	0.2		1952	0.6
10 0255	3.6		**25** 0231	3.5
0836	0.0		0803	0.4
TH 1528	3.3		F 1509	3.1
2056	0.4		2035	0.6
11 0340	3.5		**26** 0307	3.5
0933	0.1		0847	0.4
F 1618	3.2		SA 1552	3.0
2153	0.6		2122	0.6
12 0427	3.3		**27** 0346	3.4
1038	0.3		0937	0.5
SA 1712	3.0		SU 1637	3.0
◑ 2254	0.8		2213	0.7
13 0524	3.1		**28** 0430	3.3
1147	0.4		1033	0.5
SU 1815	2.8		M 1729	2.9
			◑ 2309	0.8
14 0001	0.9		**29** 0521	3.2
0636	3.0		1134	0.5
M 1254	0.4		TU 1828	2.8
1930	2.7			
15 0112	1.0		**30** 0011	0.8
0758	2.9		0625	3.1
TU 1354	0.4		W 1238	0.5
2042	2.8		1936	2.8
			31 0117	0.8
			0741	3.1
			TH 1342	0.4
			2050	2.9

JUNE

Time	m		Time	m
1 0222	0.6		**16** 0328	0.8
0856	3.2		1014	3.0
F 1441	0.3		SA 1546	0.5
2154	3.1		2226	3.1
2 0322	0.4		**17** 0414	0.7
1001	3.3		1102	3.0
SA 1537	0.2		SU 1629	0.5
2250	3.2		2312	3.2
3 0416	0.2		**18** 0454	0.6
1059	3.4		1145	3.1
SU 1629	0.1		M 1709	0.5
2340	3.4		2352	3.3
4 0506	0.0		**19** 0530	0.5
1154	3.4		1223	3.1
M 1719	0.1		TU 1746	0.5
○			●	
5 0028	3.5		**20** 0027	3.4
0554	-0.1		0602	0.5
TU 1248	3.4		W 1300	3.1
1808	0.2		1821	0.5
6 0114	3.6		**21** 0101	3.5
0642	-0.2		0634	0.4
W 1341	3.4		TH 1336	3.1
1858	0.2		1856	0.5
7 0159	3.6		**22** 0134	3.6
0730	-0.1		0708	0.4
TH 1431	3.3		F 1412	3.1
1949	0.3		1934	0.5
8 0243	3.6		**23** 0210	3.6
0820	-0.1		0745	0.3
F 1520	3.2		SA 1451	3.1
2039	0.4		2016	0.5
9 0327	3.5		**24** 0248	3.6
0912	0.1		0828	0.3
SA 1607	3.1		SU 1532	3.1
2130	0.5		2101	0.5
10 0412	3.4		**25** 0328	3.6
1007	0.2		0915	0.3
SU 1654	3.0		M 1615	3.1
2222	0.7		2149	0.5
11 0501	3.3		**26** 0410	3.5
1007	0.3		1007	0.3
M 1743	2.9		TU 1701	3.1
◑ 2317	0.8		2241	0.6
12 0556	3.1		**27** 0457	3.4
1210	0.5		1103	0.4
TU 1834	2.9		W 1751	3.0
			◑ 2338	0.7
13 0019	0.9		**28** 0552	3.2
0658	2.9		1205	0.4
W 1311	0.5		TH 1850	2.9
1929	2.8			
14 0127	1.0		**29** 0042	0.7
0809	2.9		0700	3.1
TH 1408	0.6		F 1310	0.5
2031	2.9		2005	2.9
15 0232	0.9		**30** 0152	0.7
0917	2.9		0822	3.1
F 1459	0.5		SA 1415	0.5
2133	2.9		2124	3.0

JULY

Time	m		Time	m
1 0301	0.5		**16** 0349	0.8
0940	3.1		1036	2.9
SU 1518	0.4		M 1606	0.7
2229	3.2		2243	3.2
2 0402	0.3		**17** 0434	0.7
1046	3.2		1124	3.0
M 1615	0.3		TU 1649	0.6
2325	3.3		2328	3.3
3 0455	0.1		**18** 0512	0.5
1145	3.3		1205	3.0
TU 1708	0.3		W 1727	0.5
○				
4 0015	3.5		**19** 0005	3.4
0543	-0.1		0546	0.4
W 1240	3.3		TH 1244	3.1
1757	0.3		● 1801	0.5
5 0102	3.6		**20** 0039	3.5
0630	-0.1		0617	0.4
TH 1332	3.3		F 1319	3.1
1844	0.3		1836	0.5
6 0146	3.6		**21** 0113	3.6
0714	-0.1		0649	0.3
F 1420	3.2		SA 1355	3.1
1930	0.3		1912	0.4
7 0229	3.6		**22** 0151	3.6
0759	0.0		0724	0.2
SA 1504	3.2		SU 1431	3.2
2015	0.4		1953	0.4
8 0310	3.6		**23** 0230	3.7
0843	0.1		0805	0.2
SU 1544	3.2		M 1510	3.2
2059	0.5		2036	0.4
9 0350	3.5		**24** 0310	3.7
0930	0.2		0850	0.2
M 1623	3.1		TU 1550	3.2
2144	0.5		2123	0.4
10 0431	3.4		**25** 0351	3.6
1020	0.4		0939	0.3
TU 1703	3.1		W 1632	3.2
2230	0.7		2214	0.5
11 0514	3.2		**26** 0435	3.5
1115	0.5		1034	0.4
W 1745	3.0		TH 1717	3.1
◑ 2322	0.8		◑ 2310	0.6
12 0601	3.0		**27** 0524	3.3
1217	0.7		1135	0.5
TH 1831	2.9		F 1810	3.0
13 0023	1.0		**28** 0015	0.7
0657	2.8		0624	3.1
F 1323	0.8		SA 1245	0.7
1925	2.9		1924	2.9
14 0140	1.1		**29** 0132	0.7
0809	2.7		0752	2.9
SA 1424	0.8		SU 1400	0.7
2031	2.9		2103	2.9
15 0253	1.0		**30** 0249	0.6
0933	2.8		0934	3.0
SU 1518	0.7		M 1510	0.6
2144	3.0		2218	3.1
			31 0354	0.4
			1046	3.1
			TU 1609	0.5
			2315	3.4

AUGUST

Time	m		Time	m
1 0447	0.1		**16** 0448	0.5
1142	3.2		1145	3.1
W 1700	0.4		TH 1703	0.5
			2339	3.4
2 0003	3.5		**17** 0522	0.4
0533	0.0		1223	3.1
TH 1233	3.2		F 1737	0.4
○ 1745	0.3			
3 0049	3.6		**18** 0015	3.5
0615	-0.1		0553	0.3
F 1319	3.2		SA 1258	3.2
1828	0.3		1810	0.4
4 0131	3.7		**19** 0052	3.6
0655	0.0		0625	0.2
SA 1400	3.2		SU 1333	3.2
1908	0.3		1847	0.3
5 0210	3.6		**20** 0131	3.7
0733	0.0		0701	0.1
SU 1436	3.2		M 1408	3.3
1946	0.4		1928	0.3
6 0247	3.6		**21** 0211	3.8
0811	0.1		0741	0.1
M 1510	3.2		TU 1446	3.3
2024	0.4		2011	0.3
7 0322	3.5		**22** 0252	3.8
0850	0.3		0825	0.1
TU 1545	3.2		W 1524	3.4
2103	0.5		2058	0.3
8 0358	3.4		**23** 0333	3.7
0933	0.4		0913	0.3
W 1622	3.2		TH 1605	3.3
2145	0.6		2150	0.4
9 0435	3.2		**24** 0415	3.5
1021	0.6		1007	0.5
TH 1701	3.1		F 1649	3.2
◑ 2230	0.8		◑ 2248	0.6
10 0517	3.0		**25** 0502	3.3
1118	0.8		1111	0.7
F 1745	3.0		SA 1741	3.1
2325	1.0		2358	0.7
11 0607	2.8		**26** 0600	3.0
1229	1.0		1229	0.9
SA 1836	2.9		SU 1855	2.9
12 0039	1.2		**27** 0124	0.8
0711	2.6		0737	2.8
SU 1348	1.0		M 1355	0.9
1938	2.9		2054	2.9
13 0215	1.1		**28** 0244	0.6
0843	2.6		0943	2.9
M 1452	0.9		TU 1506	0.8
2058	2.9		2208	3.2
14 0321	0.9		**29** 0345	0.4
1013	2.8		1045	3.1
TU 1543	0.8		W 1602	0.6
2211	3.1		2301	3.4
15 0409	0.7		**30** 0435	0.2
1104	3.0		1134	3.2
W 1626	0.6		TH 1649	0.5
2300	3.3		2348	3.6
			31 0518	0.0
			1217	3.3
			F 1731	0.4
			○	

Chart Datum: 1·62 metres below Ordnance Datum (Newlyn)
HAT is 3·9 metres above Chart Datum

SCOTLAND – GREENOCK
LAT 55°57'N   LONG 4°46'W
TIMES AND HEIGHTS OF HIGH AND LOW WATERS

Dates in amber are **SPRINGS**
Dates in yellow are **NEAPS**

2012

SEPTEMBER

Day	Time	m	Time	m	Time	m	Time	m
1 SA	0031	3.6	0556	0.0	1257	3.3	1808	0.4
2 SU	0111	3.6	0632	0.1	1331	3.3	1842	0.4
3 M	0147	3.6	0704	0.2	1402	3.3	1915	0.4
4 TU	0221	3.6	0738	0.3	1434	3.3	1948	0.4
5 W	0253	3.5	0813	0.4	1508	3.4	2025	0.5
6 TH	0327	3.4	0851	0.5	1544	3.4	2104	0.6
7 F	0403	3.3	0934	0.7	1622	3.3	2147	0.8
8 SA	0442	3.1	1024	1.0	1704	3.1	2237	1.0 ◑
9 SU	0530	2.8	1131	1.2	1754	3.0	2345	1.2
10 M	0633	2.6	1301	1.2	1855	2.9		
11 TU	0125	1.2	0800	2.6	1419	1.1	2011	2.9
12 W	0246	1.0	0944	2.8	1513	0.9	2131	3.1
13 TH	0337	0.8	1037	3.0	1557	0.7	2226	3.3
14 F	0417	0.5	1118	3.1	1634	0.5	2308	3.4
15 SA	0451	0.3	1156	3.2	1709	0.4	2348	3.6
16 SU	0524	0.2	1231	3.3	1745	0.3 ●		
17 M	0028	3.7	0559	0.1	1307	3.4	1823	0.3
18 TU	0111	3.7	0637	0.1	1344	3.4	1904	0.2
19 W	0153	3.8	0719	0.1	1422	3.5	1949	0.2
20 TH	0236	3.8	0804	0.2	1501	3.5	2037	0.3
21 F	0318	3.7	0853	0.4	1543	3.5	2131	0.4
22 SA	0401	3.5	0948	0.6	1628	3.3	2233	0.6 ◐
23 SU	0449	3.2	1056	0.9	1721	3.1	2352	0.7
24 M	0549	2.9	1222	1.1	1842	3.0		
25 TU	0117	0.7	0758	2.8	1347	1.1	2038	3.0
26 W	0229	0.6	0936	2.9	1454	0.9	2148	3.3
27 TH	0327	0.4	1030	3.1	1547	0.6	2240	3.5
28 F	0415	0.2	1114	3.3	1632	0.5	2325	3.6
29 SA	0457	0.1	1153	3.3	1712	0.5		
30 SU	0007	3.6	0533	0.2	1228	3.4	1746	0.4 ○

OCTOBER

Day	Time	m	Time	m	Time	m	Time	m
1 M	0046	3.6	0606	0.2	1259	3.4	1817	0.5
2 TU	0121	3.6	0637	0.3	1328	3.4	1846	0.5
3 W	0153	3.5	0708	0.4	1400	3.5	1917	0.5
4 TH	0225	3.5	0741	0.5	1434	3.5	1952	0.5
5 F	0259	3.4	0818	0.6	1509	3.5	2031	0.6
6 SA	0335	3.3	0858	0.8	1546	3.4	2113	0.8
7 SU	0415	3.1	0944	1.0	1627	3.3	2202	1.0
8 M	0502	2.9	1042	1.2	1715	3.1	2304	1.1 ◑
9 TU	0602	2.7	1201	1.3	1814	3.0		
10 W	0026	1.2	0722	2.7	1328	1.3	1925	3.0
11 TH	0154	1.0	0901	2.8	1432	1.1	2042	3.1
12 F	0253	0.8	1001	3.0	1520	0.8	2144	3.3
13 SA	0338	0.5	1046	3.2	1602	0.6	2234	3.5
14 SU	0417	0.3	1125	3.4	1641	0.4	2319	3.6
15 M	0455	0.2	1203	3.4	1720	0.3 ●		
16 TU	0005	3.7	0534	0.1	1242	3.5	1801	0.2
17 W	0052	3.8	0616	0.1	1321	3.6	1845	0.1
18 TH	0137	3.8	0701	0.2	1402	3.7	1932	0.2
19 F	0222	3.8	0748	0.3	1444	3.7	2022	0.2
20 SA	0307	3.7	0839	0.5	1527	3.6	2118	0.4
21 SU	0354	3.5	0936	0.8	1614	3.5	2223	0.6
22 M	0445	3.2	1044	1.0	1711	3.3	2341	0.7
23 TU	0552	2.9	1205	1.2	1830	3.1		
24 W	0058	0.7	0743	2.9	1323	1.1	2007	3.1
25 TH	0204	0.6	0907	3.0	1429	1.0	2118	3.3
26 F	0300	0.5	1001	3.2	1523	0.8	2212	3.4
27 SA	0348	0.4	1044	3.3	1609	0.7	2258	3.5
28 SU	0431	0.3	1123	3.4	1649	0.6	2341	3.6 ●
29 M	0509	0.4	1157	3.4	1724	0.4 ○		
30 TU	0020	3.5	0542	0.4	1228	3.5	1754	0.4
31 W	0055	3.5	0613	0.5	1300	3.5	1823	0.6

NOVEMBER

Day	Time	m	Time	m	Time	m	Time	m
1 TH	0128	3.5	0644	0.6	1332	3.7	1854	0.6
2 F	0201	3.4	0718	0.7	1406	3.7	1928	0.6
3 SA	0236	3.4	0754	0.7	1441	3.7	2006	0.7
4 SU	0313	3.3	0834	0.9	1517	3.6	2049	0.8
5 M	0353	3.2	0919	1.0	1556	3.5	2137	0.9
6 TU	0439	3.0	1011	1.2	1641	3.3	2233	1.0 ◐
7 W	0533	2.9	1114	1.3	1735	3.2	2339	1.0 ◑
8 TH	0641	2.8	1226	1.3	1840	3.1		
9 F	0052	1.0	0803	2.9	1337	1.2	1953	3.2
10 SA	0159	0.8	0915	3.1	1437	1.0	2102	3.3
11 SU	0255	0.6	1008	3.2	1528	0.7	2200	3.5
12 M	0343	0.4	1054	3.4	1614	0.5	2253	3.6
13 TU	0429	0.3	1137	3.5	1659	0.3	2344	3.7 ●
14 W	0514	0.2	1220	3.7	1744	0.2		
15 TH	0034	3.7	0559	0.2	1303	3.7	1830	0.1
16 F	0124	3.7	0646	0.3	1347	3.8	1918	0.1
17 SA	0213	3.7	0736	0.4	1431	3.8	2009	0.2
18 SU	0301	3.6	0827	0.6	1516	3.7	2105	0.3
19 M	0350	3.4	0923	0.8	1605	3.6	2206	0.5
20 TU	0443	3.2	1023	1.0	1659	3.4	2315	0.7 ◑
21 W	0544	3.1	1132	1.1	1805	3.3		
22 TH	0026	0.7	0657	3.0	1246	1.2	1922	3.2
23 F	0130	0.6	0815	3.0	1354	1.1	2036	3.2
24 SA	0228	0.6	0917	3.1	1453	1.0	2137	3.3
25 SU	0318	0.6	1007	3.2	1543	0.8	2229	3.4
26 M	0403	0.5	1050	3.4	1626	0.7	2314	3.4
27 TU	0444	0.5	1128	3.5	1704	0.7	2356	3.4
28 W	0521	0.6	1202	3.6	1737	0.7 ○		
29 TH	0033	3.4	0554	0.6	1236	3.7	1807	0.7
30 F	0108	3.4	0627	0.7	1310	3.7	1838	0.7

DECEMBER

Day	Time	m	Time	m	Time	m	Time	m
1 SA	0142	3.4	0701	0.7	1343	3.8	1911	0.7
2 SU	0217	3.4	0736	0.8	1418	3.8	1947	0.7
3 M	0254	3.3	0815	0.8	1454	3.7	2028	0.7
4 TU	0334	3.3	0858	0.9	1533	3.6	2113	0.7
5 W	0417	3.2	0946	1.0	1615	3.5	2204	0.8
6 TH	0504	3.1	1039	1.1	1703	3.4	2301	0.8 ◑
7 F	0558	3.0	1139	1.1	1758	3.3		
8 SA	0004	0.8	0704	3.0	1246	1.1	1905	3.3
9 SU	0110	0.8	0820	3.0	1354	1.0	2020	3.3
10 M	0215	0.7	0929	3.2	1456	0.8	2130	3.4
11 TU	0313	0.5	1026	3.3	1551	0.6	2232	3.5
12 W	0407	0.4	1116	3.5	1642	0.3	2328	3.6
13 TH	0457	0.3	1203	3.7	1730	0.2 ●		
14 F	0022	3.6	0546	0.3	1250	3.8	1818	0.1
15 SA	0115	3.6	0634	0.3	1336	3.9	1906	0.1
16 SU	0206	3.6	0723	0.4	1421	3.9	1955	0.1
17 M	0254	3.5	0812	0.5	1506	3.8	2046	0.2
18 TU	0341	3.4	0902	0.6	1552	3.7	2140	0.3
19 W	0428	3.3	0954	0.8	1640	3.6	2238	0.5
20 TH	0515	3.2	1050	0.9	1732	3.4	2342	0.6 ◑
21 F	0606	3.1	1155	1.1	1829	3.2		
22 SA	0048	0.8	0702	3.0	1308	1.1	1936	3.1
23 SU	0151	0.8	0809	3.0	1416	1.1	2050	3.1
24 M	0246	0.8	0918	3.1	1514	1.0	2157	3.1
25 TU	0336	0.7	1015	3.2	1603	0.9	2251	3.2
26 W	0421	0.7	1102	3.4	1645	0.9	2337	3.2
27 TH	0502	0.7	1142	3.5	1721	0.7		
28 F	0017	3.3	0539	0.7	1219	3.6	1754	0.7 ○
29 SA	0054	3.3	0613	0.7	1252	3.7	1825	0.7
30 SU	0128	3.3	0646	0.7	1324	3.7	1856	0.6
31 M	0202	3.3	0719	0.7	1358	3.7	1929	0.6

Chart Datum: 1·62 metres below Ordnance Datum (Newlyn)
HAT is 3·9 metres above Chart Datum

TIDES

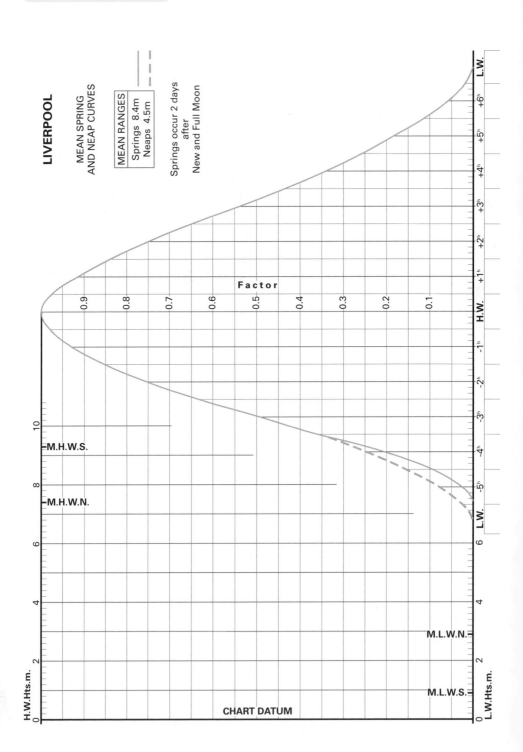

LIVERPOOL

MEAN SPRING
AND NEAP CURVES

MEAN RANGES
Springs 8.4m
Neaps 4.5m

Springs occur 2 days
after
New and Full Moon

Factor

0.9 0.8 0.7 0.6 0.5 0.4 0.3 0.2 0.1

L.W. +6ʰ +5ʰ +4ʰ +3ʰ +2ʰ +1ʰ H.W. -1ʰ -2ʰ -3ʰ -4ʰ -5ʰ L.W.

M.H.W.S.
M.H.W.N.

H.W.Hts.m.

M.L.W.N.
M.L.W.S.

L.W.Hts.m.

CHART DATUM

LIVERPOOL (GLADSTONE DOCK)

LAT 53°27'N   LONG 3°01'W

TIMES AND HEIGHTS OF HIGH AND LOW WATERS

Dates in amber are **SPRINGS**
Dates in yellow are **NEAPS**

2012

JANUARY

Day	Time	m	Time	m	Time	m	Time	m
1 SU	0354	7.7	1032	3.2	1619	7.9	◐ 2306	3.1
2 M	0450	7.4	1128	3.5	1719	7.5		
3 TU	0005	3.3	0557	7.2	1239	3.6	1827	7.4
4 W	0115	3.3	0704	7.0	1352	3.5	1937	7.5
5 TH	0219	3.2	0814	7.6	1453	3.1	2037	7.7
6 F	0313	2.8	0906	8.0	1545	2.7	2127	8.1
7 SA	0400	2.5	0949	8.4	1631	2.3	2209	8.4
8 SU	0443	2.2	1027	8.7	1715	1.9	2248	8.7
9 M	0525	1.9	1104	9.0	1757	1.6	○ 2325	8.9
10 TU	0605	1.6	1140	9.2	1838	1.4		
11 W	0002	9.1	0645	1.5	1218	9.4	1918	1.3
12 TH	0041	9.2	0725	1.4	1256	9.4	1958	1.3
13 F	0121	9.2	0804	1.5	1336	9.4	2037	1.4
14 SA	0203	9.0	0843	1.7	1418	9.2	2116	1.6
15 SU	0247	8.8	0924	2.0	1505	8.9	2200	1.9
16 M	0337	8.4	1012	2.3	1559	8.6	2252	2.3
17 TU	0436	8.1	1112	2.6	1705	8.2		
18 W	0000	2.6	0549	7.9	1228	2.8	1825	8.0
19 TH	0122	2.7	0708	7.9	1354	2.7	1946	8.0
20 F	0240	2.5	0821	8.0	1513	2.3	2057	8.4
21 SA	0346	2.1	0923	8.7	1619	1.8	2156	8.7
22 SU	0444	1.7	1016	9.1	1716	1.4	2246	9.0
23 M	0534	1.4	1102	9.4	1804	1.1	● 2330	9.2
24 TU	0618	1.3	1144	9.6	1847	1.0		
25 W	0010	9.2	0657	1.2	1223	9.6	1925	1.0
26 TH	0047	9.1	0733	1.4	1259	9.5	1959	1.2
27 F	0120	8.9	0806	1.6	1333	9.2	2030	1.6
28 SA	0153	8.7	0836	2.0	1408	8.9	2058	2.0
29 SU	0227	8.4	0905	2.4	1444	8.5	2126	2.4
30 M	0304	8.0	0939	2.8	1526	8.0	2201	2.8
31 TU	0348	7.5	1022	3.2	1616	7.5	◐ 2248	3.3

FEBRUARY

Day	Time	m	Time	m	Time	m	Time	m
1 W	0447	7.1	1124	3.6	1724	7.1	2359	3.6
2 TH	0605	7.0	1251	3.7	1845	7.0		
3 F	0125	3.6	0728	7.1	1413	3.4	2002	7.3
4 SA	0237	3.2	0834	7.6	1516	2.9	2102	7.7
5 SU	0334	2.7	0924	8.1	1609	2.3	2148	8.2
6 M	0423	2.2	1006	8.6	1657	1.8	2228	8.7
7 TU	0508	1.7	1044	9.1	1741	1.3	○ 2306	9.1
8 W	0551	1.4	1121	9.4	1823	1.0	2344	9.4
9 TH	0632	1.1	1159	9.7	1903	0.8		
10 F	0022	9.5	0711	0.9	1238	9.8	1942	0.7
11 SA	0102	9.5	0749	0.9	1318	9.7	2019	0.9
12 SU	0142	9.4	0827	1.2	1359	9.5	2056	1.2
13 M	0225	9.1	0906	1.5	1444	9.1	2136	1.7
14 TU	0312	8.6	0951	2.0	1536	8.6	◐ 2225	2.3
15 W	0410	8.1	1049	2.5	1643	8.0	2332	2.8
16 TH	0525	7.7	1209	2.9	1810	7.6		
17 F	0102	3.0	0651	7.7	1345	2.8	1939	7.7
18 SA	0229	2.8	0811	8.0	1508	2.4	2054	8.1
19 SU	0339	2.3	0915	8.5	1614	1.8	2150	8.5
20 M	0435	1.8	1005	8.9	1706	1.4	2235	8.9
21 TU	0522	1.5	1048	9.3	1749	1.1	● 2314	9.1
22 W	0601	1.3	1125	9.4	1826	1.0	2349	9.2
23 TH	0636	1.2	1200	9.5	1859	1.0		
24 F	0020	9.1	0707	1.2	1233	9.4	1927	1.2
25 SA	0051	9.0	0736	1.4	1304	9.2	1954	1.4
26 SU	0120	8.8	0803	1.9	1336	9.0	2019	1.7
27 M	0151	8.6	0827	2.0	1408	8.6	2046	2.1
28 TU	0223	8.2	0902	2.4	1443	8.1	2117	2.6
29 W	0259	7.8	0939	2.9	1525	7.6	2158	3.1

MARCH

Day	Time	m	Time	m	Time	m	Time	m
1 TH	0347	7.3	1031	3.4	1623	7.1	2257	3.5
2 F	0459	6.9	1151	3.6	1748	6.8		
3 SA	0027	3.7	0633	6.9	1328	3.4	1919	7.0
4 SU	0156	3.4	0753	7.4	1442	2.9	2028	7.5
5 M	0302	2.8	0850	8.0	1541	2.2	2119	8.2
6 TU	0357	2.2	0936	8.6	1631	1.6	2201	8.7
7 W	0445	1.6	1017	9.1	1718	1.1	2241	9.2
8 TH	0530	1.1	1056	9.6	1801	0.7	○ 2320	9.6
9 F	0612	0.8	1135	9.9	1842	0.4	2359	9.8
10 SA	0653	0.6	1216	10.0	1921	0.4		
11 SU	0040	9.8	0732	0.6	1258	9.9	1959	0.6
12 M	0121	9.6	0811	0.8	1341	9.6	2037	1.1
13 TU	0205	9.2	0852	1.3	1427	9.1	2117	1.6
14 W	0253	8.5	0938	1.8	1521	8.5	2207	2.3
15 TH	0352	8.0	1038	2.4	1631	7.8	◐ 2315	2.9
16 F	0509	7.7	1201	2.8	1759	7.4		
17 SA	0048	3.1	0635	7.6	1336	2.7	1929	7.5
18 SU	0215	2.8	0754	7.9	1455	2.3	2041	8.0
19 M	0324	2.4	0857	8.4	1557	1.8	2133	8.4
20 TU	0417	1.9	0945	8.8	1645	1.5	2215	8.7
21 W	0500	1.6	1025	9.0	1724	1.3	2250	8.9
22 TH	0536	1.4	1101	9.2	1757	1.2	● 2322	9.0
23 F	0609	1.3	1133	9.3	1827	1.2	2352	9.1
24 SA	0638	1.3	1205	9.2	1854	1.3		
25 SU	0021	9.0	0706	1.4	1236	9.1	1920	1.4
26 M	0051	8.9	0732	1.5	1307	8.9	1946	1.7
27 TU	0120	8.7	0804	1.8	1339	8.5	2015	2.0
28 W	0151	8.4	0835	2.2	1413	8.2	2047	2.4
29 TH	0225	8.0	0912	2.6	1452	7.7	2126	2.9
30 F	0308	7.6	0959	3.0	1545	7.3	◐ 2219	3.3
31 SA	0411	7.2	1108	3.3	1700	7.0	2337	3.6

APRIL

Day	Time	m	Time	m	Time	m	Time	m
1 SU	0539	7.1	1240	3.3	1828	7.1		
2 M	0108	3.4	0703	7.4	1401	2.8	1944	7.5
3 TU	0222	2.8	0807	7.9	1504	2.1	2041	8.2
4 W	0322	2.2	0859	8.6	1559	1.5	2128	8.8
5 TH	0415	1.6	0944	9.1	1648	1.0	2211	9.3
6 F	0503	1.1	1028	9.6	1734	0.6	○ 2253	9.6
7 SA	0549	0.7	1111	9.9	1817	0.4	2335	9.8
8 SU	0633	0.5	1155	10.0	1859	0.4		
9 M	0018	9.9	0715	0.5	1240	9.8	1939	0.6
10 TU	0103	9.7	0757	0.7	1327	9.5	2020	1.1
11 W	0149	9.3	0842	1.1	1416	9.0	2104	1.7
12 TH	0239	8.8	0932	1.7	1512	8.4	2155	2.3
13 F	0339	8.3	1033	2.2	1621	7.8	◐ 2303	2.8
14 SA	0452	7.9	1151	2.5	1741	7.5		
15 SU	0027	3.0	0610	7.7	1314	2.5	1903	7.5
16 M	0147	2.9	0725	7.9	1426	2.3	2013	7.8
17 TU	0254	2.5	0827	8.2	1525	2.0	2105	8.2
18 W	0347	2.1	0916	8.5	1612	1.8	2146	8.5
19 TH	0430	1.9	0956	8.7	1650	1.6	2221	8.7
20 F	0506	1.7	1032	8.9	1723	1.5	2253	8.8
21 SA	0538	1.5	1106	9.0	1753	1.5	● 2324	8.9
22 SU	0609	1.5	1138	9.0	1821	1.5	2354	8.9
23 M	0640	1.5	1211	8.9	1850	1.5		
24 TU	0024	8.8	0710	1.6	1243	8.7	1919	1.7
25 W	0055	8.7	0742	1.8	1316	8.5	1951	2.0
26 TH	0127	8.5	0816	2.0	1351	8.2	2026	2.3
27 F	0203	8.2	0854	2.4	1432	7.9	2106	2.7
28 SA	0246	7.9	0940	2.7	1522	7.6	2155	3.0
29 SU	0343	7.6	1040	2.9	1626	7.3	◐ 2301	3.2
30 M	0457	7.4	1156	2.9	1743	7.4		

Chart Datum: 4·93 metres below Ordnance Datum (Newlyn)
HAT is 10·4m above Chart Datum

TIDES

TIME ZONE (UT)
For Summer Time add ONE hour in **non-shaded** areas

LIVERPOOL (GLADSTONE DOCK)
LAT 53°27'N   LONG 3°01'W
TIMES AND HEIGHTS OF HIGH AND LOW WATERS

Dates in amber are **SPRINGS**
Dates in yellow are **NEAPS**

2012

MAY

Time	m		Time	m
1 TU 0020 / 0614 / 1314 / 1856	3.1 / 7.6 / 2.6 / 7.7		**16** W 0210 / 0745 / 1440 / 2026	2.8 / 8.0 / 2.3 / 7.9
2 W 0136 / 0722 / 1422 / 1959	2.7 / 8.0 / 2.1 / 8.2		**17** TH 0305 / 0838 / 1530 / 2111	2.5 / 8.1 / 2.2 / 8.2
3 TH 0242 / 0820 / 1522 / 2053	2.2 / 8.6 / 1.6 / 8.8		**18** F 0352 / 0923 / 1611 / 2150	2.3 / 8.3 / 2.0 / 8.4
4 F 0341 / 0912 / 1616 / 2141	1.7 / 9.1 / 1.1 / 9.2		**19** SA 0432 / 1003 / 1647 / 2224	2.0 / 8.5 / 1.9 / 8.6
5 SA 0435 / 1001 / 1706 / 2228	1.2 / 9.5 / 0.8 / 9.6		**20** SU 0508 / 1040 / 1720 / ● 2257	1.8 / 8.6 / 1.8 / 8.7
6 SU 0525 / 1049 / 1753 / ○ 2314	0.8 / 9.7 / 0.6 / 9.8		**21** M 0543 / 1115 / 1752 / 2330	1.7 / 8.7 / 1.7 / 8.8
7 M 0614 / 1137 / 1839	0.6 / 9.8 / 0.6		**22** TU 0616 / 1149 / 1825	1.6 / 8.7 / 1.7
8 TU 0000 / 0700 / 1226 / 1922	9.8 / 0.5 / 9.6 / 0.8		**23** W 0003 / 0650 / 1224 / 1858	8.8 / 1.6 / 8.6 / 1.8
9 W 0047 / 0747 / 1316 / 2007	9.6 / 0.7 / 9.3 / 1.2		**24** TH 0036 / 0726 / 1259 / 1934	8.7 / 1.7 / 8.5 / 1.9
10 TH 0136 / 0835 / 1407 / 2053	9.4 / 1.0 / 8.9 / 1.7		**25** F 0111 / 0803 / 1336 / 2011	8.6 / 1.9 / 8.4 / 2.1
11 F 0227 / 0926 / 1502 / 2144	9.0 / 1.5 / 8.4 / 2.2		**26** SA 0148 / 0843 / 1417 / 2052	8.4 / 2.1 / 8.1 / 2.4
12 SA 0324 / 1023 / 1602 / ◗ 2244	8.5 / 1.9 / 7.9 / 2.6		**27** SU 0230 / 0926 / 1503 / 2138	8.2 / 2.3 / 8.0 / 2.6
13 SU 0427 / 1128 / 1709 / 2353	8.1 / 2.3 / 7.6 / 2.9		**28** M 0321 / 1018 / 1559 / ◗ 2234	8.1 / 2.4 / 7.8 / 2.8
14 M 0535 / 1236 / 1821	7.8 / 2.5 / 7.5		**29** TU 0422 / 1119 / 1704 / 2339	7.9 / 2.5 / 7.8 / 2.8
15 TU 0104 / 0642 / 1342 / 1929	2.9 / 7.8 / 2.5 / 7.6		**30** W 0531 / 1228 / 1813	8.0 / 2.4 / 7.9
			31 TH 0050 / 0640 / 1340 / 1920	2.6 / 8.2 / 2.1 / 8.2

JUNE

Time	m		Time	m
1 F 0202 / 0745 / 1446 / 2021	2.3 / 8.5 / 1.8 / 8.6		**16** SA 0312 / 0850 / 1530 / 2118	2.7 / 7.9 / 2.5 / 8.1
2 SA 0308 / 0845 / 1546 / 2116	1.9 / 8.9 / 1.4 / 9.0		**17** SU 0359 / 0936 / 1612 / 2158	2.4 / 8.1 / 2.3 / 8.4
3 SU 0409 / 0940 / 1641 / 2207	1.4 / 9.2 / 1.1 / 9.4		**18** M 0441 / 1017 / 1651 / 2235	2.1 / 8.3 / 2.1 / 8.6
4 M 0506 / 1033 / 1733 / ○ 2257	1.0 / 9.4 / 0.9 / 9.6		**19** TU 0520 / 1054 / 1728 / ● 2310	1.9 / 8.5 / 1.9 / 8.7
5 TU 0559 / 1125 / 1822 / 2346	0.8 / 9.5 / 0.9 / 9.7		**20** W 0558 / 1130 / 1805 / 2345	1.7 / 8.6 / 1.8 / 8.8
6 W 0650 / 1216 / 1909	0.8 / 9.4 / 0.9		**21** TH 0636 / 1206 / 1843	1.6 / 8.7 / 1.7
7 TH 0035 / 0738 / 1306 / 1955	9.6 / 0.7 / 9.2 / 1.2		**22** F 0019 / 0714 / 1243 / 1920	8.9 / 1.5 / 8.7 / 1.7
8 F 0123 / 0826 / 1354 / 2040	9.4 / 0.9 / 8.9 / 1.5		**23** SA 0056 / 0752 / 1321 / 1959	8.9 / 1.6 / 8.7 / 1.8
9 SA 0211 / 0913 / 1442 / 2126	9.1 / 1.3 / 8.5 / 2.0		**24** SU 0134 / 0831 / 1400 / 2038	8.8 / 1.7 / 8.6 / 1.9
10 SU 0301 / 1001 / 1532 / 2215	8.8 / 1.7 / 8.1 / 2.4		**25** M 0214 / 0912 / 1444 / 2121	8.7 / 1.8 / 8.4 / 2.1
11 M 0353 / 1052 / 1626 / ◗ 2309	8.4 / 2.2 / 7.8 / 2.8		**26** TU 0300 / 0955 / 1533 / 2208	8.5 / 2.0 / 8.2 / 2.3
12 TU 0450 / 1147 / 1727	8.2 / 2.5 / 7.5		**27** W 0352 / 1047 / 1630 / ◗ 2305	8.4 / 2.2 / 8.1 / 2.5
13 W 0011 / 0551 / 1247 / 1832	3.0 / 7.7 / 2.7 / 7.4		**28** TH 0454 / 1149 / 1736	8.2 / 2.3 / 8.0
14 TH 0116 / 0655 / 1347 / 1936	3.1 / 7.7 / 2.8 / 7.5		**29** F 0012 / 0605 / 1302 / 1847	2.6 / 8.2 / 2.3 / 8.1
15 F 0218 / 0756 / 1442 / 2032	2.9 / 7.7 / 2.7 / 7.8		**30** SA 0129 / 0718 / 1416 / 1956	2.4 / 8.3 / 2.1 / 8.4

JULY

Time	m		Time	m
1 SU 0244 / 0827 / 1523 / 2058	2.1 / 8.5 / 1.8 / 8.8		**16** M 0328 / 0911 / 1542 / 2134	2.7 / 7.8 / 2.6 / 8.2
2 M 0352 / 0929 / 1624 / 2154	1.7 / 8.8 / 1.5 / 9.1		**17** TU 0416 / 0956 / 1627 / 2214	2.3 / 8.2 / 2.3 / 8.5
3 TU 0454 / 1025 / 1719 / ○ 2246	1.3 / 9.1 / 1.2 / 9.4		**18** W 0500 / 1035 / 1708 / 2251	2.0 / 8.4 / 2.0 / 8.8
4 W 0549 / 1117 / 1810 / 2335	0.9 / 9.3 / 1.1 / 9.6		**19** TH 0541 / 1112 / 1748 / ● 2326	1.7 / 8.7 / 1.7 / 9.0
5 TH 0640 / 1205 / 1857	0.7 / 9.3 / 1.0		**20** F 0621 / 1147 / 1828	1.4 / 8.9 / 1.5
6 F 0021 / 0726 / 1251 / 1940	9.6 / 0.7 / 9.2 / 1.1		**21** SA 0001 / 0700 / 1224 / 1907	9.2 / 1.3 / 9.0 / 1.4
7 SA 0106 / 0810 / 1354 / 2021	9.5 / 0.9 / 9.0 / 1.4		**22** SU 0038 / 0739 / 1302 / 1945	9.2 / 1.2 / 9.0 / 1.4
8 SU 0148 / 0850 / 1414 / 2100	9.3 / 1.2 / 8.7 / 1.8		**23** M 0115 / 0816 / 1341 / 2023	9.2 / 1.3 / 9.0 / 1.5
9 M 0230 / 0929 / 1455 / 2139	8.9 / 1.7 / 8.3 / 2.2		**24** TU 0155 / 0854 / 1422 / 2102	9.1 / 1.4 / 8.8 / 1.8
10 TU 0313 / 1007 / 1538 / 2220	8.5 / 2.2 / 7.9 / 2.7		**25** W 0237 / 0933 / 1507 / 2145	8.9 / 1.7 / 8.5 / 2.1
11 W 0400 / 1049 / 1629 / ◗ 2310	8.1 / 2.6 / 7.6 / 3.1		**26** TH 0326 / 1018 / 1601 / ◗ 2238	8.6 / 2.1 / 8.2 / 2.4
12 TH 0456 / 1140 / 1730 / 2345	7.7 / 3.0 / 7.3 / 2.6		**27** F 0425 / 1117 / 1707 / 2345	8.3 / 2.4 / 8.0 / 2.6
13 F 0013 / 0601 / 1246 / 1841	3.3 / 7.4 / 3.2 / 7.2		**28** SA 0541 / 1234 / 1826	8.0 / 2.6 / 7.9
14 SA 0124 / 0712 / 1353 / 1950	3.3 / 7.3 / 3.1 / 7.4		**29** SU 0108 / 0703 / 1357 / 1942	2.6 / 7.9 / 2.6 / 8.1
15 SU 0232 / 0817 / 1452 / 2047	3.1 / 7.5 / 2.9 / 7.8		**30** M 0232 / 0820 / 1510 / 2049	2.3 / 8.2 / 2.2 / 8.6
			31 TU 0345 / 0925 / 1613 / 2147	1.9 / 8.6 / 1.8 / 9.0

AUGUST

Time	m		Time	m
1 W 0447 / 1020 / 1709 / 2237	1.4 / 8.9 / 1.4 / 9.4		**16** TH 0438 / 1013 / 1648 / 2227	1.9 / 8.5 / 1.9 / 8.9
2 TH 0540 / 1107 / 1757 / ○ 2322	1.0 / 9.2 / 1.2 / 9.6		**17** F 0521 / 1049 / 1730 / ● 2303	1.5 / 8.9 / 1.5 / 9.2
3 F 0627 / 1150 / 1840	0.8 / 9.3 / 1.1		**18** SA 0602 / 1125 / 1811 / 2338	1.2 / 9.2 / 1.3 / 9.5
4 SA 0003 / 0708 / 1230 / 1919	9.7 / 0.7 / 9.2 / 1.1		**19** SU 0642 / 1201 / 1850	0.9 / 9.4 / 1.1
5 SU 0043 / 0745 / 1306 / 1955	9.6 / 0.9 / 9.1 / 1.3		**20** M 0015 / 0720 / 1239 / 1928	9.6 / 0.8 / 9.4 / 1.1
6 M 0119 / 0819 / 1340 / 2028	9.4 / 1.2 / 8.8 / 1.7		**21** TU 0054 / 0757 / 1318 / 2005	9.6 / 0.9 / 9.3 / 1.2
7 TU 0155 / 0850 / 1415 / 2100	9.0 / 1.7 / 8.5 / 2.1		**22** W 0133 / 0833 / 1359 / 2044	9.4 / 1.2 / 9.1 / 1.5
8 W 0232 / 0919 / 1452 / 2133	8.6 / 2.1 / 8.1 / 2.6		**23** TH 0216 / 0911 / 1444 / 2126	9.1 / 1.6 / 8.7 / 1.9
9 TH 0312 / 0951 / 1535 / ◗ 2213	8.1 / 2.6 / 7.7 / 3.0		**24** F 0305 / 0956 / 1538 / ◗ 2219	8.7 / 2.1 / 8.3 / 2.4
10 F 0402 / 1033 / 1631 / 2309	7.6 / 3.1 / 7.3 / 3.4		**25** SA 0407 / 1055 / 1648 / 2331	8.1 / 2.6 / 7.9 / 2.7
11 SA 0506 / 1136 / 1745	7.2 / 3.5 / 7.1		**26** SU 0529 / 1218 / 1812	7.7 / 2.9 / 7.8
12 SU 0030 / 0625 / 1300 / 1907	3.6 / 7.0 / 3.5 / 7.2		**27** M 0102 / 0659 / 1348 / 1934	2.8 / 7.7 / 2.8 / 8.0
13 M 0153 / 0744 / 1415 / 2016	3.4 / 7.2 / 3.3 / 7.6		**28** TU 0229 / 0819 / 1503 / 2042	2.4 / 8.0 / 2.4 / 8.5
14 TU 0258 / 0846 / 1514 / 2108	2.9 / 7.6 / 2.8 / 8.1		**29** W 0340 / 0921 / 1605 / 2137	1.9 / 8.5 / 1.9 / 9.0
15 W 0351 / 0933 / 1603 / 2150	2.4 / 8.1 / 2.3 / 8.5		**30** TH 0438 / 1010 / 1656 / 2223	1.4 / 8.9 / 1.5 / 9.4
			31 F 0525 / 1052 / 1740 / ○ 2303	1.1 / 9.1 / 1.3 / 9.6

Chart Datum: 4·93 metres below Ordnance Datum (Newlyn)
HAT is 10·4m above Chart Datum

LIVERPOOL (GLADSTONE DOCK)
LAT 53°27'N LONG 3°01'W
TIMES AND HEIGHTS OF HIGH AND LOW WATERS

2012

SEPTEMBER

Time	m		Time	m
1 SA	0606 0.9 / 1129 9.3 / 1818 1.1 / 2340 9.6	**16** SU	0537 1.0 / 1058 9.4 / 1748 1.1 / ●2312 9.7	
2 SU	0642 0.9 / 1203 9.2 / 1853 1.2	**17** M	0618 0.7 / 1135 9.7 / 1829 0.9 / 2351 9.9	
3 M	0015 9.5 / 0714 1.1 / 1236 9.1 / 1925 1.4	**18** TU	0657 0.7 / 1215 9.7 / 1909 0.9	
4 TU	0048 9.3 / 0743 1.4 / 1306 8.9 / 1954 1.7	**19** W	0031 9.8 / 0735 0.8 / 1256 9.6 / 1948 1.0	
5 W	0121 9.0 / 0810 1.7 / 1337 8.7 / 2023 2.1	**20** TH	0114 9.6 / 0813 1.1 / 1339 9.3 / 2029 1.4	
6 TH	0155 8.6 / 0836 2.1 / 1411 8.3 / 2053 2.5	**21** F	0200 9.2 / 0853 1.7 / 1426 8.9 / 2114 1.9	
7 F	0231 8.2 / 0906 2.6 / 1449 7.9 / 2129 2.9	**22** SA	0252 8.6 / 0940 2.3 / 1523 8.4 / ◐2210 2.4	
8 SA	0314 7.7 / 0944 3.1 / 1537 7.4 / ◐2219 3.4	**23** SU	0358 8.6 / 1043 2.8 / 1636 8.0 / 2327 2.7	
9 SU	0412 7.1 / 1040 3.6 / 1647 7.1 / 2335 3.7	**24** M	0522 7.6 / 1209 3.1 / 1801 7.8	
10 M	0533 6.8 / 1203 3.8 / 1818 7.0	**25** TU	0059 2.7 / 0652 7.6 / 1338 2.9 / 1920 8.1	
11 TU	0109 3.5 / 0703 7.0 / 1333 3.5 / 1937 7.4	**26** W	0220 2.3 / 0809 8.0 / 1450 2.5 / 2027 8.5	
12 W	0223 3.0 / 0813 7.5 / 1441 3.0 / 2034 8.0	**27** TH	0325 1.9 / 0906 8.5 / 1548 2.0 / 2119 8.9	
13 TH	0320 2.4 / 0903 8.1 / 1534 2.4 / 2118 8.5	**28** F	0418 1.5 / 0952 8.8 / 1636 1.7 / 2202 9.2	
14 F	0410 1.7 / 0943 8.6 / 1622 1.9 / 2157 9.0	**29** SA	0502 1.3 / 1030 9.1 / 1716 1.5 / 2240 9.4	
15 SA	0454 1.3 / 1021 9.1 / 1706 1.4 / 2234 9.4	**30** SU	0538 1.2 / 1104 9.2 / 1751 1.4 / ○2315 9.4	

OCTOBER

Time	m		Time	m
1 M	0611 1.2 / 1135 9.2 / 1824 1.4 / 2347 9.4	**16** TU	0552 0.7 / 1110 9.8 / 1808 0.8 / 2329 10.0	
2 TU	0640 1.4 / 1205 9.1 / 1854 1.5	**17** W	0634 0.7 / 1152 9.9 / 1851 0.8	
3 W	0019 9.2 / 0707 1.6 / 1235 9.0 / 1923 1.7	**18** TH	0013 9.9 / 0715 0.8 / 1237 9.8 / 1934 0.9	
4 TH	0052 9.0 / 0733 1.6 / 1306 8.8 / 1952 2.0	**19** F	0059 9.6 / 0757 1.2 / 1323 9.5 / 2019 1.3	
5 F	0124 8.6 / 0801 2.2 / 1338 8.5 / 2023 2.4	**20** SA	0149 9.2 / 0840 1.7 / 1413 9.1 / 2108 1.7	
6 SA	0159 8.2 / 0833 2.6 / 1413 8.1 / 2059 2.8	**21** SU	0244 8.6 / 0930 2.3 / 1512 8.6 / 2208 2.2	
7 SU	0239 7.8 / 0911 3.0 / 1456 7.7 / 2146 3.2	**22** M	0350 8.0 / 1034 2.8 / 1622 8.2 / ◐2322 2.6	
8 M	0330 7.3 / 1002 3.5 / 1556 7.3 / ◐2252 3.5	**23** TU	0508 7.7 / 1154 3.1 / 1740 8.0	
9 TU	0442 7.0 / 1114 3.7 / 1722 7.1	**24** W	0042 2.6 / 0630 7.7 / 1309 3.2 / 1855 8.1	
10 W	0020 3.5 / 0610 7.0 / 1244 3.6 / 1845 7.4	**25** TH	0155 2.4 / 0744 8.0 / 1424 2.6 / 2000 8.4	
11 TH	0140 3.0 / 0720 7.5 / 1359 3.1 / 1949 7.9	**26** F	0258 2.1 / 0841 8.3 / 1521 2.3 / 2053 8.7	
12 F	0242 2.4 / 0822 8.1 / 1458 2.5 / 2039 8.5	**27** SA	0349 1.8 / 0926 8.6 / 1608 2.0 / 2137 8.8	
13 SA	0335 1.8 / 0908 8.7 / 1550 1.9 / 2123 9.1	**28** SU	0431 1.7 / 1004 8.9 / 1648 1.8 / 2215 9.1	
14 SU	0410 1.3 / 0949 9.2 / 1638 1.4 / 2205 9.5	**29** M	0507 1.6 / 1037 9.0 / 1723 1.7 / ○2249 9.1	
15 M	0509 0.9 / 1030 9.6 / 1724 1.1 / ●2246 9.8	**30** TU	0538 1.6 / 1109 9.1 / 1756 1.7 / 2323 9.1	
		31 W	0607 1.6 / 1139 9.1 / 1827 1.6 / 2355 9.0	

NOVEMBER

Time	m		Time	m
1 TH	0636 1.7 / 1210 9.0 / 1857 1.8	**16** F	0000 9.8 / 0659 0.9 / 1222 9.9 / 1924 0.9	
2 F	0028 8.9 / 0704 1.9 / 1241 8.9 / 1928 2.0	**17** SA	0050 9.6 / 0744 1.2 / 1311 9.7 / 2012 1.1	
3 SA	0101 8.6 / 0735 2.2 / 1313 8.6 / 2002 2.3	**18** SU	0141 9.2 / 0831 1.6 / 1402 9.3 / 2104 1.5	
4 SU	0136 8.3 / 0810 2.5 / 1348 8.3 / 2039 2.6	**19** M	0235 8.7 / 0921 2.1 / 1458 8.9 / 2159 1.9	
5 M	0215 8.0 / 0848 2.9 / 1429 8.0 / 2124 2.9	**20** TU	0334 8.2 / 1019 2.6 / 1600 8.5 / ◐2302 2.3	
6 TU	0302 7.6 / 0935 3.2 / 1521 7.7 / 2220 3.2	**21** W	0440 7.9 / 1125 2.9 / 1707 8.2	
7 W	0401 7.4 / 1037 3.5 / 1630 7.5 / ◐2332 3.2	**22** TH	0009 2.6 / 0551 7.7 / 1236 3.0 / 1815 8.1	
8 TH	0515 7.3 / 1152 3.5 / 1748 7.6	**23** F	0116 2.6 / 0703 7.8 / 1344 2.9 / 1922 8.1	
9 F	0049 3.0 / 0630 7.6 / 1309 3.2 / 1857 7.9	**24** SA	0218 2.5 / 0805 8.0 / 1445 2.7 / 2020 8.3	
10 SA	0157 2.5 / 0735 8.1 / 1416 2.7 / 1957 8.5	**25** SU	0312 2.3 / 0855 8.3 / 1536 2.4 / 2108 8.5	
11 SU	0257 2.0 / 0830 8.6 / 1515 2.1 / 2049 9.0	**26** M	0357 2.2 / 0937 8.5 / 1619 2.2 / 2150 8.7	
12 M	0350 1.5 / 0918 9.1 / 1609 1.6 / 2137 9.4	**27** TU	0434 2.1 / 1013 8.7 / 1657 2.1 / 2227 8.8	
13 TU	0440 1.1 / 1004 9.6 / 1700 1.2 / ●2224 9.7	**28** W	0508 2.0 / 1046 8.9 / 1732 1.9 / ○2302 8.9	
14 W	0528 0.9 / 1049 9.8 / 1749 0.9 / 2311 9.9	**29** TH	0540 1.9 / 1119 9.0 / 1805 1.9 / 2336 8.9	
15 TH	0614 0.8 / 1135 9.9 / 1837 0.8	**30** F	0611 1.9 / 1151 9.0 / 1838 1.9	

DECEMBER

Time	m		Time	m
1 SA	0010 8.8 / 0643 1.9 / 1223 8.9 / 1912 1.9	**16** SU	0041 9.6 / 0733 1.1 / 1300 9.8 / 2004 0.9	
2 SU	0044 8.7 / 0717 2.1 / 1257 8.8 / 1947 2.1	**17** M	0130 9.3 / 0819 1.4 / 1349 9.6 / 2052 1.2	
3 M	0120 8.5 / 0753 2.2 / 1331 8.6 / 2025 2.3	**18** TU	0219 8.9 / 0906 1.8 / 1438 9.2 / 2140 1.6	
4 TU	0157 8.3 / 0832 2.5 / 1410 8.4 / 2106 2.5	**19** W	0308 8.5 / 0953 2.3 / 1529 8.8 / 2230 2.1	
5 W	0239 8.1 / 0915 2.8 / 1454 8.2 / 2153 2.7	**20** TH	0400 8.1 / 1046 2.7 / 1624 8.3 / ◐2324 2.5	
6 TH	0329 7.8 / 1006 3.0 / 1549 8.0 / ◑2249 2.8	**21** F	0500 7.7 / 1146 3.1 / 1726 8.0	
7 F	0429 7.7 / 1107 3.1 / 1655 7.9 / 2356 2.8	**22** SA	0024 2.9 / 0606 7.5 / 1253 3.2 / 1832 7.8	
8 SA	0538 7.7 / 1218 3.1 / 1806 8.0	**23** SU	0129 3.0 / 0717 7.6 / 1400 3.1 / 1939 7.8	
9 SU	0109 2.6 / 0649 8.0 / 1332 2.8 / 1915 8.3	**24** M	0229 2.9 / 0819 7.8 / 1500 2.9 / 2038 8.0	
10 M	0218 2.3 / 0753 8.4 / 1441 2.3 / 2018 8.7	**25** TU	0321 2.7 / 0909 8.1 / 1550 2.6 / 2127 8.2	
11 TU	0320 1.8 / 0851 8.9 / 1543 1.8 / 2115 9.1	**26** W	0405 2.5 / 0951 8.4 / 1634 2.3 / 2209 8.4	
12 W	0416 1.4 / 0944 9.3 / 1640 1.4 / 2209 9.4	**27** TH	0443 2.2 / 1028 8.7 / 1713 2.1 / 2246 8.6	
13 TH	0509 1.1 / 1034 9.7 / 1735 1.0 / ●2301 9.6	**28** F	0519 2.1 / 1102 8.9 / 1749 1.9 / ○2321 8.8	
14 F	0559 1.0 / 1123 9.9 / 1826 0.8 / 2351 9.7	**29** SA	0553 1.9 / 1135 9.2 / 1824 1.8 / 2355 8.8	
15 SA	0647 0.9 / 1211 9.9 / 1916 0.7	**30** SU	0628 1.8 / 1208 9.1 / 1900 1.7	
		31 M	0028 8.8 / 0704 1.8 / 1242 9.0 / 1935 1.7	

Chart Datum: 4·93 metres below Ordnance Datum (Newlyn)
HAT is 10·4m above Chart Datum

TIDES

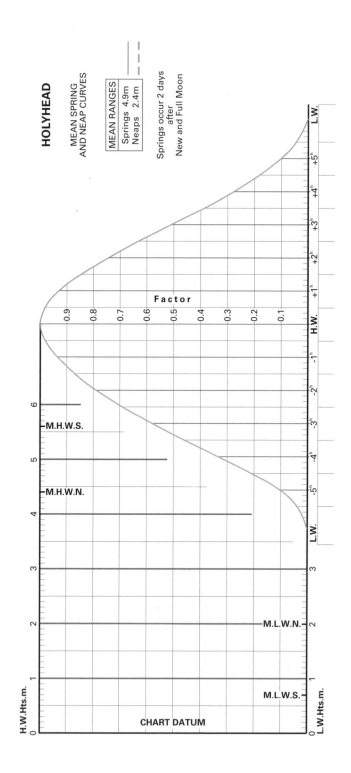

HOLYHEAD

MEAN SPRING
AND NEAP CURVES

MEAN RANGES
Springs 4.9m
Neaps 2.4m

Springs occur 2 days
after
New and Full Moon

WALES – HOLYHEAD

LAT 53°19′N LONG 4°37′W

TIMES AND HEIGHTS OF HIGH AND LOW WATERS

Dates in amber are **SPRINGS**
Dates in yellow are **NEAPS**

2012

JANUARY

Day	Time m	Time m	Time m	Time m	Day	Time m	Time m	Time m	Time m
1 SU	0319 4.6	0923 2.1	1534 4.8	☽2159 2.0	16 M	0254 5.0	0857 1.5	1515 5.2	◖2140 1.4
2 M	0418 4.4	1025 2.3	1635 4.6	2302 2.1	17 TU	0356 4.8	1003 1.7	1616 5.0	2252 1.6
3 TU	0528 4.4	1137 2.4	1746 4.5		18 W	0512 4.8	1122 1.8	1746 4.9	
4 W	0009 2.2	0639 4.5	1246 2.3	1856 4.6	19 TH	0008 1.7	0631 4.8	1241 1.7	1907 4.9
5 TH	0111 2.1	0739 4.7	1346 2.1	1956 4.7	20 F	0121 1.6	0741 5.1	1353 1.5	2016 5.1
6 F	0203 1.9	0827 4.9	1435 1.8	2044 4.9	21 SA	0223 1.4	0839 5.3	1453 1.2	2112 5.3
7 SA	0247 1.7	0907 5.1	1516 1.5	2125 5.1	22 SU	0315 1.2	0928 5.6	1543 0.9	2159 5.4
8 SU	0325 1.5	0943 5.3	1553 1.3	2202 5.2	23 M	0401 1.0	1012 5.8	1628 0.7	●2241 5.5
9 M	0402 1.3	1017 5.5	1631 1.1	○2238 5.4	24 TU	0442 0.8	1053 5.9	1708 0.6	2321 5.5
10 TU	0438 1.1	1053 5.7	1707 0.9	2315 5.5	25 W	0520 0.8	1132 5.9	1747 0.7	2358 5.4
11 W	0514 1.0	1130 5.8	1745 0.8	2354 5.5	26 TH	0557 0.9	1210 5.8	1823 0.8	
12 TH	0553 0.9	1209 5.8	1824 0.8		27 F	0034 5.3	0633 1.0	1246 5.6	1858 1.0
13 F	0034 5.5	0632 1.0	1250 5.7	1905 0.9	28 SA	0109 5.2	0709 1.3	1322 5.4	1934 1.3
14 SA	0116 5.4	0715 1.1	1333 5.6	1950 1.0	29 SU	0144 5.0	0747 1.5	1358 5.1	2013 1.6
15 SU	0202 5.2	0802 1.3	1420 5.5	2040 1.2	30 M	0222 4.7	0830 1.8	1440 4.9	2056 1.9
					31 TU	0308 4.5	0920 2.1	1531 4.7	◖2150 2.1

FEBRUARY

Day	Time m	Time m	Time m	Time m	Day	Time m	Time m	Time m	Time m
1 W	0410 4.3	1027 2.4	1641 4.3	2301 2.3	16 TH	0446 4.7	1105 1.8	1736 4.6	2353 1.9
2 TH	0532 4.3	1151 2.4	1807 4.3		17 F	0616 4.7	1233 1.7	1908 4.7	
3 F	0022 2.3	0654 4.4	1309 2.2	1925 4.4	18 SA	0113 1.8	0733 4.9	1350 1.5	2017 4.9
4 SA	0131 2.1	0757 4.7	1408 1.9	2022 4.7	19 SU	0217 1.5	0832 5.2	1448 1.2	2108 5.1
5 SU	0222 1.8	0843 5.0	1454 1.5	2106 4.9	20 M	0307 1.2	0918 5.4	1534 0.9	2149 5.3
6 M	0304 1.5	0921 5.3	1533 1.2	2143 5.2	21 TU	0348 1.0	0958 5.6	1613 0.7	●2225 5.4
7 TU	0342 1.2	0957 5.5	1610 0.9	○2219 5.4	22 W	0425 0.8	1034 5.7	1648 0.7	2259 5.5
8 W	0418 0.9	1033 5.8	1646 0.6	2255 5.6	23 TH	0459 0.7	1109 5.8	1721 0.7	2331 5.4
9 TH	0455 0.7	1110 5.9	1723 0.5	2333 5.7	24 F	0532 0.8	1143 5.7	1753 0.8	
10 F	0533 0.6	1148 6.0	1802 0.4		25 SA	0003 5.4	0604 0.9	1216 5.6	1824 0.9
11 SA	0012 5.7	0612 0.6	1229 6.0	1842 0.5	26 SU	0034 5.3	0637 1.1	1249 5.4	1856 1.2
12 SU	0054 5.6	0654 0.7	1312 5.8	1926 0.7	27 M	0105 5.1	0712 1.3	1322 5.2	1930 1.4
13 M	0137 5.4	0740 0.9	1358 5.5	2014 1.1	28 TU	0139 4.9	0750 1.6	1359 4.9	2009 1.7
14 TU	0227 5.1	0834 1.3	1452 5.2	◖2113 1.4	29 W	0218 4.7	0834 1.9	1444 4.6	2056 2.0
15 W	0327 4.9	0940 1.6	1603 4.8	2227 1.8					

MARCH

Day	Time m	Time m	Time m	Time m	Day	Time m	Time m	Time m	Time m
1 TH	0309 4.4	0933 2.2	1546 4.3	◖2200 2.3	16 F	0428 4.6	1056 1.7	1733 4.5	2339 2.0
2 F	0425 4.2	1055 2.3	1717 4.1	2327 2.4	17 SA	0600 4.6	1224 1.7	1902 4.6	
3 SA	0601 4.3	1225 2.2	1849 4.3		18 SU	0059 1.8	0718 4.8	1338 1.4	2006 4.8
4 SU	0051 2.2	0717 4.5	1333 1.8	1953 4.6	19 M	0202 1.6	0815 5.1	1432 1.2	2053 5.0
5 M	0151 1.8	0810 4.8	1423 1.4	2039 4.9	20 TU	0250 1.3	0900 5.3	1514 1.0	2130 5.2
6 TU	0236 1.4	0852 5.2	1504 1.0	2117 5.2	21 W	0329 1.0	0937 5.5	1550 0.8	2202 5.3
7 W	0316 1.0	0930 5.5	1542 0.7	2153 5.5	22 TH	0403 0.9	1011 5.5	1622 0.8	●2233 5.4
8 TH	0353 0.7	1007 5.8	1620 0.4	○2230 5.7	23 F	0435 0.8	1044 5.6	1652 0.8	2303 5.4
9 F	0431 0.4	1046 6.0	1658 0.2	2309 5.8	24 SA	0506 0.8	1116 5.5	1722 0.8	2333 5.4
10 SA	0510 0.3	1126 6.1	1738 0.2	2349 5.8	25 SU	0538 0.9	1148 5.4	1752 1.0	
11 SU	0552 0.3	1208 6.0	1820 0.4		26 M	0003 5.3	0609 1.0	1220 5.3	1823 1.1
12 M	0031 5.7	0635 0.6	1254 5.8	1904 0.6	27 TU	0035 5.2	0643 1.2	1254 5.1	1857 1.4
13 TU	0117 5.5	0724 0.7	1343 5.5	1955 1.0	28 W	0108 5.0	0720 1.5	1330 4.9	1934 1.6
14 W	0207 5.2	0819 1.1	1440 5.0	2054 1.5	29 TH	0145 4.8	0803 1.7	1413 4.6	2018 1.9
15 TH	0308 4.9	0929 1.5	1555 4.7	◖2211 1.9	30 F	0232 4.6	0857 2.0	1509 4.3	◖2117 2.2
					31 SA	0336 4.3	1010 2.1	1632 4.2	2237 2.3

APRIL

Day	Time m	Time m	Time m	Time m	Day	Time m	Time m	Time m	Time m
1 SU	0506 4.3	1136 2.0	1804 4.3		16 M	0032 1.9	0649 4.8	1310 1.5	1940 4.7
2 M	0003 2.2	0628 4.5	1249 1.7	1913 4.5	17 TU	0135 1.7	0747 4.9	1404 1.3	2027 4.9
3 TU	0110 1.8	0728 4.8	1344 1.3	2003 4.9	18 W	0223 1.4	0832 5.1	1447 1.1	2103 5.0
4 W	0201 1.4	0816 5.2	1429 0.9	2045 5.2	19 TH	0303 1.2	0910 5.2	1522 1.0	2136 5.2
5 TH	0244 1.0	0858 5.5	1511 0.6	2125 5.5	20 F	0338 1.1	0945 5.3	1554 1.0	2206 5.3
6 F	0325 0.6	0939 5.8	1551 0.3	○2204 5.8	21 SA	0411 1.0	1018 5.4	1624 0.9	●2236 5.3
7 SA	0406 0.3	1021 6.0	1632 0.2	2245 5.9	22 SU	0442 0.9	1051 5.3	1654 1.0	2307 5.4
8 SU	0449 0.2	1105 6.0	1715 0.2	2328 5.9	23 M	0514 1.0	1123 5.3	1725 1.1	2338 5.3
9 M	0534 0.2	1151 5.9	1800 0.4		24 TU	0547 1.1	1157 5.2	1757 1.2	
10 TU	0013 5.8	0621 0.4	1240 5.7	1848 0.7	25 W	0010 5.2	0622 1.2	1232 5.0	1831 1.4
11 W	0101 5.6	0713 0.7	1333 5.3	1940 1.1	26 TH	0045 5.1	0659 1.4	1310 4.9	1909 1.6
12 TH	0153 5.3	0812 1.0	1434 4.9	2041 1.5	27 F	0124 4.9	0742 1.6	1353 4.7	1953 1.8
13 F	0255 5.0	0921 1.4	1549 4.6	◖2155 1.8	28 SA	0209 4.7	0833 1.7	1446 4.5	2048 2.0
14 SA	0411 4.8	1041 1.6	1717 4.5	2316 2.0	29 SU	0306 4.6	0937 1.8	1555 4.3	◖2158 2.1
15 SU	0534 4.7	1200 1.6	1839 4.5		30 M	0419 4.5	1050 1.8	1717 4.4	2315 2.0

Chart Datum: 3·05 metres below Ordnance Datum (Newlyn)
HAT is 6·3m above Chart Datum

TIDES

TIME ZONE (UT)	WALES – HOLYHEAD	Dates in amber are SPRINGS
For Summer Time add ONE hour in non-shaded areas	LAT 53°19'N LONG 4°37'W	Dates in yellow are NEAPS

2012

TIMES AND HEIGHTS OF HIGH AND LOW WATERS

MAY

Day	Time m	Time m		Day	Time m	Time m
1 TU	0537 4.6 / 1201 1.6 / 1827 4.6			16 W	0056 1.8 / 0708 4.8 / 1326 1.5 / 1951 4.7	
2 W	0024 1.8 / 0642 4.8 / 1301 1.3 / 1923 4.9			17 TH	0150 1.7 / 0758 4.9 / 1412 1.4 / 2032 4.9	
3 TH	0122 1.4 / 0737 5.1 / 1353 0.9 / 2012 5.2			18 F	0234 1.5 / 0841 5.0 / 1451 1.3 / 2108 5.0	
4 F	0212 1.0 / 0826 5.5 / 1440 0.6 / 2056 5.5			19 SA	0312 1.3 / 0919 5.1 / 1526 1.2 / 2141 5.2	
5 SA	0258 0.7 / 0913 5.7 / 1525 0.4 / 2140 5.7			20 SU	0348 1.2 / 0954 5.1 / 1558 1.2 / 2212 5.3	
6 SU	0344 0.4 / 1001 5.9 / 1611 0.3 / 2224 5.9			21 M	0421 1.1 / 1028 5.2 / 1630 1.2 / 2244 5.3	
7 M	0431 0.3 / 1049 5.9 / 1657 0.4 / 2311 5.9			22 TU	0455 1.1 / 1103 5.2 / 1702 1.2 / 2317 5.3	
8 TU	0520 0.3 / 1139 5.8 / 1745 0.5 / 2358 5.8			23 W	0529 1.1 / 1138 5.1 / 1737 1.2 / 2351 5.3	
9 W	0611 0.4 / 1230 5.6 / 1835 0.8			24 TH	0606 1.1 / 1214 5.0 / 1813 1.3	
10 TH	0048 5.7 / 0705 0.6 / 1325 5.3 / 1927 1.1			25 F	0028 5.2 / 0644 1.2 / 1254 4.9 / 1851 1.4	
11 F	0141 5.4 / 0802 0.9 / 1424 5.0 / 2025 1.4			26 SA	0108 5.1 / 0725 1.3 / 1337 4.8 / 1935 1.6	
12 SA	0240 5.2 / 0905 1.2 / 1530 4.7 / 2130 1.7			27 SU	0151 5.0 / 0813 1.4 / 1426 4.7 / 2025 1.7	
13 SU	0345 4.9 / 1014 1.4 / 1644 4.5 / 2242 1.9			28 M	0242 4.9 / 0908 1.5 / 1524 4.6 / 2125 1.8	
14 M	0456 4.8 / 1124 1.6 / 1758 4.5 / 2352 1.9			29 TU	0342 4.8 / 1011 1.5 / 1632 4.6 / 2233 1.8	
15 TU	0607 4.7 / 1229 1.6 / 1901 4.6			30 W	0451 4.8 / 1118 1.4 / 1742 4.7 / 2342 1.7	
				31 TH	0600 4.9 / 1222 1.3 / 1845 4.9	

JUNE

Day	Time m		Day	Time m
1 F	0045 1.5 / 0702 5.1 / 1321 1.0 / 1941 5.1		16 SA	0202 1.8 / 0810 4.7 / 1419 1.6 / 2040 4.9
2 SA	0143 1.2 / 0800 5.3 / 1415 0.8 / 2032 5.4		17 SU	0247 1.6 / 0854 4.8 / 1459 1.5 / 2117 5.0
3 SU	0237 0.9 / 0854 5.6 / 1505 0.7 / 2121 5.6		18 M	0326 1.4 / 0933 5.0 / 1535 1.4 / 2151 5.2
4 M	0329 0.6 / 0947 5.7 / 1555 0.6 / 2209 5.8		19 TU	0403 1.3 / 1010 5.0 / 1609 1.3 / 2225 5.3
5 TU	0420 0.4 / 1038 5.7 / 1644 0.6 / 2257 5.9		20 W	0438 1.1 / 1045 5.1 / 1644 1.2 / 2259 5.4
6 W	0511 0.4 / 1129 5.6 / 1733 0.6 / 2346 5.9		21 TH	0513 1.1 / 1121 5.1 / 1719 1.2 / 2334 5.4
7 TH	0602 0.4 / 1220 5.5 / 1821 0.8		22 F	0550 1.0 / 1158 5.1 / 1756 1.2
8 F	0035 5.8 / 0652 0.6 / 1311 5.3 / 1910 1.0		23 SA	0012 5.4 / 0627 1.0 / 1237 5.1 / 1834 1.2
9 SA	0125 5.6 / 0744 0.8 / 1403 5.0 / 2002 1.3		24 SU	0051 5.3 / 0707 1.1 / 1318 5.0 / 1916 1.3
10 SU	0216 5.3 / 0838 1.1 / 1458 4.8 / 2056 1.6		25 M	0133 5.3 / 0750 1.1 / 1403 4.9 / 2002 1.4
11 M	0310 5.1 / 0935 1.4 / 1557 4.6 / 2157 1.8		26 TU	0218 5.2 / 0839 1.2 / 1453 4.8 / 2054 1.5
12 TU	0409 4.8 / 1036 1.6 / 1701 4.4 / 2303 2.0		27 W	0311 5.0 / 0935 1.3 / 1552 4.8 / 2156 1.6
13 W	0513 4.6 / 1138 1.8 / 1807 4.4		28 TH	0413 4.9 / 1040 1.4 / 1701 4.7 / 2306 1.7
14 TH	0008 2.0 / 0618 4.6 / 1239 1.8 / 1907 4.5		29 F	0525 4.9 / 1149 1.4 / 1812 4.8
15 F	0109 1.9 / 0718 4.6 / 1333 1.7 / 1957 4.7		30 SA	0017 1.5 / 0637 5.0 / 1256 1.3 / 1917 5.0

JULY

Day	Time m		Day	Time m
1 SU	0124 1.3 / 0745 5.1 / 1419 1.1 / 2016 5.3		16 M	0222 1.8 / 0832 4.7 / 1434 1.7 / 2054 4.9
2 M	0225 1.0 / 0845 5.3 / 1453 0.9 / 2108 5.5		17 TU	0305 1.5 / 0914 4.9 / 1514 1.5 / 2131 5.1
3 TU	0321 0.8 / 0939 5.5 / 1545 0.8 / 2158 5.7		18 W	0343 1.3 / 0951 5.0 / 1550 1.3 / 2205 5.3
4 W	0413 0.5 / 1030 5.5 / 1633 0.7 / 2245 5.9		19 TH	0419 1.1 / 1026 5.2 / 1625 1.1 / 2240 5.5
5 TH	0501 0.4 / 1118 5.6 / 1719 0.7 / 2331 5.9		20 F	0454 0.9 / 1101 5.3 / 1700 1.0 / 2315 5.6
6 F	0548 0.4 / 1204 5.5 / 1803 0.8		21 SA	0529 0.8 / 1138 5.3 / 1736 0.9 / 2352 5.6
7 SA	0017 5.8 / 0633 0.6 / 1249 5.3 / 1847 0.9		22 SU	0606 0.8 / 1215 5.3 / 1814 0.9
8 SU	0101 5.7 / 0717 0.8 / 1332 5.1 / 1931 1.2		23 M	0030 5.6 / 0644 0.8 / 1255 5.3 / 1853 1.0
9 M	0145 5.4 / 0802 1.1 / 1416 4.9 / 2017 1.4		24 TU	0110 5.5 / 0725 0.9 / 1338 5.2 / 1937 1.1
10 TU	0229 5.1 / 0848 1.4 / 1503 4.7 / 2107 1.7		25 W	0154 5.4 / 0811 1.1 / 1425 5.0 / 2027 1.3
11 W	0318 4.8 / 0939 1.7 / 1557 4.5 / 2205 2.0		26 TH	0243 5.2 / 0904 1.3 / 1520 4.9 / 2127 1.5
12 TH	0414 4.6 / 1038 1.9 / 1701 4.4 / 2313 2.2		27 F	0344 5.0 / 1009 1.5 / 1629 4.8 / 2240 1.7
13 F	0521 4.4 / 1144 2.1 / 1812 4.4		28 SA	0501 4.8 / 1126 1.6 / 1749 4.8
14 SA	0024 2.2 / 0633 4.4 / 1250 2.0 / 1918 4.5		29 SU	0000 1.7 / 0626 4.8 / 1242 1.6 / 1903 4.9
15 SU	0128 2.0 / 0740 4.5 / 1347 1.9 / 2011 4.7		30 M	0116 1.5 / 0741 4.9 / 1349 1.4 / 2007 5.2
			31 TU	0221 1.2 / 0843 5.2 / 1447 1.1 / 2100 5.5

AUGUST

Day	Time m		Day	Time m
1 W	0316 0.8 / 0934 5.3 / 1536 0.9 / 2147 5.7		16 TH	0319 1.2 / 0929 5.1 / 1526 1.3 / 2141 5.4
2 TH	0404 0.6 / 1019 5.5 / 1620 0.8 / 2231 5.9		17 F	0354 1.0 / 1003 5.3 / 1601 1.0 / 2215 5.6
3 F	0447 0.5 / 1101 5.5 / 1701 0.7 / 2312 5.9		18 SA	0429 0.7 / 1037 5.4 / 1636 0.8 / 2250 5.8
4 SA	0528 0.5 / 1141 5.5 / 1740 0.7 / 2353 5.8		19 SU	0504 0.6 / 1113 5.6 / 1712 0.7 / 2327 5.9
5 SU	0607 0.6 / 1219 5.4 / 1819 0.9		20 M	0540 0.5 / 1150 5.6 / 1750 0.7
6 M	0032 5.7 / 0644 0.8 / 1257 5.2 / 1857 1.1		21 TU	0006 5.8 / 0618 0.6 / 1231 5.5 / 1830 0.8
7 TU	0110 5.4 / 0722 1.1 / 1334 5.0 / 1936 1.4		22 W	0047 5.7 / 0700 0.8 / 1313 5.6 / 1914 0.9
8 W	0148 5.2 / 0801 1.4 / 1412 4.8 / 2019 1.7		23 TH	0132 5.5 / 0746 1.0 / 1400 5.2 / 2005 1.2
9 TH	0229 4.9 / 0844 1.7 / 1457 4.6 / 2109 2.0		24 F	0223 5.2 / 0840 1.1 / 1456 5.0 / 2107 1.5
10 F	0319 4.6 / 0936 2.0 / 1555 4.4 / 2214 2.2		25 SA	0327 4.9 / 0948 1.2 / 1608 4.8 / 2226 1.7
11 SU	0425 4.3 / 1043 2.3 / 1711 4.3 / 2335 2.3		26 SU	0453 4.7 / 1112 1.8 / 1735 4.7 / 2354 1.7
12 SU	0548 4.2 / 1202 2.3 / 1834 4.4		27 M	0627 4.7 / 1234 1.8 / 1856 4.9
13 M	0052 2.2 / 0708 4.4 / 1313 2.1 / 1940 4.6		28 TU	0113 1.5 / 0742 4.9 / 1343 1.5 / 1959 5.2
14 TU	0154 1.9 / 0808 4.6 / 1407 1.9 / 2028 4.9		29 W	0217 1.2 / 0839 5.2 / 1438 1.3 / 2050 5.5
15 W	0240 1.6 / 0852 4.8 / 1450 1.6 / 2106 5.2		30 TH	0307 0.9 / 0924 5.3 / 1523 1.0 / 2133 5.7
			31 F	0349 0.7 / 1003 5.4 / 1602 0.8 / 2212 5.8

Chart Datum: 3·05 metres below Ordnance Datum (Newlyn)
HAT is 6·3m above Chart Datum

WALES – HOLYHEAD

LAT 53°19'N LONG 4°37'W

Dates in amber are **SPRINGS**
Dates in yellow are **NEAPS**

2012

TIMES AND HEIGHTS OF HIGH AND LOW WATERS

SEPTEMBER

Day	Time m	Time m	Time m	Time m	Day	Time m	Time m	Time m	Time m
1 SA	0427 0.6	1039 5.5	1639 0.7	2249 5.8	16 SU	0359 0.6	1010 5.6	1609 0.7	2223 5.9
2 SU	0502 0.6	1114 5.5	1715 0.8	2326 5.8	17 M	0435 0.4	1046 5.8	1647 0.5	2302 6.0
3 M	0536 0.7	1148 5.4	1749 0.9		18 TU	0514 0.4	1125 5.8	1727 0.5	2343 6.0
4 TU	0001 5.6	0609 0.9	1221 5.3	1824 1.1	19 W	0554 0.5	1207 5.8	1810 0.6	
5 W	0036 5.4	0643 1.2	1254 5.2	1900 1.4	20 TH	0027 5.8	0637 0.7	1252 5.6	1857 0.9
6 TH	0111 5.2	0718 1.4	1329 5.0	1939 1.6	21 F	0115 5.6	0726 1.1	1341 5.4	1951 1.2
7 F	0148 4.9	0757 1.7	1409 4.7	2025 2.0	22 SA	0210 5.2	0823 1.5	1439 5.1	2057 1.5
8 SA	0233 4.6	0844 2.1	1500 4.5	2124 2.2	23 SU	0320 4.8	0935 1.8	1555 4.8	2220 1.7
9 SU	0334 4.3	0946 2.4	1612 4.3	2243 2.4	24 M	0453 4.6	1101 2.0	1724 4.8	2348 1.7
10 M	0502 4.2	1109 2.5	1743 4.4		25 TU	0625 4.7	1223 1.9	1843 5.0	
11 TU	0011 2.3	0632 4.3	1233 2.3	1859 4.6	26 W	0104 1.5	0734 4.9	1330 1.7	1945 5.2
12 W	0118 1.9	0737 4.6	1333 2.0	1953 4.9	27 TH	0204 1.2	0826 5.1	1422 1.4	2033 5.5
13 TH	0207 1.6	0823 4.9	1418 1.6	2034 5.2	28 F	0250 1.0	0907 5.3	1505 1.1	2113 5.6
14 F	0247 1.2	0900 5.2	1457 1.3	2111 5.5	29 SA	0328 0.9	0942 5.4	1542 1.0	2150 5.7
15 SA	0324 0.9	0935 5.4	1533 0.9	2146 5.7	30 SU	0403 0.8	1014 5.5	1616 0.9	2225 5.7

OCTOBER

Day	Time m	Time m	Time m	Time m	Day	Time m	Time m	Time m	Time m
1 M	0435 0.8	1046 5.5	1649 0.9	2259 5.7	16 TU	0409 0.4	1021 5.9	1624 0.5	2239 6.1
2 TU	0506 0.9	1118 5.5	1722 1.0	2332 5.6	17 W	0450 0.4	1103 6.0	1708 0.5	2324 6.0
3 W	0537 1.1	1149 5.4	1756 1.2		18 TH	0534 0.5	1147 5.9	1755 0.6	
4 TH	0005 5.4	0609 1.3	1222 5.3	1830 1.4	19 F	0012 5.9	0620 0.8	1235 5.8	1845 0.8
5 F	0040 5.2	0643 1.5	1255 5.1	1908 1.6	20 SA	0105 5.5	0712 1.1	1327 5.5	1943 1.1
6 SA	0117 4.9	0720 1.8	1333 4.9	1952 1.9	21 SU	0203 5.2	0811 1.5	1427 5.3	2050 1.4
7 SU	0200 4.7	0804 2.1	1420 4.7	2046 2.1	22 M	0315 4.8	0922 1.6	1540 5.0	2208 1.6
8 M	0255 4.4	0901 2.3	1522 4.5	2156 2.3	23 TU	0442 4.7	1042 2.0	1702 4.9	2328 1.7
9 TU	0415 4.3	1017 2.5	1648 4.4	2320 2.2	24 W	0605 4.7	1159 2.0	1818 5.0	
10 W	0545 4.3	1142 2.4	1809 4.6		25 TH	0040 1.6	0712 4.9	1306 1.8	1920 5.2
11 TH	0031 2.0	0654 4.6	1250 2.1	1909 4.9	26 F	0139 1.4	0803 5.1	1359 1.6	2010 5.3
12 F	0126 1.6	0744 4.9	1340 1.7	1956 5.2	27 SA	0225 1.2	0844 5.2	1442 1.4	2050 5.4
13 SA	0210 1.2	0826 5.2	1423 1.3	2037 5.5	28 SU	0304 1.1	0918 5.4	1520 1.2	2127 5.5
14 SU	0250 0.9	0904 5.5	1503 0.9	2117 5.8	29 M	0337 1.0	0950 5.5	1554 1.1	2201 5.5
15 M	0329 0.6	0942 5.8	1543 0.7	2157 6.0	30 TU	0409 1.1	1021 5.5	1627 1.1	2235 5.5
					31 W	0439 1.1	1052 5.5	1700 1.2	2308 5.5

NOVEMBER

Day	Time m	Time m	Time m	Time m	Day	Time m	Time m	Time m	Time m
1 TH	0510 1.2	1124 5.5	1733 1.3	2341 5.3	16 F	0519 0.6	1133 6.1	1745 0.5	
2 F	0543 1.3	1156 5.4	1808 1.4		17 SA	0003 5.8	0608 0.8	1223 5.9	1837 0.7
3 SA	0016 5.2	0616 1.5	1231 5.3	1845 1.6	18 SU	0056 5.6	0700 1.1	1315 5.7	1934 1.0
4 SU	0054 5.0	0654 1.7	1309 5.1	1927 1.7	19 M	0154 5.2	0756 1.4	1412 5.5	2036 1.3
5 M	0136 4.8	0736 2.0	1352 4.9	2016 1.9	20 TU	0259 5.0	0859 1.8	1516 5.2	2143 1.5
6 TU	0226 4.6	0827 2.2	1446 4.8	2116 2.1	21 W	0412 4.7	1010 2.0	1627 5.0	2254 1.7
7 W	0331 4.4	0932 2.3	1555 4.7	2227 2.1	22 TH	0527 4.7	1122 2.0	1740 5.0	
8 TH	0451 4.5	1048 2.3	1713 4.7	2338 1.9	23 F	0003 1.7	0635 4.8	1230 2.0	1845 5.0
9 F	0604 4.6	1159 2.1	1820 4.9		24 SA	0104 1.7	0731 4.9	1328 1.8	1940 5.1
10 SA	0039 1.6	0702 4.9	1259 1.8	1915 5.2	25 SU	0154 1.6	0816 5.1	1417 1.7	2025 5.2
11 SU	0131 1.3	0751 5.2	1349 1.4	2004 5.5	26 M	0237 1.5	0854 5.2	1458 1.5	2105 5.3
12 M	0218 1.0	0835 5.5	1435 1.0	2050 5.8	27 TU	0313 1.4	0929 5.3	1535 1.4	2141 5.3
13 TU	0302 0.7	0917 5.8	1521 0.8	2136 6.0	28 W	0346 1.3	1001 5.4	1610 1.3	2216 5.4
14 W	0347 0.6	1001 6.0	1607 0.6	2223 6.0	29 TH	0418 1.3	1032 5.5	1643 1.3	2249 5.3
15 TH	0432 0.5	1046 6.1	1655 0.5	2312 6.0	30 F	0450 1.3	1104 5.5	1717 1.3	2323 5.3

DECEMBER

Day	Time m	Time m	Time m	Time m	Day	Time m	Time m	Time m	Time m
1 SA	0523 1.4	1137 5.5	1752 1.3	2358 5.2	16 SU	0556 0.8	1210 6.1	1827 0.6	
2 SU	0557 1.4	1212 5.4	1828 1.4		17 M	0044 5.6	0645 1.0	1300 5.9	1918 0.8
3 M	0036 5.1	0634 1.6	1250 5.3	1907 1.5	18 TU	0135 5.4	0735 1.2	1350 5.7	2011 1.1
4 TU	0116 5.0	0714 1.7	1331 5.2	1951 1.6	19 W	0229 5.1	0829 1.5	1444 5.4	2107 1.4
5 W	0201 4.8	0800 1.9	1417 5.0	2041 1.7	20 TH	0327 4.8	0928 1.8	1543 5.1	2208 1.7
6 TH	0254 4.7	0854 2.0	1512 4.9	2140 1.8	21 F	0432 4.6	1034 2.0	1648 4.9	2314 1.9
7 F	0357 4.6	0958 2.1	1618 4.9	2246 1.8	22 SA	0543 4.6	1144 2.1	1757 4.7	
8 SA	0509 4.7	1109 2.0	1729 4.9	2353 1.6	23 SU	0018 1.9	0649 4.6	1250 2.1	1903 4.7
9 SU	0617 4.9	1217 1.8	1836 5.1		24 M	0118 1.9	0745 4.8	1349 2.0	1959 4.8
10 M	0054 1.4	0717 5.1	1318 1.5	1936 5.3	25 TU	0209 1.8	0831 5.0	1437 1.8	2045 5.1
11 TU	0150 1.2	0809 5.4	1413 1.2	2030 5.6	26 W	0251 1.7	0909 5.2	1518 1.6	2125 5.1
12 W	0242 0.9	0858 5.7	1505 0.9	2122 5.8	27 TH	0328 1.5	0944 5.3	1555 1.4	2201 5.2
13 TH	0331 0.7	0946 5.9	1556 0.6	2213 5.9	28 F	0401 1.4	1016 5.5	1628 1.3	2234 5.3
14 F	0420 0.7	1033 6.1	1646 0.5	2303 5.9	29 SA	0433 1.3	1048 5.5	1702 1.2	2308 5.3
15 SA	0508 0.7	1121 6.1	1736 0.5	2353 5.8	30 SU	0506 1.2	1121 5.6	1736 1.1	2342 5.3
					31 M	0540 1.2	1156 5.6	1811 1.1	

Chart Datum: 3·05 metres below Ordnance Datum (Newlyn)
HAT is 6·3m above Chart Datum

TIDES

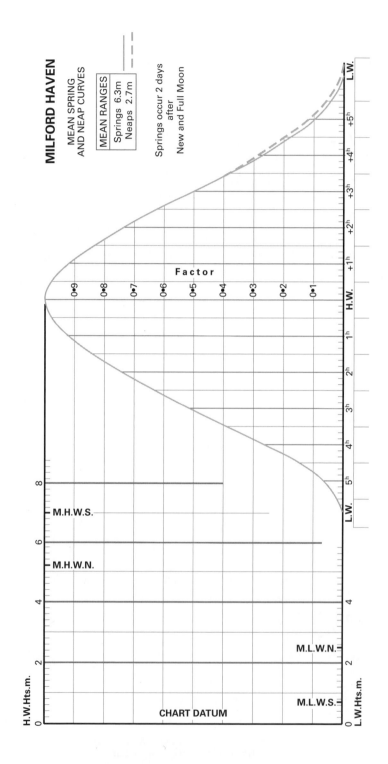

MILFORD HAVEN

MEAN SPRING
AND NEAP CURVES

MEAN RANGES	
Springs 6.3m	
Neaps 2.7m	---

Springs occur 2 days
after
New and Full Moon

Factor

0·9 0·8 0·7 0·6 0·5 0·4 0·3 0·2 0·1

H.W.   +1ʰ +2ʰ +3ʰ +4ʰ +5ʰ L.W.

1ʰ 2ʰ 3ʰ 4ʰ 5ʰ L.W.

H.W.Hts.m.

M.H.W.S.

M.H.W.N.

L.W.Hts.m.

M.L.W.N.

M.L.W.S.

CHART DATUM

WALES – MILFORD HAVEN

LAT 51°42'N   LONG 5°03'W

Dates in amber are **SPRINGS**
Dates in yellow are **NEAPS**

2012

TIMES AND HEIGHTS OF HIGH AND LOW WATERS

JANUARY

#	Time	m	#	Time	m
1 SU ☽	0459 / 1112 / 1731 / 2336	2.3 / 5.7 / 2.3 / 5.4	**16** M	0447 / 1058 / 1719 / 2330	1.6 / 6.3 / 1.8 / 5.9
2 M	0554 / 1208 / 1831	2.6 / 5.4 / 2.6	**17** TU	0545 / 1200 / 1825	2.0 / 5.9 / 2.1
3 TU	0040 / 0704 / 1318 / 1942	5.2 / 2.7 / 5.3 / 2.6	**18** W	0039 / 0702 / 1316 / 1949	5.7 / 2.2 / 5.7 / 2.2
4 W	0158 / 0823 / 1431 / 2054	5.2 / 2.7 / 5.3 / 2.5	**19** TH	0200 / 0829 / 1437 / 2112	5.7 / 2.1 / 5.7 / 2.0
5 TH	0307 / 0931 / 1534 / 2154	5.4 / 2.5 / 5.5 / 2.2	**20** F	0318 / 0947 / 1553 / 2220	5.9 / 1.8 / 6.0 / 1.7
6 F	0402 / 1025 / 1626 / 2242	5.7 / 2.1 / 5.8 / 1.9	**21** SA	0425 / 1050 / 1656 / 2316	6.3 / 1.5 / 6.3 / 1.3
7 SA	0448 / 1109 / 1710 / 2324	6.1 / 1.8 / 6.1 / 1.6	**22** SU	0521 / 1143 / 1747	6.7 / 1.1 / 6.7
8 SU	0529 / 1150 / 1750	6.4 / 1.5 / 6.4	**23** M ●	0004 / 0607 / 1230 / 1831	1.0 / 7.0 / 0.8 / 6.9
9 M ○	0003 / 0607 / 1228 / 1828	1.4 / 6.7 / 1.3 / 6.6	**24** TU	0048 / 0650 / 1312 / 1911	0.9 / 7.2 / 0.7 / 6.9
10 TU	0041 / 0644 / 1306 / 1906	1.2 / 6.9 / 1.1 / 6.8	**25** W	0127 / 0729 / 1349 / 1948	0.8 / 7.2 / 0.7 / 6.9
11 W	0119 / 0722 / 1344 / 1944	1.0 / 7.0 / 0.9 / 6.9	**26** TH	0203 / 0805 / 1424 / 2022	0.9 / 7.1 / 0.9 / 6.7
12 TH	0158 / 0801 / 1423 / 2023	0.9 / 7.1 / 0.9 / 6.8	**27** F	0236 / 0840 / 1457 / 2055	1.0 / 6.9 / 1.1 / 6.5
13 F	0237 / 0841 / 1502 / 2104	1.0 / 7.0 / 1.0 / 6.7	**28** SA	0308 / 0913 / 1527 / 2127	1.3 / 6.6 / 1.4 / 6.2
14 SA	0317 / 0922 / 1543 / 2147	1.1 / 6.9 / 1.2 / 6.5	**29** SU	0338 / 0946 / 1558 / 2200	1.6 / 6.3 / 1.7 / 5.9
15 SU	0359 / 1007 / 1627 / 2234	1.3 / 6.6 / 1.5 / 6.2	**30** M	0410 / 1022 / 1633 / 2238	2.0 / 5.9 / 2.0 / 5.6
			31 TU ☽	0449 / 1105 / 1718 / 2326	2.3 / 5.5 / 2.5 / 5.2

FEBRUARY

#	Time	m	#	Time	m
1 W	0545 / 1203 / 1825	2.7 / 5.1 / 2.7	**16**	0012 / 0638 / 1253 / 1927	5.6 / 2.2 / 5.4 / 2.4
2 TH	0037 / 0713 / 1327 / 1956	5.0 / 2.9 / 5.0 / 2.8	**17** F	0141 / 0818 / 1426 / 2102	5.4 / 2.3 / 5.4 / 2.2
3 F	0214 / 0847 / 1455 / 2116	5.0 / 2.7 / 5.1 / 2.5	**18** SA	0309 / 0941 / 1549 / 2212	5.7 / 1.9 / 5.7 / 1.8
4 SA	0330 / 0956 / 1559 / 2215	5.4 / 2.3 / 5.5 / 2.1	**19** SU	0418 / 1043 / 1648 / 2307	6.1 / 1.5 / 6.2 / 1.4
5 SU	0423 / 1046 / 1647 / 2301	5.8 / 1.9 / 6.0 / 1.7	**20** M	0510 / 1133 / 1734 / 2351	6.6 / 1.1 / 6.5 / 1.0
6 M	0507 / 1129 / 1730 / 2343	6.3 / 1.4 / 6.4 / 1.2	**21** TU ●	0553 / 1214 / 1814	6.9 / 0.8 / 6.8
7 TU ○	0547 / 1209 / 1809	6.7 / 1.0 / 6.7	**22** W	0030 / 0631 / 1251 / 1850	0.8 / 7.1 / 0.7 / 6.9
8 W	0023 / 0626 / 1248 / 1848	0.9 / 7.0 / 0.7 / 7.0	**23** TH	0105 / 0706 / 1324 / 1923	0.7 / 7.1 / 0.7 / 6.9
9 TH	0102 / 0705 / 1327 / 1926	0.6 / 7.3 / 0.5 / 7.2	**24** F	0138 / 0739 / 1355 / 1954	0.8 / 7.1 / 0.8 / 6.8
10 F	0141 / 0744 / 1406 / 2006	0.5 / 7.4 / 0.5 / 7.2	**25** SA	0208 / 0810 / 1425 / 2023	0.9 / 6.9 / 1.0 / 6.7
11 SA	0220 / 0823 / 1444 / 2045	0.5 / 7.3 / 0.6 / 7.1	**26** SU	0236 / 0840 / 1452 / 2051	1.1 / 6.7 / 1.2 / 6.4
12 SU	0300 / 0904 / 1523 / 2126	0.7 / 7.1 / 0.8 / 6.8	**27** M	0304 / 0910 / 1520 / 2121	1.4 / 6.4 / 1.5 / 6.1
13 M	0340 / 0947 / 1605 / 2210	1.0 / 6.8 / 1.2 / 6.4	**28** TU	0333 / 0941 / 1550 / 2153	1.7 / 6.0 / 1.9 / 5.8
14 TU ☽	0425 / 1035 / 1652 / 2303	1.4 / 6.3 / 1.7 / 5.9	**29** W	0406 / 1018 / 1627 / 2234	2.1 / 5.6 / 2.3 / 5.4
15 W	0520 / 1134 / 1755	1.9 / 5.8 / 2.1			

MARCH

#	Time	m	#	Time	m
1 TH ☽	0451 / 1106 / 1719 / 2333	2.5 / 5.1 / 2.7 / 5.0	**16** F	0626 / 1238 / 1913	2.2 / 5.3 / 2.5
2 F	0603 / 1221 / 1852	2.8 / 4.8 / 2.9	**17** SA	0125 / 0806 / 1414 / 2047	5.4 / 2.3 / 5.3 / 2.3
3 SA	0106 / 0756 / 1406 / 2032	4.9 / 2.8 / 4.9 / 2.7	**18** SU	0253 / 0927 / 1534 / 2156	5.6 / 1.9 / 5.6 / 1.9
4 SU	0247 / 0918 / 1524 / 2141	5.2 / 2.4 / 5.3 / 2.2	**19** M	0359 / 1026 / 1629 / 2248	6.1 / 1.5 / 6.1 / 1.4
5 M	0350 / 1015 / 1618 / 2232	5.7 / 1.9 / 5.9 / 1.7	**20** TU	0449 / 1111 / 1713 / 2329	6.5 / 1.2 / 6.4 / 1.1
6 TU	0437 / 1101 / 1702 / 2317	6.2 / 1.3 / 6.4 / 1.1	**21** W	0530 / 1149 / 1750	6.7 / 1.0 / 6.7
7 W	0520 / 1143 / 1744 / 2359	6.8 / 0.8 / 6.9 / 0.7	**22** TH ●	0005 / 0606 / 1224 / 1823	0.9 / 6.9 / 0.8 / 6.8
8 TH ○	0601 / 1224 / 1824	7.2 / 0.5 / 7.2	**23** F	0039 / 0639 / 1255 / 1854	0.8 / 6.9 / 0.8 / 6.8
9 F	0040 / 0642 / 1305 / 1904	0.4 / 7.5 / 0.3 / 7.4	**24** SA	0110 / 0710 / 1325 / 1924	0.8 / 6.9 / 0.8 / 6.8
10 SA	0121 / 0722 / 1345 / 1944	0.2 / 7.6 / 0.2 / 7.4	**25** SU	0139 / 0740 / 1353 / 1952	0.9 / 6.8 / 1.0 / 6.7
11 SU	0201 / 0803 / 1424 / 2024	0.2 / 7.5 / 0.4 / 7.3	**26** M	0207 / 0809 / 1421 / 2020	1.1 / 6.6 / 1.2 / 6.5
12 M	0242 / 0845 / 1504 / 2106	0.4 / 7.2 / 0.7 / 7.0	**27** TU	0235 / 0839 / 1449 / 2049	1.3 / 6.4 / 1.5 / 6.2
13 TU	0323 / 0928 / 1545 / 2151	0.8 / 6.8 / 1.2 / 6.5	**28** W	0305 / 0909 / 1519 / 2121	1.6 / 6.0 / 1.8 / 5.9
14 W	0409 / 1017 / 1633 / 2245	1.3 / 6.1 / 1.7 / 6.0	**29** TH	0339 / 0945 / 1555 / 2200	2.0 / 5.7 / 2.1 / 5.6
15 TH ☽	0505 / 1117 / 1737 / 2355	1.8 / 5.6 / 2.2 / 5.5	**30** F ☽	0421 / 1030 / 1642 / 2253	2.3 / 5.3 / 2.5 / 5.2
			31 SA	0522 / 1138 / 1757	2.6 / 5.0 / 2.7

APRIL

#	Time	m	#	Time	m
1 SU	0014 / 0702 / 1312 / 1942	5.0 / 2.7 / 4.9 / 2.6	**16** M	0222 / 0856 / 1502 / 2126	5.6 / 2.0 / 5.5 / 2.0
2 M	0152 / 0831 / 1439 / 2058	5.2 / 2.3 / 5.3 / 2.2	**17** TU	0327 / 0954 / 1558 / 2217	5.9 / 1.7 / 5.9 / 1.6
3 TU	0306 / 0935 / 1539 / 2156	5.7 / 1.8 / 5.8 / 1.7	**18** W	0418 / 1039 / 1642 / 2259	6.2 / 1.4 / 6.2 / 1.4
4 W	0400 / 1026 / 1628 / 2245	6.2 / 1.3 / 6.4 / 1.1	**19** TH	0500 / 1117 / 1720 / 2336	6.5 / 1.2 / 6.4 / 1.2
5 TH	0448 / 1112 / 1713 / 2331	6.8 / 0.8 / 6.9 / 0.7	**20** F	0537 / 1152 / 1754	6.6 / 1.1 / 6.6
6 F ○	0533 / 1157 / 1757	7.2 / 0.4 / 7.3	**21** SA ●	0009 / 0610 / 1225 / 1825	1.1 / 6.7 / 1.0 / 6.7
7 SA	0015 / 0616 / 1240 / 1839	0.4 / 7.5 / 0.2 / 7.5	**22** SU	0042 / 0642 / 1256 / 1856	1.1 / 6.7 / 1.0 / 6.7
8 SU	0059 / 0700 / 1323 / 1922	0.2 / 7.6 / 0.2 / 7.5	**23** M	0112 / 0713 / 1326 / 1925	1.1 / 6.6 / 1.1 / 6.6
9 M	0142 / 0744 / 1405 / 2006	0.2 / 7.4 / 0.4 / 7.3	**24** TU	0142 / 0743 / 1355 / 1955	1.2 / 6.5 / 1.3 / 6.5
10 TU	0226 / 0828 / 1447 / 2050	0.4 / 7.1 / 0.7 / 7.0	**25** W	0213 / 0814 / 1426 / 2026	1.4 / 6.3 / 1.5 / 6.3
11 W	0311 / 0915 / 1531 / 2138	0.8 / 6.7 / 1.2 / 6.6	**26** TH	0245 / 0847 / 1458 / 2100	1.6 / 6.1 / 1.7 / 6.1
12 TH	0359 / 1005 / 1621 / 2233	1.3 / 6.2 / 1.7 / 6.1	**27** F	0321 / 0924 / 1536 / 2140	1.8 / 5.8 / 2.0 / 5.8
13 F ☽	0457 / 1105 / 1725 / 2340	1.8 / 5.6 / 2.2 / 5.7	**28** SA	0404 / 1010 / 1623 / 2232	2.1 / 5.5 / 2.3 / 5.5
14 SA	0614 / 1220 / 1852	2.1 / 5.3 / 2.4	**29** SU ☽	0500 / 1111 / 1726 / 2341	2.3 / 5.2 / 2.5 / 5.4
15 SU	0101 / 0741 / 1347 / 2018	5.5 / 2.2 / 5.3 / 2.3	**30** M	0617 / 1229 / 1852	2.4 / 5.2 / 2.4

Chart Datum: 3·71 metres below Ordnance Datum (Newlyn)
HAT is 7·9m above Chart Datum

TIDES

TIDES

TIME ZONE (UT)
For Summer Time add ONE hour in **non-shaded areas**

WALES – MILFORD HAVEN
LAT 51°42'N   LONG 5°03'W
TIMES AND HEIGHTS OF HIGH AND LOW WATERS

Dates in amber are **SPRINGS**
Dates in yellow are **NEAPS**

2012

MAY

Day	Time m	Day	Time m
1 TU	0102 5.4 / 0741 2.2 / 1349 5.4 / 2011 2.1	**16** W	0243 5.7 / 0909 1.9 / 1515 5.7 / 2137 1.9
2 W	0218 5.8 / 0850 1.8 / 1456 5.9 / 2115 1.7	**17** TH	0338 5.9 / 0959 1.7 / 1605 5.9 / 2223 1.7
3 TH	0320 6.2 / 0948 1.3 / 1552 6.4 / 2210 1.2	**18** F	0424 6.1 / 1042 1.6 / 1647 6.2 / 2304 1.5
4 F	0414 6.7 / 1040 0.9 / 1642 6.8 / 2302 0.8	**19** SA	0505 6.3 / 1120 1.4 / 1724 6.3 / 2341 1.4
5 SA	0504 7.1 / 1129 0.6 / 1730 7.2 / 2351 0.5	**20** SU	0542 6.4 / 1155 1.3 / 1759 6.5 / ●
6 SU	0553 7.3 / 1216 0.4 / 1817 7.4 / ○	**21** M	0016 1.3 / 0617 6.4 / 1229 1.3 / 1831 6.5
7 M	0039 0.3 / 0641 7.4 / 1303 0.4 / 1904 7.4	**22** TU	0050 1.3 / 0650 6.5 / 1302 1.3 / 1904 6.6
8 TU	0126 0.3 / 0728 7.3 / 1349 0.5 / 1951 7.3	**23** W	0123 1.3 / 0723 6.4 / 1335 1.3 / 1936 6.5
9 W	0214 0.5 / 0816 7.0 / 1434 0.8 / 2038 7.1	**24** TH	0156 1.4 / 0757 6.3 / 1409 1.4 / 2010 6.4
10 TH	0301 0.8 / 0904 6.6 / 1520 1.2 / 2127 6.7	**25** F	0231 1.5 / 0833 6.2 / 1444 1.6 / 2047 6.3
11 F	0351 1.2 / 0954 6.2 / 1610 1.6 / 2220 6.3	**26** SA	0310 1.6 / 0911 6.0 / 1524 1.7 / 2128 6.1
12 SA	0446 1.6 / 1049 5.8 / 1708 2.0 / ◑ 2319 5.9	**27** SU	0352 1.8 / 0956 5.8 / 1609 1.9 / 2217 5.9
13 SU	0549 2.0 / 1152 5.5 / 1818 2.2	**28** M	0442 1.9 / 1050 5.6 / 1703 2.1 / ◑ 2316 5.8
14 M	0026 5.7 / 0700 2.1 / 1305 5.3 / 1933 2.3	**29** TU	0543 2.0 / 1154 5.5 / 1810 2.1
15 TU	0138 5.6 / 0809 2.1 / 1415 5.4 / 2041 2.2	**30** W	0023 5.7 / 0654 2.0 / 1305 5.6 / 1925 2.0
		31 TH	0135 5.9 / 0806 1.8 / 1415 5.9 / 2035 1.8

JUNE

Day	Time m	Day	Time m
1 F	0242 6.2 / 0911 1.5 / 1517 6.2 / 2139 1.4	**16** SA	0347 5.7 / 1005 1.9 / 1613 5.8 / 2233 1.9
2 SA	0343 6.5 / 1011 1.2 / 1615 6.6 / 2237 1.1	**17** SU	0435 5.7 / 1049 1.7 / 1656 6.1 / 2315 1.7
3 SU	0441 6.8 / 1106 0.9 / 1709 7.0 / 2331 0.8	**18** M	0517 6.1 / 1130 1.6 / 1735 6.3 / 2354 1.5
4 M	0535 7.0 / 1158 0.7 / 1800 7.2 / ○	**19** TU	0556 6.3 / 1207 1.4 / 1812 6.5 / ●
5 TU	0024 0.6 / 0626 7.1 / 1248 0.6 / 1850 7.3	**20** W	0031 1.4 / 0631 6.4 / 1243 1.3 / 1846 6.6
6 W	0114 0.5 / 0716 7.1 / 1336 0.7 / 1939 7.3	**21** TH	0106 1.3 / 0707 6.4 / 1318 1.3 / 1922 6.6
7 TH	0203 0.6 / 0804 6.9 / 1422 0.8 / 2026 7.1	**22** F	0142 1.2 / 0743 6.4 / 1354 1.2 / 1957 6.6
8 F	0250 0.8 / 0851 6.7 / 1507 1.1 / 2113 6.8	**23** SA	0219 1.2 / 0820 6.4 / 1432 1.3 / 2035 6.6
9 SA	0337 1.1 / 0937 6.3 / 1553 1.4 / 2200 6.5	**24** SU	0257 1.3 / 0859 6.3 / 1511 1.4 / 2115 6.5
10 SU	0423 1.4 / 1024 6.0 / 1641 1.8 / 2249 6.1	**25** M	0338 1.4 / 0941 6.2 / 1553 1.6 / 2200 6.3
11 M	0513 1.8 / 1115 5.7 / 1734 2.1 / ◑ 2343 5.8	**26** TU	0422 1.6 / 1028 6.0 / 1640 1.7 / 2250 6.1
12 TU	0608 2.1 / 1213 5.4 / 1835 2.3	**27** W	0513 1.7 / 1123 5.8 / 1737 1.9 / ◑ 2350 6.0
13 W	0044 5.6 / 0709 2.2 / 1319 5.3 / 1942 2.4	**28** TH	0614 1.9 / 1228 5.7 / 1845 2.0
14 TH	0150 5.5 / 0814 2.2 / 1424 5.4 / 2048 2.3	**29** F	0058 5.9 / 0727 1.9 / 1340 5.8 / 2002 1.9
15 F	0252 5.6 / 0914 2.1 / 1523 5.6 / 2145 2.1	**30** SA	0212 5.9 / 0842 1.8 / 1451 6.0 / 2115 1.7

JULY

Day	Time m	Day	Time m
1 SU	0322 6.2 / 0951 1.5 / 1556 6.3 / 2221 1.3	**16** M	0407 5.6 / 1022 2.0 / 1632 5.9 / 2252 1.9
2 M	0426 6.4 / 1051 1.2 / 1656 6.7 / 2320 1.0	**17** TU	0454 5.9 / 1106 1.7 / 1714 6.2 / 2334 1.6
3 TU	0525 6.7 / 1145 0.9 / 1750 7.0 / ○	**18** W	0535 6.2 / 1146 1.4 / 1752 6.5
4 W	0013 0.7 / 0617 6.9 / 1236 0.8 / 1839 7.2	**19** TH	0012 1.3 / 0613 6.4 / 1224 1.2 / ● 1828 6.7
5 TH	0103 0.6 / 0705 7.0 / 1323 0.7 / 1926 7.3	**20** F	0049 1.1 / 0649 6.6 / 1301 1.1 / 1905 6.8
6 F	0150 0.6 / 0750 6.9 / 1407 0.8 / 2010 7.2	**21** SA	0126 1.0 / 0726 6.7 / 1338 1.0 / 1941 6.9
7 SA	0233 0.7 / 0832 6.8 / 1448 1.0 / 2052 7.0	**22** SU	0203 0.9 / 0803 6.7 / 1416 0.9 / 2019 6.9
8 SU	0313 1.0 / 0912 6.5 / 1527 1.2 / 2132 6.7	**23** M	0240 0.9 / 0841 6.6 / 1454 1.0 / 2058 6.8
9 M	0352 1.3 / 0951 6.2 / 1606 1.6 / 2212 6.3	**24** TU	0319 1.1 / 0921 6.5 / 1534 1.2 / 2139 6.6
10 TU	0431 1.7 / 1032 5.8 / 1646 1.9 / 2256 5.9	**25** W	0400 1.3 / 1004 6.3 / 1618 1.5 / 2226 6.3
11 W	0513 2.0 / 1117 5.5 / 1734 2.3 / ◑ 2345 5.6	**26** TH	0445 1.6 / 1055 6.0 / 1709 1.8 / ◑ 2321 6.0
12 TH	0605 2.3 / 1213 5.3 / 1835 2.5	**27** F	0542 1.9 / 1157 5.7 / 1815 2.0
13 F	0048 5.5 / 0710 2.5 / 1326 5.2 / 1950 2.6	**28** SA	0030 5.7 / 0658 2.1 / 1314 5.6 / 1941 2.1
14 SA	0202 5.2 / 0823 2.5 / 1440 5.3 / 2105 2.5	**29** SU	0152 5.7 / 0825 2.1 / 1435 5.8 / 2105 1.9
15 SU	0311 5.4 / 0929 2.3 / 1542 5.6 / 2204 2.2	**30** M	0312 5.8 / 0941 1.8 / 1548 6.2 / 2215 1.5
		31 TU	0421 6.2 / 1043 1.4 / 1649 6.6 / 2313 1.1

AUGUST

Day	Time m	Day	Time m
1 W	0518 6.6 / 1136 1.0 / 1741 7.0	**16** TH	0512 6.2 / 1123 1.4 / 1729 6.6 / 2349 1.2
2 TH	0004 0.8 / 0606 6.8 / 1224 0.8 / ○ 1827 7.2	**17** F	0550 6.6 / 1202 1.1 / 1806 6.9
3 F	0049 0.6 / 0649 7.0 / 1306 0.7 / 1909 7.3	**18** SA	0027 0.9 / 0627 6.8 / 1240 0.8 / 1843 7.1
4 SA	0130 0.6 / 0729 7.0 / 1345 0.7 / 1948 7.2	**19** SU	0105 0.7 / 0704 7.0 / 1318 0.7 / 1920 7.2
5 SU	0208 0.7 / 0806 6.9 / 1422 0.9 / 2024 7.0	**20** M	0142 0.6 / 0742 7.1 / 1356 0.6 / 1958 7.2
6 M	0243 0.9 / 0841 6.6 / 1456 1.1 / 2059 6.7	**21** TU	0220 0.7 / 0820 7.0 / 1435 0.8 / 2038 7.1
7 TU	0316 1.2 / 0914 6.4 / 1528 1.5 / 2134 6.4	**22** W	0258 0.9 / 0859 6.8 / 1514 1.0 / 2119 6.8
8 W	0348 1.6 / 0948 6.0 / 1600 1.8 / 2209 6.0	**23** TH	0338 1.2 / 0942 6.5 / 1557 1.4 / 2204 6.4
9 TH	0421 2.0 / 1025 5.7 / 1638 2.2 / ◑ 2251 5.6	**24** F	0423 1.6 / 1032 6.1 / 1649 1.8 / ◑ 2259 5.9
10 F	0503 2.3 / 1112 5.3 / 1729 2.6 / 2345 5.2	**25** SA	0519 2.0 / 1135 5.7 / 1758 2.2
11 SA	0604 2.7 / 1217 5.0 / 1850 2.8	**26** SU	0012 5.5 / 0641 2.3 / 1259 5.5 / 1934 2.3
12 SU	0103 5.0 / 0730 2.8 / 1352 5.0 / 2024 2.7	**27** M	0143 5.4 / 0819 2.3 / 1428 5.7 / 2102 2.0
13 M	0234 5.1 / 0853 2.6 / 1510 5.3 / 2136 2.4	**28** TU	0310 5.9 / 0936 1.9 / 1543 6.1 / 2210 1.6
14 TU	0341 5.4 / 0955 2.2 / 1606 5.8 / 2228 2.0	**29** W	0416 6.1 / 1036 1.5 / 1640 6.6 / 2304 1.2
15 W	0430 5.8 / 1042 1.8 / 1650 6.2 / 2311 1.6	**30** TH	0507 6.5 / 1124 1.1 / 1727 7.0 / 2349 0.9
		31 F	0550 6.8 / 1206 0.8 / 1809 7.2 / ○

Chart Datum: 3·71 metres below Ordnance Datum (Newlyn)
HAT is 7·9m above Chart Datum

WALES – MILFORD HAVEN
LAT 51°42'N   LONG 5°03'W
TIMES AND HEIGHTS OF HIGH AND LOW WATERS
2012

SEPTEMBER

	Time	m		Time	m
1 SA	0029	0.7	**16** SU	0001	0.8
	0629	7.0		0600	7.1
	1244	0.7		1216	0.7
	1846	7.2	●	1817	7.4
2 SU	0105	0.7	**17** M	0040	0.8
	0704	7.0		0639	7.3
	1319	0.8		1255	0.5
	1921	7.2		1857	7.5
3 M	0138	0.8	**18** TU	0119	0.5
	0737	6.9		0718	7.4
	1352	0.9		1335	0.5
	1954	7.0		1937	7.5
4 TU	0210	1.0	**19** W	0158	0.5
	0808	6.7		0758	7.3
	1423	1.1		1416	0.6
	2025	6.8		2018	7.3
5 W	0239	1.2	**20** TH	0238	0.8
	0838	6.5		0840	7.0
	1452	1.4		1458	0.9
	2056	6.4		2101	6.9
6 TH	0308	1.6	**21** F	0320	1.2
	0909	6.2		0924	6.4
	1521	1.8		1543	1.4
	2129	6.1		2149	6.4
7 F	0338	1.9	**22** SA	0406	1.7
	0942	5.8		1016	6.2
	1555	2.2		1637	1.8
	2205	5.6	◑	2247	5.9
8 SA	0414	2.3	**23** SU	0506	2.2
	1022	5.5		1123	5.8
	1634	2.6		1752	2.2
◑	2253	5.2			
9 SU	0505	2.7	**24** M	0002	5.4
	1120	5.1		0635	2.5
	1750	2.9		1249	5.6
				1930	2.3
10 M	0004	4.9	**25** TU	0136	5.4
	0633	2.9		0812	2.4
	1250	4.9		1418	5.4
	1939	2.9		2054	2.0
11 TU	0149	4.9	**26** W	0300	5.7
	0813	2.8		0925	2.0
	1431	5.2		1529	6.2
	2101	2.5		2157	1.6
12 W	0308	5.3	**27** TH	0401	6.1
	0922	2.3		1020	1.5
	1533	5.7		1623	6.6
	2157	2.0		2246	1.3
13 TH	0400	5.8	**28** F	0448	6.5
	1012	1.8		1105	1.2
	1619	6.2		1707	6.9
	2241	1.5		2327	1.0
14 F	0443	6.3	**29** SA	0528	6.8
	1055	1.4		1144	1.0
	1700	6.7		1746	7.1
	2321	1.1			
15 SA	0522	6.8	**30** SU	0003	0.9
	1135	1.0		0604	6.9
	1739	7.1		1219	0.9
			○	1820	7.1

OCTOBER

	Time	m		Time	m
1 M	0037	0.9	**16** TU	0015	0.5
	0637	7.0		0614	7.5
	1252	0.9		1233	0.5
	1853	7.0		1834	7.6
2 TU	0108	0.9	**17** W	0057	0.5
	0708	6.9		0657	7.5
	1323	1.0		1316	0.5
	1924	6.9		1918	7.5
3 W	0138	1.1	**18** TH	0140	0.6
	0737	6.8		0740	7.4
	1353	1.2		1400	0.6
	1954	6.7		2002	7.3
4 TH	0207	1.3	**19** F	0222	0.8
	0807	6.6		0825	7.2
	1421	1.5		1446	0.9
	2025	6.4		2049	6.9
5 F	0235	1.6	**20** SA	0307	1.2
	0836	6.3		0913	6.8
	1451	1.8		1535	1.3
	2056	6.1		2139	6.4
6 SA	0305	1.9	**21** SU	0357	1.7
	0909	6.0		1007	6.3
	1525	2.1		1631	1.8
	2131	5.7		2238	5.9
7 SU	0341	2.3	**22** M	0458	2.2
	0947	5.7		1112	5.9
	1607	2.5		1745	2.2
	2216	5.3	◑	2350	5.5
8 M	0427	2.6	**23** TU	0621	2.4
	1039	5.4		1230	5.7
	1707	2.8		1912	2.3
◑	2320	5.0			
9 TU	0539	2.9	**24** W	0114	5.4
	1156	5.1		0749	2.4
	1846	2.9		1352	5.8
				2029	2.1
10 W	0051	4.9	**25** TH	0233	5.7
	0723	2.8		0900	2.1
	1334	5.2		1501	6.1
	2014	2.6		2130	1.8
11 TH	0221	5.3	**26** F	0334	6.0
	0839	2.5		0955	1.8
	1448	5.7		1555	6.4
	2116	2.1		2219	1.5
12 F	0320	5.8	**27** SA	0422	6.4
	0935	2.0		1039	1.5
	1540	6.2		1640	6.7
	2206	1.6		2259	1.3
13 SA	0408	6.3	**28** SU	0502	6.6
	1023	1.4		1118	1.3
	1626	6.7		1719	6.8
	2250	1.1		2335	1.2
14 SU	0451	6.8	**29** M	0538	6.7
	1107	1.0		1153	1.2
	1709	7.1		1755	6.9
	2332	0.8	○		
15 M	0533	7.2	**30** TU	0008	1.2
	1150	0.7		0610	6.8
	1752	7.4		1226	1.2
●				1827	6.8
			31 W	0041	1.2
				0642	6.8
				1258	1.3
				1859	6.8

NOVEMBER

	Time	m		Time	m
1 TH	0111	1.3	**16** F	0125	0.6
	0712	6.8		0727	7.5
	1329	1.4		1349	0.6
	1930	6.6		1951	7.3
2 F	0141	1.4	**17** SA	0211	0.8
	0742	6.6		0814	7.3
	1359	1.5		1438	0.8
	2001	6.4		2040	6.9
3 SA	0211	1.6	**18** SU	0258	1.2
	0813	6.5		0904	7.0
	1431	1.8		1528	1.2
	2034	6.2		2131	6.5
4 SU	0244	1.9	**19** M	0348	1.6
	0847	6.2		0956	6.6
	1506	2.0		1622	1.6
	2109	5.9		2225	6.1
5 M	0320	2.1	**20** TU	0444	2.0
	0925	5.9		1054	6.2
	1547	2.3		1724	2.0
	2152	5.6	◑	2326	5.7
6 TU	0404	2.4	**21** W	0551	2.3
	1013	5.6		1159	5.9
	1640	2.5		1835	2.2
	2248	5.3			
7 W	0503	2.7	**22** TH	0036	5.5
	1117	5.4		0707	2.4
	1752	2.7		1311	5.8
○				1946	2.2
8 TH	0001	5.2	**23** F	0149	5.6
	0625	2.7		0819	2.3
	1236	5.4		1419	5.9
	1918	2.5		2050	2.1
9 F	0123	5.4	**24** SA	0254	5.8
	0747	2.5		0919	2.1
	1353	5.7		1519	6.1
	2028	2.2		2144	1.9
10 SA	0233	5.8	**25** SU	0348	6.0
	0852	2.1		1009	1.9
	1457	6.1		1609	6.3
	2126	1.7		2228	1.7
11 SU	0329	6.3	**26** M	0433	6.3
	0947	1.6		1051	1.7
	1550	6.6		1652	6.4
	2217	1.3		2308	1.6
12 M	0419	6.8	**27** TU	0513	6.5
	1038	1.2		1130	1.6
	1640	7.0		1731	6.5
	2305	0.9		2344	1.4
13 TU	0506	7.2	**28** W	0548	6.6
	1126	0.8		1205	1.5
	1728	7.3		1806	6.6
●	2352	0.7	○		
14 W	0553	7.4	**29** TH	0018	1.4
	1214	0.6		0621	6.7
	1816	7.5		1239	1.4
○				1840	6.6
15 TH	0038	0.6	**30** F	0051	1.4
	0639	7.5		0654	6.7
	1302	0.5		1312	1.4
	1903	7.4		1912	6.6

DECEMBER

	Time	m		Time	m
1 SA	0123	1.4	**16** SU	0201	0.7
	0726	6.7		0805	7.4
	1344	1.5		1429	0.7
	1945	6.5		2030	7.0
2 SU	0155	1.5	**17** M	0247	0.9
	0758	6.6		0852	7.2
	1417	1.6		1516	0.9
	2019	6.3		2116	6.7
3 M	0229	1.7	**18** TU	0333	1.3
	0833	6.4		0939	6.9
	1453	1.8		1602	1.3
	2055	6.1		2202	6.3
4 TU	0306	1.8	**19** W	0420	1.6
	0910	6.2		1027	6.5
	1532	1.9		1651	1.7
	2135	5.9		2252	6.0
5 W	0347	2.1	**20** TH	0511	2.0
	0954	6.0		1119	6.1
	1617	2.1		1745	2.1
	2223	5.7	◑	2347	5.6
6 TH	0436	2.3	**21** F	0611	2.3
	1046	5.8		1219	5.8
	1712	2.3		1847	2.3
◑	2321	5.5			
7 F	0536	2.4	**22** SA	0053	5.4
	1150	5.7		0720	2.5
	1820	2.3		1327	5.6
				1955	2.4
8 SA	0031	5.5	**23** SU	0204	5.4
	0651	2.4		0832	2.5
	1302	5.8		1434	5.6
	1936	2.2		2101	2.3
9 SU	0144	5.7	**24** M	0309	5.6
	0806	2.2		0935	2.3
	1413	6.0		1535	5.8
	2045	1.9		2156	2.1
10 M	0251	6.1	**25** TU	0404	5.9
	0913	1.8		1026	2.1
	1517	6.3		1627	6.0
	2147	1.5		2242	1.9
11 TU	0350	6.5	**26** W	0450	6.1
	1013	1.4		1109	1.8
	1616	6.7		1710	6.2
	2243	1.2		2323	1.7
12 W	0445	6.9	**27** TH	0530	6.4
	1108	1.0		1148	1.6
	1711	7.0		1749	6.4
	2335	0.9			
13 TH	0538	7.2	**28** F	0000	1.5
	1201	0.7		0605	6.6
	1804	7.2		1224	1.5
●			○	1824	6.5
14 F	0025	0.7	**29** SA	0035	1.6
	0628	7.5		0639	6.7
	1252	0.6		1258	1.4
	1854	7.3		1858	6.6
15 SA	0114	0.6	**30** SU	0108	1.3
	0717	7.5		0712	6.7
	1341	0.5		1331	1.3
	1942	7.2		1931	6.6
			31 M	0142	1.3
				0745	6.8
				1405	1.3
				2005	6.5

Chart Datum: 3·71 metres below Ordnance Datum (Newlyn)
HAT is 7·9m above Chart Datum

TIDES

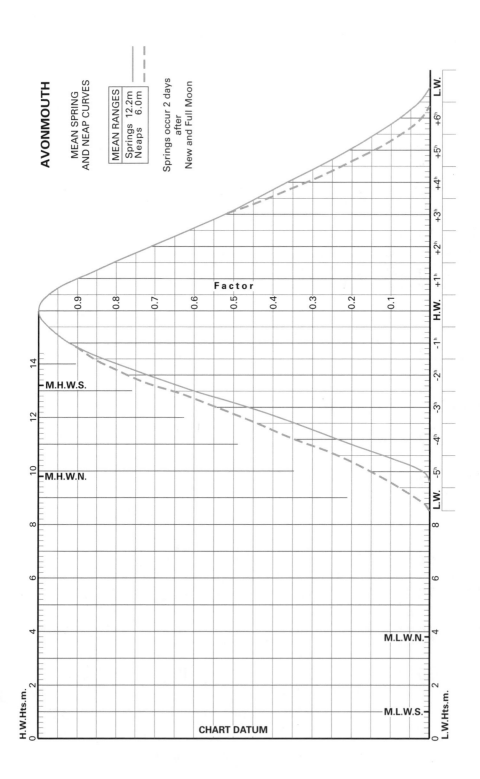

AVONMOUTH

MEAN SPRING
AND NEAP CURVES

MEAN RANGES
Springs 12.2m
Neaps 6.0m

Springs occur 2 days
after
New and Full Moon

Factor

0.9
0.8
0.7
0.6
0.5
0.4
0.3
0.2
0.1

H.W.Hts.m.

L.W.Hts.m.

M.H.W.S.
M.H.W.N.
M.L.W.N.
M.L.W.S.

CHART DATUM

H.W.

L.W.

L.W.

AVONMOUTH

LAT 51°30'N   LONG 2°44'W

TIMES AND HEIGHTS OF HIGH AND LOW WATERS

2012

JANUARY

Time m   Time m

1 0544 3.0 / 1153 10.8 / SU 1815 3.0 ☽
16 0547 2.2 / 1149 11.9 / M 1810 2.4 ☾

2 0010 10.4 / 0628 3.4 / M 1245 10.2 / 1904 3.4
17 0015 11.3 / 0634 2.7 / TU 1246 11.2 / 1900 3.0

3 0107 9.9 / 0726 3.8 / TU 1354 9.9 / 2006 3.7
18 0120 10.7 / 0736 3.3 / W 1402 10.6 / 2015 3.6

4 0224 9.8 / 0838 3.9 / W 1510 10.0 / 2120 3.6
19 0248 10.4 / 0925 3.6 / TH 1531 10.6 / 2216 3.5

5 0340 10.1 / 0957 3.6 / TH 1615 10.4 / 2234 3.1
20 0411 10.8 / 1053 3.0 / F 1646 11.2 / 2329 2.8

6 0441 10.8 / 1108 3.0 / F 1711 11.1 / 2337 2.5
21 0518 11.6 / 1158 2.3 / SA 1747 11.9

7 0533 11.5 / 1206 2.4 / SA 1800 11.7
22 0029 2.0 / 0613 12.5 / SU 1256 1.6 / 1840 12.6

8 0031 2.0 / 0618 12.2 / SU 1259 2.0 / 1844 12.2
23 0124 1.4 / 0702 13.2 / M 1349 1.1 / ● 1928 13.1

9 0121 1.7 / 0701 12.6 / M 1348 1.8 / ○ 1928 12.5
24 0214 1.0 / 0747 13.5 / TU 1438 0.8 / 2012 13.3

10 0209 1.6 / 0743 12.9 / TU 1436 1.8 / 2009 12.7
25 0259 0.9 / 0829 13.6 / W 1521 0.9 / 2052 13.2

11 0253 1.6 / 0823 13.0 / W 1518 1.6 / 2049 12.8
26 0338 1.1 / 0907 13.4 / TH 1556 1.2 / 2126 12.9

12 0331 1.6 / 0902 13.1 / TH 1554 1.8 / 2127 12.8
27 0407 1.5 / 0940 13.0 / F 1622 1.6 / 2155 12.5

13 0404 1.6 / 0941 13.1 / F 1625 1.8 / 2205 12.7
28 0425 1.9 / 1009 12.5 / SA 1640 1.9 / 2221 12.0

14 0435 1.7 / 1020 12.9 / SA 1654 1.8 / 2244 12.5
29 0442 2.1 / 1037 11.9 / SU 1701 2.1 / 2249 11.5

15 0509 1.8 / 1102 12.5 / SU 1729 2.0 / 2326 12.0
30 0507 2.4 / 1107 11.2 / M 1730 2.5 / 2321 10.9

31 0540 2.8 / 1144 10.5 / TU 1808 3.0 ☽

FEBRUARY

Time m   Time m

1 0002 10.2 / 0624 3.4 / W 1236 9.8 / 1902 3.6
16 0048 10.5 / 0702 3.4 / TH 1336 10.2 / 1934 3.9

2 0104 9.6 / 0733 4.0 / TH 1357 9.4 / 2023 4.0
17 0226 9.9 / 0901 3.9 / F 1517 10.0 / 2200 3.9

3 0237 9.5 / 0905 4.1 / F 1531 9.7 / 2149 3.7
18 0357 10.4 / 1039 3.3 / SA 1634 10.7 / 2314 3.0

4 0403 10.1 / 1028 3.5 / SA 1641 10.6 / 2303 3.0
19 0506 11.3 / 1143 2.3 / SU 1736 11.6

5 0506 11.0 / 1138 2.7 / SU 1737 11.4
20 0012 2.0 / 0600 12.3 / M 1238 1.5 / 1826 12.5

6 0006 2.2 / 0556 11.9 / M 1237 2.1 / 1825 12.2
21 0104 1.2 / 0647 13.1 / TU 1329 0.9 / ● 1911 13.1

7 0102 1.7 / 0642 12.7 / TU 1332 1.7 / ○ 1909 12.7
22 0153 0.8 / 0730 13.5 / W 1416 0.6 / 1952 13.3

8 0153 1.4 / 0725 13.2 / W 1422 1.4 / 1952 13.1
23 0237 0.7 / 0808 13.6 / TH 1458 0.7 / 2028 13.3

9 0241 1.2 / 0807 13.5 / TH 1507 1.2 / 2033 13.4
24 0316 0.8 / 0843 13.4 / F 1532 1.0 / 2059 13.0

10 0322 1.1 / 0847 13.7 / F 1546 1.2 / 2111 13.5
25 0345 1.3 / 0913 13.0 / SA 1557 1.4 / 2125 12.6

11 0357 1.1 / 0926 13.7 / SA 1616 1.2 / 2148 13.4
26 0402 1.7 / 0939 12.5 / SU 1611 1.8 / 2149 12.2

12 0426 1.1 / 1004 13.5 / SU 1642 1.4 / 2225 13.0
27 0413 1.9 / 1004 12.0 / M 1627 1.9 / 2214 11.8

13 0454 1.4 / 1044 12.9 / M 1709 1.7 / 2305 12.4
28 0433 2.0 / 1026 11.3 / TU 1651 2.2 / 2241 11.3

14 0526 1.8 / 1127 12.1 / TU 1743 2.3 / ☽ 2349 11.5
29 0502 2.4 / 1101 10.8 / W 1723 2.6 / 2316 10.6

15 0607 2.6 / 1218 11.1 / W 1828 3.1

MARCH

Time m   Time m

1 0538 3.0 / 1144 10.0 / TH 1807 3.4 ☽
16 0030 10.4 / 0644 3.5 / F 1322 9.9 / 1914 4.1

2 0007 9.8 / 0632 3.8 / F 1250 9.3 / 1919 4.1
17 0214 9.8 / 0845 4.0 / SA 1503 9.8 / 2143 4.0

3 0128 9.3 / 0809 4.2 / SA 1438 9.3 / 2105 4.1
18 0339 10.3 / 1019 3.3 / SU 1616 10.5 / 2252 3.0

4 0320 9.7 / 0950 3.8 / SU 1610 10.1 / 2231 3.3
19 0444 11.2 / 1120 2.3 / M 1714 11.5 / 2347 2.0

5 0435 10.7 / 1110 2.9 / M 1711 11.2 / 2340 2.4
20 0538 12.1 / 1212 1.5 / TU 1803 12.3

6 0531 11.8 / 1214 2.1 / TU 1801 12.2
21 0037 1.2 / 0623 12.8 / W 1301 0.9 / 1845 12.9

7 0038 1.7 / 0618 12.7 / W 1310 1.5 / 1846 13.0
22 0124 0.8 / 0704 13.2 / TH 1346 0.7 / ● 1924 13.1

8 0132 1.2 / 0703 13.4 / TH 1401 1.1 / ○ 1929 13.5
23 0208 0.7 / 0741 13.2 / F 1427 0.7 / 1958 13.1

9 0220 0.9 / 0746 13.9 / F 1447 0.8 / 2011 13.8
24 0247 0.9 / 0814 13.0 / SA 1503 1.0 / 2028 12.8

10 0303 0.6 / 0827 14.1 / SA 1526 0.7 / 2050 13.9
25 0318 1.3 / 0844 12.7 / SU 1529 1.5 / 2055 12.5

11 0340 0.6 / 0901 14.1 / SU 1558 0.9 / 2128 13.8
26 0337 1.7 / 0910 12.3 / M 1543 1.8 / 2119 12.2

12 0411 0.8 / 0947 13.7 / M 1625 1.2 / 2206 13.3
27 0347 1.9 / 0935 11.9 / TU 1557 1.9 / 2143 11.9

13 0439 1.1 / 1026 13.0 / TU 1651 1.6 / 2245 12.5
28 0406 1.9 / 1000 11.5 / W 1621 2.0 / 2211 11.5

14 0509 1.7 / 1108 12.0 / W 1722 2.3 / 2330 11.5
29 0434 2.2 / 1032 11.0 / TH 1652 2.4 / 2247 10.9

15 0548 2.6 / 1200 10.8 / TH 1805 3.2 ☽
30 0510 2.7 / 1114 10.3 / F 1733 3.1 / ○ 2336 10.2

31 0558 3.4 / 1214 9.6 / SA 1833 3.8

APRIL

Time m   Time m

1 0045 9.7 / 0716 3.9 / SU 1341 9.4 / 2015 4.1
16 0311 10.4 / 0943 3.2 / M 1544 10.5 / 2218 3.1

2 0224 9.7 / 0905 3.8 / M 1527 10.0 / 2151 3.5
17 0412 11.0 / 1044 2.5 / TU 1641 11.2 / 2313 2.3

3 0355 10.6 / 1033 3.0 / TU 1637 11.0 / 2306 2.6
18 0505 11.8 / 1137 1.8 / W 1730 12.0

4 0457 11.7 / 1142 2.1 / W 1731 12.1
19 0003 1.6 / 0551 12.3 / TH 1226 1.3 / 1813 12.5

5 0007 1.8 / 0549 12.7 / TH 1240 1.5 / 1818 13.0
20 0050 1.2 / 0632 12.7 / F 1311 1.1 / 1851 12.7

6 0102 1.1 / 0636 13.5 / F 1332 1.0 / ○ 1903 13.7
21 0134 1.1 / 0710 12.7 / SA 1353 1.1 / ● 1926 12.7

7 0152 0.7 / 0721 13.9 / SA 1419 0.7 / 1946 14.0
22 0214 1.2 / 0744 12.6 / SU 1430 1.3 / 1958 12.6

8 0238 0.4 / 0805 14.2 / SU 1501 0.6 / 2028 14.1
23 0247 1.5 / 0816 12.4 / M 1459 1.6 / 2027 12.4

9 0319 0.4 / 0848 14.1 / M 1538 0.7 / 2109 13.9
24 0312 1.8 / 0845 12.1 / TU 1519 1.8 / 2055 12.1

10 0354 0.6 / 0930 13.7 / TU 1609 1.1 / 2150 13.3
25 0327 2.0 / 0913 11.8 / W 1536 1.9 / 2121 11.9

11 0427 1.1 / 1012 12.9 / W 1638 1.7 / 2231 12.5
26 0348 2.0 / 0941 11.5 / TH 1602 2.0 / 2151 11.6

12 0500 1.7 / 1056 11.9 / TH 1711 2.4 / 2318 11.5
27 0418 2.1 / 1015 11.2 / F 1635 2.3 / 2229 11.2

13 0540 2.5 / 1149 10.8 / F 1755 3.3 ☽
28 0455 2.5 / 1058 10.7 / SA 1716 2.8 / 2318 10.7

14 0021 10.5 / 0637 3.3 / SA 1309 10.0 / 1905 4.0
29 0542 2.9 / 1153 10.2 / SU 1812 3.3 ☽

15 0156 10.0 / 0812 3.7 / SU 1437 9.9 / 2108 3.9
30 0021 10.3 / 0648 3.4 / M 1306 9.9 / 1931 3.6

TIDES

Chart Datum: 6·50 metres below Ordnance Datum (Newlyn)
HAT is 14·7m above Chart Datum

AVONMOUTH

LAT 51°30'N   LONG 2°44'W

TIMES AND HEIGHTS OF HIGH AND LOW WATERS

2012

TIME ZONE (UT)
For Summer Time add ONE hour in **non-shaded areas**

Dates in amber are **SPRINGS**
Dates in yellow are **NEAPS**

MAY

Day					Day				
1 TU	0140 10.2	0816 3.4	1433 10.2	2105 3.3	**16** W	0332 10.8	0952 2.9	1559 10.8	2228 2.9
2 W	0306 10.7	0946 2.9	1553 11.0	2225 2.6	**17** TH	0425 11.2	1052 2.4	1650 11.3	2322 2.3
3 TH	0418 11.6	1102 2.3	1655 12.0	2331 1.9	**18** F	0513 11.6	1144 2.0	1736 11.8	
4 F	0517 12.5	1205 1.6	1748 12.9		**19** SA	0011 1.8	0557 12.0	1232 1.6	1816 12.2
5 SA	0030 1.2	0608 13.2	1301 1.1	1836 13.5	**20** SU ●	0057 1.6	0637 12.1	1316 1.5	1854 12.3
6 SU ○	0123 0.8	0657 13.7	1351 0.8	1922 13.9	**21** M	0139 1.6	0715 12.2	1357 1.5	1930 12.4
7 M	0213 0.5	0745 13.9	1438 0.7	2008 14.0	**22** TU	0218 1.7	0751 12.1	1433 1.7	2004 12.3
8 TU	0259 0.5	0831 13.8	1519 0.8	2052 13.8	**23** W	0251 1.9	0826 12.0	1502 1.9	2037 12.1
9 W	0340 0.6	0917 13.5	1557 1.2	2136 13.3	**24** TH	0317 2.1	0859 11.8	1526 2.0	2108 12.0
10 TH	0418 1.1	1002 12.8	1631 1.7	2221 12.6	**25** F	0341 2.1	0931 11.7	1553 2.1	2142 11.8
11 F	0455 1.7	1047 12.0	1706 2.3	2309 11.7	**26** SA	0411 2.2	1007 11.5	1627 2.2	2221 11.6
12 SA ◐	0535 2.3	1138 11.1	1748 3.0		**27** SU	0449 2.3	1049 11.2	1709 2.4	2307 11.3
13 SU	0006 10.9	0624 2.9	1242 10.4	1844 3.5	**28** M ◐	0534 2.5	1138 10.9	1759 2.8	
14 M	0122 10.4	0726 3.3	1357 10.1	1959 3.7	**29** TU	0002 11.0	0629 2.8	1238 10.7	1901 3.0
15 TU	0232 10.9	0840 3.2	1502 10.3	2124 3.4	**30** W	0109 10.8	0736 2.9	1349 10.6	2019 3.1
					31 TH	0224 11.0	0857 2.9	1508 11.0	2143 2.7

JUNE

Day					Day				
1 F	0339 11.4	1022 2.5	1620 11.6	2258 2.2	**16** SA	0432 10.9	1053 2.6	1656 11.1	2327 2.5
2 SA	0446 12.1	1133 2.0	1720 12.4		**17** SU	0522 11.3	1150 2.2	1743 11.7	
3 SU	0001 1.6	0544 12.7	1233 1.5	1813 13.1	**18** M	0019 2.1	0606 11.7	1241 1.8	1825 12.0
4 M ○	0059 1.1	0638 13.2	1328 1.1	1903 13.6	**19** TU ●	0107 1.9	0649 11.9	1327 1.7	1906 12.3
5 TU	0153 0.8	0728 13.5	1420 0.9	1952 13.7	**20** W	0152 1.8	0730 12.0	1411 1.7	1945 12.3
6 W	0244 0.7	0818 13.5	1507 0.9	2039 13.7	**21** TH	0234 1.9	0809 12.1	1450 1.8	2023 12.3
7 TH	0330 0.7	0905 13.3	1549 1.1	2125 13.3	**22** F	0312 2.0	0847 12.0	1523 2.0	2059 12.3
8 F	0412 1.0	0951 12.9	1626 1.6	2209 12.8	**23** SA	0343 2.1	0923 12.0	1553 2.0	2134 12.2
9 SA	0449 1.5	1034 12.3	1659 2.0	2253 12.1	**24** SU	0412 2.1	0959 12.0	1624 2.0	2212 12.1
10 SU	0524 2.0	1117 11.6	1733 2.5	2339 11.4	**25** M	0445 2.1	1038 11.8	1701 2.1	2255 11.9
11 M ◐	0601 2.4	1203 10.9	1813 3.0		**26** TU	0524 2.1	1122 11.6	1744 2.3	2343 11.6
12 TU ◐	0033 10.8	0645 2.8	1258 10.4	1902 3.3	**27** W	0609 2.3	1212 11.3	1835 2.6	
13 W	0137 10.4	0736 3.1	1403 10.2	2003 3.5	**28** TH ◐	0040 11.3	0703 2.6	1314 10.9	1938 2.9
14 TH	0241 10.3	0837 3.2	1507 10.3	2113 3.4	**29** F	0149 11.0	0811 3.0	1430 10.8	2104 3.0
15 F	0339 10.5	0946 3.0	1604 10.6	2227 3.0	**30** SA	0308 11.1	0947 3.0	1550 11.2	2232 2.6

JULY

Day					Day				
1 SU	0422 11.5	1109 2.5	1658 11.8	2341 2.0	**16** M	0449 10.7	1112 2.7	1713 11.2	2346 2.5
2 M	0527 12.1	1214 1.9	1757 12.6		**17** TU	0541 11.4	1210 2.1	1802 11.9	
3 TU ○	0042 1.4	0624 12.7	1313 1.4	1849 13.2	**18** W	0040 2.0	0627 11.9	1303 1.8	1845 12.3
4 W ●	0139 1.0	0716 13.1	1407 1.0	1939 13.6	**19** TH ●	0132 1.8	0710 12.2	1353 1.7	1927 12.6
5 TH	0232 0.7	0806 13.3	1456 0.9	2026 13.7	**20** F	0220 1.8	0753 12.4	1439 1.7	2007 12.7
6 F	0320 0.7	0852 13.3	1540 1.0	2111 13.5	**21** SA	0305 1.8	0833 12.5	1519 1.7	2046 12.8
7 SA	0402 0.9	0935 13.1	1617 1.3	2152 13.1	**22** SU	0342 1.8	0910 12.5	1552 1.7	2122 12.8
8 SU	0437 1.3	1013 12.6	1646 1.7	2230 12.5	**23** M	0412 1.8	0946 12.5	1620 1.7	2159 12.7
9 M	0504 1.7	1048 12.0	1709 2.2	2305 11.8	**24** TU	0438 1.8	1023 12.4	1650 1.8	2238 12.5
10 TU	0530 2.1	1121 11.4	1738 2.6	2341 11.1	**25** W	0508 1.9	1102 12.1	1725 2.0	2322 12.0
11 W ◐	0603 2.5	1158 10.7	1815 3.0		**26** TH ◐	0546 2.2	1148 11.6	1808 2.4	
12 TH ◐	0027 10.4	0645 3.0	1248 10.2	1905 3.5	**27** F	0013 11.4	0631 2.7	1244 10.9	1902 3.0
13 F	0129 9.9	0741 3.4	1357 9.8	2011 3.8	**28** SA	0120 10.8	0732 3.3	1402 10.5	2031 3.5
14 SA	0243 9.8	0848 3.5	1513 10.0	2127 3.6	**29** SU	0247 10.5	0925 3.5	1531 10.6	2217 3.2
15 SU	0351 10.2	1002 3.2	1619 10.5	2243 3.1	**30** M	0409 10.9	1055 2.9	1645 11.4	2329 2.4
					31 TU	0517 11.7	1201 2.1	1746 12.3	

AUGUST

Day					Day				
1 W	0030 1.6	0614 12.5	1259 1.4	1838 13.1	**16** TH	0018 2.1	0605 11.9	1241 1.8	1824 12.5
2 TH ○	0126 1.0	0704 13.1	1353 0.9	1926 13.6	**17** F ●	0112 1.7	0649 12.5	1334 1.6	1906 12.9
3 F	0217 0.6	0751 13.4	1441 0.7	2011 13.8	**18** SA	0203 1.5	0732 12.8	1422 1.4	1947 13.2
4 SA	0304 0.5	0834 13.4	1524 0.7	2052 13.6	**19** SU	0249 1.4	0812 13.0	1505 1.4	2027 13.3
5 SU	0344 0.7	0913 13.2	1600 1.1	2128 13.3	**20** M	0329 1.4	0850 13.1	1541 1.4	2104 13.4
6 M	0416 1.2	0946 12.7	1625 1.6	2200 12.7	**21** TU	0401 1.5	0927 13.0	1610 1.5	2142 13.2
7 TU	0438 1.7	1014 12.2	1641 2.0	2228 12.0	**22** W	0425 1.6	1003 12.8	1636 1.6	2220 12.9
8 W	0456 2.1	1041 11.6	1701 2.4	2257 11.3	**23** TH	0450 1.9	1042 12.4	1706 1.9	2302 12.2
9 TH	0521 2.4	1111 11.0	1730 2.8	2331 10.6	**24** F ◐	0522 2.2	1125 11.7	1744 2.5	2350 11.3
10 F	0556 2.9	1150 10.3	1810 3.4		**25** SA	0603 2.9	1220 10.8	1835 3.3	
11 SA ◐	0019 9.8	0643 3.5	1247 9.7	1912 4.0	**26** SU ◐	0058 10.3	0702 3.7	1346 10.1	2015 4.0
12 SU	0138 9.3	0758 3.9	1420 9.5	2041 4.2	**27** M	0239 10.0	0923 4.0	1523 10.4	2210 3.4
13 M	0313 9.5	0922 3.8	1545 10.0	2207 3.6	**28** TU	0402 10.6	1046 3.4	1635 11.2	2317 2.4
14 TU	0422 10.3	1040 3.1	1647 10.9	2320 2.8	**29** W	0507 11.5	1147 2.5	1734 12.3	
15 W	0517 11.2	1144 2.4	1738 11.8		**30** TH	0014 1.5	0600 12.5	1241 1.3	1823 13.1
					31 F ○	0106 0.8	0647 13.1	1331 0.8	1908 13.7

Chart Datum: 6·50 metres below Ordnance Datum (Newlyn)
HAT is 14·7m above Chart Datum

AVONMOUTH

LAT 51°30'N   LONG 2°44'W

TIMES AND HEIGHTS OF HIGH AND LOW WATERS

Dates in amber are **SPRINGS**
Dates in yellow are **NEAPS**

2012

SEPTEMBER

Day	Time m	Time m	Time m	Time m
1 SA	0155 0.5	0730 13.4	1418 0.6	1949 13.8
2 SU	0240 0.5	0810 13.4	1500 0.7	2027 13.6
3 M	0319 0.7	0845 13.2	1535 1.0	2100 13.2
4 TU	0349 1.3	0914 12.7	1559 1.7	2128 12.7
5 W	0408 1.8	0940 12.3	1610 2.1	2153 12.1
6 TH	0421 2.1	1004 11.8	1626 2.3	2219 11.4
7 F	0441 2.4	1031 11.2	1651 2.7	2247 10.7
8 SA	0510 2.8	1103 10.5	1724 3.2	◑ 2326 9.9
9 SU	0550 3.5	1150 9.8	1813 4.0	
10 M	0029 9.2	0657 4.2	1313 9.2	1950 4.5
11 TU	0229 9.1	0842 4.2	1510 9.6	2132 4.0
12 W	0352 9.9	1008 3.5	1618 10.6	2253 3.1
13 TH	0450 11.0	1118 2.6	1711 11.7	2354 2.2
14 F	0539 12.0	1215 1.9	1758 12.6	
15 SA	0047 1.6	0624 12.7	1309 1.5	1841 13.2
16 SU	0138 1.3	0706 13.2	1358 1.2	● 1923 13.6
17 M	0225 1.1	0747 13.5	1442 1.1	2004 13.8
18 TU	0306 1.1	0827 13.6	1520 1.1	2044 13.8
19 W	0340 1.2	0905 13.5	1553 1.2	2123 13.6
20 TH	0408 1.5	0944 13.2	1622 1.5	2203 13.0
21 F	0433 1.9	1024 12.6	1652 2.0	2245 12.2
22 SA	0504 2.4	1108 11.7	1728 2.7	◐ 2334 11.1
23 SU	0544 3.2	1205 10.7	1821 3.6	
24 M	0047 10.1	0646 4.0	1341 10.0	2014 4.1
25 TU	0232 9.9	0914 4.1	1511 10.4	2154 3.4
26 W	0347 10.6	1027 3.1	1617 11.3	2256 2.4
27 TH	0447 11.5	1123 2.1	1713 12.3	2349 1.5
28 F	0538 12.4	1214 1.3	1801 13.0	
29 SA	0038 0.9	0623 13.0	1303 0.9	1843 13.5
30 SU	0126 0.6	0703 13.3	1348 0.7	○ 1922 13.6

OCTOBER

Day	Time m	Time m	Time m	Time m
1 M	0209 0.6	0740 13.3	1430 0.9	1958 13.4
2 TU	0248 0.9	0813 13.0	1505 1.3	2030 13.0
3 W	0319 1.4	0842 12.7	1530 1.8	2058 12.5
4 TH	0338 1.9	0908 12.3	1542 2.2	2123 12.0
5 F	0350 2.2	0933 11.8	1557 2.4	2148 11.5
6 SA	0410 2.4	0959 11.4	1622 2.6	2216 10.9
7 SU	0438 2.7	1031 10.8	1654 3.0	2254 10.3
8 M	0515 3.3	1116 10.1	1738 3.7	◐ 2349 9.5
9 TU	0610 4.0	1222 9.5	1850 4.3	
10 W	0118 9.2	0747 4.4	1412 9.6	2044 4.2
11 TH	0310 9.8	0926 3.8	1538 10.4	2212 3.4
12 F	0416 10.8	1041 3.0	1637 11.5	2320 2.5
13 SA	0508 11.9	1142 2.1	1727 12.5	
14 SU	0016 1.8	0554 12.8	1237 1.5	1813 13.3
15 M	0107 1.3	0638 13.4	1327 1.1	● 1857 13.8
16 TU	0155 1.0	0721 13.8	1414 0.9	1941 14.0
17 W	0239 0.9	0803 13.9	1457 0.9	2024 14.0
18 TH	0317 1.0	0845 13.8	1535 1.0	2107 13.7
19 F	0351 1.4	0927 13.4	1610 1.4	2150 13.1
20 SA	0423 1.8	1010 12.7	1644 1.9	2234 12.2
21 SU	0456 2.5	1057 11.8	1724 2.6	2325 11.2
22 M	0537 3.2	1156 10.9	1818 3.4	
23 TU	0037 10.3	0641 4.0	1327 10.4	1948 3.8
24 W	0210 10.1	0842 4.0	1446 10.6	2120 3.4
25 TH	0319 10.6	0955 3.3	1548 11.2	2223 2.7
26 F	0417 11.3	1052 2.5	1642 12.0	2317 1.9
27 SA	0508 12.0	1142 1.8	1731 12.6	
28 SU	0005 1.4	0552 12.6	1230 1.3	1814 13.0
29 M	0052 1.1	0633 12.9	1315 1.2	1853 13.1
30 TU	0135 1.0	0710 13.0	1357 1.3	1929 13.0
31 W	0215 1.2	0744 12.8	1434 1.6	2003 12.7

NOVEMBER

Day	Time m	Time m	Time m	Time m
1 TH	0248 1.6	0815 12.6	1503 2.0	2033 12.3
2 F	0312 2.0	0843 12.3	1522 2.3	2102 12.0
3 SA	0329 2.2	0910 11.9	1538 2.4	2129 11.6
4 SU	0350 2.4	0939 11.6	1604 2.6	2159 11.2
5 M	0420 2.6	1013 11.1	1638 2.8	2237 10.7
6 TU	0457 3.0	1056 10.7	1721 3.3	2327 10.2
7 W	0546 3.5	1154 10.2	1819 3.8	
8 TH	0033 9.8	0656 4.0	1310 10.0	1943 4.0
9 F	0201 9.9	0830 3.9	1440 10.4	2117 3.6
10 SA	0327 10.6	0954 3.2	1553 11.3	2235 2.8
11 SU	0430 11.6	1103 2.5	1652 12.2	2339 2.1
12 M	0523 12.5	1203 1.8	1745 13.0	
13 TU	0034 1.5	0611 13.3	1257 1.2	● 1833 13.6
14 W	0126 1.1	0658 13.8	1348 0.9	1920 14.0
15 TH	0214 0.9	0744 14.0	1436 0.8	2007 14.0
16 F	0258 1.0	0829 14.0	1520 0.9	2054 13.8
17 SA	0339 1.2	0915 13.6	1601 1.2	2139 13.2
18 SU	0417 1.7	1000 13.0	1640 1.7	2226 12.5
19 M	0453 2.2	1048 12.3	1721 2.3	2315 11.7
20 TU	0533 2.9	1143 11.5	1807 2.9	◐
21 W	0014 10.9	0623 3.5	1254 10.8	1905 3.4
22 TH	0129 10.4	0733 3.8	1408 10.7	2020 3.5
23 F	0239 10.4	0901 3.7	1510 10.9	2133 3.2
24 SA	0338 10.8	1009 3.2	1606 11.3	2234 2.7
25 SU	0431 11.3	1104 2.6	1648 11.8	2327 2.2
26 M	0519 11.9	1154 2.1	1743 12.2	
27 TU	0016 1.7	0602 12.3	1241 1.8	1824 12.4
28 W	0101 1.5	0641 12.6	1324 1.7	○ 1903 12.5
29 TH	0143 1.5	0718 12.6	1404 1.8	1939 12.4
30 F	0221 1.6	0753 12.5	1440 2.0	2014 12.2

DECEMBER

Day	Time m	Time m	Time m	Time m
1 SA	0253 1.9	0826 12.3	1509 2.3	2047 12.0
2 SU	0318 2.2	0857 12.1	1531 2.4	2118 11.8
3 M	0340 2.3	0928 11.9	1557 2.5	2150 11.5
4 TU	0410 2.4	1003 11.6	1630 2.6	2227 11.3
5 W	0447 2.6	1043 11.3	1710 2.8	2310 10.9
6 TH	0531 2.9	1133 11.0	1758 3.1	◐
7 F	0004 10.6	0624 3.3	1233 10.7	1857 3.3
8 SA	0109 10.4	0733 3.6	1345 10.7	2013 3.5
9 SU	0228 10.6	0900 3.4	1504 11.1	2146 3.2
10 M	0348 11.2	1024 2.9	1617 11.7	2304 2.6
11 TU	0453 12.0	1132 2.2	1719 12.5	
12 W	0007 1.9	0548 12.9	1232 1.5	1813 13.2
13 TH	0103 1.3	0639 13.5	1328 1.1	● 1905 13.6
14 F	0156 1.0	0728 13.9	1421 0.8	1955 13.8
15 SA	0245 0.9	0816 14.0	1510 0.7	2043 13.8
16 SU	0331 1.0	0903 13.9	1554 0.9	2129 13.5
17 M	0411 1.3	0949 13.5	1634 1.3	2213 13.0
18 TU	0447 1.8	1033 12.9	1710 1.7	2256 12.3
19 W	0519 2.3	1118 12.1	1745 2.3	2340 11.5
20 TH	0554 2.8	1208 11.3	1824 2.8	◐
21 F	0031 10.8	0637 3.3	1310 10.8	1912 3.3
22 SA	0137 10.3	0733 3.7	1419 10.4	2011 3.5
23 SU	0247 10.2	0844 3.8	1522 10.5	2125 3.5
24 M	0349 10.5	1009 3.5	1619 10.8	2239 3.1
25 TU	0443 11.0	1114 2.9	1711 11.3	2337 2.5
26 W	0532 11.6	1206 2.4	1757 11.8	
27 TH	0027 2.0	0615 12.1	1254 2.0	1839 12.1
28 F	0114 1.7	0656 12.4	1339 1.9	○ 1920 12.3
29 SA	0158 1.6	0734 12.5	1422 1.9	1958 12.3
30 SU	0238 1.8	0811 12.5	1500 2.1	2035 12.2
31 M	0312 1.9	0846 12.4	1532 2.2	2108 12.1

Chart Datum: 6·50 metres below Ordnance Datum (Newlyn)
HAT is 14·7m above Chart Datum

TIDES

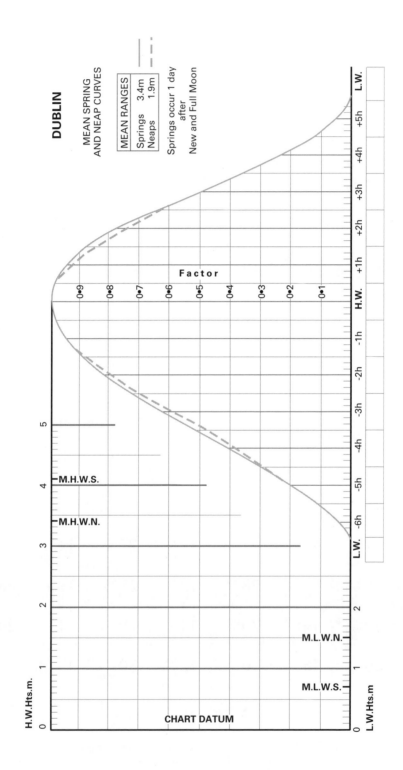

DUBLIN

MEAN SPRING
AND NEAP CURVES

MEAN RANGES	
Springs	3.4m
Neaps	1.9m

Springs occur 1 day
after
New and Full Moon

Factor

TIME ZONE (UT)
For Summer Time add ONE hour in **non-shaded areas**

IRELAND – DUBLIN (NORTH WALL)
LAT 53°21'N LONG 6°13'W
TIMES AND HEIGHTS OF HIGH AND LOW WATERS

Dates in amber are **SPRINGS**
Dates in yellow are **NEAPS**

2012

JANUARY

Time m	Time m
1 SU 0459 3.4 / 1030 1.5 / 1708 3.6 / ◑ 2303 1.4	**16** 0420 3.7 / 0956 1.1 / M 1642 3.9 / 2240 1.0
2 M 0601 3.3 / 1131 1.6 / 1813 3.4	**17** 0522 3.6 / 1103 1.3 / TU 1748 3.7 / 2348 1.1
3 TU 0003 1.5 / 0702 3.4 / 1237 1.6 / 1917 3.4	**18** 0634 3.6 / 1220 1.4 / W 1905 3.7
4 W 0109 1.6 / 0800 3.4 / 1345 1.6 / 2018 3.4	**19** 0103 1.2 / 0747 3.6 / TH 1340 1.3 / 2023 3.7
5 TH 0215 1.5 / 0853 3.6 / 1445 1.5 / 2112 3.5	**20** 0217 1.2 / 0856 3.8 / F 1452 1.1 / 2133 3.7
6 F 0307 1.4 / 0940 3.7 / 1532 1.3 / 2159 3.6	**21** 0320 1.1 / 0955 3.9 / SA 1551 0.9 / 2232 3.8
7 SA 0346 1.3 / 1021 3.8 / 1610 1.2 / 2240 3.7	**22** 0411 0.9 / 1047 4.1 / SU 1639 0.7 / 2322 3.9
8 SU 0419 1.2 / 1057 3.9 / 1644 1.0 / 2316 3.8	**23** 0454 0.8 / 1131 4.2 / M 1722 0.6 ●
9 M 0450 1.0 / 1130 4.0 / 1716 1.0 / ○ 2350 3.8	**24** 0004 3.9 / 0532 0.7 / TU 1209 4.2 / 1801 0.5
10 TU 0522 0.9 / 1204 4.1 / 1751 0.7	**25** 0040 3.9 / 0609 0.7 / W 1245 4.2 / 1839 0.5
11 W 0026 3.9 / 0556 0.8 / 1242 4.2 / 1828 0.6	**26** 0114 3.8 / 0645 0.7 / TH 1321 4.1 / 1917 0.6
12 TH 0106 3.9 / 0635 0.8 / 1323 4.2 / 1910 0.5	**27** 0149 3.7 / 0724 0.8 / F 1359 4.0 / 1955 0.7
13 F 0149 3.9 / 0718 0.8 / 1408 4.2 / 1956 0.6	**28** 0227 3.7 / 0805 0.9 / SA 1440 3.9 / 2036 0.9
14 SA 0235 3.9 / 0805 0.9 / 1455 4.1 / 2046 0.8	**29** 0309 3.6 / 0851 1.1 / SU 1523 3.7 / 2118 1.1
15 SU 0325 3.8 / 0857 1.0 / 1546 4.0 / 2140 0.8	**30** 0354 3.4 / 0941 1.3 / M 1611 3.5 / 2206 1.3
	31 0449 3.3 / 1039 1.5 / TU 1708 3.3 / ◑ 2302 1.5

FEBRUARY

Time m	Time m
1 W 0601 3.2 / 1144 1.6 / 1823 3.2	**16** 0609 3.5 / 1203 1.3 / TH 1857 3.5
2 TH 0009 1.7 / 0713 3.2 / 1255 1.6 / 1938 3.2	**17** 0043 1.4 / 0731 3.5 / F 1331 1.3 / 2019 3.5
3 F 0122 1.7 / 0816 3.3 / 1406 1.5 / 2041 3.3	**18** 0206 1.3 / 0845 3.7 / SA 1446 1.1 / 2130 3.6
4 SA 0232 1.6 / 0910 3.5 / 1503 1.3 / 2134 3.4	**19** 0311 1.2 / 0948 3.8 / SU 1543 0.9 / 2228 3.7
5 SU 0321 1.3 / 0955 3.7 / 1545 1.1 / 2217 3.6	**20** 0400 1.0 / 1039 4.0 / M 1628 0.7 / 2314 3.8
6 M 0356 1.1 / 1033 3.9 / 1619 0.8 / 2254 3.8	**21** 0441 0.8 / 1122 4.1 / TU 1707 0.6 / ● 2352 3.8
7 TU 0428 0.9 / 1107 4.0 / 1653 0.6 / ○ 2327 3.9	**22** 0517 0.7 / 1156 4.1 / W 1743 0.5
8 W 0501 0.7 / 1141 4.0 / 1728 0.4	**23** 0020 3.8 / 0550 0.6 / TH 1225 4.1 / 1816 0.3
9 TH 0002 4.0 / 0535 0.5 / 1218 4.3 / 1805 0.3	**24** 0045 3.8 / 0623 0.6 / F 1255 4.0 / 1848 0.6
10 F 0040 4.1 / 0613 0.5 / 1259 4.3 / 1846 0.3	**25** 0115 3.7 / 0657 0.7 / SA 1330 4.0 / 1921 0.7
11 SA 0121 4.1 / 0655 0.5 / 1343 4.3 / 1931 0.3	**26** 0148 3.7 / 0733 0.8 / SU 1407 3.8 / 1954 0.8
12 SU 0206 4.0 / 0741 0.6 / 1431 4.1 / 2020 0.5	**27** 0225 3.6 / 0811 0.9 / M 1447 3.7 / 2030 1.0
13 M 0255 3.9 / 0833 0.8 / 1522 4.0 / 2113 0.7	**28** 0305 3.5 / 0854 1.1 / TU 1530 3.5 / 2109 1.2
14 TU 0349 3.8 / 0932 1.0 / 1620 3.8 / ◑ 2212 1.0	**29** 0351 3.4 / 0945 1.3 / W 1620 3.3 / 2158 1.4
15 W 0451 3.6 / 1041 1.2 / 1730 3.6 / 2322 1.2	

MARCH

Time m	Time m
1 TH 0448 3.2 / 1053 1.5 / 1725 3.1 / ◑ 2311 1.6	**16** 0551 3.5 / 1150 1.2 / F 1850 3.4
2 F 0611 3.1 / 1208 1.6 / 1855 3.0	**17** 0023 1.4 / 0714 3.5 / SA 1318 1.2 / 2010 3.4
3 SA 0034 1.7 / 0733 3.2 / 1322 1.5 / 2008 3.1	**18** 0148 1.4 / 0828 3.6 / SU 1430 1.0 / 2119 3.5
4 SU 0150 1.6 / 0835 3.3 / 1425 1.2 / 2105 3.3	**19** 0252 1.2 / 0932 3.8 / M 1525 0.8 / 2213 3.6
5 M 0247 1.3 / 0923 3.6 / 1512 0.9 / 2149 3.6	**20** 0341 1.0 / 1023 3.9 / TU 1608 0.7 / 2257 3.7
6 TU 0328 1.0 / 1004 3.8 / 1550 0.6 / 2226 3.8	**21** 0421 0.8 / 1105 3.9 / W 1646 0.6 / 2332 3.7
7 W 0402 0.7 / 1040 4.0 / 1626 0.3 / 2301 3.9	**22** 0457 0.7 / 1137 3.9 / TH 1720 0.6 / ● 2357 3.7
8 TH 0437 0.5 / 1116 4.2 / 1703 0.2 / ○ 2336 4.1	**23** 0530 0.6 / 1203 3.9 / F 1751 0.6
9 F 0513 0.3 / 1155 4.3 / 1742 0.1	**24** 0018 3.7 / 0601 0.6 / SA 1232 3.9 / 1820 0.7
10 SA 0013 4.1 / 0552 0.2 / 1237 4.3 / 1823 0.1	**25** 0045 3.7 / 0633 0.6 / SU 1304 3.8 / 1848 0.7
11 SU 0055 4.2 / 0635 0.2 / 1322 4.3 / 1908 0.2	**26** 0117 3.7 / 0706 0.7 / M 1340 3.8 / 1918 0.8
12 M 0141 4.1 / 0722 0.4 / 1412 4.1 / 1957 0.5	**27** 0152 3.7 / 0741 0.8 / TU 1419 3.6 / 1952 1.0
13 TU 0230 4.0 / 0816 0.6 / 1506 3.9 / 2051 0.8	**28** 0232 3.6 / 0821 1.0 / W 1502 3.5 / 2032 1.2
14 W 0325 3.8 / 0918 0.8 / 1608 3.7 / 2152 1.1	**29** 0317 3.5 / 0908 1.1 / TH 1551 3.3 / 2120 1.4
15 TH 0429 3.6 / 1029 1.0 / 1725 3.5 / ◑ 2302 1.3	**30** 0409 3.3 / 1009 1.3 / F 1649 3.1 / ◑ 2223 1.5
	31 0514 3.2 / 1125 1.4 / SA 1806 3.1 / 2348 1.6

APRIL

Time m	Time m
1 SU 0638 3.1 / 1238 1.3 / 1926 3.1	**16** 0116 1.4 / 0802 3.6 / M 1401 1.0 / 2054 3.5
2 M 0104 1.5 / 0749 3.3 / 1342 1.1 / 2026 3.3	**17** 0222 1.3 / 0905 3.7 / TU 1456 0.9 / 2147 3.8
3 TU 0205 1.3 / 0844 3.5 / 1434 0.8 / 2114 3.6	**18** 0313 1.1 / 0957 3.8 / W 1541 0.8 / 2230 3.7
4 W 0252 1.0 / 0929 3.8 / 1518 0.5 / 2154 3.8	**19** 0355 0.9 / 1039 3.8 / TH 1619 0.7 / 2303 3.7
5 TH 0333 0.7 / 1011 4.0 / 1558 0.2 / 2232 4.0	**20** 0433 0.8 / 1112 3.8 / F 1653 0.7 / 2329 3.7
6 F 0412 0.4 / 1052 4.2 / 1638 0.1 / ○ 2310 4.1	**21** 0508 0.7 / 1141 3.8 / SA 1725 0.7 / ● 2353 3.7
7 SA 0452 0.2 / 1134 4.3 / 1719 0.0 / 2350 4.2	**22** 0541 0.7 / 1210 3.8 / SU 1753 0.8
8 SU 0534 0.1 / 1219 4.3 / 1802 0.1	**23** 0019 3.8 / 0612 0.7 / M 1242 3.7 / 1820 0.8
9 M 0033 4.2 / 0619 0.2 / 1307 4.2 / 1848 0.3	**24** 0051 3.8 / 0643 0.8 / TU 1318 3.7 / 1850 0.9
10 TU 0121 4.1 / 0709 0.3 / 1400 4.1 / 1939 0.5	**25** 0128 3.7 / 0718 0.8 / W 1357 3.6 / 1925 1.0
11 W 0212 4.0 / 0806 0.5 / 1458 3.9 / 2034 0.8	**26** 0208 3.7 / 0758 0.9 / TH 1441 3.5 / 2007 1.1
12 TH 0309 3.9 / 0910 0.7 / 1604 3.7 / 2135 1.1	**27** 0253 3.6 / 0846 1.0 / F 1529 3.4 / 2055 1.3
13 F 0415 3.7 / 1018 0.9 / 1717 3.5 / ◐ 2242 1.3	**28** 0343 3.4 / 0942 1.1 / SA 1623 3.3 / 2153 1.4
14 SA 0534 3.6 / 1132 1.0 / 1834 3.4 / 2357 1.4	**29** 0441 3.3 / 1047 1.3 / SU 1726 3.2 / ◐ 2303 1.5
15 SU 0651 3.5 / 1252 1.1 / 1948 3.4	**30** 0548 3.3 / 1156 1.1 / M 1836 3.3

Chart Datum: 0·20 metres above Ordnance Datum (Dublin)
HAT is 4·5m above Chart Datum

TIDES

TIME ZONE (UT)
For Summer Time add ONE hour in **non-shaded areas**

IRELAND – DUBLIN (NORTH WALL)

LAT 53°21′N LONG 6°13′W

TIMES AND HEIGHTS OF HIGH AND LOW WATERS

Dates in amber are **SPRINGS**
Dates in yellow are **NEAPS**

2012

MAY

Date	Day	Time	m	Time	m	Time	m	Time	m
1	TU	0016	1.4	0657	3.4	1300	1.0	1939	3.4
2	W	0120	1.2	0759	3.6	1356	0.7	2033	3.6
3	TH	0214	1.0	0853	3.8	1446	0.5	2121	3.8
4	F	0302	0.7	0942	4.0	1532	0.3	2205	4.0
5	SA	0348	0.5	1030	4.1	1616	0.2	2248	4.1
6	SU	0433	0.3	1118	4.2	1701	0.2	○ 2332	4.2
7	M	0520	0.2	1206	4.2	1746	0.3		
8	TU	0018	4.2	0608	0.2	1258	4.1	1833	0.4
9	W	0107	4.2	0700	0.3	1352	4.0	1923	0.6
10	TH	0159	4.1	0757	0.5	1450	3.8	2018	0.9
11	F	0256	4.0	0858	0.6	1552	3.7	2116	1.1
12	SA	0400	3.8	1001	0.8	1658	3.5	◑ 2217	1.3
13	SU	0510	3.7	1106	0.9	1806	3.4	2323	1.4
14	M	0620	3.6	1215	1.0	1913	3.4		
15	TU	0034	1.4	0726	3.6	1323	1.1	2015	3.5
16	W	0142	1.3	0827	3.6	1421	1.0	2109	3.5
17	TH	0239	1.2	0921	3.7	1509	1.0	2153	3.6
18	F	0326	1.1	1005	3.7	1550	1.0	2229	3.7
19	SA	0407	1.0	1043	3.7	1626	0.9	2300	3.7
20	SU	0444	0.9	1117	3.7	1658	0.9	● 2329	3.8
21	M	0519	0.9	1149	3.7	1728	0.9	2358	3.8
22	TU	0552	0.9	1221	3.7	1756	1.0		
23	W	0029	3.8	0623	0.9	1257	3.7	1826	1.0
24	TH	0106	3.8	0657	0.9	1337	3.6	1903	1.0
25	F	0148	3.8	0738	0.9	1420	3.6	1945	1.1
26	SA	0233	3.7	0825	0.9	1507	3.5	2033	1.2
27	SU	0321	3.7	0917	0.9	1558	3.5	2126	1.2
28	M	0414	3.6	1015	1.0	1653	3.4	◐ 2226	1.3
29	TU	0512	3.6	1116	0.9	1754	3.4	2331	1.3
30	W	0615	3.6	1219	0.9	1856	3.5		
31	TH	0036	1.2	0719	3.7	1320	0.8	1956	3.6

JUNE

Date	Day	Time	m	Time	m	Time	m	Time	m
1	F	0138	1.1	0821	3.8	1417	0.7	2051	3.8
2	SA	0236	0.9	0919	3.9	1510	0.5	2143	4.0
3	SU	0329	0.7	1014	4.1	1559	0.5	2232	4.1
4	M	0420	0.5	1106	4.1	1647	0.4	○ 2319	4.2
5	TU	0510	0.4	1157	4.1	1733	0.5		
6	W	0006	4.2	0600	0.3	1248	4.1	1819	0.5
7	TH	0054	4.2	0651	0.4	1340	4.0	1907	0.7
8	F	0144	4.2	0744	0.5	1433	3.8	1957	0.8
9	SA	0238	4.0	0839	0.6	1528	3.7	2051	1.0
10	SU	0334	3.9	0935	0.8	1626	3.5	2146	1.2
11	M	0435	3.8	1032	0.9	1726	3.4	◑ 2245	1.3
12	TU	0539	3.6	1131	1.1	1827	3.4	2347	1.4
13	W	0643	3.6	1234	1.2	1926	3.4		
14	TH	0053	1.4	0743	3.5	1337	1.3	2021	3.5
15	F	0158	1.4	0839	3.5	1432	1.3	2110	3.5
16	SA	0254	1.3	0929	3.6	1519	1.2	2153	3.6
17	SU	0341	1.2	1013	3.6	1559	1.2	2231	3.7
18	M	0421	1.1	1052	3.6	1633	1.1	2305	3.8
19	TU	0457	1.0	1127	3.7	1704	1.0	● 2337	3.9
20	W	0529	0.9	1201	3.7	1733	1.0		
21	TH	0009	3.9	0601	0.9	1236	3.7	1804	1.0
22	F	0045	3.9	0635	0.8	1315	3.7	1841	0.9
23	SA	0126	3.9	0715	0.8	1357	3.7	1922	0.9
24	SU	0209	3.9	0800	0.8	1442	3.7	2008	1.0
25	M	0256	3.9	0850	0.8	1530	3.7	2058	1.0
26	TU	0346	3.9	0943	0.8	1621	3.6	2153	1.1
27	W	0440	3.8	1041	0.9	1718	3.6	◐ 2253	1.2
28	TH	0540	3.7	1143	0.9	1821	3.6		
29	F	0000	1.2	0648	3.7	1249	0.9	1926	3.6
30	SA	0110	1.2	0758	3.8	1354	0.9	2030	3.8

JULY

Date	Day	Time	m	Time	m	Time	m	Time	m
1	SU	0218	1.0	0905	3.8	1454	0.8	2128	3.9
2	M	0319	0.8	1005	3.9	1548	0.7	2221	4.1
3	TU	0415	0.6	1059	4.0	1637	0.6	○ 2309	4.2
4	W	0505	0.5	1149	4.0	1722	0.6	2354	4.2
5	TH	0552	0.4	1236	4.0	1805	0.6		
6	F	0038	4.3	0638	0.4	1322	3.9	1847	0.7
7	SA	0123	4.2	0724	0.5	1407	3.8	1932	0.8
8	SU	0209	4.1	0812	0.6	1453	3.7	2020	0.9
9	M	0258	4.0	0901	0.8	1542	3.6	2110	1.1
10	TU	0350	3.8	0952	1.0	1635	3.4	2205	1.3
11	W	0447	3.6	1044	1.2	1733	3.4	◑ 2302	1.4
12	TH	0552	3.5	1141	1.3	1834	3.3		
13	F	0005	1.5	0657	3.4	1243	1.5	1934	3.4
14	SA	0112	1.5	0759	3.4	1348	1.5	2030	3.5
15	SU	0221	1.5	0856	3.4	1447	1.4	2120	3.6
16	M	0316	1.3	0946	3.5	1532	1.3	2204	3.7
17	TU	0358	1.2	1028	3.6	1609	1.2	2242	3.8
18	W	0433	1.0	1106	3.7	1640	1.0	2315	3.9
19	TH	0505	0.9	1139	3.8	1710	0.9	● 2347	4.0
20	F	0536	0.7	1212	3.8	1742	0.8		
21	SA	0021	4.1	0610	0.6	1249	3.9	1817	0.8
22	SU	0100	4.1	0649	0.6	1330	3.9	1857	0.7
23	M	0143	4.1	0733	0.6	1413	3.9	1941	0.8
24	TU	0229	4.1	0821	0.6	1500	3.8	2029	0.9
25	W	0318	4.0	0913	0.7	1550	3.8	2123	1.0
26	TH	0411	3.9	1010	0.9	1646	3.7	◐ 2224	1.1
27	F	0513	3.7	1114	1.0	1751	3.6	2335	1.3
28	SA	0627	3.6	1225	1.1	1905	3.6		
29	SU	0054	1.3	0747	3.6	1338	1.2	2016	3.7
30	M	0211	1.1	0900	3.7	1445	1.1	2120	3.9
31	TU	0317	0.9	1002	3.8	1541	0.9	2214	4.0

AUGUST

Date	Day	Time	m	Time	m	Time	m	Time	m
1	W	0412	0.7	1056	3.9	1628	0.8	2301	4.2
2	TH	0458	0.5	1141	4.0	1709	0.7	○ 2342	4.2
3	F	0540	0.4	1221	3.9	1748	0.6		
4	SA	0019	4.2	0619	0.4	1258	3.9	1825	0.6
5	SU	0057	4.2	0659	0.5	1334	3.8	1904	0.7
6	M	0137	4.1	0739	0.6	1413	3.7	1947	0.8
7	TU	0219	4.0	0822	0.8	1454	3.6	2033	1.0
8	W	0304	3.8	0907	1.0	1540	3.5	2123	1.2
9	TH	0354	3.6	0957	1.2	1632	3.4	◑ 2219	1.4
10	F	0454	3.4	1052	1.4	1738	3.3	2322	1.5
11	SA	0610	3.2	1154	1.6	1850	3.3		
12	SU	0030	1.6	0723	3.2	1303	1.6	1954	3.4
13	M	0144	1.5	0826	3.3	1413	1.5	2050	3.5
14	TU	0248	1.4	0920	3.4	1505	1.4	2138	3.7
15	W	0332	1.1	1005	3.6	1543	1.2	2217	3.9
16	TH	0407	0.9	1042	3.7	1615	1.0	2250	4.0
17	F	0438	0.7	1115	3.8	1645	0.8	● 2322	4.1
18	SA	0509	0.5	1147	3.9	1717	0.6	2356	4.2
19	SU	0544	0.4	1222	4.0	1753	0.6		
20	M	0033	4.3	0622	0.4	1301	4.0	1831	0.5
21	TU	0116	4.3	0705	0.4	1344	4.0	1915	0.6
22	W	0202	4.2	0752	0.5	1431	4.0	2004	0.7
23	TH	0252	4.1	0845	0.7	1522	3.9	2100	0.9
24	F	0348	3.9	0945	1.0	1619	3.7	◐ 2205	1.1
25	SA	0454	3.7	1052	1.2	1728	3.6	2321	1.3
26	SU	0620	3.5	1208	1.3	1851	3.6		
27	M	0047	1.3	0744	3.5	1327	1.3	2007	3.7
28	TU	0209	1.1	0858	3.6	1435	1.2	2112	3.9
29	W	0312	0.9	0959	3.8	1530	1.0	2207	4.0
30	TH	0402	0.7	1049	3.9	1614	0.8	2252	4.1
31	F	0444	0.5	1131	3.9	1653	0.7	○ 2329	4.2

Chart Datum: 0·20 metres above Ordnance Datum (Dublin)
HAT is 4·5m above Chart Datum

TIME ZONE (UT)	IRELAND – DUBLIN (NORTH WALL)	Dates in amber are SPRINGS
For Summer Time add ONE hour in **non-shaded areas**	LAT 53°21′N LONG 6°13′W	Dates in yellow are NEAPS
	TIMES AND HEIGHTS OF HIGH AND LOW WATERS	2012

SEPTEMBER

Time m   Time m

1 0522 0.5 / 1204 3.9 / SA 1729 0.6
16 0442 0.3 / 1120 4.1 / SU 1653 0.5 / ● 2330 4.3

2 0000 4.2 / 0557 0.5 / SU 1233 3.9 / 1803 0.6
17 0518 0.2 / 1155 4.1 / M 1730 0.4

3 0032 4.1 / 0631 0.6 / M 1302 3.8 / 1839 0.7
18 0009 4.4 / 0557 0.2 / TU 1235 4.2 / 1810 0.4

4 0107 4.0 / 0705 0.7 / TU 1336 3.8 / 1916 0.8
19 0052 4.3 / 0640 0.3 / W 1318 4.1 / 1855 0.5

5 0146 3.9 / 0742 0.9 / W 1414 3.7 / 1958 0.9
20 0140 4.2 / 0728 0.5 / TH 1407 4.1 / 1946 0.7

6 0228 3.8 / 0822 1.0 / TH 1455 3.6 / 2044 1.1
21 0233 4.0 / 0822 0.8 / F 1500 3.9 / 2045 0.9

7 0313 3.6 / 0907 1.3 / F 1541 3.5 / 2137 1.3
22 0334 3.8 / 0925 1.1 / SA 1600 3.8 / ◑ 2154 1.1

8 0406 3.4 / 1003 1.5 / SA 1638 3.3 / ◑ 2242 1.5
23 0449 3.6 / 1034 1.3 / SU 1714 3.7 / 2313 1.2

9 0518 3.2 / 1110 1.7 / SU 1758 3.2 / 2352 1.6
24 0616 3.5 / 1152 1.4 / M 1837 3.6

10 0646 3.1 / 1222 1.7 / M 1916 3.3
25 0039 1.2 / 0737 3.5 / TU 1312 1.4 / 1952 3.7

11 0105 1.5 / 0756 3.2 / TU 1335 1.6 / 2017 3.4
26 0157 1.1 / 0849 3.6 / W 1419 1.3 / 2058 3.9

12 0212 1.3 / 0853 3.6 / W 1432 1.4 / 2107 3.6
27 0257 0.9 / 0946 3.8 / TH 1511 1.1 / 2153 4.0

13 0259 1.1 / 0938 3.6 / TH 1513 1.2 / 2147 3.8
28 0344 0.7 / 1034 3.9 / F 1555 0.9 / 2237 4.1

14 0336 0.8 / 1015 3.8 / F 1546 0.9 / 2222 4.0
29 0424 0.6 / 1113 3.9 / SA 1634 0.8 / 2313 4.1

15 0409 0.5 / 1047 3.9 / SA 1619 0.7 / 2255 4.2
30 0501 0.6 / 1144 3.9 / SU 1710 0.7 / ○ 2341 4.1

OCTOBER

Time m   Time m

1 0534 0.6 / 1208 3.9 / M 1744 0.7
16 0455 0.2 / 1131 4.3 / TU 1710 0.3 / 2350 4.4

2 0010 4.0 / 0604 0.7 / TU 1235 3.9 / 1817 0.7
17 0536 0.2 / 1213 4.3 / W 1754 0.3

3 0043 4.0 / 0635 0.8 / W 1307 3.8 / 1852 0.8
18 0036 4.3 / 0620 0.4 / TH 1259 4.3 / 1841 0.4

4 0120 3.9 / 0707 0.9 / TH 1343 3.8 / 1930 0.9
19 0127 4.2 / 0709 0.6 / F 1349 4.2 / 1935 0.6

5 0200 3.7 / 0742 1.1 / F 1423 3.7 / 2012 1.1
20 0223 4.0 / 0805 0.9 / SA 1444 4.0 / 2036 0.9

6 0244 3.6 / 0823 1.3 / SA 1507 3.6 / 2101 1.3
21 0328 3.8 / 0907 1.1 / SU 1547 3.9 / 2144 1.0

7 0334 3.4 / 0914 1.5 / SU 1558 3.4 / 2202 1.4
22 0444 3.6 / 1015 1.4 / M 1700 3.8 / ◑ 2258 1.1

8 0436 3.2 / 1024 1.7 / M 1702 3.3 / ◑ 2312 1.5
23 0602 3.5 / 1129 1.5 / TU 1817 3.7

9 0559 3.1 / 1141 1.7 / TU 1823 3.3
24 0017 1.2 / 0718 3.6 / W 1245 1.5 / 1928 3.8

10 0023 1.5 / 0716 3.2 / W 1252 1.7 / 1933 3.4
25 0132 1.1 / 0826 3.7 / TH 1352 1.4 / 2033 3.9

11 0127 1.3 / 0816 3.4 / TH 1350 1.5 / 2027 3.6
26 0232 1.0 / 0923 3.8 / F 1447 1.2 / 2129 4.0

12 0219 1.0 / 0903 3.6 / F 1436 1.2 / 2111 3.8
27 0320 0.9 / 1010 3.9 / SA 1533 1.0 / 2215 4.0

13 0301 0.7 / 0942 3.8 / SA 1515 0.9 / 2150 4.1
28 0401 0.8 / 1049 3.9 / SU 1614 0.9 / 2252 4.0

14 0339 0.5 / 1017 4.0 / SU 1552 0.7 / 2229 4.2
29 0437 0.8 / 1120 3.9 / M 1651 0.9 / ○ 2323 4.0

15 0416 0.3 / 1053 4.2 / M 1630 0.5 / ● 2308 4.3
30 0511 0.8 / 1146 3.9 / TU 1726 0.8 / 2352 3.9

31 0541 0.9 / 1213 3.9 / W 1800 0.8

NOVEMBER

Time m   Time m

1 0024 3.9 / 0609 0.9 / TH 1245 3.9 / 1833 0.9
16 0027 4.3 / 0605 0.5 / F 1245 4.4 / 1832 0.4

2 0100 3.8 / 0639 1.0 / F 1319 3.9 / 1908 1.0
17 0119 4.2 / 0654 0.7 / SA 1336 4.3 / 1926 0.5

3 0138 3.7 / 0713 1.1 / SA 1358 3.8 / 1947 1.1
18 0216 4.0 / 0748 0.9 / SU 1431 4.2 / 2025 0.7

4 0221 3.6 / 0752 1.3 / SU 1441 3.7 / 2031 1.2
19 0319 3.8 / 0851 1.1 / M 1532 4.1 / 2127 0.9

5 0309 3.5 / 0839 1.4 / M 1529 3.6 / 2124 1.3
20 0426 3.7 / 0951 1.3 / TU 1638 3.9 / ◐ 2233 1.0

6 0404 3.4 / 0937 1.6 / TU 1623 3.5 / 2226 1.4
21 0536 3.6 / 1058 1.5 / W 1747 3.8 / 2343 1.1

7 0508 3.3 / 1048 1.7 / W 1726 3.4 / ◐ 2334 1.3
22 0645 3.6 / 1208 1.5 / TH 1855 3.8

8 0620 3.3 / 1200 1.6 / TH 1834 3.5
23 0054 1.2 / 0750 3.6 / F 1317 1.5 / 1959 3.8

9 0038 1.2 / 0725 3.4 / F 1303 1.5 / 1935 3.6
24 0159 1.2 / 0848 3.7 / SA 1418 1.4 / 2057 3.8

10 0135 1.0 / 0819 3.6 / SA 1356 1.3 / 2029 3.8
25 0252 1.1 / 0938 3.8 / SU 1509 1.2 / 2147 3.8

11 0225 0.8 / 0905 3.9 / SU 1443 1.0 / 2118 4.0
26 0336 1.1 / 1019 3.9 / M 1553 1.1 / 2228 3.8

12 0310 0.6 / 0948 4.1 / M 1527 0.7 / 2205 4.2
27 0415 1.0 / 1053 3.9 / TU 1633 1.0 / 2303 3.8

13 0353 0.4 / 1030 4.2 / TU 1611 0.5 / ● 2251 4.3
28 0449 1.0 / 1124 4.0 / W 1709 1.0 / ○ 2335 3.8

14 0436 0.3 / 1113 4.3 / W 1656 0.4 / 2338 4.3
29 0520 1.0 / 1154 4.0 / TH 1744 1.0

15 0520 0.4 / 1157 4.4 / TH 1743 0.4
30 0008 3.8 / 0548 1.1 / F 1225 4.0 / 1816 1.0

DECEMBER

Time m   Time m

1 0042 3.8 / 0617 1.1 / SA 1259 4.0 / 1849 1.0
16 0110 4.2 / 0640 0.7 / SU 1322 4.4 / 1914 0.4

2 0119 3.7 / 0649 1.1 / SU 1336 3.9 / 1924 1.0
17 0203 4.1 / 0730 0.8 / M 1414 4.3 / 2007 0.5

3 0159 3.7 / 0727 1.2 / M 1418 3.9 / 2005 1.0
18 0258 3.9 / 0823 1.0 / TU 1509 4.1 / 2102 0.7

4 0244 3.6 / 0810 1.3 / TU 1503 3.8 / 2051 1.1
19 0357 3.7 / 0920 1.2 / W 1607 4.0 / 2159 0.9

5 0333 3.6 / 0900 1.4 / W 1551 3.7 / 2143 1.1
20 0458 3.6 / 1020 1.4 / TH 1709 3.8 / ◐ 2259 1.1

6 0427 3.5 / 0957 1.5 / TH 1644 3.6 / ◐ 2242 1.2
21 0601 3.5 / 1124 1.5 / F 1813 3.7

7 0527 3.5 / 1102 1.5 / F 1743 3.6 / 2346 1.2
22 0005 1.3 / 0703 3.5 / SA 1233 1.5 / 1916 3.6

8 0631 3.5 / 1210 1.5 / SA 1847 3.7
23 0115 1.4 / 0803 3.6 / SU 1343 1.5 / 2018 3.6

9 0050 1.1 / 0733 3.6 / SU 1315 1.3 / 1950 3.8
24 0220 1.4 / 0858 3.7 / M 1444 1.4 / 2113 3.6

10 0150 0.9 / 0830 3.8 / M 1413 1.1 / 2051 3.9
25 0312 1.3 / 0945 3.8 / TU 1534 1.3 / 2201 3.6

11 0245 0.8 / 0923 4.0 / TU 1507 0.9 / 2147 4.1
26 0354 1.2 / 1026 3.9 / W 1616 1.2 / 2242 3.7

12 0335 0.6 / 1012 4.2 / W 1558 0.7 / 2239 4.2
27 0429 1.2 / 1102 3.9 / TH 1652 1.1 / 2318 3.7

13 0423 0.5 / 1059 4.3 / TH 1647 0.5 / ● 2330 4.2
28 0501 1.1 / 1135 4.0 / F 1726 1.0 / ○ 2351 3.7

14 0508 0.5 / 1146 4.4 / F 1735 0.4
29 0529 1.1 / 1206 4.0 / SA 1757 0.9

15 0019 4.2 / 0553 0.5 / SA 1233 4.4 / 1824 0.4
30 0022 3.8 / 0556 1.0 / SU 1237 4.0 / 1826 0.9

31 0056 3.8 / 0626 1.0 / M 1313 4.0 / 1859 0.8

Chart Datum: 0·20 metres above Ordnance Datum (Dublin)
HAT is 4·5m above Chart Datum

TIDES

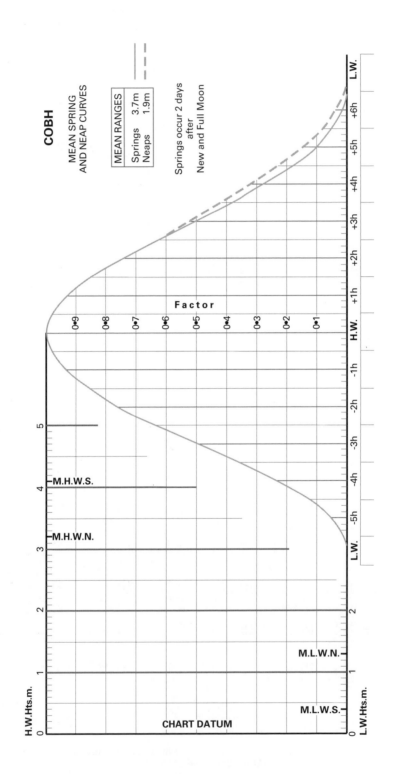

COBH

MEAN SPRING AND NEAP CURVES

MEAN RANGES	
Springs	3.7m
Neaps	1.9m

Springs occur 2 days after New and Full Moon

Factor

M.H.W.S.

M.H.W.N.

CHART DATUM

M.L.W.N.

M.L.W.S.

H.W.Hts.m.

L.W.Hts.m.

IRELAND – COBH

LAT 51°51'N LONG 8°18'W

TIMES AND HEIGHTS OF HIGH AND LOW WATERS

Dates in amber are **SPRINGS**
Dates in yellow are **NEAPS**

2012

JANUARY

Day	Time m		Day	Time m	
1 SU	0442 1.1 / 1030 3.5 / 1703 1.3 / ◐ 2244 3.4		**16** M	0415 0.9 / 1015 3.8 / 1643 1.0 / ◓ 2238 3.7	
2 M	0535 1.3 / 1123 3.4 / 1759 1.4 / 2342 3.3		**17** TU	0513 1.1 / 1113 3.6 / 1746 1.2 / 2341 3.6	
3 TU	0635 1.4 / 1225 3.4 / 1901 1.4		**18** W	0621 1.2 / 1221 3.5 / 1901 1.2	
4 W	0052 3.3 / 0737 1.4 / 1334 3.4 / 2004 1.4		**19** TH	0055 3.5 / 0739 1.2 / 1339 3.5 / 2021 1.1	
5 TH	0203 3.4 / 0838 1.3 / 1437 3.5 / 2103 1.2		**20** F	0216 3.6 / 0901 1.1 / 1455 3.6 / 2135 0.9	
6 F	0305 3.6 / 0934 1.2 / 1532 3.6 / 2156 1.1		**21** SA	0329 3.8 / 1010 0.8 / 1600 3.8 / 2235 0.7	
7 SA	0357 3.7 / 1024 1.0 / 1620 3.8 / 2241 0.9		**22** SU	0429 4.0 / 1106 0.6 / 1654 4.0 / 2326 0.5	
8 SU	0443 3.9 / 1108 0.8 / 1702 3.9 / 2321 0.8		**23** M	0518 4.2 / 1152 0.5 / 1739 4.1 ●	
9 M	0523 4.0 / 1147 0.7 / 1740 4.0 / ○ 2358 0.6		**24** TU	0009 0.4 / 0601 4.3 / 1233 0.4 / 1819 4.1	
10 TU	0601 4.1 / 1224 0.7 / 1816 4.1		**25** W	0049 0.4 / 0640 4.3 / 1310 0.5 / 1855 4.1	
11 W	0035 0.6 / 0637 4.2 / 1302 0.6 / 1852 4.1		**26** TH	0126 0.4 / 0717 4.2 / 1345 0.6 / 1929 4.0	
12 TH	0114 0.6 / 0715 4.2 / 1341 0.7 / 1930 4.1		**27** F	0201 0.5 / 0752 4.1 / 1419 0.7 / 2002 3.9	
13 F	0155 0.6 / 0755 4.1 / 1421 0.7 / 2011 4.0		**28** SA	0236 0.7 / 0827 3.9 / 1453 0.8 / 2036 3.8	
14 SA	0238 0.7 / 0838 4.1 / 1505 0.8 / 2056 3.9		**29** SU	0312 0.9 / 0903 3.8 / 1528 1.0 / 2113 3.7	
15 SU	0325 0.8 / 0924 4.0 / 1551 0.9 / 2144 3.8		**30** M	0350 1.0 / 0941 3.6 / 1607 1.2 / 2154 3.5	
			31 TU	0435 1.2 / 1024 3.5 / 1655 1.3 / ◐ 2244 3.4	

FEBRUARY

Day	Time m		Day	Time m	
1 W	0533 1.4 / 1117 3.3 / 1759 1.5 / 2346 3.2		**16** TH	0554 1.1 / 1156 3.3 / 1834 1.2	
2 TH	0642 1.5 / 1228 3.2 / 1912 1.5		**17** F	0034 3.3 / 0719 1.2 / 1323 3.2 / 2005 1.2	
3 F	0107 3.2 / 0753 1.4 / 1353 3.3 / 2023 1.4		**18** SA	0206 3.4 / 0853 1.1 / 1447 3.4 / 2127 1.0	
4 SA	0229 3.4 / 0900 1.3 / 1503 3.4 / 2126 1.2		**19** SU	0321 3.6 / 1004 0.8 / 1551 3.6 / 2227 0.7	
5 SU	0331 3.6 / 0958 1.0 / 1557 3.6 / 2218 0.9		**20** M	0418 3.9 / 1056 0.6 / 1642 3.9 / 2314 0.4	
6 M	0420 3.8 / 1047 0.8 / 1642 3.8 / 2301 0.7		**21** TU	0503 4.1 / 1138 0.4 / 1724 4.0 / ● 2354 0.3	
7 TU	0502 4.0 / 1128 0.6 / 1722 4.0 / ○ 2340 0.4		**22** W	0543 4.2 / 1215 0.4 / 1801 4.1	
8 W	0541 4.1 / 1206 0.5 / 1759 4.1		**23** TH	0029 0.3 / 0618 4.2 / 1248 0.4 / 1833 4.1	
9 TH	0017 0.4 / 0618 4.2 / 1244 0.4 / 1835 4.1		**24** F	0101 0.4 / 0651 4.1 / 1317 0.5 / 1903 4.0	
10 F	0055 0.3 / 0656 4.2 / 1322 0.4 / 1912 4.1		**25** SA	0131 0.5 / 0722 4.0 / 1346 0.6 / 1932 4.0	
11 SA	0135 0.3 / 0735 4.2 / 1401 0.4 / 1952 4.1		**26** SU	0201 0.6 / 0753 3.9 / 1415 0.7 / 2003 3.9	
12 SU	0218 0.4 / 0817 4.1 / 1443 0.5 / 2034 4.0		**27** M	0233 0.8 / 0825 3.8 / 1446 0.9 / 2037 3.8	
13 M	0302 0.5 / 0901 4.0 / 1527 0.7 / 2120 3.9		**28** TU	0307 1.0 / 0859 3.7 / 1521 1.1 / 2115 3.6	
14 TU	0351 0.7 / 0949 3.8 / 1617 0.9 / ◐ 2211 3.7		**29** W	0348 1.1 / 0939 3.5 / 1604 1.2 / 2200 3.4	
15 W	0447 0.9 / 1045 3.5 / 1717 1.1 / 2314 3.5				

MARCH

Day	Time m		Day	Time m	
1 TH	0441 1.3 / 1028 3.3 / 1704 1.4 / ◐ 2257 3.2		**16** F	0538 1.1 / 1139 3.2 / 1819 1.2	
2 F	0553 1.5 / 1132 3.1 / 1822 1.5		**17** SA	0022 3.1 / 0705 1.2 / 1311 3.1 / 1952 1.1	
3 SA	0013 3.1 / 0711 1.4 / 1259 3.1 / 1941 1.4		**18** SU	0154 3.3 / 0840 1.0 / 1432 3.3 / 2112 0.9	
4 SU	0144 3.2 / 0823 1.3 / 1426 3.3 / 2049 1.2		**19** M	0303 3.5 / 0946 0.8 / 1533 3.5 / 2210 0.6	
5 M	0256 3.5 / 0925 1.0 / 1527 3.5 / 2146 0.9		**20** TU	0357 3.8 / 1030 0.4 / 1621 3.8 / 2255 0.4	
6 TU	0349 3.7 / 1017 0.7 / 1614 3.8 / 2233 0.6		**21** W	0441 4.0 / 1116 0.4 / 1702 3.9 / 2333 0.4	
7 W	0433 4.0 / 1102 0.5 / 1655 4.0 / 2315 0.4		**22** TH	0519 4.1 / 1151 0.4 / 1738 4.0 ●	
8 TH	0514 4.1 / 1142 0.3 / 1735 4.1 / ○ 2354 0.2		**23** F	0005 0.4 / 0553 4.1 / 1222 0.4 / 1809 4.0	
9 F	0554 4.2 / 1221 0.2 / 1813 4.2		**24** SA	0034 0.4 / 0624 4.0 / 1248 0.5 / 1836 4.0	
10 SA	0034 0.1 / 0633 4.3 / 1301 0.2 / 1852 4.2		**25** SU	0101 0.5 / 0653 4.0 / 1314 0.6 / 1904 3.9	
11 SU	0116 0.1 / 0714 4.2 / 1342 0.2 / 1933 4.2		**26** M	0129 0.6 / 0721 3.9 / 1342 0.7 / 1934 3.9	
12 M	0159 0.2 / 0757 4.1 / 1424 0.3 / 2015 4.1		**27** TU	0200 0.8 / 0751 3.8 / 1413 0.8 / 2007 3.8	
13 TU	0245 0.4 / 0841 3.9 / 1510 0.5 / 2101 3.9		**28** W	0234 0.9 / 0826 3.7 / 1448 1.0 / 2044 3.7	
14 W	0334 0.6 / 0930 3.7 / 1600 0.8 / 2153 3.6		**29** TH	0315 1.1 / 0905 3.5 / 1531 1.1 / 2128 3.5	
15 TH	0430 0.8 / 1026 3.4 / 1701 1.0 / ◐ 2257 3.4		**30** F	0405 1.2 / 0953 3.3 / 1626 1.3 / ◐ 2222 3.3	
			31 SA	0512 1.4 / 1055 3.2 / 1740 1.4 / 2331 3.2	

APRIL

Day	Time m		Day	Time m	
1 SU	0630 1.4 / 1212 3.1 / 1859 1.3		**16** M	0128 3.3 / 0811 0.9 / 1404 3.3 / 2043 0.8	
2 M	0054 3.2 / 0743 1.2 / 1336 3.2 / 2008 1.1		**17** TU	0233 3.5 / 0914 0.6 / 1503 3.5 / 2139 0.7	
3 TU	0210 3.4 / 0846 0.9 / 1444 3.5 / 2108 0.8		**18** W	0326 3.7 / 1004 0.6 / 1551 3.7 / 2226 0.5	
4 W	0309 3.7 / 0941 0.6 / 1537 3.7 / 2200 0.5		**19** TH	0410 3.8 / 1046 0.5 / 1633 3.8 / 2304 0.5	
5 TH	0358 3.9 / 1030 0.4 / 1623 4.0 / 2247 0.3		**20** F	0450 3.9 / 1122 0.5 / 1710 3.9 / 2337 0.5	
6 F	0444 4.1 / 1114 0.2 / 1707 4.1 / ○ 2331 0.1		**21** SA	0525 3.9 / 1152 0.5 / 1742 3.9 ●	
7 SA	0528 4.2 / 1159 0.1 / 1750 4.2		**22** SU	0006 0.5 / 0556 3.9 / 1220 0.6 / 1811 3.9	
8 SU	0015 0.1 / 0611 4.2 / 1242 0.1 / 1833 4.3		**23** M	0033 0.6 / 0626 3.9 / 1247 0.6 / 1839 3.9	
9 M	0100 0.1 / 0655 4.2 / 1326 0.1 / 1916 4.2		**24** TU	0102 0.7 / 0655 3.8 / 1316 0.7 / 1910 3.8	
10 TU	0145 0.1 / 0741 4.1 / 1412 0.2 / 2001 4.1		**25** W	0135 0.8 / 0726 3.8 / 1349 0.8 / 1944 3.8	
11 W	0233 0.3 / 0827 3.9 / 1500 0.4 / 2050 3.9		**26** TH	0211 0.9 / 0802 3.7 / 1427 0.9 / 2022 3.7	
12 TH	0324 0.5 / 0918 3.6 / 1552 0.6 / 2143 3.6		**27** F	0253 1.0 / 0843 3.6 / 1511 1.0 / 2106 3.6	
13 F	0421 0.8 / 1015 3.4 / 1653 0.9 / ◐ 2247 3.4		**28** SA	0342 1.1 / 0931 3.4 / 1604 1.2 / 2159 3.5	
14 SA	0527 1.0 / 1125 3.2 / 1806 1.0		**29** SU	0442 1.2 / 1029 3.3 / 1708 1.2 / ◐ 2301 3.4	
15 SU	0006 3.3 / 0648 1.0 / 1248 3.1 / 1929 1.0		**30** M	0552 1.2 / 1137 3.2 / 1819 1.2	

Chart Datum: 0·13 metres above Ordnance Datum (Dublin)
HAT is 4·5m above Chart Datum

TIDES

341

TIME ZONE (UT)
For Summer Time add ONE hour in **non-shaded areas**

IRELAND – COBH
LAT 51°51'N   LONG 8°18'W
TIMES AND HEIGHTS OF HIGH AND LOW WATERS

Dates in amber are **SPRINGS**
Dates in yellow are **NEAPS**

2012

MAY

Day	Time m	Time m	Time m	Time m		Day	Time m	Time m	Time m	Time m
1 TU	0013 3.4	0702 1.1	1251 3.3	1928 1.0		**16** W	0152 3.4	0829 0.9	1421 3.4	2057 0.8
2 W	0125 3.5	0806 0.9	1358 3.5	2030 0.8		**17** TH	0246 3.5	0921 0.8	1512 3.5	2146 0.7
3 TH	0227 3.7	0905 0.7	1457 3.8	2126 0.6		**18** F	0333 3.6	1007 0.7	1558 3.7	2229 0.7
4 F	0323 3.9	0959 0.4	1551 4.0	2220 0.3		**19** SA	0416 3.7	1047 0.7	1638 3.8	2306 0.7
5 SA	0415 4.0	1050 0.3	1641 4.1	2310 0.2		**20** SU	0455 3.8	1122 0.7	1715 3.8	● 2338 0.7
6 SU	0505 4.1	1139 0.1	1730 4.2	○ 2359 0.1		**21** M	0531 3.8	1153 0.7	1748 3.9	
7 M	0554 4.2	1227 0.1	1817 4.3			**22** TU	0008 0.7	0603 3.8	1224 0.7	1820 3.9
8 TU	0047 0.1	0641 4.1	1314 0.1	1903 4.2		**23** W	0041 0.7	0635 3.8	1257 0.7	1852 3.9
9 W	0135 0.2	0728 4.0	1402 0.2	1951 4.1		**24** TH	0116 0.8	0708 3.8	1332 0.8	1928 3.8
10 TH	0224 0.3	0817 3.9	1452 0.4	2040 3.9		**25** F	0154 0.8	0745 3.7	1412 0.8	2007 3.8
11 F	0316 0.5	0907 3.7	1544 0.6	2133 3.7		**26** SA	0237 0.9	0827 3.7	1456 0.9	2050 3.7
12 SA	0410 0.7	1001 3.5	1641 0.7	◗ 2231 3.5		**27** SU	0324 1.0	0914 3.6	1545 1.0	2140 3.6
13 SU	0511 0.9	1102 3.3	1745 0.9	2337 3.3		**28** M	0416 1.0	1007 3.5	1641 1.0	◗ 2236 3.6
14 M	0619 1.0	1211 3.2	1854 0.9			**29** TU	0516 1.1	1107 3.5	1743 1.0	2338 3.6
15 TU	0048 3.3	0727 1.0	1321 3.3	2000 0.9		**30** W	0622 1.0	1212 3.5	1850 1.0	
						31 TH	0045 3.6	0728 0.9	1318 3.6	1954 0.8

JUNE

Day	Time m	Time m	Time m	Time m		Day	Time m	Time m	Time m	Time m
1 F	0150 3.7	0831 0.8	1421 3.8	2057 0.7		**16** SA	0253 3.5	0924 1.0	1519 3.5	2149 0.9
2 SA	0252 3.8	0932 0.6	1522 3.9	2157 0.5		**17** SU	0342 3.6	1012 0.9	1607 3.7	2234 0.8
3 SU	0351 3.9	1029 0.4	1619 4.1	2254 0.3		**18** M	0428 3.7	1053 0.8	1650 3.9	2312 0.8
4 M	0447 4.0	1123 0.3	1714 4.2	○ 2346 0.2		**19** TU	0508 3.8	1130 0.7	1728 3.8	● 2348 0.7
5 TU	0539 4.1	1214 0.2	1804 4.2			**20** W	0545 3.8	1204 0.7	1804 3.9	
6 W	0036 0.2	0628 4.1	1303 0.2	1852 4.2		**21** TH	0023 0.7	0620 3.8	1240 0.7	1838 3.9
7 TH	0124 0.2	0716 4.0	1351 0.2	1939 4.1		**22** F	0100 0.7	0654 3.8	1316 0.7	1913 3.9
8 F	0212 0.3	0803 3.9	1439 0.3	2026 4.0		**23** SA	0138 0.7	0731 3.8	1356 0.7	1952 3.9
9 SA	0301 0.5	0850 3.7	1527 0.5	2114 3.8		**24** SU	0219 0.8	0812 3.8	1438 0.7	2034 3.9
10 SU	0350 0.6	0938 3.6	1618 0.7	2204 3.6		**25** M	0303 0.8	0856 3.8	1524 0.8	2119 3.8
11 M	0442 0.8	1028 3.4	1711 0.8	◗ 2258 3.5		**26** TU	0350 0.9	0944 3.7	1613 0.9	2210 3.7
12 TU	0537 1.0	1125 3.3	1809 1.0	◗ 2357 3.4		**27** W	0443 1.0	1037 3.6	1709 0.9	◗ 2307 3.7
13 W	0636 1.0	1226 3.3	1908 1.0			**28** TH	0543 1.0	1138 3.6	1813 1.0	
14 TH	0100 3.3	0735 1.1	1329 3.3	2006 1.0		**29** F	0010 3.6	0651 0.9	1244 3.6	1921 0.9
15 F	0159 3.4	0831 0.9	1427 3.4	2100 1.0		**30** SA	0119 3.6	0801 0.9	1353 3.7	2031 0.8

JULY

Day	Time m	Time m	Time m	Time m		Day	Time m	Time m	Time m	Time m
1 SU	0228 3.7	0909 0.8	1501 3.8	2139 0.7		**16** M	0311 3.5	0938 1.0	1539 3.6	2204 0.9
2 M	0333 3.8	1013 0.6	1605 3.9	2241 0.5		**17** TU	0402 3.6	1027 0.9	1626 3.7	2249 0.8
3 TU	0434 3.9	1110 0.4	1702 4.1	○ 2335 0.3		**18** W	0447 3.7	1108 0.7	1708 3.9	2328 0.7
4 W	0527 4.0	1201 0.2	1752 4.2			**19** TH	0526 3.8	1145 0.6	1745 3.9	●
5 TH	0024 0.2	0615 4.1	1249 0.2	1838 4.2		**20** F	0004 0.6	0602 3.9	1220 0.6	1820 4.0
6 F	0110 0.2	0700 4.0	1334 0.2	1922 4.1		**21** SA	0041 0.6	0637 3.9	1256 0.5	1855 4.0
7 SA	0154 0.3	0743 4.0	1418 0.3	2004 4.0		**22** SU	0118 0.6	0713 3.9	1335 0.5	1932 4.0
8 SU	0237 0.5	0824 3.8	1501 0.5	2046 3.9		**23** M	0158 0.6	0752 3.9	1416 0.6	2012 4.0
9 M	0320 0.6	0905 3.7	1544 0.6	2128 3.7		**24** TU	0239 0.7	0834 3.9	1500 0.6	2056 3.9
10 TU	0403 0.8	0947 3.6	1628 0.8	2212 3.5		**25** W	0324 0.7	0919 3.8	1547 0.7	2143 3.8
11 W	0449 1.0	1032 3.4	1717 1.0	◗ 2301 3.4		**26** TH	0412 0.9	1009 3.7	1639 0.9	◗ 2237 3.7
12 TH	0540 1.1	1125 3.3	1812 1.1	2359 3.3		**27** F	0510 1.0	1108 3.6	1741 1.0	2340 3.5
13 F	0638 1.2	1226 3.3	1912 1.2			**28** SA	0619 1.1	1216 3.5	1854 1.1	
14 SA	0106 3.3	0740 1.2	1339 3.3	2012 1.2		**29** SU	0055 3.4	0737 1.1	1334 3.5	2013 1.0
15 SU	0213 3.3	0841 1.2	1444 3.4	2111 1.1		**30** M	0213 3.5	0855 0.9	1450 3.7	2129 0.8
						31 TU	0324 3.7	1003 0.7	1556 3.9	2233 0.6

AUGUST

Day	Time m	Time m	Time m	Time m		Day	Time m	Time m	Time m	Time m
1 W	0424 3.9	1100 0.4	1651 4.1	2324 0.4		**16** TH	0423 3.7	1043 0.7	1643 3.9	2304 0.6
2 TH	0514 4.0	1148 0.3	1738 4.2	○		**17** F	0503 3.9	1120 0.5	1721 4.0	● 2341 0.5
3 F	0009 0.3	0559 4.1	1232 0.2	1820 4.2		**18** SA	0539 4.0	1156 0.4	1757 4.1	
4 SA	0050 0.3	0639 4.1	1312 0.2	1859 4.2		**19** SU	0018 0.4	0614 4.0	1233 0.4	1832 4.1
5 SU	0129 0.4	0717 4.0	1350 0.3	1936 4.1		**20** M	0055 0.4	0651 4.0	1312 0.4	1909 4.1
6 M	0205 0.5	0753 3.9	1427 0.5	2012 3.9		**21** TU	0134 0.4	0729 4.0	1353 0.4	1949 4.1
7 TU	0242 0.6	0828 3.8	1504 0.7	2049 3.8		**22** W	0215 0.5	0810 4.0	1436 0.5	2032 4.0
8 W	0318 0.6	0905 3.6	1541 0.9	2127 3.6		**23** TH	0300 0.6	0855 3.9	1523 0.7	2119 3.8
9 TH	0357 1.0	0945 3.5	1623 1.1	◗ 2208 3.5		**24** F	0349 0.8	0946 3.7	1616 0.8	◗ 2213 3.6
10 F	0443 1.2	1031 3.3	1715 1.2	2258 3.3		**25** SA	0446 1.0	1045 3.5	1718 1.0	2318 3.4
11 SA	0541 1.3	1130 3.2	1819 1.4			**26** SU	0558 1.1	1158 3.4	1835 1.1	
12 SU	0005 3.2	0651 1.4	1248 3.1	1928 1.4		**27** M	0040 3.3	0723 1.1	1327 3.4	2004 1.1
13 M	0129 3.2	0801 1.3	1410 3.3	2035 1.2		**28** TU	0206 3.4	0847 0.9	1446 3.6	2124 0.8
14 TU	0241 3.3	0905 1.1	1512 3.5	2134 1.0		**29** W	0316 3.6	0955 0.7	1547 3.8	2223 0.6
15 W	0337 3.5	0959 0.9	1601 3.7	2223 0.8		**30** TH	0412 3.8	1048 0.5	1637 4.1	2311 0.4
						31 F	0459 4.0	1132 0.3	1720 4.2	○ 2351 0.3

Chart Datum: 0·13 metres above Ordnance Datum (Dublin)
HAT is 4·5m above Chart Datum

TIME ZONE (UT)	IRELAND – COBH	Dates in amber are SPRINGS
For Summer Time add ONE hour in non-shaded areas	LAT 51°51'N LONG 8°18'W	Dates in yellow are NEAPS
	TIMES AND HEIGHTS OF HIGH AND LOW WATERS	2012

SEPTEMBER

Time	m		Time	m
1 0540 1211 SA 1758	4.1 0.2 4.2	**16** 0511 1130 SU 1729 ● 2353	4.1 0.3 4.2 0.3
2 0026 0616 SU 1246 1833	0.3 4.1 0.3 4.2	**17** 0549 1209 M 1808	4.2 0.3 4.2
3 0100 0649 M 1319 1905	0.4 4.0 0.4 4.1	**18** 0032 0627 TU 1250 1847	0.3 4.2 0.3 4.2
4 0131 0720 TU 1350 1937	0.5 4.0 0.6 3.9	**19** 0113 0708 W 1332 1928	0.3 4.1 0.3 4.1
5 0202 0752 W 1422 2010	0.7 3.8 0.7 3.8	**20** 0156 0751 TH 1418 2013	0.4 4.1 0.4 4.0
6 0234 0826 TH 1456 2044	0.9 3.7 0.9 3.7	**21** 0242 0838 F 1507 2101	0.6 3.9 0.6 3.8
7 0309 0904 F 1535 2123	1.0 3.6 1.1 3.6	**22** 0334 0930 SA 1601 ◐ 2156	0.8 3.7 0.9 3.5
8 0352 0948 SA 1624 ◖ 2210	1.2 3.4 1.2 3.3	**23** 0433 1032 SU 1705 2304	1.0 3.5 1.1 3.3
9 0449 1043 SU 1730 2311	1.4 3.2 1.4 3.2	**24** 0547 1150 M 1825	1.1 3.3 1.2
10 0604 1155 M 1846	1.5 3.1 1.5	**25** 0030 0715 TU 1320 1959	3.2 1.1 3.4 1.1
11 0034 0721 TU 1328 1958	3.1 1.4 3.2 1.3	**26** 0156 0838 W 1434 2112	3.4 0.9 3.6 0.9
12 0204 0829 W 1439 2100	3.3 1.2 3.4 1.1	**27** 0302 0940 TH 1530 2206	3.6 0.7 3.8 0.6
13 0304 0924 TH 1530 2151	3.5 0.9 3.7 0.8	**28** 0354 1030 F 1617 2250	3.8 0.5 4.0 0.5
14 0351 1011 F 1612 2235	3.8 0.7 3.9 0.6	**29** 0438 1111 SA 1658 2328	4.0 0.4 4.1 0.4
15 0433 1052 SA 1651 2315	3.9 0.5 4.1 0.4	**30** 0517 1147 SU 1734 ○	4.1 0.4 4.2

OCTOBER

Time	m		Time	m
1 0001 0551 M 1219 1806	0.5 4.1 0.4 4.1	**16** 0525 1149 TU 1745	4.3 0.2 4.3
2 0030 0621 TU 1248 1836	0.5 4.0 0.6 4.0	**17** 0013 0607 W 1233 1828	0.3 4.3 0.2 4.3
3 0058 0650 W 1316 1905	0.6 4.0 0.7 3.9	**18** 0057 0651 TH 1319 1913	0.3 4.3 0.3 4.2
4 0126 0720 TH 1346 1935	0.8 3.9 0.8 3.9	**19** 0143 0737 F 1406 1959	0.4 4.1 0.4 4.0
5 0156 0754 F 1419 2009	0.9 3.8 1.0 3.7	**20** 0232 0827 SA 1457 2050	0.5 4.0 0.6 3.8
6 0231 0831 SA 1458 2047	1.1 3.6 1.2 3.6	**21** 0325 0921 SU 1552 2146	0.7 3.8 0.8 3.6
7 0314 0915 SU 1546 2133	1.2 3.5 1.3 3.4	**22** 0425 1023 M 1656 ◖ 2252	0.9 3.6 1.1 3.4
8 0409 1007 M 1648 ◖ 2231	1.4 3.3 1.5 3.3	**23** 0537 1138 TU 1814	1.1 3.4 1.2
9 0520 1113 TU 1804 2345	1.5 3.2 1.5 3.2	**24** 0012 0700 W 1300 1939	3.3 1.1 3.4 1.1
10 0638 1234 W 1918	1.4 3.3 1.4	**25** 0133 0815 TH 1408 2046	3.4 0.9 3.6 0.9
11 0110 0747 TH 1351 2021	3.3 1.2 3.4 1.1	**26** 0236 0915 F 1503 2139	3.6 0.8 3.8 0.8
12 0220 0846 F 1448 2115	3.5 1.0 3.7 0.9	**27** 0328 1004 SA 1550 2224	3.8 0.6 3.9 0.7
13 0312 0936 SA 1536 2203	3.8 0.7 3.9 0.6	**28** 0412 1046 SU 1631 2301	3.9 0.4 4.0 0.6
14 0358 1022 SU 1620 2248	4.0 0.5 4.1 0.4	**29** 0451 1122 M 1707 ○ 2334	4.0 0.4 4.1 0.6
15 0442 1106 M 1703 ● 2331	4.2 0.3 4.3 0.3	**30** 0526 1153 TU 1740	4.0 0.6 4.1
			31 0002 0556 W 1221 1810	0.7 4.0 0.7 4.0

NOVEMBER

Time	m		Time	m
1 0029 0626 TH 1249 1839	0.7 4.0 0.8 4.0	**16** 0046 0640 F 1310 1901	0.3 4.3 0.3 4.2
2 0057 0656 F 1319 1909	0.8 3.9 0.9 3.9	**17** 0134 0728 SA 1359 1949	0.3 4.2 0.4 4.1
3 0129 0730 SA 1354 1943	0.9 3.9 1.0 3.8	**18** 0223 0818 SU 1449 2039	0.5 4.1 0.6 3.9
4 0206 0807 SU 1433 2022	1.0 3.8 1.1 3.7	**19** 0316 0911 M 1543 2133	0.6 3.9 0.8 3.7
5 0249 0850 M 1520 2107	1.2 3.7 1.3 3.6	**20** 0413 1008 TU 1642 ◖ 2232	0.8 3.7 1.0 3.5
6 0341 0941 TU 1616 2202	1.3 3.5 1.4 3.5	**21** 0516 1112 W 1749 2339	1.0 3.6 1.1 3.4
7 0443 1040 W 1723 ◖ 2307	1.4 3.4 1.4 3.4	**22** 0627 1221 TH 1901	1.1 3.5 1.2
8 0554 1148 TH 1835	1.4 3.4 1.4	**23** 0052 0737 F 1329 2007	3.4 1.0 3.5 1.1
9 0020 0703 F 1259 1941	3.4 1.3 3.6 1.2	**24** 0158 0838 SA 1426 2102	3.5 1.0 3.6 1.0
10 0130 0806 SA 1403 2039	3.6 1.1 3.7 1.0	**25** 0253 0930 SU 1516 2150	3.6 0.9 3.8 0.9
11 0231 0903 SU 1458 2133	3.8 0.8 3.9 0.7	**26** 0341 1015 M 1600 2232	3.8 0.8 3.9 0.8
12 0325 0956 M 1550 2224	4.0 0.6 4.1 0.5	**27** 0424 1055 TU 1641 2308	3.9 0.6 3.9 0.7
13 0415 1046 TU 1639 ● 2312	4.2 0.4 4.2 0.4	**28** 0502 1129 W 1717 ○ 2339	4.0 0.6 4.0 0.6
14 0504 1135 W 1727 2359	4.3 0.3 4.3 0.3	**29** 0537 1159 TH 1750	4.0 0.6 4.0
15 0552 1222 TH 1814	4.4 0.3 4.3	**30** 0008 0608 F 1230 1821	0.8 4.0 0.9 4.0

DECEMBER

Time	m		Time	m
1 0038 0640 SA 1302 1852	0.8 4.0 0.9 4.0	**16** 0123 0718 SU 1349 1937	0.3 4.3 0.4 4.1
2 0112 0714 SU 1337 1926	0.9 4.0 1.0 3.9	**17** 0211 0805 M 1436 2024	0.4 4.1 0.5 4.0
3 0149 0751 M 1417 2004	1.0 3.9 1.1 3.8	**18** 0300 0853 TU 1525 2111	0.5 4.0 0.7 3.8
4 0231 0832 TU 1500 2047	1.1 3.8 1.2 3.7	**19** 0350 0943 W 1615 2200	0.7 3.8 0.9 3.6
5 0319 0918 W 1549 2137	1.2 3.8 1.3 3.7	**20** 0443 1035 TH 1709 ◖ 2254	0.9 3.7 1.1 3.5
6 0412 1010 TH 1645 ◖ 2234	1.2 3.7 1.3 3.6	**21** 0542 1132 F 1809 2356	1.1 3.5 1.2 3.4
7 0512 1109 F 1749 2337	1.3 3.6 1.3 3.6	**22** 0645 1235 SA 1913	1.2 3.4 1.3
8 0619 1214 SA 1858	1.3 3.7 1.3	**23** 0104 0748 SU 1339 2014	3.4 1.2 3.5 1.2
9 0045 0726 SU 1320 2003	3.6 1.2 3.7 1.1	**24** 0210 0847 M 1437 2111	3.4 1.2 3.5 1.2
10 0152 0831 M 1424 2105	3.8 1.0 3.9 0.9	**25** 0306 0941 TU 1529 2202	3.6 1.1 3.7 1.0
11 0254 0932 TU 1524 2203	3.9 0.8 4.0 0.7	**26** 0356 1028 W 1616 2244	3.8 1.0 3.8 0.9
12 0354 1030 W 1621 2257	4.1 0.6 4.1 0.5	**27** 0440 1108 TH 1658 2320	3.9 0.9 3.9 0.8
13 0449 1124 TH 1714 ● 2348	4.3 0.4 4.2 0.3	**28** 0519 1142 F 1735 ○ 2352	4.0 0.9 4.0 0.8
14 0541 1213 F 1804	4.4 0.4 4.3	**29** 0555 1214 SA 1808	4.1 0.9 4.0
15 0036 0630 SA 1302 1851	0.3 4.4 0.3 4.2	**30** 0023 0627 SU 1248 1839	0.8 4.1 0.8 4.0
			31 0057 0700 M 1322 1912	0.8 4.1 0.9 4.0

Chart Datum: 0·13 metres above Ordnance Datum (Dublin)
HAT is 4·5m above Chart Datum

TIDES

343

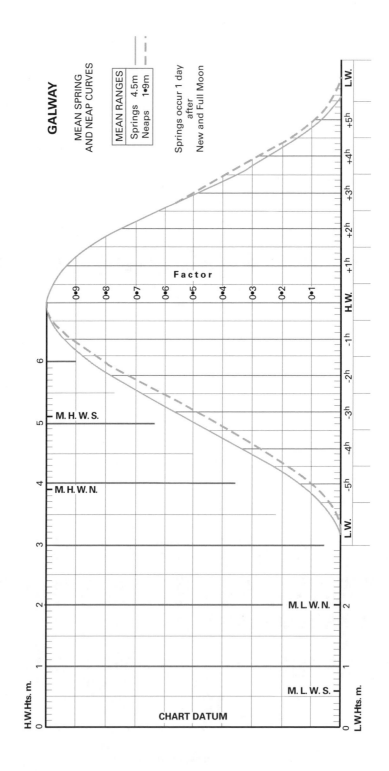

GALWAY

MEAN SPRING
AND NEAP CURVES

MEAN RANGES

Springs 4.5m
Neaps 1•9m

Springs occur 1 day
after
New and Full Moon

Factor

0•9 0•8 0•7 0•6 0•5 0•4 0•3 0•2 0•1

H.W.Hts. m.

M. H. W. S.

M. H. W. N.

M. L. W. N.

M. L. W. S.

CHART DATUM

L.W.Hts. m.

L.W.

H.W.

L.W.

TIME ZONE (UT)	IRELAND – GALWAY	Dates in amber are **SPRINGS**
For Summer Time add ONE hour in **non-shaded areas**	LAT 53°16′N LONG 9°03′W	Dates in yellow are NEAPS
	TIMES AND HEIGHTS OF HIGH AND LOW WATERS	**2012**

JANUARY

#	Time m	#	Time m
1	0355 1.9 / 1022 4.1 / SU 1612 1.8 / ☽ 2305 3.9	16	0329 1.5 / 1001 4.4 / M 1557 1.4 / ☽ 2247 4.3
2	0503 2.1 / 1116 3.9 / M 1715 2.0	17	0433 1.7 / 1107 4.3 / TU 1703 1.7 / 2355 4.2
3	0005 3.8 / 0613 2.2 / TU 1826 2.1	18	0549 1.8 / 1222 4.1 / W 1835 1.7
4	0113 3.9 / 0719 2.1 / W 1334 3.8 / 1936 2.0	19	0109 4.3 / 0715 1.7 / TH 1344 4.2 / 1959 1.6
5	0218 4.0 / 0818 1.9 / TH 1440 3.9 / 2031 1.8	20	0219 4.5 / 0826 1.4 / F 1453 4.4 / 2056 1.4
6	0308 4.2 / 0906 1.6 / F 1530 4.1 / 2116 1.6	21	0317 4.7 / 0920 1.1 / SA 1548 4.6 / 2143 1.1
7	0349 4.4 / 0949 1.4 / SA 1612 4.3 / 2157 1.4	22	0407 4.9 / 1008 0.8 / SU 1636 4.8 / 2227 0.9
8	0428 4.6 / 1029 1.1 / SU 1651 4.5 / 2236 1.1	23	0453 5.1 / 1051 0.6 / M 1721 4.9 / ● 2309 0.8
9	0506 4.7 / 1107 0.9 / M 1730 4.7 / ☽ 2314 1.0	24	0538 5.2 / 1132 0.5 / TU 1803 4.9 / 2349 0.7
10	0544 4.9 / 1143 0.7 / TU 1809 4.6 / 2351 0.8	25	0620 5.2 / 1211 0.5 / W 1844 4.9
11	0623 5.0 / 1218 0.6 / W 1848 4.9	26	0027 0.7 / 0700 5.1 / TH 1248 0.5 / 1922 4.8
12	0029 0.8 / 0701 5.0 / TH 1255 0.5 / 1926 4.9	27	0105 0.8 / 0739 5.0 / F 1323 0.7 / 2001 4.6
13	0109 0.8 / 0739 5.0 / F 1333 0.6 / 2007 4.8	28	0142 1.0 / 0817 4.7 / SA 1359 0.9 / 2039 4.4
14	0151 1.0 / 0818 4.9 / SA 1415 0.8 / 2052 4.6	29	0221 1.3 / 0855 4.4 / SU 1436 1.3 / 2120 4.2
15	0237 1.2 / 0904 4.7 / SU 1502 1.1 / 2145 4.4	30	0304 1.6 / 0936 4.2 / M 1517 1.6 / 2205 3.9
		31	0356 1.9 / 1021 3.9 / TU 1606 1.9 / ☽ 2256 3.7

FEBRUARY

#	Time m	#	Time m
1	0514 2.1 / 1114 3.6 / W 1719 2.1 / 2357 3.6	16	0525 1.7 / 1208 3.9 / TH 1818 1.9
2	0640 2.2 / 1222 3.5 / TH 1857 2.1	17	0054 4.0 / 0702 1.7 / F 1338 3.9 / 1951 1.7
3	0132 3.6 / 0750 2.0 / F 1409 3.6 / 2007 1.9	18	0211 4.2 / 0820 1.5 / SA 1448 4.2 / 2048 1.4
4	0248 3.9 / 0845 1.7 / SA 1512 3.9 / 2058 1.6	19	0308 4.5 / 0913 1.1 / SU 1539 4.5 / 2132 1.1
5	0333 4.1 / 0930 1.3 / SU 1555 4.2 / 2140 1.3	20	0356 4.8 / 0956 0.8 / M 1623 4.7 / 2212 0.9
6	0412 4.4 / 1010 0.9 / M 1634 4.5 / 2220 0.9	21	0440 5.0 / 1035 0.6 / TU 1704 4.8 / ● 2251 0.7
7	0449 4.7 / 1048 0.6 / TU 1712 4.7 / ○ 2258 0.7	22	0521 5.1 / 1112 0.5 / W 1743 4.9 / 2329 0.6
8	0527 4.9 / 1124 0.4 / W 1749 4.9 / 2335 0.4	23	0601 5.1 / 1147 0.4 / TH 1821 4.9
9	0605 5.1 / 1159 0.2 / TH 1827 5.1	24	0005 0.6 / 0638 5.1 / F 1221 0.5 / 1856 4.9
10	0012 0.3 / 0642 5.2 / F 1236 0.2 / 1904 5.1	25	0040 0.7 / 0714 4.9 / SA 1253 0.6 / 1931 4.7
11	0051 0.4 / 0720 5.1 / SA 1313 0.3 / 1942 5.0	26	0113 0.8 / 0749 4.7 / SU 1326 0.9 / 2005 4.5
12	0131 0.5 / 0759 5.0 / SU 1353 0.6 / 2023 4.7	27	0148 1.1 / 0823 4.4 / M 1359 1.2 / 2039 4.2
13	0215 0.8 / 0842 4.7 / M 1437 0.9 / 2112 4.5	28	0223 1.4 / 0900 4.2 / TU 1434 1.5 / 2118 4.0
14	0305 1.2 / 0937 4.4 / TU 1529 1.4 / ☽ 2215 4.2	29	0303 1.8 / 0943 3.9 / W 1513 1.8 / 2207 3.7
15	0406 1.5 / 1046 4.1 / W 1636 1.7 / 2330 4.0		

MARCH

#	Time m	#	Time m
1	0357 2.0 / 1036 3.6 / TH 1606 2.1 / ☽ 2304 3.6	16	0510 1.7 / 1158 3.8 / F 1806 1.9
2	0601 2.0 / 1138 3.5 / F 1820 2.2	17	0039 3.9 / 0646 1.7 / SA 1326 3.9 / 1935 1.8
3	0012 3.5 / 0717 2.0 / SA 1318 3.5 / 1939 2.0	18	0154 4.1 / 0806 1.4 / SU 1433 4.1 / 2032 1.5
4	0217 3.7 / 0816 1.7 / SU 1447 3.8 / 2033 1.7	19	0251 4.4 / 0856 1.2 / M 1522 4.4 / 2114 1.2
5	0308 4.0 / 0903 1.3 / M 1531 4.2 / 2116 1.2	20	0337 4.7 / 0935 0.9 / TU 1603 4.6 / 2152 0.9
6	0347 4.4 / 0943 0.8 / TU 1609 4.5 / 2156 0.8	21	0419 4.8 / 1012 0.7 / W 1642 4.8 / 2229 0.7
7	0425 4.7 / 1022 0.5 / W 1646 4.8 / 2235 0.5	22	0459 4.9 / 1047 0.6 / TH 1719 4.9 / ● 2306 0.6
8	0503 5.0 / 1059 0.2 / TH 1724 5.1 / ○ 2313 0.2	23	0537 5.0 / 1121 0.6 / F 1754 4.9 / 2341 0.6
9	0542 5.2 / 1135 0.0 / F 1802 5.2 / 2351 0.1	24	0614 4.9 / 1152 0.6 / SA 1829 4.8
10	0622 5.3 / 1212 0.0 / SA 1840 5.3	25	0014 0.7 / 0648 4.8 / SU 1223 0.8 / 1901 4.7
11	0030 0.1 / 0701 5.2 / SU 1251 0.1 / 1918 5.1	26	0046 0.9 / 0723 4.7 / M 1254 1.0 / 1934 4.5
12	0112 0.3 / 0739 4.8 / M 1332 0.5 / 2000 4.9	27	0119 1.1 / 0757 4.4 / TU 1327 1.2 / 2008 4.3
13	0156 0.6 / 0826 4.5 / TU 1416 0.9 / 2048 4.5	28	0153 1.3 / 0833 4.2 / W 1401 1.5 / 2046 4.1
14	0246 1.0 / 0921 4.3 / W 1508 1.4 / 2150 4.2	29	0232 1.6 / 0917 3.9 / TH 1441 1.8 / 2133 3.9
15	0347 1.4 / 1032 4.0 / TH 1619 1.8 / ☽ 2311 3.9	30	0319 1.9 / 1009 3.7 / F 1531 2.1 / ☽ 2230 3.7
		31	0441 2.1 / 1108 3.6 / SA 1652 2.3 / 2332 3.6

APRIL

#	Time m	#	Time m
1	0639 2.0 / 1219 3.6 / SU 1902 2.1	16	0126 4.1 / 0732 1.5 / M 1407 4.1 / 2004 1.6
2	0048 3.7 / 0739 1.7 / M 1358 3.8 / 1959 1.7	17	0224 4.3 / 0827 1.3 / TU 1457 4.4 / 2048 1.3
3	0222 4.0 / 0829 1.3 / TU 1454 4.2 / 2046 1.3	18	0312 4.5 / 0908 1.1 / W 1538 4.6 / 2127 1.1
4	0311 4.4 / 0912 0.9 / W 1535 4.6 / 2128 0.8	19	0354 4.7 / 0945 1.0 / TH 1616 4.7 / 2205 0.9
5	0353 4.7 / 0952 0.5 / TH 1614 5.0 / 2208 0.4	20	0433 4.7 / 1020 0.9 / F 1652 4.8 / 2242 0.8
6	0434 5.0 / 1031 0.2 / F 1654 5.2 / ○ 2248 0.2	21	0511 4.8 / 1053 0.9 / SA 1726 4.8 / ● 2317 0.8
7	0517 5.3 / 1110 0.1 / SA 1735 5.4 / 2329 0.0	22	0548 4.7 / 1124 0.9 / SU 1800 4.8 / 2350 0.9
8	0559 5.3 / 1150 0.1 / SU 1816 5.4	23	0623 4.7 / 1155 1.0 / M 1834 4.7
9	0011 0.0 / 0642 5.3 / M 1231 0.2 / 1858 5.3	24	0023 1.0 / 0658 4.6 / TU 1227 1.1 / 1908 4.6
10	0055 0.2 / 0726 5.1 / TU 1313 0.5 / 1942 5.0	25	0056 1.1 / 0734 4.4 / W 1301 1.3 / 1943 4.4
11	0141 0.5 / 0813 4.7 / W 1359 1.0 / 2031 4.7	26	0132 1.3 / 0812 4.2 / TH 1337 1.5 / 2021 4.2
12	0232 0.9 / 0909 4.3 / TH 1453 1.4 / 2133 4.3	27	0211 1.5 / 0855 4.1 / F 1419 1.7 / 2107 4.1
13	0333 1.3 / 1019 4.0 / F 1605 1.8 / ☽ 2253 4.0	28	0258 1.7 / 0945 3.9 / SA 1509 2.0 / 2202 3.9
14	0452 1.6 / 1140 3.9 / SA 1742 1.9	29	0358 1.8 / 1042 3.8 / SU 1616 2.1 / ☽ 2302 3.9
15	0015 4.0 / 0617 1.6 / SU 1301 3.9 / 1903 1.8	30	0540 1.8 / 1144 3.8 / M 1808 2.0

TIDES

Chart Datum: 0·20 metres above Ordnance Datum (Dublin)
HAT is 5·6m above Chart Datum

TIME ZONE (UT)
For Summer Time add ONE hour in **non-shaded areas**

IRELAND – GALWAY
LAT 53°16'N   LONG 9°03'W
TIMES AND HEIGHTS OF HIGH AND LOW WATERS

Dates in amber are **SPRINGS**
Dates in yellow are **NEAPS**

2012

MAY

Time	m		Time	m
1 TU 0005 / 0653 / 1254 / 1918	3.9 / 1.6 / 4.0 / 1.7	**16** W	0149 / 0745 / 1424 / 2017	4.2 / 1.5 / 4.2 / 1.5
2 W 0118 / 0750 / 1404 / 2011	4.1 / 1.3 / 4.3 / 1.4	**17** TH	0241 / 0834 / 1509 / 2100	4.3 / 1.4 / 4.4 / 1.3
3 TH 0226 / 0838 / 1456 / 2057	4.4 / 1.0 / 4.7 / 0.9	**18** F	0325 / 0915 / 1548 / 2140	4.4 / 1.3 / 4.5 / 1.2
4 F 0318 / 0922 / 1542 / 2141	4.7 / 0.7 / 5.0 / 0.6	**19** SA	0406 / 0951 / 1624 / 2218	4.5 / 1.2 / 4.6 / 1.1
5 SA 0406 / 1004 / 1625 / 2224	5.0 / 0.4 / 5.3 / 0.3	**20** SU	0445 / 1026 / 1658 / 2255	4.5 / 1.2 / 4.7 / 1.0
6 SU 0453 / 1046 / 1710 / 2309	5.2 / 0.3 / 5.4 / 0.2	**21** M	0523 / 1059 / 1733 / 2330	4.6 / 1.1 / 4.7 / 1.0
7 M 0540 / 1129 / 1755 / 2354	5.3 / 0.3 / 5.4 / 0.1	**22** TU	0600 / 1132 / 1809	4.6 / 1.1 / 4.7
8 TU 0627 / 1213 / 1841	5.2 / 0.4 / 5.3	**23** W	0005 / 0637 / 1207 / 1845	1.0 / 4.5 / 1.2 / 4.6
9 W 0040 / 0713 / 1259 / 1928	0.3 / 5.1 / 0.7 / 5.1	**24** TH	0040 / 0715 / 1242 / 1922	1.1 / 4.5 / 1.3 / 4.5
10 TH 0128 / 0802 / 1346 / 2019	0.5 / 4.8 / 1.0 / 4.8	**25** F	0116 / 0754 / 1321 / 2001	1.2 / 4.4 / 1.4 / 4.4
11 F 0219 / 0856 / 1438 / 2118	0.8 / 4.4 / 1.4 / 4.5	**26** SA	0156 / 0835 / 1403 / 2044	1.3 / 4.3 / 1.5 / 4.3
12 SA 0316 / 0959 / 1544 / 2228	1.2 / 4.1 / 1.7 / 4.2	**27** SU	0240 / 0922 / 1452 / 2135	1.4 / 4.2 / 1.7 / 4.2
13 SU 0424 / 1110 / 1705 / 2340	1.4 / 4.0 / 1.9 / 4.1	**28** M	0332 / 1015 / 1550 / 2233	1.5 / 4.1 / 1.8 / 4.1
14 M 0537 / 1221 / 1821	1.6 / 3.9 / 1.9	**29** TU	0434 / 1112 / 1701 / 2333	1.6 / 4.1 / 1.9 / 4.2
15 TU 0047 / 0645 / 1329 / 1925	4.1 / 1.6 / 4.0 / 1.7	**30** W	0547 / 1213 / 1824	1.6 / 4.2 / 1.7

JUNE

Time	m		Time	m
1 F 0147 / 0803 / 1421 / 2028	4.4 / 1.2 / 4.7 / 1.1	**16** SA	0255 / 0842 / 1520 / 2116	4.0 / 1.6 / 4.2 / 1.4
2 SA 0249 / 0855 / 1514 / 2118	4.7 / 1.0 / 4.9 / 0.8	**17** SU	0340 / 0924 / 1558 / 2156	4.2 / 1.5 / 4.4 / 1.2
3 SU 0343 / 0942 / 1603 / 2205	4.9 / 0.7 / 5.2 / 0.5	**18** M	0421 / 1003 / 1635 / 2235	4.3 / 1.3 / 4.5 / 1.1
4 M 0434 / 1028 / 1651 / 2253	5.0 / 0.6 / 5.3 / 0.3	**19** TU	0501 / 1040 / 1711 / 2313	4.4 / 1.2 / 4.6 / 1.0
5 TU 0524 / 1114 / 1739 / 2340	5.1 / 0.5 / 5.4 / 0.2	**20** W	0540 / 1116 / 1749 / 2350	4.5 / 1.1 / 4.7 / 0.9
6 W 0613 / 1159 / 1828	5.1 / 0.6 / 5.3	**21** TH	0619 / 1152 / 1826	4.5 / 1.1 / 4.7
7 TH 0027 / 0700 / 1245 / 1915	0.3 / 5.0 / 0.7 / 5.1	**22** F	0025 / 0657 / 1229 / 1903	0.8 / 4.6 / 1.1 / 4.7
8 F 0114 / 0748 / 1331 / 2004	0.4 / 4.8 / 0.9 / 4.9	**23** SA	0101 / 0735 / 1306 / 1941	0.9 / 4.6 / 1.1 / 4.6
9 SA 0201 / 0837 / 1418 / 2056	0.7 / 4.6 / 1.2 / 4.6	**24** SU	0139 / 0814 / 1347 / 2021	0.9 / 4.5 / 1.2 / 4.5
10 SU 0251 / 0931 / 1512 / 2155	1.0 / 4.3 / 1.5 / 4.3	**25** M	0220 / 0856 / 1432 / 2108	1.0 / 4.4 / 1.4 / 4.4
11 M 0346 / 1030 / 1618 / 2257	1.3 / 4.1 / 1.8 / 4.1	**26** TU	0306 / 0945 / 1523 / 2203	1.2 / 4.3 / 1.5 / 4.3
12 TU 0448 / 1108 / 1731 / 2359	1.5 / 3.9 / 1.9 / 4.0	**27** W	0359 / 1039 / 1624 / 2304	1.3 / 4.2 / 1.6 / 4.2
13 W 0552 / 1236 / 1839	1.7 / 3.9 / 1.9	**28** TH	0501 / 1139 / 1736	1.5 / 4.2 / 1.7
14 TH 0102 / 0655 / 1340 / 1940	3.9 / 1.7 / 4.0 / 1.7	**29** F	0009 / 0613 / 1246 / 1856	4.2 / 1.5 / 4.3 / 1.5
15 F 0203 / 0754 / 1436 / 2032	4.0 / 1.7 / 4.1 / 1.6	**30** SA	0121 / 0732 / 1355 / 2006	4.3 / 1.4 / 4.5 / 1.3

JULY

Time	m		Time	m
1 SU 0230 / 0835 / 1455 / 2102	4.4 / 1.2 / 4.7 / 0.9	**16** M	0319 / 0900 / 1539 / 2136	3.9 / 1.6 / 4.2 / 1.3
2 M 0329 / 0927 / 1548 / 2153	4.6 / 1.0 / 5.0 / 0.7	**17** TU	0403 / 0943 / 1617 / 2215	4.1 / 1.4 / 4.4 / 1.0
3 TU 0422 / 1014 / 1638 / 2241	4.8 / 0.8 / 5.2 / 0.4	**18** W	0443 / 1022 / 1653 / 2253	4.3 / 1.2 / 4.5 / 0.8
4 W 0512 / 1100 / 1727 / 2327	5.0 / 0.6 / 5.3 / 0.3	**19** TH	0522 / 1100 / 1730 / 2330	4.5 / 1.0 / 4.7 / 0.6
5 TH 0600 / 1145 / 1814	5.0 / 0.6 / 5.3	**20** F	0600 / 1136 / 1807	4.6 / 0.8 / 4.8
6 F 0012 / 0645 / 1228 / 1859	0.3 / 5.0 / 0.6 / 5.2	**21** SA	0006 / 0636 / 1212 / 1843	0.5 / 4.7 / 0.7 / 4.8
7 SA 0055 / 0729 / 1310 / 1944	0.3 / 4.9 / 0.8 / 5.0	**22** SU	0041 / 0713 / 1248 / 1919	0.5 / 4.8 / 0.7 / 4.8
8 SU 0137 / 0813 / 1352 / 2030	0.5 / 4.7 / 1.0 / 4.7	**23** M	0117 / 0750 / 1327 / 1956	0.6 / 4.7 / 0.8 / 4.7
9 M 0220 / 0858 / 1437 / 2118	0.8 / 4.4 / 1.3 / 4.4	**24** TU	0156 / 0828 / 1409 / 2038	0.7 / 4.6 / 1.0 / 4.6
10 TU 0305 / 0946 / 1528 / 2210	1.2 / 4.2 / 1.6 / 4.1	**25** W	0239 / 0912 / 1457 / 2132	1.0 / 4.4 / 1.2 / 4.4
11 W 0356 / 1037 / 1633 / 2306	1.5 / 3.9 / 1.9 / 3.9	**26** TH	0330 / 1006 / 1554 / 2237	1.2 / 4.3 / 1.5 / 4.2
12 TH 0455 / 1134 / 1749	1.8 / 3.8 / 2.0	**27** F	0429 / 1108 / 1704 / 2347	1.5 / 4.2 / 1.7 / 4.1
13 F 0007 / 0602 / 1241 / 1901	3.7 / 1.9 / 3.7 / 1.9	**28** SA	0543 / 1220 / 1833	1.7 / 4.2 / 1.6
14 SA 0118 / 0706 / 1357 / 2004	3.7 / 1.9 / 3.8 / 1.8	**29** SU	0105 / 0715 / 1339 / 1956	4.1 / 1.6 / 4.3 / 1.4
15 SU 0221 / 0811 / 1456 / 2054	3.7 / 1.8 / 4.0 / 1.5	**30** M	0221 / 0823 / 1446 / 2055	4.2 / 1.4 / 4.6 / 1.1
		31 TU	0321 / 0916 / 1540 / 2143	4.5 / 1.1 / 4.8 / 0.7

AUGUST

Time	m		Time	m
1 W 0412 / 1002 / 1628 / 2228	4.7 / 0.9 / 5.1 / 0.5	**16** TH	0421 / 1001 / 1633 / 2229	4.4 / 1.1 / 4.6 / 0.7
2 TH 0459 / 1045 / 1713 / 2311	4.9 / 0.7 / 5.2 / 0.3	**17** F	0459 / 1038 / 1708 / 2305	4.6 / 0.8 / 4.8 / 0.4
3 F 0543 / 1127 / 1757 / 2352	5.0 / 0.6 / 5.2 / 0.3	**18** SA	0535 / 1115 / 1744 / 2340	4.8 / 0.6 / 5.0 / 0.3
4 SA 0626 / 1207 / 1839	5.0 / 0.5 / 5.2	**19** SU	0611 / 1150 / 1819	4.9 / 0.4 / 5.0
5 SU 0031 / 0706 / 1246 / 1920	0.3 / 4.9 / 0.6 / 5.0	**20** M	0015 / 0647 / 1227 / 1855	0.3 / 5.0 / 0.4 / 5.0
6 M 0109 / 0745 / 1323 / 2000	0.5 / 4.7 / 0.8 / 4.8	**21** TU	0052 / 0723 / 1305 / 1932	0.3 / 4.9 / 0.5 / 4.9
7 TU 0146 / 0823 / 1402 / 2041	0.8 / 4.5 / 1.1 / 4.4	**22** W	0131 / 0800 / 1346 / 2013	0.6 / 4.8 / 0.7 / 4.7
8 W 0225 / 0903 / 1443 / 2125	1.1 / 4.3 / 1.5 / 4.1	**23** TH	0214 / 0842 / 1432 / 2106	0.9 / 4.6 / 1.1 / 4.4
9 TH 0308 / 0945 / 1534 / 2214	1.5 / 4.0 / 1.8 / 3.8	**24** F	0303 / 0935 / 1528 / 2215	1.3 / 4.3 / 1.4 / 4.1
10 F 0359 / 1032 / 1653 / 2311	1.8 / 3.8 / 2.0 / 3.6	**25** SA	0404 / 1043 / 1640 / 2334	1.6 / 4.1 / 1.7 / 3.9
11 SA 0513 / 1128 / 1824	2.0 / 3.6 / 2.1	**26** SU	0529 / 1204 / 1823	1.8 / 4.0 / 1.7
12 SU 0024 / 0635 / 1302 / 1935	3.5 / 2.1 / 3.6 / 1.9	**27** M	0059 / 0707 / 1331 / 1952	4.0 / 1.8 / 4.2 / 1.5
13 M 0158 / 0743 / 1435 / 2030	3.6 / 2.0 / 3.8 / 1.6	**28** TU	0215 / 0812 / 1438 / 2047	4.2 / 1.5 / 4.5 / 1.1
14 TU 0300 / 0836 / 1521 / 2113	3.8 / 1.7 / 4.1 / 1.3	**29** W	0312 / 0902 / 1529 / 2131	4.5 / 1.2 / 4.8 / 0.8
15 W 0343 / 0920 / 1558 / 2151	4.1 / 1.4 / 4.3 / 0.9	**30** TH	0358 / 0945 / 1613 / 2211	4.7 / 0.9 / 5.0 / 0.5
		31 F	0441 / 1026 / 1656 / 2249	4.9 / 0.7 / 5.2 / 0.4

Chart Datum: 0·20 metres above Ordnance Datum (Dublin)
HAT is 5·6m above Chart Datum

IRELAND – GALWAY

LAT 53°16'N   LONG 9°03'W

TIMES AND HEIGHTS OF HIGH AND LOW WATERS

SEPTEMBER

Day	Time m	Day	Time m
1 SA	0522 5.0 / 1105 0.6 / 1737 5.2 / 2327 0.4	16 SU	0504 5.0 / 1049 0.4 / 1716 5.2 / ● 2313 0.2
2 SU	0601 5.0 / 1143 0.6 / 1816 5.2	17 M	0541 5.0 / 1126 0.3 / 1753 5.3 / 2349 0.2
3 M	0003 0.5 / 0639 4.9 / 1219 0.6 / 1853 5.0	18 TU	0619 5.2 / 1204 0.3 / 1832 5.2
4 TU	0038 0.6 / 0715 4.8 / 1254 0.8 / 1930 4.8	19 W	0027 0.3 / 0656 5.2 / 1244 0.4 / 1912 5.1
5 W	0112 0.9 / 0750 4.6 / 1328 1.1 / 2007 4.5	20 TH	0108 0.6 / 0736 5.0 / 1326 0.6 / 1956 4.8
6 TH	0147 1.2 / 0825 4.4 / 1405 1.4 / 2047 4.2	21 F	0151 0.9 / 0820 4.7 / 1413 1.0 / 2049 4.5
7 F	0224 1.6 / 0903 4.1 / 1445 1.8 / 2133 3.9	22 SA	0242 1.4 / 0914 4.4 / 1509 1.4 / ◐ 2200 4.1
8 SA	0307 1.9 / 0948 3.9 / 1540 2.1 / ◑ 2228 3.6	23 SU	0347 1.8 / 1025 4.2 / 1624 1.7 / 2324 4.0
9 SU	0411 2.2 / 1041 3.7 / 1747 2.2 / 2333 3.5	24 M	0525 2.0 / 1152 4.1 / 1814 1.8
10 M	0606 2.3 / 1144 3.6 / 1902 2.0	25 TU	0049 4.0 / 0654 1.9 / 1317 4.2 / 1940 1.5
11 TU	0118 3.6 / 0714 2.1 / 1400 3.7 / 1958 1.7	26 W	0202 4.3 / 0755 1.6 / 1421 4.5 / 2032 1.2
12 W	0232 3.8 / 0808 1.8 / 1453 4.0 / 2043 1.4	27 TH	0255 4.6 / 0843 1.3 / 1511 4.8 / 2112 0.9
13 TH	0315 4.1 / 0854 1.4 / 1531 4.4 / 2123 1.0	28 F	0338 4.8 / 0925 1.0 / 1554 5.0 / 2149 0.8
14 F	0352 4.5 / 0934 1.1 / 1605 4.7 / 2200 0.6	29 SA	0419 4.9 / 1004 0.8 / 1634 5.1 / 2225 0.7
15 SA	0428 4.8 / 1012 0.7 / 1640 4.9 / 2237 0.4	30 SU	0457 5.0 / 1042 0.7 / 1713 5.2 / ○ 2300 0.6

OCTOBER

Day	Time m	Day	Time m
1 M	0534 5.0 / 1119 0.7 / 1750 5.1 / 2334 0.7	16 TU	0510 5.4 / 1102 0.3 / 1729 5.4 / 2324 0.3
2 TU	0610 5.0 / 1153 0.8 / 1827 5.0	17 W	0552 5.5 / 1143 0.2 / 1812 5.4
3 W	0006 0.9 / 0645 4.9 / 1226 1.0 / 1902 4.8	18 TH	0005 0.4 / 0634 5.4 / 1226 0.3 / 1856 5.2
4 TH	0039 1.1 / 0719 4.7 / 1300 1.2 / 1939 4.5	19 F	0049 0.7 / 0717 5.2 / 1311 0.6 / 1944 4.9
5 F	0113 1.4 / 0754 4.5 / 1334 1.5 / 2017 4.3	20 SA	0135 1.0 / 0805 4.9 / 1359 0.9 / 2039 4.6
6 SA	0149 1.7 / 0832 4.3 / 1412 1.7 / 2102 4.0	21 SU	0227 1.5 / 0900 4.6 / 1455 1.3 / 2147 4.3
7 SU	0230 2.0 / 0915 4.0 / 1457 2.0 / 2156 3.8	22 M	0334 1.9 / 1010 4.3 / 1607 1.7 / ◐ 2307 4.1
8 M	0322 2.3 / 1008 3.9 / 1622 2.2 / ◑ 2257 3.7	23 TU	0507 2.0 / 1132 4.2 / 1745 1.8
9 TU	0525 2.4 / 1106 3.8 / 1821 2.1	24 W	0027 4.1 / 0628 1.9 / 1250 4.3 / 1910 1.6
10 W	0009 3.7 / 0639 2.2 / 1212 3.8 / 1919 1.9	25 TH	0137 4.3 / 0730 1.7 / 1355 4.5 / 2006 1.4
11 TH	0140 3.9 / 0730 1.9 / 1356 4.0 / 2008 1.5	26 F	0230 4.6 / 0820 1.5 / 1447 4.7 / 2048 1.2
12 F	0234 4.3 / 0827 1.6 / 1449 4.4 / 2050 1.1	27 SA	0314 4.8 / 0902 1.3 / 1531 4.9 / 2124 1.1
13 SA	0315 4.6 / 0904 1.2 / 1529 4.7 / 2130 0.8	28 SU	0354 4.9 / 0942 1.1 / 1611 5.0 / 2200 1.0
14 SU	0353 4.9 / 0944 0.8 / 1607 5.1 / 2207 0.5	29 M	0431 5.0 / 1020 1.0 / 1649 5.0 / ○ 2234 1.0
15 M	0431 5.2 / 1023 0.5 / 1647 5.3 / ● 2245 0.3	30 TU	0507 5.0 / 1056 1.0 / 1725 5.0 / 2306 1.1
		31 W	0542 4.9 / 1130 1.0 / 1802 4.9 / 2338 1.2

NOVEMBER

Day	Time m	Day	Time m
1 TH	0618 4.9 / 1204 1.1 / 1838 4.8	16 F	0617 5.5 / 1212 0.3 / 1845 5.3
2 F	0012 1.3 / 0653 4.8 / 1238 1.3 / 1915 4.6	17 SA	0034 0.7 / 0704 5.4 / 1259 0.5 / 1933 5.0
3 SA	0047 1.5 / 0729 4.6 / 1313 1.4 / 1955 4.4	18 SU	0122 1.0 / 0753 5.1 / 1347 0.8 / 2027 4.7
4 SU	0125 1.7 / 0807 4.4 / 1351 1.6 / 2038 4.2	19 M	0214 1.4 / 0847 4.8 / 1440 1.2 / 2129 4.4
5 M	0206 2.0 / 0848 4.3 / 1434 1.8 / 2128 4.0	20 TU	0315 1.7 / 0950 4.5 / 1542 1.5 / ◐ 2240 4.2
6 TU	0255 2.2 / 0937 4.1 / 1528 2.0 / 2225 3.9	21 W	0431 2.0 / 1101 4.3 / 1659 1.7 / 2351 4.2
7 W	0400 2.3 / 1032 4.1 / 1655 2.1 / ◑ 2326 4.0	22 TH	0550 2.0 / 1211 4.3 / 1821 1.8
8 TH	0544 2.3 / 1131 4.1 / 1829 1.9	23 F	0059 4.3 / 0655 1.9 / 1318 4.3 / 1928 1.7
9 F	0030 4.1 / 0651 2.0 / 1236 4.2 / 1926 1.7	24 SA	0159 4.4 / 0751 1.7 / 1416 4.4 / 2018 1.6
10 SA	0137 4.4 / 0745 1.7 / 1349 4.4 / 2015 1.3	25 SU	0248 4.6 / 0838 1.6 / 1505 4.5 / 2059 1.4
11 SU	0231 4.7 / 0833 1.3 / 1448 4.7 / 2058 1.0	26 M	0329 4.7 / 0920 1.4 / 1547 4.6 / 2136 1.4
12 M	0317 5.0 / 0916 1.0 / 1537 5.1 / 2140 0.7	27 TU	0407 4.8 / 1000 1.3 / 1626 4.8 / 2210 1.3
13 TU	0401 5.3 / 0959 0.6 / 1623 5.3 / ● 2221 0.5	28 W	0443 4.8 / 1037 1.2 / 1703 4.7 / ○ 2244 1.3
14 W	0445 5.5 / 1042 0.4 / 1710 5.4 / 2304 0.5	29 TH	0519 4.8 / 1113 1.2 / 1741 4.7 / 2318 1.3
15 TH	0531 5.6 / 1127 0.3 / 1757 5.4 / 2348 0.5	30 F	0555 4.8 / 1148 1.2 / 1819 4.7 / 2353 1.3

DECEMBER

Day	Time m	Day	Time m
1 SA	0633 4.8 / 1223 1.2 / 1857 4.6	16 SU	0022 0.7 / 0653 5.4 / 1247 0.4 / 1921 5.1
2 SU	0029 1.4 / 0709 4.7 / 1258 1.3 / 1935 4.5	17 M	0109 0.9 / 0740 5.2 / 1333 0.6 / 2010 4.8
3 M	0108 1.6 / 0746 4.6 / 1335 1.4 / 2016 4.4	18 TU	0156 1.1 / 0830 5.0 / 1420 0.9 / 2104 4.6
4 TU	0148 1.7 / 0825 4.5 / 1415 1.5 / 2101 4.3	19 W	0248 1.5 / 0923 4.7 / 1511 1.3 / 2203 4.3
5 W	0233 1.9 / 0908 4.4 / 1501 1.6 / 2152 4.2	20 TH	0348 1.8 / 1023 4.4 / 1609 1.6 / ◐ 2307 4.1
6 TH	0326 2.0 / 0959 4.3 / 1556 1.8 / ◑ 2248 4.2	21 F	0459 1.9 / 1125 4.2 / 1719 1.8
7 F	0429 2.1 / 1055 4.3 / 1702 1.8 / 2347 4.2	22 SA	0012 4.1 / 0610 2.0 / 1231 4.0 / 1834 1.9
8 SA	0545 2.0 / 1155 4.3 / 1823 1.7	23 SU	0118 4.1 / 0715 2.0 / 1338 4.0 / 1941 1.9
9 SU	0049 4.4 / 0659 1.8 / 1304 4.4 / 1935 1.5	24 M	0218 4.2 / 0812 1.8 / 1437 4.1 / 2032 1.7
10 M	0152 4.6 / 0800 1.5 / 1414 4.6 / 2030 1.2	25 TU	0306 4.3 / 0900 1.6 / 1525 4.3 / 2114 1.6
11 TU	0248 4.9 / 0853 1.1 / 1513 4.9 / 2118 1.0	26 W	0348 4.5 / 0942 1.4 / 1607 4.4 / 2152 1.4
12 W	0339 5.2 / 0941 0.8 / 1606 5.1 / 2203 0.8	27 TH	0425 4.6 / 1021 1.3 / 1646 4.5 / 2228 1.3
13 TH	0427 5.4 / 1028 0.5 / 1656 5.3 / ● 2249 0.6	28 F	0502 4.7 / 1059 1.1 / 1724 4.6 / ○ 2305 1.2
14 F	0516 5.5 / 1115 0.4 / 1745 5.3 / 2336 0.6	29 SA	0539 4.8 / 1135 1.0 / 1802 4.7 / 2341 1.2
15 SA	0605 5.5 / 1201 0.3 / 1834 5.3	30 SU	0616 4.8 / 1210 0.9 / 1840 4.7
		31 M	0016 1.1 / 0652 4.8 / 1244 0.9 / 1916 4.7

Chart Datum: 0·20 metres above Ordnance Datum (Dublin)
HAT is 5·6m above Chart Datum

TIDES

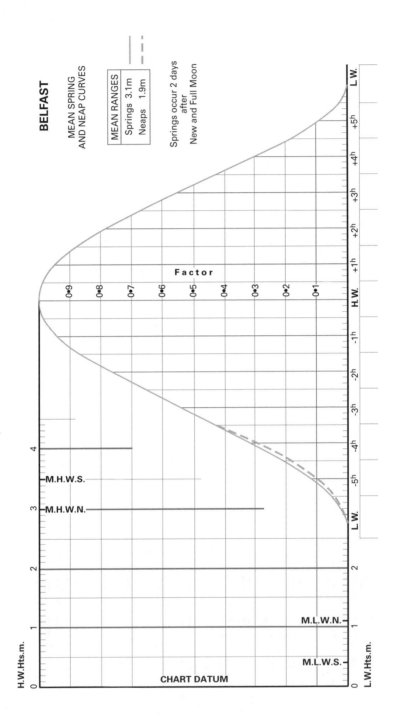

BELFAST

MEAN SPRING
AND NEAP CURVES

MEAN RANGES
Springs 3.1m
Neaps 1.9m

Springs occur 2 days
after
New and Full Moon

Factor

0·9
0·8
0·7
0·6
0·5
0·4
0·3
0·2
0·1

+5ʰ +4ʰ +3ʰ +2ʰ +1ʰ H.W. -1ʰ -2ʰ -3ʰ -4ʰ -5ʰ L.W. L.W.

H.W.Hts.m.

M.H.W.S.
M.H.W.N.

M.L.W.N.
M.L.W.S.

CHART DATUM

L.W.Hts.m.

NORTHERN IRELAND – BELFAST

LAT 54°36′N   LONG 5°55′W

TIMES AND HEIGHTS OF HIGH AND LOW WATERS

Dates in amber are **SPRINGS**
Dates in yellow are **NEAPS**

2012

JANUARY

Time	m		Time	m
1 0416	3.1	**16** 0338	3.2	
1001	1.1	0947	0.9	
SU 1630	3.3	M 1606	3.5	
☽ 2256	1.0	☽ 2218	0.7	
2 0507	3.0	**17** 0438	3.1	
1100	1.2	1051	1.0	
M 1723	3.1	TU 1710	3.4	
		2326	0.8	
3 0000	1.1	**18** 0548	3.1	
0600	3.0	1211	1.0	
TU 1212	1.3	W 1825	3.2	
1822	3.0			
4 0101	1.1	**19** 0045	0.9	
0700	3.0	0710	3.1	
W 1321	1.3	TH 1333	1.0	
1929	3.0	1947	3.2	
5 0156	1.1	**20** 0157	0.9	
0806	3.1	0926	3.2	
TH 1420	1.2	F 1441	0.8	
2043	3.0	2056	3.3	
6 0247	1.0	**21** 0258	0.8	
0906	3.3	0926	3.4	
F 1510	1.0	SA 1540	0.6	
2137	3.1	2153	3.3	
7 0331	0.9	**22** 0351	0.7	
0954	3.4	1017	3.5	
SA 1553	0.9	SU 1631	0.5	
2220	3.2	2243	3.4	
8 0411	0.8	**23** 0438	0.7	
1034	3.5	1103	3.7	
SU 1632	0.7	M 1716	0.4	
2256	3.3	● 2328	3.4	
9 0449	0.8	**24** 0521	0.7	
1108	3.6	1146	3.7	
M 1710	0.6	TU 1758	0.4	
○ 2325	3.3			
10 0527	0.7	**25** 0011	3.3	
1137	3.6	0600	0.7	
TU 1748	0.5	W 1228	3.7	
2350	3.3	1836	0.4	
11 0605	0.7	**26** 0052	3.3	
1210	3.7	0638	0.7	
W 1826	0.5	TH 1307	3.7	
		1913	0.5	
12 0026	3.3	**27** 0131	3.2	
0643	0.7	0713	0.7	
TH 1249	3.7	F 1346	3.6	
1904	0.4	1947	0.6	
13 0109	3.3	**28** 0211	3.2	
0723	0.7	0749	0.8	
F 1333	3.7	SA 1425	3.5	
1946	0.4	2022	0.7	
14 0155	3.3	**29** 0251	3.2	
0806	0.8	0828	0.8	
SA 1420	3.7	SU 1506	3.4	
2031	0.5	2101	0.8	
15 0245	3.2	**30** 0335	3.1	
0854	0.8	0911	0.9	
SU 1510	3.6	M 1550	3.3	
2121	0.6	2146	0.9	
		31 0422	3.1	
		1000	1.1	
		TU 1639	3.1	
		☽ 2243	1.1	

FEBRUARY

Time	m		Time	m
1 0515	3.0	**16** 0523	3.0	
1104	1.2	1158	0.9	
W 1736	2.9	TH 1812	3.0	
2 0009	1.2	**17** 0030	1.0	
0612	2.9	0656	3.0	
TH 1236	1.3	F 1323	0.9	
1839	2.8	1941	3.0	
3 0121	1.2	**18** 0147	1.0	
0717	2.9	0816	3.1	
F 1348	1.2	SA 1434	0.7	
1956	2.8	2050	3.1	
4 0218	1.1	**19** 0251	0.9	
0829	3.1	0916	3.3	
SA 1444	1.0	SU 1534	0.5	
2113	2.9	2144	3.2	
5 0307	0.9	**20** 0344	0.7	
0926	3.2	1005	3.5	
SU 1531	0.8	M 1622	0.4	
2158	3.1	2230	3.2	
6 0350	0.8	**21** 0428	0.6	
1007	3.4	1049	3.6	
M 1612	0.6	TU 1703	0.3	
2232	3.2	● 2312	3.2	
7 0429	0.6	**22** 0506	0.6	
1040	3.5	1130	3.6	
TU 1650	0.4	W 1739	0.3	
○ 2300	3.2	2351	3.2	
8 0507	0.6	**23** 0541	0.6	
1112	3.6	1207	3.6	
W 1727	0.3	TH 1812	0.4	
2329	3.3			
9 0544	0.5	**24** 0027	3.2	
1147	3.7	0612	0.6	
TH 1804	0.3	F 1243	3.5	
		1842	0.5	
10 0005	3.3	**25** 0101	3.2	
0622	0.5	0643	0.6	
F 1229	3.7	SA 1318	3.5	
1843	0.4	1911	0.6	
11 0048	3.3	**26** 0137	3.2	
0701	0.5	0716	0.6	
SA 1314	3.8	SU 1353	3.4	
1924	0.3	1943	0.6	
12 0134	3.3	**27** 0214	3.2	
0744	0.5	0752	0.6	
SU 1402	3.7	M 1430	3.3	
2008	0.3	2019	0.7	
13 0222	3.3	**28** 0255	3.2	
0831	0.5	0833	0.7	
M 1453	3.6	TU 1510	3.2	
2057	0.5	2059	0.9	
14 0314	3.2	**29** 0339	3.1	
0924	0.7	0918	0.9	
TU 1548	3.4	W 1557	3.0	
2152	0.7	2148	1.0	
15 0412	3.1			
1029	0.8			
W 1652	3.2			
2302	0.9			

MARCH

Time	m		Time	m
1 0430	3.0	**16** 0507	3.0	
1014	1.1	1150	0.8	
TH 1654	2.8	F 1807	2.9	
☽ 2256	1.2			
2 0529	2.9	**17** 0015	1.1	
1140	1.2	0641	2.9	
F 1800	2.7	SA 1311	0.7	
		1930	2.9	
3 0044	1.2	**18** 0133	1.0	
0633	2.8	0758	3.1	
SA 1315	1.1	SU 1421	0.6	
1910	2.7	2035	3.0	
4 0148	1.1	**19** 0239	0.9	
0740	2.9	0857	3.2	
SU 1415	0.9	M 1520	0.5	
2029	2.8	2126	3.1	
5 0241	0.9	**20** 0332	0.8	
0843	3.1	0945	3.4	
M 1504	0.6	TU 1605	0.4	
2122	3.0	2210	3.2	
6 0326	0.7	**21** 0413	0.6	
0929	3.3	1028	3.4	
TU 1546	0.4	W 1642	0.3	
2157	3.1	2250	3.2	
7 0406	0.6	**22** 0447	0.6	
1007	3.5	1108	3.4	
W 1624	0.3	TH 1713	0.4	
2230	3.2	● 2327	3.2	
8 0443	0.4	**23** 0518	0.6	
1045	3.6	1144	3.4	
TH 1701	0.2	F 1743	0.5	
○ 2306	3.3			
9 0520	0.4	**24** 0000	3.2	
1125	3.7	0547	0.6	
F 1739	0.1	SA 1217	3.4	
2345	3.4	1811	0.5	
10 0558	0.3	**25** 0031	3.3	
1210	3.7	0616	0.6	
SA 1818	0.1	SU 1248	3.3	
		1839	0.6	
11 0029	3.4	**26** 0104	3.3	
0639	0.3	0648	0.5	
SU 1258	3.7	M 1321	3.3	
1901	0.2	1910	0.6	
12 0117	3.4	**27** 0140	3.3	
0723	0.6	0723	0.6	
M 1348	3.7	TU 1356	3.2	
1946	0.4	1946	0.7	
13 0206	3.4	**28** 0218	3.3	
0812	0.6	0802	0.6	
TU 1441	3.5	W 1434	3.1	
2036	0.5	2026	0.8	
14 0258	3.3	**29** 0258	3.2	
0907	0.6	0846	0.8	
W 1538	3.3	TH 1519	3.0	
2133	0.8	2112	1.0	
15 0356	3.1	**30** 0346	3.1	
1017	0.7	0938	0.9	
TH 1644	3.1	F 1617	2.8	
☽ 2245	1.0	☽ 2210	1.2	
		31 0445	2.9	
		1046	1.0	
		SA 1725	2.7	
		2349	1.2	

APRIL

Time	m		Time	m
1 0551	2.8	**16** 0106	1.1	
1234	1.0	0730	3.1	
SU 1834	2.7	M 1356	0.6	
		2009	3.0	
2 0112	1.1	**17** 0213	0.9	
0657	2.9	0829	3.2	
M 1339	0.8	TU 1452	0.5	
1940	2.8	2100	3.0	
3 0208	1.0	**18** 0307	0.8	
0758	3.1	0919	3.3	
TU 1430	0.6	W 1537	0.4	
2036	2.9	2144	3.1	
4 0256	0.8	**19** 0350	0.7	
0850	3.3	1002	3.3	
W 1514	0.4	TH 1613	0.5	
2121	3.2	2223	3.2	
5 0337	0.6	**20** 0424	0.7	
0936	3.5	1042	3.3	
TH 1554	0.2	F 1644	0.5	
2202	3.3	2259	3.2	
6 0416	0.4	**21** 0454	0.6	
1020	3.6	1118	3.3	
F 1632	0.1	SA 1713	0.6	
○ 2243	3.4	● 2332	3.3	
7 0455	0.3	**22** 0524	0.6	
1105	3.7	1149	3.3	
SA 1712	0.1	SU 1743	0.6	
2327	3.5			
8 0536	0.2	**23** 0002	3.3	
1153	3.7	0554	0.6	
SU 1755	0.2	M 1219	3.2	
		1813	0.7	
9 0014	3.5	**24** 0036	3.4	
0620	0.2	0626	0.6	
M 1245	3.7	TU 1251	3.2	
1840	0.3	1845	0.7	
10 0104	3.5	**25** 0111	3.4	
0708	0.2	0701	0.6	
TU 1338	3.6	W 1325	3.2	
1928	0.4	1921	0.8	
11 0155	3.5	**26** 0147	3.4	
0759	0.3	0739	0.6	
W 1432	3.4	TH 1404	3.1	
2021	0.6	2002	0.8	
12 0247	3.4	**27** 0225	3.3	
0857	0.4	0823	0.7	
TH 1530	3.2	F 1449	3.0	
2119	0.8	2048	1.0	
13 0344	3.3	**28** 0309	3.2	
1009	0.6	0912	0.8	
F 1636	3.0	SA 1544	2.9	
☽ 2231	0.9	2142	1.1	
14 0451	3.1	**29** 0403	3.1	
1134	0.7	1013	0.8	
SA 1754	2.9	SU 1651	2.8	
2352	1.1	☽ 2249	1.2	
15 0615	3.0	**30** 0508	3.0	
1248	0.6	1129	0.8	
SU 1909	2.9	M 1758	2.8	

Chart Datum: 2·01 metres below Ordnance Datum (Belfast)
HAT is 3·9m above Chart Datum

TIDES

TIDES

TIME ZONE (UT)
For Summer Time add ONE hour in **non-shaded areas**

NORTHERN IRELAND – BELFAST
LAT 54°36'N   LONG 5°55'W
TIMES AND HEIGHTS OF HIGH AND LOW WATERS

Dates in amber are **SPRINGS**
Dates in yellow are **NEAPS**

2012

MAY

Time	m	Time	m
1 TU 0014 / 0615 / 1251 / 1901	1.1 / 3.0 / 0.7 / 2.9	**16** W 0131 / 0754 / 1412 / 2026	1.0 / 3.1 / 0.6 / 3.0
2 W 0124 / 0718 / 1349 / 1957	1.0 / 3.2 / 0.5 / 3.0	**17** TH 0228 / 0847 / 1459 / 2112	1.0 / 3.2 / 0.6 / 3.1
3 TH 0218 / 0816 / 1437 / 2048	0.8 / 3.3 / 0.4 / 3.2	**18** F 0317 / 0934 / 1539 / 2153	0.9 / 3.2 / 0.6 / 3.2
4 F 0306 / 0908 / 1522 / 2136	0.6 / 3.5 / 0.3 / 3.4	**19** SA 0356 / 1015 / 1613 / 2230	0.8 / 3.2 / 0.7 / 3.3
5 SA 0350 / 0958 / 1605 / 2222	0.5 / 3.6 / 0.2 / 3.5	**20** SU 0431 / 1051 / 1646 / ● 2305	0.7 / 3.2 / 0.7 / 3.4
6 SU 0434 / 1047 / 1649 / ○ 2311	0.3 / 3.7 / 0.2 / 3.6	**21** M 0503 / 1125 / 1719 / 2339	0.7 / 3.2 / 0.7 / 3.4
7 M 0520 / 1138 / 1735	0.2 / 3.7 / 0.3	**22** TU 0536 / 1155 / 1752	0.7 / 3.2 / 0.7
8 TU 0000 / 0607 / 1231 / 1823	3.6 / 0.2 / 3.6 / 0.4	**23** W 0011 / 0609 / 1225 / 1827	3.5 / 0.6 / 3.2 / 0.8
9 W 0052 / 0657 / 1325 / 1914	3.6 / 0.2 / 3.5 / 0.5	**24** TH 0045 / 0644 / 1258 / 1904	3.5 / 0.6 / 3.2 / 0.8
10 TH 0143 / 0750 / 1420 / 2008	3.6 / 0.3 / 3.4 / 0.7	**25** F 0120 / 0722 / 1337 / 1945	3.5 / 0.6 / 3.1 / 0.8
11 F 0234 / 0848 / 1517 / 2106	3.5 / 0.4 / 3.2 / 0.8	**26** SA 0159 / 0804 / 1422 / 2029	3.4 / 0.6 / 3.1 / 0.9
12 SA 0328 / 0956 / 1619 / ◑ 2211	3.4 / 0.5 / 3.1 / 1.0	**27** SU 0242 / 0851 / 1514 / 2119	3.4 / 0.6 / 3.0 / 1.0
13 SU 0427 / 1108 / 1727 / 2320	3.3 / 0.6 / 2.9 / 1.1	**28** M 0332 / 0945 / 1613 / ◑ 2215	3.3 / 0.7 / 2.9 / 1.0
14 M 0537 / 1215 / 1835	3.1 / 0.6 / 2.9	**29** TU 0429 / 1047 / 1717 / 2319	3.2 / 0.7 / 2.9 / 1.0
15 TU 0027 / 0651 / 1317 / 1934	1.1 / 3.1 / 0.6 / 3.0	**30** W 0533 / 1155 / 1821	0.7 / 3.2 / 3.0
		31 TH 0029 / 0640 / 1303 / 1921	1.0 / 3.2 / 0.6 / 3.1

JUNE

Time	m	Time	m
1 F 0138 / 0744 / 1402 / 2019	0.9 / 3.3 / 0.5 / 3.2	**16** SA 0239 / 0903 / 1504 / 2121	1.0 / 3.1 / 0.8 / 3.2
2 SA 0237 / 0844 / 1455 / 2113	0.7 / 3.5 / 0.4 / 3.4	**17** SU 0327 / 0948 / 1544 / 2203	0.9 / 3.1 / 0.8 / 3.3
3 SU 0331 / 0940 / 1545 / 2205	0.5 / 3.6 / 0.4 / 3.5	**18** M 0407 / 1028 / 1621 / 2241	0.8 / 3.1 / 0.8 / 3.4
4 M 0421 / 1032 / 1633 / ○ 2256	0.4 / 3.6 / 0.4 / 3.6	**19** TU 0443 / 1104 / 1657 / ● 2317	0.7 / 3.2 / 0.7 / 3.4
5 TU 0510 / 1124 / 1722 / 2346	0.3 / 3.6 / 0.4 / 3.7	**20** W 0518 / 1136 / 1733 / 2349	0.7 / 3.2 / 0.7 / 3.5
6 W 0559 / 1216 / 1811	0.2 / 3.5 / 0.5	**21** TH 0553 / 1201 / 1810	0.6 / 3.2 / 0.7
7 TH 0037 / 0649 / 1310 / 1901	3.7 / 0.2 / 3.4 / 0.6	**22** F 0019 / 0629 / 1232 / 1847	3.5 / 0.5 / 3.2 / 0.8
8 F 0127 / 0740 / 1402 / 1953	3.7 / 0.3 / 3.3 / 0.7	**23** SA 0054 / 0706 / 1311 / 1927	3.5 / 0.5 / 3.2 / 0.8
9 SA 0216 / 0833 / 1456 / 2046	3.6 / 0.4 / 3.2 / 0.8	**24** SU 0133 / 0745 / 1356 / 2009	3.5 / 0.5 / 3.1 / 0.8
10 SU 0306 / 0931 / 1550 / 2141	3.5 / 0.5 / 3.1 / 0.9	**25** M 0217 / 0828 / 1444 / 2054	3.5 / 0.5 / 3.1 / 0.8
11 M 0357 / 1032 / 1645 / ◑ 2240	3.4 / 0.6 / 3.0 / 1.0	**26** TU 0305 / 0917 / 1538 / 2145	3.5 / 0.5 / 3.1 / 0.9
12 TU 0451 / 1134 / 1743 / ◑ 2342	3.2 / 0.7 / 3.0 / 1.1	**27** W 0358 / 1013 / 1637 / 2243	3.4 / 0.6 / 3.0 / 0.9
13 W 0551 / 1232 / 1842	3.1 / 0.8 / 3.0	**28** TH 0458 / 1115 / 1741 / 2350	3.3 / 0.7 / 3.0 / 0.9
14 TH 0044 / 0701 / 1327 / 1940	1.1 / 3.0 / 0.8 / 3.0	**29** F 0606 / 1226 / 1848	3.3 / 0.7 / 3.1
15 F 0144 / 0808 / 1418 / 2033	1.1 / 3.0 / 0.8 / 3.1	**30** SA 0107 / 0718 / 1337 / 1954	0.9 / 3.3 / 0.7 / 3.2

JULY

Time	m	Time	m
1 SU 0219 / 0827 / 1438 / 2057	0.8 / 3.3 / 0.6 / 3.3	**16** M 0257 / 0924 / 1517 / 2136	1.0 / 3.0 / 0.9 / 3.3
2 M 0319 / 0928 / 1533 / 2153	0.6 / 3.4 / 0.5 / 3.5	**17** TU 0342 / 1008 / 1557 / 2218	0.8 / 3.1 / 0.8 / 3.4
3 TU 0413 / 1022 / 1623 / ○ 2244	0.4 / 3.5 / 0.5 / 3.6	**18** W 0421 / 1044 / 1635 / 2253	0.7 / 3.1 / 0.7 / 3.4
4 W 0503 / 1112 / 1711 / 2333	0.3 / 3.5 / 0.5 / 3.7	**19** TH 0457 / 1115 / 1712 / ● 2322	0.6 / 3.2 / 0.7 / 3.5
5 TH 0551 / 1202 / 1758	0.2 / 3.4 / 0.6	**20** F 0533 / 1136 / 1749 / 2350	0.5 / 3.2 / 0.7 / 3.5
6 F 0021 / 0637 / 1251 / 1844	3.7 / 0.2 / 3.4 / 0.6	**21** SA 0609 / 1205 / 1826	0.4 / 3.2 / 0.7
7 SA 0108 / 0723 / 1339 / 1930	3.7 / 0.3 / 3.3 / 0.7	**22** SU 0026 / 0645 / 1245 / 1904	3.6 / 0.4 / 3.2 / 0.7
8 SU 0153 / 0808 / 1427 / 2015	3.6 / 0.4 / 3.2 / 0.8	**23** M 0108 / 0722 / 1329 / 1944	3.6 / 0.4 / 3.2 / 0.7
9 M 0238 / 0854 / 1513 / 2100	3.6 / 0.5 / 3.1 / 0.8	**24** TU 0153 / 0804 / 1417 / 2028	3.6 / 0.4 / 3.2 / 0.7
10 TU 0323 / 0943 / 1600 / 2149	3.4 / 0.7 / 3.1 / 0.9	**25** W 0241 / 0850 / 1508 / 2117	3.6 / 0.5 / 3.2 / 0.8
11 W 0410 / 1039 / 1648 / ◑ 2245	3.3 / 0.8 / 3.0 / 1.0	**26** TH 0333 / 0942 / 1605 / ◑ 2213	3.5 / 0.6 / 3.1 / 0.8
12 TH 0500 / 1141 / 1739 / 2352	3.1 / 0.9 / 3.0 / 1.1	**27** F 0432 / 1043 / 1709 / 2323	3.3 / 0.7 / 3.1 / 0.9
13 F 0556 / 1242 / 1835	2.9 / 1.0 / 3.0	**28** SA 0541 / 1158 / 1821	3.2 / 0.8 / 3.1
14 SA 0100 / 0702 / 1339 / 1940	1.2 / 2.9 / 1.0 / 3.1	**29** SU 0053 / 0700 / 1322 / 1940	0.9 / 3.1 / 0.9 / 3.1
15 SU 0203 / 0827 / 1431 / 2045	1.1 / 2.9 / 1.0 / 3.1	**30** M 0209 / 0819 / 1429 / 2049	0.8 / 3.2 / 0.8 / 3.3
		31 TU 0312 / 0922 / 1525 / 2145	0.6 / 3.3 / 0.7 / 3.5

AUGUST

Time	m	Time	m
1 W 0406 / 1015 / 1614 / 2234	0.4 / 3.4 / 0.6 / 3.6	**16** TH 0356 / 1019 / 1611 / 2221	0.6 / 3.1 / 0.7 / 3.4
2 TH 0454 / 1102 / 1659 / ○ 2319	0.3 / 3.4 / 0.6 / 3.7	**17** F 0433 / 1046 / 1648 / ● 2250	0.5 / 3.2 / 0.6 / 3.5
3 F 0538 / 1146 / 1742	0.2 / 3.3 / 0.6	**18** SA 0508 / 1109 / 1724 / 2322	0.4 / 3.2 / 0.6 / 3.6
4 SA 0003 / 0618 / 1230 / 1821	3.7 / 0.3 / 3.3 / 0.6	**19** SU 0543 / 1140 / 1800	0.3 / 3.3 / 0.6
5 SU 0046 / 0657 / 1312 / 1900	3.6 / 0.4 / 3.3 / 0.7	**20** M 0001 / 0619 / 1220 / 1837	3.7 / 0.3 / 3.3 / 0.6
6 M 0127 / 0733 / 1353 / 1937	3.6 / 0.5 / 3.2 / 0.8	**21** TU 0044 / 0657 / 1304 / 1918	3.7 / 0.3 / 3.3 / 0.6
7 TU 0207 / 0808 / 1435 / 2016	3.5 / 0.6 / 3.2 / 0.8	**22** W 0131 / 0738 / 1352 / 2003	3.7 / 0.4 / 3.3 / 0.6
8 W 0248 / 0845 / 1518 / 2058	3.4 / 0.7 / 3.2 / 0.9	**23** TH 0220 / 0824 / 1443 / 2053	3.6 / 0.5 / 3.3 / 0.7
9 TH 0331 / 0928 / 1604 / ◑ 2145	3.3 / 0.9 / 3.1 / 1.0	**24** F 0313 / 0916 / 1540 / ◑ 2152	3.5 / 0.7 / 3.3 / 0.8
10 F 0419 / 1022 / 1655 / 2246	3.1 / 1.0 / 3.1 / 1.1	**25** SA 0414 / 1018 / 1646 / 2310	3.3 / 0.8 / 3.1 / 0.9
11 SA 0513 / 1148 / 1750	2.9 / 1.2 / 3.0	**26** SU 0527 / 1141 / 1806	3.1 / 1.0 / 3.0
12 SU 0015 / 0614 / 1301 / 1851	1.2 / 2.8 / 1.2 / 3.0	**27** M 0047 / 0656 / 1312 / 1934	0.9 / 3.0 / 1.0 / 3.1
13 M 0128 / 0729 / 1359 / 2000	1.2 / 2.7 / 1.1 / 3.1	**28** TU 0202 / 0816 / 1420 / 2042	0.8 / 3.1 / 0.9 / 3.3
14 TU 0227 / 0859 / 1449 / 2104	1.0 / 2.9 / 1.0 / 3.2	**29** W 0305 / 0915 / 1516 / 2135	0.6 / 3.2 / 0.8 / 3.5
15 W 0315 / 0944 / 1532 / 2147	0.8 / 3.0 / 0.8 / 3.3	**30** TH 0357 / 1004 / 1603 / 2221	0.4 / 3.3 / 0.7 / 3.6
		31 F 0441 / 1047 / 1644 / ○ 2303	0.3 / 3.3 / 0.6 / 3.6

Chart Datum: 2·01 metres below Ordnance Datum (Belfast)
HAT is 3·9m above Chart Datum

TIME ZONE (UT)
For Summer Time add ONE hour in **non-shaded areas**

NORTHERN IRELAND – BELFAST
LAT 54°36'N   LONG 5°55'W
TIMES AND HEIGHTS OF HIGH AND LOW WATERS

Dates in amber are **SPRINGS**
Dates in yellow are **NEAPS**

2012

SEPTEMBER

Day	Time m		Day	Time m
1 SA	0520 0.3 / 1127 3.3 / 1721 0.6 / 2343 3.6		**16**	0439 0.3 / 1043 3.4 / 1656 0.5 / ● 2257 3.7
2 SU	0554 0.4 / 1205 3.3 / 1755 0.7		**17** M	0514 0.3 / 1118 3.4 / 1733 0.5 / 2339 3.8
3 M	0021 3.6 / 0625 0.5 / 1242 3.3 / 1827 0.7		**18** TU	0552 0.3 / 1159 3.5 / 1812 0.5
4 TU	0058 3.5 / 0655 0.6 / 1319 3.3 / 1900 0.7		**19** W	0025 3.8 / 0632 0.3 / 1244 3.5 / 1855 0.5
5 W	0134 3.4 / 0726 0.7 / 1358 3.3 / 1937 0.8		**20** TH	0115 3.7 / 0716 0.4 / 1333 3.5 / 1943 0.5
6 TH	0213 3.3 / 0801 0.8 / 1439 3.3 / 2017 0.8		**21** F	0207 3.6 / 0804 0.5 / 1426 3.4 / 2036 0.6
7 F	0254 3.2 / 0840 0.9 / 1524 3.2 / 2102 0.9		**22** SA	0303 3.4 / 0858 0.6 / 1524 3.3 / ◑ 2139 0.8
8 SA	0340 3.1 / 0927 1.1 / 1614 3.1 / ◐ 2156 1.1		**23** SU	0407 3.2 / 1002 1.0 / 1633 3.2 / 2306 0.9
9 SU	0434 2.9 / 1029 1.3 / 1710 3.0 / 2316 1.2		**24** M	0523 3.0 / 1130 1.2 / 1757 3.1
10 M	0537 2.7 / 1219 1.3 / 1811 3.0		**25** TU	0037 0.9 / 0651 3.0 / 1259 1.2 / 1921 3.2
11 TU	0052 1.2 / 0646 2.7 / 1327 1.2 / 1915 3.0		**26** W	0150 0.7 / 0803 3.1 / 1408 1.0 / 2025 3.3
12 W	0154 1.0 / 0808 2.8 / 1420 1.1 / 2018 3.2		**27** TH	0252 0.6 / 0858 3.2 / 1504 0.9 / 2117 3.5
13 TH	0244 0.8 / 0907 3.0 / 1505 0.9 / 2107 3.3		**28** F	0342 0.5 / 0945 3.3 / 1549 0.8 / 2202 3.6
14 F	0326 0.6 / 0942 3.2 / 1544 0.7 / 2145 3.5		**29** SA	0422 0.4 / 1027 3.3 / 1626 0.7 / 2243 3.6
15 SA	0404 0.4 / 1013 3.3 / 1621 0.6 / 2220 3.6		**30** SU	0456 0.5 / 1105 3.4 / 1658 0.7 / ○ 2321 3.5

OCTOBER

Day	Time m		Day	Time m
1 M	0526 0.6 / 1140 3.4 / 1729 0.7 / 2356 3.5		**16** TU	0446 0.3 / 1100 3.6 / 1709 0.5 / 2323 3.8
2 TU	0554 0.7 / 1213 3.4 / 1759 0.7		**17** W	0527 0.3 / 1144 3.7 / 1752 0.4
3 W	0028 3.4 / 0622 0.7 / 1247 3.4 / 1831 0.7		**18** TH	0013 3.8 / 0611 0.4 / 1232 3.7 / 1838 0.4
4 TH	0102 3.4 / 0652 0.8 / 1324 3.5 / 1906 0.8		**19** F	0106 3.7 / 0658 0.5 / 1324 3.6 / 1929 0.5
5 F	0139 3.3 / 0727 0.9 / 1404 3.4 / 1945 0.8		**20** SA	0200 3.6 / 0749 0.7 / 1417 3.6 / 2025 0.6
6 SA	0219 3.2 / 0806 1.0 / 1446 3.4 / 2029 0.9		**21** SU	0258 3.4 / 0845 0.9 / 1515 3.5 / 2131 0.7
7 SU	0303 3.1 / 0852 1.1 / 1534 3.2 / ◐ 2120 1.1		**22** M	0402 3.2 / 0951 1.1 / 1621 3.3 / ◑ 2256 0.8
8 M	0358 2.9 / 0947 1.3 / 1630 3.1 / ◐ 2224 1.2		**23** TU	0515 3.1 / 1112 1.2 / 1739 3.2
9 TU	0503 2.8 / 1108 1.4 / 1732 3.0		**24** W	0017 0.8 / 0633 3.0 / 1234 1.2 / 1856 3.3
10 W	0002 1.2 / 0610 2.8 / 1246 1.3 / 1835 3.1		**25** TH	0126 0.8 / 0739 3.1 / 1343 1.1 / 1959 3.4
11 TH	0114 1.0 / 0717 2.9 / 1344 1.1 / 1935 3.2		**26** F	0226 0.7 / 0833 3.2 / 1441 1.0 / 2052 3.4
12 F	0207 0.8 / 0816 3.1 / 1432 1.0 / 2027 3.4		**27** SA	0316 0.6 / 0920 3.3 / 1527 0.9 / 2139 3.5
13 SA	0251 0.6 / 0902 3.3 / 1514 0.8 / 2113 3.6		**28** SU	0355 0.6 / 1002 3.4 / 1604 0.8 / ● 2221 3.5
14 SU	0330 0.5 / 0942 3.4 / 1552 0.7 / 2155 3.7		**29** M	0428 0.7 / 1041 3.4 / 1636 0.8 / ○ 2259 3.5
15 M	0408 0.4 / 1020 3.5 / 1629 0.5 / ● 2237 3.8		**30** TU	0457 0.8 / 1116 3.5 / 1707 0.8 / ● 2333 3.4
			31 W	0527 0.8 / 1147 3.5 / 1738 0.8

NOVEMBER

Day	Time m		Day	Time m
1 TH	0003 3.4 / 0556 0.9 / 1220 3.6 / 1809 0.8		**16** F	0002 3.8 / 0555 0.5 / 1223 3.8 / 1828 0.4
2 F	0035 3.4 / 0628 0.9 / 1256 3.6 / 1844 0.8		**17** SA	0056 3.7 / 0645 0.6 / 1315 3.8 / 1920 0.5
3 SA	0111 3.3 / 0703 0.9 / 1333 3.6 / 1922 0.8		**18** SU	0151 3.6 / 0737 0.8 / 1408 3.7 / 2016 0.5
4 SU	0148 3.3 / 0742 1.0 / 1413 3.5 / 2005 0.9		**19** M	0248 3.4 / 0833 0.9 / 1503 3.6 / 2119 0.6
5 M	0230 3.2 / 0827 1.1 / 1455 3.4 / 2053 1.0		**20** TU	0348 3.3 / 0934 1.1 / 1602 3.5 / ◑ 2232 0.7
6 TU	0321 3.0 / 0919 1.2 / 1546 3.3 / 2149 1.0		**21** W	0454 3.2 / 1044 1.2 / 1709 3.4 / 2344 0.8
7 W	0425 2.9 / 1021 1.3 / 1647 3.2 / ◐ 2256 1.1		**22** TH	0602 3.1 / 1156 1.2 / 1821 3.3
8 TH	0532 2.9 / 1137 1.4 / 1752 3.2		**23** F	0048 0.8 / 0705 3.1 / 1303 1.2 / 1926 3.3
9 F	0013 1.0 / 0636 3.0 / 1253 1.3 / 1853 3.4		**24** SA	0147 0.8 / 0802 3.2 / 1404 1.1 / 2024 3.3
10 SA	0118 0.9 / 0734 3.1 / 1351 1.1 / 1951 3.4		**25** SU	0239 0.8 / 0852 3.3 / 1456 1.0 / 2114 3.4
11 SU	0210 0.7 / 0826 3.3 / 1440 0.9 / 2043 3.6		**26** M	0322 0.8 / 0936 3.4 / 1540 1.0 / 2159 3.4
12 M	0256 0.6 / 0913 3.5 / 1525 0.7 / 2133 3.7		**27** TU	0359 0.9 / 1017 3.5 / 1616 0.9 / 2239 3.4
13 TU	0339 0.5 / 0959 3.6 / 1608 0.6 / ● 2221 3.8		**28** W	0432 0.9 / 1054 3.6 / 1649 0.9 / ○ 2314 3.4
14 W	0423 0.4 / 1045 3.7 / 1653 0.5 / 2311 3.8		**29** TH	0505 0.9 / 1128 3.6 / 1722 0.8 / 2346 3.3
15 TH	0508 0.5 / 1133 3.8 / 1739 0.4		**30** F	0537 1.0 / 1201 3.6 / 1755 0.8

DECEMBER

Day	Time m		Day	Time m
1 SA	0016 3.3 / 0611 0.9 / 1234 3.7 / 1829 0.8		**16** SU	0043 3.6 / 0633 0.6 / 1302 3.9 / 1911 0.4
2 SU	0047 3.3 / 0647 0.9 / 1308 3.6 / 1906 0.8		**17** M	0137 3.6 / 0723 0.7 / 1353 3.8 / 2003 0.4
3 M	0121 3.3 / 0725 1.0 / 1343 3.6 / 1946 0.8		**18** TU	0230 3.4 / 0815 0.8 / 1444 3.7 / 2058 0.5
4 TU	0201 3.2 / 0807 1.0 / 1423 3.5 / 2029 0.8		**19** W	0324 3.3 / 0909 0.9 / 1536 3.6 / 2159 0.7
5 W	0247 3.1 / 0853 1.1 / 1509 3.5 / 2119 0.9		**20** TH	0419 3.2 / 1007 1.1 / 1630 3.5 / ◑ 2302 0.8
6 TH	0340 3.1 / 0946 1.2 / 1602 3.4 / ◑ 2215 0.9		**21** F	0516 3.1 / 1112 1.2 / 1729 3.3
7 F	0442 3.0 / 1046 1.2 / 1703 3.3 / 2318 0.9		**22** SA	0004 0.9 / 0617 3.1 / 1218 1.2 / 1838 3.2
8 SA	0549 3.1 / 1154 1.2 / 1810 3.3		**23** SU	0102 1.0 / 0720 3.1 / 1321 1.2 / 1948 3.1
9 SU	0025 0.9 / 0652 3.1 / 1306 1.1 / 1915 3.4		**24** M	0158 1.0 / 0819 3.2 / 1421 1.1 / 2048 3.2
10 M	0131 0.8 / 0752 3.3 / 1409 1.0 / 2017 3.5		**25** TU	0248 1.0 / 0910 3.3 / 1513 1.0 / 2138 3.2
11 TU	0228 0.7 / 0849 3.4 / 1505 0.8 / 2114 3.6		**26** W	0332 0.9 / 0955 3.4 / 1555 0.9 / 2220 3.2
12 W	0319 0.6 / 0941 3.6 / 1555 0.6 / 2207 3.7		**27** TH	0410 0.9 / 1035 3.5 / 1632 0.8 / 2259 3.3
13 TH	0408 0.5 / 1032 3.7 / 1644 0.5 / ● 2259 3.7		**28** F	0445 0.9 / 1112 3.6 / 1705 0.8 / ○ 2333 3.3
14 F	0456 0.5 / 1121 3.8 / 1732 0.4 / 2351 3.7		**29** SA	0520 0.8 / 1145 3.6 / 1740 0.7
15 SA	0544 0.6 / 1212 3.8 / 1821 0.3		**30** SU	0002 3.3 / 0554 0.8 / 1215 3.6 / 1814 0.7
			31 M	0024 3.2 / 0631 0.8 / 1242 3.6 / 1850 0.6

TIDES

Chart Datum: 2·01 metres below Ordnance Datum (Belfast)
HAT is 3·9m above Chart Datum

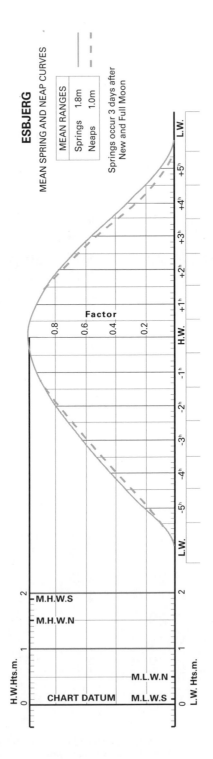

ESBJERG

MEAN SPRING AND NEAP CURVES

MEAN RANGES	
Springs	1.8m
Neaps	1.0m

Springs occur 3 days after
New and Full Moon

TIME ZONE -0100
(Danish Standard Time)
Subtract 1 hour for UT
For Danish Summer Time add
ONE hour in **non-shaded areas**

DENMARK – ESBJERG

LAT 55°28'N   LONG 8°26'E

TIMES AND HEIGHTS OF HIGH AND LOW WATERS

Dates in amber are **SPRINGS**
Dates in yellow are **NEAPS**

2012

JANUARY

Day	Time m	Time m	Time m	Time m
1 SU ☽	0115 0.4	0742 1.9	1354 0.5	2015 1.7
2 M	0203 0.5	0833 1.9	1445 0.5	2110 1.7
3 TU	0258 0.5	0933 1.8	1542 0.6	2212 1.7
4 W	0403 0.6	1037 1.8	1648 0.6	2316 1.7
5 TH	0516 0.6	1142 1.8	1752 0.5	
6 F	0017 1.8	0623 0.5	1242 1.8	1848 0.5
7 SA	0112 1.8	0718 0.5	1336 1.8	1934 0.5
8 SU	0201 1.9	0803 0.4	1425 1.8	2015 0.4
9 M ○	0245 1.9	0844 0.3	1509 1.8	2059 0.4
10 TU	0324 2.0	0922 0.3	1550 1.8	2131 0.3
11 W	0401 2.0	1000 0.2	1627 1.8	2209 0.3
12 TH	0436 2.0	1039 0.2	1705 1.8	2249 0.2
13 F	0513 2.0	1120 0.1	1742 1.8	2331 0.2
14 SA	0551 2.1	1203 0.1	1822 1.8	
15 SU	0015 0.2	0635 2.0	1248 0.2	1906 1.8
16 M	0102 0.2	0723 2.0	1337 0.2	1957 1.7
17 TU	0154 0.2	0820 1.9	1432 0.3	2056 1.7
18 W	0253 0.3	0927 1.9	1533 0.4	2206 1.7
19 TH	0401 0.4	1045 1.8	1644 0.4	2321 1.7
20 F	0518 0.4	1201 1.8	1756 0.4	
21 SA	0031 1.8	0631 0.5	1309 1.8	1859 0.4
22 SU	0133 1.9	0733 0.2	1409 1.8	1954 0.3
23 M	0227 1.9	0827 0.2	1502 1.8	2042 0.3
24 TU	0316 2.0	0915 0.1	1547 1.8	2126 0.2
25 W	0400 2.0	0959 0.1	1627 1.7	2207 0.2
26 TH	0439 2.0	1039 0.1	1703 1.7	2245 0.2
27 F	0515 2.0	1118 0.2	1736 1.7	2323 0.2
28 SA	0548 1.9	1154 0.2	1808 1.7	
29 SU	0000 0.2	0621 1.9	1230 0.3	1841 1.7
30 M	0038 0.3	0657 1.8	1306 0.4	1919 1.7
31 TU ☽	0119 0.3	0739 1.8	1347 0.4	2005 1.7

FEBRUARY

Day	Time m	Time m	Time m	Time m
1 W	0205 0.4	0830 1.7	1435 0.5	2101 1.6
2 TH	0300 0.5	0933 1.7	1533 0.5	2210 1.6
3 F	0409 0.5	1048 1.6	1646 0.5	2324 1.7
4 SA	0533 0.5	1200 1.6	1801 0.5	
5 SU	0030 1.7	0642 0.4	1303 1.7	1900 0.4
6 M	0127 1.8	0735 0.3	1358 1.7	1948 0.3
7 TU ○	0217 1.8	0819 0.2	1446 1.8	2030 0.2
8 W	0301 1.9	0900 0.1	1529 1.8	2110 0.2
9 TH	0341 2.0	0939 0.0	1609 1.8	2150 0.1
10 F	0420 2.0	1019 0.0	1647 1.8	2230 0.0
11 SA	0458 2.0	1100 0.0	1724 1.8	2312 0.0
12 SU	0538 2.0	1142 0.0	1803 1.7	2355 0.0
13 M	0621 2.0	1226 0.1	1845 1.7	
14 TU ☽	0042 0.0	0708 1.9	1313 0.2	1932 1.7
15 W	0133 0.1	0804 1.8	1406 0.3	2030 1.6
16 TH	0231 0.2	0912 1.7	1506 0.4	2142 1.6
17 F	0342 0.3	1033 1.6	1621 0.4	2302 1.6
18 SA	0507 0.3	1151 1.6	1740 0.4	
19 SU	0015 1.7	0622 0.2	1259 1.6	1845 0.3
20 M	0118 1.8	0723 0.1	1356 1.7	1939 0.2
21 TU ●	0212 1.9	0813 0.1	1445 1.7	2025 0.1
22 W	0300 1.9	0858 0.0	1528 1.7	2108 0.1
23 TH	0342 1.9	0939 0.0	1605 1.7	2147 0.1
24 F	0418 1.9	1015 0.1	1637 1.7	2223 0.1
25 SA	0451 1.9	1049 0.1	1706 1.7	2257 0.1
26 SU	0520 1.8	1121 0.2	1733 1.7	2330 0.1
27 M	0548 1.8	1151 0.2	1800 1.7	2355 0.0
28 TU	0004 0.1	0618 1.7	1224 0.3	1833 1.7
29 W	0041 0.2	0655 1.7	1302 0.3	1914 1.6

MARCH

Day	Time m	Time m	Time m	Time m
1 TH ☽	0124 0.2	0742 1.6	1345 0.3	2004 1.6
2 F	0214 0.3	0839 1.6	1439 0.4	2106 1.6
3 SA	0316 0.4	0952 1.5	1546 0.4	2224 1.6
4 SU	0439 0.4	1117 1.5	1709 0.4	2344 1.6
5 M	0601 0.3	1228 1.6	1821 0.3	
6 TU	0049 1.7	0701 0.2	1327 1.6	1915 0.2
7 W	0144 1.8	0749 0.1	1418 1.7	2003 0.1
8 TH ○	0233 1.9	0833 0.0	1503 1.7	2046 0.0
9 F	0317 1.9	0915 -0.1	1545 1.7	2127 -0.1
10 SA	0359 1.9	0956 -0.1	1624 1.7	2209 -0.1
11 SU	0440 1.9	1036 -0.1	1703 1.7	2252 -0.2
12 M	0521 1.9	1118 -0.1	1742 1.7	2336 -0.1
13 TU	0606 1.8	1203 0.0	1823 1.7	
14 W	0023 -0.1	0654 1.7	1249 0.1	1911 1.6
15 TH ☽	0115 0.0	0751 1.6	1342 0.2	2009 1.6
16 F	0215 0.1	0903 1.5	1444 0.4	2123 1.6
17 SA	0330 0.2	1023 1.5	1602 0.4	2244 1.6
18 SU	0457 0.2	1137 1.5	1722 0.3	2356 1.7
19 M	0608 0.1	1241 1.6	1826 0.2	
20 TU	0057 1.7	0705 0.0	1336 1.6	1918 0.1
21 W	0151 1.8	0753 0.0	1423 1.7	2005 0.0
22 TH	0239 1.8	0836 0.0	1504 1.7	2046 0.0
23 F	0320 1.8	0915 0.0	1540 1.7	2124 0.0
24 SA	0355 1.8	0949 0.1	1611 1.7	2159 0.0
25 SU	0426 1.7	1020 0.1	1638 1.6	2231 0.0
26 M	0453 1.7	1048 0.1	1703 1.6	2302 0.0
27 TU	0518 1.6	1118 0.1	1727 1.6	2335 0.1
28 W	0546 1.6	1149 0.1	1757 1.6	
29 TH	0011 0.1	0621 1.6	1227 0.2	1836 1.6
30 F ☽	0053 0.1	0706 1.5	1310 0.2	1924 1.6
31 SA	0142 0.2	0801 1.5	1402 0.3	2021 1.6

APRIL

Day	Time m	Time m	Time m	Time m
1 SU	0242 0.2	0910 1.4	1506 0.3	2131 1.6
2 M	0356 0.3	1033 1.4	1623 0.3	2254 1.6
3 TU	0517 0.2	1150 1.5	1739 0.3	
4 W	0008 1.6	0623 0.1	1253 1.6	1840 0.2
5 TH	0109 1.7	0716 0.0	1347 1.6	1932 0.1
6 F ○	0202 1.8	0803 -0.1	1435 1.7	2019 -0.1
7 SA	0251 1.8	0848 -0.2	1518 1.7	2104 -0.2
8 SU	0336 1.8	0931 -0.2	1600 1.7	2148 -0.2
9 M	0421 1.8	1014 -0.1	1641 1.7	2233 -0.2
10 TU	0506 1.8	1057 -0.1	1721 1.7	2318 -0.2
11 W	0551 1.7	1141 0.0	1805 1.7	
12 TH	0007 -0.1	0642 1.6	1228 0.1	1854 1.6
13 F ☽	0100 0.0	0740 1.5	1321 0.2	1952 1.6
14 SA	0202 0.1	0849 1.4	1423 0.3	2103 1.6
15 SU	0316 0.2	1003 1.4	1539 0.3	2220 1.6
16 M	0437 0.1	1112 1.4	1655 0.3	2329 1.6
17 TU	0544 0.1	1213 1.5	1759 0.2	
18 W	0030 1.7	0639 0.0	1306 1.6	1853 0.1
19 TH	0124 1.8	0727 0.0	1354 1.6	1941 0.0
20 F	0212 1.8	0810 0.0	1436 1.7	2024 0.0
21 SA ●	0254 1.7	0848 0.0	1513 1.7	2102 0.0
22 SU	0330 1.7	0922 0.0	1546 1.6	2136 0.0
23 M	0402 1.6	0951 0.1	1614 1.6	2208 0.0
24 TU	0430 1.6	1020 0.1	1639 1.6	2239 0.0
25 W	0455 1.5	1049 0.1	1703 1.6	2312 0.0
26 TH	0523 1.5	1123 0.1	1733 1.6	2348 0.1
27 F	0558 1.5	1200 0.1	1809 1.7	
28 SA ☽	0030 0.1	0642 1.6	1245 0.1	1855 1.7
29 SU	0119 0.1	0735 1.5	1336 0.2	1949 1.6
30 M	0216 0.1	0839 1.4	1436 0.2	2054 1.6

Chart Datum: 0·69 metres below Dansk Normal Null
HAT is 2·2 metres above Chart Datum

TIDES

TIDES

DENMARK – ESBJERG

LAT 55°28'N LONG 8°26'E

TIMES AND HEIGHTS OF HIGH AND LOW WATERS

TIME ZONE -0100
(Danish Standard Time)
Subtract 1 hour for UT
For Danish Summer Time add
ONE hour in **non-shaded areas**

Dates in amber are **SPRINGS**
Dates in yellow are **NEAPS**

2012

MAY

Day	Time	m	Time	m	Time	m	Time	m
1 TU	0323	0.1	0954	1.4	1545	0.2	2209	1.6
2 W	0436	0.1	1110	1.5	1658	0.2	2327	1.6
3 TH	0544	0.0	1216	1.5	1804	0.1		
4 F	0033	1.7	0642	0.0	1314	1.6	1901	0.0
5 SA	0133	1.7	0734	-0.1	1406	1.6	1954	-0.1
6 SU ○	0227	1.8	0822	-0.1	1454	1.7	2042	-0.2
7 M	0317	1.8	0908	-0.1	1538	1.7	2130	-0.2
8 TU	0405	1.7	0952	-0.1	1621	1.7	2217	-0.2
9 W	0451	1.7	1037	0.0	1705	1.7	2305	-0.2
10 TH	0539	1.6	1122	0.0	1750	1.7	2354	-0.1
11 F	0630	1.5	1210	0.1	1839	1.7		
12 SA ◐	0047	0.0	0725	1.4	1301	0.2	1935	1.7
13 SU	0145	0.1	0826	1.4	1400	0.2	2039	1.6
14 M	0252	0.1	0932	1.4	1506	0.3	2147	1.6
15 TU	0404	0.1	1036	1.4	1618	0.3	2254	1.6
16 W	0510	0.1	1136	1.5	1725	0.2	2355	1.7
17 TH	0607	0.1	1230	1.6	1823	0.1		
18 F	0050	1.7	0657	0.1	1320	1.6	1914	0.1
19 SA ○	0140	1.7	0742	0.0	1406	1.7	1959	0.0
20 SU	0225	1.7	0821	0.0	1446	1.7	2039	0.0
21 M ●	0305	1.6	0856	0.1	1522	1.7	2115	0.1
22 TU	0339	1.6	0927	0.1	1553	1.7	2148	0.1
23 W	0410	1.5	0957	0.1	1621	1.7	2220	0.1
24 TH	0439	1.5	1028	0.1	1648	1.7	2254	0.1
25 F	0509	1.5	1103	0.1	1717	1.7	2332	0.0
26 SA	0545	1.5	1142	0.1	1753	1.7		
27 SU	0014	0.0	0626	1.5	1226	0.1	1836	1.7
28 M ◑	0101	0.0	0715	1.5	1315	0.1	1927	1.7
29 TU	0154	0.0	0812	1.5	1411	0.2	2025	1.7
30 W	0254	0.1	0918	1.5	1513	0.2	2134	1.7
31 TH	0359	0.1	1030	1.5	1621	0.2	2249	1.7

JUNE

Day	Time	m	Time	m	Time	m	Time	m
1 F	0506	0.1	1139	1.5	1730	0.1		
2 SA	0002	1.7	0609	0.1	1242	1.6	1833	0.1
3 SU	0107	1.7	0707	0.0	1339	1.6	1931	0.0
4 M ○	0206	1.7	0759	0.0	1432	1.7	2025	-0.1
5 TU	0300	1.7	0848	0.0	1521	1.7	2115	-0.1
6 W	0351	1.7	0935	0.0	1606	1.8	2204	-0.1
7 TH	0439	1.6	1021	0.0	1651	1.8	2252	-0.1
8 F	0526	1.6	1106	0.1	1736	1.8	2340	-0.1
9 SA	0612	1.5	1151	0.1	1822	1.8		
10 SU	0030	0.0	0700	1.5	1239	0.1	1912	1.7
11 M ◐	0121	0.1	0752	1.4	1330	0.2	2006	1.7
12 TU	0217	0.1	0848	1.4	1427	0.2	2106	1.7
13 W	0318	0.2	0948	1.5	1531	0.3	2209	1.7
14 TH	0424	0.2	1049	1.5	1641	0.3	2312	1.6
15 F	0526	0.2	1148	1.6	1746	0.2		
16 SA	0011	1.6	0621	0.2	1242	1.6	1844	0.2
17 SU	0105	1.6	0710	0.2	1332	1.7	1934	0.2
18 M	0154	1.6	0753	0.2	1418	1.7	2018	0.2
19 TU ●	0239	1.6	0831	0.2	1458	1.7	2056	0.1
20 W	0318	1.6	0905	0.2	1533	1.7	2130	0.1
21 TH	0354	1.6	0937	0.2	1606	1.7	2204	0.1
22 F	0427	1.6	1011	0.2	1636	1.8	2239	0.1
23 SA	0500	1.6	1047	0.1	1706	1.8	2317	0.0
24 SU	0534	1.6	1127	0.1	1742	1.8	2358	0.0
25 M	0612	1.6	1209	0.1	1822	1.8		
26 TU	0042	0.0	0657	1.6	1256	0.1	1909	1.8
27 W ◐	0132	0.0	0747	1.6	1347	0.1	2003	1.8
28 TH	0225	0.1	0845	1.5	1444	0.2	2106	1.8
29 F	0326	0.2	0952	1.5	1548	0.2	2220	1.7
30 SA	0432	0.2	1105	1.5	1700	0.2	2337	1.7

JULY

Day	Time	m	Time	m	Time	m	Time	m
1 SU	0541	0.2	1215	1.6	1811	0.2		
2 M	0049	1.7	0645	0.2	1318	1.6	1915	0.1
3 TU ○	0152	1.7	0742	0.2	1415	1.7	2012	0.0
4 W	0249	1.7	0833	0.1	1506	1.8	2104	0.0
5 TH	0340	1.7	0920	0.1	1554	1.9	2152	0.0
6 F	0426	1.7	1005	0.1	1638	1.9	2238	0.0
7 SA	0509	1.6	1048	0.1	1720	1.9	2322	0.0
8 SU	0550	1.6	1130	0.1	1801	1.9		
9 M	0006	0.1	0630	1.6	1214	0.1	1843	1.8
10 TU	0050	0.1	0712	1.6	1258	0.2	1928	1.8
11 W ◐	0136	0.2	0758	1.5	1345	0.2	2018	1.7
12 TH	0224	0.3	0851	1.5	1439	0.3	2115	1.7
13 F	0321	0.4	0951	1.5	1543	0.4	2219	1.6
14 SA	0427	0.4	1056	1.6	1658	0.4	2324	1.6
15 SU	0536	0.4	1158	1.6	1809	0.4		
16 M	0026	1.6	0634	0.4	1255	1.7	1906	0.3
17 TU	0121	1.7	0723	0.3	1346	1.7	1954	0.3
18 W	0211	1.7	0805	0.3	1431	1.8	2034	0.2
19 TH ●	0255	1.7	0842	0.2	1512	1.8	2110	0.2
20 F	0335	1.7	0918	0.2	1547	1.9	2145	0.1
21 SA	0411	1.7	0953	0.2	1621	1.9	2221	0.1
22 SU	0445	1.7	1030	0.1	1654	1.9	2259	0.0
23 M	0521	1.7	1109	0.1	1730	1.9	2339	0.0
24 TU	0557	1.7	1151	0.1	1809	2.0		
25 W	0022	0.0	0637	1.7	1236	0.1	1853	1.9
26 TH ◐	0108	0.1	0723	1.7	1324	0.1	1945	1.9
27 F	0159	0.2	0815	1.7	1419	0.2	2045	1.8
28 SA	0256	0.3	0920	1.6	1522	0.3	2200	1.7
29 SU	0403	0.4	1037	1.6	1637	0.3	2322	1.7
30 M	0518	0.4	1154	1.7	1757	0.3		
31 TU	0037	1.7	0627	0.4	1302	1.8	1904	0.2

AUGUST

Day	Time	m	Time	m	Time	m	Time	m
1 W	0142	1.7	0727	0.3	1401	1.9	2002	0.1
2 TH ○	0237	1.8	0818	0.2	1453	1.9	2052	0.1
3 F	0326	1.8	0904	0.2	1539	2.0	2137	0.0
4 SA	0409	1.8	0948	0.1	1621	2.0	2220	0.1
5 SU	0447	1.7	1028	0.1	1700	2.0	2300	0.1
6 M	0522	1.7	1107	0.1	1736	2.0	2337	0.2
7 TU	0556	1.7	1146	0.2	1812	1.9		
8 W	0015	0.2	0630	1.7	1225	0.2	1848	1.9
9 TH	0052	0.3	0706	1.7	1306	0.3	1929	1.8
10 F	0133	0.4	0750	1.7	1351	0.4	2017	1.7
11 SA	0218	0.5	0843	1.7	1444	0.5	2117	1.7
12 SU	0314	0.5	0950	1.7	1552	0.5	2230	1.6
13 M	0427	0.6	1104	1.7	1720	0.5	2342	1.6
14 TU	0547	0.6	1212	1.7	1830	0.5		
15 W	0045	1.7	0647	0.5	1309	1.8	1922	0.4
16 TH	0140	1.7	0734	0.4	1400	1.9	2006	0.3
17 F ●	0228	1.8	0815	0.3	1444	1.9	2045	0.2
18 SA	0311	1.8	0854	0.2	1524	2.0	2121	0.2
19 SU	0350	1.8	0932	0.2	1601	2.0	2159	0.1
20 M	0427	1.9	1010	0.1	1638	2.1	2238	0.1
21 TU	0502	1.9	1050	0.1	1715	2.1	2318	0.1
22 W	0538	1.8	1132	0.1	1755	2.0		
23 TH	0000	0.1	0617	1.8	1216	0.1	1839	2.0
24 F ◑	0045	0.2	0700	1.8	1304	0.2	1930	1.9
25 SA	0134	0.3	0752	1.8	1359	0.3	2033	1.8
26 SU	0231	0.4	0857	1.7	1504	0.4	2151	1.7
27 M	0339	0.5	1018	1.7	1624	0.4	2314	1.7
28 TU	0500	0.5	1139	1.8	1747	0.4		
29 W	0027	1.7	0612	0.5	1247	1.9	1853	0.3
30 TH	0129	1.8	0711	0.3	1345	2.0	1948	0.2
31 F ○	0221	1.8	0801	0.3	1436	2.1	2035	0.1

Chart Datum: 0·69 metres below Dansk Normal Null
HAT is 2·2 metres above Chart Datum

TIME ZONE -0100
(Danish Standard Time)
Subtract 1 hour for UT
For Danish Summer Time add ONE hour in **non-shaded areas**

DENMARK – ESBJERG

LAT 55°28'N   LONG 8°26'E

TIMES AND HEIGHTS OF HIGH AND LOW WATERS

Dates in amber are **SPRINGS**
Dates in yellow are **NEAPS**

2012

SEPTEMBER

Time m	Time m
1 0307 1.9 / 0846 0.2 / SA 1521 2.1 / 2118 0.1	**16** 0242 1.9 / 0827 0.3 / SU 1457 2.1 / ● 2054 0.2
2 0347 1.9 / 0927 0.2 / SU 1602 2.1 / 2157 0.2	**17** 0324 2.0 / 0907 0.2 / M 1538 2.1 / 2134 0.1
3 0422 1.9 / 1006 0.2 / M 1637 2.1 / 2233 0.2	**18** 0403 2.0 / 0948 0.1 / TU 1618 2.1 / 2214 0.1
4 0454 1.9 / 1043 0.2 / TU 1709 2.0 / 2307 0.3	**19** 0441 2.0 / 1030 0.1 / W 1659 2.1 / 2255 0.2
5 0523 1.9 / 1118 0.2 / W 1739 1.9 / 2339 0.4	**20** 0518 2.0 / 1113 0.1 / TH 1741 2.1 / 2338 0.2
6 0551 1.9 / 1153 0.3 / TH 1810 1.9	**21** 0558 2.0 / 1158 0.2 / F 1827 2.0
7 0012 0.4 / 0622 1.8 / F 1230 0.4 / 1845 1.8	**22** 0023 0.3 / 0642 1.9 / SA 1248 0.2 / ◑ 1921 1.9
8 0048 0.5 / 0700 1.8 / SA 1310 0.4 / ◗ 1927 1.8	**23** 0113 0.5 / 0736 1.9 / SU 1344 0.4 / 2025 1.9
9 0130 0.5 / 0747 1.8 / SU 1357 0.5 / 2021 1.7	**24** 0210 0.6 / 0842 1.9 / M 1451 0.5 / 2144 1.8
10 0219 0.6 / 0845 1.8 / M 1457 0.6 / 2131 1.7	**25** 0321 0.6 / 1003 1.9 / TU 1615 0.6 / 2303 1.8
11 0322 0.7 / 1000 1.8 / TU 1616 0.6 / 2253 1.7	**26** 0442 0.6 / 1121 1.9 / W 1733 0.4
12 0445 0.7 / 1120 1.8 / W 1742 0.6	**27** 0010 1.8 / 0553 0.6 / TH 1227 2.0 / 1836 0.3
13 0006 1.7 / 0600 0.6 / TH 1227 1.9 / 1842 0.5	**28** 0109 1.9 / 0651 0.4 / F 1325 2.1 / 1927 0.3
14 0106 1.8 / 0657 0.5 / F 1323 2.0 / 1931 0.3	**29** 0159 1.9 / 0741 0.3 / SA 1415 2.1 / 2013 0.3
15 0157 1.9 / 0744 0.4 / SA 1412 2.0 / 2014 0.3	**30** 0243 2.0 / 0825 0.3 / SU 1500 2.1 / ○ 2054 0.2

OCTOBER

Time m	Time m
1 0322 2.0 / 0906 0.2 / M 1539 2.1 / 2132 0.3	**16** 0257 2.0 / 0842 0.2 / TU 1515 2.2 / 2109 0.2
2 0357 2.0 / 0944 0.3 / TU 1614 2.1 / 2206 0.3	**17** 0339 2.1 / 0927 0.2 / W 1559 2.1 / 2151 0.2
3 0427 2.0 / 1019 0.3 / W 1644 2.0 / 2237 0.4	**18** 0420 2.1 / 1011 0.2 / TH 1643 2.1 / 2234 0.3
4 0454 2.0 / 1052 0.3 / TH 1711 1.9 / 2306 0.4	**19** 0500 2.1 / 1057 0.2 / F 1729 2.0 / 2318 0.3
5 0519 2.0 / 1124 0.4 / F 1738 1.9 / 2338 0.5	**20** 0542 2.0 / 1144 0.2 / SA 1818 2.0
6 0547 2.0 / 1200 0.4 / SA 1810 1.9	**21** 0004 0.4 / 0629 2.0 / SU 1235 0.3 / 1912 1.9
7 0012 0.5 / 0622 1.9 / SU 1239 0.5 / 1851 1.8	**22** 0055 0.5 / 0724 2.0 / M 1333 0.4 / ◑ 2017 1.9
8 0053 0.5 / 0706 1.9 / M 1324 0.5 / ◗ 1942 1.8	**23** 0152 0.6 / 0830 2.0 / TU 1439 0.5 / 2129 1.8
9 0141 0.6 / 0800 1.9 / TU 1419 0.6 / 2045 1.8	**24** 0300 0.7 / 0944 2.0 / W 1557 0.5 / 2240 1.8
10 0240 0.7 / 0904 1.9 / W 1528 0.6 / 2203 1.8	**25** 0417 0.6 / 1057 2.0 / TH 1710 0.4 / 2344 1.9
11 0352 0.7 / 1023 1.9 / TH 1647 0.6 / 2321 1.8	**26** 0527 0.6 / 1201 2.1 / F 1810 0.4
12 0509 0.6 / 1139 1.9 / F 1757 0.5	**27** 0041 1.9 / 0626 0.5 / SA 1258 2.1 / 1902 0.4
13 0027 1.8 / 0615 0.5 / SA 1242 2.0 / 1852 0.4	**28** 0131 2.0 / 0717 0.4 / SU 1350 2.1 / 1948 0.3
14 0122 1.9 / 0709 0.4 / SU 1338 2.1 / 1941 0.3	**29** 0216 2.0 / 0803 0.3 / M 1435 2.1 / ○ 2030 0.3
15 0212 2.0 / 0757 0.3 / M 1428 2.1 / ● 2026 0.2	**30** 0257 2.1 / 0845 0.3 / TU 1515 2.1 / 2107 0.4
	31 0333 2.0 / 0924 0.3 / W 1551 2.0 / 2140 0.4

NOVEMBER

Time m	Time m
1 0403 2.0 / 0957 0.4 / TH 1621 1.9 / 2210 0.5	**16** 0401 2.1 / 0955 0.2 / F 1630 2.0 / 2215 0.3
2 0430 2.0 / 1030 0.4 / F 1648 1.9 / 2239 0.5	**17** 0445 2.1 / 1043 0.2 / SA 1718 2.0 / 2301 0.4
3 0455 2.0 / 1102 0.4 / SA 1715 1.9 / 2310 0.5	**18** 0530 2.1 / 1132 0.2 / SU 1807 1.9 / 2348 0.4
4 0522 2.0 / 1136 0.4 / SU 1745 1.9 / 2346 0.5	**19** 0618 2.1 / 1223 0.3 / M 1900 1.9
5 0555 2.0 / 1215 0.4 / M 1824 1.8	**20** 0038 0.5 / 0710 2.1 / TU 1318 0.4 / ◑ 1958 1.8
6 0027 0.5 / 0637 2.0 / TU 1300 0.5 / 1912 1.8	**21** 0133 0.5 / 0810 2.0 / W 1420 0.4 / 2102 1.8
7 0114 0.5 / 0727 2.0 / W 1352 0.5 / ◑ 2010 1.8	**22** 0234 0.6 / 0916 2.0 / TH 1527 0.5 / 2206 1.8
8 0209 0.6 / 0825 2.0 / TH 1453 0.5 / 2118 1.8	**23** 0343 0.6 / 1024 2.0 / F 1636 0.5 / 2308 1.8
9 0313 0.6 / 0934 2.0 / F 1601 0.5 / 2234 1.8	**24** 0453 0.5 / 1128 2.0 / SA 1739 0.4
10 0424 0.6 / 1051 2.0 / SA 1711 0.5 / 2344 1.9	**25** 0006 1.9 / 0556 0.5 / SU 1227 2.1 / 1833 0.4
11 0533 0.5 / 1202 2.0 / SU 1813 0.4	**26** 0058 2.0 / 0651 0.4 / M 1320 2.1 / 1921 0.4
12 0045 1.9 / 0634 0.4 / M 1304 2.1 / 1908 0.3	**27** 0146 2.0 / 0741 0.4 / TU 1408 2.0 / 2005 0.4
13 0140 2.0 / 0729 0.4 / TU 1400 2.1 / ● 1957 0.3	**28** 0230 2.0 / 0825 0.4 / W 1451 2.0 / ○ 2043 0.4
14 0230 2.0 / 0819 0.3 / W 1453 2.1 / 2045 0.3	**29** 0309 2.0 / 0905 0.4 / TH 1529 1.9 / 2117 0.4
15 0316 2.1 / 0908 0.2 / TH 1542 2.1 / 2130 0.3	**30** 0343 2.0 / 0939 0.4 / F 1602 1.9 / 2148 0.5

DECEMBER

Time m	Time m
1 0412 2.0 / 1012 0.4 / SA 1631 1.8 / 2218 0.5	**16** 0432 2.1 / 1031 0.3 / SU 1706 1.9 / 2245 0.3
2 0439 2.0 / 1043 0.4 / SU 1659 1.8 / 2250 0.5	**17** 0517 2.1 / 1118 0.2 / M 1752 1.8 / 2331 0.3
3 0506 2.0 / 1118 0.4 / M 1730 1.8 / 2326 0.4	**18** 0603 2.1 / 1207 0.2 / TU 1839 1.8
4 0537 2.0 / 1157 0.4 / TU 1806 1.8	**19** 0018 0.4 / 0651 2.1 / W 1257 0.3 / 1930 1.8
5 0006 0.4 / 0616 2.1 / W 1239 0.4 / 1850 1.8	**20** 0108 0.4 / 0743 2.0 / TH 1351 0.4 / ◑ 2024 1.7
6 0052 0.4 / 0702 2.1 / TH 1328 0.4 / ◑ 1942 1.8	**21** 0202 0.5 / 0841 2.0 / F 1448 0.4 / 2122 1.7
7 0143 0.4 / 0755 2.0 / F 1423 0.4 / 2041 1.8	**22** 0303 0.5 / 0944 2.0 / SA 1552 0.5 / 2224 1.8
8 0241 0.5 / 0857 2.0 / SA 1524 0.4 / 2149 1.8	**23** 0411 0.5 / 1048 1.9 / SU 1658 0.5 / 2324 1.8
9 0345 0.5 / 1009 2.0 / SU 1630 0.4 / 2301 1.8	**24** 0521 0.5 / 1149 1.9 / M 1759 0.5
10 0454 0.5 / 1124 2.0 / M 1736 0.5	**25** 0021 1.9 / 0624 0.5 / TU 1246 1.9 / 1852 0.4
11 0009 1.9 / 0602 0.4 / TU 1235 2.0 / 1838 0.4	**26** 0114 1.9 / 0718 0.4 / W 1338 1.9 / 1939 0.4
12 0111 1.9 / 0704 0.4 / W 1338 2.0 / 1933 0.3	**27** 0202 2.0 / 0806 0.4 / TH 1425 1.9 / 2020 0.4
13 0206 2.0 / 0800 0.3 / TH 1436 2.0 / 2024 0.3	**28** 0245 2.0 / 0847 0.4 / F 1506 1.8 / ○ 2056 0.4
14 0257 2.0 / 0853 0.2 / F 1529 2.0 / 2113 0.3	**29** 0323 2.0 / 0922 0.4 / SA 1543 1.8 / 2127 0.4
15 0346 2.1 / 0942 0.2 / SA 1618 1.9 / 2159 0.3	**30** 0355 2.0 / 0954 0.4 / SU 1615 1.8 / 2200 0.4
	31 0424 2.0 / 1027 0.3 / M 1646 1.8 / 2233 0.3

Chart Datum: 0·69 metres below Dansk Normal Null
HAT is 2·2 metres above Chart Datum

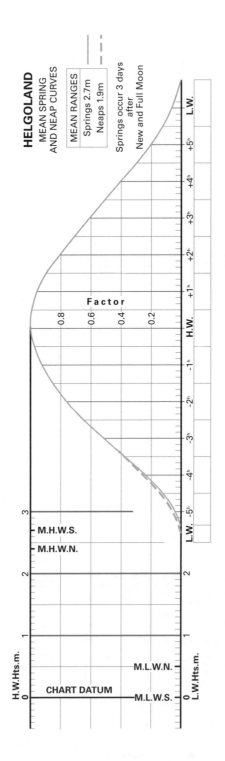

HELGOLAND
MEAN SPRING
AND NEAP CURVES

MEAN RANGES
Springs 2.7m
Neaps 1.9m

Springs occur 3 days
after
New and Full Moon

TIME ZONE -0100
(German Standard Time)
Subtract 1 hour for UT
For German Summer Time add
ONE hour in **non-shaded areas**

GERMANY – HELGOLAND

LAT 54°11'N   LONG 7°53'E

TIMES AND HEIGHTS OF HIGH AND LOW WATERS

Dates in amber are **SPRINGS**
Dates in yellow are **NEAPS**

2012

JANUARY

Time	m		Time	m
1 SU 0430 / 1115 / 1656 / ☽2325	3.1 / 0.9 / 2.8 / 0.9	**16** M 0414 / 1104 / 1647 / 2322	3.3 / 0.7 / 3.0 / 0.8	
2 M 0515 / 1157 / 1745	3.0 / 0.9 / 2.8	**17** TU 0504 / 1151 / 1739	3.2 / 0.7 / 2.9	
3 TU 0019 / 0610 / 1253 / 1845	1.0 / 2.9 / 0.9 / 2.7	**18** W 0018 / 0605 / 1252 / 1845	0.9 / 3.1 / 0.8 / 2.9	
4 W 0128 / 0717 / 1401 / 1955	1.0 / 2.8 / 0.9 / 2.8	**19** TH 0131 / 0720 / 1410 / 2002	0.9 / 3.0 / 0.9 / 2.9	
5 TH 0243 / 0828 / 1510 / 2103	1.0 / 2.8 / 0.9 / 2.9	**20** F 0254 / 0841 / 1531 / 2119	0.9 / 3.0 / 0.9 / 3.0	
6 F 0351 / 0931 / 1611 / 2202	0.9 / 2.9 / 0.8 / 3.0	**21** SA 0414 / 0958 / 1644 / 2228	0.7 / 3.0 / 0.8 / 3.1	
7 SA 0447 / 1027 / 1705 / 2252	0.8 / 2.9 / 0.8 / 3.1	**22** SU 0522 / 1102 / 1744 / 2325	0.6 / 3.0 / 0.7 / 3.2	
8 SU 0536 / 1116 / 1752 / 2335	0.7 / 3.0 / 0.7 / 3.1	**23** M 0618 / 1155 / 1834 ●	0.5 / 3.0 / 0.6	
9 M 0621 / 1201 / 1836 ○	0.7 / 3.0 / 0.7	**24** TU 0012 / 0705 / 1240 / 1919	3.3 / 0.5 / 3.1 / 0.6	
10 TU 0017 / 0704 / 1243 / 1918	3.2 / 0.6 / 3.0 / 0.7	**25** W 0054 / 0748 / 1322 / 2001	3.3 / 0.5 / 3.0 / 0.6	
11 W 0057 / 0747 / 1323 / 1957	3.3 / 0.6 / 3.1 / 0.6	**26** TH 0135 / 0829 / 1402 / 2039	3.3 / 0.5 / 3.1 / 0.5	
12 TH 0135 / 0826 / 1400 / 2033	3.3 / 0.5 / 3.1 / 0.5	**27** F 0214 / 0906 / 1437 / 2111	3.3 / 0.5 / 3.0 / 0.5	
13 F 0209 / 0902 / 1436 / 2108	3.3 / 0.5 / 3.0 / 0.5	**28** SA 0248 / 0936 / 1508 / 2139	3.3 / 0.6 / 3.0 / 0.5	
14 SA 0246 / 0940 / 1516 / 2149	3.3 / 0.5 / 3.0 / 0.6	**29** SU 0320 / 1004 / 1538 / 2209	3.2 / 0.7 / 3.0 / 0.7	
15 SU 0327 / 1022 / 1601 / 2234	3.3 / 0.6 / 3.0 / 0.7	**30** M 0352 / 1031 / 1609 / 2242	3.1 / 0.8 / 2.9 / 0.8	
		31 TU 0426 / 1100 / 1645 / ☽2321	3.0 / 0.9 / 2.9 / 0.9	

FEBRUARY

Time	m		Time	m
1 W 0508 / 1143 / 1735	2.8 / 0.9 / 2.8	**16** TH 0541 / 1226 / 1816	3.0 / 0.8 / 2.9	
2 TH 0019 / 0609 / 1249 / 1845	0.9 / 2.7 / 1.0 / 2.7	**17** F 0109 / 0658 / 1347 / 1940	0.8 / 2.9 / 0.9 / 2.9	
3 F 0138 / 0727 / 1411 / 2008	1.0 / 2.7 / 1.0 / 2.8	**18** SA 0239 / 0829 / 1518 / 2107	0.8 / 2.8 / 0.9 / 3.0	
4 SA 0302 / 0849 / 1531 / 2124	0.9 / 2.7 / 0.9 / 2.9	**19** SU 0407 / 0952 / 1636 / 2220	0.8 / 2.9 / 0.8 / 3.1	
5 SU 0414 / 0959 / 1638 / 2226	0.8 / 2.8 / 0.8 / 3.0	**20** M 0516 / 1057 / 1735 / 2315	0.6 / 2.9 / 0.7 / 3.2	
6 M 0513 / 1056 / 1732 / 2314	0.7 / 3.0 / 0.7 / 3.1	**21** TU 0608 / 1145 / 1822 / ●2359	0.5 / 3.0 / 0.6 / 3.3	
7 TU 0602 / 1144 / 1820 / ○2357	0.6 / 3.0 / 0.7 / 3.2	**22** W 0651 / 1225 / 1904	0.5 / 3.0 / 0.5	
8 W 0647 / 1225 / 1902	0.5 / 3.1 / 0.6	**23** TH 0038 / 0729 / 1302 / 1942	3.3 / 0.5 / 3.1 / 0.4	
9 TH 0037 / 0730 / 1305 / 1942	3.3 / 0.4 / 3.1 / 0.5	**24** F 0114 / 0805 / 1336 / 2015	3.3 / 0.5 / 3.1 / 0.5	
10 F 0116 / 0810 / 1342 / 2019	3.3 / 0.4 / 3.1 / 0.4	**25** SA 0148 / 0836 / 1407 / 2045	3.3 / 0.5 / 3.1 / 0.5	
11 SA 0153 / 0847 / 1420 / 2057	3.3 / 0.3 / 3.1 / 0.3	**26** SU 0219 / 0903 / 1436 / 2113	3.2 / 0.5 / 3.0 / 0.4	
12 SU 0232 / 0926 / 1459 / 2138	3.3 / 0.3 / 3.0 / 0.4	**27** M 0249 / 0930 / 1504 / 2142	3.1 / 0.6 / 3.0 / 0.5	
13 M 0314 / 1006 / 1542 / 2221	3.3 / 0.5 / 3.0 / 0.5	**28** TU 0319 / 0955 / 1532 / 2209	3.0 / 0.6 / 3.0 / 0.6	
14 TU 0358 / 1045 / 1625 / ☽2304	3.3 / 0.6 / 3.0 / 0.6	**29** W 0348 / 1019 / 1600 / 2238	2.9 / 0.7 / 2.9 / 0.7	
15 W 0445 / 1127 / 1713 / 2356	3.2 / 0.7 / 2.9 / 0.7			

MARCH

Time	m		Time	m
1 TH 0422 / 1051 / 1640 / ☽2324	2.8 / 0.8 / 2.8 / 0.8	**16** F 0527 / 1207 / 1757	2.8 / 0.8 / 2.9	
2 F 0514 / 1149 / 1745	2.6 / 0.9 / 2.7	**17** SA 0054 / 0645 / 1330 / 1922	0.7 / 2.7 / 0.9 / 2.9	
3 SA 0039 / 0632 / 1315 / 1913	0.9 / 2.6 / 0.9 / 2.7	**18** SU 0227 / 0818 / 1504 / 2053	0.7 / 2.7 / 0.9 / 3.0	
4 SU 0212 / 0805 / 1449 / 2042	0.9 / 2.7 / 0.9 / 2.8	**19** M 0357 / 0943 / 1624 / 2207	0.7 / 2.8 / 0.8 / 3.1	
5 M 0338 / 0927 / 1607 / 2153	0.8 / 2.8 / 0.8 / 3.0	**20** TU 0503 / 1043 / 1719 / 2257	0.6 / 2.9 / 0.6 / 3.2	
6 TU 0445 / 1029 / 1707 / 2246	0.6 / 2.9 / 0.7 / 3.1	**21** W 0548 / 1127 / 1801 / 2336	0.5 / 3.0 / 0.5 / 3.2	
7 W 0537 / 1118 / 1756 / 2330	0.5 / 3.0 / 0.6 / 3.2	**22** TH 0626 / 1200 / 1840 ●	0.4 / 3.0 / 0.4	
8 TH 0623 / 1200 / 1840 ○	0.4 / 3.1 / 0.5	**23** F 0013 / 0702 / 1235 / 1917	3.2 / 0.4 / 3.0 / 0.4	
9 F 0010 / 0704 / 1239 / 1921	3.3 / 0.3 / 3.1 / 0.3	**24** SA 0048 / 0735 / 1308 / 1949	3.1 / 0.4 / 3.0 / 0.4	
10 SA 0051 / 0746 / 1318 / 2001	3.3 / 0.2 / 3.1 / 0.2	**25** SU 0120 / 0804 / 1337 / 2019	3.1 / 0.4 / 3.0 / 0.4	
11 SU 0133 / 0827 / 1358 / 2042	3.3 / 0.3 / 3.1 / 0.2	**26** M 0150 / 0832 / 1406 / 2048	3.1 / 0.5 / 3.0 / 0.4	
12 M 0216 / 0908 / 1439 / 2124	3.2 / 0.3 / 3.1 / 0.3	**27** TU 0221 / 0900 / 1434 / 2117	3.0 / 0.5 / 3.0 / 0.4	
13 TU 0259 / 0948 / 1521 / 2207	3.2 / 0.4 / 3.0 / 0.3	**28** W 0252 / 0927 / 1503 / 2145	2.9 / 0.5 / 3.0 / 0.4	
14 W 0343 / 1027 / 1604 / 2250	3.2 / 0.5 / 3.0 / 0.5	**29** TH 0321 / 0951 / 1531 / 2211	2.9 / 0.6 / 2.9 / 0.5	
15 TH 0430 / 1109 / 1652 / ☽2342	3.0 / 0.7 / 2.9 / 0.6	**30** F 0353 / 1019 / 1606 / 2250	2.7 / 0.7 / 2.8 / 0.7	
		31 SA 0439 / 1109 / 1703 / 2356	2.6 / 0.8 / 2.7 / 0.8	

APRIL

Time	m		Time	m
1 SU 0550 / 1230 / 1825	2.6 / 0.9 / 2.7	**16** M 0208 / 0758 / 1440 / 2028	0.6 / 2.6 / 0.8 / 3.0	
2 M 0126 / 0721 / 1405 / 1955	0.8 / 2.6 / 0.9 / 2.8	**17** TU 0333 / 0918 / 1557 / 2139	0.6 / 2.7 / 0.7 / 3.0	
3 TU 0256 / 0847 / 1528 / 2112	0.7 / 2.8 / 0.8 / 3.0	**18** W 0435 / 1015 / 1651 / 2227	0.5 / 2.8 / 0.6 / 3.1	
4 W 0408 / 0953 / 1632 / 2210	0.5 / 2.9 / 0.6 / 3.1	**19** TH 0516 / 1053 / 1730 / 2304	0.4 / 2.9 / 0.5 / 3.1	
5 TH 0503 / 1043 / 1724 / 2257	0.3 / 3.0 / 0.5 / 3.2	**20** F 0551 / 1128 / 1809 / 2343	0.4 / 2.9 / 0.4 / 3.1	
6 F 0551 / 1127 / 1811 / ○2342	0.3 / 3.0 / 0.4 / 3.2	**21** SA 0629 / 1205 / 1848 ●	0.4 / 3.0 / 0.4	
7 SA 0635 / 1209 / 1856	0.2 / 3.1 / 0.3	**22** SU 0020 / 0704 / 1239 / 1923	3.0 / 0.4 / 3.0 / 0.3	
8 SU 0026 / 0719 / 1251 / 1940	3.2 / 0.2 / 3.1 / 0.2	**23** M 0054 / 0735 / 1309 / 1954	3.0 / 0.4 / 3.1 / 0.3	
9 M 0112 / 0804 / 1335 / 2025	3.2 / 0.2 / 3.1 / 0.2	**24** TU 0125 / 0804 / 1338 / 2025	3.0 / 0.4 / 3.1 / 0.3	
10 TU 0158 / 0849 / 1418 / 2110	3.2 / 0.3 / 3.1 / 0.2	**25** W 0157 / 0834 / 1409 / 2056	2.9 / 0.4 / 3.0 / 0.3	
11 W 0245 / 0931 / 1501 / 2154	3.1 / 0.4 / 3.1 / 0.2	**26** TH 0230 / 0904 / 1441 / 2126	2.9 / 0.4 / 3.0 / 0.4	
12 TH 0331 / 1011 / 1546 / 2240	3.0 / 0.5 / 3.0 / 0.3	**27** F 0303 / 0933 / 1513 / 2156	2.8 / 0.5 / 3.0 / 0.5	
13 F 0419 / 1055 / 1637 / ☽2332	2.9 / 0.6 / 3.0 / 0.5	**28** SA 0338 / 1004 / 1549 / 2235	2.8 / 0.6 / 2.9 / 0.6	
14 SA 0518 / 1153 / 1741	2.7 / 0.7 / 2.9	**29** SU 0421 / 1048 / 1638 / ☽2331	2.7 / 0.7 / 2.9 / 0.7	
15 SU 0042 / 0632 / 1311 / 1902	0.6 / 2.6 / 0.8 / 2.9	**30** M 0521 / 1156 / 1747	2.6 / 0.8 / 2.9	

Chart Datum: 1·68 metres below Normal Null (German reference level)
HAT is 3·0 metres above Chart Datum

TIDES

TIDES

TIME ZONE -0100
(German Standard Time)
Subtract 1 hour for UT
For German Summer Time add
ONE hour in **non-shaded areas**

GERMANY – HELGOLAND
LAT 54°11′N   LONG 7°53′E
TIMES AND HEIGHTS OF HIGH AND LOW WATERS

Dates in amber are **SPRINGS**
Dates in yellow are **NEAPS**

2012

MAY

Day	Time m	Day	Time m
1 TU	0048 0.7 / 0640 2.7 / 1321 0.8 / 1909 2.9	16 W	0248 0.6 / 0832 2.7 / 1511 0.7 / 2054 3.0
2 W	0211 0.6 / 0800 2.8 / 1443 0.7 / 2025 3.0	17 TH	0349 0.5 / 0930 2.7 / 1609 0.6 / 2146 3.0
3 TH	0322 0.5 / 0908 2.9 / 1550 0.6 / 2128 3.1	18 F	0433 0.5 / 1014 2.8 / 1654 0.5 / 2228 3.0
4 F	0421 0.3 / 1003 3.0 / 1647 0.5 / 2223 3.1	19 SA	0512 0.4 / 1053 2.9 / 1736 0.5 / 2310 3.0
5 SA	0516 0.3 / 1053 3.0 / 1742 0.4 / 2314 3.2	20 SU	0554 0.4 / 1134 3.0 / 1819 0.4 / 2352 3.0
6 SU	0607 0.2 / 1141 3.1 / 1832 0.3 / O	21 M	0634 0.4 / 1211 3.0 / 1857 0.4 / ●
7 M	0003 3.2 / 0655 0.2 / 1227 3.1 / 1920 0.2	22 TU	0029 2.9 / 0709 0.4 / 1245 3.1 / 1932 0.4
8 TU	0051 3.2 / 0742 0.2 / 1313 3.1 / 2009 0.2	23 W	0103 2.9 / 0741 0.4 / 1317 3.1 / 2006 0.4
9 W	0141 3.1 / 0829 0.3 / 1400 3.2 / 2058 0.2	24 TH	0138 2.9 / 0815 0.5 / 1351 3.1 / 2039 0.4
10 TH	0232 3.0 / 0915 0.3 / 1447 3.1 / 2145 0.2	25 F	0213 2.9 / 0847 0.5 / 1425 3.1 / 2112 0.4
11 F	0321 2.9 / 0957 0.4 / 1533 3.1 / 2231 0.3	26 SA	0250 2.9 / 0920 0.5 / 1500 3.1 / 2148 0.5
12 SA	0411 2.8 / 1043 0.5 / 1624 3.1 / ◑ 2322 0.4	27 SU	0328 2.9 / 0955 0.6 / 1538 3.1 / 2228 0.5
13 SU	0506 2.7 / 1136 0.7 / 1723 3.0	28 M	0410 2.8 / 1038 0.7 / 1623 3.0 / ◑ 2317 0.6
14 M	0023 0.6 / 0609 2.7 / 1242 0.7 / 1832 2.9	29 TU	0501 2.8 / 1134 0.7 / 1719 3.0
15 TU	0134 0.6 / 0721 2.6 / 1358 0.7 / 1947 2.9	30 W	0016 0.6 / 0604 2.8 / 1243 0.7 / 1828 3.0
		31 TH	0125 0.6 / 0714 2.8 / 1357 0.7 / 1940 3.0

JUNE

Day	Time m	Day	Time m
1 F	0235 0.6 / 0822 2.9 / 1507 0.7 / 2049 3.1	16 SA	0343 0.6 / 0929 2.8 / 1615 0.6 / 2151 2.9
2 SA	0341 0.5 / 0924 3.0 / 1613 0.5 / 2152 3.1	17 SU	0433 0.6 / 1018 2.9 / 1705 0.6 / 2239 2.9
3 SU	0444 0.4 / 1022 3.0 / 1716 0.4 / 2251 3.1	18 M	0521 0.5 / 1104 3.0 / 1751 0.5 / 2325 2.9
4 M	0543 0.3 / 1118 3.1 / 1813 0.3 / O 2345 3.1	19 TU	0606 0.5 / 1146 3.1 / 1833 0.5 / ●
5 TU	0635 0.3 / 1208 3.1 / 1905 0.2	20 W	0007 3.0 / 0646 0.5 / 1224 3.1 / 1912 0.5
6 W	0036 3.1 / 0724 0.3 / 1256 3.2 / 1956 0.2	21 TH	0045 3.0 / 0723 0.5 / 1301 3.2 / 1949 0.5
7 TH	0128 3.0 / 0813 0.4 / 1346 3.2 / 2047 0.2	22 F	0123 3.0 / 0800 0.5 / 1336 3.2 / 2026 0.5
8 F	0220 3.0 / 0900 0.4 / 1435 3.2 / 2135 0.3	23 SA	0159 3.0 / 0833 0.5 / 1410 3.2 / 2100 0.5
9 SA	0309 2.9 / 0944 0.4 / 1521 3.2 / 2220 0.3	24 SU	0235 3.0 / 0907 0.5 / 1446 3.2 / 2137 0.5
10 SU	0356 2.8 / 1026 0.5 / 1607 3.2 / 2305 0.5	25 M	0314 2.9 / 0946 0.6 / 1526 3.2 / 2219 0.5
11 M	0443 2.8 / 1112 0.6 / 1657 3.1 / ◑ 2352 0.6	26 TU	0358 2.9 / 1029 0.6 / 1610 3.2 / 2303 0.6
12 TU	0534 2.7 / 1204 0.7 / 1752 3.0	27 W	0444 2.9 / 1117 0.7 / 1659 3.1 / ◑ 2349 0.6
13 W	0045 0.6 / 0630 2.7 / 1304 0.7 / 1853 2.9	28 TH	0535 2.9 / 1212 0.7 / 1756 3.1
14 TH	0145 0.6 / 0731 2.7 / 1412 0.7 / 1957 2.9	29 F	0046 0.6 / 0635 2.9 / 1319 0.8 / 1904 3.1
15 F	0247 0.6 / 0833 2.7 / 1518 0.7 / 2058 2.9	30 SA	0155 0.7 / 0744 3.0 / 1433 0.7 / 2017 3.1

JULY

Day	Time m	Day	Time m
1 SU	0309 0.6 / 0854 3.0 / 1547 0.6 / 2129 3.1	16 M	0355 0.7 / 0943 2.9 / 1633 0.7 / 2211 2.9
2 M	0420 0.5 / 1001 3.1 / 1657 0.4 / 2235 3.0	17 TU	0451 0.7 / 1037 3.0 / 1724 0.6 / 2302 3.0
3 TU	0525 0.5 / 1102 3.1 / 1800 0.3 / O 2334 3.0	18 W	0541 0.6 / 1124 3.1 / 1810 0.6 / 2348 3.0
4 W	0621 0.4 / 1156 3.2 / 1854 0.3	19 TH	0626 0.6 / 1205 3.2 / 1852 0.6 / ●
5 TH	0026 3.1 / 0711 0.4 / 1245 3.3 / 1944 0.3	20 F	0029 3.1 / 0707 0.6 / 1243 3.3 / 1933 0.5
6 F	0116 3.1 / 0759 0.4 / 1333 3.3 / 2034 0.3	21 SA	0107 3.1 / 0744 0.6 / 1319 3.3 / 2010 0.5
7 SA	0206 3.1 / 0845 0.4 / 1420 3.4 / 2120 0.4	22 SU	0142 3.1 / 0819 0.6 / 1353 3.3 / 2044 0.5
8 SU	0251 3.0 / 0926 0.4 / 1503 3.3 / 2200 0.4	23 M	0217 3.1 / 0853 0.6 / 1428 3.3 / 2121 0.5
9 M	0331 2.9 / 1003 0.5 / 1542 3.2 / 2236 0.5	24 TU	0256 3.0 / 0932 0.5 / 1509 3.3 / 2202 0.5
10 TU	0410 2.9 / 1040 0.6 / 1623 3.2 / 2311 0.7	25 W	0340 3.0 / 1016 0.6 / 1554 3.2 / 2244 0.6
11 W	0450 2.9 / 1120 0.6 / 1706 3.1 / ◑ 2349 0.8	26 TH	0425 3.0 / 1100 0.6 / 1641 3.2 / ◑ 2325 0.7
12 TH	0534 2.8 / 1207 0.8 / 1755 2.9	27 F	0510 3.0 / 1148 0.7 / 1732 3.1
13 F	0037 0.8 / 0626 2.8 / 1308 0.8 / 1855 2.8	28 SA	0016 0.7 / 0605 2.9 / 1250 0.8 / 1837 3.0
14 SA	0139 0.8 / 0731 2.8 / 1420 0.8 / 2005 2.8	29 SU	0126 0.8 / 0716 3.0 / 1410 0.8 / 1957 3.0
15 SU	0249 0.8 / 0840 2.8 / 1532 0.8 / 2112 2.8	30 M	0248 0.8 / 0835 3.0 / 1534 0.7 / 2118 3.0
		31 TU	0407 0.7 / 0950 3.1 / 1648 0.5 / 2229 3.0

AUGUST

Day	Time m	Day	Time m
1 W	0514 0.6 / 1053 3.2 / 1751 0.4 / 2327 3.0	16 TH	0517 0.7 / 1100 3.1 / 1746 0.6 / 2326 3.0
2 TH	0610 0.5 / 1147 3.3 / 1843 0.4 / O	17 F	0604 0.7 / 1141 3.2 / 1829 0.6 / ●
3 F	0017 3.1 / 0659 0.5 / 1233 3.3 / 1931 0.4	18 SA	0007 3.1 / 0645 0.6 / 1219 3.3 / 1909 0.5
4 SA	0102 3.1 / 0744 0.5 / 1317 3.4 / 2015 0.4	19 SU	0044 3.1 / 0724 0.5 / 1256 3.3 / 1947 0.5
5 SU	0145 3.1 / 0826 0.5 / 1359 3.4 / 2055 0.5	20 M	0120 3.1 / 0800 0.5 / 1331 3.3 / 2023 0.4
6 M	0224 3.1 / 0901 0.5 / 1437 3.3 / 2129 0.5	21 TU	0156 3.1 / 0835 0.4 / 1408 3.3 / 2100 0.5
7 TU	0259 3.0 / 0933 0.5 / 1512 3.3 / 2159 0.6	22 W	0234 3.1 / 0915 0.5 / 1450 3.3 / 2141 0.5
8 W	0332 3.0 / 1006 0.6 / 1546 3.2 / 2228 0.8	23 TH	0317 3.1 / 0959 0.5 / 1535 3.3 / 2222 0.7
9 TH	0406 3.0 / 1039 0.8 / 1622 3.1 / ◑ 2258 0.9	24 F	0401 3.1 / 1042 0.6 / 1621 3.2 / ◑ 2303 0.7
10 F	0441 2.9 / 1117 0.9 / 1701 2.9 / 2335 0.9	25 SA	0446 3.0 / 1129 0.7 / 1713 3.0 / 2353 0.8
11 SA	0525 2.8 / 1207 0.9 / 1755 2.8	26 SU	0542 2.9 / 1233 0.8 / 1822 2.9
12 SU	0034 0.9 / 0628 2.8 / 1320 0.9 / 1909 2.7	27 M	0107 0.9 / 0659 2.9 / 1358 0.8 / 1949 2.8
13 M	0152 0.9 / 0748 2.8 / 1444 0.9 / 2031 2.7	28 TU	0237 1.0 / 0826 3.0 / 1529 0.8 / 2116 2.9
14 TU	0314 0.9 / 0907 2.9 / 1559 0.8 / 2143 2.8	29 W	0402 0.9 / 0945 3.1 / 1645 0.6 / 2227 3.0
15 W	0423 0.8 / 1010 3.0 / 1658 0.7 / 2240 2.9	30 TH	0506 0.7 / 1045 3.2 / 1741 0.5 / 2319 3.0
		31 F	0557 0.6 / 1133 3.3 / 1827 0.5 / O

Chart Datum: 1·68 metres below Normal Null (German reference level)
HAT is 3·0 metres above Chart Datum

TIME ZONE -0100
(German Standard Time)
Subtract 1 hour for UT
For German Summer Time add
ONE hour in **non-shaded areas**

GERMANY – HELGOLAND

LAT 54°11′N   LONG 7°53′E

TIMES AND HEIGHTS OF HIGH AND LOW WATERS

Dates in amber are **SPRINGS**
Dates in yellow are **NEAPS**

2012

SEPTEMBER

Day	Time m	Time m	Time m	Time m
1 SA	0002 3.1	0642 0.6	1215 3.3	1909 0.5
2 SU	0042 3.1	0723 0.5	1255 3.3	1948 0.5
3 M	0119 3.1	0800 0.5	1332 3.3	2023 0.6
4 TU	0153 3.1	0833 0.5	1407 3.3	2053 0.6
5 W	0224 3.1	0903 0.6	1439 3.2	2121 0.7
6 TH	0255 3.1	0933 0.6	1511 3.1	2148 0.8
7 F	0325 3.0	1004 0.7	1543 3.0	2215 0.8
8 SA ☽	0357 3.0	1035 0.8	1618 2.9	2246 0.9
9 SU	0435 2.9	1116 0.9	1706 2.7	2337 1.0
10 M	0534 2.8	1224 1.0	1818 2.6	
11 TU	0057 1.1	0656 2.8	1353 1.0	1946 2.7
12 W	0230 1.0	0824 2.8	1519 0.9	2109 2.8
13 TH	0349 0.9	0936 3.0	1627 0.7	2212 2.9
14 F	0448 0.8	1029 3.1	1716 0.6	2258 3.0
15 SA	0535 0.7	1110 3.2	1759 0.5	2338 3.1
16 SU ●	0617 0.6	1150 3.3	1839 0.5	
17 M	0015 3.1	0657 0.5	1229 3.3	1919 0.4
18 TU	0053 3.1	0736 0.4	1308 3.3	1959 0.4
19 W	0132 3.2	0816 0.4	1349 3.3	2039 0.5
20 TH	0212 3.1	0857 0.4	1431 3.3	2120 0.5
21 F	0254 3.1	0941 0.5	1516 3.2	2200 0.7
22 SA ☽	0337 3.1	1025 0.6	1604 3.1	2243 0.8
23 SU	0426 3.1	1115 0.7	1659 2.9	2337 0.9
24 M	0526 3.0	1221 0.8	1813 2.8	
25 TU	0053 1.0	0646 3.0	1349 0.9	1943 2.7
26 W	0227 1.0	0817 3.0	1522 0.8	2112 2.8
27 TH	0352 1.0	0936 3.2	1635 0.7	2218 2.9
28 F	0454 0.8	1031 3.2	1724 0.6	2302 3.0
29 SA	0537 0.7	1111 3.2	1802 0.5	2338 3.0
30 SU ○	0616 0.6	1150 3.2	1840 0.5	

OCTOBER

Day	Time m	Time m	Time m	Time m
1 M	0015 3.1	0656 0.5	1228 3.2	1917 0.5
2 TU	0051 3.1	0733 0.5	1305 3.2	1950 0.6
3 W	0123 3.1	0805 0.6	1338 3.2	2019 0.6
4 TH	0153 3.1	0835 0.6	1409 3.1	2047 0.7
5 F	0221 3.1	0905 0.6	1441 3.0	2115 0.7
6 SA	0251 3.1	0933 0.6	1512 2.9	2142 0.8
7 SU	0323 3.0	1002 0.7	1546 2.8	2211 0.9
8 M ☽	0359 2.9	1040 0.9	1630 2.7	2256 1.0
9 TU	0451 2.8	1139 1.0	1734 2.6	
10 W	0009 1.1	0607 2.8	1303 1.0	1859 2.7
11 TH	0140 1.1	0734 2.9	1432 0.9	2025 2.8
12 F	0305 1.0	0851 3.0	1544 0.7	2132 2.9
13 SA	0409 0.8	0949 3.1	1637 0.6	2221 3.0
14 SU	0459 0.7	1035 3.2	1723 0.5	2303 3.1
15 M ●	0544 0.6	1118 3.2	1807 0.5	2344 3.1
16 TU	0629 0.5	1202 3.2	1851 0.4	
17 W	0025 3.2	0713 0.4	1246 3.3	1935 0.5
18 TH	0107 3.2	0757 0.4	1331 3.2	2020 0.5
19 F	0151 3.2	0842 0.4	1416 3.2	2102 0.6
20 SA	0234 3.2	0927 0.5	1502 3.1	2143 0.6
21 SU	0319 3.1	1013 0.6	1551 3.0	2227 0.8
22 M ☽	0410 3.1	1104 0.7	1649 2.8	2322 0.9
23 TU	0512 3.0	1210 0.8	1801 2.7	
24 W	0036 1.0	0630 3.0	1332 0.9	1926 2.7
25 TH	0204 1.0	0756 3.0	1500 0.8	2049 2.7
26 F	0327 0.9	0912 3.1	1610 0.7	2153 2.9
27 SA	0427 0.8	1006 3.1	1655 0.6	2235 2.9
28 SU	0509 0.7	1045 3.1	1730 0.6	2309 3.0
29 M ○	0548 0.6	1122 3.1	1807 0.6	2346 3.0
30 TU ●	0628 0.6	1202 3.1	1845 0.6	
31 W	0023 3.1	0707 0.5	1239 3.0	1919 0.6

NOVEMBER

Day	Time m	Time m	Time m	Time m
1 TH	0056 3.1	0740 0.5	1312 3.0	1950 0.6
2 F	0126 3.1	0811 0.6	1344 3.0	2020 0.6
3 SA	0156 3.1	0841 0.6	1417 2.9	2049 0.7
4 SU	0227 3.1	0910 0.6	1450 2.9	2118 0.7
5 M	0259 3.1	0941 0.7	1524 2.8	2148 0.9
6 TU ☽	0335 3.0	1017 0.9	1605 2.8	2229 1.0
7 W	0420 3.0	1108 1.0	1659 2.7	2329 1.1
8 TH	0523 2.9	1218 1.0	1812 2.7	
9 F	0049 1.1	0640 2.9	1338 0.9	1932 2.8
10 SA	0211 1.0	0758 3.0	1451 0.8	2042 2.9
11 SU	0321 0.9	0903 3.1	1552 0.6	2139 3.0
12 M	0419 0.8	0958 3.1	1645 0.5	2228 3.1
13 TU ●	0512 0.6	1049 3.2	1737 0.5	2315 3.1
14 W	0603 0.5	1138 3.2	1826 0.5	
15 TH	0000 3.1	0652 0.4	1225 3.2	1914 0.5
16 F	0046 3.2	0740 0.4	1315 3.2	2002 0.5
17 SA	0133 3.2	0830 0.4	1405 3.1	2048 0.5
18 SU	0221 3.2	0918 0.4	1454 3.0	2131 0.6
19 M	0307 3.2	1005 0.5	1542 2.9	2215 0.7
20 TU ☽	0357 3.2	1055 0.6	1636 2.9	2307 0.8
21 W	0455 3.1	1153 0.8	1738 2.7	
22 TH	0010 0.9	0602 3.0	1301 0.8	1850 2.7
23 F	0124 0.9	0716 3.0	1415 0.8	2004 2.7
24 SA	0240 0.9	0829 3.0	1522 0.8	2108 2.8
25 SU	0346 0.9	0928 3.0	1614 0.7	2158 2.9
26 M	0436 0.8	1014 3.0	1656 0.7	2239 3.0
27 TU	0520 0.7	1056 3.0	1737 0.6	2319 3.0
28 W ○	0603 0.6	1138 3.0	1817 0.6	
29 TH	0643 0.6	1217 3.0	1854 0.5	
30 F	0033 3.1	0718 0.5	1251 2.9	1927 0.6

DECEMBER

Day	Time m	Time m	Time m	Time m
1 SA	0106 3.1	0751 0.6	1325 3.0	1959 0.6
2 SU	0138 3.2	0824 0.6	1400 3.0	2031 0.7
3 M	0211 3.2	0855 0.6	1433 2.9	2101 0.7
4 TU	0242 3.2	0927 0.7	1508 2.9	2134 0.8
5 W	0317 3.1	1003 0.8	1546 2.9	2212 0.9
6 TH ☽	0357 3.1	1047 0.9	1632 2.8	2300 1.0
7 F	0448 3.0	1140 0.9	1729 2.8	
8 SA	0003 1.0	0552 3.0	1245 0.9	1838 2.8
9 SU	0117 1.0	0704 3.0	1356 0.8	1949 2.9
10 M	0231 1.0	0817 3.1	1506 0.7	2056 3.0
11 TU	0340 0.8	0923 3.1	1611 0.6	2156 3.0
12 W	0444 0.6	1024 3.1	1712 0.5	2251 3.1
13 TH ●	0544 0.5	1119 3.1	1807 0.5	2343 3.1
14 F	0637 0.4	1211 3.1	1857 0.5	
15 SA	0031 3.2	0728 0.3	1303 3.1	1947 0.6
16 SU	0121 3.3	0820 0.3	1356 3.1	2037 0.5
17 M	0211 3.3	0911 0.4	1445 3.0	2122 0.5
18 TU	0258 3.3	0956 0.4	1531 2.9	2203 0.6
19 W	0343 3.2	1040 0.5	1616 2.9	2246 0.7
20 TH ☽	0431 3.2	1125 0.7	1705 2.8	2334 0.8
21 F	0524 3.1	1215 0.8	1800 2.7	
22 SA	0031 0.9	0624 2.9	1313 0.9	1902 2.9
23 SU	0139 0.9	0731 2.9	1418 0.9	2009 2.7
24 M	0252 0.9	0839 2.9	1523 0.8	2112 2.8
25 TU	0358 0.8	0939 2.9	1619 0.8	2207 2.9
26 W	0453 0.8	1030 2.9	1709 0.7	2254 3.0
27 TH	0540 0.7	1116 2.9	1753 0.7	2336 3.1
28 F ○	0621 0.6	1157 2.9	1833 0.6	
29 SA	0014 3.1	0659 0.6	1235 2.9	1909 0.6
30 SU	0050 3.2	0735 0.6	1311 3.0	1945 0.6
31 M	0124 3.2	0810 0.6	1345 3.0	2017 0.6

Chart Datum: 1·68 metres below Normal Null (German reference level)
HAT is 3·0 metres above Chart Datum

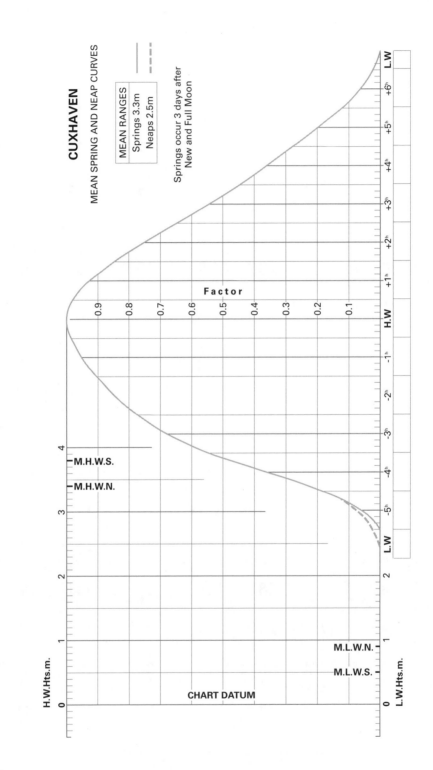

CUXHAVEN

MEAN SPRING AND NEAP CURVES

MEAN RANGES
Springs 3.3m
Neaps 2.5m

Springs occur 3 days after
New and Full Moon

TIME ZONE -0100
(German Standard Time)
Subtract 1 hour for UT
For German Summer Time add ONE hour in **non-shaded areas**

GERMANY – CUXHAVEN

LAT 53°52'N   LONG 8°43'E

TIMES AND HEIGHTS OF HIGH AND LOW WATERS

Dates in amber are **SPRINGS**
Dates in yellow are **NEAPS**

2012

JANUARY

Day	Times (m)
1 SU ◑	0000 0.7 / 0542 3.6 / 1235 0.8 / 1810 3.2
2 M	0038 0.9 / 0626 3.5 / 1315 0.9 / 1857 3.2
3 TU	0129 0.9 / 0720 3.4 / 1408 0.9 / 1958 3.2
4 W	0238 1.0 / 0827 3.3 / 1515 0.9 / 2107 3.2
5 TH	0355 0.9 / 0938 3.3 / 1626 0.9 / 2214 3.3
6 F	0507 0.9 / 1044 3.3 / 1730 0.8 / 2313 3.4
7 SA	0606 0.7 / 1140 3.4 / 1825 0.7
8 SU	0003 3.5 / 0658 0.7 / 1229 3.5 / 1915 0.7
9 M ○	0048 3.6 / 0745 0.6 / 1314 3.5 / 1959 0.7
10 TU	0130 3.8 / 0830 0.6 / 1356 3.6 / 2042 0.6
11 W	0211 3.8 / 0913 0.6 / 1437 3.6 / 2123 0.6
12 TH	0249 3.9 / 0953 0.6 / 1514 3.6 / 2159 0.5
13 F	0324 3.9 / 1027 0.4 / 1551 3.5 / 2233 0.5
14 SA	0400 3.9 / 1103 0.5 / 1630 3.5 / 2311 0.5
15 SU	0442 3.9 / 1145 0.5 / 1714 3.5 / 2354 0.6
16 M ◑	0527 3.8 / 1228 0.7 / 1800 3.5
17 TU	0040 0.7 / 0615 3.7 / 1313 0.7 / 1852 3.4
18 W	0134 0.8 / 0715 3.6 / 1412 0.8 / 1957 3.4
19 TH	0246 0.9 / 0830 3.5 / 1528 0.9 / 2114 3.5
20 F	0410 0.9 / 0952 3.5 / 1651 0.8 / 2230 3.6
21 SA	0533 0.7 / 1109 3.5 / 1806 0.7 / 2338 3.6
22 SU	0644 0.6 / 1215 3.5 / 1909 0.6
23 M ●	0036 3.7 / 0741 0.5 / 1309 3.6 / 2000 0.5
24 TU	0124 3.8 / 0828 0.5 / 1354 3.6 / 2044 0.5
25 W	0206 3.8 / 0911 0.5 / 1436 3.7 / 2125 0.5
26 TH	0246 3.9 / 0952 0.5 / 1516 3.7 / 2203 0.5
27 F	0324 3.9 / 1028 0.5 / 1551 3.6 / 2233 0.5
28 SA	0359 3.9 / 1059 0.5 / 1622 3.6 / 2300 0.5
29 SU	0432 3.8 / 1126 0.6 / 1653 3.4 / 2327 0.6
30 M	0504 3.7 / 1152 0.7 / 1723 3.4 / 2356 0.7
31 TU ◑	0537 3.5 / 1218 0.8 / 1757 3.3

FEBRUARY

Day	Times (m)
1 W	0031 0.8 / 0618 3.3 / 1256 0.9 / 1847 3.2
2 TH	0125 0.9 / 0718 3.2 / 1358 0.9 / 1957 3.2
3 F	0244 0.9 / 0837 3.2 / 1521 0.9 / 2117 3.3
4 SA	0412 0.9 / 0959 3.2 / 1644 0.8 / 2232 3.4
5 SU	0529 0.8 / 1109 3.4 / 1755 0.6 / 2334 3.5
6 M	0632 0.6 / 1206 3.5 / 1853 0.5
7 TU ○	0025 3.7 / 0725 0.6 / 1255 3.6 / 1943 0.6
8 W	0109 3.8 / 0812 0.6 / 1337 3.6 / 2027 0.6
9 TH	0150 3.9 / 0855 0.4 / 1416 3.6 / 2107 0.4
10 F	0228 3.9 / 0935 0.3 / 1454 3.7 / 2144 0.3
11 SA	0305 3.9 / 1011 0.3 / 1531 3.6 / 2219 0.3
12 SU	0343 3.9 / 1048 0.3 / 1611 3.6 / 2258 0.4
13 M	0426 3.9 / 1129 0.5 / 1654 3.6 / 2340 0.5
14 TU ◑	0510 3.8 / 1209 0.6 / 1738 3.6
15 W	0021 0.6 / 0556 3.7 / 1248 0.7 / 1825 3.5
16 TH	0109 0.7 / 0652 3.5 / 1342 0.8 / 1928 3.4
17 F	0219 0.8 / 0809 3.4 / 1500 0.9 / 2050 3.4
18 SA	0351 0.8 / 0939 3.4 / 1633 0.9 / 2216 3.6
19 SU	0523 0.7 / 1103 3.4 / 1755 0.8 / 2329 3.7
20 M	0636 0.6 / 1208 3.5 / 1858 0.6
21 TU ●	0025 3.8 / 0730 0.5 / 1257 3.6 / 1947 0.5
22 W	0110 3.8 / 0812 0.5 / 1338 3.6 / 2028 0.5
23 TH	0148 3.8 / 0850 0.4 / 1414 3.7 / 2104 0.4
24 F	0223 3.9 / 0925 0.4 / 1448 3.7 / 2137 0.4
25 SA	0256 3.9 / 0957 0.4 / 1518 3.6 / 2206 0.4
26 SU	0328 3.8 / 1024 0.4 / 1547 3.6 / 2232 0.4
27 M	0400 3.7 / 1050 0.5 / 1616 3.6 / 2259 0.5
28 TU	0431 3.6 / 1114 0.6 / 1645 3.6 / 2324 0.5
29 W ◑	0500 3.5 / 1135 0.7 / 1713 3.4 / 2349 0.6

MARCH

Day	Times (m)
1 TH ●	0532 3.3 / 1202 0.7 / 1751 3.3
2 F	0029 0.8 / 0622 3.1 / 1255 0.8 / 1855 3.2
3 SA	0141 0.9 / 0740 3.1 / 1420 0.9 / 2021 3.2
4 SU	0317 0.9 / 0912 3.2 / 1557 0.9 / 2148 3.4
5 M	0449 0.7 / 1035 3.3 / 1721 0.8 / 2300 3.6
6 TU	0602 0.6 / 1139 3.5 / 1827 0.7 / 2355 3.7
7 W	0659 0.4 / 1228 3.6 / 1919 0.6
8 TH ○	0041 3.8 / 0746 0.3 / 1311 3.6 / 2003 0.4
9 F	0122 3.9 / 0827 0.2 / 1350 3.7 / 2044 0.3
10 SA	0202 3.9 / 0908 0.2 / 1428 3.7 / 2123 0.2
11 SU	0243 3.9 / 0949 0.2 / 1509 3.7 / 2202 0.2
12 M	0325 3.9 / 1030 0.3 / 1551 3.7 / 2243 0.2
13 TU	0410 3.9 / 1111 0.4 / 1634 3.6 / 2325 0.3
14 W	0456 3.8 / 1149 0.5 / 1717 3.6
15 TH ◑	0006 0.4 / 0543 3.6 / 1227 0.6 / 1805 3.5
16 F	0053 0.5 / 0639 3.4 / 1319 0.7 / 1908 3.4
17 SA	0202 0.7 / 0756 3.2 / 1439 0.8 / 2032 3.4
18 SU	0336 0.7 / 0929 3.3 / 1615 0.9 / 2202 3.6
19 M	0512 0.7 / 1053 3.4 / 1740 0.8 / 2315 3.7
20 TU	0623 0.6 / 1154 3.5 / 1840 0.6
21 W	0006 3.8 / 0712 0.2 / 1236 3.6 / 1923 0.5
22 TH ●	0045 3.8 / 0746 0.4 / 1311 3.6 / 2001 0.4
23 F	0121 3.8 / 0821 0.4 / 1346 3.6 / 2037 0.3
24 SA	0156 3.8 / 0854 0.3 / 1417 3.7 / 2109 0.3
25 SU	0228 3.8 / 0923 0.4 / 1446 3.7 / 2138 0.4
26 M	0300 3.7 / 0951 0.4 / 1515 3.6 / 2206 0.3
27 TU	0332 3.6 / 1017 0.4 / 1545 3.6 / 2234 0.3
28 W	0404 3.5 / 1044 0.4 / 1615 3.5 / 2300 0.4
29 TH	0433 3.4 / 1106 0.5 / 1643 3.5 / 2324 0.5
30 F ◑	0504 3.3 / 1131 0.6 / 1717 3.3 / 2357 0.6
31 SA	0548 3.2 / 1215 0.7 / 1813 3.3

APRIL

Day	Times (m)
1 SU	0059 0.7 / 0659 3.1 / 1334 0.8 / 1934 3.3
2 M	0230 0.8 / 0829 3.2 / 1512 0.8 / 2103 3.4
3 TU	0406 0.6 / 0956 3.3 / 1642 0.7 / 2219 3.6
4 W	0524 0.5 / 1103 3.5 / 1751 0.6 / 2318 3.7
5 TH	0623 0.3 / 1154 3.6 / 1846 0.5
6 F ○	0008 3.8 / 0712 0.2 / 1239 3.7 / 1934 0.3
7 SA	0053 3.8 / 0757 0.2 / 1321 3.7 / 2018 0.2
8 SU	0136 3.9 / 0840 0.1 / 1403 3.7 / 2100 0.2
9 M	0222 3.9 / 0924 0.2 / 1447 3.7 / 2144 0.1
10 TU	0309 3.8 / 1009 0.3 / 1532 3.7 / 2228 0.2
11 W	0357 3.7 / 1052 0.3 / 1616 3.7 / 2312 0.2
12 TH	0445 3.6 / 1131 0.4 / 1700 3.6 / 2356 0.3
13 F ◑	0534 3.4 / 1211 0.6 / 1750 3.6
14 SA	0045 0.5 / 0631 3.3 / 1303 0.7 / 1853 3.5
15 SU	0151 0.6 / 0744 3.2 / 1418 0.8 / 2012 3.4
16 M	0317 0.6 / 0910 3.2 / 1549 0.8 / 2137 3.5
17 TU	0446 0.6 / 1029 3.3 / 1711 0.7 / 2248 3.7
18 W	0554 0.5 / 1125 3.4 / 1808 0.5 / 2336 3.7
19 TH	0636 0.4 / 1203 3.5 / 1849 0.4
20 F	0013 3.7 / 0710 0.4 / 1238 3.5 / 1928 0.4
21 SA ●	0051 3.7 / 0746 0.3 / 1314 3.6 / 2008 0.3
22 SU	0129 3.6 / 0821 0.3 / 1348 3.6 / 2043 0.3
23 M	0204 3.6 / 0852 0.3 / 1419 3.7 / 2114 0.3
24 TU	0236 3.6 / 0921 0.3 / 1449 3.7 / 2143 0.3
25 W	0308 3.6 / 0951 0.4 / 1520 3.6 / 2213 0.3
26 TH	0342 3.5 / 1020 0.4 / 1553 3.6 / 2243 0.3
27 F	0416 3.4 / 1049 0.5 / 1626 3.6 / 2312 0.4
28 SA	0451 3.4 / 1118 0.6 / 1701 3.5 / 2347 0.5
29 SU ◑	0533 3.3 / 1159 0.7 / 1750 3.4
30 M	0039 0.6 / 0633 3.2 / 1304 0.8 / 1859 3.4

TIDES

Chart Datum: 2·06 metres below Normal Null (German reference level)
HAT is 4·1 metres above Chart Datum

TIME ZONE -0100	GERMANY – CUXHAVEN	Dates in amber are **SPRINGS**

TIME ZONE -0100
(German Standard Time)
Subtract 1 hour for UT
For German Summer Time add
ONE hour in **non-shaded areas**

GERMANY – CUXHAVEN
LAT 53°52'N   LONG 8°43'E
TIMES AND HEIGHTS OF HIGH AND LOW WATERS

Dates in amber are **SPRINGS**
Dates in yellow are **NEAPS**

2012

MAY

	Time	m		Time	m
1 TU	0156 0752 1431 2020	0.6 3.2 0.8 3.5	**16** W	0400 0945 1622 2203	0.5 3.2 0.6 3.6
2 W	0321 0912 1557 2135	0.6 3.4 0.7 3.4	**17** TH	0505 1042 1723 2256	0.5 3.3 0.6 3.6
3 TH	0438 1021 1708 2238	0.5 3.5 0.6 3.7	**18** F	0552 1125 1810 2338	0.4 3.4 0.5 3.6
4 F	0540 1116 1808 2333	0.3 3.6 0.5 3.8	**19** SA	0631 1204 1854	0.4 3.5 0.4
5 SA	0636 1207 1903	0.3 3.7 0.3	**20** SU	0021 0711 1244 1938	3.6 0.4 3.6 0.4
6 SU ○	0025 0728 1255 1953	3.8 0.2 3.7 0.2	**21** M ●	0104 0751 1322 2018	3.6 0.2 3.6 0.2
7 M	0115 0815 1341 2040	3.8 0.2 3.7 0.2	**22** TU	0143 0826 1356 2052	3.5 0.3 3.7 0.2
8 TU	0204 0901 1427 2128	3.8 0.2 3.8 0.2	**23** W	0217 0859 1430 2125	3.5 0.4 3.7 0.3
9 W	0255 0950 1514 2216	3.8 0.3 3.8 0.2	**24** TH	0251 0932 1503 2158	3.5 0.4 3.7 0.4
10 TH	0346 1035 1601 2303	3.6 0.3 3.7 0.3	**25** F	0327 1005 1538 2231	3.5 0.4 3.7 0.4
11 F	0436 1117 1648 2349	3.5 0.4 3.7 0.3	**26** SA	0404 1038 1614 2306	3.5 0.5 3.7 0.5
12 SA ☽	0526 1159 1738	3.4 0.5 3.7	**27** SU	0443 1113 1653 2345	3.4 0.6 3.7 0.5
13 SU	0038 0620 1248 1836	0.4 3.3 0.7 3.6	**28** M ☽	0526 1154 1737	3.4 0.6 3.6
14 M	0136 0722 1351 1944	0.5 3.2 0.7 3.5	**29** TU	0031 0617 1247 1834	0.6 3.3 0.7 3.6
15 TU	0245 0834 1507 2057	0.6 3.1 0.7 3.5	**30** W	0130 0719 1356 1942	0.6 3.3 0.7 3.6
			31 TH	0240 0830 1512 2053	0.6 3.4 0.7 3.7

JUNE

	Time	m		Time	m
1 F	0352 0938 1625 2200	0.6 3.5 0.7 3.7	**16** SA	0459 1043 1729 2304	0.6 3.4 0.6 3.5
2 SA	0459 1040 1732 2303	0.5 3.6 0.5 3.7	**17** SU	0551 1131 1822 2353	0.5 3.5 0.5 3.5
3 SU	0604 1137 1836	0.4 3.7 0.4	**18** M	0639 1216 1910	0.5 3.6 0.5
4 M ○	0003 0703 1233 1934	3.7 0.3 3.7 0.2	**19** TU ●	0040 0724 1259 1954	3.5 0.5 3.6 0.5
5 TU	0100 0756 1324 2026	3.7 0.2 3.8 0.2	**20** W	0123 0805 1338 2034	3.5 0.5 3.7 0.4
6 W	0152 0844 1412 2115	3.7 0.3 3.8 0.2	**21** TH	0202 0843 1415 2112	3.6 0.5 3.8 0.5
7 TH	0244 0934 1501 2206	3.7 0.3 3.9 0.2	**22** F	0239 0920 1451 2149	3.6 0.5 3.9 0.5
8 F	0336 1023 1549 2255	3.6 0.4 3.9 0.3	**23** SA	0315 0955 1525 2222	3.6 0.5 3.9 0.5
9 SA	0425 1106 1636 2340	3.5 0.4 3.8 0.3	**24** SU	0351 1029 1601 2257	3.6 0.5 3.8 0.5
10 SU	0512 1146 1722	3.4 0.5 3.8	**25** M	0430 1106 1641 2339	3.5 0.6 3.8 0.5
11 M ☾	0024 0559 1227 1811	0.4 3.4 0.6 3.7	**26** TU	0514 1149 1726	3.5 0.6 3.8
12 TU	0110 0648 1315 1904	0.5 3.3 0.7 3.6	**27** W ☾	0023 0601 1234 1814	0.6 3.5 0.6 3.7
13 W	0200 0744 1413 2004	0.6 3.2 0.7 3.5	**28** TH	0110 0652 1328 1911	0.6 3.5 0.7 3.7
14 TH	0258 0846 1521 2108	0.6 3.2 0.7 3.5	**29** F	0206 0753 1434 2018	0.6 3.5 0.8 3.7
15 F	0401 0948 1630 2210	0.6 3.3 0.7 3.5	**30** SA	0313 0902 1549 2130	0.7 3.5 0.7 3.7

JULY

	Time	m		Time	m
1 SU	0427 1010 1705 2242	0.6 3.6 0.6 3.6	**16** M	0510 1058 1749 2327	0.7 3.5 0.7 3.4
2 M	0539 1116 1817 2350	0.5 3.6 0.4 3.4	**17** TU	0610 1151 1843	0.6 3.6 0.6
3 TU ○	0646 1217 1921	0.4 3.7 0.3	**18** W	0018 0701 1237 1931	3.5 0.6 3.8 0.6
4 W	0051 0743 1312 2016	3.6 0.4 3.8 0.3	**19** TH ●	0105 0747 1320 2016	3.6 0.6 3.8 0.5
5 TH	0144 0834 1401 2106	3.7 0.4 3.9 0.3	**20** F	0146 0829 1359 2058	3.6 0.6 3.9 0.5
6 F	0235 0922 1449 2155	3.7 0.4 3.9 0.4	**21** SA	0224 0908 1436 2135	3.7 0.5 3.9 0.5
7 SA	0324 1009 1535 2241	3.7 0.5 4.0 0.4	**22** SU	0259 0943 1509 2208	3.7 0.5 3.9 0.5
8 SU	0408 1049 1617 2321	3.6 0.5 3.9 0.4	**23** M	0333 1016 1544 2242	3.6 0.5 3.9 0.5
9 M	0448 1124 1658 2357	3.5 0.5 3.9 0.5	**24** TU	0411 1053 1624 2324	3.6 0.5 3.9 0.5
10 TU	0526 1158 1738	3.4 0.6 3.8	**25** W	0455 1137 1710	3.6 0.6 3.9
11 W ☾	0033 0605 1234 1820	0.6 3.4 0.7 3.7	**26** TH ☾	0008 0541 1220 1755	0.6 3.6 0.6 3.8
12 TH	0108 0648 1318 1908	0.7 3.3 0.8 3.5	**27** F	0050 0628 1305 1846	0.7 3.6 0.7 3.7
13 F	0152 0742 1416 2009	0.8 3.3 0.8 3.4	**28** SA	0138 0724 1406 1953	0.7 3.6 0.8 3.6
14 SA	0251 0847 1529 2119	0.8 3.3 0.8 3.3	**29** SU	0245 0834 1525 2113	0.8 3.5 0.8 3.5
15 SU	0402 0956 1644 2228	0.8 3.4 0.7 3.4	**30** M	0406 0952 1651 2234	0.8 3.5 0.7 3.5
			31 TU	0526 1105 1809 2345	0.7 3.7 0.5 3.6

AUGUST

	Time	m		Time	m
1 W	0636 1208 1913	0.6 3.8 0.4	**16** TH	0638 1214 1908	0.7 3.7 0.6
2 TH ○	0045 0735 1303 2007	3.6 0.5 3.9 0.4	**17** F ●	0043 0727 1257 1954	3.6 0.7 3.8 0.6
3 F	0136 0824 1350 2053	3.7 0.5 3.9 0.4	**18** SA	0124 0810 1336 2035	3.7 0.6 3.9 0.5
4 SA	0222 0909 1433 2137	3.7 0.5 4.0 0.5	**19** SU	0201 0849 1413 2113	3.7 0.5 3.9 0.5
5 SU	0304 0950 1514 2217	3.7 0.5 4.0 0.5	**20** M	0236 0925 1448 2148	3.7 0.5 3.9 0.5
6 M	0342 1025 1552 2251	3.7 0.5 4.0 0.5	**21** TU	0311 0959 1524 2223	3.7 0.5 3.9 0.5
7 TU	0416 1055 1627 2321	3.6 0.5 3.9 0.6	**22** W	0350 1037 1605 2303	3.5 0.5 3.9 0.6
8 W	0448 1125 1702 2350	3.6 0.5 3.8 0.7	**23** TH	0433 1120 1651 2347	3.7 0.6 3.9 0.6
9 TH ☾	0521 1156 1737	3.6 0.8 3.7	**24** F	0518 1203 1737	3.7 0.6 3.8
10 F	0018 0556 1229 1816	0.9 3.4 0.8 3.5	**25** SA	0027 0605 1247 1829	0.8 3.6 0.7 3.6
11 SA	0051 0641 1316 1910	0.9 3.3 0.9 3.3	**26** SU	0115 0701 1347 1938	0.8 3.5 0.8 3.4
12 SU	0144 0745 1427 2024	1.0 3.3 0.9 3.2	**27** M	0224 0816 1512 2106	0.9 3.5 0.9 3.4
13 M	0302 0905 1553 2146	0.9 3.3 0.9 3.2	**28** TU	0354 0943 1647 2233	1.0 3.6 0.8 3.5
14 TU	0427 1022 1713 2259	0.9 3.4 0.8 3.3	**29** W	0522 1101 1807 2344	0.9 3.7 0.7 3.5
15 W	0540 1124 1817 2356	0.9 3.5 0.7 3.5	**30** TH	0630 1201 1905	0.7 3.9 0.7
			31 F ○	0037 0722 1249 1951	3.6 0.6 3.9 0.5

Chart Datum: 2·06 metres below Normal Null (German reference level)
HAT is 4·1 metres above Chart Datum

TIME ZONE -0100
(German Standard Time)
Subtract 1 hour for UT
For German Summer Time add
ONE hour in **non-shaded areas**

GERMANY – CUXHAVEN

LAT 53°52′N   LONG 8°43′E

TIMES AND HEIGHTS OF HIGH AND LOW WATERS

Dates in amber are **SPRINGS**
Dates in yellow are **NEAPS**

2012

SEPTEMBER

Day	Time	m	Day	Time	m
1 SA	0120 / 0807 / 1331 / 2032	3.6 / 0.5 / 3.9 / 0.5	16 SU	0055 / 0744 / 1306 / ● 2005	3.6 / 0.6 / 3.8 / 0.5
2 SU	0200 / 0847 / 1410 / 2111	3.7 / 0.5 / 3.9 / 0.5	17 M	0132 / 0824 / 1345 / 2045	3.7 / 0.5 / 3.9 / 0.4
3 M	0237 / 0924 / 1447 / 2146	3.7 / 0.5 / 3.9 / 0.5	18 TU	0209 / 0902 / 1424 / 2124	3.7 / 0.4 / 3.9 / 0.4
4 TU	0311 / 0956 / 1522 / 2216	3.7 / 0.6 / 3.9 / 0.6	19 W	0248 / 0940 / 1504 / 2203	3.8 / 0.4 / 3.9 / 0.5
5 W	0341 / 1025 / 1555 / 2243	3.7 / 0.6 / 3.8 / 0.7	20 TH	0328 / 1020 / 1548 / 2243	3.7 / 0.4 / 3.8 / 0.6
6 TH	0411 / 1053 / 1628 / 2310	3.6 / 0.6 / 3.7 / 0.8	21 F	0411 / 1103 / 1634 / 2324	3.7 / 0.5 / 3.8 / 0.7
7 F	0441 / 1121 / 1700 / 2335	3.6 / 0.7 / 3.6 / 0.9	22 SA	0456 / 1146 / 1722 / ☾	3.7 / 0.6 / 3.6
8 SA	0512 / 1149 / 1733 / ☽	3.5 / 0.8 / 3.4	23 SU	0005 / 0544 / 1234 / 1817	0.8 / 3.6 / 0.7 / 3.4
9 SU	0002 / 0550 / 1226 / 1820	0.9 / 3.4 / 0.9 / 3.2	24 M	0056 / 0644 / 1336 / 1929	0.9 / 3.5 / 0.8 / 3.3
10 M	0048 / 0649 / 1330 / 1932	1.0 / 3.3 / 1.0 / 3.1	25 TU	0209 / 0803 / 1504 / 2059	1.0 / 3.4 / 0.9 / 3.3
11 TU	0206 / 0811 / 1501 / 2101	1.1 / 3.3 / 1.0 / 3.2	26 W	0343 / 0933 / 1641 / 2228	1.0 / 3.6 / 0.8 / 3.3
12 W	0340 / 0938 / 1633 / 2224	1.0 / 3.4 / 0.9 / 3.3	27 TH	0513 / 1052 / 1759 / 2335	1.0 / 3.7 / 0.7 / 3.5
13 TH	0506 / 1050 / 1746 / 2328	0.9 / 3.5 / 0.7 / 3.4	28 F	0618 / 1147 / 1850	0.8 / 3.8 / 0.6
14 F	0610 / 1143 / 1839	0.8 / 3.6 / 0.6	29 SA	0019 / 0702 / 1227 / 1927	3.6 / 0.7 / 3.8 / 0.5
15 SA	0014 / 0700 / 1226 / 1924	3.6 / 0.7 / 3.8 / 0.5	30 SU	0056 / 0741 / 1304 / ○ 2003	3.6 / 0.6 / 3.8 / 0.5

OCTOBER

Day	Time	m	Day	Time	m
1 M	0132 / 0820 / 1343 / 2040	3.6 / 0.5 / 3.8 / 0.5	16 TU	0102 / 0756 / 1317 / 2016	3.7 / 0.5 / 3.8 / 0.4
2 TU	0207 / 0857 / 1419 / 2113	3.7 / 0.5 / 3.8 / 0.6	17 W	0143 / 0838 / 1401 / 2059	3.7 / 0.4 / 3.8 / 0.4
3 W	0239 / 0929 / 1453 / 2142	3.7 / 0.5 / 3.7 / 0.6	18 TH	0225 / 0922 / 1447 / 2144	3.8 / 0.4 / 3.8 / 0.5
4 TH	0308 / 0958 / 1526 / 2209	3.7 / 0.6 / 3.6 / 0.6	19 F	0309 / 1006 / 1534 / 2226	3.8 / 0.4 / 3.7 / 0.6
5 F	0337 / 1025 / 1558 / 2235	3.6 / 0.6 / 3.5 / 0.7	20 SA	0353 / 1050 / 1622 / 2306	3.7 / 0.5 / 3.6 / 0.6
6 SA	0407 / 1052 / 1629 / 2301	3.6 / 0.6 / 3.4 / 0.8	21 SU	0437 / 1133 / 1711 / 2349	3.7 / 0.6 / 3.5 / 0.6
7 SU	0438 / 1119 / 1701 / 2328	3.5 / 0.8 / 3.3 / 0.9	22 M	0527 / 1225 / 1807 / ☾	3.6 / 0.7 / 3.3
8 M	0513 / 1153 / 1743 / ☽	3.4 / 0.9 / 3.2	23 TU	0040 / 0629 / 1327 / 1916	0.9 / 3.5 / 0.8 / 3.2
9 TU	0009 / 0604 / 1249 / 1848	1.1 / 3.3 / 1.0 / 3.1	24 W	0151 / 0745 / 1449 / 2040	1.0 / 3.5 / 0.9 / 3.2
10 W	0119 / 0720 / 1412 / 2013	1.1 / 3.3 / 1.0 / 3.1	25 TH	0319 / 0910 / 1618 / 2204	1.0 / 3.5 / 0.8 / 3.2
11 TH	0252 / 0848 / 1546 / 2140	1.1 / 3.4 / 0.9 / 3.3	26 F	0446 / 1026 / 1733 / 2308	1.0 / 3.6 / 0.7 / 3.3
12 F	0422 / 1005 / 1704 / 2248	1.0 / 3.5 / 0.7 / 3.4	27 SA	0550 / 1104 / 1821 / 2351	0.8 / 3.5 / 0.6 / 0.6
13 SA	0531 / 1104 / 1801 / 2338	0.8 / 3.6 / 0.5 / 3.5	28 SU	0633 / 1158 / 1855 ●	0.7 / 3.7 / 0.6
14 SU	0625 / 1151 / 1848	0.7 / 3.7 / 0.5	29 M	0025 / 0711 / 1235 / ○ 1931	3.5 / 0.6 / 3.7 / 0.6
15 M	0020 / 0712 / 1234 / ● 1933	3.6 / 0.6 / 3.8 / 0.5	30 TU	0101 / 0752 / 1316 / 2008	3.6 / 0.6 / 3.6 / 0.6
			31 W	0138 / 0831 / 1354 / 2042	3.6 / 0.5 / 3.6 / 0.5

NOVEMBER

Day	Time	m	Day	Time	m
1 TH	0210 / 0904 / 1428 / 2112	3.6 / 0.5 / 3.5 / 0.6	16 F	0204 / 0905 / 1432 / 2126	3.7 / 0.4 / 3.7 / 0.5
2 F	0241 / 0934 / 1501 / 2141	3.6 / 0.5 / 3.5 / 0.6	17 SA	0251 / 0955 / 1524 / 2213	3.8 / 0.4 / 3.7 / 0.5
3 SA	0311 / 1003 / 1533 / 2210	3.6 / 0.5 / 3.4 / 0.6	18 SU	0338 / 1042 / 1614 / 2256	3.8 / 0.4 / 3.5 / 0.6
4 SU	0342 / 1032 / 1606 / 2238	3.6 / 0.6 / 3.4 / 0.7	19 M	0425 / 1128 / 1703 / 2338	3.7 / 0.5 / 3.4 / 0.7
5 M	0414 / 1101 / 1640 / 2308	3.6 / 0.7 / 3.3 / 0.9	20 TU	0514 / 1217 / 1755 / ◐	3.7 / 0.6 / 3.3
6 TU	0449 / 1135 / 1720 / 2346	3.5 / 0.9 / 3.3 / 1.0	21 W	0025 / 0610 / 1312 / 1854	0.8 / 3.6 / 0.8 / 3.2
7 W	0533 / 1222 / 1814 / ◐	3.5 / 1.0 / 3.2	22 TH	0125 / 0715 / 1419 / 2003	0.9 / 3.5 / 0.8 / 3.1
8 TH	0044 / 0636 / 1331 / 1926	1.1 / 3.4 / 1.0 / 3.2	23 F	0237 / 0828 / 1533 / 2116	0.9 / 3.5 / 0.8 / 3.1
9 F	0203 / 0754 / 1453 / 2047	1.1 / 3.4 / 0.9 / 3.3	24 SA	0356 / 0940 / 1643 / 2222	0.9 / 3.5 / 0.8 / 3.2
10 SA	0329 / 0912 / 1611 / 2159	1.0 / 3.5 / 0.8 / 3.4	25 SU	0505 / 1040 / 1737 / 2312	0.8 / 3.6 / 0.7 / 3.4
11 SU	0443 / 1017 / 1715 / 2256	0.9 / 3.6 / 0.6 / 3.5	26 M	0558 / 1127 / 1819 / 2353	0.8 / 3.5 / 0.7 / 3.5
12 M	0544 / 1112 / 1811 / 2346	0.8 / 3.7 / 0.5 / 3.6	27 TU	0643 / 1209 / 1900	0.7 / 3.5 / 0.6
13 TU	0639 / 1204 / 1903 ●	0.6 / 3.7 / 0.5	28 W	0033 / 0726 / 1252 / ○ 1940	3.5 / 0.6 / 3.5 / 0.6
14 W	0033 / 0730 / 1253 / 1951	3.6 / 0.5 / 3.7 / 0.4	29 TH	0112 / 0807 / 1332 / 2017	3.6 / 0.5 / 3.4 / 0.5
15 TH	0118 / 0818 / 1341 / 2038	3.7 / 0.4 / 3.7 / 0.4	30 F	0147 / 0842 / 1408 / 2050	3.6 / 0.5 / 3.4 / 0.5

DECEMBER

Day	Time	m	Day	Time	m
1 SA	0220 / 0916 / 1442 / 2122	3.6 / 0.5 / 3.5 / 0.6	16 SU	0237 / 0945 / 1513 / 2204	3.8 / 0.4 / 3.6 / 0.5
2 SU	0253 / 0949 / 1516 / 2154	3.7 / 0.6 / 3.5 / 0.6	17 M	0327 / 1035 / 1604 / 2248	3.9 / 0.4 / 3.6 / 0.5
3 M	0326 / 1019 / 1550 / 2224	3.7 / 0.6 / 3.4 / 0.7	18 TU	0413 / 1121 / 1650 / 2327	3.8 / 0.4 / 3.5 / 0.6
4 TU	0358 / 1050 / 1624 / 2255	3.7 / 0.7 / 3.4 / 0.8	19 W	0458 / 1203 / 1734	3.8 / 0.5 / 3.3
5 W	0432 / 1124 / 1702 / 2332	3.7 / 0.8 / 3.4 / 0.9	20 TH	0006 / 0545 / 1247 / ◑ 1821	0.7 / 3.7 / 0.5 / 3.2
6 TH	0512 / 1205 / 1747 / ◐	3.6 / 0.9 / 3.3	21 F	0050 / 0636 / 1335 / 1912	0.8 / 3.6 / 0.6 / 3.1
7 F	0019 / 0601 / 1257 / 1844	1.0 / 3.6 / 0.9 / 3.3	22 SA	0144 / 0734 / 1430 / 2013	0.8 / 3.4 / 0.7 / 3.1
8 SA	0121 / 0705 / 1402 / 1953	1.0 / 3.5 / 0.9 / 3.3	23 SU	0251 / 0841 / 1535 / 2120	0.9 / 3.4 / 0.9 / 3.2
9 SU	0235 / 0817 / 1516 / 2106	1.0 / 3.5 / 0.8 / 3.4	24 M	0406 / 0949 / 1641 / 2224	0.9 / 3.4 / 0.8 / 3.3
10 M	0351 / 0929 / 1628 / 2212	1.0 / 3.6 / 0.7 / 3.5	25 TU	0516 / 1051 / 1740 / 2319	0.8 / 3.4 / 0.8 / 3.4
11 TU	0502 / 1035 / 1735 / 2312	0.8 / 3.6 / 0.6 / 3.5	26 W	0613 / 1144 / 1831	0.7 / 3.4 / 0.7
12 W	0608 / 1137 / 1837	0.6 / 3.6 / 0.5	27 TH	0007 / 0702 / 1230 / 1916	3.5 / 0.7 / 3.4 / 0.6
13 TH	0007 / 0709 / 1234 / ● 1932	3.6 / 0.4 / 3.6 / 0.4	28 F	0049 / 0745 / 1313 / ○ 1956	3.6 / 0.6 / 3.4 / 0.6
14 F	0059 / 0802 / 1327 / 2022	3.7 / 0.3 / 3.6 / 0.4	29 SA	0127 / 0823 / 1350 / 2032	3.6 / 0.5 / 3.4 / 0.6
15 SA	0148 / 0853 / 1420 / 2113	3.7 / 0.3 / 3.6 / 0.5	30 SU	0203 / 0901 / 1426 / 2109	3.7 / 0.6 / 3.5 / 0.6
			31 M	0238 / 0937 / 1501 / 2142	3.7 / 0.6 / 3.5 / 0.6

Chart Datum: 2·06 metres below Normal Null (German reference level)
HAT is 4·1 metres above Chart Datum

TIDES

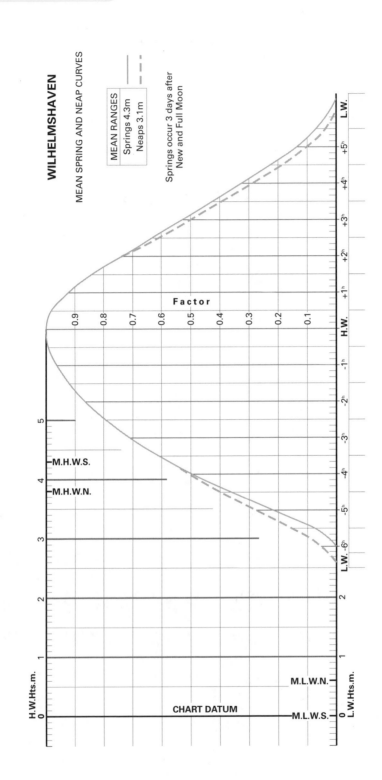

TIME ZONE -0100
(German Standard Time)
Subtract 1 hour for UT
For German Summer Time add
ONE hour in **non-shaded areas**

GERMANY – WILHELMSHAVEN

LAT 53°31′N   LONG 8°09′E

TIMES AND HEIGHTS OF HIGH AND LOW WATERS

Dates in amber are **SPRINGS**
Dates in yellow are **NEAPS**

2012

JANUARY

Time	m		Time	m
1 0525	4.6	**16** 0513	4.8
1140	0.9	1133	0.7
SU 1747	4.1	M 1744	4.4
◐ 2342	1.1	2345	0.9
2 0607	4.4	**17** 0601	4.7
1219	1.0	1216	0.8
M 1833	4.1	TU 1833	4.4
3 0032	1.2	**18** 0035	1.0
0700	4.3	0700	4.6
TU 1310	1.1	W 1313	1.0
1934	4.1	1936	4.3
4 0139	1.2	**19** 0144	1.1
0807	4.2	0814	4.5
W 1416	1.2	TH 1427	1.1
2045	4.2	2053	4.4
5 0255	1.2	**20** 0307	1.1
0919	4.3	0936	4.4
TH 1527	1.1	F 1549	1.0
2153	4.3	2212	4.5
6 0407	1.1	**21** 0429	0.9
1024	4.3	1054	4.4
F 1632	1.0	SA 1705	0.9
2253	4.4	2323	4.6
7 0507	0.9	**22** 0541	0.7
1121	4.3	1201	4.5
SA 1729	0.9	SU 1811	0.7
2345	4.5		
8 0600	0.8	**23** 0023	4.8
1212	4.4	0640	0.6
SU 1820	0.8	M 1256	4.5
		● 1906	0.6
9 0032	4.6	**24** 0112	4.8
0648	0.7	0730	0.6
M 1259	4.5	TU 1343	4.6
○ 1906	0.8	1951	0.6
10 0115	4.7	**25** 0155	4.8
0735	0.7	0815	0.5
TU 1342	4.5	W 1426	4.6
1950	0.8	2033	0.6
11 0157	4.8	**26** 0236	4.9
0820	0.6	0857	0.5
W 1423	4.6	TH 1505	4.6
2032	0.7	2110	0.5
12 0236	4.9	**27** 0314	4.9
0901	0.6	0935	0.5
TH 1501	4.6	F 1538	4.6
2108	0.6	2139	0.5
13 0311	4.9	**28** 0347	4.8
0935	0.5	1006	0.5
F 1538	4.5	SA 1607	4.4
2141	0.6	2205	0.5
14 0348	4.9	**29** 0418	4.7
1010	0.5	1034	0.6
SA 1617	4.4	SU 1634	4.4
2219	0.6	2233	0.7
15 0429	4.9	**30** 0449	4.6
1051	0.6	1100	0.8
SU 1700	4.4	M 1703	4.3
2301	0.8	2302	0.9
		31 0519	4.5
		1126	0.9
		TU 1736	4.2
		◐ 2336	1.0

FEBRUARY

Time	m		Time	m
1 0559	4.3	**16** 0011	0.8
1202	1.1	0639	4.4
W 1825	4.1	TH 1244	0.9
		1909	4.3
2 0028	1.2	**17** 0117	1.0
0659	4.1	0755	4.3
TH 1302	1.2	F 1400	1.1
1936	4.1	2032	4.3
3 0145	1.2	**18** 0247	1.0
0819	4.1	0925	4.3
F 1424	1.2	SA 1532	1.1
2058	4.2	2200	4.5
4 0311	1.2	**19** 0419	0.9
0941	4.1	1049	4.3
SA 1547	1.1	SU 1656	1.0
2215	4.3	2315	4.6
5 0428	1.0	**20** 0534	0.7
1052	4.3	1156	4.4
SU 1658	1.0	M 1802	0.8
2319	4.5		
6 0532	0.8	**21** 0013	4.7
1151	4.4	0630	0.6
M 1757	0.9	TU 1247	4.5
		● 1853	0.6
7 0011	4.7	**22** 0059	4.8
0627	0.7	0716	0.5
TU 1241	4.5	W 1329	4.6
○ 1849	0.8	1935	0.5
8 0057	4.8	**23** 0140	4.8
0716	0.6	0756	0.5
W 1326	4.6	TH 1406	4.6
1935	0.7	2012	0.5
9 0139	4.9	**24** 0216	4.9
0802	0.5	0833	0.4
TH 1407	4.6	F 1440	4.6
2016	0.5	2045	0.5
10 0219	4.9	**25** 0249	4.9
0843	0.4	0905	0.4
F 1445	4.6	SA 1509	4.6
2053	0.4	2113	0.4
11 0257	4.9	**26** 0320	4.8
0920	0.3	0934	0.5
SA 1523	4.6	SU 1535	4.5
2128	0.3	2139	0.4
12 0335	4.9	**27** 0350	4.7
0957	0.4	1000	0.6
SU 1602	4.5	M 1602	4.6
2206	0.4	2206	0.4
13 0417	4.9	**28** 0418	4.6
1037	0.5	1025	0.7
M 1644	4.5	TU 1629	4.6
2247	0.5	2231	0.4
14 0500	4.8	**29** 0445	4.4
1116	0.6	1045	0.8
TU 1724	4.5	W 1656	4.3
◐ 2326	0.7	2255	0.8
15 0544	4.7		
1153	0.7		
W 1808	4.4		

MARCH

Time	m		Time	m
1 0515	4.2	**16** 0628	4.3
1111	0.9	1222	0.9
TH 1734	4.2	F 1853	4.3
◐ 2334	0.9		
2 0606	4.0	**17** 0101	0.8
1202	1.1	0744	4.1
F 1838	4.1	SA 1340	1.1
		2018	4.3
3 0043	1.1	**18** 0232	0.9
0725	4.0	0916	4.1
SA 1325	1.2	SU 1516	1.1
2006	4.1	2149	4.5
4 0216	1.1	**19** 0408	0.9
0857	4.0	1042	4.3
SU 1500	1.1	M 1643	0.9
2135	4.3	2304	4.6
5 0348	0.9	**20** 0521	0.7
1021	4.2	1145	4.4
M 1624	1.0	TU 1744	0.7
2249	4.5	2356	4.7
6 0501	0.7	**21** 0611	0.5
1126	4.4	1229	4.5
TU 1730	0.8	W 1828	0.6
2346	4.7		
7 0600	0.5	**22** 0037	4.8
1218	4.5	0650	0.5
W 1824	0.7	TH 1305	4.5
		● 1907	0.4
8 0033	4.8	**23** 0116	4.7
0650	0.4	0728	0.4
TH 1304	4.6	F 1340	4.6
○ 1911	0.5	1944	0.4
9 0116	4.9	**24** 0152	4.7
0735	0.3	0802	0.4
F 1345	4.6	SA 1412	4.6
1953	0.4	2017	0.4
10 0157	4.9	**25** 0224	4.7
0818	0.2	0832	0.4
SA 1425	4.7	SU 1441	4.6
2032	0.2	2046	0.4
11 0239	4.9	**26** 0254	4.7
0900	0.2	0901	0.4
SU 1505	4.7	M 1508	4.6
2112	0.2	2113	0.4
12 0321	4.9	**27** 0324	4.6
0940	0.3	0928	0.5
M 1546	4.6	TU 1535	4.6
2152	0.3	2140	0.4
13 0405	4.8	**28** 0354	4.5
1019	0.4	0953	0.5
TU 1626	4.6	W 1603	4.5
2231	0.4	2206	0.4
14 0449	4.7	**29** 0421	4.4
1057	0.5	1016	0.6
W 1707	4.5	TH 1630	4.4
2311	0.5	2231	0.6
15 0533	4.5	**30** 0449	4.2
1133	0.7	1040	0.7
TH 1751	4.4	F 1703	4.3
◐ 2355	0.7	2303	0.7
		31 0533	4.0
		1124	0.9
		SA 1759	4.2

APRIL

Time	m		Time	m
1 0002	0.9	**16** 0215	0.8
0645	3.9	0858	4.1
SU 1240	1.1	M 1451	1.0
1922	4.2	2128	4.4
2 0131	1.0	**17** 0344	0.7
0816	4.0	1019	4.2
M 1416	1.1	TU 1614	0.9
2053	4.3	2240	4.6
3 0305	0.8	**18** 0453	0.6
0944	4.2	1118	4.3
TU 1544	0.9	W 1712	0.6
2212	4.5	2329	4.7
4 0423	0.6	**19** 0538	0.5
1053	4.4	1158	4.4
W 1653	0.8	TH 1753	0.5
2313	4.7		
5 0524	0.4	**20** 0007	4.7
1147	4.5	0614	0.4
TH 1750	0.6	F 1233	4.5
		1833	0.4
6 0003	4.8	**21** 0046	4.6
0617	0.3	0653	0.4
F 1235	4.6	SA 1310	4.6
○ 1841	0.4	● 1914	0.4
7 0049	4.8	**22** 0126	4.6
0705	0.2	0729	0.4
SA 1320	4.7	SU 1344	4.6
1926	0.3	1950	0.3
8 0134	4.9	**23** 0200	4.6
0750	0.1	0801	0.4
SU 1402	4.7	M 1415	4.6
2009	0.2	2021	0.3
9 0220	4.9	**24** 0232	4.6
0836	0.2	0831	0.5
M 1445	4.7	TU 1444	4.7
2053	0.1	2050	0.4
10 0307	4.8	**25** 0303	4.5
0920	0.2	0901	0.4
TU 1528	4.7	W 1514	4.6
2136	0.2	2119	0.3
11 0354	4.7	**26** 0335	4.4
1001	0.3	0930	0.5
W 1611	4.6	TH 1544	4.6
2217	0.2	2149	0.4
12 0440	4.5	**27** 0406	4.3
1038	0.5	0958	0.6
TH 1653	4.6	F 1615	4.5
2259	0.4	2220	0.5
13 0526	4.4	**28** 0438	4.3
1117	0.7	1027	0.7
F 1740	4.5	SA 1650	4.5
◐ 2346	0.5	2254	0.6
14 0621	4.2	**29** 0519	4.1
1207	0.8	1109	0.8
SA 1841	4.4	SU 1738	4.4
		◐ 2345	0.7
15 0050	0.7	**30** 0619	0.9
0732	4.1	1212	0.9
SU 1320	1.0	M 1848	4.3
2001	4.3		

Chart Datum: 2·7 metres below Normal Null (German reference level)
HAT is 5·1 metres above Chart Datum

TIDES

TIDES

TIME ZONE -0100
(German Standard Time)
Subtract 1 hour for UT
For German Summer Time add
ONE hour in **non-shaded areas**

GERMANY – WILHELMSHAVEN

LAT 53°31'N   LONG 8°09'E

TIMES AND HEIGHTS OF HIGH AND LOW WATERS

Dates in amber are **SPRINGS**
Dates in yellow are **NEAPS**

2012

MAY

Date	Time m	Time m	Time m	Time m
1 TU	0058 0.8	0739 4.1	1336 1.0	2011 4.4
2 W	0222 0.7	0902 4.2	1500 0.9	2128 4.5
3 TH	0339 0.6	1012 4.4	1611 0.7	2233 4.7
4 F	0443 0.4	1110 4.5	1712 0.6	2330 4.7
5 SA	0541 0.3	1204 4.6	1809 0.4	
6 SU	0024 4.8	0636 0.2	1254 4.7	○ 1901 0.2
7 M	0114 4.8	0725 0.1	1341 4.7	1948 0.1
8 TU	0203 4.8	0813 0.2	1426 4.8	2035 0.1
9 W	0253 4.7	0900 0.3	1512 4.8	2122 0.1
10 TH	0343 4.6	0944 0.3	1557 4.7	2207 0.2
11 F	0432 4.4	1024 0.4	1642 4.7	2251 0.3
12 SA	0519 4.3	1105 0.6	1730 4.6	◑ 2340 0.5
13 SU	0610 4.2	1153 0.8	1826 4.5	
14 M	0038 0.6	0710 4.1	1254 0.9	1933 4.4
15 TU	0146 0.7	0821 4.0	1409 0.9	2048 4.4
16 W	0301 0.7	0933 4.1	1525 0.8	2157 4.5
17 TH	0406 0.6	1033 4.3	1626 0.6	2250 4.5
18 F	0454 0.5	1118 4.4	1713 0.5	2332 4.6
19 SA	0535 0.5	1158 4.5	1759 0.5	
20 SU	0015 4.5	0618 0.5	1238 4.6	1844 0.5
21 M	0059 4.5	0659 0.4	1317 4.6	● 1925 0.4
22 TU	0138 4.5	0735 0.4	1352 4.7	1959 0.4
23 W	0212 4.5	0809 0.4	1425 4.7	2033 0.4
24 TH	0246 4.5	0843 0.5	1458 4.7	2106 0.4
25 F	0321 4.5	0916 0.5	1531 4.7	2140 0.4
26 SA	0355 4.4	0948 0.6	1605 4.7	2216 0.5
27 SU	0431 4.3	1023 0.6	1642 4.7	2255 0.6
28 M	0512 4.3		1727 4.6	◑ 2339 0.6
29 TU	0603 4.2	1156 0.8	1823 4.5	
30 W	0035 0.7	0707 4.2	1302 0.8	1932 4.5
31 TH	0143 0.7	0819 4.3	1417 0.8	2044 4.6

JUNE

Date	Time m	Time m	Time m	Time m
1 F	0255 0.6	0928 4.4	1529 0.8	2153 4.7
2 SA	0403 0.5	1032 4.5	1636 0.6	2259 4.7
3 SU	0508 0.4	1133 4.6	1741 0.6	
4 M	0001 4.7	0610 0.3	1231 4.7	○ 1840 0.3
5 TU	0058 4.7	0705 0.2	1323 4.8	1932 0.2
6 W	0150 4.7	0755 0.3	1410 4.8	2022 0.2
7 TH	0242 4.6	0844 0.3	1458 4.9	2112 0.2
8 F	0333 4.6	0931 0.4	1546 4.9	2200 0.2
9 SA	0421 4.4	1012 0.4	1630 4.8	2244 0.3
10 SU	0505 4.3	1051 0.5	1714 4.8	2328 0.4
11 M	0548 4.2	1133 0.7	1801 4.6 ◑	
12 TU	0015 0.6	0634 4.2	1220 0.8	1854 4.5
13 W	0105 0.7	0728 4.1	1317 0.8	1954 4.4
14 TH	0203 0.7	0831 4.1	1425 0.8	2059 4.4
15 F	0305 0.7	0935 4.2	1533 0.8	2202 4.4
16 SA	0404 0.7	1032 4.4	1633 0.7	2256 4.5
17 SU	0457 0.6	1122 4.5	1727 0.6	2345 4.5
18 M	0546 0.6	1208 4.5	1816 0.6	
19 TU	0032 4.5	0633 0.5	1252 4.6	● 1901 0.5
20 W	0116 4.5	0715 0.5	1331 4.7	1942 0.5
21 TH	0155 4.5	0755 0.5	1409 4.8	2022 0.5
22 F	0233 4.6	0833 0.6	1445 4.9	2059 0.5
23 SA	0308 4.6	0908 0.6	1519 4.9	2133 0.5
24 SU	0343 4.5	0941 0.6	1553 4.8	2209 0.5
25 M	0420 4.4	1018 0.6	1632 4.8	2249 0.6
26 TU	0503 4.4	1059 0.7	1716 4.8	2332 0.6
27 W	0548 4.4	1144 0.7	1803 4.7 ◐	
28 TH	0017 0.6	0638 4.4	1235 0.8	1900 4.7
29 F	0111 0.7	0739 4.4	1340 0.9	2007 4.6
30 SA	0218 0.8	0848 4.5	1454 0.8	2121 4.6

JULY

Date	Time m	Time m	Time m	Time m
1 SU	0331 0.7	1000 4.5	1609 0.7	2235 4.6
2 M	0443 0.6	1109 4.6	1721 0.5	2345 4.6
3 TU	0552 0.5	1213 4.7	1826 0.4 ○	
4 W	0047 4.6	0652 0.4	1309 4.8	1922 0.3
5 TH	0141 4.6	0745 0.4	1358 4.9	2013 0.3
6 F	0231 4.6	0834 0.4	1445 5.0	2103 0.3
7 SA	0319 4.6	0919 0.4	1531 5.0	2149 0.3
8 SU	0402 4.5	0958 0.4	1612 4.9	2229 0.4
9 M	0440 4.4	1031 0.5	1650 4.8	2305 0.5
10 TU	0515 4.4	1105 0.7	1728 4.7	2342 0.7
11 W	0550 4.3	1142 0.8	1808 4.6 ◑	
12 TH	0018 0.8	0631 4.2	1225 0.9	1855 4.4 ◐
13 F	0101 0.9	0723 4.2	1322 1.0	1955 4.3
14 SA	0159 1.0	0830 4.2	1434 1.0	2106 4.3
15 SU	0309 1.0	0941 4.3	1549 0.9	2216 4.3
16 M	0418 0.8	1045 4.4	1654 0.7	2316 4.4
17 TU	0518 0.7	1140 4.5	1750 0.7	
18 W	0008 4.4	0611 0.7	1228 4.6	1840 0.6
19 TH	0055 4.5	0659 0.7	1311 4.8	● 1926 0.6
20 F	0138 4.6	0743 0.7	1352 4.9	2009 0.6
21 SA	0217 4.7	0823 0.6	1429 5.0	2048 0.5
22 SU	0252 4.7	0858 0.6	1503 4.9	2121 0.5
23 M	0326 4.6	0930 0.5	1537 4.9	2154 0.5
24 TU	0404 4.5	1006 0.6	1616 4.9	2235 0.6
25 W	0446 4.5	1048 0.6	1700 4.9	2319 0.6
26 TH	0529 4.5	1130 0.7	1744 4.8	◐ 2359 0.7
27 F	0612 4.5		1834 4.6	
28 SA	0045 0.8	0706 4.4	1311 0.9	1940 4.5
29 SU	0149 0.9	0818 4.4	1428 0.9	2100 4.5
30 M	0309 1.0	0939 4.5	1554 0.8	2222 4.5
31 TU	0430 0.8	1055 4.6	1712 0.6	2336 4.5

AUGUST

Date	Time m	Time m	Time m	Time m
1 W	0543 0.7	1201 4.7	1818 0.5	
2 TH	0038 4.6	0645 0.6	1256 4.9	○ 1913 0.4
3 F	0130 4.6	0736 0.5	1344 4.9	2002 0.4
4 SA	0216 4.7	0821 0.5	1428 5.0	2047 0.4
5 SU	0258 4.7	0901 0.5	1509 5.0	2128 0.4
6 M	0334 4.6	0936 0.5	1546 5.0	2203 0.5
7 TU	0406 4.5	1005 0.6	1619 4.8	2234 0.6
8 W	0435 4.5	1034 0.7	1651 4.7	2303 0.8
9 TH	0505 4.4	1106 0.8	1723 4.6	◑ 2331 0.9
10 F	0538 4.4	1139 1.0	1800 4.4	
11 SA	0004 1.0	0621 4.2	1223 1.1	1853 4.2
12 SU	0055 1.1	0725 4.2	1333 1.2	2008 4.1
13 M	0211 1.2	0846 4.2	1458 1.1	2131 4.2
14 TU	0336 1.1	1005 4.3	1618 1.0	2245 4.3
15 W	0449 0.9	1111 4.5	1723 0.8	2343 4.4
16 TH	0548 0.6	1202 4.6	1816 0.7	
17 F	0031 4.5	0638 0.8	1247 4.8	● 1904 0.6
18 SA	0115 4.6	0724 0.7	1327 4.9	1947 0.5
19 SU	0154 4.7	0804 0.6	1405 4.9	2026 0.5
20 M	0230 4.7	0839 0.5	1441 4.9	2102 0.5
21 TU	0305 4.7	0913 0.5	1517 4.9	2136 0.5
22 W	0343 4.7	0950 0.6	1557 4.9	2216 0.6
23 TH	0424 4.6	1031 0.6	1641 4.9	2258 0.7
24 F	0506 4.6	1112 0.7	1725 4.7	◐ 2337 0.7
25 SA	0548 4.5	1153 0.8	1815 4.5	
26 SU	0021 0.9	0642 4.4	1250 0.9	1923 4.3
27 M	0128 1.1	0758 4.4	1413 1.0	2050 4.3
28 TU	0257 1.2	0927 4.5	1547 0.9	2218 4.4
29 W	0426 1.1	1048 4.6	1709 0.7	2331 4.5
30 TH	0538 0.9	1150 4.8	1810 0.6	
31 F	0026 4.5	0633 0.7	1240 4.9	○ 1859 0.5

Chart Datum: 2·7 metres below Normal Null (German reference level)
HAT is 5·1 metres above Chart Datum

TIME ZONE -0100
(German Standard Time)
Subtract 1 hour for UT
For German Summer Time add
ONE hour in **non-shaded areas**

GERMANY – WILHELMSHAVEN

LAT 53°31'N   LONG 8°09'E

TIMES AND HEIGHTS OF HIGH AND LOW WATERS

Dates in amber are **SPRINGS**
Dates in yellow are **NEAPS**

2012

SEPTEMBER

Time	m	Time	m
1 0112 0719 SA 1324 1943	4.6 0.6 4.9 0.5	**16** 0044 0654 SU 1256 ● 1916	4.6 0.7 4.8 0.5
2 0152 0759 SU 1404 2022	4.6 0.5 4.9 0.5	**17** 0124 0736 M 1336 1957	4.7 0.6 4.9 0.5
3 0229 0835 M 1441 2058	4.7 0.5 4.9 0.5	**18** 0203 0815 TU 1416 2038	4.7 0.5 4.9 0.5
4 0302 0908 TU 1514 2129	4.7 0.6 4.9 0.6	**19** 0241 0853 W 1457 2117	4.7 0.4 4.9 0.5
5 0330 0936 W 1546 2157	4.6 0.6 4.8 0.7	**20** 0321 0932 TH 1539 2155	4.7 0.5 4.8 0.6
6 0357 1003 TH 1616 2224	0.6 0.6 4.6 0.8	**21** 0402 1012 F 1623 2234	4.6 0.6 4.7 0.7
7 0425 1031 F 1644 2248	4.5 0.8 4.5 0.9	**22** 0443 1053 SA 1709 ◑ 2314	4.5 0.7 4.6 0.9
8 0454 1058 SA 1715 ◑ 2315	4.4 0.9 4.3 1.1	**23** 0527 1137 SU 1801	4.4 0.8 4.3
9 0531 1134 SU 1800 2359	4.3 1.1 4.1 1.2	**24** 0001 0624 M 1237 1911	1.1 4.4 0.9 4.2
10 0628 1236 M 1912	4.2 1.2 4.0	**25** 0111 0743 TU 1402 2040	1.2 4.4 1.1 4.1
11 0114 0751 TU 1405 2042	1.3 4.2 1.3 4.0	**26** 0245 0915 W 1538 2210	1.3 4.5 1.0 4.3
12 0248 0920 W 1536 2207	1.3 4.3 1.1 4.2	**27** 0417 1036 TH 1659 2319	1.2 4.6 0.8 4.4
13 0413 1034 TH 1649 2312	1.1 4.4 0.8 4.4	**28** 0524 1133 F 1753	0.9 4.8 0.7
14 0517 1130 F 1744	0.9 4.6 0.7	**29** 0006 0610 SA 1215 1833	4.5 0.7 4.8 0.6
15 0001 0608 SA 1214 1832	4.5 0.8 4.7 0.6	**30** 0044 0649 SU 1255 ○ 1912	4.5 0.6 4.8 0.6

OCTOBER

Time	m	Time	m
1 0121 0729 M 1335 1949	4.6 0.6 4.8 0.6	**16** 0052 0705 TU 1306 1927	4.7 0.6 4.8 0.5
2 0157 0806 TU 1411 2023	4.6 0.5 4.8 0.6	**17** 0134 0749 W 1352 2012	4.7 0.5 4.8 0.5
3 0229 0838 W 1443 2053	4.6 0.6 4.7 0.6	**18** 0217 0832 TH 1438 2056	4.7 0.4 4.8 0.5
4 0256 0907 TH 1514 2121	4.7 0.6 4.6 0.7	**19** 0300 0915 F 1524 2137	4.7 0.4 4.7 0.6
5 0324 0933 F 1544 2147	4.6 0.6 4.5 0.8	**20** 0343 0957 SA 1610 2214	4.7 0.5 4.6 0.7
6 0352 1000 SA 1613 2212	4.5 0.7 4.4 0.9	**21** 0425 1038 SU 1657 2255	4.6 0.6 4.4 0.9
7 0420 1027 SU 1642 2239	4.5 0.9 4.3 1.1	**22** 0512 1125 M 1751 ◑ 2344	4.6 0.8 4.2 1.1
8 0454 1101 M 1722 ◑ 2319	4.3 1.1 4.1 1.2	**23** 0610 1226 TU 1858	4.5 1.0 4.1
9 0544 1154 TU 1826	4.2 1.3 4.0	**24** 0052 0725 W 1345 2020	1.2 4.4 1.1 4.0
10 0026 0700 W 1315 1952	1.4 4.2 1.3 4.0	**25** 0220 0851 TH 1514 2144	1.3 4.4 1.0 4.1
11 0157 0828 TH 1447 2120	1.4 4.3 1.1 4.2	**26** 0347 1009 F 1630 2250	1.2 4.6 0.9 4.3
12 0325 0947 F 1604 2230	1.2 4.4 0.9 4.3	**27** 0453 1105 SA 1721 2334	1.0 4.7 0.7 4.4
13 0434 1048 SA 1703 2322	1.0 4.6 0.7 4.5	**28** 0536 1145 SU 1758 ●	0.9 4.7 0.7
14 0529 1136 SU 1754	0.9 4.6 0.6	**29** 0010 0615 M 1224 ○ 1836	4.5 0.7 4.6 0.4
15 0008 0618 M 1222 ● 1842	4.6 0.7 4.7 0.5	**30** 0047 0657 TU 1305 1915	4.5 0.7 4.6 0.6
		31 0125 0737 W 1343 1950	4.6 0.6 4.7 0.6

NOVEMBER

Time	m	Time	m
1 0158 0811 TH 1416 2020	4.6 0.6 4.5 0.6	**16** 0154 0811 F 1421 2035	4.7 0.4 4.7 0.5
2 0228 0841 F 1447 2050	4.6 0.6 4.5 0.7	**17** 0241 0859 SA 1512 2121	4.8 0.4 4.6 0.6
3 0257 0909 SA 1519 2119	4.6 0.6 4.4 0.7	**18** 0328 0946 SU 1601 2202	4.8 0.4 4.4 0.6
4 0327 0937 SU 1549 2146	4.6 0.7 4.3 0.9	**19** 0413 1029 M 1648 2241	4.7 0.5 4.3 0.8
5 0357 1008 M 1620 2216	4.6 0.8 4.2 1.0	**20** 0459 1118 TU 1738 ◐ 2327	4.7 0.7 4.2 0.9
6 0430 1042 TU 1657 2254	4.5 1.0 4.2 1.2	**21** 0553 1211 W 1835	4.6 0.9 4.1
7 0514 1128 W 1751 ◐ 2350	4.4 1.2 4.1 1.3	**22** 0025 0657 TH 1316 1942	1.1 4.4 1.0 4.0
8 0616 1233 TH 1904	4.3 1.2 4.1	**23** 0136 0809 F 1428 2055	1.2 4.4 1.0 4.0
9 0106 0735 F 1353 2025	1.4 4.3 1.1 4.2	**24** 0254 0922 SA 1539 2201	1.2 4.4 0.9 4.2
10 0230 0853 SA 1511 2139	1.3 4.4 1.0 4.3	**25** 0404 1023 SU 1635 2253	1.0 4.5 0.9 4.3
11 0343 0959 SU 1616 2238	1.1 4.6 0.9 4.4	**26** 0457 1111 M 1720 2335	0.9 4.5 0.8 4.5
12 0445 1056 M 1713 2331	0.9 4.6 0.6 4.5	**27** 0543 1154 TU 1802	0.8 4.5 0.8
13 0541 1150 TU 1808 ●	0.8 4.7 0.6	**28** 0016 0629 W 1237 ○ 1845	4.5 0.7 4.5 0.7
14 0021 0635 W 1241 ○ 1859	4.6 0.7 4.7 0.5	**29** 0056 0711 TH 1318 1922	4.6 0.7 4.4 0.6
15 0109 0723 TH 1331 1947	4.7 0.4 4.7 0.5	**30** 0133 0747 F 1353 1955	4.6 0.6 4.4 0.6

DECEMBER

Time	m	Time	m
1 0206 0821 SA 1427 2029	4.7 0.6 4.4 0.7	**16** 0227 0847 SU 1502 2110	4.8 0.4 4.6 0.6
2 0239 0854 SU 1500 2102	4.7 0.7 4.4 0.7	**17** 0316 0937 M 1552 2153	4.9 0.5 4.5 0.5
3 0310 0925 M 1532 2131	4.7 0.7 4.4 0.8	**18** 0401 1022 TU 1636 2229	4.8 0.4 4.4 0.6
4 0341 0957 TU 1604 2203	4.7 0.8 4.3 0.9	**19** 0445 1103 W 1718 2307	4.8 0.6 4.3 0.8
5 0414 1032 W 1641 2239	4.6 0.9 4.3 1.0	**20** 0530 1147 TH 1802 ◐ 2351	4.7 0.7 4.3 0.9
6 0454 1111 TH 1725 ◑ 2324	4.6 1.0 4.2 1.1	**21** 0619 1235 F 1851	4.5 0.9 4.1
7 0543 1200 F 1822	4.5 1.2 4.2	**22** 0044 0716 SA 1329 1951	1.1 4.3 1.0 4.0
8 0023 0646 SA 1303 1931	1.2 4.5 1.1 4.2	**23** 0150 0822 SU 1432 2059	1.1 4.3 1.1 4.1
9 0134 0758 SU 1415 2044	1.2 4.5 1.1 4.3	**24** 0304 0931 M 1539 2204	1.1 4.3 1.1 4.3
10 0250 0910 M 1527 2152	1.2 4.5 0.9 4.4	**25** 0414 1033 TU 1639 2301	1.0 4.4 1.0 4.4
11 0401 1019 TU 1634 2255	1.0 4.6 0.8 4.5	**26** 0512 1126 W 1732 2349	0.9 4.4 0.9 4.5
12 0507 1123 W 1738 2355	0.8 4.6 0.6 4.6	**27** 0603 1214 TH 1819	0.8 4.4 0.8
13 0609 1222 TH 1836 ●	0.6 4.6 0.5	**28** 0032 0647 F 1257 ○ 1901	4.6 0.7 4.4 0.7
14 0048 0703 F 1316 1928	4.7 0.4 4.6 0.5	**29** 0112 0727 SA 1335 1939	4.6 0.7 4.4 0.7
15 0138 0755 SA 1409 2020	4.7 0.4 4.6 0.5	**30** 0149 0806 SU 1411 2016	4.7 0.7 4.5 0.7
		31 0224 0843 M 1445 2050	4.8 0.7 4.5 0.7

Chart Datum: 2·7 metres below Normal Null (German reference level)
HAT is 5·1 metres above Chart Datum

TIDES

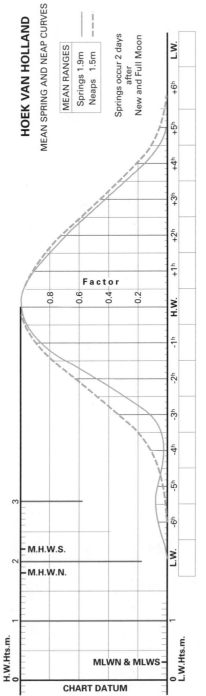

HOEK VAN HOLLAND

MEAN SPRING AND NEAP CURVES

MEAN RANGES
Springs 1.9m
Neaps 1.5m

Springs occur 2 days after New and Full Moon

Note - Double LWs often occur.
The predictions are for the lower
LW which is usually the first.

TIME ZONE –0100
(Dutch Standard Time)
Subtract 1 hour for UT
For Dutch Summer Time add
ONE hour in **non-shaded areas**

NETHERLANDS – HOEK VAN HOLLAND

LAT 51°59'N   LONG 4°07'E

TIMES AND HEIGHTS OF HIGH AND LOW WATERS

Dates in amber are **SPRINGS**
Dates in yellow are **NEAPS**

2012

JANUARY

Time	m	Time	m
1 0120	0.6	**16** 0224	0.5
0749	2.0	0729	2.0
SU 1324	0.2	M 1249	0.1
☾ 2026	2.0	☽ 1959	2.2
2 0226	0.5	**17** 0215	0.5
0846	1.9	0835	2.0
M 1425	0.3	TU 1404	0.2
2126	1.9	2105	2.1
3 0334	0.5	**18** 0305	0.5
0944	1.8	0940	1.9
TU 1630	0.4	W 1526	0.2
2234	1.8	2220	2.0
4 0456	0.5	**19** 0355	0.5
1116	1.8	1056	1.9
W 1736	0.4	TH 1635	0.3
2355	1.8	2340	1.9
5 0556	0.5	**20** 0510	0.4
1205	1.8	1205	2.0
TH 1815	0.4	F 1734	0.4
6 0050	1.9	**21** 0046	2.0
0634	0.4	0616	0.4
F 1306	1.9	SA 1305	2.1
1904	0.4	1834	0.4
7 0136	2.0	**22** 0138	2.0
0704	0.4	0649	0.3
SA 1345	2.0	SU 1357	2.2
1940	0.5	2154	0.5
8 0204	2.0	**23** 0228	2.1
0734	0.4	0731	0.2
SU 1414	2.1	M 1445	2.3
2004	0.5	● 2225	0.5
9 0246	2.1	**24** 0315	2.1
0759	0.3	0809	0.2
M 1455	2.2	TU 1525	2.3
○ 2014	0.5	2314	0.6
10 0314	2.1	**25** 0355	2.2
0829	0.3	0856	0.1
TU 1535	2.3	W 1607	2.4
2300	0.5		
11 0355	2.1	**26** 0004	0.6
0906	0.2	0435	2.2
W 1609	2.4	TH 0929	0.1
2350	0.4	1648	2.3
12 0435	2.1	**27** 0105	0.5
0935	0.2	0515	2.2
TH 1647	2.4	F 1015	0.1
		1735	2.3
13 0036	0.4	**28** 0156	0.5
0511	2.1	0555	2.1
F 1018	0.2	SA 1059	0.1
1727	2.3	1816	2.2
14 0127	0.4	**29** 0220	0.5
0555	2.0	0630	2.1
SA 1106	0.1	SU 1150	0.1
1811	2.3	1849	2.1
15 0200	0.5	**30** 0030	0.5
0638	2.0	0710	2.0
SU 1144	0.1	M 1239	0.2
1901	2.2	1935	2.0
		31 0115	0.4
		0755	2.0
		TU 1334	0.2
		☾ 2026	1.9

FEBRUARY

Time	m	Time	m
1 0204	0.4	**16** 0245	0.3
0856	1.8	0916	1.9
W 1424	0.3	TH 1525	0.3
2125	1.8	2153	1.8
2 0420	0.4	**17** 0356	0.4
1006	1.7	1035	1.9
TH 1700	0.4	F 1624	0.4
2245	1.7	2323	1.7
3 0515	0.4	**18** 0445	0.4
1125	1.7	1155	1.9
F 1754	0.4	SA 1957	0.4
4 0010	1.7	**19** 0039	1.8
0614	0.4	0835	0.3
SA 1236	1.8	SU 1305	2.1
1850	0.4	2125	0.4
5 0105	1.8	**20** 0135	1.9
0706	0.4	0935	0.2
SU 1326	2.0	M 1349	2.2
2110	0.4	2200	0.4
6 0149	1.9	**21** 0225	2.0
0935	0.3	1026	0.3
M 1354	2.1	TU 1428	2.2
2200	0.4	● 2215	0.5
7 0225	2.0	**22** 0305	2.1
0735	0.3	0756	0.2
TU 1436	2.2	W 1508	2.3
○ 2224	0.5	2306	0.5
8 0255	2.1	**23** 0335	2.1
0806	0.2	0829	0.1
W 1509	2.3	TH 1547	2.3
2256	0.5	2335	0.5
9 0336	2.1	**24** 0415	2.2
0835	0.2	0906	0.1
TH 1545	2.4	F 1626	2.3
2325	0.4	2125	0.5
10 0415	2.1	**25** 0448	2.2
0911	0.1	1306	0.1
F 1626	2.4	SA 1701	2.2
		2205	0.5
11 0016	0.4	**26** 0519	2.2
0449	2.1	1325	0.2
SA 0955	0.1	SU 1735	2.1
1707	2.4	2244	0.4
12 0056	0.4	**27** 0556	2.1
0531	2.1	1103	0.2
SU 1035	0.1	M 1804	2.0
1753	2.3	2325	0.4
13 0125	0.4	**28** 0625	2.1
0615	2.1	1154	0.2
M 1129	0.1	TU 1845	2.0
1837	2.2		
14 0145	0.4	**29** 0025	0.3
0701	2.1	0659	0.2
TU 1300	0.1	W 1254	0.2
☽ 1935	2.1	1914	1.9
15 0206	0.4		
0759	2.0		
W 1405	0.2		
2039	1.9		

MARCH

Time	m	Time	m
1 0136	0.3	**16** 0225	0.2
0755	1.9	0900	1.9
TH 1354	0.3	F 1505	0.3
☾ 2015	1.7	2156	1.7
2 0215	0.3	**17** 0330	0.2
0925	1.7	1030	1.9
F 1635	0.4	SA 1810	0.4
2156	1.6	2319	1.7
3 0505	0.3	**18** 0445	0.3
1046	1.7	1149	1.9
SA 1734	0.4	SU 1950	0.4
2315	1.6		
4 0544	0.3	**19** 0024	1.8
1155	1.8	0815	0.2
SU 1825	0.4	M 1255	2.1
		2055	0.3
5 0023	1.7	**20** 0119	1.9
0637	0.3	0914	0.1
M 1249	2.0	TU 1336	2.1
2037	0.4	2147	0.4
6 0114	1.9	**21** 0205	2.0
0904	0.3	0954	0.1
TU 1329	2.1	W 1410	2.2
2135	0.3	2210	0.4
7 0155	2.0	**22** 0238	2.1
0705	0.3	1034	0.2
W 1405	2.2	TH 1448	2.2
2220	0.4	● 2240	0.5
8 0229	2.1	**23** 0316	2.1
0731	0.2	0816	0.2
TH 1446	2.3	F 1526	2.2
○ 2246	0.4	2326	0.4
9 0305	2.1	**24** 0348	2.2
0805	0.1	1146	0.2
F 1526	2.4	SA 1558	2.2
2304	0.4		
10 0346	2.2	**25** 0006	0.4
0848	0.1	0417	2.2
SA 1606	2.4	SU 1220	0.2
2355	0.4	1636	2.1
11 0425	2.2	**26** 0025	0.3
0929	0.1	0456	2.2
SU 1645	2.3	M 1254	0.2
		1708	2.1
12 0046	0.3	**27** 0055	0.3
0507	2.1	0526	2.1
M 1018	0.1	TU 1305	0.2
1732	2.2	1735	2.0
13 0121	0.3	**28** 0125	0.3
0551	2.1	0556	2.1
TU 1315	0.1	W 1119	0.3
1817	2.1	1805	2.0
14 0130	0.3	**29** 0145	0.3
0639	2.2	0626	2.1
W 1315	0.1	TH 1230	0.3
1908	2.0	1839	1.9
15 0125	0.2	**30** 0035	0.2
0735	2.1	0705	2.0
TH 1405	0.2	F 1340	0.3
☾ 2014	1.8	☽ 1929	1.8
		31 0150	0.2
		0805	1.8
		SA 1450	0.4
		2115	1.6

APRIL

Time	m	Time	m
1 0446	0.3	**16** 0420	0.2
1006	1.8	1124	2.0
SU 1710	0.4	M 1905	0.3
2236	1.6		
2 0536	0.3	**17** 0006	1.8
1104	1.8	0746	0.1
M 1824	0.3	TU 1225	2.1
2346	1.7	2040	0.3
3 0640	0.3	**18** 0055	1.9
1209	2.0	0844	0.1
TU 2026	0.3	W 1308	2.1
		2125	0.3
4 0034	1.8	**19** 0134	2.0
0846	0.2	0940	0.2
W 1255	2.1	TH 1355	2.1
2126	0.3	2145	0.4
5 0125	1.9	**20** 0216	2.0
0625	0.2	0724	0.2
TH 1335	2.3	F 1425	2.1
2206	0.3	2220	0.4
6 0158	2.1	**21** 0249	2.1
0706	0.1	0759	0.2
F 1417	2.3	SA 1458	2.1
○ 2236	0.4	● 2019	0.3
7 0239	2.2	**22** 0319	2.1
0746	0.1	1040	0.2
SA 1457	2.4	SU 1535	2.1
2006	0.3	2336	0.3
8 0321	2.2	**23** 0348	2.2
0826	0.1	1130	0.2
SU 1541	2.3	M 1609	2.1
2048	0.3	2355	0.2
9 0402	2.3	**24** 0425	2.2
0910	0.1	1205	0.2
M 1626	2.3	TU 1646	2.0
2136	0.3		
10 0445	2.3	**25** 0025	0.2
0959	0.2	0455	2.1
TU 1707	2.1	W 1244	0.3
2221	0.2	1709	2.0
11 0531	2.3	**26** 0115	0.2
1254	0.2	0528	2.1
W 1757	2.0	TH 1315	0.3
2324	0.2	1746	1.9
12 0625	2.2	**27** 0155	0.2
1310	0.2	0558	2.0
TH 1855	1.9	F 1400	0.3
		1815	1.9
13 0100	0.1	**28** 0010	0.2
0719	2.1	0639	2.0
F 1350	0.2	SA 1420	0.3
☽ 2003	1.7	1905	1.8
14 0154	0.1	**29** 0105	0.2
0845	2.0	0740	2.0
SA 1450	0.3	SU 1510	0.4
2130	1.7	☾ 2030	1.7
15 0254	0.1	**30** 0205	0.2
1015	1.9	0915	1.9
SU 1755	0.4	M 1637	0.4
2306	1.7	2150	1.7

Chart Datum: 0·92 metres below NAP Datum
HAT is 2·5 metres above Chart Datum

TIDES

TIDES

TIME ZONE -0100
(Dutch Standard Time)
Subtract 1 hour for UT
For Dutch Summer Time add
ONE hour in **non-shaded areas**

NETHERLANDS – HOEK VAN HOLLAND

LAT 51°59'N   LONG 4°07'E

TIMES AND HEIGHTS OF HIGH AND LOW WATERS

Dates in amber are **SPRINGS**
Dates in yellow are **NEAPS**

2012

MAY

Day	Time m	Time m	Time m	Time m		Day	Time m	Time m	Time m	Time m
1	0314 0.2	1025 1.9	TU 1800 0.4	2255 1.7		**16**	0656 0.1	1155 2.0	W 1935 0.3	
2	0415 0.2	1124 2.1	W 1956 0.3	2355 1.8		**17**	0025 1.9	0750 0.2	TH 1246 2.0	2044 0.3
3	0510 0.2	1219 2.2	TH 2056 0.3			**18**	0104 1.9	0640 0.2	F 1330 2.0	2135 0.3
4	0048 2.0	0556 0.1	F 1306 2.3	2125 0.3		**19**	0145 2.0	0715 0.3	SA 1406 2.0	1934 0.3
5	0128 2.1	0634 0.1	SA 1353 2.3	1908 0.3		**20**	0218 2.0	0755 0.3	SU 1439 2.0	2010 0.3
6	0215 2.2	0722 0.1	SU 1437 2.3	O 1945 0.3		**21**	0255 2.1	0920 0.3	M 1516 2.0	● 2034 0.2
7	0258 2.3	0806 0.2	M 1520 2.2	2030 0.2		**22**	0325 2.1	1040 0.3	TU 1548 2.1	2330 0.2
8	0346 2.3	0851 0.2	TU 1607 2.1	2116 0.2		**23**	0401 2.2	1140 0.3	W 1619 2.0	
9	0428 2.3	1245 0.3	W 1656 2.0	2205 0.1		**24**	0015 0.1	0436 2.1	TH 1226 0.3	1655 2.0
10	0515 2.3	1330 0.3	TH 1745 1.9	2310 0.1		**25**	0055 0.1	0510 2.1	F 1255 0.3	1725 1.9
11	0609 2.2	1330 0.3	F 1845 1.9			**26**	0135 0.1	0546 2.1	SA 1356 0.3	1805 1.9
12	0014 0.0	0715 2.1	SA 1325 0.3	◑ 1955 1.8		**27**	0225 0.1	0626 2.1	SU 1436 0.3	1856 1.8
13	0115 2.0	0825 2.0	SU 1425 0.4	2055 1.7		**28**	0024 0.1	0715 2.0	M 1514 0.4	◐ 2000 1.7
14	0235 2.0	0940 2.0	M 1736 0.4	2215 1.7		**29**	0135 0.1	0835 2.0	TU 1614 0.4	2110 1.7
15	0345 0.1	1100 2.0	TU 1836 0.3	2330 1.8		**30**	0235 0.1	0946 2.0	W 1545 0.4	2215 1.8
						31	0335 0.1	1044 2.1	TH 1625 0.4	2315 1.9

JUNE

Day	Time m	Time m	Time m	Time m		Day	Time m	Time m	Time m	Time m
1	0424 0.1	1150 2.2	F 2015 0.3			**16**	0036 1.8	0614 0.3	SA 1305 1.9	1834 0.3
2	0015 2.0	0530 0.1	SA 1241 2.2	1806 0.3		**17**	0119 1.9	0654 0.3	SU 1346 2.0	1915 0.3
3	0106 2.1	0625 0.2	SU 1331 2.2	1844 0.3		**18**	0200 2.0	0734 0.3	M 1425 2.0	1944 0.3
4	0152 2.2	0704 0.2	M 1418 2.2	O 1935 0.2		**19**	0236 2.0	0824 0.4	TU 1455 2.0	● 2024 0.2
5	0241 2.3	0755 0.3	TU 1507 2.1	2016 0.2		**20**	0305 2.1	0940 0.4	W 1529 2.0	2044 0.2
6	0327 2.3	0841 0.4	W 1555 2.1	2106 0.1		**21**	0346 2.2	1055 0.4	TH 1606 2.0	2356 0.2
7	0415 2.3	1235 0.4	TH 1648 2.0	2156 0.1		**22**	0418 2.2	1145 0.4	F 1639 2.0	2150 0.2
8	0502 2.3	1336 0.4	F 1735 2.0	2245 0.0		**23**	0448 2.2	1240 0.3	SA 1715 1.9	2225 0.2
9	0556 2.2	1426 0.4	SA 1838 1.9	2345 0.0		**24**	0529 2.2	1325 0.3	SU 1755 1.9	2301 0.1
10	0656 2.2	1515 0.4	SU 1925 1.9			**25**	0609 2.2	1416 0.4	M 1835 1.9	2350 0.1
11	0044 0.0	0756 2.1	M 1345 0.4	◑ 2020 1.8		**26**	0655 2.1	1455 0.4	TU 1923 1.8	
12	0154 0.0	0855 2.0	TU 1450 0.4	2115 1.8		**27**	0034 0.1	0755 2.1	W 1510 0.4	◐ 2029 1.9
13	0305 0.1	1016 1.9	W 1606 0.4	2246 1.8		**28**	0154 0.1	0906 2.1	TH 1516 0.4	2135 1.9
14	0414 0.2	1115 1.9	TH 1655 0.4	2339 1.8		**29**	0310 0.1	1016 2.1	F 1554 0.4	2246 1.9
15	0524 0.2	1215 1.9	F 1744 0.4			**30**	0405 0.2	1120 2.1	SA 1645 0.4	2350 2.0

JULY

Day	Time m	Time m	Time m	Time m		Day	Time m	Time m	Time m	Time m
1	0515 0.2	1222 2.1	SU 1750 0.3			**16**	0056 1.8	0644 0.4	M 1325 1.9	1854 0.3
2	0045 2.1	0615 0.3	M 1317 2.1	1835 0.3		**17**	0133 1.9	0730 0.4	TU 1416 1.9	1935 0.3
3	0138 2.2	0706 0.3	TU 1408 2.1	O 1919 0.2		**18**	0215 2.0	0755 0.4	W 1434 2.0	2000 0.3
4	0227 2.2	0749 0.4	W 1459 2.1	2005 0.2		**19**	0245 2.1	0830 0.5	TH 1504 2.0	● 2020 0.2
5	0316 2.3	0829 0.5	TH 1546 2.1	2046 0.1		**20**	0326 2.2	1040 0.5	F 1546 2.1	2044 0.2
6	0400 2.3	1215 0.5	F 1630 2.1	2129 0.1		**21**	0355 2.3	1136 0.4	SA 1619 2.1	2119 0.2
7	0447 2.3	1316 0.5	SA 1719 2.1	2220 0.0		**22**	0431 2.3	1205 0.4	SU 1655 2.0	2155 0.2
8	0536 2.3	1354 0.5	SU 1801 2.0	2304 0.0		**23**	0508 2.3	1254 0.4	M 1728 2.0	2236 0.1
9	0625 2.2	1456 0.5	M 1849 2.0			**24**	0549 2.3	1340 0.4	TU 1816 2.0	2319 0.1
10	0004 0.1	0715 2.1	TU 1310 0.5	1940 2.0		**25**	0635 2.2	1420 0.4	W 1900 2.0	
11	0115 0.1	0805 2.0	W 1405 0.4	◑ 2025 1.9		**26**	0015 0.1	0726 2.2	TH 1425 0.4	◐ 1951 2.0
12	0217 0.2	0906 2.0	TH 1455 0.4	2125 1.8		**27**	0125 0.1	0829 2.1	F 1445 0.4	2059 2.0
13	0350 0.2	1004 1.8	F 1624 0.4	2245 1.7		**28**	0244 0.2	0934 2.0	SA 1535 0.4	2215 1.9
14	0455 0.3	1135 1.8	SA 1715 0.4	2355 1.8		**29**	0406 0.3	1056 1.9	SU 1634 0.4	2329 2.0
15	0554 0.3	1235 1.8	SU 1815 0.3			**30**	0504 0.4	1209 1.9	M 1734 0.3	
						31	0036 2.0	0610 0.4	TU 1315 2.0	1825 0.3

AUGUST

Day	Time m	Time m	Time m	Time m		Day	Time m	Time m	Time m	Time m
1	0128 2.2	0655 0.5	W 1406 2.0	1910 0.2		**16**	0149 2.1	0955 0.5	TH 1416 2.0	1924 0.3
2	0219 2.3	0735 0.5	TH 1448 2.1	O 1945 0.2		**17**	0225 2.2	0744 0.5	F 1446 2.1	● 1950 0.3
3	0305 2.3	1105 0.6	F 1531 2.1	2026 0.1		**18**	0255 2.3	0815 0.5	SA 1515 2.1	2015 0.2
4	0346 2.3	1155 0.6	SA 1610 2.2	2106 0.1		**19**	0329 2.4	1054 0.5	SU 1555 2.2	2056 0.2
5	0427 2.3	1245 0.6	SU 1650 2.2	2149 0.1		**20**	0407 2.4	1145 0.5	M 1629 2.2	2130 0.2
6	0508 2.3	1335 0.5	M 1736 2.1	2235 0.1		**21**	0445 2.4	1235 0.5	TU 1707 2.2	2209 0.2
7	0556 2.2	1420 0.5	TU 1815 2.1	2325 0.2		**22**	0525 2.3	1315 0.5	W 1747 2.2	2255 0.2
8	0636 2.1	1155 0.5	W 1855 2.1			**23**	0612 2.1	1355 0.5	TH 1836 2.1	2344 0.2
9	0014 0.2	0715 2.0	TH 1255 0.4	◑ 1935 2.0		**24**	0659 2.4	1400 0.4	F 1921 2.1	◐
10	0115 0.3	0805 1.9	F 1344 0.4	2024 1.9		**25**	0156 0.3	0759 2.0	SA 1414 0.4	2029 2.0
11	0250 0.4	0906 1.8	SA 1606 0.4	2133 1.7		**26**	0256 0.3	0915 1.9	SU 1504 0.4	2200 1.9
12	0446 0.4	1014 1.7	SU 1654 0.4	2310 1.7		**27**	0355 0.4	1034 1.8	M 1614 0.4	2325 1.9
13	0535 0.4	1200 1.7	M 1755 0.4			**28**	0726 0.5	1205 1.8	TU 1724 0.4	
14	0015 1.8	0630 0.4	TU 1253 1.8	1834 0.3		**29**	0029 2.1	0840 0.5	W 1303 1.9	2106 0.3
15	0116 2.0	0714 0.5	W 1346 1.9	1904 0.3		**30**	0125 2.2	0934 0.5	TH 1356 2.0	1849 0.3
						31	0206 2.3	1000 0.6	F 1435 2.1	O 1929 0.2

Chart Datum: 0·92 metres below NAP Datum
HAT is 2·5 metres above Chart Datum

TIME ZONE -0100
(Dutch Standard Time)
Subtract 1 hour for UT
For Dutch Summer Time add
ONE hour in **non-shaded areas**

LAT 51°59'N   LONG 4°07'E

TIMES AND HEIGHTS OF HIGH AND LOW WATERS

Dates in amber are **SPRINGS**
Dates in yellow are **NEAPS**

2012

SEPTEMBER

Time	m	Time	m
1 0245	2.3	**16** 0225	2.4
1034	0.6	0739	0.5
SA 1515	2.2	SU 1447	2.2
2008	0.2	● 1950	0.2
2 0326	2.3	**17** 0300	2.5
0830	0.6	0815	0.5
SU 1548	2.2	M 1526	2.3
2046	0.2	2025	0.2
3 0406	2.3	**18** 0340	2.5
0905	0.6	0846	0.5
M 1628	2.3	TU 1602	2.3
2126	0.2	2106	0.2
4 0445	2.3	**19** 0423	2.4
1254	0.5	0925	0.5
TU 1701	2.2	W 1642	2.3
2159	0.3	2145	0.2
5 0521	2.2	**20** 0505	2.4
1025	0.5	1004	0.5
W 1735	2.2	TH 1725	2.3
2244	0.3	2235	0.3
6 0555	2.1	**21** 0547	2.2
1103	0.5	1054	0.4
TH 1811	2.2	F 1810	2.3
2346	0.4		
7 0635	2.0	**22** 0107	0.4
1154	0.4	0637	2.1
F 1850	2.1	SA 1240	0.4
		◑ 1906	2.2
8 0024	0.4	**23** 0145	0.4
0716	1.9	0734	1.9
SA 1300	0.4	SU 1345	0.4
1925	1.9	2009	2.0
9 0124	0.4	**24** 0235	0.4
0754	1.8	0854	1.8
SU 1354	0.4	M 1450	0.4
2056	1.8	2145	2.0
10 0415	0.5	**25** 0334	0.5
0920	1.7	1035	1.7
M 1640	0.4	TU 1554	0.4
2205	1.7	2304	2.0
11 0515	0.5	**26** 0705	0.5
1044	1.6	1206	1.8
TU 1725	0.4	W 1925	0.3
2334	1.8		
12 0610	0.5	**27** 0014	2.1
1214	1.7	0825	0.5
W 1815	0.4	TH 1256	2.0
		2056	0.3
13 0033	2.0	**28** 0105	2.2
0750	0.5	0930	0.5
TH 1310	1.9	F 1335	2.1
1850	0.4	2146	0.3
14 0120	2.2	**29** 0149	2.3
0915	0.5	0950	0.6
F 1339	2.0	SA 1415	2.1
1855	0.4	1916	0.3
15 0148	2.3	**30** 0227	2.3
1016	0.5	1014	0.6
SA 1416	2.1	SU 1448	2.2
1915	0.3	○ 1944	0.3

OCTOBER

Time	m	Time	m
1 0306	2.3	**16** 0235	2.5
0810	0.6	0750	0.5
M 1526	2.3	TU 1458	2.4
2026	0.3	2006	0.2
2 0341	2.3	**17** 0317	2.5
0846	0.5	0821	0.4
TU 1558	2.3	W 1538	2.4
2054	0.4	2045	0.3
3 0418	2.3	**18** 0401	2.4
0915	0.5	0906	0.4
W 1635	2.3	TH 1620	2.4
2135	0.4	2129	0.3
4 0456	2.2	**19** 0445	2.3
0955	0.5	0955	0.4
TH 1705	2.3	F 1706	2.4
2215	0.5	2226	0.4
5 0526	2.1	**20** 0531	2.2
1034	0.4	1050	0.3
F 1734	2.2	SA 1750	2.3
2254	0.5		
6 0551	0.4	**21** 0050	0.5
1115	0.4	0621	2.1
SA 1816	2.1	SU 1154	0.3
2350	0.5	1850	2.2
7 0626	2.0	**22** 0124	0.5
1204	0.4	0725	1.9
SU 1843	2.1	M 1326	0.3
		◑ 1954	2.1
8 0104	0.5	**23** 0215	0.5
0705	1.9	0856	1.8
M 1326	0.4	TU 1419	0.3
◑ 1934	1.9	2125	2.0
9 0220	0.6	**24** 0535	0.6
0835	1.7	1015	1.8
TU 1415	0.5	W 1534	0.3
2136	1.8	2245	2.1
10 0456	0.6	**25** 0650	0.5
0955	1.7	1124	1.8
W 1716	0.4	TH 1855	0.3
2256	1.9		
11 0550	0.6	**26** 0000	2.2
1104	1.7	0755	0.5
TH 1804	0.4	F 1225	2.0
2355	2.1	2014	0.3
12 0755	0.5	**27** 0045	2.2
1213	1.9	0905	0.5
F 2010	0.4	SA 1308	2.1
		2105	0.3
13 0039	2.2	**28** 0129	2.3
0906	0.5	0940	0.5
SA 1259	2.0	SU 1348	2.1
1809	0.4	1905	0.4
14 0116	2.3	**29** 0205	2.4
0945	0.5	1005	0.6
SU 1339	2.2	M 1429	2.2
1846	0.3	○ 1939	0.4
15 0156	2.5	**30** 0245	2.3
0715	0.5	0754	0.5
M 1417	2.3	TU 1458	2.3
● 1922	0.3	2026	0.4
		31 0319	2.3
		0829	0.5
		W 1535	2.3
		2044	0.5

NOVEMBER

Time	m	Time	m
1 0355	2.2	**16** 0345	2.3
0859	0.4	0856	0.3
TH 1608	2.3	F 1606	2.4
2340	0.5	2115	0.4
2 0430	2.2	**17** 0427	2.2
0933	0.4	0939	0.3
F 1646	2.3	SA 1651	2.4
		2216	0.5
3 0030	0.5	**18** 0518	2.1
0454	2.1	1036	0.2
SA 1015	0.4	SU 1741	2.4
1715	2.2	2314	0.6
4 0100	0.6	**19** 0616	2.0
0530	2.1	1135	0.2
SU 1106	0.4	M 1839	2.3
1745	2.2		
5 0125	0.6	**20** 0100	0.6
0605	2.0	0715	2.0
M 1134	0.3	TU 1245	0.2
1821	2.1	◑ 1950	2.2
6 0050	0.6	**21** 0155	0.6
0646	1.9	0814	1.9
TU 1246	0.3	W 1355	0.2
1915	2.1	2055	2.1
7 0150	0.6	**22** 0510	0.6
0744	1.8	0935	1.8
W 1346	0.4	TH 1455	0.3
◑ 2034	2.0	2214	2.1
8 0400	0.6	**23** 0626	0.6
0915	1.8	1055	1.9
TH 1435	0.4	F 1830	0.3
2155	2.0	2325	2.1
9 0520	0.6	**24** 0725	0.5
1026	1.8	1149	1.9
F 1556	0.4	SA 1930	0.3
2305	2.1		
10 0700	0.6	**25** 0019	2.1
1136	1.9	0830	0.5
SA 1645	0.4	SU 1245	2.0
		2030	0.4
11 0000	2.2	**26** 0105	2.2
0831	0.5	0926	0.5
SU 1226	2.0	M 1325	2.1
1736	0.3	1854	0.4
12 0046	2.3	**27** 0149	2.2
0925	0.5	0945	0.5
M 1308	2.2	TU 1408	2.2
1820	0.3	1944	0.4
13 0129	2.4	**28** 0230	2.2
0645	0.5	0745	0.4
TU 1351	2.3	W 1439	2.2
● 1859	0.3	○ 2015	0.5
14 0215	2.4	**29** 0306	2.2
0725	0.4	0805	0.4
W 1436	2.4	TH 1517	2.2
1946	0.3	2144	0.5
15 0257	2.4	**30** 0335	2.2
0805	0.4	0854	0.4
TH 1519	2.4	F 1549	2.3
2029	0.4	2247	0.5

DECEMBER

Time	m	Time	m
1 0409	2.2	**16** 0421	2.2
0925	0.3	0925	0.2
SA 1625	2.3	SU 1638	2.4
2347	0.5	2155	0.6
2 0446	2.1	**17** 0508	2.1
0953	0.3	1015	0.1
SU 1700	2.3	M 1729	2.4
3 0046	0.5	**18** 0135	0.6
0515	2.1	0558	2.1
M 1025	0.3	TU 1104	0.1
1729	2.2	1818	2.3
4 0120	0.5	**19** 0005	0.6
0549	2.0	0655	2.1
TU 1115	0.3	W 1216	0.1
1806	2.2	1914	2.2
5 0206	0.6	**20** 0105	0.6
0625	2.0	0750	2.0
W 1206	0.3	TH 1304	0.1
1855	2.2	◑ 2025	2.1
6 0230	0.6	**21** 0204	0.6
0719	1.9	0843	1.9
TH 1250	0.2	F 1425	0.2
◑ 1949	2.1	2124	2.0
7 0230	0.6	**22** 0310	0.6
0836	1.9	1000	1.9
F 1400	0.3	SA 1535	0.3
2110	2.1	2245	2.0
8 0310	0.6	**23** 0414	0.6
0934	1.9	1116	1.9
SA 1506	0.3	SU 1706	0.3
2218	2.2	2350	2.0
9 0354	0.6	**24** 0514	0.5
1046	1.9	1216	1.9
SU 1606	0.3	M 1754	0.4
2320	2.2		
10 0454	0.5	**25** 0046	2.0
1145	2.0	0615	0.5
M 1705	0.3	TU 1305	2.0
		1850	0.4
11 0015	2.3	**26** 0135	2.0
0534	0.5	0654	0.4
TU 1246	2.2	W 1349	2.0
1800	0.3	1925	0.5
12 0110	2.3	**27** 0215	2.1
0629	0.4	0734	0.4
W 1328	2.3	TH 1425	2.1
1850	0.4	2014	0.5
13 0155	2.3	**28** 0244	2.1
0715	0.4	0815	0.4
TH 1417	2.4	F 1459	2.2
● 1935	0.4	○ 2050	0.5
14 0245	2.3	**29** 0326	2.1
0756	0.3	0834	0.5
F 1506	2.4	SA 1528	2.2
2026	0.5	2220	0.5
15 0336	2.2	**30** 0356	2.1
0839	0.2	0905	0.3
SA 1551	2.4	SU 1608	2.3
2105	0.5	2324	0.5
		31 0424	2.1
		0935	0.3
		M 1639	2.3

Chart Datum: 0·92 metres below NAP Datum
HAT is 2·5 metres above Chart Datum

TIDES

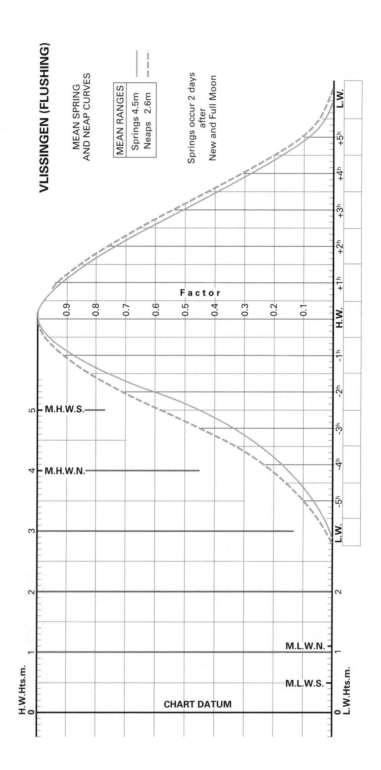

VLISSINGEN (FLUSHING)

MEAN SPRING
AND NEAP CURVES

MEAN RANGES

Springs 4.5m
Neaps 2.6m

Springs occur 2 days
after
New and Full Moon

TIME ZONE -0100
(Dutch Standard Time)
Subtract 1 hour for UT
For Dutch Summer Time add
ONE hour in **non-shaded areas**

NETHERLANDS – VLISSINGEN

LAT 51°27'N   LONG 3°36'E

TIMES AND HEIGHTS OF HIGH AND LOW WATERS

Dates in amber are **SPRINGS**
Dates in yellow are **NEAPS**

2012

JANUARY

Day	Time m	Time m	Time m	Time m	Day	Time m	Time m	Time m	Time m
1 SU	0046 1.2	0706 4.4	1325 0.9	◑1935 4.3	**16** M	0036 0.9	0638 4.6	1316 0.6	◐1915 4.6
2 M	0133 1.3	0749 4.2	1414 1.1	2029 4.1	**17** TU	0130 1.0	0742 4.5	1416 0.8	2026 4.4
3 TU	0250 1.4	0856 4.0	1525 1.0	2146 3.9	**18** W	0236 1.1	0852 4.3	1515 0.9	2132 4.3
4 W	0354 1.4	1016 3.9	1635 1.0	2301 4.0	**19** TH	0346 1.1	1006 4.3	1630 1.0	2248 4.3
5 TH	0506 1.3	1120 4.0	1736 1.2	2357 4.2	**20** F	0510 1.1	1118 4.4	1750 1.0	2355 4.4
6 F	0605 1.2	1216 4.2	1826 1.1		**21** SA	0619 0.9	1226 4.6	1848 0.9	
7 SA	0040 4.4	0649 1.0	1256 4.4	1905 1.0	**22** SU	0050 4.6	0720 0.6	1316 4.8	1935 0.8
8 SU	0116 4.5	0729 0.9	1336 4.6	1946 0.9	**23** M	0141 4.8	0806 0.5	1400 5.0	●2017 0.8
9 M	0155 4.7	0812 0.7	1408 4.8	○2022 0.8	**24** TU	0225 4.9	0852 0.4	1446 5.1	2059 0.8
10 TU	0232 4.8	0855 0.6	1447 5.0	2102 0.8	**25** W	0307 5.0	0935 0.3	1525 5.1	2138 0.8
11 W	0306 4.9	0936 0.5	1526 5.0	2146 0.7	**26** TH	0347 5.0	1011 0.4	1607 5.0	2216 0.8
12 TH	0343 4.9	1021 0.4	1600 5.1	2229 0.8	**27** F	0425 5.0	1050 0.4	1645 4.9	2252 0.9
13 F	0422 4.9	1102 0.4	1642 5.0	2311 0.8	**28** SA	0501 4.9	1126 0.5	1722 4.7	2325 0.9
14 SA	0506 4.8	1145 0.5	1727 4.9	2352 0.9	**29** SU	0537 4.7	1156 0.7	1758 4.5	
15 SU	0550 4.5	1225 0.5	1815 4.8		**30** M	0000 1.0	0615 4.5	1224 0.8	1846 4.3
					31 TU	0036 1.1	0655 4.3	1310 1.0	◑1936 4.1

FEBRUARY

Day	Time m	Time m	Time m	Time m	Day	Time m	Time m	Time m	Time m
1 W	0126 1.3	0755 4.1	1404 1.2	2036 3.9	**16** TH	0216 1.0	0825 4.3	1449 1.0	2115 4.1
2 TH	0316 1.4	0906 3.8	1545 1.3	2145 3.8	**17** F	0330 1.1	0950 4.2	1615 1.1	2235 4.1
3 F	0426 1.4	1035 3.8	1656 1.4	2316 3.9	**18** SA	0506 1.0	1116 4.3	1734 1.1	2349 4.3
4 SA	0524 1.2	1146 4.1	1755 1.1		**19** SU	0620 0.8	1225 4.5	1839 0.9	
5 SU	0016 4.2	0625 1.0	1235 4.4	1846 1.0	**20** M	0048 4.5	0716 0.6	1308 4.8	1926 0.9
6 M	0058 4.4	0715 0.8	1312 4.6	1926 0.9	**21** TU	0131 4.7	0756 0.4	1350 4.9	●2008 0.8
7 TU	0132 4.7	0755 0.7	1348 4.8	○2006 0.8	**22** W	0206 4.9	0838 0.4	1429 5.0	2041 0.8
8 W	0207 4.8	0832 0.5	1425 5.0	2045 0.7	**23** TH	0245 5.0	0913 0.3	1505 5.0	2116 0.7
9 TH	0246 5.0	0915 0.4	1501 5.2	2126 0.6	**24** F	0321 5.0	0950 0.4	1540 5.0	2156 0.7
10 F	0323 5.0	0958 0.3	1540 5.2	2211 0.6	**25** SA	0356 5.0	1021 0.4	1617 4.9	2226 0.7
11 SA	0400 5.0	1042 0.3	1621 5.1	2256 0.6	**26** SU	0428 4.9	1055 0.5	1649 4.8	2258 0.8
12 SU	0443 5.0	1122 0.3	1705 5.0	2336 0.7	**27** M	0502 4.8	1126 0.7	1721 4.6	2326 0.8
13 M	0525 4.9	1206 0.4	1755 4.8		**28** TU	0535 4.6	1151 0.8	1756 4.4	2356 0.9
14 TU	0021 0.7	0615 4.8	1252 0.5	◑1849 4.6	**29** W	0609 4.4	1220 0.9	1836 4.2	
15 W	0105 0.8	0715 4.5	1345 0.7	1958 4.3					

MARCH

Day	Time m	Time m	Time m	Time m	Day	Time m	Time m	Time m	Time m
1 TH	0036 1.0	0656 4.2	1306 1.1	◑1935 4.0	**16** F	0158 0.8	0811 4.3	1436 1.0	2056 4.0
2 F	0123 1.2	0804 3.9	1430 1.3	2050 3.8	**17** SA	0315 1.0	0940 4.1	1555 1.2	2225 4.0
3 SA	0345 1.3	0945 3.8	1626 1.3	2226 3.8	**18** SU	0456 0.9	1105 4.3	1736 1.1	2335 4.2
4 SU	0456 1.2	1111 4.0	1725 1.1	2334 4.1	**19** M	0610 0.7	1209 4.6	1829 0.9	
5 M	0555 1.0	1205 4.4	1820 1.0		**20** TU	0028 4.5	0654 0.5	1255 4.7	1915 0.9
6 TU	0028 4.4	0650 0.8	1248 4.7	1906 0.8	**21** W	0110 4.7	0739 0.4	1336 4.8	1945 0.8
7 W	0106 4.6	0729 0.6	1322 4.9	1946 0.7	**22** TH	0148 4.8	0816 0.4	1409 4.9	●2019 0.7
8 TH	0140 4.8	0809 0.4	1359 5.1	○2026 0.6	**23** F	0222 4.9	0848 0.4	1442 4.9	2055 0.7
9 F	0218 5.0	0856 0.3	1436 5.2	2106 0.5	**24** SA	0255 5.0	0926 0.4	1513 4.9	2131 0.6
10 SA	0256 5.1	0935 0.2	1547 5.3	2148 0.5	**25** SU	0327 5.0	0956 0.5	1547 4.8	2206 0.6
11 SU	0335 5.2	1018 0.2	1559 5.2	2232 0.5	**26** M	0402 4.9	1025 0.6	1617 4.7	2236 0.7
12 M	0419 5.1	1100 0.2	1645 5.0	2316 0.5	**27** TU	0431 4.8	1056 0.7	1650 4.6	2258 0.7
13 TU	0505 5.0	1146 0.4	1732 4.8	2359 0.5	**28** W	0505 4.7	1115 0.8	1720 4.5	2326 0.8
14 W	0553 4.8	1230 0.5	1826 4.5		**29** TH	0536 4.5	1151 0.9	1756 4.3	
15 TH	0055 0.7	0658 4.5	1326 0.8	◑1935 4.2	**30** F	0006 0.9	0611 4.3	1229 1.0	◑1839 4.1
					31 SA	0055 1.0	0714 4.0	1340 1.2	2016 3.8

APRIL

Day	Time m	Time m	Time m	Time m	Day	Time m	Time m	Time m	Time m
1 SU	0240 1.2	0900 3.9	1540 1.3	2136 3.8	**16** M	0441 0.7	1039 4.3	1710 1.1	2312 4.2
2 M	0416 1.1	1026 4.1	1645 1.1	2256 4.0	**17** TU	0546 0.6	1146 4.5	1816 0.9	
3 TU	0520 0.9	1125 4.4	1742 1.0	2350 4.3	**18** W	0006 4.4	0638 0.5	1228 4.7	1849 0.9
4 W	0616 0.7	1211 4.7	1830 0.8		**19** TH	0045 4.6	0715 0.5	1308 4.7	1925 0.8
5 TH	0032 4.6	0700 0.5	1252 5.0	1912 0.6	**20** F	0122 4.7	0750 0.5	1346 4.8	1955 0.7
6 F	0111 4.9	0742 0.4	1333 5.1	○1959 0.5	**21** SA	0157 4.8	0819 0.5	1417 4.8	●2030 0.6
7 SA	0151 5.1	0827 0.2	1414 5.2	2042 0.4	**22** SU	0230 4.7	0852 0.5	1447 4.8	2106 0.6
8 SU	0234 5.2	0910 0.2	1456 5.2	2127 0.4	**23** M	0301 4.9	0926 0.6	1519 4.8	2140 0.6
9 M	0315 5.2	0953 0.2	1539 5.1	2213 0.3	**24** TU	0335 4.9	1001 0.6	1551 4.7	2216 0.6
10 TU	0359 5.2	1038 0.3	1626 5.0	2258 0.4	**25** W	0406 4.8	1026 0.7	1622 4.6	2240 0.7
11 W	0446 5.1	1122 0.4	1715 4.7	2345 0.4	**26** TH	0437 4.7	1055 0.8	1656 4.5	2316 0.7
12 TH	0538 4.8	1210 0.6	1811 4.5		**27** F	0511 4.6	1125 0.9	1728 4.4	2356 0.8
13 F	0035 0.5	0646 4.6	1301 0.8	◑1926 4.2	**28** SA	0555 4.4	1216 1.0	1815 4.2	
14 SA	0146 0.7	0759 4.4	1416 1.1	2035 4.0	**29** SU	0045 0.9	0656 4.2	1304 1.1	◑1936 4.0
15 SU	0306 0.8	0926 4.2	1545 1.1	2206 4.0	**30** M	0206 1.0	0826 4.1	1424 1.2	2058 4.0

Chart Datum: 2·56 metres below NAP Datum
HAT is 5·4 metres above Chart Datum

TIDES

TIDES

TIME ZONE -0100
(Dutch Standard Time)
Subtract 1 hour for UT
For Dutch Summer Time add
ONE hour in **non-shaded areas**

NETHERLANDS – VLISSINGEN
LAT 51°27'N LONG 3°36'E
TIMES AND HEIGHTS OF HIGH AND LOW WATERS

Dates in amber are **SPRINGS**
Dates in yellow are **NEAPS**

2012

MAY

Day	Time m	Time m	Time m	Time m
1 TU	0331 0.9	0938 4.2	1554 1.0	2206 4.1
2 W	0436 0.8	1041 4.5	1706 1.0	2308 4.4
3 TH	0536 0.6	1136 4.7	1756 0.8	2357 4.6
4 F	0626 0.5	1222 5.0	1846 0.6	
5 SA	0046 4.9	0716 0.4	1306 5.1	1936 0.5
6 SU	0126 5.1	0802 0.3	1353 5.2	○ 2022 0.4
7 M	0211 5.2	0848 0.3	1436 5.2	2110 0.3
8 TU	0257 5.2	0933 0.3	1526 5.1	2155 0.3
9 W	0345 5.2	1018 0.4	1612 4.9	2246 0.3
10 TH	0436 5.0	1102 0.6	1702 4.7	2329 0.3
11 F	0531 4.9	1150 0.7	1759 4.5	
12 SA	0026 0.4	0636 4.7	1239 0.9	◑ 1906 4.4
13 SU	0125 0.5	0740 4.5	1345 1.0	2005 4.2
14 M	0235 0.6	0849 4.3	1454 1.1	2126 4.1
15 TU	0355 0.7	1005 4.3	1624 1.1	2236 4.2
16 W	0510 0.7	1110 4.4	1736 1.0	2336 4.3
17 TH	0606 0.6	1159 4.5	1820 0.9	
18 F	0018 4.4	0647 0.7	1241 4.6	1856 0.9
19 SA	0056 4.5	0721 0.7	1320 4.6	1930 0.8
20 SU	0131 4.6	0752 0.7	1351 4.7	2005 0.7
21 M	0205 4.7	0826 0.7	1426 4.7	● 2039 0.6
22 TU	0237 4.8	0855 0.7	1457 4.7	2120 0.6
23 W	0310 4.8	0935 0.7	1531 4.7	2158 0.6
24 TH	0345 4.8	1006 0.8	1606 4.6	2230 0.6
25 F	0417 4.7	1040 0.8	1642 4.5	2308 0.7
26 SA	0455 4.6	1115 0.9	1718 4.4	2346 0.7
27 SU	0539 4.5	1155 1.0	1805 4.3	
28 M	0035 0.7	0636 4.4	1245 1.0	◑ 1911 4.2
29 TU	0136 0.8	0745 4.4	1355 1.1	2015 4.2
30 W	0234 0.8	0855 4.4	1510 1.0	2126 4.2
31 TH	0345 0.7	0959 4.5	1616 1.0	2231 4.4

JUNE

Day	Time m	Time m	Time m	Time m
1 F	0444 0.6	1102 4.7	1720 0.8	2327 4.6
2 SA	0557 0.6	1156 4.9	1820 0.7	
3 SU	0018 4.8	0650 0.5	1246 5.0	1916 0.5
4 M	0106 5.0	0740 0.4	1335 5.0	○ 2005 0.4
5 TU	0156 5.1	0828 0.4	1423 5.0	2056 0.3
6 W	0245 5.2	0915 0.5	1510 5.0	2141 0.2
7 TH	0333 5.1	1000 0.6	1600 4.9	2229 0.2
8 F	0425 5.1	1041 0.7	1651 4.8	2318 0.3
9 SA	0517 4.9	1130 0.8	1741 4.7	
10 SU	0008 0.3	0615 4.8	1215 0.9	1836 4.5
11 M	0055 0.5	0705 4.6	1309 1.0	◑ 1930 4.4
12 TU	0156 0.6	0805 4.4	1416 1.1	2036 4.2
13 W	0306 0.7	0926 4.2	1519 1.1	2146 4.1
14 TH	0416 0.6	1026 4.2	1625 1.1	2250 4.2
15 F	0515 0.9	1125 4.3	1736 1.1	2345 4.2
16 SA	0606 0.9	1216 4.4	1826 1.0	
17 SU	0035 4.4	0646 0.9	1255 4.5	1906 0.9
18 M	0112 4.5	0722 0.8	1331 4.6	1945 0.8
19 TU	0148 4.6	0801 0.8	1406 4.6	● 2022 0.7
20 W	0221 4.7	0836 0.8	1438 4.7	2106 0.6
21 TH	0257 4.8	0909 0.8	1515 4.7	2145 0.5
22 F	0327 4.8	0945 0.8	1551 4.7	2219 0.5
23 SA	0406 4.8	1028 0.8	1626 4.6	2306 0.5
24 SU	0442 4.8	1106 0.8	1702 4.6	2339 0.6
25 M	0522 4.7	1146 0.9	1745 4.5	
26 TU	0026 0.6	0611 4.6	1231 1.0	1840 4.4
27 W	0116 0.6	0711 4.6	1331 1.0	◑ 1939 4.4
28 TH	0210 0.7	0820 4.5	1430 1.0	2046 4.4
29 F	0310 0.7	0926 4.5	1535 1.0	2156 4.4
30 SA	0415 0.7	1031 4.6	1656 0.9	2259 4.5

JULY

Day	Time m	Time m	Time m	Time m
1 SU	0531 0.7	1136 4.6	1800 0.8	
2 M	0002 4.7	0630 0.6	1232 4.8	1859 0.6
3 TU	0055 4.9	0726 0.6	1326 4.9	○ 1953 0.4
4 W	0146 5.0	0812 0.6	1416 4.9	2041 0.3
5 TH	0236 5.1	0858 0.6	1459 5.0	2129 0.3
6 F	0320 5.1	0942 0.7	1547 5.0	2216 0.3
7 SA	0407 5.1	1026 0.8	1629 4.9	2255 0.3
8 SU	0456 5.0	1106 0.8	1717 4.9	2339 0.4
9 M	0541 4.8	1146 0.9	1759 4.7	
10 TU	0026 0.5	0629 4.6	1235 1.0	1845 4.5
11 W	0110 0.6	0720 4.6	1326 1.1	◑ 1936 4.3
12 TH	0205 0.8	0816 4.2	1424 1.2	2035 4.1
13 F	0310 1.0	0926 4.2	1535 1.2	2149 4.0
14 SA	0404 1.1	1046 4.0	1650 1.2	2306 4.0
15 SU	0514 1.1	1146 4.1	1750 1.1	
16 M	0006 4.2	0616 1.0	1236 4.3	1839 1.0
17 TU	0056 4.4	0706 1.0	1311 4.5	1925 0.8
18 W	0125 4.6	0735 0.9	1348 4.6	2005 0.7
19 TH	0206 4.7	0816 0.8	1426 4.7	● 2039 0.6
20 F	0236 4.9	0849 0.8	1455 4.8	2119 0.5
21 SA	0311 5.0	0930 0.8	1527 4.9	2205 0.4
22 SU	0347 5.0	1010 0.8	1607 4.8	2245 0.4
23 M	0422 5.0	1052 0.8	1642 4.8	2325 0.5
24 TU	0506 4.9	1136 0.8	1725 4.7	
25 W	0005 0.5	0547 4.8	1216 0.9	1808 4.6
26 TH	0055 0.6	0646 4.7	1306 0.9	◑ 1908 4.5
27 F	0146 0.7	0746 4.5	1359 1.0	2015 4.4
28 SA	0234 0.8	0855 4.4	1504 1.0	2128 4.3
29 SU	0344 0.9	1010 4.3	1630 1.0	2245 4.4
30 M	0516 0.9	1126 4.4	1750 0.9	2356 4.6
31 TU	0621 0.9	1225 4.6	1852 0.6	

AUGUST

Day	Time m	Time m	Time m	Time m
1 W	0049 4.8	0715 0.8	1315 4.8	1945 0.5
2 TH	0137 5.0	0800 0.8	1400 4.9	○ 2028 0.3
3 F	0222 5.1	0842 0.8	1445 5.0	2116 0.3
4 SA	0305 5.1	0922 0.8	1526 5.1	2155 0.3
5 SU	0347 5.1	1002 0.8	1605 5.0	2236 0.4
6 M	0427 5.0	1041 0.8	1646 5.0	2312 0.5
7 TU	0507 4.9	1116 0.9	1726 4.8	2346 0.6
8 W	0548 4.7	1156 1.0	1805 4.6	
9 TH	0025 0.8	0629 4.4	1230 1.1	◑ 1845 4.4
10 F	0106 1.0	0715 4.2	1314 1.2	1935 4.1
11 SA	0216 1.2	0809 4.0	1455 1.4	2045 3.9
12 SU	0336 1.3	0936 3.8	1610 1.3	2226 3.8
13 M	0434 1.3	1109 3.9	1716 1.2	2336 4.1
14 TU	0546 1.2	1205 4.2	1821 1.1	
15 W	0025 4.3	0636 1.1	1248 4.4	1906 0.9
16 TH	0106 4.6	0711 1.0	1326 4.6	1946 0.7
17 F	0138 4.8	0750 0.9	1356 4.8	● 2020 0.3
18 SA	0212 5.0	0828 0.8	1427 4.9	2058 0.5
19 SU	0245 5.1	0908 0.7	1503 5.0	2138 0.4
20 M	0322 5.2	0948 0.7	1540 5.1	2220 0.4
21 TU	0359 5.1	1030 0.7	1619 5.0	2302 0.4
22 W	0440 5.1	1112 0.7	1701 5.0	2346 0.5
23 TH	0525 4.9	1156 1.0	1746 4.8	
24 F	0028 0.6	0615 4.7	1242 0.9	◑ 1837 4.6
25 SA	0116 0.8	0721 4.4	1334 1.0	1950 4.4
26 SU	0215 1.0	0832 4.2	1456 1.1	2110 4.3
27 M	0336 1.1	0958 4.1	1614 1.1	2236 4.3
28 TU	0506 1.1	1116 4.3	1748 0.9	2345 4.5
29 W	0612 1.0	1216 4.5	1846 0.7	
30 TH	0040 4.8	0706 0.9	1306 4.8	1936 0.5
31 F	0127 5.0	0746 0.9	1346 4.9	○ 2017 0.4

Chart Datum: 2·56 metres below NAP Datum
HAT is 5·4 metres above Chart Datum

TIME ZONE -0100
(Dutch Standard Time)
Subtract 1 hour for UT
For Dutch Summer Time add
ONE hour in **non-shaded areas**

NETHERLANDS – VLISSINGEN

LAT 51°27'N   LONG 3°36'E

TIMES AND HEIGHTS OF HIGH AND LOW WATERS

Dates in amber are **SPRINGS**
Dates in yellow are **NEAPS**

2012

SEPTEMBER

Time	m		Time	m
1 0207	5.1	**16** 0142	5.1	
0826	0.8	0802	0.8	
SA 1423	5.0	SU 1359	5.0	
2055	0.4	● 2030	0.5	
2 0246	5.1	**17** 0218	5.3	
0859	0.8	0842	0.7	
SU 1500	5.0	M 1435	5.2	
2132	0.4	2112	0.4	
3 0322	5.1	**18** 0256	5.3	
0938	0.8	0923	0.6	
M 1536	5.1	TU 1516	5.2	
2208	0.5	2156	0.4	
4 0358	5.0	**19** 0335	5.3	
1012	0.8	1005	0.6	
TU 1615	5.0	W 1556	5.2	
2239	0.6	2236	0.4	
5 0436	4.8	**20** 0417	5.1	
1046	0.9	1052	0.6	
W 1649	4.9	TH 1635	5.1	
2312	0.8	2318	0.5	
6 0509	4.7	**21** 0503	4.9	
1118	1.0	1136	0.7	
TH 1726	4.7	F 1723	5.0	
2340	0.9			
7 0542	4.5	**22** 0002	0.7	
1145	1.0	0555	4.7	
F 1800	4.5	SA 1225	0.8	
		◑ 1819	4.7	
8 0010	1.1	**23** 0056	0.9	
0622	4.3	0700	4.4	
SA 1220	1.2	SU 1326	0.9	
◑ 1846	4.2	1936	4.4	
9 0044	1.3	**24** 0200	1.1	
0716	4.0	0818	4.1	
SU 1315	1.4	M 1445	1.1	
1955	3.9	2100	4.3	
10 0234	1.5	**25** 0326	1.3	
0830	3.8	0939	4.0	
M 1530	1.4	TU 1615	1.0	
2120	3.8	2226	4.3	
11 0406	1.4	**26** 0507	1.3	
0959	3.8	1106	0.2	
TU 1640	1.3	W 1740	0.8	
2255	4.0	2335	4.6	
12 0510	1.3	**27** 0605	1.1	
1126	4.0	1206	4.5	
W 1745	1.1	TH 1835	0.6	
2356	4.3			
13 0606	1.1	**28** 0029	4.8	
1215	4.4	0655	1.0	
TH 1835	0.9	F 1247	4.7	
		1918	0.5	
14 0036	4.7	**29** 0108	4.9	
0646	1.0	0730	0.9	
F 1256	4.6	SA 1325	4.9	
1915	0.7	1958	0.5	
15 0109	4.9	**30** 0147	5.0	
0722	0.9	0805	0.6	
SA 1326	4.9	SU 1400	5.0	
1949	0.6	○ 2029	0.5	

OCTOBER

Time	m		Time	m
1 0222	5.0	**16** 0153	5.3	
0838	0.8	0819	0.6	
M 1437	5.1	TU 1409	5.3	
2105	0.6	2045	0.4	
2 0256	5.0	**17** 0233	5.3	
0912	0.8	0902	0.6	
TU 1511	5.1	W 1451	5.3	
2138	0.6	2128	0.4	
3 0331	5.0	**18** 0316	5.3	
0948	0.8	0946	0.5	
W 1545	5.0	TH 1535	5.3	
2210	0.7	2212	0.5	
4 0405	4.9	**19** 0359	5.1	
1020	0.8	1032	0.6	
TH 1617	4.9	F 1621	5.2	
2240	0.9	2257	0.6	
5 0435	4.7	**20** 0446	4.9	
1045	0.9	1120	0.6	
F 1652	4.8	SA 1709	5.0	
2306	1.0	2342	0.8	
6 0505	4.5	**21** 0541	4.6	
1112	1.0	1210	0.7	
SA 1725	4.6	SU 1805	4.7	
2336	1.1			
7 0542	4.4	**22** 0036	1.0	
1145	1.1	0645	4.4	
SU 1754	4.4	M 1309	0.8	
		◑ 1925	4.5	
8 0005	1.3	**23** 0140	1.2	
0626	4.1	0800	4.2	
M 1236	1.2	TU 1425	0.9	
◑ 1900	4.1	2039	4.4	
9 0105	1.5	**24** 0254	1.4	
0747	3.9	0920	4.1	
TU 1354	1.4	W 1606	1.0	
2035	3.9	2205	4.4	
10 0326	1.5	**25** 0446	1.3	
0906	3.8	1035	4.2	
W 1555	1.3	TH 1721	0.8	
2156	4.0	2315	4.6	
11 0430	1.4	**26** 0546	1.2	
1024	4.0	1135	4.5	
TH 1706	1.1	F 1816	0.7	
2306	4.4			
12 0526	1.2	**27** 0006	4.7	
1130	4.3	0630	1.1	
F 1755	0.9	SA 1225	4.6	
2355	4.7	1855	0.7	
13 0610	1.0	**28** 0045	4.8	
1211	4.6	0708	1.0	
SA 1836	0.8	SU 1305	4.8	
		1929	0.7	
14 0036	5.0	**29** 0126	4.9	
0649	0.9	0739	0.9	
SU 1253	4.9	M 1338	4.9	
1918	0.6	○ 2006	0.7	
15 0112	5.2	**30** 0158	4.9	
0736	0.7	0816	0.8	
M 1331	5.1	TU 1412	4.9	
● 2002	0.5	2039	0.7	
		31 0232	4.9	
		0851	0.8	
		W 1445	5.0	
		2110	0.8	

NOVEMBER

Time	m		Time	m
1 0305	4.9	**16** 0258	5.2	
0926	0.8	0930	0.5	
TH 1518	5.0	F 1519	5.3	
2142	0.8	2152	0.6	
2 0339	4.8	**17** 0345	5.1	
0955	0.8	1018	0.5	
F 1556	4.9	SA 1608	5.2	
2209	0.9	2238	0.7	
3 0412	4.7	**18** 0437	4.9	
1030	0.9	1105	0.5	
SA 1625	4.8	SU 1659	5.0	
2235	1.0	2321	0.9	
4 0445	4.6	**19** 0528	4.7	
1055	0.9	1156	0.6	
SU 1659	4.6	M 1759	4.8	
2305	1.1			
5 0518	4.4	**20** 0012	1.0	
1125	1.0	0629	4.5	
M 1735	4.5	TU 1255	0.7	
2346	1.2	◐ 1906	4.6	
6 0555	4.3	**21** 0109	1.2	
1216	1.1	0736	4.4	
TU 1826	4.3	W 1400	0.8	
		2016	4.5	
7 0040	1.3	**22** 0220	1.3	
0654	4.1	0846	4.2	
W 1314	1.2	TH 1515	0.9	
◑ 1951	4.2	2126	4.4	
8 0143	1.5	**23** 0345	1.4	
0820	4.0	0956	4.2	
TH 1455	1.2	F 1640	0.9	
2107	4.2	2238	4.4	
9 0336	1.4	**24** 0505	1.3	
0935	4.1	1105	4.3	
F 1554	1.1	SA 1740	0.9	
2216	4.4	2335	4.5	
10 0429	1.2	**25** 0605	1.2	
1039	4.3	1155	4.5	
SA 1659	0.9	SU 1826	0.8	
2309	4.7			
11 0526	1.1	**26** 0026	4.6	
1135	4.6	0636	1.1	
SU 1801	0.8	M 1239	4.6	
2359	4.9	1902	0.9	
12 0616	0.9	**27** 0102	4.7	
1219	4.9	0718	1.0	
M 1848	0.6	TU 1317	4.7	
		1936	0.9	
13 0045	5.1	**28** 0142	4.7	
0709	0.7	0756	0.9	
TU 1305	5.1	W 1356	4.8	
● 1935	0.5	○ 2010	0.9	
14 0128	5.2	**29** 0215	4.8	
0756	0.6	0831	0.8	
W 1347	5.3	TH 1428	4.8	
2023	0.5	2046	0.8	
15 0213	5.2	**30** 0248	4.8	
0842	0.5	0905	0.7	
TH 1434	5.3	F 1501	5.0	
2107	0.5	2116	0.9	

DECEMBER

Time	m		Time	m
1 0318	4.8	**16** 0335	5.0	
0939	0.7	1007	0.4	
SA 1536	4.9	SU 1556	5.2	
2150	0.9	2218	0.8	
2 0355	4.7	**17** 0423	5.0	
1016	0.8	1051	0.4	
SU 1607	4.9	M 1646	5.1	
2226	1.0	2306	0.9	
3 0428	4.6	**18** 0512	4.9	
1045	0.8	1139	0.4	
M 1646	4.7	TU 1741	5.0	
2255	1.1	2350	1.0	
4 0506	4.5	**19** 0606	4.7	
1115	0.9	1230	0.5	
TU 1719	4.6	W 1836	4.8	
2336	1.1			
5 0539	4.4	**20** 0040	1.1	
1205	0.9	0700	4.6	
W 1806	4.5	TH 1314	0.7	
		◑ 1935	4.5	
6 0016	1.2	**21** 0136	1.2	
0629	4.3	0756	4.4	
TH 1256	0.9	F 1414	0.8	
◑ 1906	4.4	2040	4.3	
7 0115	1.2	**22** 0239	1.3	
0735	4.2	0906	4.2	
F 1355	1.0	SA 1525	1.0	
2021	4.4	2156	4.2	
8 0219	1.3	**23** 0355	1.3	
0845	4.2	1020	4.1	
SA 1505	1.0	SU 1644	1.1	
2125	4.5	2300	4.2	
9 0329	1.2	**24** 0505	1.3	
0955	4.4	1126	4.2	
SU 1615	0.9	M 1756	1.1	
2229	4.6	2356	4.3	
10 0440	1.1	**25** 0615	1.2	
1057	4.6	1215	4.3	
M 1720	0.8	TU 1836	1.0	
2330	4.8			
11 0548	0.9	**26** 0045	4.4	
1151	4.8	0656	1.0	
TU 1820	0.7	W 1301	4.5	
		1916	1.0	
12 0023	4.9	**27** 0126	4.5	
0646	0.8	0736	0.9	
W 1246	5.0	TH 1339	4.6	
1912	0.6	1946	1.0	
13 0110	5.0	**28** 0159	4.6	
0741	0.6	0816	0.8	
TH 1331	5.1	F 1411	4.7	
● 2002	0.6	○ 2019	0.9	
14 0159	5.1	**29** 0232	4.7	
0830	0.5	0851	0.6	
F 1418	5.2	SA 1446	4.8	
2051	0.6	2055	0.8	
15 0246	5.1	**30** 0302	4.8	
0915	0.4	0925	0.6	
SA 1506	5.2	SU 1517	4.9	
2136	0.7	2136	0.9	
		31 0335	4.8	
		1002	0.6	
		M 1556	4.9	
		2206	0.9	

Chart Datum: 2·56 metres below NAP Datum
HAT is 5·4 metres above Chart Datum

TIDES

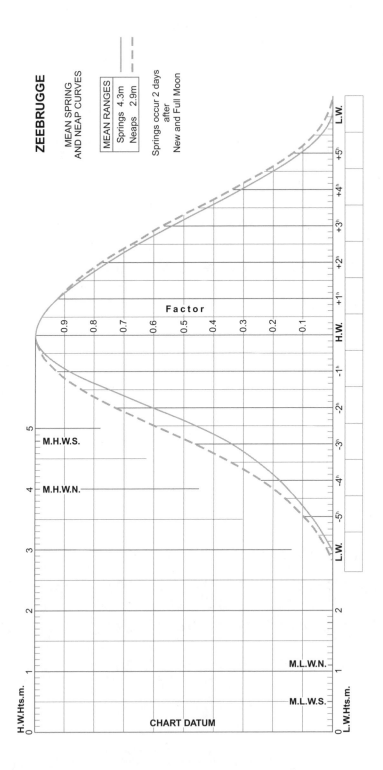

ZEEBRUGGE

MEAN SPRING
AND NEAP CURVES

MEAN RANGES
Springs 4.3m
Neaps 2.9m

Springs occur 2 days
after
New and Full Moon

Factor

0.9
0.8
0.7
0.6
0.5
0.4
0.3
0.2
0.1

H.W.

M.H.W.S.

M.H.W.N.

L.W.

M.L.W.N.

M.L.W.S.

CHART DATUM

H.W.Hts.m.

L.W.Hts.m.

TIME ZONE -0100
(Belgian Standard Time)
Subtract 1 hour for UT
For Belgian Summer Time add
ONE hour in **non-shaded areas**

BELGIUM – ZEEBRUGGE

LAT 51°21'N   LONG 3°12'E

TIMES AND HEIGHTS OF HIGH AND LOW WATERS

Dates in amber are **SPRINGS**
Dates in yellow are **NEAPS**

2012

	JANUARY			FEBRUARY			MARCH			APRIL	
	Time m	Time m		Time m	Time m		Time m	Time m		Time m	Time m

JANUARY

1 0029 1.2 / 0639 4.2 / SU 1314 4.1 / ☽ 1915 4.1 **16** 0010 0.9 / 0615 4.5 / M 1247 0.6 / 1852 4.5

2 0130 1.3 / 0738 4.0 / M 1416 4.1 / 2017 4.0 **17** 0108 1.0 / 0717 4.4 / TU 1349 0.8 / 1959 4.3

3 0242 1.4 / 0844 3.9 / TU 1519 4.2 / 2124 3.9 **18** 0217 1.2 / 0828 4.2 / W 1501 0.9 / 2113 4.1

4 0351 1.4 / 0953 3.8 / W 1619 1.2 / 2231 3.9 **19** 0337 1.2 / 0946 4.1 / TH 1615 1.0 / 2230 4.1

5 0455 1.3 / 1058 3.9 / TH 1716 1.2 / 2330 4.0 **20** 0454 1.1 / 1102 4.2 / F 1725 1.0 / 2340 4.2

6 0551 1.2 / 1152 4.1 / F 1803 1.1 **21** 0601 0.9 / 1206 4.4 / SA 1824 0.9

7 0018 4.2 / 0633 1.0 / SA 1235 4.2 / 1840 1.1 **22** 0033 4.4 / 0653 0.7 / SU 1255 4.6 / 1912 0.9

8 0056 4.3 / 0707 0.9 / SU 1311 4.4 / 1913 1.0 **23** 0116 4.5 / 0737 0.6 / M 1337 4.7 / ● 1953 0.8

9 0129 4.4 / 0739 0.8 / M 1344 4.5 / ○ 1948 0.9 **24** 0155 4.6 / 0817 0.4 / TU 1416 4.8 / 2031 0.8

10 0200 4.5 / 0814 0.6 / TU 1417 4.7 / 2025 0.8 **25** 0233 4.7 / 0857 0.3 / W 1456 4.9 / 2110 0.7

11 0233 4.6 / 0853 0.5 / W 1454 4.8 / 2106 0.7 **26** 0312 4.8 / 0937 0.3 / TH 1536 4.8 / 2148 0.7

12 0310 4.7 / 0934 0.4 / TH 1534 4.9 / 2148 0.7 **27** 0352 4.8 / 1017 0.3 / F 1617 4.8 / 2226 0.7

13 0351 4.8 / 1018 0.4 / F 1617 4.9 / 2233 0.7 **28** 0432 4.7 / 1057 0.4 / SA 1657 4.6 / 2303 0.8

14 0434 4.7 / 1104 0.4 / SA 1703 4.8 / 2319 0.8 **29** 0511 4.6 / 1136 0.6 / SU 1738 4.4 / 2339 1.0

15 0522 4.7 / 1153 0.5 / SU 1754 4.7 **30** 0551 4.4 / 1214 0.9 / M 1818 4.2

31 0018 1.2 / 0633 4.1 / TU 1259 1.1 / ☽ 1906 3.9

FEBRUARY

1 0110 1.4 / 0728 3.8 / W 1417 1.4 / 2013 3.7 **16** 0150 1.1 / 0801 4.1 / TH 1437 1.1 / 2050 3.9

2 0259 1.5 / 0848 3.6 / TH 1533 1.4 / 2136 3.6 **17** 0317 1.2 / 0930 4.0 / F 1558 1.2 / 2218 3.8

3 0413 1.5 / 1011 3.6 / F 1635 1.4 / 2250 3.7 **18** 0440 1.1 / 1056 4.1 / SA 1713 1.1 / 2331 4.0

4 0514 1.3 / 1117 3.8 / SA 1729 1.3 / 2346 3.9 **19** 0549 0.9 / 1159 4.3 / SU 1814 1.0

5 0603 1.1 / 1207 4.1 / SU 1813 1.1 **20** 0023 4.3 / 0641 0.7 / M 1245 4.5 / 1859 0.9

6 0028 4.2 / 0642 0.9 / M 1245 4.4 / 1850 1.0 **21** 0102 4.5 / 0722 0.5 / TU 1323 4.7 / ● 1936 0.8

7 0102 4.4 / 0718 0.7 / TU 1320 4.6 / ○ 1928 0.8 **22** 0138 4.6 / 0800 0.4 / W 1359 4.8 / 2012 0.7

8 0136 4.6 / 0755 0.5 / W 1356 4.8 / 2007 0.6 **23** 0213 4.7 / 0836 0.3 / TH 1435 4.8 / 2047 0.6

9 0212 4.8 / 0835 0.3 / TH 1435 5.0 / 2049 0.5 **24** 0250 4.8 / 0913 0.3 / F 1512 4.8 / 2122 0.6

10 0251 4.9 / 0918 0.2 / F 1515 5.0 / 2133 0.5 **25** 0326 4.8 / 0949 0.3 / SA 1549 4.8 / 2157 0.6

11 0332 5.0 / 1001 0.2 / SA 1558 5.0 / 2217 0.5 **26** 0402 4.7 / 1024 0.4 / SU 1624 4.6 / 2230 0.7

12 0415 4.9 / 1046 0.2 / SU 1643 4.9 / 2301 0.6 **27** 0436 4.6 / 1055 0.6 / M 1657 4.4 / 2300 0.9

13 0501 4.8 / 1132 0.4 / M 1731 4.7 / 2348 0.8 **28** 0508 4.4 / 1124 0.8 / TU 1728 4.2 / 2332 1.0

14 0551 4.6 / 1221 0.6 / TU 1824 4.4 / ☽ **29** 0543 4.2 / 1157 1.1 / W 1804 4.0

15 0040 1.0 / 0649 4.4 / W 1321 0.9 / 1929 4.1

MARCH

1 0010 1.2 / 0625 4.0 / TH 1240 1.3 / ☽ 1852 3.8 **16** 0131 1.1 / 0743 4.0 / F 1417 1.2 / 2030 3.7

2 0106 1.5 / 0728 3.7 / F 1431 1.5 / 2022 3.5 **17** 0259 1.1 / 0915 3.9 / SA 1538 1.3 / 2159 3.8

3 0327 1.5 / 0916 3.6 / SA 1553 1.5 / 2201 3.6 **18** 0418 1.0 / 1040 4.1 / SU 1654 1.2 / 2311 4.0

4 0432 1.3 / 1035 3.8 / SU 1651 1.3 / 2306 3.8 **19** 0527 0.8 / 1142 4.3 / M 1756 1.0 / 2359 4.3

5 0525 1.1 / 1131 4.1 / M 1740 1.1 / 2353 4.1 **20** 0620 0.6 / 1227 4.5 / TU 1840 0.9

6 0610 0.8 / 1214 4.4 / TU 1824 0.9 **21** 0042 4.5 / 0702 0.5 / W 1304 4.6 / 1916 0.8

7 0032 4.4 / 0651 0.5 / W 1254 4.7 / 1905 0.7 **22** 0117 4.6 / 0738 0.4 / TH 1338 4.7 / ● 1950 0.7

8 0110 4.7 / 0732 0.3 / TH 1332 4.9 / ○ 1947 0.5 **23** 0152 4.7 / 0813 0.3 / F 1413 4.8 / 2023 0.6

9 0149 4.9 / 0814 0.2 / F 1412 5.1 / 2030 0.4 **24** 0226 4.8 / 0847 0.3 / SA 1448 4.7 / 2056 0.5

10 0229 5.0 / 0858 0.1 / SA 1454 5.1 / 2114 0.4 **25** 0301 4.8 / 0919 0.4 / SU 1522 4.7 / 2128 0.6

11 0312 5.1 / 0942 0.1 / SU 1537 5.0 / 2158 0.4 **26** 0334 4.7 / 0950 0.5 / M 1553 4.5 / 2159 0.6

12 0355 5.0 / 1026 0.2 / M 1622 4.8 / 2242 0.5 **27** 0404 4.6 / 1019 0.7 / TU 1621 4.4 / 2229 0.7

13 0441 4.9 / 1111 0.4 / TU 1709 4.6 / 2328 0.7 **28** 0434 4.4 / 1048 0.8 / W 1650 4.3 / 2300 0.9

14 0530 4.6 / 1159 0.7 / W 1801 4.3 **29** 0507 4.3 / 1119 1.0 / TH 1725 4.1 / 2336 1.0

15 0020 0.9 / 0628 4.3 / TH 1258 1.0 / ☽ 1905 4.0 **30** 0549 4.1 / 1200 1.2 / F 1811 3.9

31 0026 1.2 / 0647 3.9 / SA 1304 1.4 / 1921 3.6

APRIL

1 0233 1.4 / 0823 3.7 / SU 1508 1.4 / 2110 3.6 **16** 0347 0.9 / 1010 4.1 / M 1621 1.2 / 2239 4.0

2 0348 1.2 / 0951 3.9 / M 1612 1.3 / 2221 3.8 **17** 0455 0.8 / 1113 4.3 / TU 1727 1.0 / 2333 4.2

3 0445 1.0 / 1052 4.2 / TU 1705 1.0 / 2315 4.1 **18** 0552 0.6 / 1201 4.5 / W 1816 0.9

4 0535 0.7 / 1141 4.5 / W 1754 0.8 / 2359 4.5 **19** 0017 4.4 / 0637 0.5 / TH 1240 4.6 / 1854 0.8

5 0622 0.4 / 1225 4.8 / TH 1840 0.6 **20** 0054 4.5 / 0714 0.5 / F 1316 4.6 / 1928 0.7

6 0042 4.7 / 0707 0.3 / F 1307 5.0 / ○ 1925 0.4 **21** 0130 4.6 / 0748 0.5 / SA 1351 4.6 / ● 1959 0.6

7 0124 5.0 / 0751 0.1 / SA 1350 5.1 / 2010 0.3 **22** 0204 4.6 / 0819 0.5 / SU 1424 4.5 / 2031 0.6

8 0207 5.1 / 0836 0.1 / SU 1433 5.0 / 2055 0.3 **23** 0237 4.6 / 0850 0.6 / M 1456 4.5 / 2102 0.6

9 0251 5.1 / 0921 0.2 / M 1517 4.9 / 2139 0.4 **24** 0308 4.5 / 0919 0.7 / TU 1524 4.4 / 2133 0.6

10 0336 5.0 / 1006 0.3 / TU 1602 4.7 / 2224 0.5 **25** 0337 4.5 / 0949 0.8 / W 1552 4.4 / 2205 0.7

11 0423 4.8 / 1051 0.5 / W 1650 4.5 / 2311 0.6 **26** 0408 4.4 / 1020 0.9 / TH 1623 4.3 / 2238 0.8

12 0514 4.6 / 1140 0.8 / TH 1743 4.2 **27** 0443 4.4 / 1054 1.0 / F 1700 4.2 / 2316 0.9

13 0005 0.8 / 0613 4.3 / F 1240 1.0 / ☽ 1847 3.9 **28** 0527 4.3 / 1137 1.1 / SA 1747 4.0

14 0117 0.9 / 0727 4.1 / SA 1355 1.2 / 2007 3.8 **29** 0006 1.0 / 0624 4.1 / SU 1237 1.3 / ☽ 1853 3.9

15 0235 1.0 / 0852 4.0 / SU 1510 1.3 / 2128 3.8 **30** 0137 1.1 / 0746 4.0 / M 1418 1.3 / 2024 3.8

Chart Datum: 0·19 metres below TAW Datum
HAT is 5·6 metres above Chart Datum

TIDES

TIDES

TIME ZONE -0100
(Belgian Standard Time)
Subtract 1 hour for UT
For Belgian Summer Time add
ONE hour in **non-shaded areas**

BELGIUM – ZEEBRUGGE

LAT 51°21'N   LONG 3°12'E

TIMES AND HEIGHTS OF HIGH AND LOW WATERS

Dates in amber are **SPRINGS**
Dates in yellow are **NEAPS**

2012

MAY

Time	m		Time	m
1 TU	0304 1.0 / 0908 4.1 / 1531 1.2 / 2138 4.0	**16** W	0415 0.8 / 1034 4.2 / 1648 1.1 / 2257 4.2	
2 W	0405 0.8 / 1013 4.3 / 1630 1.0 / 2237 4.2	**17** TH	0516 0.7 / 1128 4.3 / 1745 1.0 / 2347 4.3	
3 TH	0500 0.6 / 1108 4.5 / 1724 0.8 / 2329 4.5	**18** F	0607 0.7 / 1213 4.4 / 1830 0.9	
4 F	0552 0.4 / 1157 4.7 / 1815 0.6	**19** SA	0030 4.4 / 0648 0.7 / 1253 4.5 / 1906 0.8	
5 SA	0016 4.7 / 0641 0.3 / 1243 4.9 / 1903 0.5	**20** SU	0108 4.4 / 0722 0.7 / 1330 4.5 / 1938 0.7	
6 SU ○	0102 4.9 / 0729 0.3 / 1328 4.9 / 1950 0.4	**21** M ●	0143 4.5 / 0752 0.7 / 1403 4.4 / 2039 0.7	
7 M	0148 5.0 / 0815 0.3 / 1413 4.9 / 2036 0.4	**22** TU	0215 4.4 / 0821 0.8 / 1433 4.4 / 2039 0.7	
8 TU	0234 5.0 / 0901 0.4 / 1459 4.8 / 2122 0.4	**23** W	0245 4.4 / 0852 0.8 / 1501 4.4 / 2111 0.7	
9 W	0320 4.9 / 0946 0.5 / 1545 4.6 / 2209 0.4	**24** TH	0315 4.4 / 0924 0.8 / 1530 4.3 / 2146 0.7	
10 TH	0409 4.8 / 1033 0.7 / 1634 4.4 / 2258 0.5	**25** F	0349 4.5 / 0959 0.9 / 1604 4.3 / 2222 0.7	
11 F	0500 4.6 / 1122 0.8 / 1726 4.3 / 2352 0.6	**26** SA	0427 4.5 / 1037 0.9 / 1644 4.3 / 2304 0.7	
12 SA ☽	0558 4.4 / 1219 1.0 / 1826 4.1	**27** SU	0512 4.4 / 1122 1.0 / 1732 4.2 / 2356 0.8	
13 SU	0057 0.7 / 0705 4.2 / 1326 1.2 / 1936 3.9	**28** M ☾	0607 4.3 / 1220 1.1 / 1831 4.1	
14 M	0205 0.8 / 0818 4.1 / 1435 1.2 / 2049 3.9	**29** TU	0105 0.8 / 0715 4.3 / 1335 1.1 / 1945 4.1	
15 TU	0311 0.6 / 0930 4.1 / 1542 1.2 / 2157 4.0	**30** W	0221 0.8 / 0829 4.3 / 1450 1.1 / 2057 4.1	
		31 TH	0326 0.7 / 0936 4.4 / 1554 1.0 / 2201 4.3	

JUNE

Time	m		Time	m
1 F	0426 0.6 / 1036 4.5 / 1655 0.8 / 2300 4.4	**16** SA	0532 0.9 / 1144 4.2 / 1802 1.0	
2 SA	0524 0.5 / 1132 4.6 / 1752 0.7 / 2354 4.6	**17** SU	0004 4.2 / 0619 0.9 / 1229 4.3 / 1844 0.9	
3 SU	0619 0.5 / 1223 4.7 / 1845 0.6	**18** M	0046 4.3 / 0655 0.9 / 1308 4.3 / 1917 0.8	
4 M ○	0044 4.7 / 0709 0.5 / 1311 4.7 / 1934 0.5	**19** TU ●	0123 4.3 / 0725 0.9 / 1341 4.4 / 1947 0.8	
5 TU	0132 4.8 / 0757 0.5 / 1358 4.7 / 2021 0.4	**20** W	0155 4.4 / 0755 0.9 / 1411 4.4 / 2018 0.7	
6 W	0219 4.8 / 0842 0.5 / 1443 4.7 / 2107 0.4	**21** TH	0225 4.4 / 0828 0.8 / 1440 4.4 / 2053 0.6	
7 TH	0306 4.8 / 0928 0.6 / 1529 4.6 / 2154 0.3	**22** F	0257 4.5 / 0904 0.8 / 1512 4.5 / 2130 0.6	
8 F	0354 4.8 / 1014 0.7 / 1616 4.5 / 2242 0.4	**23** SA	0333 4.6 / 0942 0.8 / 1548 4.5 / 2210 0.5	
9 SA	0444 4.7 / 1101 0.8 / 1705 4.4 / 2333 0.4	**24** SU	0413 4.7 / 1024 0.8 / 1629 4.5 / 2254 0.5	
10 SU	0537 4.5 / 1153 0.9 / 1759 4.3	**25** M	0457 4.7 / 1109 0.8 / 1715 4.5 / 2343 0.5	
11 M ☾	0029 0.6 / 0635 4.4 / 1250 1.1 / 1859 4.2	**26** TU	0548 4.6 / 1201 0.9 / 1809 4.4	
12 TU	0130 0.7 / 0738 4.2 / 1354 1.2 / 2004 4.0	**27** W ☾	0039 0.6 / 0646 4.5 / 1301 1.0 / 1911 4.4	
13 W	0232 0.8 / 0843 4.1 / 1459 1.2 / 2110 4.0	**28** TH	0143 0.6 / 0753 4.4 / 1410 1.0 / 2020 4.3	
14 TH	0334 0.9 / 0948 4.1 / 1605 1.2 / 2215 4.0	**29** F	0250 0.7 / 0901 4.3 / 1521 1.0 / 2129 4.3	
15 F	0435 0.9 / 1050 4.1 / 1708 1.1 / 2314 4.1	**30** SA	0357 0.7 / 1008 4.3 / 1630 1.0 / 2236 4.3	

JULY

Time	m		Time	m
1 SU	0501 0.7 / 1112 4.4 / 1734 0.8 / 2338 4.5	**16** M	0546 1.1 / 1201 4.1 / 1818 1.0	
2 M	0601 0.7 / 1209 4.4 / 1831 0.7	**17** TU	0021 4.2 / 0626 1.1 / 1243 4.2 / 1854 0.9	
3 TU ○	0032 4.6 / 0654 0.7 / 1259 4.5 / 1921 0.6	**18** W	0059 4.3 / 0659 1.0 / 1316 4.3 / 1925 0.8	
4 W	0121 4.7 / 0741 0.7 / 1344 4.6 / 2007 0.4	**19** TH ●	0131 4.5 / 0731 0.9 / 1347 4.4 / 1957 0.6	
5 TH	0206 4.8 / 0825 0.7 / 1427 4.7 / 2052 0.3	**20** F	0203 4.6 / 0806 0.8 / 1418 4.6 / 2034 0.5	
6 F	0251 4.9 / 0909 0.7 / 1511 4.7 / 2136 0.3	**21** SA	0237 4.7 / 0845 0.7 / 1452 4.7 / 2113 0.4	
7 SA	0336 4.9 / 0952 0.7 / 1555 4.7 / 2222 0.3	**22** SU	0315 4.9 / 0926 0.6 / 1530 4.8 / 2155 0.3	
8 SU	0422 4.8 / 1037 0.7 / 1640 4.7 / 2308 0.3	**23** M	0355 4.9 / 1009 0.6 / 1612 4.8 / 2239 0.3	
9 M	0509 4.7 / 1122 0.8 / 1728 4.6 / 2357 0.5	**24** TU	0438 4.9 / 1054 0.7 / 1656 4.8 / 2325 0.4	
10 TU	0559 4.5 / 1209 1.0 / 1818 4.4	**25** W	0525 4.8 / 1141 0.8 / 1745 4.7	
11 W ☾	0049 0.7 / 0652 4.3 / 1303 1.1 / 1914 4.2	**26** TH ☾	0014 0.5 / 0618 4.6 / 1233 0.9 / 1841 4.5	
12 TH	0147 0.9 / 0751 4.1 / 1411 1.3 / 2017 4.0	**27** F	0111 0.7 / 0719 4.4 / 1336 1.0 / 1947 4.4	
13 F	0251 1.1 / 0857 3.9 / 1522 1.3 / 2126 3.9	**28** SA	0219 0.8 / 0829 4.2 / 1453 1.1 / 2102 4.2	
14 SA	0354 1.2 / 1006 3.9 / 1629 1.3 / 2235 3.9	**29** SU	0333 0.9 / 0946 4.1 / 1610 1.1 / 2219 4.2	
15 SU	0453 1.2 / 1109 4.0 / 1729 1.2 / 2334 4.0	**30** M	0444 0.9 / 1059 4.2 / 1720 0.9 / 2328 4.4	
		31 TU	0547 0.9 / 1159 4.3 / 1820 0.7	

AUGUST

Time	m		Time	m
1 W	0024 4.6 / 0641 0.9 / 1247 4.5 / 1909 0.6	**16** TH	0030 4.4 / 0631 1.0 / 1247 4.4 / 1859 0.7	
2 TH ○	0110 4.8 / 0726 0.8 / 1329 4.6 / 1952 0.4	**17** F	0104 4.6 / 0707 0.8 / 1319 4.6 / 1934 0.5	
3 F	0151 4.8 / 0807 0.7 / 1409 4.8 / 2034 0.3	**18** SA	0138 4.8 / 0745 0.7 / 1353 4.8 / 2012 0.4	
4 SA	0232 4.9 / 0848 0.7 / 1450 4.9 / 2115 0.2	**19** SU	0215 5.0 / 0826 0.6 / 1430 5.0 / 2054 0.2	
5 SU	0314 5.0 / 0928 0.6 / 1531 4.9 / 2157 0.2	**20** M	0253 5.1 / 0908 0.5 / 1510 5.0 / 2136 0.2	
6 M	0356 4.9 / 1009 0.6 / 1613 4.9 / 2239 0.3	**21** TU	0334 5.1 / 0951 0.5 / 1551 5.0 / 2220 0.3	
7 TU	0439 4.8 / 1049 0.7 / 1655 4.7 / 2320 0.5	**22** W	0417 5.0 / 1035 0.6 / 1635 5.0 / 2304 0.4	
8 W	0522 4.6 / 1128 0.9 / 1737 4.5 / 2359 0.7	**23** TH	0502 4.8 / 1120 0.7 / 1722 4.8 / 2351 0.6	
9 TH ☾	0604 4.4 / 1207 1.1 / 1821 4.3	**24** F ☾	0552 4.6 / 1209 0.8 / 1815 4.6	
10 F	0045 1.0 / 0651 4.1 / 1256 1.3 / 1913 4.0	**25** SA	0045 0.8 / 0650 4.3 / 1310 1.1 / 1920 4.3	
11 SA	0153 1.3 / 0753 3.8 / 1433 1.5 / 2026 3.8	**26** SU	0155 1.0 / 0804 4.1 / 1432 1.2 / 2043 4.1	
12 SU	0311 1.4 / 0913 3.7 / 1549 1.4 / 2149 3.7	**27** M	0314 1.1 / 0929 4.0 / 1554 1.1 / 2209 4.2	
13 M	0414 1.4 / 1028 3.8 / 1651 1.3 / 2258 3.9	**28** TU	0429 1.1 / 1048 4.1 / 1706 0.9 / 2320 4.4	
14 TU	0509 1.3 / 1127 4.0 / 1743 1.1 / 2350 4.1	**29** W	0535 1.0 / 1148 4.3 / 1806 0.7	
15 W	0554 1.2 / 1211 4.2 / 1824 0.9	**30** TH	0013 4.6 / 0627 0.8 / 1233 4.5 / 1853 0.5	
		31 F ○	0056 4.8 / 0709 0.8 / 1312 4.7 / 1934 0.4	

Chart Datum: 0·19 metres below TAW Datum
HAT is 5·6 metres above Chart Datum

TIME ZONE -0100
(Belgian Standard Time)
Subtract 1 hour for UT
For Belgian Summer Time add
ONE hour in **non-shaded areas**

BELGIUM – ZEEBRUGGE

LAT 51°21'N   LONG 3°12'E

TIMES AND HEIGHTS OF HIGH AND LOW WATERS

Dates in amber are **SPRINGS**
Dates in yellow are **NEAPS**

2012

SEPTEMBER

#	Time	m		#	Time	m
1 SA	0134 / 0748 / 1350 / 2013	4.9 / 0.7 / 5.0 / 0.3		**16** SU	0112 / 0723 / 1328 / ● 1949	5.0 / 0.6 / 5.0 / 0.3
2 SU	0212 / 0826 / 1428 / 2052	5.0 / 0.6 / 5.0 / 0.3		**17** M	0150 / 0805 / 1407 / 2032	5.2 / 0.4 / 5.2 / 0.2
3 M	0251 / 0903 / 1507 / 2130	5.0 / 0.6 / 5.0 / 0.3		**18** TU	0231 / 0849 / 1448 / 2115	5.3 / 0.4 / 5.2 / 0.2
4 TU	0330 / 0941 / 1546 / 2208	5.0 / 0.6 / 4.9 / 0.4		**19** W	0313 / 0932 / 1531 / 2159	5.2 / 0.4 / 5.2 / 0.3
5 W	0409 / 1017 / 1623 / 2243	4.8 / 0.7 / 4.8 / 0.6		**20** TH	0356 / 1016 / 1615 / 2243	5.0 / 0.5 / 5.0 / 0.5
6 TH	0445 / 1050 / 1658 / 2314	4.6 / 0.8 / 4.6 / 0.8		**21** F	0441 / 1101 / 1702 / 2330	4.8 / 0.7 / 4.8 / 0.7
7 F	0519 / 1123 / 1733 / 2347	4.4 / 1.0 / 4.4 / 1.1		**22** SA	0530 / 1150 / 1756 / ●	4.5 / 0.9 / 4.6
8 SA	0554 / 1159 / 1814 / ◐	4.2 / 1.2 / 4.1		**23** SU	0024 / 0628 / 1252 / 1903	1.0 / 4.2 / 1.0 / 4.3
9 SU	0027 / 0638 / 1251 / 1912	1.3 / 3.9 / 1.4 / 3.8		**24** M	0136 / 0745 / 1416 / 2029	1.2 / 4.0 / 1.1 / 4.1
10 M	0205 / 0800 / 1506 / 2054	1.6 / 3.7 / 1.5 / 3.7		**25** TU	0257 / 0913 / 1536 / 2155	1.3 / 3.9 / 1.1 / 4.2
11 TU	0333 / 0939 / 1610 / 2214	1.5 / 3.7 / 1.4 / 3.9		**26** W	0410 / 1030 / 1646 / 2305	1.2 / 4.1 / 0.9 / 4.4
12 W	0430 / 1045 / 1704 / 2312	1.4 / 3.9 / 1.1 / 4.2		**27** TH	0517 / 1129 / 1747 / 2357	1.1 / 4.4 / 0.7 / 4.7
13 TH	0520 / 1134 / 1749 / 2356	1.2 / 4.2 / 0.9 / 4.5		**28** F	0610 / 1215 / 1834	0.9 / 4.6 / 0.5
14 F	0602 / 1214 / 1829	1.0 / 4.5 / 0.6		**29** SA	0038 / 0651 / 1253 / 1914	4.8 / 0.8 / 4.8 / 0.4
15 SA	0034 / 0642 / 1250 / 1908	4.8 / 0.8 / 4.8 / 0.4		**30** SU	0116 / 0728 / 1330 / ○ 1951	4.9 / 0.7 / 4.9 / 0.4

OCTOBER

#	Time	m		#	Time	m
1 M	0152 / 0804 / 1407 / 2028	5.0 / 0.6 / 5.0 / 0.4		**16** TU	0127 / 0745 / 1345 / 2010	5.2 / 0.4 / 5.2 / 0.2
2 TU	0229 / 0839 / 1444 / 2103	5.0 / 0.6 / 5.0 / 0.4		**17** W	0209 / 0830 / 1428 / 2055	5.2 / 0.4 / 5.2 / 0.3
3 W	0305 / 0914 / 1520 / 2136	4.9 / 0.6 / 4.9 / 0.6		**18** TH	0252 / 0914 / 1512 / 2139	5.1 / 0.4 / 5.2 / 0.4
4 TH	0340 / 0947 / 1553 / 2207	4.7 / 0.7 / 4.7 / 0.7		**19** F	0337 / 0959 / 1558 / 2225	4.9 / 0.5 / 5.0 / 0.6
5 F	0411 / 1018 / 1625 / 2236	4.6 / 0.8 / 4.6 / 0.9		**20** SA	0423 / 1046 / 1647 / 2312	4.7 / 0.6 / 4.8 / 0.8
6 SA	0441 / 1046 / 1657 / 2307	4.4 / 0.9 / 4.4 / 1.1		**21** SU	0513 / 1137 / 1742	4.5 / 0.8 / 4.6
7 SU	0513 / 1124 / 1735 / 2345	4.2 / 1.1 / 4.2 / 1.3		**22** M	0007 / 0612 / 1240 / ◐ 1850	1.1 / 4.2 / 0.9 / 4.3
8 M	0554 / 1209 / 1827 / ◐	4.0 / 1.3 / 4.0		**23** TU	0117 / 0727 / 1357 / 2011	1.3 / 4.0 / 1.0 / 4.2
9 TU	0040 / 0656 / 1404 / 1955	1.5 / 3.8 / 1.5 / 3.9		**24** W	0233 / 0848 / 1510 / 2132	1.3 / 4.0 / 1.0 / 4.3
10 W	0245 / 0843 / 1527 / 2126	1.6 / 3.7 / 1.3 / 4.0		**25** TH	0344 / 1003 / 1619 / 2241	1.3 / 4.1 / 0.8 / 4.4
11 TH	0350 / 0958 / 1623 / 2230	1.4 / 3.9 / 1.1 / 4.2		**26** F	0452 / 1104 / 1721 / 2335	1.1 / 4.4 / 0.7 / 4.6
12 F	0443 / 1053 / 1712 / 2320	1.2 / 4.2 / 0.8 / 4.6		**27** SA	0549 / 1153 / 1812	1.0 / 4.6 / 0.6
13 SA	0531 / 1139 / 1758	0.9 / 4.6 / 0.6		**28** SU	0019 / 0633 / 1234 / 1854	4.8 / 0.8 / 4.7 / 0.5
14 SU	0004 / 0616 / 1221 / 1842	4.9 / 0.7 / 4.9 / 0.4		**29** M	0057 / 0710 / 1312 / ○ 1931	4.8 / 0.8 / 4.8 / 0.5
15 M	0045 / 0701 / 1303 / ● 1926	5.1 / 0.5 / 5.1 / 0.3		**30** TU	0134 / 0745 / 1349 / 2005	4.8 / 0.7 / 4.8 / 0.6
				31 W	0209 / 0818 / 1424 / 2037	4.8 / 0.7 / 4.8 / 0.7

NOVEMBER

#	Time	m		#	Time	m
1 TH	0244 / 0851 / 1457 / 2107	4.7 / 0.7 / 4.7 / 0.8		**16** F	0235 / 0859 / 1457 / 2122	5.0 / 0.4 / 5.1 / 0.5
2 F	0315 / 0922 / 1529 / 2137	4.6 / 0.7 / 4.6 / 0.9		**17** SA	0321 / 0945 / 1544 / 2208	4.8 / 0.5 / 5.0 / 0.7
3 SA	0344 / 0953 / 1558 / 2207	4.5 / 0.8 / 4.4 / 1.0		**18** SU	0408 / 1033 / 1634 / 2256	4.7 / 0.5 / 4.8 / 0.9
4 SU	0412 / 1025 / 1631 / 2240	4.4 / 0.9 / 4.5 / 1.1		**19** M	0458 / 1125 / 1729 / 2350	4.5 / 0.6 / 4.6 / 1.0
5 M	0446 / 1101 / 1710 / 2318	4.3 / 1.0 / 4.4 / 1.2		**20** TU	0555 / 1225 / 1832 / ◐	4.3 / 0.7 / 4.4
6 TU	0528 / 1146 / 1801	4.2 / 1.1 / 4.2		**21** W	0052 / 0701 / 1332 / 1944	1.2 / 4.2 / 0.8 / 4.3
7 W	0010 / 0625 / 1257 / ◐ 1913	1.4 / 4.0 / 1.2 / 4.1		**22** TH	0201 / 0814 / 1439 / 2057	1.3 / 4.1 / 0.9 / 4.3
8 TH	0139 / 0749 / 1438 / 2039	1.5 / 3.9 / 1.2 / 4.1		**23** F	0310 / 0926 / 1546 / 2206	1.3 / 4.1 / 0.9 / 4.3
9 F	0306 / 0910 / 1541 / 2147	1.4 / 4.0 / 1.0 / 4.3		**24** SA	0420 / 1032 / 1651 / 2307	1.2 / 4.3 / 0.8 / 4.5
10 SA	0406 / 1012 / 1636 / 2244	1.2 / 4.3 / 0.8 / 4.6		**25** SU	0524 / 1128 / 1748 / 2357	1.1 / 4.4 / 0.8 / 4.6
11 SU	0500 / 1106 / 1728 / 2334	1.0 / 4.4 / 0.6 / 4.8		**26** M	0615 / 1215 / 1834	0.9 / 4.6 / 0.7
12 M	0551 / 1154 / 1817	0.8 / 4.8 / 0.5		**27** TU	0040 / 0655 / 1256 / 1912	4.6 / 0.8 / 4.6 / 0.8
13 TU	0021 / 0640 / 1240 / ● 1904	5.0 / 0.6 / 5.0 / 0.4		**28** W	0118 / 0730 / 1333 / ○ 1944	4.6 / 0.8 / 4.6 / 0.8
14 W	0106 / 0727 / 1325 / 1951	5.1 / 0.5 / 5.1 / 0.4		**29** TH	0153 / 0801 / 1407 / 2013	4.6 / 0.9 / 4.6 / 0.9
15 TH	0150 / 0813 / 1411 / 2036	5.0 / 0.6 / 5.1 / 0.4		**30** F	0225 / 0831 / 1439 / 2042	4.6 / 0.7 / 4.6 / 0.9

DECEMBER

#	Time	m		#	Time	m
1 SA	0254 / 0901 / 1508 / 2112	4.5 / 0.7 / 4.6 / 0.9		**16** SU	0306 / 0932 / 1531 / 2152	4.8 / 0.4 / 5.0 / 0.7
2 SU	0322 / 0934 / 1539 / 2145	4.5 / 0.7 / 4.5 / 1.0		**17** M	0353 / 1019 / 1619 / 2238	4.7 / 0.4 / 4.9 / 0.8
3 M	0352 / 1008 / 1613 / 2220	4.5 / 0.8 / 4.6 / 1.0		**18** TU	0441 / 1109 / 1711 / 2328	4.7 / 0.4 / 4.7 / 0.9
4 TU	0428 / 1046 / 1653 / 2301	4.4 / 0.8 / 4.5 / 1.1		**19** W	0533 / 1202 / 1807	4.5 / 0.5 / 4.6
5 W	0510 / 1131 / 1741 / 2350	4.4 / 0.9 / 4.5 / 1.2		**20** TH	0022 / 0630 / 1300 / ◐ 1908	1.1 / 4.4 / 0.7 / 4.4
6 TH	0602 / 1230 / 1842 / ◐	4.3 / 0.9 / 4.4		**21** F	0123 / 0734 / 1403 / 2015	1.2 / 4.2 / 0.8 / 4.2
7 F	0055 / 0708 / 1346 / 1954	1.2 / 4.2 / 1.0 / 4.3		**22** SA	0231 / 0842 / 1509 / 2124	1.3 / 4.1 / 0.9 / 4.1
8 SA	0216 / 0823 / 1458 / 2105	1.3 / 4.0 / 0.9 / 4.4		**23** SU	0342 / 0952 / 1615 / 2232	1.3 / 4.1 / 1.0 / 4.2
9 SU	0327 / 0932 / 1600 / 2208	1.2 / 4.3 / 0.8 / 4.5		**24** M	0453 / 1059 / 1719 / 2331	1.2 / 4.2 / 1.0 / 4.3
10 M	0430 / 1033 / 1659 / 2307	1.0 / 4.4 / 0.7 / 4.6		**25** TU	0554 / 1154 / 1813	1.1 / 4.3 / 1.0
11 TU	0528 / 1130 / 1755 / 2359	0.9 / 4.6 / 0.6 / 4.7		**26** W	0020 / 0641 / 1240 / 1854	4.4 / 1.0 / 4.4 / 1.0
12 W	0623 / 1222 / 1846	0.7 / 4.8 / 0.6		**27** TH	0101 / 0718 / 1318 / 1925	4.4 / 0.9 / 4.4 / 1.0
13 TH	0049 / 0712 / 1310 / ● 1934	4.8 / 0.6 / 4.9 / 0.6		**28** F	0136 / 0747 / 1351 / ○ 1951	4.4 / 0.8 / 4.5 / 1.0
14 F	0136 / 0800 / 1357 / 2020	4.9 / 0.5 / 5.0 / 0.6		**29** SA	0207 / 0814 / 1420 / 2019	4.5 / 0.8 / 4.5 / 0.9
15 SA	0221 / 0846 / 1444 / 2106	4.8 / 0.4 / 5.0 / 0.6		**30** SU	0234 / 0843 / 1450 / 2051	4.5 / 0.7 / 4.6 / 0.9
				31 M	0303 / 0917 / 1521 / 2127	4.5 / 0.6 / 4.6 / 0.8

Chart Datum: 0·19 metres below TAW Datum
HAT is 5·6 metres above Chart Datum

TIDES

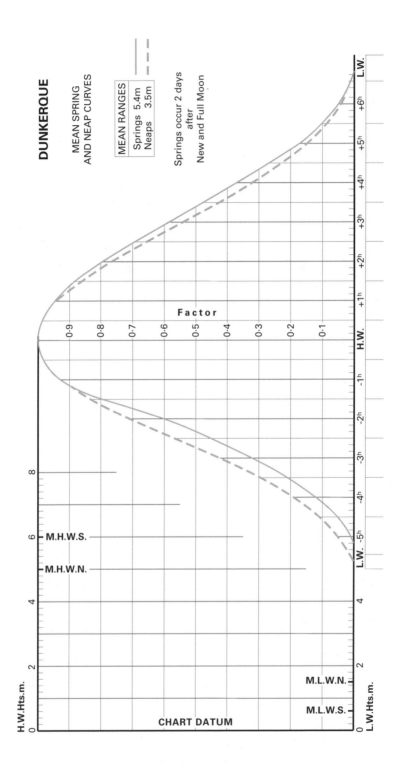

DUNKERQUE

MEAN SPRING
AND NEAP CURVES

MEAN RANGES
Springs 5.4m
Neaps 3.5m

Springs occur 2 days
after
New and Full Moon

Factor

0·9 0·8 0·7 0·6 0·5 0·4 0·3 0·2 0·1

H.W.

L.W.

M.H.W.S.

M.H.W.N.

M.L.W.N.

M.L.W.S.

CHART DATUM

H.W.Hts.m.

L.W.Hts.m.

8

6

4

2

0

TIME ZONE -0100
(French Standard Time)
Subtract 1 hour for UT
For French Summer Time add
ONE hour in **non-shaded areas**

FRANCE – DUNKERQUE

LAT 51°03'N   LONG 2°22'E

TIMES AND HEIGHTS OF HIGH AND LOW WATERS

Dates in amber are **SPRINGS**
Dates in yellow are **NEAPS**

2012

JANUARY

Time	m	Time	m
1 0002	1.5	**16** 0509	5.6
0529	5.2	1216	0.9
SU 1232	1.3	M 1748	5.5
◑ 1807	5.1	○	
2 0049	1.7	**17** 0036	1.3
0624	5.0	0610	5.4
M 1328	1.5	TU 1317	1.1
1908	4.9	1853	5.3
3 0154	1.8	**18** 0146	1.4
0733	4.8	0722	5.3
TU 1435	1.7	W 1431	1.3
2020	4.7	2011	5.1
4 0305	1.8	**19** 0305	1.5
0849	4.8	0847	5.2
W 1542	1.7	TH 1550	1.3
2128	4.8	2135	5.2
5 0412	1.7	**20** 0426	1.4
0955	4.9	1008	5.3
TH 1646	1.6	F 1708	1.1
2227	5.0	2245	5.4
6 0513	1.5	**21** 0540	1.1
1051	5.1	1113	5.6
F 1741	1.4	SA 1811	1.0
2316	5.2	2341	5.6
7 0603	1.3	**22** 0638	0.8
1137	5.3	1205	5.8
SA 1826	1.2	SU 1902	0.8
2358	5.4		
8 0645	1.1	**23** 0027	5.8
1215	5.6	0725	0.6
SU 1905	1.1	M 1251	6.0
		● 1946	0.7
9 0034	5.6	**24** 0108	5.9
0725	0.9	0809	0.5
M 1250	5.8	TU 1332	6.0
○ 1944	0.9	2026	0.7
10 0108	5.8	**25** 0146	6.0
0804	0.7	0849	0.5
TU 1326	5.9	W 1411	6.0
2023	0.8	2104	0.7
11 0143	5.9	**26** 0223	6.0
0843	0.6	0927	0.5
W 1403	6.0	TH 1449	6.0
2102	0.8	2139	0.8
12 0220	5.9	**27** 0258	5.9
0924	0.5	1002	0.6
TH 1442	6.0	F 1524	5.8
2141	0.8	2212	0.9
13 0257	5.9	**28** 0332	5.8
1004	0.5	1035	0.7
F 1521	6.0	SA 1558	5.7
2220	0.8	2246	1.0
14 0335	5.8	**29** 0407	5.6
1044	0.6	1108	0.9
SA 1603	5.8	SU 1633	5.5
2300	0.9	2319	1.2
15 0418	5.8	**30** 0445	5.4
1127	0.7	1142	1.2
SU 1651	5.7	M 1714	5.2
2344	1.1	2357	1.4
		31 0529	5.2
		1224	1.4
		TU 1804	4.9
		◑	

FEBRUARY

Time	m	Time	m
1 0045	1.7	**16** 0121	1.4
0627	4.8	0703	5.2
W 1323	1.7	TH 1409	1.4
1909	4.6	1954	4.9
2 0153	1.9	**17** 0246	1.5
0742	4.6	0837	5.0
TH 1441	1.9	F 1537	1.4
2029	4.5	2126	4.9
3 0316	1.9	**18** 0417	1.4
0906	4.6	1003	5.2
F 1559	1.8	SA 1701	1.3
2146	4.7	2237	5.2
4 0433	1.7	**19** 0532	1.1
1018	4.9	1107	5.4
SA 1709	1.5	SU 1801	1.0
2248	5.0	2333	5.4
5 0536	1.4	**20** 0627	0.8
1112	5.2	1158	5.7
SU 1802	1.3	M 1848	0.9
2336	5.3		
6 0624	1.0	**21** 0015	5.6
1155	5.5	0711	0.6
M 1845	1.0	TU 1238	5.8
		● 1928	0.8
7 0015	5.6	**22** 0051	5.8
0705	0.8	0751	0.5
TU 1232	5.8	W 1314	5.9
○ 1925	0.8	2005	0.7
8 0049	5.8	**23** 0124	5.9
0745	0.5	0828	0.4
W 1307	6.0	TH 1348	6.0
2004	0.7	2039	0.7
9 0123	6.0	**24** 0158	6.0
0825	0.4	0902	0.5
TH 1343	6.1	F 1422	5.9
2043	0.6	2112	0.7
10 0158	6.1	**25** 0230	5.9
0905	0.3	0933	0.5
F 1420	6.1	SA 1453	5.9
2122	0.5	2142	0.8
11 0234	6.1	**26** 0301	5.9
0947	0.3	1004	0.7
SA 1459	6.1	SU 1523	5.7
2201	0.6	2214	0.9
12 0313	6.1	**27** 0333	5.7
1026	0.3	1033	0.8
SU 1541	6.0	M 1555	5.6
2241	0.7	2244	1.1
13 0357	6.0	**28** 0406	5.6
1108	0.5	1102	1.0
M 1628	5.8	TU 1630	5.3
2323	0.9	2316	1.2
14 0447	5.8	**29** 0444	5.3
1154	0.8	1138	1.3
TU 1723	5.5	W 1713	5.0
◑		2356	1.5
15 0013	1.1		
0548	5.5		
W 1252	1.1		
1830	5.2		

MARCH

Time	m	Time	m
1 0535	4.9	**16** 0107	1.3
1226	1.6	0651	5.1
TH 1817	4.7	F 1357	1.5
◑		1939	4.8
2 0053	1.8	**17** 0234	1.4
0651	4.6	0828	4.9
F 1337	1.9	SA 1525	1.5
1937	4.5	2112	4.8
3 0215	1.9	**18** 0405	1.4
0817	4.5	0950	5.1
SA 1508	1.9	SU 1646	1.3
2100	4.5	2221	5.1
4 0347	1.8	**19** 0516	1.0
0939	4.7	1052	5.4
SU 1631	1.6	M 1743	1.1
2214	4.8	2314	5.3
5 0502	1.4	**20** 0608	0.8
1042	5.1	1140	5.6
M 1733	1.3	TU 1828	0.9
2307	5.2	2354	5.5
6 0556	1.0	**21** 0650	0.6
1128	5.5	1217	5.7
TU 1819	0.9	W 1906	0.8
2349	5.6		
7 0640	0.7	**22** 0027	5.7
1207	5.8	0727	0.6
W 1900	0.7	TH 1250	5.8
		● 1940	0.7
8 0023	5.8	**23** 0100	5.8
0722	0.4	0801	0.5
TH 1242	6.0	F 1322	5.9
○ 1940	0.6	2012	0.7
9 0057	6.0	**24** 0132	5.6
0802	0.2	0833	0.6
F 1318	6.2	SA 1354	5.9
2020	0.4	2044	0.7
10 0133	6.2	**25** 0202	5.6
0842	0.1	0904	0.6
SA 1356	6.2	SU 1423	5.8
2100	0.4	2114	0.7
11 0212	6.2	**26** 0232	5.9
0924	0.1	0934	0.7
SU 1437	6.2	M 1452	5.8
2141	0.4	2146	0.8
12 0253	6.2	**27** 0303	5.8
1007	0.3	1003	0.8
M 1521	6.1	TU 1522	5.6
2222	0.5	2215	0.9
13 0339	6.1	**28** 0335	5.6
1049	0.5	1032	1.0
TU 1610	5.8	W 1555	5.4
2306	0.7	2247	1.1
14 0432	5.8	**29** 0410	5.3
1136	0.8	1106	1.2
W 1706	5.5	TH 1633	5.1
2358	1.0	2326	1.3
15 0535	5.5	**30** 0455	5.0
1237	1.2	1151	1.5
TH 1813	5.1	F 1735	4.8
◑		◑	
		31 0018	1.6
		0614	4.7
		SA 1254	1.8
		1857	4.5

APRIL

Time	m	Time	m
1 0129	1.7	**16** 0339	1.3
0734	4.6	0925	5.0
SU 1418	1.8	M 1617	1.4
2014	4.6	2151	5.0
2 0300	1.6	**17** 0448	1.0
0854	4.8	1024	5.3
M 1546	1.6	TU 1715	1.2
2131	4.8	2242	5.2
3 0420	1.3	**18** 0541	0.9
1003	5.1	1110	5.4
TU 1655	1.2	W 1800	1.0
2230	5.2	2323	5.4
4 0521	0.9	**19** 0623	0.8
1054	5.5	1149	5.6
W 1747	0.9	TH 1838	0.9
2314	5.6		
5 0610	0.6	**20** 0000	5.6
1135	5.8	0659	0.7
TH 1831	0.7	F 1223	5.7
2351	5.8	1912	0.8
6 0654	0.4	**21** 0035	5.7
1213	6.0	0731	0.7
F 1913	0.5	SA 1256	5.7
○		● 1944	0.8
7 0028	6.1	**22** 0107	5.8
0737	0.2	0803	0.7
SA 1251	6.2	SU 1327	5.8
1955	0.4	2017	0.7
8 0108	6.2	**23** 0137	5.8
0819	0.2	0835	0.7
SU 1333	6.2	M 1356	5.8
2038	0.3	2049	0.7
9 0151	6.3	**24** 0208	5.8
0902	0.2	0908	0.8
M 1417	6.2	TU 1426	5.7
2122	0.3	2123	0.8
10 0237	6.3	**25** 0241	5.7
0947	0.3	0939	0.9
TU 1506	6.0	W 1500	5.6
2200	0.4	2155	0.9
11 0328	6.1	**26** 0316	5.6
1034	0.5	1010	1.0
W 1557	5.8	TH 1535	5.4
2255	0.7	2229	1.0
12 0424	5.8	**27** 0354	5.4
1125	0.9	1046	1.2
TH 1654	5.5	F 1615	5.2
2349	0.9	2308	1.2
13 0526	5.5	**28** 0440	5.1
1224	1.2	1131	1.4
F 1758	5.1	SA 1712	4.9
◑		2358	1.3
14 0057	1.2	**29** 0547	4.9
0639	5.1	1228	1.6
SA 1341	1.5	SU 1822	4.8
1919	4.8	◑	
15 0218	1.3	**30** 0100	1.4
0809	5.0	0656	4.9
SU 1503	1.5	M 1338	1.6
2045	4.8	1930	4.8

Chart Datum: 2·69 metres below IGN Datum
HAT is 6·4 metres above Chart Datum

TIDES

TIDES

TIME ZONE -0100
(French Standard Time)
Subtract 1 hour for UT
For French Summer Time add
ONE hour in **non-shaded areas**

FRANCE – DUNKERQUE
LAT 51°03'N   LONG 2°22'E
TIMES AND HEIGHTS OF HIGH AND LOW WATERS

Dates in amber are **SPRINGS**
Dates in yellow are **NEAPS**

2012

MAY

Time	m		Time	m
1 0218	1.4	**16** 0406	1.1
0807	5.0	0944	5.1
TU 1459	1.5	W 1634	1.3
2040	4.9	2203	5.1
2 0336	1.2	**17** 0503	1.0
0916	5.2	1033	5.3
W 1611	1.2	TH 1725	1.2
2144	5.2	2250	5.3
3 0441	0.9	**18** 0550	1.0
1014	5.5	1117	5.4
TH 1710	1.0	F 1807	1.1
2235	5.5	2332	5.4
4 0536	0.6	**19** 0628	0.9
1101	5.8	1156	5.5
F 1801	0.7	SA 1844	1.0
2319	5.8		
5 0626	0.4	**20** 0011	5.5
1144	6.0	0702	0.9
SA 1848	0.6	SU 1232	5.6
		1918	0.9
6 0003	6.1	**21** 0045	5.6
0712	0.3	0736	0.9
SU 1228	6.1	M 1304	5.6
○ 1934	0.5	● 1953	0.8
7 0048	6.2	**22** 0117	5.7
0759	0.4	0811	0.9
M 1315	6.2	TU 1334	5.7
2020	0.4	2029	0.8
8 0136	6.3	**23** 0149	5.7
0845	0.3	0846	0.9
TU 1403	6.1	W 1408	5.7
2107	0.3	2105	0.8
9 0227	6.2	**24** 0225	5.7
0932	0.4	0921	0.9
W 1455	6.0	TH 1445	5.6
2155	0.4	2140	0.9
10 0321	6.1	**25** 0304	5.6
1021	0.6	0956	1.0
TH 1548	5.8	F 1524	5.5
2245	0.6	2217	0.9
11 0417	5.8	**26** 0345	5.5
1112	0.9	1033	1.1
F 1641	5.5	SA 1605	5.3
2339	0.8	2257	1.0
12 0514	5.5	**27** 0430	5.3
1209	1.2	1117	1.2
SA 1738	5.2	SU 1652	5.2
◐		2343	1.1
13 0040	1.0	**28** 0522	5.2
0618	5.2	1206	1.3
SU 1314	1.4	M 1748	5.1
1847	5.0	◑	
14 0149	1.2	**29** 0037	1.1
0735	5.0	0621	5.2
M 1424	1.5	TU 1305	1.4
2005	4.9	1848	5.0
15 0259	1.2	**30** 0141	1.1
0846	5.0	0724	5.2
TU 1533	1.5	W 1416	1.4
2110	5.0	1952	5.0
		31 0255	1.1
		0830	5.3
		TH 1529	1.2
		2058	5.3

JUNE

Time	m		Time	m
1 0403	0.9	**16** 0510	1.2
0935	5.5	1044	5.2
F 1635	1.0	SA 1734	1.2
2200	5.5	2304	5.2
2 0505	0.7	**17** 0557	1.2
1032	5.7	1130	5.3
SA 1733	0.8	SU 1818	1.1
2255	5.8	2348	5.4
3 0601	0.6	**18** 0637	1.1
1124	5.9	1210	5.4
SU 1827	0.7	M 1856	1.0
2346	6.0		
4 0654	0.5	**19** 0027	5.5
1214	6.0	0714	1.0
M 1918	0.5	TU 1245	5.5
○		● 1933	0.9
5 0037	6.1	**20** 0101	5.6
0744	0.5	0750	0.9
TU 1304	6.0	W 1318	5.6
2008	0.4	2011	0.8
6 0128	6.2	**21** 0134	5.7
0833	0.5	0828	0.9
W 1354	6.0	TH 1352	5.7
2057	0.3	2048	0.7
7 0221	6.2	**22** 0211	5.8
0920	0.6	0906	0.7
TH 1445	6.0	F 1430	5.7
2145	0.4	2127	0.7
8 0313	6.1	**23** 0250	5.7
1008	0.7	0943	0.9
F 1534	5.8	SA 1508	5.7
2233	0.5	2204	0.7
9 0404	5.9	**24** 0329	5.7
1055	0.9	1020	1.0
SA 1622	5.6	SU 1546	5.5
2321	0.7	2243	0.7
10 0454	5.6	**25** 0409	5.6
1143	1.1	1100	1.0
SU 1710	5.4	M 1625	5.4
		2325	0.8
11 0012	0.9	**26** 0454	5.5
0547	5.4	1143	1.1
M 1235	1.3	TU 1713	5.4
◑ 1805	5.2		
12 0107	1.1	**27** 0013	0.9
0648	5.1	0547	5.4
TU 1334	1.5	W 1235	1.2
1910	5.0	◑ 1810	5.3
13 0208	1.2	**28** 0110	1.0
0754	5.0	0647	5.4
W 1437	1.5	TH 1338	1.3
2019	4.9	1914	5.3
14 0311	1.3	**29** 0220	1.0
0857	5.0	0753	5.3
TH 1540	1.5	F 1453	1.3
2120	5.0	2023	5.3
15 0413	1.3	**30** 0331	1.0
0953	5.0	0906	5.4
F 1641	1.4	SA 1605	1.2
2215	5.1	2137	5.4

JULY

Time	m		Time	m
1 0441	0.9	**16** 0527	1.4
1016	5.5	1104	5.1
SU 1714	1.0	M 1754	1.3
2244	5.6	2327	5.2
2 0546	0.8	**17** 0615	1.2
1116	5.7	1149	5.3
M 1816	0.8	TU 1837	1.1
2342	5.9		
3 0643	0.7	**18** 0008	5.4
1209	5.8	0654	1.1
TU 1910	0.6	W 1227	5.5
○		1914	0.9
4 0033	6.0	**19** 0043	5.6
0734	0.6	0731	1.0
W 1258	5.9	TH 1300	5.7
1959	0.4	● 1952	0.7
5 0123	6.1	**20** 0117	5.8
0821	0.6	0809	0.9
TH 1344	6.0	F 1333	5.8
2046	0.3	2030	0.6
6 0210	6.1	**21** 0152	5.9
0906	0.6	0847	0.8
F 1429	6.0	SA 1408	5.8
2131	0.3	2108	0.5
7 0257	6.1	**22** 0229	5.9
0949	0.7	0925	0.8
SA 1513	5.9	SU 1444	5.8
2214	0.4	2148	0.5
8 0342	5.9	**23** 0305	5.9
1030	0.9	1002	0.8
SU 1554	5.8	M 1518	5.8
2256	0.6	2225	0.5
9 0424	5.7	**24** 0342	5.8
1110	1.0	1040	0.9
M 1636	5.6	TU 1556	5.7
2337	0.8	2305	0.6
10 0507	5.5	**25** 0425	5.7
1151	1.2	1120	1.0
TU 1719	5.4	W 1642	5.6
		2349	0.8
11 0021	1.0	**26** 0517	5.6
0547	5.2	1207	1.1
W 1239	1.4	TH 1739	5.5
◑ 1811	5.1	◑	
12 0112	1.3	**27** 0042	0.9
0650	5.0	0620	5.4
TH 1336	1.6	F 1308	1.3
1915	4.9	1846	5.4
13 0213	1.5	**28** 0151	1.1
0758	4.8	0727	5.2
F 1444	1.7	SA 1426	1.4
2029	4.8	2003	5.2
14 0319	1.6	**29** 0309	1.2
0907	4.8	0851	5.2
SA 1553	1.6	SU 1546	1.3
2137	4.8	2131	5.3
15 0426	1.5	**30** 0427	1.1
1010	4.9	1011	5.3
SU 1700	1.5	M 1705	1.1
2236	5.0	2243	5.6
		31 0539	1.0
		1114	5.5
		TU 1810	0.8
		2340	5.8

AUGUST

Time	m		Time	m
1 0636	0.8	**16** 0632	1.1
1204	5.8	1204	5.5
W 1902	0.6	TH 1852	0.8
2 0028	6.0	**17** 0021	5.7
0723	0.7	0709	0.9
TH 1247	5.9	F 1237	5.8
○ 1948	0.4	● 1929	0.6
3 0112	6.1	**18** 0054	5.9
0806	0.7	0746	0.8
F 1327	6.0	SA 1309	5.9
2030	0.3	2008	0.5
4 0153	6.1	**19** 0127	6.0
0846	0.7	0824	0.7
SA 1406	6.0	SU 1341	6.0
2111	0.4	2045	0.4
5 0233	6.1	**20** 0201	6.1
0925	0.7	0902	0.6
SU 1445	6.0	M 1415	6.0
2149	0.5	2125	0.4
6 0312	5.9	**21** 0237	6.1
1001	0.8	0940	0.7
M 1522	5.9	TU 1451	6.0
2225	0.6	2204	0.4
7 0348	5.8	**22** 0316	6.0
1035	1.0	1018	0.7
TU 1558	5.7	W 1531	6.0
2300	0.8	2244	0.6
8 0425	5.6	**23** 0400	5.9
1112	1.1	1058	0.9
W 1636	5.5	TH 1618	5.8
2336	1.1	2327	0.8
9 0504	5.3	**24** 0452	5.6
1150	1.3	1145	1.1
TH 1720	5.3	F 1717	5.6
◑		◑	
10 0017	1.3	**25** 0019	1.0
0552	5.0	0556	5.4
F 1237	1.6	SA 1246	1.3
1816	4.9	1829	5.3
11 0112	1.6	**26** 0131	1.3
0654	4.7	0711	5.1
SA 1343	1.8	SU 1409	1.5
1929	4.7	1955	5.1
12 0225	1.8	**27** 0256	1.4
0811	4.6	0845	5.0
SU 1503	1.9	M 1537	1.4
2052	4.6	2128	5.2
13 0343	1.8	**28** 0421	1.3
0930	4.7	1005	5.2
M 1622	1.7	TU 1659	1.1
2205	4.8	2238	5.5
14 0455	1.6	**29** 0531	1.1
1034	5.0	1105	5.5
TU 1726	1.4	W 1800	0.8
2301	5.2	2332	5.8
15 0550	1.3	**30** 0623	0.9
1124	5.3	1152	5.7
W 1813	1.1	TH 1848	0.6
2345	5.5		
		31 0016	6.0
		0706	0.8
		F 1230	5.9
		○ 1930	0.5

Chart Datum: 2·69 metres below IGN Datum
HAT is 6·4 metres above Chart Datum

TIME ZONE -0100
(French Standard Time)
Subtract 1 hour for UT
For French Summer Time add
ONE hour in **non-shaded areas**

FRANCE – DUNKERQUE

LAT 51°03'N   LONG 2°22'E

TIMES AND HEIGHTS OF HIGH AND LOW WATERS

Dates in amber are **SPRINGS**
Dates in yellow are **NEAPS**

2012

SEPTEMBER

Time	m		Time	m
1 SA	0054 6.1 / 0746 0.8 / 1305 6.0 / 2009 0.4	**16** SU		0025 6.0 / 0719 0.7 / 1238 6.0 / ● 1941 0.4
2 SU	0129 6.1 / 0822 0.7 / 1340 6.0 / 2045 0.5	**17** M		0057 6.2 / 0758 0.6 / 1311 6.2 / 2020 0.3
3 M	0204 6.1 / 0857 0.8 / 1415 6.0 / 2119 0.6	**18** TU		0133 6.2 / 0837 0.6 / 1347 6.2 / 2101 0.3
4 TU	0239 6.0 / 0930 0.8 / 1449 6.0 / 2152 0.7	**19** W		0211 6.2 / 0917 0.6 / 1427 6.1 / 2142 0.4
5 W	0311 5.8 / 1003 0.9 / 1522 5.8 / 2224 0.9	**20** TH		0253 6.1 / 0958 0.7 / 1511 6.1 / 2224 0.6
6 TH	0344 5.7 / 1035 1.1 / 1557 5.6 / 2255 1.1	**21** F		0340 5.9 / 1041 0.8 / 1602 5.9 / 2309 0.9
7 F	0419 5.4 / 1109 1.3 / 1636 5.3 / 2331 1.4	**22** SA		0435 5.7 / 1130 1.1 / 1705 5.6 / ☾
8 SA	0503 5.1 / 1149 1.6 / 1729 5.0 / ◐	**23** SU		0003 1.2 / 0541 5.3 / 1234 1.4 / 1818 5.3
9 SU	0017 1.7 / 0604 4.8 / 1244 1.8 / 1841 4.7	**24** M		0119 1.5 / 0659 5.0 / 1400 1.5 / 1948 5.1
10 M	0124 2.0 / 0720 4.5 / 1405 2.0 / 2002 4.6	**25** TU		0247 1.6 / 0835 5.0 / 1529 1.4 / 2118 5.2
11 TU	0253 2.0 / 0842 4.6 / 1537 1.8 / 2125 4.8	**26** W		0411 1.4 / 0951 5.2 / 1646 1.1 / 2224 5.5
12 W	0417 1.8 / 0957 4.9 / 1650 1.5 / 2228 5.1	**27** TH		0516 1.2 / 1048 5.5 / 1744 0.8 / 2316 5.7
13 TH	0517 1.4 / 1052 5.3 / 1742 1.1 / 2315 5.5	**28** F		0605 1.0 / 1132 5.7 / 1829 0.6 / 2356 5.9
14 F	0603 1.1 / 1134 5.6 / 1824 0.8 / 2352 5.8	**29** SA		0645 0.9 / 1207 5.9 / 1908 0.6
15 SA	0642 0.9 / 1208 5.8 / 1903 0.6	**30** SU		0030 6.0 / 0722 0.9 / 1240 6.0 / ○ 1944 0.6

OCTOBER

Time	m		Time	m
1 M	0103 6.0 / 0756 0.8 / 1313 6.0 / 2017 0.6	**16** TU		0028 6.2 / 0732 0.6 / 1244 6.3 / 1955 0.4
2 TU	0136 6.0 / 0828 0.8 / 1347 6.0 / 2049 0.7	**17** W		0107 6.3 / 0814 0.6 / 1325 6.4 / 2037 0.4
3 W	0207 6.0 / 0901 0.9 / 1418 6.0 / 2121 0.8	**18** TH		0150 6.3 / 0857 0.6 / 1409 6.4 / 2122 0.5
4 TH	0237 5.9 / 0934 0.9 / 1450 5.8 / 2152 1.0	**19** F		0236 6.2 / 0941 0.6 / 1458 6.2 / 2209 0.7
5 F	0309 5.7 / 1005 1.1 / 1523 5.7 / 2222 1.2	**20** SA		0326 6.0 / 1029 0.8 / 1554 6.0 / 2257 1.0
6 SA	0343 5.5 / 1037 1.3 / 1601 5.4 / 2255 1.5	**21** SU		0423 5.7 / 1122 1.0 / 1656 5.7 / 2354 1.3
7 SU	0423 5.2 / 1115 1.5 / 1649 5.1 / 2338 1.7	**22** M		0526 5.4 / 1226 1.3 / 1806 5.4 / ☾
8 M	0521 4.9 / 1204 1.7 / 1801 4.8 / ◐	**23** TU		0107 1.6 / 0640 5.1 / 1346 1.4 / 1932 5.2
9 TU	0036 2.0 / 0637 4.6 / 1311 1.9 / 1916 4.7	**24** W		0228 1.7 / 0811 5.0 / 1508 1.4 / 2055 5.2
10 W	0154 2.0 / 0752 4.6 / 1442 1.9 / 2034 4.8	**25** TH		0346 1.5 / 0923 5.2 / 1621 1.2 / 2158 5.4
11 TH	0326 1.9 / 0908 4.8 / 1603 1.5 / 2144 5.1	**26** F		0450 1.3 / 1019 5.4 / 1719 0.9 / 2249 5.6
12 F	0435 1.5 / 1010 5.2 / 1703 1.1 / 2236 5.5	**27** SA		0540 1.2 / 1105 5.6 / 1805 0.8 / 2330 5.8
13 SA	0527 1.2 / 1056 5.6 / 1750 0.8 / 2317 5.8	**28** SU		0621 1.0 / 1141 5.7 / 1844 0.8
14 SU	0610 0.9 / 1132 5.8 / 1833 0.6 / 2352 6.1	**29** M		0005 5.8 / 0657 0.9 / 1216 5.8 / ○ 1918 0.8
15 M	0651 0.8 / 1207 6.1 / 1914 0.4 ●	**30** TU		0038 5.9 / 0730 0.9 / 1250 5.9 / 1950 0.5
		31 W		0110 5.9 / 0803 0.9 / 1322 5.9 / 2022 0.9

NOVEMBER

Time	m		Time	m
1 TH	0140 5.9 / 0836 0.9 / 1353 5.9 / 2054 1.0	**16** F		0135 6.3 / 0842 0.5 / 1358 6.4 / 2106 0.5
2 F	0210 5.8 / 0910 1.0 / 1425 5.8 / 2126 1.1	**17** SA		0224 6.2 / 0930 0.5 / 1451 6.3 / 2154 0.7
3 SA	0243 5.7 / 0942 1.1 / 1501 5.7 / 2158 1.2	**18** SU		0316 6.0 / 1020 0.7 / 1545 6.1 / 2244 1.0
4 SU	0319 5.6 / 1015 1.2 / 1539 5.5 / 2231 1.4	**19** M		0409 5.8 / 1112 0.9 / 1643 5.8 / 2339 1.3
5 M	0357 5.3 / 1052 1.4 / 1623 5.2 / 2312 1.6	**20** TU		0505 5.5 / 1211 1.1 / 1745 5.5 / ☽
6 TU	0446 5.1 / 1138 1.5 / 1724 5.0	**21** W		0042 1.5 / 0610 5.2 / 1319 1.3 / 1901 5.2
7 W	0003 1.8 / 0555 4.9 / 1235 1.7 / ☽ 1833 4.9	**22** TH		0152 1.6 / 0730 5.1 / 1431 1.4 / 2017 5.2
8 TH	0107 1.9 / 0703 4.8 / 1346 1.7 / 1941 4.9	**23** F		0303 1.6 / 0842 5.1 / 1541 1.3 / 2120 5.2
9 F	0226 1.8 / 0811 4.9 / 1510 1.5 / 2049 5.2	**24** SA		0410 1.5 / 0941 5.2 / 1644 1.2 / 2213 5.4
10 SA	0344 1.6 / 0917 5.2 / 1617 1.2 / 2150 5.5	**25** SU		0507 1.4 / 1031 5.4 / 1735 1.1 / 2259 5.5
11 SU	0445 1.3 / 1012 5.5 / 1713 0.9 / 2239 5.8	**26** M		0554 1.2 / 1115 5.5 / 1818 1.0 / 2340 5.6
12 M	0537 1.0 / 1057 5.8 / 1803 0.7 / 2321 6.0	**27** TU		0633 1.1 / 1155 5.6 / 1854 1.0
13 TU	0624 0.8 / 1139 6.1 / 1849 0.5 ●	**28** W		0017 5.7 / 0708 1.0 / 1231 5.7 / ○ 1926 1.0
14 W	0004 6.2 / 0709 0.7 / 1223 6.3 / 1934 0.5	**29** TH		0051 5.8 / 0742 1.0 / 1305 5.8 / 1959 1.0
15 TH	0048 6.3 / 0755 0.6 / 1309 6.4 / 2020 0.5	**30** F		0121 5.8 / 0816 0.9 / 1336 5.8 / 2033 1.0

DECEMBER

Time	m		Time	m
1 SA	0151 5.8 / 0850 0.9 / 1409 5.8 / 2107 1.1	**16** SU		0214 6.2 / 0920 0.6 / 1442 6.3 / 2143 0.7
2 SU	0225 5.8 / 0926 1.0 / 1445 5.8 / 2141 1.2	**17** M		0302 6.0 / 1009 0.5 / 1533 6.1 / 2230 0.9
3 M	0302 5.7 / 0959 1.0 / 1523 5.6 / 2215 1.3	**18** TU		0350 5.9 / 1057 0.7 / 1623 5.9 / 2317 1.1
4 TU	0339 5.5 / 1036 1.1 / 1603 5.5 / 2253 1.4	**19** W		0438 5.6 / 1146 0.9 / 1715 5.6
5 W	0418 5.3 / 1117 1.2 / 1649 5.3 / 2337 1.5	**20** TH		0007 1.3 / 0530 5.4 / 1240 1.1 / ☽ 1814 5.3
6 TH	0508 5.2 / 1206 1.3 / 1747 5.2	**21** F		0103 1.5 / 0633 5.2 / 1340 1.3 / 1923 5.1
7 F	0030 1.6 / 0611 5.1 / 1304 1.4 / 1851 5.2	**22** SA		0206 1.7 / 0747 5.0 / 1445 1.5 / 2031 5.0
8 SA	0134 1.6 / 0716 5.1 / 1417 1.4 / 1956 5.0	**23** SU		0313 1.7 / 0855 5.0 / 1553 1.5 / 2132 5.0
9 SU	0250 1.6 / 0822 5.2 / 1532 1.2 / 2102 5.4	**24** M		0422 1.6 / 0955 5.1 / 1658 1.4 / 2227 5.1
10 M	0402 1.4 / 0928 5.4 / 1637 1.0 / 2204 5.6	**25** TU		0523 1.4 / 1049 5.2 / 1751 1.3 / 2316 5.3
11 TU	0505 1.1 / 1028 5.7 / 1735 0.8 / 2259 5.9	**26** W		0611 1.3 / 1136 5.4 / 1832 1.2 / 2359 5.5
12 W	0601 0.9 / 1121 6.0 / 1829 0.6 / 2349 6.0	**27** TH		0650 1.1 / 1216 5.5 / 1907 1.1
13 TH	0653 0.7 / 1211 6.2 / 1919 0.6 ●	**28** F		0035 5.6 / 0724 1.0 / 1251 5.7 / ○ 1941 1.0
14 F	0037 6.2 / 0743 0.5 / 1301 6.3 / 2008 0.5	**29** SA		0106 5.7 / 0759 0.9 / 1321 5.8 / 2015 1.0
15 SA	0125 6.2 / 0832 0.6 / 1351 6.4 / 2056 0.6	**30** SU		0136 5.8 / 0835 0.8 / 1354 5.8 / 2051 1.0
		31 M		0209 5.8 / 0909 0.8 / 1429 5.9 / 2125 1.0

Chart Datum: 2·69 metres below IGN Datum
HAT is 6·4 metres above Chart Datum

TIDES

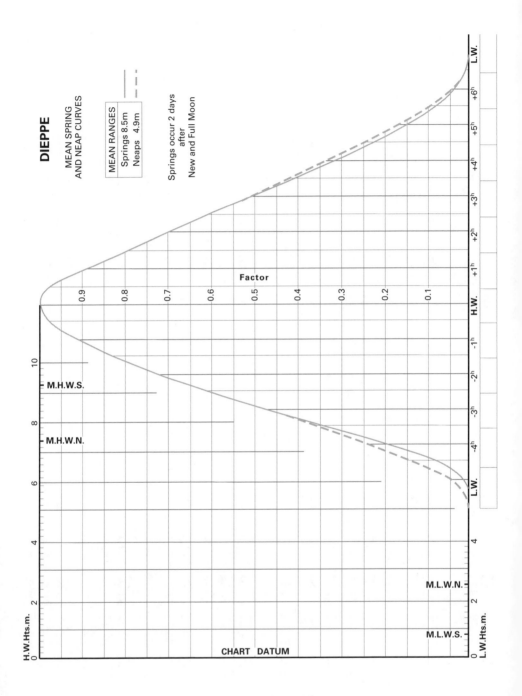

DIEPPE

MEAN SPRING
AND NEAP CURVES

MEAN RANGES
Springs 8.5m
Neaps 4.9m

Springs occur 2 days
after
New and Full Moon

Factor

0.9
0.8
0.7
0.6
0.5
0.4
0.3
0.2
0.1

H.W.Hts.m.

M.H.W.S.

M.H.W.N.

M.L.W.N.

M.L.W.S.

CHART DATUM

L.W.Hts.m.

H.W.

L.W.

TIME ZONE -0100
(French Standard Time)
Subtract 1 hour for UT
For French Summer Time add
ONE hour in **non-shaded areas**

FRANCE – DIEPPE

LAT 49°56'N   LONG 1°05'E

TIMES AND HEIGHTS OF HIGH AND LOW WATERS

Dates in amber are **SPRINGS**
Dates in yellow are **NEAPS**

2012

JANUARY

Day	Time	m	Time	m	Time	m	Time	m
1 SU ◗	0424	7.8	1109	2.5	1645	7.5	2328	2.5
2 M	0512	7.4	1159	2.8	1740	7.1		
3 TU	0022	2.9	0614	7.1	1303	3.0	1852	6.8
4 W	0131	3.0	0731	7.0	1419	2.9	2009	7.0
5 TH	0249	2.9	0840	7.3	1530	2.6	2112	7.3
6 F	0356	2.5	0935	7.7	1627	2.2	2202	7.8
7 SA	0449	2.1	1021	8.1	1715	1.8	2246	8.1
8 SU	0534	1.8	1103	8.5	1759	1.5	2327	8.6
9 M ○	0616	1.5	1142	8.8	1841	1.2		
10 TU	0006	8.8	0657	1.3	1240	9.0	1922	1.0
11 W	0045	9.0	0737	1.2	1300	9.2	2002	0.9
12 TH	0124	9.1	0817	1.1	1339	9.2	2041	0.9
13 F	0203	9.1	0857	1.1	1419	9.1	2119	1.0
14 SA	0244	9.0	0936	1.2	1500	8.9	2157	1.2
15 SU	0325	8.8	1017	1.5	1543	8.6	2237	1.5
16 M	0410	8.5	1102	1.7	1633	8.2	2325	1.8
17 TU	0505	8.1	1156	2.0	1736	7.8		
18 W	0025	2.2	0615	7.8	1307	2.2	1855	7.6
19 TH	0145	2.4	0737	7.8	1432	2.2	2018	7.7
20 F	0310	2.2	0854	8.0	1551	1.8	2132	8.1
21 SA	0422	1.8	1001	8.5	1657	1.4	2233	8.5
22 SU	0524	1.5	1056	8.9	1755	1.1	2324	8.9
23 M ●	0619	1.2	1143	9.2	1846	0.8		
24 TU	0008	9.2	0706	1.0	1226	9.3	1930	0.7
25 W	0049	9.3	0746	0.9	1305	9.4	2010	0.7
26 TH	0125	9.2	0823	0.9	1341	9.3	2042	0.9
27 F	0200	9.1	0854	1.0	1416	9.1	2111	1.1
28 SA	0233	8.9	0922	1.4	1449	8.7	2136	1.4
29 SU	0305	8.5	0949	1.8	1521	8.3	2203	1.8
30 M	0336	8.1	1020	2.1	1553	7.8	2236	2.3
31 TU ◗	0410	7.6	1100	2.6	1634	7.2	2319	2.7

FEBRUARY

Day	Time	m	Time	m	Time	m	Time	m
1 W	0458	7.1	1152	3.0	1734	6.7		
2 TH	0018	3.1	0613	6.7	1305	3.2	1909	6.5
3 F	0141	3.3	0752	6.8	1438	3.0	2036	6.9
4 SA	0313	2.9	0903	7.3	1553	2.5	2136	7.5
5 SU	0419	2.3	0957	7.9	1649	1.9	2224	8.1
6 M	0510	1.8	1042	8.4	1738	1.4	2307	8.6
7 TU ○	0557	1.4	1124	8.9	1825	1.0	2348	9.0
8 W	0642	1.0	1204	9.2	1909	0.7		
9 TH	0028	9.3	0725	0.8	1244	9.5	1950	0.6
10 F	0107	9.5	0806	0.6	1323	9.6	2029	0.6
11 SA	0146	9.5	0845	0.6	1403	9.6	2106	0.5
12 SU	0225	9.4	0923	0.8	1443	9.3	2142	0.8
13 M	0305	9.2	1000	1.0	1524	8.9	2219	1.2
14 TU ◗	0347	8.6	1042	1.4	1611	8.4	2303	1.7
15 W	0438	8.1	1134	1.9	1712	7.7		
16 TH	0001	2.3	0548	7.6	1243	2.3	1836	7.3
17 F	0124	2.6	0721	7.4	1415	2.4	2012	7.4
18 SA	0258	2.5	0849	7.7	1543	2.0	2130	7.9
19 SU	0417	2.0	0956	8.2	1653	1.5	2227	8.4
20 M	0520	1.5	1048	8.7	1749	1.1	2313	8.8
21 TU ●	0610	1.2	1131	9.1	1834	0.9	2352	9.1
22 W	0650	1.0	1209	9.3	1910	0.7		
23 TH	0028	9.2	0726	0.9	1243	9.3	1946	0.7
24 F	0100	9.2	0757	0.9	1316	9.3	2013	0.8
25 SA	0132	9.2	0826	1.0	1347	9.1	2040	1.0
26 SU	0201	9.0	0852	1.2	1417	8.8	2104	1.3
27 M	0229	8.7	0916	1.5	1445	8.5	2128	1.6
28 TU	0256	8.3	0943	1.9	1514	8.0	2157	2.1
29 W ◗	0329	7.9	1017	2.3	1549	7.5	2235	2.6

MARCH

Day	Time	m	Time	m	Time	m	Time	m
1 TH ◗	0406	7.3	1103	2.8	1638	6.9	2327	3.1
2 F	0507	6.7	1206	3.1	1800	6.5		
3 SA	0042	3.3	0650	6.5	1338	3.2	1953	6.7
4 SU	0223	3.1	0825	7.0	1511	2.6	2103	7.3
5 M	0342	2.4	0926	7.7	1617	2.0	2155	8.0
6 TU	0440	1.8	1015	8.4	1711	1.4	2241	8.6
7 W	0531	1.2	1059	8.9	1801	0.9	2324	9.1
8 TH ○	0620	0.8	1141	9.4	1848	0.5		
9 F	0005	9.5	0706	0.5	1222	9.7	1931	0.3
10 SA	0045	9.7	0748	0.4	1303	9.8	2011	0.2
11 SU	0125	9.8	0828	0.3	1344	9.8	2048	0.4
12 M	0205	9.7	0906	0.5	1425	9.5	2125	0.7
13 TU	0245	9.3	0944	0.8	1508	9.0	2203	1.2
14 W	0328	8.8	1026	1.3	1556	8.3	2247	1.8
15 TH ◗	0420	8.1	1118	1.9	1657	7.6	2346	2.4
16 F	0531	7.4	1228	2.4	1824	7.2		
17 SA	0111	2.7	0707	7.2	1404	2.4	2001	7.3
18 SU	0246	2.5	0837	7.5	1531	2.0	2115	7.8
19 M	0405	2.0	0940	8.1	1638	1.6	2208	8.4
20 TU	0503	1.5	1029	8.6	1729	1.2	2251	8.8
21 W	0549	1.2	1110	8.9	1810	1.0	2328	9.0
22 TH ●	0626	1.1	1145	9.1	1843	0.9		
23 F	0001	9.1	0658	1.0	1218	9.1	1916	0.9
24 SA	0032	9.1	0728	1.0	1248	9.1	1943	0.9
25 SU	0101	9.1	0757	1.0	1319	9.0	2010	1.0
26 M	0130	9.0	0823	1.2	1348	8.8	2035	1.3
27 TU	0158	8.7	0848	1.4	1417	8.5	2100	1.6
28 W	0226	8.4	0915	1.7	1446	8.1	2129	2.0
29 TH	0256	8.0	0948	2.1	1521	7.6	2205	2.4
30 F ◗	0335	7.5	1031	2.5	1607	7.1	2255	2.9
31 SA	0430	7.0	1129	2.9	1717	6.7		

APRIL

Day	Time	m	Time	m	Time	m	Time	m
1 SU	0004	3.1	0556	6.7	1251	3.0	1901	6.8
2 M	0134	3.0	0736	7.0	1424	2.6	2021	7.3
3 TU	0258	2.4	0845	7.6	1536	1.9	2119	8.0
4 W	0402	1.7	0940	8.3	1636	1.3	2208	8.7
5 TH	0459	1.2	1029	8.9	1730	0.8	2254	9.2
6 F ○	0551	0.8	1114	9.4	1820	0.5	2338	9.6
7 SA	0641	0.5	1158	9.7	1906	0.3		
8 SU	0021	9.8	0727	0.3	1242	9.8	1949	0.3
9 M	0103	9.8	0809	0.3	1325	9.8	2030	0.4
10 TU	0145	9.7	0850	0.4	1409	9.5	2109	0.7
11 W	0229	9.3	0931	0.8	1455	9.0	2149	1.2
12 TH	0314	8.8	1015	1.3	1545	8.3	2236	1.8
13 F ◗	0408	8.1	1107	1.8	1647	7.7	2336	2.3
14 SA	0517	7.5	1215	2.3	1805	7.3		
15 SU	0054	2.6	0641	7.2	1340	2.4	1932	7.3
16 M	0218	2.5	0806	7.4	1458	2.1	2044	7.7
17 TU	0331	2.1	0911	7.9	1603	1.8	2138	8.2
18 W	0429	1.7	1000	8.3	1654	1.5	2221	8.5
19 TH	0515	1.4	1041	8.6	1735	1.3	2258	8.7
20 F	0553	1.3	1117	8.7	1810	1.3	2331	8.8
21 SA ●	0626	1.2	1149	8.8	1843	1.1		
22 SU	0002	8.9	0659	1.1	1221	8.9	1913	1.1
23 M	0033	8.9	0729	1.1	1253	8.8	1943	1.2
24 TU	0103	8.9	0759	1.2	1324	8.7	2011	1.4
25 W	0133	8.7	0827	1.3	1354	8.5	2039	1.6
26 TH	0203	8.5	0856	1.6	1427	8.2	2110	1.9
27 F	0237	8.1	0930	1.9	1504	7.9	2148	2.2
28 SA ◗	0318	7.7	1012	2.2	1550	7.5	2236	2.5
29 SU	0409	7.3	1106	2.5	1651	7.1	2338	2.7
30 M	0520	7.1	1216	2.6	1813	7.1		

Chart Datum: 4·43 metres below IGN Datum
HAT is 10·1 metres above Chart Datum

TIDES

TIDES

TIME ZONE -0100
(French Standard Time)
Subtract 1 hour for UT
For French Summer Time add
ONE hour in **non-shaded areas**

FRANCE – DIEPPE

LAT 49°56'N   LONG 1°05'E

TIMES AND HEIGHTS OF HIGH AND LOW WATERS

Dates in amber are **SPRINGS**
Dates in yellow are **NEAPS**

2012

MAY

Time	m		Time	m
1 0054	2.7	**16** 0239	2.3
0645	7.2	0826	7.5
TU 1337	2.4	W 1510	2.1
1932	7.5	2056	7.8
2 0213	2.3	**17** 0339	2.0
0759	7.7	0922	7.8
W 1452	1.9	TH 1606	1.9
2037	8.1	2144	8.1
3 0322	1.7	**18** 0431	1.8
0901	8.3	1007	8.1
TH 1557	1.4	F 1653	1.7
2132	8.7	2225	8.4
4 0423	1.2	**19** 0515	1.6
0956	8.8	1046	8.3
F 1655	1.0	SA 1734	1.5
2223	9.1	2301	8.5
5 0520	0.8	**20** 0554	1.4
1046	9.2	1122	8.5
SA 1750	0.7	SU 1811	1.4
2311	9.5	2335	8.6
6 0614	0.6	**21** 0631	1.3
1135	9.5	1157	8.6
SU 1840	0.5	M 1846	1.4
○ 2357	9.7	●	
7 0704	0.4	**22** 0008	8.7
1222	9.7	0705	1.3
M 1928	0.4	TU 1231	8.7
		1919	1.4
8 0043	9.7	**23** 0041	8.7
0751	0.3	0738	1.3
TU 1309	9.6	W 1304	8.6
2012	0.6	1952	1.4
9 0129	9.6	**24** 0114	8.7
0836	0.5	0810	1.3
W 1356	9.4	TH 1339	8.6
2056	0.8	2024	1.5
10 0215	9.3	**25** 0149	8.5
0920	0.7	0844	1.4
TH 1444	9.0	F 1415	8.4
2139	1.2	2059	1.7
11 0303	8.8	**26** 0226	8.3
1006	1.2	0920	1.6
F 1535	8.5	SA 1454	8.2
2227	1.7	2138	1.9
12 0355	8.2	**27** 0307	8.1
1056	1.6	1002	1.9
SA 1631	8.0	SU 1538	7.9
◗ 2321	2.1	2223	2.1
13 0455	7.7	**28** 0354	7.8
1154	2.0	1050	2.1
SU 1734	7.6	M 1631	7.7
		◗ 2316	2.3
14 0025	2.4	**29** 0452	7.6
0602	7.4	1147	2.2
M 1259	2.3	TU 1734	7.6
1844	7.4		
15 0133	2.4	**30** 0019	2.3
0716	7.3	0601	7.6
TU 1407	2.3	W 1255	2.1
1956	7.5	1846	7.7
		31 0130	2.1
		0714	7.8
		TH 1409	1.9
		1955	8.1

JUNE

Time	m		Time	m
1 0242	1.8	**16** 0346	2.2
0823	8.2	0931	7.6
F 1519	1.5	SA 1613	2.1
2057	8.5	2150	7.9
2 0349	1.4	**17** 0439	1.9
0925	8.6	1017	7.9
SA 1623	1.2	SU 1702	1.9
2154	8.9	2233	8.2
3 0451	1.0	**18** 0525	1.7
1022	9.0	1058	8.2
SU 1722	0.9	M 1744	1.7
2248	9.2	2311	8.4
4 0550	0.7	**19** 0606	1.5
1116	9.3	1136	8.4
M 1817	0.8	TU 1823	1.5
○ 2339	9.4	● 2348	8.6
5 0645	0.6	**20** 0645	1.4
1207	9.4	1213	8.6
TU 1909	0.7	W 1900	1.4
6 0028	9.5	**21** 0024	8.7
0736	0.5	0722	1.3
W 1257	9.4	TH 1249	8.7
1958	0.7	1936	1.4
7 0116	9.5	**22** 0100	8.8
0825	0.5	0758	1.2
TH 1345	9.3	F 1325	8.7
2044	0.9	2013	1.4
8 0203	9.3	**23** 0137	8.8
0910	0.7	0835	1.2
F 1432	9.1	SA 1403	8.7
2129	1.1	2050	1.4
9 0249	8.9	**24** 0215	8.7
0954	1.0	0913	1.3
SA 1518	8.7	SU 1442	8.6
2212	1.5	2129	1.5
10 0336	8.5	**25** 0255	8.5
1036	1.4	0952	1.4
SU 1605	8.3	M 1523	8.4
2256	1.9	2210	1.7
11 0425	8.0	**26** 0338	8.3
1121	1.8	1033	1.6
M 1655	7.9	TU 1609	8.2
◗ 2344	2.2	2255	1.8
12 0518	7.6	**27** 0427	8.1
1211	2.2	1121	1.8
TU 1751	7.5	W 1701	8.0
		◗ 2349	2.0
13 0040	2.4	**28** 0525	7.9
0619	7.3	1220	1.9
W 1308	2.4	TH 1805	7.9
1855	7.4		
14 0141	2.5	**29** 0053	2.0
0728	7.2	0637	7.8
TH 1411	2.4	F 1330	2.0
2002	7.4	1918	8.0
15 0246	2.4	**30** 0208	1.9
0835	7.4	0753	8.0
F 1515	2.3	SA 1448	1.8
2102	7.6	2029	8.3

JULY

Time	m		Time	m
1 0323	1.6	**16** 0407	2.2
0903	8.3	0949	7.6
SU 1558	1.5	M 1634	2.2
2134	8.6	2207	7.9
2 0430	1.3	**17** 0459	1.9
1007	8.6	1035	8.0
M 1701	1.2	TU 1721	1.8
2233	9.0	2250	8.3
3 0533	1.0	**18** 0544	1.6
1105	9.0	1116	8.4
TU 1800	1.0	W 1803	1.6
○ 2327	9.2	2329	8.6
4 0632	0.7	**19** 0627	1.3
1158	9.2	1155	8.7
W 1856	0.9	TH 1843	1.4
		●	
5 0017	9.4	**20** 0007	8.8
0726	0.6	0707	1.1
TH 1246	9.4	F 1232	8.9
1946	0.8	1922	1.2
6 0104	9.4	**21** 0044	9.0
0814	0.6	0747	1.0
F 1331	9.4	SA 1309	9.0
2031	0.8	2001	1.1
7 0147	9.3	**22** 0122	9.1
0856	0.7	0825	0.9
SA 1413	9.2	SU 1347	9.1
2111	1.0	2039	1.1
8 0229	9.1	**23** 0200	9.1
0933	0.9	0902	0.9
SU 1453	8.9	M 1425	9.0
2147	1.3	2116	1.1
9 0309	8.7	**24** 0238	8.9
1007	1.3	0938	1.1
M 1533	8.6	TU 1504	8.9
2221	1.7	2154	1.3
10 0349	8.3	**25** 0319	8.7
1041	1.7	1015	1.3
TU 1612	8.1	W 1545	8.6
2258	2.1	2235	1.5
11 0431	7.8	**26** 0403	8.4
1119	2.1	1058	1.6
W 1657	7.7	TH 1633	8.3
◗ 2343	2.4	◗ 2324	1.8
12 0521	7.3	**27** 0457	8.0
1204	2.5	1151	2.0
TH 1752	7.3	F 1733	7.9
13 0040	2.7	**28** 0025	2.1
0625	6.9	0609	7.7
F 1310	2.8	SA 1301	2.2
1902	7.1	1851	7.8
14 0151	2.8	**29** 0143	2.1
0744	6.9	0734	7.7
SA 1425	2.8	SU 1427	2.2
2017	7.2	2013	7.9
15 0304	2.6	**30** 0307	1.9
0854	7.2	0854	8.0
SU 1536	2.5	M 1544	1.8
2118	7.5	2125	8.3
		31 0420	1.5
		1003	8.4
		TU 1651	1.5
		2227	8.8

AUGUST

Time	m		Time	m
1 0525	1.1	**16** 0520	1.6
1059	8.9	1053	8.5
W 1752	1.1	TH 1740	1.5
2319	9.1	2307	8.7
2 0622	0.8	**17** 0605	1.2
1148	9.2	1133	8.8
TH 1845	0.9	F 1823	1.2
○		● 2346	9.0
3 0006	9.4	**18** 0648	0.9
0711	0.7	1211	9.1
F 1231	9.4	SA 1904	1.0
1931	0.8		
4 0047	9.4	**19** 0024	9.3
0756	0.6	0729	0.7
SA 1311	9.4	SU 1248	9.3
2011	0.8	1944	0.8
5 0126	9.4	**20** 0102	9.4
0834	0.7	0807	0.7
SU 1348	9.3	M 1326	9.4
2046	1.0	2023	0.8
6 0203	9.2	**21** 0140	9.4
0904	0.9	0844	0.7
M 1423	9.1	TU 1404	9.4
2116	1.2	2100	0.8
7 0238	8.9	**22** 0219	9.3
0932	1.3	0920	0.9
TU 1457	8.7	W 1442	9.2
2143	1.6	2136	1.0
8 0312	8.4	**23** 0259	9.0
0958	1.7	0956	1.2
W 1530	8.3	TH 1523	8.8
2213	2.0	2216	1.4
9 0346	7.9	**24** 0343	8.5
1029	2.1	1037	1.6
TH 1604	7.8	F 1609	8.4
◗ 2250	2.4	◗ 2303	1.8
10 0425	7.4	**25** 0437	8.0
1110	2.6	1131	2.1
F 1649	7.2	SA 1711	7.8
2339	2.9		
11 0520	6.8	**26** 0005	2.2
1207	3.1	0553	7.5
SA 1756	6.8	SU 1245	2.5
		1836	7.5
12 0048	3.1	**27** 0131	2.4
0648	6.6	0727	7.4
SU 1329	3.2	M 1418	2.4
1930	6.8	2006	7.7
13 0219	3.0	**28** 0304	2.1
0819	6.8	0853	7.8
M 1458	2.9	TU 1539	2.0
2046	7.2	2122	8.2
14 0335	2.6	**29** 0416	1.6
0922	7.5	0958	8.4
TU 1605	2.4	W 1647	1.5
2141	7.7	2220	8.7
15 0432	2.0	**30** 0519	1.2
1010	8.0	1049	8.9
W 1655	1.9	TH 1743	1.2
2226	8.3	2307	9.1
		31 0610	0.9
		1132	9.2
		F 1830	1.0
		○ 2349	9.3

Chart Datum: 4·43 metres below IGN Datum
HAT is 10·1 metres above Chart Datum

FRANCE – DIEPPE

LAT 49°56'N   LONG 1°05'E

TIMES AND HEIGHTS OF HIGH AND LOW WATERS

Dates in amber are **SPRINGS**
Dates in yellow are **NEAPS**

2012

SEPTEMBER

Day	Time m		Day	Time m	
1 SA	0652 0.8	1211 9.4 / 1909 0.9	16 SU	0622 0.8	1144 9.4 / 1841 0.8 / ● 2359 9.5
2 SU	0026 9.4	0730 0.7 / 1246 9.4 / 1944 0.9	17 M	0705 0.8	1223 9.6 / 1923 0.6
3 M	0101 9.3	0803 0.8 / 1319 9.3 / 2015 1.0	18 TU	0039 9.6	0746 0.5 / 1302 9.7 / 2003 0.6
4 TU	0134 9.2	0830 1.0 / 1351 9.1 / 2042 1.2	19 W	0119 9.7	0824 0.6 / 1341 9.6 / 2041 0.7
5 W	0205 8.9	0856 1.3 / 1421 8.8 / 2108 1.5	20 TH	0159 9.5	0901 0.8 / 1422 9.4 / 2119 0.9
6 TH	0236 8.5	0920 1.7 / 1450 8.4 / 2134 1.9	21 F	0242 9.1	0939 1.2 / 1504 8.9 / 2201 1.3
7 F	0306 8.0	0948 2.2 / 1520 7.9 / 2206 2.4	22 SA	0328 8.5	1022 1.8 / 1553 8.3 / ◑ 2249 1.8
8 SA	0339 7.5	1025 2.7 / 1558 7.3 / ◑ 2249 2.8	23 SU	0425 7.9	1118 2.3 / 1658 7.7 / 2354 2.3
9 SU	0426 6.9	1116 3.2 / 1656 6.8 / 2351 3.2	24 M	0545 7.4	1237 2.7 / 1826 7.4
10 M	0544 6.5	1231 3.4 / 1833 6.6	25 TU	0124 2.5	0720 7.4 / 1411 2.5 / 1957 7.6
11 TU	0122 3.3	0736 6.7 / 1412 3.2 / 2008 6.9	26 W	0254 2.1	0842 7.9 / 1530 2.0 / 2108 8.1
12 W	0255 2.8	0847 7.3 / 1528 2.6 / 2108 7.6	27 TH	0405 1.6	0941 8.4 / 1633 1.5 / 2203 8.7
13 TH	0358 2.1	0939 8.0 / 1622 1.9 / 2156 8.3	28 F	0502 1.2	1029 8.9 / 1724 1.2 / 2247 9.0
14 F	0449 1.6	1023 8.6 / 1710 1.4 / 2239 8.8	29 SA	0547 1.0	1109 9.1 / 1806 1.1 / 2326 9.2
15 SA	0537 1.1	1104 9.0 / 1756 1.1 / 2320 9.2	30 SU	0625 1.0	1145 9.2 / 1842 1.0 / ○

OCTOBER

Day	Time m		Day	Time m	
1 M	0001 9.2	0700 1.0 / 1218 9.3 / 1913 1.1	16 TU	0638 0.6	1156 9.7 / 1859 0.6
2 TU	0033 9.2	0729 1.1 / 1248 9.2 / 1943 1.1	17 W	0016 9.7	0722 0.6 / 1238 9.8 / 1943 0.5
3 W	0104 9.1	0757 1.2 / 1319 9.1 / 2012 1.3	18 TH	0059 9.7	0804 0.6 / 1321 9.7 / 2024 0.7
4 TH	0135 8.9	0824 1.4 / 1348 8.8 / 2038 1.5	19 F	0143 9.6	0844 0.9 / 1404 9.5 / 2106 0.9
5 F	0205 8.5	0849 1.8 / 1417 8.4 / 2103 1.9	20 SA	0229 9.2	0926 1.3 / 1451 9.0 / 2150 1.3
6 SA	0234 8.1	0917 2.2 / 1446 8.0 / 2134 2.3	21 SU	0318 8.6	1013 1.8 / 1543 8.4 / 2241 1.8
7 SU	0307 7.7	0952 2.6 / 1523 7.5 / 2214 2.7	22 M	0418 8.0	1111 2.3 / 1648 7.8 / ◑ 2346 2.3
8 M	0351 7.2	1039 3.1 / 1615 7.0 / ◑ 2309 3.1	23 TU	0532 7.5	1227 2.6 / 1807 7.5
9 TU	0457 6.7	1146 3.4 / 1735 6.7	24 W	0107 2.4	0655 7.5 / 1350 2.5 / 1930 7.6
10 W	0028 3.2	0638 6.7 / 1316 3.3 / 1915 6.9	25 TH	0228 2.2	0813 7.8 / 1504 2.1 / 2041 7.9
11 TH	0202 2.9	0801 7.2 / 1441 2.7 / 2025 7.5	26 F	0336 1.9	0913 8.3 / 1605 1.7 / 2136 8.4
12 F	0315 2.3	0859 7.9 / 1542 2.0 / 2118 8.2	27 SA	0431 1.6	0959 8.7 / 1655 1.5 / 2221 8.7
13 SA	0412 1.6	0947 8.5 / 1635 1.4 / 2206 8.8	28 SU	0516 1.4	1041 8.9 / 1736 1.3 / 2300 8.9
14 SU	0503 1.1	1032 9.1 / 1725 1.0 / 2250 9.2	29 M	0552 1.3	1117 9.0 / 1811 1.3 / ○ 2334 8.9
15 M	0552 0.8	1114 9.5 / 1813 0.7 / ● 2333 9.6	30 TU	0627 1.3	1149 9.0 / 1844 1.2
			31 W	0006 9.0	0658 1.3 / 1220 9.0 / 1916 1.2

NOVEMBER

Day	Time m		Day	Time m	
1 TH	0038 8.9	0729 1.4 / 1251 8.9 / 1946 1.3	16 F	0043 9.7	0747 0.7 / 1305 9.7 / 2011 0.6
2 F	0110 8.8	0759 1.6 / 1322 8.8 / 2015 1.5	17 SA	0131 9.6	0832 0.9 / 1352 9.5 / 2057 0.8
3 SA	0141 8.6	0826 1.8 / 1352 8.5 / 2042 1.8	18 SU	0219 9.2	0918 1.2 / 1440 9.1 / 2143 1.2
4 SU	0212 8.3	0856 2.1 / 1424 8.2 / 2114 2.1	19 M	0309 8.8	1006 1.7 / 1532 8.6 / 2232 1.6
5 M	0247 7.9	0931 2.4 / 1501 7.8 / 2152 2.4	20 TU	0404 8.3	1059 2.1 / 1630 8.1 / ◑ 2329 2.0
6 TU	0329 7.5	1016 2.8 / 1549 7.4 / 2241 2.7	21 W	0505 7.8	1201 2.4 / 1734 7.7
7 W	0425 7.2	1114 3.0 / 1653 7.1 / ◑ 2346 2.9	22 TH	0033 2.3	0614 7.6 / 1310 2.5 / 1846 7.5
8 TH	0541 7.0	1226 3.0 / 1814 7.1	23 F	0143 2.4	0727 7.6 / 1419 2.4 / 1959 7.6
9 F	0105 2.8	0704 7.3 / 1346 2.7 / 1932 7.3	24 SA	0249 2.3	0834 7.9 / 1523 2.2 / 2101 7.9
10 SA	0223 2.4	0812 7.9 / 1457 2.1 / 2035 8.1	25 SU	0349 2.0	0927 8.2 / 1617 1.9 / 2150 8.2
11 SU	0330 1.8	0908 8.5 / 1558 1.6 / 2130 8.6	26 M	0438 1.8	1011 8.4 / 1703 1.7 / 2232 8.4
12 M	0427 1.3	0958 9.0 / 1654 1.1 / 2220 9.1	27 TU	0520 1.7	1049 8.6 / 1742 1.5 / 2309 8.6
13 TU	0521 1.0	1046 9.4 / 1746 0.8 / ● 2309 9.3	28 W	0559 1.6	1124 8.8 / 1818 1.4 / ○ 2343 8.7
14 W	0612 0.7	1132 9.7 / 1837 0.6 / 2356 9.7	29 TH	0633 1.5	1157 8.8 / 1853 1.4
15 TH	0701 0.7	1218 9.8 / 1925 0.5	30 F	0017 8.7	0707 1.5 / 1230 8.8 / 1927 1.4

DECEMBER

Day	Time m		Day	Time m	
1 SA	0050 8.7	0739 1.6 / 1302 8.8 / 1958 1.4	16 SU	0120 9.6	0823 0.8 / 1341 9.6 / 2049 0.6
2 SU	0124 8.7	0810 1.7 / 1335 8.7 / 2029 1.6	17 M	0208 9.4	0909 1.0 / 1428 9.3 / 2134 0.9
3 M	0157 8.5	0843 1.9 / 1410 8.4 / 2102 1.8	18 TU	0255 9.0	0953 1.4 / 1515 8.9 / 2216 1.3
4 TU	0233 8.3	0918 2.1 / 1447 8.2 / 2139 2.0	19 W	0341 8.6	1037 1.8 / 1603 8.4 / 2259 1.8
5 W	0313 8.0	0959 2.3 / 1530 7.9 / 2221 2.2	20 TH	0430 8.1	1124 2.2 / 1654 7.9 / ◑ 2346 2.2
6 TH	0400 7.7	1047 2.5 / 1621 7.6 / ◑ 2313 2.4	21 F	0524 7.7	1217 2.5 / 1753 7.4
7 F	0457 7.5	1146 2.6 / 1723 7.5	22 SA	0042 2.5	0628 7.4 / 1320 2.7 / 1902 7.2
8 SA	0016 2.5	0607 7.5 / 1254 2.5 / 1838 7.5	23 SU	0147 2.7	0740 7.4 / 1429 2.6 / 2016 7.3
9 SU	0129 2.4	0721 7.8 / 1409 2.2 / 1951 7.9	24 M	0259 2.6	0847 7.6 / 1535 2.4 / 2117 7.6
10 M	0245 2.0	0828 8.3 / 1521 1.8 / 2056 8.4	25 TU	0400 2.3	0940 7.9 / 1630 2.1 / 2206 7.9
11 TU	0353 1.6	0927 8.8 / 1624 1.3 / 2155 8.8	26 W	0451 2.0	1024 8.2 / 1717 1.8 / 2247 8.2
12 W	0454 1.2	1022 9.2 / 1723 0.9 / 2249 9.2	27 TH	0535 1.8	1102 8.5 / 1758 1.5 / 2324 8.5
13 TH	0550 0.9	1114 9.5 / 1818 0.7 / ● 2341 9.5	28 F	0614 1.6	1138 8.7 / 1836 1.4 / ○
14 F	0643 0.8	1204 9.7 / 1912 0.5	29 SA	0000 8.6	0650 1.5 / 1213 8.8 / 1911 1.3
15 SA	0032 9.6	0735 0.7 / 1253 9.7 / 2002 0.5	30 SU	0035 8.8	0724 1.4 / 1247 8.9 / 1946 1.3
			31 M	0109 8.8	0758 1.4 / 1322 8.9 / 2019 1.3

Chart Datum: 4·43 metres below IGN Datum
HAT is 10·1 metres above Chart Datum

TIDES

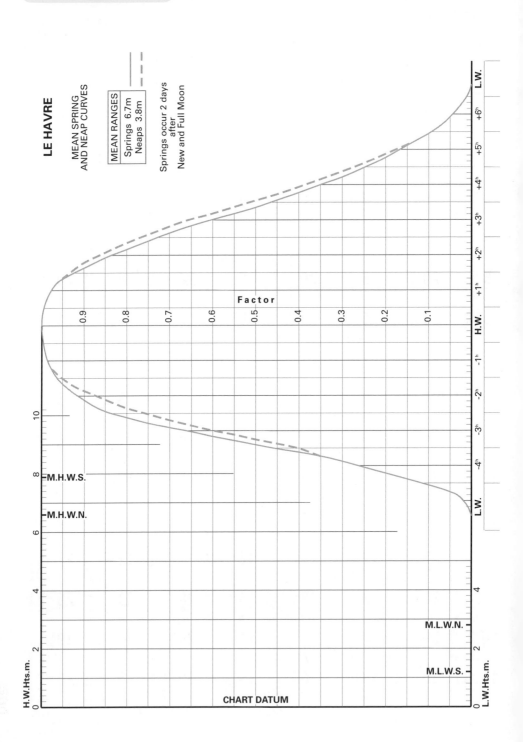

LE HAVRE
MEAN SPRING
AND NEAP CURVES

MEAN RANGES
Springs 6.7m
Neaps 3.8m

Springs occur 2 days
after
New and Full Moon

Factor

0.9
0.8
0.7
0.6
0.5
0.4
0.3
0.2
0.1

H.W.

+1ʰ
+2ʰ
+3ʰ
+4ʰ
+5ʰ
+6ʰ
L.W.

-1ʰ
-2ʰ
-3ʰ
-4ʰ
L.W.

H.W.Hts.m.

10

8 M.H.W.S.

M.H.W.N.

6

4

2

0 CHART DATUM

M.L.W.N.

M.L.W.S.

L.W.Hts.m.

TIME ZONE -0100
(French Standard Time)
Subtract 1 hour for UT
For French Summer Time add
ONE hour in **non-shaded areas**

FRANCE – LE HAVRE

LAT 49°29'N   LONG 0°07'E

TIMES AND HEIGHTS OF HIGH AND LOW WATERS

Dates in amber are **SPRINGS**
Dates in yellow are **NEAPS**

2012

JANUARY

Time m	Time m
1 0331 6.8 / 1018 2.8 / SU 1547 6.7 / ☽2235 2.8	**16** 0317 7.3 / 1011 2.1 / M 1534 7.2 / 2235 2.2
2 0422 6.6 / 1105 3.1 / M 1647 6.4 / 2326 3.1	**17** 0413 7.1 / 1104 2.4 / TU 1640 6.9 / 2334 2.5
3 0529 6.4 / 1205 3.3 / TU 1801 6.3	**18** 0527 6.9 / 1213 2.6 / W 1804 6.8
4 0032 3.3 / 0642 6.5 / W 1323 3.2 / 1917 6.3	**19** 0053 2.7 / 0646 7.0 / TH 1340 2.6 / 1927 6.9
5 0155 3.2 / 0747 6.6 / TH 1440 2.9 / 2019 6.6	**20** 0221 2.5 / 0800 7.2 / F 1500 2.2 / 2040 7.2
6 0305 2.9 / 0839 6.9 / F 1538 2.5 / 2108 6.9	**21** 0333 2.2 / 0904 7.4 / SA 1608 1.8 / 2138 7.4
7 0359 2.5 / 0923 7.2 / SA 1626 2.2 / 2151 7.2	**22** 0437 1.8 / 0956 7.7 / SU 1710 1.5 / 2227 7.7
8 0444 2.2 / 1003 7.4 / SU 1708 1.9 / 2230 7.4	**23** 0534 1.6 / 1042 7.8 / M 1802 1.2 / 2310 7.8
9 0527 1.9 / 1040 7.6 / M 1752 1.6 / ○2308 7.6	**24** 0621 1.4 / 1124 7.9 / TU 1844 1.1 / 2350 7.8
10 0608 1.7 / 1118 7.8 / TU 1833 1.4 / 2346 7.7	**25** 0700 1.3 / 1203 8.0 / W 1920 1.1
11 0649 1.5 / 1156 7.9 / W 1913 1.2	**26** 0027 7.8 / 0734 1.4 / TH 1239 7.9 / 1952 1.2
12 0025 7.7 / 0729 1.5 / TH 1236 7.9 / 1953 1.2	**27** 0102 7.7 / 0805 1.5 / F 1314 7.7 / 2021 1.5
13 0105 7.7 / 0809 1.5 / F 1317 7.8 / 2031 1.3	**28** 0136 7.5 / 0834 1.8 / SA 1348 7.5 / 2047 1.8
14 0147 7.6 / 0901 1.6 / SA 1359 7.7 / 2108 1.5	**29** 0208 7.3 / 0901 2.1 / SU 1420 7.2 / 2112 2.2
15 0230 7.5 / 0927 1.8 / SU 1443 7.5 / 2148 1.8	**30** 0239 7.0 / 0929 2.5 / M 1453 6.9 / 2141 2.6
	31 0314 6.7 / 1004 2.9 / TU 1535 6.5 / ☽2222 3.0

FEBRUARY

Time m	Time m
1 0404 6.4 / 1055 3.2 / W 1640 6.2 / 2320 3.4	**16** 0459 6.8 / 1147 2.7 / TH 1749 6.6
2 0526 6.2 / 1205 3.4 / TH 1821 6.1	**17** 0030 2.9 / 0630 6.7 / F 1321 2.8 / 1922 6.7
3 0043 3.5 / 0701 6.3 / F 1342 3.3 / 1944 6.3	**18** 0208 2.8 / 0753 6.9 / SA 1452 2.4 / 2036 7.0
4 0221 3.2 / 0808 6.6 / SA 1502 2.8 / 2042 6.7	**19** 0330 2.4 / 0857 7.2 / SU 1610 1.9 / 2130 7.3
5 0330 2.7 / 0859 6.9 / SU 1600 2.3 / 2129 7.1	**20** 0437 1.9 / 0946 7.5 / M 1709 1.5 / 2214 7.5
6 0423 2.2 / 0942 7.3 / M 1651 1.8 / 2210 7.4	**21** 0527 1.6 / 1027 7.7 / TU 1752 1.3 / ●2252 7.7
7 0510 1.8 / 1022 7.6 / TU 1737 1.4 / ○2249 7.6	**22** 0606 1.4 / 1105 7.8 / W 1825 1.1 / 2328 7.8
8 0555 1.4 / 1101 7.9 / W 1820 1.1 / 2328 7.8	**23** 0639 1.3 / 1139 7.9 / TH 1856 1.0
9 0637 1.2 / 1140 8.0 / TH 1901 0.9	**24** 0000 7.8 / 0709 1.3 / F 1214 7.9 / 1924 1.2
10 0008 8.0 / 0718 1.0 / F 1221 8.1 / 1940 0.8	**25** 0032 7.7 / 0737 1.4 / SA 1245 7.8 / 1951 1.4
11 0048 8.0 / 0756 1.0 / SA 1302 8.1 / 2017 0.9	**26** 0103 7.6 / 0803 1.6 / SU 1317 7.6 / 2014 1.7
12 0129 7.9 / 0827 1.1 / SU 1343 7.9 / 2053 1.2	**27** 0132 7.4 / 0827 1.9 / M 1345 7.3 / 2037 2.0
13 0210 7.7 / 0911 1.4 / M 1426 7.6 / 2129 1.6	**28** 0157 7.2 / 0851 2.2 / TU 1414 7.0 / 2102 2.4
14 0253 7.4 / 0951 1.9 / TU 1514 7.2 / ☽2212 2.1	**29** 0228 6.9 / 0922 2.6 / W 1451 6.6 / 2137 2.9
15 0345 7.1 / 1040 2.3 / W 1618 6.8 / 2308 2.6	

MARCH

Time m	Time m
1 0311 6.5 / 1005 3.0 / TH 1545 6.2 / ☽2229 3.3	**16** 0440 6.7 / 1131 2.7 / F 1739 6.5
2 0415 6.2 / 1109 3.4 / F 1713 6.0 / 2347 3.5	**17** 0017 3.0 / 0615 6.5 / SA 1308 2.8 / 1912 6.6
3 0603 6.1 / 1244 3.4 / SA 1903 6.1	**18** 0158 2.9 / 0739 6.7 / SU 1441 2.4 / 2023 6.9
4 0134 3.4 / 0730 6.4 / SU 1420 2.9 / 2010 6.5	**19** 0320 2.4 / 0840 7.0 / M 1556 2.0 / 2112 7.2
5 0255 2.8 / 0828 6.8 / M 1527 2.3 / 2101 7.0	**20** 0421 1.9 / 0926 7.3 / TU 1648 1.6 / 2152 7.4
6 0354 2.2 / 0915 7.2 / TU 1623 1.7 / 2144 7.4	**21** 0506 1.6 / 1006 7.5 / W 1728 1.4 / 2228 7.6
7 0446 1.6 / 0957 7.6 / W 1713 1.2 / 2225 7.7	**22** 0541 1.4 / 1041 7.7 / TH 1757 1.3 / ●2300 7.7
8 0533 1.2 / 1038 7.9 / TH 1759 0.9 / ○2305 8.2	**23** 0611 1.3 / 1113 7.7 / F 1826 1.3 / 2331 7.7
9 0618 0.9 / 1120 8.1 / F 1841 0.6 / 2346 8.1	**24** 0641 1.3 / 1145 7.7 / SA 1854 1.3
10 0659 0.7 / 1202 8.2 / SA 1921 0.6	**25** 0002 7.7 / 0709 1.4 / SU 1217 7.7 / 1920 1.4
11 0027 8.2 / 0739 0.7 / SU 1244 8.2 / 1959 0.7	**26** 0032 7.6 / 0734 1.5 / M 1249 7.5 / 1945 1.7
12 0108 8.1 / 0817 0.9 / M 1327 8.0 / 2036 1.1	**27** 0100 7.4 / 0759 1.7 / TU 1318 7.3 / 2008 2.0
13 0150 7.8 / 0855 1.2 / TU 1411 7.6 / 2112 1.6	**28** 0127 7.3 / 0824 2.0 / W 1348 7.0 / 2035 2.3
14 0233 7.5 / 0934 1.7 / W 1500 7.2 / 2154 2.2	**29** 0159 7.0 / 0854 2.4 / TH 1426 6.7 / 2108 2.7
15 0325 7.1 / 1022 2.3 / TH 1606 6.7 / ☽2251 2.7	**30** 0241 6.6 / 0933 2.8 / F 1517 6.4 / ☽2155 3.1
	31 0339 6.3 / 1029 3.1 / SA 1629 6.1 / 2306 3.4

APRIL

Time m	Time m
1 0505 6.1 / 1158 3.2 / SU 1816 6.2	**16** 0128 2.8 / 0709 6.6 / M 1404 2.5 / 1954 6.8
2 0049 3.3 / 0643 6.3 / M 1334 2.8 / 1929 6.6	**17** 0242 2.5 / 0812 6.8 / TU 1515 2.2 / 2044 7.1
3 0212 2.7 / 0748 6.7 / TU 1446 2.3 / 2024 7.0	**18** 0343 2.1 / 0859 7.1 / W 1608 1.9 / 2124 7.3
4 0316 2.1 / 0841 7.2 / W 1546 1.7 / 2112 7.5	**19** 0429 1.8 / 0939 7.3 / TH 1646 1.7 / 2159 7.4
5 0412 1.6 / 0927 7.6 / TH 1641 1.2 / 2156 7.8	**20** 0506 1.6 / 1014 7.5 / F 1721 1.6 / 2231 7.5
6 0505 1.1 / 1012 7.9 / F 1731 0.9 / ○2239 8.0	**21** 0539 1.5 / 1047 7.6 / SA 1753 1.5 / ●2302 7.6
7 0553 0.8 / 1057 8.1 / SA 1817 0.6 / 2322 8.2	**22** 0611 1.5 / 1119 7.5 / SU 1824 1.5 / 2333 7.6
8 0638 0.6 / 1142 8.2 / SU 1900 0.6	**23** 0641 1.5 / 1153 7.5 / M 1852 1.6
9 0005 8.2 / 0721 0.6 / M 1227 8.1 / 1941 0.8	**24** 0004 7.5 / 0708 1.5 / TU 1225 7.4 / 1919 1.8
10 0049 8.1 / 0801 0.8 / TU 1312 7.9 / 2020 1.1	**25** 0034 7.4 / 0736 1.7 / W 1257 7.3 / 1947 2.0
11 0132 7.8 / 0841 1.1 / W 1359 7.6 / 2100 1.6	**26** 0105 7.3 / 0805 1.9 / TH 1332 7.1 / 2017 2.2
12 0218 7.5 / 0923 1.6 / TH 1451 7.1 / 2144 2.2	**27** 0141 7.1 / 0836 2.2 / F 1412 6.8 / 2052 2.6
13 0311 7.0 / 1012 2.2 / F 1557 6.7 / ☽2243 2.7	**28** 0224 6.8 / 0914 2.5 / SA 1500 6.6 / 2136 2.9
14 0423 6.6 / 1120 2.6 / SA 1720 6.5	**29** 0317 6.5 / 1006 2.7 / SU 1602 6.4 / ☽2240 3.1
15 0004 2.9 / 0549 6.5 / SU 1244 2.7 / 1845 6.6	**30** 0425 6.4 / 1121 2.9 / M 1726 6.4

Chart Datum: 4·38 metres below IGN Datum
HAT is 8·4 metres above Chart Datum

TIDES

TIME ZONE -0100
(French Standard Time)
Subtract 1 hour for UT
For French Summer Time add
ONE hour in **non-shaded areas**

FRANCE – LE HAVRE
LAT 49°29'N   LONG 0°07'E
TIMES AND HEIGHTS OF HIGH AND LOW WATERS

Dates in amber are **SPRINGS**
Dates in yellow are **NEAPS**

2012

MAY

Day	Time m	Time m	Time m	Time m
1 TU	0006 3.0	0551 6.5	1248 2.7	1844 6.7
16 W	0147 2.6	0729 6.7	1412 2.5	2004 6.9
2 W	0126 2.6	0703 6.8	1401 2.2	1944 7.1
17 TH	0247 2.4	0824 6.9	1509 2.3	2049 7.1
3 TH	0234 2.1	0802 7.2	1505 1.8	2036 7.5
18 F	0341 2.2	0908 7.1	1559 2.1	2127 7.3
4 F	0336 1.6	0855 7.5	1605 1.4	2125 7.8
19 SA	0426 1.9	0946 7.2	1643 1.9	2202 7.4
5 SA	0433 1.2	0946 7.8	1700 1.0	2212 8.0
20 SU	0507 1.8	1022 7.3	1721 1.8	2235 7.5
6 SU	0527 0.9	1035 8.0	1751 0.8	○2259 8.1
21 M	0543 1.7	1057 7.4	1755 1.8	●2308 7.5
7 M	0616 0.7	1124 8.1	1839 0.8	2345 8.1
22 TU	0615 1.6	1132 7.4	1827 1.8	2342 7.5
8 TU	0703 0.7	1212 8.0	1924 0.9	
23 W	0647 1.6	1206 7.4	1859 1.8	
9 W	0032 8.0	0748 0.8	1300 7.9	2008 1.2
24 TH	0014 7.5	0719 1.6	1241 7.3	1932 1.9
10 TH	0118 7.8	0832 1.1	1349 7.6	2051 1.6
25 F	0049 7.4	0752 1.7	1318 7.2	2006 2.1
11 F	0206 7.5	0916 1.5	1441 7.2	2138 2.1
26 SA	0128 7.2	0827 1.9	1359 7.1	2044 2.3
12 SA	0258 7.1	1004 2.0	1539 6.9	◐2232 2.5
27 SU	0211 7.1	0906 2.1	1445 6.9	2128 2.5
13 SU	0359 6.8	1101 2.4	1646 6.7	2336 2.7
28 M	0259 6.9	0953 2.3	1538 6.8	◑2222 2.6
14 M	0509 6.6	1205 2.6	1758 6.6	
29 TU	0355 6.8	1053 2.5	1643 6.7	2330 2.7
15 TU	0042 2.8	0621 6.6	1310 2.6	1908 6.7
30 W	0505 6.7	1204 2.4	1757 6.8	
31 TH	0042 2.5	0619 6.8	1317 2.2	1903 7.1

JUNE

Day	Time m	Time m	Time m	Time m
1 F	0154 2.2	0726 7.1	1428 1.9	2002 7.4
16 SA	0256 2.5	0836 6.8	1517 2.5	2056 7.0
2 SA	0302 1.8	0827 7.4	1533 1.6	2057 7.7
17 SU	0349 2.3	0921 7.0	1608 2.3	2135 7.2
3 SU	0405 1.4	0924 7.6	1633 1.3	2150 7.9
18 M	0435 2.0	1000 7.1	1652 2.1	2212 7.3
4 M	0503 1.1	1019 7.8	1729 1.1	○2241 8.0
19 TU	0517 1.8	1037 7.3	1732 1.9	●2248 7.4
5 TU	0558 0.9	1110 7.9	1822 1.1	2330 8.0
20 W	0554 1.7	1114 7.3	1808 1.8	2323 7.5
6 W	0649 0.8	1200 7.9	1911 1.1	
21 TH	0631 1.6	1150 7.4	1845 1.8	2358 7.5
7 TH	0018 8.0	0737 0.8	1249 7.8	1957 1.3
22 F	0707 1.5	1227 7.4	1922 1.7	
8 F	0105 7.8	0821 1.0	1336 7.6	2041 1.5
23 SA	0035 7.5	0744 1.5	1305 7.4	2000 1.8
9 SA	0151 7.6	0904 1.4	1423 7.4	2124 1.9
24 SU	0115 7.4	0822 1.6	1345 7.3	2039 1.9
10 SU	0237 7.3	0946 1.8	1511 7.1	2208 2.2
25 M	0156 7.4	0900 1.8	1428 7.2	2119 2.1
11 M	0326 7.0	1029 2.2	1603 6.8	◐2255 2.6
26 TU	0240 7.2	0941 1.9	1515 7.1	2205 2.2
12 TU	0422 6.7	1117 2.5	1701 6.7	2350 2.8
27 W	0329 7.1	1029 2.1	1608 7.0	◐2259 2.4
13 W	0525 6.5	1213 2.7	1806 6.6	
28 TH	0428 6.9	1127 2.3	1715 7.0	
14 TH	0051 2.8	0633 6.5	1315 2.8	1912 6.7
29 F	0004 2.4	0543 6.9	1238 2.3	1827 7.0
15 F	0155 2.7	0741 6.6	1419 2.7	2009 6.8
30 SA	0119 2.3	0659 7.0	1357 2.2	1935 7.2

JULY

Day	Time m	Time m	Time m	Time m
1 SU	0236 2.0	0808 7.2	1508 1.9	2038 7.5
16 M	0315 2.6	0856 6.7	1538 2.6	2111 7.0
2 M	0342 1.6	0912 7.5	1612 1.6	2136 7.7
17 TU	0408 2.2	0939 7.0	1628 2.2	2151 7.3
3 TU	0445 1.3	1009 7.7	1712 1.4	○2229 7.9
18 W	0454 1.9	1018 7.3	1712 2.0	2229 7.4
4 W	0544 1.1	1100 7.8	1809 1.2	2317 8.0
19 TH	0537 1.6	1055 7.4	1753 1.8	●2305 7.6
5 TH	0638 0.9	1148 7.9	1900 1.2	
20 F	0617 1.4	1132 7.5	1833 1.6	2342 7.7
6 F	0004 8.0	0725 0.9	1233 7.9	1944 1.2
21 SA	0656 1.3	1210 7.6	1911 1.5	
7 SA	0047 7.9	0806 1.0	1316 7.7	2023 1.4
22 SU	0020 7.7	0734 1.2	1248 7.7	1950 1.4
8 SU	0129 7.7	0843 1.3	1357 7.5	2059 1.7
23 M	0059 7.7	0811 1.3	1328 7.6	2027 1.5
9 M	0209 7.5	0916 1.6	1436 7.3	2133 2.1
24 TU	0139 7.6	0847 1.4	1409 7.5	2105 1.7
10 TU	0250 7.2	0949 2.1	1517 7.0	2209 2.4
25 W	0221 7.5	0925 1.7	1451 7.4	2145 1.9
11 W	0334 6.8	1024 2.5	1603 6.7	◐2251 2.8
26 TH	0306 7.2	1006 2.0	1539 7.2	◐2233 2.2
12 TH	0427 6.5	1102 2.8	1702 6.5	2347 3.0
27 F	0402 7.0	1058 2.3	1642 7.0	2334 2.4
13 F	0534 6.3	1211 3.1	1813 6.4	
28 SA	0519 6.8	1208 2.6	1802 6.9	
14 SA	0058 3.1	0653 6.3	1327 3.1	1926 6.5
29 SU	0054 2.5	0644 6.8	1336 2.5	1920 7.1
15 SU	0213 2.9	0803 6.5	1440 2.9	2025 6.7
30 M	0218 2.2	0802 7.1	1453 2.2	2030 7.3
31 TU	0329 1.8	0908 7.4	1601 1.9	2128 7.6

AUGUST

Day	Time m	Time m	Time m	Time m
1 W	0436 1.5	1002 7.6	1705 1.6	2218 7.8
16 TH	0431 1.9	0955 7.3	1651 1.9	2206 7.5
2 TH	0537 1.2	1049 7.8	1801 1.3	○2303 8.0
17 F	0517 1.5	1033 7.6	1734 1.6	●2244 7.7
3 F	0626 1.0	1132 7.9	1846 1.2	2345 8.0
18 SA	0559 1.3	1110 7.7	1815 1.3	2322 7.9
4 SA	0707 0.9	1212 7.9	1923 1.2	
19 SU	0639 1.1	1148 7.8	1855 1.2	
5 SU	0025 8.0	0742 1.0	1249 7.8	1957 1.3
20 M	0000 8.0	0717 1.0	1227 7.9	1933 1.1
6 M	0102 7.8	0813 1.3	1325 7.6	2027 1.6
21 TU	0040 8.0	0754 1.0	1307 7.9	2011 1.1
7 TU	0138 7.6	0841 1.6	1359 7.4	2055 1.9
22 W	0121 7.9	0830 1.2	1347 7.8	2048 1.4
8 W	0213 7.3	0907 2.0	1433 7.1	2123 2.3
23 TH	0203 7.6	0906 1.6	1429 7.5	2126 1.8
9 TH	0248 6.9	0934 2.5	1508 6.8	◐2156 2.7
24 F	0248 7.3	0945 2.0	1516 7.2	◑2211 2.2
10 F	0330 6.6	1011 2.9	1555 6.5	2242 3.1
25 SA	0345 7.0	1036 2.5	1620 6.9	2312 2.6
11 SA	0431 6.2	1106 3.3	1709 6.2	2352 3.4
26 SU	0507 6.7	1149 2.8	1748 6.8	
12 SU	0604 6.1	1228 3.5	1842 6.2	
27 M	0039 2.7	0640 6.7	1326 2.8	1913 6.9
13 M	0127 3.2	0728 6.2	1404 3.2	1953 6.5
28 TU	0211 2.4	0800 7.0	1448 2.4	2024 7.2
14 TU	0244 2.8	0829 6.6	1511 2.8	2045 6.9
29 W	0326 1.9	0902 7.3	1559 1.9	2119 7.5
15 W	0341 2.3	0915 7.0	1604 2.3	2128 7.2
30 TH	0432 1.5	0949 7.6	1659 1.6	2204 7.8
31 F	0527 1.2	1031 7.8	1746 1.3	○2245 7.9

Chart Datum: 4·38 metres below IGN Datum
HAT is 8·4 metres above Chart Datum

TIME ZONE -0100
(French Standard Time)
Subtract 1 hour for UT
For French Summer Time add ONE hour in **non-shaded areas**

TIMES AND HEIGHTS OF HIGH AND LOW WATERS

Dates in amber are **SPRINGS**
Dates in yellow are **NEAPS**

2012

SEPTEMBER

Date	Time	m	Date	Time	m
1 SA	0607	1.1	**16** SU	0533	1.1
	1109	7.8		1044	7.9
	1823	1.3		1752	1.2
	2322	8.0	●	2257	8.0
2 SU	0641	1.1	**17** M	0615	0.9
	1145	7.9		1123	8.0
	1856	1.4		1833	1.0
	2358	7.9		2338	8.1
3 M	0711	1.2	**18** TU	0655	0.8
	1219	7.8		1203	8.1
	1926	1.4		1913	0.9
4 TU	0032	7.8	**19** W	0020	8.1
	0740	1.4		0734	0.9
	1252	7.7		1248	8.1
	1954	1.6		1953	1.0
5 W	0106	7.6	**20** TH	0102	8.0
	0805	1.7		0812	1.2
	1323	7.5		1326	7.9
	2019	1.9		2031	1.3
6 TH	0138	7.3	**21** F	0146	7.7
	0829	2.1		0849	1.6
	1352	7.2		1409	7.6
	2044	2.3		2110	1.7
7 F	0209	7.0	**22** SA	0235	7.3
	0854	2.6		0930	2.1
	1422	6.9		1459	7.2
	2112	2.7	◑	2156	2.2
8 SA	0244	6.6	**23** SU	0335	6.9
	0926	3.0		1022	2.6
	1502	6.6		1606	6.9
◑ 2153		3.1		2259	2.6
9 SU	0336	6.3	**24** M	0502	6.6
	1015	3.3		1142	3.0
	1603	6.2		1737	6.7
	2255	3.4			
10 M	0504	6.0	**25** TU	0034	2.8
	1131	3.6		0634	6.7
	1749	6.1		1323	2.9
				1902	6.8
11 TU	0033	3.4	**26** W	0205	2.4
	0650	6.1		0751	7.0
	1321	3.5		1441	2.4
	1915	6.3		2011	7.1
12 W	0207	3.0	**27** TH	0318	2.0
	0755	6.6		0846	7.3
	1438	2.9		1546	2.0
	2012	6.8		2102	7.5
13 TH	0309	2.4	**28** F	0417	1.6
	0844	7.0		0930	7.6
	1533	2.3		1639	1.7
	2058	7.2		2144	7.7
14 F	0401	1.9	**29** SA	0503	1.4
	0926	7.4		1008	7.7
	1622	1.8		1720	1.5
	2139	7.6		2222	7.8
15 SA	0449	1.5	**30** SU	0537	1.4
	1005	7.7		1043	7.8
	1708	1.5		1754	1.4
	2218	7.9	○	2257	7.9

OCTOBER

Date	Time	m	Date	Time	m
1 M	0609	1.3	**16** TU	0548	0.9
	1116	7.8		1057	8.1
	1825	1.4		1810	0.9
	2331	7.8		2316	8.2
2 TU	0639	1.4	**17** W	0632	0.9
	1148	7.8		1139	8.2
	1855	1.5		1854	0.8
3 W	0003	7.7	**18** TH	0001	8.2
	0707	1.6		0715	1.0
	1219	7.7		1223	8.1
	1923	1.6		1936	0.9
4 TH	0036	7.6	**19** F	0047	8.0
	0734	1.8		0756	1.2
	1249	7.5		1307	7.9
	1949	1.9		2018	1.2
5 F	0108	7.3	**20** SA	0134	7.7
	0758	2.1		0837	1.7
	1317	7.3		1354	7.6
	2014	2.2		2100	1.7
6 SA	0138	7.0	**21** SU	0225	7.3
	0824	2.5		0921	2.2
	1347	7.0		1446	7.3
	2042	2.6		2148	2.1
7 SU	0213	6.7	**22** M	0327	6.9
	0856	2.9		1017	2.7
	1426	6.7		1553	6.9
	2119	2.9	◑	2253	2.6
8 M	0301	6.4	**23** TU	0448	6.7
	0940	3.3		1135	2.9
	1522	6.3		1716	6.7
◑ 2212		3.3			
9 TU	0411	6.2	**24** W	0019	2.7
	1046	3.6		0611	6.7
	1643	6.2		1302	2.9
	2338	3.4		1836	6.9
10 W	0600	6.2	**25** TH	0139	2.5
	1228	3.5		0725	6.9
	1825	6.3		1415	2.5
				1945	7.2
11 TH	0117	3.1	**26** F	0246	2.2
	0713	6.5		0821	7.2
	1353	3.0		1516	2.2
	1930	6.7		2038	7.3
12 F	0227	2.5	**27** SA	0343	2.0
	0806	7.0		0904	7.4
	1454	2.4		1607	1.9
	2021	7.2		2121	7.5
13 SA	0323	2.0	**28** SU	0426	1.8
	0851	7.4		0942	7.6
	1547	1.9		1647	1.7
	2106	7.6	●	2159	7.6
14 SU	0414	1.5	**29** M	0502	1.7
	0933	7.8		1022	7.8
	1637	1.4		1722	1.6
	2149	7.9	○	2233	7.7
15 M	0502	1.2	**30** TU	0536	1.6
	1015	8.0		1048	7.7
	1725	1.1		1755	1.6
●	2232	8.1		2306	7.7
			31 W	0608	1.7
				1119	7.7
				1827	1.6
				2339	7.6

NOVEMBER

Date	Time	m	Date	Time	m
1 TH	0639	1.8	**16** F	0658	1.0
	1150	7.6		1206	8.2
	1857	1.7		1923	0.9
2 F	0012	7.5	**17** SA	0035	8.0
	0708	1.9		0744	1.3
	1221	7.5		1253	8.0
	1924	1.9		2009	1.1
3 SA	0044	7.3	**18** SU	0124	7.8
	0736	2.2		0829	1.6
	1251	7.4		1342	7.7
	1953	2.1		2054	1.5
4 SU	0116	7.1	**19** M	0216	7.5
	0805	2.4		0917	2.0
	1324	7.1		1433	7.4
	2022	2.4		2143	1.9
5 M	0153	6.9	**20** TU	0313	7.1
	0837	2.7		1009	2.5
	1404	6.9		1532	7.0
	2058	2.7	◑	2238	2.3
6 TU	0239	6.6	**21** W	0418	6.9
	0918	3.0		1111	2.8
	1454	6.6		1640	6.8
	2144	3.0		2343	2.6
7 W	0336	6.5	**22** TH	0529	6.7
	1015	3.3		1220	2.9
	1557	6.4		1753	6.7
◑ 2252		3.1			
8 TH	0455	6.4	**23** F	0051	2.7
	1134	3.3		0641	6.8
	1720	6.4		1329	2.8
				1905	6.8
9 F	0017	3.0	**24** SA	0157	2.6
	0620	6.6		0744	7.0
	1257	3.0		1432	2.5
	1839	6.7		2006	6.9
10 SA	0134	2.6	**25** SU	0256	2.4
	0721	7.0		0834	7.2
	1408	2.5		1526	2.3
	1939	7.1		2055	7.2
11 SU	0240	2.1	**26** M	0346	2.2
	0813	7.4		0915	7.4
	1509	2.0		1612	2.1
	2031	7.4		2135	7.3
12 M	0338	1.7	**27** TU	0428	2.1
	0900	7.7		0951	7.5
	1605	1.5		1652	1.9
	2121	7.7		2212	7.4
13 TU	0432	1.3	**28** W	0507	1.9
	0946	8.0		1024	7.6
	1659	1.2		1729	1.8
●	2209	8.0	○	2246	7.5
14 W	0523	1.1	**29** TH	0543	1.9
	1032	8.1		1056	7.6
	1749	0.9		1804	1.7
	2257	8.1		2319	7.5
15 TH	0612	1.0	**30** F	0617	1.9
	1119	8.2		1128	7.6
	1837	0.8		1836	1.7
	2346	8.1		2353	7.5

DECEMBER

Date	Time	m	Date	Time	m
1 SA	0648	2.0	**16** SU	0024	8.1
	1201	7.6		0736	1.2
	1907	1.8		1241	8.1
				2001	1.0
2 SU	0026	7.4	**17** M	0112	7.9
	0720	2.1		0822	1.5
	1233	7.5		1328	7.9
	1939	1.9		2045	1.2
3 M	0100	7.3	**18** TU	0200	7.6
	0752	2.2		0905	1.7
	1308	7.4		1415	7.6
	2012	2.1		2127	1.6
4 TU	0138	7.1	**19** W	0247	7.3
	0827	2.4		0948	2.1
	1347	7.2		1503	7.2
	2047	2.3		2209	2.1
5 W	0220	7.0	**20** TH	0337	7.0
	0906	2.6		1033	2.5
	1432	7.0		1556	6.9
	2128	2.5	◑	2255	2.5
6 TH	0308	6.8	**21** F	0434	6.8
	0953	2.8		1125	2.8
	1523	6.8		1657	6.7
◑ 2220		2.7		2349	2.8
7 F	0406	6.7	**22** SA	0540	6.7
	1053	2.9		1228	3.0
	1625	6.6		1809	6.5
	2325	2.8			
8 SA	0519	6.7	**23** SU	0055	3.0
	1202	2.9		0652	6.7
	1742	6.7		1338	3.0
				1924	6.6
9 SU	0038	2.7	**24** M	0205	2.9
	0632	6.9		0757	6.9
	1318	2.6		1443	2.7
	1856	6.9		2026	6.7
10 M	0155	2.4	**25** TU	0307	2.7
	0734	7.2		0847	7.0
	1432	2.2		1539	2.4
	1959	7.2		2113	7.0
11 TU	0304	2.0	**26** W	0358	2.4
	0831	7.6		0927	7.2
	1537	1.7		1626	2.2
	2058	7.6		2152	7.2
12 W	0405	1.6	**27** TH	0443	2.2
	0923	7.8		1003	7.4
	1636	1.3		1708	1.9
	2152	7.8		2228	7.3
13 TH	0502	1.3	**28** F	0523	2.0
	1015	8.0		1037	7.5
	1731	1.0		1746	1.8
●	2244	8.0	○	2302	7.4
14 F	0556	1.1	**29** SA	0600	1.9
	1104	8.2		1111	7.6
	1824	0.8		1822	1.6
	2335	8.1		2336	7.5
15 SA	0647	1.1	**30** SU	0634	1.8
	1153	8.2		1144	7.6
	1914	0.8		1856	1.6
			31 M	0010	7.5
				0709	1.8
				1218	7.7
				1930	1.6

Chart Datum: 4·38 metres below IGN Datum
HAT is 8·4 metres above Chart Datum

TIDES

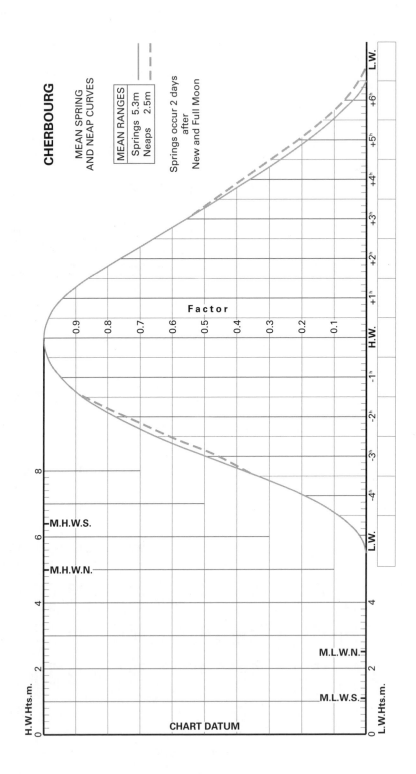

CHERBOURG

MEAN SPRING
AND NEAP CURVES

MEAN RANGES	
Springs	5.3m
Neaps	2.5m

Springs occur 2 days
after
New and Full Moon

TIME ZONE -0100
(French Standard Time)
Subtract 1 hour for UT
For French Summer Time add
ONE hour in **non-shaded areas**

FRANCE – CHERBOURG

LAT 49°39'N   LONG 1°38'W

TIMES AND HEIGHTS OF HIGH AND LOW WATERS

Dates in amber are **SPRINGS**
Dates in yellow are **NEAPS**

2012

JANUARY

Day					Day				
1 SU ◐	0126 5.2	0813 2.5	1344 5.2	2034 2.5	**16** M	0115 5.7	0802 1.9	1331 5.6	2029 1.9
2 M	0216 5.0	0908 2.8	1441 4.9	2131 2.7	**17** TU	0201 5.5	0901 2.2	1434 5.4	2134 2.2
3 TU	0320 4.9	1018 2.9	1553 4.8	2244 2.8	**18** W	0322 5.3	1015 2.3	1557 5.2	2254 2.3
4 W	0436 4.9	1134 2.8	1711 4.8	2357 2.7	**19** TH	0445 5.3	1138 2.2	1724 5.3	
5 TH	0544 5.1	1240 2.5	1817 5.1		**20** F	0016 2.2	0600 5.6	1254 2.0	1838 5.5
6 F	0058 2.5	0639 5.4	1332 2.2	1908 5.4	**21** SA	0125 1.9	0703 5.9	1357 1.6	1939 5.8
7 SA	0148 2.2	0725 5.7	1416 1.9	1952 5.6	**22** SU	0222 1.7	0758 6.2	1451 1.3	2031 6.1
8 SU	0231 1.9	0806 5.9	1457 1.6	2033 5.9	**23** M ●	0312 1.6	0846 6.4	1537 1.1	2115 6.2
9 M ○	0311 1.7	0845 6.1	1536 1.4	2111 6.1	**24** TU	0357 1.3	0929 6.5	1619 1.0	2155 6.3
10 TU	0351 1.5	0922 6.3	1615 1.2	2149 6.2	**25** W	0436 1.2	1008 6.5	1657 1.0	2231 6.3
11 W	0430 1.4	1000 6.4	1654 1.1	2228 6.2	**26** TH	0513 1.3	1044 6.4	1732 1.1	2304 6.2
12 TH	0509 1.3	1040 6.4	1732 1.1	2308 6.2	**27** F	0546 1.4	1117 6.3	1804 1.3	2336 6.0
13 F	0548 1.3	1119 6.3	1811 1.1	2348 6.1	**28** SA	0619 1.6	1149 6.0	1834 1.6	
14 SA	0629 1.5	1159 6.2	1852 1.3		**29** SU	0005 5.8	0650 1.9	1219 5.7	1905 1.9
15 SU	0030 5.9	0713 1.7	1242 5.9	1937 1.6	**30** M	0035 5.8	0725 2.2	1252 5.3	1940 2.3
					31 TU	0111 5.2	0806 2.6	1334 5.0	2023 2.6

FEBRUARY

Day					Day				
1 W	0201 4.9	0902 2.8	1437 4.7	2126 2.9	**16** TH	0252 5.2	0951 2.4	1542 5.0	2235 2.6
2 TH	0318 4.7	1024 2.9	1613 4.6	2256 2.9	**17** F	0428 5.1	1125 2.4	1721 5.0	
3 F	0456 4.8	1153 2.8	1743 4.8		**18** SA	0008 2.4	0552 5.3	1248 2.1	1837 5.3
4 SA	0020 2.7	0608 5.1	1300 2.4	1843 5.1	**19** SU	0120 2.1	0658 5.7	1351 1.7	1934 5.7
5 SU	0121 2.4	0701 5.4	1351 2.0	1931 5.5	**20** M	0216 1.7	0750 6.0	1441 1.4	2020 6.0
6 M	0209 2.0	0746 5.8	1436 1.6	2014 5.9	**21** TU ●	0302 1.5	0834 6.3	1524 1.1	2059 6.2
7 TU ○	0252 1.6	0827 6.2	1517 1.2	2054 6.1	**22** W	0341 1.3	0913 6.4	1600 1.0	2134 6.3
8 W	0334 1.3	0907 6.4	1558 0.9	2134 6.3	**23** TH	0417 1.2	0947 6.5	1634 1.0	2206 6.3
9 TH	0414 1.0	0947 6.6	1637 0.7	2214 6.5	**24** F	0449 1.2	1020 6.4	1704 1.0	2235 6.2
10 F	0454 0.9	1026 6.7	1716 0.7	2253 6.5	**25** SA	0519 1.3	1050 6.3	1733 1.2	2303 6.1
11 SA	0533 0.9	1105 6.6	1754 0.8	2331 6.4	**26** SU	0548 1.4	1118 6.0	1801 1.5	2329 5.9
12 SU	0612 1.0	1144 6.4	1834 1.0		**27** M	0617 1.7	1145 5.7	1829 1.8	2354 5.6
13 M	0010 6.2	0654 1.3	1224 6.1	1916 1.4	**28** TU	0647 2.0	1212 5.4	1900 2.1	
14 TU ◐	0050 5.9	0740 1.7	1310 5.7	2005 1.9	**29** W	0024 5.3	0722 2.3	1248 5.1	1937 2.5
15 W	0141 5.5	0836 2.1	1411 5.2	2108 2.3					

MARCH

Day					Day				
1 TH ◐	0103 5.0	0808 2.6	1340 4.7	2030 2.8	**16** F	0233 5.1	0937 2.4	1534 4.8	2225 2.7
2 F	0210 4.7	0919 2.9	1511 4.5	2155 3.0	**17** SA	0412 5.0	1114 2.4	1715 4.9	2358 2.5
3 SA	0358 4.6	1058 2.8	1704 4.6	2336 2.8	**18** SU	0538 5.2	1235 2.1	1826 5.3	
4 SU	0531 4.9	1221 2.5	1813 5.0		**19** M	0107 2.2	0642 5.5	1335 1.8	1917 5.6
5 M	0048 2.4	0631 5.3	1320 2.0	1904 5.4	**20** TU	0200 1.8	0731 5.9	1422 1.5	1958 5.9
6 TU	0141 1.9	0719 5.7	1408 1.5	1948 5.9	**21** W	0242 1.5	0809 6.1	1501 1.3	2034 6.1
7 W	0227 1.5	0803 6.2	1452 1.1	2031 6.2	**22** TH ●	0319 1.3	0849 6.3	1535 1.1	2107 6.2
8 TH ○	0311 1.1	0846 6.5	1534 0.7	2113 6.5	**23** F	0352 1.2	0923 6.3	1606 1.1	2137 6.2
9 F	0353 0.6	0928 6.7	1615 0.5	2153 6.7	**24** SA	0423 1.2	0954 6.3	1635 1.2	2206 6.2
10 SA	0434 0.6	1009 6.8	1655 0.5	2233 6.7	**25** SU	0452 1.2	1022 6.2	1703 1.3	2232 6.1
11 SU	0514 0.6	1049 6.7	1735 0.6	2311 6.6	**26** M	0520 1.4	1050 6.0	1731 1.5	2257 5.9
12 M	0555 0.8	1128 6.5	1815 1.0	2350 6.3	**27** TU	0548 1.6	1117 5.8	1759 1.8	2324 5.7
13 TU	0637 1.1	1209 6.1	1858 1.6		**28** W	0618 1.8	1146 5.5	1829 2.1	2354 5.4
14 W	0031 5.9	0723 1.6	1256 5.6	1948 2.0	**29** TH	0652 2.1	1221 5.1	1906 2.4	
15 TH ◐	0121 5.5	0820 2.0	1358 5.1	2053 2.5	**30** F ◐	0032 5.1	0735 2.4	1310 4.8	1956 2.7
					31 SA	0128 4.8	0838 2.7	1428 4.6	2113 2.9

APRIL

Day					Day				
1 SU	0303 4.6	1007 2.7	1615 4.6	2249 2.8	**16** M	0507 5.1	1203 2.2	1754 5.2	
2 M	0441 4.8	1134 2.4	1733 5.0		**17** TU	0037 2.2	0610 5.4	1301 1.9	1845 5.5
3 TU	0007 2.4	0550 5.2	1240 2.0	1828 5.4	**18** W	0130 1.9	0700 5.6	1349 1.7	1926 5.7
4 W	0106 1.9	0643 5.7	1333 1.5	1916 5.9	**19** TH	0213 1.7	0743 5.8	1429 1.5	2003 5.9
5 TH	0156 1.4	0732 6.1	1421 1.1	2002 6.3	**20** F	0251 1.5	0821 6.0	1504 1.4	2037 6.0
6 F ○	0243 1.0	0819 6.5	1507 0.7	2046 6.5	**21** SA ●	0325 1.4	0856 6.1	1536 1.4	2109 6.1
7 SA	0329 0.7	0904 6.7	1551 0.6	2129 6.7	**22** SU	0356 1.4	0928 6.0	1607 1.4	2137 6.1
8 SU	0412 0.6	0949 6.8	1634 0.5	2211 6.7	**23** M	0426 1.4	0958 6.0	1636 1.5	2205 6.0
9 M	0455 0.5	1032 6.7	1716 0.7	2252 6.6	**24** TU	0456 1.4	1027 5.9	1706 1.6	2233 5.9
10 TU	0539 0.7	1115 6.5	1759 1.0	2333 6.4	**25** W	0526 1.6	1057 5.7	1736 1.8	2304 5.8
11 W	0623 1.0	1159 6.1	1845 1.5		**26** TH	0558 1.7	1130 5.5	1809 2.0	2339 5.5
12 TH	0017 6.0	0712 1.5	1248 5.6	1937 2.0	**27** F	0633 1.9	1209 5.3	1847 2.3	
13 F ◐	0108 5.5	0809 2.0	1351 5.1	2043 2.5	**28** SA	0019 5.3	0717 2.2	1256 5.0	1938 2.5
14 SA	0217 5.1	0923 2.3	1518 4.9	2208 2.7	**29** SU ◐	0112 5.0	0814 2.4	1401 4.8	2046 2.7
15 SU	0347 5.0	1049 2.3	1647 4.9	2331 2.5	**30** M	0225 4.9	0928 2.4	1525 4.8	2207 2.6

Chart Datum: 3·33 metres below IGN Datum
HAT is 7·0 metres above Chart Datum

TIDES

TIDES

TIME ZONE -0100
(French Standard Time)
Subtract 1 hour for UT
For French Summer Time add
ONE hour in **non-shaded areas**

FRANCE – CHERBOURG
LAT 49°39'N   LONG 1°38'W
TIMES AND HEIGHTS OF HIGH AND LOW WATERS

Dates in amber are **SPRINGS**
Dates in yellow are **NEAPS**

2012

MAY				JUNE				JULY				AUGUST			
Time	m	Time	m	Time	m	Time	m	Time	m	Time	m	Time	m	Time	m

MAY

1 TU 0348 4.9 / 1047 2.3 / 1644 5.0 / 2323 2.3
16 W 0523 5.2 / 1214 2.1 / 1800 5.3

2 W 0501 5.2 / 1156 1.9 / 1746 5.4
17 TH 0048 2.2 / 0620 5.3 / 1306 2.0 / 1848 5.5

3 TH 0027 1.9 / 0602 5.6 / 1255 1.5 / 1839 5.8
18 F 0137 2.0 / 0708 5.5 / 1352 1.8 / 1929 5.7

4 F 0123 1.5 / 0658 6.0 / 1349 1.2 / 1929 6.2
19 SA 0219 1.8 / 0751 5.7 / 1431 1.7 / 2007 5.8

5 SA 0215 1.1 / 0751 6.3 / 1439 0.9 / 2018 6.5
20 SU 0257 1.6 / 0830 5.8 / 1507 1.7 / 2042 5.9

6 SU 0304 0.8 / 0841 6.5 / 1527 0.8 / ○ 2105 6.7
21 M 0331 1.5 / 0905 5.8 / ● 1541 1.6 / 2114 6.0

7 M 0352 0.7 / 0930 6.6 / 1614 0.8 / 2150 6.7
22 TU 0404 1.5 / 0937 5.8 / 1614 1.6 / 2145 6.0

8 TU 0439 0.6 / 1017 6.6 / 1700 0.9 / 2235 6.6
23 W 0437 1.5 / 1009 5.8 / 1647 1.7 / 2217 5.9

9 W 0526 0.8 / 1104 6.3 / 1746 1.2 / 2320 6.4
24 TH 0510 1.5 / 1043 5.7 / 1721 1.8 / 2252 5.8

10 TH 0613 1.0 / 1150 6.0 / 1834 1.6
25 F 0545 1.6 / 1120 5.6 / 1756 1.9 / 2329 5.7

11 F 0006 6.0 / 0702 1.4 / 1250 5.6 / 1926 2.0
26 SA 0622 1.7 / 1200 5.4 / 1836 2.1

12 SA 0057 5.6 / 0756 1.8 / 1336 5.3 / ◑ 2026 2.3
27 SU 0011 5.5 / 0704 1.9 / 1245 5.3 / 1924 2.2

13 SU 0156 5.3 / 0858 2.1 / 1444 5.0 / 2136 2.5
28 M 0058 5.3 / 0755 2.0 / 1339 5.1 / ◓ 2023 2.4

14 M 0307 5.1 / 1007 2.3 / 1557 5.0 / 2247 2.5
29 TU 0155 5.2 / 0855 2.1 / 1443 5.1 / 2130 2.4

15 TU 0419 5.0 / 1114 2.3 / 1704 5.1 / 2352 2.4
30 W 0302 5.2 / 1004 2.1 / 1555 5.2 / 2241 2.2

31 TH 0414 5.3 / 1114 1.9 / 1703 5.4 / 2349 2.0

JUNE

1 F 0524 5.5 / 1220 1.7 / 1804 5.7
16 SA 0058 2.3 / 0633 5.2 / 1314 2.2 / 1856 5.4

2 SA 0052 1.6 / 0628 5.8 / 1320 1.4 / 1901 6.1
17 SU 0147 2.0 / 0723 5.4 / 1401 2.0 / 1940 5.6

3 SU 0150 1.3 / 0727 6.1 / 1416 1.2 / 1954 6.3
18 M 0230 1.8 / 0806 5.6 / 1442 1.9 / 2019 5.8

4 M 0245 1.0 / 0824 6.3 / 1508 1.0 / ○ 2045 6.5
19 TU 0309 1.7 / 0845 5.7 / 1520 1.8 / ● 2054 5.9

5 TU 0337 0.8 / 0916 6.4 / 1559 1.0 / 2135 6.6
20 W 0345 1.5 / 0921 5.8 / 1556 1.7 / 2129 6.0

6 W 0427 0.7 / 1006 6.4 / 1647 1.1 / 2222 6.5
21 TH 0421 1.4 / 0955 5.8 / 1632 1.6 / 2203 6.0

7 TH 0515 0.8 / 1054 6.3 / 1735 1.2 / 2309 6.4
22 F 0457 1.4 / 1031 5.9 / 1708 1.6 / 2240 6.0

8 F 0601 1.0 / 1139 6.1 / 1821 1.5 / 2354 6.1
23 SA 0533 1.4 / 1109 5.8 / 1746 1.7 / 2319 6.0

9 SA 0648 1.3 / 1224 5.8 / 1909 1.8
24 SU 0610 1.4 / 1149 5.7 / 1825 1.7 / 2359 5.8

10 SU 0039 5.8 / 0734 1.6 / 1310 5.5 / 1958 2.1
25 M 0650 1.5 / 1230 5.6 / 1909 1.9

11 M 0127 5.5 / 0823 1.9 / 1400 5.2 / ◑ 2052 2.4
26 TU 0041 5.7 / 0735 1.7 / 1315 5.5 / 1959 2.0

12 TU 0221 5.2 / 0916 2.2 / 1458 5.0 / 2153 2.5
27 W 0129 5.5 / 0826 1.8 / 1408 5.3 / ◑ 2058 2.2

13 W 0322 5.0 / 1016 2.4 / 1602 5.0 / 2258 2.6
28 TH 0226 5.3 / 0928 2.0 / 1512 5.1 / 2205 2.2

14 TH 0429 4.9 / 1120 2.4 / 1708 5.1
29 F 0336 5.3 / 1039 2.0 / 1626 5.4 / 2318 2.1

15 F 0002 2.4 / 0535 5.0 / 1220 2.3 / 1806 5.2
30 SA 0455 5.4 / 1151 1.9 / 1737 5.6

JULY

1 SU 0029 1.8 / 0609 5.6 / 1259 1.7 / 1841 5.9
16 M 0118 2.3 / 0658 5.2 / 1334 2.3 / 1915 5.5

2 M 0133 1.5 / 0715 5.8 / 1400 1.5 / 1939 6.2
17 TU 0205 2.0 / 0744 5.4 / 1419 2.0 / 1957 5.7

3 TU 0232 1.2 / 0814 6.1 / 1456 1.3 / ○ 2033 6.4
18 W 0247 1.7 / 0825 5.7 / 1500 1.8 / 2036 5.9

4 W 0326 1.0 / 0907 6.3 / 1547 1.2 / 2124 6.5
19 TH 0326 1.5 / 0903 5.8 / ● 1538 1.6 / 2113 6.1

5 TH 0416 0.8 / 0956 6.3 / 1635 1.1 / 2211 6.5
20 F 0403 1.3 / 0940 6.0 / 1616 1.4 / 2149 6.2

6 F 0502 0.8 / 1040 6.3 / 1720 1.2 / 2254 6.5
21 SA 0441 1.1 / 1016 6.1 / 1653 1.3 / 2226 6.3

7 SA 0545 0.9 / 1121 6.2 / 1802 1.4 / 2335 6.3
22 SU 0517 1.1 / 1054 6.1 / 1731 1.3 / 2304 6.2

8 SU 0625 1.2 / 1200 6.0 / 1842 1.6
23 M 0554 1.1 / 1132 6.0 / 1809 1.4 / 2343 6.1

9 M 0014 6.0 / 0703 1.5 / 1237 5.7 / 1922 1.9
24 TU 0632 1.2 / 1211 5.9 / 1850 1.5

10 TU 0053 5.7 / 0741 1.8 / 1315 5.4 / 2004 2.2
25 W 0022 5.9 / 0713 1.4 / 1251 5.7 / 1935 1.8

11 W 0134 5.3 / 0823 2.2 / 1359 5.1 / ◑ 2055 2.5
26 TH 0105 5.7 / 0800 1.7 / 1338 5.5 / ◑ 2029 2.0

12 TH 0224 5.0 / 0910 2.5 / 1456 4.9 / 2158 2.7
27 F 0159 5.4 / 0858 2.0 / 1438 5.3 / 2136 2.2

13 F 0330 4.8 / 1020 2.7 / 1609 4.9 / 2312 2.7
28 SA 0311 5.2 / 1011 2.2 / 1559 5.3 / 2257 2.2

14 SA 0449 4.7 / 1134 2.7 / 1725 5.0
29 SU 0442 5.2 / 1134 2.2 / 1722 5.4

15 SU 0021 2.5 / 0601 4.9 / 1240 2.5 / 1826 5.2
30 M 0016 2.0 / 0603 5.4 / 1249 2.0 / 1832 5.7

31 TU 0125 1.7 / 0711 5.7 / 1352 1.7 / 1932 6.1

AUGUST

1 W 0224 1.3 / 0808 6.0 / 1447 1.4 / 2025 6.3
16 TH 0222 1.7 / 0802 5.7 / 1437 1.7 / 2013 6.0

2 TH 0316 1.0 / 0858 6.2 / 1536 1.2 / ○ 2112 6.5
17 F 0302 1.4 / 0841 6.0 / 1516 1.4 / ○ 2052 6.3

3 F 0402 0.9 / 0941 6.3 / 1620 1.1 / 2155 6.6
18 SA 0341 1.1 / 0919 6.2 / 1555 1.2 / 2130 6.4

4 SA 0443 0.8 / 1020 6.3 / 1659 1.1 / 2233 6.5
19 SU 0419 0.9 / 0956 6.3 / 1633 1.1 / 2207 6.5

5 SU 0521 0.9 / 1055 6.2 / 1736 1.3 / 2309 6.4
20 M 0456 0.8 / 1034 6.4 / 1711 1.0 / 2245 6.5

6 M 0555 1.1 / 1128 6.1 / 1810 1.5 / 2343 6.1
21 TU 0533 0.9 / 1111 6.3 / 1749 1.1 / 2324 6.4

7 TU 0627 1.4 / 1159 5.8 / 1843 1.8
22 W 0611 1.1 / 1148 6.2 / 1829 1.3

8 W 0015 5.8 / 0659 1.8 / 1230 5.6 / 1918 2.1
23 TH 0002 6.1 / 0651 1.4 / 1227 5.9 / 1913 1.6

9 TH 0048 5.4 / 0733 2.2 / 1304 5.2 / ◑ 1959 2.5
24 F 0046 5.8 / 0737 1.8 / 1313 5.6 / ◓ 2006 2.0

10 F 0128 5.0 / 0815 2.5 / 1349 4.9 / 2054 2.8
25 SA 0140 5.4 / 0836 2.2 / 1415 5.3 / 2116 2.3

11 SA 0227 4.7 / 0916 2.8 / 1502 4.7 / 2215 2.9
26 SU 0300 5.1 / 0956 2.5 / 1545 5.1 / 2247 2.4

12 SU 0400 4.5 / 1043 2.9 / 1641 4.7 / 2342 2.8
27 M 0442 5.0 / 1128 2.5 / 1716 5.3

13 M 0531 4.7 / 1206 2.8 / 1756 5.0
28 TU 0012 2.1 / 0604 5.3 / 1245 2.1 / 1827 5.7

14 TU 0048 2.4 / 0633 5.0 / 1307 2.4 / 1849 5.3
29 W 0119 1.7 / 0707 5.7 / 1345 1.8 / 1924 6.0

15 W 0139 2.1 / 0720 5.4 / 1355 2.1 / 1933 5.7
30 TH 0214 1.4 / 0757 6.0 / 1436 1.5 / 2012 6.3

31 F 0301 1.1 / 0840 6.2 / 1520 1.3 / ○ 2054 6.5

Chart Datum: 3·33 metres below IGN Datum
HAT is 7·0 metres above Chart Datum

TIME ZONE -0100
(French Standard Time)
Subtract 1 hour for UT
For French Summer Time add
ONE hour in **non-shaded areas**

FRANCE – CHERBOURG

LAT 49°39'N   LONG 1°38'W

TIMES AND HEIGHTS OF HIGH AND LOW WATERS

Dates in amber are **SPRINGS**
Dates in yellow are **NEAPS**

2012

SEPTEMBER

Day	Time m	Time m	Time m	Time m		Day	Time m	Time m	Time m	Time m
1 SA	0342 1.0	0918 6.3	1558 1.2	2132 6.6		16 SU	0313 1.0	0852 6.4	1529 1.0	●2105 6.6
2 SU	0418 1.0	0953 6.4	1633 1.2	2207 6.5		17 M	0352 0.8	0931 6.6	1609 0.9	2145 6.7
3 M	0451 1.0	1024 6.3	1706 1.3	2239 6.3		18 TU	0432 0.7	1009 6.6	1649 0.8	2224 6.7
4 TU	0522 1.2	1054 6.1	1736 1.5	2309 6.1		19 W	0510 0.8	1047 6.6	1729 0.9	2304 6.5
5 W	0551 1.5	1121 5.9	1806 1.7	2338 5.8		20 TH	0550 1.1	1126 6.4	1810 1.2	2346 6.2
6 TH	0620 1.8	1147 5.7	1837 2.0			21 F	0632 1.5	1207 6.1	1856 1.6	
7 F	0007 5.4	0651 2.2	1217 5.4	1913 2.4		22 SA	0032 5.8	0721 1.9	1255 5.7	◐1951 2.0
8 SA	0041 5.1	0728 2.6	1256 5.0	◐1959 2.7		23 SU	0130 5.3	0823 2.4	1400 5.3	2105 2.4
9 SU	0133 4.7	0820 2.9	1358 4.7	2112 3.0		24 M	0257 5.0	0949 2.7	1534 5.1	2240 2.4
10 M	0302 4.5	0946 3.1	1544 4.6	2253 2.9		25 TU	0439 5.0	1123 2.6	1705 5.3	
11 TU	0454 4.6	1126 2.9	1718 4.9			26 W	0003 2.2	0555 5.3	1223 2.3	1813 5.6
12 W	0011 2.6	0601 5.0	1234 2.5	1816 5.3		27 TH	0105 1.8	0651 5.7	1331 1.9	1906 6.0
13 TH	0105 2.1	0649 5.4	1324 2.1	1902 5.7		28 F	0155 1.5	0736 6.0	1417 1.6	1951 6.2
14 F	0150 1.7	0732 5.8	1408 1.7	1944 6.1		29 SA	0238 1.3	0815 6.2	1457 1.4	2030 6.4
15 SA	0232 1.3	0812 6.1	1449 1.3	2025 6.4		30 SU	0315 1.2	0850 6.3	1533 1.3	○2106 6.4

OCTOBER

Day	Time m	Time m	Time m	Time m		Day	Time m	Time m	Time m	Time m
1 M	0349 1.2	0922 6.3	1606 1.3	2138 6.4		16 TU	0325 0.8	0902 6.7	1546 0.8	2121 6.8
2 TU	0420 1.3	0952 6.3	1636 1.4	2209 6.3		17 W	0408 0.8	0944 6.8	1628 0.8	2204 6.7
3 W	0450 1.4	1020 6.2	1706 1.5	2238 6.1		18 TH	0450 0.9	1025 6.7	1711 0.9	2248 6.6
4 TH	0519 1.6	1046 6.0	1735 1.7	2305 5.8		19 F	0533 1.2	1107 6.5	1756 1.1	2333 6.2
5 F	0547 1.9	1112 5.8	1805 2.0	2334 5.5		20 SA	0619 1.6	1152 6.2	1845 1.5	
6 SA	0618 2.2	1143 5.5	1839 2.3			21 SU	0023 5.8	0710 2.0	1242 5.8	1941 2.0
7 SU	0009 5.2	0653 2.6	1219 5.2	1921 2.6		22 M	0123 5.4	0814 2.5	1347 5.4	◐2054 2.3
8 M	0057 4.8	0741 2.9	1316 4.9	◐2021 2.9		23 TU	0246 5.1	0937 2.7	1513 5.2	2221 2.4
9 TU	0213 4.6	0855 3.1	1444 4.7	2152 2.9		24 W	0416 5.1	1102 2.6	1638 5.2	2337 2.2
10 W	0359 4.6	1033 3.0	1623 4.8	2321 2.6		25 TH	0527 5.3	1210 2.3	1744 5.5	
11 TH	0517 5.0	1150 2.6	1731 5.2			26 F	0038 2.0	0621 5.6	1305 2.0	1837 5.8
12 F	0023 2.2	0610 5.4	1246 2.2	1823 5.6		27 SA	0127 1.7	0706 5.9	1351 1.8	1922 6.0
13 SA	0113 1.7	0655 5.8	1334 1.7	1909 6.1		28 SU	0209 1.6	0745 6.1	1431 1.6	2002 6.2
14 SU	0159 1.3	0738 6.2	1419 1.3	1954 6.4		29 M	0246 1.5	0820 6.2	1506 1.5	○2038 6.2
15 M	0242 1.0	0821 6.5	1502 1.0	●2037 6.7		30 TU	0320 1.5	0853 6.2	1539 1.5	2112 6.2
						31 W	0352 1.5	0923 6.2	1611 1.5	2143 6.1

NOVEMBER

Day	Time m	Time m	Time m	Time m		Day	Time m	Time m	Time m	Time m
1 TH	0423 1.6	0951 6.1	1641 1.6	2212 6.0		16 F	0434 1.0	1008 6.8	1658 0.8	2236 6.5
2 F	0453 1.8	1019 6.0	1712 1.7	2241 5.8		17 SA	0520 1.2	1053 6.6	1746 1.1	2324 6.3
3 SA	0523 2.0	1048 5.8	1743 1.9	2313 5.6		18 SU	0609 1.5	1140 6.3	1835 1.4	
4 SU	0555 2.2	1121 5.6	1816 2.1	2350 5.3		19 M	0014 5.9	0700 1.9	1231 5.9	1930 1.8
5 M	0631 2.4	1200 5.4	1856 2.4			20 TU	0110 5.5	0759 2.3	1329 5.6	◐2031 2.1
6 TU	0035 5.1	0716 2.7	1250 5.1	1948 2.6		21 W	0216 5.2	0907 2.6	1437 5.3	2141 2.3
7 W	0137 4.9	0818 2.9	1358 4.9	◐2059 2.7		22 TH	0329 5.1	1021 2.6	1551 5.2	2253 2.4
8 TH	0258 4.8	0938 2.9	1520 4.9	2221 2.6		23 F	0439 5.2	1130 2.5	1700 5.3	2356 2.3
9 F	0419 5.0	1057 2.6	1635 5.2	2333 2.3		24 SA	0539 5.4	1229 2.3	1759 5.4	
10 SA	0522 5.4	1203 2.2	1737 5.5			25 SU	0050 2.1	0629 5.6	1319 2.1	1850 5.6
11 SU	0032 1.9	0615 5.8	1258 1.8	1831 5.9		26 M	0136 2.0	0712 5.8	1403 1.9	1934 5.8
12 M	0124 1.5	0703 6.2	1349 1.4	1922 6.3		27 TU	0217 1.8	0751 6.0	1441 1.7	2013 5.9
13 TU	0213 1.2	0750 6.5	1437 1.1	●2012 6.6		28 W	0254 1.8	0827 6.1	1517 1.6	○2049 6.0
14 W	0301 1.0	0836 6.7	1525 0.9	2100 6.6		29 TH	0329 1.7	0900 6.1	1550 1.6	2122 6.0
15 TH	0348 0.9	0922 6.8	1611 0.8	2148 6.7		30 F	0402 1.7	0930 6.1	1622 1.6	2153 6.0

DECEMBER

Day	Time m	Time m	Time m	Time m		Day	Time m	Time m	Time m	Time m
1 SA	0434 1.8	1001 6.1	1655 1.6	2225 5.9		16 SU	0510 1.1	1043 6.7	1736 0.9	2314 6.4
2 SU	0507 1.9	1033 6.0	1728 1.7	2259 5.7		17 M	0557 1.4	1129 6.4	1823 1.2	
3 M	0540 2.0	1108 5.8	1802 1.8	2336 5.6		18 TU	0000 6.1	0644 1.7	1215 6.1	1909 1.5
4 TU	0616 2.2	1146 5.6	1840 2.0			19 W	0046 5.8	0733 2.0	1302 5.8	1957 1.9
5 W	0018 5.4	0658 2.3	1229 5.4	1924 2.2		20 TH	0134 5.4	0824 2.4	1353 5.4	◑2049 2.2
6 TH	0107 5.2	0749 2.5	1321 5.3	◑2019 2.3		21 F	0230 5.2	0924 2.6	1453 5.1	2150 2.5
7 F	0208 5.1	0852 2.6	1425 5.2	2126 2.4		22 SA	0335 5.1	1033 2.7	1603 5.0	2259 2.6
8 SA	0318 5.1	1004 2.5	1538 5.2	2240 2.3		23 SU	0444 5.1	1142 2.6	1714 5.0	
9 SU	0430 5.3	1117 2.3	1651 5.4	2350 2.0		24 M	0005 2.5	0548 5.2	1244 2.4	1817 5.2
10 M	0534 5.6	1223 2.0	1757 5.6			25 TU	0102 2.4	0641 5.5	1335 2.2	1908 5.4
11 TU	0052 1.7	0632 6.0	1322 1.6	1857 6.1		26 W	0151 2.2	0726 5.7	1419 1.9	1952 5.7
12 W	0149 1.4	0725 6.3	1417 1.2	1953 6.3		27 TH	0233 2.0	0806 5.9	1457 1.7	2031 5.8
13 TH	0242 1.2	0817 6.6	1509 0.9	●2047 6.5		28 F	0310 1.8	0842 6.0	1533 1.6	○2106 5.9
14 F	0333 1.0	0907 6.7	1600 0.8	2138 6.6		29 SA	0345 1.7	0915 6.1	1607 1.5	2139 6.0
15 SA	0422 1.0	0956 6.8	1648 0.8	2227 6.5		30 SU	0419 1.7	0947 6.2	1641 1.4	2211 6.0
						31 M	0453 1.8	1021 6.2	1714 1.4	2246 5.9

Chart Datum: 3·33 metres below IGN Datum
HAT is 7·0 metres above Chart Datum

TIDES

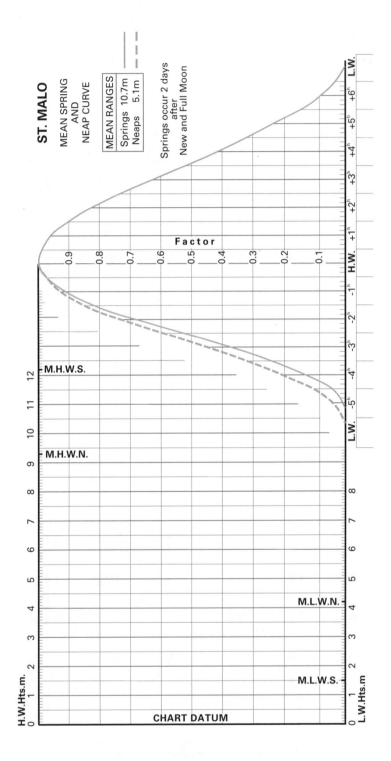

ST. MALO

MEAN SPRING
AND
NEAP CURVE

MEAN RANGES	
Springs	10.7m
Neaps	5.1m

Springs occur 2 days
after
New and Full Moon

Factor

TIME ZONE -0100
(French Standard Time)
Subtract 1 hour for UT
For French Summer Time add
ONE hour in **non-shaded areas**

FRANCE – ST MALO

LAT 48°38'N   LONG 2°02'W

TIMES AND HEIGHTS OF HIGH AND LOW WATERS

Dates in amber are **SPRINGS**
Dates in yellow are **NEAPS**

2012

JANUARY

Time m	Time m
1 0614 4.1 / 1148 9.5 / SU 1838 4.2 ◔	**16** 0613 3.0 / 1143 10.6 / M 1839 3.2
2 0013 9.2 / 0658 4.6 / M 1240 9.0 / 1928 4.6	**17** 0014 10.1 / 0705 3.6 / TU 1241 10.0 / 1938 3.7
3 0114 8.8 / 0803 4.9 / TU 1355 8.6 / 2040 4.8	**18** 0122 9.6 / 0815 3.9 / W 1359 9.6 / 2057 4.0
4 0238 8.8 / 0925 4.8 / W 1519 8.8 / 2159 4.6	**19** 0249 9.6 / 0941 3.8 / TH 1530 9.6 / 2223 3.7
5 0352 9.2 / 1037 4.4 / TH 1626 9.2 / 2304 4.1	**20** 0411 10.0 / 1103 3.3 / F 1647 10.1 / 2340 3.1
6 0449 9.8 / 1134 3.8 / F 1718 9.8 / 2357 3.5	**21** 0519 10.7 / 1213 2.6 / SA 1750 10.8
7 0536 10.4 / 1224 3.2 / SA 1803 10.4	**22** 0044 2.5 / 0614 11.4 / SU 1313 2.0 / 1842 11.4
8 0045 2.9 / 0619 11.0 / SU 1310 2.7 / 1845 10.9	**23** 0138 2.0 / 0702 11.9 / M 1404 1.6 / 1928 11.8 ●
9 0129 2.5 / 0659 11.4 / M 1354 2.2 / 1925 11.3 ○	**24** 0224 1.6 / 0745 12.3 / TU 1448 1.3 / 2009 12.0
10 0212 2.1 / 0738 11.8 / TU 1437 1.9 / 2004 11.6	**25** 0305 1.5 / 0824 12.4 / W 1527 1.3 / 2045 12.0
11 0254 1.9 / 0817 12.1 / W 1519 1.7 / 2042 11.8	**26** 0340 1.6 / 0900 12.2 / TH 1601 1.5 / 2119 11.8
12 0334 1.7 / 0856 12.2 / TH 1558 1.6 / 2121 11.8	**27** 0412 1.9 / 0932 11.9 / F 1630 1.9 / 2149 11.4
13 0413 1.8 / 0935 12.1 / F 1637 1.8 / 2200 11.6	**28** 0439 2.4 / 1002 11.3 / SA 1656 2.5 / 2218 10.9
14 0451 2.0 / 1014 11.8 / SA 1714 2.1 / 2239 11.2	**29** 0503 3.0 / 1031 10.7 / SU 1720 3.2 / 2247 10.3
15 0530 2.5 / 1056 11.2 / SU 1753 2.6 / 2322 10.6	**30** 0527 3.7 / 1100 9.9 / M 1746 3.9 / 2317 9.6
	31 0558 4.3 / 1134 9.2 / TU 1822 4.5 / 2358 9.0 ◑

FEBRUARY

Time m	Time m
1 0645 4.9 / 1229 8.5 / W 1919 5.0	**16** 0051 9.4 / 0749 4.1 / TH 1336 9.1 / 2033 4.4 ◑
2 0111 8.4 / 0802 5.2 / TH 1412 8.2 / 2051 5.1	**17** 0230 9.1 / 0924 4.2 / F 1521 9.1 / 2212 4.2
3 0302 8.5 / 0946 5.0 / F 1551 8.6 / 2224 4.7	**18** 0404 9.6 / 1056 3.6 / SA 1643 9.8 / 2334 3.4
4 0418 9.1 / 1101 4.2 / SA 1654 9.3 / 2329 3.9	**19** 0511 10.4 / 1207 2.8 / SU 1742 10.6
5 0513 10.0 / 1159 3.4 / SU 1743 10.1	**20** 0035 2.6 / 0603 11.2 / M 1302 2.1 / 1829 11.2
6 0022 3.1 / 0559 10.8 / M 1250 2.6 / 1828 10.9	**21** 0125 2.0 / 0647 11.8 / TU 1349 1.6 / 1910 11.7 ●
7 0111 2.4 / 0643 11.5 / TU 1339 2.0 / 1909 11.5 ○	**22** 0208 1.6 / 0727 12.2 / W 1429 1.4 / 1947 12.0
8 0158 1.8 / 0724 12.1 / W 1425 1.5 / 1950 12.0	**23** 0244 1.5 / 0803 12.3 / TH 1503 1.3 / 2021 12.1
9 0242 1.3 / 0803 12.6 / TH 1508 1.1 / 2029 12.4	**24** 0316 1.5 / 0835 12.3 / F 1533 1.5 / 2051 12.0
10 0324 1.1 / 0843 12.8 / F 1548 0.9 / 2107 12.5	**25** 0344 1.7 / 0905 12.0 / SA 1600 1.8 / 2118 11.7
11 0403 1.0 / 0921 12.7 / SA 1625 1.1 / 2144 12.3	**26** 0409 2.1 / 0932 11.5 / SU 1623 2.3 / 2145 11.2
12 0439 1.3 / 0959 12.3 / SU 1700 1.6 / 2221 11.8	**27** 0430 2.7 / 0957 10.9 / M 1644 2.9 / 2209 10.6
13 0515 1.9 / 1037 11.7 / M 1735 2.3 / 2300 11.0	**28** 0451 3.3 / 1021 10.2 / TU 1707 3.6 / 2235 10.0
14 0553 2.7 / 1120 10.8 / TU 1815 3.1 / 2346 10.2 ◑	**29** 0517 3.9 / 1048 9.5 / W 1737 4.3 / 2306 9.3
15 0640 3.5 / 1214 9.8 / W 1910 3.9	

MARCH

Time m	Time m
1 0555 4.6 / 1128 8.7 / TH 1824 4.9 / 2359 8.6 ◔	**16** 0033 9.4 / 0733 4.1 / F 1323 8.9 / 2018 4.6
2 0657 5.1 / 1254 8.1 / F 1943 5.3	**17** 0214 9.0 / 0911 4.3 / SA 1510 9.0 / 2200 4.3
3 0156 8.2 / 0843 5.2 / SA 1509 8.3 / 2136 5.0	**18** 0348 9.4 / 1042 3.7 / SU 1628 9.6 / 2318 3.5
4 0342 8.8 / 1022 4.5 / SU 1623 9.1 / 2255 4.1	**19** 0452 10.2 / 1148 2.9 / M 1722 10.5
5 0443 9.7 / 1128 3.5 / M 1716 10.1 / 2354 3.2	**20** 0015 2.8 / 0541 11.0 / TU 1240 2.3 / 1806 11.1
6 0533 10.7 / 1224 2.6 / TU 1803 11.0	**21** 0101 2.2 / 0623 11.6 / W 1323 1.9 / 1845 11.6
7 0047 2.3 / 0619 11.6 / W 1316 1.8 / 1846 11.8	**22** 0141 1.9 / 0701 11.9 / TH 1400 1.7 / 1920 11.8 ●
8 0137 1.5 / 0702 12.4 / TH 1405 1.1 / 1928 12.4 ○	**23** 0216 1.7 / 0736 12.0 / F 1433 1.6 / 1952 11.9
9 0224 0.9 / 0744 12.9 / F 1449 0.7 / 2008 12.8	**24** 0247 1.7 / 0807 12.0 / SA 1502 1.7 / 2021 11.9
10 0307 0.6 / 0823 13.1 / SA 1530 0.6 / 2046 12.9	**25** 0314 1.8 / 0836 11.8 / SU 1528 1.9 / 2047 11.7
11 0346 0.6 / 0902 13.0 / SU 1608 0.8 / 2124 12.7	**26** 0339 2.1 / 0902 11.5 / M 1552 2.3 / 2113 11.4
12 0424 1.0 / 0941 12.6 / M 1643 1.4 / 2201 12.1	**27** 0402 2.5 / 0928 11.0 / TU 1614 2.8 / 2138 10.9
13 0500 1.6 / 1020 11.8 / TU 1718 2.2 / 2240 11.2	**28** 0424 3.0 / 0953 10.4 / W 1638 3.4 / 2205 10.3
14 0538 2.5 / 1103 10.7 / W 1757 3.2 / 2326 10.3	**29** 0451 3.6 / 1021 9.7 / TH 1709 4.0 / 2237 9.6
15 0625 3.4 / 1157 9.7 / TH 1852 4.1 ◑	**30** 0527 4.2 / 1100 9.0 / F 1752 4.6 / 2325 8.9 ◑
	31 0622 4.7 / 1210 8.4 / SA 1901 5.1

APRIL

Time m	Time m
1 0058 8.5 / 0750 4.9 / SU 1416 8.4 / 2044 5.0	**16** 0315 9.4 / 1008 3.8 / M 1556 9.5 / 2243 3.7
2 0252 8.8 / 0933 4.4 / M 1541 9.1 / 2212 4.2	**17** 0419 10.0 / 1112 3.2 / TU 1649 10.2 / 2339 3.1
3 0403 9.7 / 1048 3.5 / TU 1640 10.0 / 2317 3.2	**18** 0509 10.6 / 1203 2.7 / W 1733 10.8
4 0458 10.7 / 1149 2.6 / W 1730 11.0	**19** 0026 2.6 / 0552 11.1 / TH 1246 2.4 / 1813 11.2
5 0015 2.3 / 0547 11.6 / TH 1245 1.7 / 1816 11.9	**20** 0106 2.3 / 0631 11.4 / F 1324 2.2 / 1848 11.5
6 0108 1.5 / 0634 12.4 / F 1337 1.1 / 1900 12.5 ○	**21** 0142 2.1 / 0707 11.5 / SA 1358 2.1 / 1921 11.6 ●
7 0158 0.9 / 0719 12.9 / SA 1424 0.7 / 1942 12.9	**22** 0214 2.1 / 0739 11.6 / SU 1429 2.0 / 1951 11.7
8 0245 0.6 / 0801 13.1 / SU 1508 0.6 / 2023 13.0	**23** 0244 2.1 / 0808 11.5 / M 1457 2.2 / 2019 11.6
9 0327 0.5 / 0843 13.0 / M 1548 0.8 / 2104 12.8	**24** 0312 2.2 / 0837 11.3 / TU 1525 2.4 / 2047 11.4
10 0407 0.9 / 0924 12.5 / TU 1625 1.4 / 2144 12.2	**25** 0339 2.5 / 0905 11.0 / W 1552 2.7 / 2116 11.0
11 0446 1.5 / 1006 11.7 / W 1703 2.3 / 2226 11.3	**26** 0406 2.8 / 0935 10.5 / TH 1620 3.2 / 2147 10.6
12 0527 2.4 / 1052 10.7 / TH 1746 3.2 / 2314 10.4	**27** 0437 3.3 / 1008 10.0 / F 1653 3.7 / 2223 10.0
13 0615 3.3 / 1148 9.7 / F 1841 4.0 ◑	**28** 0514 3.8 / 1050 9.4 / SA 1737 4.2 / 2312 9.4
14 0020 9.5 / 0721 4.0 / SA 1306 9.0 / 2000 4.5	**29** 0606 4.2 / 1153 8.9 / SU 1838 4.6 ◑
15 0148 9.1 / 0846 4.2 / SU 1441 9.0 / 2130 4.3	**30** 0025 9.1 / 0717 4.4 / M 1324 8.8 / 2001 4.6

Chart Datum: 6·29 metres below IGN Datum
HAT is 13·6 metres above Chart Datum

TIDES

TIME ZONE -0100
(French Standard Time)
Subtract 1 hour for UT
For French Summer Time add
ONE hour in **non-shaded areas**

FRANCE – ST MALO
LAT 48°38'N   LONG 2°02'W
TIMES AND HEIGHTS OF HIGH AND LOW WATERS

Dates in amber are **SPRINGS**
Dates in yellow are **NEAPS**

2012

MAY

Time m	Time m
1 TU 0156 9.2 / 0844 4.1 / 1449 9.3 / 2125 4.1	**16** W 0334 9.6 / 1020 3.7 / 1606 9.8 / 2251 3.7
2 W 0314 9.8 / 1002 3.5 / 1556 10.1 / 2235 3.2	**17** TH 0430 10.0 / 1115 3.4 / 1655 10.3 / 2342 3.3
3 TH 0416 10.6 / 1109 2.7 / 1652 10.9 / 2338 2.4	**18** F 0517 10.4 / 1203 3.0 / 1738 10.7
4 F 0512 11.4 / 1210 1.9 / 1743 11.7	**19** SA 0027 2.9 / 0559 10.7 / 1245 2.7 / 1816 11.0
5 SA 0036 1.7 / 0604 12.1 / 1307 1.4 / 1831 12.3	**20** SU 0107 2.6 / 0637 11.0 / 1323 2.5 / 1851 11.3
6 SU 0131 1.1 / 0653 12.5 / 1358 1.0 / 1917 12.7 ○	**21** M 0143 2.5 / 0712 11.1 / 1359 2.4 / 1924 11.4 ●
7 M 0221 0.8 / 0741 12.7 / 1445 0.9 / 2002 12.8	**22** TU 0217 2.4 / 0745 11.1 / 1432 2.4 / 1956 11.4
8 TU 0308 0.8 / 0826 12.6 / 1529 1.1 / 2047 12.7	**23** W 0250 2.4 / 0817 11.1 / 1504 2.5 / 2028 11.4
9 W 0352 1.0 / 0911 12.2 / 1611 1.6 / 2130 12.2	**24** TH 0322 2.4 / 0850 11.0 / 1536 2.6 / 2101 11.2
10 TH 0435 1.5 / 0954 11.6 / 1653 2.2 / 2215 11.5	**25** F 0355 2.6 / 0924 10.8 / 1609 2.9 / 2137 10.9
11 F 0518 2.2 / 1041 10.8 / 1736 3.0 / 2304 10.7	**26** SA 0429 2.9 / 1002 10.4 / 1646 3.2 / 2216 10.5
12 SA 0605 3.0 / 1132 10.0 / 1827 3.7 ◐	**27** SU 0508 3.2 / 1045 10.0 / 1729 3.6 / 2303 10.1
13 SU 0000 9.9 / 0700 3.7 / 1235 9.4 / 1930 4.2	**28** M 0555 3.6 / 1137 9.6 / 1821 3.9 ◐
14 M 0108 9.4 / 0806 4.0 / 1351 9.1 / 2042 4.3	**29** TU 0001 9.8 / 0652 3.8 / 1243 9.4 / 1926 4.0
15 TU 0225 9.2 / 0916 4.0 / 1506 9.3 / 2152 4.1	**30** W 0111 9.7 / 0803 3.8 / 1357 9.6 / 2041 3.9
	31 TH 0224 9.9 / 0919 3.5 / 1509 10.0 / 2155 3.4

JUNE

Time m	Time m
1 F 0335 10.4 / 1031 3.0 / 1613 10.7 / 2303 2.7	**16** SA 0440 9.7 / 1120 3.7 / 1703 10.1 / 2348 3.5
2 SA 0438 11.0 / 1137 2.4 / 1712 11.4	**17** SU 0529 10.1 / 1209 3.3 / 1747 10.5
3 SU 0006 2.1 / 0538 11.5 / 1238 1.9 / 1807 11.9	**18** M 0034 3.1 / 0612 10.5 / 1253 3.0 / 1826 10.9
4 M 0106 1.5 / 0633 12.0 / 1335 1.5 / 1858 12.3 ○	**19** TU 0116 2.8 / 0651 10.8 / 1334 2.7 / 1903 11.2 ●
5 TU 0202 1.2 / 0725 12.2 / 1427 1.3 / 1947 12.5	**20** W 0155 2.5 / 0727 11.0 / 1412 2.5 / 1939 11.4
6 W 0253 1.0 / 0814 12.3 / 1514 1.4 / 2034 12.5	**21** TH 0233 2.4 / 0803 11.1 / 1449 2.4 / 2014 11.5
7 TH 0340 1.1 / 0901 12.1 / 1559 1.6 / 2119 12.2	**22** F 0310 2.3 / 0839 11.2 / 1525 2.4 / 2050 11.6
8 F 0424 1.5 / 0945 11.7 / 1641 2.1 / 2203 11.7	**23** SA 0347 2.3 / 0915 11.2 / 1602 2.4 / 2128 11.5
9 SA 0506 2.0 / 1027 11.1 / 1722 2.7 / 2246 11.1	**24** SU 0424 2.4 / 0953 11.0 / 1639 2.6 / 2207 11.2
10 SU 0548 2.7 / 1110 10.5 / 1804 3.3 / 2331 10.4	**25** M 0502 2.6 / 1034 10.7 / 1719 2.9 / 2249 10.8
11 M 0630 3.3 / 1156 9.8 / 1850 3.9 ◐	**26** TU 0543 3.0 / 1118 10.4 / 1803 3.3 / 2337 10.4
12 TU 0021 9.7 / 0717 3.9 / 1251 9.4 / 1944 4.3	**27** W 0629 3.3 / 1210 10.0 / 1856 3.6 ◐
13 W 0123 9.3 / 0814 4.2 / 1400 9.1 / 2050 4.5	**28** TH 0034 10.1 / 0727 3.6 / 1314 9.8 / 2002 3.7
14 TH 0235 9.1 / 0919 4.3 / 1511 9.3 / 2156 4.3	**29** F 0144 9.9 / 0839 3.6 / 1428 9.9 / 2119 3.6
15 F 0343 9.3 / 1023 4.0 / 1613 9.6 / 2257 3.9	**30** SA 0300 10.1 / 0957 3.4 / 1542 10.3 / 2235 3.1

JULY

Time m	Time m
1 SU 0415 10.4 / 1111 2.9 / 1651 10.9 / 2345 2.5	**16** M 0502 9.6 / 1139 3.8 / 1721 10.1
2 M 0521 11.0 / 1219 2.4 / 1752 11.5	**17** TU 0007 3.4 / 0549 10.2 / 1228 3.3 / 1805 10.7
3 TU 0050 2.0 / 0622 11.5 / 1319 1.9 / 1847 12.0 ○	**18** W 0053 2.9 / 0631 10.6 / 1313 2.8 / 1845 11.2
4 W 0148 1.5 / 0715 11.9 / 1414 1.6 / 1936 12.4	**19** TH 0137 2.5 / 0711 11.1 / 1355 2.4 / 1923 11.6 ●
5 TH 0241 1.2 / 0804 12.1 / 1502 1.5 / 2022 12.5	**20** F 0219 2.2 / 0748 11.4 / 1435 2.1 / 2000 11.9
6 F 0328 1.2 / 0848 12.1 / 1546 1.5 / 2104 12.4	**21** SA 0259 1.9 / 0825 11.6 / 1515 1.9 / 2037 12.1
7 SA 0410 1.4 / 0928 11.9 / 1625 1.8 / 2144 12.0	**22** SU 0338 1.8 / 0902 11.7 / 1552 1.9 / 2115 12.1
8 SU 0447 1.8 / 1005 11.5 / 1700 2.3 / 2221 11.4	**23** M 0415 1.8 / 0939 11.7 / 1629 2.0 / 2152 11.9
9 M 0521 2.4 / 1040 10.9 / 1732 3.0 / 2257 10.7	**24** TU 0450 2.1 / 1016 11.4 / 1705 2.3 / 2231 11.5
10 TU 0553 3.1 / 1117 10.3 / 1804 3.7 / 2334 10.0	**25** W 0526 2.5 / 1055 10.9 / 1744 2.8 / 2313 10.9
11 W 0626 3.8 / 1157 9.7 / 1843 4.3 ◐	**26** TH 0606 3.0 / 1140 10.4 / 1829 3.4 ◐
12 TH 0020 9.3 / 0709 4.3 / 1248 9.1 / 1938 4.7	**27** F 0004 10.3 / 0657 3.6 / 1238 9.9 / 1930 3.8
13 F 0124 8.8 / 0811 4.7 / 1402 8.8 / 2056 4.8	**28** SA 0112 9.7 / 0807 3.9 / 1357 9.6 / 2052 3.9
14 SA 0230 8.7 / 0930 4.7 / 1527 9.0 / 2213 4.5	**29** SU 0240 9.6 / 0935 3.9 / 1525 9.8 / 2219 3.5
15 SU 0405 9.0 / 1041 4.3 / 1631 9.5 / 2315 4.0	**30** M 0405 9.9 / 1058 3.4 / 1642 10.5 / 2335 2.9
	31 TU 0516 10.6 / 1209 2.8 / 1744 11.2

AUGUST

Time m	Time m
1 W 0041 2.2 / 0614 11.3 / 1310 2.1 / 1837 11.9	**16** TH 0030 2.9 / 0608 10.7 / 1250 2.7 / 1823 11.3
2 TH 0138 1.6 / 0704 11.8 / 1402 1.7 / 1923 12.3 ○	**17** F 0116 2.3 / 0649 11.3 / 1335 2.2 / 1903 11.9 ●
3 F 0228 1.3 / 0748 12.1 / 1447 1.5 / 2005 12.5	**18** SA 0201 1.9 / 0728 11.8 / 1418 1.8 / 1941 12.3
4 SA 0311 1.2 / 0828 12.2 / 1527 1.5 / 2043 12.5	**19** SU 0243 1.5 / 0806 12.1 / 1459 1.5 / 2019 12.6
5 SU 0348 1.4 / 0904 12.1 / 1601 1.7 / 2118 12.2	**20** M 0322 1.3 / 0843 12.3 / 1538 1.4 / 2056 12.6
6 M 0420 1.7 / 0936 11.7 / 1630 2.2 / 2150 11.7	**21** TU 0359 1.4 / 0919 12.3 / 1614 1.5 / 2133 12.4
7 TU 0447 2.3 / 1007 11.2 / 1655 2.8 / 2220 11.0	**22** W 0434 1.7 / 0955 11.9 / 1649 1.9 / 2211 11.9
8 W 0512 3.0 / 1037 10.6 / 1719 3.5 / 2250 10.2	**23** TH 0508 2.3 / 1033 11.3 / 1725 2.6 / 2251 11.1
9 TH 0536 3.7 / 1107 9.9 / 1747 4.2 / 2324 9.4	**24** F 0545 3.0 / 1116 10.6 / 1808 3.3 / 2341 10.2 ◑
10 F 0609 4.4 / 1146 9.2 / 1829 4.8	**25** SA 0633 3.7 / 1213 9.8 / 1908 4.0
11 SA 0014 8.7 / 0701 5.0 / 1250 8.6 / 1941 5.2	**26** SU 0052 9.4 / 0746 4.3 / 1340 9.4 / 2038 4.2
12 SU 0149 8.3 / 0826 5.2 / 1437 8.5 / 2126 5.1	**27** M 0233 9.2 / 0925 4.3 / 1518 9.6 / 2213 3.8
13 M 0331 8.5 / 1003 4.9 / 1559 9.1 / 2244 4.4	**28** TU 0402 9.7 / 1053 3.7 / 1635 10.3 / 2330 3.0
14 TU 0436 9.2 / 1110 4.2 / 1655 9.9 / 2341 3.7	**29** W 0509 10.5 / 1202 2.8 / 1733 11.2
15 W 0525 10.0 / 1202 3.4 / 1741 10.6	**30** TH 0031 2.2 / 0601 11.3 / 1257 2.2 / 1821 11.9
	31 F 0123 1.7 / 0646 11.8 / 1345 1.7 / 1904 12.3 ○

Chart Datum: 6·29 metres below IGN Datum
HAT is 13·6 metres above Chart Datum

TIME ZONE -0100
(French Standard Time)
Subtract 1 hour for UT
For French Summer Time add
ONE hour in **non-shaded areas**

FRANCE – ST MALO

LAT 48°38'N   LONG 2°02'W

TIMES AND HEIGHTS OF HIGH AND LOW WATERS

Dates in amber are **SPRINGS**
Dates in yellow are **NEAPS**

2012

SEPTEMBER

Day	Time m	Time m	Time m	Time m
1 SA	0207 1.4	0726 12.1	1425 1.5	1943 12.5
2 SU	0245 1.4	0802 12.2	1500 1.6	2017 12.4
3 M	0318 1.5	0835 12.1	1530 1.8	2049 12.2
4 TU	0346 1.8	0904 11.9	1557 2.1	2118 11.7
5 W	0411 2.3	0932 11.4	1619 2.7	2145 11.1
6 TH	0432 2.9	0958 10.8	1640 3.3	2211 10.4
7 F	0454 3.6	1024 10.2	1704 4.0	2238 9.6
8 SA ◐	0523 4.3	1056 9.4	1740 4.6	2317 8.8
9 SU	0607 5.0	1146 8.7	1838 5.2	
10 M	0039 8.2	0720 5.4	1336 8.3	2021 5.3
11 TU	0250 8.3	0914 5.2	1520 8.8	2204 4.7
12 W	0403 9.0	1034 4.4	1621 9.7	2308 3.8
13 TH	0455 10.0	1131 3.5	1710 10.6	
14 F	0000 2.9	0539 10.9	1221 2.7	1755 11.5
15 SA	0049 2.2	0622 11.6	1309 2.0	1837 12.2
16 SU ●	0136 1.6	0702 12.2	1355 1.5	1917 12.7
17 M	0220 1.2	0741 12.6	1438 1.1	1957 12.9
18 TU	0301 1.0	0819 12.8	1519 1.0	2035 12.9
19 W	0340 1.1	0857 12.7	1556 1.2	2114 12.6
20 TH	0415 1.5	0934 12.3	1633 1.7	2153 12.0
21 F	0451 2.2	1014 11.6	1710 2.4	2235 11.1
22 SA ◑	0529 3.0	1058 10.7	1755 3.3	2326 10.1
23 SU	0620 3.9	1158 9.8	1857 4.0	
24 M	0041 9.3	0737 4.5	1329 9.3	2029 4.3
25 TU	0225 9.1	0917 4.4	1506 9.5	2204 3.8
26 W	0351 9.7	1041 3.7	1619 10.3	2315 3.1
27 TH	0451 10.5	1143 2.9	1713 11.1	
28 F	0011 2.4	0539 11.2	1235 2.3	1758 11.7
29 SA	0058 1.9	0621 11.7	1318 1.9	1839 12.1
30 SU ○	0139 1.7	0658 12.0	1356 1.8	1916 12.2

OCTOBER

Day	Time m	Time m	Time m	Time m
1 M	0214 1.7	0733 12.1	1429 1.8	1949 12.2
2 TU	0244 1.8	0804 12.0	1458 1.9	2019 12.0
3 W	0312 2.0	0831 11.8	1524 2.2	2047 11.6
4 TH	0337 2.4	0859 11.5	1548 2.6	2113 11.1
5 F	0400 2.9	0925 11.0	1611 3.2	2140 10.5
6 SA	0424 3.5	0952 10.4	1636 3.7	2208 9.8
7 SU	0452 4.1	1023 9.7	1710 4.3	2244 9.1
8 M ◐	0533 4.7	1108 9.0	1800 4.9	2348 8.5
9 TU	0637 5.2	1234 8.5	1921 5.1	
10 W	0153 8.4	0814 5.2	1429 8.8	2107 4.8
11 TH	0318 9.0	0946 4.5	1539 9.6	2223 3.9
12 F	0416 9.9	1051 3.6	1633 10.5	2322 3.0
13 SA	0504 10.9	1145 2.7	1721 11.4	
14 SU	0015 2.2	0549 11.7	1238 1.9	1807 12.2
15 M ●	0106 1.5	0632 12.3	1327 1.3	1850 12.7
16 TU	0154 1.1	0714 12.8	1414 1.0	1933 13.0
17 W	0238 0.9	0755 13.0	1458 0.9	2015 13.0
18 TH	0320 1.1	0836 12.9	1540 1.1	2057 12.7
19 F	0359 1.5	0917 12.4	1620 1.6	2140 12.0
20 SA	0438 2.2	1000 11.7	1702 2.3	2225 11.1
21 SU	0521 3.0	1048 10.8	1749 3.1	2319 10.2
22 M ◑	0614 3.8	1149 10.0	1851 3.8	
23 TU	0028 9.4	0726 4.4	1310 9.4	2011 4.1
24 W	0200 9.2	0854 4.4	1438 9.5	2135 3.9
25 TH	0322 9.6	1011 3.9	1550 10.1	2244 3.3
26 F	0422 10.3	1112 3.2	1644 10.7	2339 2.8
27 SA	0510 10.9	1203 2.7	1730 11.2	
28 SU	0025 2.4	0551 11.4	1246 2.4	1811 11.5
29 M ○	0105 2.2	0629 11.7	1324 2.2	1848 11.7
30 TU	0140 2.1	0703 11.8	1357 2.1	1922 11.7
31 W	0212 2.1	0735 11.8	1428 2.2	1953 11.6

NOVEMBER

Day	Time m	Time m	Time m	Time m
1 TH	0241 2.2	0803 11.7	1457 2.3	2022 11.4
2 F	0310 2.5	0832 11.5	1525 2.6	2050 11.1
3 SA	0337 2.8	0901 11.2	1552 3.0	2120 10.7
4 SU	0405 3.3	0932 10.7	1620 3.4	2152 10.1
5 M	0436 3.8	1006 10.1	1655 3.9	2230 9.6
6 TU ◐	0516 4.3	1050 9.6	1741 4.3	2324 9.0
7 W	0611 4.7	1154 9.1	1845 4.6	
8 TH	0050 8.8	0726 4.8	1324 9.1	2008 4.5
9 F	0220 9.1	0851 4.4	1446 9.5	2131 4.0
10 SA	0328 9.8	1004 3.7	1548 10.3	2239 3.2
11 SU	0424 10.7	1107 2.8	1644 11.1	2339 2.4
12 M	0515 11.5	1205 2.1	1736 11.9	
13 TU ●	0035 1.7	0603 12.2	1300 1.5	1825 12.4
14 W	0128 1.3	0650 12.7	1352 1.1	1912 12.7
15 TH	0217 1.1	0735 12.9	1441 0.9	1959 12.8
16 F	0303 1.1	0820 12.9	1527 1.0	2045 12.5
17 SA	0347 1.4	0906 12.5	1612 1.4	2130 12.0
18 SU	0431 2.0	0951 11.9	1657 2.0	2217 11.3
19 M	0516 2.7	1040 11.1	1744 2.7	2307 10.5
20 TU ◑	0605 3.4	1133 10.4	1836 3.4	
21 W	0004 9.8	0703 4.0	1237 9.7	1938 3.9
22 TH	0117 9.4	0812 4.3	1352 9.5	2048 4.0
23 F	0235 9.4	0924 4.2	1507 9.6	2156 3.8
24 SA	0341 9.8	1029 3.8	1608 10.0	2255 3.5
25 SU	0435 10.3	1124 3.3	1659 10.4	2346 3.1
26 M	0521 10.8	1211 3.0	1744 10.8	
27 TU	0030 2.8	0601 11.1	1252 2.7	1824 11.1
28 W ○	0109 2.5	0638 11.4	1329 2.5	1859 11.3
29 TH	0145 2.4	0712 11.5	1404 2.4	1933 11.3
30 F	0218 2.4	0743 11.5	1437 2.4	2005 11.2

DECEMBER

Day	Time m	Time m	Time m	Time m
1 SA	0251 2.5	0815 11.5	1509 2.5	2036 11.1
2 SU	0323 2.6	0847 11.3	1541 2.7	2109 10.9
3 M	0355 2.9	0920 11.1	1613 2.9	2143 10.6
4 TU	0428 3.2	0956 10.7	1648 3.3	2221 10.2
5 W	0506 3.6	1037 10.2	1729 3.6	2306 9.7
6 TH ◐	0552 4.0	1127 9.8	1819 3.9	
7 F	0004 9.4	0650 4.2	1231 9.6	1923 4.1
8 SA	0118 9.3	0800 4.2	1347 9.6	2039 3.9
9 SU	0235 9.4	0918 3.8	1502 10.0	2156 3.4
10 M	0343 10.3	1030 3.2	1609 10.7	2305 2.8
11 TU	0444 11.0	1135 2.4	1709 11.3	
12 W	0008 2.1	0539 11.8	1237 1.8	1806 11.9
13 TH ●	0106 1.6	0632 12.3	1334 1.3	1859 12.3
14 F	0201 1.3	0723 12.7	1428 0.9	1950 12.5
15 SA	0252 1.1	0811 12.8	1518 0.9	2038 12.5
16 SU	0339 1.2	0857 12.7	1605 1.1	2124 12.2
17 M	0423 1.6	0942 12.2	1649 1.5	2207 11.6
18 TU	0506 2.2	1026 11.6	1731 2.2	2249 10.9
19 W	0547 2.9	1110 10.8	1812 3.0	2333 10.2
20 TH ◑	0630 3.6	1157 10.1	1857 3.6	
21 F	0024 9.6	0720 4.2	1255 9.4	1950 4.2
22 SA	0130 9.2	0823 4.5	1408 9.1	2055 4.4
23 SU	0248 9.2	0934 4.4	1525 9.2	2204 4.2
24 M	0357 9.6	1041 4.1	1628 9.6	2306 3.8
25 TU	0452 10.0	1137 3.6	1719 10.1	2358 3.4
26 W	0537 10.5	1225 3.1	1803 10.5	
27 TH	0043 2.9	0618 10.9	1307 2.7	1842 10.8
28 F ○	0124 2.6	0655 11.3	1347 2.4	1919 11.1
29 SA	0202 2.3	0729 11.5	1424 2.3	1953 11.2
30 SU	0238 2.3	0803 11.6	1459 2.2	2026 11.3
31 M	0313 2.3	0837 11.7	1534 2.2	2100 11.3

Chart Datum: 6·29 metres below IGN Datum
HAT is 13·6 metres above Chart Datum

TIDES

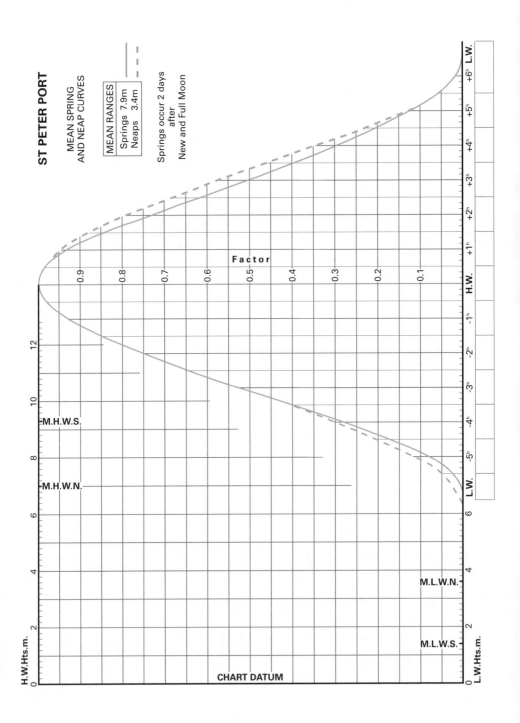

ST PETER PORT

MEAN SPRING
AND NEAP CURVES

MEAN RANGES
Springs 7.9m
Neaps   3.4m

Springs occur 2 days
after
New and Full Moon

Factor

0.9 0.8 0.7 0.6 0.5 0.4 0.3 0.2 0.1

M.H.W.S.

M.H.W.N.

M.L.W.N.

M.L.W.S.

CHART DATUM

H.W.Hts.m.

L.W.Hts.m.

L.W.

H.W.

L.W.

CHANNEL ISLES – ST PETER PORT

LAT 49°27'N   LONG 2°31'W

TIMES AND HEIGHTS OF HIGH AND LOW WATERS

Dates in amber are **SPRINGS**
Dates in yellow are **NEAPS**

2012

JANUARY

Day	Time m	Day	Time m
1 SU	0517 3.4 / 1120 7.4 / 1747 3.4 / ☽2343 7.1	**16** M	0507 2.6 / 1112 8.1 / 1736 2.7 / 2343 7.7
2 M	0607 3.8 / 1213 7.0 / 1840 3.7	**17** TU	0605 3.0 / 1213 7.6 / 1839 3.1
3 TU	0044 6.8 / 0713 4.0 / 1323 6.8 / 1946 3.9	**18** W	0053 7.4 / 0722 3.3 / 1333 7.3 / 2003 3.3
4 W	0201 6.8 / 0827 4.0 / 1440 6.9 / 2056 3.7	**19** TH	0223 7.4 / 0855 3.2 / 1503 7.4 / 2134 3.1
5 TH	0313 7.1 / 0937 3.6 / 1545 7.2 / 2159 3.4	**20** F	0343 7.7 / 1015 2.8 / 1618 7.8 / 2245 2.7
6 F	0410 7.5 / 1034 3.2 / 1638 7.6 / 2253 3.0	**21** SA	0447 8.3 / 1117 2.2 / 1717 8.3 / 2342 2.2
7 SA	0458 8.0 / 1123 2.7 / 1725 8.0 / 2339 2.6	**22** SU	0540 8.8 / 1210 1.7 / 1808 8.7
8 SU	0542 8.4 / 1207 2.3 / 1809 8.3	**23** M	0031 1.7 / 0626 9.2 / 1257 1.3 / 1853 9.0
9 M	0023 2.2 / 0623 8.8 / 1211 1.9 / ○1850 8.6	**24** TU	0116 1.4 / 0710 9.5 / 1340 1.1 / 1934 9.4
10 TU	0105 1.9 / 0703 9.0 / 1331 1.6 / 1930 8.8	**25** W	0156 1.3 / 0750 9.6 / 1419 1.0 / 2012 9.2
11 W	0145 1.7 / 0742 9.2 / 1410 1.5 / 2008 8.9	**26** TH	0233 1.3 / 0826 9.4 / 1454 1.2 / 2045 9.0
12 TH	0223 1.6 / 0820 9.2 / 1448 1.5 / 2045 8.9	**27** F	0305 1.6 / 0859 9.1 / 1526 1.6 / 2116 8.7
13 F	0301 1.6 / 0859 9.2 / 1526 1.6 / 2123 8.8	**28** SA	0334 2.0 / 0929 8.7 / 1554 2.0 / 2144 8.3
14 SA	0339 1.8 / 0939 8.9 / 1604 1.8 / 2204 8.5	**29** SU	0401 2.4 / 0959 8.2 / 1621 2.6 / 2214 7.9
15 SU	0420 2.2 / 1022 8.6 / 1646 2.2 / 2249 8.2	**30** M	0429 2.9 / 1031 7.6 / 1650 3.1 / 2247 7.4
		31 TU	0502 3.5 / 1110 7.1 / 1729 3.6 / ☽2330 6.9

FEBRUARY

Day	Time m	Day	Time m
1 W	0555 3.9 / 1206 6.7 / 1831 4.0	**16** TH	0021 7.2 / 0655 3.4 / 1311 7.0 / 1939 3.6
2 TH	0037 6.6 / 0720 4.1 / 1334 6.5 / 1957 4.1	**17** F	0203 7.0 / 0843 3.4 / 1456 7.0 / 2126 3.4
3 F	0216 6.6 / 0848 3.9 / 1506 6.7 / 2118 3.8	**18** SA	0334 7.4 / 1008 3.0 / 1612 7.5 / 2237 2.9
4 SA	0336 7.1 / 1002 3.5 / 1613 7.2 / 2224 3.3	**19** SU	0437 8.0 / 1107 2.3 / 1708 8.1 / 2331 2.3
5 SU	0434 7.6 / 1059 2.8 / 1705 7.7 / 2318 2.6	**20** M	0527 8.6 / 1156 1.7 / 1754 8.6
6 M	0522 8.2 / 1148 2.2 / 1751 8.3	**21** TU	0016 1.7 / 0610 9.1 / 1240 1.3 / ●1834 9.0
7 TU	0006 2.1 / 0606 8.8 / 1214 1.7 / ○1834 8.8	**22** W	0058 1.3 / 0650 9.4 / 1319 1.0 / 1912 9.2
8 W	0050 1.6 / 0648 9.2 / 1316 1.2 / 1914 9.1	**23** TH	0135 1.1 / 0728 9.5 / 1355 1.0 / 1947 9.3
9 TH	0131 1.2 / 0728 9.6 / 1356 0.9 / 1953 9.4	**24** F	0208 1.2 / 0801 9.4 / 1426 1.1 / 2017 9.2
10 F	0210 1.0 / 0806 9.7 / 1434 0.8 / 2030 9.4	**25** SA	0238 1.3 / 0832 9.2 / 1454 1.4 / 2045 8.9
11 SA	0248 1.0 / 0845 9.6 / 1510 1.0 / 2107 9.3	**26** SU	0304 1.7 / 0859 8.8 / 1519 1.8 / 2111 8.6
12 SU	0325 1.2 / 0923 9.4 / 1546 1.3 / 2144 9.0	**27** M	0327 2.1 / 0926 8.3 / 1542 2.3 / 2137 8.1
13 M	0402 1.6 / 1003 8.8 / 1625 1.9 / 2225 8.4	**28** TU	0351 2.5 / 0954 7.8 / 1607 2.9 / 2205 7.6
14 TU	0445 2.2 / 1048 8.2 / 1710 2.6 / ☽2314 7.8	**29** W	0418 3.1 / 1026 7.3 / 1639 3.4 / 2240 7.2
15 W	0538 2.9 / 1146 7.5 / 1809 3.2		

MARCH

Day	Time m	Day	Time m
1 TH	0458 3.6 / 1111 6.8 / 1728 3.9 / ☽2334 6.7	**16** F	0001 7.2 / 0640 3.4 / 1258 6.8 / 1924 3.8
2 F	0609 4.0 / 1226 6.4 / 1857 4.1	**17** SA	0146 6.9 / 0831 3.5 / 1445 6.9 / 2113 3.5
3 SA	0105 6.5 / 0801 4.0 / 1420 6.5 / 2037 3.9	**18** SU	0317 7.3 / 0952 3.0 / 1556 7.4 / 2220 3.0
4 SU	0254 6.8 / 0926 3.5 / 1543 7.0 / 2153 3.4	**19** M	0417 7.8 / 1047 2.4 / 1647 7.9 / 2309 2.4
5 M	0404 7.4 / 1031 2.8 / 1639 7.6 / 2252 2.7	**20** TU	0505 8.4 / 1132 1.9 / 1730 8.5 / 2352 1.8
6 TU	0456 8.1 / 1123 2.1 / 1726 8.3 / 2342 1.9	**21** W	0547 8.9 / 1213 1.5 / 1809 8.8
7 W	0542 8.8 / 1209 1.4 / 1810 8.9	**22** TH	0031 1.5 / 0625 9.2 / 1251 1.2 / ●1844 9.1
8 TH	0027 1.3 / 0625 9.4 / 1253 0.9 / ○1851 9.4	**23** F	0108 1.3 / 0701 9.3 / 1325 1.2 / 1917 9.2
9 F	0111 0.8 / 0707 9.8 / 1334 0.6 / 1931 9.7	**24** SA	0140 1.2 / 0733 9.3 / 1355 1.3 / 1947 9.1
10 SA	0151 0.5 / 0747 10.0 / 1413 0.4 / 2010 9.8	**25** SU	0208 1.4 / 0803 9.1 / 1422 1.5 / 2015 8.9
11 SU	0230 0.5 / 0831 9.7 / 1451 0.7 / 2047 9.6	**26** M	0234 1.7 / 0831 8.7 / 1447 1.9 / 2041 8.6
12 M	0308 0.8 / 0906 9.5 / 1528 1.1 / 2125 9.2	**27** TU	0258 2.0 / 0858 8.3 / 1511 2.3 / 2107 8.2
13 TU	0347 1.3 / 0946 8.9 / 1607 1.8 / 2206 8.6	**28** W	0322 2.5 / 0925 7.9 / 1536 2.8 / 2135 7.8
14 W	0429 2.0 / 1031 8.1 / 1651 2.6 / 2254 7.8	**29** TH	0350 2.9 / 0957 7.4 / 1608 3.2 / 2209 7.4
15 TH	0522 2.8 / 1129 7.3 / 1751 3.3 / ☽	**30** F	0428 3.4 / 1041 6.9 / 1654 3.7 / ☽2300 6.9
		31 SA	0528 3.8 / 1148 6.6 / 1809 4.0

APRIL

Day	Time m	Day	Time m
1 SU	0017 6.7 / 0712 3.9 / 1953 3.9	**16** M	0244 7.2 / 0919 3.0 / 1523 7.3 / 2148 3.1
2 M	0159 6.8 / 0845 3.5 / 1500 7.0 / 2115 3.4	**17** TU	0345 7.6 / 1014 2.6 / 1615 7.8 / 2238 2.6
3 TU	0321 7.4 / 0954 2.8 / 1602 7.6 / 2218 2.6	**18** W	0434 8.1 / 1100 2.2 / 1658 8.2 / 2321 2.2
4 W	0420 8.1 / 1049 2.1 / 1654 8.3 / 2311 1.9	**19** TH	0516 8.5 / 1140 1.9 / 1737 8.6
5 TH	0511 8.8 / 1139 1.4 / 1740 9.0	**20** F	0000 1.8 / 0554 8.7 / 1218 1.7 / 1812 8.8
6 F	0000 1.2 / 0558 9.4 / 1226 0.9 / ○1824 9.5	**21** SA	0036 1.6 / 0631 8.9 / 1252 1.6 / ●1846 9.0
7 SA	0046 0.7 / 0643 9.8 / 1310 0.5 / 1907 9.8	**22** SU	0109 1.6 / 0704 8.9 / 1323 1.6 / 1918 8.9
8 SU	0130 0.4 / 0726 9.9 / 1352 0.5 / 1948 9.9	**23** M	0139 1.6 / 0736 8.8 / 1352 1.7 / 1947 8.8
9 M	0212 0.4 / 0809 9.8 / 1432 0.7 / 2029 9.7	**24** TU	0207 1.8 / 0806 8.6 / 1420 2.0 / 2016 8.6
10 TU	0253 0.7 / 0850 9.5 / 1512 1.1 / 2109 9.3	**25** W	0235 2.1 / 0835 8.3 / 1447 2.3 / 2044 8.3
11 W	0334 1.2 / 0933 8.8 / 1553 1.8 / 2152 8.7	**26** TH	0303 2.4 / 0905 7.9 / 1516 2.7 / 2114 8.0
12 TH	0420 1.8 / 1021 8.1 / 1640 2.6 / 2242 7.9	**27** F	0334 2.8 / 0940 7.5 / 1551 3.1 / 2152 7.6
13 F	0515 2.7 / 1119 7.4 / 1740 3.3 / ☽2347 7.3	**28** SA	0413 3.1 / 1025 7.2 / 1636 3.4 / 2242 7.3
14 SA	0629 3.3 / 1241 6.9 / 1906 3.7	**29** SU	0510 3.4 / 1125 6.9 / 1741 3.7 / ☽2349 7.1
15 SU	0118 7.0 / 0802 3.3 / 1414 6.9 / 2041 3.5	**30** M	0631 3.5 / 1244 6.9 / 1908 3.6

Chart Datum: 5·06 metres below Ordnance Datum (Local)
HAT is 10·3 metres above Chart Datum

TIDES

TIME ZONE (UT)
For Summer Time add ONE hour in **non-shaded areas**

CHANNEL ISLES – ST PETER PORT
LAT 49°27′N   LONG 2°31′W
TIMES AND HEIGHTS OF HIGH AND LOW WATERS

Dates in amber are **SPRINGS**
Dates in yellow are **NEAPS**

2012

MAY

Time	m	Time	m	Time	m	Time	m
1 0110	7.1	**16** 0301	7.3				
0758	3.3	0929	3.0				
TU 1408	7.1	W 1532	7.4				
2031	3.2	2157	3.0				
2 0232	7.5	**17** 0355	7.6				
0911	2.7	1019	2.7				
W 1518	7.7	TH 1619	7.8				
2139	2.6	2244	2.7				
3 0339	8.1	**18** 0440	7.9				
1012	2.1	1102	2.4				
TH 1616	8.3	F 1700	8.2				
2238	2.0	2325	2.4				
4 0437	8.7	**19** 0522	8.2				
1106	1.6	1142	2.2				
F 1708	8.9	SA 1739	8.4				
2331	1.4						
5 0530	9.2	**20** 0003	2.1				
1157	1.1	0600	8.4				
SA 1757	9.4	SU 1219	2.0				
		● 1815	8.6				
6 0021	0.9	**21** 0039	2.0				
0619	9.5	0637	8.5				
SU 1246	0.8	M 1253	2.0				
○ 1844	9.7	1850	8.7				
7 0109	0.6	**22** 0113	1.9				
0707	9.7	0712	8.5				
M 1332	0.7	TU 1326	2.0				
1929	9.8	1924	8.7				
8 0156	0.6	**23** 0145	1.9				
0753	9.6	0746	8.4				
TU 1416	0.9	W 1359	2.1				
2013	9.7	1956	8.6				
9 0241	0.8	**24** 0218	2.1				
0839	9.3	0819	8.3				
W 1500	1.2	TH 1431	2.3				
2057	9.3	2028	8.4				
10 0326	1.2	**25** 0250	2.3				
0924	8.8	0852	8.1				
TH 1544	1.8	F 1504	2.5				
2142	8.8	2102	8.2				
11 0413	1.8	**26** 0325	2.5				
1012	8.2	0930	7.8				
F 1632	2.4	SA 1541	2.8				
2231	8.2	2142	8.0				
12 0505	2.4	**27** 0406	2.7				
1106	7.6	1013	7.6				
SA 1726	3.0	SU 1625	3.0				
☽ 2328	7.6	2229	7.7				
13 0606	2.9	**28** 0456	2.9				
1210	7.2	1106	7.4				
SU 1833	3.4	M 1721	3.2				
		☽ 2327	7.6				
14 0038	7.2	**29** 0559	3.1				
0717	3.2	1210	7.3				
M 1325	7.0	TU 1829	3.3				
1950	3.5						
15 0154	7.2	**30** 0034	7.5				
0829	3.2	0712	3.0				
TU 1435	7.1	W 1322	7.4				
2101	3.4	1946	3.1				
		31 0148	7.7				
		0827	2.8				
		TH 1435	7.7				
		2100	2.7				

JUNE

Time	m	Time	m
1 0301	8.0	**16** 0401	7.4
0935	2.4	1020	3.0
F 1541	8.2	SA 1623	7.7
2206	2.2	2248	2.9
2 0407	8.4	**17** 0449	7.7
1037	1.9	1106	2.7
SA 1640	8.7	SU 1707	8.0
2306	1.7	2331	2.6
3 0506	8.8	**18** 0533	8.0
1134	1.5	1148	2.4
SU 1734	9.1	M 1749	8.3
4 0001	1.3	**19** 0011	2.3
0601	9.1	0613	8.2
M 1227	1.2	TU 1228	2.2
○ 1825	9.4	● 1828	8.5
5 0054	0.9	**20** 0051	2.1
0653	9.3	0653	8.4
TU 1317	1.1	W 1306	2.1
1914	9.6	1905	8.6
6 0143	0.8	**21** 0129	1.9
0742	9.4	0731	8.4
W 1405	1.1	TH 1343	2.0
2001	9.6	1941	8.7
7 0231	0.8	**22** 0205	1.9
0829	9.2	0807	8.4
TH 1450	1.3	F 1419	2.1
2046	9.4	2016	8.7
8 0316	1.1	**23** 0241	2.0
0914	8.9	0842	8.4
F 1534	1.6	SA 1455	2.2
2130	9.0	2052	8.6
9 0401	1.6	**24** 0317	2.1
0958	8.5	0919	8.2
SA 1618	2.1	SU 1532	2.3
2214	8.5	2131	8.4
10 0446	2.1	**25** 0356	2.2
1043	8.0	1000	8.1
SU 1703	2.7	M 1613	2.5
2300	7.9	2214	8.2
11 0534	2.6	**26** 0439	2.5
1131	7.5	1046	7.9
M 1753	3.2	TU 1700	2.7
☽ 2352	7.5	2304	8.0
12 0627	3.1	**27** 0530	2.7
1226	7.2	1139	7.7
TU 1850	3.5	W 1757	2.9
		●	
13 0052	7.1	**28** 0003	7.8
0725	3.3	0632	2.9
W 1330	7.0	TH 1244	7.6
1955	3.6	1907	3.0
14 0200	7.0	**29** 0113	7.6
0828	3.4	0747	2.9
TH 1435	7.1	F 1359	7.6
2101	3.5	2026	2.9
15 0306	7.1	**30** 0231	7.7
0928	3.3	0905	2.7
F 1533	7.4	SA 1514	7.9
2159	3.2	2142	2.6

JULY

Time	m	Time	m
1 0346	8.0	**16** 0420	7.3
1016	2.4	1033	3.1
SU 1621	8.3	M 1640	7.7
2249	2.1	2303	2.9
2 0452	8.4	**17** 0509	7.7
1119	2.0	1122	2.7
M 1720	8.8	TU 1726	8.1
2348	1.6	2349	2.4
3 0550	8.8	**18** 0554	8.1
1215	1.6	1207	2.3
TU 1813	9.2	W 1808	8.5
○			
4 0043	1.2	**19** 0032	2.1
0642	9.1	0635	8.4
W 1307	1.3	TH 1249	2.0
1902	9.5	● 1848	8.8
5 0133	0.9	**20** 0113	1.8
0731	9.3	0715	8.6
TH 1354	1.1	F 1329	1.8
1948	9.6	1926	9.0
6 0219	0.8	**21** 0152	1.6
0816	9.3	0753	8.8
F 1438	1.2	SA 1407	1.7
2031	9.5	2003	9.1
7 0301	1.0	**22** 0229	1.5
0857	9.1	0828	8.8
SA 1518	1.4	SU 1444	1.6
2111	9.2	2040	9.1
8 0341	1.3	**23** 0304	1.6
0935	8.8	0904	8.8
SU 1555	1.8	M 1520	1.8
2149	8.8	2117	8.9
9 0418	1.9	**24** 0341	1.8
1012	8.3	0942	8.6
M 1631	2.4	TU 1557	2.0
2226	8.2	2157	8.7
10 0455	2.4	**25** 0419	2.1
1049	7.8	1023	8.3
TU 1708	2.9	W 1639	2.3
2305	7.7	2241	8.3
11 0534	3.0	**26** 0504	2.5
1130	7.4	1112	7.9
W 1751	3.4	TH 1729	2.7
☽ 2351	7.2	☽ 2335	7.8
12 0622	3.5	**27** 0601	2.9
1221	7.0	1212	7.6
TH 1847	3.8	F 1836	3.1
13 0051	6.8	**28** 0045	7.4
0722	3.7	0717	3.2
F 1329	6.8	SA 1332	7.4
1956	3.9	2003	3.2
14 0208	6.7	**29** 0213	7.3
0830	3.7	0848	3.2
SA 1443	6.9	SU 1459	7.6
2108	3.7	2131	2.9
15 0321	6.9	**30** 0339	7.6
0937	3.5	1008	2.8
SU 1547	7.3	M 1612	8.1
2211	3.3	2242	2.3
		31 0446	8.1
		1112	2.3
		TU 1711	8.6
		2341	1.8

AUGUST

Time	m	Time	m
1 0542	8.6	**16** 0532	8.1
1206	1.7	1146	2.3
W 1802	9.1	TH 1747	8.6
2 0032	1.3	**17** 0012	1.9
0630	9.0	0614	8.6
TH 1254	1.3	F 1230	1.8
○ 1848	9.5	● 1828	9.0
3 0118	0.9	**18** 0054	1.5
0715	9.3	0654	9.0
F 1338	1.1	SA 1311	1.4
1931	9.7	1907	9.3
4 0200	0.8	**19** 0133	1.2
0756	9.4	0732	9.2
SA 1418	1.1	SU 1350	1.2
2011	9.6	1945	9.5
5 0239	0.9	**20** 0210	1.1
0833	9.3	0809	9.2
SU 1454	1.3	M 1427	1.2
2046	9.4	2022	9.5
6 0313	1.0	**21** 0246	1.1
0906	9.0	0845	9.2
M 1527	1.7	TU 1503	1.3
2119	8.9	2059	9.3
7 0344	1.8	**22** 0322	1.4
0936	8.5	0921	9.0
TU 1556	2.2	W 1539	1.6
2149	8.4	2138	9.0
8 0413	2.4	**23** 0359	1.9
1006	8.0	1001	8.6
W 1624	2.7	TH 1619	2.1
2220	7.8	2220	8.4
9 0442	3.0	**24** 0442	2.5
1039	7.5	1047	8.0
TH 1655	3.3	F 1708	2.7
○ 2256	7.2	☾ 2313	7.1
10 0518	3.5	**25** 0537	3.1
1119	7.1	1148	7.5
F 1741	3.8	SA 1816	3.3
2346	6.8		
11 0617	3.9	**26** 0026	7.1
1220	6.7	0659	3.6
SA 1857	4.1	SU 1318	7.2
		1954	3.5
12 0107	6.5	**27** 0210	7.0
0738	4.1	0845	3.5
SU 1351	6.6	M 1454	7.4
2023	4.0	2130	3.1
13 0243	6.6	**28** 0338	7.5
0858	3.9	1004	3.0
M 1514	7.0	TU 1605	8.0
2139	3.6	2236	2.5
14 0354	7.1	**29** 0439	8.1
1005	3.4	1102	2.3
TU 1614	7.5	W 1659	8.6
2239	3.0	2328	1.8
15 0447	7.6	**30** 0529	8.6
1059	2.8	1151	1.8
W 1703	8.0	TH 1746	9.1
2328	2.4		
		31 0014	1.3
		0612	9.1
		F 1236	1.4
		○ 1829	9.5

Chart Datum: 5·06 metres below Ordnance Datum (Local)
HAT is 10·3 metres above Chart Datum

CHANNEL ISLES – ST PETER PORT

LAT 49°27'N   LONG 2°31'W

TIMES AND HEIGHTS OF HIGH AND LOW WATERS

Dates in amber are **SPRINGS**
Dates in yellow are **NEAPS**

2012

SEPTEMBER

	Time	m		Time	m
1 SA	0057 / 0652 / 1316 / 1908	1.0 / 9.3 / 1.1 / 9.6	**16** SU	0028 / 0628 / 1247 / 1843	1.3 / 9.2 / 1.2 / 9.6
2 SU	0136 / 0729 / 1353 / 1945	1.0 / 9.4 / 1.1 / 9.6	**17** M	0109 / 0707 / 1328 / 1923	1.0 / 9.6 / 0.9 / 9.8
3 M	0210 / 0803 / 1426 / 2017	1.1 / 9.3 / 1.3 / 9.4	**18** TU	0148 / 0745 / 1407 / 2002	0.8 / 9.7 / 0.8 / 9.8
4 TU	0241 / 0833 / 1454 / 2047	1.4 / 9.1 / 1.7 / 9.0	**19** W	0226 / 0823 / 1445 / 2041	0.9 / 9.6 / 1.0 / 9.6
5 W	0308 / 0900 / 1520 / 2114	1.8 / 8.7 / 2.1 / 8.5	**20** TH	0303 / 0902 / 1523 / 2121	1.3 / 9.3 / 1.4 / 9.1
6 TH	0332 / 0927 / 1544 / 2142	2.4 / 8.2 / 2.7 / 7.9	**21** F	0341 / 0943 / 1605 / 2204	1.8 / 8.8 / 2.0 / 8.4
7 F	0356 / 0956 / 1610 / 2213	2.9 / 7.7 / 3.2 / 7.4	**22** SA	0425 / 1030 / 1655 / 2258	2.5 / 8.1 / 2.7 / 7.6
8 SA	0426 / 1030 / 1645 / 2255	3.5 / 7.2 / 3.6 / 6.8	**23** SU	0523 / 1134 / 1807	3.3 / 7.5 / 3.4
9 SU	0512 / 1121 / 1752	4.0 / 6.8 / 4.2	**24** M	0018 / 0651 / 1309 / 1949	7.1 / 3.7 / 7.1 / 3.5
10 M	0005 / 0644 / 1252 / 1940	6.4 / 4.3 / 6.5 / 4.2	**25** TU	0207 / 0839 / 1443 / 2119	7.0 / 3.6 / 7.4 / 3.1
11 TU	0202 / 0820 / 1436 / 2106	6.5 / 4.1 / 6.8 / 3.8	**26** W	0327 / 0951 / 1549 / 2219	7.5 / 3.1 / 8.0 / 2.5
12 W	0325 / 0953 / 1544 / 2210	7.0 / 3.2 / 7.4 / 3.1	**27** TH	0422 / 1044 / 1640 / 2308	8.1 / 2.4 / 8.5 / 2.0
13 TH	0419 / 1031 / 1635 / 2300	7.6 / 2.9 / 8.0 / 2.4	**28** F	0507 / 1130 / 1724 / 2350	8.6 / 1.9 / 9.0 / 1.6
14 F	0505 / 1119 / 1720 / 2345	8.2 / 2.3 / 8.7 / 1.8	**29** SA	0547 / 1211 / 1805	9.0 / 1.6 / 9.3
15 SA	0547 / 1204 / 1803	8.8 / 1.7 / 9.2	**30** SU	0030 / 0625 / 1250 / 1842 ○	1.3 / 9.3 / 1.4 / 9.4

OCTOBER

	Time	m		Time	m
1 M	0106 / 0700 / 1324 / 1916	1.3 / 9.3 / 1.4 / 9.4	**16** TU	0043 / 0641 / 1305 / 1900	1.0 / 9.7 / 0.9 / 9.9
2 TU	0139 / 0732 / 1355 / 1948	1.4 / 9.3 / 1.5 / 9.2	**17** W	0126 / 0723 / 1347 / 1943	0.8 / 9.9 / 0.8 / 9.9
3 W	0208 / 0801 / 1423 / 2016	1.6 / 9.1 / 1.8 / 8.9	**18** TH	0207 / 0804 / 1429 / 2025	0.9 / 9.8 / 0.9 / 9.6
4 TH	0234 / 0828 / 1448 / 2044	2.0 / 8.7 / 2.2 / 8.5	**19** F	0247 / 0846 / 1511 / 2108	1.3 / 9.5 / 1.3 / 9.1
5 F	0258 / 0855 / 1512 / 2111	2.4 / 8.3 / 2.6 / 8.0	**20** SA	0329 / 0930 / 1557 / 2155	1.8 / 8.9 / 1.9 / 8.4
6 SA	0323 / 0923 / 1539 / 2142	2.9 / 7.9 / 3.1 / 7.5	**21** SU	0416 / 1020 / 1650 / 2251	2.5 / 8.3 / 2.6 / 7.7
7 SU	0352 / 0956 / 1613 / 2222	3.4 / 7.4 / 3.6 / 7.0	**22** M	0515 / 1123 / 1759	3.2 / 7.6 / 3.2
8 M	0435 / 1044 / 1708 / 2324	3.9 / 7.0 / 4.0 / 6.6	**23** TU	0006 / 0638 / 1249 / 1928	7.2 / 3.7 / 7.3 / 3.4
9 TU	0549 / 1159 / 1849	4.3 / 6.7 / 4.2	**24** W	0142 / 0813 / 1415 / 2050	7.1 / 3.6 / 7.4 / 3.2
10 W	0105 / 0735 / 1343 / 2022	6.5 / 4.2 / 6.8 / 3.8	**25** TH	0258 / 0924 / 1521 / 2151	7.4 / 3.2 / 7.8 / 2.8
11 TH	0241 / 0855 / 1501 / 2131	6.9 / 3.7 / 7.3 / 3.2	**26** F	0353 / 1017 / 1612 / 2239	7.9 / 2.7 / 8.2 / 2.4
12 F	0342 / 0956 / 1558 / 2226	7.6 / 3.0 / 8.0 / 2.5	**27** SA	0438 / 1102 / 1656 / 2321	8.4 / 2.3 / 8.6 / 2.0
13 SA	0431 / 1048 / 1647 / 2314	8.3 / 2.3 / 8.7 / 1.9	**28** SU	0518 / 1143 / 1737	8.7 / 2.0 / 8.9
14 SU	0516 / 1135 / 1733 / 2359	8.9 / 1.7 / 9.2 / 1.3	**29** M	0000 / 0555 / 1221 / 1814 ○	1.8 / 9.0 / 1.8 / 9.0
15 M	0559 / 1221 / 1818 ●	9.4 / 1.2 / 9.7	**30** TU	0036 / 0629 / 1255 / 1848	1.7 / 9.1 / 1.7 / 9.1
			31 W	0108 / 0702 / 1327 / 1921	1.8 / 9.1 / 1.8 / 9.0

NOVEMBER

	Time	m		Time	m
1 TH	0138 / 0733 / 1356 / 1951	1.9 / 9.0 / 2.0 / 8.8	**16** F	0152 / 0749 / 1418 / 2014	1.0 / 9.9 / 0.9 / 9.6
2 F	0206 / 0802 / 1424 / 2021	2.1 / 8.8 / 2.3 / 8.4	**17** SA	0237 / 0834 / 1504 / 2100	1.3 / 9.6 / 1.2 / 9.2
3 SA	0233 / 0830 / 1451 / 2050	2.5 / 8.4 / 2.6 / 8.1	**18** SU	0322 / 0921 / 1551 / 2148	1.7 / 9.2 / 1.7 / 8.6
4 SU	0301 / 0900 / 1521 / 2123	2.9 / 8.1 / 3.0 / 7.7	**19** M	0409 / 1010 / 1642 / 2240	2.3 / 8.6 / 2.3 / 8.0
5 M	0333 / 0935 / 1557 / 2202	3.3 / 7.7 / 3.4 / 7.3	**20** TU	0503 / 1106 / 1740 / 2341 ☾	2.9 / 8.0 / 2.8 / 7.5
6 TU	0415 / 1021 / 1647 / 2257	3.7 / 7.3 / 3.7 / 7.0	**21** W	0608 / 1213 / 1849	3.4 / 7.6 / 3.2
7 W	0515 / 1124 / 1759	4.0 / 7.1 / 3.8	**22** TH	0055 / 0726 / 1330 / 2002	7.2 / 3.6 / 7.4 / 3.3
8 TH	0012 / 0640 / 1245 / 1928	6.8 / 4.0 / 7.1 / 3.7	**23** F	0212 / 0841 / 1440 / 2109	7.3 / 3.5 / 7.5 / 3.2
9 F	0141 / 0806 / 1408 / 2044	7.1 / 3.7 / 7.4 / 3.3	**24** SA	0315 / 0941 / 1537 / 2203	7.5 / 3.1 / 7.7 / 2.9
10 SA	0254 / 0915 / 1515 / 2146	7.6 / 3.1 / 7.9 / 2.7	**25** SU	0404 / 1031 / 1625 / 2249	7.9 / 2.9 / 8.0 / 2.6
11 SU	0352 / 1013 / 1612 / 2241	8.2 / 2.5 / 8.5 / 2.1	**26** M	0447 / 1114 / 1708 / 2329	8.3 / 2.6 / 8.3 / 2.4
12 M	0443 / 1106 / 1704 / 2331	8.8 / 1.9 / 9.0 / 1.6	**27** TU	0526 / 1153 / 1747	8.6 / 2.3 / 8.5
13 TU	0532 / 1156 / 1754 ●	9.3 / 1.3 / 9.4	**28** W	0006 / 0602 / 1229 / 1824 ○	2.2 / 8.8 / 2.1 / 8.7
14 W	0019 / 0618 / 1245 / 1841 ○	1.2 / 9.7 / 1.0 / 9.7	**29** TH	0041 / 0637 / 1303 / 1859	2.1 / 8.9 / 2.1 / 8.7
15 TH	0107 / 0704 / 1332 / 1928	1.0 / 9.9 / 0.8 / 9.7	**30** F	0114 / 0711 / 1335 / 1933	2.1 / 8.9 / 2.1 / 8.6

DECEMBER

	Time	m		Time	m
1 SA	0145 / 0743 / 1407 / 2005	2.2 / 8.8 / 2.2 / 8.5	**16** SU	0228 / 0825 / 1456 / 2051	1.1 / 9.8 / 0.9 / 9.3
2 SU	0217 / 0815 / 1439 / 2037	2.4 / 8.6 / 2.4 / 8.2	**17** M	0313 / 0910 / 1541 / 2135	1.4 / 9.5 / 1.3 / 8.9
3 M	0249 / 0847 / 1511 / 2111	2.6 / 8.3 / 2.6 / 8.0	**18** TU	0357 / 0954 / 1625 / 2219	1.9 / 9.0 / 1.8 / 8.4
4 TU	0323 / 0923 / 1547 / 2149	2.9 / 8.1 / 2.9 / 7.7	**19** W	0441 / 1040 / 1711 / 2306	2.4 / 8.4 / 2.4 / 7.9
5 W	0402 / 1005 / 1630 / 2235	3.2 / 7.8 / 3.1 / 7.5	**20** TH	0530 / 1130 / 1801 / 2359 ☾	3.0 / 7.8 / 3.0 / 7.4
6 TH	0450 / 1057 / 1724 / 2333 ☽	3.5 / 7.6 / 3.3 / 7.3	**21** F	0626 / 1230 / 1859	3.5 / 7.3 / 3.4
7 F	0553 / 1201 / 1832	3.6 / 7.4 / 3.4	**22** SA	0104 / 0734 / 1341 / 2005	7.1 / 3.8 / 7.1 / 3.6
8 SA	0044 / 0710 / 1315 / 1949	7.3 / 3.6 / 7.5 / 3.3	**23** SU	0218 / 0849 / 1452 / 2114	7.1 / 3.7 / 7.1 / 3.5
9 SU	0202 / 0830 / 1431 / 2104	7.0 / 3.2 / 7.7 / 2.9	**24** M	0324 / 0952 / 1552 / 2211	7.3 / 3.5 / 7.4 / 3.3
10 M	0313 / 0939 / 1539 / 2209	8.0 / 2.7 / 8.2 / 2.4	**25** TU	0415 / 1043 / 1641 / 2259	7.7 / 3.1 / 7.7 / 2.9
11 TU	0414 / 1041 / 1640 / 2308	8.5 / 2.2 / 8.6 / 1.9	**26** W	0459 / 1127 / 1724 / 2341	8.1 / 2.7 / 8.0 / 2.6
12 W	0510 / 1137 / 1736	9.0 / 1.6 / 9.1	**27** TH	0540 / 1207 / 1804	8.4 / 2.4 / 8.3
13 TH	0002 / 0601 / 1231 / 1828 ●	1.5 / 9.5 / 1.2 / 9.4	**28** F	0019 / 0618 / 1245 / 1842 ○	2.3 / 8.7 / 2.2 / 8.5
14 F	0053 / 0651 / 1321 / 1918	1.2 / 9.8 / 0.9 / 9.6	**29** SA	0056 / 0655 / 1321 / 1919	2.4 / 8.8 / 2.0 / 8.6
15 SA	0142 / 0738 / 1410 / 2005	1.1 / 9.9 / 0.8 / 9.5	**30** SU	0131 / 0730 / 1355 / 1954	2.4 / 8.9 / 2.0 / 8.6
			31 M	0205 / 0803 / 1429 / 2027	2.1 / 8.8 / 2.0 / 8.5

Chart Datum: 5·06 metres below Ordnance Datum (Local)
HAT is 10·3 metres above Chart Datum

TIDES

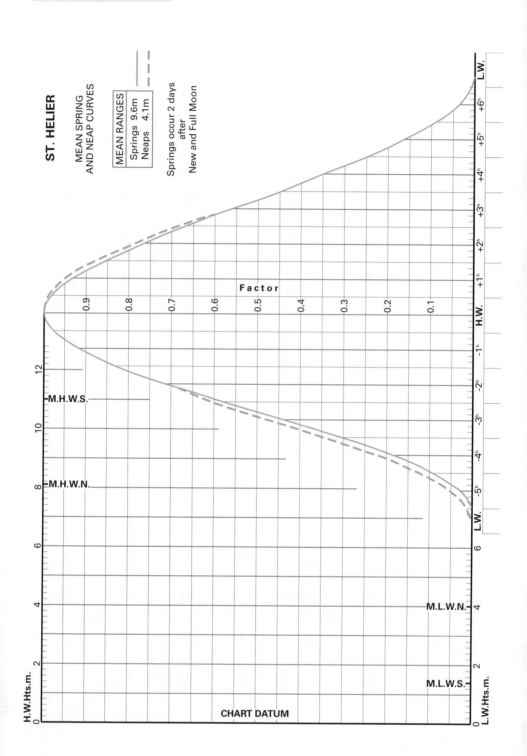

ST. HELIER

MEAN SPRING AND NEAP CURVES

MEAN RANGES
Springs 9.6m
Neaps 4.1m

Springs occur 2 days
after
New and Full Moon

Factor

0.9 0.8 0.7 0.6 0.5 0.4 0.3 0.2 0.1

L.W. +6ʰ +5ʰ +4ʰ +3ʰ +2ʰ +1ʰ H.W. -1ʰ -2ʰ -3ʰ -4ʰ -5ʰ L.W. 6

12

M.H.W.S.

10

M.H.W.N.

8

6

4

M.L.W.N.

2

M.L.W.S.

H.W.Hts.m. 0

CHART DATUM

L.W.Hts.m. 0

CHANNEL ISLES – ST HELIER

LAT 49°11'N   LONG 2°07'W

TIMES AND HEIGHTS OF HIGH AND LOW WATERS

Dates in amber are **SPRINGS**
Dates in yellow are **NEAPS**

2012

JANUARY

Time	m		Time	m
1 SU 0518 / 1106 / 1745 / ◑2332	3.7 / 8.6 / 3.8 / 8.3	**16** M	0514 / 1059 / 1740 / ◐2330	2.7 / 9.6 / 2.9 / 9.1
2 M 0606 / 1202 / 1839	4.2 / 8.1 / 4.2	**17** TU	0609 / 1156 / 1841	3.2 / 8.9 / 3.4
3 TU 0037 / 0712 / 1320 / 1951	7.9 / 4.5 / 7.8 / 4.3	**18** W	0037 / 0721 / 1313 / 2002	8.6 / 3.6 / 8.5 / 3.6
4 W 0158 / 0834 / 1440 / 2108	7.9 / 4.4 / 8.0 / 4.1	**19** TH	0203 / 0847 / 1443 / 2128	8.6 / 3.5 / 8.6 / 3.4
5 TH 0309 / 0946 / 1543 / 2211	8.3 / 4.0 / 8.4 / 3.7	**20** F	0327 / 1009 / 1604 / 2244	8.9 / 3.0 / 9.0 / 2.9
6 F 0404 / 1043 / 1634 / 2304	8.8 / 3.4 / 8.9 / 3.2	**21** SA	0436 / 1118 / 1707 / 2347	9.6 / 2.4 / 9.7 / 2.3
7 SA 0451 / 1131 / 1718 / 2350	9.3 / 2.9 / 9.4 / 2.7	**22** SU	0531 / 1217 / 1759	10.3 / 1.8 / 10.2
8 SU 0533 / 1216 / 1800	9.8 / 2.4 / 9.8	**23** M	0040 / 0619 / 1308 / ●1844	1.8 / 10.8 / 1.4 / 10.6
9 M 0034 / 0612 / 1259 / ○1839	2.3 / 10.3 / 2.0 / 10.2	**24** TU	0127 / 0702 / 1351 / 1925	1.5 / 11.1 / 1.2 / 10.8
10 TU 0115 / 0652 / 1340 / 1918	2.0 / 10.6 / 1.7 / 10.5	**25** W	0207 / 0741 / 1430 / 2001	1.4 / 11.2 / 1.2 / 10.8
11 W 0154 / 0731 / 1418 / 1958	1.8 / 10.9 / 1.6 / 10.7	**26** TH	0243 / 0816 / 1502 / 2034	1.5 / 11.0 / 1.4 / 10.6
12 TH 0232 / 0811 / 1456 / 2037	1.6 / 10.9 / 1.5 / 10.7	**27** F	0313 / 0848 / 1531 / 2104	1.8 / 10.7 / 1.8 / 10.3
13 F 0310 / 0850 / 1534 / 2116	1.6 / 10.9 / 1.6 / 10.5	**28** SA	0340 / 0918 / 1557 / 2133	2.2 / 10.2 / 2.2 / 9.8
14 SA 0349 / 0931 / 1612 / 2156	1.8 / 10.6 / 1.9 / 10.1	**29** SU	0406 / 0947 / 1623 / 2201	2.7 / 9.6 / 2.8 / 9.2
15 SU 0430 / 1012 / 1653 / 2239	2.2 / 10.2 / 2.3 / 9.6	**30** M	0433 / 1017 / 1652 / 2234	3.2 / 9.0 / 3.4 / 8.6
		31 TU	0507 / 1054 / 1732 / ◑2318	3.8 / 8.3 / 4.0 / 8.0

FEBRUARY

Time	m		Time	m
1 W 0557 / 1151 / 1832	4.4 / 7.7 / 4.5	**16** TH	0006 / 0654 / 1248 / 1937	8.5 / 3.7 / 8.1 / 4.0
2 TH 0030 / 0716 / 1331 / 2002	7.6 / 4.7 / 7.4 / 4.6	**17** F	0141 / 0832 / 1434 / 2118	8.2 / 3.8 / 8.1 / 3.8
3 F 0214 / 0855 / 1504 / 2131	7.7 / 4.5 / 7.7 / 4.2	**18** SA	0318 / 1002 / 1600 / 2238	8.6 / 3.2 / 8.7 / 3.1
4 SA 0330 / 1010 / 1607 / 2235	8.2 / 3.8 / 8.4 / 3.5	**19** SU	0427 / 1111 / 1659 / 2338	9.3 / 2.5 / 9.5 / 2.3
5 SU 0425 / 1106 / 1656 / 2328	8.9 / 3.0 / 9.1 / 2.8	**20** M	0520 / 1206 / 1747	10.1 / 1.8 / 10.1
6 M 0512 / 1156 / 1741	9.7 / 2.3 / 9.8	**21** TU	0027 / 0604 / 1252 / ●1827	1.8 / 10.7 / 1.4 / 10.6
7 TU 0015 / 0555 / 1243 / ○1822	2.1 / 10.3 / 1.8 / 10.4	**22** W	0110 / 0643 / 1332 / 1904	1.5 / 11.0 / 1.2 / 10.8
8 W 0100 / 0637 / 1326 / 1903	1.6 / 10.9 / 1.3 / 10.9	**23** TH	0146 / 0719 / 1405 / 1936	1.3 / 11.1 / 1.2 / 10.9
9 TH 0142 / 0717 / 1406 / 1943	1.2 / 11.3 / 1.0 / 10.7	**24** F	0217 / 0751 / 1434 / 2006	1.4 / 11.0 / 1.3 / 10.8
10 F 0221 / 0757 / 1444 / 2022	1.0 / 11.5 / 0.8 / 11.3	**25** SA	0244 / 0821 / 1459 / 2033	1.5 / 10.8 / 1.6 / 10.5
11 SA 0259 / 0837 / 1521 / 2100	1.0 / 11.5 / 0.9 / 11.1	**26** SU	0309 / 0848 / 1523 / 2059	1.8 / 10.4 / 2.0 / 10.1
12 SU 0336 / 0915 / 1557 / 2138	1.2 / 11.1 / 1.3 / 10.6	**27** M	0333 / 0913 / 1548 / 2123	2.3 / 9.8 / 2.5 / 9.6
13 M 0414 / 0954 / 1634 / 2217	1.7 / 10.5 / 2.0 / 10.0	**28** TU	0358 / 0938 / 1614 / 2149	2.9 / 9.2 / 3.1 / 9.0
14 TU 0454 / 1036 / 1716 / ◑2302	2.3 / 9.7 / 2.8 / 9.2	**29** W	0427 / 1006 / 1646 / 2222	3.5 / 8.5 / 3.8 / 8.3
15 W 0544 / 1130 / 1812	3.1 / 8.8 / 3.5			

MARCH

Time	m		Time	m
1 TH 0506 / 1047 / 1734 / ◑2316	4.1 / 7.8 / 4.4 / 7.7	**16** F	0641 / 1236 / 1924	3.7 / 7.9 / 4.1
2 F 0612 / 1211 / 1858	4.6 / 7.3 / 4.7	**17** SA	0127 / 0820 / 1425 / 2106	8.0 / 3.8 / 8.0 / 3.9
3 SA 0103 / 0755 / 1418 / 2043	7.4 / 4.6 / 7.4 / 4.5	**18** SU	0303 / 0948 / 1545 / 2222	8.5 / 3.3 / 8.6 / 3.1
4 SU 0248 / 0929 / 1534 / 2201	7.9 / 4.0 / 8.2 / 3.7	**19** M	0409 / 1052 / 1640 / 2318	9.2 / 2.5 / 9.4 / 2.4
5 M 0353 / 1035 / 1628 / 2259	8.7 / 3.1 / 9.1 / 2.8	**20** TU	0459 / 1143 / 1724	9.9 / 1.9 / 10.0
6 TU 0445 / 1129 / 1716 / 2350	9.6 / 2.3 / 9.9 / 2.0	**21** W	0004 / 0541 / 1226 / 1802	1.9 / 10.4 / 1.6 / 10.4
7 W 0531 / 1218 / 1800	10.4 / 1.5 / 10.6	**22** TH	0045 / 0619 / 1303 / ●1837	1.6 / 10.7 / 1.4 / 10.7
8 TH 0038 / 0615 / 1304 / ○1842	1.3 / 11.1 / 1.0 / 11.2	**23** F	0119 / 0653 / 1334 / 1908	1.5 / 10.8 / 1.4 / 10.8
9 F 0122 / 0658 / 1347 / 1922	0.9 / 11.6 / 0.6 / 11.6	**24** SA	0148 / 0724 / 1402 / 1936	1.5 / 10.8 / 1.5 / 10.7
10 SA 0204 / 0739 / 1426 / 2002	0.6 / 11.8 / 0.5 / 11.6	**25** SU	0214 / 0752 / 1428 / 2003	1.6 / 10.7 / 1.6 / 10.6
11 SU 0243 / 0819 / 1504 / 2041	0.5 / 11.7 / 0.7 / 11.4	**26** M	0240 / 0819 / 1454 / 2028	1.8 / 10.3 / 1.9 / 10.2
12 M 0321 / 0859 / 1540 / 2119	0.8 / 11.3 / 1.2 / 10.9	**27** TU	0306 / 0844 / 1519 / 2053	2.1 / 9.9 / 2.4 / 9.8
13 TU 0359 / 0938 / 1617 / 2158	1.4 / 10.5 / 1.9 / 10.1	**28** W	0332 / 0909 / 1546 / 2118	2.7 / 9.3 / 3.0 / 9.2
14 W 0439 / 1020 / 1659 / 2243	2.2 / 9.6 / 2.8 / 9.2	**29** TH	0401 / 0936 / 1617 / 2149	3.2 / 8.7 / 3.6 / 8.6
15 TH 0529 / 1114 / 1755 / ◑2347	3.0 / 8.6 / 3.6 / 8.4	**30** F	0437 / 1015 / 1701 / ◑2238	3.6 / 8.0 / 4.2 / 8.0
		31 SA	0534 / 1127 / 1813	4.3 / 7.5 / 4.5

APRIL

Time	m		Time	m
1 SU 0008 / 0704 / 1324 / 1952	7.6 / 4.4 / 7.5 / 4.4	**16** M	0231 / 0915 / 1511 / 2149	8.5 / 3.3 / 8.6 / 3.3
2 M 0158 / 0841 / 1452 / 2119	7.9 / 3.9 / 8.2 / 3.7	**17** TU	0336 / 1017 / 1607 / 2245	9.0 / 2.8 / 9.2 / 2.7
3 TU 0313 / 0955 / 1553 / 2223	8.7 / 3.1 / 9.1 / 2.8	**18** W	0428 / 1108 / 1652 / 2331	9.6 / 2.3 / 9.7 / 2.3
4 W 0411 / 1054 / 1644 / 2318	9.6 / 2.2 / 9.9 / 2.0	**19** TH	0511 / 1151 / 1731	10.0 / 2.0 / 10.1
5 TH 0502 / 1146 / 1731	10.5 / 1.5 / 10.7	**20** F	0011 / 0549 / 1228 / 1805	2.0 / 10.3 / 1.9 / 10.4
6 F 0009 / 0549 / 1236 / ○1816	1.3 / 11.1 / 1.0 / 11.3	**21** SA	0046 / 0623 / 1300 / ●1837	1.9 / 10.4 / 1.8 / 10.5
7 SA 0057 / 0634 / 1322 / 1859	0.8 / 11.6 / 0.6 / 11.7	**22** SU	0117 / 0655 / 1330 / 1907	1.8 / 10.4 / 1.8 / 10.5
8 SU 0142 / 0718 / 1405 / 1941	0.5 / 11.8 / 0.5 / 11.7	**23** M	0146 / 0725 / 1359 / 1935	1.8 / 10.4 / 1.9 / 10.4
9 M 0224 / 0801 / 1445 / 2022	0.5 / 11.6 / 0.7 / 11.5	**24** TU	0215 / 0754 / 1428 / 2003	1.9 / 10.2 / 2.1 / 10.2
10 TU 0306 / 0843 / 1525 / 2102	0.8 / 11.2 / 1.2 / 10.9	**25** W	0244 / 0822 / 1457 / 2030	2.2 / 9.8 / 2.4 / 9.9
11 W 0347 / 0925 / 1605 / 2144	1.4 / 10.4 / 2.0 / 10.1	**26** TH	0313 / 0851 / 1527 / 2100	2.5 / 9.4 / 2.9 / 9.4
12 TH 0430 / 1011 / 1650 / 2232	2.1 / 9.5 / 2.6 / 9.3	**27** F	0345 / 0923 / 1601 / 2135	3.0 / 8.9 / 3.3 / 8.9
13 F 0522 / 1106 / 1747 / ◑2335	3.0 / 8.6 / 3.6 / 8.5	**28** SA	0423 / 1005 / 1644 / 2224	3.4 / 8.4 / 3.8 / 8.4
14 SA 0630 / 1223 / 1908	3.6 / 8.1 / 4.0	**29** SU	0515 / 1108 / 1746 / ◑2337	3.8 / 8.0 / 4.1 / 8.1
15 SU 0104 / 0756 / 1356 / 2037	8.2 / 3.7 / 8.1 / 3.9	**30** M	0627 / 1236 / 1908	3.9 / 7.9 / 4.1

Chart Datum: 5·88 metres below Ordnance Datum (Local)
HAT is 12·2 metres above Chart Datum

TIDES

TIME ZONE (UT)
For Summer Time add ONE hour in **non-shaded areas**

CHANNEL ISLES – ST HELIER
LAT 49°11'N   LONG 2°07'W
TIMES AND HEIGHTS OF HIGH AND LOW WATERS

Dates in amber are **SPRINGS**
Dates in yellow are **NEAPS**

2012

MAY

Day	Time m	Day	Time m
1 TU	0107 8.2 / 0752 3.7 / 1402 8.4 / 2032 3.6	16 W	0251 8.7 / 0929 3.2 / 1522 8.8 / 2200 3.2
2 W	0227 8.8 / 0909 3.1 / 1510 9.1 / 2142 2.9	17 TH	0347 9.1 / 1023 2.9 / 1612 9.3 / 2250 2.9
3 TH	0332 9.5 / 1013 2.4 / 1607 9.9 / 2242 2.1	18 F	0435 9.4 / 1109 2.6 / 1655 9.6 / 2333 2.6
4 F	0428 10.3 / 1111 1.7 / 1700 10.6 / 2337 1.5	19 SA	0516 9.7 / 1150 2.4 / 1733 9.9
5 SA	0521 10.9 / 1205 1.2 / 1749 11.1	20 SU	0011 2.3 / 0554 9.9 / 1227 2.3 / 1807 10.1
6 SU	0030 1.0 / 0610 11.3 / 1256 0.9 / 1835 11.5	21 M	0048 2.2 / 0628 10.0 / 1302 2.1 / 1840 10.3
7 M	0120 0.7 / 0658 11.5 / 1344 0.8 / 1921 11.6	22 TU	0122 2.1 / 0702 10.1 / 1336 2.1 / 1912 10.3
8 TU	0208 0.7 / 0745 11.4 / 1429 1.0 / 2006 11.4	23 W	0155 2.1 / 0734 10.0 / 1408 2.2 / 1944 10.2
9 W	0253 0.9 / 0831 11.0 / 1513 1.4 / 2050 10.9	24 TH	0227 2.2 / 0807 9.9 / 1441 2.4 / 2016 10.1
10 TH	0338 1.4 / 0916 10.3 / 1557 2.0 / 2134 10.3	25 F	0300 2.3 / 0841 9.6 / 1514 2.6 / 2051 9.8
11 F	0424 2.0 / 1002 9.6 / 1643 2.7 / 2222 9.5	26 SA	0335 2.6 / 0918 9.3 / 1551 2.9 / 2130 9.4
12 SA	0513 2.7 / 1053 8.9 / 1734 3.3 / 2317 8.9	27 SU	0414 2.9 / 1001 8.9 / 1634 3.2 / 2217 9.1
13 SU	0610 3.3 / 1155 8.4 / 1838 3.8	28 M	0501 3.2 / 1054 8.6 / 1727 3.5 / 2315 8.8
14 M	0026 8.5 / 0717 3.5 / 1309 8.2 / 1951 3.8	29 TU	0600 3.4 / 1159 8.5 / 1833 3.6
15 TU	0143 8.4 / 0826 3.5 / 1421 8.4 / 2100 3.6	30 W	0025 8.7 / 0709 3.4 / 1314 8.6 / 1947 3.4
		31 TH	0141 8.9 / 0824 3.1 / 1426 9.0 / 2100 3.0

JUNE

Day	Time m	Day	Time m
1 F	0252 9.4 / 0934 2.6 / 1531 9.6 / 2207 2.4	16 SA	0356 8.8 / 1026 3.3 / 1618 9.1 / 2255 3.1
2 SA	0357 9.9 / 1038 2.1 / 1630 10.2 / 2309 1.8	17 SU	0445 9.1 / 1114 2.9 / 1702 9.5 / 2340 2.7
3 SU	0456 10.4 / 1138 1.7 / 1725 10.8	18 M	0527 9.5 / 1157 2.6 / 1741 9.8
4 M	0007 1.4 / 0551 10.8 / 1235 1.4 / 1817 11.2	19 TU	0022 2.4 / 0605 9.7 / 1238 2.4 / 1818 10.1
5 TU	0103 1.0 / 0643 11.0 / 1328 1.2 / 1906 11.3	20 W	0102 2.2 / 0643 9.6 / 1317 2.2 / 1854 10.2
6 W	0155 0.9 / 0733 11.1 / 1417 1.2 / 1953 11.3	21 TH	0139 2.1 / 0719 10.0 / 1353 2.1 / 1929 10.4
7 TH	0244 1.0 / 0820 10.9 / 1503 1.4 / 2038 11.0	22 F	0215 2.0 / 0755 10.1 / 1429 2.1 / 2006 10.4
8 F	0329 1.3 / 0904 10.5 / 1547 1.8 / 2122 10.5	23 SA	0251 2.0 / 0832 10.0 / 1504 2.2 / 2043 10.3
9 SA	0413 1.8 / 0947 9.9 / 1629 2.4 / 2204 9.9	24 SU	0327 2.1 / 0910 9.9 / 1542 2.3 / 2123 10.1
10 SU	0455 2.4 / 1030 9.3 / 1711 3.0 / 2249 9.3	25 M	0405 2.3 / 0951 9.6 / 1623 2.6 / 2205 9.7
11 M	0538 3.0 / 1117 8.8 / 1757 3.5 / 2341 8.7	26 TU	0447 2.6 / 1035 9.3 / 1709 2.9 / 2253 9.4
12 TU	0626 3.4 / 1212 8.4 / 1852 3.8	27 W	0535 2.9 / 1128 9.0 / 1803 3.2 / 2351 9.0
13 W	0044 8.4 / 0724 3.7 / 1319 8.3 / 1958 3.9	28 TH	0634 3.2 / 1232 8.8 / 1910 3.3
14 TH	0154 8.3 / 0828 3.7 / 1427 8.4 / 2105 3.8	29 F	0101 8.9 / 0745 3.2 / 1346 8.9 / 2025 3.2
15 F	0300 8.5 / 0931 3.6 / 1527 8.7 / 2204 3.5	30 SA	0219 9.0 / 0902 3.0 / 1501 9.2 / 2140 2.8

JULY

Day	Time m	Day	Time m
1 SU	0333 9.4 / 1015 2.6 / 1610 9.8 / 2249 2.2	16 M	0417 8.7 / 1043 3.3 / 1634 9.1 / 2313 3.0
2 M	0440 9.9 / 1121 2.1 / 1710 10.4 / 2353 1.7	17 TU	0504 9.2 / 1132 2.9 / 1718 9.6
3 TU	0540 10.4 / 1221 1.7 / 1805 10.9	18 W	0000 2.5 / 0545 9.6 / 1218 2.4 / 1758 10.0
4 W	0052 1.3 / 0633 10.7 / 1317 1.4 / 1854 11.2	19 TH	0044 2.2 / 0625 10.0 / 1300 2.1 / 1837 10.4
5 TH	0145 1.0 / 0721 10.9 / 1406 1.3 / 1940 11.3	20 F	0125 1.9 / 0703 10.3 / 1339 1.9 / 1915 10.7
6 F	0232 1.0 / 0806 10.9 / 1450 1.3 / 2023 11.1	21 SA	0203 1.7 / 0741 10.5 / 1417 1.7 / 1953 10.8
7 SA	0314 1.1 / 0846 10.7 / 1530 1.6 / 2102 10.8	22 SU	0240 1.5 / 0818 10.6 / 1453 1.7 / 2031 10.9
8 SU	0352 1.6 / 0923 10.3 / 1605 2.1 / 2139 10.2	23 M	0316 1.5 / 0856 10.5 / 1530 1.7 / 2109 10.7
9 M	0426 2.1 / 0958 9.7 / 1638 2.6 / 2215 9.6	24 TU	0352 1.7 / 0934 10.2 / 1609 2.0 / 2149 10.3
10 TU	0458 2.7 / 1030 9.2 / 1712 3.2 / 2253 9.0	25 W	0430 2.1 / 1014 9.8 / 1650 2.5 / 2231 9.7
11 W	0533 3.3 / 1116 8.6 / 1752 3.8 / 2342 8.4	26 TH	0512 2.6 / 1059 9.3 / 1738 3.0 / 2322 9.1
12 TH	0618 3.8 / 1212 8.2 / 1847 4.2	27 F	0605 3.2 / 1158 8.8 / 1840 3.4
13 F	0048 7.9 / 0719 4.1 / 1325 8.0 / 2001 4.3	28 SA	0030 8.7 / 0715 3.5 / 1316 8.6 / 2001 3.5
14 SA	0210 7.9 / 0836 4.1 / 1442 8.2 / 2118 4.0	29 SU	0157 8.5 / 0842 3.5 / 1444 8.8 / 2126 3.2
15 SU	0320 8.2 / 0946 3.8 / 1544 8.6 / 2221 3.6	30 M	0324 8.9 / 1004 3.0 / 1600 9.4 / 2241 2.5
		31 TU	0435 9.5 / 1113 2.4 / 1702 10.1 / 2346 1.9

AUGUST

Day	Time m	Day	Time m
1 W	0533 10.2 / 1213 1.8 / 1755 10.7	16 TH	0523 9.7 / 1155 2.4 / 1737 10.2
2 TH	0042 1.3 / 0622 10.7 / 1305 1.4 / 1841 11.2	17 F	0022 2.0 / 0604 10.2 / 1240 1.9 / 1817 10.7
3 F	0131 1.0 / 0706 10.9 / 1350 1.2 / 1923 11.3	18 SA	0105 1.6 / 0643 10.7 / 1321 1.5 / 1856 11.1
4 SA	0214 1.0 / 0745 11.0 / 1430 1.3 / 2001 11.3	19 SU	0146 1.3 / 0721 11.0 / 1400 1.3 / 1935 11.3
5 SU	0251 1.1 / 0821 10.9 / 1504 1.5 / 2036 11.0	20 M	0223 1.1 / 0759 11.1 / 1438 1.2 / 2014 11.4
6 M	0323 1.5 / 0853 10.5 / 1534 1.9 / 2108 10.5	21 TU	0259 1.1 / 0837 11.0 / 1515 1.3 / 2052 11.1
7 TU	0351 2.0 / 0923 10.0 / 1601 2.4 / 2138 9.8	22 W	0335 1.4 / 0914 10.7 / 1552 1.7 / 2130 10.6
8 W	0417 2.6 / 0952 9.5 / 1628 3.0 / 2208 9.1	23 TH	0412 1.9 / 0952 10.1 / 1632 2.3 / 2211 9.9
9 TH	0445 3.2 / 1024 8.8 / 1700 3.7 / 2244 8.4	24 F	0452 2.6 / 1035 9.4 / 1718 2.9 / 2300 9.0
10 F	0521 3.9 / 1105 8.2 / 1745 4.2 / 2336 7.8	25 SA	0543 3.3 / 1133 8.7 / 1821 3.6
11 SA	0615 4.4 / 1211 7.7 / 1856 4.6	26 SU	0010 8.3 / 0658 3.9 / 1259 8.3 / 1950 3.8
12 SU	0111 7.4 / 0737 4.6 / 1354 7.7 / 2031 4.5	27 M	0151 8.1 / 0835 3.8 / 1440 8.5 / 2122 3.4
13 M	0247 7.7 / 0908 4.3 / 1513 8.2 / 2149 3.9	28 TU	0324 8.6 / 1000 3.2 / 1555 9.3 / 2237 2.6
14 TU	0351 8.3 / 1015 3.7 / 1609 8.8 / 2247 3.2	29 W	0430 9.4 / 1106 2.5 / 1652 10.1 / 2336 1.9
15 W	0440 9.0 / 1108 3.0 / 1655 9.5 / 2336 2.5	30 TH	0521 10.2 / 1200 1.8 / 1740 10.7
		31 F	0026 1.4 / 0605 10.7 / 1247 1.5 / 1822 11.1

Chart Datum: 5·88 metres below Ordnance Datum (Local)
HAT is 12·2 metres above Chart Datum

TIME ZONE (UT)
For Summer Time add ONE hour in non-shaded areas

CHANNEL ISLES – ST HELIER
LAT 49°11'N   LONG 2°07'W
TIMES AND HEIGHTS OF HIGH AND LOW WATERS

Dates in amber are SPRINGS
Dates in yellow are NEAPS

2012

SEPTEMBER

Day	Time m	Time m	Time m	Time m	Day	Time m	Time m	Time m	Time m
1 SA	0111 1.1	0644 11.0	1328 1.3	1900 11.3	16 SU	0039 1.4	0618 11.0	1257 1.3	1833 11.4 ●
2 SU	0148 1.1	0719 11.0	1403 1.4	1935 11.2	17 M	0122 1.0	0658 11.4	1339 1.0	1914 11.7
3 M	0220 1.3	0751 10.9	1432 1.5	2007 11.0	18 TU	0201 0.9	0737 11.5	1418 0.9	1954 11.6
4 TU	0248 1.6	0820 10.7	1459 1.9	2035 10.5	19 W	0239 0.9	0816 11.4	1457 1.1	2034 11.3
5 W	0313 2.0	0847 10.3	1524 2.3	2102 10.0	20 TH	0317 1.3	0854 11.0	1536 1.5	2114 10.7
6 TH	0338 2.5	0913 9.7	1549 2.9	2128 9.3	21 F	0355 1.9	0934 10.3	1617 2.2	2156 9.8
7 F	0404 3.2	0939 9.1	1618 3.6	2157 8.6	22 SA	0437 2.7	1018 9.5	1705 3.0	2247 8.9 ☽
8 SA	0436 3.8	1012 8.4	1657 4.2	2237 7.8 ☽	23 SU	0530 3.5	1118 8.7	1812 3.6	
9 SU	0523 4.5	1104 7.8	1801 4.7	2359 7.3	24 M	0002 8.2	0650 4.1	1250 8.2	1944 3.8
10 M	0642 4.8	1250 7.4	1939 4.7		25 TU	0148 8.1	0829 3.9	1431 8.5	2113 3.4
11 TU	0208 7.4	0824 4.6	1437 7.9	2112 4.2	26 W	0314 8.7	0949 3.3	1541 9.3	2221 2.7
12 W	0321 8.1	0942 3.9	1538 8.7	2215 3.4	27 TH	0413 9.4	1049 2.5	1634 10.0	2316 2.0
13 TH	0412 9.0	1038 3.1	1626 9.5	2307 2.6	28 F	0500 10.1	1139 2.0	1719 10.6	
14 F	0456 9.8	1127 2.3	1710 10.3	2354 1.9	29 SA	0002 1.6	0541 10.6	1222 1.7	1758 10.9
15 SA	0538 10.5	1213 1.7	1753 10.9		30 SU	0042 1.5	0617 10.8	1300 1.6	1834 11.0 ○

OCTOBER

Day	Time m	Time m	Time m	Time m	Day	Time m	Time m	Time m	Time m
1 M	0117 1.5	0650 10.9	1331 1.6	1907 11.0	16 TU	0054 1.0	0633 11.5	1315 0.9	1852 11.7
2 TU	0146 1.4	0720 10.9	1359 1.7	1937 10.8	17 W	0138 0.9	0715 11.7	1358 0.8	1935 11.7
3 W	0213 1.8	0748 10.7	1426 2.0	2005 10.5	18 TH	0220 1.0	0756 11.5	1440 1.0	2018 11.3
4 TH	0239 2.1	0815 10.4	1452 2.3	2031 10.0	19 F	0301 1.4	0838 11.1	1523 1.4	2101 10.7
5 F	0306 2.6	0840 9.9	1519 2.8	2057 9.4	20 SA	0342 2.0	0921 10.4	1608 2.1	2147 9.8
6 SA	0333 3.1	0906 9.3	1548 3.4	2125 8.7	21 SU	0428 2.8	1009 9.6	1659 2.9	2241 9.0
7 SU	0404 3.8	0937 8.7	1624 4.0	2201 8.1	22 M	0524 3.5	1108 8.9	1805 3.5	2351 8.4
8 M	0447 4.4	1021 8.0	1720 4.5	2307 7.5 ☽	23 TU	0639 4.0	1231 8.4	1927 3.7	
9 TU	0556 4.8	1146 7.6	1847 4.7		24 W	0123 8.2	0806 3.9	1402 8.6	2047 3.4
10 W	0107 7.4	0732 4.7	1342 7.8	2022 4.3	25 TH	0244 8.6	0921 3.4	1512 9.1	2152 2.9
11 TH	0237 8.0	0858 4.1	1456 8.5	2134 3.5	26 F	0344 9.3	1020 2.9	1606 9.7	2245 2.4
12 F	0334 8.9	1001 3.2	1550 9.4	2230 2.7	27 SA	0431 9.8	1109 2.4	1651 10.1	2330 2.1
13 SA	0422 9.8	1053 2.4	1638 10.3	2321 1.9	28 SU	0512 10.2	1152 2.1	1731 10.4	
14 SU	0507 10.5	1142 1.7	1724 11.0		29 M	0009 2.0	0548 10.5	1229 2.0	1807 10.6 ○
15 M	0008 1.4	0550 11.1	1230 1.2	1808 11.5 ●	30 TU	0044 1.9	0621 10.6	1301 2.0	1840 10.6
					31 W	0114 2.0	0652 10.7	1333 2.2	1911 10.5

NOVEMBER

Day	Time m	Time m	Time m	Time m	Day	Time m	Time m	Time m	Time m
1 TH	0143 2.0	0721 10.6	1359 2.1	1940 10.3	16 F	0203 1.1	0741 11.6	1428 1.0	2006 11.2
2 F	0212 2.2	0749 10.4	1428 2.3	2009 10.0	17 SA	0249 1.4	0827 11.2	1515 1.3	2053 10.7
3 SA	0241 2.6	0817 10.0	1458 2.7	2037 9.5	18 SU	0334 1.9	0912 10.7	1602 1.9	2139 10.1
4 SU	0311 3.0	0846 9.6	1529 3.2	2108 9.0	19 M	0421 2.5	0959 10.0	1652 2.5	2229 9.3
5 M	0344 3.5	0919 9.1	1605 3.6	2146 8.5	20 TU	0513 3.2	1052 9.3	1747 3.1	2327 8.7 ☽
6 TU	0425 4.0	1002 8.5	1653 4.1	2240 8.0	21 W	0613 3.7	1156 8.7	1852 3.5	
7 W	0522 4.4	1106 8.1	1802 4.3 ○		22 TH	0037 8.4	0725 3.9	1313 8.5	2002 3.6
8 TH	0003 7.8	0640 4.5	1236 8.1	1925 4.2	23 F	0153 8.5	0837 3.8	1426 8.7	2108 3.4
9 F	0136 8.1	0805 4.1	1401 8.5	2044 3.6	24 SA	0300 8.8	0940 3.4	1528 9.1	2205 3.1
10 SA	0246 8.8	0916 3.4	1507 9.2	2148 2.9	25 SU	0354 9.3	1034 3.0	1619 9.5	2254 2.8
11 SU	0343 9.6	1016 2.6	1602 10.0	2245 2.2	26 M	0440 9.7	1119 2.7	1702 9.8	2336 2.5
12 M	0434 10.3	1110 1.9	1654 10.7	2337 1.6	27 TU	0520 10.0	1158 2.5	1741 10.0	
13 TU	0522 11.0	1202 1.4	1744 11.2 ●		28 W	0013 2.4	0555 10.2	1234 2.3	1816 10.1
14 W	0028 1.3	0609 11.4	1252 1.0	1832 11.5 ○	29 TH	0048 2.3	0628 10.4	1308 2.2	1850 10.2
15 TH	0117 1.1	0656 11.6	1341 0.9	1919 11.5	30 F	0121 2.2	0700 10.4	1340 2.2	1922 10.1

DECEMBER

Day	Time m	Time m	Time m	Time m	Day	Time m	Time m	Time m	Time m
1 SA	0153 2.3	0731 10.4	1412 2.3	1954 10.0	16 SU	0240 1.2	0817 11.4	1507 1.0	2043 10.9
2 SU	0225 2.4	0803 10.2	1444 2.5	2026 9.8	17 M	0326 1.6	0901 11.0	1552 1.5	2126 10.4
3 M	0257 2.7	0835 9.9	1517 2.7	2100 9.5	18 TU	0409 2.1	0944 10.4	1635 2.0	2209 9.8
4 TU	0331 3.0	0910 9.6	1553 3.1	2137 9.1	19 W	0451 2.7	1027 9.8	1718 2.7	2253 9.2
5 W	0410 3.4	0950 9.2	1635 3.4	2222 8.7	20 TH	0536 3.3	1115 9.1	1805 3.3	2343 8.6 ☽
6 TH	0457 3.7	1040 8.8	1727 3.7	2320 8.4	21 F	0629 3.8	1213 8.5	1901 3.7	
7 F	0557 3.9	1145 8.6	1833 3.8		22 SA	0048 8.3	0734 4.1	1326 8.3	2008 3.9
8 SA	0033 8.4	0710 3.9	1302 8.6	1949 3.6	23 SU	0203 8.3	0847 4.0	1440 8.3	2116 3.8
9 SU	0151 8.7	0828 3.6	1419 9.0	2104 3.2	24 M	0311 8.6	0952 3.7	1544 8.7	2215 3.5
10 M	0301 9.2	0938 3.0	1527 9.6	2210 2.6	25 TU	0407 9.0	1047 3.3	1635 9.0	2305 3.1
11 TU	0403 9.9	1041 2.3	1628 10.2	2311 2.0	26 W	0453 9.4	1132 2.9	1719 9.4	2348 2.7
12 W	0459 10.6	1140 1.7	1725 10.7		27 TH	0533 9.8	1213 2.5	1758 9.8	
13 TH	0007 1.6	0552 11.1	1236 1.2	1818 11.1 ●	28 F	0028 2.5	0609 10.1	1251 2.3	1833 10.0 ○
14 F	0102 1.3	0642 11.5	1329 0.9	1909 11.3	29 SA	0105 2.3	0644 10.3	1327 2.1	1908 10.1
15 SA	0153 1.1	0730 11.6	1420 0.9	1957 11.2	30 SU	0140 2.2	0718 10.4	1402 2.1	1941 10.2
					31 M	0214 2.1	0751 10.5	1435 2.1	2015 10.2

Chart Datum: 5·88 metres below Ordnance Datum (Local)
HAT is 12·2 metres above Chart Datum

TIDES

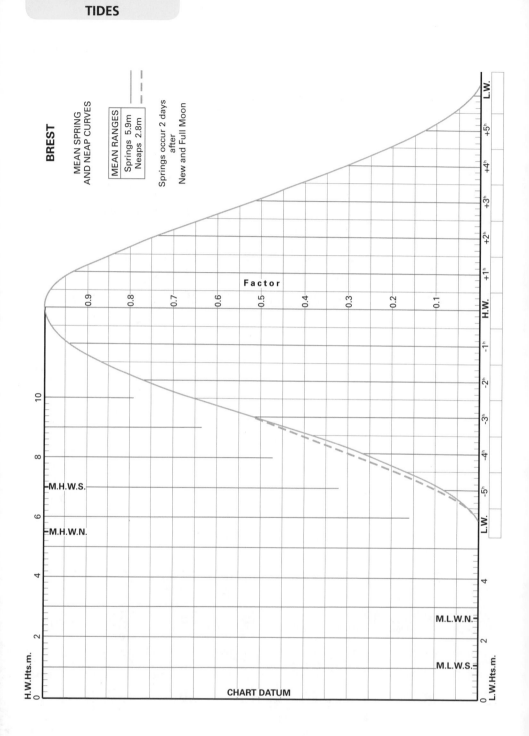

BREST

MEAN SPRING
AND NEAP CURVES

MEAN RANGES
Springs 5.9m
Neaps 2.8m

Springs occur 2 days
after
New and Full Moon

Factor

TIME ZONE -0100
(French Standard Time)
Subtract 1 hour for UT
For French Summer Time add
ONE hour in **non-shaded areas**

FRANCE – BREST

LAT 48°23'N   LONG 4°30'W

TIMES AND HEIGHTS OF HIGH AND LOW WATERS

Dates in amber are **SPRINGS**
Dates in yellow are **NEAPS**

2012

JANUARY

Day	Time	m	Time	m	Time	m	Time	m
1 SU ☽	0404	2.7	1001	5.7	1630	2.7	2230	5.4
16 M	0346	2.0	0947	6.2	1618	2.1	2223	6.0
2 M	0459	2.9	1100	5.4	1728	2.9	2336	5.3
17 TU	0445	2.3	1050	5.9	1723	2.4	2332	5.8
3 TU	0604	3.1	1211	5.3	1835	3.0		
18 W	0556	2.4	1208	5.7	1838	2.5		
4 W	0048	5.3	0716	3.0	1322	5.4	1943	2.9
19 TH	0052	5.8	0716	2.4	1333	5.8	1956	2.3
5 TH	0154	5.5	0821	2.8	1424	5.6	2041	2.6
20 F	0209	6.1	0832	2.1	1445	6.1	2103	2.0
6 F	0249	5.8	0913	2.5	1514	5.9	2129	2.3
21 SA	0313	6.5	0935	1.7	1543	6.4	2200	1.7
7 SA	0334	6.1	0958	2.1	1557	6.2	2211	2.0
22 SU	0406	6.8	1028	1.4	1632	6.7	2249	1.4
8 SU	0415	6.4	1038	1.8	1637	6.4	2251	1.8
23 M	0453	7.1	1115	1.1	1716	6.9	2334	1.2
9 M ○	0454	6.7	1117	1.6	1715	6.6	2330	1.6
24 TU	0536	7.2	1157	1.0	1756	7.0		
10 TU	0531	6.9	1155	1.4	1753	6.8		
25 W	0015	1.2	0615	7.2	1236	1.1	1832	6.9
11 W	0008	1.4	0609	7.0	1233	1.3	1831	6.9
26 TH	0053	1.2	0650	7.1	1312	1.2	1906	6.7
12 TH	0047	1.3	0648	7.1	1312	1.2	1910	6.8
27 F	0128	1.4	0724	6.9	1346	1.5	1938	6.5
13 F	0128	1.4	0727	7.0	1353	1.3	1951	6.7
28 SA	0203	1.7	0756	6.6	1420	1.8	2010	6.2
14 SA	0210	1.5	0809	6.8	1436	1.5	2035	6.5
29 SU	0238	2.0	0829	6.2	1455	2.2	2045	5.9
15 SU	0255	1.7	0854	6.6	1524	1.8	2125	6.2
30 M	0315	2.4	0906	5.8	1534	2.6	2126	5.5
31 TU ☽	0358	2.8	0952	5.4	1621	2.9	2221	5.2

FEBRUARY

Day	Time	m	Time	m	Time	m	Time	m
1 W	0455	3.1	1058	5.1	1727	3.1	2339	5.1
16 TH	0535	2.5	1148	5.5	1819	2.7		
2 TH	0611	3.2	1225	5.0	1847	3.1		
17 F	0036	5.6	0703	2.6	1326	5.5	1947	2.6
3 F	0103	5.2	0735	3.0	1348	5.2	2003	2.9
18 SA	0201	5.9	0825	2.3	1441	5.9	2057	2.2
4 SA	0215	5.5	0843	2.7	1449	5.6	2101	2.5
19 SU	0305	6.3	0928	1.9	1535	6.3	2151	1.8
5 SU	0308	5.9	0933	2.2	1536	6.0	2148	2.1
20 M	0355	6.7	1017	1.5	1620	6.6	2237	1.4
6 M	0353	6.3	1016	1.8	1617	6.4	2230	1.7
21 TU ●	0439	7.0	1100	1.2	1700	6.8	2317	1.2
7 TU ○	0434	6.7	1057	1.4	1656	6.8	2310	1.3
22 W	0517	7.1	1138	1.1	1735	6.9	2354	1.2
8 W	0513	7.1	1136	1.1	1735	7.0	2350	1.1
23 TH	0552	7.2	1211	1.1	1806	7.0		
9 TH	0552	7.3	1215	0.9	1813	7.2		
24 F	0027	1.2	0623	7.1	1244	1.2	1836	6.8
10 F	0030	0.9	0631	7.4	1254	0.8	1851	7.2
25 SA	0059	1.3	0653	6.9	1314	1.4	1905	6.7
11 SA	0110	0.9	0710	7.4	1334	0.9	1931	7.1
26 SU	0131	1.6	0723	6.7	1345	1.7	1934	6.4
12 SU	0152	1.0	0751	7.1	1416	1.2	2013	6.8
27 M	0202	1.9	0753	6.3	1415	2.0	2004	6.1
13 M	0236	1.4	0834	6.8	1502	1.6	2100	6.4
28 TU	0235	2.2	0825	5.9	1449	2.4	2039	5.7
14 TU ☽	0325	1.8	0924	6.3	1554	2.1	2156	6.0
29 W	0313	2.6	0903	5.5	1530	2.8	2124	5.4
15 W	0423	2.2	1026	5.8	1658	2.5	2307	5.7

MARCH

Day	Time	m	Time	m	Time	m	Time	m
1 TH ☽	0401	2.9	0958	5.2	1627	3.1	2234	5.1
16 F	0521	2.5	1137	5.3	1805	2.8		
2 F	0509	3.2	1124	4.9	1748	3.2		
17 SA	0023	5.5	0650	2.6	1314	5.4	1934	2.6
3 SA	0007	5.1	0640	3.1	1302	5.1	1918	3.0
18 SU	0146	5.8	0810	2.3	1426	5.8	2041	2.2
4 SU	0132	5.3	0803	2.8	1415	5.5	2026	2.6
19 M	0247	6.2	0910	1.9	1517	6.2	2133	1.8
5 M	0235	5.8	0901	2.3	1507	6.0	2118	2.1
20 TU	0335	6.5	0957	1.6	1600	6.5	2216	1.5
6 TU	0324	6.3	0948	1.7	1550	6.5	2203	1.6
21 W	0416	6.8	1037	1.4	1636	6.7	2254	1.4
7 W	0408	6.8	1031	1.2	1631	6.9	2246	1.1
22 TH ●	0452	6.9	1112	1.3	1709	6.8	2328	1.3
8 TH ○	0449	7.2	1112	0.8	1711	7.3	2328	0.8
23 F	0524	7.0	1144	1.3	1738	6.9		
9 F	0530	7.5	1152	0.6	1750	7.5		
24 SA	0000	1.3	0555	6.9	1214	1.3	1807	6.8
10 SA	0009	0.6	0610	7.6	1233	0.6	1830	7.5
25 SU	0031	1.4	0624	6.8	1244	1.5	1835	6.7
11 SU	0051	0.6	0653	7.6	1314	0.7	1911	7.3
26 M	0101	1.6	0653	6.6	1313	1.7	1903	6.5
12 M	0134	0.8	0733	7.3	1357	1.1	1954	7.0
27 TU	0132	1.8	0723	6.3	1344	2.0	1933	6.2
13 TU	0219	1.2	0817	6.8	1443	1.6	2041	6.5
28 W	0205	2.1	0755	6.0	1417	2.3	2007	5.9
14 W	0309	1.7	0908	6.2	1535	2.1	2138	6.0
29 TH	0242	2.4	0833	5.6	1457	2.6	2050	5.6
15 TH ☽	0408	2.2	1011	5.7	1641	2.6	2252	5.6
30 F ☽	0327	2.7	0924	5.3	1549	2.9	2152	5.3
31 SA	0428	3.0	1040	5.1	1701	3.1	2318	5.2

APRIL

Day	Time	m	Time	m	Time	m	Time	m
1 SU	0550	3.0	1212	5.1	1829	3.0		
16 M	0115	5.7	0740	2.4	1355	5.7	2012	2.3
2 M	0043	5.4	0715	2.7	1331	5.5	1944	2.6
17 TU	0216	6.0	0839	2.1	1448	6.0	2104	2.0
3 TU	0153	5.8	0820	2.2	1429	6.0	2042	2.1
18 W	0305	6.3	0927	1.9	1530	6.3	2148	1.8
4 W	0248	6.3	0913	1.7	1518	6.5	2132	1.5
19 TH	0346	6.5	1007	1.7	1607	6.5	2226	1.6
5 TH	0336	6.8	1000	1.2	1602	7.0	2218	1.0
20 F	0423	6.6	1043	1.6	1640	6.6	2300	1.5
6 F ○	0422	7.2	1044	0.8	1645	7.4	2303	0.7
21 SA ●	0456	6.7	1115	1.5	1710	6.7	2333	1.5
7 SA	0506	7.5	1128	0.6	1727	7.6	2347	0.5
22 SU	0527	6.7	1146	1.5	1740	6.7		
8 SU	0549	7.6	1211	0.5	1809	7.6		
23 M	0004	1.5	0558	6.6	1217	1.6	1810	6.7
9 M	0032	0.5	0633	7.5	1255	0.7	1852	7.4
24 TU	0036	1.6	0629	6.5	1248	1.7	1840	6.5
10 TU	0117	0.7	0717	7.2	1340	1.1	1938	7.1
25 W	0108	1.8	0701	6.3	1320	1.9	1911	6.3
11 W	0205	1.1	0804	6.7	1428	1.6	2028	6.6
26 TH	0142	2.0	0735	6.0	1355	2.2	1947	6.1
12 TH	0257	1.6	0857	6.2	1521	2.1	2126	6.1
27 F	0221	2.3	0815	5.8	1435	2.5	2031	5.8
13 F ☽	0356	2.1	1000	5.7	1626	2.5	2238	5.7
28 SA	0306	2.5	0905	5.5	1525	2.7	2128	5.5
14 SA	0506	2.4	1115	5.4	1745	2.7	2359	5.6
29 SU ☽	0402	2.7	1011	5.3	1628	2.8	2240	5.4
15 SU	0625	2.5	1245	5.4	1906	2.6		
30 M	0511	2.7	1128	5.3	1744	2.8	2358	5.5

Chart Datum: 3·64 metres below IGN Datum
HAT is 7·9 metres above Chart Datum

TIDES

TIDES

TIME ZONE -0100
-(French Standard Time)
Subtract 1 hour for UT
For French Summer Time add
ONE hour in **non-shaded areas**

FRANCE – BREST
LAT 48°23'N   LONG 4°30'W
TIMES AND HEIGHTS OF HIGH AND LOW WATERS

Dates in amber are **SPRINGS**
Dates in yellow are **NEAPS**

2012

MAY

Day	Time m	Day	Time m
1 TU	0627 2.5 / 1243 5.6 / 1859 2.5	16 W	0133 5.8 / 0756 2.4 / 1406 5.7 / 2027 2.3
2 W	0108 5.8 / 0736 2.2 / 1347 6.0 / 2003 2.1	17 TH	0226 5.9 / 0848 2.2 / 1454 6.0 / 2114 2.1
3 TH	0209 6.3 / 0835 1.7 / 1442 6.5 / 2058 1.6	18 F	0312 6.1 / 0932 2.0 / 1535 6.2 / 2155 1.9
4 F	0304 6.7 / 0928 1.3 / 1532 6.9 / 2150 1.1	19 SA	0352 6.2 / 1011 1.9 / 1611 6.4 / 2233 1.8
5 SA	0354 7.1 / 1017 0.9 / 1619 7.3 / 2239 0.8	20 SU	0428 6.4 / 1046 1.8 / 1644 6.5 / 2308 1.7
6 SU	0443 7.3 / 1105 0.7 / 1706 7.5 / ○ 2327 0.6	21 M	0503 6.4 / 1120 1.7 / ● 1717 6.6 / 2342 1.7
7 M	0530 7.4 / 1151 0.7 / 1752 7.5	22 TU	0537 6.4 / 1154 1.7 / 1749 6.6
8 TU	0015 0.6 / 0617 7.3 / 1238 0.9 / 1838 7.4	23 W	0016 1.7 / 0611 6.4 / 1227 1.8 / 1822 6.5
9 W	0104 0.8 / 0705 7.0 / 1325 1.2 / 1926 7.1	24 TH	0050 1.8 / 0645 6.3 / 1302 1.9 / 1857 6.4
10 TH	0153 1.1 / 0754 6.6 / 1414 1.6 / 2016 6.7	25 F	0126 1.9 / 0722 6.1 / 1339 2.0 / 1934 6.3
11 F	0244 1.5 / 0845 6.2 / 1507 2.0 / 2112 6.3	26 SA	0205 2.0 / 0802 6.0 / 1420 2.2 / 2017 6.1
12 SA	0340 2.0 / 0943 5.8 / 1607 2.4 / ◐ 2214 5.9	27 SU	0249 2.2 / 0849 5.8 / 1507 2.3 / 2108 5.9
13 SU	0441 2.3 / 1049 5.6 / 1714 2.6 / 2322 5.7	28 M	0340 2.3 / 0945 5.6 / 1602 2.5 / ◑ 2209 5.8
14 M	0548 2.5 / 1200 5.4 / 1825 2.6	29 TU	0439 2.4 / 1050 5.6 / 1707 2.5 / 2317 5.7
15 TU	0031 5.7 / 0655 2.5 / 1308 5.5 / 1931 2.5	30 W	0546 2.3 / 1158 5.7 / 1817 2.4
		31 TH	0026 5.9 / 0654 2.1 / 1305 6.0 / 1925 2.1

JUNE

Day	Time m	Day	Time m
1 F	0132 6.2 / 0759 1.8 / 1407 6.3 / 2027 1.7	16 SA	0236 5.7 / 0855 2.4 / 1501 5.9 / 2125 2.3
2 SA	0234 6.5 / 0858 1.5 / 1505 6.7 / 2125 1.3	17 SU	0323 5.9 / 0940 2.2 / 1543 6.1 / 2207 2.1
3 SU	0331 6.8 / 0953 1.2 / 1558 7.0 / 2220 1.0	18 M	0404 6.1 / 1020 2.0 / 1621 6.3 / 2245 1.9
4 M	0425 7.0 / 1046 1.0 / 1649 7.3 / ○ 2312 0.8	19 TU	0442 6.2 / 1058 1.9 / 1657 6.4 / ● 2322 1.7
5 TU	0516 7.1 / 1136 1.0 / 1738 7.4	20 W	0519 6.3 / 1134 1.8 / 1733 6.5 / 2358 1.6
6 W	0002 0.8 / 0605 7.1 / 1224 1.0 / 1826 7.3	21 TH	0554 6.4 / 1210 1.7 / 1808 6.6
7 TH	0051 0.9 / 0653 6.9 / 1312 1.2 / 1914 7.1	22 F	0034 1.6 / 0631 6.4 / 1246 1.7 / 1844 6.6
8 F	0139 1.1 / 0740 6.7 / 1359 1.5 / 2001 6.8	23 SA	0110 1.6 / 0708 6.4 / 1324 1.7 / 1922 6.5
9 SA	0227 1.4 / 0826 6.3 / 1448 1.8 / 2049 6.4	24 SU	0149 1.7 / 0747 6.3 / 1404 1.8 / 2002 6.4
10 SU	0316 1.8 / 0915 6.0 / 1538 2.2 / 2140 6.1	25 M	0231 1.8 / 0830 6.1 / 1448 2.0 / 2048 6.2
11 M	0407 2.1 / 1008 5.7 / 1633 2.5 / ◑ 2236 5.8	26 TU	0317 1.9 / 0919 6.0 / 1537 2.1 / 2140 6.1
12 TU	0502 2.4 / 1106 5.5 / 1734 2.6 / 2337 5.6	27 W	0410 2.1 / 1015 5.9 / 1635 2.3 / ◐ 2241 5.9
13 W	0602 2.6 / 1211 5.4 / 1838 2.7	28 TH	0511 2.2 / 1120 5.8 / 1741 2.3 / 2349 5.9
14 TH	0040 5.5 / 0704 2.6 / 1315 5.5 / 1941 2.6	29 F	0619 2.2 / 1229 5.9 / 1852 2.2
15 F	0142 5.6 / 0803 2.5 / 1413 5.7 / 2037 2.5	30 SA	0102 6.0 / 0729 2.1 / 1340 6.1 / 2003 1.9

JULY

Day	Time m	Day	Time m
1 SU	0213 6.2 / 0836 1.8 / 1446 6.5 / 2108 1.6	16 M	0256 5.6 / 0911 2.4 / 1517 5.9 / 2142 2.2
2 M	0316 6.5 / 0937 1.5 / 1554 6.8 / 2207 1.3	17 TU	0342 5.8 / 0956 2.1 / 1559 6.2 / 2223 1.9
3 TU	0413 6.7 / 1032 1.3 / 1638 7.1 / ○ 2300 1.0	18 W	0422 6.2 / 1036 1.9 / 1638 6.4 / 2302 1.7
4 W	0504 6.9 / 1123 1.1 / 1727 7.2 / 2350 0.9	19 TH	0500 6.4 / 1114 1.7 / ● 1715 6.7 / 2339 1.5
5 TH	0552 7.0 / 1211 1.1 / 1813 7.3	20 F	0536 6.6 / 1151 1.5 / 1751 6.8
6 F	0036 0.9 / 0637 6.9 / 1256 1.1 / 1857 7.2	21 SA	0015 1.3 / 0613 6.7 / 1228 1.4 / 1828 6.9
7 SA	0120 1.0 / 0719 6.7 / 1339 1.3 / 1938 6.9	22 SU	0052 1.3 / 0649 6.7 / 1306 1.4 / 1905 6.9
8 SU	0202 1.3 / 0759 6.5 / 1421 1.6 / 2018 6.6	23 M	0130 1.3 / 0727 6.7 / 1345 1.4 / 1944 6.8
9 M	0244 1.7 / 0838 6.1 / 1503 2.0 / 2059 6.2	24 TU	0210 1.4 / 0808 6.5 / 1428 1.6 / 2026 6.6
10 TU	0326 2.1 / 0920 5.8 / 1548 2.3 / 2144 5.8	25 W	0254 1.7 / 0853 6.3 / 1515 1.8 / 2114 6.3
11 W	0411 2.4 / 1008 5.5 / 1639 2.7 / ◑ 2237 5.5	26 TH	0343 1.9 / 0945 6.0 / 1609 2.1 / ◐ 2211 6.0
12 TH	0504 2.7 / 1108 5.3 / 1740 2.9 / 2342 5.3	27 F	0441 2.2 / 1049 5.8 / 1713 2.3 / 2321 5.7
13 F	0607 2.9 / 1218 5.2 / 1849 2.9	28 SA	0551 2.4 / 1203 5.8 / 1829 2.4
14 SA	0053 5.2 / 0715 2.9 / 1328 5.4 / 1957 2.8	29 SU	0042 5.7 / 0709 2.4 / 1324 5.9 / 1949 2.2
15 SU	0200 5.4 / 0819 2.7 / 1429 5.6 / 2055 2.5	30 M	0203 5.9 / 0824 2.1 / 1436 6.3 / 2100 1.8
		31 TU	0310 6.2 / 0928 1.8 / 1536 6.7 / 2158 1.4

AUGUST

Day	Time m	Day	Time m
1 W	0404 6.6 / 1022 1.4 / 1627 7.0 / 2249 1.1	16 TH	0358 6.6 / 1011 1.8 / 1614 6.5 / 2238 1.6
2 TH	0452 6.8 / 1110 1.2 / 1713 7.2 / ○ 2335 0.9	17 F	0437 6.6 / 1050 1.5 / 1652 6.8 / ● 2316 1.3
3 F	0536 6.9 / 1154 1.1 / 1755 7.3	18 SA	0514 6.8 / 1129 1.3 / 1730 7.1 / 2353 1.1
4 SA	0017 0.9 / 0615 6.9 / 1235 1.1 / 1833 7.2	19 SU	0550 7.0 / 1207 1.1 / 1807 7.2
5 SU	0056 1.0 / 0651 6.8 / 1313 1.3 / 1909 7.0	20 M	0030 1.0 / 0627 7.1 / 1245 1.0 / 1844 7.2
6 M	0132 1.3 / 0725 6.6 / 1349 1.5 / 1943 6.7	21 TU	0109 1.0 / 0705 7.0 / 1325 1.1 / 1923 7.1
7 TU	0207 1.6 / 0758 6.3 / 1425 1.9 / 2017 6.3	22 W	0149 1.2 / 0745 6.8 / 1408 1.4 / 2005 6.8
8 W	0243 2.0 / 0832 6.0 / 1503 2.3 / 2053 5.9	23 TH	0232 1.5 / 0829 6.5 / 1455 1.7 / 2052 6.4
9 TH	0321 2.4 / 0912 5.6 / 1546 2.7 / ◑ 2138 5.5	24 F	0321 1.9 / 0922 6.1 / 1549 2.1 / ◐ 2150 5.9
10 F	0407 2.8 / 1004 5.3 / 1641 3.0 / 2240 5.1	25 SA	0419 2.3 / 1027 5.8 / 1655 2.4 / 2304 5.6
11 SA	0507 3.0 / 1117 5.1 / 1753 3.1	26 SU	0534 2.6 / 1150 5.7 / 1818 2.5
12 SU	0001 5.0 / 0624 3.1 / 1241 5.1 / 1915 3.0	27 M	0036 5.5 / 0701 2.6 / 1319 5.8 / 1944 2.3
13 M	0124 5.1 / 0741 2.9 / 1354 5.4 / 2024 2.7	28 TU	0201 5.8 / 0819 2.3 / 1430 6.2 / 2053 1.9
14 TU	0229 5.5 / 0842 2.6 / 1449 5.8 / 2115 2.3	29 W	0303 6.2 / 0919 1.8 / 1525 6.6 / 2148 1.5
15 W	0317 5.8 / 0929 2.2 / 1534 6.2 / 2158 1.9	30 TH	0353 6.5 / 1009 1.5 / 1612 7.0 / 2234 1.2
		31 F	0436 6.8 / 1053 1.2 / 1654 7.2 / ○ 2316 1.1

Chart Datum: 3·64 metres below IGN Datum
HAT is 7·9 metres above Chart Datum

TIME ZONE -0100
(French Standard Time)
Subtract 1 hour for UT
For French Summer Time add
ONE hour in **non-shaded areas**

FRANCE – BREST

LAT 48°23'N   LONG 4°30'W

TIMES AND HEIGHTS OF HIGH AND LOW WATERS

Dates in amber are **SPRINGS**
Dates in yellow are **NEAPS**

2012

SEPTEMBER

Day	Time m		Day	Time m	
1 SA	0514 6.9 / 1133 1.1 / 1731 7.2 / 2353 1.0		**16** SU	0447 7.1 / 1103 1.1 / 1705 7.3 / 2328 0.9 ●	
2 SU	0549 7.0 / 1209 1.2 / 1805 7.1		**17** M	0525 7.3 / 1143 0.9 / 1744 7.5	
3 M	0027 1.2 / 0620 6.9 / 1243 1.3 / 1837 7.0		**18** TU	0007 0.8 / 0604 7.4 / 1224 0.8 / 1823 7.4	
4 TU	0100 1.4 / 0650 6.7 / 1316 1.5 / 1908 6.7		**19** W	0047 0.9 / 0643 7.3 / 1306 0.9 / 1904 7.2	
5 W	0131 1.7 / 0720 6.5 / 1349 1.9 / 1939 6.4		**20** TH	0129 1.1 / 0725 7.1 / 1351 1.2 / 1948 6.9	
6 TH	0203 2.0 / 0751 6.1 / 1423 2.2 / 2012 6.0		**21** F	0214 1.5 / 0812 6.7 / 1440 1.6 / 2037 6.4	
7 F	0237 2.4 / 0826 5.8 / 1501 2.6 / 2050 5.6		**22** SA	0304 2.0 / 0906 6.2 / 1536 2.1 / 2138 5.9 ☽	
8 SA	0317 2.8 / 0910 5.4 / 1549 3.0 / 2144 5.2 ☽		**23** SU	0405 2.5 / 1016 5.8 / 1645 2.5 / 2257 5.5	
9 SU	0411 3.1 / 1017 5.1 / 1657 3.2 / 2308 5.0		**24** M	0524 2.7 / 1143 5.7 / 1811 2.6	
10 M	0529 3.2 / 1149 5.1 / 1825 3.2		**25** TU	0031 5.5 / 0653 2.7 / 1309 5.9 / 1934 2.4	
11 TU	0041 5.0 / 0657 3.1 / 1313 5.3 / 1945 2.9		**26** W	0150 5.8 / 0807 2.3 / 1415 6.2 / 2038 2.0	
12 W	0154 5.4 / 0806 2.7 / 1415 5.7 / 2042 2.4		**27** TH	0247 6.2 / 0904 1.9 / 1507 6.6 / 2129 1.6	
13 TH	0246 5.9 / 0857 2.2 / 1503 6.2 / 2127 1.9		**28** F	0334 6.5 / 0945 1.5 / 1551 6.9 / 2213 1.4	
14 F	0329 6.3 / 0942 1.8 / 1545 6.7 / 2209 1.5		**29** SA	0414 6.8 / 1032 1.4 / 1630 7.0 / 2251 1.3	
15 SA	0409 6.7 / 1023 1.4 / 1626 7.0 / 2248 1.1		**30** SU	0449 6.9 / 1109 1.3 / 1705 7.1 / 2326 1.3 ○	

OCTOBER

Day	Time m		Day	Time m	
1 M	0521 6.9 / 1143 1.3 / 1737 7.0 / 2358 1.3		**16** TU	0501 7.5 / 1121 0.8 / 1722 7.6 / 2344 0.7	
2 TU	0551 6.9 / 1215 1.4 / 1807 6.9		**17** W	0543 7.6 / 1205 0.7 / 1805 7.5	
3 W	0029 1.5 / 0620 6.8 / 1246 1.6 / 1838 6.7		**18** TH	0028 0.8 / 0626 7.5 / 1250 0.9 / 1849 7.3	
4 TH	0059 1.7 / 0649 6.6 / 1318 1.9 / 1908 6.4		**19** F	0113 1.1 / 0711 7.2 / 1337 1.2 / 1937 6.9	
5 F	0131 2.0 / 0720 6.3 / 1351 2.2 / 1941 6.0		**20** SA	0200 1.5 / 0759 6.8 / 1429 1.6 / 2029 6.4	
6 SA	0204 2.4 / 0753 6.0 / 1428 2.5 / 2018 5.7		**21** SU	0253 2.0 / 0857 6.3 / 1526 2.0 / 2130 5.9	
7 SU	0242 2.7 / 0834 5.6 / 1513 2.9 / 2107 5.3		**22** M	0355 2.5 / 1005 6.0 / 1634 2.4 / 2246 5.6 ☽	
8 M	0332 3.0 / 0933 5.2 / 1612 3.1 / 2221 5.1 ☽		**23** TU	0510 2.7 / 1126 5.8 / 1753 2.5	
9 TU	0440 3.2 / 1057 5.2 / 1732 3.1 / 2352 5.1		**24** W	0010 5.5 / 0632 2.7 / 1244 5.9 / 1909 2.4	
10 W	0605 3.1 / 1224 5.3 / 1856 2.9		**25** TH	0124 5.8 / 0742 2.4 / 1349 6.1 / 2011 2.1	
11 TH	0109 5.4 / 0722 2.8 / 1332 5.7 / 2000 2.4		**26** F	0221 6.1 / 0839 2.1 / 1441 6.4 / 2103 1.9	
12 F	0207 5.9 / 0826 2.3 / 1426 6.4 / 2050 1.9		**27** SA	0307 6.4 / 0926 1.8 / 1525 6.6 / 2146 1.7	
13 SA	0254 6.4 / 0909 1.8 / 1513 6.7 / 2136 1.5		**28** SU	0348 6.6 / 1007 1.6 / 1604 6.8 / 2224 1.6	
14 SU	0338 6.9 / 0954 1.3 / 1557 7.1 / 2219 1.1		**29** M	0423 6.8 / 1044 1.6 / 1639 6.8 / 2259 1.5 ○	
15 M	0420 7.2 / 1038 1.0 / 1639 7.4 / 2302 0.8 ●		**30** TU	0455 6.8 / 1118 1.6 / 1711 6.8 / 2331 1.6	
			31 W	0526 6.8 / 1150 1.6 / 1743 6.7	

NOVEMBER

Day	Time m		Day	Time m	
1 TH	0003 1.7 / 0556 6.8 / 1222 1.7 / 1815 6.6		**16** F	0012 0.9 / 0613 7.5 / 1238 0.8 / 1839 7.3	
2 F	0035 1.8 / 0627 6.6 / 1255 1.9 / 1847 6.4		**17** SA	0100 1.1 / 0701 7.3 / 1327 1.1 / 1928 6.9	
3 SA	0107 2.0 / 0658 6.4 / 1329 2.1 / 1920 6.1		**18** SU	0149 1.4 / 0751 7.0 / 1418 1.4 / 2020 6.5	
4 SU	0141 2.3 / 0732 6.2 / 1405 2.4 / 1958 5.8		**19** M	0242 1.9 / 0846 6.6 / 1513 1.8 / 2116 6.1	
5 M	0219 2.5 / 0812 5.9 / 1448 2.6 / 2044 5.6		**20** TU	0339 2.2 / 0946 6.2 / 1614 2.2 / 2221 5.8 ☽	
6 TU	0305 2.8 / 0904 5.6 / 1540 2.8 / 2146 5.3		**21** W	0444 2.5 / 1053 5.9 / 1721 2.5 / 2332 5.6	
7 W	0403 3.0 / 1012 5.5 / 1646 2.9 / 2302 5.3		**22** TH	0555 2.7 / 1204 5.8 / 1830 2.5	
8 TH	0515 3.0 / 1131 5.5 / 1802 2.8		**23** F	0042 5.6 / 0704 2.6 / 1310 5.9 / 1934 2.4	
9 F	0017 5.5 / 0631 2.8 / 1243 5.8 / 1912 2.5		**24** SA	0144 5.8 / 0805 2.4 / 1408 6.0 / 2029 2.2	
10 SA	0121 5.9 / 0737 2.4 / 1345 6.2 / 2010 2.0		**25** SU	0236 6.1 / 0857 2.2 / 1456 6.2 / 2117 2.1	
11 SU	0217 6.3 / 0833 1.9 / 1439 6.6 / 2102 1.6		**26** M	0320 6.3 / 0941 2.0 / 1538 6.4 / 2158 1.9	
12 M	0307 6.8 / 0925 1.4 / 1529 7.0 / 2151 1.2		**27** TU	0358 6.5 / 1019 1.8 / 1616 6.5 / 2234 1.8	
13 TU	0354 7.2 / 1014 1.1 / 1617 7.3 / 2239 0.9 ●		**28** W	0433 6.6 / 1056 1.8 / 1651 6.6 / 2309 1.8 ○	
14 W	0441 7.5 / 1102 0.8 / 1704 7.5 / 2326 0.8		**29** TH	0506 6.7 / 1131 1.7 / 1725 6.6 / 2342 1.8	
15 TH	0527 7.6 / 1150 0.7 / 1751 7.5		**30** F	0539 6.7 / 1204 1.7 / 1758 6.5	

DECEMBER

Day	Time m		Day	Time m	
1 SA	0016 1.8 / 0611 6.7 / 1238 1.8 / 1832 6.4		**16** SU	0049 1.0 / 0652 7.5 / 1316 0.9 / 1917 7.0	
2 SU	0050 1.9 / 0644 6.6 / 1312 1.9 / 1906 6.3		**17** M	0137 1.2 / 0739 7.2 / 1404 1.2 / 2004 6.7	
3 M	0124 2.1 / 0719 6.4 / 1348 2.1 / 1943 6.1		**18** TU	0225 1.6 / 0827 6.8 / 1453 1.6 / 2052 6.3	
4 TU	0202 2.2 / 0757 6.2 / 1428 2.3 / 2026 5.9		**19** W	0315 2.0 / 0916 6.4 / 1543 2.0 / 2144 5.9	
5 W	0245 2.4 / 0842 6.0 / 1514 2.4 / 2116 5.7		**20** TH	0409 2.3 / 1010 6.0 / 1638 2.4 / 2242 5.6 ☽	
6 TH	0334 2.6 / 0937 5.8 / 1609 2.6 / 2218 5.6		**21** F	0508 2.6 / 1112 5.7 / 1739 2.6 / 2348 5.5	
7 F	0434 2.7 / 1042 5.7 / 1714 2.6 / 2326 5.6		**22** SA	0614 2.8 / 1219 5.6 / 1845 2.7	
8 SA	0542 2.7 / 1153 5.8 / 1823 2.5		**23** SU	0056 5.5 / 0722 2.7 / 1327 5.6 / 1949 2.6	
9 SU	0035 5.8 / 0653 2.4 / 1303 6.0 / 1930 2.2		**24** M	0200 5.7 / 0824 2.6 / 1426 5.8 / 2045 2.5	
10 M	0139 6.2 / 0759 2.1 / 1407 6.4 / 2031 1.8		**25** TU	0252 5.9 / 0916 2.3 / 1515 6.0 / 2132 2.2	
11 TU	0239 6.6 / 0859 1.6 / 1506 6.8 / 2128 1.4		**26** W	0336 6.2 / 0959 2.1 / 1557 6.2 / 2213 2.0	
12 W	0334 7.0 / 0955 1.2 / 1600 7.1 / 2221 1.1		**27** TH	0415 6.4 / 1038 1.9 / 1634 6.4 / 2250 1.9	
13 TH	0425 7.3 / 1047 0.9 / 1651 7.3 / 2311 1.0 ●		**28** F	0450 6.6 / 1114 1.8 / 1709 6.5 / 2325 1.8 ○	
14 F	0515 7.5 / 1138 0.7 / 1741 7.4 / 2359 1.7		**29** SA	0524 6.7 / 1148 1.7 / 1744 6.6	
15 SA	0001 0.9 / 0604 7.6 / 1227 0.7 / 1829 7.3		**30** SU	0558 6.8 / 1222 1.6 / 1818 6.6	
			31 M	0034 1.7 / 0632 6.8 / 1257 1.6 / 1852 6.5	

Chart Datum: 3·64 metres below IGN Datum
HAT is 7·9 metres above Chart Datum

TIDES

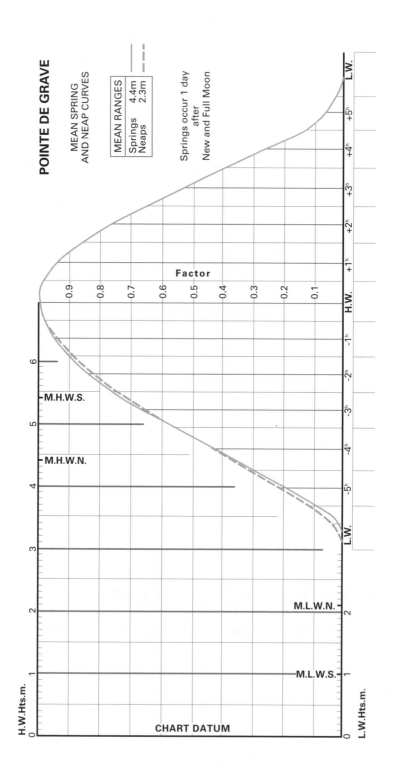

POINTE DE GRAVE

MEAN SPRING
AND NEAP CURVES

MEAN RANGES	
Springs	4.4m
Neaps	2.3m

Springs occur 1 day
after
New and Full Moon

Factor

0.9
0.8
0.7
0.6
0.5
0.4
0.3
0.2
0.1

H.W.
-1ʰ
-2ʰ
-3ʰ
-4ʰ
-5ʰ
L.W.

+1ʰ +2ʰ +3ʰ +4ʰ +5ʰ L.W.

M.H.W.S.
M.H.W.N.

M.L.W.N.
M.L.W.S.

CHART DATUM

H.W.Hts.m.

L.W.Hts.m.

TIME ZONE -0100
(French Standard Time)
Subtract 1 hour for UT
For French Summer Time add
ONE hour in **non-shaded areas**

FRANCE – POINTE DE GRAVE

LAT 45°34'N   LONG 1°04'W

TIMES AND HEIGHTS OF HIGH AND LOW WATERS

Dates in amber are **SPRINGS**
Dates in yellow are **NEAPS**

2012

JANUARY

Day	Time m	Day	Time m
1 SU ◑	0354 2.1 / 1020 4.4 / 1620 2.1 / 2258 4.2	**16** M	0331 1.6 / 1009 4.8 / 1604 1.7 / 2248 4.6
2 M	0453 2.3 / 1123 4.2 / 1722 2.3	**17** TU	0432 1.8 / 1121 4.6 / 1711 1.9
3 TU	0010 4.1 / 0600 2.3 / 1236 4.2 / 1831 2.3	**18** W	0006 4.5 / 0544 1.9 / 1245 4.5 / 1827 2.0
4 W	0122 4.2 / 0707 2.3 / 1348 4.2 / 1936 2.2	**19** TH	0124 4.6 / 0702 1.9 / 1403 4.6 / 1943 1.9
5 TH	0221 4.4 / 0808 2.2 / 1445 4.4 / 2031 2.1	**20** F	0231 4.8 / 0817 1.7 / 1508 4.8 / 2051 1.7
6 F	0307 4.6 / 0859 2.0 / 1531 4.6 / 2117 1.9	**21** SA	0328 5.0 / 0922 1.5 / 1603 5.0 / 2147 1.4
7 SA	0347 4.8 / 0944 1.8 / 1612 4.8 / 2158 1.7	**22** SU	0419 5.2 / 1016 1.3 / 1650 5.1 / 2236 1.2
8 SU	0425 5.0 / 1025 1.6 / 1650 4.9 / 2238 1.5	**23** M ●	0505 5.4 / 1103 1.1 / 1733 5.2 / 2321 1.1
9 M ○	0502 5.1 / 1105 1.4 / 1727 5.1 / 2317 1.4	**24** TU	0546 5.5 / 1146 1.0 / 1811 5.2
10 TU	0540 5.3 / 1145 1.3 / 1804 5.1 / 2356 1.3	**25** W	0002 1.1 / 0625 5.4 / 1225 1.1 / 1846 5.1
11 W	0617 5.3 / 1224 1.2 / 1842 5.2	**26** TH	0040 1.2 / 0700 5.3 / 1301 1.2 / 1918 5.0
12 TH	0036 1.2 / 0657 5.3 / 1303 1.2 / 1921 5.1	**27** F	0116 1.3 / 0733 5.2 / 1335 1.3 / 1947 4.8
13 F	0115 1.3 / 0738 5.2 / 1342 1.3 / 2003 5.0	**28** SA	0151 1.4 / 0804 5.0 / 1409 1.5 / 2018 4.7
14 SA	0156 1.3 / 0822 5.2 / 1424 1.4 / 2049 4.9	**29** SU	0226 1.7 / 0839 4.7 / 1444 1.8 / 2055 4.5
15 SU	0240 1.5 / 0911 5.0 / 1510 1.5 / 2143 4.7	**30** M	0305 1.9 / 0921 4.5 / 1524 2.0 / 2144 4.2
		31 TU ◑	0352 2.2 / 1016 4.2 / 1614 2.3 / 2253 4.1

FEBRUARY

Day	Time m	Day	Time m
1 W	0456 2.4 / 1132 4.0 / 1727 2.4	**16** TH	0526 2.0 / 1236 4.3 / 1809 2.1
2 TH	0020 4.0 / 0616 2.4 / 1302 4.0 / 1849 2.4	**17** F	0113 4.5 / 0654 2.0 / 1400 4.4 / 1936 2.0
3 F	0141 4.1 / 0732 2.3 / 1415 4.2 / 1958 2.3	**18** SA	0225 4.7 / 0814 1.8 / 1505 4.6 / 2045 1.8
4 SA	0239 4.4 / 0833 2.1 / 1508 4.4 / 2052 2.0	**19** SU	0322 4.9 / 0915 1.5 / 1557 4.8 / 2138 1.5
5 SU	0324 4.7 / 0922 1.8 / 1551 4.7 / 2137 1.7	**20** M	0409 5.1 / 1005 1.3 / 1639 5.0 / 2224 1.3
6 M	0405 4.9 / 1006 1.5 / 1630 4.9 / 2219 1.5	**21** TU ●	0450 5.3 / 1047 1.1 / 1715 5.1 / 2305 1.1
7 TU ○	0443 5.2 / 1047 1.3 / 1708 5.2 / 2300 1.2	**22** W	0526 5.4 / 1126 1.1 / 1748 5.1 / 2342 1.1
8 W	0522 5.4 / 1127 1.1 / 1745 5.3 / 2340 1.1	**23** TH	0559 5.4 / 1202 1.1 / 1817 5.1
9 TH	0600 5.5 / 1207 1.0 / 1823 5.4	**24** F	0017 1.1 / 0630 5.3 / 1234 1.2 / 1844 5.1
10 F	0020 1.0 / 0640 5.5 / 1245 0.9 / 1902 5.4	**25** SA	0049 1.2 / 0659 5.2 / 1304 1.3 / 1911 5.0
11 SA	0059 1.0 / 0721 5.5 / 1324 1.0 / 1943 5.3	**26** SU	0119 1.4 / 0728 5.0 / 1334 1.5 / 1940 4.8
12 SU	0139 1.0 / 0804 5.3 / 1404 1.2 / 2026 5.1	**27** M	0150 1.5 / 0800 4.8 / 1404 1.7 / 2012 4.6
13 M	0221 1.2 / 0851 5.1 / 1447 1.4 / 2116 4.8	**28** TU	0222 1.8 / 0836 4.5 / 1437 1.9 / 2050 4.4
14 TU ◐	0310 1.5 / 0946 4.7 / 1539 1.7 / 2219 4.6	**29** W	0300 2.0 / 0922 4.2 / 1517 2.2 / 2144 4.1
15 W	0409 1.7 / 1100 4.4 / 1645 2.0 / 2345 4.4		

MARCH

Day	Time m	Day	Time m
1 TH ◑	0351 2.3 / 1030 4.0 / 1617 2.4 / 2308 4.0	**16** F	0511 2.0 / 1229 4.2 / 1754 2.2
2 F	0515 2.5 / 1208 3.9 / 1753 2.5	**17** SA	0100 4.4 / 0641 2.0 / 1350 4.3 / 1921 2.1
3 SA	0047 4.0 / 0649 2.4 / 1335 4.1 / 1917 2.4	**18** SU	0211 4.6 / 0759 1.8 / 1454 4.8 / 2028 1.8
4 SU	0159 4.3 / 0759 2.1 / 1434 4.4 / 2018 2.1	**19** M	0307 4.8 / 0857 1.6 / 1540 4.8 / 2119 1.5
5 M	0252 4.6 / 0852 1.8 / 1521 4.7 / 2108 1.7	**20** TU	0351 5.0 / 0943 1.4 / 1618 5.0 / 2203 1.3
6 TU	0337 4.9 / 0939 1.5 / 1602 5.0 / 2153 1.4	**21** W	0427 5.1 / 1024 1.2 / 1650 5.0 / 2242 1.2
7 W	0418 5.2 / 1021 1.2 / 1642 5.2 / 2236 1.1	**22** TH	0500 5.2 / 1100 1.2 / 1719 5.1 / 2317 1.2
8 TH ○	0459 5.5 / 1103 1.0 / 1721 5.4 / 2318 0.9	**23** F	0530 5.2 / 1133 1.2 / 1746 5.1 / 2349 1.2
9 F	0539 5.6 / 1143 0.8 / 1801 5.5 / 2359 0.8	**24** SA	0559 5.2 / 1203 1.2 / 1813 5.1
10 SA	0620 5.7 / 1223 0.8 / 1841 5.5	**25** SU	0020 1.2 / 0628 5.1 / 1232 1.3 / 1841 5.0
11 SU	0040 0.8 / 0703 5.6 / 1303 0.9 / 1923 5.4	**26** M	0049 1.3 / 0658 5.0 / 1300 1.5 / 1910 4.9
12 M	0121 0.9 / 0747 5.4 / 1343 1.1 / 2007 5.2	**27** TU	0118 1.5 / 0730 4.8 / 1330 1.6 / 1941 4.7
13 TU	0204 1.1 / 0835 5.0 / 1427 1.4 / 2058 4.9	**28** W	0149 1.7 / 0805 4.6 / 1402 1.8 / 2017 4.5
14 W	0253 1.4 / 0931 4.7 / 1519 1.7 / 2201 4.5	**29** TH	0225 1.9 / 0848 4.3 / 1442 2.1 / 2105 4.3
15 TH ◑	0352 1.7 / 1050 4.3 / 1626 2.0 / 2330 4.4	**30** F ◑	0312 2.1 / 0949 4.1 / 1535 2.3 / 2214 4.1
		31 SA	0420 2.3 / 1117 4.0 / 1656 2.4 / 2346 4.1

APRIL

Day	Time m	Day	Time m
1 SU	0555 2.3 / 1246 4.1 / 1825 2.3	**16** M	0142 4.5 / 0728 1.9 / 1426 4.5 / 1957 1.9
2 M	0109 4.3 / 0712 2.1 / 1351 4.2 / 1933 2.1	**17** TU	0238 4.7 / 0826 1.7 / 1511 4.6 / 2050 1.6
3 TU	0211 4.6 / 0812 1.8 / 1443 4.7 / 2030 1.7	**18** W	0322 4.8 / 0913 1.5 / 1548 4.8 / 2134 1.5
4 W	0302 4.9 / 0903 1.4 / 1529 5.0 / 2120 1.4	**19** TH	0358 4.9 / 0953 1.4 / 1619 4.9 / 2213 1.4
5 TH	0348 5.2 / 0949 1.1 / 1613 5.3 / 2207 1.1	**20** F	0431 5.0 / 1029 1.4 / 1648 5.0 / 2248 1.3
6 F ○	0433 5.5 / 1034 0.9 / 1655 5.5 / 2253 0.8	**21** SA ●	0502 5.1 / 1101 1.3 / 1718 5.0 / 2320 1.3
7 SA	0517 5.6 / 1117 0.8 / 1738 5.6 / 2337 0.7	**22** SU	0533 5.1 / 1132 1.3 / 1747 5.1 / 2351 1.3
8 SU	0601 5.7 / 1200 0.8 / 1821 5.6	**23** M	0604 5.0 / 1202 1.4 / 1817 5.0
9 M	0020 0.7 / 0646 5.5 / 1242 0.9 / 1906 5.5	**24** TU	0022 1.4 / 0636 4.9 / 1233 1.5 / 1847 4.9
10 TU	0104 0.8 / 0733 5.3 / 1325 1.1 / 1953 5.3	**25** W	0054 1.5 / 0709 4.8 / 1304 1.6 / 1920 4.8
11 W	0149 1.0 / 0823 5.0 / 1410 1.4 / 2046 5.0	**26** TH	0127 1.6 / 0745 4.6 / 1339 1.7 / 1958 4.7
12 TH	0239 1.3 / 0922 4.6 / 1503 1.7 / 2149 4.7	**27** F	0204 1.7 / 0829 4.4 / 1420 1.9 / 2045 4.5
13 F ◑	0337 1.6 / 1040 4.3 / 1609 2.0 / 2311 4.5	**28** SA	0250 1.9 / 0925 4.2 / 1511 2.1 / 2145 4.4
14 SA	0451 1.9 / 1209 4.2 / 1730 2.1	**29** SU ◑	0349 2.1 / 1037 4.2 / 1618 2.2 / 2300 4.3
15 SU	0033 4.4 / 0614 2.0 / 1325 4.3 / 1851 2.0	**30** M	0506 2.1 / 1156 4.2 / 1735 2.2

Chart Datum: 2·83 metres below IGN Datum
HAT is 6·1 metres above Chart Datum

TIDES

TIME ZONE -0100
(French Standard Time)
Subtract 1 hour for UT
For French Summer Time add ONE hour in **non-shaded areas**

FRANCE – POINTE DE GRAVE
LAT 45°34'N   LONG 1°04'W
TIMES AND HEIGHTS OF HIGH AND LOW WATERS

Dates in amber are **SPRINGS**
Dates in yellow are **NEAPS**

2012

MAY

Time m	Time m
1 0017 4.4 / 0620 2.0 / TU 1305 4.4 / 1845 2.0	**16** 0155 4.5 / 0745 1.8 / W 1432 4.5 / 2012 1.8
2 0126 4.6 / 0725 1.7 / W 1403 4.6 / 1947 1.7	**17** 0244 4.6 / 0836 1.7 / TH 1512 4.6 / 2100 1.7
3 0225 4.9 / 0823 1.4 / TH 1455 5.0 / 2044 1.4	**18** 0325 4.7 / 0919 1.6 / F 1547 4.7 / 2142 1.6
4 0318 5.2 / 0915 1.2 / F 1543 5.3 / 2137 1.1	**19** 0402 4.8 / 0957 1.5 / SA 1620 4.9 / 2219 1.5
5 0408 5.4 / 1005 1.0 / SA 1630 5.5 / 2227 0.9	**20** 0437 4.8 / 1031 1.5 / SU 1652 4.9 / 2253 1.4
6 0456 5.5 / 1052 0.8 / SU 1717 5.6 / ○ 2316 0.7	**21** 0512 4.9 / 1104 1.4 / M 1725 5.0 / ● 2327 1.4
7 0544 5.5 / 1138 0.8 / M 1805 5.6	**22** 0546 4.9 / 1138 1.4 / TU 1758 5.0
8 0002 0.7 / 0633 5.4 / TU 1223 0.9 / 1853 5.5	**23** 0001 1.4 / 0620 4.8 / W 1212 1.5 / 1831 5.0
9 0049 0.8 / 0722 5.2 / W 1309 1.1 / 1943 5.3	**24** 0036 1.4 / 0655 4.8 / TH 1247 1.5 / 1906 4.9
10 0136 1.0 / 0813 4.9 / TH 1356 1.3 / 2035 5.1	**25** 0112 1.5 / 0732 4.7 / F 1324 1.6 / 1945 4.8
11 0225 1.2 / 0910 4.6 / F 1447 1.6 / 2134 4.8	**26** 0151 1.6 / 0814 4.6 / SA 1405 1.7 / 2030 4.7
12 0319 1.5 / 1017 4.4 / SA 1547 1.8 / ◑ 2240 4.6	**27** 0234 1.7 / 0905 4.5 / SU 1452 1.8 / 2124 4.6
13 0422 1.8 / 1130 4.2 / SU 1656 2.0 / 2350 4.5	**28** 0326 1.8 / 1005 4.4 / M 1549 1.9 / ◑ 2226 4.5
14 0532 1.9 / 1241 4.2 / M 1808 2.0	**29** 0427 1.8 / 1113 4.4 / TU 1654 1.9 / 2335 4.5
15 0056 4.4 / 0642 1.9 / TU 1343 4.3 / 1915 1.9	**30** 0535 1.8 / 1221 4.5 / W 1802 1.8
	31 0045 4.6 / 0641 1.7 / TH 1326 4.7 / 1908 1.6

JUNE

Time m	Time m
1 0151 4.8 / 0745 1.5 / F 1424 4.9 / 2010 1.4	**16** 0251 4.4 / 0844 1.8 / SA 1516 4.6 / 2110 1.8
2 0252 5.0 / 0844 1.3 / SA 1519 5.1 / 2110 1.2	**17** 0336 4.5 / 0927 1.7 / SU 1554 4.7 / 2152 1.6
3 0348 5.2 / 0940 1.1 / SU 1610 5.3 / 2206 1.0	**18** 0416 4.7 / 1006 1.6 / M 1631 4.8 / 2231 1.5
4 0440 5.3 / 1032 1.0 / M 1701 5.5 / ○ 2259 0.8	**19** 0453 4.8 / 1042 1.5 / TU 1706 4.9 / ● 2308 1.4
5 0531 5.3 / 1121 0.9 / TU 1751 5.5 / 2349 0.8	**20** 0529 4.8 / 1119 1.4 / W 1741 5.0 / 2345 1.3
6 0621 5.3 / 1209 1.0 / W 1841 5.5	**21** 0605 4.9 / 1155 1.4 / TH 1816 5.0
7 0036 0.8 / 0710 5.2 / TH 1255 1.1 / 1930 5.3	**22** 0022 1.3 / 0640 4.9 / F 1232 1.4 / 1853 5.0
8 0123 1.0 / 0759 4.9 / F 1341 1.2 / 2019 5.1	**23** 0059 1.3 / 0717 4.8 / SA 1310 1.4 / 1932 5.0
9 0208 1.2 / 0847 4.7 / SA 1428 1.4 / 2108 4.9	**24** 0138 1.4 / 0758 4.8 / SU 1350 1.5 / 2014 4.9
10 0256 1.4 / 0939 4.5 / SU 1519 1.7 / 2200 4.7	**25** 0218 1.4 / 0843 4.7 / M 1433 1.5 / 2102 4.8
11 0347 1.6 / 1035 4.3 / M 1616 1.8 / ◑ 2255 4.4	**26** 0303 1.5 / 0935 4.6 / TU 1522 1.6 / 2157 4.7
12 0444 1.9 / 1138 4.2 / TU 1719 2.0 / 2356 4.3	**27** 0355 1.6 / 1035 4.5 / W 1620 1.7 / ◑ 2301 4.6
13 0548 2.0 / 1244 4.2 / W 1825 2.0	**28** 0457 1.7 / 1143 4.5 / TH 1727 1.7
14 0059 4.3 / 0654 2.0 / TH 1344 4.3 / 1928 2.0	**29** 0012 4.6 / 0605 1.7 / F 1255 4.6 / 1837 1.7
15 0159 4.3 / 0753 1.9 / F 1434 4.4 / 2023 1.9	**30** 0126 4.7 / 0715 1.6 / SA 1402 4.8 / 1946 1.5

JULY

Time m	Time m
1 0234 4.8 / 0822 1.4 / SU 1502 5.0 / 2052 1.3	**16** 0311 4.4 / 0900 1.8 / M 1531 4.6 / 2129 1.7
2 0334 5.0 / 0923 1.3 / M 1557 5.2 / 2153 1.1	**17** 0355 4.5 / 0943 1.7 / TU 1610 4.8 / 2210 1.5
3 0429 5.1 / 1018 1.1 / TU 1649 5.4 / ○ 2247 0.9	**18** 0434 4.7 / 1023 1.5 / W 1646 4.9 / 2250 1.4
4 0520 5.2 / 1109 1.0 / W 1738 5.5 / 2337 0.8	**19** 0510 4.9 / 1101 1.3 / TH 1722 5.1 / ● 2328 1.2
5 0608 5.2 / 1156 1.0 / TH 1826 5.5	**20** 0546 5.0 / 1139 1.2 / F 1758 5.2
6 0023 0.8 / 0653 5.1 / F 1241 1.0 / 1910 5.4	**21** 0006 1.2 / 0622 5.0 / SA 1217 1.2 / 1835 5.2
7 0106 0.9 / 0735 5.0 / SA 1323 1.1 / 1952 5.2	**22** 0043 1.1 / 0658 5.0 / SU 1254 1.2 / 1914 5.2
8 0147 1.1 / 0814 4.8 / SU 1404 1.3 / 2032 4.9	**23** 0120 1.1 / 0737 5.0 / M 1333 1.2 / 1955 5.1
9 0227 1.3 / 0852 4.6 / M 1447 1.5 / 2112 4.7	**24** 0158 1.2 / 0819 4.9 / TU 1413 1.3 / 2040 5.0
10 0309 1.6 / 0933 4.4 / TU 1534 1.8 / 2158 4.4	**25** 0240 1.3 / 0907 4.7 / W 1459 1.4 / 2132 4.8
11 0356 1.8 / 1027 4.2 / W 1628 2.0 / ◑ 2254 4.2	**26** 0328 1.5 / 1004 4.6 / TH 1553 1.6 / ◑ 2234 4.6
12 0452 2.0 / 1134 4.1 / TH 1732 2.1	**27** 0426 1.7 / 1113 4.5 / F 1700 1.7 / 2350 4.5
13 0001 4.1 / 0559 2.2 / F 1249 4.1 / 1842 2.2	**28** 0538 1.8 / 1235 4.5 / SA 1817 1.8
14 0114 4.1 / 0708 2.1 / SA 1346 4.2 / 1947 2.1	**29** 0113 4.5 / 0656 1.8 / SU 1350 4.6 / 1934 1.6
15 0220 4.2 / 0810 2.0 / SU 1448 4.4 / 2042 1.9	**30** 0226 4.6 / 0811 1.6 / M 1453 4.9 / 2045 1.2
	31 0328 4.8 / 0915 1.4 / TU 1548 5.1 / 2145 1.2

AUGUST

Time m	Time m
1 0421 5.0 / 1009 1.2 / W 1637 5.3 / 2237 1.0	**16** 0408 4.8 / 1000 1.5 / TH 1623 5.0 / 2228 1.3
2 0507 5.1 / 1057 1.0 / TH 1723 5.4 / ○ 2323 0.9	**17** 0446 5.0 / 1040 1.3 / F 1659 5.2 / ● 2306 1.1
3 0550 5.1 / 1141 1.0 / F 1805 5.4	**18** 0522 5.1 / 1119 1.1 / SA 1736 5.3 / 2345 1.0
4 0005 0.9 / 0629 5.1 / SA 1222 1.0 / 1843 5.3	**19** 0559 5.2 / 1157 1.0 / SU 1814 5.4
5 0044 1.0 / 0703 5.0 / SU 1300 1.1 / 1918 5.2	**20** 0022 1.0 / 0636 5.2 / M 1235 1.0 / 1853 5.4
6 0120 1.1 / 0735 4.8 / M 1336 1.2 / 1951 5.0	**21** 0059 1.0 / 0715 5.2 / TU 1313 1.0 / 1934 5.3
7 0155 1.3 / 0805 4.7 / TU 1412 1.5 / 2025 4.7	**22** 0137 1.1 / 0756 5.1 / W 1354 1.2 / 2020 5.1
8 0230 1.6 / 0839 4.5 / W 1451 1.7 / 2105 4.5	**23** 0218 1.3 / 0843 4.9 / TH 1439 1.4 / 2112 4.8
9 0309 1.8 / 0924 4.3 / TH 1536 2.0 / ◑ 2157 4.2	**24** 0305 1.5 / 0940 4.6 / F 1533 1.6 / ◑ 2216 4.5
10 0356 2.1 / 1027 4.1 / F 1636 2.2 / 2307 4.0	**25** 0404 1.8 / 1054 4.4 / SA 1642 1.8 / 2342 4.3
11 0501 2.3 / 1152 4.0 / SA 1755 2.3	**26** 0521 2.0 / 1227 4.4 / SU 1808 1.9
12 0031 3.9 / 0622 2.3 / SU 1316 4.1 / 1911 2.2	**27** 0112 4.4 / 0648 2.0 / M 1345 4.6 / 1931 1.5
13 0148 4.1 / 0735 2.2 / M 1418 4.3 / 2014 2.0	**28** 0224 4.5 / 0806 1.8 / TU 1447 4.9 / 2040 1.5
14 0245 4.3 / 0832 2.0 / TU 1505 4.5 / 2104 1.8	**29** 0321 4.8 / 0906 1.5 / W 1538 5.1 / 2135 1.3
15 0329 4.5 / 0919 1.7 / W 1545 4.8 / 2147 1.5	**30** 0409 4.9 / 0956 1.2 / TH 1623 5.3 / 2221 1.1
	31 0450 5.1 / 1041 1.1 / F 1702 5.4 / ○ 2303 1.0

Chart Datum: 2·83 metres below IGN Datum
HAT is 6·1 metres above Chart Datum

TIME ZONE -0100
(French Standard Time)
Subtract 1 hour for UT
For French Summer Time add
ONE hour in **non-shaded areas**

FRANCE – POINTE DE GRAVE
LAT 45°34'N   LONG 1°04'W
TIMES AND HEIGHTS OF HIGH AND LOW WATERS

Dates in amber are **SPRINGS**
Dates in yellow are **NEAPS**

2012

SEPTEMBER

Day	Time	m	Time	m	Time	m	Time	m
1 SA	0526	5.1	1121	1.0	1739	5.4	2342	1.0
16 SU	0455	5.3	1054	1.0	1712	5.5	● 2319	0.9
2 SU	0559	5.1	1158	1.0	1812	5.3		
17 M	0533	5.4	1134	0.9	1752	5.6	2358	0.8
3 M	0017	1.1	0629	5.1	1233	1.1	1843	5.2
18 TU	0613	5.5	1214	0.9	1833	5.5		
4 TU	0049	1.2	0656	5.0	1305	1.3	1913	5.0
19 W	0037	0.9	0654	5.4	1254	0.9	1917	5.4
5 W	0120	1.4	0725	4.8	1337	1.5	1945	4.8
20 TH	0117	1.1	0738	5.2	1337	1.1	2004	5.1
6 TH	0152	1.6	0757	4.6	1410	1.7	2022	4.5
21 F	0200	1.3	0826	5.0	1424	1.3	2059	4.8
7 F	0226	1.8	0836	4.4	1448	2.0	2108	4.2
22 SA	0249	1.6	0926	4.7	1519	1.6	☽ 2209	4.5
8 SA	0306	2.1	0929	4.2	1538	2.3	◐ 2216	4.0
23 SU	0349	1.9	1047	4.6	1631	1.9	2344	4.3
9 SU	0401	2.4	1051	4.0	1659	2.4	2348	3.9
24 M	0509	2.1	1220	4.5	1759	2.0		
10 M	0530	2.5	1227	4.0	1831	2.4		
25 TU	0109	4.4	0638	2.1	1335	4.7	1921	1.8
11 TU	0111	4.0	0654	2.4	1340	4.2	1939	2.1
26 W	0215	4.6	0752	1.8	1434	4.9	2025	1.6
12 W	0211	4.3	0756	2.1	1432	4.5	2032	1.8
27 TH	0308	4.8	0849	1.6	1523	5.1	2115	1.4
13 TH	0257	4.6	0846	1.8	1515	4.8	2117	1.5
28 F	0350	4.9	0937	1.3	1603	5.2	2159	1.2
14 F	0338	4.9	0931	1.2	1554	5.1	2159	1.3
29 SA	0426	5.1	1019	1.2	1638	5.3	2238	1.2
15 SA	0417	5.1	1013	1.2	1633	5.4	2239	1.1
30 SU	0458	5.1	1057	1.2	1711	5.3	○ 2314	1.2

OCTOBER

Day	Time	m	Time	m	Time	m	Time	m
1 M	0528	5.1	1132	1.2	1742	5.3	2347	1.2
16 TU	0510	5.6	1110	0.9	1732	5.7	2333	0.9
2 TU	0557	5.1	1204	1.3	1812	5.2		
17 W	0553	5.6	1154	0.8	1817	5.6		
3 W	0017	1.3	0625	5.0	1238	1.4	1842	5.0
18 TH	0016	0.9	0638	5.5	1238	0.9	1904	5.4
4 TH	0047	1.5	0655	4.8	1306	1.5	1914	4.8
19 F	0059	1.1	0726	5.4	1323	1.1	1954	5.1
5 F	0118	1.7	0727	4.6	1338	1.7	1950	4.6
20 SA	0145	1.3	0818	5.1	1412	1.3	2052	4.8
6 SA	0151	1.9	0803	4.4	1414	2.0	2034	4.3
21 SU	0236	1.6	0919	4.9	1508	1.6	2206	4.5
7 SU	0230	2.1	0849	4.3	1458	2.2	2135	4.1
22 M	0337	1.9	1038	4.6	1617	1.9	☽ 2334	4.4
8 M	0320	2.3	0957	4.2	1604	2.4	◐ 2301	4.0
23 TU	0453	2.1	1201	4.6	1738	2.0		
9 TU	0434	2.5	1129	4.1	1738	2.4		
24 W	0051	4.4	0614	2.1	1313	4.7	1855	1.9
10 W	0025	4.1	0602	2.4	1250	4.3	1853	2.2
25 TH	0154	4.6	0726	1.9	1412	4.8	1958	1.7
11 TH	0128	4.4	0710	2.2	1350	4.6	1951	1.9
26 F	0245	4.7	0823	1.7	1500	5.0	2049	1.6
12 F	0219	4.7	0806	1.9	1439	4.9	2039	1.6
27 SA	0326	4.9	0911	1.5	1539	5.1	2132	1.5
13 SA	0304	5.0	0855	1.6	1524	5.2	2125	1.3
28 SU	0400	5.0	0953	1.4	1613	5.1	● 2211	1.4
14 SU	0346	5.2	0941	1.3	1607	5.4	2208	1.1
29 M	0431	5.1	1031	1.4	1646	5.2	○ 2245	1.4
15 M	0428	5.4	1026	5.6	1649	5.6	● 2251	0.9
30 TU	0501	5.1	1105	1.4	1718	5.1	2317	1.4
31 W	0532	5.1	1137	1.4	1749	5.1	2349	1.5

NOVEMBER

Day	Time	m	Time	m	Time	m	Time	m
1 TH	0602	5.1	1209	1.5	1821	5.0		
16 F	0626	5.6	1225	0.9	1855	5.4		
2 F	0020	1.6	0633	5.0	1241	1.6	1854	4.8
17 SA	0045	1.1	0717	5.5	1312	1.0	1947	5.2
3 SA	0052	1.7	0706	4.9	1315	1.7	1930	4.7
18 SU	0133	1.3	0810	5.3	1401	1.3	2044	4.9
4 SU	0127	1.8	0742	4.7	1351	1.9	2012	4.5
19 M	0224	1.6	0909	5.0	1455	1.5	2150	4.6
5 M	0206	2.0	0826	4.5	1434	2.1	2106	4.3
20 TU	0320	1.8	1015	4.8	1554	1.8	☽ 2304	4.4
6 TU	0253	2.2	0923	4.4	1529	2.2	2216	4.2
21 W	0426	2.0	1127	4.6	1703	2.0		
7 W	0354	2.3	1036	4.3	1642	2.3	◐ 2333	4.2
22 TH	0016	4.4	0537	2.1	1236	4.6	1815	2.0
8 TH	0508	2.3	1154	4.4	1758	2.2		
23 F	0121	4.5	0648	2.0	1338	4.6	1922	1.9
9 F	0041	4.4	0619	2.2	1303	4.6	1902	2.0
24 SA	0214	4.6	0750	1.9	1431	4.7	2017	1.8
10 SA	0139	4.7	0720	1.9	1401	4.9	1958	1.7
25 SU	0258	4.7	0842	1.8	1514	4.8	2104	1.7
11 SU	0230	5.0	0817	1.6	1453	5.1	2049	1.4
26 M	0335	4.9	0927	1.7	1551	4.9	2144	1.6
12 M	0318	5.2	0910	1.3	1542	5.4	2138	1.2
27 TU	0408	5.0	1006	1.6	1626	5.0	2220	1.6
13 TU	0404	5.5	1000	1.1	1630	5.5	● 2226	1.0
28 W	0441	5.1	1042	1.5	1701	5.0	○ 2253	1.5
14 W	0451	5.6	1049	0.9	1717	5.6	2313	0.9
29 TH	0514	5.1	1116	1.5	1734	5.0	2327	1.5
15 TH	0538	5.7	1137	0.8	1806	5.6	2359	1.0
30 F	0546	5.1	1150	1.5	1808	5.0		

DECEMBER

Day	Time	m	Time	m	Time	m	Time	m
1 SA	0000	1.6	0619	5.1	1224	1.5	1841	4.9
16 SU	0034	1.0	0707	5.6	1302	0.9	1936	5.2
2 SU	0034	1.6	0652	5.0	1259	1.6	1917	4.8
17 M	0121	1.2	0757	5.4	1348	1.1	2026	5.0
3 M	0110	1.7	0728	4.9	1336	1.7	1956	4.7
18 TU	0208	1.4	0847	5.2	1435	1.4	2119	4.7
4 TU	0148	1.8	0809	4.8	1416	1.8	2042	4.5
19 W	0257	1.6	0940	4.9	1525	1.6	2216	4.5
5 W	0231	1.9	0858	4.7	1502	2.0	2138	4.4
20 TH	0352	1.8	1038	4.6	1621	1.9	☽ 2321	4.3
6 TH	0322	2.1	0957	4.6	1558	2.1	◐ 2243	4.4
21 F	0453	2.0	1142	4.5	1725	2.1		
7 F	0423	2.1	1104	4.5	1705	2.1	2352	4.5
22 SA	0030	4.3	0602	2.1	1251	4.4	1835	2.1
8 SA	0531	2.1	1216	4.6	1813	2.0		
23 SU	0134	4.4	0710	2.1	1355	4.4	1940	2.1
9 SU	0058	4.6	0638	1.9	1325	4.8	1917	1.8
24 M	0227	4.5	0811	2.0	1448	4.5	2035	2.0
10 M	0159	4.9	0742	1.7	1427	5.0	2017	1.5
25 TU	0311	4.6	0902	1.9	1532	4.6	2120	1.8
11 TU	0254	5.1	0842	1.4	1524	5.2	2113	1.3
26 W	0349	4.8	0946	1.7	1611	4.8	2159	1.7
12 W	0346	5.4	0940	1.2	1616	5.4	2207	1.1
27 TH	0425	4.9	1024	1.6	1647	4.9	2235	1.6
13 TH	0437	5.6	1034	1.0	1707	5.5	● 2258	1.0
28 F	0459	5.0	1100	1.5	1721	5.0	○ 2310	1.5
14 F	0527	5.7	1125	0.9	1757	5.5	2347	1.0
29 SA	0533	5.1	1135	1.5	1755	5.0	2345	1.5
15 SA	0617	5.7	1214	0.8	1846	5.4		
30 SU	0606	5.1	1210	1.4	1828	5.0		
31 M	0020	1.5	0639	5.1	1246	1.4	1902	5.0

Chart Datum: 2·83 metres below IGN Datum
HAT is 6·1 metres above Chart Datum

TIDES